T0137013

Lecture Notes in Computer Science　　12711

More information about this subseries at http://www.springer.com/series/7410

Juan A. Garay (Ed.)

Public-Key Cryptography – PKC 2021

24th IACR International Conference
on Practice and Theory of Public Key Cryptography
Virtual Event, May 10–13, 2021
Proceedings, Part II

Springer

Editor
Juan A. Garay 🆔
Texas A&M University
College Station, TX, USA

ISSN 0302-9743   ISSN 1611-3349   (electronic)
Lecture Notes in Computer Science
ISBN 978-3-030-75247-7   ISBN 978-3-030-75248-4   (eBook)
https://doi.org/10.1007/978-3-030-75248-4

LNCS Sublibrary: SL4 – Security and Cryptology

This Springer imprint is published by the registered company Springer Nature Switzerland AG
The registered company address is: Gewerbestrasse 11, 6330 Cham, Switzerland

Preface

The 24th International Conference on Practice and Theory of Public-Key Cryptography (PKC 2021) was held virtually over Zoom from May 10th to May 13th, 2021. It was supposed to take place in Edinburgh, Scotland, but due to COVID-19 this was not possible. The conference is organized annually by the International Association for Cryptologic Research (IACR), and is the main annual conference with an explicit focus on public-key cryptography. Given NIST's efforts on standardization of post-quantum cryptography, this year constructions and cryptanalysis in this area were specially encouraged. These proceedings are comprised of two volumes and include the 52 papers that were selected by the Program Committee (PC), as well as a one-page abstract corresponding to one of the two invited talks, which reflect this year's focus.

The 52 accepted papers were selected out of a total of 156 received submissions. Submissions were assigned to at least three reviewers, while submissions by PC members received at least four reviews. Due to time constraints, the review period this year did not include a rebuttal step, where the authors get a chance to preview their papers' preliminary reviews. The review process, however, was fairly interactive, as in a large number of occasions reviewers posed questions to the authors. Six of the accepted papers were first conditionally accepted and received an additional round of reviewing; in addition, two of the papers were "soft merged" due to the similarity of results and shared one presentation slot.

Given the high number and quality of the submissions, the reviewing and paper selection process was a challenging task and I am deeply grateful to the members of the PC for their high dedication and thorough work. In addition to the PC members, many external reviewers joined the review process in their particular areas of expertise. We were fortunate to have this knowledgeable and energetic team of experts, and I am deeply grateful to all of them for their contributions. The submissions included two papers with which I had a conflict of interest (they were authored by current and/or close collaborators). For these two papers I abstained from the management of the discussion and delegated this task to a PC member. Many thanks to Hoeteck Wee and Vassilis Zikas, respectively, for their help in managing these two papers.

The paper submission, review and discussion processes were effectively and efficiently made possible by the Web-Submission-and-Review software, written by Shai Halevi, and hosted by the IACR. As always, many thanks to Shai for his assistance with the system's various features.

This year the program was further enriched by two invited talks by Léo Ducas (CWI, the Netherlands; "Lattices and Factoring") and Eike Kiltz (Ruhr-Universität Bochum, Germany; "How Provably Secure are (EC)DSA Signatures?"). My special thanks to Lèo and Eike for accepting the invitation and great presentations.

I am also grateful for their predisposition, availability, and efforts (unfortunately not fully realized when we decided to go virtual) to Markulf Kohlweiss and Petros Wallden, who served as General Co-chairs, and to Dimitris Karakostas (all from The

University of Edinburgh), who managed the conference's website. I finally thank all the authors who submitted papers to this conference, and all the conference attendees who made this event a truly intellectually stimulating one through their active (albeit remote) participation.

Next time, Edinburgh!

March 2021   Juan A. Garay

PKC 2021

The 24th International Conference on Practice and Theory of Public-Key Cryptography

Virtual Event
May 10–13, 2021

Organized in cooperation with IACR

General Chairs

Markulf Kohlweiss   The University of Edinburgh, UK
Petros Wallden   The University of Edinburgh, UK

Program Chair

Juan A. Garay   Texas A&M University, USA

Program Committee

Daniel Apon	NIST, USA
Christian Badertscher	IOHK, Switzerland
Saikrishna Badrinarayanan	Visa Research, USA
Manuel Barbosa	University of Porto, Portugal
Paulo Barreto	University of Washington-Tacoma, USA
Fabrice Benhamouda	Algorand Foundation, USA
Michele Ciampi	The University of Edinburgh, UK
Yi Deng	Chinese Academy of Sciences, China
Yfke Dulek	QuSoft and CWI, the Netherlands
Marc Joye	Zama, France
Shuichi Katsumata	AIST, Japan
Lisa Kohl	CWI, the Netherlands
Venkata Koppula	IIT Delhi, India
Changmin Lee	KIAS, South Korea
Feng-Hao Liu	Florida Atlantic University, USA
Vadim Lyubashevsky	IBM Research, Switzerland
Giulio Malavolta	Max Planck Institute, Germany
Mary Maller	Ethereum Foundation, UK
Takahiro Matsuda	AIST, Japan
Peihan Miao	University of Illinois at Chicago, USA
David Naccache	ENS, France
Adam O'Neill	University of Massachusetts Amherst, USA
Cristina Onete	University of Limoges and XLIM, France

Giorgos Panagiotakos	University of Athens, Greece
Alice Pellet-Mary	KUL, Belgium
Christophe Petit	University of Birmingham, UK
Bertram Poettering	IBM Research, Switzerland
Melissa Rossi	ANSSI, France
Olivier Sanders	Orange Labs, France
Berry Schoenmakers	TU Eindhoven, the Netherlands
Fang Song	Portland State University, USA
Akshayaram Srinivasan	Tata Institute of Fundamental Research, India
Qiang Tang	The University of Sydney, Australia
Hoeteck Wee	NTT Research and ENS, France
Vassilis Zikas	Purdue University, USA

Sponsoring Institutions

The Scottish Informatics and Computer Science Alliance (SICSA) Cyber Nexus
INPUT|OUTPUT
DFINITY

External Reviewers

Behzad Abdolmaleki
Ojaswi Acharya
Thomas Attema
Nuttapong Attrapadung
Reza Azarderakhsh
Karim Baghery
Shi Bai
James Bartusek
Andrea Basso
Carsten Baum
Ward Beullens
Olivier Blazy
Charlotte Bonte
Jonathan Bootle
Pedro Branco
Konstantinos Brazitikos
Xavier Bultel
Sèbastien Canard
Wouter Castryk
Jie Chen
Long Chen
Yu Chen
Benoit Chevallier-Mames
Wonhee Cho

Jérémy Chotard
Ran Cohen
Orel Cosseron
Geoffroy Couteau
Daniele Cozzo
Gareth Davies
Yi Deng
Jintai Ding
Ehsan Ebrahimi
Keita Emura
Thomas Espitau
Leo Fan
Antonio Faonio
Thibauld Feneuil
Hanwen Feng
Weiqi Feng
Luca De Feo
Rex Fernando
Ben Fisch
Boris Fouotsa
Pierre-Alain Fouque
Phillip Gajland
Chaya Ganesh
Rachit Garg

Romain Gay
Nicholas Genise
Riddhi Ghosal
Huijing Gong
Junqing Gong
Rishab Goyal
Vipul Goyal
François Gérard
Mohammad Hajiabadi
Shai Halevi
Mike Hamburg
Kyoohyung Han
Patrick Harasser
Brett Hemenway
Julia Hesse
Minki Hhan
Seungwan Hong
Yuncong Hu
Andreas Hlsing
Muhammad Ishaq
David Jao
Sam Jaques
Stanislaw Jarecki
Dingding Jia

Zhengzhong Jin
Daniel Jost
Bhavana Kanukurthi
Harish Karthikeyan
John Kelsey
Dongwoo Kim
Duhyeong Kim
Jiseung Kim
Fuyuki Kitagawa
Susumu Kiyoshima
Michael Klooss
Yashvanth Kondi
Brian Koziel
Hugo Krawczyk
Mukul Kulkarni
Nishant Kumar
Pèter Kutas
Fabien Laguillaumie
Qiqi Lai
Russel Lai
Anja Lehmann
Chengyu Lin
Xi Lin
Yanyan Liu
Chen-Da Liu-Zhang
George Lu
Steve Lu
Yun Lu
Zhenliang Lu
Fermi Ma
Shunli Ma
Gilles Macario-Rat
Christian Majenz
Nathan Manohar
Ange Martinelli
Simon-Philipp Merz
Romy Minko
Dustin Moody

Hiraku Morita
Michael Naehrig
Anderson Nascimento
Khoa Nguyen
Ngoc Khanh Nguyen
Anca Nitulescu
Martha Hovd Norberg
Hiroshi Onuki
Michele Orr
Jiaxin Pan
Bo Pang
Louiza Papachristodoulou
Sikhar Patranabis
Geovandro Pereira
Ray Perlner
Federico Pintore
Bernardo Portela
Youming Qiao
Tian Qiu
Willy Quach
Srinivasan Raghuraman
Divya Ravi
Lo Robert
Angela Robinson
Miruna Rosca
Paul Rösler
Yusuke Sakai
Dimitris Sakavalas
Peter Scholl
Jacob Schuldt
Rebecca Schwerdt
Toon Segers
Gregor Seiler
Yannick Seurin
Akash Shah
Sina Shiehian
Luisa Siniscalchi
Daniel Smith-Tone

Yongha Son
Yongsoo Song
Florian Speelman
Martijn Stam
Yiru Sun
Katsuyuki Takashima
Samuel Tap
Aravind Thyagarajan
Song Tian
Jacques Traoré
Yiannis Tselekounis
Bogdan Ursu
Prashant Vasudevan
Hendrik Waldner
Alexandre Wallet
Hailong Wang
Luping Wang
Yuyu Wang
Zhedong Wang
Charlotte Weitkämper
Weiqiang Wen
Benjamin Wesolowski
David Wu
Keita Xagawa
Tiancheng Xie
Anshu Yadav
Sophia Yakoubov
Shota Yamada
Takashi Yamakawa
Avishay Yanai
Kazuki Yoneyama
Aaram Yun
Thomas Zacharias
Mohammad Zaheri
Cong Zhang
Jiaheng Zhang
Kai Zhang
Yongjun Zhao

Lattices and Factoring
(Abstract of Invited Talk)

Léo Ducas

Cryptology Group, Centrum Wiskunde & Informatica, Amsterdam,
The Netherlands

Abstract. In this talk, I would like to re-popularize two dual ideas that relate Lattices and Factoring. Such a connection may appear surprising at first, but is only one logarithm away: after all, factoring is nothing more than a *multiplicative* knapsack problem, i.e. a subset product problem, where the weights are given by the set of small enough primes.

The first of the two ideas, we owe to Schnorr (1991) and to Adleman (1995). It consists in finding close or short vectors in a carefully crafted lattice, in the hope that they will provide so-called factoring relations. While this idea does not appear to lead to faster factoring algorithms, it remains fascinating and has in fact lead to other major results. Indeed, the Schnorr-Adleman lattice plays a key role in the proof by Ajtai (1998) of the NP-hardness of the shortest vector problem.

The second idea, due to Chor and Rivest (1988) shows a reverse connection: constructing the lattice this time using *discrete* logarithms, they instead solve the bounded distance decoding (BDD) problem through easy factoring instances. Revisiting their idea, Pierrot and I (2018) showed that this was a quite close to an optimal construction for solving BDD in polynomial time. It was in fact the best known such construction until some recent work by Peikert and Mook (2020).

I wish to conclude with an invitation to explore the cryptographic potential of other lattices than the random q-ary lattices—the lattices underlying the Learning with Error problem (LWE) and the Short Integer Solution problem (SIS). While SIS and LWE have shown to be very convenient for constructing the most advanced schemes and protocols, I believe that more general lattices have a yet untapped potential for cryptography.

Contents – Part II

Cryptographic Protocols

Attacks and Cryptanalysis

Contents – Part I

Cryptographic Primitives and Schemes

More Efficient Digital Signatures with Tight Multi-user Security

Denis Diemert$^{(\boxtimes)}$, Kai Gellert, Tibor Jager, and Lin Lyu

Bergische Universität Wuppertal, Wuppertal, Germany
{denis.diemert,kai.gellert,tibor.jager,lin.lyu}@uni-wuppertal.de

Abstract. We construct the currently most efficient signature schemes with tight *multi-user* security against *adaptive* corruptions. It is the first *generic* construction of such schemes, based on lossy identification schemes (Abdalla et al.; JoC 2016), and the first to achieve *strong* existential unforgeability. It also has significantly more compact signatures than the previously most efficient construction by Gjøsteen and Jager (CRYPTO 2018). When instantiated based on the decisional Diffie–Hellman assumption, a signature consists of only three exponents.

We propose a new variant of the generic construction of signatures from *sequential OR-proofs* by Abe, Ohkubo, and Suzuki (ASIACRYPT 2002) and Fischlin, Harasser, and Janson (EUROCRYPT 2020). In comparison to Fischlin et al., who focus on constructing signatures in the non-programmable random oracle model (NPROM), we aim to achieve tight security against adaptive corruptions, maximize efficiency, and to directly achieve *strong* existential unforgeability (also in the NPROM). This yields a slightly different construction and we use slightly different and additional properties of the lossy identification scheme.

Signatures with tight multi-user security against adaptive corruptions are a commonly-used standard building block for tightly-secure authenticated key exchange protocols. We also show how our construction improves the efficiency of all existing tightly-secure AKE protocols.

1 Introduction

The commonly accepted standard security goal for digital signatures is *existential unforgeability under adaptive chosen message attacks* (EUF-CMA). This security model considers a *single-user* setting, in the sense that the adversary has access to a single public key and its goal is to forge a signature with respect to this key. A stronger security notion is EUF-CMA-security in the *multi-user* setting with *adaptive corruptions* (MU-EUF-CMA^{corr}). In this security model, the adversary has access to multiple public keys, and it is allowed to adaptively *corrupt* certain users, and thus obtain their secret keys. The goal of the adversary is to forge a signature with respect to the public key of an *uncorrupted* user.

Supported by the European Research Council (ERC) under the European Union's Horizon 2020 research and innovation programme, grant agreement 802823.

© International Association for Cryptologic Research 2021
J. A. Garay (Ed.): PKC 2021, LNCS 12711, pp. 1–31, 2021.
https://doi.org/10.1007/978-3-030-75248-4_1

A straightforward argument, which essentially guesses the user for which the adversary creates a forgery at the beginning of the security experiment, shows that EUF-CMA security implies MU-EUF-CMA^{corr} security. However, this guessing incurs a linear security loss in the number of users, and thus cannot achieve *tight* MU-EUF-CMA^{corr} security.

The question how tightly MU-EUF-CMA^{corr}-secure signatures can be constructed, and how efficient these constructions can be, is interesting for different reasons. Most importantly, MU-EUF-CMA^{corr} security seems to reflect the security requirements of many applications that use digital signatures as building blocks more directly than EUF-CMA security. This holds in particular for many constructions of authenticated key exchange protocols (AKE) that use signing keys as long-term keys to authenticate protocol messages. Standard AKE security models, such as the well-known Bellare–Rogaway [8] or the Canetti–Krawczyk [10] model and their countless variants and refinements, allow for adaptive corruption of users, which then translates to adaptive corruptions of secret keys. Therefore Bader et al. [5] introduced the notion of MU-EUF-CMA^{corr} as a building block to construct the first tightly-secure AKE protocol. This security model was subsequently used to construct more efficient tightly-secure AKE protocols [23,28,34], or to prove tight security of real-world protocols [14,15]. Note that tight security is particularly interesting for AKE, due to the pervasive and large-scale use of such protocols in practice (e.g., the TLS Handshake is an AKE protocol). Furthermore, we consider the goal of understanding if, how, and how efficiently strong security notions for digital signatures such as MU-EUF-CMA^{corr} can be achieved with tight security proofs also as a general and foundational research question in cryptography.

The Difficulty of Constructing Tightly MU-EUF-CMA^{corr}-*Secure Signatures.* The already mentioned straightforward reduction showing that EUF-CMA security implies MU-EUF-CMA^{corr} security guesses the user for which the adversary creates a forgery. Note that this user must not be corrupted by a successful adversary. Hence, the reduction can define this user's public key as the public key obtained from the EUF-CMA experiment. The keys of all users are generated by the reduction itself, such that it knows all corresponding secret keys. On the one hand, this enables the reduction to respond to all corruption queries made by the adversary, provided that it has guessed correctly. On the other hand, this makes the reduction lossy, since it may fail if the reduction did not guess correctly.

A reduction proving MU-EUF-CMA^{corr} security *tightly* (under some complexity assumption) has to avoid such a guessing argument. However, note that this implies that the reduction must satisfy the following two properties simultaneously:

1. It has to know the secret keys of all users, in order to be able to respond to a corruption query for any user, without the need to guess uncorrupted users.
2. At the same time, the reduction has to be able to extract a solution to the underlying assumed-to-be-hard computational problem, while knowing the secret key of the corresponding instance of the signature scheme.

Since these two properties seem to contradict each other, one might think that tight MU-EUF-CMA^{corr} security is impossible to achieve. Indeed, one can even prove formally that MU-EUF-CMA^{corr} security is not tightly achievable [6] (under non-interactive assumptions[1]), however, this impossibility result holds only for signature schemes satisfying certain properties. While most schemes indeed satisfy these properties, and thus seem not able to achieve tight MU-EUF-CMA^{corr} security, there are some constructions that circumvent this impossibility result.

Known Constructions of Tightly MU-EUF-CMA^{corr}-*Secure Signatures.* To our best knowledge, there are only a few schemes with tight MU-EUF-CMA^{corr} security under non-interactive hardness assumptions (cf. Table 1). Bader et al. (BHJKL) [5] describe a scheme with constant security loss ("fully-tight"), but it uses the tree-based scheme from [27] as a building block and therefore has rather large signatures. The scheme is proven secure in the standard model, using pairings. Bader et al. also describe a second scheme with constant-size signatures, which is also based on pairings and in the standard model, but which has a linear security loss in the security parameter ("almost-tight") and has linear-sized public keys. The currently most efficient tightly MU-EUF-CMA^{corr}-secure scheme is due to Gjøsteen and Jager (GJ) [23]. It has constant-size signatures and keys, as well as a constant security loss, in the random oracle model. The security proof requires "programming" of the random oracle in the sense of [19].

Strong Existential Unforgeability. Currently there exists no signature scheme with tight multi-user security under adaptive corruptions that achieves *strong* existential unforgeability. Here "strong" unforgeability refers to a security model where the adversary is considered to successfully break the security of a signature scheme, even if it outputs a *new* signature for a message for which it has already received a signature in the security experiment. Hence, strong unforgeability essentially guarantees that signatures additionally are "non-malleable", in the sense that an adversary is not able to efficiently derive a new valid signature σ^* for a message m when it is already given another valid signature σ for m, where $\sigma \neq \sigma^*$.

Strong unforgeability is particularly useful for the construction of authenticated key exchange protocols where partnering is defined over *"matching conversations"*, as introduced by Bellare and Rogaway [8]. Intuitively, matching conversations formalize "authentication" for AKE protocols, by requiring that a communicating party must "accept" a protocol session (and thus derive a key for use in a higher-layer application protocol) only if there exists a unique partner oracle to which it has a matching conversation, that is, which has sent and received exactly the same sequence of messages that the accepting oracle has received and sent.

Consider for instance the "signed Diffie–Hellman" AKE protocol. Standard existential unforgeability of the signature scheme is not sufficient to achieve security in the sense of matching conversations, because this security notion does

---

[1] One can always prove tight MU-EUF-CMA^{corr} security under the interactive assumption that the scheme is MU-EUF-CMA^{corr} secure.

Table 1. Comparison of existing tightly-secure signature schemes in the multi-user setting with adaptive corruptions. "BHJKL 1" refers to the generic construction from [5] instantiated with the scheme from [27], "BHJKL 2" is the new scheme constructed in [5]. $|\sigma|$ indicates the size of a signature and $|pk|$ the size of public keys, where $|\mathbb{G}|$ is the size of an element of the underlying group $\mathbb{G}$, $|q|$ is the size of the binary representation of an integer in the discrete interval $[0, q-1]$, where q is order of $\mathbb{G}$, and λ is the security parameter. The column "Setting" indicates whether pairings/the Programmable Random Oracle (PRO) model/the Non-Programmable Random Oracle (NPRO) model is used. The column "sEUF" refers to whether the scheme is proven *strongly* existentially unforgeable.

Scheme	$|\sigma|$	$|pk|$	Loss	Assumption	Setting	sEUF
BHJKL 1 [5,27]	$\mathcal{O}(\lambda)|\mathbb{G}|$	$\mathcal{O}(1)|\mathbb{G}|$	$\mathcal{O}(1)$	DLIN	Pairings	–
BHJKL 2 [5]	$3|\mathbb{G}|$	$\mathcal{O}(\lambda)|\mathbb{G}|$	$\mathcal{O}(\lambda)$	SXDH	Pairings	–
GJ [23]	$2|\mathbb{G}| + 2\lambda + 4|q|$	$2|\mathbb{G}|$	$\mathcal{O}(1)$	DDH	PRO	–
Ours	$3|q|$	$4|\mathbb{G}|$	$\mathcal{O}(1)$	Lossy ID	NPRO	✓

not guarantee that signatures are non-malleable. Hence, an adversary might, for instance, be able to efficiently re-randomize probabilistic signatures, and thus always be able to break matching conversations efficiently. This is a commonly overlooked mistake in many security proofs for AKE protocols [33]. Therefore Bader et al. [5] need to construct a more complex protocol that additionally requires strongly-unforgeable one-time signatures to achieve security in the sense of matching conversations. Gjøsteen and Jager [23] had to rely on the weaker partnering notion defined by Li and Schäge [33] in order to deal with potential malleability of signatures.

Hence, strongly-unforgeable digital signatures are particularly desirable in the context of AKE protocols, in order to achieve the strong notion of "matching conversation" security from [8].

Our Contributions. We construct strongly MU-EUF-CMA^{corr}-secure digital signature schemes, based on *lossy identification schemes* as defined by Abdalla et al. [2,3] and *sequential OR-proofs* as considered by Abe et al. [4] and Fischlin et al. [18]. This construction provides the following properties:

- It is the first *generic* construction of MU-EUF-CMA^{corr}-secure digital signatures, which can be instantiated from any concrete hardness assumption that gives rise to suitable lossy identification schemes. This includes instantiations from the decisional Diffie–Hellman (DDH) assumption, and the ϕ-Hiding assumption.
- It is the first construction of MU-EUF-CMA^{corr}-secure digital signatures that achieves *strong* existential unforgeability. Here we use "uniqueness" of the lossy identification scheme in the sense of [2,3].
- When instantiated under the DDH assumption, a signature consists of only three elements of $\mathbb{Z}_q$, where q is the order of the underlying algebraic group.

For comparison, Schnorr signatures [36] and ECDSA [16], for instance, have signatures consisting of two elements of $\mathbb{Z}_q$, but do not enjoy tight security proofs (not even in the single-user setting) [17,20–22,35,37]. In case of Schnorr signatures [36], security can be based on the weaker discrete logarithm assumption, though. Katz-Wang signatures [29] also consist of two $\mathbb{Z}_q$-elements and have tight security in the single-user setting, but not in the multi-user setting with adaptive corruptions.

- Similar to the work by Fischlin et al. [18], the proof does not rely on *programming* a random oracle, but holds in the *non-programmable* random oracle model [19]. This yields the first efficient and tightly multi-user secure signature scheme that does not require a programmable random oracle.

Our construction is almost identical to the construction based on sequential OR-proofs (as opposed to "parallel" OR-proofs in the sense of [13]), which was originally described by Abe et al. [4]. Fischlin, Harasser, and Janson [18] formally analyzed this construction and showed that it implies EUF-CMA-secure digital signatures based on lossy identification schemes. Their main focus is to achieve security in the non-programmable random oracle model [19], since the classical construction of signatures from lossy identification schemes [2,3] requires a programmable random oracle.

We observe that this approach also gives rise to tightly-secure signatures in a multi-user model with adaptive corruptions, by slightly modifying the construction. Due to the fact that the reduction is always in possession of a correctly distributed secret key for all users, it can both (i) respond to singing-queries and (ii) respond to corruption-queries without the need to guess in the MU-EUF-CMA^{corr} security experiment.

Also, our security proof is based on slightly different and additional properties of the lossy identification scheme. We use that a sequential OR-proof is *perfectly* witness indistinguishable when both instances of the lossy identification scheme are in non-lossy mode. This enables us to argue that the adversary receives no information about the random bit b chosen by the key generation algorithm of one user, such that the probability that the adversary creates a forgery with respect to sk_{1-b} is $1/2$. This enables us then to construct a distinguisher for the lossy identification scheme with only constant security loss.

Another difference to the proof by Fischlin et al. [18] is that we directly achieve *strong* unforgeability by leveraging *uniqueness* of lossy identification schemes, as defined by Abdalla et al. [2,3]. Also, their construction does not yet leverage "commitment-recoverability" of a lossy identification scheme, such that their DDH-based instantiation consists of four elements of $\mathbb{Z}_q$.

In particular, Table 2 shows that our scheme does not only improve the overall performance of all the presented protocols, but it also enables the protocols by GJ and LLGW to catch up to the communication complexity of JKRS. This means that when instantiated with our signature scheme, the constructions by GJ, LLGW, and JKRS achieve the same communication complexity. This observation suggests that especially constructions that exchange two or more signatures will benefit from an instantiation with our new signature scheme.

Table 2. Comparison of existing tightly-secure AKE protocols when instantiated with parameters for "128-bit security" (i.e., $\lambda = 128$). The columns **Comm.** count the values exchanged during execution of the protocol with an abstract signature scheme, when instantiated with the GJ signature scheme [23], and when instantiated with our DDH-based signature scheme respectively. $\mathbb{G}$ is the number of group elements, H the number of hashes or MACs, Sig. the number of signatures, $\mathbb{Z}_q$ the number of exponents, and "other" the amount of additional data in bits (nonces are 2λ-bit strings). The columns **Bytes** contain the total amount of data in bytes when instantiating $\mathbb{G}$ with the NIST P256 curve.

Protocol	Comm. $(\mathbb{G}, H, \text{Sig.}, \text{other})$	With GJ Sigs.		With our scheme	
		Comm. $(\mathbb{G}, H, \mathbb{Z}_q, \text{other})$	Bytes	Comm. $(\mathbb{G}, H, \mathbb{Z}_q, \text{other})$	Bytes
GJ [23]	$(2, 1, 2, 0)$	$(6, 1, 8, 4\lambda)$	544	$(2, 1, 6, 0)$	288
TLS 1.3 [14,15]	$(2, 2, 2, 512)$	$(6, 2, 8, 4\lambda + 512)$	640	$(2, 2, 6, 512)$	384
SIGMA-I [14,32]	$(2, 2, 2, 512)$	$(6, 2, 8, 4\lambda + 512)$	640	$(2, 2, 6, 512)$	384
LLGW [34]	$(3, 0, 2, 0)$	$(7, 0, 8, 4\lambda)$	544	$(3, 0, 6, 0)$	288
JKRS [28]	$(5, 1, 1, 0)$	$(7, 1, 4, 2\lambda)$	416	$(5, 1, 3, 0)$	288

Applications to Tightly-Secure AKE Protocols. Since tightly MU-EUF-CMA^{corr}-secure signatures are commonly used to construct tightly-secure AKE protocols, let us consider the impact of our scheme on the performance of known protocols. Since the performance gain obtained by the signature scheme has already been discussed, we focus here only on the *communication complexity* of the considered protocols, that is, the number of bits exchanged when running the protocol. Table 2 shows the impact of our signature schemes on known AKE protocols with tight security proofs. We compare instantiations with the signature scheme by Gjøsteen and Jager [23] to instantiations with our signature scheme. Note that the Gjøsteen–Jager scheme is also based on the DDH assumption, and so are the considered protocols (except for TLS 1.3 and Sigma, which are based on the *strong* Diffie–Hellman assumption).

We omit the protocol by Bader et al. [5], since it is more of a standard-model feasibility result, which does not aim for maximal efficiency. Their protocol has a communication complexity of $O(\lambda)$ group elements when instantiated with constant security loss, and 14 group elements plus 4 exponents when instantiated with their "almost-tight" signature scheme with a security loss of $O(\lambda)$. Cohn-Gordon et al. [12] construct a protocol which entirely avoids signatures and aims to achieve tightness, however, they achieve only a *linear* security loss and also show that this is optimal for the class of protocols they consider.

Outline. The remainder of this work is organized as follows. In the next section, we introduce standard definitions for signatures and their security. In Sect. 3, we recall lossy identification schemes and their security properties. The generic construction of our signature scheme from any lossy identification scheme alongside a security proof is presented in Sect. 4. We conclude our work with a detailed discussion on possible instantiations of our scheme in Sect. 5.

2   Preliminaries

For strings a and b, we denote the concatenation of these strings by $a \parallel b$. For an integer $n \in \mathbb{N}$, we denote the set of integers ranging from 1 to n by $[n] := \{1,\ldots,n\}$. For a set $X = \{x_1, x_2, \ldots\}$, we use $(v_i)_{i \in X}$ as a shorthand for the tuple $(v_{x_1}, v_{x_2}, \ldots)$. We denote the operation of assigning a value y to a variable x by $x := y$. If S is a finite set, we denote by $x \xleftarrow{\$} S$ the operation of sampling a value uniformly at random from set S and assigning it to variable x.

2.1   Digital Signatures

We recall the standard definition of a *digital signature scheme* by Goldwasser, Micali, and Rivest [24] and its standard security notion.

Definition 1. *A* digital signature scheme *is a triple of algorithms* Sig = (Gen, Sign, Vrfy) *such that*

1. Gen *is the randomized key generation algorithm generating a public (verification) key pk and a secret (signing) key sk.*
2. Sign(sk, m) *is the randomized signing algorithm outputting a signature σ on input of a message $m \in M$ and a signing key sk.*
3. Vrfy(pk, m, σ) *is the deterministic verification algorithm outputting either 0 or 1.*

We say that a digital signature scheme Sig *is ρ-correct if for $(pk, sk) \xleftarrow{\$}$ Gen, and any $m \in M$, it holds that*

$$\Pr[\mathsf{Vrfy}\,(pk, m, \mathsf{Sign}(sk, m)) = 1] \geq \rho.$$

And we say Sig *is* perfectly correct *if it is 1-correct.*

Definition 2. *Let* Sig = (Gen, Sign, Vrfy) *be a signature scheme and let $N \in \mathbb{N}$ be the number of users. Consider the following experiment* $\mathsf{Exp}_{\mathsf{Sig},N}^{\mathsf{MU\text{-}sEUF\text{-}CMA}^{\mathsf{corr}}}(\mathcal{A})$ *played between a challenger and an adversary $\mathcal{A}$:*

1. *The challenger generates a key pair $(pk^{(i)}, sk^{(i)}) \xleftarrow{\$}$ Gen for each user $i \in [N]$, initializes the set of corrupted users $\mathcal{Q}^{\mathsf{corr}} := \emptyset$, and N sets of chosen-message queries $\mathcal{Q}^{(1)}, \ldots, \mathcal{Q}^{(N)} := \emptyset$ issued by the adversary. Subsequently, it hands $(pk^{(i)})_{i \in [N]}$ to $\mathcal{A}$ as input.*
2. *The adversary may adaptively issue signature queries $(i, m) \in [N] \times M$ to the challenger. The challenger replies to each query with a signature $\sigma \xleftarrow{\$}$ Sign$(sk^{(i)}, m)$ and adds (m, σ) to $\mathcal{Q}^{(i)}$. Moreover, the adversary may adaptively issue corrupt queries Corrupt(i) for some $i \in [N]$. In this case, the challenger adds i to $\mathcal{Q}^{\mathsf{corr}}$ and forwards $sk^{(i)}$ to the adversary. We call each user $i \in \mathcal{Q}^{\mathsf{corr}}$ corrupted.*

3. *Finally, the adversary outputs a tuple (i^*, m^*, σ^*). The challenger checks whether $\mathsf{Vrfy}(pk^{(i^*)}, m^*, \sigma^*) = 1$, $i^* \notin \mathcal{Q}^{\mathsf{corr}}$ and $(m^*, \sigma^*) \notin \mathcal{Q}^{(i^*)}$. If all of these conditions hold, the experiment outputs 1 and 0 otherwise.*

We denote the advantage of an adversary $\mathcal{A}$ in breaking the strong existential unforgeability under an adaptive chosen-message attack in the multi-user setting with adaptive corruptions ($\mathsf{MU\text{-}sEUF\text{-}CMA}^{\mathsf{corr}}$) for Sig by

$$\mathsf{Adv}_{\mathsf{Sig},N}^{\mathsf{MU\text{-}sEUF\text{-}CMA}^{\mathsf{corr}}}(\mathcal{A}) := \Pr\left[\mathsf{Exp}_{\mathsf{Sig},N}^{\mathsf{MU\text{-}sEUF\text{-}CMA}^{\mathsf{corr}}}(\mathcal{A}) = 1\right]$$

where $\mathsf{Exp}_{\mathsf{Sig},N}^{\mathsf{MU\text{-}sEUF\text{-}CMA}^{\mathsf{corr}}}(\mathcal{A})$ is as defined as above.

3   Lossy Identification Schemes

We adapt the definitions of a *lossy identification scheme* [2,3,30].

Definition 3. *A* lossy identification scheme *is a five-tuple* $\mathsf{LID} = (\mathsf{LID.Gen}, \mathsf{LID.LossyGen}, \mathsf{LID.Prove}, \mathsf{LID.Vrfy}, \mathsf{LID.Sim})$ *of probabilistic polynomial-time algorithms with the following properties.*

- *$\mathsf{LID.Gen}$ is the normal key generation algorithm. It outputs a public verification key pk and a secret key sk.*
- *$\mathsf{LID.LossyGen}$ is a lossy key generation algorithm that takes the security parameter and outputs a lossy verification key pk.*
- *$\mathsf{LID.Prove}$ is the prover algorithm that is split into two algorithms:*
  - *$(\mathsf{cmt}, \mathsf{st}) \xleftarrow{\$} \mathsf{LID.Prove}_1(sk)$ is a probabilistic algorithm that takes as input the secret key and returns a commitment cmt and a state st.*
  - *$\mathsf{resp} \leftarrow \mathsf{LID.Prove}_2(sk, \mathsf{cmt}, \mathsf{ch}, \mathsf{st})$ is a deterministic algorithm[2] that takes as input a secret key sk, a commitment cmt, a challenge ch, a state st, and returns a response resp.*
- *$\mathsf{LID.Vrfy}(pk, \mathsf{cmt}, \mathsf{ch}, \mathsf{resp})$ is a deterministic verification algorithm that takes a public key, and a conversation transcript (i.e., a commitment, a challenge, and a response) as input and outputs a bit, where 1 indicates that the proof is "accepted" and 0 that it is "rejected".*
- *$\mathsf{cmt} \leftarrow \mathsf{LID.Sim}(pk, \mathsf{ch}, \mathsf{resp})$ is a deterministic algorithm that takes a public key pk, a challenge ch, and a response resp as inputs and outputs a commitment cmt.*

We assume that a public key pk implicitly defines two sets, the set of challenges CSet and the set of responses RSet.

---

[2] All known instantiations of lossy identification schemes have a deterministic $\mathsf{LID.Prove}_2$ algorithm. However, if a new instantiation requires randomness, then it can be "forwarded" from $\mathsf{LID.Prove}_1$ in the state variable st. Therefore the requirement that $\mathsf{LID.Prove}_2$ is deterministic is without loss of generality, and only made to simplify our security analysis.

Definition 4. *Let* LID $=$ (LID.Gen, LID.LossyGen, LID.Prove, LID.Vrfy, LID.Sim) *be defined as above. We call* LID *lossy when the following properties hold:*

- Completeness of normal keys. *We call* LID ρ-complete, *if*

$$
\Pr \left[\text{LID.Vrfy}(pk, \text{cmt}, \text{ch}, \text{resp}) = 1 : \begin{array}{l} (pk, sk) \xleftarrow{\$} \text{LID.Gen} \\ (\text{cmt}, \text{st}) \xleftarrow{\$} \text{LID.Prove}_1(sk) \\ \text{ch} \xleftarrow{\$} \text{CSet} \\ \text{resp} \xleftarrow{\$} \text{LID.Prove}_2(sk, \text{cmt}, \text{ch}, \text{st}) \end{array} \right] \geq \rho.
$$

We call LID *perfectly-complete, if it is 1-complete.*
- Simulatability of transcripts. *We call* LID ε_s-simulatable if for $(pk, sk) \xleftarrow{\$}$ LID.Gen, $(\text{ch}, \text{resp}) \xleftarrow{\$}$ CSet $\times$ RSet, *the distribution of the transcript* $(\text{cmt}, \text{ch}, \text{resp})$ *where* $\text{cmt} \leftarrow$ LID.Sim$(pk, \text{ch}, \text{resp})$ *is statistically indistinguishable from honestly generated transcript (with a statistical distance up to ε_s) and we have that* LID.Vrfy$(pk, \text{cmt}, \text{ch}, \text{resp}) = 1$. *If $\varepsilon_s = 0$, we call* LID *perfectly simulatable.*
  Note that this simulatability property is different from the original definition in [2] where the simulator simulates the whole transcript.
- Indistinguishability of keys. *This definition is a generalization of the standard key indistinguishability definition of a lossy identification scheme extended to N instances. For any integer $N > 0$, we define the advantage of an adversary $\mathcal{A}$ breaking the N-key-indistinguishability of* LID *as* $\text{Adv}_{\text{LID},N}^{\text{MU-IND-KEY}}(\mathcal{A}) :=$

$$
\left| \Pr\left[\mathcal{A}(pk^{(1)}, \cdots, pk^{(N)}) = 1 \right] - \Pr\left[\mathcal{A}(pk'^{(1)}, \cdots, pk'^{(N)}) = 1 \right] \right|,
$$

where $(pk^{(i)}, sk^{(i)}) \xleftarrow{\$}$ LID.Gen *and* $pk'^{(i)} \xleftarrow{\$}$ LID.LossyGen *for all* $i \in [N]$.
- Lossiness. *Consider the following security experiment* $\text{Exp}_{\text{LID}}^{\text{IMPERSONATE}}(\mathcal{A})$ *described below, played between a challenger and an adversary $\mathcal{A}$:*
  1. *The challenger generates a lossy verification key* $pk \xleftarrow{\$}$ LID.LossyGen *and sends it to the adversary $\mathcal{A}$.*
  2. *The adversary $\mathcal{A}$ may now compute a commitment* cmt *and send it to the challenger. The challenger responds with a random challenge* $\text{ch} \xleftarrow{\$}$ CSet.
  3. *Eventually, the adversary $\mathcal{A}$ outputs a response* resp. *The challenger outputs* LID.Vrfy$(pk, \text{cmt}, \text{ch}, \text{resp})$.

  We call LID ε_ℓ-lossy *if no computationally unrestricted adversary $\mathcal{A}$ wins the above security game with probability*

$$
\Pr[\text{Exp}_{\text{LID}}^{\text{IMPERSONATE}}(\mathcal{A}) = 1] \geq \varepsilon_\ell.
$$

Below are two more properties for lossy identification schemes defined in [2,3].

Definition 5. *Let* $pk \xleftarrow{\$}$ LID.LossyGen *be a lossy public key and let* $(\text{cmt}, \text{ch}, \text{resp})$ *be any transcript which makes* LID.Vrfy$(pk, \text{cmt}, \text{ch}, \text{resp}) = 1$. *We say* LID *is ε_u-unique with respect to lossy keys if the probability that there exists* $\text{resp}' \neq \text{resp}$ *such that* LID.Vrfy$(pk, \text{cmt}, \text{ch}, \text{resp}') = 1$ *is at most ε_u, and perfectly unique with respect to lossy keys if $\varepsilon_u = 0$.*

Definition 6. *Let $(pk, sk) \xleftarrow{\$} \mathsf{LID.Gen}$ be any honestly generated key pair and $\mathcal{C}(sk) := \{\mathsf{LID.Prove}_1(sk)\}$ be the set of commitments associated to sk. We define the* min-entropy with respect to LID *as*

$$\alpha := -\log_2 \left(\max_{sk, \mathsf{cmt} \in \mathcal{C}(sk)} \Pr\left[\mathsf{LID.Prove}_1(sk) = \mathsf{cmt}\right] \right)$$

Below is another property for lossy identification schemes defined in [30].

Definition 7. *A lossy identification scheme* LID *is* commitment-recoverable *if the algorithm* $\mathsf{LID.Vrfy}(pk, \mathsf{cmt}, \mathsf{ch}, \mathsf{resp})$ *first recomputes a commitment* $\mathsf{cmt}' = \mathsf{LID.Sim}(pk, \mathsf{ch}, \mathsf{resp})$ *and then outputs 1 if and only if* $\mathsf{cmt}' = \mathsf{cmt}$.

Below, we define a new property for lossy identification schemes which requires that the LID.Sim algorithm is injective with respect to the input challenge.

Definition 8. *A lossy identification scheme* LID *has an* injective simulator *if for any* $(pk, sk) \xleftarrow{\$} \mathsf{LID.Gen}$, *any response* $\mathsf{resp} \in \mathsf{RSet}$, *any* $\mathsf{ch} \neq \mathsf{ch}'$, *it holds that* $\mathsf{LID.Sim}(pk, \mathsf{ch}, \mathsf{resp}) \neq \mathsf{LID.Sim}(pk, \mathsf{ch}', \mathsf{resp})$.

In Sect. 5 we give a detailed discussion which of the existing lossy identification schemes [1–3, 26, 29] satisfy which of the above properties.

4   Construction and Security of Our Signature Scheme

Let $\mathsf{LID} = (\mathsf{LID.Gen}, \mathsf{LID.LossyGen}, \mathsf{LID.Prove}, \mathsf{LID.Vrfy}, \mathsf{LID.Sim})$ be a lossy identification scheme and let $\mathsf{H} \colon \{0,1\}^* \to \mathsf{CSet}$ be a hash function mapping finite-length bitstrings to the set of challenges CSet. Consider the following digital signature scheme $\mathsf{Sig} = (\mathsf{Gen}, \mathsf{Sign}, \mathsf{Vrfy})$.

Key generation. The key generation algorithm Gen samples a bit $b \xleftarrow{\$} \{0,1\}$ and two independent key pairs $(pk_0, sk_0) \xleftarrow{\$} \mathsf{LID.Gen}$ and $(pk_1, sk_1) \xleftarrow{\$} \mathsf{LID.Gen}$. Then it sets

$$pk := (pk_0, pk_1) \qquad \text{and} \qquad sk := (b, sk_b)$$

Note that the secret key consists only of sk_b and the other key sk_{1-b} is discarded.

Signing. The signing algorithm Sign takes as input $sk = (b, sk_b)$ and a message $m \in \{0,1\}^*$. Then it proceeds as follows.

1. It first computes $(\mathsf{cmt}_b, \mathsf{st}_b) \xleftarrow{\$} \mathsf{LID.Prove}_1(sk_b)$ and sets

$$\mathsf{ch}_{1-b} := \mathsf{H}(m, \mathsf{cmt}_b)$$

Note that the ch_{1-b} is derived from cmt_b and m.

2. It generates the simulated transcript by choosing $\mathsf{resp}_{1-b} \xleftarrow{\$} \mathsf{RSet}$ and

$$\mathsf{cmt}_{1-b} := \mathsf{LID.Sim}(pk_{1-b}, \mathsf{ch}_{1-b}, \mathsf{resp}_{1-b})$$

using the simulator.

3. Finally, it computes

$$\mathsf{ch}_b := \mathsf{H}(m, \mathsf{cmt}_{1-b}) \quad \text{and} \quad \mathsf{resp}_b := \mathsf{LID.Prove}_2(sk_b, \mathsf{ch}_b, \mathsf{cmt}_b, \mathsf{st}_b)$$

and outputs the signature $\sigma := (\mathsf{ch}_0, \mathsf{resp}_0, \mathsf{resp}_1)$. Note that ch_1 is not included in the signature.

Verification. The verification algorithm Vrfy takes as input a public key $pk = (pk_0, pk_1)$, a message $m \in \{0,1\}^*$, and a signature $\sigma = (\mathsf{ch}_0, \mathsf{resp}_0, \mathsf{resp}_1)$. It first recovers

$$\mathsf{cmt}_0 := \mathsf{LID.Sim}(pk_0, \mathsf{ch}_0, \mathsf{resp}_0)$$

From cmt_0 it can then compute

$$\mathsf{ch}_1 := \mathsf{H}(m, \mathsf{cmt}_0)$$

and then recover

$$\mathsf{cmt}_1 := \mathsf{LID.Sim}(pk_1, \mathsf{ch}_1, \mathsf{resp}_1)$$

Finally, the reduction outputs 1 if and only if $\mathsf{ch}_0 = \mathsf{H}(m, \mathsf{cmt}_1)$.

One can easily verify that the above construction Sig is perfectly correct if LID is commitment-recoverable and perfectly complete. Also, note that, even though algorithm $\mathsf{LID.Vrfy}$ is not used in algorithm Vrfy, we have that $\mathsf{Vrfy}(pk, m, \sigma) = 1$ implies that $\mathsf{LID.Vrfy}(pk_j, \mathsf{cmt}_j, \mathsf{ch}_j, \mathsf{resp}_j) = 1$ for both $j \in \{0,1\}$. This is directly implied by our definition of the lossy identification scheme's simulatability of transcripts.

Theorem 9. *If* H *is modeled as a random oracle and* LID *is commitment-recoverable, perfectly simulatable,* ε_ℓ*-lossy,* ε_u*-unique, has* α*-bit min-entropy and has an injective simulator, then for each adversary* $\mathcal{A}$ *with running time* $t_{\mathcal{A}}$ *breaking the* MU-sEUF-CMA^{corr} *security of the above signature scheme* Sig, *we can construct an adversary* $\mathcal{B}$ *with running time* $t_{\mathcal{B}} \approx t_{\mathcal{A}}$ *such that*

$$\mathsf{Adv}_{\mathsf{Sig},N}^{\mathsf{MU\text{-}sEUF\text{-}CMA}^{\mathsf{corr}}}(\mathcal{A}) \leq 4 \cdot \mathsf{Adv}_{\mathsf{LID},N}^{\mathsf{MU\text{-}IND\text{-}KEY}}(\mathcal{B}) + \frac{2q_{\mathsf{S}}q_{\mathsf{H}}}{2^\alpha} + \frac{2}{|\mathsf{CSet}|} + 2\varepsilon_u + 2Nq_{\mathsf{H}}^2\varepsilon_\ell,$$

where q_{S} *is the number of signing queries and* q_{H} *is the number of hash queries.*

Proof. We prove Theorem 9 through a sequence of games. See Table 3 for an intuitive overview of our proof. In the sequel, let X_i denote the event that the experiment outputs 1 in Game i.

Game 0. This is the original security experiment $\mathsf{Exp}_{\mathsf{Sig},N}^{\mathsf{MU\text{-}sEUF\text{-}CMA}^{\mathsf{corr}}}(\mathcal{A})$. In this experiment, adversary $\mathcal{A}$ is provided with oracles Sign and $\mathsf{Corrupt}$ from the security experiment, as well as a hash oracle H since we are working in the random oracle model. In the following, it will be useful to specify the implementation of this game explicitly:

Table 3. Overview of the sequence of games used in the proof of Theorem 9.

Game #	Changes	Remark
0	–	The MU-sEUF-CMA^{corr} game
1	We rule out repeating commitments cmt	This ensures that every signing query makes fresh hash queries
2	We ensure the two hash queries in the final verification have been made before.	We will need this in Game 4
3	We exclude the case where $(\mathsf{cmt}_0^*, \mathsf{cmt}_1^*)$ is re-used from a signing query	The adversary does not use "implicit" knowledge of the secret bit $b^{(i^*)}$
4	The adversary can only win if hash query "$(1 - b^{(i^*)})$" is made first	$b^{(i^*)}$ is perfectly hidden, prepa-ration to achieve statistically small winning probability
5	We make all "$(1 - b^{(i)})$" public keys lossy	This game has statistically small winning probability for any adversary

- The game initializes the chosen-message sets $\mathcal{Q}^{(1)}, \ldots, \mathcal{Q}^{(N)} := \emptyset$, the set of corrupted users $\mathcal{Q}^{corr} := \emptyset$ and an implementation of the random oracle $\mathcal{L} := \emptyset$. It then runs the signature key generation algorithm Gen N times to get the key pair $(pk^{(i)}, sk^{(i)})$ for each $i \in [N]$. More precisely, the game samples a bit $b^{(i)} \xleftarrow{\$} \{0,1\}$ and two independent key pairs $(pk_0^{(i)}, sk_0^{(i)}) \xleftarrow{\$}$ LID.Gen and $(pk_1^{(i)}, sk_1^{(i)}) \xleftarrow{\$}$ LID.Gen. Then it sets $pk^{(i)} := (pk_0^{(i)}, pk_1^{(i)})$ and stores $(pk^{(i)}, b^{(i)}, sk_0^{(i)}, sk_1^{(i)})$. Finally, it runs adversary $\mathcal{A}$ with input $(pk^{(i)})_{i \in [N]}$. In the following proof, to simplify the notation, we will use $pk_b^{(i)}, pk_{1-b}^{(i)}, sk_b^{(i)}, sk_{1-b}^{(i)}$ to denote $pk_{b^{(i)}}^{(i)}, pk_{1-b^{(i)}}^{(i)}, sk_{b^{(i)}}^{(i)}, sk_{1-b^{(i)}}^{(i)}$ respectively.
- $H(x)$. When the adversary or the simulation of the experiment make a hash oracle query for some $x \in \{0,1\}^*$, the game checks whether $(x, y) \in \mathcal{L}$ for some $y \in \mathsf{CSet}$. If it does, the game returns y. Otherwise the game selects $y \xleftarrow{\$} \mathsf{CSet}$, logs (x, y) into set $\mathcal{L}$ and returns y.
- $\mathsf{Sign}(i, m)$. When the adversary queries the signing oracle with user i and message m, the game first sets $b := b^{(i)}$, then computes

$$(\mathsf{cmt}_b, \mathsf{st}_b) \xleftarrow{\$} \mathsf{LID.Prove}_1(sk_b^{(i)})$$

and sets $\mathsf{ch}_{1-b} := H(m, \mathsf{cmt}_b)$ by making a hash query. Then, the game chooses $\mathsf{resp}_{1-b} \xleftarrow{\$} \mathsf{RSet}$ and uses the simulator to compute $\mathsf{cmt}_{1-b} := \mathsf{LID.Sim}(pk_{1-b}^{(i)}, \mathsf{ch}_{1-b}, \mathsf{resp}_{1-b})$. Finally, the game queries hash oracle to get $\mathsf{ch}_b := H(m, \mathsf{cmt}_{1-b})$ and then uses $\mathsf{LID.Prove}_2$ to compute

$$\mathsf{resp}_b := \mathsf{LID.Prove}_2(sk_b^{(i)}, \mathsf{ch}_b, \mathsf{cmt}_b, \mathsf{st}_b).$$

The game outputs signature $\sigma := (\mathsf{ch}_0, \mathsf{resp}_0, \mathsf{resp}_1)$ to $\mathcal{A}$ and logs the pair (m, σ) in set $\mathcal{Q}^{(i)}$.

- Corrupt(i). When the adversary $\mathcal{A}$ queries the Corrupt oracle for the secret key of user i, the game returns $sk^{(i)} := (b^{(i)}, sk_b^{(i)})$ to the adversary and logs i in the set $\mathcal{Q}^{\mathsf{corr}}$.
- Finally, when adversary $\mathcal{A}$ outputs a forgery attempt (i^*, m^*, σ^*), the game outputs 1 if and only if $\mathsf{Vrfy}(pk^{(i^*)}, m^*, \sigma^*) = 1$, $i^* \notin \mathcal{Q}^{\mathsf{corr}}$, and $(m^*, \sigma^*) \notin \mathcal{Q}^{(i^*)}$ hold. More precisely, for $\sigma^* = (\mathsf{ch}_0^*, \mathsf{resp}_0^*, \mathsf{resp}_1^*)$, the game recovers $\mathsf{cmt}_0^* := \mathsf{LID.Sim}(pk_0^{(i^*)}, \mathsf{ch}_0^*, \mathsf{resp}_0^*)$ and queries the hash oracle to get $\mathsf{ch}_1^* := \mathsf{H}(m^*, \mathsf{cmt}_0^*)$. Then it recovers $\mathsf{cmt}_1^* := \mathsf{LID.Sim}(pk_1^{(i^*)}, \mathsf{ch}_1^*, \mathsf{resp}_1^*)$ and queries the hash oracle to get $\mathsf{ch}^* := \mathsf{H}(m^*, \mathsf{cmt}_1^*)$. Finally, the game outputs 1 if and only if $\mathsf{ch}_0^* = \mathsf{ch}^*$, $i^* \notin \mathcal{Q}^{\mathsf{corr}}$ and $(m^*, \sigma^*) \notin \mathcal{Q}^{(i^*)}$.

It is clear that $\Pr[X_0] = \mathsf{Adv}_{\mathsf{Sig},N}^{\mathsf{MU\text{-}sEUF\text{-}CMA}^{\mathsf{corr}}}(\mathcal{A})$.

Game 1. Game 1 is the same with Game 0 except with one change. Denote with cmtColl the event that there exists a signing query $\mathsf{Sign}(i, m)$ such that at least one of the two hash queries $\mathsf{H}(m, \mathsf{cmt}_{b^{(i)}})$ and $\mathsf{H}(m, \mathsf{cmt}_{1-b^{(i)}})$ made in this signing query has been made before.

Game 1 outputs 0 when cmtColl happens. In other words, X_1 happens if and only if $X_0 \wedge \neg\mathsf{cmtColl}$ happens. We can prove the following lemma.

Lemma 10.
$$\Pr[X_1] \geq \Pr[X_0] - \frac{2q_{\mathsf{S}}q_{\mathsf{H}}}{2^\alpha}$$

where q_{S} is the number of signing queries made by $\mathcal{A}$ and q_{H} is the number of hash queries made in Game 0.

Proof. To prove Lemma 10, we divide the event cmtColl into two subevents.

- There exists a signing query $\mathsf{Sign}(i, m)$ such that $\mathsf{H}(m, \mathsf{cmt}_{b^{(i)}})$ has been made before. If this happens, then $\mathsf{cmt}_{b^{(i)}}$ is the output of $\mathsf{LID.Prove}_1(sk^{(i)})$ for any signing query. Since LID has α-bit min-entropy (cf. Definition 6), the probability that this happens is at most $q_{\mathsf{S}}q_{\mathsf{H}}/2^\alpha$ by a union bound.
- There exists a signing query $\mathsf{Sign}(i, m)$ such that $\mathsf{H}(m, \mathsf{cmt}_{1-b^{(i)}})$ has been made before. Note that $\mathsf{cmt}_{1-b^{(i)}}$ is the output of

$$\mathsf{LID.Sim}(pk_{1-b}^{(i)}, \mathsf{ch}_{1-b^{(i)}}, \mathsf{resp}_{1-b^{(i)}})$$

where $\mathsf{ch}_{1-b^{(i)}} = \mathsf{H}(m, \mathsf{cmt}_{b^{(i)}})$. Since LID.Sim is deterministic, we know that $\mathsf{cmt}_{1-b^{(i)}}$ is determined by $pk_{1-b}^{(i)}, m, \mathsf{cmt}_{b^{(i)}}$ and $\mathsf{resp}_{1-b^{(i)}}$. Furthermore, since LID.Sim is injective with respect to challenges (cf. Definition 8), we know that the entropy of $\mathsf{cmt}_{1-b^{(i)}}$ in any fixed signing query is at least the entropy of $\mathsf{cmt}_{b^{(i)}}$ in that query. Thus, we obtain that the probability that this subevent happens is at most $q_{\mathsf{S}}q_{\mathsf{H}}/2^\alpha$.

Thus, we have that $\Pr[\mathsf{cmtColl}] \leq 2q_{\mathsf{S}}q_{\mathsf{H}}/2^\alpha$ and Lemma 10 follows.   □

Remark 11. Note that, from Game 1 on, the hash queries $H(m, cmt_{b(i)})$ and $H(m, cmt_{1-b(i)})$ are not made before any signing query $Sign(i, m)$ if the game finally outputs 1. This implies that each signing query uses independent and uniformly random $ch_{1-b(i)}$ and $ch_{b(i)}$, and they are not known to the adversary at that time.

Game 2. Game 2 differs from Game 1 only in the way the game checks the winning condition. More precisely, Game 1 issues two hash queries $H(m^*, cmt_0^*)$ and $H(m^*, cmt_1^*)$ to check the validity of a forgery attempt (i^*, m^*, σ^*). In the following, we call the former $H(m^*, cmt_0^*)$ a "0-query" and the latter $H(m^*, cmt_1^*)$ a "1-query". Let Both denote the event that both a 0-query and a 1-query have been made by the signing oracle or by the adversary before submitting the forgery attempt (i^*, m^*, σ^*).

Game 2 outputs 0 if event Both does *not* happen. In other words, X_2 happens if and only if $X_1 \wedge$ Both happens. We can prove the following lemma.

Lemma 12. $\Pr[X_2] \geq \Pr[X_1] - 2/|CSet|$.

Proof. We know that $\Pr[X_1] = \Pr[X_1 \wedge \neg Both] + \Pr[X_2]$. We will prove that $\Pr[X_1 \wedge \neg Both] \leq 2/|CSet|$ and the lemma follows. Note that

$$\Pr[X_1 \wedge \neg Both] \leq \Pr[X_1 \wedge 1\text{-query is never made}] + \Pr[X_1 \wedge 0\text{-query is never made}]$$

- $X_1 \wedge 1$-query is never made: Event X_1 implies that $Vrfy(pk^{(i^*)}, m^*, \sigma^*) = 1$. This further implies that the value ch_0^* (chosen by the adversary) equals the 1-query hash result $ch^* = H(m^*, cmt_1^*)$, which is a random element in CSet. Since the 1-query is never made at this time, the adversary has no knowledge about this value, which yields

$$\Pr[X_1 \wedge 1\text{-query is never made}] \leq \frac{1}{|CSet|}.$$

- $X_1 \wedge 0$-query is never made: The 0-query value $ch_1^* = H(m^*, cmt_0^*)$ is used to recover $cmt_1^* = LID.Sim(pk_1^{(i^*)}, ch_1^*, resp_1^*)$. Since the 0-query is not made at that time, the adversary has no knowledge about ch_1^* except that it is a random element in CSet. Together with the fact that algorithm LID.Sim is injective (cf. Definition 8), the adversary only knows that cmt_1^* is uniformly distributed over a set of size $|CSet|$. To make the verification pass, the adversary would need to select ch_0^* which equals to $H(m^*, cmt_1^*)$. However, there are $|CSet|$ possible values for cmt_1^* so that this can happen with probability at most $1/|CSet|$. Thus,

$$\Pr[X_1 \wedge 0\text{-query is never made}] \leq \frac{1}{|CSet|}.$$

Putting both together, we have $\Pr[X_1 \wedge \neg Both] \leq 2/|CSet|$. $\square$

Game 3. Game 3 is exactly the same as Game 2, except for one change. We denote by ImplicitUsage the event that the first 0-query and the first 1-query are made in a signing query $\mathsf{Sign}(i^*, m^*)$, and the pair $(\mathsf{cmt}_0^*, \mathsf{cmt}_1^*)$ equals to the pair $(\mathsf{cmt}_0, \mathsf{cmt}_1)$, which is generated in this signing query. Game 3 outputs 0 if event ImplicitUsage happens.

Hence, X_3 happens if and only if $X_2 \wedge \neg\mathsf{ImplicitUsage}$ happens. We prove the following lemma.

Lemma 13. *We can construct an adversary $\mathcal{B}$ with running time $t_{\mathcal{B}} \approx t_{\mathcal{A}}$ such that*

$$\Pr[X_3] \geq \Pr[X_2] - 2 \cdot \mathsf{Adv}_{\mathsf{LID},N}^{\mathsf{MU\text{-}IND\text{-}KEY}}(\mathcal{B}) - 2\varepsilon_u.$$

Remark 14. Note that this proof can be potentially simplified if we define the uniqueness property of LID with respect to normal public keys. However, this would introduce a non-standard LID property compared to the standard LID definition by Abdalla et al. [2,3].

Proof. We know that $\Pr[X_2] = \Pr[X_2 \wedge \mathsf{ImplicitUsage}] + \Pr[X_3]$. We will prove that $\Pr[X_2 \wedge \mathsf{ImplicitUsage}] \leq 2\mathsf{Adv}_{\mathsf{LID},N}^{\mathsf{MU\text{-}IND\text{-}KEY}}(\mathcal{B}) + 2\varepsilon_u$ such that the above lemma follows.

Note that ImplicitUsage implies that

$$\mathsf{ch}_j = \mathsf{H}(m^*, \mathsf{cmt}_{1-j}) = \mathsf{H}(m^*, \mathsf{cmt}_{1-j}^*) = \mathsf{ch}_j^*$$

for $j \in \{0, 1\}$. Together with the fact that $(m^*, \sigma^*) \notin \mathcal{Q}^{(i^*)}$, we must have that $(\mathsf{resp}_0^*, \mathsf{resp}_1^*) \neq (\mathsf{resp}_0, \mathsf{resp}_1)$. Then two subcases are possible.

- $X_2 \wedge \mathsf{ImplicitUsage} \wedge (\mathsf{resp}_{1-b^{(i^*)}}^* = \mathsf{resp}_{1-b^{(i^*)}}) \wedge (\mathsf{resp}_{b^{(i^*)}}^* \neq \mathsf{resp}_{b^{(i^*)}})$. This subcase intuitively implies that the adversary successfully guesses the bit $b^{(i^*)}$, since the adversary has to choose $\mathsf{resp}_0^*, \mathsf{resp}_1^*$ such that $\mathsf{resp}_{1-b^{(i^*)}}^*$ is equal and $\mathsf{resp}_{b^{(i^*)}}^*$ is unequal. However, in Game 2, the secret bit $b^{(i^*)}$ is perfectly hidden to the adversary due to the following facts.
  - The public key $pk^{(i^*)}$ is independent of $b^{(i^*)}$.
  - User i^* is not corrupted (or otherwise the forgery is invalid, anyway), so the bit $b^{(i^*)}$ is not leaked through corruptions.
  - The signature σ returned by oracle $\mathsf{Sign}(i^*, m)$ is independent of bit $b^{(i^*)}$. The reason is that X_2 implies that cmtColl does not happen. As shown in Remark 11, each $\mathsf{Sign}(i^*, m)$ query will use uniformly random $\mathsf{ch}_{1-b^{(i^*)}}$ and $\mathsf{ch}_{b^{(i^*)}}$. Thus, the signature essentially contains the two transcripts

$$(\mathsf{cmt}_{b^{(i^*)}}, \mathsf{ch}_{b^{(i^*)}}, \mathsf{resp}_{b^{(i^*)}}) \quad \text{and} \quad (\mathsf{cmt}_{1-b^{(i^*)}}, \mathsf{ch}_{1-b^{(i^*)}}, \mathsf{resp}_{1-b^{(i^*)}})$$

Note that the $b^{(i^*)}$ transcript is an "honestly generated" transcript and the $(1-b^{(i^*)})$ transcript is a "simulated" transcript with uniformly random $\mathsf{ch}_{1-b^{(i^*)}}$ and $\mathsf{resp}_{1-b^{(i^*)}}$. Due to the perfect simulatability of LID, we know that these two transcripts are perfectly identically distributed. Thus, $\mathcal{A}$ gains no information about $b^{(i^*)}$ through signatures.

In summary, we conclude that this subcase happens with probability

$$\frac{1}{2} \Pr[X_2 \wedge \mathsf{ImplicitUsage}].$$

- $X_2 \wedge \mathsf{ImplicitUsage} \wedge (\mathsf{resp}^*_{1-b^{(i^*)}} \neq \mathsf{resp}_{1-b^{(i^*)}})$. For this subcase, we can prove the following claim.

Claim. We can construct an adversary $\mathcal{B}$ with running time $t_\mathcal{B} \approx t_\mathcal{A}$ such that

$$\Pr[X_2 \wedge \mathsf{ImplicitUsage} \wedge (\mathsf{resp}^*_{1-b^{(i^*)}} \neq \mathsf{resp}_{1-b^{(i^*)}})] \leq \mathsf{Adv}^{\mathsf{MU\text{-}IND\text{-}KEY}}_{\mathsf{LID},N}(\mathcal{B}) + \varepsilon_u.$$

Proof. To prove this claim, we define a new intermediate game Game 2', which is exactly the same as Game 2, except that we choose a lossy public key $pk^{(i)}_{1-b} \xleftarrow{\$} \mathsf{LID.LossyGen}$ for every user $i \in [N]$ in Game 2'. We can build an adversary $\mathcal{B}$ with running time $t_\mathcal{B} \approx t_\mathcal{A}$ such that

$$\left| \begin{aligned} &\Pr[X_2 \wedge \mathsf{ImplicitUsage} \wedge (\mathsf{resp}^*_{1-b^{(i^*)}} \neq \mathsf{resp}_{1-b^{(i^*)}})] \\ &- \Pr[X_{2'} \wedge \mathsf{ImplicitUsage} \wedge (\mathsf{resp}^*_{1-b^{(i^*)}} \neq \mathsf{resp}_{1-b^{(i^*)}})] \end{aligned} \right| \leq \mathsf{Adv}^{\mathsf{MU\text{-}IND\text{-}KEY}}_{\mathsf{LID},N}(\mathcal{B}) \tag{1}$$

The construction of $\mathcal{B}$ using $\mathcal{A}$ is straightforward. It receives $(pk'_i)_{i \in [N]}$, which is either generated by algorithm $\mathsf{LID.Gen}$ or by $\mathsf{LID.LossyGen}$. Then, it simulates Game 2 for the adversary $\mathcal{A}$ and sets $pk^{(i)}_{1-b} := pk'_i$ for all $i \in [N]$. Note that, in Game 2, the secret key $sk^{(i)}_{1-b}$ is not used for any user i. So $\mathcal{B}$ is able to simulate the game perfectly. Finally, $\mathcal{B}$ outputs 1 if and only if $\mathcal{A}$ wins and $\mathsf{ImplicitUsage} \wedge (\mathsf{resp}^*_{1-b^{(i^*)}} \neq \mathsf{resp}_{1-b^{(i^*)}})$ happens. It is clear that $\mathcal{B}$ perfectly simulates Game 2 if it receives normal public keys and $\mathcal{B}$ perfectly simulates Game 2' if it receives lossy public keys. Thus, Eq. (1) follows.

Now in Game 2', the key $pk^{(i^*)}_{1-b}$ is lossy. Since $X_{2'}$ implies that σ^* is a valid signature with respect to m^*, we know that

$$\mathsf{LID.Vrfy}(pk^{(i^*)}_{1-b}, \mathsf{cmt}^*_{1-b^{(i^*)}}, \mathsf{ch}^*_{1-b^{(i^*)}}, \mathsf{resp}^*_{1-b^{(i^*)}}) = 1.$$

Since the signing oracle $\mathsf{Sign}(i^*, m^*)$ also outputs valid signature σ for m^*, we have that

$$\mathsf{LID.Vrfy}(pk^{(i^*)}_{1-b}, \mathsf{cmt}_{1-b^{(i^*)}}, \mathsf{ch}_{1-b^{(i^*)}}, \mathsf{resp}_{1-b^{(i^*)}}) = 1.$$

In this subcase, we have $(\mathsf{cmt}_{1-b^{(i^*)}}, \mathsf{ch}_{1-b^{(i^*)}}) = (\mathsf{cmt}^*_{1-b^{(i^*)}}, \mathsf{ch}^*_{1-b^{(i^*)}})$ and $\mathsf{resp}_{1-b^{(i^*)}} \neq \mathsf{resp}^*_{1-b^{(i^*)}}$. Due to the uniqueness property of LID with respect to lossy public keys, we must have

$$\Pr[X_{2'} \wedge \mathsf{ImplicitUsage} \wedge (\mathsf{resp}^*_{1-b^{(i^*)}} \neq \mathsf{resp}_{1-b^{(i^*)}})] \leq \varepsilon_u.$$

Applying Eq. (1) to the obtained bounds, the claim follows. □

Putting both subcases together, we obtain that

$$\Pr[X_2 \wedge \mathsf{ImplicitUsage}] \leq \frac{1}{2} \Pr[X_2 \wedge \mathsf{ImplicitUsage}] + \mathsf{Adv}_{\mathsf{LID},N}^{\mathsf{MU\text{-}IND\text{-}KEY}}(\mathcal{B}) + \varepsilon_u,$$

which implies that $\Pr[X_2 \wedge \mathsf{ImplicitUsage}] \leq 2\mathsf{Adv}_{\mathsf{LID},N}^{\mathsf{MU\text{-}IND\text{-}KEY}}(\mathcal{B}) + 2\varepsilon_u.$ □

Game 4. Game 4 further modifies the winning condition. We denote Before as the event that Both happens and the first $(1 - b^{(i^*)})$-query is made before the first $b^{(i^*)}$-query is made. Game 4 outputs 0 if event Before does not happen.

Hence, X_4 happens if and only if $X_3 \wedge$ Before happens. We can prove the following lemma.

Lemma 15. $\Pr[X_4] \geq 1/2 \cdot \Pr[X_3].$

Proof. Since we know that event Both happens, we can divide X_3 into three subcases.

- Both the first 0-query and the first 1-query are made in *one and the same* signing query $\mathsf{Sign}(i^*, m^*)$.
  In this subcase, we have that two hash queries $\{\mathsf{H}(m^*, \mathsf{cmt}_0^*), \mathsf{H}(m^*, \mathsf{cmt}_1^*)\}$ made by the final verification algorithm have the same input as the two hash queries $\{\mathsf{H}(m^*, \mathsf{cmt}_0), \mathsf{H}(m^*, \mathsf{cmt}_1)\}$ made by the signing oracle. We know that X_3 implies that ImplicitUsage does not happen, so we must have that $(\mathsf{cmt}_0^*, \mathsf{cmt}_1^*) = (\mathsf{cmt}_1, \mathsf{cmt}_0)$. Since the signing algorithm always makes a $\mathsf{H}(m^*, \mathsf{cmt}_{b^{(i^*)}})$ query before $\mathsf{H}(m, \mathsf{cmt}_{1-b^{(i^*)}})$, we have that event Before always happens in this subcase.
- Both the first 0-query and the first 1-query are made in one signing query $\mathsf{Sign}(i', m^*)$ for some $i' \neq i^*$.
  In this subcase, the $b^{(i')}$-query is made first and Before happens if and only if $b^{(i')} = 1 - b^{(i^*)}$.
- The first 0-query and the first 1-query are not made in exactly one signing query. In other words, they lie in different signing queries or at least one of them is made by the adversary.
  In this subcase, the adversary $\mathcal{A}$ actually has full control which one is queried first. Suppose the β-query is made first for some implicit bit $\beta \in \{0, 1\}$ chosen by the adversary. Then, event Before happens if and only if $\beta = b^{(i^*)}$.

Similar to the proof of Lemma 13, we can show that the bit $b^{(i^*)}$ is perfectly hidden to the adversary. So if the second or the third subcase happens, the probability that Before happens is $1/2$. Together with the fact that Before always happen in the first subcase, Lemma 15 follows.   □

Game 5. In this game, we change the generation of the key $pk_{1-b}^{(i)}$. Namely, the key generation in Game 5 is exactly as in Game 4 except that we choose lossy public keys $pk_{1-b}^{(i)} \xleftarrow{\$} \mathsf{LID.LossyGen}$ for every user $i \in [N]$ in Game 5.

Lemma 16. *We can construct an adversary $\mathcal{B}$ with running time $t_{\mathcal{B}} \approx t_{\mathcal{A}}$ such that*

$$|\Pr[X_4] - \Pr[X_5]| \leq \mathsf{Adv}_{\mathsf{LID},N}^{\mathsf{MU\text{-}IND\text{-}KEY}}(\mathcal{B}).$$

Proof. The proof of the lemma is straightforward. We can construct $\mathcal{B}$ using $\mathcal{A}$ as a subroutine. $\mathcal{B}$ receives as input $(pk'_i)_{i \in [N]}$, which is either generated by algorithm $\mathsf{LID.Gen}$ or by $\mathsf{LID.LossyGen}$. Then, it simulates Game 5 for the adversary $\mathcal{A}$ and set $pk_{1-b}^{(i)} := pk'_i$ for all $i \in [N]$. $\qquad\square$

Finally, we can prove the following lemma.

Lemma 17.
$$\Pr[X_5] \leq N \cdot q_{\mathsf{H}}^2 \cdot \varepsilon_\ell$$

where q_{H} is the number of hash queries made in Game 5.

Note that the lossiness of LID guarantees that ε_ℓ is *statistically* negligible (even for computationally *unbounded* adversaries). Hence, the multiplicative term $N \cdot q_{\mathsf{H}}^2$ does not break the tightness of our signature scheme. It will convenient to prove this claim by reduction.

Proof. To prove this lemma, we build an adversary $\mathcal{B}$ against the lossiness of LID. On getting a lossy public key $pk \xleftarrow{\$} \mathsf{LID.LossyGen}$, $\mathcal{B}$ uniformly selects $i' \xleftarrow{\$} [N], j_1 \xleftarrow{\$} [q_{\mathsf{H}} - 1]$ and $j_2 \xleftarrow{\$} \{j_1 + 1, \cdots, q_{\mathsf{H}}\}$. Then $\mathcal{B}$ generates all the public keys for $\mathcal{A}$ according to Game 5 except that it sets $pk_{1-b}^{(i')} := pk$. Then $\mathcal{B}$ invokes $\mathcal{A}$ and answers all the queries according to Game 5 with the following exceptions.

- In the j_1-th hash query $\mathsf{H}(m, \mathsf{cmt})$, $\mathcal{B}$ submits cmt to its own challenger and get back $\mathsf{ch} \xleftarrow{\$} \mathsf{CSet}$.
- In the j_2-th hash query $\mathsf{H}(m, \mathsf{cmt}')$, $\mathcal{B}$ returns ch as response and logs $((m, \mathsf{cmt}'), \mathsf{ch})$ into the hash list $\mathcal{L}$.

After $\mathcal{A}$ submits the forgery attempt $(i^*, m^*, \sigma^* = (\mathsf{ch}_0^*, \mathsf{resp}_0^*, \mathsf{resp}_1^*))$, $\mathcal{B}$ checks whether all the following events happen:

- X_5 happens,
- $i' = i^*$,
- the first $(1 - b^{(i^*)})$-query is exactly the j_1-th hash query,
- the first $b^{(i^*)}$-query is exactly the j_2-th hash query.

If all of these events happen, $\mathcal{B}$ outputs $\mathsf{resp}_{1-b^{(i^*)}}^*$ to its own challenger. Otherwise, $\mathcal{B}$ halts and outputs nothing.

The probability that $\mathcal{B}$ does not halt is at least $\Pr[X_5]/(N \cdot q_{\mathsf{H}}^2)$. We will show that in this case

$$\mathsf{LID.Vrfy}(pk, \mathsf{cmt}, \mathsf{ch}, \mathsf{resp}_{1-b^{(i^*)}}^*) = 1,$$

and hence $\mathcal{B}$ wins the lossiness game. This is implied by the following facts.

- $i' = i^*$ indicates that $pk = pk_{1-b}^{(i^*)}$.
- The j_1-th hash query is the first $(1 - b^{(i^*)})$-query indicates that $\mathsf{cmt} = \mathsf{cmt}_{1-b^{(i^*)}}^*$.
- The j_2-th hash query is the first $b^{(i^*)}$-query indicates that $\mathsf{ch} = \mathsf{ch}_{1-b^{(i^*)}}^*$.
- X_3 happens indicates that $\mathsf{Vrfy}(pk^{(i^*)}, m^*, \sigma^*) = 1$, which further indicates that

$$\mathsf{LID.Vrfy}(pk_{1-b}^{(i^*)}, \mathsf{cmt}_{1-b^{(i^*)}}^*, \mathsf{ch}_{1-b^{(i^*)}}^*, \mathsf{resp}_{1-b^{(i^*)}}^*) = 1.$$

Thus, we have that $\Pr[X_5]/(N \cdot q_{\mathsf{H}}^2) \leq \Pr[\mathcal{B}\text{ wins}] \leq \varepsilon_\ell$ and Lemma 17 follows.
□

Theorem 9 now follows.
□

5 Instantiations of Our Scheme

In the previous section we identified the necessary properties of the underlying lossy identification scheme. We now continue to discuss how suitable schemes can be instantiated based on concrete hardness assumptions. The constructions described in this section are derived from [1–3,29] and are well-known. The purpose of this section is to argue and justify that these constructions indeed satisfy all properties required for our signature scheme.

5.1 Instantiation Based on Decisional Diffie–Hellman

The well-known DDH-based lossy identification scheme uses the standard Sigma protocol to prove equality of discrete logarithms by Chaum et al. [11] (cf. Fig. 1) as foundation, which was used by Katz and Wang [29] to build tightly-secure signatures (in the single-user setting without corruptions).

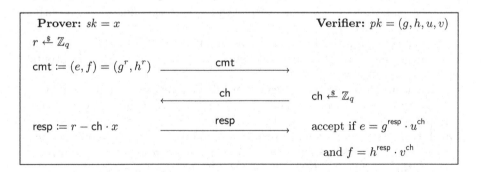

Fig. 1. The DDH-based identification scheme [11].

The DDH Problem. Let $(\mathbb{G}, g, q)$ be a cyclic group of prime order q and generator g. Further, let $h \in \mathbb{G}$. We denote the set of *DDH tuples* in $\mathbb{G}$ with respect to g and h as

$$\mathsf{DDH}(\mathbb{G}, g, h) := \{(u, v) \in \mathbb{G}^2 : \log_g u = \log_h v\}$$

and the set of *"non-DDH tuples"* as

$$\overline{\mathsf{DDH}(\mathbb{G}, g, h)} := \mathbb{G}^2 \setminus \mathsf{DDH}(\mathbb{G}, g, h).$$

Definition 18. *Let $(\mathbb{G}, g, q)$ be a cyclic group of prime order q and generator g. Further, let $h \xleftarrow{\$} \mathbb{G}$. We define the advantage of an algorithm $\mathcal{B}$ in solving the DDH problem in $\mathbb{G}$ with respect to (g, h) as*

$$\mathsf{Adv}^{\mathsf{DDH}}_{\mathbb{G}, g, h}(\mathcal{B}) := |\Pr\left[\mathcal{B}(\mathbb{G}, g, h, u, v) = 1\right] - \Pr\left[\mathcal{B}(\mathbb{G}, g, h, \overline{u}, \overline{v}) = 1\right]|$$

where $(u, v) \xleftarrow{\$} \mathsf{DDH}(\mathbb{G}, g, h)$ and $(\overline{u}, \overline{v}) \xleftarrow{\$} \overline{\mathsf{DDH}(\mathbb{G}, g, h)}$ are chosen uniformly random.

A DDH-Based LID Scheme. Let $(\mathbb{G}, g, q)$ be a cyclic group of prime order q and generator g and let $h \in \mathbb{G}$. We define the lossy identification scheme LID = (LID.Gen, LID.LossyGen, LID.Prove, LID.Vrfy, LID.Sim) based on the protocol presented above as follows:

Key generation. The algorithm LID.Gen chooses a value $x \xleftarrow{\$} \mathbb{Z}_q$ uniformly at random. It sets $pk := (g, h, u, v) = (g, h, g^x, h^x)$ and $sk := x$, and outputs (pk, sk).

Lossy key generation. The algorithm LID.LossyGen chooses two group elements $u, v \xleftarrow{\$} \mathbb{G}$ uniformly and independently at random. It outputs $pk := (g, h, u, v)$.

Proving. The algorithm LID.Prove is split up into the following two algorithms:
  1. The algorithm LID.Prove$_1$ takes as input a secret key $sk = x$, chooses a random value $r \xleftarrow{\$} \mathbb{Z}_q$, and computes a commitment cmt $:= (e, f) = (g^r, h^r)$, where g, h are the value of the pk corresponding to sk. It outputs (cmt, st) with st $:= r$.
  2. The algorithm LID.Prove$_2$ takes as input a secret key $sk = x$, a commitment cmt $= (e, f)$, a challenge ch $\in \mathbb{Z}_q$, a state st $= r$, and outputs a response resp $:= r - \text{ch} \cdot x$.

Verification. The verification algorithm LID.Vrfy takes as input a public key $pk = (g, h, u, v)$, a commitment cmt $= (e, f)$, a challenge ch $\in \mathbb{Z}_q$, and a response resp $\in \mathbb{Z}_q$. It outputs 1 if and only if $e = g^{\mathsf{resp}} \cdot u^{\mathsf{ch}}$ and $f = h^{\mathsf{resp}} \cdot v^{\mathsf{ch}}$.

Simulation. The simulation algorithm LID.Sim takes as input a public key $pk = (g, h, u, v)$, a challenge ch $\in \mathbb{Z}_q$, and a response resp $\in \mathbb{Z}_q$. It outputs a commitment cmt $= (e, f) = (g^{\mathsf{resp}} \cdot u^{\mathsf{ch}}, h^{\mathsf{resp}} \cdot v^{\mathsf{ch}})$.

Remark 19. Note that an honest public key generated with LID.Gen is of the form $pk = (g, h, u, v)$ such that $(u, v) \in \mathsf{DDH}(\mathbb{G}, g, h)$, whereas a lossy public key generated with LID.LossyGen is of the form $pk = (g, h, u, v)$ such that $(u, v) \notin \mathsf{DDH}(\mathbb{G}, g, h)$ with high probability.

Theorem 20. *The scheme* LID *defined above is lossy with*

$$\rho = 1, \quad \varepsilon_s = 0, \quad \varepsilon_\ell \le 1/q,$$

and from any efficient adversary $\mathcal{A}$ *we can construct an efficient adversary* $\mathcal{B}$ *such that*

$$\mathsf{Adv}_{\mathsf{LID},N}^{\mathsf{MU\text{-}IND\text{-}KEY}}(\mathcal{A}) \le \mathsf{Adv}_{\mathbb{G},g}^{\mathsf{DDH}}(\mathcal{B}).$$

Furthermore, LID *is perfectly unique with respect to lossy keys (i.e.,* $\varepsilon_u = 0$*),* LID *has* α*-bit min-entropy with* $\alpha = \log_2(q)$*,* LID *is commitment-recoverable, and* LID *has an injective simulator.*

The proof of this theorem is rather standard and implicitly contained in the aforementioned prior works. For completeness, we provide a sketch in Appendix A.

Concrete Instantiation. We can now use the DDH-based lossy identification scheme to describe an explicit instantiation of our signature scheme based on the DDH assumption, in order to assess its concrete performance. Let $\mathbb{G}$ be a group of prime order p with generator g, let $h \xleftarrow{\$} \mathbb{G}$ be a random generator and let $\mathsf{H} \colon \{0,1\}^* \to \mathbb{Z}_p$ be a hash function. We construct a digital signature scheme $\mathsf{Sig} = (\mathsf{Gen}, \mathsf{Sign}, \mathsf{Vrfy})$ as follows.

Key generation. The key generation Gen algorithm samples $x_0, x_1 \xleftarrow{\$} \mathbb{Z}_p$, $b \xleftarrow{\$} \{0,1\}$. Then it sets

$$pk := (u_0, v_0, u_1, v_1) = (g^{x_0}, h^{x_0}, g^{x_1}, h^{x_1}) \quad \text{and} \quad sk := (b, x_b).$$

Signing. The signing algorithm Sign takes as input $sk = (b, x_b)$ and a message $m \in \{0,1\}^*$. Then it proceeds as follows.

1. It first chooses a random value $r \xleftarrow{\$} \mathbb{Z}_p$, and sets $(e_b, f_b) := (g^r, h^r)$ and

$$\mathsf{ch}_{1-b} := \mathsf{H}(m, e_b, f_b).$$

2. Then it samples a value $\mathsf{resp}_{1-b} \xleftarrow{\$} \mathbb{Z}_p$ and computes

$$e_{1-b} = g^{\mathsf{resp}_{1-b}} u_{1-b}^{\mathsf{ch}_{1-b}} \quad \text{and} \quad f_{1-b} = h^{\mathsf{resp}_{1-b}} v_{1-b}^{\mathsf{ch}_{1-b}}.$$

3. Finally, it computes

$$\mathsf{ch}_b := \mathsf{H}(m, e_{1-b}, f_{1-b}) \quad \text{and} \quad \mathsf{resp}_b := r - \mathsf{ch}_b \cdot x_b$$

and outputs the signature $\sigma := (\mathsf{ch}_0, \mathsf{resp}_0, \mathsf{resp}_1) \in \mathbb{Z}_p^3$.

Verification. The verification algorithm takes as input a public key $pk := (u_0, v_0, u_1, v_1)$, a message $m \in \{0,1\}^*$, and a signature $\sigma = (\mathsf{ch}_0, \mathsf{resp}_0, \mathsf{resp}_1)$. If first computes

$$e_0 = g^{\mathsf{resp}_0} u_0^{\mathsf{ch}_0} \quad \text{and} \quad f_0 = h^{\mathsf{resp}_0} v_0^{\mathsf{ch}_0}.$$

From (e_0, f_0) it is then able to compute

$$\mathsf{ch}_1 := \mathsf{H}(m, e_0, f_0)$$

and then

$$e_1 = g^{\mathsf{resp}_1} \cdot u_1^{\mathsf{ch}_1} \qquad \text{and} \qquad f_1 = h^{\mathsf{resp}_1} \cdot v_1^{\mathsf{ch}_1}.$$

Finally, the algorithm outputs 1 if and only if

$$\mathsf{ch}_0 = \mathsf{H}(m, e_1, f_1).$$

Note that public keys are $pk \in \mathbb{G}^4$, secret keys are $sk \in \{0,1\} \times \mathbb{Z}_p$, and signatures are $\sigma \in \mathbb{Z}_p^3$.

5.2   Instantiation from the ϕ-Hiding Assumption

Another possible instantiation is based on the Guillou–Quisquater (GQ) identification scheme [25], which proves that an element $U = S^e \bmod N$ is an e-th residue (cf. Fig. 2). Abdalla et al. [1] describe a lossy version of the GQ scheme, based on the ϕ-hiding assumption. We observe that we can build a lossy identification scheme on a weaker assumption, which is implied by ϕ-hiding.

In order to achieve tightness in a multi-user setting, we will need a common setup, which is shared across all users. This setup consists of a public tuple (N, e) where $N = p \cdot q$ is the product of two large random primes and e a uniformly random prime of length $\ell_e \leq \lambda/4$ that divides $p - 1$. The factors p and q need to remain secret, so we assume that (N, e) either was generated by a trusted party, or by running a secure multi-party computation protocol with multiple parties.

The Guillou–Quisquater LID Scheme. We define the lossy identification scheme $\mathsf{LID} = (\mathsf{LID.Gen}, \mathsf{LID.LossyGen}, \mathsf{LID.Prove}, \mathsf{LID.Vrfy}, \mathsf{LID.Sim})$ based on the protocol presented above as follows:

Common setup. The common system parameters are a tuple (N, e) where $N = p \cdot q$ is the product of two distinct primes p, q of length $\lambda/2$ and e is random prime of length $\ell_e \leq \lambda/4$ such that e divides $p - 1$.
  Note that the parameters (N, e) are always in "lossy mode", and not switched from an "injective" pair (N, e) where e is coprime to $\phi(N) = (p-1)(q-1)$ to "lossy" in the security proof, as common in other works.

Key generation. The algorithm $\mathsf{LID.Gen}$ samples $S \xleftarrow{\$} \mathbb{Z}_N^*$ and computes $U = S^e$. It sets $pk = (N, e, U)$ and $sk = (N, e, S)$, where (N, e) are from the common parameters.

Lossy key generation. The lossy key generation algorithm $\mathsf{LID.LossyGen}$ samples U uniformly at random from the e-th non-residues modulo N.[3]

---

[3] This is indeed efficiently possible as $U \xleftarrow{\$} \mathbb{Z}_N^*$ is a not an e-th residue with probability $1 - 1/e$ and we can efficiently check whether a given U is an e-th residue when the factorization of N is known [1].

Proving. The algorithm LID.Prove is split up into the following two algorithms:

1. The algorithm $\mathsf{LID.Prove_1}$ takes as input a secret key $sk = (N, e, S)$, chooses a random value $r \xleftarrow{\$} \mathbb{Z}_N^*$, and computes a commitment $\mathsf{cmt} := r^e \bmod N$. It outputs $(\mathsf{cmt}, \mathsf{st})$ with $\mathsf{st} := r$.
2. The algorithm $\mathsf{LID.Prove_2}$ takes as input a secret key $sk = (N, e, S)$, a commitment cmt, a challenge $\mathsf{ch} \in \{0, \ldots, 2^{\ell_e} - 1\}$, a state $\mathsf{st} = r$, and outputs a response $\mathsf{resp} := r \cdot S^{\mathsf{ch}} \bmod N$.

Verification. The verification algorithm LID.Vrfy takes as input a public key $pk = (N, e, U)$, a commitment cmt, a challenge ch, and a response resp. It outputs 1 if and only if $\mathsf{resp} \neq 0 \bmod N$ and $\mathsf{resp}^e = \mathsf{cmt} \cdot U^{\mathsf{ch}}$.

Simulation. The simulation algorithm LID.Sim takes as input a public key $pk = (N, e, U)$, a challenge ch, and a response resp. It outputs a commitment $\mathsf{cmt} = \mathsf{resp}^e / U^{\mathsf{ch}}$.

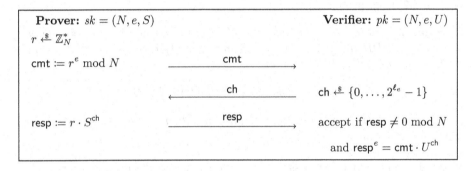

Fig. 2. The Guillou–Quisquater identification scheme [25].

Theorem 21. *The scheme* LID *defined above is lossy with*

$$\rho = 1, \quad \varepsilon_s = 0, \quad \varepsilon_\ell \leq 1/2^{\ell_e},$$

and from any efficient adversary $\mathcal{A}$ we can construct an efficient adversary $\mathcal{B}$ such that

$$\mathsf{Adv}_{\mathsf{LID},n}^{\mathsf{MU\text{-}IND\text{-}KEY}}(\mathcal{A}) \leq \mathsf{Adv}^{n\text{-}\mathsf{HR}}(\mathcal{B}).$$

Furthermore, LID *is perfectly unique with respect to lossy keys (i.e., $\varepsilon_u = 0$),* LID *has α-bit min-entropy with $\alpha \geq \lambda - 2$,* LID *is commitment-recoverable, and* LID *has an injective simulator.*

The above theorem has been proven in [1] for most of its statements. What is left is a proof for n-key-indistinguishability, which we provide in Appendix B.

5.3 On Instantiations of Lossy ID Schemes from Other Assumptions

There also exist lossy identification schemes based on the decisional short discrete logarithm problem, the ring LWE problem, and the subset sum problem (all due to Abdalla et al. [2,3]). However, they do not directly translate to a tight multi-user signature scheme that is existentially unforgeable with adaptive corruptions.

Our security proof requires tight multi-instance security of the underlying hardness assumption. While, for example, the DDH-based scheme satisfies this via its self-reducibility property, it is not obvious how schemes based on, for example, lattices or subset sum achieve this notion in a *tight* manner.

A   Proof of Theorem 20

Random Self-reducibility of DDH. It is well-known that the DDH problem is random self-reducible, which we summarize in the following lemma. See [7, Lemma 5.2] for a proof.

Lemma 22. *There exists an efficient algorithm* ReRand *that takes as input* (g, h) *and a DDH instance* $(u, v) \in \mathbb{G}^2$ *and an integer* N, *and outputs* N *new DDH instances* $(u^{(i)}, v^{(i)})$ *such that*

$$(u, v) \in \mathsf{DDH}(\mathbb{G}, g, h) \iff (u^{(i)}, v^{(i)}) \in \mathsf{DDH}(\mathbb{G}, g, h)$$

for all $i \in [N]$. *The running time of this algorithm mainly consists of* $\mathcal{O}(N)$ *exponentiations in* $\mathbb{G}$.

Proof. To show that LID is lossy, we need to show that it satisfies all properties presented in Definition 4.

Completeness of normal keys. We claim that the above scheme is perfectly-complete. To prove this, we show that for any honest transcript it holds that $\mathsf{LID.Vrfy}(pk, \mathsf{cmt}, \mathsf{ch}, \mathsf{resp}) = 1$. Let $(pk, sk) \xleftarrow{\$} \mathsf{LID.Gen}$ be an (honest) key pair and let $(\mathsf{cmt}, \mathsf{ch}, \mathsf{resp})$ be an honest transcript, that is, $\mathsf{ch} \xleftarrow{\$} \mathsf{CSet}$, $(\mathsf{cmt}, \mathsf{st}) \xleftarrow{\$} \mathsf{LID.Prove}_1(sk)$ and $\mathsf{resp} := \mathsf{LID.Prove}_2(sk, \mathsf{cmt}, \mathsf{ch}, \mathsf{st})$. By definition of the scheme, we have $pk = (g, h, u, v)$ with $(u, v) \in \mathsf{DDH}(\mathbb{G}, g, h)$ and $sk = x$ and $\mathsf{cmt} = (e, f) = (g^r, h^r)$ and $\mathsf{resp} = r - \mathsf{ch} \cdot x$. Further, $\mathsf{LID.Vrfy}(pk, \mathsf{cmt}, \mathsf{ch}, \mathsf{resp}) = 1$ if and only if $e = g^{\mathsf{resp}} \cdot u^{\mathsf{ch}}$ and $f = h^{\mathsf{resp}} \cdot v^{\mathsf{ch}}$. Observe that

$$g^{\mathsf{resp}} \cdot u^{\mathsf{ch}} = g^{r - \mathsf{ch} \cdot x} \cdot g^{\mathsf{ch} \cdot x} = g^r = e.$$

An analogous equation holds for f if g is replaced by h. Hence, $\mathsf{LID.Vrfy}$ outputs 1 for every honest transcript.

Simulatability of transcripts. We claim that the above scheme is perfectly simulatable. To show this, we need to argue that the two distributions

$$\left\{ (\mathsf{cmt}, \mathsf{ch}, \mathsf{resp}) : \begin{array}{l} (\mathsf{cmt}, \mathsf{st}) \xleftarrow{\$} \mathsf{LID.Prove}_1(sk) \\ \mathsf{ch} \xleftarrow{\$} \mathbb{Z}_q \\ \mathsf{resp} := \mathsf{LID.Prove}_2(sk, \mathsf{ch}, \mathsf{cmt}, \mathsf{st}) \end{array} \right\}$$

and

$$
\left\{
(\mathsf{cmt}, \mathsf{ch}, \mathsf{resp}) :
\begin{array}{l}
\mathsf{ch} \xleftarrow{\$} \mathbb{Z}_q \\
\mathsf{resp} \xleftarrow{\$} \mathbb{Z}_q \\
\mathsf{cmt} := \mathsf{LID}.\mathsf{Sim}(pk, \mathsf{ch}, \mathsf{resp})
\end{array}
\right\}
$$

are identical. Recall that we have $pk = (g, h, u, v)$ with $(u, v) \in \mathsf{DDH}(\mathbb{G}, g, h)$, $sk = x$, $\mathsf{cmt} = (e, f) = (g^r, h^r)$ with $\mathsf{st} = r \xleftarrow{\$} \mathbb{Z}_q$, and $\mathsf{resp} = r - \mathsf{ch} \cdot x$ for an honest transcript (i.e., in the former distribution). Thus, we have that $\mathsf{cmt} = (e, f)$ is uniformly distributed over $\mathbb{G}^2$. Consequently, since $r \xleftarrow{\$} \mathbb{Z}_q$ and $\mathsf{ch} \xleftarrow{\$} \mathbb{Z}_q$, we also have that the response resp is distributed uniformly and independently (of cmt and ch) over $\mathbb{Z}_q$.

We will now take a look at the later distribution. Note that ch and resp are both uniformly random elements over $\mathbb{Z}_p$. It remains to show that cmt in the simulated transcript is distributed uniformly over $\mathbb{G}^2$.

Recall that $\mathsf{cmt} := \mathsf{LID}.\mathsf{Sim}(pk, \mathsf{ch}, \mathsf{resp})$ is defined as $\mathsf{cmt} := (e, f) = (g^{\mathsf{resp}} \cdot u^{\mathsf{ch}}, h^{\mathsf{resp}} \cdot v^{\mathsf{ch}})$. Observe that $\log_g(e) = \mathsf{resp} + \mathsf{ch} \cdot x$ and $\log_g(f) = \log_g(h) \cdot (\mathsf{resp} + \mathsf{ch} \cdot x)$. Since $\mathsf{ch} \xleftarrow{\$} \mathbb{Z}_q$ and $\mathsf{resp} \xleftarrow{\$} \mathbb{Z}_q$, we have that both $\log_g(e)$ and $\log_g(f)$ are distributed uniformly and independently (of ch and resp) over $\mathbb{Z}_q$ and thus (e, f) is distributed uniformly over $\mathbb{G}^2$. Note that e, f are not distributed independently of each other (as it is the case in the honest transcript).

Indistinguishability of keys. As already remarked above, honest keys contain a DDH tuple, whereas lossy keys contain a non-DDH tuple. Therefore, we claim that for every adversary $\mathcal{A}$ trying to distinguish honest from lossy keys of LID, we can construct an adversary $\mathcal{B}$ such that

$$
\mathsf{Adv}_{\mathsf{LID}, N}^{\mathsf{MU\text{-}IND\text{-}KEY}}(\mathcal{A}) \leq \mathsf{Adv}_{\mathbb{G}, g}^{\mathsf{DDH}}(\mathcal{B}).
$$

To prove this claim, we give a construction of $\mathcal{B}$ running $\mathcal{A}$ as a subroutine. The adversary $\mathcal{B}$ receives a tuple (g, h, u, v) such that (u, v) either is a DDH tuple (i.e., $(u, v) \in \mathsf{DDH}(\mathbb{G}, g, h)$) or not. Then, it uses the algorithm of Lemma 22 to re-randomize (u, v) into N tuples $(u^{(i)}, v^{(i)})_{i \in [N]} \xleftarrow{\$} \mathsf{ReRand}(g, h, u, v, N)$ such that

$$
(u, v) \in \mathsf{DDH}(\mathbb{G}, g, h) \iff \forall i \in [N] : (u^{(i)}, v^{(i)}) \in \mathsf{DDH}(\mathbb{G}, g, h)
$$

and hands $(pk_i = (g, h, u^{(i)}, v^{(i)}))_{i \in [N]}$ to $\mathcal{A}$ as input. When $\mathcal{A}$ halts and outputs a bit b, $\mathcal{B}$ halts and outputs b as well.

Observe that by Lemma 22, we have

$$
\Pr[\mathcal{B}(g, h, u, v) = 1] \geq \Pr[\mathcal{A}(pk^{(1)}, \ldots, pk^{(N)})]
$$

with $(u, v) \xleftarrow{\$} \mathsf{DDH}(\mathbb{G}, g, h)$, $(u^{(i)}, v^{(i)})_{i \in [N]} \xleftarrow{\$} \mathsf{ReRand}(g, h, u, v, N)$, and $pk^{(i)} := (g, h, u^{(i)}, v^{(i)})$. Further, we have

$$
\Pr[\mathcal{B}(g, h, \bar{u}, \bar{v}) = 1] \geq \Pr[\mathcal{A}(pk'^{(1)}, \ldots, pk'^{(N)})]
$$

with $(\bar{u}, \bar{v}) \xleftarrow{\$} \overline{\mathsf{DDH}(\mathbb{G}, g, h)}$, $(\bar{u}^{(i)}, \bar{v}^{(i)}) \xleftarrow{\$} \mathsf{ReRand}(g, h, \bar{u}, \bar{v})$ for every $i \in [N]$, and $pk'^{(i)} := (g, h, \bar{u}^{(i)}, \bar{v}^{(i)})$. In conclusion, we have

$$\mathsf{Adv}_{\mathsf{LID}, N}^{\mathsf{MU\text{-}IND\text{-}KEY}}(\mathcal{A}) \leq \mathsf{Adv}_{\mathbb{G}, g}^{\mathsf{DDH}}(\mathcal{B}).$$

Lossiness. We claim that the above scheme LID is $1/q$-lossy. To show this, we first recall a classical result showing the soundness of the protocol to "prove DDH tuples" by Chaum et al. presented above. Namely, we claim that if $\log_g(u) \neq \log_h(v)$ holds for the public key $pk = (g, h, u, v)$ (i.e., pk is a lossy key and $(u, v) \notin \mathsf{DDH}(\mathbb{G}, g, h)$), for any commitment cmt there can only be at most one challenge ch such that the transcript is valid. We prove this statement by contradiction.

Let $\mathcal{A}$ be an unbounded adversary that on input of a lossy public key $pk \xleftarrow{\$}$ LID.LossyGen, outputs commitment $\mathsf{cmt} = (e, f)$. We now show that $\mathcal{A}$ can only output a correct resp for *one* ch such that $\mathsf{LID.Vrfy}(pk, \mathsf{cmt}, \mathsf{ch}, \mathsf{resp}) = 1$. Suppose that $\mathcal{A}$ was able to come up with two responses resp_1 and resp_2 for two different challenge $\mathsf{ch}_1 \neq \mathsf{ch}_2$ such that $\mathsf{LID.Vrfy}(pk, \mathsf{cmt}, \mathsf{ch}_1, \mathsf{resp}_1) = 1$ and $\mathsf{LID.Vrfy}(pk, \mathsf{cmt}, \mathsf{ch}_2, \mathsf{resp}_2) = 1$ holds. This implies by the definition of LID.Vrfy that

$$e = g^{\mathsf{resp}_1} u^{\mathsf{ch}_1} = g^{\mathsf{resp}_2} u^{\mathsf{ch}_2} \qquad \text{and} \qquad f = h^{\mathsf{resp}_1} v^{\mathsf{ch}_1} = h^{\mathsf{resp}_2} v^{\mathsf{ch}_2}.$$

Equivalently, we get by using the assumption that $\mathsf{ch}_1 \neq \mathsf{ch}_2$:

$$\log_g(u) = \frac{(\mathsf{resp}_1 - \mathsf{resp}_2)}{\mathsf{ch}_2 - \mathsf{ch}_1} \qquad \text{and} \qquad \log_h(v) = \frac{(\mathsf{resp}_1 - \mathsf{resp}_2)}{\mathsf{ch}_2 - \mathsf{ch}_1}.$$

However, this is a contraction to the assumption that $\log_g(u) \neq \log_h(v)$. Thus, pk must be a lossy key.

Using this, we have that for every commitment $\mathcal{A}$ outputs, there can only be at most one challenge ch such that the adversary generated a valid transcript. Note that we have an unbounded adversary and based on cmt and ch it can compute a response. As there is only one challenge for cmt output by $\mathcal{A}$ and the challenge is chosen uniformly at random, the adversary can only win with a probability of at most $1/q$.

Uniqueness with respect to lossy keys. Let $pk = (g, h, u, v)$ with $(u, v) \notin \mathsf{DDH}(\mathbb{G}, g, h)$ and $(\mathsf{cmt}, \mathsf{ch}, \mathsf{resp})$ with $\mathsf{LID.Vrfy}(pk, \mathsf{cmt}, \mathsf{ch}, \mathsf{resp}) = 1$. Suppose that there is a $\mathsf{resp}' \neq \mathsf{resp}$ such that $\mathsf{LID.Vrfy}(pk, \mathsf{cmt}, \mathsf{ch}, \mathsf{resp}') = 1$. In this case, we have for $\mathsf{cmt} = (e, f)$ that

$$e = g^{\mathsf{resp}} u^{\mathsf{ch}} = g^{\mathsf{resp}'} u^{\mathsf{ch}} \qquad \text{and} \qquad f = h^{\mathsf{resp}} v^{\mathsf{ch}} = h^{\mathsf{resp}'} v^{\mathsf{ch}}.$$

However, this implies that

$$g^{\mathsf{resp}} = g^{\mathsf{resp}'} \qquad \text{and} \qquad h^{\mathsf{resp}} = h^{\mathsf{resp}'},$$

which implies that $\mathsf{resp} = \mathsf{resp}'$, contradicting the initial assumption.

Min-entropy. For any secret key sk, the commitment $\mathsf{cmt} \xleftarrow{\$} \mathsf{LID.Prove}_1(sk)$ equals (g^r, h^r) for $r \xleftarrow{\$} \mathbb{Z}_q$, which is independent of sk. So the min-entropy of cmt is $\alpha = \log_2(q)$.

Commitment-recoverable. The verification algorithm of LID first recovers a commitment using the simulator and then compares the result with the commitment in the transcript. So LID is commitment-recoverable.

Injective simulator. For any normal public key $pk = (g, h, u, v)$, any response resp and any challenge $\mathsf{ch} \neq \mathsf{ch}'$, we have that

$$\mathsf{LID.Sim}(pk, \mathsf{ch}, \mathsf{resp}) = (g^{\mathsf{resp}} u^{\mathsf{ch}}, h^{\mathsf{resp}} v^{\mathsf{ch}}),$$

$$\mathsf{LID.Sim}(pk, \mathsf{ch}', \mathsf{resp}) = (g^{\mathsf{resp}} u^{\mathsf{ch}'}, h^{\mathsf{resp}} v^{\mathsf{ch}'}).$$

Thus, if the above two pairs are equal, we must have that $(u^{\mathsf{ch}}, v^{\mathsf{ch}}) = (u^{\mathsf{ch}'}, v^{\mathsf{ch}'})$. That implies $\mathsf{ch} = \mathsf{ch}'$.

$\square$

B   Proof of Theorem 21

The following definition is from [1].

Definition 23 (RSA modulus generation algorithm). *Let ℓ_N be a positive integer and let RSA_{ℓ_N} be the set of all tuples (N, p_1, p_2) such that $N = p_1 p_2$ is a ℓ_N-bit number and p_1, p_2 are two distinct primes in the set of $\ell_N/2$-bit primes $\mathbb{P}_{\ell_N/2}$. Let R be any relation on p_1 and p_2, define $\mathsf{RSA}_{\ell_N}[R] := \{(N, p_1, p_2) \in \mathsf{RSA}_{\ell_N} \mid R(p_1, p_2) = 1\}$.*

We can use it to define the n-fold higher residuosity assumption as well as the ϕ-hiding assumption [1,9,31].

Definition 24 (n-fold higher residuosity assumption). *Let e be a random prime of length $\ell_e \leq \ell_N/4$ and*

$$(N, p_1, p_2) \xleftarrow{\$} \mathsf{RSA}_{\ell_N}[p_1 = 1 \bmod e]$$

and let $\mathsf{HR}_N[e] := \{g^e \bmod N \mid g \in \mathbb{Z}_N^*\}$ be the set of e-th residues modulo N. We define the advantage of any $\mathcal{A}$ in solving the higher residuosity problem as

$$\mathsf{Adv}^{n\text{-}\mathsf{HR}}(\mathcal{A}) := |\Pr[\mathcal{A}(N, e, y_1, \ldots, y_n) = 1] - \Pr[\mathcal{A}(N, e, y_1', \ldots, y_n') = 1]|,$$

where $y_1, \ldots, y_n \xleftarrow{\$} \mathsf{HR}_N[e]$ and $y_1', \ldots, y_n' \xleftarrow{\$} \mathbb{Z}_N^* \setminus \mathsf{HR}_N[e]$. The e-residuosity problem is (t, ε)-hard if for any $\mathcal{A}$ with running time at most t, $\mathsf{Adv}^{n\text{-}\mathsf{HR}}(\mathcal{A})$ is at most ε.

We prove the following lemma.

Lemma 25. *For any adversary $\mathcal{A}$ with running time $t_{\mathcal{A}}$ against the n-key-indistinguishability of LID in Fig. 2, we can construct an adversary $\mathcal{B}$ with running time $t_{\mathcal{B}} \approx t_{\mathcal{A}}$ such that*

$$\mathsf{Adv}_{\mathsf{LID},n}^{\mathsf{MU\text{-}IND\text{-}KEY}}(\mathcal{A}) \leq \mathsf{Adv}^{n\text{-}\mathsf{HR}}(\mathcal{B}).$$

Proof. The proof is a straightforward reduction. $\mathcal{B}$ receives $(N, e, y_1, \ldots, y_n)$ as input and defines the common parameters as (N, e) and

$$\left(pk^{(1)}, \cdots, pk^{(n)}\right) = (y_1, \ldots, y_n).$$

Note that this defines real keys if the y_i are e-th residues, and lossy keys if the y_i are e-th non-residues.   □

Finally, we can show that the n-fold higher residuosity assumption is tightly implied by the ϕ-hiding assumption, for any polynomially-bounded n.

Definition 26 (ϕ-hiding assumption [1,9,31]). *Let $c \leq 1/4$ be a constant. For any adversary $\mathcal{A}$, define the advantage of $\mathcal{A}$ in solving the ϕ-hiding problem to be*

$$\mathsf{Adv}^{\phi H}(\mathcal{A}) := |\Pr[\mathcal{A}(N, e) = 1] - \Pr[\mathcal{A}(N', e) = 1]|,$$

where $e \xleftarrow{\$} \mathbb{P}_{c\ell_N}$, $(N, p_1, p_2) \xleftarrow{\$} \mathsf{RSA}_{\ell_N}[\gcd(e, \phi(N)) = 1]$ and $(N', p'_1, p'_2) \xleftarrow{\$} \mathsf{RSA}_{\ell_N}[p'_1 = 1 \bmod e]$. The ϕ-hiding problem is (t, ε)-hard if for any $\mathcal{A}$ with running time at most t, $\mathsf{Adv}^{\phi H}(\mathcal{A})$ is at most ε.

Lemma 27. *For any adversary $\mathcal{A}$ with running time $t_{\mathcal{A}}$ we can construct an adversary $\mathcal{B}$ with running time $t_{\mathcal{B}} \approx t_{\mathcal{A}}$ such that*

$$\mathsf{Adv}^{n\text{-}HR}(\mathcal{A}) \leq 2 \cdot \mathsf{Adv}^{\phi H}(\mathcal{B}).$$

Proof. First, we have that

$$\begin{aligned}
\mathsf{Adv}^{n\text{-}HR}(\mathcal{A}) &= |\Pr[\mathcal{A}(N, e, y_1, \ldots, y_n) = 1] - \Pr[\mathcal{A}(N, e, y'_1, \ldots, y'_n) = 1]| \\
&\leq |\Pr[\mathcal{A}(N, e, y_1, \ldots, y_n) = 1] - \Pr[\mathcal{A}(N', e, y'_1, \ldots, y'_n) = 1]| \\
&\quad + |\Pr[\mathcal{A}(N', e, y'_1, \ldots, y'_n) = 1] - \Pr[\mathcal{A}(N, e, y'_1, \ldots, y'_n) = 1]|,
\end{aligned}$$

where $(N, p_1, p_2) \xleftarrow{\$} \mathsf{RSA}_{\ell_N}[\gcd(e, \phi(N)) = 1]$ and $(N', p'_1, p'_2) \xleftarrow{\$} \mathsf{RSA}_{\ell_N}[p'_1 = 1 \bmod e]$. We can prove the following claim.

Claim. $|\Pr[\mathcal{A}(N, e, y_1, \ldots, y_n) = 1] - \Pr[\mathcal{A}(N', e, y'_1, \ldots, y'_n) = 1]| \leq \mathsf{Adv}^{\phi H}(\mathcal{B})$.

The proof is again a very straightforward reduction. $\mathcal{B}$ receives as input (N, e). It samples $x_1, \ldots, x_n \xleftarrow{\$} \mathbb{Z}_N$ uniformly random and then defines $y_i := x_i^e \bmod N$ for $i \in \{1, \ldots, n\}$. Then it runs $\mathcal{A}$ on input $(N, e, y_1, \ldots, y_n)$ and returns whatever $\mathcal{A}$ returns.

Note that if (N, e) is a "lossy" key, so that $e \mid \phi(N)$, then the y_i are random e-th residues. However, if $\gcd(e, \phi(N)) = 1$, then all y_i are random e-th non-residues, since the map $x \mapsto x^e \bmod N$ is a permutation.

Using a similar idea, we can prove that

Claim. $|\Pr[\mathcal{A}(N', e, y'_1, \ldots, y'_n) = 1] - \Pr[\mathcal{A}(N, e, y'_1, \ldots, y'_n) = 1]| \leq \mathsf{Adv}^{\phi H}(\mathcal{B})$.

Putting the two claims together, we have that $\mathsf{Adv}^{n\text{-}HR}(\mathcal{A}) \leq 2\mathsf{Adv}^{\phi H}(\mathcal{B})$ and Lemma 27 follows.   □

References

1. Abdalla, M., Ben Hamouda, F., Pointcheval, D.: Tighter reductions for forward-secure signature schemes. In: Kurosawa, K., Hanaoka, G. (eds.) PKC 2013. LNCS, vol. 7778, pp. 292–311. Springer, Heidelberg (2013). https://doi.org/10.1007/978-3-642-36362-7_19
2. Abdalla, M., Fouque, P.-A., Lyubashevsky, V., Tibouchi, M.: Tightly-secure signatures from lossy identification schemes. In: Pointcheval, D., Johansson, T. (eds.) EUROCRYPT 2012. LNCS, vol. 7237, pp. 572–590. Springer, Heidelberg (2012). https://doi.org/10.1007/978-3-642-29011-4_34
3. Abdalla, M., Fouque, P.-A., Lyubashevsky, V., Tibouchi, M.: Tightly secure signatures from lossy identification schemes. J. Cryptol. **29**(3), 597–631 (2016)
4. Abe, M., Ohkubo, M., Suzuki, K.: 1-out-of-n signatures from a variety of keys. In: Zheng, Y. (ed.) ASIACRYPT 2002. LNCS, vol. 2501, pp. 415–432. Springer, Heidelberg (2002). https://doi.org/10.1007/3-540-36178-2_26
5. Bader, C., Hofheinz, D., Jager, T., Kiltz, E., Li, Y.: Tightly-secure authenticated key exchange. In: Dodis, Y., Nielsen, J.B. (eds.) TCC 2015, Part I. LNCS, vol. 9014, pp. 629–658. Springer, Heidelberg (2015). https://doi.org/10.1007/978-3-662-46494-6_26
6. Bader, C., Jager, T., Li, Y., Schäge, S.: On the impossibility of tight cryptographic reductions. In: Fischlin, M., Coron, J.-S. (eds.) EUROCRYPT 2016, Part II. LNCS, vol. 9666, pp. 273–304. Springer, Heidelberg (2016). https://doi.org/10.1007/978-3-662-49896-5_10
7. Bellare, M., Boldyreva, A., Micali, S.: Public-key encryption in a multi-user setting: security proofs and improvements. In: Preneel, B. (ed.) EUROCRYPT 2000. LNCS, vol. 1807, pp. 259–274. Springer, Heidelberg (2000). https://doi.org/10.1007/3-540-45539-6_18
8. Bellare, M., Rogaway, P.: Entity authentication and key distribution. In: Stinson, D.R. (ed.) CRYPTO 1993. LNCS, vol. 773, pp. 232–249. Springer, Heidelberg (1994). https://doi.org/10.1007/3-540-48329-2_21
9. Cachin, C., Micali, S., Stadler, M.: Computationally private information retrieval with polylogarithmic communication. In: Stern, J. (ed.) EUROCRYPT 1999. LNCS, vol. 1592, pp. 402–414. Springer, Heidelberg (1999). https://doi.org/10.1007/3-540-48910-X_28
10. Canetti, R., Krawczyk, H.: Analysis of key-exchange protocols and their use for building secure channels. In: Pfitzmann, B. (ed.) EUROCRYPT 2001. LNCS, vol. 2045, pp. 453–474. Springer, Heidelberg (2001). https://doi.org/10.1007/3-540-44987-6_28
11. Chaum, D., Evertse, J.-H., van de Graaf, J.: An improved protocol for demonstrating possession of discrete logarithms and some generalizations. In: Chaum, D., Price, W.L. (eds.) EUROCRYPT 1987. LNCS, vol. 304, pp. 127–141. Springer, Heidelberg (1988). https://doi.org/10.1007/3-540-39118-5_13
12. Cohn-Gordon, K., Cremers, C., Gjøsteen, K., Jacobsen, H., Jager, T.: Highly efficient key exchange protocols with optimal tightness. In: Boldyreva, A., Micciancio, D. (eds.) CRYPTO 2019, Part II. LNCS, vol. 11694, pp. 767–797. Springer, Cham (2019). https://doi.org/10.1007/978-3-030-26954-8_25
13. Cramer, R., Damgård, I., Schoenmakers, B.: Proofs of partial knowledge and simplified design of witness hiding protocols. In: Desmedt, Y.G. (ed.) CRYPTO 1994. LNCS, vol. 839, pp. 174–187. Springer, Heidelberg (1994). https://doi.org/10.1007/3-540-48658-5_19

14. Davis, H., Günther, F.: Tighter proofs for the sigma and TLS 1.3 key exchange protocols. Cryptology ePrint Archive, Report 2020/1029 (2020). https://eprint.iacr.org/2020/1029

15. Diemert, D., Jager, T.: On the tight security of TLS 1.3: theoretically-sound cryptographic parameters for real-world deployments. Cryptology ePrint Archive, Report 2020/726; to appear in the Journal of Cryptology (2020). https://eprint.iacr.org/2020/726

16. Digital Signature Standard (DSS). National Institute of Standards and Technology (NIST), FIPS PUB 186-3, U.S. Department of Commerce (2009). http://csrc.nist.gov/publications/fips/fips186-3/fips_186-3.pdf

17. Fersch, M., Kiltz, E., Poettering, B.: On the provable security of (EC)DSA signatures. In: Weippl, E.R., Katzenbeisser, S., Kruegel, C., Myers, A.C., Halevi, S (eds.) ACM CCS 2016, pp. 1651–1662. ACM Press, October 2016

18. Fischlin, M., Harasser, P., Janson, C.: Signatures from sequential-OR proofs. In: Canteaut, A., Ishai, Y. (eds.) EUROCRYPT 2020, Part III. LNCS, vol. 12107, pp. 212–244. Springer, Cham (2020). https://doi.org/10.1007/978-3-030-45727-3_8

19. Fischlin, M., Lehmann, A., Ristenpart, T., Shrimpton, T., Stam, M., Tessaro, S.: Random oracles with(out) programmability. In: Abe, M. (ed.) ASIACRYPT 2010. LNCS, vol. 6477, pp. 303–320. Springer, Heidelberg (2010). https://doi.org/10.1007/978-3-642-17373-8_18

20. Fleischhacker, N., Jager, T., Schröder, D.: On tight security proofs for Schnorr signatures. In: Sarkar, P., Iwata, T. (eds.) ASIACRYPT 2014, Part I. LNCS, vol. 8873, pp. 512–531. Springer, Heidelberg (2014). https://doi.org/10.1007/978-3-662-45611-8_27

21. Fleischhacker, N., Jager, T., Schröder, D.: On tight security proofs for Schnorr signatures. J. Cryptol. 32(2), 566–599 (2019)

22. Garg, S., Bhaskar, R., Lokam, S.V.: Improved bounds on security reductions for discrete log based signatures. In: Wagner, D. (ed.) CRYPTO 2008. LNCS, vol. 5157, pp. 93–107. Springer, Heidelberg (2008). https://doi.org/10.1007/978-3-540-85174-5_6

23. Gjøsteen, K., Jager, T.: Practical and tightly-secure digital signatures and authenticated key exchange. In: Shacham, H., Boldyreva, A. (eds.) CRYPTO 2018, Part II. LNCS, vol. 10992, pp. 95–125. Springer, Cham (2018). https://doi.org/10.1007/978-3-319-96881-0_4

24. Goldwasser, S., Micali, S., Rivest, R.L.: A digital signature scheme secure against adaptive chosen-message attacks. SIAM J. Comput. 17(2), 281–308 (1988)

25. Guillou, L.C., Quisquater, J.-J.: A "paradoxical" indentity-based signature scheme resulting from zero-knowledge. In: Goldwasser, S. (ed.) CRYPTO 1988. LNCS, vol. 403, pp. 216–231. Springer, New York (1990). https://doi.org/10.1007/0-387-34799-2_16

26. Hasegawa, S., Isobe, S.: Lossy identification schemes from decisional RSA. In: International Symposium on Information Theory and its Applications, ISITA 2014, Melbourne, Australia, 26–29 October 2014, pp. 143–147. IEEE (2014)

27. Hofheinz, D., Jager, T.: Tightly secure signatures and public-key encryption. In: Safavi-Naini, R., Canetti, R. (eds.) CRYPTO 2012. LNCS, vol. 7417, pp. 590–607. Springer, Heidelberg (2012). https://doi.org/10.1007/978-3-642-32009-5_35

28. Jager, T., Kiltz, E., Riepel, D., Schäge, S.: Tightly-secure authenticated key exchange, revisited. Cryptology ePrint Archive, Report 2020/1279 (2020). https://eprint.iacr.org/2020/1279

29. Katz, J., Wang, N.: Efficiency improvements for signature schemes with tight security reductions. In: Jajodia, S., Atluri, V., Jaeger, T. (eds.) ACM CCS 2003, pp. 155–164. ACM Press, October 2003

30. Kiltz, E., Masny, D., Pan, J.: Optimal security proofs for signatures from identification schemes. In: Robshaw, M., Katz, J. (eds.) CRYPTO 2016, Part II. LNCS, vol. 9815, pp. 33–61. Springer, Heidelberg (2016). https://doi.org/10.1007/978-3-662-53008-5_2

31. Kiltz, E., O'Neill, A., Smith, A.: Instantiability of RSA-OAEP under chosen-plaintext attack. In: Rabin, T. (ed.) CRYPTO 2010. LNCS, vol. 6223, pp. 295–313. Springer, Heidelberg (2010). https://doi.org/10.1007/978-3-642-14623-7_16

32. Krawczyk, H.: SIGMA: the "SIGn-and-MAc" approach to authenticated Diffie-Hellman and its use in the IKE protocols. In: Boneh, D. (ed.) CRYPTO 2003. LNCS, vol. 2729, pp. 400–425. Springer, Heidelberg (2003). https://doi.org/10.1007/978-3-540-45146-4_24

33. Li, Y., Schäge, S.: No-match attacks and robust partnering definitions: defining trivial attacks for security protocols is not trivial. In: Thuraisingham, B.M., Evans, D., Malkin, T., Xu, D. (eds.) ACM CCS 2017, pp. 1343–1360. ACM Press, October/November 2017

34. Liu, X., Liu, S., Gu, D., Weng, J.: Two-pass authenticated key exchange with explicit authentication and tight security. In: Moriai, S., Wang, H. (eds.) ASIACRYPT 2020, Part II. LNCS, vol. 12492, pp. 785–814. Springer, Cham (2020). https://doi.org/10.1007/978-3-030-64834-3_27

35. Paillier, P., Vergnaud, D.: Discrete-log-based signatures may not be equivalent to discrete log. In: Roy, B. (ed.) ASIACRYPT 2005. LNCS, vol. 3788, pp. 1–20. Springer, Heidelberg (2005). https://doi.org/10.1007/11593447_1

36. Schnorr, C.P.: Efficient identification and signatures for smart cards. In: Brassard, G. (ed.) CRYPTO 1989. LNCS, vol. 435, pp. 239–252. Springer, New York (1990). https://doi.org/10.1007/0-387-34805-0_22

37. Seurin, Y.: On the exact security of Schnorr-type signatures in the random oracle model. In: Pointcheval, D., Johansson, T. (eds.) EUROCRYPT 2012. LNCS, vol. 7237, pp. 554–571. Springer, Heidelberg (2012). https://doi.org/10.1007/978-3-642-29011-4_33

Multiparty Cardinality Testing for Threshold Private Intersection

Pedro Branco[1]([✉]), Nico Döttling[2], and Sihang Pu[2]

[1] IT, IST - University of Lisbon, Lisbon, Portugal
[2] Helmholtz Center for Information Security (CISPA), Saarbrücken, Germany

Abstract. Threshold Private Set Intersection (PSI) allows multiple parties to compute the intersection of their input sets if and only if the intersection is larger than $n - t$, where n is the size of each set and t is some threshold. The main appeal of this primitive is that, in contrast to standard PSI, known upper-bounds on the communication complexity only depend on the threshold t and not on the sizes of the input sets. Current threshold PSI protocols split themselves into two components: A Cardinality Testing phase, where parties decide if the intersection is larger than some threshold; and a PSI phase, where the intersection is computed. The main source of inefficiency of threshold PSI is the former part.

In this work, we present a new Cardinality Testing protocol that allows N parties to check if the intersection of their input sets is larger than $n - t$. The protocol incurs in $\tilde{\mathcal{O}}(Nt^2)$ communication complexity. We thus obtain a Threshold PSI scheme for N parties with communication complexity $\tilde{\mathcal{O}}(Nt^2)$.

1 Introduction

Suppose Alice holds a set S_A and Bob a set S_B. Private set intersection (PSI) is a cryptographic primitive that allows each party to learn the intersection $S_A \cap S_B$ and nothing else. In particular, Alice gets no information about $S_B \setminus S_A$ (and vice-versa). The problem has attracted a lot of attention through the years, with an extended line of work proposing solutions in a variety of different settings (e.g., [11–13,15–17,21,25–27,31–36]). Also, numerous applications have been proposed for PSI such as contact discovery, advertising, etc. (see for example [22] and references therein). More recently, PSI has also been proposed as a solution for private contact tracing (e.g., [2]).

Threshold PSI. In this work, we focus on a special setting of PSI called *Threshold PSI*. Here, the parties involved in the protocol learn the output if the size of the intersection between the input sets of the parties is very large, say larger than $n - t$, where n is the size of the input sets and t is some *threshold* such that $t \ll n$; Otherwise, they learn nothing about the intersection. This is in contrast

J. A. Garay (Ed.): PKC 2021, LNCS 12711, pp. 32–60, 2021.
https://doi.org/10.1007/978-3-030-75248-4_2

with standard PSI where the parties always get the intersection, no matter its size.

The main reason for considering this problem (apart from its numerous applications which we discuss next) is that the amount of communication needed is much smaller than for standard PSI: In particular, there are threshold PSI protocols whose communication complexity depends only on the threshold t and not on the size of the input sets as for standard PSI [17].

Despite its theoretical and practical appeal, there are just a few works that consider this problem [16,17,20], and just one of them achieves communication complexity independent of n [17], in the two party setting.

1.1 Applications of Threshold PSI

A wide number of applications has been suggested for threshold PSI in previous works such as applications to dating apps or biometric authentication mechanisms [17].

One of the most interesting applications for threshold PSI is its use in carpooling (or ridesharing) apps. Suppose two (or more) parties are using a carpooling app, which allows them to share a vehicle if their routes have a large intersection. However, due to privacy issues, they do not want to make their itinerary public. Threshold PSI solves this problem in a simple way [20]: The parties can engage in a threshold PSI protocol, learn the intersection of the routes and, if the intersection is large enough, share a vehicle. Otherwise, they learn nothing and their privacy is maintained.

PSI Using Threshold PSI. Most of current protocols for threshold PSI (including ours) are splitted into two parts: i) a *Cardinality Testing*, where parties decide if the intersection is larger than $n - t$; and ii) secure computation of the intersection of the input sets (which we refer to as the PSI part). The communication complexity of these two parts should depend only on the threshold t and not on the input sets' size n.

Threshold PSI protocols of this form can be used to efficiently compute the intersection, even when no threshold on the intersection is known a priori by the parties, by doing an exponential search for the *right* threshold. In this case, parties can proceed as follows:

1. Run a Cardinality Testing for some t (say $t = 1$).
2. If it succeeds, perform the PSI part. Else, run again the Cardinality Test for $t = 2t$.
3. Repeat Step 2 until the Cardinality Testing succeeds for some threshold t and the set intersection is computed.

By following this blueprint, parties are sure that they overshoot the right threshold by a factor of at most 2. That is, if the intersection is larger than $n - t'$, then the Cardinality Testing will succeed for t such that $t \geq t' > t/2$. Thus, they can compute the intersection incurring only in a factor of 2 overhead over the best insecure protocol. In other words, PSI protocols can be computed with communication complexity depending on the size of the intersection, and not on the size of the sets.

This approach can be useful in scenarios where parties suspect that the intersection is large but they do not know exactly how large it is.

1.2   Our Contributions

In the following, N denotes the number of parties in a multi-party protocol and t is the threshold in a threshold PSI protocol. Below, we briefly describe our results.

Multi-party Cardinality Testing. We develop a new Cardinality Testing scheme that allows N parties to check if the intersection of their input sets, each having size n, is larger than $n - t$ for some threshold $t \ll n$. The protocol needs $\tilde{\mathcal{O}}(Nt^2)$ bits of information to be exchanged.

Along the way, we develop new protocols to securely compute linear algebra related functions (such as compute the rank of an encrypted matrix, invert an encrypted matrix or even solve an encrypted linear system). Our protocols build on ideas of previous works [24,29], except that our protocols are specially crafted for the multi-party case. Technically, we rely heavily on Threshold Public-Key Encryption schemes which are additively homomorphic (such schemes can be constructed from DDH [14], DCR [30], or from several pairings assumptions [3,4]) to perform linear operations.

Multi-party Threshold PSI. We then show how our Cardinality Testing protocol can be used to build a Threshold PSI protocol in the multi-party setting. Our construction achieves communication complexity of $\tilde{\mathcal{O}}(Nt^2)$.

Concurrent Work. Recently, Ghosh and Simkin [18] updated their paper with a generalization to the multi-party case which is similar to the one presented in this paper in Sect. 4. However, they leave as a major open problem the design of a new Cardinality Testing that extends nicely to multiple parties, a problem on which we make relevant advances in this work.

In a concurrent work, Badrinarayanan *et al.* [1] also proposed new protocols for threshold PSI in the multi-party setting. Their results complement ours. In particular, they propose an FHE-based approach to solve the same problem as we do with a communication complexity of $\mathcal{O}(Nt)$, where N is the number of parties and t is the threshold. However, we remark that the goal of our work was to reduce the assumptions needed for threshold PSI. They also propose a TPKE-based protocol that solves a slightly different problem: the parties learn the intersection if and only if the set difference among the sets is large, that is, $|\left(\cup_{i=1}^{N} S_i\right) \setminus \left(\cap_{i=1}^{N} S_i\right)|$ is large[1], which is denoted as $\mathcal{F}_{\mathsf{TPSI\text{-}int}}$ in [1]. This

---

[1] It is a slightly different problem from the one we solve in this work. Here, we want to disclosure the intersection $\cap_{i=1}^{N} S_i$ if $|\cap_{i=1}^{N} S_i| \geq n - t$, which is denoted as $\mathcal{F}_{\mathsf{TPSI\text{-}diff}}$ in [1].

protocol achieves communication complexity of $\tilde{\mathcal{O}}(Nt)$. They achieve that result using completely different techniques from ones used in this work. Namely, they noticed that computing the determinant of a Hankel matrix can be done in sublinear time in the size of the matrix. This implies that the cardinality testing of [17] can actually be realized in time $\tilde{\mathcal{O}}(Nt)$.

1.3   Technical Outline

We now give a high-level overview of the techniques we use to achieve the results discussed above.

Threshold PSI: The Protocol of [17]. Consider two parties Alice and Bob, with their respective input sets S_A and S_B of size n. Suppose that they want to know the intersection $S_A \cap S_B$ iff $|S_A \cap S_B| \geq n - t$ for some threshold $t \ll n$. To compute the intersection, both parties encode their sets into polynomials $P_A(x) = \prod_i^n (x - a_i)$ and $P_B(x) = \prod_i^n (x - b_i)$ over a large finite field $\mathbb{F}$, where $a_i \in S_A$ and $b_i \in S_B$. The main observation of Ghosh and Simkin [17] is that *set reconciliation techniques* (developed by Minsky et al. [28]) can be applied in this scenario: if $|S_A \cap S_B| \geq n - t$, then

$$\frac{P_A(x)}{P_B(x)} = \frac{P_{A \cap B}(x)}{P_{A \cap B}(x)} \frac{P_{A \setminus B}(x)}{P_{B \setminus A}(x)} = \frac{P_{A \setminus B}(x)}{P_{B \setminus A}(x)}$$

and, moreover, $\deg P_{A \setminus B} = \deg P_{B \setminus A} = t$. Hence, Alice and Bob just need to (securely) compute $\mathcal{O}(t)$ evaluation points of the rational function $P_A(x)/P_B(x) = P_{A \setminus B}(x)/P_{B \setminus A}(x)$ and, after interpolating over these points, Bob can recover the denominator (which reveals the intersection).

Of course, Bob should not be able to recover the numerator $P_{A \setminus B}$, otherwise security is compromised. So, [17] used an Oblivious Linear Evaluation (OLE) scheme to *mask* the numerator with a random polynomial that hides $P_{A \setminus B}$ from Bob.

This protocol is only secure if Alice and Bob are absolutely sure that $|S_A \cap S_B| \geq n - t$. Otherwise, additional information could be leaked about the respective inputs. Consequently, Alice and Bob should perform a *Cardinality Testing* protocol, which reveals if $|S_A \cap S_B| \geq n - t$ and nothing else.

Limitations of the Protocol when Extending to the Multi-party Setting. It turns out that the main source of inefficiency when extending Ghosh and Simkin protocol to the multi-party setting is the Cardinality Testing they use. In [17], Alice and Bob encode their sets into polynomials $Q_A(X) = \sum_i^n x^{a_i}$ and $Q_B(X) = \sum_i^n x^{b_i}$, respectively, where $a_i \in S_A$ and $b_i \in S_B$. Then, they can check if $\tilde{Q}(x) = Q_A(x) - Q_B(x)$ is a *sparse* polynomial. If it is, we conclude that the set $(S_A \cup S_B) \setminus (S_A \cap S_B)$ is small. By disposing $\mathcal{O}(t)$ evaluations of the polynomial $\tilde{Q}(x)$ in a Hankel matrix [19] and securely computing its determinant (via a generic secure linear algebra protocol from [24]), both parties can determine if $|S_A \cap S_B| \geq n - t$. The total communication complexity of this protocol is $\mathcal{O}(t^2)$.[2]

However, if we were to *naively* extend this approach to the multi-party setting, we would have N parties computing, say,

$$\tilde{Q}(x) = NQ_1(x) - Q_2(x) - \cdots - Q_N(x)$$

which is a sparse polynomial only if N is small. Moreover, if we were to compute the sparsity of this polynomial using the same approach, we would have a protocol with communication complexity $\mathcal{O}((Nt)^2)$.

Our Approach. Given the state of affairs presented in the previous section, it seems we need to take a different approach from the one of [17] if we want to design an efficient threshold PSI protocol for multiple parties.

Interlude: Secure Linear Algebra. Recall that in the setting of *secure linear algebra* (as in [29] and [24]), there are two parties, one holding an encryption of a matrix $\mathsf{Enc}(\mathsf{pk}, \mathbf{M})$ and the other one holding the corresponding secret key sk. Their goal is to compute an encryption of a (linear algebra related) function of the matrix $\mathbf{M}$, such as the rank, the determinant of $\mathbf{M}$, or, most importantly, find a solution $\mathbf{x}$ for the linear system $\mathbf{Mx} = \mathbf{y}$ where both $\mathbf{M}$ and $\mathbf{y}$ are encrypted. We can easily extend this problem to the multi-party case: Consider N parties, $\mathsf{P}_1, \ldots, \mathsf{P}_N$, each one holding a share of the secret key of a threshold PKE scheme. Additionally, P_1 has an encrypted matrix. The goal of all the parties is to compute an encryption of a (linear algebra related) function of the encrypted matrix.

We observe that the protocols for secure linear algebra presented in [24] can be extended to the multiparty setting by replacing the use of an (additively homomorphic) PKE and garbled circuits for an (additively homomorphic) threshold PKE[3]. Hence, our protocols allow N parties to solve a linear system of the form $\mathbf{Mx} = \mathbf{y}$ under the hood of a threshold PKE scheme.

Cardinality Testing via Degree Test of a Rational Function. Consider again the encodings $P_{S_i}(x) = \prod_j^n (x - a_j^{(i)})$ where $a_j^{(i)} \in S_i$, for N different sets, and the rational function[4]

$$\frac{P_{S_1} + \cdots + P_{S_N}}{P_{S_1}} = \frac{P_{S_1 \backslash (\cap_{j=1}^N S_j)} + \cdots + P_{S_N \backslash (\cap_{j=1}^N S_j)}}{P_{S_1 \backslash (\cap_{j=1}^N S_j)}}.$$

---

[2] Given this, we conclude that the communication complexity of the threshold PSI protocol of [17] is dominated by this Cardinality Testing protocol.

[3] We need a bit-conversion protocol such as [37] to convert between binary circuits and algebra operations.

[4] We actually need to randomize the polynomials in the numerator to guarantee correctness, that is, we need to multiply each term in the numerator by a uniformly chosen element. This is in contrast with the two-party setting where correctness holds even without randomizing the numerator. However, we omit this step for simplicity.

Note that, if the intersection $\cap S_i$ is larger than $n - t$, then $\deg P_{S_1 \setminus (\cap_{j=1}^N S_j)} = \cdots = \deg P_{S_N \setminus (\cap_{j=1}^N S_j)} \leq t$.

Therefore, the Cardinality Testing boils down to the following problem: Given a rational function $f(x) = \tilde{P}_1(x)/\tilde{P}_2(x)$, can we securely decide if $\deg \tilde{P}_1 = \deg \tilde{P}_2 \leq t$ having access to $\mathcal{O}(t)$ evaluation points of $f(x)$?

Our crucial observation is that, if we interpolate two different rational functions f_V and f_W on different two support sets $V = \{v_i, f(v_i)\}$ and $W = \{w_i, f(w_i)\}$ each one of size $2t$, then we have:

1. $f_V = f_W$ if $\deg P_1 = \deg P_2 \leq t$
2. $f_V \neq f_W$ if $\deg P_1 = \deg P_2 > t$

except with negligible probability over the uniform choice of v_i, w_i.

Moreover, interpolating a rational function can be reduced to solving a linear system of equations. Hence, by using the Secure Linear Algebra tools developed before, we can perform the *degree test* revealing nothing else than the output. In other words, we can decide if the size of the intersection is smaller than $n - t$ while revealing no additional information about the parties' input sets.

Security of the Protocol. We prove security of our Cardinality Testing in the UC framework [7]. However, there is a subtle issue in our security proof. Namely, our secure linear algebra protocols cannot be proven UC-secure since the inputs are encrypted under a public key which, in the UC setting, needs to come from somewhere.

We solve this problem by using the Externalized UC framework [8]. In this framework, the secure linear algebra ideal functionalities all share a common setup which, in our case, is the public key (and the corresponding secret key shares). We prove security of our secure linear algebra protocols in this setting.

Since the secure linear algebra protocols are secure if they all share the same public key, then, on the Cardinality Testing, we just need to create this public key and share it over these functionalities. Thus, we prove standard UC-security of our Cardinality Testing.

Badrinarayanan et al. [1] also encounter the same problem as we did and they opted to not prove security of each subprotocol individually, but rather prove security only for their main protocol (where the public key is created and shared among these smaller protocols).

Multi-party PSI. Having developed a Cardinality Testing, we can now focus on securely computing the intersection. In fact, our protocol for computing the intersection can be seen as a *generalization* of Gosh and Simkin protocol [17]. Again, by encoding the sets as above (that is, $P_{S_i}(x) = \prod_j^n (x - a_j^{(i)})$ where $a_j^{(i)} \in S_j$ and S_j is the set of party P_j) and knowing that the intersection is larger than $n - t$, parties can securely compute the rational function[5] $(P_{S_1} + \cdots + P_{S_N})/P_{S_1}$.

---

[5] Again, we omit the randomization of the polynomials. Actually, without randomization, these methods (including [17]) are exactly the same as the technique for set reconciliation problem in [28].

By interpolating the rational function on any $\mathcal{O}(t)$ points, party P_1 can recover the denominator and compute the intersection.

The main difference between our protocol and the one in [17] is that we replace the OLE calls used in [17] by a threshold additively homomorphic PKE scheme (which can be seen as the multi-party replacement of OLE).

1.4   Other Related Work

Oblivious Linear Algebra. Cramer and Damgård [9] proposed a constant-round protocol to securely solve a linear system of unknown rank over a finite field. Since they were mainly focused on round-optimality, the communication cost of their proposal is $\Omega(t^3)$ for $\mathcal{O}(t^2)$ input size. Bouman et al. [5] recently constructed a secure linear algebra protocol for multiple parties, however they focused on computational complexity.

Other secure linear algebra schemes in the two-party setting were presented by Nissim and Weinreb in [29] and Kiltz et al. in [24]. In the following, consider (square) matrices of size t over a field $\mathbb{F}$. These two works take different approaches: [29] obliviously solves linear algebra related problems directly via Gaussian elimination in $\mathcal{O}(t^2)$ communication complexity, for a square matrix of size t. However, their approach has an error probability that decreases polynomially with t. In other words, the error probability is only sufficiently small when applied to linear system with large matrices. Whereas [24] has error probability decreases polynomially with $|\mathbb{F}|$, which is negligible when $\mathbb{F}$ is of exponentially size.[6]

2   Preliminaries

If S is a finite set, then $x \leftarrow_\$ S$ denotes an element x sampled from S according to a uniform distribution and $|S|$ denotes the cardinality of S. If $\mathcal{A}$ is an algorithm, $y \leftarrow \mathcal{A}(x)$ denotes the output y after running $\mathcal{A}$ on input x. For $N \in \mathbb{N}$, we define $[N] = \{1, \ldots, N\}$.

Given two distributions D_1, D_2, we say that they are computationally indistinguishable, denoted as $D_1 \approx D_2$, if no probabilistic polynomial-time (PPT) algorithm is able to distinguish them.

Throughout this work, we denote the security parameter by λ.

---

[6] This is important to us since, in the threshols PSI setting, $t \ll n$ where t is the threshold and n is the set size. Kiltz et al. solve linear algebra problems via minimal polynomials, and use adaptors between garbled circuits and additive homomorphic encryption to reduce round complexity. In this work, we extend Kiltz's protocol to the multiparty case without using garbled circuits (otherwise the circuit size would depend on number of parties) while preserving the same communication complexity for each party ($\mathcal{O}(t^2)$).

2.1   Threshold Public-Key Encryption

We present some ideal functionalities regarding threshold public-key encryption (TPKE) schemes. In the following, N is the number of parties.

Let $\mathcal{F}_{\mathsf{Gen}}$ be the ideal functionality that distributes a secret share of the secret key and the corresponding public key. That is, on input $(\mathsf{sid}, \mathsf{P}_i)$, $\mathcal{F}_{\mathsf{Gen}}$ outputs $(\mathsf{pk}, \mathsf{sk}_i)$ to each party party where $(\mathsf{pk}, \mathsf{sk}_1, \ldots, \mathsf{sk}_N) \leftarrow \mathsf{TPKE.Gen}(1^\lambda, N)$.

Moreover, we define the functionality $\mathcal{F}_{\mathsf{DecZero}}$, which allows N parties, each of them holding a secret share sk_i, to learn if a ciphertext is an encryption of 0 and nothing else. That is, $\mathcal{F}_{\mathsf{DecZero}}$ receives as input a ciphertext c and the secret shares of each of the parties. It outputs 0, if $0 \leftarrow \mathsf{Dec}(\mathsf{sk}, \ldots \mathsf{Dec}(\mathsf{sk}_N, c) \ldots)$, and 1 otherwise. Note that these functionalities can be securely realized on varies PKE schemes such as El Gamal PKE or Pailler[7] PKE [21].

We also assume that the underlying TPKE (or plain PKE) is always additively homomorphic, unless stated otherwise (see Supplementary Material A.1).

2.2   UC Framework and Ideal Functionalities

In this work, we use the UC framework by Canetti [7] to analyze the security of our protocols.[8] Throughout this work, we only consider semi-honest adversaries, unless stated otherwise. We denote the underlying environment by $\mathcal{Z}$. For a protocol π and a real-world adversary $\mathcal{A}$, we denote the real-world ensemble by $\mathsf{EXEC}_{\pi, \mathcal{A}, \mathcal{Z}}$ Similarly, for an ideal functionality $\mathcal{F}$ and a simulator Sim, we denote the ideal-world ensemble by $\mathsf{IDEAL}_{\mathcal{F}, \mathsf{Sim}, \mathcal{Z}}$.

Definition 1. *We say that a protocol π UC-realizes $\mathcal{F}$ if for every PPT adversary $\mathcal{A}$ there is a PPT simulator Sim such that for all PPT environments $\mathcal{Z}$,*

$$\mathsf{IDEAL}_{\mathcal{F}, \mathsf{Sim}, \mathcal{Z}} \approx \mathsf{EXEC}_{\pi, \mathcal{A}, \mathcal{Z}}$$

where $\mathcal{F}$ is an ideal functionality.

In the following, we present some ideal functionalities that will be recurrent for the rest of the paper.

Multi-party Threshold Private Set Intersection. This ideal functionality implements the multi-party version of the functionality above. Here, each of the N parties input a set and they learn the intersection if and only if the intersection is large enough.

---

[7] We will assume the message space of Paillier's cryptosystem as a field as also mentioned in [24].

[8] We refer the reader to [7] for a detailed explanation of the framework.

$\mathcal{F}_{\mathsf{MTPSI}}$ **functionality**

Parameters: $\mathsf{sid}, N, t \in \mathbb{N}$ known to both parties.

- Upon receiving $(\mathsf{sid}, \mathsf{P}_i, S_i)$ from party P_i, $\mathcal{F}_{\mathsf{MTPSI}}$ stores S_i and ignores future messages from P_i with the same sid.
- Once $\mathcal{F}_{\mathsf{MTPSI}}$ has stored all inputs S_i, for $i \in [n]$, it does the following: If $|S_1 \setminus (\cap_{i=2}^N S_i)| \leq t$, $\mathcal{F}_{\mathsf{MTPSI}}$ outputs $S_\cap = \cap_{i=1}^N S_i$. Else, it outputs $\bot$.

Externalized UC Protocol with Global Setup. We introduce a notion of protocol emulation from [8], called externalized UC emulation (EUC), which is a simplified version of UC with global setup (GUC).

Definition 2 (EUC-Emulation [8]). *We say that π EUC-realizes $\mathcal{F}$ with respect to shared functionality $\bar{\mathcal{G}}$ (or, in shorthand, that π $\bar{\mathcal{G}}$-EUC-emulates ϕ) if for any PPT adversary $\mathcal{A}$ there exists a PPT adversary Sim such that for any shared functionality $\bar{\mathcal{G}}$, we have:*

$$\mathsf{IDEAL}^{\bar{\mathcal{G}}}_{\mathcal{F},\mathsf{Sim},\mathcal{Z}} \approx \mathsf{EXEC}^{\bar{\mathcal{G}}}_{\pi,\mathcal{A},\mathcal{Z}}$$

Notice that the formalism implies that the shared functionality $\bar{\mathcal{G}}$ exists both in the model for executing π and also in the model for executing the ideal protocol for $\mathcal{F}$, $\mathsf{IDEAL}_{\mathcal{F}}$.

We remark that the notion of $\bar{\mathcal{G}}$-EUC-emulation can be naturally extended to protocols that use several different shared functionalities (instead of only one).

2.3 Polynomials and Interpolation

We present a series of results that will be useful to analyze correctness and security of the protocols presented in this work.

The following lemma show how we can mask a polynomial of degree less than t using a uniformly random polynomial.

Lemma 1 ([25]). *Let $\mathbb{F}_p$ be a prime order field, $P(x), Q(x)$ be two polynomials over $\mathbb{F}_p$ such that $\deg P = \deg Q = d \leq t$ and $\gcd(P, Q) = 1$. Let $R_1, R_2 \leftarrow_\$ \mathbb{F}_p$ such that $\deg R_1 = \deg R_2 = t$. Then $U(x) = P(x)R_1(x) + Q(x)R_2(x)$ is a uniformly random polynomial with $\deg U \leq 2t$.*

Note that this result also applies for multiple polynomials as long as they don't share a common factor (referring to Theorem 2 and Theorem 3 of [25] for more details).

We say that f is a rational function if $f(x) = \frac{P(x)}{Q(x)}$ for two polynomials P and Q.

The next two lemmata show that we can recover a rational function via interpolation and that this function is unique.

Lemma 2 ([28]). *Let $f(x) = P(x)/Q(x)$ be rational function where $\deg P(x) = m$ and $\deg Q(x) = n$. Then $f(x)$ can be uniquely recovered (up to constants) via interpolation from $m + n + 1$ points. In particular, if $P(x)$ and $Q(x)$ are monic, $f(x)$ can be uniquely recovered from $m + n$ points.*

Lemma 3 ([28]). *Choose V to be a support set[9] of cardinality $m_1 + m_2 + 1$. Then, there is a unique rational function $f(x) = P(x)/Q(x)$ that can be interpolated from V, and $P(x)$ has degree at most m_1 and $Q(x)$ has degree at most m_2.*

3   Oblivious Degree Test for Rational Functions

Suppose we have a rational function $f(x) = P(x)/Q(x)$ where $P(x)$ and $Q(x)$ are two polynomials with the same degree. In this section, we present a protocol that allows several parties to check if $\deg P(x) = \deg Q(x) \leq t$ for some threshold $t \in Z$. To this end, and inspired by the works of [24,29], we present a multi-party protocol to obliviously solve a linear system $\mathbf{Mx} = \mathbf{y}$ over a finite field $\mathbb{F}$ with communication complexity $O(t^2 k \lambda N)$, where $\mathbf{M} \in \mathbb{F}^{t \times t}$, $\log |\mathbb{F}| = k$ and N is the number of parties involved in the protocol.

3.1   Oblivious Linear Algebra

In this section, we state the Secure Linear Algebra protocols that we need to build our degree test protocol. For the sake of briefness, the protocols are presented in Appendix B. These protocol all have the following form: There is a public key of a TPKE that encrypts a matrix $\mathbf{M}$ and every party involved in the protocol has a share of the secret key.

Note that if we let parties P_i input their encrypted matrix $\mathsf{Enc}(\mathbf{M})$, then the ideal functionality $\mathcal{F}$ has to know the secret key (by receiving secret key shares from all parties), otherwise $\mathcal{F}$ cannot compute the corresponding function correctly. However, this will cause an unexpected problem in security proof as mentioned in our introduction and [1]: The environment $\mathcal{Z}$ will learn the secret key as well since it can choose inputs for all parties. We fix this by relying on global UC framework where exists a shared functionality $\bar{\mathcal{G}}$ in charge of distributing key pairs ($\mathcal{F}_{\mathsf{Gen}}$ from Sect. 2.1).

Oblivious Matrix Multiplication. We begin by presenting the ideal functionality for a multi-party protocol to jointly compute the product of two matrices, under a TPKE. The protocol is presented in Appendix B.1.

---

[9] A support set is a set of pairs (x, y).

Ideal Functionality. The ideal functionality for oblivious matrix multiplication is presented below.

$\mathcal{F}_{\mathsf{OMM}}$ functionality

Parameters: sid, $N, q, t \in \mathbb{N}$ and $\mathbb{F}$, where $\mathbb{F}$ is a field of order q, known to the N parties involved in the protocol.

Global Setup: pk public-key of a threshold PKE scheme and sk_i distributed to each party P_i via $\mathcal{F}_{\mathsf{Gen}}$.

– Upon receiving $(\mathsf{sid}, \mathsf{P}_1, \mathsf{Enc}(\mathsf{pk}, \mathbf{M}_l), \mathsf{Enc}(\mathsf{pk}, \mathbf{M}_r))$ from party P_1 (where $\mathbf{M}_l, \mathbf{M}_r \in \mathbb{F}^{t \times t}$), $\mathcal{F}_{\mathsf{OMM}}$ outputs $\mathsf{Enc}(\mathsf{pk}, \mathbf{M}_l \cdot \mathbf{M}_r)$ to P_1 and $(\mathsf{Enc}(\mathsf{pk}, \mathbf{M}_l), \mathsf{Enc}(\mathsf{pk}, \mathbf{M}_r), \mathsf{Enc}(\mathsf{pk}, \mathbf{M}_l \cdot \mathbf{M}_r))$ to all other parties P_i, for $i = 2, \ldots, N$.

Securely Compute the Rank of a Matrix. We present the ideal functionality to obliviously compute the rank of an encrypted matrix. The protocol is presented in Appendix B.2.

Ideal Functionality. The ideal functionality of oblivious rank computation is defined below.

$\mathcal{F}_{\mathsf{ORank}}$ functionality

Parameters: sid, $N, q, t \in \mathbb{N}$ and $\mathbb{F}$, where $\mathbb{F}$ is a field of order q, known to the N parties involved in the protocol.

Global Setup: pk public-key of a threshold PKE scheme and sk_i distributed to each party P_i via $\mathcal{F}_{\mathsf{Gen}}$.

– Upon receiving $(\mathsf{sid}, \mathsf{P}_1, \mathsf{Enc}(\mathsf{pk}, \mathbf{M}))$ from party P_1 (where $\mathbf{M} \in \mathbb{F}^{t \times t}$), $\mathcal{F}_{\mathsf{ORank}}$ outputs $\mathsf{Enc}(\mathsf{pk}, \mathsf{rank}(\mathbf{M}))$ to P_1 and $(\mathsf{Enc}(\mathsf{pk}, \mathbf{M}), \mathsf{Enc}(\mathsf{pk}, \mathsf{rank}(\mathbf{M})))$ to all other parties P_i, for $i = 2, \ldots, N$.

Oblivious Linear System Solver. We now show how N parties can securely solve a linear system using the multiplication protocol above. We follow the ideas from [24] to reduce the problem to minimal polynomials, and the only difference is we focus on multiparty setting.

The protocol is presented in Appendix B.5. Informally, we evaluate an arithmetic circuit following the ideas of [10], and for the unary representation, a binary-conversion protocol [37] is required. All of above protocols can be based on Paillier cryptosystem.

Ideal Functionality. We give an ideal functionality of oblivious linear system solver for multiparty as follows.

$\mathcal{F}_{\mathsf{OLS}}$ functionality

Parameters: sid, $N, q, t \in \mathbb{N}$ and $\mathbb{F}$, where $\mathbb{F}$ is a field of order q , known to the N parties involved in the protocol. pk public-key of a threshold PKE scheme.

Global Setup: pk public-key of a threshold PKE scheme and sk_i distributed to each party P_i via $\mathcal{F}_{\mathsf{Gen}}$.

- Upon receiving $(\mathsf{sid}, \mathsf{P}_1, \mathsf{Enc}(\mathsf{pk}, \mathbf{M}), \mathsf{Enc}(\mathsf{pk}, \mathbf{y}))$ from party P_1 (assuming there is a solution $\mathbf{x}$ for $\mathbf{Mx} = \mathbf{y}$), $\mathcal{F}_{\mathsf{OLS}}$ outputs $\mathsf{Enc}(\mathsf{pk}, \mathbf{x})$ such that $\mathbf{Mx} = \mathbf{y}$.

3.2 Oblivious Degree Test

We now present the main protocol of this section and the one that will be using in the construction of threshold PSI. Given a rational function $P(x)/Q(x)$ (for two polynomials $P(x)$ and $Q(x)$ with the same degree) and two support sets V_1, V_2, the protocol allows us to test if the degree of the polynomials is less than some threshold t. Of course, we can do this using generic approaches like garbled circuits. However, we are interested in solutions with communication complexity depending on t (even when the degree of $P(x)$ or $Q(x)$ is much larger than t).

Ideal Functionality. The ideal functionality for degree test of rational functions is presented below.

$\mathcal{F}_{\mathsf{SDT}}$ functionality

Parameters: sid, $N, q, n, t \in \mathbb{N}$, $\mathbb{F}$ is a field of order q and t is a predefined threshold, known to the N parties involved in the protocol. pk public-key of a threshold PKE scheme. $\alpha_1, \ldots, \alpha_{4t+2} \leftarrow_{\$} \mathbb{F}$ known to the N parties.

Global Setup: pk public-key of a threshold PKE scheme and sk_i distributed to each party P_i via $\mathcal{F}_{\mathsf{Gen}}$.

- Upon receiving $(\mathsf{sid}, \mathsf{P}_1, \mathsf{Enc}(\mathsf{pk}, f_1), \ldots, \mathsf{Enc}(\mathsf{pk}, f_{4t+2}))$ from party P_1 (where $f_i = P_1(\alpha_i)/P_2(\alpha_i)$, and P_1, P_2 are two co-prime polynomials with same degree t' (additionally, P_2 is monic), $\mathcal{F}_{\mathsf{SDT}}$ outputs 0 if $t' \leq t$; otherwise it outputs 1.

Protocol. We present the Protocol 1 for secure degree test which we denote by
secDT. The main idea of the protocol is to interpolate the rational function on
two different support sets and check if the result is the same in both experiments.

Recall that interpolating a rational function boils down to solve a linear
equation. We can thus use the secure linear algebra tools developed to allow the
parties to securely solve a linear equation.

Also recall that two rational functions $C_v^{(1)}/C_v^{(2)} = C_w^{(1)}/C_w^{(2)}$ are equivalent
if $C_v^{(1)}C_w^{(2)} - C_w^{(1)}C_v^{(2)} = 0$. Thus, in the end, parties just need to securely check
if $C_v^{(1)}C_w^{(2)} - C_w^{(1)}C_v^{(2)}$ is equal to 0.

Comments. Suppose that, for an interpolation point α_i, the rational function
$f(x) = P(x)/Q(x)$ is well-defined but $Q(\alpha_i) = P(\alpha_i) = 0$ such that we cannot compute $f(\alpha_i)$ by division. In this case[12], the parties evaluate $\tilde{P}(x) =
P(x)/(x - \alpha_i)$ and $\tilde{Q}(x) = Q(x)/(x - \alpha_i)$ on α_i and set $f(\alpha_i) = \tilde{P}(\alpha_i)/\tilde{Q}(\alpha_i)$.
These points are called *tagged values* and this strategy is used in [28]. In
more details, instead of using $\mathsf{Enc}(\mathsf{pk}, f_i)$ for α_i, we will use a tagged pair
$\left(\mathsf{Enc}\left(\mathsf{pk}, s_i^{(1)}\right), \mathsf{Enc}\left(\mathsf{pk}, s_i^{(2)}\right)\right)$ where $s_i^{(1)} = \frac{P_1(\alpha_i)}{x - \alpha_i}$ and $s_i^{(2)} = \frac{P_2(\alpha_i)}{x - \alpha_i}$. Corre-
spondingly, replace each row of $\mathsf{Enc}(\mathsf{pk}, \mathbf{M}_r)$ and $\mathsf{Enc}(\mathsf{pk}, \mathbf{y}_r)$ with

$$\mathsf{Enc}\left(\mathsf{pk}, \left[s_i^{(2)}r_i^t \ \ldots \ s_i^{(2)} -s_i^{(1)}r_i^{t-1} \ \ldots \ -s_i^{(1)}\right]\right)$$

and $\mathsf{Enc}\left(\mathsf{pk}, \left[s_i^{(1)}r_i^t\right]\right)$, respectively.

Also, note that the protocol easily generalizes to rational functions $f(x) =
P(x)/Q(x)$ with $\deg P \neq \deg Q$ (which is actually what we use in the follow-
ing sections). We present the version where $\deg P = \deg Q$ for simplicity. In
fact, the case where $\deg P \neq \deg Q$ can be reduced to the presented case by
multiplying the least degree polynomial by a uniformly chosen $R(x)$ of degree
$\max\{\deg P(x) - \deg Q(X), \deg Q(x) - \deg P(x)\}$.

Moreover, if $t' > t$, the linear system for rational interpolation might be
unsolvable. In this case, there is no solution which means we cannot interpolate
an appropriate rational function on certain support set. Therefore, the parties
just return 0.

Analysis. We analyze correctness, security and communication complexity of
the protocol. We begin the analysis with the following auxiliary lemma.

Lemma 4. *Let* $\mathbb{F}$ *be a field with* $|\mathbb{F}| = \omega(2^{\log \lambda})$. *Let* $V = \{(v_i, f(v_i))|\forall i \in
[1, 2t + 1]\}$ *and* $W = \{(w_i, f(w_i))|\forall i \in [1, 2t + 1]\}$ *be two support sets each of*

---

[10] Note that this is the linear system that we need to solve in order to perform rational
interpolation [28].

[11] The polynomial multiplication can be expressed as matrix multiplication.

[12] In the case that only $Q(\alpha_i) = 0$, use a different tagged pair $(\mathsf{Enc}(\mathsf{pk}, s_i^{(1)}), \mathsf{Enc}(\mathsf{pk}, 0))$,
and this can be noticed by the party who owns polynomial $Q(x)$. In our PSI setting,
it is party P_1.

Protocol 1 Secure Degree Test secDT

Setup: Each party has a secret key share sk_i for a public key pk of a TPKE $\mathsf{TPKE} = (\mathsf{Gen}, \mathsf{Enc}, \mathsf{Dec})$. The parties have access to the ideal functionalities $\mathcal{F}_{\mathsf{ORank}}$, $\mathcal{F}_{\mathsf{OLS}}$, $\mathcal{F}_{\mathsf{OMM}}$ and $\mathcal{F}_{\mathsf{DecZero}}$. The values $\{\alpha_1, \ldots, \alpha_{4t+2}\} \leftarrow_{\$} \mathbb{F}^{4t+2}$ are public, from which also sampling a random point $\alpha^* \leftarrow_{\$} \{\alpha_1, \ldots, \alpha_{4t+2}\}$.

Input: Party P_1 inputs $\{(\alpha_1, \mathsf{Enc}(\mathsf{pk}, f_1)), \ldots, (\alpha_{4t+2}, \mathsf{Enc}(\mathsf{pk}, f_{4t+2}))\}$, where $f_i = \frac{P_1(\alpha_i)}{P_2(\alpha_i)}$, where $P_1(x), P_2(x)$ are two polynomials with degree $\deg(P_1) = \deg(P_2) = t' = \mathsf{poly}(\log|\mathbb{F}|)$ and such that $P_2(\alpha_i) \neq 0$ for all $i \in [2t]$.

1: P_1 sets $\{(\alpha_j, \mathsf{Enc}(\mathsf{pk}, f_j))\}_{j \in [2t+1]} = \{(v_j, \mathsf{Enc}(\mathsf{pk}, f_{v,j}))\}_{j \in [2t+1]}$, and $\{(\alpha_j, \mathsf{Enc}(\mathsf{pk}, f_j))\}_{j \in \{2t+2, \ldots, 4t+2\}} = \{(w_j, \mathsf{Enc}(f_{w,j}))\}_{j \in [2t+1]}$. It homomorphically generates an encrypted linear system consisting of

$$\mathsf{Enc}(\mathsf{pk}, \mathbf{M}_r) = \mathsf{Enc}\left(\mathsf{pk}, \begin{bmatrix} r_1^t & \cdots & 1 & -f_{r,1} \cdot r_1^{t-1} & \cdots & -f_{r,1} \\ \vdots & & \vdots & \vdots & & \vdots \\ r_{2t+1}^t & \cdots & 1 & -f_{r,2t+1} \cdot r_{2t+1}^{t-1} & \cdots & -f_{r,2t+1} \end{bmatrix}\right)$$

and

$$\mathsf{Enc}(\mathsf{pk}, \mathbf{y}_r) = \mathsf{Enc}\left(\mathsf{pk}, \begin{bmatrix} f_{r,1} \cdot r_1^t \\ \vdots \\ f_{r,2t+1} \cdot r_{2t+1}^t \end{bmatrix}\right)$$

for $r = \{v, w\}$.[10] Here $\mathbf{M}_r$ is a square matrix with dimension $2t + 1$ and $\mathbf{y}_r$ a $2t + 1$-sized vector.

2: All parties jointly compute $\mathsf{Enc}(\mathsf{pk}, \mathrm{rank}(\mathbf{M}_r) - \mathrm{rank}([\mathbf{M}_r\|\mathbf{y}])$ for $r \in \{v, w\}$ through two invocations of $\mathcal{F}_{\mathsf{ORank}}$ and mutually decrypt the ciphertext via $\mathcal{F}_{\mathsf{DecZero}}$. If the result is different from 0, they abort the protocol.

3: All parties mutually solve the two linear systems above using $\mathcal{F}_{\mathsf{OLS}}$ such that each party gets $\mathsf{Enc}\left(\mathsf{pk}, \left(\mathbf{c}_v^{(1)}\|\mathbf{c}_v^{(2)}\right)\right)$ and $\mathsf{Enc}\left(\mathsf{pk}, \left(\mathbf{c}_w^{(1)}\|\mathbf{c}_w^{(2)}\right)\right)$, where $\mathbf{M}_r\begin{bmatrix} \mathbf{c}_r^{(1)} \\ \mathbf{c}_r^{(2)} \end{bmatrix} = \mathbf{y}_r$, for $r \in \{v, w\}$. Besides, $\mathbf{c}_r^{(1)}$ and $\mathbf{c}_r^{(2)}$ are $t + 1$- and t-sized vectors, respectively.

4: All parties compute the polynomials $C_r^{(1)}(x) = \sum_{j=0}^{t} \mathbf{c}_{r,j}^{(1)} x^{t-j}$, and $C_r^{(2)}(x) = x^t + \sum_{j=1}^{t} \mathbf{c}_{r,j-1}^{(2)} x^{t-j}$, for $r \in \{v, w\}$, then compute

$$\mathsf{Enc}(\mathsf{pk}, z) = \mathsf{Enc}(\mathsf{pk}, C_v^{(1)}(x) \cdot C_w^{(2)}(x) - C_w^{(1)}(x) \cdot C_v^{(2)}(x))$$

by invoking $\mathcal{F}_{\mathsf{OMM}}$.[11] Here $C_r^{(b)}(x)$ are evaluated on a random selected point $\alpha^* \leftarrow_{\$} \{\alpha_1, \ldots, \alpha_{4t+2}\}$.

5: All parties jointly use $\mathcal{F}_{\mathsf{DecZero}}$ to check if $z = 0$. If it is, output 1. Otherwise, output 0.

---

them with $2t + 1$ elements over a field $\mathbb{F}$, with $w_i \leftarrow_{\$} \mathbb{F}$, and $f(x) := \frac{P(x)}{Q(x)}$ is some unknown reduced rational function (i.e., $P(x), Q(x)$ are co-prime), where $\deg(P) = \deg(Q) = t'$ and $t < t'$ where $t, t' \in \mathsf{poly}(\lambda)$. We also require $Q(x)$ to be monic (to fit in our application). Additionally, assume that $Q(v_i) \neq 0$ and $Q(w_i) \neq 0$ for every $i \in [2t + 1]$.

If we recover two rational function $f_V(x), f_W(x)$ by interpolation on V, W, respectively, then

$$\Pr\left[f_V(x) = f_W(x)\right] \leq \mathsf{negl}(\lambda)$$

over the choice of v_i, w_i.

Proof. Let $f_V(x) = A(x)/B(x)$ the rational function recovered by rational interpolation over the support set V and let $f(x) = P(x)/Q(x)$ be the rational function interpolated over any $2t' + 1$ interpolation points. We have that $f_V(v_i) = f(v_i)$ for all $i \in [2t + 1]$ and hence

$$\frac{A(v_i)}{B(v_i)} = \frac{P(v_i)}{Q(v_i)} \Leftrightarrow A(v_i)Q(v_i) = P(v_i)B(v_i).$$

Since $\gcd(P(x), Q(x)) = 1$, then the polynomial $\tilde{P}(x) = A(x)Q(x) - P(x)B(x)$ is different from the null polynomial (as $\deg(P) = t' > t = \deg(A)$). Moreover, v_i is a root of $\tilde{P}(x)$, for all $i \in [2t + 1]$, and $\deg \tilde{P}(x) \leq t + t'$ (which means that $\tilde{P}(x)$ has at most $t + t'$ roots).

Analogously, let $f_W = C(x)/D(x)$ be the rational function resulting from interpolating over the support set W and let $\tilde{Q}(x) = C(x)Q(x) - D(x)P(x)$. We have that $\tilde{Q}(w_i) = 0$ for all $i \in [2t + 1]$. Hence, if $f_V(x) = f_W(x)$, then we have that the points w_i are also roots of $\tilde{P}(x)$. But, since the points w_i are chosen uniformly at random from $\mathbb{F}$ (which is of exponential size when compared to t, t'), then there is a negligible probability that all w_i's are roots of $\tilde{P}(x)$.

Concretely,

$$\Pr\left[f_V = f_W\right] \leq \Pr\left[\tilde{P}(w_i) = 0 \forall i[2t + 1]\right]$$

$$= \prod_i^{2t+1} \Pr\left[\tilde{P}(w_i) = 0\right] \leq \left(\frac{\deg \tilde{P}}{|\mathbb{F}|}\right)^{2t+1}$$

which is negligible for $|\mathbb{F}| \in \omega(2^{\log \lambda})$.   □

Theorem 1 (Correctness). *The protocol* secDT *is correct.*

Proof. The protocol interpolates two polynomials from two different support sets. Then, it checks if the two interpolated polynomials are the same by computing

$$C_v^{(1)}(x) \cdot C_w^{(2)}(x) - C_w^{(1)}(x) \cdot C_v^{(2)}(x))$$

which should be equal to 0 if $C_v^{(1)}(x)/C_v^{(2)}(x) = C_w^{(1)}(x)/C_w^{(2)}(x)$.

If $t' \leq t$, then by Lemma 3, there is a unique rational function can be recovered thus the final output of the algorithm should be 1. On the other hand, if $t' > t$, the linear system can be either unsolvable or solvable but yielding two different solutions with overwhelming probability by Lemma 4. In this case, the protocol outputs 0.   □

Theorem 2. *The protocol* secDT *EUC-securely realizes* $\mathcal{F}_{\mathsf{SDT}}$ *with shared ideal functionality* $\mathcal{F}_{\mathsf{Gen}}$ *in the* $(\mathcal{F}_{\mathsf{ORank}}, \mathcal{F}_{\mathsf{OMM}}, \mathcal{F}_{\mathsf{OLS}}, \mathcal{F}_{\mathsf{DecZero}})$-*hybrid model against semi-honest adversaries corrupting at most* $N - 1$ *parties, given that* TPKE *is IND-CPA.*

Proof (Sketch). The simulator sends the corrupted parties' input to the ideal functionality and obtains the output (either 0 or 1). Then, it simulates the ideal functionalities $(\mathcal{F}_{\mathsf{ORank}}, \mathcal{F}_{\mathsf{OMM}}, \mathcal{F}_{\mathsf{OLS}}, \mathcal{F}_{\mathsf{DecZero}})$ so that the output in the real-world execution is the same as in the ideal-world execution. In particular, the simulator is able to recover the secret key shares via $\mathcal{F}_{\mathsf{ORank}}, \mathcal{F}_{\mathsf{OMM}}, \mathcal{F}_{\mathsf{OLS}}$ and, thus, simulate $\mathcal{F}_{\mathsf{DecZero}}$ in the right way.

Indistinguishability of executions holds given that TPKE is IND-CPA.   □

Communication Complexity. When we instantiate $\mathcal{F}_{\mathsf{OLS}}$ with the protocol from the previous section, the communication complexity of secDT is $\mathcal{O}(Nt^2)$.

4   Multi-party Threshold Private Set Intersection

We present our protocol for Threshold PSI in the multi-party setting. Our protocol to privately compute the intersection can be seen as a generalization of Ghosh and Simkin protocol [17] where we replace the OLE by a TPKE (which fits nicer in a multi-party setting). The main difference between our protocol and theirs is in the cardinality test protocol used.

We begin by presenting the protocol to securely compute a cardinality testing between N sets. Then, we plug everything together in a PSI protocol.

4.1   Secure Cardinality Testing

Ideal Functionality. The ideal functionality for Secure Cardinality Testing receives the sets from all the parties and outputs 1 if and only if the intersection between these sets is larger than some threshold. Else, no information is disclosed. The ideal functionality for multi-party cardinality testing is given as follows.

$\mathcal{F}_{\mathsf{MPCT}}$ **functionality**

Parameters: sid, $N, n, t \in \mathbb{N}$ known to both parties.

- Upon receiving $(\mathsf{sid}, \mathsf{P}_i, S_i)$ from party P_i, $\mathcal{F}_{\mathsf{MPCT}}$ stores S_i and ignores future messages from P_i with the same sid;
- Once $\mathcal{F}_{\mathsf{MPCT}}$ has stored all inputs S_i, for $i \in [N]$, it does the following: If $|S_\cap| \geq n - t$, $\mathcal{F}_{\mathsf{MPCT}}$ outputs 1 to all parties, where $|S_\cap| = \cap_{i=1}^{N} S_i$. Else, it returns 0.

Protocol 2 Private Cardinality Test for Multi-party MPCT

Setup: Values $\alpha_1, \ldots, \alpha_{4t+2} \leftarrow_\$ \mathbb{F}$, threshold $t \in \mathbb{N}$ and N parties. Functionalities $\mathcal{F}_{\mathsf{Gen}}$ and $\mathcal{F}_{\mathsf{SDT}}$, and a IND-CPA TPKE $\mathsf{TPKE} = (\mathsf{Gen}, \mathsf{Enc}, \mathsf{Dec})$.

Input: Each party P^i inputs a set $S_i = \{a_i^{(1)}, \ldots, a_i^{(n)}\} \in \mathbb{F}^n$.

1: Each party P_i sends request $(\mathsf{sid}, \mathsf{request}_i)$ to $\mathcal{F}_{\mathsf{Gen}}$ and receives a secret key share sk_i and a public key pk, which is known to every party involved in the protocol.

2: Each party P_i encodes its set as a polynomial $P_i(x) = \prod_{j=1}^n (x - a_i^{(j)})$ and evaluates it on $4t + 2$ points. That is, it computes $P_i(\alpha_1), \ldots, P_i(\alpha_{4t+2})$. It encrypts the points, that is, $c_i^{(j)} \leftarrow \mathsf{Enc}(\mathsf{pk}, r_i \cdot P_i(\alpha_j))$ for a uniformly chosen $r_i \leftarrow_\$ \mathbb{F}$. Finally, it broadcasts $\{c_i^{(j)}\}_{j \in [4t+2]}$.

3: Party P_1 computes $d^{(j)} = (\sum_{i=1}^N c_i^{(j)})/P_1(\alpha_j)$ for each $j \in [4t+2]$. Then, sends $\{\alpha_j, d^{(j)}\}_j$ for every j, and sk_1 to the ideal functionality $\mathcal{F}_{\mathsf{SDT}}$.[13] Each party P_i, for $i = 2, \ldots, N$, send sk_i to $\mathcal{F}_{\mathsf{SDT}}$ to check if the degree of the numerator (and the denominator) is at most t.

4: Upon receiving $b \in \{0, 1\}$ from the ideal functionality $\mathcal{F}_{\mathsf{SDT}}$, every party outputs b.

Protocol. We introduce our multiparty Protocol 2 (based on degree test protocol). In the following, $\mathcal{F}_{\mathsf{Gen}}$ be the ideal functionality defined in Sect. 2.1 and $\mathcal{F}_{\mathsf{SDT}}$ be the functionality defined in Sect. 3.2.

Analysis. We now proceed to the analysis of the protocol described above.

Lemma 5. *Given n characteristic polynomials with same degree from $\mathbb{F}[x]$, denoted as $P_1(x), \ldots, P_n(x)$, we argue that, for any j, $P'(x) = \sum_{i=1}^n r_i \cdot P_i(x)$ and $P_j(x)$ are relatively prime with probability $1 - \mathsf{negl}(\log |\mathbb{F}|)$ if $P_1(x), \ldots, P_n(x)$ are mutually relatively prime, where $r_i \leftarrow_\$ \mathbb{F}$ is a uniformly random element.*

Proof. Supposing there is a common divisor of two polynomials $P'(x)$ and $P_j(x)$, since $P_j(x)$ is a characteristic polynomial, we denote $(x - s)$ the common divisor. Therefore, we have $P'(s) = 0$ which can be represented as $\sum_{i=1}^n r_i \cdot P_i(s) = 0$. However, from the mutually relative primality of $P_1(x), \ldots, P_n(x)$, we know that $P_i(s)$ cannot be zero simultaneously which means there exists at least one i^* to make $P_{i^*}(s) \neq 0$. Moreover, r_i are all sampled uniformly from $\mathbb{F}$, the weighted sum of r_i will not be zero with all but negligible probability. This is a contradiction. Therefore, $P'(x)$ and $P_j(x)$ will share a common divisor only with negligible probability. $\qquad\square$

Theorem 3 (Correctness). *The protocol MPCT described above is correct.*

Proof. Note that the encryption $d^{(j)}$ computed by party P_1 are equal to

$$d^{(j)} = \mathsf{Enc}\left(\mathsf{pk}, \left(\sum_{i=1}^N r_i \cdot P_i(\alpha_j)\right) / P_1(\alpha_j)\right).$$

---

[13] Here, $\mathcal{F}_{\mathsf{SDT}}$ has shared functionality $\mathcal{F}_{\mathsf{Gen}}$.

Also, observe that

$$\frac{\sum_{i=1}^{N} r_i \cdot P_i(\alpha_j)}{P_1(\alpha_j)} = \frac{P_{\cap_i S_i}(\alpha_j) \cdot \sum_i^N r_i \cdot P_{S_i \backslash (\cap_{k \neq i} S_k)}(\alpha_j)}{P_{\cap_i S_i}(\alpha_j) \cdot P_{S_1 \backslash (\cap_{k \neq 1} S_k)}}$$

$$= \frac{\sum_i^N r_i \cdot P_{S_i \backslash (\cap_{k \neq i} S_k)}(\alpha_j)}{P_{S_1 \backslash (\cap_{k \neq 1} S_k)}(\alpha_j)},$$

in this way, we make the numerator and denominator relatively prime except with negligible probability by Lemma 5.

Observe that $\deg \sum_i^N r_i \cdot P_{S_i \backslash (\cap_{k \neq i} S_k)}(x) \leq t$ and $\deg P_{S_1 \backslash (\cap_{k \neq 1} S_k)}(x) \leq t$ if and only if $S_\cap \geq n - t$. Hence, by the correctness of $\mathcal{F}_{\mathsf{SDT}}$, the protocol outputs 1 if $S_\cap \geq n - t$, and 0 otherwise. □

Theorem 4. *The protocol* MPCT *securely realizes functionality* $\mathcal{F}_{\mathsf{MPCT}}$ *in the* $(\mathcal{F}_{\mathsf{Gen}}, \mathcal{F}_{\mathsf{SDT}})$*-hybrid model against any semi-honest adversaries corrupting up to* $N - 1$ *parties, given that* TPKE *is IND-CPA.*

Proof. Assume that the adversary is corrupting $N - k$ parties in the protocol, for $k = 1, \ldots, N - 1$. The simulator creates the secret keys and the public key of a threshold PKE in the setup phase while simulating $\mathcal{F}_{\mathsf{Gen}}$ and distributes the secret keys between every party. The simulator Sim takes the inputs (which are sets of size n, say $S_{i_1}, \ldots, S_{i_{N-k}}$) of the corrupted parties and send them to the ideal functionality $\mathcal{F}_{\mathsf{MPCT}}$. It receives the output b from the ideal functionality. If $b = 0$, the simulator chooses k uniformly chosen sets such that $| \cap_{i=1}^N S_i | < n - t$ and proceed the simulation as the honest parties would do. If $b = 1$, the simulator chooses k uniformly chosen random sets such that $| \cap_{i=1}^N S_i | \geq n - t$ and proceed the simulation as the honest parties would do. Note that it can simulate the ideal functionality $\mathcal{F}_{\mathsf{SDT}}$ since it knows all the secret keys of the threshold PKE.

Indistinguishability of executions follows immediately from the IND-CPA property of the underlying threshold PKE scheme. □

Communication Complexity. When we instantiate the $\mathcal{F}_{\mathsf{SDT}}$ with the protocol from the previous section, each party broadcasts $\tilde{\mathcal{O}}(t^2)$. Hence, the total communication complexity is $\tilde{\mathcal{O}}(Nt^2)$, assuming a broadcast channel.

4.2   Multi-party Threshold Private Set Intersection Protocol

In this section, we extend Ghosh and Simkin protocol [17] to the multi-party setting using TPKE. We make use of the cardinality testing designed above to get the Protocol 3.

Analysis. We now proceed to the analysis of the protocol described above. We start by analyzing the correctness of the protocol and then its security.

Theorem 5 (Correctness). *The protocol* MTPSI *is correct.*

Protocol 3 Multi-Party Threshold PSI MTPSI

Setup: Given public parameters as follows: Values $\alpha_1, \ldots, \alpha_{3t+1} \leftarrow_\$ \mathbb{F}$, threshold $t \in \mathbb{N}$ and N parties. Functionalities $\mathcal{F}_{\mathsf{Gen}}$ and $\mathcal{F}_{\mathsf{MPCT}}$, and a threshold additively PKE $\mathsf{TPKE} = (\mathsf{Gen}, \mathsf{Enc}, \mathsf{Dec})$.

Input: Each party P_i inputs a set $S_i = \{a_i^{(1)}, \ldots, a_i^{(n)}\} \in \mathbb{F}^n$.

1: Each party P_i sends its set S_i to $\mathcal{F}_{\mathsf{MPCT}}$. If the functionality $\mathcal{F}_{\mathsf{MPCT}}$ outputs 0, then every party P_i outputs $\perp$ and terminates the protocol.

2: Each party P_i sends request $(\mathsf{sid}, \mathsf{request}_i)$ to $\mathcal{F}_{\mathsf{Gen}}$ and receives a secret key share sk_i and a public key pk, which is known to every party involved in the protocol.

3: **for all** Party P_i **do**

4:     It encodes its set as a polynomial $P_i(x) = \prod_{j=1}^n (x - a_i^{(j)})$ and evaluates it on $3t + 1$ points. That is, it computes $P_i(\alpha_1), \ldots, P_i(\alpha_{3t+1})$.

5:     It samples $R_i(x) \leftarrow_\$ \mathbb{F}[x]$ such that $\deg R_i(x) = t$.

6:     It encrypts these points using pk, that is, it computes $c_i^{(j)} = \mathsf{Enc}(\mathsf{pk}, R_i(\alpha_j) \cdot P_i(\alpha_j))$ for every $j \in [3t + 1]$.

7:     It broadcasts $\{c_i^{(j)}\}_{j \in [3t+1]}$.

8: **end for**

9: Party P_1 adds the ciphertexts to get $d^{(j)} = \sum_i^N c_i^{(j)}$ for each $j \in [3t + 1]$. It broadcasts $\{d^{(j)}\}_{j \in [3t+1]}$.

10: They mutually decrypt $\{d^{(j)}\}_{j \in [3t+1]}$ to learn $V^{(j)} \leftarrow \mathsf{Dec}(\mathsf{sk}, d_N^{(j)})$ for $j \in [3t+1]$.

11: P_1 computes the points $\tilde{V}^{(j)} = V^{(j)}/P_1(\alpha_j)$ for $j \in [3t + 1]$.

12: P_1 interpolates a rational function using the pairs of points $(\alpha_j, \tilde{V}^{(j)})$.

13: P_1 recovers the polynomial $P_{S_1 \setminus (\cap_i S_i)}(x)$ in the denominator.

14: P_1 evaluates $P_{S_1 \setminus \cap_i S_i}(x)$ on every point of its set $\{a_1^{(1)}, \ldots, a_1^{(n)}\}$ to compute $\cap_i S_i$. That is, whenever $P_{S_1 \setminus \cap_i S_i}(a_1^j) \neq 0$, then $a_1^j \in \cap_i S_i$.

15: It broadcasts the output $\cap_i S_i$.

Proof. Assume that $|S_1 \setminus (\cap_{i=2}^N S_i)| \leq t$ (note that this condition is guaranteed after resorting to the functionality $\mathcal{F}_{\mathsf{MPCT}}$ in the first step of the protocol). After the execution of the protocol, party P_1 obtains the points $V^{(j)} = \sum_i^N P_i(\alpha_j) \cdot R_i(\alpha_j)$. Then,

$$
\begin{aligned}
\tilde{V}^{(j)} &= \frac{V^{(j)}}{P_1(\alpha_j)} = \frac{\sum_i^N P_i(\alpha_j) \cdot R_i(\alpha_j)}{P_1(\alpha_j)} \\
&= \frac{P_{\cap_i S_i}(\alpha_j) \cdot \sum_i^N P_{S_i \setminus (\cap_{k \neq i} S_k)}(\alpha_j) \cdot R_i(\alpha_j)}{P_{\cap_i S_i}(\alpha_j) \cdot P_{S_1 \setminus (\cap_{k \neq 1} S_k)}(\alpha_j)} \\
&= \frac{\sum_i^N P_{S_i \setminus (\cap_{k \neq i} S_k)}(\alpha_j) \cdot R_i(\alpha_j)}{P_{S_1 \setminus (\cap_{k \neq 1} S_k)}(\alpha_j)}.
\end{aligned}
$$

Since P_1 has $3t + 1$ evaluated points of the rational function above, then it can interpolate a rational function to recover the polynomial $P_{S_1 \setminus (\cap_{k \neq 1} S_k)}$. This is possible because of Lemma 2 and the fact that

$$
\deg \left(\sum_i^N P_{S_i \setminus (\cap_{k \neq i} S_k)}(\alpha_j) \cdot R_i(\alpha_j) \right) \leq 2t \quad \text{and} \quad \deg \left(P_{S_1 \setminus (\cap_{k \neq 1} S_k)}(\alpha_j) \right) \leq t.
$$

Having computed the polynomial $P_{S_1 \setminus (\cap_{k \neq 1} S_k)}$, party P_1 can compute the intersection because the roots of this polynomial are exactly the elements in $S_1 \setminus (\cap_{k \neq 1} S_k)$.   □

Theorem 6. *The protocol* MTPSI *securely realizes functionality* $\mathcal{F}_{\mathsf{MTPSI}}$ *in the* $(\mathcal{F}_{\mathsf{Gen}}, \mathcal{F}_{\mathsf{MPCT}})$*-hybrid model against any semi-honest adversary corrupting up to* $N - 1$ *parties.*

Proof. Let $\mathcal{A}$ be an adversary corrupting up to k parties involved in the protocol, for any $k \in [N-1]$. Let $\mathsf{P}_{i_1}, \ldots, \mathsf{P}_{i_k}$ be the corrupted parties. The simulator Sim works as follows:

1. It sends the inputs of the corrupted parties, $S_{i_1}, \ldots, S_{i_k}$, to the ideal functionality $\mathcal{F}_{\mathsf{MTPSI}}$. Sim either receives $\perp$ or $\cap_i S_i$ from the ideal functionality $\mathcal{F}_{\mathsf{MTPSI}}$.
2. Sim waits for $\mathcal{A}$ to send the corrupted parties' inputs to the ideal functionality $\mathcal{F}_{\mathsf{MPCT}}$. If Sim has received $\perp$ from $\mathcal{F}_{\mathsf{MPCT}}$, then Sim leaks 0 to $\mathcal{A}$ (and $\mathcal{Z}$) and terminates the protocol. Else, Sim leaks 1 and continues.
3. Sim waits for $\mathcal{A}$ to send a request $(\mathsf{sid}, \mathsf{request}_{i_j})$ for each of the corrupted parties (that is, for $j \in [k]$) to $\mathcal{F}_{\mathsf{Gen}}$. Upon receiving such requests, Sim generates $(\mathsf{pk}, \mathsf{sk}_1, \ldots, \mathsf{sk}_N) \leftarrow \mathsf{Gen}(1^\lambda, N)$ and returns $(\mathsf{pk}, \mathsf{sk}_{i_j})$ for each of the requests.
4. For each party P_ℓ such that $\ell \neq i_j$ (where $j \in [k]$), Sim picks a random polynomial $U_\ell(x)$ of degree $n - |\cap_i S_i| + t$ and sends $\mathsf{Enc}(\mathsf{pk}, R_\ell(\alpha_j) \cdot P_{\cap_i S_i}(\alpha_j) \cdot U_\ell(\alpha_j))$, where $R_\ell(x)$ is chosen uniformly at random such that $\deg R_\ell(x) = t$. From now on, Sim simulates the dummy parties as in the protocol.

We now argue that both the simulation and the real-world scheme are indistinguishable from the point-of-view of any environment $\mathcal{Z}$. In the real-world scheme, party P_1 obtains the polynomial

$$V(x) = P_{\cap_i S_i}(x) \cdot \sum_i^N P_{S_i \setminus (\cap_{k \neq i} S_k)}(x) \cdot R_i(x)$$

evaluated in $3t + 1$ points. Assume that P_1 is corrupted by $\mathcal{A}$. Even in this case, there is an index ℓ for which $\mathcal{A}$ does not know the polynomial $R_\ell(x)$. More precisely, we have that

$$V(x) = P_{\cap_i S_i}(x) \cdot \left(\left(\sum_{i \neq \ell} P_{S_i \setminus (\cap_{k \neq i} S_k)}(x) \cdot R_i(x) \right) + P_{S_\ell \setminus (\cap_{k \neq \ell} S_k)}(x) \cdot R_\ell(x) \right).$$

First, note that

$$\deg \left(\sum_{i \neq \ell} P_{S_i \setminus (\cap_{k \neq i} S_k)}(x) \cdot R_i(x) \right) = \deg P_{S_\ell \setminus (\cap_{k \neq \ell} S_k)}(x) \cdot R_\ell(x)$$

$$= n - |\cap_i S_i| + t \leq 2t.$$

Moreover, we have for any $i \in [N]$ that $\deg P_{S_i \setminus (\cap_{k \neq i} S_k)} \leq t$, $\deg R_i(x) = t$ and $\gcd \left(P_{S_i \setminus (\cap_{k \neq i} S_k)}, P_{S_j \setminus (\cap_{k \neq j} S_k)} \right) = 1$ for any $j \neq i$. Hence, by Lemma 1, we can build a sequence of hybrids where we replace $V(x)$ by the polynomial $V'(x) = P_{\cap_i S_i}(x) \cdot U(x)$, where $\deg U(x) = n - |\cap_i S_i| + t$, as in the ideal-world execution. Indistinguishability of executions follows. □

Communication Complexity. When we instantiate the ideal functionality $\mathcal{F}_{\mathsf{MPCT}}$ with the protocol from the previous section the scheme has communication complexity $\tilde{\mathcal{O}}(Nt^2)$.

Acknowledgment. *Pedro Branco:* Part of this work was done while the author was at CISPA. The author is supported by DP-PMI and FCT (Portugal) through the grant PD/BD/135181/2017. This work is supported by Security and Quantum Information Group of Instituto de Telecomunicações, by the Fundação para a Ciência e a Tecnologia (FCT) through national funds, by FEDER, COMPETE 2020, and by Regional Operational Program of Lisbon, under UIDB/50008/2020.

Nico Döttling: Part of this work was done while visiting Simons Institute, Berkeley, California. This work is partially funded by the Helmholtz Association within the project "Trustworthy Federated Data Analytics" (TFDA) (funding number ZT-I-OO1 4).

Sihang Pu: Part of this work was done while visiting Simons Institute, Berkeley, California.

A   Preliminaries Cont'd

A.1   Threshold Public-Key Encryption

In this work, we will use Public-Key Encryption schemes and a variant of it: Threshold Public-key Encryption. We now define Threshold Public-key Encryption. Such schemes can be instantiated from several hardness assumptions such as DDH, DCR or pairing-based assumptions [21].

Definition 3 (Threshold Public-Key Encryption). *A Threshold Public-Key Encryption (TPKE) scheme is defined by the following algorithms:*

- $(\mathsf{pk}, \mathsf{sk}_1, \ldots, \mathsf{sk}_N) \leftarrow \mathsf{Gen}(1^\lambda, N)$ *takes as input a security parameter. It outputs a public key* pk *and* N *secret keys* $(\mathsf{sk}_1, \ldots, \mathsf{sk}_N)$.
- $c \leftarrow \mathsf{Enc}(\mathsf{pk}, m)$ *takes as input a public key* pk *and a message* $m \in \{0,1\}^*$. *It outputs a ciphertext* c.
- $c' \leftarrow \mathsf{Dec}(\mathsf{sk}_i, c)$ *takes as input one of the secret keys* sk_i *and a ciphertext. It outputs a share decryption* c' *of* c.

Correctness. For any $N \in \mathbb{N}$ and any permutation $\pi : [N] \to [N]$, we have that

$$\Pr \left[m \leftarrow \mathsf{Dec}(\mathsf{sk}_{\pi(N)}, \mathsf{Dec}(\mathsf{sk}_{\pi(N-1)}, \ldots \mathsf{Dec}(\mathsf{sk}_{\pi(1)}, \mathsf{Enc}(\mathsf{pk}, m)) \ldots)) \right] = 1$$

where $(\mathsf{pk}, \mathsf{sk}_1, \ldots, \mathsf{sk}_N) \leftarrow \mathsf{Gen}(1^\lambda, N)$.

IND-CPA Security. For any $N \in \mathbb{N}$, any permutation $\pi : [N] \to [N]$ and any adversary $\mathcal{A}$, we require that

$$\Pr\left[b \leftarrow \mathcal{A}(c, \text{st}) : \begin{array}{c} (\text{pk}, \text{sk}_1, \ldots, \text{sk}_N) \leftarrow \text{Gen}(1^\lambda, N) \\ (m_0, m_1, \text{st}) \leftarrow \mathcal{A}\left(\text{pk}, \text{sk}_{\pi(1)}, \ldots, \text{sk}_{\pi(k)}\right) \\ b \leftarrow_{\$} \{0,1\} \\ c \leftarrow \text{Enc}(\text{pk}, m_b) \end{array} \right] \leq \text{negl}(\lambda)$$

for any $k < N$.

Additive Homomorphism. We also assume that the TPKE (or plain PKE) is homomorphic for additive operation.[14] That is, for all $(\text{pk}, \text{sk}_1, \ldots, \text{sk}_N) \leftarrow \text{Gen}(1^\lambda, N)$, we can define two groups $(\mathcal{M}, \oplus), (\mathcal{C}, \otimes)$ such that, given two ciphertexts $c_1 \leftarrow \text{Enc}(\text{pk}, m_1)$ and $c_2 \leftarrow \text{Enc}(\text{pk}, m_2)$, we require that

$$c_1 \otimes c_2 = \text{Enc}(\text{pk}, m_1 \oplus m_2).$$

By abuse of notation, we usually denote the operations of $\mathcal{M}$ and $\mathcal{C}$ as $+$.

A.2   Linear Algebra

We first introduce minimal polynomials of a sequence and of a matrix. Then we present how they can be used to solve linear algebra related problems.

Minimal Polynomial of a Matrix. The minimal polynomial of a sequence $\mathfrak{a}$ is the least degree polynomial m such that $\langle m \rangle = Ann(\mathfrak{a})$ where $Ann(\mathfrak{a})$ is the annihilator ideal of $\mathfrak{a}$ (that is, the ideal such that every element f of $Ann(\mathfrak{a})$ satisfies $f \cdot \mathfrak{a} = 0$).

Lemma 6 (Lemma 3 in [24]). *Let $\mathbf{A} \in \mathbb{F}^{n \times n}$ and let $m_{\mathbf{A}}$ be the minimal polynomial of matrix $\mathbf{A}$. For $\mathbf{u}, \mathbf{v} \leftarrow_{\$} \mathbb{F}^n$, we have $m_{\mathbf{A}} = m_{\mathfrak{a}'}$ with probability at least $1 - 2\deg(m_{\mathbf{A}})/|\mathbb{F}|$, where $\mathfrak{a}' = (\mathbf{u}^\top \mathbf{A}^i \mathbf{v})_{i \in \mathbb{N}}$. Moreover, $m_{\mathfrak{a}'}$ can be calculated using a Boolean circuit of size $\mathcal{O}(nk \log n \log k \log \log k)$ where $k = \log |\mathbb{F}|$.*

Compute the Rank of a Matrix and Solve a Linear System

Lemma 7 ([23]). *Let $\mathbf{A} \in \mathbb{F}^{n \times n}$ of (unknown) rank r. Let $\mathbf{U}$ and $\mathbf{L}$ be randomly chosen unit upper triangular and lower triangular Toeplitz matrices in $\mathbb{F}^{n \times n}$, and let $\mathbf{B} = \mathbf{U A L}$. Let us denote the $i \times i$ leading principal of $\mathbf{B}$ by $\mathbf{B}_i$. The probability that $\det(\mathbf{B}_i) \neq 0$ for all $1 \leq i \leq r$ is greater than $1 - n^2/|\mathbb{F}|$.*

Lemma 8 ([23]). *Let $\mathbf{B} \in \mathbb{F}^{n \times n}$ with leading invertible principals up to $\mathbf{B}_r$ where r is the (unknown) rank of $\mathbf{B}$. Let $\mathbf{X}$ be a randomly chosen diagonal matrix in $\mathbb{F}^{n \times n}$. Then, $r = \deg(m_{\mathbf{XB}}) - 1$ with probability greater than $1 - n^2/|\mathbb{F}|$.*

---

[14] From now on, we always assume that PKE and TPKE used in this work fulfill this property, unless stated otherwise.

B   Oblivious Linear Algebra

B.1   Oblivious Matrix Multiplication

Protocol. The following Protocol 4 allows several parties to jointly compute the (encrypted) product of two encrypted matrices. Note that the protocol can also be used to compute the encryption of the product of two encrypted values in $\mathbb{F}$.

Protocol 4 Secure Multiplication secMult

Setup: Each party P_i has a secret share sk_i of a secret key for a public key pk of a TPKE scheme $\mathsf{TPKE} = (\mathsf{Gen}, \mathsf{Enc}, \mathsf{Dec})$.

Input: Party P_1 inputs $\mathsf{Enc}(\mathsf{pk}, \mathbf{M}_l)$ and $\mathsf{Enc}(\mathsf{pk}, \mathbf{M}_r)$, where $\mathbf{M}_l, \mathbf{M}_r \in \mathbb{F}^{t \times t}$.

Goal: Every one knows the product $\mathsf{Enc}(\mathbf{M}_l \cdot \mathbf{M}_r)$.

1: **for all** party P_i **do**
2:     It samples two random matrices $\mathbf{R}_l^{(i)}, \mathbf{R}_r^{(i)} \leftarrow_{\$} \mathbb{F}^{t \times t}$.
3:     It computes $c_l^{(i)} = \mathsf{Enc}(\mathsf{pk}, \mathbf{R}_l^{(i)})$, $c_l^{(i)} = \mathsf{Enc}(\mathsf{pk}, \mathbf{R}_r^{(i)})$, $d_r^{(i)} = \mathsf{Enc}(\mathsf{pk}, \mathbf{M}_l \cdot \mathbf{R}_r^{(i)})$, $d_l^{(i)} = \mathsf{Enc}(\mathsf{pk}, \mathbf{R}_l^{(i)} \cdot \mathbf{M}_r)$.
4:     It broadcasts $\{c_l^{(i)}, c_r^{(i)}, d_l^{(i)}, d_r^{(i)}\}$.
5: **end for**
6: Each party P_i computes $\tilde{c}^{(i)} = \mathsf{Enc}(\mathsf{pk}, \sum_{j \neq i} \mathbf{R}_l^{(i)} \cdot \mathbf{R}_r^{(j)})$ (using $c_r^{(j)}$ and $\mathbf{R}_l^{(i)}$) and broadcasts $\tilde{c}^{(i)}$.
7: All parties mutually decrypt i) $\mathsf{Enc}(\mathbf{M}'_l) := \mathsf{Enc}(\mathsf{pk}, \mathbf{M}_l) + \sum_j c_l^{(j)}$ (to obtain $\mathbf{M}'_l \in \mathbb{F}^{t \times t}$), ii) $\mathsf{Enc}(\mathbf{M}'_r) := \mathsf{Enc}(\mathsf{pk}, \mathbf{M}_r) + \sum_j c_r^{(j)}$ (to obtain $\mathbf{M}'_r \in \mathbb{F}^{t \times t}$)
8: **for all** party P_i **do**
9:     It computes $\tilde{d} = \mathsf{Enc}(\mathsf{pk}, \mathbf{M}'_l \cdot \mathbf{M}'_r)$.
10:     It outputs $e = \tilde{d} - \sum_j d_l^{(j)} - \sum_j d_r^{(j)} - \sum_j \tilde{c}^{(j)}$
11: **end for**

Analysis. We proceed to the analysis of the protocol described above.

Lemma 9 (Correctness). *The protocol* secMult *is correct.*

Proof The correctness is straightforward.   □

Lemma 10 (Security). *The protocol* secMult *securely EUC-realizes* $\mathcal{F}_{\mathsf{OMM}}$ *with shared ideal functionality* $\mathcal{F}_{\mathsf{Gen}}$ *against semi-honest adversaries corrupting up to* $N - 1$ *parties, given that* TPKE *is IND-CPA.*

Proof (Sketch). Assume that the adversary corrupts $N - k$ parties. The simulator takes the inputs from these parties and send them to the ideal functionality. Upon receiving the encrypted value $\mathsf{Enc}(\mathsf{pk}, \mathbf{M}_l \cdot \mathbf{M}_r)$, it simulates the protocol as the honest parties would do.

We now prove that no set of at most $N - 1$ colluding parties can extract information about $\mathbf{M}_l, \mathbf{M}_r$. First, observe that any set of $N - 1$ parties cannot extract any information about encrypted values that are not decrypted during the protocol (because there is always a missing secret key share) given that TPKE is IND-CPA. Second, we analyze the matrix $\mathbf{M}'_l$ (which is decrypted during the protocol). We have that $\mathbf{M}'_l = \mathbf{M}_l + \sum_j \mathbf{R}_l^{(j)}$. Hence, there is always at least one matrix $\mathbf{R}_l^{(\ell)}$ which is unknown to the adversary and that perfectly hides the matrix $\mathbf{M}_l$ (the same happens $\mathbf{M}'_r$. $\hfill\square$

Complexity. The communication complexity of the protocol is dominated by the messages carrying the (encrypted) matrix. Hence, assuming a broadcast channel between the parties, the protocol has communication complexity of $\mathcal{O}(Nt^2)$ where t is the size of the input matrices and N the number of parties involved in the protocol.

B.2   Compute the Rank of a Matrix

Protocol. We present this protocol in the full version of this paper in [6].

Complexity. Each party broadcasts $\mathcal{O}(t^2 k \log t)$ bits of information, where $k = \log |\mathbb{F}|$. To see this, note that the communication of the protocol is dominated by the computation of the circuit that computes the degree of $\mathfrak{a}$ and this can be implemented with communication cost of $\mathcal{O}(t^2 k \log t)$ [24]. Assuming a broadcast channel, the communication complexity is $\tilde{\mathcal{O}}(Nt^2)$.

B.3   Invert a Matrix

In this section, we present and analyze a protocol that allows N parties to invert an encrypted matrix. In this setting, each of the N parties holds a secret share of a public key pk of a TPKE. Given an encrypted matrix, they want to compute an encryption of the inverse of this matrix.

Ideal Functionality. The ideal functionality of oblivious rank computation is defined below.

$\mathcal{F}_{\mathsf{OInv}}$ functionality

Parameters: sid, $N, q, t \in \mathbb{N}$ and $\mathbb{F}$, where $\mathbb{F}$ is a field of order q, known to the N parties involved in the protocol. pk public-key of a threshold PKE scheme.

- Upon receiving $(\mathsf{sid}, P_1, \mathsf{Enc}(\mathsf{pk}, \mathbf{M}))$ from party P_1 (where $\mathbf{M} \in \mathbb{F}^{t \times t}$ is a non-singular matrix), $\mathcal{F}_{\mathsf{ORank}}$ outputs $\mathsf{Enc}(\mathsf{pk}, \mathbf{M}^{-1})$ to P_1 and $(\mathsf{Enc}(\mathsf{pk}, \mathbf{M}), \mathsf{Enc}(\mathsf{pk}, \mathbf{M}^{-1}))$ to all other parties P_i, for $i = 2, \ldots, N$.

Protocol. This protocol allows N parties to jointly compute the encryption of the inverse of a matrix, given that this matrix is non-singular. Please refer to the full version of this paper in [6] to see details.

Analysis. The proofs of the following lemmas follow the same lines as the proofs in the analysis of secMult protocol. We state the lemmas but omit the proofs for briefness.

Lemma 11. *The protocol* secInv *is correct.*

Lemma 12. *The protocol* secInv *securely EUC-realizes* $\mathcal{F}_{\mathsf{OInv}}$ *with shared ideal functionality* $\mathcal{F}_{\mathsf{Gen}}$ *against semi-honest adversaries corrupting up to* $N-1$ *parties, given that* TPKE *is IND-CPA.*

Complexity. Each party broadcasts $\mathcal{O}(t^2)$ bits of information. The communication complexity of the protocol is $\mathcal{O}(Nt^2)$, assuming a broadcast channel.

B.4   Secure Unary Representation

Following [24], we present a protocol that allows to securely compute the unary representation of a matrix.

Ideal Functionality. The ideal functionality for Secure Unary Representation is given below.

$\mathcal{F}_{\mathsf{SUR}}$ functionality

Parameters: sid, $N, q, t \in \mathbb{N}$ and $\mathbb{F}$, where $\mathbb{F}$ is a field of order q, known to the N parties involved in the protocol. pk public-key of a threshold PKE scheme.

- Upon receiving $(\mathsf{sid}, \mathsf{P}_1, \mathsf{Enc}(\mathsf{pk}, r))$ from party P_1 (where $r \in \mathbb{F}$ and $r \leq t$), $\mathcal{F}_{\mathsf{SUR}}$ computes $(\mathsf{Enc}(\mathsf{pk}, \delta_1), \ldots, \mathsf{Enc}(\mathsf{pk}, \delta_t))$ such that $\delta_i = 1$ if $i \leq r$, and $\delta_i = 0$ otherwise. The functionality outputs $(\mathsf{Enc}(\mathsf{pk}, \delta_1), \ldots, \mathsf{Enc}(\mathsf{pk}, \delta_t))$ to P_1 and $(\mathsf{Enc}(\mathsf{pk}, r), (\mathsf{Enc}(\mathsf{pk}, \delta_1), \ldots, \mathsf{Enc}(\mathsf{pk}, \delta_t)))$ to all other parties P_i, for $i = 2, \ldots, N$.

Protocol. A protocol for secure unary representation can be implemented with the help of a binary-conversion protocol [37]. That is, given $\mathsf{Enc}(\mathsf{pk}, r)$, all parties jointly compute $\mathsf{Enc}(\mathsf{pk}, \delta_i)$, where $\delta_i = 1$, if $i \leq r$, and $\delta_i = 0$ otherwise, via a Boolean circuit (which can be securely implemented based on Paillier cryptosystem).

Communication Complexity. We can calculate the result using a Boolean circuit of size $O(r \log t)$, thus the communication complexity is $O(Nr \log t)$.

Protocol 5 Secure Linear Solve secLS

Setup: Each party has a secret key share sk_i for a public key pk of a TPKE TPKE = (Gen, Enc, Dec). The parties have access to the ideal functionalities $\mathcal{F}_{ORank}$, $\mathcal{F}_{OInv}$ and $\mathcal{F}_{SUR}$.

Input: Party P_1 inputs $Enc(pk, \mathbf{M})$ where $\mathbf{M} \in \mathbb{F}^{t \times t}$ is a non-singular matrix.

1: All parties jointly compute an encryption of the rank $Enc(pk, r)$ of $\mathbf{M}$ via the ideal functionality $\mathcal{F}_{ORank}$.

2: Set $Enc(pk, \mathbf{M}') := Enc(pk, \mathbf{M})$ and $Enc(pk, \mathbf{y}') := Enc(pk, \mathbf{y})$.

3: **for** i from 1 to N **do**

4:   P_i samples two non-singular matrices $\mathbf{R}_i, \mathbf{Q}_i$ from $\mathbb{F}^{t \times t}$. It calculates $Enc(pk, \mathbf{M}') = Enc(pk, \mathbf{R}_i \mathbf{M}' \mathbf{Q}_i)$ and $Enc(pk, \mathbf{y}') = Enc(pk, \mathbf{R}_i \mathbf{y}')$. P_i broadcasts $Enc(pk, \mathbf{M}'), Enc(pk, \mathbf{y}')$.

5: **end for**

6: All the parties jointly compute $Enc(\delta_1), \ldots, Enc(\delta_t)$ by invoking $\mathcal{F}_{SUR}$ on input $Enc(pk, r)$. They set $Enc(pk, \Delta) := Enc \left(pk, \begin{bmatrix} \delta_1 & \ldots & 0 \\ \vdots & \ddots & \vdots \\ 0 & \ldots & \delta_t \end{bmatrix} \right)$. Finally, they compute $Enc(pk, \mathbf{N}) := Enc(pk, \mathbf{M}' \cdot \Delta + \mathbf{I}_t - \Delta)$, where $\mathbf{I}_t \in \mathbb{F}^{t \times t}$ is the identity matrix.

7: All the parties jointly compute $Enc(\mathbf{N}^{-1})$ by invoking $\mathcal{F}_{OInv}$ on input $Enc(pk, \mathbf{N})$.

8: Each party P^i samples $\mathbf{u}_i \leftarrow_\$ \mathbb{F}^t$ and broadcasts $(Enc(pk, \mathbf{M}' \mathbf{u}_i), Enc(pk, \mathbf{u}_i))$.

9: All parties jointly compute $Enc(pk, \mathbf{u}') = Enc(pk, \mathbf{N}^{-1} \mathbf{y}'_r)$ by invoking $\mathcal{F}_{OMM}$, where $Enc(pk, \mathbf{y}'_r) = Enc(pk, (\mathbf{y}' + \sum_j \mathbf{M}' \mathbf{u}_j) \Delta)$. Then they set $Enc(pk, \mathbf{x}) = Enc(pk, (\sum_j \mathbf{u}_j) - \mathbf{u}')$.

10: **for** i from N to 1 **do**

11:   P_i calculates $Enc(pk, \mathbf{x}) = Enc(pk, \mathbf{Q}_i^{-1} \mathbf{x})$. P_i broadcasts $Enc(pk, \mathbf{x})$.

12: **end for**

13: P_1 outputs $Enc(pk, \mathbf{x})$.

B.5 Solve a Linear System

Protocol. We now present the Protocol 5 that allows multiple parties to solve an encrypted linear system. In the following, we assume that the system has at least one solution (note that this can be guaranteed using the secRank protocol).

Lemma 13 (Correctness). *The protocol secLS is correct.*

Proof. The proof follows directly from [23, 24]. □

Lemma 14. *The protocol secLS securely EUC-realizes $\mathcal{F}_{OLS}$ with shared ideal functionality $\mathcal{F}_{Gen}$ in the $(\mathcal{F}_{ORank}, \mathcal{F}_{OInv}, \mathcal{F}_{SUR})$-hybrid model against semi-honest adversaries corrupting up to $N-1$ parties, given that TPKE is IND-CPA.*

Communication Complexity. Each party broadcasts $\mathcal{O}(t^2 k \log t)$ bits of information where $k = |\mathbb{F}|$. The total communication complexity is $\tilde{\mathcal{O}}(t^2)$.

References

1. Badrinarayanan, S., Miao, P., Raghuraman, S., Rindal, P.: Multi-party threshold private set intersection with sublinear communication. In: PKC 2021 (2021)

2. Berke, A., Bakker, M., Vepakomma, P., Larson, K., Pentland, A.S.: Assessing disease exposure risk with location data: a proposal for cryptographic preservation of privacy (2020). https://arxiv.org/abs/2003.14412
3. Boneh, D., Boyen, X., Shacham, H.: Short group signatures. In: Franklin, M. (ed.) CRYPTO 2004. LNCS, vol. 3152, pp. 41–55. Springer, Heidelberg (2004). https://doi.org/10.1007/978-3-540-28628-8_3
4. Boneh, D., Goh, E.-J., Nissim, K.: Evaluating 2-DNF formulas on ciphertexts. In: Kilian, J. (ed.) TCC 2005. LNCS, vol. 3378, pp. 325–341. Springer, Heidelberg (2005). https://doi.org/10.1007/978-3-540-30576-7_18
5. Bouman, N.J., de Vreede, N.: New protocols for secure linear algebra: pivoting-free elimination and fast block-recursive matrix decomposition. IACR Cryptology ePrint Archive 2018/703 (2018)
6. Branco, P., Döttling, N., Pu, S.: Multiparty cardinality testing for threshold private set intersection. Cryptology ePrint Archive, Report 2020/1307 (2020). https://eprint.iacr.org/2020/1307
7. Canetti, R.: Universally composable security: a new paradigm for cryptographic protocols. In: 42nd Annual Symposium on Foundations of Computer Science, Las Vegas, NV, USA, 14–17 October 2001, pp. 136–145. IEEE Computer Society Press. https://doi.org/10.1109/SFCS.2001.959888
8. Canetti, R., Dodis, Y., Pass, R., Walfish, S.: Universally composable security with global setup. In: Vadhan, S.P. (ed.) TCC 2007. LNCS, vol. 4392, pp. 61–85. Springer, Heidelberg (2007). https://doi.org/10.1007/978-3-540-70936-7_4
9. Cramer, R., Damgård, I.: Secure distributed linear algebra in a constant number of rounds. In: Kilian, J. (ed.) CRYPTO 2001. LNCS, vol. 2139, pp. 119–136. Springer, Heidelberg (2001). https://doi.org/10.1007/3-540-44647-8_7
10. Cramer, R., Damgård, I., Nielsen, J.B.: Multiparty computation from threshold homomorphic encryption. In: Pfitzmann, B. (ed.) EUROCRYPT 2001. LNCS, vol. 2045, pp. 280–300. Springer, Heidelberg (2001). https://doi.org/10.1007/3-540-44987-6_18
11. Dachman-Soled, D., Malkin, T., Raykova, M., Yung, M.: Efficient robust private set intersection. In: Abdalla, M., Pointcheval, D., Fouque, P.-A., Vergnaud, D. (eds.) ACNS 2009. LNCS, vol. 5536, pp. 125–142. Springer, Heidelberg (2009). https://doi.org/10.1007/978-3-642-01957-9_8
12. De Cristofaro, E., Kim, J., Tsudik, G.: Linear-complexity private set intersection protocols secure in malicious model. In: Abe, M. (ed.) ASIACRYPT 2010. LNCS, vol. 6477, pp. 213–231. Springer, Heidelberg (2010). https://doi.org/10.1007/978-3-642-17373-8_13
13. Dong, C., Chen, L., Wen, Z.: When private set intersection meets big data: an efficient and scalable protocol. In: Sadeghi, A.R., Gligor, V.D., Yung, M. (eds.) ACM CCS 2013: 20th Conference on Computer and Communications Security, Berlin, Germany, 4–8 November 2013, pp. 789–800. ACM Press (2013). https://doi.org/10.1145/2508859.2516701
14. Elgamal, T.: A public key cryptosystem and a signature scheme based on discrete logarithms. IEEE Trans. Inf. Theory **31**(4), 469–472 (1985)
15. Freedman, M.J., Nissim, K., Pinkas, B.: Efficient private matching and set intersection. In: Cachin, C., Camenisch, J.L. (eds.) EUROCRYPT 2004. LNCS, vol. 3027, pp. 1–19. Springer, Heidelberg (2004). https://doi.org/10.1007/978-3-540-24676-3_1

16. Ghosh, S., Nilges, T.: An algebraic approach to maliciously secure private set intersection. In: Ishai, Y., Rijmen, V. (eds.) EUROCRYPT 2019, Part III. LNCS, vol. 11478, pp. 154–185. Springer, Cham (2019). https://doi.org/10.1007/978-3-030-17659-4_6

17. Ghosh, S., Simkin, M.: The communication complexity of threshold private set intersection. In: Boldyreva, A., Micciancio, D. (eds.) CRYPTO 2019, Part II. LNCS, vol. 11693, pp. 3–29. Springer, Cham (2019). https://doi.org/10.1007/978-3-030-26951-7_1

18. Ghosh, S., Simkin, M.: The communication complexity of threshold private set intersection. Cryptology ePrint Archive, Report 2019/175 (2019). https://eprint.iacr.org/2019/175

19. Grigorescu, E., Jung, K., Rubinfeld, R.: A local decision test for sparse polynomials. Inf. Process. Lett. **110**(20), 898–901 (2010). https://doi.org/10.1016/j.ipl.2010.07.012

20. Hallgren, P., Orlandi, C., Sabelfeld, A.: Privatepool: privacy-preserving ridesharing. In: 2017 IEEE 30th Computer Security Foundations Symposium (CSF), pp. 276–291 (2017)

21. Hazay, C., Venkitasubramaniam, M.: Scalable multi-party private set-intersection. In: Fehr, S. (ed.) PKC 2017, Part I. LNCS, vol. 10174, pp. 175–203. Springer, Heidelberg (2017). https://doi.org/10.1007/978-3-662-54365-8_8

22. Ion, M., Kreuter, B., Nergiz, E., Patel, S., Saxena, S., Seth, K., Shanahan, D., Yung, M.: Private intersection-sum protocol with applications to attributing aggregate ad conversions. Cryptology ePrint Archive, Report 2017/738 (2017). http://eprint.iacr.org/2017/738

23. Kaltofen, E., David Saunders, B.: On Wiedemann's method of solving sparse linear systems. In: Mattson, H.F., Mora, T., Rao, T.R.N. (eds.) AAECC 1991. LNCS, vol. 539, pp. 29–38. Springer, Heidelberg (1991). https://doi.org/10.1007/3-540-54522-0_93

24. Kiltz, E., Mohassel, P., Weinreb, E., Franklin, M.: Secure linear algebra using linearly recurrent sequences. In: Vadhan, S.P. (ed.) TCC 2007. LNCS, vol. 4392, pp. 291–310. Springer, Heidelberg (2007). https://doi.org/10.1007/978-3-540-70936-7_16

25. Kissner, L., Song, D.: Privacy-preserving set operations. In: Shoup, V. (ed.) CRYPTO 2005. LNCS, vol. 3621, pp. 241–257. Springer, Heidelberg (2005). https://doi.org/10.1007/11535218_15

26. Kolesnikov, V., Kumaresan, R., Rosulek, M., Trieu, N.: Efficient batched oblivious PRF with applications to private set intersection. In: Weippl, E.R., Katzenbeisser, S., Kruegel, C., Myers, A.C., Halevi, S. (eds.) ACM CCS 2016: 23rd Conference on Computer and Communications Security, Vienna, Austria, 24–28 October 2016, pp. 818–829. ACM Press (2016). https://doi.org/10.1145/2976749.2978381

27. Meadows, C.: A more efficient cryptographic matchmaking protocol for use in the absence of a continuously available third party. In: 1986 IEEE Symposium on Security and Privacy, pp. 134–134 (1986)

28. Minsky, Y., Trachtenberg, A., Zippel, R.: Set reconciliation with nearly optimal communication complexity. IEEE Trans. Inf. Theory **49**(9), 2213–2218 (2003). https://doi.org/10.1109/TIT.2003.815784

29. Nissim, K., Weinreb, E.: Communication efficient secure linear algebra. In: Halevi, S., Rabin, T. (eds.) TCC 2006. LNCS, vol. 3876, pp. 522–541. Springer, Heidelberg (2006). https://doi.org/10.1007/11681878_27

30. Paillier, P.: Public-key cryptosystems based on composite degree residuosity classes. In: Stern, J. (ed.) EUROCRYPT 1999. LNCS, vol. 1592, pp. 223–238. Springer, Heidelberg (1999). https://doi.org/10.1007/3-540-48910-X_16

31. Pinkas, B., Rosulek, M., Trieu, N., Yanai, A.: SpOT-light: lightweight private set intersection from sparse OT extension. In: Boldyreva, A., Micciancio, D. (eds.) CRYPTO 2019, Part III. LNCS, vol. 11694, pp. 401–431. Springer, Cham (2019). https://doi.org/10.1007/978-3-030-26954-8_13

32. Pinkas, B., Schneider, T., Segev, G., Zohner, M.: Phasing: private set intersection using permutation-based hashing. In: Jung, J., Holz, T. (eds.) USENIX Security 2015: 24th USENIX Security Symposium, Washington, DC, USA, 12–14 August 2015, pp. 515–530. USENIX Association (2015)

33. Pinkas, B., Schneider, T., Weinert, C., Wieder, U.: Efficient circuit-based PSI via cuckoo hashing. In: Nielsen, J.B., Rijmen, V. (eds.) EUROCRYPT 2018, Part III. LNCS, vol. 10822, pp. 125–157. Springer, Cham (2018). https://doi.org/10.1007/978-3-319-78372-7_5

34. Pinkas, B., Schneider, T., Zohner, M.: Faster private set intersection based on OT extension. In: Fu, K., Jung, J. (eds.) USENIX Security 2014: 23rd USENIX Security Symposium, San Diego, CA, USA, 20–22 August 2014, pp. 797–812. USENIX Association (2014)

35. Rindal, P., Rosulek, M.: Improved private set intersection against malicious adversaries. In: Coron, J.-S., Nielsen, J.B. (eds.) EUROCRYPT 2017, Part I. LNCS, vol. 10210, pp. 235–259. Springer, Cham (2017). https://doi.org/10.1007/978-3-319-56620-7_9

36. Rindal, P., Rosulek, M.: Malicious-secure private set intersection via dual execution. In: Thuraisingham, B.M., Evans, D., Malkin, T., Xu, D. (eds.) ACM CCS 2017: 24th Conference on Computer and Communications Security, Dallas, TX, USA, 31 October–2 November 2017, pp. 1229–1242. ACM Press (2017). https://doi.org/10.1145/3133956.3134044

37. Schoenmakers, B., Tuyls, P.: Efficient binary conversion for Paillier encrypted values. In: Vaudenay, S. (ed.) EUROCRYPT 2006. LNCS, vol. 4004, pp. 522–537. Springer, Heidelberg (2006). https://doi.org/10.1007/11761679_31

Verifiable Random Functions
with Optimal Tightness

David Niehues$^{(\boxtimes)}$ (iD)

Paderborn University, Paderborn, Germany
david.niehues@uni-paderborn.de

Abstract. Verifiable random functions (VRFs), introduced by Micali, Rabin and Vadhan (FOCS'99), are the public-key equivalent of pseudorandom functions. A public verification key and proofs accompanying the output enable all parties to verify the correctness of the output. However, all known standard model VRFs have a reduction loss that is much worse than what one would expect from known optimal constructions of closely related primitives like unique signatures. We show that:

1. Every security proof for a VRF that relies on a non-interactive assumption has to lose a factor of Q, where Q is the number of adversarial queries. To that end, we extend the meta-reduction technique of Bader *et al.* (EUROCRYPT'16) to also cover VRFs.
2. This raises the question: Is this bound optimal? We answer this question in the affirmative by presenting the first VRF with a reduction from the non-interactive qDBDHI assumption to the security of VRF that achieves this optimal loss.

We thus paint a complete picture of the achievability of tight verifiable random functions: We show that a security loss of Q is unavoidable and present the first construction that achieves this bound.

1 Introduction

Verifiable Random Functions (VRFs), introduced by Micali, Rabin and Vadhan in [41], can be thought of as the public key equivalent of pseudorandom functions (PRFs). That is, a secret key sk always comes together with a public verification key vk. The secret key sk allows the evaluation of the verifiable random function $F_{sk}(X)$ on input X and obtain the pseudorandom output Y. In contrast to pseudorandom functions, however, a verifiable random function also produces a non-interactive proof of correctness π. Together with vk, the proof π allows everyone to verify that Y is the output of $F_{sk}(X)$. We require two security properties from VRFs: *unique provability* and *pseudorandomness*. Unique provability means that for every verification key vk and every VRF input X, there is a *unique* Y for which a proof π exists such that the verification algorithm

This work was partially supported by the German Research Foundation (DFG) within the Collaborative Research Centre On-The-Fly Computing (GZ: SFB 901/3) under the project number 160364472.

J. A. Garay (Ed.): PKC 2021, LNCS 12711, pp. 61–91, 2021.
https://doi.org/10.1007/978-3-030-75248-4_3

accepts. However, note that there might be multiple valid proofs π verifying the correctness of Y with respect to vk and X. Further, we (informally) say that a VRF is pseudorandom if there is no efficient adversary that can distinguish a VRF output without the accompanying proof from a uniformly random element of the range of the VRF. In addition to these properties, Hofheinz and Jager introduced the notion of *VRFs with all desired properties* [27]. Namely, we say that a VRF possesses *all desired properties* if it fulfills all requirements above, has an exponentially sized domain, is secure even in presence of an adaptive the adversary is proven secure under a non-interactive complexity assumption. In this work, we only consider VRFs that have all desired properties.

Applications of VRFs. VRFs have found a wide range of applications in theory in practice. One of the most notable ones is the recent application of VRFs in *proof of stake* consensus mechanisms, like the ones used in the Algorand Blockchain [23], the Cardano Blockchain [6,21] and the DFINITY Blockchain [4]. Further applications are in *key transparency systems* like CONIKS [40], where VRFs prevent the enumeration of all users that have keys in the system. Similarly, VRFs are used in the proposed *DNSSEC extension NSECv5* [49], where they provably prevent zone enumeration attacks in the authenticated denial of existence mechanism of DNSSEC [24].

Tightness. Following the reductionist approach to security, we relate the difficulty of breaking the security of a cryptographic scheme to the difficulty of solving an underlying hard problem. Let λ be the security parameter and consider a reduction showing that any adversary that breaks the security of a cryptographic scheme in time $t(\lambda)$ with probability $\epsilon(\lambda)$ implies an algorithm that solves the underlying hard problem with probability $\epsilon'(\lambda)$ in time $t'(\lambda)$ with $t'(\lambda) \geq t(\lambda)$ and $\epsilon'(\lambda) \leq \epsilon(\lambda)$. We then say that the reduction *loses* a factor $\ell(\lambda)$ if $t'(\lambda))/\epsilon'(\lambda) \geq \ell(\lambda)t(\lambda)/\epsilon(\lambda)$ for all $\lambda \in \mathbb{N}$. We say that a reduction is *tight* if ℓ is a constant, *i.e.* if the quality of the reduction does not depend on the security parameter.

The loss of a reduction is of particular practical importance when deciding on the key sizes to use for cryptographic schemes. For simplicity, assume that we have a reduction with $\epsilon'(\lambda) = \epsilon(\lambda)$ and $t'(\lambda) = \ell(\lambda)t(\lambda)$ and let $t_{\mathsf{opt}}(\lambda)$ denote the time the fastest algorithm takes to solve an instance of the hardness assumption. Then, if we want to rule out the existence of an adversary that breaks the security of the scheme faster than t_{adv}, we have to choose the security parameter large enough such that $t_{\mathsf{opt}}(\lambda)/\ell(\lambda) \geq t_{\mathsf{adv}}$. Hence, if ℓ is large, then λ has to be rather large in order to guarantee that any adversary that breaks the security of the scheme has runtime at least t_{adv}. However, a large security parameter also implies large keys, which negatively affects the real-world efficiency of the scheme. On the positive side, this means that if we are able to construct a tight reduction, this allows us to use *small key sizes and guarantee security* against all adversaries with runtime at most t_{adv}. This approach to security is also known as concrete security and is more thoroughly discussed in [8].

Impossibility of Tight Reductions. Unfortunately, we know that tight reductions can not exist for some primitives. Coron presented the first result of this kind in 2002 for unique signatures [19], in which he showed that every security reduction for unique signatures loses at least a factor of $\approx Q$, where Q is the number of adaptive signature queries made by the forger. He achieved this result by introducing the *meta-reduction technique.* That is, one shows that a tight reduction can not exist by proving that any tight reduction would be able to solve the underling hard problem without the help of an adversary. Subsequently, the technique has been successfully used to prove the same lower bound for the loss of security reductions for efficiently re-randomizable signatures by Hofheinz *et al.* [28] and later on to an even wider classes of primitives by Bader *et al.* [5]. Most recently the Coron's technique has been extended by further works. First, Morgan and Pass extended Coron's technique to also incorporate interactive complexity assumptions and reductions that execute several instances of an adversary in parallel. However, since the result applies to a wider class of reductions and complexity assumptions, the lower bound on the loss is only $\sqrt{Q}$ instead of Q. Then Morgan*et al.* applied the technique to MACs and PRFs [43].

Even though VRFs are closely related to unique signatures, none of the lower bounds on the loss mentioned above applies to VRFs in general because the non-interactive proofs of VRFs do not need to be unique, nor do they need to be re-randomizable. For example, the VRF by Bitansky does not have unique proofs [10]. Hence, in contrast to a remark in [42], a VRF does not immediately imply a unique signature, but only a signature with a unique component.

Circumventing Tightness Lower Bounds. Despite all the lower bounds on the loss of reductions to the security of unique signatures, Guo *et al.* showed in [25] that reductions circumventing the lower bounds are possible by making heavy use of the programmability of a random oracle. However, this technique is only applicable in the random oracle model and can not be adapted in the standard model to the best of our knowledge.

Moreover, the tightness lower bounds have also been circumvented in the standard model by making the signatures non-randomizable [2,11,20,26,37,47]. Kakvi and Kiltz even describe a tightly secure unique signature scheme by using a public key in the reduction that allows for non-unique signatures and is indistinguishable from an honestly generated public key [35].

Furthermore, for identity based encryption – a primitive that is closely related to VRFs [1] – Wee and Chen [17] describe a scheme that can proven secure with a reduction whose loss depends only on the security parameter and not on the number of queries made by the adversary. In 2016, Boyen and Li then presented the first tightly secure construction in [16]. Similar to our approach in this work, they homomorphically evaluate a pseudorandom function in the reduction. However, they use it in order to apply the technique of Katz and Wang to construct tightly secure signatures by making the signatures non-re-randomizable [37].

However, the techniques above are not applicable to VRFs. Replacing the verification with an indistinguishable verification key that allows for non-unique signatures is not possible due to the strong uniqueness requirement. Moreover, our meta reduction makes no assumptions about the re-randomizability of the proof of correctness produced by a VRF evaluation. Hence, making the proofs of correct evaluation non-rerandomizable can not allow for tighter reductions. Thus, to the best of our knowledge the only avenues to achieve tighter reductions for VRFs would be either to use the random oracle model, to prove the security from an interactive assumption or to use a reduction that can run several instances of an adversary in parallel. However, for the latter two approaches, it seems unlikely to achieve a loss better than $\sqrt{Q}$ due to the lower bound by Morgan and Pass [42].

Our Contributions. In this paper, we study the tightness of reductions from non-interactive complexity assumptions to the security of verifiable random functions.

1. We first extend the lower bound for the loss of re-randomizable signatures from Bader *et al.* [5] to verifiable *unpredictable* functions (VUFs), which differ from VRFs in that the output only has to be unpredictable instead of pseudorandom. Since this is a weaker requirement, the theorem for VUFs also implies the same bound for reductions to the security of VRFs. Concretely, we prove that any reduction from a non-interactive complexity assumption to the unpredictability of a VUF loses a factor of at least Q.
2. We present a VRF and a reduction from the non-interactive q-DBDHI assumption to the adaptive pseudorandomness of the VRF that achieves this bound. The VRF is based on the VRF by Yamada [51,52].

1.1   Notation

We introduce some notation before giving a technical overview of our work. For this, let $a, b, c \in \mathbb{N}$ with $a \leq b \leq c$. We then let $[c] := \{1, \ldots, c\}$. Analogously, we let $[a, c] := \{a, \ldots, c\}$ and $[c \setminus b] := [c] \setminus \{b\}$. Also, for any finite set S, we denote drawing a uniformly random element y from S by $y \xleftarrow{\$} S$. Further, for a probabilistic algorithm $\mathcal{A}$ that uses k bits of randomness and takes some input x, we write $\mathcal{A}(x; \rho_{\mathcal{A}})$ for the execution of $\mathcal{A}$ on input x with fixed random bits $\rho_{\mathcal{A}} \in \{0,1\}^k$. Analogously, we write $a \xleftarrow{\$} \mathcal{A}(x)$ for executing $\mathcal{A}$ on input x with uniformly random bits and assigning the result to a. Finally, we will view the time to execute the security experiment as part of the runtime of an adversary that is executed in the security experiment. We do so as to not worsen the runtime of a reduction by accounting it runtime for simulating the security experiment for the adversary.

1.2   Technical Overview

Before presenting our results, we give a short overview over our techniques below. We first describe how we prove the lower bound for the loss of VRFs and then describe our construction attaining this bound.

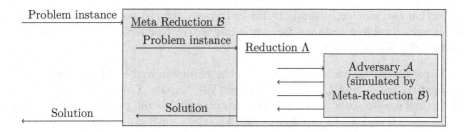

Fig. 1. The meta-reduction technique of Coron [19].

Bounding the Tightness of VRFs. We first extend the meta-reduction of Bader *et al.* to VRFs and thus show that any reduction from a non-interactive complexity assumption to the security of a VRF necessarily loses a factor of at least Q, where Q is the number of queries made by the adversary. The results by Bader *et al.* do not cover VRFs and VUFs because their theorems only apply to *re-randomizable* signatures/relations[1]. However, VRFs and VUFs do not fall into this class of primitives because their non-interactive proofs are not necessarily re-randomizable. In order to explain how we extend their technique, we shortly revisit Coron's meta-reduction technique depicted in Fig. 1. A *meta-reduction* can be thought of as a reduction against a reduction. That is, the meta-reduction $\mathcal{B}$ simulates a hypothetical adversary $\mathcal{A}$ for a reduction Λ. Since the meta-reduction is constructed to have a polynomial runtime and simulates the hypothetical adversary, it is actually the reduction Λ that solves the instance of the hardness assumption. This allows us to show that any reduction with a certain tightness is able to break the underlying hardness assumption without the help of any adversary and therefore contradicts the hardness assumption.

In their proof, Bader *et al.* use the re-randomizability/uniqueness of the signatures that Λ produces for $\mathcal{A}$ in order to solve the challenge when simulating $\mathcal{A}$. We extend their technique to VRF/VUFs by showing that it is sufficient if the part of the signature that the adversary has to provide for the challenge, in the case of VUFs the unpredictable value Y, is unique or re-randomizable.

For simplicity, we prove the theorem for VUFs: this automatically implies the same bound for VRFs because every VRF is also a VUF. Following Bader *et al.*, we consider a very weak security model in which the number of queries Q is fixed a priori. Further, the adversary is presented with Q uniformly random and pairwise distinct inputs $X_1, \ldots, X_Q$ and has to choose a challenge X^* from these. For all other inputs, the adversary is then given the VUF output and proof. Finally, the adversary has to output the VUF value for the challenge input and wins if the output is correct. We refer to this very weak security as *weak-selective unpredictability*. We describe a hypothetical adversary that breaks the adaptive pseudorandomness with certainty and then show that our meta-

---

[1] Note that unique signatures are re-randomizable because, given a unique signature for a message, it is trivial to sample from all signatures for that message since there is only that one signature.

reduction can efficiently simulate this adversary for the reduction. Informally, on input a problem instance for a non-interactive complexity assumption, the meta-reduction Λ behaves as follows.

1. It passes on the problem instance to the reduction and lets it output a verification key vk and Q pairwise different VUF inputs $X_1, \ldots, X_Q$.
2. It then iterates over all $j \in [Q]$ and executes the second part of the reduction as if it chose j as the challenge and lets the reduction produce all pairs of VUF output and proof except for the j'th pair. It then verifies them and saves them if they are correct with respect to vk and the corresponding input.
3. Finally, it chooses $j^* \xleftarrow{\$} [Q]$ and passes on the correct VUF output for X_{j^*} to the reduction. We formally prove in Sect. 2 that the meta-reduction indeed has learned the correct VUF output for X_{j^*} from the reduction with probability at least $1/Q$.
4. When the reduction then outputs the solution to the underlying problem instance, the meta-reduction outputs this solution as well.

Overall, we can then show that the meta-reduction takes time at most $\mathcal{B} = Q \cdot t_\Lambda + Q(Q+1)t_{\text{Vfy}}$ and has a success probability at least $\epsilon_\Lambda - 1/Q$, where t_Λ and ϵ_Λ are the runtime and the success probability of the reduction and t_{Vfy} is the time it takes to verify a VUF output. Now we can follow that Λ has a loss of at least $\ell = (\epsilon_N + 1/Q)^{-1}$, where ϵ_N is the largest probability any algorithm running in time $t_\mathcal{B}$ has in breaking the hardness assumption. Since the hardness assumption implies that ϵ_N is negligibly small, we have that $\ell \approx Q$.

While the meta-reduction above is only applicable to reductions that execute the adversary exactly once, our proof of the lower bound on the loss of VRFs in Sect. 2, like the one by like Bader *et al.*, also applies to reductions that can sequentially rewind the adversary.

On the Difficulty of Constructing Tightly Secure VRFs. As Table 1 shows, known security proofs for VRFs in the standard model are significantly more lossy than the lower bound Q. This raises the question:

Do verifiable random functions with a loss of Q exist?

In consequence, such a VRF would show that a loss of Q is indeed optimal.

We proceed by explaining why all previous constructions have a loss much worse than Q and then give an overview over our approach that achieves the optimal tightness. They all have in common that the reduction makes a guess in the very beginning and then has to abort and output a random bit depending on the queries and the challenge of the adversary. Let succ-red be the event that the reduction solves the underlying hardness assumption and let abort be the event that the reduction aborts and outputs a random bit. For a clear exposition, we assume that the reduction always succeeds when it does not abort and the

Table 1. We compare the loss of previous VRFs with all desired properties. For the variables, let $|\pi|$ denotes the size of the proofs of the VRF and ϵ, t and Q the advantage, runtime and number of queries made by the adversary the reduction is run against. Further, there are three values that depend on the error correcting code used in the construction: the function $\tau(\epsilon) > 1$ and the constants $\nu > 1$ and $c \leq 1/2$. Note that the full version [14] of [15] has been updated with the bound stated above.

Schemes	Security loss
Hohenberger and Waters [29]	$\mathcal{O}(\lambda Q/\epsilon)$
Boneh *et al.* Sec. 7 in [15]	$(Q\lambda)^{\tau(\epsilon)}$
Jager [31]	$\mathcal{O}(Q^\nu/\epsilon^{\nu+1})$
Hofheinz and Jager [27]	$\mathcal{O}(\lambda \log(\lambda) Q^{2/c}/\epsilon^3)$
Yamada Sec 6.1 in [52]	$\mathcal{O}(Q^\nu/\epsilon^{\nu+1})$
Yamada Sec. 6.2 in [52]	$\mathcal{O}(Q^\nu/\epsilon^{\nu+1})$
Yamada App. C in [51]	$\mathcal{O}(\lambda^2 Q/\epsilon^2)$
Katsumata Sec. 5.1 in [36]	$\mathcal{O}(Q^\nu/\epsilon^{\nu+1})$
Kastumata Sec. 5.3 in [36]	$\mathcal{O}(Q^\nu/\epsilon^{\nu+1})$
Rosie [46]	$\mathcal{O}(\lambda \log(\lambda) Q^{2/c}/\epsilon^3)$
Kohl [38]	$\mathcal{O}(|\pi| \log(\lambda) Q^{2/\nu}/\epsilon^3)$
Kohl [38]	$\mathcal{O}(|\pi| \log(\lambda) Q^{2+2/\nu}/\epsilon^3)$
Jager and Niehues [34]	$\mathcal{O}(t^3/\epsilon^2)$
Jager *et al.* [32]	$\mathcal{O}(t^3/\epsilon^2)$
Sect. 4	$\mathcal{O}(Q)$

adversary succeeds. We then have that

$$\Pr[\text{succ-red}] = \Pr[\text{succ-red} \wedge \text{abort}] + \Pr[\text{succ-red} \wedge \neg\text{abort}]$$

$$= \frac{1}{2}(1 - \Pr[\neg\text{abort}]) + \Pr[\text{succ-red} \wedge \neg\text{abort}]$$

$$= \frac{1}{2} + \Pr[\text{succ-red} \wedge \neg\text{abort}] - \frac{\Pr[\neg\text{abort}]}{2}.$$

This shows that, in contrast to computational security experiments/hardness assumptions, where a lower bound would suffice, we need upper and lower bounds on $\Pr[\text{abort}]$ that are close to each other in order prove the security of a VRF. Waters used the *artificial abort technique* to prove close lower and upper bounds on $\Pr[\neg\text{abort}]$ [50]. That is, the reduction estimates the probability of aborting over all possible choices it can make in the very beginning for the sequence of queries made by the adversary and then aborts with a probability that ensures that the reduction always aborts with almost the same probability. However, the estimation step in the reduction is computationally expensive. Bellare and Ristenpart addressed this issue with a more thorough analysis and by making $\Pr[\neg\text{abort}]$ slightly smaller [9]. Jager then applied Bellare's and Ristenpart's technique to admissible hash functions (AHFs) and introduced *balanced admissible hash functions* [31]. But in conclusion, none of the techniques known so far achieves the optimal loss of Q.

A Reduction with Optimal Tightness. We next answer the question stated above in the affirmative by presenting a VRF with a reduction that only loses a factor of Q. To do so, we have to address the issue raised above: that the success probability for the partitioning argument depends on the sequence of queries made by the adversary. We achieve this by passing every query and the challenge of the adversary through a pseudorandom function (PRF). Further, we utilize a property of the VRF Yamada introduced in [51, Appendix C]. This VRF allows the reduction to homomorphically embed an arbitrary NAND circuit of polynomial size and logarithmic depth in the VRF. The idea here is that the reduction can embed an arbitrary NAND-circuit in the VRF such that it can answer all queries by the adversary for which the circuit evaluates to 0 and can extract a solution to the underlying hard problem whenever the circuit evaluates to 1. In particular, the homomorphic evaluation hides selected parts of the circuit inputs, all internal states of the circuit and the output of the circuit from the adversary.

We use these properties to homomorphically evaluate a PRF. Since the adversary does not learn any internal states or outputs of the PRF, we thus have that the outputs of the PRF are distributed as if they were the outputs of a random function. In particular, we then have that the outputs of the PRF are distributed uniformly and independent of each other. We show in Sect. 3 that it then suffices for the reduction to guess $\lceil \log(Q) \rceil + 1$ bits of the PRF output of the challenge. Then the probability that the following two events both occur is at least $1/8Q$:

1. The PRF output of the challenge matches the guess.
2. The guess does not match the PRF output for any of the adversary's queries.

Further, viewing the PRF outputs as the output of a truly random function, the probability for the reduction to succeeds is independent of the probability of the adversary breaking the security of the VRF. Ultimately, this yields a VRF, which has a loss of Q plus the loss of the PRF.

2   Impossibility of VRFs and VUFs with Tight Reductions

In this section, we prove that any reduction from a non-interactive complexity assumption to the security of a VUF or VRF unavoidably loses a factor of Q. To do so, we first formally introduce VUFs and VRFs and their accompanying security notions. We then introduce a very weak security notion for VUFs and prove that even for this notion, every reduction form a non-interactive complexity assumption to it necessarily loses a factor of Q.

2.1 Syntax of Verifiable Random Functions (VRFs) and Verifiable Unpredictable Functions (VUFs)

Formally, a VRF or VUF consists of algorithms (Gen, Eval, Vfy) with the following syntax.

- $(\mathsf{vk}, \mathsf{sk}) \xleftarrow{\$} \mathsf{Gen}(1^\lambda)$ takes as input the security parameter λ and outputs a key pair $(\mathsf{vk}, \mathsf{sk})$. We say that sk is the *secret key* and vk is the *verification key*.
- $(Y, \pi) \xleftarrow{\$} \mathsf{Eval}(\mathsf{sk}, X)$ takes as input a secret key sk and $X \in \{0,1\}^\lambda$, and outputs a function value $Y \in \mathcal{Y}$, where $\mathcal{Y}$ is a finite set, and a proof π. We write $V_{\mathsf{sk}}(X)$ to denote the function value Y computed by Eval on input (sk, X).
- $\mathsf{Vfy}(\mathsf{vk}, X, Y, \pi) \in \{0,1\}$ takes as input a verification key vk, $X \in \{0,1\}^\lambda$, $Y \in \mathcal{Y}$, and proof π, and outputs a bit.

Note that VRFs and VUFs share a common syntax. The only difference is in the achieved security properties. We first define security for VRFs and then describe how the definition has to be adapted for VUFs.

$$
\begin{array}{|l|}
\hline
G^{\mathcal{VRF}}_{(\mathcal{A}_1, \mathcal{A}_2)}(\lambda) \\
\hline
(\mathsf{vk}, \mathsf{sk}) \xleftarrow{\$} \mathsf{Gen}(1^\lambda);\; \rho_\mathcal{A} \xleftarrow{\$} \{0,1\}^\lambda \\
(X^*, \mathsf{st}) \xleftarrow{\$} \mathcal{A}_1^{\mathsf{Eval}(\mathsf{sk}, \cdot)}(\mathsf{vk}; \rho_\mathcal{A}) \\
Y_0 := \mathsf{Eval}(\mathsf{sk}, X^*) \\
Y_1 \xleftarrow{\$} \mathcal{Y} \\
b \xleftarrow{\$} \{0,1\} \\
b' := \mathcal{A}_2^{\mathsf{Eval}(\mathsf{sk}, \cdot)}(Y_b, \mathsf{st}) \\
\text{return } b == b' \\
\hline
\end{array}
$$

Fig. 2. The security experiment specifying pseudorandomness of verifiable random functions.

Definition 1. $\mathcal{VRF} = (\mathsf{Gen}, \mathsf{Eval}, \mathsf{Vfy})$ *is a* secure *verifiable random function (VRF) if it fulfills following requirements.*

Correctness. *For all* $(\mathsf{vk}, \mathsf{sk}) \xleftarrow{\$} \mathsf{Gen}(1^\lambda)$ *and* $X \in \{0,1\}^\lambda$ *holds: if* $(Y, \pi) \xleftarrow{\$} \mathsf{Eval}(\mathsf{sk}, X)$, *then* $\mathsf{Vfy}(\mathsf{vk}, X, Y, \pi) = 1$. *Further, the algorithms* Gen, Eval, Vfy *are polynomial-time.*

Unique provability. *For all* $\mathsf{vk} \in \{0,1\}^*$ *and all* $X \in \{0,1\}^\lambda$, *there does not exist any* $Y_0, \pi_0, Y_1, \pi_1 \in \{0,1\}^*$ *such that* $Y_0 \neq Y_1$ *and it holds that* $\mathsf{Vfy}(\mathsf{vk}, X, Y_0, \pi_0) = \mathsf{Vfy}(\mathsf{vk}, X, Y_1, \pi_1) = 1$.

$$\boxed{\begin{array}{l}
\text{weak-selective-Unpredictability}^{Q,\mathcal{VUF}}_{(\mathcal{A}_1,\mathcal{A}_2)}(\lambda)\\
\hline
(\mathsf{vk},\mathsf{sk}) \xleftarrow{\$} \mathsf{Gen}(1^\lambda); \rho_{\mathcal{A}} \xleftarrow{\$} \{0,1\}^\lambda\\
(X_1,\ldots,X_Q) \xleftarrow{\$} \{0,1\}^\lambda \text{ s.t. } X_i \neq X_j \text{ for all } i \neq j\\
(Y_i,\pi_i) \xleftarrow{\$} \mathsf{Eval}(\mathsf{sk},X_i)\\
(j,\mathsf{st}) \xleftarrow{\$} \mathcal{A}_1(\mathsf{vk},(X_i)_{i\in[Q];\rho_{\mathcal{A}}})\\
Y^* \xleftarrow{\$} \mathcal{A}_2((Y_i,\pi_i,\mathsf{st})_{i\in[Q\setminus j]})\\
\text{return } Y^* == Y_j
\end{array}}$$

Fig. 3. The security experiment specifying weak selective pseudorandomness.

Pseudorandomness. *Consider an attacker* $\mathcal{A} = (\mathcal{A}_1,\mathcal{A}_2)$ *with access (via oracle queries) to* $\mathsf{Eval}(\mathsf{sk},\cdot)$ *in the pseudorandomness game depicted in Fig. 2. Let* $\mathcal{Q} = (X_1,\ldots,X_Q)$ *be the oracle queries made by* $\mathcal{A}_1$ *and* $\mathcal{A}_2$, *then we say that* $\mathcal{A}$ *is* legitimate *if there is no* $\rho_{\mathcal{A}} \in \{0,1\}^\lambda$ *such that there exists* $i \in [Q]$ *with* $X_i = X^*$, *where* X_i *is the* i*'th query to* Eval *made by* $\mathcal{A}$. *We define the advantage of* $\mathcal{A}$ *in breaking the pseudorandomness of* $\mathcal{VRF}$ *as*

$$\mathsf{Adv}^{\mathcal{VRF}}_{\mathcal{A}}(\lambda) := \left| \Pr\left[G^{\mathcal{VRF}}_{(\mathcal{A}_1,\mathcal{A}_2)}(\lambda) = 1 \right] - 1/2 \right|.$$

We require the same security properties from VUFs as the properties we require from VRFs in Definition 1, with the exception that we require the weaker property of *unpredictability* instead of pseudorandomness from VUFs. This property can be formalized just like pseudorandomness just that the adversary has to output the correct Y^* instead of distinguishing it from a random element as depicted in Fig. 2. We do not give a formal definition since it is very similar to VRFs, and we use the notion of weak select unpredictability, which is defined in Sect. 2.2, in our proof.

2.2   Lower Tightness Bounds for VUFs

We begin by introducing the very weak security notion of *weak-selective unpredictability*. In this security model, all queries and the challenge are uniformly random and pairwise different. We formally define it as follows.

Definition 2. *Let* $\mathcal{VUF} = (\mathsf{Gen},\mathsf{Eval},\mathsf{Vfy})$ *be a verifiable unpredictable function and let* $t : \mathbb{N} \to \mathbb{N}, \epsilon : \mathbb{N} \to [0,1]$. *For an adversary* $\mathcal{A} = (\mathcal{A}_1,\mathcal{A}_2)$, *we say that* $\mathcal{A}$ (t,Q,ϵ)-*breaks the weak selective pseudorandomness of* $\mathcal{VUF}$ *if* $\mathcal{A}$ *runs in time* t *and*

$$\mathsf{Adv}^{\mathcal{VUF}}_{\mathcal{A}_1,\mathcal{A}_2}(\lambda) := \Pr\left[\text{weak-selective-Unpredictability}^{Q,\mathcal{VUF}}_{\mathcal{A}_1,\mathcal{A}_2}(\lambda) = 1 \right] = \epsilon(\lambda)$$

where $\text{weak-selective-Unpredictability}^{Q,\mathcal{VUF}}_{(\mathcal{A}_1,\mathcal{A}_2)}(\lambda)$ *is the security experiment depicted in Fig. 3.*

Note that any verifiable random function fulfilling the requirements of Definition 1 has also weak-selective unpredictability. Hence, ruling out a tight reduction from weak selective unpredictability to a class of hardness assumptions, also rules out tight reductions from pseudorandomness to that class of hardness assumptions. We thus prove a lower bound on the loss of any reduction from any non-interactive complexity assumption to the weak selective unpredictability of a VUF, where the reduction my sequentially repeat the execution of the adversary.

Following [3,5], we define a non-interactive complexity assumption as a triple $N = (\mathsf{T}, \mathsf{V}, \mathsf{U})$ of Turing machines (TMs). While the TM T generates a problem instance and V verifies the correctness of a solution, the TM U represents a trivial adversary to compare an actual adversary against. For example, a trivial adversary against the DDH assumption would just output random bit as its guess. We formally define non-interactive complexity assumptions as follows.

Definition 3. *A non-interactive complexity assumption $N = (\mathsf{T}, \mathsf{V}, \mathsf{U})$ consist of three Turing machines. The instance generation machine $(c, w) \xleftarrow{\$} \mathsf{T}(1^\lambda)$ takes the security parameter as input and outputs a problem instance c and a witness w. U is a probabilistic polynomial-time Turing machine, which takes c as input and outputs a candidate solution s. The verification Turing machine V takes as input (c, w) and a candidate solution s. If $\mathsf{V}(c, w, s) = 1$, then we say that s is a correct solution to the challenge c.*

$$
\begin{array}{|l|}
\hline
\mathsf{NICA}_{\mathcal{A}}^{N}(\lambda) \\
\hline
(c, w) \xleftarrow{\$} \mathsf{T}(1^\lambda); \rho_{\mathcal{A}} \xleftarrow{\$} \{0, 1\}^\lambda \\
s \xleftarrow{\$} \mathcal{A}(c; \rho_{\mathcal{A}}) \\
\text{return } \mathsf{V}(c, w, s) \\
\hline
\end{array}
$$

Fig. 4. The generic security experiment for a non-interactive complexity assumption $N = (\mathsf{T}, \mathsf{V}, \mathsf{U})$ between the challenger and an adversary $\mathcal{A}$.

Definition 4. *Let $N = (\mathsf{T}, \mathsf{V}, \mathsf{U})$ be a non-interactive complexity assumption and let NICA be the security experiment depicted in Fig. 4. For functions $t : \mathbb{N} \to \mathbb{N}, \epsilon : \mathbb{N} \to [0, 1]$ and a probabilistic Turing machine $\mathcal{B}$ running in time $t(\lambda)$, we say that $\mathcal{B}$ (t, ϵ)-breaks N if*

$$
\left| \Pr\left[\mathsf{NICA}_{\mathcal{B}}^{N}(\lambda) = 1 \right] - \Pr\left[\mathsf{NICA}_{\mathsf{U}}^{N}(\lambda) = 1 \right] \right| \geq \epsilon(\lambda),
$$

where the probabilities are taken over the randomness consumed by T and the random choices of ρ_{U} and $\rho_{\mathcal{B}}$ in the security experiments $\mathsf{NICA}_{\mathcal{B}}^{n}(\lambda)$ and $\mathsf{NICA}_{\mathsf{U}}^{n}(\lambda)$.

$$
\begin{array}{|l|}
\hline
r\text{-}\Lambda^{\mathcal{A}}(c, \rho_\Lambda) \\
\hline
\mathsf{st}_{\Lambda_{1,1}} \overset{\$}{\leftarrow} \Lambda_1(c; \rho_0) \\
\textbf{For } 1 \le \ell \le r \textbf{ do:} \\
\quad (\mathsf{vk}^\ell, (X_i^\ell)_{i \in [Q]}, \rho_\mathcal{A}, \mathsf{st}_{\Lambda_{\ell,2}}) \overset{\$}{\leftarrow} \Lambda_{\ell,1}(\mathsf{st}_{\Lambda,1}) \\
\quad (j^{*\ell}, \mathsf{st}_\mathcal{A}) \overset{\$}{\leftarrow} \mathcal{A}_1(\mathsf{vk}^\ell, (X_i^\ell)_{i \in [Q]}; \rho_\mathcal{A}) \\
\quad ((Y_i^\ell, \pi_i^\ell)_{i \in [Q\setminus j^{*\ell}]}, \mathsf{st}_{\Lambda_{\ell,3}}) \overset{\$}{\leftarrow} \Lambda_{\ell,2}(j^{*\ell}, \mathsf{st}_{\Lambda_{\ell,2}}) \\
\quad Y_{j^{*\ell}}^\ell \overset{\$}{\leftarrow} \mathcal{A}_2((Y_i^\ell, \pi_i^\ell)_{i \in [Q\setminus j^{*\ell}]}, \mathsf{st}_\mathcal{A}) \\
\quad \mathsf{st}_{\Lambda_{\ell+1,1}} \overset{\$}{\leftarrow} \Lambda_{\ell,3}\left(Y_{j^{*\ell}}^\ell, j^{*\ell}, \mathsf{st}_{\Lambda_{\ell,3}}\right) \\
s \overset{\$}{\leftarrow} \Lambda_3(\mathsf{st}_{\Lambda r+1,1}) \\
\hline
\end{array}
$$

Fig. 5. Description of the Turing r-$\Lambda^{\mathcal{A}}$ machine built from an adversary $\mathcal{A} = (\mathcal{A}_1, \mathcal{A}_2)$ against the weak selective unpredictability of a verifiable unpredictable function and a reduction $(\Lambda_1, (\Lambda_{\ell,1}, \Lambda_{\ell,2}, \Lambda_{\ell,3})_{\ell \in [r]}, \Lambda_3)$.

Bader *et al.* prove lower bounds for simple reductions as well as for reductions that can sequentially rewind the adversary [5]. Since the latter class of reduction include the former class, we directly prove the lower bound on the loss for the larger class of reductions. Following Bader *et al.*, we view a reduction that sequentially rewinds an adversary up to $r \in \mathbb{N}$ times as a $3r + 2$-tuple of Turing machines. That is, one TM that initializes the reduction, one to produce a solution in the end and three for each execution of the adversary. For an adversary $\mathcal{A} = (\mathcal{A}_1, \mathcal{A}_2)$ against the weak selective unpredictability of a verifiable unpredictable function $\mathcal{VUF}$, we let r-$\Lambda^{\mathcal{A}}$ be the Turing machine depicted in Fig. 5.

Definition 5 (Def. 6 in [5]). *For a verifiable unpredictable function $\mathcal{VUF}$, we say that a Turing machine r-$\Lambda = (\Lambda_1, (\Lambda_{\ell,1}, \Lambda_{\ell,2}, \Lambda_{\ell,3})_{\ell \in [r]}, \Lambda_3)$ is an r-simple $(t_\Lambda, Q, \epsilon_\Lambda, \epsilon_\mathcal{A})$-reduction from breaking the non-interactive complexity assumption $N = (\mathsf{T}, \mathsf{V}, \mathsf{U})$ to breaking the weak selective unpredictability of $\mathcal{VUF}$ if for any TM $\mathcal{A}$ that $(t_\mathcal{A}, Q, \epsilon_\mathcal{A})$-breaks the weak selective unpredictability of $\mathcal{VUF}$, TM r-$\Lambda^{\mathcal{A}}$ as defined in Fig. 5 $(t_\Lambda + rt_\mathcal{A}, \epsilon_\Lambda)$ breaks N.*

Furthermore, we define the loss of a reduction as the factor that $(t_\Lambda(\lambda) + rt_\mathcal{A}(\lambda))/\epsilon_\Lambda(\lambda)$ is larger than $t_\mathcal{A}(\lambda)/\epsilon_\mathcal{A}(\lambda)$. We formalize this in the following definition.

Definition 6. *For a verifiable unpredictable function $\mathcal{VUF}$, a non-interactive complexity assumption N, a function $\ell : \mathbb{N} \to \mathbb{N}$ and a reduction Λ, we say that Λ loses ℓ, if there exists an adversary $\mathcal{A}$ that $(t_\mathcal{A}, Q, \epsilon_\mathcal{A})$ breaks the weak selective unpredictability of $\mathcal{VUF}$ such that $\Lambda^{\mathcal{A}}$ $(t_\Lambda + r \cdot t_\mathcal{A}, \epsilon_\mathcal{A})$-breaks N where*

$$
\frac{t_\Lambda(\lambda) + rt_\mathcal{A}(\lambda)}{\epsilon_\Lambda(\lambda)} \ge \ell(\lambda) \cdot \frac{t_\mathcal{A}(\lambda)}{\epsilon_\mathcal{A}(\lambda)}.
$$

After introducing the needed notations and notions, we can now state our theorem regarding the loss of VRFs and VUFs.

Theorem 1. *Let* $N = (\mathsf{T}, \mathsf{V}, \mathsf{U})$ *be a non-interactive complexity assumption,* $Q, r \in \mathsf{poly}(\lambda)$ *and let* $\mathcal{VUF}$ *be a verifiable unpredictable function. Then for any* r-*simple* $(t_\Lambda, Q, \epsilon_\Lambda, 1)$-*reduction* Λ *from breaking* N *to breaking the weak selective unpredictability of* $\mathcal{VUF}$ *there exists a TM* $\mathcal{B}$ *that* $(t_\mathcal{B}, \epsilon_\mathcal{B})$-*breaks* N, *where*

$$t_\mathcal{B} \leq r \cdot Q \cdot t_\Lambda + r \cdot Q \cdot (Q - 1) \cdot t_{\mathsf{Vfy}}$$
$$\epsilon_\mathcal{B} \geq \epsilon_\Lambda - \frac{r}{Q}.$$

Here, t_{Vfy} *is time needed to run the algorithm* Vfy *of* $\mathcal{VUF}$.

Note that the theorem also applies to adversaries with $\epsilon_\Lambda < 1$, as we discuss after the proof of Theorem 1. However, before proving Theorem 1, we show that it implies that every r-simple reduction Λ from a non-interactive complexity assumption N has at least a loss of $\approx Q$. For $t_N := t_\mathcal{B} = r \cdot Q \cdot t_\Lambda + r \cdot Q \cdot (Q-1) \cdot t_{\mathsf{Vfy}}$, let ϵ_N be the largest probability such that there exists an algorithm that (t_N, ϵ_N)-breaks N. We then have that $\epsilon_N \geq \epsilon_\mathcal{B}$ and by Theorem 1, we have that $\epsilon_\Lambda \leq \epsilon_\mathcal{B} + r/Q \leq \epsilon_N + r/Q$. We can then conclude that

$$\frac{t_\Lambda + r \cdot t_\Lambda}{\epsilon_\Lambda} \geq \frac{r \cdot t_\Lambda}{\epsilon_N + r/Q} = (\epsilon_N + r/Q)^{-1} \cdot r \cdot \frac{t_\Lambda}{1} = (\epsilon_N + r/Q)^{-1} \cdot r \cdot \frac{t_\Lambda}{\epsilon_\Lambda}.$$

This means that Λ loses at least a factor of $\ell = r/(\epsilon_N + r/Q)$. Further, if ϵ_N is very small, which it is supposed to be for a good complexity assumption, then $\ell \approx Q$.

Proof. Our proof is structured like the proofs in [5, 28, 39] and thus first describes a hypothetical adversary that breaks the weak selective unpredictability of $\mathcal{VUF}$ with certainty and then describes a meta reduction that perfectly and efficiently simulates this adversary towards Λ.

The Hypothetical Adversary $\mathcal{A}$. The hypothetical adversary $\mathcal{A} = (\mathcal{A}_1, \mathcal{A}_2)$ consists of the following two procedures.

$\mathcal{A}_1(\mathsf{vk}, (X_i)_{i \in [Q]}; \rho_\mathcal{A})$ samples $j \xleftarrow{\$} [Q]$ and outputs (j, st) with the state $\mathsf{st} = (\mathsf{vk}, (X_i)_{i \in [Q]}, j)$.

$\mathcal{A}_2((Y_i, \pi_i)_{i \in [Q \setminus j]}, \mathsf{st})$ first parses the state st as $(\mathsf{vk}, (X_i)_{i \in [Q]}, j)$ and then checks whether $\mathsf{Vfy}(\mathsf{vk}, X_i, Y_i, \pi_i) = 1$ for all $i \in [Q \setminus j]$. If there is i^* such that $\mathsf{Vfy}(\mathsf{vk}, X_i, Y_i, \pi_i) = 0$, it aborts with result $\perp$. Otherwise, it computes $Y^* \in \mathcal{Y}$ such that there exists $\pi \in \{0, 1\}^*$ with $\mathsf{Vfy}(\mathsf{vk}, X_j, Y^*, \pi) = 1$. The existence of such a Y^* is guaranteed by the correctness of $\mathcal{VUF}$.

Observe that $\mathcal{A}$ breaks the weak selective unpredictability of $\mathcal{VUF}$ with certainty because a correct VUF produces only valid pairs of outputs and proofs, but $\mathcal{A}_2$ may not be efficiently computable. However, we show that $\mathcal{B}$ can efficiently simulate $\mathcal{A}$ nonetheless.

The Meta-reduction $\mathcal{B}$. We now describe the meta-reduction $\mathcal{B}$ that simulates $\mathcal{A}$ r times for $\Lambda = (\Lambda_1, (\Lambda_{\ell,1}, \Lambda_{\ell,2}, \Lambda_{\ell,3})_{\ell \in [r]}, \Lambda_3)$. $\mathcal{B}$'s goal in this is to break N and is therefore called on input c, where $(c, w) \xleftarrow{\$} \mathsf{T}(1^\lambda)$.

i. $\mathcal{B}$ receives c as input. It samples randomness $\rho_\Lambda \xleftarrow{\$} \{0, 1\}^\lambda$ and executes $\mathsf{st}_{\Lambda_{1,1}} = \Lambda_1(c, \rho_\Lambda)$. If Λ_1 does not output $\mathsf{st}_{\Lambda_{1,1}}$, then $\mathcal{B}$ aborts and outputs $\perp$. Since the randomness of Λ_1 is fixed, we view all subroutines of Λ as deterministic. Note that Λ_1 can pass on random coins to the other subroutines via $\mathsf{st}_{\Lambda_{1,1}}$.

ii. Next, $\mathcal{B}$ sequentially simulates $\mathcal{A}$ r times for Λ. That is, for all $1 \leq \ell \leq r$ it does the following.

   a) Initialize an empty array A^ℓ with Q places, that is $A^\ell[i] = \perp$ for all $i \in [Q]$.

   b) Run $(\mathsf{vk}^\ell, (X_i^\ell)_{i \in [Q]}, \rho_\mathcal{A}, \mathsf{st}_{\Lambda_{\ell,2}}) = \Lambda_{\ell,1}(\mathsf{st}_{\Lambda_{\ell,1}})$. If $\Lambda_{\ell,1}$ does not produce such an output, then $\mathcal{B}$ aborts and outputs $\perp$.

   c) Then $\mathcal{B}$ runs $((Y_{i,j}^\ell, \pi_{i,j}^\ell)_{i \in [Q] \setminus j}, \mathsf{st}_{\Lambda_{3,\ell}}) = \Lambda_{\ell,2}(j, \mathsf{st}_{\Lambda_{\ell,2}})$ for all $j \in [Q]$. If $\Lambda_{\ell,2}$ only produces correct outputs with respect to vk^ℓ, that is if

$$\bigwedge_{i \in [Q \setminus \ell]} \mathsf{Vfy}(\mathsf{vk}^\ell, X_i^\ell, Y_{i,j}^\ell, \pi_{i,j}^\ell) = 1,$$

then $\mathcal{B}$ sets $A^\ell[i] := Y_{i,j}^\ell$ for all $i \in [Q \setminus j]$.

   d) $\mathcal{B}$ then samples $j^{*\ell} \xleftarrow{\$} [Q]$. It then proceeds in one of the following cases:
      1. If $\Lambda_{\ell,2}(j^{*\ell}, \mathsf{st}_{\Lambda_{\ell,2}})$ produced any invalid pair of output and proof, that is, if there exists $i \in [Q \setminus j^{*\ell}]$ such that it holds that the Vfy rejects, that is $\mathsf{Vfy}(\mathsf{vk}^\ell, X_i^\ell, Y_{i,j^{*\ell}}^\ell, \pi_{i,j^{*\ell}}^\ell) = 0$, then $\mathcal{B}$ aborts and outputs $\perp$.
      2. Otherwise, $\mathcal{B}$ sets $Y^* := A^\ell[j^{*\ell}]$.

   e) Set $\mathsf{st}_{\Lambda_{\ell+1,1}} := \Lambda_{\ell,3}(Y^*, \mathsf{st}_{\Lambda_{\ell,3}})$

iii. Finally, $\mathcal{B}$ runs $s \xleftarrow{\$} \Lambda_3(\mathsf{st}_{\Lambda_{r+1,1}})$ and outputs s.

Success Probability of $\mathcal{B}$. In order to analyze the success probability of $\mathcal{B}$, we compare the simulation of $\mathcal{A}$ by $\mathcal{B}$ with the description of $\mathcal{A}$. Note that $\mathcal{A}_1$ samples j uniformly at random and $\mathcal{A}_2$ aborts if it is given an invalid pair of output and proof. $\mathcal{B}$ also samples $j^{*\ell}$ uniformly at random from $[Q]$ and aborts if $\Lambda_{\ell,2}(j^{*\ell}, \mathsf{st}_{\Lambda_{\ell,2}})$ produced any invalid pair of output and proof, just like $\mathcal{A}$. However, we are only guaranteed that $A^\ell[j^{*\ell}]$ contains the correct output of $\mathcal{VUF}$ for X_i^ℓ if there is $j' \in [Q \setminus j^{*\ell}]$ such that $\Lambda_{\ell,2}(j', \mathsf{st}_{\ell,2})$ outputs only correct pairs of outputs and proofs, *i.e.*, if this is not the case the simulation of $\mathcal{A}$ by $\mathcal{B}$ deviates from $\mathcal{A}$'s behavior. Below, we formally prove that $\mathcal{B}$ perfectly simulates $\mathcal{A}$ unless the event described above occurs and upper bound the probability that it occurs by r/Q.

Let $\mathsf{st}_{\Lambda_{\ell,2}}$ be the unique state computed by $\Lambda_{\ell,1}$ and let $j^{*\ell} \in [Q]$ be the unique index that $\Lambda_{\ell,3}$ is executed with. Note that these values are well-defined in both $\mathsf{NICA}_N^{\Lambda^\mathcal{A}}(\lambda)$ and $\mathsf{NICA}_N^\mathcal{B}(\lambda)$. Now, define the event all-valid$(\mathsf{st}_{\Lambda_{\ell,2}}, j)$ as the event that $\Lambda_{\ell,2}$ outputs only valid pairs of outputs and proofs. That is

$$\text{all-valid}(\mathsf{st}_{\Lambda_{\ell,2}}, j) = \begin{cases} 1 & \text{if } \mathsf{Vfy}(\mathsf{vk}^\ell, X_i^\ell, Y_{i,j}^\ell, \pi_{i,j}^\ell) = 1 \text{ for all } i \in [Q \setminus j] \\ 0 & \text{otherwise,} \end{cases}$$

where $(Y_{i,j}^\ell, \pi_{i,j}^\ell)_{i \in [Q \setminus j]} = \Lambda_{\ell,2}(\mathsf{st}_{\Lambda_{\ell,2}}, j)$. Recalling the case in which $\mathcal{B}$'s simulation deviates the hypothetical adversary $\mathcal{A}$, we define the event $\mathsf{bad}(\ell) := \mathsf{all\text{-}valid}(\mathsf{st}_{\Lambda_{\ell,2}}, j^{*\ell}) \bigwedge_{j \in [Q \setminus j^{*\ell}]} \neg \mathsf{all\text{-}valid}(\mathsf{st}_{\Lambda_{\ell,2}}, j)$, that is the event that $\Lambda_{\ell,2}$ returned only valid pairs of outputs and proofs for $j = j^{*\ell}$ in the ℓ'th simulation of $\mathcal{A}$. Further, we let $\mathsf{bad} := \bigvee_{\ell \in [r]} \mathsf{bad}(\ell)$ be the event that $\mathsf{bad}(\ell)$ occurs for any $\ell \in [r]$.

Next, let $\mathsf{S}(\mathcal{F})$ denote the event that $\mathsf{NICA}_N^{\mathcal{F}}(\lambda) = 1$ for some adversary $\mathcal{F}$ against the non-interactive complexity assumption N. Then we observe the following:

$$\Pr\left[\mathsf{S}(r\text{-}\Lambda^{\mathcal{A}})\right] - \Pr\left[\mathsf{S}(\mathcal{B})\right]$$
$$= \Pr\left[\mathsf{S}(r\text{-}\Lambda^{\mathcal{A}}) \wedge \mathsf{bad}\right] + \Pr\left[\mathsf{S}(r\text{-}\Lambda^{\mathcal{A}}) \wedge \neg\mathsf{bad}\right] - \Pr\left[\mathsf{S}(\mathcal{B}) \wedge \mathsf{bad}\right] - \Pr\left[\mathsf{S}(\mathcal{B}) \wedge \neg\mathsf{bad}\right]$$
$$\leq \Pr\left[\mathsf{S}(r\text{-}\Lambda^{\mathcal{A}}) \wedge \neg\mathsf{bad}\right] - \Pr\left[\mathsf{S}(\mathcal{B}) \wedge \neg\mathsf{bad}\right] + \Pr\left[\mathsf{bad}\right]$$

Therefore, we proceed by showing two things:

1. $\Pr\left[\mathsf{S}(r\text{-}\Lambda^{\mathcal{A}}) \wedge \neg\mathsf{bad}\right] = \Pr\left[\mathsf{S}(\mathcal{B}) \wedge \neg\mathsf{bad}\right]$
2. $\Pr\left[\mathsf{bad}\right] \leq r/Q$

In order to prove the first statement, we consider two cases in which $\mathcal{A}$ outputs either $\perp$ or the correct output of $\mathcal{VUF}$ for input X_j^ℓ under verification key vk^ℓ. These are the two cases that $\mathcal{B}$ distinguishes in step ii. d).

1. In the first case $\Lambda_{\ell,2}(j^{*\ell}, \mathsf{st}_{\Lambda_{\ell,2}})$ outputs $(Y_{i,j^{*\ell}}^\ell, \pi_{i,j^{*\ell}}^\ell)_{i \in [Q \setminus j^{*\ell}]}$ such that there is $i \in [Q \setminus j^{*\ell}]$ with $\mathsf{Vfy}(\mathsf{vk}^\ell, X_i^\ell, Y_{i,j^{*\ell}}^\ell, \pi_{i,j^{*\ell}}^\ell) = 0$. Note that in this case, $\mathcal{A}_2$ aborts and outputs $\perp$. $\mathcal{B}$ also aborts and outputs $\perp$ in step ii. d) in the first case.

2. In the second case no such $i \in [Q \setminus j^{*\ell}]$ exists for the output of $\Lambda_{\ell,2}(j^{*\ell}, \mathsf{st}_{\Lambda_{\ell,2}})$. Hence, we have $\mathsf{all\text{-}valid}(\mathsf{st}_{\Lambda_{\ell,2}}, j^{*\ell}) = 1$. Furthermore, since we assumed that bad does not happen, we have that there is also $j \in [Q \setminus j^{*\ell}]$ with $\mathsf{all\text{-}valid}(\mathsf{st}_{\Lambda_{\ell,2}}, j) = 1$ and therefore $A^\ell[j^{*\ell}]$ contains the correct $\mathcal{VUF}$ output, which $\mathcal{B}$ passes on to $\Lambda_{\ell,3}$. Since $\mathcal{A}$ also outputs the correct $\mathcal{VUF}$ value in this case, the two outputs are distributed identically.

We therefore have $\Pr\left[\mathsf{S}(r\text{-}\Lambda^{\mathcal{A}}) \wedge \neg\mathsf{bad}\right] = \Pr\left[\mathsf{S}(\mathcal{B}) \wedge \neg\mathsf{bad}\right]$.

Next, we show that $\Pr\left[\mathsf{bad}\right] \leq r/Q$. For this, consider a fixed $\ell \in [r]$ and observe that $\mathsf{bad}(\ell)$ can occur only if there is a unique index $j \in [Q]$ such that $\mathsf{all\text{-}valid}(\mathsf{st}_{\ell,2}, j) = 1$. Hence, the probability that $\mathcal{B}$ draws $j^{*\ell} = j$ in step ii. d) in the ℓ'th round is $1/Q$. We therefore have that $\Pr\left[\mathsf{bad}(\ell)\right] = 1/Q$, and it follows by the union bound that $\Pr\left[\mathsf{bad}\right] \leq r/Q$. Summing up, we have shown that.

$$\Pr\left[\mathsf{S}(r\text{-}\Lambda^{\mathcal{A}})\right] - \Pr\left[\mathsf{S}(\mathcal{B})\right] \leq \Pr\left[\mathsf{bad}\right] \leq r/Q \iff \epsilon_{\mathcal{A}} \leq \epsilon_{\mathcal{B}} - r/Q$$

It is now only left to compute the running time of $\mathcal{B}$. For this, note that $\mathcal{B}$ executes the algorithms $\Lambda_{\ell,2}$ Q times for each $\ell \in [r]$ and other algorithms of Λ only once. Furthermore, $\mathcal{B}$ executes Vfy $r \cdot Q \cdot (Q-1)$ times. Overall, we therefore conclude that

$$t_{\mathcal{B}} \leq r \cdot Q \cdot t_{\Lambda} + r \cdot Q \cdot (Q-1) \cdot t_{\mathsf{Vfy}},$$

where t_{Vfy} is the time it takes to execute Vfy. This concludes the proof.

Non-perfect Adversaries. We only considered adversaries that always break the weak selective unpredictability of the VUF in the theorem above. However, the hypothetical adversary $\mathcal{A}$ and the meta-reduction can also simulate adversaries with arbitrary $\epsilon_{\mathcal{A}} \in [0,1]$ by just aborting with probability $1 - \epsilon_{\mathcal{A}}$ in the simulation of $\mathcal{A}$.

3   A Reduction Strategy with Optimal Tightness

Now that we showed that every reduction from a non-interactive complexity assumption to the pseudorandomness or unpredictability of a VRF or VUF loses at least a factor of Q, we present a VRF together with a reduction, which attains this bound up to a small constant factor. We achieve this by describing a *partitioning proof strategy*. In these types of proofs, the reduction partitions the input space of the VRF in a controlled set and an uncontrolled set and embeds this partitioning into the verification key. The reduction is then able to answer evaluation queries for inputs in the controlled set and can extract a solution to the underlying complexity assumption if the challenge is in the uncontrolled set. This type of proof has also been used in most of the previous VRFs that do not rely on the random oracle heuristic, for example [31,36,38,52]. In this section, we describe how the reduction chooses this partition. We discuss the embedding of the partitioning in the VRF in Sect. 4.

Optimal Partitioning. In order to make a partitioning argument with optimal tightness for VRFs, we need to decouple the probability that the partitioning succeeds from the queries and the challenge, which are chosen by the adversary. We achieve this by passing every input of the adversary through a pseudorandom function. This ensures that the outputs are distributed independently and uniformly at random for pairwise different inputs. We formally define a PRF as follows.

Definition 7. *For functions $t, m, n : \mathbb{N} \to \mathbb{N}$ and $\epsilon : \mathbb{N} \to [0,1]$, we say that a function $\mathsf{PRF} : \{0,1\}^{m(\lambda)} \times \{0,1\}^{\lambda} \to \{0,1\}^{n(\lambda)}$ is an (t, ϵ)-secure Pseudorandom Function if it holds for every algorithm $\mathcal{D}$ running in time $t(\lambda)$ that*

$$\left| \Pr_{\mathsf{K}^{\mathsf{PRF}} \xleftarrow{\$} \{0,1\}^m} \left[\mathcal{D}^{\mathsf{PRF}(\mathsf{K}^{\mathsf{PRF}}, \cdot)}(1^{\lambda}) = 1 \right] - \Pr_{F \xleftarrow{\$} \mathcal{F}_{\lambda, n(\lambda)}} \left[\mathcal{D}^{F(\cdot)} = 1 \right] \right| \le \epsilon(\lambda),$$

where $\mathcal{F}_{\lambda, n(\lambda)} = \{F : \{0,1\}^{\lambda} \to \{0,1\}^{n(\lambda)}\}$ is the set of all functions from $\{0,1\}^{\lambda}$ to $\{0,1\}^{n(\lambda)}$.

For a clear exposition, assume that all queries by the adversary and the challenge are passed through a truly random function. We later on replace this truly random function with a PRF. If the PRF is secure, then this does only make a negligible difference in the success probability.

   We use the outputs X' of the truly random function for partitioning in the following way. The reduction draws η uniformly random bits $\mathsf{K}^{\mathsf{part}}$ for some carefully chosen $\eta \in [n(\lambda)]$. It then defines the uncontrolled set, *i.e.*, the set of inputs for which the reduction can extract a solution but not answer evaluation queries, as the set of all inputs whose PRF output match $\mathsf{K}^{\mathsf{part}}$ on the first η bits. We formalize this partitioning as the following function F.

Definition 8. *For $X' \in \{0,1\}^{n(\lambda)}$ and $\mathsf{K}^{\mathsf{part}} \in \{0,1\}^{\eta}$, we define*

$$\mathsf{F}(X', \mathsf{K}^{\mathsf{part}}) := \begin{cases} 1 & \text{if } X'_{|\eta} = \mathsf{K}^{\mathsf{part}} \\ 0 & \text{otherwise,} \end{cases}$$

where $X'_{|\eta}$ denotes the first η bits of X'.

Such a function F has been used in many previous partitioning arguments, *e.g.* [22,27,31,36,52], but has its origin in [13, Sec. 4.1] as *biased binary pseudorandom function*.

Let $\mathsf{TRF} \xleftarrow{\$} \mathcal{F}_{\lambda,n(\lambda)}$ be a truly random function and let $X_1, \ldots, X_Q, X^* \in \{0,1\}^{\lambda}$ be arbitrary with $X_i \neq X_j$ and $X_i \neq X^*$ for all $i \neq j$. We then let $X'_i := \mathsf{TRF}(X_i)$ and $X^{*'} := \mathsf{TRF}(X^*)$. Observe that we then have that all X'_i and $X^{*'}$ are independent and uniformly random in $\{0,1\}^{n(\lambda)}$. We show in the following Lemma that for $\eta = \lceil \log(Q) \rceil + 1$ and $\mathsf{K}^{\mathsf{part}} \xleftarrow{\$} \{0,1\}^{\eta}$, where Q is the number of evaluation queries made by the adversary, we have that $\mathsf{F}(X'_i, \mathsf{K}^{\mathsf{part}}) = 0$ for all $i \in [Q]$ and $\mathsf{F}(X^{*'}, \mathsf{K}^{\mathsf{part}}) = 1$ with probability at least $1/(8Q)$. That means, the partitioning argument has optimal tightness for VRFs up to a small constant factor. We later on show that since a pseudorandom function is indistinguishable from a truly random function, we can efficiently apply this in our construction.

Lemma 1. *Let $Q = Q(\lambda)$ be a polynomial, let $\eta = \eta(\lambda) := \lceil \log(Q) \rceil + 1$ and let $X'_1, \ldots, X'_Q, X^{*'}$ be as above. For $\mathsf{K}^{\mathsf{part}} \xleftarrow{\$} \{0,1\}^{\eta}$, we then have that*

$$\Pr\left[\mathsf{F}(X'_i, \mathsf{K}^{\mathsf{part}}) = 0 \text{ for all } 0 \leq i \leq Q \text{ and } \mathsf{F}(X^{*'}, \mathsf{K}^{\mathsf{part}}) = 1\right] \geq 1/(8Q).$$

Proof. We start by lower bound the probability from the lemma as follows.

$$\Pr\left[\mathsf{F}(X'_i, \mathsf{K}^{\mathsf{part}}) = 0 \text{ for all } 0 \leq i \leq Q \text{ and } \mathsf{F}(X^{*'}, \mathsf{K}^{\mathsf{part}}) = 1\right]$$

$$= \Pr\left[\mathsf{F}(X'_i, \mathsf{K}^{\mathsf{part}}) = 0 \text{ for all } 0 \leq i \leq Q \mid \mathsf{F}(X^{*'}, \mathsf{K}^{\mathsf{part}}) = 1\right] \Pr\left[\mathsf{F}(X^{*'}, \mathsf{K}^{\mathsf{part}}) = 1\right]$$

$$= \left(\prod_{i=1}^{Q} \Pr\left[\mathsf{F}(X'_i, \mathsf{K}^{\mathsf{part}}) \mid \mathsf{F}(X^{*'}, \mathsf{K}^{\mathsf{part}}) = 1\right]\right) \Pr\left[\mathsf{F}(X^{*'}, \mathsf{K}^{\mathsf{part}}) = 1\right] \tag{1}$$

$$= \left(1 - \left(\frac{1}{2}\right)^{\eta}\right)^{Q} \Pr\left[\mathsf{F}(X^{*'}, \mathsf{K}^{\mathsf{part}}) = 1\right]$$

$$\geq \left(1 - \left(\frac{1}{2}\right)^{\eta} Q\right) \Pr\left[\mathsf{F}_{\mathsf{K}}(X^{*'}, \mathsf{K}^{\mathsf{part}}) = 1\right] \tag{2}$$

$$= \left(1 - \left(\frac{1}{2}\right)^{\eta} Q\right) \left(\frac{1}{2}\right)^{\eta}$$

Observe that Eq. (1) holds because all X_i' and $X^{*'}$ are stochastically independent and that Eq. (2) follows from Bernoulli's inequality. Next, notice that since $\eta = \lceil \log(Q) \rceil + 1$ we have that $\left(\frac{1}{2}\right)^{\eta} \geq \left(\frac{1}{2}\right)^{\log(Q)+2} = \frac{1}{4Q}$ and $-\left(\frac{1}{2}\right)^{\eta} \geq -\left(\frac{1}{2}\right)^{\log(Q)+1} = -\frac{1}{2Q}$. We can therefore conclude the proof as follows.

$$\Pr\left[\mathsf{F}(X_i, \mathsf{K}^{\mathsf{part}}) = 0 \text{ for all } 0 \leq i \leq Q \text{ and } \mathsf{F}(X^*, \mathsf{K}^{\mathsf{part}}) = 1\right]$$

$$\geq \left(1 - \left(\frac{1}{2}\right)^{\eta} Q\right)\left(\frac{1}{2}\right)^{\eta} \geq \left(1 - \frac{1}{2Q}Q\right)\frac{1}{4Q} = \frac{1}{2}\frac{1}{4Q} = \frac{1}{8Q}$$

Note that Lemma 1 only holds if all X_i' and $X^{*'}$ are distributed independently and uniformly at random in $\{0,1\}^n$, e.g., if $X_i' = \mathsf{TRF}(X_i)$ for all $i \in [Q]$ and $X^{*'} = \mathsf{TRF}(X^*)$. Observe that we stated our argument for a truly random function instead of a PRF and our construction in Sect. 4 uses a PRF. We therefore define the function G, which uses a pseudorandom function instead of a truly random function.

Definition 9. *For* $X \in \{0,1\}^{\lambda}, \mathsf{K}^{\mathsf{PRF}} \in \{0,1\}^m$ *and* $\mathsf{K}^{\mathsf{part}} \in \{0,1\}^n$, *we define*

$$\mathsf{G}(X, \mathsf{K}^{\mathsf{PRF}}, \mathsf{K}^{\mathsf{part}}) := \mathsf{F}(\mathsf{PRF}(\mathsf{K}^{\mathsf{PRF}}, X), \mathsf{K}^{\mathsf{part}}).$$

Intuitively, Lemma 1 also applies to G and adversarially chosen X_i and X^* because the outputs of the pseudorandom function are indistinguishable from the outputs of a truly random function. Hence, any adversary that is able to efficiently make queries to the PRF such that the probability in Lemma 1 differs significantly from the probability for a truly random function would also be able to distinguish the pseudorandom function from a truly random function. We show that this also holds formally as part of the security proof of the pseudorandomness of VRF in Sect. 4.1.

4   Verifiable Random Functions with Optimal Tightness

In order to embed the partitioning argument we described in Sect. 3 into a VRF, we use the verifiable random function that Yamada describes in [51, Appendix C]. This is the full version of [52]. This VRF is well-suited for our purposes, because it enables us to embed the homomorphic evaluation of arbitrary NAND-circuits in the reduction such that the reduction can answer all queries for inputs on which the circuit evaluates to zero and can extract a solution to the underlying complexity assumption for all inputs for which the circuit evaluates to 1. At the same time, the embedding of the circuit hides some input bits, all internal states and the output of the circuit from the adversary. We use this property to embed the homomorphic evaluation of G from Definition 9. We first describe bilinear group generators, which we require in the VRF construction and then describe how we model NAND circuits. Finally, we describe the VRF.

Bilinear Group Generators. We shortly introduce (certified) bilinear group generators, which were originally described in [27]. These allow us to define complexity assumptions relative to the way the bilinear group is chosen end ensure that every group element has a unique encoding, which is required for the unique provability of our construction.

Definition 10. *A* Bilinear Group Generator *is a probabilistic polynomial-time algorithm* GrpGen *that takes as input a security parameter* λ *(in unary) and outputs* $\Pi = (p, \mathbb{G}, \mathbb{G}_T, \circ, \circ_T, e, \phi(1)) \xleftarrow{\$} \mathsf{GrpGen}(1^\lambda)$ *such that the following requirements are satisfied.*

1. *p is a prime and $\log(p) \in \Omega(k)$*
2. *$\mathbb{G}$ and $\mathbb{G}_T$ are subsets of $\{0,1\}^*$, defined by algorithmic descriptions of maps $\phi : \mathbb{Z}_p \to \mathbb{G}$ and $\phi_T : \mathbb{Z}_p \to \mathbb{G}_T$.*
3. *$\circ$ and $\circ_T$ are algorithmic descriptions of efficiently computable (in the security parameter) maps $\circ : \mathbb{G} \times \mathbb{G} \to \mathbb{G}$ and $\circ_T : \mathbb{G}_T \times \mathbb{G}_T \to \mathbb{G}_T$, such that*
   a) *$(\mathbb{G}, \circ)$ and $(\mathbb{G}_T, \circ_T)$ form algebraic groups,*
   b) *ϕ is a group isomorphism from $(\mathbb{Z}_p, +)$ to $(\mathbb{G}, \circ)$ and*
   c) *ϕ_T is a group isomorphism from $(\mathbb{Z}_p, +)$ to $(\mathbb{G}_T, \circ_T)$.*
4. *e is an algorithmic description of an efficiently computable (in the security parameter) bilinear map $e : \mathbb{G} \times \mathbb{G} \to \mathbb{G}_T$. We require that e is non-degenerate, that is,*

$$x \neq 0 \Rightarrow e(\phi(x), \phi(x)) \neq \phi_T(0).$$

Definition 11. *We say that group generator* GrpGen *is certified, if there exist deterministic polynomial-time (in the security parameter) algorithms* GrpVfy *and* GrpElemVfy *with the following properties.*

Parameter Validation. *Given the security parameter (in unary) and a string Π, which is not necessarily generated by* GrpGen*, algorithm* $\mathsf{GrpVfy}(1^\lambda, \Pi)$ *outputs 1 if and only if Π has the form*

$$\Pi = (p, \mathbb{G}, \mathbb{G}_T, \circ, \circ_T, e, \phi(1))$$

and all requirements from Definition 10 are satisfied.

Recognition and Unique Representation of Elements of $\mathbb{G}$. *Further, we require that each element in $\mathbb{G}$ has a unique representation, which can be efficiently recognized. That is, on input the security parameter (in unary) and two strings Π and s,* $\mathsf{GrpElemVfy}(1^\lambda, \Pi, s)$ *outputs 1 if and only if* $\mathsf{GrpVfy}(1^\lambda, \Pi) = 1$, *and it holds that $s = \phi(x)$ for some $x \in \mathbb{Z}_p$. Here $\phi : \mathbb{Z}_p \to \mathbb{G}$ denotes the fixed group isomorphism contained in Π to specify the representation of elements of $\mathbb{G}$.*

NAND Circuits. Before describing our construction, we require a formal definition of NAND circuits. The type of circuits we consider take two types of inputs: public inputs and secret inputs. For the function G, which we want to embed in the VRF, we can think of the public input as a VRF input $X \in \{0,1\}^\lambda$ and of the secret input as the PRF key $\mathsf{K}^{\mathsf{PRF}}$ and the partitioning key $\mathsf{K}^{\mathsf{part}}$. Like

Yamada, we roughly follow the notation of [7] when describing NAND circuits. That is, we assign an index to each input bit and to each gate, beginning with the public input bits, continuing with the secret inputs bits and finally indexing the gates. Formally, if there are $k \in \mathbb{N}$ inputs of which $k_{pub} \in [k]$ are public input bits and $k_{sec} = k - k_{pub}$ are secret input bits, then we set $\mathcal{P} := [k_{pub}]$ and $\mathcal{S} := [k_{pub} + 1, k_{pub} + k_{sec}]$ as the respective index sets for the public and secret input bits.

For a NAND circuit $C : \{0,1\}^{|\mathcal{P}|+|\mathcal{S}|} \to \{0,1\}$ with c many gates and $|\mathcal{P}| + |\mathcal{S}|$ many input bits, we assign an index $j \in \mathcal{C} := [|\mathcal{P}| + |\mathcal{S}| + 1, |\mathcal{P}| + |\mathcal{S}| + c]$ to each gate. Further, we formalize the wiring of the circuit with the functions $\mathsf{in}_1, \mathsf{in}_2 : \mathcal{C} \to \mathcal{P} \cup \mathcal{S} \cup \mathcal{C}$ that represent the input wires of a gate. We require that for all $j \in \mathcal{C}$ it holds that $\mathsf{in}_1(j) < j$ and $\mathsf{in}_2(j) < j$. This condition ensures that the circuit does not contain any circles.

Since we only consider circuits with a single output bit, we assume without loss of generality that the output of the gate with index $|\mathcal{P}| + |\mathcal{S}| + |\mathcal{C}|$ outputs the overall output of the circuit. Furthermore, we define the depth of a gate j as the maximal distance from any input gate to j. Consequentially, we define the depth of a circuit C as the depth of the gate with index $|\mathcal{P}| + |\mathcal{S}| + |\mathcal{C}|$.

Evaluating a Circuit. For a circuit C in the notation above with public inputs $\mathbf{p} = (p_j)_{j \in \mathcal{P}}$, secret inputs $\mathbf{s} = (s_j)_{j \in \mathcal{S}}$, gates with indexes in $\mathcal{C}$ and the wiring encoded by $\mathsf{in}^1, \mathsf{in}^2 : \mathcal{C} \to \mathcal{P} \cup \mathcal{S} \cup \mathcal{C}$, we define the function value $: \mathcal{P} \cup \mathcal{S} \cup \mathcal{C} \to \{0,1\}$ as follows. For all $j \in \mathcal{P}$ we set $\mathsf{value}(j) := p_j$ and for all $j \in \mathcal{S}$ as $\mathsf{value}(j) := s_j$. Further, for all $j \in \mathcal{C}$, we set $\mathsf{value}(j) := \mathsf{value}(\mathsf{in}^1(j))\mathsf{NAND}\mathsf{value}(\mathsf{in}^2(j))$. In order to evaluate a circuit on input $\mathbf{p} \in \{0,1\}^{|\mathcal{P}|}$ and $\mathbf{s} \in \{0,1\}^{|\mathcal{S}|}$, we compute $\mathsf{value}(|\mathcal{P}| + |\mathcal{S}| + |\mathcal{C}|)$ since the gate with index $|\mathcal{P}| + |\mathcal{S}| + |\mathcal{C}|$ outputs the overall output of C. Note that the evaluation of the circuit is well-defined because we have that for all $j \in \mathcal{C}$ it holds that $\mathsf{in}^1(j) < j$ and $\mathsf{in}^2(j) < j$.

Representing G as a Circuit. For our construction, we need to represent G from Definition 9 as a NAND-circuit. However, given the plain definition of G, the number of input bits of the circuit depends on $\eta(\lambda)$, which in turn depends on the number Q of Eval queries made by the adversary. We address this by adapting the encoding of K^{part}. Namely, we let $\mathsf{PrtSmp}(1^\lambda, Q(\lambda))$ be the algorithm that samples $\mathsf{K}^{match} \xleftarrow{\$} \{0,1\}^{n(\lambda)}$, computes $\eta := \lceil \log(Q(\lambda)) \rceil + 1$ sets $\mathsf{K}^{fixing} = 1^\eta || 0^{n(\lambda)-\eta(\lambda)}$ and outputs $\mathsf{K}^{part} = (\mathsf{K}^{match}, \mathsf{K}^{fixing}) \in (\{0,1\}^{n(\lambda)})^2$. We then adapt the function $\mathsf{F}(X', \mathsf{K}^{part})$ to compare X and K^{match} on all positions where K^{fixing} is 1 and output 1 if they match on all such positions and 0 otherwise. These adaptations do not change the output of F or G but ensure that the NAND-circuit representing G only depends on λ and not on Q. Note that it would be possible to encode K^{fixing} more efficiently, but we use this encoding for simplicity.

Construction. We assume that the NAND-circuits for the function G for different security parameters are publicly known, and we denote the circuit for G with security parameter λ by $C_{\mathsf{G},\lambda}$. For our construction, we have that $\mathcal{P} = [\lambda]$, since the public input of G is $X \in \{0,1\}^\lambda$. Furthermore, we set $\mathcal{S}^{\mathsf{PRF}} := [|\mathcal{P}| + 1, |\mathcal{P}| + m(\lambda)]$ for the indexes of the bits of $\mathsf{K}^{\mathsf{PRF}} \in \{0,1\}^{m(\lambda)}$, $\mathcal{S}^{\mathsf{part}} := [|\mathcal{P}| + |\mathcal{S}^{\mathsf{PRF}}| + 1, |\mathcal{P}| + |\mathcal{S}^{\mathsf{PRF}}| + 2n(\lambda)]$ for the indexes of $\mathsf{K}^{\mathsf{match}} \in \{0,1\}^{2n(\lambda)}$, and $\mathcal{S} := \mathcal{S}^{\mathsf{PRF}} \cup \mathcal{S}^{\mathsf{part}}$. Finally, we assume that the function $\mathsf{in}_\lambda^1, \mathsf{in}_\lambda^2 : \mathcal{C} \to \mathcal{P} \cup \mathcal{S} \cup \mathcal{C}$ encode the wiring of $C_{\mathsf{G},\lambda}$ and that $|\mathcal{P}| + |\mathcal{S}| + |\mathcal{C}|$ is the index of the output gate. For simplicity, we set $\mathsf{out} := |\mathcal{P}| + |\mathcal{S}| + |\mathcal{C}|$.

$\mathsf{Gen}(1^\lambda)$ first generates a group description $\Pi \xleftarrow{\$} \mathsf{GrpGen}(1^\lambda)$ and samples uniformly random group generators $g, h \xleftarrow{\$} \mathbb{G} \setminus \{0\}$, $w_0 \xleftarrow{\$} \mathbb{Z}_p^*$ and $w_j \xleftarrow{\$} \mathbb{Z}_p$ for all $j \in \mathcal{S}$. It then sets $W_0 := g^{w_0}$, $W_j := g^{w_j}$ for all $j \in \mathcal{S}$ and outputs

$$\mathsf{vk} := \left(\Pi, g, h, W_0, (W_j)_{j \in \mathcal{S}} \right) \qquad \text{and} \qquad \mathsf{sk} := \left(w_0, (w_j)_{j \in \mathcal{S}} \right).$$

$\mathsf{Eval}(\mathsf{sk}, X)$ parses $X \in \{0,1\}^\lambda$ as $(X_1, \ldots, X_\lambda)$ and sets

$$\theta_j := \begin{cases} X_j & \text{if } j \in \mathcal{P} \\ w_j & \text{if } j \in \mathcal{S} \end{cases}$$

for all $j \in \mathcal{P} \cup \mathcal{S}$. For all $j \in \mathcal{C}$, it sets

$$\theta_j := 1 - \theta_{\mathsf{in}_\lambda^1(j)} \theta_{\mathsf{in}_\lambda^2(j)}.$$

It then sets $\pi_0 := g^{\theta_{\mathsf{out}}/w_0}$ and $\pi_j := g^{\theta_j}$ for all $j \in \mathcal{C}$ and outputs

$$Y := e(g, h)^{\theta_{\mathsf{out}}/w_0} \qquad \text{and} \qquad \pi := (\pi_0, (\pi_j)_{j \in \mathcal{C}}).$$

$\mathsf{Vfy}(\mathsf{vk}, X, Y, \pi)$ first verifies that vk has the form $(\Pi, g, h, W_0, (W_j)_{j \in \mathcal{S}})$ and that π has the form $(\pi_0, (\pi_j)_{j \in \mathcal{C}})$. It then verifies the group description by running $\mathsf{GrpVfy}(1^\lambda, \Pi)$ and then verifies all group elements in vk, π and Y by running $\mathsf{GrpElemVfy}(1^\lambda, \Pi, s)$ for all $s \in \{g, h, Y, \pi_0, \pi_{|\mathcal{P}|+|\mathcal{S}|+1}, \ldots, \pi_{|\mathcal{P}|+|\mathcal{S}|+|\mathcal{C}|}\}$. Vfy outputs 0 if any of the checks fails. Next, the algorithm verifies the correctness of Y in respect to vk, X and π by setting $\pi_j := g^{X_j}$ for all $j \in \mathcal{P}$ and $\pi_j := W_j$ for all $i \in \mathcal{S}$ and performing the following steps.

1. It checks whether $e(g, \pi_j) = e(g, g) \left(e(\pi_{\mathsf{in}_\lambda^1(j)}, \pi_{\mathsf{in}_\lambda^2(j)}) \right)^{-1}$ for all $j \in \mathcal{C}$.
2. It checks whether $e(\pi_0, W_0) = e(\pi_{\mathsf{out}}, g)$.
3. It checks whether $e(\pi_0, h) = Y$.

If any of the checks above fail, then Vfy outputs 0. Otherwise, it outputs 1.

The proofs for correctness and unique provability closely follow the respective proofs by Yamada [51]. We therefore only present them in the full version [45, Section 4.1]. Before proving the pseudorandomness of the VRF, we shortly discuss the instantiation with concrete PRFs and the effect on the efficiency.

Instantiation. In order to instantiate the $\mathcal{VRF}$, we need that G can be represented by a circuit of polynomial size and logarithmic depth. While this is certainly possible for the comparison of the PRF output with $\mathsf{K}^{\mathsf{match}}$, we also require a PRF that can be computed by such a NAND circuit. The Naor-Reingold PRF is an example of such a PRF that is also provably secure under the DDH assumption [44]. However, we can further optimize the efficiency by using the adaptation of the Naor-Reingold PRF in [33, Section 5.1]. This PRF has secret keys of size $\omega(\log(\lambda))$. Further, we can change the encoding of $\mathsf{K}^{\mathsf{match}}$ and $\mathsf{K}^{\mathsf{fixing}}$ to also consist of only $\omega(\log(\lambda))$ many bits. This would bring the size of the public verification key down to $\omega(\log(\lambda))$, would however only hold for λ large enough. We can further optimize the size of the proofs by applying the technique of [30], which allows to reduce the circuit size of every PRF to $\mathcal{O}(\lambda)$ at the cost of reducing the output length to $\lambda^{1/c}$ for some constant $c > 0$ that depends on the PRF. However, the smaller output length is no issue, since $\lambda^{1/c}$ is larger than $\lceil \log(Q(\lambda)) \rceil + 1 = \mathcal{O}(\log(\lambda))$ for large enough λ, because Q is polynomial in λ. This technique therefore reduces the size of proofs to $\mathcal{O}(\lambda)$.

4.1   Proof of Pseudorandomness

The security of our VRF is based on the decisional q-bilinear Diffie-Hellman inversion assumption that we formally introduce below.

Definition 12 (Definition 4 in [12]). *For a bilinear group generator* GrpGen, *an algorithm* $\mathcal{B}$ *and* $q \in \mathbb{N}$, *let* $G_{\mathcal{B}}^{q\text{-DBDHI}}(\lambda)$ *be the following game. The challenger runs* $\Pi \xleftarrow{\$} \mathsf{GrpGen}(1^{\lambda})$, *samples* $g, h \xleftarrow{\$} \mathbb{G}$, $\alpha \xleftarrow{\$} \mathbb{Z}_p^*$ *and* $b \xleftarrow{\$} \{0,1\}$. *Then it defines* $T_0 := e(g,h)^{1/\alpha}$ *and* $T_1 \xleftarrow{\$} \mathbb{G}_T$. *Finally, it runs* $b' \xleftarrow{\$} \mathcal{B}(\Pi, g, h, g^{\alpha}, \ldots, g^{\alpha^q}, T_b)$, *and outputs* 1 *if* $b = b'$, *and* 0 *otherwise. We denote with*

$$\mathsf{Adv}_{\mathcal{B}}^{q\text{-DBDHI}}(\lambda) := \left| \Pr\left[G_{\mathcal{B}}^{q\text{-DBDHI}}(\lambda) = 1 \right] - 1/2 \right|$$

the advantage of $\mathcal{B}$ *in breaking the* q-DBDHI-*assumption for groups generated by* GrpGen, *where the probability is taken over the randomness of the challenger and* $\mathcal{B}$. *For functions* $t : \mathbb{N} \to \mathbb{N}$ *and* $\epsilon : \mathbb{N} \to [0,1]$, *we say that* $\mathcal{B}$ (t, ϵ)-*breaks the* q-DBDHI *assumption relative to* GrpGen, *if* $\mathsf{Adv}_{\mathcal{B}}^{q\text{-DBDHI}}(\lambda) = \epsilon(\lambda)$ *and* $\mathcal{B}$ *runs in time* $t(\lambda)$.

Note that the assumption falls in the category of non-interactive complexity assumptions from Definition 3. Based on this assumption, we can formulate the theorem for the pseudorandomness of our VRF.

Theorem 2. *Let* $\mathcal{VRF} = (\mathsf{Gen}, \mathsf{Eval}, \mathsf{Vfy})$ *be the verifiable random function above, then for every legitimate adversary* $\mathcal{A} = (\mathcal{A}_1, \mathcal{A}_2)$ *that* $(t_{\mathcal{A}}, \epsilon_{\mathcal{A}})$ *breaks the pseudorandomness of* $\mathcal{VRF}$ *and makes* $Q(\lambda)$ *queries to* Eval *for some* polynomial $Q : \mathbb{N} \to \mathbb{N}$, *there exists an algorithm $\mathcal{B}$ that $(t_\mathcal{B}, \epsilon_\mathcal{B})$-breaks the q-DBDHI assumption relative to* GrpGen *used in* $\mathcal{VRF}$ *with*

$$t_\mathcal{B}(\lambda) = t_\mathcal{A}(\lambda), \qquad \epsilon_\mathcal{B}(\lambda) \geq \frac{\epsilon_\mathcal{A}(\lambda)}{8Q(\lambda)} - \epsilon_{\mathsf{PRF}}(\lambda) - \mathsf{negl}(\lambda) \qquad and \qquad q := 2^d,$$

where d is the depth of the circuit for G, ϵ_{PRF} *is the largest advantage any algorithm with runtime $t_\mathcal{A}(\lambda)$ that makes $Q(\lambda)$ queries to its oracle has in breaking the security of the* PRF *used in* $\mathcal{VRF}$ *and* $\mathsf{negl}(\lambda)$ *is a negligible function. In particular:* $\mathcal{VRF}$ *achieves the optimal tightness, since $\epsilon_{\mathsf{PRF}}(\lambda)$ is negligible if the construction is instantiated with a* PRF *with a security reduction loss of at most $Q(\lambda)$.*

Remark 1. Note that the requirement of a loss of at most Q for the PRF is fulfilled by *e.g.* the Naor-Reingold PRF [44] or the PRFs by Jager*et al.* [33].

Proof. Since Eval is deterministic, $\mathcal{A}$ can not learn anything by making the same query to Eval twice. We therefor assume without loss of generality that $\mathcal{A}$ makes only pairwise distinct queries to Eval. Further, we set $Q := Q(\lambda), n := n(\lambda), m := m(\lambda)$ and $\epsilon_\mathcal{A} := \epsilon_\mathcal{A}(\lambda)$ in order to simplify notation.

We prove Theorem 2 with a sequence of games argument [48]. We denote the event that Game i outputs 1 by E_i. The first part of the proof will focus on our technique of using a PRF for partitioning. The second part of the proof follows the proof by Yamada [51, Theorem 6] and we provide it mostly for completeness.

Game 0. This is the original security experiment from Definition 1 and we therefore have that

$$\left| \Pr\left[E_0\right] - \frac{1}{2} \right| = \epsilon_\mathcal{A}$$

holds by definition.

Game 1. In this game, the challenger first runs the game as before. But, before outputting a result, it samples $X'_i \xleftarrow{\$} \{0,1\}^n$ uniformly and independently at random for each query $X_i \in \{0,1\}^\lambda$ to Eval by $\mathcal{A}$ and $X^{*'} \xleftarrow{\$} \{0,1\}^n$ for the challenge $X^* \in \{0,1\}^\lambda$. Observe that this perfectly emulates the process of evaluating a truly random function on the queries and the challenge because we assumed without loss generality that all queries and the challenge are pairwise distinct. Further, it sets $\eta := \lceil \log Q \rceil + 1$ and samples $\mathsf{K}^{\mathsf{part}} \xleftarrow{\$} \mathsf{PrtSmp}(1^\lambda, Q)$. It then aborts and outputs a random bit if $\mathsf{F}(X'_i, \mathsf{K}^{\mathsf{part}}) = 1$ for any $i \in [Q]$ or if $\mathsf{F}(X^{*'}, \mathsf{K}^{\mathsf{part}}) = 0$. We denote the occurrence of any of the two abort conditions by the event bad. We next show that

$$\left|\Pr\left[E_1\right] - \Pr\left[E_0\right]\right| = \epsilon_\mathcal{A}(1 - \Pr\left[\mathsf{bad}\right]) \leq \epsilon_\mathcal{A}\left(1 - \frac{1}{8Q}\right).$$

We use later that $\Pr[\neg\text{bad}] \geq 1/(8Q)$, which follows from Lemma 1 and will in the end yield the loss stated in Theorem 2. We have the following.

$$
\begin{aligned}
|\Pr[E_1] - \Pr[E_0]| &= |\Pr[E_1 \mid \text{bad}]\Pr[\text{bad}] + \Pr[E_1 \mid \neg\text{bad}]\Pr[\neg\text{bad}] - \Pr[E_0]| \\
&= \left| \frac{1}{2}(1 - \Pr[\neg\text{bad}]) + \Pr[E_1 \mid \neg\text{bad}]\Pr[\neg\text{bad}] - \Pr[E_0] \right| \\
&= \left| \frac{1}{2} + \Pr[\neg\text{bad}]\left(\Pr[E_1 \mid \neg\text{bad}] - \frac{1}{2}\right) - \Pr[E_0] \right| \\
&= \left| \frac{1}{2} + \Pr[\neg\text{bad}]\left(\Pr[E_0] - \frac{1}{2}\right) - \Pr[E_0] \right| \qquad (3) \\
&= \left| \Pr[\neg\text{bad}]\left(\Pr[E_0] - \frac{1}{2}\right) - \left(\Pr[E_0] - \frac{1}{2}\right) \right| \\
&= \left| \left(\Pr[E_0] - \frac{1}{2}\right)(\Pr[\neg\text{bad}] - 1) \right| \\
&= \left| \Pr[E_0] - \frac{1}{2} \right| \cdot |\Pr[\neg\text{bad}] - 1| \\
&= \epsilon_{\mathcal{A}} \cdot (1 - \Pr[\neg\text{bad}])
\end{aligned}
$$

Note that Eq. (3) holds because $\Pr[E_1 \mid \neg\text{bad}] = \Pr[E_0 \mid \neg\text{bad}]$ and the event $\neg\text{bad}$ is independent of E_0. The independence holds because X^* and all X_i' are drawn at random. Note that it is this independence together with the independence between the different X_i' and X^* that allows us to achieve the optimal tightness in contrast to the other approaches discussed in the introduction.

Further, by Lemma 1, we have that $\Pr[\neg\text{bad}] \geq 1/(8Q)$ holds and therefore

$$
|E_1 - E_0| = \epsilon_{\mathcal{A}}(1 - \Pr[\neg\text{bad}]) \leq \epsilon_{\mathcal{A}}\left(1 - \frac{1}{8Q}\right).
$$

Game 2. In this game, the challenger only changes the way it computes $X^{*'}$ and X_i' for all $i \in [Q]$. The challenger samples $\mathsf{K}^{\mathsf{PRF}} \xleftarrow{\$} \{0,1\}^m$ and aborts and outputs a random bit if $\mathsf{G}(X_i, \mathsf{K}^{\mathsf{PRF}}, \mathsf{K}^{\mathsf{part}}) = 1$ or if $\mathsf{G}(X^*, \mathsf{K}^{\mathsf{PRF}}, \mathsf{K}^{\mathsf{part}}) = 0$. The only difference to Game 1 is that G sets $X^{*'} := \mathsf{PRF}(\mathsf{K}^{\mathsf{PRF}}, X^*)$ and $X_i' := \mathsf{PRF}(\mathsf{K}^{\mathsf{PRF}}, X_i)$ instead of drawing them uniformly at random.

Informally, every algorithm distinguishing Game 2 from Game 1 with advantage ϵ implies a distinguisher for PRF with advantage ϵ. We describe a distinguisher $\mathcal{B}_{\mathsf{PRF}}$ for PRF that is based on Game 2 and Game 1 and achieves exactly this: $\mathcal{B}_{\mathsf{PRF}}(\lambda)$ with access to either a $\mathsf{PRF}(\mathsf{K}^{\mathsf{PRF}}, \cdot)$ or a truly random function $F \xleftarrow{\$} \mathcal{F}_{\lambda, n(\lambda)}$ as oracle first runs $(\mathsf{vk}, \mathsf{sk}) \xleftarrow{\$} \mathsf{Gen}(1^\lambda)$ and uses sk to answer all queries and the challenge by $\mathcal{A}$. After $\mathcal{A}$ submits its guess b', $\mathcal{B}_{\mathsf{PRF}}$ queries its oracle on X_i and by that obtains X_i' for all $i \in [Q]$. Analogously, it queries its oracle on X^* and by that obtains $X^{*'}$. It then samples $\mathsf{K}^{\mathsf{part}} \xleftarrow{\$} \mathsf{PrtSmp}(1^\lambda, Q)$ and aborts and outputs a random bit if $F(X^{*'}, \mathsf{K}^{\mathsf{part}}) = 0$ or $F(X_i', \mathsf{K}^{\mathsf{part}}) = 1$ for some $i \in [Q]$. Otherwise, $\mathcal{B}_{\mathsf{PRF}}$ outputs 1 if $\mathcal{A}$'s guess is correct and 0 otherwise.

Note that $\mathcal{B}$ has exactly the same runtime as $\mathcal{A}$ and that the probability that it outputs 1 is identical to $\Pr[E_2]$ if its oracle is the pseudorandom function. Analogously, if its oracle is a truly random function, then its output is 1 with probability $\Pr[E_1]$. We therefore have

$$|\Pr[E_2] - \Pr[E_1]| =$$

$$\left| \Pr_{\mathsf{K}^{\mathsf{PRF}} \xleftarrow{\$} \{0,1\}^m} \left[\mathcal{B}_{\mathsf{PRF}}^{\mathsf{PRF}(\mathsf{K}^{\mathsf{PRF}},\cdot)}(1^\lambda) = 1 \right] - \Pr_{F \xleftarrow{\$} \mathcal{F}_{\lambda,n(\lambda)}} \left[\mathcal{B}_{\mathsf{PRF}}^{F(\cdot)} = 1 \right] \right| \leq \epsilon_{\mathsf{PRF}}.$$

Game 3. In this game, the challenger samples $\mathsf{K}^{\mathsf{PRF}} \xleftarrow{\$} \{0,1\}^m$ and the partitioning key $\mathsf{K}^{\mathsf{part}} \xleftarrow{\$} \mathsf{PrtSmp}(1^\lambda, Q)$ in the very beginning and aborts and outputs a random bit as soon as $\mathcal{A}$ makes an Eval query X_i with $\mathsf{G}(X_i, \mathsf{K}^{\mathsf{PRF}}, \mathsf{K}^{\mathsf{part}}) = 1$ or if it holds for $\mathcal{A}$'s challenge X^* that $\mathsf{G}(X^*, \mathsf{K}^{\mathsf{PRF}}, \mathsf{K}^{\mathsf{part}}) = 0$. Since this is just a conceptual change, we have that

$$\Pr[E_3] = \Pr[E_2].$$

From here on, the proof mostly follows the proof by Yamada [51, Appendix C] and we present it here for completeness.

Game 4. In this game, we change the way the w_j are chosen. That is, the challenger samples the partitioning key $\mathsf{K}^{\mathsf{part}} \xleftarrow{\$} \mathsf{PrtSmp}(1^\lambda, Q)$ with $\mathsf{K}^{\mathsf{part}} \in \{0,1\}^{|\mathcal{S}^{\mathsf{part}}|}$ and $\mathsf{K}^{\mathsf{PRF}} \xleftarrow{\$} \{0,1\}^{|\mathcal{S}^{\mathsf{PRF}}|}$. For all $j \in \mathcal{S}$ it sets $s_j := \mathsf{K}^{\mathsf{PRF}}_{j-|\mathcal{P}|}$ for all $j \in \mathcal{S}^{\mathsf{PRF}}$ and $s_j := \mathsf{K}^{\mathsf{part}}_{j-|\mathcal{P}|-|\mathcal{S}^{\mathsf{PRF}}|}$ for all $j \in \mathcal{S}^{\mathsf{part}}$. The challenger then samples $\alpha \xleftarrow{\$} \mathbb{Z}_p^*$, and $\tilde{w}_j \xleftarrow{\$} \mathbb{Z}_p^*$ for all $j \in \mathcal{S}$. It then sets

$$w_0 := \tilde{w}_0 \alpha \qquad \text{and} \qquad w_j := \tilde{w}_j \cdot \alpha + s_j \qquad \text{for all } j \in \mathcal{S}.$$

Note that the $\tilde{w}_j$ are drawn from $\mathbb{Z}_p^*$ and not from $\mathbb{Z}_p$ like the w_j in the previous game. This slightly changes the distributions of the w_j. However, the overall statistical distance is at most $|\mathcal{S}|/p$, which is negligible because $p = \Omega(2^\lambda)$ by Definition 10. We therefore have that

$$|E_4 - E_3| = \mathsf{negl}(\lambda).$$

Before proceeding to the next game, we introduce additional notation. That is, for all $X \in \{0,1\}^\lambda$ and all $j \in \mathcal{P} \cup \mathcal{S} \cup \mathcal{C}$, we let

$$\mathsf{P}_{X,j}(\mathsf{Z}) := \begin{cases} X_j & \text{if } j \in \mathcal{P}, \\ \tilde{w}_i \mathsf{Z} + s_j & \text{if } j \in \mathcal{S} \text{ and} \\ 1 - \mathsf{P}_{X,\mathsf{in}_\lambda^1(j)}(\mathsf{Z}) \mathsf{P}_{X,\mathsf{in}_\lambda^2(j)}(\mathsf{Z}) & \text{if } j \in \mathcal{C}. \end{cases}$$

Note that by the definition of w_j form Game 3, we have that $\mathsf{P}_{X,j}(\alpha) = \theta_j$. In order to proceed to the next game, we require the following lemma by Yamada.

Lemma 2 (Lemma 16 in [51]). *There exists* $R_X(Z) \in \mathbb{Z}_p[Z]$ *with* $\deg(R(Z)) \leq \deg(P_{X,\text{out}}(Z)) \leq 2^d$, *where* d *is the depth of the circuit for the function* G, *and*

$$P_{X,\text{out}}(Z) = G(X, K^{\text{PRF}}, K^{\text{part}}) + Z \cdot R_X(Z).$$

We provide proof in the full version [45, Appendix A] for completeness.

Game 5. With Lemma 2 at our hands, we change how the challenger answers $\mathcal{A}$'s queries to Eval in this game. As in the previous game, the challenger aborts and outputs a random bit if $G(X_i, K^{\text{PRF}}, K^{\text{part}}) = 1$ for any query X_i by $\mathcal{A}$. Otherwise, the challenger computes and outputs

$$Y := e\left(g^{R_X(\alpha)/\tilde{w}_0}, h\right), \qquad \pi := \left(\pi_0 = g^{R_X(\alpha)/\tilde{w}_0}, \left(\pi_j := g^{P_{X,j}(\alpha)}\right)_{j \in \mathcal{C}}\right).$$

Observe that Y and π are distributed exactly as in Game 4. This holds for all π_j because $P_{X,j}(Z)$ is defined exactly as P_j in the definition of Eval above, just with w_j defined as in Game 4. Further, it holds for π_0 and Y because

$$\frac{R_X(\alpha)}{\tilde{w}_0} = \frac{\alpha \cdot R_X(\alpha)}{\alpha \cdot \tilde{w}_0} = \frac{G(X, K^{\text{PRF}}, K^{\text{part}}) + \alpha \cdot R_X(\alpha)}{\alpha \cdot \tilde{w}_0} = \frac{P_{X,\text{out}}(\alpha)}{w_0},$$

where the last equality follows from Lemma 2. We therefore have that

$$\Pr[E_5] = \Pr[E_4].$$

Game 6. In this game, we change how the challenger answers to $\mathcal{A}$'s challenge X^*. As in the previous game, the challenger aborts and outputs a random bit if $G(X^*, K^{\text{PRF}}, K^{\text{part}}) = 0$. Otherwise, the challenger computes $R_{X^*}(\alpha)$ and sets

$$Y_0 := \left(e(g,h)^{1/\alpha} \cdot e\left(g^{R_{X^*}(\alpha)}, h\right)\right)^{1/\tilde{w}_0} = e\left(g^{(1+\alpha R_{X^*}(\alpha))/(\tilde{w}_0 \alpha)}, h\right)$$

$$= e\left(g^{(G(X^*, K^{\text{PRF}}, K^{\text{part}}) + \alpha R_{X^*}(\alpha))/(\tilde{w}_0 \alpha)}, h\right) = e\left(g^{P_{X^*,\text{out}}(\alpha)/w_0}, h\right)$$

Then, the challenger samples a uniformly random bit b and $Y_1 \xleftarrow{\$} \mathbb{G}_T$ and outputs Y_b to $\mathcal{A}$. Again, observe that $P_{X^*,\text{out}}(\alpha)$ is, relative to w_j as defined in Game 4, distributed exactly as θ_{out} in the definition of Eval . We therefore have that

$$\Pr[E_6] = \Pr[E_5].$$

We now claim that there is an algorithm $\mathcal{B}$ that runs in time $t_{\mathcal{A}}$ and solves the q-DBDHI problem probability $\Pr[E_6]$.

Lemma 3. *Let* $d \in \mathbb{N}$ *be the depth of the* $C_{G,\lambda}$, *then there is an algorithm* $\mathcal{B}$ *with run time* $t_{\mathcal{B}} \approx t_{\mathcal{A}}$ *that on input a* q-DBDHI *instance with* $q = 2^d$ *perfectly simulates Game 6 such that* $\Pr\left[G_{\mathcal{B}}^{q\text{-DBDHI}}(\lambda) = 1\right] = \Pr[E_6]$.

Due to space limitations and since the proof very closely follows the respective proof by Yamada, we only provide it in the full version [45]. By Lemma 3 and the (in)equalities we derived above we have that

$$
\epsilon_{\mathcal{A}} = \left| \Pr\left[E_0\right] - \frac{1}{2} \right| \le |\Pr\left[E_0\right] - \Pr\left[E_1\right]| + \left| \Pr\left[E_1\right] - \frac{1}{2} \right|
$$

$$
\le \epsilon_{\mathcal{A}} \left(1 - \frac{1}{8Q}\right) + \left| \Pr\left[E_1\right] - \frac{1}{2} \right|
$$

$$
\le \epsilon_{\mathcal{A}} \left(1 - \frac{1}{8Q}\right) + \epsilon_{\mathsf{PRF}} + \left| \Pr\left[E_2\right] - \frac{1}{2} \right|
$$

$$
= \epsilon_{\mathcal{A}} \left(1 - \frac{1}{8Q}\right) + \epsilon_{\mathsf{PRF}} + \left| \Pr\left[E_3\right] - \frac{1}{2} \right|
$$

$$
\le \epsilon_{\mathcal{A}} \left(1 - \frac{1}{8Q}\right) + \epsilon_{\mathsf{PRF}} + \mathsf{negl}(\lambda) + \left| \Pr\left[E_4\right] - \frac{1}{2} \right|
$$

$$
= \epsilon_{\mathcal{A}} \left(1 - \frac{1}{8Q}\right) + \epsilon_{\mathsf{PRF}} + \mathsf{negl}(\lambda) + \left| \Pr\left[E_6\right] - \frac{1}{2} \right|
$$

$$
= \epsilon_{\mathcal{A}} \left(1 - \frac{1}{8Q}\right) + \epsilon_{\mathsf{PRF}} + \mathsf{negl}(\lambda) + \epsilon_{\mathcal{B}}
$$

Rearranging the terms, we have that

$$
\epsilon_{\mathcal{B}} \ge \frac{\epsilon_{\mathcal{A}}}{8Q} - \epsilon_{\mathsf{PRF}} - \mathsf{negl}(\lambda).
$$

This concludes the proof of Theorem 2.

5 Conclusion

We have settled the question: What is the optimal tightness an adaptively secure VRF can achieve? We did so by showing that every reduction from a non-interactive complexity assumption that can sequentially rewind the adversary a constant number of times necessarily loses a factor of $\approx Q$. Further, we constructed the first VRF with a reduction that has this optimal tightness. The takeaway message is that the optimal loss for adaptively secure VRFs is Q and that it is possible to construct VRFs that attain this bound.

Our main technical contributions are:

1. The extension of the lower bound for the loss of reductions by Bader et al. [5] to VRFs and VUFs in Sect. 2.
2. Further, we presented a new partitioning strategy that achieves this optimal tightness even in the context of decisional security notions and complexity assumptions.
3. Finally, we show that this partitioning strategy can be applied in Yamada's VRF and thus yields a VRF in the standard model with optimal tightness. This also shows that the lower bound on the loss of reductions from a non-interactive complexity assumption to the security of a VRF that we present is optimal.

However, there are still some open questions. The technique of Bader *et al.*, and therefore also our results, only applies to non-interactive complexity assumptions and reductions that sequentially rewind adversaries. While this result covers already a large class of assumptions and reductions, it does not cover interactive assumptions and reductions that can run several instances of the adversary in parallel. Morgan and Pass show a lower bound of $\sqrt{Q}$ for the loss of reductions to the unforgeability of unique signatures from interactive assumptions [42]. It seems plausible that their technique could be extended to also cover VRFs and VUFs.

Another open question is whether there are VRFs with an optimally tight reduction that have key and proof sizes comparable to constructions with non-optimal tightness (see *e.g.* [38] or [36] for recent comparisons). Furthermore, the q-DBDHI assumption with a polynomial q is not a standard assumption and gets stronger with q [18]. It would therefore be preferable to construct an efficient VRF with optimal tightness from a standard assumption, like the VRFs in [27,38,46].

Acknowledgments. I would like to thank Yuval Ishai for the helpful discussion. Further, I would like to thank my advisor Tibor Jager for his support and helpful feedback.

References

1. Abdalla, M., Catalano, D., Fiore, D.: Verifiable random functions: relations to identity-based key encapsulation and new constructions. J. Cryptol. **27**(3), 544–593 (2014)

2. Abdalla, M., Fouque, P.-A., Lyubashevsky, V., Tibouchi, M.: Tightly-secure signatures from lossy identification schemes. In: Pointcheval, D., Johansson, T. (eds.) EUROCRYPT 2012. LNCS, vol. 7237, pp. 572–590. Springer, Heidelberg (2012). https://doi.org/10.1007/978-3-642-29011-4_34

3. Abe, M., Groth, J., Ohkubo, M.: Separating short structure-preserving signatures from non-interactive assumptions. In: Lee, D.H., Wang, X. (eds.) ASIACRYPT 2011. LNCS, vol. 7073, pp. 628–646. Springer, Heidelberg (2011). https://doi.org/10.1007/978-3-642-25385-0_34

4. Abraham, I., Malkhi, D., Nayak, K., Ren, L.: Dfinity consensus, explored. Cryptology ePrint Archive, Report 2018/1153 (2018). https://eprint.iacr.org/2018/1153

5. Bader, C., Jager, T., Li, Y., Schäge, S.: On the impossibility of tight cryptographic reductions. In: Fischlin, M., Coron, J.-S. (eds.) EUROCRYPT 2016, Part II. LNCS, vol. 9666, pp. 273–304. Springer, Heidelberg (2016). https://doi.org/10.1007/978-3-662-49896-5_10

6. Badertscher, C., Gazi, P., Kiayias, A., Russell, A., Zikas, V.: Ouroboros genesis: composable proof-of-stake blockchains with dynamic availability. In: ACM CCS 2018 (2018)

7. Bellare, M., Hoang, V.T., Rogaway, P.: Foundations of garbled circuits. In: ACM CCS 2012 (2012)

8. Bellare, M., Ristenpart, T.: Simulation without the artificial abort: simplified proof and improved concrete security for waters' IBE scheme. Cryptology ePrint Archive, Report 2009/084 (2009). http://eprint.iacr.org/2009/084

9. Bellare, M., Ristenpart, T.: Simulation without the artificial abort: simplified proof and improved concrete security for waters' IBE scheme. In: Joux, A. (ed.) EURO-CRYPT 2009. LNCS, vol. 5479, pp. 407–424. Springer, Heidelberg (2009). https://doi.org/10.1007/978-3-642-01001-9_24

10. Bitansky, N.: Verifiable random functions from non-interactive witness-indistinguishable proofs. J. Cryptol. **33**, 459–493 (2019)

11. Blazy, O., Kakvi, S.A., Kiltz, E., Pan, J.: Tightly-secure signatures from chameleon hash functions. In: Katz, J. (ed.) PKC 2015. LNCS, vol. 9020, pp. 256–279. Springer, Heidelberg (2015). https://doi.org/10.1007/978-3-662-46447-2_12

12. Boneh, D., Boyen, X.: Efficient selective-ID secure identity-based encryption without random oracles. In: Cachin, C., Camenisch, J.L. (eds.) EUROCRYPT 2004. LNCS, vol. 3027, pp. 223–238. Springer, Heidelberg (2004). https://doi.org/10.1007/978-3-540-24676-3_14

13. Boneh, D., Boyen, X.: Secure identity based encryption without random oracles. In: Franklin, M. (ed.) CRYPTO 2004. LNCS, vol. 3152, pp. 443–459. Springer, Heidelberg (2004). https://doi.org/10.1007/978-3-540-28628-8_27

14. Boneh, D., Montgomery, H.W., Raghunathan, A.: Algebraic pseudorandom functions with improved efficiency from the augmented cascade. https://crypto.stanford.edu/~dabo/pubs/papers/algebprf.pdf. Accessed 12 Nov 2020

15. Boneh, D., Montgomery, H.W., Raghunathan, A.: Algebraic pseudorandom functions with improved efficiency from the augmented cascade. In: ACM CCS 2010 (2010)

16. Boyen, X., Li, Q.: Towards tightly secure lattice short signature and id-based encryption. In: Cheon, J.H., Takagi, T. (eds.) ASIACRYPT 2016, Part II. LNCS, vol. 10032, pp. 404–434. Springer, Heidelberg (2016). https://doi.org/10.1007/978-3-662-53890-6_14

17. Chen, J., Wee, H.: Fully, (almost) tightly secure IBE and dual system groups. In: Canetti, R., Garay, J.A. (eds.) CRYPTO 2013, Part II. LNCS, vol. 8043, pp. 435–460. Springer, Heidelberg (2013). https://doi.org/10.1007/978-3-642-40084-1_25

18. Cheon, J.H.: Discrete logarithm problems with auxiliary inputs. J. Cryptol. **23**(3), 457–476 (2010)

19. Coron, J.-S.: Optimal security proofs for PSS and other signature schemes. In: Knudsen, L.R. (ed.) EUROCRYPT 2002. LNCS, vol. 2332, pp. 272–287. Springer, Heidelberg (2002). https://doi.org/10.1007/3-540-46035-7_18

20. Cramer, R., Damgård, I.: New generation of secure and practical RSA-based signatures. In: Koblitz, N. (ed.) CRYPTO 1996. LNCS, vol. 1109, pp. 173–185. Springer, Heidelberg (1996). https://doi.org/10.1007/3-540-68697-5_14

21. David, B., Gaži, P., Kiayias, A., Russell, A.: Ouroboros Praos: an adaptively-secure, semi-synchronous proof-of-stake blockchain. In: Nielsen, J.B., Rijmen, V. (eds.) EUROCRYPT 2018, Part II. LNCS, vol. 10821, pp. 66–98. Springer, Cham (2018). https://doi.org/10.1007/978-3-319-78375-8_3

22. Davidson, A., Katsumata, S., Nishimaki, R., Yamada, S., Yamakawa, T.: Adaptively secure constrained pseudorandom functions in the standard model. In: Micciancio, D., Ristenpart, T. (eds.) CRYPTO 2020, Part I. LNCS, vol. 12170, pp. 559–589. Springer, Cham (2020). https://doi.org/10.1007/978-3-030-56784-2_19

23. Gilad, Y., Hemo, R., Micali, S., Vlachos, G., Zeldovich, N.: Algorand: scaling byzantine agreements for cryptocurrencies. In: Proceedings of the 26th Symposium on Operating Systems Principles, Shanghai, China, 28–31 October 2017 (2017)

24. Goldberg, S., Naor, M., Papadopoulos, D., Reyzin, L., Vasant, S., Ziv, A.: NSEC5: provably preventing DNSSEC zone enumeration. In: NDSS 2015 (2015)

25. Guo, F., Chen, R., Susilo, W., Lai, J., Yang, G., Mu, Y.: Optimal security reductions for unique signatures: bypassing impossibilities with a counterexample. In: Katz, J., Shacham, H. (eds.) CRYPTO 2017, Part II. LNCS, vol. 10402, pp. 517–547. Springer, Cham (2017). https://doi.org/10.1007/978-3-319-63715-0_18

26. Hofheinz, D., Jager, T.: Tightly secure signatures and public-key encryption. In: Safavi-Naini, R., Canetti, R. (eds.) CRYPTO 2012. LNCS, vol. 7417, pp. 590–607. Springer, Heidelberg (2012). https://doi.org/10.1007/978-3-642-32009-5_35

27. Hofheinz, D., Jager, T.: Verifiable random functions from standard assumptions. In: Kushilevitz, E., Malkin, T. (eds.) TCC 2016, Part I. LNCS, vol. 9562, pp. 336–362. Springer, Heidelberg (2016). https://doi.org/10.1007/978-3-662-49096-9_14

28. Hofheinz, D., Jager, T., Knapp, E.: Waters signatures with optimal security reduction. In: Fischlin, M., Buchmann, J., Manulis, M. (eds.) PKC 2012. LNCS, vol. 7293, pp. 66–83. Springer, Heidelberg (2012). https://doi.org/10.1007/978-3-642-30057-8_5

29. Hohenberger, S., Waters, B.: Constructing verifiable random functions with large input spaces. In: Gilbert, H. (ed.) EUROCRYPT 2010. LNCS, vol. 6110, pp. 656–672. Springer, Heidelberg (2010). https://doi.org/10.1007/978-3-642-13190-5_33

30. Ishai, Y., Kushilevitz, E., Ostrovsky, R., Sahai, A.: Cryptography with constant computational overhead. In: 40th ACM STOC (2008)

31. Jager, T.: Verifiable random functions from weaker assumptions. In: Dodis, Y., Nielsen, J.B. (eds.) TCC 2015, Part II. LNCS, vol. 9015, pp. 121–143. Springer, Heidelberg (2015). https://doi.org/10.1007/978-3-662-46497-7_5

32. Jager, T., Kurek, R., Niehues, D.: Efficient adaptively-secure IB-KEMs and VRFs via near-collision resistance. Cryptology ePrint Archive, Report 2021/160 (2021). https://eprint.iacr.org/2021/160

33. Jager, T., Kurek, R., Pan, J.: Simple and more efficient PRFs with tight security from LWE and matrix-DDH. In: Peyrin, T., Galbraith, S. (eds.) ASIACRYPT 2018, Part III. LNCS, vol. 11274, pp. 490–518. Springer, Cham (2018). https://doi.org/10.1007/978-3-030-03332-3_18

34. Jager, T., Niehues, D.: On the real-world instantiability of admissible hash functions and efficient verifiable random functions. In: Paterson, K.G., Stebila, D. (eds.) SAC 2019. LNCS, vol. 11959, pp. 303–332. Springer, Cham (2020). https://doi.org/10.1007/978-3-030-38471-5_13

35. Kakvi, S.A., Kiltz, E.: Optimal security proofs for full domain hash, revisited. In: Pointcheval, D., Johansson, T. (eds.) EUROCRYPT 2012. LNCS, vol. 7237, pp. 537–553. Springer, Heidelberg (2012). https://doi.org/10.1007/978-3-642-29011-4_32

36. Katsumata, S.: On the untapped potential of encoding predicates by arithmetic circuits and their applications. In: Takagi, T., Peyrin, T. (eds.) ASIACRYPT 2017, Part III. LNCS, vol. 10626, pp. 95–125. Springer, Cham (2017). https://doi.org/10.1007/978-3-319-70700-6_4

37. Katz, J., Wang, N.: Efficiency improvements for signature schemes with tight security reductions. In: ACM CCS (2003)

38. Kohl, L.: Hunting and gathering – verifiable random functions from standard assumptions with short proofs. In: Lin, D., Sako, K. (eds.) PKC 2019, Part II. LNCS, vol. 11443, pp. 408–437. Springer, Cham (2019). https://doi.org/10.1007/978-3-030-17259-6_14

39. Lewko, A., Waters, B.: Why proving HIBE systems secure is difficult. In: Nguyen, P.Q., Oswald, E. (eds.) EUROCRYPT 2014. LNCS, vol. 8441, pp. 58–76. Springer, Heidelberg (2014). https://doi.org/10.1007/978-3-642-55220-5_4

40. Melara, M.S., Blankstein, A., Bonneau, J., Felten, E.W., Freedman, M.J.: CONIKS: bringing key transparency to end users. In: USENIX Security 2015 (2015)
41. Micali, S., Rabin, M.O., Vadhan, S.P.: Verifiable random functions. In: 40th FOCS (1999)
42. Morgan, A., Pass, R.: On the security loss of unique signatures. In: Beimel, A., Dziembowski, S. (eds.) TCC 2018, Part I. LNCS, vol. 11239, pp. 507–536. Springer, Cham (2018). https://doi.org/10.1007/978-3-030-03807-6_19
43. Morgan, A., Pass, R., Shi, E.: On the adaptive security of MACs and PRFs. In: Moriai, S., Wang, H. (eds.) ASIACRYPT 2020, Part I. LNCS, vol. 12491, pp. 724–753. Springer, Cham (2020). https://doi.org/10.1007/978-3-030-64837-4_24
44. Naor, M., Reingold, O.: Number-theoretic constructions of efficient pseudo-random functions. In: 38th FOCS (1997)
45. Niehues, D.: Verifiable random functions with optimal tightness. Cryptology ePrintArchive, Report 2021/217 (2021). https://eprint.iacr.org/2021/217
46. Roşie, R.: Adaptive-secure VRFs with shorter keys from static assumptions. In: Camenisch, J., Papadimitratos, P. (eds.) CANS 2018. LNCS, vol. 11124, pp. 440–459. Springer, Cham (2018). https://doi.org/10.1007/978-3-030-00434-7_22
47. Schäge, S.: Tight proofs for signature schemes without random oracles. In: Paterson, K.G. (ed.) EUROCRYPT 2011. LNCS, vol. 6632, pp. 189–206. Springer, Heidelberg (2011). https://doi.org/10.1007/978-3-642-20465-4_12
48. Shoup, V.: Sequences of games: a tool for taming complexity in security proofs. Cryptology ePrint Archive, Report 2004/332 (2004). http://eprint.iacr.org/2004/332
49. Včelák, J., Goldberg, S., Papadopoulos, D., Huque, S., Lawrence, D.C.: NSEC5, DNSSEC Authenticated Denial of Existence. Internet-Draft draft-vcelak-nsec5-08, Internet Engineering Task Force (2018)
50. Waters, B.: Efficient identity-based encryption without random oracles. In: Cramer, R. (ed.) EUROCRYPT 2005. LNCS, vol. 3494, pp. 114–127. Springer, Heidelberg (2005). https://doi.org/10.1007/11426639_7
51. Yamada, S.: Asymptotically compact adaptively secure lattice IBEs and verifiable random functions via generalized partitioning techniques. Cryptology ePrint Archive, Report 2017/096 (2017). http://eprint.iacr.org/2017/096
52. Yamada, S.: Asymptotically compact adaptively secure lattice IBEs and verifiable random functions via generalized partitioning techniques. In: Katz, J., Shacham, H. (eds.) CRYPTO 2017, Part III. LNCS, vol. 10403, pp. 161–193. Springer, Cham (2017). https://doi.org/10.1007/978-3-319-63697-9_6

A Geometric Approach to Homomorphic Secret Sharing

Yuval Ishai[1], Russell W. F. Lai[2(✉)], and Giulio Malavolta[3]

[1] Technion, Haifa, Israel
[2] Friedrich-Alexander-Universität Erlangen-Nürnberg, Erlangen, Germany
russell.lai@cs.fau.de
[3] Max Planck Institute for Security and Privacy, Bochum, Germany

Abstract. An (n, m, t)-homomorphic secret sharing (HSS) scheme allows n clients to share their inputs across m servers, such that the inputs are hidden from any t colluding servers, and moreover the servers can evaluate functions over the inputs *locally* by mapping their input shares to *compact* output shares. Such compactness makes HSS a useful building block for communication-efficient secure multi-party computation (MPC).

In this work, we propose a simple compiler for HSS evaluating multivariate polynomials based on two building blocks: (1) homomorphic encryption for linear functions or low-degree polynomials, and (2) information-theoretic HSS for low-degree polynomials. Our compiler leverages the power of the first building block towards improving the parameters of the second.

We use our compiler to generalize and improve on the HSS scheme of Lai, Malavolta, and Schröder [ASIACRYPT'18], which is only efficient when the number of servers is at most logarithmic in the security parameter. In contrast, we obtain efficient schemes for polynomials of higher degrees and an arbitrary number of servers. This application of our general compiler extends techniques that were developed in the context of information-theoretic private information retrieval (Woodruff and Yekhanin [CCC'05]), which use partial derivatives and Hermite interpolation to support the computation of polynomials of higher degrees.

In addition to the above, we propose a new application of HSS to MPC with preprocessing. By pushing the computation of some HSS servers to a preprocessing phase, we obtain communication-efficient MPC protocols for low-degree polynomials that use fewer parties than previous protocols based on the same assumptions. The online communication of these protocols is linear in the input size, independently of the description size of the polynomial.

1 Introduction

In lightweight secure multi-party computation (MPC) protocols, communication is usually the bottleneck for efficiency. For example, typical protocols based on oblivious-transfer (OT) have a communication complexity linear in the circuit

© International Association for Cryptologic Research 2021
J. A. Garay (Ed.): PKC 2021, LNCS 12711, pp. 92–119, 2021.
https://doi.org/10.1007/978-3-030-75248-4_4

size of the function being computed. A promising approach to bypass this barrier is homomorphic secret sharing (HSS) for multivariate polynomials, which enables low communication MPC protocols, while retaining practical efficiency. In this work, we study this problem and present a set of new lightweight techniques to maximize the degree of polynomials supported by HSS without increasing the communication cost.

1.1 Homomorphic Secret Sharing

An (n, m, t)-HSS scheme allows n input clients to share their secret inputs $(x_1, \ldots, x_n)$ to m non-communicating servers, such that the latter can homomorphically evaluate any admissible public function f over the shares, and produce the output shares $(y_1, \ldots, y_m)$. Using these, an output client can recover $f(x_1, \ldots, x_n)$. Shares of HSS should be much shorter, or ideally of size independent of the size of the description of the function f being computed. This non-trivial feature distinguishes HSS from OT-based MPC. As for ordinary threshold secret sharing schemes, security requires that the servers cannot learn anything about the inputs assuming at most t of them are corrupt.

HSS was conceived [10] as a lightweight alternative to fully-homomorphic encryption (FHE) [23] and it leverages the non-collusion of the servers to achieve better efficiency. Indeed, any homomorphic encryption for a function class $\mathcal{F}$ can be seen as an $(n, 1, 1)$-HSS for the same class. Due to the distributed setting, homomorphic secret sharing can be constructed from assumptions that do not imply a fully homomorphic encryption scheme, such as the intractability of the Diffie-Hellman (DDH) problem [20], or even information-theoretically.

Boyle et al. [10] proposed a DDH-based $(n, 2, 1)$-HSS scheme for branching programs, where the reconstruction function is simply the addition of output shares. This enables many important applications, such as low-communication 2-party computation, efficient round-optimal multiparty computation protocols, and 2-server private-information retrieval. See [12] for a comprehensive discussion on the matter. One drawback of the scheme is that its correctness holds only for an inverse polynomial probability. Amplifications through parallel repetition results in a loss of concrete efficiency.

Boyle, Kohl, and Scholl [13] proposed a counterpart of [10] based on the learning with errors (LWE) assumption with negligible error. Similar to FHE, their scheme is only concretely efficient in an amortized sense and only for SIMD[1]-style computations. Boyle *et al.* [9] proposed an $(n, 2, 1)$-HSS scheme for constant-degree polynomials based on the learning parity with noise (LPN) assumption. The scheme does not apply to the multi-input setting, *i.e.*, the entire input must come from a single party, and the share size $O(\lambda^d)$ (as opposed to the trivial $O(n^d)$) grows exponentially with the degree d.

In a different line of work originated by Catalano and Fiore [15], Lai, Mala-volta, and Schröder (LMS) [31] considered a variant of the HSS model, where the reconstruction function is not necessarily linear. While this notion is strictly weaker than that considered by Boyle *et al.* [10], it is still useful in some context

---

[1] Single-Instruction-Multiple-Data.

to "amplify" the homomorphic capability of some encryption schemes, leveraging the existence of multiple non-colluding servers. They proposed a construction of $(n, m, 1)$-HSS for degree $d < (k + 1)m$ polynomials using only a homomorphic encryption scheme for degree k polynomials (k-HE), for any $k \geq 1$. The LMS construction [31] focused on the case $t = 1$. Their discussion of how the construction can be extended to $t > 1$ was non-constructive. A constructive version for general $t \geq 1$ was proposed in [35]. The main shortcoming of LMS [31,35] is that it is only efficient for a small number of servers, i.e., $m = O(\log \lambda)$, where λ is the security parameter. This is due to the difficulty of the combinatorial problem of assigning monomials of the expanded form of $\prod_{\ell \in [d]}(\sum_{i \in [n]} X_i)$ to m servers so that each monomial is computed by exactly one server.

1.2   Power of Low-Degree Polynomials

The homomorphic computation of low-degree polynomials enables several interesting applications, that we discuss below.

1. *Private Information Retrieval:* An m-server private information retrieval (PIR) protocol allows a client to retrieve the entry of a certain database (stored by all servers) without revealing which entry he is interested in. HSS offers a natural implementation of PIR by allowing the client to secret share the index across all servers, who can homomorphically evaluate the index selection function and return the corresponding entry of the database to the client. It is a well-known fact that the index selection function can be expressed as a low-degree polynomial (logarithmic in the size of the database).
2. *Private Queries:* In the context of private queries, even a few extra degrees of computation turn out to be useful. Instead of the simple index selection, the servers can answer more complex queries, such as conjunctive statements [6]. As a concrete example, a client can query how many database entries contain a 1 at positions (i, j), without revealing the indices (i, j), by just adding a single degree to the polynomial homomorphically evaluated by the servers. See [3] for an elaborate discussion on the matter. Other examples of useful queries computable with low-degree polynomials include pattern matching over unsorted databases [1,2].
3. *Machine Learning:* HSS for low-degree polynomials can be used to securely compute repeated linear operations, such as matrix multiplication (for small amounts of matrices). These operations are recurrent for many interesting tasks, such as the secure computation of the training phase (*e.g.,* [26]) and classification phase of (*e.g.,* [8]) of machine learning.
4. *Biometrics:* In applications of biometrics it is often required to compare or compute the distance of two data points. These tasks, such as the comparison of two integers [33], Hamming distance [38], and edit distance [16], can be represented as the computation of low-degree polynomials.
5. *Statistical Analysis:* Low-degree polynomials allow one to compute statistics over private data, such as low-order moments, correlations, and linear regressions. See, e.g. [15] and references therein.

1.3   Our Results

The starting point of this work is the observation that the LMS construction can be viewed more abstractly as compiling an information-theoretic (IT) HSS scheme into its computational counterpart using k-HE. In their case, the IT HSS scheme consisted of the so called CNF secret sharing scheme [29], consequently, the inefficiency of their scheme for $m = \Omega(\log \lambda)$ servers is essentially due to the difficulty of evaluating CNF shares, which in turn is related to the #P-hard problem of computing the permanent of matrices [27]. With this view, it is natural to ask if the CNF scheme can be replaced with another IT HSS scheme, so that its (k-HE-compiled) computational variant is efficient for $m = \mathsf{poly}(\lambda)$ servers.

Generic Compiler from IT HSS to HSS Using HE. In this work, we answer the above question positively. Specifically, we propose a generic compiler based on homomorphic encryption that compiles a certain class of IT HSS for degree-d polynomials into their computational counterpart with less client computation (and hence shorter output shares). In other words, for a fixed client computation cost, the computational variant supports higher degrees.

Theorem 1 (Informal). *Let $k, \ell \in \mathbb{N}$ be constants with $k \leq \ell$, and $d < \frac{(\ell+1)m}{t}$. Suppose there exists an IT (n, m, t)-HSS for degree-d polynomials satisfying certain structural properties, and a CPA-secure k-HE scheme. Further suppose that the IT HSS scheme has recovery information size ρ, input share size α, output share size β, server computation σ, and client computation γ. Then there exists an (n, m, t)-HSS for degree-d polynomials with the following efficiency measures:*

- *Recovery information size $\rho' = \rho$*
- *Input share size $\alpha' = \rho + \alpha$*
- *Output share size $\beta' = \rho^{\ell-k}$*
- *Server computation $\sigma' = \sigma + \beta\rho^{\ell}$*
- *Client computation $\gamma' = m\rho^{\ell-k}$*

All $\mathsf{poly}(\lambda)$ factors contributed by the ciphertext size and $\log |\mathbb{F}|$ are omitted.

For $k = \ell$, when the base IT HSS scheme is instantiated with the CNF scheme[2], we recover the LMS schemes [31,35].

Theorem 1 might seem confusing at first glance – Our compiler turns a degree-d IT HSS into another degree-d computational HSS. What is the gain? We highlight that the output share size of the resulting HSS is independent of that of the base HSS, which could be much larger. From another perspective, for a fixed communication cost, the compiled (computational) HSS supports a higher degree than the base (IT) HSS.

More concretely, as we will see later in Corollary 1 (setting $\ell = k + 1$), with $O(n) \cdot \mathsf{poly}(\lambda)$ communication, the compiled HSS supports degree $< (k+2)m/t$

---

[2] More rigorously, the LMS construction can be seen as compiling the "first-order CNF scheme" which we define in Sect. 4.

with m servers, instead of $< 2m/t$ by the base HSS. Note that the supported degree is proportional to km, i.e., the expressiveness of k-HE is amplified *multiplicatively* by the number of servers m.

Generalizations of Existing Compatible IT HSS. In search of a substitute of the CNF scheme, we observe that implicit in the work of Woodruff and Yekhanin [37] lies an IT HSS, which was implicitly used to construct information-theoretic secure multi-party computation protocols [3]. This scheme, which we denote by WY_1 (first-order Woodruff-Yekhanin HSS), can be seen as a generalization of the well-known Shamir secret sharing scheme [36], which we denote by WY_0.

To recall, in the Shamir secret sharing scheme, a secret $\mathbf{x} \in \mathbb{F}^n$ is shared into $(\mathbf{s}_1, \ldots, \mathbf{s}_m) = (\varphi(1), \ldots, \varphi(m))$ for some degree-t polynomial φ with $\varphi(0) = \mathbf{x}$. To evaluate a degree-d polynomial f, where $d < \frac{m}{t}$, server j sends $f(\mathbf{s}_j) = (f \circ \varphi)(j)$ to the output client. Since $f \circ \varphi$ is a polynomial of degree at most $dt < m$, the output client can recover $f(\mathbf{x}) = (f \circ \varphi)(0)$ by Lagrange interpolation. Notice that the Shamir secret sharing scheme is *compact* in the sense that, while an input share is of length n, an output share is of constant length. The latter is in some sense "wasteful", since increasing the output share length to n (which we refer to as *balanced*), does not increase the overall asymptotic communication complexity. To utilize this "wasted" space, the idea of Woodruff and Yekhanin is to let the servers further compute the n first-order derivatives of f evaluated at $\mathbf{s}_j$. Since m additional data points are available, the degree of f can now be as high as $d < \frac{2m}{t}$, and $f(\mathbf{x}) = (f \circ \varphi)(0)$ can be recovered by Hermite interpolation.

Our idea to further increase the degree of the supported polynomials is to let the servers compute even higher-order derivatives.[3] With some routine calculation one can show that the output share size is $O(n^\ell)$ if derivatives of up to the ℓ-th order are evaluated and sent to the output client. While this does not necessarily help in a standalone use of the HSS scheme, since it increases the overall communication complexity (and also client computation), it turns out that the increased communication can be brought back down again using the k-HE-based compiler, so that the resulting scheme is balanced or even compact.

Theorem 2 (Informal). *For any constant $\ell \in \mathbb{N}$ and $d < \frac{(\ell+1)m}{t}$, there exists an IT (n, m, t)-HSS scheme WY_ℓ for degree-d polynomials with the following efficiency measures:*

- *Recovery information size $\rho = n$*
- *Input share size $\alpha = n$*
- *Output share size $\beta = n^\ell$*
- *Server computation $\sigma = |f|n^{\ell-1}$*
- *Client computation $\gamma = mn^\ell$*

---

[3] The idea of generalizing the approach of Woodroof and Yekhanin to higher order derivatives was already explored in the context of locally decodable codes [30] although in very different parameter settings. To the best of our knowledge, its application in cryptography is new to this work.

Table 1. Comparison of HSS schemes. Computation complexities for CNF_ℓ and CNF_ℓ + k-HE are rough (over)estimations. The LMS scheme [31,35] achieves the efficiency reported in the "$\mathsf{CNF}_\ell + k$-HE" column with $\ell = k$. Factors of $\mathsf{poly}(\lambda)$ contributed by $\log|\mathbb{F}|$ and k-HE ciphertext size are omitted.

Scheme	CNF_ℓ	$\mathsf{CNF}_\ell + k$-HE	WY_ℓ	$\mathsf{WY}_\ell + k$-HE
Security	IT	Comp.	IT	Comp.
Max degree d (Exclusive)	$(\ell+1)m/t$			
Recovery info. size ρ	$m^t n$	$m^t n$	ℓn	ℓn
Input share size α	$m^t n$	$m^t n$	n	ℓn
Output share size β	$(m^t n)^\ell$	$(m^t n)^{\ell-k}$	n^ℓ	$(\ell n)^{\ell-k}$
Server computation σ	$(m^t n)^d$	$(m^t n)^d$	$|f|n^{\ell-1}$	$|f|n^{\ell-1} + (\ell n^2)^\ell$
Client computation γ	$\ell m(m^t n)^\ell$	$m(m^t n)^{\ell-k}$	$\ell m(\ell n)^\ell$	$m(\ell n)^{\ell-k}$

Furthermore, WY_ℓ satisfies the structural requirements of the k-HE-based compiler. All $\log|\mathbb{F}|$ factors are omitted.

Implications. When WY_ℓ is compiled with the k-HE based compiler, we obtain the following result.

Corollary 1 (Informal). *Let $k, \ell \in \mathbb{N}$ be constants with $k \leq \ell$, and $d < \frac{(\ell+1)m}{t}$. Suppose there exists a CPA-secure k-HE scheme. Then there exists an (n, m, t)-HSS for degree-d polynomials with the following efficiency measures:*

- *Recovery information size $\rho' = n$*
- *Input share size $\alpha' = n$*
- *Output share size $\beta' = n^{\ell-k}$*
- *Server computation $\sigma' = |f|n^{\ell-1} + n^{2\ell}$*
- *Client computation $\gamma' = mn^{\ell-k}$*

All $\mathsf{poly}(\lambda)$ factors contributed by the ciphertext size and $\log|\mathbb{F}|$ are omitted.

As shown in Table 1, if we treat ℓ as a constant, the k-HE-compiled WY_ℓ scheme strictly outperforms the k-HE-compiled CNF_ℓ scheme ($\ell = 1$ in LMS [31,35]) in all parameters. We are mostly interested in the setting where the communication is *balanced*, in the sense that the input share size is comparable to the output share size. From Corollary 1, this can be achieved by setting $\ell = k+1$.

In Table 2, we highlight some practically interesting parameters for the k-HE-compiled WY_ℓ scheme. For a fixed communication cost $n \cdot \mathsf{poly}(\lambda)$, we state the relation between k, $\ell = k+1$ (so that the HSS is balanced), the corruption threshold t, the number of servers m, and the degree d of supported polynomials. The degree d reported for each setting of (t, m) is generally higher than that

Table 2. Some practically interesting parameters for our HSS schemes for polynomials using k-HE for $k = 1, 2$ and linear communication. The first six rows are obtained by setting $k = 1$ and $\ell = 2$ in $\mathsf{WY}_\ell + k$-HE. The last six rows are obtained by setting $k = 2$ and $\ell = 3$.

Corruption t	# Servers m	Max degree d (Inclusive)
1	2	5
1	3	8
1	4	11
2	3	4
2	4	5
3	4	3
1	2	7
1	3	11
1	4	15
2	3	5
2	4	7
3	4	5

supported by LMS [31] ($t = 1$) and [35] ($t \geq 1$) by an additive factor of m/t, since they did not consider balanced HSS schemes. We focus on small $k = O(1)$ since for such values of k it is not known how a k-HE can be bootstrapped [23] into an FHE. For $k \in \{1, 2\}$, k-HE can be realized based on assumptions that are not known to imply FHE: For polynomials whose outputs are contained in a polynomial-size space, the ElGamal encryption [21] is a 1-HE based on the decisional Diffie Hellman (DDH) assumption, and the BGN encryption [7] is a 2-HE based on the subgroup decision assumption. For large outputs, the Paillier encryption [34] and Damgård–Jurik encryption [19] are 1-HE based on the decisional composite residuosity assumption. The additive variant of ElGamal [14] is a 1-HE based on DDH in groups with a discrete-logarithm-easy subgroup. For general $k = O(1)$, k-HE can be construction from the learning with errors assumption with smaller parameters than those which imply FHE, and therefore are concretely efficient.

Application to MPC with Preprocessing. In typical (n, m, t)-HSS schemes, including ones constructed in this work, there exists $p < m$ such that any p input shares are distributed uniformly over an efficiently sampleable space. In other words, the input shares of any, say the first, p parties contain no information about the input $(x_1, \ldots, x_n)$, and can be generated in a preprocessing phase even before the inputs $(x_1, \ldots, x_n)$ are known. We formalize this as the p-preprocessing property, and show that the WY_ℓ scheme its k-HE-compiled counterpart support $\left\lfloor \frac{t}{\ell+1} \right\rfloor$-preprocessing.

We then show that, given a general purpose MPC protocol (whose communication cost might be linear in the function description size), an HSS for polynomials with p-preprocessing can be compiled into a communication-efficient MPC for polynomials with preprocessing. Our technique generalizes the approach taken in [5] for obtaining 2-party MPC with preprocessing from 3-server PIR.

Recall that an MPC protocol with preprocessing is split into two phases – a preprocessing phase and an online phase. In the preprocessing phase, a trusted party performs an input-independent preprocessing on the function f, and distributes shares of the preprocessing result to the m participants. Alternatively, the trusted party can be emulated by an MPC among the m parties. Then, in the online phase, the m parties collectively receive their online inputs $(x_1, \ldots, x_n)$, where each party either possesses a share or a disjoint subset of entries of $(x_1, \ldots, x_n)$, and interact in an online MPC protocol to compute $f(x_1, \ldots, x_n)$. The hope is that, by exploiting the offline preprocessing, the online communication cost can be reduced such that it is independent of the description size of f.

Our idea is to push the work of the first p servers in an HSS scheme with p-preprocessing to the preprocessing phase of the MPC protocol, and thereby reduce the minimal necessary number of parties required to run the protocol. The MPC preprocessing first generates the inputs shares of the first p HSS servers, which can be done independently of the input. It then homomorphically evaluates f on the p input shares to produce p output shares. The input and output shares of the first p HSS servers are then secret shared among the m MPC participants.

In the online phase, the m MPC participants receive their respective inputs $(x_1, \ldots, x_n)$ and engage in an MPC protocol to generate the remaining input shares. Naturally, the j-th participant gets the $(p + j)$-th HSS input share. Each participant can then proceed to homomorphically evaluate f on their input shares, and then engage in another MPC to recover the computation result from all output shares.

Note that the two MPC sub-protocols run in the online phase are computing functions whose circuit size is comparable to the input size, independently of $|f|$. For degree d polynomials, $|f|$ can be of size $O(n^d)$. Our MPC protocol therefore potentially achieves an exponential improvement over general-purpose MPC, without using heavy tools such as FHE.

In the case where t is a multiple of $\ell + 1$, when instantiated with the k-HE-compiled WY_ℓ scheme and, say, an OT-based MPC, we obtain an m party MPC protocol with preprocessing for degree-d polynomials, where $d < \frac{(\ell+1)m}{t} + 1$, i.e., the degree grows by 1 compared to a direct use of HSS without increasing the number of participants. The online communication is $mn^{\ell-k} \cdot \mathsf{poly}(\lambda)$. As long as $|f| = \omega(mn^{\ell-k})$, which holds for the vast majority of n-variate polynomials of degree $d < \frac{(\ell+1)m}{t} + 1$, our preprocessing MPC achieves a communication complexity sublinear in $|f|$. Due to the requirement that t is a multiple of $\ell + 1$, the preprocessing technique seems to be more suited to the setting where t is large

Table 3. Some practically interesting parameters for our MPC protocols with preprocessing with $n \cdot \text{poly}(\lambda)$ communication, based on HE for linear or quadratic functions.

Corruption t	# Parties m	Max degree d (Inclusive)	Base scheme
3	4	4	$\text{WY}_2 + 1\text{-HE}$
3	5	5	$\text{WY}_2 + 1\text{-HE}$
3	6	6	$\text{WY}_2 + 1\text{-HE}$
4	5	5	$\text{WY}_3 + 2\text{-HE}$
4	6	6	$\text{WY}_3 + 2\text{-HE}$
4	7	7	$\text{WY}_3 + 2\text{-HE}$

(close to m). In Table 3, we highlight some practically interesting parameters for the MPC protocols with preprocessing obtained via our transformation.

Beyond the computation of degree-d polynomials, our preprocessing MPC can be used as a building block in MPC for structured circuits whose "gates" compute degree-d mappings, similar to the ideas of [10,11,17] for evaluating layered circuits and circuits over low-degree gates. Some examples for useful circuits of this kind were given in [17]. These include circuits for Fast Fourier Transform (FFT), symmetric-key cryptography, and dynamic programming.

1.4 Related Work

In addition to the aforementioned related works, we point out that the task of evaluating degree-d n-variate polynomials privately was also considered in the context of maliciously-secure MPC, where the adversary is allowed to corrupt all but one parties, *i.e.*, $t = m - 1$, whereas we only consider HSS and MPC schemes in the semi-honest setting. Below we discuss the semi-honest protocols implicitly described in two maliciously-secure MPC, both of which are indirectly based on the idea of compiling an IT HSS using a k-HE (for $k = 1$), which is made explicit in this work. These schemes inherently require that the polynomial to be evaluated is represented in expanded form, and consequently has only polynomially-many monomials. In contrast, our WY-based schemes support polynomials represented by polynomial-sized arithmetic circuits.

The semi-honest part of the 2-party protocol of Franklin and Mohassel [22] is precisely the HSS obtained by compiling CNF_1 with a 1-HE in the setting where $(t, m) = (1, 2)$. They also proposed an m-party (maliciously-secure) protocol for degree-d polynomials which achieves computation and communication complexity $\text{poly}(m) \cdot n^{\lfloor d/2 \rfloor}$, which is comparable to the 1-HE compiled WY_ℓ scheme which has communication complexity $m(\ell n)^{\ell-1}$ and supports polynomials of degree at least $\ell + 1$ (c.f., Table 1).

Underneath the protocol of Dachman-Soled et al. [18] lies the following protocol for evaluating a (publicly known) monomial $\mu(x_1, \ldots, x_n)$ where $(x_1, \ldots, x_n)$ are jointly contributed by m parties. First, the monomial is split into $\mu =$

$\mu_1 \cdot \ldots \cdot \mu_m$, where $\mu_i(x_1, \ldots, x_n)$ is a monomial which depends only on the inputs of the i-th party. Party 1 encrypts the evaluation of μ_1 using a 1-HE and sends the ciphertext c_1 to Party 2. Then, for $i \in \{2, \ldots, m\}$, Party i homomorphically multiplies μ_i to the ciphertext c_{i-1} encrypting $\mu_1 \cdot \ldots \cdot \mu_{i-1}$ received from Party $i - 1$ to obtain a new ciphertext c_i. Finally, Party i sends c_i to Party $i+1$ if $i \neq m$, or to everyone if $i = m$. Based on the above incremental evaluation protocol, the (maliciously-secure) protocol of Dachman-Soled et al. [18] requires (roughly) $O(n^2 \log^2 d)$ communication and $O(n \log d)$ computation, where the logarithmic dependency on d is achieved by having each party precompute the powers-of-2 of their inputs[4]. Due to the logarithmic dependency on d and the limit of the number of monomials, their scheme seems best suited for evaluating sparse polynomials of a high degree $d = \mathsf{poly}(\lambda)$.

2 Preliminaries

Let $\lambda \in \mathbb{N}$ denote the security parameter. The set of all polynomials and negligible functions in λ are denoted by $\mathsf{poly}(\lambda)$ and $\mathsf{negl}(\lambda)$ respectively. An algorithm with input length n is PPT if it can be computed by a probabilistic Turing machine whose running time is bounded by some function $\mathsf{poly}(n)$. We use $[n]$ to denote the set $\{1, \ldots, n\}$, and $\mathbb{N}_0$ to denote the set of all non-negative integers. Given a finite set S, we denote by $x \leftarrow S$ the sampling of an element uniformly at random in S.

For simplicity, throughout this work we fix a field $\mathbb{F}$ which is sufficiently large, such that for any polynomial $f \in \mathbb{F}[X_1, \ldots, X_n]$ we will be considering, we have $\deg(f) < |\mathbb{F}| \leq 2^\lambda$. An $\mathbb{F}$ element can therefore be represented by λ bits. Let $\mathbf{e} = (e_1, \ldots, e_n) \in \mathbb{N}_0^n$ and $\mathbf{x} = (x_1, \ldots, x_n) \in \mathbb{F}^n$. We define the weight function $\mathsf{wt}(\mathbf{e}) := e_1 + \ldots + e_n$. We use $\mathbf{x}^{\mathbf{e}}$ to denote the expression $\mathbf{x}^{\mathbf{e}} := x_1^{e_1} \ldots x_n^{e_n}$.

2.1 Homomorphic Encryption for Degree-k Polynomials (k-HE)

We recall the notion of homomorphic encryption for degree-k polynomials over $\mathbb{F}$.

Definition 1 (Homomorphic Encryption). *A homomorphic encryption scheme* $\mathsf{HE} = (\mathsf{KGen}, \mathsf{Enc}, \mathsf{Eval}, \mathsf{Dec})$ *for degree-k polynomials over $\mathbb{F}$, k-HE for short, consists of the following PPT algorithms:*

- $\mathsf{KGen}(1^\lambda)$: *The* key generation *algorithm takes as input the security parameter λ and outputs the public key* pk *and the secret key* sk.
- $\mathsf{Enc}(\mathsf{pk}, \mathbf{x})$: *The* encryption *algorithm takes as input the public key* pk *and a message $\mathbf{x} \in \mathbb{F}^n$ for some $n = \mathsf{poly}(\lambda)$; it returns a ciphertext $\mathbf{c} \in \mathcal{C}^n$ in some ciphertext space $\mathcal{C}$.*
- $\mathsf{Eval}(\mathsf{pk}, f, \mathbf{c})$: *The* evaluation *algorithm takes as input the public key* pk, *(the description of) a polynomial $f \in \mathbb{F}[X_1, \ldots, X_n]$, and a ciphertext $\mathbf{c} \in \mathcal{C}^n$ for some $n = \mathsf{poly}(\lambda)$; it returns a ciphertext $c' \in \mathcal{C}$.*

---

[4] This degree reduction technique is generic and also applies to our HSS-based schemes.

$$\boxed{\begin{aligned} &\text{IND-CPA}^{b}_{\mathcal{A},\text{HE}}(1^{\lambda}): \\ \hline &(\text{pk},\text{sk}) \leftarrow \text{KGen}(1^{\lambda}) \\ &(x_0, x_1, \text{state}) \leftarrow \mathcal{A}_1(\text{pk}) \\ &c \leftarrow \text{Enc}(\text{pk}, x_b) \\ &b' \leftarrow \mathcal{A}_2(\text{state}, c) \\ &\textbf{return } b' \end{aligned}}$$

Fig. 1. IND-CPA experiment for public-key encryption

– Dec(sk, c) : *The* decryption *algorithm takes as input the private key* sk *and a ciphertext* $\mathbf{c} \in \mathcal{C}^n$ *for some* $n = \text{poly}(\lambda)$; *it returns a plaintext* $\mathbf{x} \in \mathbb{F}^n$.

We focus only on *compact* HE schemes [23], where the size of the ciphertext space $|\mathcal{C}| = \text{poly}(\lambda)$ is independent of the size of the supported polynomials.

Definition 2 (Correctness). *A k-HE scheme is said to be correct if for any $\lambda \in \mathbb{N}$, any $(\text{pk}, \text{sk}) \in \text{KGen}(1^{\lambda})$, any positive integer $n \in \text{poly}(\lambda)$, any polynomial $f \in \mathbb{F}[X_1, \ldots, X_n]$ of degree at most k, and message $x \in \mathbb{F}^n$, we have*

$$\Pr[\text{Dec}(\text{sk}, \text{Enc}(\text{pk}, \mathbf{x})) = \mathbf{x}] \geq 1 - \text{negl}(\lambda), \text{ and}$$

$$\Pr\left[\text{Dec}(\text{sk}, c) = f(x) : \begin{array}{l} \mathbf{c} \leftarrow \text{Enc}(\text{pk}, \mathbf{x}) \\ c' \leftarrow \text{Eval}(\text{pk}, f, \mathbf{c}) \end{array}\right] \geq 1 - \text{negl}(\lambda)$$

where the probability is taken over the random coins of Enc *and* Eval. *The scheme is* perfectly correct *if the above probabilities are exactly 1.*

Definition 3 (CPA-Security). *A homomorphic encryption scheme* HE *is* IND-CPA-*secure (has indistinguishable ciphertexts under chosen plaintext attack) if for any* PPT *adversary* $\mathcal{A} = (\mathcal{A}_1, \mathcal{A}_2)$

$$\left|\Pr\left[\text{IND-CPA}^0_{\mathcal{A},\text{HE}}(1^{\lambda}) = 1\right] - \Pr\left[\text{IND-CPA}^1_{\mathcal{A},\text{HE}}(1^{\lambda}) = 1\right]\right| \leq \text{negl}(\lambda)$$

where the experiment IND-CPA$^{b}_{\mathcal{A},\text{HE}}$ *is defined in Fig. 1.*

3   Definition of Homomorphic Secret Sharing

We recall the notion of homomorphic secret sharing [12]. The definitions presented here are for the variant in the public-key setup model [31]. For the definitions in the plain model, we refer to [12,31].

Definition 4 (Homomorphic Secret Sharing (HSS)). *An n-input m-server homomorphic secret sharing scheme* HSS = (KGen, Share, Eval, Dec) *for degree-d polynomials over $\mathbb{F}$ consists of the following* PPT *algorithms:*

- $(\mathsf{pk}, \mathsf{sk}) \leftarrow \mathsf{KGen}(1^\lambda)$: *On input the security parameter* 1^λ, *the* key generation *algorithm outputs a public key* pk *and a secret key* sk.

- $\begin{pmatrix} \mathsf{in}_1, \dots, \mathsf{in}_m \\ \mathsf{rec}_1, \dots, \mathsf{rec}_m \end{pmatrix} \leftarrow \mathsf{Share}(\mathsf{pk}, \mathbf{x})$: *Given a public key* pk, *and an input* $\mathbf{x} \in \mathbb{F}^n$, *the* sharing *algorithm outputs a a set of input shares* $(\mathsf{in}_1, \dots, \mathsf{in}_m)$ *where* $\mathsf{in}_j \in \{0,1\}^{\alpha \cdot \mathsf{poly}(\lambda)}$ *and their corresponding recovery information* $(\mathsf{rec}_1, \dots, \mathsf{rec}_m)$ *where* $\mathsf{rec}_j \in \{0,1\}^{\rho \cdot \mathsf{poly}(\lambda)}$.

- $\mathsf{out}_j \leftarrow \mathsf{Eval}(\mathsf{pk}, j, f, \mathsf{in}_j)$: *The* evaluation *algorithm is executed by a server* $\mathcal{S}_j$ *on inputs the public key* pk, *an index* j, *(the description of) a degree-d polynomial* f, *and a share* in_j. *Upon termination, the server* $\mathcal{S}_j$ *outputs the corresponding output share* $\mathsf{out}_j \in \{0,1\}^{\beta \cdot \mathsf{poly}(\lambda)}$.

- $y \leftarrow \mathsf{Dec}\left(\mathsf{sk}, \begin{matrix} \mathsf{out}_1, \dots, \mathsf{out}_m, \\ \mathsf{rec}_1, \dots, \mathsf{rec}_m \end{matrix}\right)$: *On input a secret key* sk, *a tuple of output shares* $(\mathsf{out}_1, \dots, \mathsf{out}_m)$, *and a tuple of recovery information* $(\mathsf{rec}_1, \dots, \mathsf{rec}_m)$, *the* decoding *algorithm outputs the result* y *of the evaluation.*

The efficiency measures $\rho = \rho(n)$, $\alpha = \alpha(n)$ *and* $\beta = \beta(n)$ *are the lengths of the recovery information, input shares, and output shares respectively (omitting* $\mathsf{poly}(\lambda)$ *factors). An HSS scheme is said to be* compact *if* $\beta = \mathsf{poly}(\lambda)$ *(independent of* n*), and* balanced *if* $\beta = O(\alpha)$.

Remark 1. In the syntax, we decide to split the recovery information into m chunks $(\mathsf{rec}_1, \dots, \mathsf{rec}_m)$, so that it is more convenient to describe the compiler in Sect. 5, and so that we can omit a factor of m from the measure ρ to reduce clutter. In general, the recovery information can be grouped into a single object rec and the definition ρ can be changed accordingly.

Remark 2. In the literature, an HSS scheme is usually defined without the recovery information $(\mathsf{rec}_1, \dots, \mathsf{rec}_m)$, i.e., $\rho = 0$. We remark that given an HSS scheme with efficiency measures (ρ, α, β), we can construct another scheme (with the same security under the same assumptions) with efficiency measures $(0, \alpha + m\rho, \beta + m\rho)$, by having the input client secret-share r to the servers and the servers relaying those shares to the output client. We use the present definition for convenience.

Remark 3. Our syntax describes a setting where a single party provides all n inputs to the Share algorithm for simplicity. In the case where the input x_i is provided by party i, we can consider an alternative syntax of Share which inputs (pk, x_i) and outputs $(\mathsf{in}_{i,j}, \mathsf{rec}_{i,j})$. The Share algorithm of all HSS schemes considered in this work can be "split" to suit the multi-input syntax.

Definition 5 (Correctness). *An* n-input m-server *HSS scheme for degree-d polynomials is* correct *if for any* $\lambda, m, n \in \mathbb{N}$, *any* $(\mathsf{pk}, \mathsf{sk}) \in \mathsf{KGen}(1^\lambda)$, *any* $f \in \mathbb{F}[X_1, \dots, X_n]$ *with* $\deg(f) \le d$, *any* n-tuple of inputs $\mathbf{x} = (x_1, \dots, x_n) \in \mathbb{F}^n$, *it holds that*

$$\begin{array}{|l|}
\hline
\text{Security}^b_{\mathcal{A},\text{HSS}}(1^\lambda): \\
\hline
(\text{pk}, \text{sk}) \leftarrow \text{KGen}(1^\lambda) \\
(\mathbf{x}_0, \mathbf{x}_1, j_1, \ldots, j_t, \text{state}) \leftarrow \mathcal{A}_0(\text{pk}) \\
\begin{pmatrix} \text{in}_1, \ldots, \text{in}_m, \\ \text{rec}_1, \ldots, \text{rec}_m \end{pmatrix} \leftarrow \text{Share}(\text{pk}, x_b) \\
b' \leftarrow \mathcal{A}_1(\text{state}, \text{in}_{j_1}, \ldots, \text{in}_{j_t}) \\
\textbf{return } b' \\
\hline
\end{array}$$

Fig. 2. Security experiments for $(*, m, t)$-HSS

$$\Pr\left[\text{Dec}\left(\text{sk}, \begin{matrix} \text{out}_1, \ldots, \text{out}_m, \\ \text{rec}_1, \ldots, \text{rec}_m \end{matrix} \right) = f(\mathbf{x}) : \begin{matrix} \begin{pmatrix} \text{in}_1, \ldots, \text{in}_m \\ \text{rec}_1, \ldots, \text{rec}_m \end{pmatrix} \in \text{Share}(\text{pk}, \mathbf{x}) \\ \forall j \in [m], \text{out}_j \in \text{Eval}(\text{pk}, j, f, \text{in}_j) \end{matrix} \right]$$
$$\geq 1 - \text{negl}(\lambda),$$

where the probability is taken over the random coins of Share *and* Eval. *The scheme is* perfectly correct *if the above probability is exactly* 1.

The security of an HSS scheme is analogous to the CPA-security of HE, and guarantees that no information about the message is disclosed to any t servers.

Definition 6 (Security). *An n-input m-server HSS scheme is t-secure if for any $\lambda \in \mathbb{N}$ there exists a negligible function* $\text{negl}(\lambda)$ *such that for any* PPT *algorithm $\mathcal{A} = (\mathcal{A}_0, \mathcal{A}_1)$,*

$$\left| \Pr\left[\text{Security}^0_{\mathcal{A},\text{HSS}} = 1 \right] - \Pr\left[\text{Security}^1_{\mathcal{A},\text{HSS}} = 1 \right] \right| < \text{negl}(\lambda)$$

where $\text{Security}^b_{\mathcal{A},\text{HSS}}$ *is defined in Fig. 2 for $b \in \{0, 1\}$.*

We use the short hand (n, m, t)-HSS to refer to n-input, m-server, t-secure homomorphic secret sharing.

Definition 7 (p-Preprocessing). *We say that an (n, m, t)-HSS scheme* HSS.(KGen, Share, Eval, Dec) *supports p-preprocessing if there exists* PPT *algorithms* (PreProc, ShareComp) *such that, for any $\lambda \in \mathbb{N}$, any $(\text{pk}, \text{sk}) \in \text{KGen}(1^\lambda)$ and any $\mathbf{x} \in \mathbb{F}^n$, the following distributions are identical:*

$$\left\{ \begin{pmatrix} \text{in}_1, \ldots, \text{in}_m \\ \text{rec}_1, \ldots, \text{rec}_m \end{pmatrix} : \begin{matrix} \begin{pmatrix} \text{in}_1, \ldots, \text{in}_p \\ \text{rec}_1, \ldots, \text{rec}_p \end{pmatrix} \leftarrow \text{PreProc}(\text{pk}, 1^n) \\ \begin{pmatrix} \text{in}_{p+1}, \ldots, \text{in}_m \\ \text{rec}_{p+1}, \ldots, \text{rec}_m \end{pmatrix} \leftarrow \text{ShareComp}\left(\text{pk}, \begin{matrix} \text{in}_1, \ldots, \text{in}_p, \\ \text{rec}_1, \ldots, \text{rec}_p, \end{matrix} \mathbf{x} \right) \end{matrix} \right\}$$
$$\equiv \left\{ \begin{pmatrix} \text{in}_1, \ldots, \text{in}_m \\ \text{rec}_1, \ldots, \text{rec}_m \end{pmatrix} : \begin{pmatrix} \text{in}_1, \ldots, \text{in}_m \\ \text{rec}_1, \ldots, \text{rec}_m \end{pmatrix} \leftarrow \text{Share}(\text{pk}, \mathbf{x}) \right\}$$

If an HSS scheme supports p-preprocessing, it means that the shares of the first p servers are independent of the input $\mathbf{x}$, and can thus be computed in a preprocessing phase when the input $\mathbf{x}$ is yet unknown.

Definition 8 (Information-Theoretic HSS). *We say that* HSS.(KGen, Share, Eval, Dec) *is information-theoretic (IT) if* KGen *outputs empty strings, and* HSS *is secure against unbounded adversaries. In such case we simply write* HSS.(Share, Eval, Dec) *to denote the HSS scheme and omit the public and secret key inputs to the algorithms* Share, Eval, *and* Dec. *In case* HSS *supports p-preprocessing, we also omit the public key input to* PreProc *and* ShareComp.

4   Information-Theoretic Homomorphic Secret Sharing

Information-theoretic HSS exists implicitly in the literature of secret sharing and private information retrieval (PIR). The simplest examples are the additive secret sharing scheme and Shamir's secret sharing scheme [36]. The former is an $(n, m, m-1)$-HSS for degree-1 polynomials, *i.e.*, linear functions, with efficiency measures while the latter is an (n, m, t)-HSS for degree-$\lfloor \frac{m-1}{t} \rfloor$ polynomials. Both schemes are compact as an output share consists of a single $\mathbb{F}$ element.

In the following, we extract two IT HSS schemes – the "CNF" scheme CNF_0 [29] and the scheme WY_1 from Woodruff and Yekhanin [37] – from the literature of private information retrieval (PIR) which are generalizations of the additive and Shamir secret sharing schemes respectively. We then present the "ℓ-th order" generalizations of the two schemes – CNF_ℓ and WY_ℓ – which aim to support higher-degree polynomials at the cost of, among other parameters, larger recovery information size and higher degree client computation. The generalizations are done in a way compatible with the compiler to be presented in Sect. 5, so that the higher degree client computation can be delegated back to the servers in the compiled schemes. While the CNF_ℓ scheme is strictly inferior to the WY_ℓ for all ℓ, we include it since compiling CNF_1 with our compiler in Sect. 5 captures the LMS scheme [31, 35].

4.1   CNF Secret Sharing

A generalization of the additive secret sharing scheme is the so called CNF secret sharing scheme [29], where CNF stands for conjunctive normal form. The scheme was first used in the context of PIR by Ishai and Kushilevitz [28].

Original Scheme CNF_0. The idea of the CNF scheme is to write $\mathbf{x} \in \mathbb{F}^n$ as a sum of random elements so that $\mathbf{x} = \sum_{\mathbf{u}} \mathbf{c_u}$, where $\mathbf{u} = (u_1, \dots, u_m) \in \{0,1\}^m$ runs through all possible choices of choosing t out of m objects. The j-th share is then defined as $\mathbf{s}_j := (\mathbf{c_u})_{\mathbf{u}:u_j=0}$, *i.e.*, all $\mathbf{c_u}$ where the j-th bit of $\mathbf{u}$ is 0. The scheme is t-secure because, given any t-subset $\{j_1, \dots, j_t\} \subseteq [m]$, there exists $\mathbf{c}_{\mathbf{u}^*}$, where $u_j^* = 1$ for all $j \in \{j_1, \dots, j_t\}$, which is not known to this subset of servers.

The CNF scheme is clearly linearly homomorphic. Thus, for evaluating a polynomial of degree d, it suffices to show how a monomial $\mathbf{x^e}$ where $\mathsf{wt}(\mathbf{e}) = d$ can be evaluated. Without loss of generality, we consider the monomial

$$x_1 \cdots x_d = \prod_{i=1}^{d} \sum_{\substack{\mathbf{u} \in \{0,1\}^m: \\ \mathsf{wt}(\mathbf{u})=t}} c_{i,\mathbf{u}} = \sum_{\substack{\mathbf{u}_1,\ldots,\mathbf{u}_d \in \{0,1\}^m: \\ \mathsf{wt}(\mathbf{u}_i)=t}} \prod_{i=1}^{d} c_{i,\mathbf{u}_i}.$$

To let the output client recover $x_1 \cdots x_d$, one way is to have (at least) one server being able to compute for each $(\mathbf{u}_1,\ldots,\mathbf{u}_d)$ the term $\prod_{i=1}^{d} c_{i,\mathbf{u}_i}$. If so, we distribute the terms so that each term is computed by exactly one server. Each server can compute the partial sum of all the terms that it is assigned, and send this sum to the output client. The latter can then sum over all partial sums and recover $x_1 \cdots x_d$.

We now examine the term $\prod_{i=1}^{d} c_{i,\mathbf{u}_i}$ for any fixed $\mathbf{u}_1,\ldots,\mathbf{u}_d \in \{0,1\}^m$ with $\mathsf{wt}(\mathbf{u}_i) = t$. Consider the string $\mathbf{u} = \mathbf{u}_1 \vee \ldots \vee \mathbf{u}_d$ obtained by bit-wise OR operations. Note that if $d \leq \frac{m-1}{t}$, we have

$$\mathsf{wt}(\mathbf{u}) \leq \sum_{i=1}^{d} \mathsf{wt}(\mathbf{u}_i) \leq \frac{m-1}{t} \cdot t < m.$$

Therefore there must exist $j^* \in [m]$ such that $\mathbf{u}_{i,j^*} = 0$ for all $i \in [d]$. That is, server j^* possesses $c_{1,\mathbf{u}_1},\ldots,c_{d,\mathbf{u}_d}$ and can thus compute the term.

Although it is information theoretically possible for the parties to compute $x_1 \cdots x_d$, there seems to be no natural way to distribute the terms among the servers. In particular, as noted in [27], when $t = 1$, $m = d+1$, and the terms are distributed greedily to the servers, then the last server would need to compute the permanent of a d-by-d matrix, which is #P-hard. The difficulty of distributing the terms limits the number of servers in [31,35] to be logarithmic in λ.

For the case $t = 1$, [27, Section 5.2] showed an alternative method of computing $x_1 \cdots x_d$ efficiently. The idea is essentially to first locally convert a CNF share into a Shamir share of the same secret, and then perform homomorphic evaluation on the Shamir share. We present here a generalization of the method for any $t < m$. Fix an arbitrary m-subset $\{\zeta_1,\ldots,\zeta_m\} \subseteq \mathbb{Z}_q$. Define the degree-$dt$ polynomial

$$p(Z) := \prod_{i=1}^{d} \sum_{\substack{\mathbf{u} \in \{0,1\}^m: \\ \mathsf{wt}(\mathbf{u})=t}} c_{i,\mathbf{u}} \prod_{j:u_j=1} (1 - Z/\zeta_j)$$

such that $p(0) = \prod_{i=1}^{d} \sum_{\substack{\mathbf{u} \in \{0,1\}^m: c_{i,\mathbf{u}} \\ \mathsf{wt}(\mathbf{u})=t}} = x_1 \cdots x_d$. Note that $p(\zeta_j)$ does not depend on the values of $c_{i,\mathbf{u}}$ where the j-th bit of $\mathbf{u}$ is 1, and can therefore be computed by the j-th server. Since the degree of p is $dt \leq m - 1$, $p(0)$ can be recovered by interpolating $p(\zeta_1),\ldots,p(\zeta_m)$.

In general, given an n-variate degree-d polynomial f, we can define

$$p_f(Z) := f\left(\sum_{\substack{\mathbf{u}\in\{0,1\}^m:\\ \mathsf{wt}(\mathbf{u})=t}} c_{1,\mathbf{u}}\prod_{j:u_j=1}(1-Z/\zeta_j),\ldots,\sum_{\substack{\mathbf{u}\in\{0,1\}^m:\\ \mathsf{wt}(\mathbf{u})=t}} c_{n,\mathbf{u}}\prod_{j:u_j=1}(1-Z/\zeta_j)\right).$$

The value $f(\mathbf{x})$ can be recovered by $f(\mathbf{x}) = p_f(0)$.

Generalized Scheme CNF_ℓ. In the above, the client is required to perform only a simple linear computation for recovery. We show that the computation of higher degree polynomials is possible, if the client is willing to perform a degree-ℓ computation for $\ell > 1$.

We first consider the naive strategy of distributing terms to servers, and discuss the interpolation-based approach later. In the former setting, it suffices to have that, for any fixed $\mathbf{u}_1,\ldots,\mathbf{u}_d \in \{0,1\}^m$ with $\mathsf{wt}(\mathbf{u}_i) = t$, there exists a server $j^* \in [m]$ and an index set I of size $|I| \geq d - \ell$ such that $u_{i,j^*} = 0$ for all $i \in I$. Server j^* can therefore compute $\prod_{i\in I} c_{i,\mathbf{u}_i}$, and leave the computation of $\prod_{i\in[d]\setminus I} c_{i,\mathbf{u}_i}$ to the output client. To compute the latter, the client would need to store locally a copy of all shares – the recovery information is the same as the input shares.

We argue that if $dt < (\ell+1)m$, then the above condition is satisfied. Suppose not, then for all $j \in [m]$, we have $|\{i \in [d] : u_{i,j} = 0\}| \leq d-\ell-1$. In other words, for all $j \in [m]$, we have $|\{i \in [d] : u_{i,j} = 1\}| \geq \ell+1$. Summing up the weights of all $\mathbf{u}_i$, we have $\sum_{i=1}^d \mathsf{wt}(\mathbf{u}_i) \geq (\ell+1)m$. By the pigeonhole principle, there must exist i^* such that

$$\mathsf{wt}(\mathbf{u}_{i^*}) \geq \frac{(\ell+1)m}{d} > \frac{(\ell+1)mt}{(\ell+1)m} = t$$

which is a contradiction as $\mathsf{wt}(\mathbf{u}_i) = t$ for all $i \in [d]$.

The CNF scheme suffers from many drawbacks. First, each input share consists of $\binom{m}{t}n$ $\mathbb{F}$ elements. It also suffers from inefficient evaluation, unless the interpolation-based evaluation is used, which makes it equivalent to the scheme presented in Sect. 4.2, except with larger input shares. Finally, the output share size is upper bounded by the number of monomials of degree at most ℓ over the variables $(c_{i,u})_{i\in[n],\mathbf{u}\in\{0,1\}^m:\mathsf{wt}(\mathbf{u})=t}$, i.e., $\binom{\binom{m}{t}n+\ell}{\ell} = O((m^t n)^\ell)$.

We next state the formal theorem about the CNF_ℓ scheme. Its proof is already written inline in the above discussion.

Theorem 3. *Let $d < \frac{(\ell+1)m}{t}$. The ℓ-th order CNF secret sharing scheme CNF_ℓ is an IT (n,m,t)-HSS for degree-d polynomials, with efficiency measures $(\rho,\alpha,\beta) = \left(m^t n, m^t n, (m^t n)^\ell\right)$.*

Similar to the $\ell = 0$ case, the above approach suffers in evaluation efficiency since there is no natural way to distribute the terms. Naturally, one would hope to use a generalization of the interpolation-based approach to achieve the same parameter $(d = \lfloor \frac{(\ell+1)m-1}{t} \rfloor)$. Indeed, in Sect. 4.2 we recall and generalize a technique by Woodruff and Yekhanin [37] of using partial derivatives and Hermite interpolation to support higher degree polynomials, which would also be applicable in CNF_ℓ. Since the resulting schemes, which we denote by WY_ℓ, are superior to CNF_ℓ in all parameters, we do not discuss applying the technique to CNF_ℓ in detail.

4.2 ℓ-th Order Woodruff-Yekhanin HSS

In an insightful work of Woodruff and Yekhanin [37], they constructed a PIR scheme which can be viewed as an (n, m, t)-HSS for degree-$\lfloor \frac{2m-1}{t} \rfloor$ polynomials, which we call the first-order Woodruff-Yekhanin HSS WY_1. The idea of the scheme is as follows.

First Order Scheme by Woodruff and Yekhanin. We begin with the sharing procedures of Shamir's scheme. To secret-share $\mathbf{x} \in \mathbb{F}^n$, the input client sample a random (vector valued) degree-t polynomial $\varphi(Z)$ so that $\varphi(0) = \mathbf{x}$. The j-th share is defined as $\mathbf{s}_j := \varphi(j)$. What differs from Shamir's scheme is that the input client also computes, as recovery information, the derivatives of φ evaluated at $j \in [m]$, denoted by $\varphi^{(1)}(j)$, $\varphi'(j)$, or $\frac{d\varphi}{dZ}(j)$.

To evaluate a polynomial f of degree $\lfloor \frac{2m-1}{t} \rfloor$ over a share $\mathbf{s}_j$, server j computes as in Shamir's scheme $f(\mathbf{s}_j) = f(\varphi(j))$. Additionally, it computes all partial derivatives of f evaluated at $\mathbf{s}_j$, denoted by $\left(\frac{\partial f}{\partial X_i}(\mathbf{s}_j) \right)_{i \in [n]}$. The j-th output share is defined as $y_j := \left(f(\mathbf{s}_j), \frac{\partial f}{\partial X_1}(\mathbf{s}_j), \dots, \frac{\partial f}{\partial X_n}(\mathbf{s}_j) \right)$.

Finally, to decode the output shares, the output client first recover $(f \circ \varphi)'(\mathbf{s}_j) = \frac{df \circ \varphi}{dZ}(\mathbf{s}_j)$ by using the chain rule of derivatives. Then, since $f \circ \varphi$ is a univariate polynomial of degree at most $2m - 1$, it is possible to recover $f(\varphi(0)) = f(x)$ from m points on $f \circ \varphi$ and m points on $(f \circ \varphi)'$ using Hermite interpolation.

The scheme of Woodruff and Yekhanin is balanced, meaning that both input and output shares consist of $O(n)$ $\mathbb{F}$ elements. The result can be seen as a trade-off between $\frac{m}{t}$ degrees and compactness, when compared to Shamir's scheme. If we view the sharing, evaluation, and decoding procedures of an HSS as one MPC protocol, then for a fixed input share size, a balanced HSS and a compact HSS would give MPC protocols with the same asymptotic communication complexity. In this sense, the extra $\frac{m}{t}$ degrees are gained for free.

Generalization to Higher Orders. Intuitively, a way to support polynomials of even higher degrees is to further sacrifice the output share size. The idea is to let the servers compute all partial derivatives of order at most ℓ, so that a polynomial of degree at most $d < \frac{(\ell+1)m}{t}$ can be supported. In a standalone application of the HSS, this would not make sense as it is "wasteful" to have a

$$WY_\ell.\text{Share}(\mathbf{x})$$

$\varphi \leftarrow (\mathbb{F}[Z])^n$ s.t. $\begin{cases}\deg(\varphi)=t \\ \varphi(0)=\mathbf{x}\end{cases}$

$\text{in}_j := \varphi(j), \forall j \in [m]$

$\text{rec}_j := \left(\varphi^{(u)}(j)\right)_{u\in[\ell]}$

$\textbf{return } \begin{pmatrix}\text{in}_1,\dots,\text{in}_m, \\ \text{rec}_1,\dots,\text{rec}_m\end{pmatrix}$

$$WY_\ell.\text{Eval}(j,f,\text{in}_j)$$

$\text{out}_j := \left(f(\mathbf{s}_j), f^{(\mathbf{e})}(\mathbf{s}_j)\right)_{\mathbf{e}\in\mathbb{N}_0^n:\text{wt}(\mathbf{e})\le\ell}$

$\textbf{return } \text{out}_j$

$$WY_\ell.\text{Dec}\begin{pmatrix}\text{out}_1,\dots,\text{out}_m, \\ \text{rec}_1,\dots,\text{rec}_m\end{pmatrix}$$

$\textbf{foreach } j\in[m], u\in[\ell] \textbf{ do}$

$\quad (f\circ\varphi)^{(u)}(\mathbf{s}_j)$

$\quad = \text{Faa-di-Bruno}[(\varphi^{(h)}(j))_{h\in[u]}]((f^{(\mathbf{e})}(\mathbf{s}_j))_{\mathbf{e}\in\mathbb{N}_0:\text{wt}(\mathbf{e})\le u})$

$y := \text{Hermite}((f(\mathbf{s}_j),(f\circ\varphi)^{(u)}(\mathbf{s}_j))_{j\in[m],u\in[\ell]})$

Fig. 3. The ℓ-th order Woodruff-Yekhanin HSS.

smaller input share size than the output share size. However, with the observation that, in our compiler constructed in Sect. 5, the output share size of the resulting HSS scheme is independent of that of the base scheme, sacrificing the output share size even more for the support of more degrees might be worth it. We therefore formalize this intuition in Fig. 3 and call the resulting scheme the ℓ-th order Woodruff-Yekhanin HSS, denoted by $WY_\ell.(\text{Share, Eval, Dec})$.

For $\mathbf{e} \in \mathbb{N}_0^n$, we use the notation $f^{(\mathbf{e})}(\mathbf{x})$ to denote the high-order partial derivative $\frac{\partial^{\text{wt}(\mathbf{e})}f}{\partial X_1^{e_1}\dots\partial X_n^{e_n}}$ evaluated at $\mathbf{x}$. For $u\in[\ell]$, we make use of a generalization of the Faa di Bruno formula [32] which expresses $(f\circ\varphi)^{(u)}(j)$ as a linear function of $(f^{(\mathbf{e})}(\mathbf{s}_j))_{\mathbf{e}\in\mathbb{N}_0^n:\text{wt}(\mathbf{e})\le u}$ with coefficients determined by degree-u polynomials of $(\varphi^{(h)}(j))_{h\in[u]}$. We denote this formula by

$$\text{Faa-di-Bruno}[(\varphi^{(h)}(j))_{h\in[u]}]((f^{(\mathbf{e})}(\mathbf{s}_j))_{\mathbf{e}\in\mathbb{N}_0:\text{wt}(\mathbf{e})\le u}).$$

Finally, we use the notation

$$\text{Hermite}((f(\mathbf{s}_j),(f\circ\varphi)^{(u)}(\mathbf{s}_j))_{j\in[m],u\in[\ell]})$$

to denote the value $f(\varphi(0))$ recovered using Hermite interpolation.

Theorem 4. Let $d < \frac{(\ell+1)m}{t}$. The ℓ-th order Woodruff-Yekhanin HSS WY_ℓ is an IT (n,m,t)-HSS for degree-d polynomials with efficiency measures $(\rho,\alpha,\beta) = (\ell n, n, n^\ell)$.

Proof. Input shares of WY_ℓ are just shares of the Shamir secret sharing scheme. Security thus follows immediately. More seriously, for any fixed t-subset of input shares $\{\text{in}_{j_1},\dots,\text{in}_{j_t}\}$ and any input $\mathbf{x}\in\mathbb{F}^n$, there exists a unique degree-t polynomial φ such that $\varphi(0)=\mathbf{x}$ and $\varphi(j)=\text{in}_j$ for all $j\in\{j_1,\dots,j_t\}$. The set $\{\text{in}_{j_1},\dots,\text{in}_{j_t}\}$ therefore contain no information about the true input.

The support of degree-d polynomials follows immediately from Hermite interpolation. Specifically, we note that the output client obtains the following $(\ell + 1)m$ data points:

$$(1, (f \circ \varphi)(1)) \quad \ldots \quad (m, (f \circ \varphi)(m))$$
$$(1, (f \circ \varphi)'(1)) \quad \ldots \quad (m, (f \circ \varphi)'(m))$$
$$\vdots \qquad \ddots \qquad \vdots$$
$$(1, (f \circ \varphi)^{(\ell)}(1)) \ldots (m, (f \circ \varphi)^{(\ell)}(m))$$

for a univariate degree-dt polynomial $f \circ \varphi$ and its derivatives. Since $dt \leq (\ell + 1)m - 1$ the client is able to recover $f(\mathbf{x}) = f(\varphi(0))$ using Hermite interpolation.

The size of a recovery information $\rho = \ell n$ and that of an input share $\alpha = n$ can be easily observed. For the size of an output share, observe that an output share consists of $\left(f(\mathbf{s}_j), f^{(\mathbf{e})}(\mathbf{s}_j)\right)_{\mathbf{e} \in \mathbb{N}_0^n : \mathsf{wt}(\mathbf{e}) \leq \ell}$. The set $\{\mathbf{e} \in \mathbb{N}_0^n : \mathsf{wt}(\mathbf{e}) \leq \ell\}$ counts the number of n-variate monomials of degree at most ℓ, and thus is of size $\binom{n+\ell}{\ell} = O(n^\ell)$. We thus have $\beta = n^\ell$.

Note that WY_0 is simply the Shamir secret sharing scheme.

Computational Complexity. We remark about the computational complexity of the servers and the output client. It is well-known, e.g., by the Baur-Strassen theorem [4] or in the field of auto-differentiation, that if a multivariate polynomial f can be computed by an arithmetic circuit of size denoted by $|f|$, then there exists a circuit of size $O(|f|)$ which computes f and all n first-order partial derivatives of f simultaneously. Applying this recursively to the n first-order partial derivatives suggests that the server computation is bounded by $O(|f| n^{\ell-1})$.

On the output client side, we note that

$$\mathsf{Faa\text{-}di\text{-}Bruno}[(\varphi^{(h)}(j))_{h \in [u]}]((f^{(\mathbf{e})}(\mathbf{s}_j))_{\mathbf{e} \in \mathbb{N}_0 : \mathsf{wt}(\mathbf{e}) \leq u})$$

is a linear function with $\binom{n+u}{u} \leq \binom{n+\ell}{\ell}$ terms, where each coefficient is a degree-u polynomial with at most $\binom{2u}{u} \leq \binom{2\ell}{\ell}$ terms. The output client needs to evaluate ℓm of these. Lastly, the Hermite interpolation is a linear function with $(\ell + 1)m$ terms. Therefore, the output client computation is bounded by $O\left(\ell m \cdot \binom{n+\ell}{\ell} \cdot \binom{2\ell}{\ell}\right) = O\left(\ell m (\ell n)^\ell\right)$. For the cases of $\ell = 1$ or $\ell = 2$, the output client computation is $O(mn)$ and $O(mn^2)$ respectively.

Preprocessing. In the Share algorithm of WY_ℓ, a degree-t polynomial φ is sampled such that the input $\mathbf{x}$ is encoded as $\varphi(0) = \mathbf{x}$. Note that φ is not determined until $t+1$ points on it or its derivatives are fixed. We can therefore exploit this property and push the sampling of $p \leq \frac{t}{\ell+1}$ shares and their corresponding recovery information, which in total consist of $p(\ell + 1) \leq t < t + 1$ points, to a preprocessing phase.

$$
\begin{array}{|ll|}
\hline
\end{array}
$$

$\mathsf{WY}_\ell.\mathsf{PreProc}(1^n)$	$\mathsf{WY}_\ell.\mathsf{ShareComp}\left(\begin{array}{l}\mathsf{in}_1,\ldots,\mathsf{in}_p,\\ \mathsf{rec}_1,\ldots,\mathsf{rec}_p,\end{array}\mathbf{x}\right)$

$p := \left\lfloor \dfrac{t}{\ell+1} \right\rfloor$

$\mathbf{s}_{0,j} \leftarrow \mathbb{F}^n, \ \forall j \in [p]$

$\mathbf{s}_{u,j} \leftarrow \mathbb{F}^n, \ \forall j \in [p], \forall u \in [\ell]$

$\mathsf{in}_j := \mathbf{s}_{0,j}, \ \forall j \in [p]$

$\mathsf{rec}_j := (\mathbf{s}_{u,j})_{j \in [p], u \in [\ell]}$

$\mathbf{return} \ \left(\begin{array}{l}\mathsf{in}_1,\ldots,\mathsf{in}_p,\\ \mathsf{rec}_1,\ldots,\mathsf{rec}_p\end{array}\right)$

// Sample φ by Hermite interpolation.

$\varphi \leftarrow (\mathbb{F}[Z])^n \ \text{s.t.} \ \begin{cases} \deg(\varphi) = t \\ \varphi(0) = \mathbf{x} \\ \varphi(j) = \mathbf{s}_{0,j} & \forall j \in [p] \\ \varphi^{(u)}(j) = \mathbf{s}_{u,j} & \forall j \in [p] \ \forall u \in [\ell] \end{cases}$

$\mathsf{in}_j := \varphi(j), \forall j \in [m] \setminus [p]$

$\mathsf{rec}_j := \left(\varphi^{(u)}(j)\right)_{j \in [p], u \in [\ell]}$

$\mathbf{return} \ \left(\begin{array}{l}\mathsf{in}_{p+1},\ldots,\mathsf{in}_m,\\ \mathsf{rec}_{p+1},\ldots,\mathsf{rec}_m\end{array}\right)$

Fig. 4. $\left\lfloor \frac{t}{\ell+1} \right\rfloor$-Preprocessing of the ℓ-th order Woodruff-Yekhanin HSS.

Theorem 5. *Let $p \le \frac{t}{\ell+1}$. The ℓ-th order Woodruff-Yekhanin HSS WY_ℓ supports p-preprocessing.*

Proof. We show that WY_ℓ supports p-preprocessing by constructing the algorithms $\mathsf{WY}_\ell.(\mathsf{PreProc}, \mathsf{ShareComp})$ in Fig. 4.

5 Compiler from IT HSS to HSS Using HE

For $d < (k+1)m$ and $m = O(\log \lambda)$, Lai, Malavolta, and Schröder [31] proposed an $(n, m, 1)$-HSS scheme for degree-d polynomials based on any k-HE scheme. Generalizing their approach, we present a compiler based on homomorphic encryption from IT HSS to HSS. Our compiler makes use of the following elementary observation. Let $f(\mathbf{X})$ be a ρ-variate degree-ℓ polynomial. For any $0 \le k \le \ell$, note that $f(\mathbf{X})$ can be written as

$$
f(\mathbf{X}) = \sum_{\substack{\mathbf{e} \in \mathbb{N}_0^\rho: \\ \mathsf{wt}(\mathbf{e}) \le \ell-k}} \mathbf{X}^{\mathbf{e}} f_{\mathbf{e}}(\mathbf{X})
$$

where $f_{\mathbf{e}}(\mathbf{X})$ is a ρ-variate degree-k polynomial. Note that $|\{\mathbf{e} \in \mathbb{N}_0^\rho : \mathsf{wt}(\mathbf{e}) \le \ell - k\}|$ is the number of ρ-variate monomials of degree at most $\ell - k$, and can be computed by $\binom{\rho+\ell-k}{\ell-k} = O(\rho^{\ell-k})$.

5.1 The Compiler

Let IT-HSS.$(\mathsf{Share}, \mathsf{Eval}, \mathsf{Dec})$ be a an IT (n, m, t)-HSS for degree-d polynomials with the following properties:

- The recovery information rec_j is a vector $\mathbf{r}_j \in \mathbb{F}^\rho$ for all $j \in [m]$.
- The output share in_j is a vector $\mathbf{y}_j \in \mathbb{F}^\beta$ for all $j \in [m]$.

$$
\begin{array}{l}
\underline{\text{HSS.KGen}(1^\lambda)} \\[4pt]
(\text{pk}, \text{sk}) \leftarrow \text{HE.KGen}(1^\lambda) \\
\textbf{return } (\text{pk}, \text{sk})
\end{array}
$$

$$
\begin{array}{l}
\underline{\text{HSS.Share}(\text{pk}, \mathbf{x})} \\[4pt]
\begin{pmatrix} \text{in}_1, \dots, \text{in}_m, \\ \mathbf{r}_1, \dots, \mathbf{r}_m \end{pmatrix} \leftarrow \text{IT-HSS.Share}(\mathbf{x}) \\[6pt]
\tilde{\mathbf{r}}_j \leftarrow \text{HE.Enc}(\text{pk}, \mathbf{r}_j), \ \forall j \in [m] \\
\text{in}'_j := (\tilde{\mathbf{r}}_j, \text{in}_j), \ \forall j \in [m] \\
\textbf{if } h > 0 \textbf{ then} \\
\quad \text{rec}_j := \mathbf{r}_j, \ \forall j \in [m] \\
\textbf{return } \begin{pmatrix} \text{in}'_1, \dots, \text{in}'_m \\ \text{rec}_1, \dots, \text{rec}_m \end{pmatrix}
\end{array}
$$

$$
\begin{array}{l}
\underline{\text{HSS.Eval}(\text{pk}, j, f, \text{in}'_j)} \\[4pt]
\mathbf{y}_j \leftarrow \text{IT-HSS.Eval}(j, f, \text{in}_j) \\
\textbf{foreach } \mathbf{e} \in \mathbb{N}_0^\rho : \text{wt}(\mathbf{e}) \le \ell - k \textbf{ do} \\
\quad \tilde{d}_{\mathbf{e},j} \leftarrow \text{HE.Eval}\left(\sum_{b=1}^{\beta} y_{j,b} \cdot \text{Dec}_{\mathbf{e},j,b}, \tilde{\mathbf{r}}_j \right) \\
\textbf{return } \text{out}'_j := (\tilde{d}_{\mathbf{e},j})_{\mathbf{e} \in \mathbb{N}_0^\rho : \text{wt}(\mathbf{e}) \le \ell - k}
\end{array}
$$

$$
\begin{array}{l}
\underline{\text{HSS.Dec}\left(\text{sk}, \begin{array}{l} \text{out}'_1, \dots, \text{out}'_m \\ \text{rec}_1, \dots, \text{rec}_m \end{array} \right)} \\[8pt]
\textbf{foreach } \mathbf{e} \in \mathbb{N}_0^\rho : \text{wt}(\mathbf{e}) \le \ell - k, j \in [m] \textbf{ do} \\
\quad d_{\mathbf{e},j} \leftarrow \text{Dec}(\text{sk}, \tilde{d}_{\mathbf{e},j}) \\
y := \sum_{\substack{\mathbf{e} \in \mathbb{N}_0^\rho: \\ \text{wt}(\mathbf{e}) \le \ell - k}} \sum_{j=1}^{m} \mathbf{r}_j^{\mathbf{e}} d_{\mathbf{e},j} \\
\textbf{return } y
\end{array}
$$

Fig. 5. Compiler from IT-HSS to HSS based on HE.

- The decoding algorithm $\text{IT-HSS.Dec}(\mathbf{y}_1, \dots, \mathbf{y}_m, \mathbf{r}_1, \dots, \mathbf{r}_m)$ is a linear function of $(\mathbf{y}_1, \dots, \mathbf{y}_m)$, where the coefficient of $\mathbf{y}_j$ is computed by a degree-ℓ polynomial of $\mathbf{r}_j$, where $\ell \ge k$. More concretely,

$$
\text{IT-HSS.Dec}(\mathbf{y}_1, \dots, \mathbf{y}_m, \mathbf{r}_1, \dots, \mathbf{r}_m)
$$

$$
= \sum_{j=1}^{m} \sum_{b=1}^{\beta} y_{j,b} \cdot \text{Dec}_{j,b}(\mathbf{r}_j)
$$

where $\text{Dec}_{j,b}$ is a degree-ℓ polynomial of $\mathbf{r}_j$

$$
= \sum_{\substack{\mathbf{e} \in \mathbb{N}_0^\rho: \\ \text{wt}(\mathbf{e}) \le \ell - k}} \sum_{j=1}^{m} \mathbf{r}_j^{\mathbf{e}} \sum_{b=1}^{\beta} y_{j,b} \cdot \text{Dec}_{\mathbf{e},j,b}(\mathbf{r}_j)
$$

where $\text{Dec}_{\mathbf{e},j,b}$ is a degree-k polynomial of $\mathbf{r}_j$.

The idea of the compiler is to delegate the computation of $\sum_{b=1}^{\beta} y_{j,b} \cdot \text{Dec}_{\mathbf{e},j,b}(\mathbf{r}_j)$ to server j by encrypting r_j with a homomorphic encryption scheme HE which supports the evaluation of degree-k polynomials. Formally, we construct an (n, m, t)-HSS for degree-d polynomials, denoted HSS.(KGen, Share, Eval, Dec), in Fig. 5.

Note that when $k = \ell$ the decoding function is simply

$$\text{IT-HSS.Dec}(\mathbf{y}_1, \ldots, \mathbf{y}_m, \mathbf{r}_1, \ldots, \mathbf{r}_m) = \sum_{j=1}^{m} \sum_{b=1}^{\beta} y_{j,b} \cdot \text{Dec}_{\mathbf{e},j,b}(\mathbf{r}_j).$$

In this case the input client does not need to store a local copy of the recovery information.

Theorem 6. *Let* IT-HSS *be an* (n, m, t)-*HSS for degree-d polynomials satisfying the above properties, and* HE *be a CPA-secure k-HE scheme, then* HSS *is an* (n, m, t)-*HSS for degree-d polynomials. If* IT-HSS *and* HE *are correct, then* HSS *is correct. If* IT-HSS *has the efficiency measures* (ρ, α, β), *then* HSS *has the efficiency measures* $(\rho', \alpha', \beta') = (\rho, \rho + \alpha, \rho^{\ell-k})$. *If* $k = \ell$, *then* $\rho' = 0$. *Note that* β' *is independent of* β.

Proof. The correctness of HSS is already proven in-line in the above discussion.

For security, note that an input share in'_j consists of an input share in_j of the underlying IT HSS scheme and an HE ciphertext $\tilde{r}_j$. We can thus prove security by a simple hybrid argument, where we consider an intermediate hybrid security experiment where the ciphertexts $\tilde{r}_j$ are replaced by ciphertexts encrypting zeros. Clearly, this hybrid experiment is indistinguishable from the security experiment for HSS, based on the CPA-security of HE. Next, we observe that the environment of the hybrid experiment can be simulated perfectly using an adversary against the security of the underlying IT HSS scheme. We can therefore conclude that the advantage of any (unbounded) adversaries in the hybrid experiment is identical to that against the security of the underlying IT HSS scheme, which is negligible.

The correctness of ρ' and α' follows from simple observations. For the correctness of β', we observe that an output share consists of $(\tilde{d}_{\mathbf{e},j})_{\mathbf{e} \in \mathbb{N}_0^{\rho}: \text{wt}(\mathbf{e}) \leq \ell-k}$, where each $\tilde{d}_{\mathbf{e},j}$ is of fixed $\text{poly}(\lambda)$ size since HE is assumed to be compact. Note that the index set $\{\mathbf{e} \in \mathbb{N}_0^{\rho} : \text{wt}(\mathbf{e}) \leq \ell - k\}$ is of size $\binom{\rho+\ell-k}{\ell-k} = O(\rho^{\ell-k})$.

5.2 Computation Complexity

The computation complexity of the compiled scheme depends on that of the base scheme. Suppose that the base scheme has server computation σ. We also assume that HE.Dec() can be computed in $\text{poly}(\lambda)$ time, and HE.Eval$(f, \cdot)$ can be computed in time $|f| \cdot \text{poly}(\lambda)$. Then, the server computation of the compiled scheme is

$$\sigma' = \sigma + \beta \binom{\rho+\ell-k}{\ell-k} \binom{\rho+k}{k} \cdot \text{poly}(\lambda) = \sigma + \beta \cdot \rho^{\ell} \cdot \text{poly}(\lambda),$$

and the client computation is $\gamma' = \binom{\rho+\ell-k}{\ell-k} m \cdot \text{poly}(\lambda) = \rho^{\ell-k} \cdot m \cdot \text{poly}(\lambda)$.

$$
\begin{array}{|ll|}
\hline
\textsf{HSS.PreProc(pk)} & \textsf{HSS.ShareComp}(\textsf{pk}, r', s'_1, \ldots, s'_p, x) \\
\hline
\end{array}
$$

HSS.PreProc(pk)	HSS.ShareComp(pk, $r', s'_1, \ldots, s'_p, x$)
$\begin{pmatrix} \mathsf{in}_1, \ldots, \mathsf{in}_p, \\ \mathbf{r}_1, \ldots, \mathbf{r}_p \end{pmatrix} \leftarrow$ IT-HSS.PreProc(1^n)	$\begin{pmatrix} \mathsf{in}_{p+1}, \ldots, \mathsf{in}_m \\ \mathbf{r}_{p+1}, \ldots, \mathbf{r}_m \end{pmatrix} \leftarrow$ IT-HSS.ShareComp $\begin{pmatrix} \mathsf{in}_1, \ldots, \mathsf{in}_p, \\ \mathbf{r}_1, \ldots, \mathbf{r}_p, \end{pmatrix} x$
$\tilde{\mathbf{r}}_j \leftarrow$ HE.Enc(pk, $\mathbf{r}_j$), $\forall j \in [p]$	$\tilde{\mathbf{r}}_j \leftarrow$ HE.Enc(pk, $\mathbf{r}_j$), $\forall j \in [m] \setminus [p]$
$\mathsf{in}'_j := (\tilde{\mathbf{r}}_j, \mathsf{in}_j)$, $\forall j \in [p]$	$\mathsf{in}'_j := (\tilde{\mathbf{r}}_j, \mathsf{in}_j)$, $\forall j \in [m] \setminus [p]$
if $h > 0$ then	if $h > 0$ then
$\quad \mathsf{rec}'_j := \mathbf{r}_j$, $\forall j \in [p]$	$\quad \mathsf{rec}'_j := \mathbf{r}_j$, $\forall j \in [m] \setminus [p]$
return $\begin{pmatrix} \mathsf{in}'_1, \ldots, \mathsf{in}'_p \\ \mathsf{rec}'_1, \ldots, \mathsf{rec}'_p \end{pmatrix}$	return $\begin{pmatrix} \mathsf{in}'_{p+1}, \ldots, \mathsf{in}'_m \\ \mathsf{rec}'_{p+1}, \ldots, \mathsf{rec}'_m \end{pmatrix}$

Fig. 6. p-Preprocessing of the Compiler from IT-HSS to HSS based on HE.

5.3 Preprocessing

We show that if the base scheme IT-HSS supports p-preprocessing and satisfies certain additional properties, then HSS p-preprocessing.

Theorem 7. *If* IT-HSS *supports p-preprocessing, then so does* HSS.

Proof. We construct the algorithms HSS.(PreProc, ShareComp) in Fig. 6.

5.4 Instantiations

Both CNF_ℓ and WY_ℓ constructed in Sect. 4 satisfy the properties required by the compiler. The main HSS scheme in [31] can be seen as the result of applying the k-HE-based compiler on the CNF_ℓ scheme in the setting with $k = \ell$. Lai, Malavolta, and Schröder [31] discussed the setting with $t > 1$, but did not provide any concrete schemes. A constructive version for general $t \geq 1$ was proposed in [35]. The approach of compiling CNF_ℓ gives concrete schemes and significantly simplifies the analysis in [31] (*c.f.*, Sect. 4.1).

As discussed in Sect. 4, CNF_ℓ is almost strictly inferior to WY_ℓ. We therefore focus on the instantiations with a linearly-homomorphic HE ($k = 1$) and the ℓ-th order Woodruff-Yekhanin IT-HSS WY_ℓ which has efficiency measures $(\rho, \alpha, \beta) = (\ell n, n, n^\ell)$ and supports polynomials of degree $d < \frac{(\ell+1)m}{t}$. When $\ell = 1$, we obtain a compact HSS with efficiency measures $(\rho', \alpha', \beta') = (0, n, 1)$ supporting polynomials of degree $d < \frac{2m}{t}$, where decoding is linear. When $\ell = 2$, we obtain a balanced HSS with efficiency measures $(\rho', \alpha', \beta') = (mn, n, n)$ supporting polynomials of degree $d < \frac{3m}{t}$, where decoding is quadratic.

6 Application to MPC with Preprocessing

In the following we show an application of HSS to multi-party computation (MPC) with preprocessing. Specifically, we show how to generically construc-tion an m-party MPC protocol for degree-d polynomials resistant against the corruption of t parties, assuming the existence of an $(n, m+p, t)$-HSS for degree-d polynomials that supports p-preprocessing. A similar result for the restricted case of 2 parties was given (implicitly) in [5]. The salient point of our construction is that the online communication complexity of the MPC scheme is independent of the size of the polynomial being computed. For certain regimes of parameters, this leads to an exponential improvement in the communication complexity of the online phase, when compared with general-purpose MPC solutions.

6.1   Protocol Description

In the following we describe our (semi-honest) MPC protocol for degree-d polynomials assuming the existence of a $(n, m + p, t)$-HSS scheme with perfect correctness and a general purpose (semi-honest) m-party MPC that is resilient against the corruption of up to t parties. For a definition of MPC and its notion of simulation-based semi-honest security, we refer to [24]. The scheme is detailed below.

Preprocessing: We assume that the (input-independent) preprocessing phase is run by a trusted party, which can be substituted by an execution of a general-purpose MPC protocol jointly executed by the m participants. The preprocessing phase proceeds as follows.

1. Generate a key for the HSS scheme via $(\mathsf{pk}, \mathsf{sk}) \leftarrow \mathsf{HSS.KGen}(1^\lambda)$.
2. Run $\mathsf{HSS.PreProc}(\mathsf{pk}, 1^n)$ to obtain $(\mathsf{in}_1, \dots, \mathsf{in}_p, \mathsf{rec}_1, \dots, \mathsf{rec}_p)$.
3. Run $\mathsf{HSS.Eval}(\mathsf{pk}, j, f, \mathsf{in}_j)$ to obtain out_j, for all $j \in [p]$.
4. Let s be the concatenation of the variables $(\mathsf{sk}, \mathsf{in}_1, \mathsf{rec}_1, \mathsf{out}_1, \dots, \mathsf{in}_p, \mathsf{rec}_p, \mathsf{out}_p)$ as defined above. The preprocessing algorithm computes an t-out-of-m[5] secret sharing of s and returns to each party the public key pk and the j-th share s_j.

Online: The online phase is jointly executed by the m participants, who collectively receive the inputs $\mathbf{x}$, *i.e.*, either $\mathbf{x}$ is secret shared among the m participants or each participant has knowledge of a disjoint subset of entries of $\mathbf{x}$. The j-th party inputs the j-th output of the preprocessing phase (pk, s_j) and its share of $\mathbf{x}$. The parties jointly compute the following function using a general-purpose MPC protocol. For simplicity we assume that the function takes as input the variable s as defined in the preprocessing, which can be obtained by running the reconstruction procedure of the t-out-of-m secret sharing scheme.

1. Run $\mathsf{HSS.ShareComp}(\mathsf{in}_1, \dots, \mathsf{in}_p, \mathsf{rec}_1, \dots, \mathsf{rec}_p, \mathbf{x})$ to obtain the tuple $(\mathsf{in}_{p+1}, \dots, \mathsf{in}_{m+p}, \mathsf{rec}_{p+1}, \dots, \mathsf{rec}_{m+p})$.
2. The j-th participant is given in_{p+j} and an t-out-of-m secret share of $\tilde{s} = (\mathsf{rec}_{p+1}, \dots, \mathsf{rec}_{m+p})$.

---

[5] We use t-out-of-m secret sharing to refer to an m-party secret sharing scheme which is resilient against t corrupt parties.

The j-th party locally computes $\mathsf{HSS.Eval}(\mathsf{pk}, p + j, f, \mathsf{in}_{p+j})$ to obtain out_{p+j}. Then the m parties engage once again in a general-purpose MPC on input the secret key sk, the output shares $(\mathsf{out}_1, \dots, \mathsf{out}_{m+p})$, and the reconstruction information $(\mathsf{rec}_1, \dots, \mathsf{rec}_{m+p})$. Whenever some information is not available to any party in plain, the MPC protocol reconstructs it from the shares.

1. Run $\mathsf{HSS.Dec}(\mathsf{sk}, \mathsf{out}_1, \dots, \mathsf{out}_{m+p}, \mathsf{rec}_1, \dots, \mathsf{rec}_{m+p}))$ and return the output to all parties.

6.2   Analysis

The security of the MPC protocol follows from a standard argument, which we sketch in the following. Observe that the view of the parties consist of the public key of the HSS scheme together with HSS shares of the input $\mathbf{x}$ and the t-out-of-m secret sharing of the variables s and $\tilde{s}$. By the semi-honest security of the MPC protocol, the MPC transcript does not reveal anything beyond the output of the computation. Thus the t-out-of-m security of the resulting MPC follows by a reduction against the HSS scheme (observe that the variables s and $\tilde{s}$ are information-theoretically hidden from the eyes of any t-subset of the participants).

We analyze the communication complexity of our protocol when instantiating the general-purpose MPC with any OT-based protocol (e.g. [25]) and the HSS scheme with k-HE-compiled variant of WY_ℓ described in Sect. 5. To reduce cluttering, we assume that t and $1 \le k \le \ell$ are constants, e.g., $t = 1$, $k = 1$, and $\ell = 1$ or 2. Recall that (compiled) WY_ℓ supports $\left\lfloor \frac{t}{\ell+1} \right\rfloor$-preprocessing. We therefore set $p = \left\lfloor \frac{t}{\ell+1} \right\rfloor = O(1)$. The communication complexity of the preprocessing phase is upper bounded by

$$(|\mathsf{HSS.KGen}| + |\mathsf{HSS.PreProc}| + p|\mathsf{HSS.Eval}(\cdot, \cdot, f, \cdot)|) \cdot \mathsf{poly}(\lambda)$$
$$= \left(1 + \ell \cdot n \cdot p + p(|f|n^{\ell-1} + (\ell n^2)^\ell)\right) \cdot \mathsf{poly}(\lambda)$$
$$= (|f|n^{\ell-1} + n^{2\ell}) \cdot \mathsf{poly}(\lambda).$$

On the other hand, the online communication is upper bounded by

$$(|\mathsf{HSS.ShareComp}| + |\mathsf{HSS.Dec}|) \cdot \mathsf{poly}(\lambda)$$
$$= \left(p \cdot nt + m(\ell \cdot n)^{\ell-k}\right) \cdot \mathsf{poly}(\lambda)$$
$$= mn^{\ell-k} \cdot \mathsf{poly}(\lambda).$$

In case t is a multiple of $\ell + 1$, the protocol allows the participants to jointly evaluate a degree d multivariate polynomial where $d < \frac{(\ell+1)m}{t} + 1$, i.e., we gain 1 degree compared to using the k-HE-compiled WY_ℓ scheme as-is. The size of the circuit representation of such a polynomial ranges from a constant to $O(n^d)$. Thus for large enough m, the communication complexity of the online phase is exponentially smaller than that of a naive implementation using a general-purpose MPC protocol. We stress that this result is obtained without relying on heavy machinery, such as fully-homomorphic encryption.

7   Conclusion

With the conceptual observation that the HSS scheme of [31] can be abstractly seen as compiling the CNF IT HSS using a k-HE, in this work we have constructed a generic compiler which turns a class of compatible IT HSS for degree-d polynomials into a computational one with more favourable parameters.

A generic compiler has many advantages. For starters, it allows instantiation with WY, which, unlike CNF, scales well with a large number of servers. In contrast, [31] using CNF becomes exponentially inefficient. Due to degree-amplification, this improvement is significant in practice as higher degrees can be supported by simply employing more servers. The preprocessing property of WY also allows application to preprocessing MPC, which was not possible with [31]. Other choices of instantiating the IT-HSS and k-HE potentially yield further improvements.

Acknowledgment. Yuval Ishai is supported by ERC Project NTSC (742754), ISF grant 2774/20, NSF-BSF grant 2015782, and BSF grant 2018393. Russell W. F. Lai is supported by the State of Bavaria at the Nuremberg Campus of Technology (NCT) – a research cooperation between the Friedrich-Alexander-Universität Erlangen-Nürnberg (FAU) and the Technische Hochschule Nürnberg Georg Simon Ohm (THN).

References

1. Akavia, A., Feldman, D., Shaul, H.: Secure search via multi-ring fully homomorphic encryption. IACR Cryptology ePrint Archive 2018/245 (2018)
2. Akavia, A., Gentry, C., Halevi, S., Leibovich, M.: Setup-free secure search on encrypted data: faster and post-processing free. Proc. Privacy Enhancing Technol. **2019**(3), 87–107 (2019)
3. Barkol, O., Ishai, Y.: Secure computation of constant-depth circuits with applications to database search problems. In: Shoup, V. (ed.) CRYPTO 2005. LNCS, vol. 3621, pp. 395–411. Springer, Heidelberg (2005). https://doi.org/10.1007/11535218_24
4. Baur, W., Strassen, V.: The complexity of partial derivatives. Theor. Comput. Sci. **22**(3), 317–330 (1983). https://doi.org/10.1016/0304-3975(83)90110-X
5. Beimel, A., Ishai, Y., Kumaresan, R., Kushilevitz, E.: On the cryptographic complexity of the worst functions. In: Lindell, Y. (ed.) TCC 2014. LNCS, vol. 8349, pp. 317–342. Springer, Heidelberg (2014). https://doi.org/10.1007/978-3-642-54242-8_14
6. Boneh, D., Gentry, C., Halevi, S., Wang, F., Wu, D.J.: Private database queries using somewhat homomorphic encryption. In: Jacobson, M., Locasto, M., Mohassel, P., Safavi-Naini, R. (eds.) ACNS 2013. LNCS, vol. 7954, pp. 102–118. Springer, Heidelberg (2013). https://doi.org/10.1007/978-3-642-38980-1_7
7. Boneh, D., Goh, E.-J., Nissim, K.: Evaluating 2-DNF formulas on ciphertexts. In: Kilian, J. (ed.) TCC 2005. LNCS, vol. 3378, pp. 325–341. Springer, Heidelberg (2005). https://doi.org/10.1007/978-3-540-30576-7_18
8. Bost, R., Popa, R.A., Tu, S., Goldwasser, S.: Machine learning classification over encrypted data. In: NDSS, vol. 4324, p. 4325 (2015)

9. Boyle, E., Couteau, G., Gilboa, N., Ishai, Y., Kohl, L., Scholl, P.: Efficient pseudorandom correlation generators: silent OT extension and more. In: Boldyreva, A., Micciancio, D. (eds.) CRYPTO 2019, Part III. LNCS, vol. 11694, pp. 489–518. Springer, Cham (2019). https://doi.org/10.1007/978-3-030-26954-8_16

10. Boyle, E., Gilboa, N., Ishai, Y.: Breaking the circuit size barrier for secure computation under DDH. In: Robshaw, M., Katz, J. (eds.) CRYPTO 2016, Part I. LNCS, vol. 9814, pp. 509–539. Springer, Heidelberg (2016). https://doi.org/10.1007/978-3-662-53018-4_19

11. Boyle, E., Gilboa, N., Ishai, Y.: Secure computation with preprocessing via function secret sharing. In: Hofheinz, D., Rosen, A. (eds.) TCC 2019, Part I. LNCS, vol. 11891, pp. 341–371. Springer, Cham (2019). https://doi.org/10.1007/978-3-030-36030-6_14

12. Boyle, E., Gilboa, N., Ishai, Y., Lin, H., Tessaro, S.: Foundations of homomorphic secret sharing. In: Karlin, A.R. (ed.) ITCS 2018, vol. 94, pp. 21:1–21:21. LIPIcs, January 2018. https://doi.org/10.4230/LIPIcs.ITCS.2018.21

13. Boyle, E., Kohl, L., Scholl, P.: Homomorphic secret sharing from lattices without FHE. In: Ishai, Y., Rijmen, V. (eds.) EUROCRYPT 2019, Part II. LNCS, vol. 11477, pp. 3–33. Springer, Cham (2019). https://doi.org/10.1007/978-3-030-17656-3_1

14. Castagnos, G., Laguillaumie, F.: Linearly homomorphic encryption from DDH. In: Nyberg, K. (ed.) CT-RSA 2015. LNCS, vol. 9048, pp. 487–505. Springer, Cham (2015). https://doi.org/10.1007/978-3-319-16715-2_26

15. Catalano, D., Fiore, D.: Using linearly-homomorphic encryption to evaluate degree-2 functions on encrypted data. In: Ray, I., Li, N., Kruegel, C. (eds.) ACM CCS 2015, pp. 1518–1529. ACM Press, October 2015. https://doi.org/10.1145/2810103.2813624

16. Cheon, J.H., Kim, M., Lauter, K.: Homomorphic computation of edit distance. In: Brenner, M., Christin, N., Johnson, B., Rohloff, K. (eds.) FC 2015. LNCS, vol. 8976, pp. 194–212. Springer, Heidelberg (2015). https://doi.org/10.1007/978-3-662-48051-9_15

17. Couteau, G.: A note on the communication complexity of multiparty computation in the correlated randomness model. In: Ishai, Y., Rijmen, V. (eds.) EUROCRYPT 2019, Part II. LNCS, vol. 11477, pp. 473–503. Springer, Cham (2019). https://doi.org/10.1007/978-3-030-17656-3_17

18. Dachman-Soled, D., Malkin, T., Raykova, M., Yung, M.: Secure efficient multiparty computing of multivariate polynomials and applications. In: Lopez, J., Tsudik, G. (eds.) ACNS 2011. LNCS, vol. 6715, pp. 130–146. Springer, Heidelberg (2011). https://doi.org/10.1007/978-3-642-21554-4_8

19. Damgård, I., Jurik, M.: A generalisation, a simplification and some applications of Paillier's probabilistic public-key system. In: Kim, K. (ed.) PKC 2001. LNCS, vol. 1992, pp. 119–136. Springer, Heidelberg (2001). https://doi.org/10.1007/3-540-44586-2_9

20. Diffie, W., Hellman, M.E.: New directions in cryptography. IEEE Trans. Inf. Theory 22(6), 644–654 (1976)

21. ElGamal, T.: A public key cryptosystem and a signature scheme based on discrete logarithms. IEEE Trans. Inf. Theory 31, 469–472 (1985)

22. Franklin, M., Mohassel, P.: Efficient and secure evaluation of multivariate polynomials and applications. In: Zhou, J., Yung, M. (eds.) ACNS 2010. LNCS, vol. 6123, pp. 236–254. Springer, Heidelberg (2010). https://doi.org/10.1007/978-3-642-13708-2_15

23. Gentry, C.: Fully homomorphic encryption using ideal lattices. In: Mitzenmacher, M. (ed.) 41st ACM STOC, pp. 169–178. ACM Press, May/June 2009. https://doi. org/10.1145/1536414.1536440
24. Goldreich, O.: Foundations of Cryptography: vol. 2, 1st edn. Basic Applications. Cambridge University Press, New York (2009)
25. Goldreich, O., Micali, S., Wigderson, A.: How to prove all NP statements in zero-knowledge and a methodology of cryptographic protocol design (extended abstract). In: Odlyzko, A.M. (ed.) CRYPTO 1986. LNCS, vol. 263, pp. 171–185. Springer, Heidelberg (1987). https://doi.org/10.1007/3-540-47721-7_11
26. Graepel, T., Lauter, K., Naehrig, M.: ML confidential: machine learning on encrypted data. In: Kwon, T., Lee, M.-K., Kwon, D. (eds.) ICISC 2012. LNCS, vol. 7839, pp. 1–21. Springer, Heidelberg (2013). https://doi.org/10.1007/978-3-642-37682-5_1
27. Harsha, P., Ishai, Y., Kilian, J., Nissim, K., Venkatesh, S.: Communication vs. computation. Comput. Complex. 16(1), 1–33 (2007). https://doi.org/10.1007/s00037-007-0224-y10.1007/s00037-007-0224-y
28. Ishai, Y., Kushilevitz, E.: Improved upper bounds on information-theoretic private information retrieval (extended abstract). In: 31st ACM STOC, pp. 79–88. ACM Press, May 1999. https://doi.org/10.1145/301250.301275
29. Ito, M., Saito, A., Nishizeki, T.: Secret sharing schemes realizing general access structure. In: Proceedings of IEEE Global Telecommunication Conference (Globecom 1987), pp. 99–102 (1987)
30. Kopparty, S., Saraf, S., Yekhanin, S.: High-rate codes with sublinear-time decoding. In: Fortnow, L., Vadhan, S.P. (eds.) 43rd ACM STOC, pp. 167–176. ACM Press, June 2011. https://doi.org/10.1145/1993636.1993660
31. Lai, R.W.F., Malavolta, G., Schröder, D.: Homomorphic secret sharing for low degree polynomials. In: Peyrin, T., Galbraith, S. (eds.) ASIACRYPT 2018, Part III. LNCS, vol. 11274, pp. 279–309. Springer, Cham (2018). https://doi.org/10.1007/978-3-030-03332-3_11
32. Mishkov, R.: Generalization of the formula of Faa di Bruno for a composite function with a vector argument. Int. J. Math. Math. Sci. 24, 481–491 (2000)
33. Naehrig, M., Lauter, K.E., Vaikuntanathan, V.: Can homomorphic encryption be practical? In: Proceedings of the 3rd ACM Cloud Computing Security Workshop, CCSW 2011, pp. 113–124. ACM (2011). https://dl.acm.org/citation.cfm?id=2046682
34. Paillier, P.: Public-key cryptosystems based on composite degree residuosity classes. In: Stern, J. (ed.) EUROCRYPT 1999. LNCS, vol. 1592, pp. 223–238. Springer, Heidelberg (1999). https://doi.org/10.1007/3-540-48910-X_16
35. Phalakarn, K., Suppakitpaisarn, V., Attrapadung, N., Matsuura, K.: Constructive t-secure homomorphic secret sharing for low degree polynomials. In: Bhargavan, K., Oswald, E., Prabhakaran, M. (eds.) INDOCRYPT 2020. LNCS, vol. 12578, pp. 763–785. Springer, Cham (2020). https://doi.org/10.1007/978-3-030-65277-7_34
36. Shamir, A.: How to share a secret. Commun. ACM 22(11), 612–613 (1979)
37. Woodruff, D., Yekhanin, S.: A geometric approach to information-theoretic private information retrieval. In: 20th Annual IEEE Conference on Computational Complexity (CCC 2005), pp. 275–284. IEEE (2005)
38. Yasuda, M., Shimoyama, T., Kogure, J., Yokoyama, K., Koshiba, T.: Packed homomorphic encryption based on ideal lattices and its application to biometrics. In: Cuzzocrea, A., Kittl, C., Simos, D.E., Weippl, E., Xu, L. (eds.) CD-ARES 2013. LNCS, vol. 8128, pp. 55–74. Springer, Heidelberg (2013). https://doi.org/10.1007/978-3-642-40588-4_5

Generic Negation of Pair Encodings

Miguel Ambrona$^{(\boxtimes)}$

NTT Secure Platform Laboratories, Tokyo, Japan
miguel.ambrona.fu@hco.ntt.co.jp

Abstract. Attribute-based encryption (ABE) is a cryptographic primitive which supports fine-grained access control on encrypted data, making it an appealing building block for many applications. Pair encodings (Attrapadung, EUROCRYPT 2014) are simple primitives that can be used for constructing fully secure ABE schemes associated to a predicate relative to the encoding. We propose a generic transformation that takes any pair encoding scheme (PES) for a predicate P and produces a PES for its negated predicate $\overline{P}$. This construction finally solves a problem that was open since 2015. Our techniques bring new insight to the expressivity and generality of PES and can be of independent interest. We also provide, to the best of our knowledge, the first pair encoding scheme for negated doubly spatial encryption (obtained with our transformation) and explore several other consequences of our results.

1 Introduction

Attribute-based encryption (ABE) is a form of public-key encryption that generalizes the traditional single-recipient variant, providing fine-grained access control on the encrypted data. In this new paradigm, ciphertexts and keys have attributes attached and the decryption ability of a key on a ciphertext is determined by a potentially complex access control policy involving these attributes. More concretely, an ABE scheme for predicate P guarantees that the decryption of a ciphertext ct_x with a secret key sk_y is successful if and only if the ciphertext attribute x and the key attribute y verify the predicate, i.e., $P(x,y) = 1$.

ABE was first conceived by Sahai and Waters [30] and later introduced by Goyal *et al.* [19]. Originally, ABE was designed in the flavour of key-policy ABE (KP-ABE), where value x is a Boolean vector, value y is a Boolean function and predicate $P(x,y)$ is defined as $y(x) \overset{?}{=} 1$. On the other hand, in the analogous version, ciphertext-policy ABE (CP-ABE), the roles of values x and y are swapped. Nowadays, the notion of ABE has been generalized and, thanks to a considerable effort by the community of cryptographers, there exist efficient schemes for a rich variety of predicates. For example, identity-based encryption (IBE) [31] can be obtained as $P(x,y) := x \overset{?}{=} y$, zero-inner product encryption (ZIPE) [23] can be obtained by setting $P(\boldsymbol{x}, \boldsymbol{y}) := \langle \boldsymbol{x}, \boldsymbol{y} \rangle \overset{?}{=} 0$, where $\boldsymbol{x}$ and $\boldsymbol{y}$ belong to some vector space; other examples are span programs [22], non-monotonic access structures [28], hierarchical IBE [26], large universe ABE [29], polynomial size circuits [18], or regular languages [33]. Despite such a great progress in the field,

© International Association for Cryptologic Research 2021
J. A. Garay (Ed.): PKC 2021, LNCS 12711, pp. 120–146, 2021.
https://doi.org/10.1007/978-3-030-75248-4_5

designing better schemes in terms of size, performance, security and expressivity became an excessively hard and tedious task. Until two astonishing works appeared in 2014.

Modular Frameworks for ABE. In 2014, Wee [34] and Attrapadung [4] independently proposed two generic and unifying frameworks for designing attribute-based encryption schemes for different predicates. Both works define a simple primitive called *encoding* and follow the dual system methodology by Lewko and Waters [25,32] to construct a compiler that, on input an encoding (for certain predicate P), produces a fully secure attribute-based encryption scheme for P. Wee defines so-called *predicate encodings*, an information-theoretic primitive inspired by linear secret sharing, while Attrapadung introduces the notion of *pair encodings*, a similar primitive that admits both information-theoretic and computational security definitions. These frameworks remarkably simplify the design and study of ABE schemes: the designer can focus on the construction of the simpler encoding (for the desired predicate), which requires weaker security properties that are more easily verifiable. In fact, the potential of this new frameworks is evidenced by the invention of new constructions and performance improvements on existing primitives. Although these frameworks were designed over composite-order groups, they were both extended, in [15] and [5] respectively, to the prime-order setting (under the Matrix-DH assumption). Subsequent works propose variations and extensions of these modular frameworks [1,2,14], some of them even redefining the core encoding primitive [24] (defining so-called *tag-based* encodings). However, note that the frameworks based on *pair encodings* are the most general and expressive[1] and they have led to breakthrough constructions such as constant-size ciphertext KP-ABE (with large universes) [4], fully-secure functional encryption for regular languages [4], constant-size ciphertext CP-ABE [1] or completely-unbounded KP-ABE for non-monotone span programs (NSP) over large universes [6]. Note that, even nowadays, it is still unknown how to construct any of these powerful schemes based on predicate encodings or tag-based encodings.

Generic Predicate Transformations. In order to further simplify the design of these encodings, a common practice is to develop techniques to modify or combine existing ones. For example, the *DUAL* transformation, that swaps the ciphertext attribute and the key attribute, or the *AND* transformation, that joins two predicates in conjunction, can be achieved for pair encodings [4,10]. Among many applications, these transformations can be used to build dual-policy attribute-based encryption (DP-ABE) [7,10]; or to enhance any encoding with direct revocation of keys by combining (in conjunction) the original encoding with, e.g., an encoding for broadcast encryption.

In the framework of [15], Ambrona *et al.* [3] designed new general transformations for the *DUAL*, *OR* and *AND* connectors and, remarkably, the *NOT* transformation (that negates the predicate of the encoding). This functionally

---

[1] In fact, it is known that *predicate encodings* are a subclass of *pair encodings* [3].

complete set of Boolean transformers provides a rich combination of predicates and arguably broadens the expressivity of the framework, however, such a negation is *limited to the framework based on predicate encodings*. Designing a similar negation transformation that is applicable to all pair encoding schemes (PES) is a very appealing problem, since it would facilitate the design of new encodings and would immediately expand the expressivity of the PES framework by applying it to all existing ones. Note that, as we have already mentioned, pair encodings have proven themselves to be significantly more expressive than any other related framework.

However, recent works have considered the problem of designing such a general negation to be intrinsically hard [2,6] (see our discussion in Sect. 3, we also refer to this section for more details about relevant related works). To the best of our knowledge, a general *NOT* transformation that is applicable to the framework of pair encodings does not exist in the literature.

1.1   Our Contribution

We pursue the study of pair encoding schemes and establish several general results that can lead to performance improvements, and new encodings that broaden their scope.

Generic Negation of Pair Encodings. We propose a generic transformation that takes any pair encoding scheme for a predicate P and produces a pair encoding scheme for its negated predicate, $\overline{P}$. Our transformation is applicable to pair encodings that follow the most recent and refined definition given in [2]. Our construction finally solves a problem that was open since 2015, when several other transformation for pair encodings (like conjunction or duality) were proposed [10], but no generic negation was provided (nor designed in subsequent works). In fact, several works had suggested that finding such a transformation was non-obvious [2,6], since it relates to the problem of generically finding a short "certificate" of security of the encoding. We elaborate on this idea in Sect. 3.

Algebraic Characterization of Pair Encodings. En route to designing our generic negation, we define an algebraic characterization of PES that brings new insight to their expressivity and generality and can be of independent interest. Our characterization allows us to express the security of a pair encoding scheme as the (in)existence of solutions to a system of matrix equations. This is the bridge that allows us to leverage Lemma 1, a very powerful result from linear algebra (commonly used in cryptography), in order to design and prove our generic negation.

New Encodings. Our generic negation facilitates the design of new pair encoding schemes. It will immediately provide us with a negated version of any encoding, something particularly useful for encodings for which a negated counterpart is not known. A relevant example of a PES with (previously) unknown negation is the case of doubly spatial encryption.

Doubly spatial encryption [20] is an important primitive that generalizes both spatial encryption and *negated spatial encryption* [8]. A negated doubly spatial encryption scheme serves as its revocation analogue and can lead to powerful generalizations in the same way that negated (standard) spatial encryption unifies existing primitives, e.g. it subsumes *non-zero-mode* inner-product encryption (IPE) [8]. In Sect. 6.1 we provide, to the best of our knowledge, the first pair encoding scheme for negated doubly spatial encryption, obtained with our transformation.

Other Implications of Our Results. We believe the results presented in this work improve our understanding of pair encodings and how expressive they are. In particular, we now know that *the set of predicates that can be expressed with PES is closed under negation*. In Sect. 6.2, we elaborate on the conclusions we could derive from this fact as well as discuss how our generic transformation can also lead to performance improvements when implementing ABE schemes. Furthermore, note that our generic negation is compatible with the very recent framework proposed by Attrapadung [6], designed to perform dynamic pair encoding compositions. We believe our new transformation complements his work, where the proposed non-monotone formulae composition was only *semi-generic* (but dynamic), because he had to rely on encodings for which a negated version was available.

2 Preliminaries

2.1 Notation

We write $s \xleftarrow{\$} S$ to denote that s is uniformly sampled from a set S. For integers m, n, we define $[m, n]$ as the range $\{m, \ldots, n\}$ and we denote by $[n]$ the range $[1, n]$. We use the same conventions for matrix-representations of linear maps on finite-dimensional spaces. For a ring R, we define vectors $\boldsymbol{v} \in R^n$ as *column* matrices, denote the transpose of a matrix A by $A^\top$ and its trace by $\mathrm{tr}(A)$. We denote by $|\boldsymbol{v}|$ the length or dimension of vector $\boldsymbol{v}$ and by v_i its i-th component, for all $i \in \{1, \ldots, |\boldsymbol{v}|\}$. Similarly, A_i denotes the i-th *row* of matrix A (we do not use this notation when the name of the matrix already contains a subindex). We denote by $\mathrm{span}(A)$ the linear *column* span of matrix A. We denote the identity matrix of dimension n by I_n, a zero vector of length n by $\boldsymbol{0}_n$ and a zero matrix of m rows and n columns by $0_{m \times n}$. We denote by $\boldsymbol{e}_i^n$ the i-th vector of the standard basis of an n-dimensional space, for all $i \in [n]$. We sometimes denote $\boldsymbol{e}_1^n$ by $\boldsymbol{1}_n$. Similarly, we denote by $1_{m \times n}$ the matrix $\boldsymbol{1}_m \boldsymbol{1}_n^\top$, i.e., *a null matrix of m rows and n columns whose component in the first row and first column is 1*. Given two matrices A and B, we denote by $A \otimes B$ their Kronecker product.

We consider a bilinear group generator $\mathcal{G}$ that takes a security parameter $\lambda \in \mathbb{N}$ and outputs the description of a bilinear group $(p, G_1, G_2, G_t, g_1, g_2, e)$ where G_1, G_2 and G_t are cyclic groups of order p (for a λ-bits prime p), g_1 and g_2 are generators of G_1 and G_2 respectively and $e : G_1 \times G_2 \to G_t$ is a (non-degenerate) bilinear map, satisfying $e(g_1^a, g_2^b) = e(g_1, g_2)^{ab}$ for all $a, b \in \mathbb{N}$. Observe that the element $g_t = e(g_1, g_2)$ generates G_t.

2.2   Attribute-Based Encryption

Attribute-based encryption (ABE) [30] is a form of of public-key encryption that supports fine-grained access control of encrypted data.

Definition 1 (Attribute-based encryption). *An ABE scheme for predicate* $P : \mathcal{X} \times \mathcal{Y} \to \{0,1\}$ *consists of four probabilistic polynomial-time algorithms:*

- Setup($1^\lambda, \mathcal{X}, \mathcal{Y}$) → (mpk, msk), *on input the security parameter* λ *and attribute universes* $\mathcal{X}, \mathcal{Y}$, *outputs a master public key and a master secret key, defining a key space* $\mathcal{K}$.

- Enc(mpk, x) → (ct$_x$, τ), *on input* mpk *and a ciphertext attribute* $x \in \mathcal{X}$, *outputs a ciphertext* ct$_x$ *and a symmetric encryption key* $\tau \in \mathcal{K}$.

- KeyGen(msk, y) → sk$_y$, *on input the master secret key and a key attribute* $y \in \mathcal{Y}$, *outputs a secret key* sk$_y$.

- Dec(mpk, sk$_y$, ct$_x$, x) → $\tau/\bot$, *on input* sk$_y$ *and* ct$_x$, *outputs a symmetric key* $\tau \in \mathcal{K}$ *if* $P(x,y) = 1$ *or* $\bot$ *otherwise.*

Correctness. For all $\lambda \in \mathbb{N}$, $x \in \mathcal{X}$ and $y \in \mathcal{Y}$ such that $P(x,y) = 1$, it holds:

$$\Pr \left[\begin{array}{c} (\mathsf{msk}, \mathsf{pk}) \leftarrow \mathsf{Setup}(1^\lambda) \\ \mathsf{sk}_y \leftarrow \mathsf{KeyGen}(\mathsf{msk}, y) \; : \; \mathsf{Dec}(\mathsf{mpk}, \mathsf{sk}_y, \mathsf{ct}_x, x) = \tau \\ (\mathsf{ct}_x, \tau) \leftarrow \mathsf{Enc}(\mathsf{mpk}, x) \end{array} \right] = 1.$$

Security. Informally, an ABE scheme is secure if no probabilistic polynomial-time (PPT) adversary can distinguish the symmetric encryption key associated to a ciphertext ct$_{x^\star}$ (for some attribute $x^\star$) from a uniformly chosen one from $\mathcal{K}$, even after requesting several secret keys for attributes y of their choice, as long as they all satisfy $P(x^\star, y) = 0$.

In this work we focus on *pair encodings* (see the next section) as a building block for constructing ABE schemes and we refer to Appendix B.1 for a formal security definition of ABE, which we do not state here. Instead, we will formally state and reason about the security requirements for pair encodings.

2.3   Pair Encodings

We consider the refined definition of pair encodings introduced by Agrawal and Chase in [2].

Definition 2 (Pair encoding). *A* pair encoding scheme *(PES) for a predicate family* $P_\kappa : \mathcal{X}_\kappa \times \mathcal{Y}_\kappa \to \{0,1\}$ *indexed by* $\kappa = (N, \mathsf{par})$ *consists of the following deterministic and efficiently computable algorithms:*

- Param(par): *on input certain parameters outputs an integer* n, *specifying the number of* common variables, *denoted by* $\boldsymbol{b} = (b_1, \ldots, b_n)$.

- EncKey(N, y): on input $N \in \mathbb{N}$ and $y \in \mathcal{Y}_{(N,\mathsf{par})}$, outputs a vector of polynomials $\boldsymbol{k} = (k_1, \ldots, k_{m_3})$ in the non-lone variables $\boldsymbol{r} = (r_1, \ldots, r_{m_1})$, the lone variables $\hat{\boldsymbol{r}} = (\alpha, \hat{r}_1, \ldots, \hat{r}_{m_2})$ and the common variables $\boldsymbol{b}$.
- EncCt(N, x): on input $N \in \mathbb{N}$ and $x \in \mathcal{X}_{(N,\mathsf{par})}$, outputs a vector of polynomials $\boldsymbol{c} = (c_1, \ldots, c_{w_3})$ in the non-lone variables $\boldsymbol{s} = (s_0, s_1, \ldots, s_{w_1-1})$, the lone variables $\hat{\boldsymbol{s}} = (\hat{s}_1, \ldots, \hat{s}_{w_2})$ and the common variables $\boldsymbol{b}$.
- Pair(N, x, y): on input $N \in \mathbb{N}$ and attributes x and y, outputs a pair of matrices (E, E') with coefficients in $\mathbb{Z}_N$ of dimensions $w_1 \times m_3$ and $w_3 \times m_1$ respectively.

We require that the following properties be satisfied:

reconstructability: *For every* $\kappa = (N, \mathsf{par})$, $x \in \mathcal{X}_\kappa$ *and* $y \in \mathcal{Y}_\kappa$ *such that* $P_\kappa(x, y) = 1$, *the following equation holds symbolically:*

$$\boldsymbol{s}^\top E \boldsymbol{k} + \boldsymbol{c}^\top E' \boldsymbol{r} = \alpha s_0,$$

where $\boldsymbol{k} \leftarrow$ EncKey(N, x), $\boldsymbol{c} \leftarrow$ EncCt(N, y) *and* $(E, E') \leftarrow$ Pair(N, x, y).

structural constraints: *The polynomials produced by* EncKey *only contain monomials of the form* α, $r_i b_j$ *or* $\hat{r}_{i'}$ *for some* $i \in [m_1]$, $j \in [n]$ *and* $i' \in [m_2]$. *On the other hand, the polynomials produced by* EncCt *only contain monomials of the form* $s_i b_j$ *or* $\hat{s}_{i'}$ *for some* $i \in [0, w_1-1]$, $j \in [n]$ *and* $i' \in [w_2]$.

security (non-reconstructability): *For all* $\kappa \in (N, \mathsf{par})$, $x \in \mathcal{X}_\kappa$ *and* $y \in \mathcal{Y}_\kappa$ *such that* $P_\kappa(x, y) = 0$, *and for every pair of matrices* E *and* E', *over* $\mathbb{Z}_N$, $\boldsymbol{s}^\top E \boldsymbol{k} + \boldsymbol{c}^\top E' \boldsymbol{r} \neq \alpha s_0$, *where* $\boldsymbol{k} \leftarrow$ EncKey(N, x) *and* $\boldsymbol{c} \leftarrow$ EncCt(N, y).

Remark 1. Observe that m_1 and w_1 represent[2] the number of non-lone variables $\boldsymbol{r}$ and $\boldsymbol{s}$ respectively; m_2 and w_2 represent the number of lone variables $\hat{\boldsymbol{r}}$ and $\hat{\boldsymbol{s}}$ respectively; and m_3 and w_3 represent the number of polynomials produced by EncKey and EncCt respectively. Also note that m_3 may depend on the key attribute y and w_3 may depend on the ciphertext attribute x. We will use this notation throughout the paper.

Agrawal and Chase [2] showed that an encoding with the non-reconstructability property (coined *non-trivially broken*) satisfies the *symbolic property*, a concept introduced by them which is a sufficient condition to build attribute-based encryption in the standard model under the so-called q-ratio assumption.

We refer to Appendix B.2 for details about how the compiler from PES to fully secure ABE works. In this work we directly reason about PES and do not need to explicitly define such a compiler. However, for the sake of understanding, we provide an intuition of how a PES can be used to create an ABE scheme in the following section.

---

[2] In some literature, the number of non-lone ciphertext variables is defined as w_1+1, since the special variable s_0 is treated separately. Observe that our vector of non-lone variables ranges from s_0 to s_{w_1-1}, this is for the sake of notation in further sections.

Example 1 (PES for identity-based encryption). The following is a pair encoding scheme for the IBE predicate $P(x,y) := x \stackrel{?}{=} y$, for $x,y \in \mathbb{Z}_N$. (With $m_1 = 1$, $m_2 = 0$, $m_3 = 2$ and $w_1 = 2$, $w_2 = 0$, $w_3 = 1$.)

$$\mathsf{EncKey}(N,y) := \{\alpha + r_1 b_1,\ r_1(y b_2 + b_3)\} \quad \mathsf{EncCt}(N,x) := \{s_0 b_1 + s_1(x b_2 + b_3)\}.$$

Furthermore, in this case Param is an algorithm that simply outputs $n = 3$ and $\mathsf{Pair}(N,x,y)$ returns matrices $E = I_2$ and $E' = -I_1$. For reconstructability, observe that $(s_0\ s_1) E \boldsymbol{k} + \boldsymbol{c}^\top E'(r_1)$ equals $s_0 \alpha + s_1 r_1(y b_2 + b_3) - s_1 r_1(x b_2 + b_3)$ which equals αs_0 whenever $x = y$, as desired.

Arguing security, i.e., non-reconstructability whenever $x \neq y$, is a little trickier. One needs to show that for all matrices $E \in \mathbb{Z}_N^{2 \times 2}$, $E' \in \mathbb{Z}_N$, the above linear combination is never equal to αs_0. This could be done by unfolding the list of polynomials in $\boldsymbol{s} \otimes \boldsymbol{k}$, $\boldsymbol{c} \otimes \boldsymbol{r}$ into a matrix A with $w_1 m_3 + w_3 m_1$ rows (as many as polynomials) and as many columns as different monomials appear in them, where the element at row i and column j of the matrix represents the coefficient of the j-th monomial in the i-th polynomial. (Let the first column be the one associated to monomial αs_0.) One could then argue security by checking that the row span of A does not contain the vector $(1\,0 \ldots 0)$ when $P(x,y) = 0$.

However, there is a simpler way of proving non-reconstructability. Simply evaluate the polynomials produced by EncKey and EncCt in:

$$b_1 \leftarrow -1 \qquad b_2, s_0, r_1, \alpha \leftarrow 1 \qquad b_3 \leftarrow -y \qquad s_1 \leftarrow (x-y)^{-1}.$$

Since all the polynomials evaluate to 0, but αs_0 evaluates to $1 \neq 0$, it must be impossible to symbolically reconstruct αs_0 with some pair of matrices E, E'. Otherwise, we would have a contradiction:

$$0 = \boldsymbol{s}^\top E \boldsymbol{0}_{m_3} + \boldsymbol{0}_{w_3}^\top E' \boldsymbol{r} = \boldsymbol{s}^\top E \boldsymbol{k}(\boldsymbol{r}, \boldsymbol{b}) + \boldsymbol{c}(\boldsymbol{s}, \boldsymbol{b})^\top E' \boldsymbol{r} = \alpha s_0 = 1.$$

The above variable substitution that vanishes all polynomials, but does not vanish polynomial αs_0 can be considered to be a short "certificate" of the security of the scheme (and it is well-defined as long as $x \neq y$). We elaborate on this interesting method for arguing security in Sect. 3. ∎

2.4   ABE from PES

The compiler from pair encodings to attribute-based encryption is defined over bilinear groups implemented as dual system groups (DSG) [2,16,17]. Here, we define a simplified version of the compiler and avoid DSG for simplicity, but note that the actual scheme produced by these compilers uses vectors of group elements where we write single group elements. We provide a complete description of the compiler from [2] in Appendix B.2.

Informally, the symmetric encryption key is computed as $\tau := g_t^{\alpha s_0}$, where s_0 is fresh randomness and g_t^α is part of the master public key. Both ciphertexts and keys are made of group elements (created based on the recipe given by the corresponding PES polynomials). It is possible to recover τ when the predicate is satisfied. More concretely, for $\boldsymbol{k} \leftarrow \mathsf{EncKey}(x)$ and $\boldsymbol{c} \leftarrow \mathsf{EncCt}(y)$, the compiler could be summarized as follows:

$$\mathsf{mpk} := \left\{ g_\mathsf{t}^\alpha, g_1^b \right\} \qquad\qquad (\mathsf{ct}_x, \tau) := \left(\left\{ g_1^s, g_1^{c(s,\hat{s},b)} \right\}, g_\mathsf{t}^{\alpha s_0} \right)$$

$$\mathsf{msk} := \left\{ \alpha, \boldsymbol{b} \right\} \qquad\qquad \mathsf{sk}_y := \left\{ g_2^r, g_2^{k(r,\hat{r},b)} \right\}$$

Decryption is done by pairing g_1^s with g_2^k, g_1^c with g_2^r, and linearly combining the resulting elements, according to the coefficients given by $\mathsf{Pair}(x,y)$, obtaining αs_0 in the exponent.

2.5   Linear Algebra Tools

In order to prove the validity of our generic negation of pair encodings, we will use a very powerful result from linear algebra that has been widely used in the literature [1–3,11]. It states that given a field K, a matrix $A \in K^{m \times n}$ and a vector $\boldsymbol{z} \in K^m$, it holds that $A\boldsymbol{v} \neq \boldsymbol{z}$ for all $\boldsymbol{v} \in K^n$ if and only if there exists a vector $\boldsymbol{w} \in K^m$ such that $\boldsymbol{w}^\top A = \boldsymbol{0}_n$ and $\boldsymbol{w}^\top \boldsymbol{z} = 1$. We refer to [11, Claim 2] for a formal proof.

Here, for the sake of presentation, we state a variant of the above result, which can be shown to be equivalent, but that facilitates its application in the proof of Lemma 2.

Lemma 1. *Let V and W be vector spaces over a field K. Let $f : V \to W$ be a linear operator and let $\boldsymbol{z} \in W$. We have that:*

$$\boldsymbol{z} \notin \mathrm{Im}(f) \quad \Leftrightarrow \quad \exists \varphi \in W^* \text{ such that } \varphi \circ f = 0 \wedge \varphi(\boldsymbol{z}) = 1.$$

Here, W^* denotes the dual space *of W, i.e., the set of all linear maps $\varphi : W \to K$.*

3   Overview of Our Generic Negation Transformation

Our starting point is the generic negation for the (less expressive) framework of *predicate encodings* from [3]. In order to achieve their transformation, Ambrona, Barthe, and Schmidt first defined an algebraic characterization of predicate encodings where the security of the encoding (previously defined as an equality between distributions) was redefined into a purely algebraic statement related to the existence of solutions to a linear system of equations. This observation allowed them to link the notions of security and non-reconstructability and define what they coined the *implicit predicate* of an encoding. This implies, in a nutshell, that all functions mapping attributes into matrices define a valid predicate encoding for a certain predicate, informally defined as all pairs of attributes (x,y) that map into matrices that lead to reconstructability.

Now that security has been proven to be equivalent to non-reconstructability, and given the simple structure of predicate encodings (which are essentially matrices over $\mathbb{Z}_p$), it is possible to find a short "witness" of non-reconstructability by simply finding a solution to a dual system of equations.[3] What we want to highlight here is that their new understanding of predicate encodings allows them to view both reconstructability and non-reconstructability as essentially the same kind of property. This suggests that one may be able to build a generic negation of predicate encodings by transposing the matrices induced by them.[4] This is in fact what the negation by Ambrona *et al.* does, but extra care is needed to make things really work.

Unfortunately, in the case of pair encodings things are not as simple. Their structure is significantly more convoluted, involving abstract polynomials that do not allow the kind of reasoning that was possible before (standard linear algebra). However, in 2017, Agrawal and Chase introduced a new security notion applicable to pair encodings called the *symbolic property* [2]. They also showed how to adapt the previous modular frameworks [1,5] to define a compiler that takes pair encodings satisfying the symbolic property and produces fully secure predicate encryption schemes under the q-ratio assumption, a new q-type assumption proposed by them that is implied by other assumptions of this kind [27]. This symbolic property can be seen as a generalization of the "trick" that we have used in Example 1 to argue the security of the encoding. The main difference is that scalar variables in the PES may be substituted by vectors or matrices (not necessarily scalars as in our example) in such a way that, after the substitution, all the polynomials evaluate to zero, but there is an extra constraint relating the inner product of the vectors that replaced the special variables that guarantees that αs_0 is non-zero. As mentioned by Attrapadung [6], the above methodology generalizes the well-known Boneh-Boyen cancellation technique for identity-based encryption [12]. What is remarkable about this idea is that the substitution can be used as a "witness" or "certificate" (as coined by the authors of [2]) of the security of the scheme. Furthermore, Agrawal and Chase also showed that any pair encoding that is *not trivially broken* satisfies the symbolic property, a result that is closely related to the algebraic characterization of privacy on predicate encodings from [3].

It may seem that after these relevant results on pair encodings, and the similarity with those in the framework of predicate encodings, we are in a position to define a generic negation transformation for pair encodings. However, the more involved structure of pair encodings makes it difficult to find and prove a valid conversion. In fact, recent works have considered the problem of designing such a general negation to be non-trivial (see [6, Appendix L.5]), since in the framework of pair encodings it is generally hard to find the mentioned *"certificates"* that can be interpreted as a short proof of security. (Note that any possible NOT transformation would, at least implicitly, use such certificates as decryption cre-

---

[3] Recall that $\forall v : Av \neq z \Leftrightarrow \exists w : A^\top w = 0 \wedge z^\top w = 1$ for all compatible A and z.

[4] That way, the witness of non-reconstructability can be used as the linear combination for decryption (reconstructability) in the negated encoding and vice versa: the solution for reconstructability can be used as the witness of security in the negated encoding.

dentials for the transformed encoding, whereas the decryption credentials of the original encoding would become the security certificate of the negated one.)

In order to construct a valid negation of pair encodings, we first need to treat them in a simplified manner, closer to linear algebra. To do so, we provide an algebraic characterization of pair encodings (Sect. 4), whose security can be expressed as a system of matrix equations, very similar to the statement $i)$ from Lemma 2. Intuitively, we split the polynomials produced by the encoding into layers, each being a matrix that corresponds to one of the (common, lone or non-lone) variables. We then show how the security of the scheme can be expressed as a linear system involving these matrices. Our characterization makes an structural assumption on the form of the pair encoding (that can be made without loss of generality and has been used in the literature for other purposes [2,6]). Namely, we assume that EncKey only produces one polynomial that depends on α, which is of the form $\alpha + r_1 b_1$. This assumption introduces a "symmetry" between the nature of key and ciphertext polynomials (now that the special variable α is out of the way) that allows us to express the security of the PES as the symmetric algebraic statement of Definition 3. The next step is to leverage Lemma 1 in order to prove our following lemma, linking the inexistence of a solution to the system in $i)$ with the existence of a solution to $ii)$. This is the main tool on which we base our negation transformation. The last (but non-trivial) step is to define a new encoding (in algebraic form) such that the solution from statement $ii)$ serves as a decryption credential for it.

Lemma 2. *Let K be a field, let $n \in \mathbb{N}$ and let $\{A_i, B_i, C_i\}_{i \in [n]}$, $\hat{A}, \hat{B}$ be matrices:*

$$A_i \in K^{\ell \times m} \qquad\qquad B_i \in K^{r \times s} \qquad\qquad C_i \in K^{r \times m}$$
$$\hat{A} \in K^{\ell \times \hat{m}} \qquad\qquad \hat{B} \in K^{\hat{r} \times s},$$

for certain $\ell, m, r, s, \hat{m}, \hat{r} \in \mathbb{N}$ and every $i \in [n]$. The following are equivalent:

i) There do not exist X, Y with $X \in K^{r \times \ell}$, $Y \in K^{s \times m}$ such that:

$$\forall i \in [n]. \ XA_i + B_iY = C_i \quad \wedge \quad X\hat{A} = 0_{r \times \hat{m}} \quad \wedge \quad \hat{B}Y = 0_{\hat{r} \times m}.$$

ii) There exist $Z_1, \ldots, Z_n \in K^{m \times r}$ and $Z_A \in K^{\hat{m} \times r}$, $Z_B \in K^{m \times \hat{r}}$ such that

$$A_1 Z_1 + \cdots + A_n Z_n + \hat{A} Z_A = 0_{\ell \times r}$$
$$\wedge \quad Z_1 B_1 + \cdots + Z_n B_n + Z_B \hat{B} = 0_{m \times s} \qquad \wedge \quad \sum_{i=1}^n \mathrm{tr}(C_i Z_i) = 1.$$

Proof. Let f be the linear map defined as

$$f : (X, Y) \mapsto (XA_1 + B_1Y, \ \ldots, \ XA_n + B_nY, \ X\hat{A}, \ \hat{B}Y).$$

Observe that the first statement of the lemma is equivalent to saying that

$$(C_1, \ldots, C_n, 0_{r \times \hat{m}}, 0_{\hat{r} \times m}) \notin \mathrm{Im}(f),$$

which, by Lemma 1 is equivalent to the existence of $\varphi : W \to K$, where in this case $W := (K^{r \times m})^n \times K^{r \times \hat{m}} \times K^{\hat{r} \times m}$, such that

$$\varphi \circ f = 0 \quad \text{and} \quad \varphi(C_1, \ldots, C_n, 0_{r \times \hat{m}}, 0_{\hat{r} \times m}) = 1,$$

which is equivalent to the existence of matrices $Z_1, \ldots, Z_n \in K^{m \times r}$ and $Z_A \in K^{\hat{m} \times r}$, $Z_B \in K^{m \times \hat{r}}$ such that

$$\forall X, Y. \quad \text{tr}\left(\sum_{i=1}^{n}(XA_i + B_i Y) Z_i\right) + \text{tr}\left(X \hat{A} Z_A\right) + \text{tr}\left(\hat{B} Y Z_B\right) = 0 \tag{1}$$

$$\text{and} \quad \text{tr}\left(C_1 Z_1 + \cdots + C_n Z_n\right) + \text{tr}\left(0_{r \times \hat{m}} Z_A\right) + \text{tr}\left(0_{\hat{r} \times m} Z_B\right) = 1, \tag{2}$$

which is equivalent to the second statement of the lemma, *quod erat demonstrandum*. To see why, note that Eq. (2) is present in both cases and observe that if the second statement of the lemma holds, then (for any X, Y) we have

$$0 = \text{tr}\left(0_{\ell \times r}\right) + \text{tr}\left(0_{m \times s}\right)$$

$$= \text{tr}\left(X\left(A_1 Z_1 + \cdots + A_n Z_n + \hat{A} Z_A\right)\right) + \text{tr}\left(\left(Z_1 B_1 + \cdots + Z_n B_n + Z_B \hat{B}\right) Y\right)$$

$$= \text{tr}\left(\sum_{i=1}^{n} X A_i Z_i\right) + \text{tr}\left(X \hat{A} Z_A\right) + \text{tr}\left(\sum_{i=1}^{n} Z_i B_i Y\right) + \text{tr}\left(Z_B \hat{B} Y\right)$$

$$\overset{\dagger}{=} \text{tr}\left(\sum_{i=1}^{n} X A_i Z_i\right) + \text{tr}\left(X \hat{A} Z_A\right) + \text{tr}\left(\sum_{i=1}^{n} B_i Y Z_i\right) + \text{tr}\left(\hat{B} Y Z_B\right)$$

$$= \text{tr}\left(\sum_{i=1}^{n}(X A_i + B_i Y) Z_i\right) + \text{tr}\left(X \hat{A} Z_A\right) + \text{tr}\left(\hat{B} Y Z_B\right),$$

where in † we have used the fact that the trace is invariant under cyclic permutations. Finally, to see the converse, note that if Eq. (1) holds for any X, Y, it must hold for $Y = 0_{s \times m}$, which would imply that for every $X \in K^{r \times \ell}$,

$$\text{tr}\left(X\left(A_1 Z_1 + \cdots + A_n Z_n + \hat{A} Z_A\right)\right) = 0,$$

but that can only happen if $A_1 Z_1 + \cdots + A_n Z_n + \hat{A} Z_A$ is the zero matrix.

Analogously, evaluating (1) on $X = 0_{r \times \ell}$, we get

$$\text{tr}\left(B_1 Y Z_1 + \cdots + B_1 Y Z_n\right) + \text{tr}\left(\hat{B} Y Z_B\right) \overset{\dagger}{=} \text{tr}\left(\left(Z_1 B_1 + \cdots + Z_n B_n + Z_B \hat{B}\right) Y\right) = 0,$$

for every $Y \in K^{s \times m}$, which can only happen if $Z_1 B_1 + \cdots + Z_n B_n + Z_B \hat{B}$ is the null matrix. □

4   Characterization of Pair Encodings

In this section we propose a characterization of pair encodings that will be used to define our generic transformation for the negated predicate.

The first step towards our characterization is to assume that only one polynomial from EncKey depends on α and is of the form $\alpha + r_1 b_1$. This assumption is without loss of generality[5], and has been utilized before in the literature [2,6]. The rest of polynomials can be expressed as $\boldsymbol{k} = B_y \boldsymbol{r} + C_y \hat{\boldsymbol{r}}$, for some matrix B_y whose terms are *linear* polynomials in $\mathbb{Z}_N[b_1, \ldots, b_n]$, and some matrix C_y with coefficients in $\mathbb{Z}_N$. Given that $\alpha + r_1 b_1$ is always present, for the sake of notation, we redefine m_3 to be the total number of polynomials produced by KeyGen excluding $\alpha + r_1 b_1$. Similarly, the polynomials from EncCt can be expressed as $\boldsymbol{c} = B'_x \boldsymbol{s} + C'_x \hat{\boldsymbol{s}}$. Such an analogy in the form of $\boldsymbol{k}$ and $\boldsymbol{c}$ (only achieved after getting rid of variable α) allows us to express the encodings in an algebraic form, amenable to be combined with different results of linear algebra.

Definition 3 (Algebraic pair encoding). *An algebraic pair encoding scheme for a predicate family $P_\kappa : \mathcal{X}_\kappa \times \mathcal{Y}_\kappa \to \{0,1\}$ indexed by $\kappa = (N, \mathsf{par})$ consists of the following deterministic and efficiently computable algorithms:*

- Param^{alg}(par)*: on input certain parameters outputs an integer $n \in \mathbb{N}$.*
- EncKey$^{\mathsf{alg}}(N, x)$*: on input $N \in \mathbb{N}$ and $x \in \mathcal{X}_{(N,\mathsf{par})}$, outputs a list of $n+1$ matrices with coefficients in $\mathbb{Z}_N$, $(B_1, \ldots, B_n, C)$, where B_j has dimension $m_3 \times m_1$, for $j \in [n]$, and C has dimension $m_3 \times m_2$.*
- EncCt$^{\mathsf{alg}}(N, y)$*: on input $N \in \mathbb{N}$ and $y \in \mathcal{Y}_{(N,\mathsf{par})}$, outputs a list of $n+1$ matrices with coefficients in $\mathbb{Z}_N$, $(B'_1, \ldots, B'_n, C')$, where B'_j has dimension $w_3 \times w_1$, for $j \in [n]$, and C' has dimension $w_3 \times w_2$.*

Furthermore, for every $\kappa = (N, \mathsf{par})$, $x \in \mathcal{X}_\kappa$ and $y \in \mathcal{Y}_\kappa$, $P_\kappa(x, y) = 1$ if and only if there exist matrices $E \in \mathbb{Z}_N^{w_1 \times m_3}$ and $E' \in \mathbb{Z}_N^{w_3 \times m_1}$ such that

$$EB_1 + B'^{\top}_1 E' = 1_{w_1 \times m_1} \qquad \wedge \qquad EC = 0_{w_1 \times m_2}$$
$$\wedge \quad EB_j + B'^{\top}_j E' = 0_{w_1 \times m_1}, \, j \in [2, n] \quad \wedge \quad C'^{\top} E' = 0_{w_2 \times m_1} \qquad (3)$$

where $(B_1, \ldots, B_n, C) \leftarrow$ EncKey$^{\mathsf{alg}}(N, x)$ and $(B'_1, \ldots, B'_n, C') \leftarrow$ EncCt^{alg} (N, y).

Theorem 1 (Characterization). *There exists a pair encoding for predicate family P_κ if and only if there exists an algebraic pair encoding for P_κ. Furthermore, there is an efficient conversion in both directions.*

The above theorem is a consequence of our following two lemmas.

Lemma 3 (From algebraic to standard). *Let* (Param^{alg}, EncKey^{alg}, EncCt^{alg}) *be an algebraic pair encoding scheme for predicate family $P_\kappa : \mathcal{X}_\kappa \times \mathcal{Y}_\kappa \to \{0,1\}$. Then, algorithms* (Param, EncKey, EncCt, Pair) *(defined below) constitute a pair encoding scheme for P_κ.*

---

[5] An easy way of arguing that this is w.l.o.g. is to apply the generic dual transformation defined in [10] twice. (Note that the dual operation is an involution and a double application of it would preserve the original predicate.).

- Param(par) := *run* $n \leftarrow$ Param^{alg}(par), *output* n *and let* $\boldsymbol{b} = (b_1, \ldots, b_n)$.
- EncKey$(N, x) :=$ *run* $(B_1, \ldots, B_n, C) \leftarrow$ EncKey$^{\mathsf{alg}}(N, x)$, *output the vector of polynomials given by* $\alpha + r_1 b_1$ *and* $(b_1 B_1 + \cdots + b_n B_n)\boldsymbol{r} + C\hat{\boldsymbol{r}}$, *where* $\boldsymbol{r} = (r_1, \ldots, r_{m_1})$ *and* $\hat{\boldsymbol{r}} = (\hat{r}_1, \ldots, \hat{r}_{m_2})$.
- EncCt$(N, y) :=$ *run* $(B'_1, \ldots, B'_n, C') \leftarrow$ EncCt$^{\mathsf{alg}}(N, y)$, *output the vector of polynomials given by* $(b_1 B'_1 + \cdots + b_n B'_n)\boldsymbol{s} + C'\hat{\boldsymbol{s}}$, *where* $\boldsymbol{s} = (s_0, \ldots, s_{w_1-1})$ *and* $\hat{\boldsymbol{s}} = (\hat{s}_1, \ldots, \hat{s}_{w_2})$.
- Pair$(N, x, y) :=$ *find matrices* (E, E') *satisfying Eq. (3), that exist if and only if* $P_\kappa(x, y) = 1$, *output* $\left((\mathbf{1}_{w_1} -E), -E'\right)$.

Proof. Observe that the structural constraints on the polynomials of EncKey and EncCt are satisfied. To see reconstructability, simply note that for any $N \in \mathbb{N}$, $x \in \mathcal{X}_\kappa$ and $y \in \mathcal{Y}_\kappa$ with $P(x, y) = 1$, and for (E, E') satisfying (3), it holds:

$$\boldsymbol{s}^\top (\mathbf{1}_{w_1} -E) \begin{pmatrix} \alpha + r_1 b_1 \\ (b_1 B_1 + \cdots + b_n B_n)\boldsymbol{r} + C\hat{\boldsymbol{r}} \end{pmatrix} - \left(\boldsymbol{s}^\top \left(b_1 {B'_1}^\top + \cdots + b_n {B'_n}^\top\right) + \hat{\boldsymbol{s}}^\top {C'}^\top\right) E'\boldsymbol{r}$$

$$= s_0(\alpha + r_1 b_1) - \boldsymbol{s} b_1 \left(\mathbf{1}_{w_1 \times m_1}\right)\boldsymbol{r} = s_0 \alpha.$$

For security, note that if the new pair encoding were trivially broken, there would exist a pair $(x, y) \in \mathcal{X}_\kappa \times \mathcal{Y}_\kappa$ with $P_\kappa(x, y) = 0$, and matrices E, E' satisfying Eq. (3). For details about this fact, we refer to the proof Lemma 4 (the part about reconstructability). □

Lemma 4 (From standard to algebraic). *Let* (Param, EncKey, EncCt, Pair) *be a pair encoding scheme[6] for predicate family* $P_\kappa : \mathcal{X}_\kappa \times \mathcal{Y}_\kappa \to \{0, 1\}$. *Then, algorithms* (Param^{alg}, EncKey^{alg}, EncCt^{alg}) *(defined below) constitute an algebraic pair encoding scheme for* P_κ.

- Param^{alg}(par) := Param(par).
- EncKey$^{\mathsf{alg}}(N, x) :=$ *run* $(\alpha + r_1 b_1, \boldsymbol{k}) \leftarrow$ EncKey(N, x), *and let* $m_3 = |\boldsymbol{k}|$. *For* $j \in [n]$, *define matrix* B_j *as the matrix whose element at the ℓ-th row and i-th column is the coefficient of monomial* $r_i b_j$ *in polynomial* k_ℓ. *Define C as the matrix whose element at the ℓ-th row and i'-th column is the coefficient of monomial* $\hat{r}_{i'}$ *in polynomial* k_ℓ, *for* $i \in [m_1]$, $i' \in [m_2]$ *and* $\ell \in [m_3]$. *Output* $(B_1, \ldots, B_n, C)$.
- EncCt$^{\mathsf{alg}}(N, y) :=$ *run* $\boldsymbol{c} \leftarrow$ EncCt(N, y). *For* $j \in [n]$, *define matrix* B'_j *as the matrix whose element at the ℓ-th row and $(i+1)$-th column is the coefficient of monomial* $s_i b_j$ *in polynomial* c_ℓ. *Define C' as the matrix whose element at the ℓ-th row and i'-th column is the coefficient of monomial* $\hat{s}_{i'}$ *in polynomial* c_ℓ, *for* $i \in [0, w_1-1]$, $i' \in [w_2]$ *and* $\ell \in [w_3]$. *Output* $(B'_1, \ldots, B'_n, C')$.

Proof. Note that the structural constraints on the PES enforce that for every $N \in \mathbb{N}$, $x \in \mathcal{X}_\kappa$ and $y \in \mathcal{Y}_\kappa$, $(\alpha + r_1 b_1, \boldsymbol{k}) \leftarrow$ EncKey(N, x), $\boldsymbol{c} \leftarrow$ EncCt(N, y), $(B_1, \ldots, B_n, C) \leftarrow$ EncKey$^{\mathsf{alg}}(N, x)$, $(B'_1, \ldots, B'_n, C') \leftarrow$ EncCt$^{\mathsf{alg}}(N, y)$, it holds:

$$\boldsymbol{k} = (b_1 B_1 + \cdots + b_n B_n)\boldsymbol{r} + C\hat{\boldsymbol{r}} \quad \text{and} \quad \boldsymbol{c} = (b_1 B'_1 + \cdots + b_n B'_n)\boldsymbol{s} + C'\hat{\boldsymbol{s}}.$$

---

[6] Recall that we are assuming, without loss of generality, that the first polynomial produced by EncKey is $\alpha + r_1 b_1$ and that α does not appear anywhere else.

Now, note that, due to reconstructability of the original encoding, for any $N \in \mathbb{N}$, $x \in \mathcal{X}_\kappa$ and $y \in \mathcal{Y}_\kappa$ such that $P(x,y) = 1$, if we let $((\boldsymbol{v}\, E)\,, E') \leftarrow \mathsf{Pair}(N, x, y)$, it holds:

$$\boldsymbol{s}^\top (\boldsymbol{v}\, E) \begin{pmatrix} \alpha + r_1 b_1 \\ \boldsymbol{k} \end{pmatrix} + \boldsymbol{c}^\top E' \boldsymbol{r} = \alpha s_0,$$

which is equivalent to $\boldsymbol{s}^\top E \boldsymbol{k} + \boldsymbol{c}^\top E' \boldsymbol{r} = -s_0 r_1 b_1 \wedge \boldsymbol{v} = 1_{w_1}$, but then:

$$\boldsymbol{s}^\top E\big((b_1 B_1 + \cdots + b_n B_n)\boldsymbol{r} + C\hat{\boldsymbol{r}}\big) + \big(\boldsymbol{s}^\top (b_1 {B'_1}^\top + \cdots + b_n {B'_n}^\top) + \hat{\boldsymbol{s}}^\top {C'}^\top\big)E'\boldsymbol{r} = -s_0 r_1 b_1$$

and because the above equality must hold **symbolically**, it must be the case that $EB_1 + B'_1 E' = 1_{w_1 \times m_1}$ and $EB_j + B'_j E' = 0_{w_1 \times m_1}$ for every $j \in [2, n]$. Moreover, $EC = 0_{w_1 \times m_2}$ and ${C'}^\top E' = 0_{w_2 \times m_1}$. Finally, note that the non-reconstructability of the original encoding enforces that the above system does not have a solution when $P_\kappa(x, y) = 0$. $\qquad\square$

5   Generic Negation of Algebraic Pair Encodings

Although the general definition of pair encodings defines polynomials with coefficients over $\mathbb{Z}_N$ for an arbitrary integer $N \in \mathbb{N}$. In this section we assume that N is a prime number and write p instead. The reason is that our transformation for the negated encoding leverages a result from linear algebra (our Lemma 2) which requires that the underlying structure be a field. Note that this restriction does not significantly weaken our result, since prime-order groups are preferred over composite over groups.

Theorem 2. *Let* $(\mathsf{Param}^{\mathsf{alg}}, \mathsf{EncKey}^{\mathsf{alg}}, \mathsf{EncCt}^{\mathsf{alg}})$ *be an algebraic pair encoding for a predicate family* $P_\kappa : \mathcal{X}_\kappa \times \mathcal{Y}_\kappa \to \{0, 1\}$. *The encoding* $(\overline{\mathsf{Pair}}, \overline{\mathsf{EncKey}}, \overline{\mathsf{EncCt}})$ *described in Fig. 1 is an algebraic pair encoding for the predicate family* $\overline{P}_\kappa$ *given by* $\overline{P}(x, y) = 1 \Leftrightarrow P(x, y) = 0$ *for all* $x \in \mathcal{X}_\kappa$, $y \in \mathcal{Y}_\kappa$.

Proof. We need to show that whenever $P(x, y) = 0$, there exist matrices $\overline{E}$ and $\overline{E}'$ of dimension $w_1 \times (1 + m_1 n + m_2)$ and $(w_1 + w_1 n + w_2) \times m_1$ respectively, with coefficients in $\mathbb{Z}_p$, such that:

$$\overline{E}\,\overline{B}_0 + \overline{B}'^{\,\top}_0 \overline{E}' = 1_{w_1 \times m_1} \qquad\qquad \wedge \qquad \overline{E}\,\overline{C} = 0_{w_1 \times m_3}$$
$$\wedge \quad \overline{E}\,\overline{B}_j + \overline{B}'^{\,\top}_j \overline{E}' = 0_{w_1 \times m_1}, j \in [n+1] \qquad \wedge \qquad \overline{C}'^{\,\top} \overline{E}' = 0_{w_3 \times m_1}, \qquad (4)$$

where $(\overline{B}_0, \ldots, \overline{B}_{n+1}, \overline{C}) \leftarrow \overline{\mathsf{EncKey}}(p, x)$, $(\overline{B}'_0, \ldots, \overline{B}'_{n+1}, \overline{C}') \leftarrow \overline{\mathsf{EncCt}}(p, y)$. Now, our original encoding guarantees that $P(x, y) = 0$ if and only if there **do not** exist matrices E, E' such that:

$$EB_1 + {B'_1}^\top E' = 1_{w_1 \times m_1} \qquad\qquad \wedge \qquad EC = 0_{w_1 \times m_2}$$
$$\wedge \quad EB_j + {B'_j}^\top E' = 0_{w_1 \times m_1}, j \in [2, n] \qquad \wedge \qquad {C'}^\top E' = 0_{w_2 \times m_1},$$

Let (Param^{alg}, EncKey^{alg}, EncCt^{alg}) be an algebraic pair encoding scheme. We define the following (algebraic) PES:

- $\overline{\mathsf{Param}}(\mathsf{par}) := \text{run } n \leftarrow \mathsf{Param}^{\mathsf{alg}}(\mathsf{par})$, output $n+2$.

- $\overline{\mathsf{EncKey}}(p, x) := \text{run } (B_1, \dots, B_n, C) \leftarrow \mathsf{EncKey}^{\mathsf{alg}}(p, x)$, and let:

$$
\bar{B}_0 := \left(\frac{\mathbf{1}_{m_1}^{\mathsf{T}}}{\frac{\mathbf{1}_{m_1 n \times m_1}}{\mathbf{0}_{m_2 \times m_1}}}\right) \quad
\bar{B}_i := \left(\frac{\mathbf{0}_{m_1}^{\mathsf{T}}}{\frac{\boldsymbol{e}_i^n \otimes I_{m_1}}{\mathbf{0}_{m_2 \times m_1}}}\right) \quad
\bar{B}_{n+1} := \left(\frac{\mathbf{1}_{m_1}^{\mathsf{T}}}{\frac{\mathbf{0}_{m_1 n \times m_1}}{\mathbf{0}_{m_2 \times m_1}}}\right) \quad
\bar{C} := \left(\frac{\mathbf{0}_{m_3}^{\mathsf{T}}}{\frac{B_1^{\mathsf{T}}}{\frac{\vdots}{\frac{B_n^{\mathsf{T}}}{C^{\mathsf{T}}}}}}\right).
$$

Output $(\bar{B}_0, \bar{B}_1, \dots, \bar{B}_{n+1}, \bar{C})$.

- $\overline{\mathsf{EncCt}}(p, y) := \text{run } (B_1', \dots, B_n', C') \leftarrow \mathsf{EncCt}^{\mathsf{alg}}(p, y)$, let $\bar{B}_0'$ be the zero matrix of $w_1(1+n)+w_2$ rows and w_1 columns and let:

$$
\bar{B}_i' := \left(\frac{\mathbf{0}_{w_1 \times w_1}}{\frac{-\boldsymbol{e}_i^n \otimes I_{w_1}}{\mathbf{0}_{w_2 \times w_1}}}\right) \quad
\bar{B}_{n+1}' := \left(\frac{I_{w_1} - \mathbf{1}_{w_1 \times w_1}}{\frac{\mathbf{0}_{w_1 n \times w_1}}{\mathbf{0}_{w_2 \times w_1}}}\right) \quad
\bar{C}' := \left(\frac{\mathbf{0}_{w_1 \times w_3}}{\frac{B_1'^{\mathsf{T}}}{\frac{\vdots}{\frac{B_n'^{\mathsf{T}}}{C'^{\mathsf{T}}}}}}\right).
$$

Output $(\bar{B}_0', \bar{B}_1', \dots, \bar{B}_{n+1}', \bar{C}')$.

Fig. 1. Generic negation of algebraic pair encoding schemes.

for $(B_1, \dots, B_n, C) \leftarrow \mathsf{EncKey}(p, x)$ and $(B_1', \dots, B_n', C') \leftarrow \mathsf{EncCt}(p, y)$. But that is equivalent, in virtue of Lemma 2, to the existence of $Z_1, \dots, Z_n \in \mathbb{Z}_p^{m_1 \times w_1}$, $Z_A \in \mathbb{Z}_p^{m_2 \times w_1}$ and $Z_B \in \mathbb{Z}_p^{m_1 \times w_2}$ such that:[7]

$$
\begin{aligned}
B_1 Z_1 + \cdots + B_n Z_n + C Z_A = \mathbf{0}_{m_3 \times w_1} \\
\wedge \quad Z_1 B_1'^{\mathsf{T}} + \cdots + Z_n B_n'^{\mathsf{T}} + Z_B C'^{\mathsf{T}} = \mathbf{0}_{m_1 \times w_3}
\end{aligned}
\quad \wedge \quad \mathrm{tr}(\mathbf{1}_{w_1 \times m_1} Z_1) = 1. \quad (5)
$$

Now, for certain $\boldsymbol{v} \in \mathbb{Z}_p^{w_1}$ and $V \in \mathbb{Z}_p^{m_1 \times w_1}$ we can consider the matrices:

$$
\bar{E} := (\boldsymbol{v} \mid Z_1^{\mathsf{T}} \dots Z_n^{\mathsf{T}} \mid Z_A^{\mathsf{T}}) \quad \text{and} \quad \bar{E}' := (V \mid Z_1 \dots Z_n \mid Z_B)^{\mathsf{T}}, \quad (6)
$$

and observe that they satisfy all the equations in (4) if we set $\boldsymbol{v}$ to be the first column of Z_1^{T} multiplied by -1 (with the exception that $v_1 = 0$) and we set V to be the null matrix except for its first row, that is set to $-\boldsymbol{v}^{\mathsf{T}}$.

---

[7] To see why, set the matrices in Lemma 2 to $A_i := B_i$, $B_i := B_i'^{\mathsf{T}}$, for $i \in [n]$ and $C_1 := \mathbf{1}_{w_1 \times m_1}$, $C_j := \mathbf{0}_{w_1 \times m_1}$ for $j \in [2, n]$. Also, $\hat{A} := C$ and $\hat{B} := C'^{\mathsf{T}}$.

To conclude, observe that the converse is also true, i.e., if the equations in (4) admit a solution, then (5) is satisfiable. To see this, note that the left-hand side equations of (4) imply that any solution to them must be of the form of (6) for certain $\boldsymbol{v}$, V, $Z_1, \ldots, Z_n, Z_A, Z_B$. Furthermore, the right-hand side equations of (4) guarantee that such matrices Z_i, for $i \in \{1, \ldots, n, A, B\}$ satisfy (5). Therefore, we have shown that $P(x, y) = 0$ iff the equations in (4) have a solution.   □

Observe that, in general, if $(m_1, m_2, m_3, w_1, w_2, w_3, n)$ are the parameters of the original encoding, our negated transformation will produce an encoding with parameters $\bar{n} = n+2$ and:

$$\bar{m}_1 = m_1 \qquad \bar{m}_2 = m_3 \qquad \bar{m}_3 = 1 + m_1 n + m_2$$
$$\bar{w}_1 = w_1 \qquad \bar{w}_2 = w_3 \qquad \bar{w}_3 = w_1(1 + n) + w_2 - 1.$$

Note that, although the negated encoding may seem to have a much larger size compared to the original one, the matrices associated to the new encoding are actually very sparse and thus, our transformation will barely impact the performance of the ABE scheme build from the negated encoding.

Furthermore, note that our generic negation is compatible with the promising dynamic pair encoding composition technique very recently proposed by Attrapadung [6]. We believe our new transformation complements his work which could only achieve non-monotone formulae composition in a semi-generic (but dynamic) manner, since the composition had to rely on encodings for which a negated version was available.

6   Consequences of Our Results

Since Attrapadung introduced the notion of pair encoding schemes and the modular framework for constructing fully secure ABE from them [4], there have been several works [1,2,6] refining this framework and proposing new encoding schemes for different predicates, that sometimes enjoy extra properties (e.g., constant ciphertext size). The community has made a significant effort on building the negated version of most of the encodings from the literature, which in some cases is significantly more involved. However, there are still encodings for which not negation is known. Our generic transformation puts an end to this situation, since we can now take any encoding and immediately obtain its negated counterpart. A relevant example of a PES with (previously) unknown negation is the case of doubly spatial encryption.

6.1   PES for Negated Doubly Spatial Encryption

Doubly spatial encryption [20] is an important primitive that generalizes both spatial encryption[8] [13] and *negated spatial encryption*, defined by Attrapadung

---

[8] Spatial encryption is already a quite powerful predicate, that generalizes hierarchical identity-based encryption (HIBE).

and Libert [8]. It can be used to capture complex predicates and build flexible revocation systems. Its relevance is evidenced by the fact that a variant of it, called key-policy over doubly spatial encryption (defined by Attrapadung [4]), generalizes KP-ABE and leads to efficient unbounded KP-ABE schemes with large universes and KP-ABE with short ciphertexts. Given a field K, the doubly spatial predicate, over sets $\mathcal{X} := K^d \times K^{d \times \ell}$ and $\mathcal{Y} := K^d \times K^{d \times \ell'}$, $P((\boldsymbol{x}, X), (\boldsymbol{y}, Y))$, is defined as 1 if and only if the affine spaces $\boldsymbol{x} + \mathrm{span}(X)$ and $\boldsymbol{y} + \mathrm{span}(Y)$ intersect.

In the same way that negated spatial encryption generalizes spatial encryption and serves as its revocation analogue, unifying existing primitives (for example, it subsumes non-zero-mode IPE), negated *doubly* spatial encryption is a more expressive and very powerful primitive that deserves our attention. However, to the best of our knowledge, there does not exist a general pair encoding scheme for negated doubly spatial encryption in the literature. Attrapadung [4] provided a pair encoding for doubly spatial encryption and a negated version, for which he had to restrict one of the attributes (originally the ciphertext attribute) to be confined to just a vector instead of a general affine space. This encoding gave birth to the first fully-secure negated spatial encryption scheme, but it is not the negated version of *doubly* spatial encryption. In the rest of this section, we describe how to obtain the first, to the best of our knowledge, pair encoding scheme for negated doubly spatial encryption without restrictions.

We start from the following PES for doubly spatial encryption (over $\mathbb{Z}_N$) from [4]. (With $m_1 = 1$, $m_2 = 0$, $m_3 = \ell'+1$ and $w_1 = 1$, $w_2 = 0$, $w_3 = \ell+1$.)

$$\mathsf{Param}(\mathsf{par}) \to d+1 \text{ and let } \boldsymbol{b} = (b_0, \boldsymbol{b}') = (b_0, b_1, \dots, b_d)$$
$$\mathsf{EncKey}(N, (\boldsymbol{y}, Y)) := \{\alpha + r_1 b_0 + r_1 \boldsymbol{y}^\top \boldsymbol{b}', \ r_1 Y^\top \boldsymbol{b}'\}$$
$$\mathsf{EncCt}(N, (\boldsymbol{x}, X)) := \{\quad s_0 b_0 + s_0 \boldsymbol{x}^\top \boldsymbol{b}', \ s_0 X^\top \boldsymbol{b}'\}.$$

We refer to [4] for a proof of security and reconstructability.

In order to apply our negated transformation to this encoding, we first need to modify it so that it satisfies our structural assumption (see the first paragraph of our Sect. 4). For this, we can apply the conversion defined by Attrapadung [6, Section 4]. If we do so, we will get and encoding with $m_1 = 2$, $m_2 = 0$, $m_3 = \ell'+1$ and $w_1 = 2$, $w_2 = 0$, $w_3 = \ell+2$ that looks as follows (after renaming some variables):

$$\mathsf{Param}(\mathsf{par}) \to d+3 \text{ and let } \boldsymbol{b} = (b_0, \boldsymbol{b}', b_{d+1}, b_{d+2}) \text{ with } \boldsymbol{b}' = (b_1, \dots, b_d)$$
$$\mathsf{EncKey}(N, (\boldsymbol{y}, Y)) := \{r_1 b_{d+2} + r_2 b_{d+1} + r_2 \boldsymbol{y}^\top \boldsymbol{b}', \ r_2 Y^\top \boldsymbol{b}'\} \text{ (also } \alpha + r_1 b_0)$$
$$\mathsf{EncCt}(N, (\boldsymbol{x}, X)) := \{s_0 b_0 + s_1 b_{d+2}, \ s_1 b_{d+1} + s_1 \boldsymbol{x}^\top \boldsymbol{b}', \ s_1 X^\top \boldsymbol{b}'\}.$$

Applying our negation transformation to the above encoding, we obtain the pair encoding described in Fig. 3 (presented in Appendix A), where we have renamed[9] some common variables for the sake of readability. In Appendix A.1

---

[9] Before applying the transformation, we rename $b_0 \mapsto t$, $b_{d+1} \mapsto u$, $b_{d+2} \mapsto v$. After the transformation, the two new common variables are named b_0 and w respectively.

PES for predicate $P((\boldsymbol{x}, X), (\boldsymbol{y}, Y)) = 1 \Leftrightarrow (\boldsymbol{x} + \mathrm{span}(X)) \cap (\boldsymbol{y} + \mathrm{span}(Y)) = \emptyset$.

Where $\mathcal{X} := \mathbb{Z}_N^d \times \mathbb{Z}_N^{d \times \ell}$ and $\mathcal{Y} := \mathbb{Z}_N^d \times \mathbb{Z}_N^{d \times \ell'}$ for integers N, d, ℓ, ℓ'.

- **Param**(par) $\rightarrow d + 4$ and let $\boldsymbol{b} = (b_0, \boldsymbol{b}', t, u, v)$ with $\boldsymbol{b}' = (b_1, \dots, b_d)$.

- **EncKey**$(N, (\boldsymbol{y}, Y)) :=$
  $\{ r_1(b_0 + t),\ r_2 u + \hat{r}_1,\ r_1 v + \hat{r}_1,\ (Y_j \hat{\boldsymbol{r}}' + r_2 b_j + \hat{r}_1 y_j)_{j \in [d]} \}$ (also $\alpha + r_1 b_0$).

- **EncCt**$(N, (\boldsymbol{x}, X)) :=$
  $\{ s_0 t - \hat{s}_1,\ s_1 v - \hat{s}_1,\ s_1 u - \hat{s}_2,\ (X_j \hat{\boldsymbol{s}}' - s_1 b_j + \hat{s}_2 x_j)_{j \in [d]} \}$.

Here, $\boldsymbol{r} := (r_1, r_2)$, $\hat{\boldsymbol{r}} := (\hat{r}_1, \hat{\boldsymbol{r}}')$ with $\hat{\boldsymbol{r}}' := (\hat{r}_2, \dots, \hat{r}_{\ell'+1})$, and $\boldsymbol{s} := (s_0, s_1)$, $\hat{\boldsymbol{s}} := (\hat{s}_1, \hat{s}_2, \hat{\boldsymbol{s}}')$ with $\hat{\boldsymbol{s}}' := (\hat{s}_3, \dots, \hat{s}_{\ell+2})$.

Fig. 2. Simplified PES for negated doubly spatial encryption.

we show how we can slightly simplify the encoding from Fig. 3 and derive the encoding that we present in Fig. 2. Our Theorem 2 guarantees that it is a valid encoding for the negated doubly spatial encryption predicate, but we provide an independent proof in Appendix A.2.

The process of applying our generic negation by hand may seem tedious (but it seems necessary if we want to give an explicit description of an encoding that is parametric in size, like the one for negated doubly spatial encryption). However, notice that this process can be easily delegated to a computer, which does not need to have an explicit definition of the negated encoding. Instead, it can start from the non-negated encoding and apply the negation on the fly.

6.2   Other Implications of Our Transformation

Expressivity of Pair Encoding Schemes. A very important and long-standing open question about pair encoding schemes is *how expressive they really are.* They have led to breakthrough constructions such as constant-size ciphertext KP-ABE (with large universes) [4], fully-secure functional encryption for regular languages [4], completely-unbounded KP-ABE for non-monotone span programs (NSP) over large universes [6]. However, it is still unknown where their limit is. We believe our results bring new insight to answer this question and improve our understanding of pair encodings and their expressivity.

For example, there exist pair encodings for regular languages, where key attributes represent deterministic finite-state automata (DFSA), ciphertext attributes represent (arbitrarily long) words, and the predicate is defined as 1 iff the automaton accepts the word. However, building ABE for context-free languages (CFL) from pairings is still an important open problem, so it would be desirable to understand whether CFL can be constructed from pair encoding schemes. Our results imply that:

The set of predicates that can be expressed with PES is closed under negation.

This tells us new non-trivial information about what predicates can be expressed with a PES. In particular, it suggests that building PES for context-free languages may be harder than we think or even impossible. Note that context-free languages are not closed under complementation [21] and, consequently, if we can build a PES for CFL, we could build a PES for a predicate class that is strictly more powerful than CFL (at least the union of CFL and coCFL[10]). Of course, this reasoning does not allow us to roundly conclude anything, but it serves as an evidence of the difficulty of this problem.

Potential Performance Improvements. Not only does our generic transformation broaden the class of predicates that can be captured by pair encoding schemes, but it also can lead to efficiency improvements in actual ABE constructions. Observe the peculiar structure of the negated encodings produced with our transformation from Fig. 1. All of the matrices associated to common variables, $\overline{B}_i$ and $\overline{B}'_i$, have a fixed structure that is independent of the key attribute and the ciphertext attribute respectively (only the part associated to lone variables is dependent on the attributes). Furthermore, observe that they are arguably sparse. We can conclude that all pair encoding schemes admit a representation (an encoding for the same predicate) in this form, since we can always apply our transformation twice, leveraging the fact that the negation is an involution. However, in many cases it may be simpler to arrive at the mentioned structure more directly, by simply applying linear combinations and variable substitutions. What is important is that such a representation always exists.

This observation opens the possibility of splitting the computation of ciphertexts and secret keys into an offline part (before the attribute value is known) and an online part (once the attribute has been determined). Observe that such a strategy can bring significant performance improvements, given that operations involving common variables require a group exponentiation per matrix coefficient (since the common variables are available in the master public key in the form of group elements, with unknown discrete logarithm)[11], whereas operations involving lone variables can be batched together, reducing the number of exponentiations (one can do linear algebra over the field $\mathbb{Z}_N$ and perform one single exponentiation at the end). This is because the value of lone variables is freshly sampled during the computation and, therefore, known. This approach would not only reduce the online encryption and key generation time, but also the total time, since the offline computation can be reused for different attributes after it has been computed once.

---

[10] We denote by coCFL the class of languages whose complement is context-free.
[11] See the ABE compiler from PES described in Appendix B.2.

7   Conclusions and Future Work

Pair encodings are a simple, yet powerful, tool for building complex fully secure attribute-based encryption schemes. In this work, we have presented a generic transformation that takes any pair encoding scheme and negates its predicate. This construction finally solves a problem that was open since 2015 [10] and that has been considered to be non-obvious by several recent works [2,6]. Along the way, we have defined new results that improve our understanding of pair encodings and can be of independent interest, including a new encoding (previously unknown) for negated doubly spatial encryption, obtained with our transformation.

We propose several directions for future work. On the theoretical side, it would be interesting to explore whether our negation transformation can lead to simpler encodings as in [3]. In their work, Ambrona *et al.* show how, applying their negation to an encoding for monotone span programs [22] and after performing some simplifications, the new encoding is more compact and leads to an ABE that is twice as fast as the original one. The fact that the encoding is negated does not spoil its usage, since span programs are closed under negation and can be tweaked to implement the original functionality. The same technique of negating the encoding also results into a successful simplification in the case of arithmetic span programs. We believe the same kind of phenomenon can occur when negating pair encodings with our technique, potentially producing simpler encodings.

A very recent work [9] provides a new framework for constructing ABE schemes that support unbounded and dynamic predicate compositions whose security is proven under the standard matrix Diffie-Hellman assumption (generalizing the result by Attrapadung [6], which achieved the same kind of composition under the q-ratio assumption). The work by Attrapadung and Tomida [9] enables generic conjunctive and disjunctive compositions (which lead to *monotone* Boolean formula compositions). Extending their techniques in order to design a generic negation under standard assumptions is a very appealing direction for future work. (Note that the negation that we have provided in this work is applicable to the framework of Agrawal and Chase [2], thus it also relies on the less standard q-ratio assumption.)

On the practical side, it would be interesting to implement and evaluate the performance improvements that we propose in Sect. 6.2, exploiting the singular structure of the encodings produced by our transformation.

Acknowledgment. I would like to express my sincere gratitude to Nuttapong Attrapadung, for very fruitful discussions at the early stages of this project, and for pointing out that the transformation described herein would lead to an encoding for negated doubly spatial encryption. I would also like to thank Mehdi Tibouchi, for his help with the formulation of Lemma 1, which led to a simple proof for Lemma 2; and Elena Gutiérrez, for her advice on automata theory, and for all her feedback. Finally, I would like to thank the anonymous reviewers of PKC 2021, for their valuable time and multiple suggestions.

A   Pair Encoding for Negated Doubly Spatial Encryption

A.1   Building the Encoding

A direct application of our negated transformation (Fig. 1) to the encoding for doubly spatial encryption from [4] (after minor modifications so that it satisfies our structural constraints) leads to the encoding from Fig. 3. This encoding can be simplified, as the following reasoning shows that not all the polynomials are needed for reconstructability.

The only way to get polynomial $s_0 r_1 b_0$ (and consequently αs_0) as a linear combination of polynomials from $L = s \otimes k \cup c \otimes r$ is through the two first polynomials in the key (multiplied by s_0): $s_0 r_1 b_0 + s_0 r_1 w$ and $s_0 r_1 b_0 + s_0 r_1 t$. For that, we need to express monomial $s_0 r_1 w$ or monomial $s_0 r_1 t$ as a linear combination of other polynomials in L. The former is impossible to obtain (since monomial $s_0 r_1 w$ does not appear in any other polynomial in L). The latter can be achieved only through polynomial $r_1 s_0 t - r_1 \hat{s}_1 \in L$. Again, that requires to arrive at polynomial $r_1 \hat{s}_1$, which is present only in $r_1 s_1 v - r_1 \hat{s}_1$. Furthermore, $r_1 s_1 v$ can only be (additionally) found in $s_1 r_1 v + s_1 \hat{r}_1$. However, $s_1 \hat{r}_1$ is present in several polynomials in L, namely: $s_1 r_2 u + s_1 \hat{r}_1$ and $s_1 (Y_j \hat{r}' + r_2 b_j + \hat{r}_1 y_j)_{j \in [d]}$. The former contains a monomial, $s_1 r_2 u$, that only additionally appears in $r_2 s_1 u - r_2 \hat{s}_2$, but $r_2 \hat{s}_2$ is only present in polynomials $r_2 (X_j \hat{s}' - s_1 b_j + \hat{s}_2 x_j)_{j \in [d]}$. Consequently, reconstructability will be possible if there exist coefficients β_j and γ_j for all $j \in [0, d]$ such that:

$$s_1 \hat{r}_1 = \beta_0 (s_1 r_2 u + s_1 \hat{r}_1) + \sum_{j \in [d]} \beta_j s_1 (Y_j \hat{r}' + r_2 b_j + \hat{r}_1 y_j)$$
$$+ \gamma_0 (r_2 s_1 u - r_2 \hat{s}_2) + \sum_{j \in [d]} \gamma_j r_2 (X_j \hat{s}' - s_1 b_j + \hat{s}_2 x_j).$$

Considering the different monomials in both sides of the equation, we deduce:

$$
\begin{array}{ll}
s_1 \hat{r}_1 : \ 1 = \beta_0 + \sum_{j \in [d]} \beta_j y_j & r_2 \hat{s}_2 : \ 0 = -\gamma_0 + \sum_{j \in [d]} \gamma_j x_j \\
s_1 r_2 u : \ 0 = \beta_0 + \gamma_0 & s_1 r_2 b_j : \ 0 = \beta_j - \gamma_j \ \ \forall j \in [d] \\
s_1 \hat{r}' : \ \mathbf{0}_{\ell'} = \sum_{j \in [d]} \beta_j Y_j & r_2 \hat{s}' : \ \mathbf{0}_\ell = \sum_{j \in [d]} \gamma_j X_j
\end{array}
$$

Consequently, reconstructability is possible if there exist coefficients β_j for all $j \in [d]$ such that:

$$1 = \sum_{j \in [d]} \beta_j (y_j - x_j) \quad \wedge \quad \mathbf{0}_{\ell'} = \sum_{j \in [d]} \beta_j Y_j \quad \wedge \quad \mathbf{0}_\ell = \sum_{j \in [d]} \beta_j X_j.$$

But this is equivalent to $y - x \notin \mathrm{span}(Y) \cup \mathrm{span}(X)$ (see Lemma 1) which holds if and only if the predicate is true, as needed.

All the polynomials in the key and the ciphertext which have not been used for reconstructability can be eliminated. Figure 2 describes the resulting encoding after this simplification.

A.2   Arguing Security

Our Theorem 2 guarantees that the encoding from Fig. 3 is secure. Note that removing polynomials cannot change security (only spoil reconstructability), so

---

PES for predicate $P((\boldsymbol{x}, X), (\boldsymbol{y}, Y)) = 1 \Leftrightarrow (\boldsymbol{x} + \mathrm{span}(X)) \cap (\boldsymbol{y} + \mathrm{span}(Y)) = \emptyset$.

Where $\mathcal{X} := \mathbb{Z}_N^d \times \mathbb{Z}_N^{d \times \ell}$ and $\mathcal{Y} := \mathbb{Z}_N^d \times \mathbb{Z}_N^{d \times \ell'}$ for integers N, d, ℓ, ℓ'.

- $\mathsf{Param}(\mathrm{par}) \to d + 5$ and let $\boldsymbol{b} = (b_0, \boldsymbol{b'}, t, u, v, w)$ with $\boldsymbol{b'} = (b_1, \dots, b_d)$.

- $\mathsf{EncKey}(N, (\boldsymbol{y}, Y)) :=$
$\{\, r_1(b_0 + w),\ r_1(b_0 + t),\ r_2 t,\ r_2 v,\ r_1 u,\ r_2 u + \hat{r}_1,\ r_1 v + \hat{r}_1,$
$(Y_j \hat{\boldsymbol{r}}' + r_2 b_j + \hat{r}_1 y_j)_{j \in [d]},\ (r_1 b_j)_{j \in [d]} \,\}$ (and also $\alpha + r_1 b_0$).

- $\mathsf{EncCt}(N, (\boldsymbol{x}, X)) :=$
$\{\, s_1 w,\ s_1 t,\ s_0 t - \hat{s}_1,\ s_1 v - \hat{s}_1,\ s_1 u - \hat{s}_2,\ s_0 u,\ s_0 v$
$(X_j \hat{\boldsymbol{s}}' - s_1 b_j + \hat{s}_2 x_j)_{j \in [d]},\ (s_0 b_j)_{j \in [d]} \,\}$.

Here, $\boldsymbol{r} := (r_1, r_2)$, $\hat{\boldsymbol{r}} := (\hat{r}_1, \hat{\boldsymbol{r}}')$ with $\hat{\boldsymbol{r}}' := (\hat{r}_2, \dots, \hat{r}_{\ell'+1})$, and $\boldsymbol{s} := (s_0, s_1)$, $\hat{\boldsymbol{s}} := (\hat{s}_1, \hat{s}_2, \hat{\boldsymbol{s}}')$ with $\hat{\boldsymbol{s}}' := (\hat{s}_3, \dots, \hat{s}_{\ell+2})$.

Fig. 3. PES for negated doubly spatial encryption.

the simpler scheme presented in the main body (Fig. 2) must also be secure. Nevertheless, we provide an independent proof of its security, for the sake of completeness.

Proof (Security of the encoding from Fig. 2). Assume the predicate is false, i.e., the affine spaces $\boldsymbol{x} + \mathrm{span}(X)$ and $\boldsymbol{y} + \mathrm{span}(Y)$ intersect. Let $\boldsymbol{z} \in \mathbb{Z}_N^d$ be a vector in their intersection and let $\boldsymbol{z}_x \in \mathbb{Z}_N^\ell$ and $\boldsymbol{z}_y \in \mathbb{Z}_N^{\ell'}$ be such that:

$$\boldsymbol{x} + X \boldsymbol{z}_x = \boldsymbol{z} = \boldsymbol{y} + Y \boldsymbol{z}_y.$$

Observe that all the polynomials in $\mathsf{EncKey}(N, (\boldsymbol{y}, Y))$ and $\mathsf{EncCt}(N, (\boldsymbol{x}, X))$ (see Fig. 2) evaluate to zero on the following substitution:

$$(\boldsymbol{b}, \hat{\boldsymbol{r}}', \hat{\boldsymbol{s}}') \leftarrow (\boldsymbol{z}, \boldsymbol{z}_y, \boldsymbol{z}_x) \quad r_1, s_1, \hat{r}_1, \hat{s}_2, u, t, \alpha \leftarrow 1 \quad b_0, s_0, r_2, \hat{s}_1, v \leftarrow -1,$$

but polynomial αs_0 evaluates to -1 ($\neq 0$). As explained in Example 1, this is an evidence of the security of the encoding.

B   Additional Definitions

B.1   Security of Attribute-Based Encryption

An ABE scheme is *adaptively secure* if there exists a negligible ϵ such that for all PPT adversaries $\mathcal{A}$, and all sufficiently large $\lambda \in \mathbb{N}$, $\mathsf{Adv}_{\mathcal{A}}^{\mathsf{ABE}}(\lambda) < \epsilon(\lambda)$, where:

$$\mathsf{Adv}_{\mathcal{A}}^{\mathsf{ABE}}(\lambda) := \Pr \begin{bmatrix} (\mathrm{mpk}, \mathrm{msk}) \leftarrow \mathsf{Setup}(1^\lambda, \mathcal{X}, \mathcal{Y}) \\ x^\star \leftarrow \mathcal{A}^{\mathsf{KeyGen}(\mathrm{msk}, \cdot)}(\mathrm{mpk}) \\ (\mathrm{ct}_{x^\star}, \tau) \leftarrow \mathsf{Enc}(\mathrm{mpk}, x^\star) \quad : b' = b \\ b \xleftarrow{\$} \{0, 1\};\ \tau_0 := \tau;\ \tau_1 \xleftarrow{\$} \mathcal{K} \\ b' \leftarrow \mathcal{A}^{\mathsf{KeyGen}(\mathrm{msk}, \cdot)}(\mathrm{ct}_{x^\star}, \tau_b) \end{bmatrix} - \frac{1}{2}$$

where the advantage is defined to be zero if some of the queries y made by $\mathcal{A}$ to the KeyGen oracle violates the condition $P(x^\star, y) = 0$.

B.2   Attribute-Based Encryption from Pair Encodings

In order to explain how to build attribute-based encryption from pair encodings, we need to introduce the notion of dual system groups (DSG) [2,16,17], since the compilers from pair encodings into ABE [1,5] rely on DSG in a black-box way.

Dual System Groups

A dual system group is a tuple of six efficiently computable algorithms:

- SampP($1^\lambda, 1^n$): on input the security parameter and an integer n, outputs public parameters pp and secret parameters sp such that:
  - The public parameters, pp, include a triple of abelian groups (G, H, G_t) (that are $\mathbb{Z}_p$-modules for some λ-bits prime p), a non-degenerate bilinear map $e : G \times H \to G_t$, an homomorphism μ (defined over H) and additional parameters required by SampP and SampH.
  - Given pp, it is possible to uniformly sample to H.
  - The secret parameters, sp, include a distinguished element $h^* \in H$ (different from the unit) and additional parameters required by $\widehat{\text{SampG}}$ and $\widehat{\text{SampH}}$.
- SampG(pp) and $\widehat{\text{SampG}}$(pp, sp) output an element from G^{n+1}.
- SampH(pp) and $\widehat{\text{SampH}}$(pp, sp) output an element from H^{n+1}.
- SampGT is a function defined from $\text{Im}(\mu)$ to G_t.

Additional conditions are required for correctness and security:

projective: For all public parameters, pp, every $h \in H$ and all coin tosses σ, it holds SampGT($\mu(h); \sigma$) = $e(g_0, h)$, where $(g_0, g_1, \ldots, g_n) \leftarrow$ SampG(pp; r).
associative: Let $(g_0, g_1, \ldots, g_n) \leftarrow$ SampG(pp), $(h_0, h_1, \ldots, h_n) \leftarrow$ SampH(pp), it holds $e(g_0, h_i) = e(g_i, h_0)$ for every $i \in [n]$.
H-subgroup: SampH(pp) is the uniform distribution over a subgroup of H^{n+1}.
orthogonality: $h^* \in \text{Kernel}(\mu)$.
non-degeneracy: For every $(h_0, h_1, \ldots, h_n) \leftarrow$ SampH(pp), $h^* \in \langle h_0 \rangle$. Furthermore, for every $(\hat{g}_0, \hat{g}_1, \ldots, \hat{g}_n) \leftarrow \widehat{\text{SampG}}$(pp, sp), $(\alpha \xleftarrow{\$} \mathbb{Z}_p;$ return $e(\hat{g}_0, h^*)^\alpha)$ is the uniform distribution over G_t.
left-subgroup indistinguishability: (pp, g) $\approx_c$ (pp, $g \cdot \hat{g}$).
right-subgroup indistinguishability: (pp, h^*, $g \cdot \hat{g}$, h) $\approx_c$ (pp, h^*, $g \cdot \hat{g}$, $h \cdot \hat{h}$).
parameter-hiding: (pp, h^*, $\hat{g}$, $\hat{h}$) $\equiv$ (pp, h^*, $\hat{g} \cdot \hat{g}'$, $\hat{h} \cdot \hat{h}'$).

Where, $\approx_c$ denotes a distinguishing probability upper-bounded by a negligible function on λ and, for any $n \in \mathbb{N}$, the above elements are sampled as:

$$(\mathsf{pp}, \mathsf{sp}) \leftarrow \mathsf{SampP}(1^\lambda, 1^n)$$

$$
\begin{array}{lll}
g \leftarrow \mathsf{SampG}(\mathsf{pp}) & \hat{g} \leftarrow \widehat{\mathsf{SampG}}(\mathsf{pp}, \mathsf{sp}) & \hat{g}' := (1_{\mathsf{G}}, \hat{g}_0^{z_1}, \dots, \hat{g}_0^{z_n}) \\
h \leftarrow \mathsf{SampG}(\mathsf{pp}) & \hat{h} \leftarrow \widehat{\mathsf{SampG}}(\mathsf{pp}, \mathsf{sp}) & \hat{h}' := (1_{\mathsf{H}}, \hat{h}_0^{z_1}, \dots, \hat{h}_0^{z_n})
\end{array}
$$

for $z_1, \dots, z_n \overset{\$}{\leftarrow} \mathbb{Z}_p$.

Remark. Observe that we have presented the version of dual system groups defined in [15]. Other works consider slightly different conditions (e.g., the non-degeneracy of [1]). However, the widely used instantiation of DSG from k-lin given in [15] also satisfies the properties of those variations.

ABE from Pair Encodings

Given a pair encoding scheme $\{\mathsf{Param}, \mathsf{EncKey}, \mathsf{EncCt}, \mathsf{Pair}\}$ (see Definition 2) for a predicate family $P_\kappa : \mathcal{X}_\kappa \times \mathcal{Y}_\kappa \to \{0, 1\}$ indexed by $\kappa = (N, \mathsf{par})$ (let $\lambda = |N|$), an attribute-based encryption scheme can be constructed as follows:

- Setup($1^\lambda, \mathcal{X}_\kappa, \mathcal{Y}_\kappa$): let $n \leftarrow \mathsf{Param}(\mathsf{par})$ and run the DSG generation algorithm $\mathsf{SampP}(1^\lambda, 1^n)$ to obtain pp and sp. Let $\mathsf{msk} \overset{\$}{\leftarrow} \mathsf{H}$ and $\mathsf{mpk} := (\mathsf{pp}, \mu(\mathsf{msk}))$. Output $(\mathsf{mpk}, \mathsf{msk})$.
- Enc(mpk, x): run $\mathsf{EncCt}(N, x)$ to obtain polynomials $c_x(s, \hat{s}, b)$. For every $\ell \in [w_3]$, let the ℓ-th polynomial in c_x be

$$\sum_{i \in [w_2]} \gamma_i^{(\ell)} \hat{s}_i + \sum_{i \in [0, w_1 - 1]} \sum_{j \in [n]} \gamma_{\{i,j\}}^{(\ell)} s_i b_j$$

for some coefficients $\gamma_i^{(\ell)}$ and $\gamma_{\{i,j\}}^{(\ell)}$ in $\mathbb{Z}_p$. Now, run SampG to produce

$$
\begin{array}{ll}
(\hat{g}_{\{i,0\}}, \hat{g}_{\{i,1\}}, \dots, \hat{g}_{\{i,n\}}) \leftarrow \mathsf{SampG}(\mathsf{pp}) & \text{for } i \in [w_2] \\
(g_{\{i,0\}}, g_{\{i,1\}}, \dots, g_{\{i,n\}}) \leftarrow \mathsf{SampG}(\mathsf{pp}) & \text{for } i \in [0, w_1 - 1] \\
(g_{\{0,0\}}, g_{\{0,1\}}, \dots, g_{\{0,n\}}) \leftarrow \mathsf{SampG}(\mathsf{pp}; \sigma) &
\end{array}
$$

Observe that we have made explicit the coin tosses, σ, used in the last sampling. Setup $\mathsf{ct}_x := \left(\mathsf{ct}_0, \mathsf{ct}_1, \dots, \mathsf{ct}_{w_1 - 1}, \widetilde{\mathsf{ct}}_1, \dots, \widetilde{\mathsf{ct}}_{w_3} \right)$ and define the symmetric encryption key as $\tau := \mathsf{SampGT}(\mu(\mathsf{msk}); \sigma)$, where $\mathsf{ct}_i := g_{\{i,0\}}$ for every $i \in [0, w_1 - 1]$; and for every $\ell \in [w_3]$, $\widetilde{\mathsf{ct}}_\ell$ is computed as

$$\widetilde{\mathsf{ct}}_\ell := \prod_{i \in [w_2]} \hat{g}_{\{i,0\}}^{\gamma_i^{(\ell)}} \cdot \prod_{i \in [0, w_1 - 1]} \prod_{j \in [n]} g_{\{i,j\}}^{\gamma_{\{i,j\}}^{(\ell)}} \cdot$$

Output (ct_x, τ).

- KeyGen(msk, y): run EncKey(N, y) to obtain polynomials $\boldsymbol{k}_y(\boldsymbol{r}, \hat{\boldsymbol{r}}, \boldsymbol{b})$. For every $\ell \in [m_3]$, let the ℓ-th polynomial in $\boldsymbol{k}_y$ be

$$\phi^{(\ell)}\alpha + \sum_{i \in [m_2]} \phi_i^{(\ell)} \hat{r}_i + \sum_{i \in [m_1]} \sum_{j \in [n]} \phi_{\{i,j\}}^{(\ell)} r_i b_j$$

for some coefficients $\phi^{(\ell)}$, $\phi_i^{(\ell)}$ and $\phi_{\{i,j\}}^{(\ell)}$ in $\mathbb{Z}_p$. Now, run SampH to produce

$$(\hat{h}_{\{i,0\}}, \hat{h}_{\{i,1\}}, \ldots, \hat{h}_{\{i,n\}}) \leftarrow \mathsf{SampH}(\mathsf{pp}) \qquad \text{for } i \in [m_2]$$
$$(h_{\{i,0\}}, h_{\{i,1\}}, \ldots, h_{\{i,n\}}) \leftarrow \mathsf{SampH}(\mathsf{pp}) \qquad \text{for } i \in [m_1]$$

Define the secret key as $\mathsf{sk}_y := \left(\mathsf{sk}_1, \ldots, \mathsf{sk}_{m_1}, \widetilde{\mathsf{sk}}_1, \ldots, \widetilde{\mathsf{sk}}_{m_3}\right)$, where $\mathsf{sk}_i := h_{\{i,0\}}$ for every $i \in [m_1]$; and for every $\ell \in [m_3]$, $\widetilde{\mathsf{sk}}_\ell$ is computed as

$$\widetilde{\mathsf{sk}}_\ell := \mathsf{msk}^{\phi^{(\ell)}} \cdot \prod_{i \in [m_2]} \hat{h}_{\{i,0\}}^{\phi_i^{(\ell)}} \cdot \prod_{i \in [m_1]} \prod_{j \in [n]} h_{\{i,j\}}^{\phi_{\{i,j\}}^{(\ell)}}.$$

Output sk_y.
- Dec(mpk, sk_y, ct_x, x): run Pair(N, x, y) to obtain matrices E, E' (note that y is assumed to be extractable from sk_y, whereas x is explicitly included as an input to Dec). Define:

$$\tau := \prod_{i \in [w_1]} \prod_{\ell \in [m_3]} e(\mathsf{ct}_{i-1}, \widetilde{\mathsf{sk}}_\ell)^{E_{i,\ell}} \cdot \prod_{\ell \in [w_3]} \prod_{i \in [m_1]} e(\widetilde{\mathsf{ct}}_\ell, \mathsf{sk}_i)^{E'_{\ell,i}}$$

Output the symmetric encryption key τ.

References

1. Agrawal, S., Chase, M.: A study of pair encodings: predicate encryption in prime order groups. In: Kushilevitz, E., Malkin, T. (eds.) TCC 2016, Part II. LNCS, vol. 9563, pp. 259–288. Springer, Heidelberg (2016). https://doi.org/10.1007/978-3-662-49099-0_10
2. Agrawal, S., Chase, M.: Simplifying design and analysis of complex predicate encryption schemes. In: Coron, J.-S., Nielsen, J.B. (eds.) EUROCRYPT 2017, Part I. LNCS, vol. 10210, pp. 627–656. Springer, Cham (2017). https://doi.org/10.1007/978-3-319-56620-7_22
3. Ambrona, M., Barthe, G., Schmidt, B.: Generic transformations of predicate encodings: constructions and applications. In: Katz, J., Shacham, H. (eds.) CRYPTO 2017, Part I. LNCS, vol. 10401, pp. 36–66. Springer, Cham (2017). https://doi.org/10.1007/978-3-319-63688-7_2
4. Attrapadung, N.: Dual system encryption via doubly selective security: framework, fully secure functional encryption for regular languages, and more. In: Nguyen, P.Q., Oswald, E. (eds.) EUROCRYPT 2014. LNCS, vol. 8441, pp. 557–577. Springer, Heidelberg (2014). https://doi.org/10.1007/978-3-642-55220-5_31

5. Attrapadung, N.: Dual system encryption framework in prime-order groups via computational pair encodings. In: Cheon, J.H., Takagi, T. (eds.) ASIACRYPT 2016, Part II. LNCS, vol. 10032, pp. 591–623. Springer, Heidelberg (2016). https://doi.org/10.1007/978-3-662-53890-6_20

6. Attrapadung, N.: Unbounded dynamic predicate compositions in attribute-based encryption. In: Ishai, Y., Rijmen, V. (eds.) EUROCRYPT 2019, Part I. LNCS, vol. 11476, pp. 34–67. Springer, Cham (2019). https://doi.org/10.1007/978-3-030-17653-2_2

7. Attrapadung, N., Imai, H.: Dual-policy attribute based encryption. In: Abdalla, M., Pointcheval, D., Fouque, P.-A., Vergnaud, D. (eds.) ACNS 2009. LNCS, vol. 5536, pp. 168–185. Springer, Heidelberg (2009). https://doi.org/10.1007/978-3-642-01957-9_11

8. Attrapadung, N., Libert, B.: Functional encryption for inner product: achieving constant-size ciphertexts with adaptive security or support for negation. In: Nguyen, P.Q., Pointcheval, D. (eds.) PKC 2010. LNCS, vol. 6056, pp. 384–402. Springer, Heidelberg (2010). https://doi.org/10.1007/978-3-642-13013-7_23

9. Attrapadung, N., Tomida, J.: Unbounded dynamic predicate compositions in ABE from standard assumptions. In: Moriai, S., Wang, H. (eds.) ASIACRYPT 2020, Part III. LNCS, vol. 12493, pp. 405–436. Springer, Cham (2020). https://doi.org/10.1007/978-3-030-64840-4_14

10. Attrapadung, N., Yamada, S.: Duality in ABE: converting attribute based encryption for dual predicate and dual policy via computational encodings. In: Nyberg, K. (ed.) CT-RSA 2015. LNCS, vol. 9048, pp. 87–105. Springer, Cham (2015). https://doi.org/10.1007/978-3-319-16715-2_5

11. Beimel, A.: Secret-sharing schemes: a survey. In: Chee, Y.M., et al. (eds.) IWCC 2011. LNCS, vol. 6639, pp. 11–46. Springer, Heidelberg (2011). https://doi.org/10.1007/978-3-642-20901-7_2

12. Boneh, D., Boyen, X.: Efficient selective identity-based encryption without random oracles. J. Cryptol. **24**(4), 659–693 (2011)

13. Boneh, D., Hamburg, M.: Generalized identity based and broadcast encryption schemes. In: Pieprzyk, J. (ed.) ASIACRYPT 2008. LNCS, vol. 5350, pp. 455–470. Springer, Heidelberg (2008). https://doi.org/10.1007/978-3-540-89255-7_28

14. Chatterjee, S., Mukherjee, S., Pandit, T.: CCA-secure predicate encryption from pair encoding in prime order groups: generic and efficient. In: Patra, A., Smart, N.P. (eds.) INDOCRYPT 2017. LNCS, vol. 10698, pp. 85–106. Springer, Cham (2017). https://doi.org/10.1007/978-3-319-71667-1_5

15. Chen, J., Gay, R., Wee, H.: Improved dual system ABE in prime-order groups via predicate encodings. In: Oswald, E., Fischlin, M. (eds.) EUROCRYPT 2015, Part II. LNCS, vol. 9057, pp. 595–624. Springer, Heidelberg (2015). https://doi.org/10.1007/978-3-662-46803-6_20

16. Chen, J., Wee, H.: Fully, (almost) tightly secure IBE and dual system groups. In: Canetti, R., Garay, J.A. (eds.) CRYPTO 2013, Part II. LNCS, vol. 8043, pp. 435–460. Springer, Heidelberg (2013). https://doi.org/10.1007/978-3-642-40084-1_25

17. Chen, J., Wee, H.: Dual system groups and its applications – compact HIBE and more. Cryptology ePrint Archive, Report 2014/265 (2014). http://eprint.iacr.org/2014/265

18. Gorbunov, S., Vaikuntanathan, V., Wee, H.: Attribute-based encryption for circuits. In: Boneh, D., Roughgarden, T., Feigenbaum, J. (eds.) 45th ACM STOC, pp. 545–554. ACM Press, June 2013

19. Goyal, V., Pandey, O., Sahai, A., Waters, B.: Attribute-based encryption for fine-grained access control of encrypted data. In: Juels, A., Wright, R.N., De Capitani di Vimercati, S. (eds.) ACM CCS 2006, pp. 89–98. ACM Press, October/November 2006. Available as Cryptology ePrint Archive Report 2006/309

20. Hamburg, M.: Spatial encryption. Cryptology ePrint Archive, Report 2011/389 (2011). http://eprint.iacr.org/2011/389

21. Hopcroft, J.E., Ullman, J.D.: Introduction to Automata Theory, Languages and Computation. Addison-Wesley, Boston (1979)

22. Karchmer, M., Wigderson, A.: On span programs. In: Proceedings of Structures in Complexity Theory, pp. 102–111 (1993)

23. Katz, J., Sahai, A., Waters, B.: Predicate encryption supporting disjunctions, polynomial equations, and inner products. In: Smart, N. (ed.) EUROCRYPT 2008. LNCS, vol. 4965, pp. 146–162. Springer, Heidelberg (2008). https://doi.org/10.1007/978-3-540-78967-3_9

24. Kim, J., Susilo, W., Guo, F., Au, M.H.: A tag based encoding: an efficient encoding for predicate encryption in prime order groups. In: Zikas, V., De Prisco, R. (eds.) SCN 2016. LNCS, vol. 9841, pp. 3–22. Springer, Cham (2016). https://doi.org/10.1007/978-3-319-44618-9_1

25. Lewko, A., Waters, B.: New techniques for dual system encryption and fully secure HIBE with short ciphertexts. In: Micciancio, D. (ed.) TCC 2010. LNCS, vol. 5978, pp. 455–479. Springer, Heidelberg (2010). https://doi.org/10.1007/978-3-642-11799-2_27

26. Lewko, A., Waters, B.: Unbounded HIBE and attribute-based encryption. In: Paterson, K.G. (ed.) EUROCRYPT 2011. LNCS, vol. 6632, pp. 547–567. Springer, Heidelberg (2011). https://doi.org/10.1007/978-3-642-20465-4_30

27. Lewko, A.B., Waters, B.: New proof methods for attribute-based encryption: achieving full security through selective techniques. In: Safavi-Naini, R., Canetti, R. (eds.) CRYPTO 2012. LNCS, vol. 7417, pp. 180–198. Springer, Heidelberg (2012). https://doi.org/10.1007/978-3-642-32009-5_12

28. Ostrovsky, R., Sahai, A., Waters, B.: Attribute-based encryption with non-monotonic access structures. In: Ning, P., De Capitani di Vimercati, S., Syverson, P.F. (eds.) ACM CCS 2007, pp. 195–203. ACM Press, October 2007

29. Rouselakis, Y., Waters, B.: Practical constructions and new proof methods for large universe attribute-based encryption. In: Sadeghi, A.-R., Gligor, V.D., Yung, M. (eds.) ACM CCS 2013, pp. 463–474. ACM Press, November 2013

30. Sahai, A., Waters, B.: Fuzzy identity-based encryption. In: Cramer, R. (ed.) EUROCRYPT 2005. LNCS, vol. 3494, pp. 457–473. Springer, Heidelberg (2005). https://doi.org/10.1007/11426639_27

31. Shamir, A.: Identity-based cryptosystems and signature schemes. In: Blakley, G.R., Chaum, D. (eds.) CRYPTO 1984. LNCS, vol. 196, pp. 47–53. Springer, Heidelberg (1985). https://doi.org/10.1007/3-540-39568-7_5

32. Waters, B.: Dual system encryption: realizing fully secure IBE and HIBE under simple assumptions. In: Halevi, S. (ed.) CRYPTO 2009. LNCS, vol. 5677, pp. 619–636. Springer, Heidelberg (2009). https://doi.org/10.1007/978-3-642-03356-8_36

33. Waters, B.: Functional encryption for regular languages. In: Safavi-Naini, R., Canetti, R. (eds.) CRYPTO 2012. LNCS, vol. 7417, pp. 218–235. Springer, Heidelberg (2012). https://doi.org/10.1007/978-3-642-32009-5_14

34. Wee, H.: Dual system encryption via predicate encodings. In: Lindell, Y. (ed.) TCC 2014. LNCS, vol. 8349, pp. 616–637. Springer, Heidelberg (2014). https://doi.org/10.1007/978-3-642-54242-8_26

On Selective-Opening Security
of Deterministic Primitives

Adam O'Neill[1]([✉]) and Mohammad Zaheri[2]

[1] College of Information and Computer Sciences, University of Massachusetts
Amherst, Amherst, USA
adamo@cs.umass.edu
[2] Snap Inc., Santa Monica, USA
mzaheri@snap.com

Abstract. Classically, selective-opening attack (SOA) has been studied
for *randomized* primitives, like randomized encryption schemes and commitments. The study of SOA for deterministic primitives, which presents
some unique challenges, was initiated by Bellare *et al.* (PKC 2015), who
showed negative results. Subsequently, Hoang *et al.* (ASIACRYPT 2016)
showed positive results in the non-programmable random oracle model.
Here we show the first positive results for SOA security of deterministic
primitives in the *standard* (RO devoid) model. Our results are:

- Any $2t$-wise independent hash function is SOA secure for an
  unbounded number of "t-correlated" messages, meaning any group
  of up to t messages are arbitrarily correlated.
- A construction of a deterministic encryption scheme with analogous
  security, combining a regular lossy trapdoor function with a $2t$-wise
  independent hash function.
- The one-more-RSA problem of Bellare *et al.* (J. Cryptology 2003),
  which can be seen as a form of SOA, is hard under the Φ-Hiding
  Assumption with large enough encryption exponent.

Somewhat surprisingly, the last result yields the first proof of RSA-based
Chaum's blind signature scheme (CRYPTO 1982), albeit for large exponent e, based on a "standard" computational assumption. Notably, it
avoids the impossibility result of Pass (STOC 2011) because lossiness of
RSA endows the scheme with non-unique signatures.

Keywords: Selective opening security · One-more RSA · Randomness
extractor · Deterministic public-key encryption · Information theoretic
setting

1 Introduction

In this paper, we study selective-opening-attack (SOA) security of some *deterministic* primitives, namely hash functions, (public-key) deterministic encryption, and trapdoor functions. In particular, we extend the work of Hoang
et al. [20] in addition to answering some open questions there. We also provide
a new analysis of Chaum's blind signature scheme [12].

Work done while M.Z. was a PhD student at Georgetown University.

J. A. Garay (Ed.): PKC 2021, LNCS 12711, pp. 147–172, 2021.
https://doi.org/10.1007/978-3-030-75248-4_6

1.1 Background and Motivation

SOA SECURITY. Roughly, SOA security of a cryptographic primitive refers to giving the adversary the power to adaptively choose instances of the primitive to corrupt and considering security of the uncorrupted instances. SOA grew out of work on non-committing and deniable primitives [6,9–11,14,16,26,27,31], which are even stronger forms of security. Namely, SOA has been studied in a line of work on public-key encryption and commitments started by Bellare, Hofheinz, and Yilek [2,3,7,19,21,22]. When considering adaptive corruption, SOA arguably captures the security one wants in practice. Here we only consider *sender* SOA (*i.e.*, sender, not receiver, corruption), which we just refer to SOA security in the remainder of the paper for simplicity.

SOA FOR DETERMINISTIC ENCRYPTION. SOA security has usually been studied for *randomized* primitives, where the parties use random coins that are given to the adversary when corrupted, in particular randomized encryption. The study of SOA for deterministic primitives, namely deterministic encryption was initiated by Bellare *et al.* [1], who showed an impossibility result wrt. a simulation based definition. Subsequently, Hoang *et al.* [20] proposed a comparison based definition and showed positive results in the non programmable random oracle (RO) model [5,25]. They left open the problem of constructions in the standard (RO devoid) model, which we study in this work. In particular, Hoang *et al.* emphasized this problem is open even for uniform and independent messages.

SOA FOR HASH FUNCTIONS. In addition to randomized encryption, SOA security has often been considered for randomized commitments. Note that a simple construction of a commitment in the RO model is $H(x\|r)$ where x is the input and r is the randomness (decommitment). Analogously to the case of encryption, we study SOA security of hash functions. This can also be seen as studying the more basic case compared to deterministic encryption, as Goyal *et al.* [18] did in the non-SOA setting. The practical motivation is *password hashing*—note some passwords may be recovered by coercion, and one would like to say something about security of the other passwords.

ONE-MORE RSA INVERSION PROBLEM. Finally, an influential problem that we cast in the framework of SOA (this problem has not been explicitly connected to SOA before as far as we are aware) is the *one-more RSA inversion problem* of Bellare *et al.* [4]. Informally, the problem asks that an adversary with many RSA challenges and an inversion oracle cannot produce more preimages than number of oracle calls. Bellare *et al.* show this leads to a proof of security of Chaum's blind signature scheme in the RO model.

CHALLENGES. For randomized primitives, a key challenge in security proofs has been that at the time the simulator prepares the challenge ciphertexts it does not know the subset that the adversary will corrupt. Compared to randomized primitives, deterministic primitives additionally presents some unique challenges in the SOA setting. To see why, say for encryption, a common strategy is for the simulator to "lie" about the randomness in order to make the message encrypt to the right ciphertext. However, in the deterministic case the adversary there is no randomness to fake.

1.2 Our Contributions

RESULTS FOR HASH FUNCTIONS. We start with the study of a more basic primitive than deterministic encryption, namely hash functions (which in some sense are the deterministic analogue of commitments). We note that SOA notion for hash functions is stronger than the one-wayness notion. We point out that the SOA adversary without any opening could simply run the one-wayness adversary on each image challenge and recover the preimages. Thus, SOA notion is strictly stronger than one-wayness. Here we show results for an unbounded number of "t-correlated" messages, meaning each set of up to t messages may be arbitrarily correlated. Namely, we show that $2t$-wise independent hash functions, which can be realized information-theoretically by a classical construction of polynomial evaluation. We also consider the notion of t-correlated messages to be interesting in its own right, and it captures a setting with password hashing where a password is correlated with a small number of others (and it is even stronger than that, in that a password may be correlated with *any* small number of others).

To show $2t$-wise independent hash functions are SOA secure, we first show that in the information theoretic setting, knowing the content of the opened messages increases the upper-bound on the adversary's advantage by at most factor of 2. This is because the messages are independent, and knowing the opened messages does not increase the adversary's advantage in guessing the unopened messages. Then, we show that for any hash key s in the set of "good hash keys", the probability of $H(s, X) = y$ is almost equally distributed over all hash value y. Therefore, we can show for any hash key s in the set of "good hash keys" and any vector of hash values, opening does not increase the upper-bound on adversary's advantage. Thus, it is only enough to bound the adversary's advantage without any opening. Note that this strategy avoids the exponential (in the number of messages) blow-up in the bound compared to the naïve strategy of guessing the subset the adversary will open.

CONSTRUCTIONS IN THE STANDARD MODEL. In the setting of deterministic encryption, it is easy to see the same strategy as above works using lossy trapdoor functions [30] that are $2t$-wise independent in the lossy mode. However, for $t > 1$ we are not aware of any such construction and highlight this as an interesting open problem.[1] Hence, we turn to building a D-SO-CPA secure scheme in the standard model. We give a new DPKE scheme using $2t$-wise independent hash functions and regular lossy trapdoor function [30], which has practical instantiations, *e.g.*, RSA is regular lossy [24]. A close variant of our scheme is shown to be D-SO-CPA secure in the NPROM [20]. The proof strategy here is very

---

[1] It is tempting to give a Paillier-based construction with a degree $2t$ polynomial in the exponent, but unfortunately the coefficients don't lie in a field so the classical proof of $2t$-wise independence does not work.

similar to the hash function case above. We start by switching to the lossy mode and then bound the adversary's advantage in the information-theoretic setting.

RESULTS FOR ONE-MORE-RSA. Bellare *et al.* [4] were first to introduce one-more-RSA problem. They show assuming hardness of the one-more-RSA inversion problem leads to a proof of security of Chaum's blind signature scheme [12] in the random oracle model. This problem is natural SOA extension of the one-wayness of RSA. Intuitively, in the one-more inversion problem, the adversary gets a number of image points and has access to the corruption oracle that allows it to get preimages for image points of its choice. It needs to produce one more correct preimage than the number of queries it makes. We show that one-more inversion problem is hard for RSA with a large enough encryption exponent e. In particular, we show that one-more inversion problem is hard for any regular lossy trapdoor function. Intuitively, we show that in the lossy mode the images are uniformly distributed. Then we show that inverting even one of the images is hard, since any preimage x is equally likely. RSA is known to be regular lossy under the Φ-Hiding Assumption [24]. Thus, by the result of [4], we obtain a security proof for Chaum's scheme.[2] Interestingly, this result avoids an impossibility result of Pass [29] because if RSA is lossy then Chaum's scheme does not have unique signatures. Analogously, in a different context, Kakvi and Kiltz [23] used non-uniqueness of RSA-FDH signatures under Φ-Hiding to show tight security, getting around an impossibility result of Coron [13].

1.3   Seeing us as Replacing Random Oracles

Another way of seeing our treatment of hash functions is as isolating a property of random oracles and realizing it in the standard model, building on a line of work in this vein started by Canetti [8]. In this context, it would be interesting to consider *adaptive* SOA security for hash functions similar to [28] who consider adaptive commitments. We leave this as another open problem. Additionally, it would be interesting to see if our results allow replacing ROs in any particular higher-level protocols.

2   Preliminaries

2.1   Notation and Conventions

For a probabilistic algorithm A, by $y \leftarrow_{\$} A(x)$ we mean that A is executed on input x and the output is assigned to y. We sometimes use $y \leftarrow A(x; r)$ to make A's random coins explicit. If A is deterministic we denote this instead by $y \leftarrow A(x)$. We denote by $[A(x)]$ the set of all possible outputs of A when run on input x. For a finite set S, we denote by $s \leftarrow_{\$} S$ the choice of a uniformly random element from S and assigning it to s.

---

[2] This glosses over an issue about regularity of lossy RSA on subdomains discussed in the body.

Let $\mathbb{N}$ denote the set of all non-negative integers. For any $n \in \mathbb{N}$ we denote by $[n]$ the set $\{1, \ldots, n\}$. For a vector $\mathbf{x}$, we denote by $|\mathbf{x}|$ its length (number of components) and by $\mathbf{x}[i]$ its i-th component. For a vector $\mathbf{x}$ of length n and any $I \subseteq [n]$, we denote by $\mathbf{x}[I]$ the vector of length $|I|$ such that $\mathbf{x}[I] = (\mathbf{x}[i])_{i \in I}$, and by $\mathbf{x}[\overline{I}]$ the vector of length $n - |I|$ such that $\mathbf{x}[\overline{I}] = (\mathbf{x}[i])_{i \notin I}$. For a string X, we denote by $|X|$ its length.

Let X, Y be random variables taking values on a common finite domain. The *statistical distance* between X and Y is given by

$$\Delta(X, Y) = \frac{1}{2} \sum_x \left| \Pr[X = x] - \Pr[Y = x] \right|.$$

We also define $\Delta(X, Y \mid S) = \frac{1}{2} \sum_{x \in S} |\Pr[X = x] - \Pr[Y = x]|$, for a set S. The *min-entropy* of a random variable X is $\mathrm{H}_\infty(X) = -\log(\max_x \Pr[X = x])$. The *average conditional min-entropy* of X given Y is

$$\widetilde{\mathrm{H}}_\infty(X|Y) = -\log(\sum_y P_Y(y) \max_x \Pr[X = x \mid Y = y]).$$

ENTROPY AFTER INFORMATION LEAKAGE. Dodis *et al.* [15] characterized the effect of auxiliary information on average min-entropy:

Lemma 1. [15] Let X, Y, Z be random variables and $\delta > 0$ be a real number.
(a) If Y has at most 2^λ possible values then we have $\widetilde{\mathrm{H}}_\infty(X \mid Z, Y) \geq \widetilde{\mathrm{H}}_\infty(X \mid Z) - \lambda$.
(b) Let S be the set of values b such that $\mathrm{H}_\infty(X \mid Y = b) \geq \widetilde{\mathrm{H}}_\infty(X \mid Y) - \log(1/\delta)$. Then it holds that $\Pr[Y \in S] \geq 1 - \delta$.

2.2 Public-Key Encryption

PUBLIC-KEY ENCRYPTION. A public-key encryption scheme PKE with message-space Msg is a tuple of algorithms (Kg, Enc, Dec) defined as follows. The key-generation algorithm Kg on input unary encoding of the security parameter 1^k outputs a public key pk and matching secret key sk. The encryption algorithm Enc on inputs a public key pk and message $m \in \mathsf{Msg}(1^k)$ outputs a ciphertext c. The deterministic decryption algorithm Dec on inputs a secret key sk and ciphertext c outputs a message m or $\perp$. We require that for all $(pk, sk) \in [\mathsf{Kg}(1^k)]$ and all $m \in \mathsf{Msg}(1^k)$, it holds that $\mathsf{Dec}(sk, (\mathsf{Enc}(pk, m))) = m$. We say that PKE is *deterministic* if Enc is deterministic.

D-SO-CPA SECURITY. Let DE = (Kg, Enc, Dec) be a D-PKE scheme. To a message sampler $\mathcal{M}$ and an adversary $A = (A.\mathrm{pg}, A.\mathrm{cor}, A.\mathrm{g}, A.\mathrm{f})$, we associate the experiment in Fig. 1 for every $k \in \mathbb{N}$. We say that DE is D-SO-CPA secure for a class $\mathcal{M}$ of efficiently resamplable message samplers and a class $\mathcal{A}$ of adversaries if for every $\mathcal{M} \in \mathcal{M}$ and any $A \in \mathcal{A}$,

$$\mathbf{Adv}_{\mathsf{DE}, A, \mathcal{M}}^{\mathrm{d\text{-}so\text{-}cpa}}(k)$$

$$= \Pr\left[\text{D-CPA1-REAL}_{\mathsf{DE}}^{A, \mathcal{M}}(k) \Rightarrow 1\right] - \Pr\left[\text{D-CPA1-IDEAL}_{\mathsf{DE}}^{A, \mathcal{M}}(k) \Rightarrow 1\right]$$

Game D-CPA1-REAL$_{\mathsf{DE}}^{A,\mathcal{M}}(k)$	**Game** D-CPA1-IDEAL$_{\mathsf{DE}}^{A,\mathcal{M}}(k)$
$param \leftarrow\!\!{}_\$ A.\mathrm{pg}(1^k)$	$param \leftarrow\!\!{}_\$ A.\mathrm{pg}(1^k)$
$(pk, sk) \leftarrow\!\!{}_\$ \mathsf{Kg}(1^k)$	$(pk, sk) \leftarrow\!\!{}_\$ \mathsf{Kg}(1^k)$
$\mathbf{m}_1 \leftarrow\!\!{}_\$ \mathcal{M}(1^k, param)$	$\mathbf{m}_1 \leftarrow\!\!{}_\$ \mathcal{M}(1^k, param)$
For $i = 1$ to $|\mathbf{m}|$ do	For $i = 1$ to $|\mathbf{m}|$ do
$\quad \mathbf{c}[i] \leftarrow \mathsf{Enc}(pk, \mathbf{m}_1[i])$	$\quad \mathbf{c}[i] \leftarrow \mathsf{Enc}(pk, \mathbf{m}_1[i])$
$(state, I) \leftarrow\!\!{}_\$ A.\mathrm{cor}(pk, \mathbf{c}, param)$	$(state, I) \leftarrow\!\!{}_\$ A.\mathrm{cor}(pk, \mathbf{c}, param)$
$\omega \leftarrow\!\!{}_\$ A.\mathrm{g}(state, \mathbf{m}_1[I], param)$	$\mathbf{m}_0 \leftarrow\!\!{}_\$ \mathsf{Resamp}_{\mathcal{M}}(1^k, \mathbf{m}_1[I], I, param)$
Return $(\omega = A.\mathrm{f}(\mathbf{m}_1, param))$	$\omega \leftarrow\!\!{}_\$ A.\mathrm{g}(state, \mathbf{m}_1[I], param)$
	Return $(\omega = A.\mathrm{f}(\mathbf{m}_0, param))$

Fig. 1. Games to define the D-SO-CPA security.

is negligible in k.

2.3 Lossy Trapdoor Functions and Their Security

LOSSY TRAPDOOR FUNCTIONS. A lossy trapdoor function [30] with domain LDom, range LRng and lossiness τ is a tuple of algorithms LT = (IKg, LKg, Eval, Inv) that work as follows. Algorithm IKg on input a unary encoding of the security parameter 1^k outputs an "injective" evaluation key ek and matching trapdoor td. Algorithm LKg on input 1^k outputs a "lossy" evaluation key lk. Algorithm Eval on inputs an (either injective or lossy) evaluation key ek and $x \in \mathsf{LDom}(k)$ outputs $y \in \mathsf{LRng}(k)$. Algorithm Inv on inputs a trapdoor td and a $y \in \mathsf{LRng}(k)$ outputs $x \in \mathsf{LDom}(k)$. We denote by $\mathsf{Img}(lk)$ the co-domain of $\mathsf{Eval}(lk, \cdot)$. We require the following properties:

Correctness: For all $k \in \mathbb{N}$, all $(ek, td) \in [\mathsf{IKg}(1^k)]$ and all $x \in \mathsf{LDom}(k)$ it holds that $\mathsf{Inv}(td, \mathsf{Eval}(ek, x)) = x$.

Key Indistinguishability: We require that for every PPT distinguisher D, the following advantage be negligible in k.

$$\mathbf{Adv}_{\mathsf{LT},D}^{\mathsf{ltdf}}(k) = \Pr\left[D(ek) \Rightarrow 1\right] - \Pr\left[D(lk) \Rightarrow 1\right].$$

where $(ek, td) \leftarrow\!\!{}_\$ \mathsf{IKg}(1^k)$ and $lk \leftarrow\!\!{}_\$ \mathsf{LKg}(1^k)$.

Lossiness: The size of the co-domain of $\mathsf{Eval}(lk, \cdot)$ is at most $|\mathsf{LRng}(k)|/2^{\tau(k)}$ for all $k \in \mathbb{N}$ and all $lk \in [\mathsf{LKg}(1^k)]$. We call τ the *lossiness* of LT.

t-WISE INDEPENDENT. Let LT be a lossy trapdoor function with domain LDom, range LRng and lossiness τ. We say LT is t-wise independent if for all $lk \in [\mathsf{LKg}(1^k)]$ and all distinct $x_1, \ldots, x_{t(k)} \in \mathsf{LDom}(k)$

$$\Delta\left((\mathsf{Eval}(lk, x_1), \ldots, \mathsf{Eval}(lk, x_{t(k)})), (U_1, \ldots, U_{t(k)})\right) = 0$$

where $lk \leftarrow\!\!{}_\$ \mathsf{LKg}(1^k)$ and $U_1, \ldots, U_{t(k)}$ are uniform and independent on $\mathsf{LRng}(k)$.

REGULARITY. Let LT be a lossy trapdoor function with domain LDom, range LRng and lossiness τ. We say LT is regular if for all $lk \in [\mathsf{LKg}(1^k)]$ and all $y \in \mathsf{Img}(lk)$, we have $\Pr[\mathsf{Eval}(lk, U) = y] = 1/\|\mathsf{Img}(lk)\|$, where U is uniform on $\mathsf{LDom}(k)$.

2.4 Hash Functions and Associated Security Notions

HASH FUNCTIONS. A *hash function* with domain HDom and range HRng is a pair of algorithms $\mathsf{H} = (\mathsf{HKg}, \mathsf{h})$ that work as follows. Algorithm HKg on input a unary encoding of the security parameter 1^k outputs a key K. Algorithm h on inputs a key K and $x \in \mathsf{HDom}(k)$ outputs $y \in \mathsf{HRng}(k)$. We say that H is *t-wise independent* if for all $k \in \mathbb{N}$ and all distinct $x_1, \ldots, x_{t(k)} \in \mathsf{HDom}(k)$

$$\Delta\left((\mathsf{h}(K, x_1), \ldots, \mathsf{h}(K, x_{t(k)})), (U_1, \ldots, U_{t(k)})\right) = 0$$

where $K \leftarrow_{\$} \mathsf{HKg}(1^k)$ and $U_1, \ldots, U_{t(k)}$ are uniform and independent in $\mathsf{HRng}(k)$.

3 Selective Opening Security for Hash Functions

Bellare, Dowsley, and Keelveedhi [1] were the first to consider selective-opening security of deterministic PKE. They propose a "simulation-based" semantic security notion, but then show that this definition is unachievable in both the standard model and the non-programmable random-oracle model. Later in [20] Hoang *et al.* introduce an alternative, "comparison-based" semantic-security notion and show that this definition is achievable in the non-programmable random-oracle model but leave it open in the standard model. In this section, we extend their definitions to hash function families and show that *t*-wise independent hash functions are selective opening secure under this notion.

3.1 Security Notion

MESSAGE SAMPLERS. A *message sampler* $\mathcal{M}$ is a PPT algorithm that takes as input the unary representation 1^k of the security parameter and a string $param \in \{0, 1\}^*$, and outputs a vector $\mathbf{m}$ of messages. We require that $\mathcal{M}$ be associated with functions v and n such that for any $param \in \{0, 1\}^*$, for any $k \in \mathbb{N}$, and any $\mathbf{m} \in [\mathcal{M}(1^k, param)]$, we have $|\mathbf{m}| = v(k)$ and $|\mathbf{m}[i]| = n(k)$, for every $i \leq |\mathbf{m}|$. Moreover, the components of $\mathbf{m}$ must be distinct. Let $\mathsf{Coins}[k]$ be the set of coins for $\mathcal{M}(1^k, \cdot)$. Define $\mathsf{Coins}[k, \mathbf{m}, I, param] = \{\omega \in \mathsf{Coins}[k] \mid \mathbf{m}[I] = \mathbf{m}'[I]$, where $\mathbf{m}' \leftarrow \mathcal{M}(1^k, param; \omega)\}$.

A message sampler $\mathcal{M}$ is (μ, d)-*correlated* if

- For any $k \in \mathbb{N}$, any $param \in \{0, 1\}^*$, every $\mathbf{m} \in [\mathcal{M}(1^k, param)]$ and any $i \in [v]$, $\mathbf{m}[i]$ have min-entropy at least μ and is independent of at least $v - d$ messages.
- Messages $\mathbf{m}[1], \ldots, \mathbf{m}[v(k)]$ must be distinct, for any $param \in \{0, 1\}^*$ and any $\mathbf{m} \in [\mathcal{M}(1^k, param)]$.

Game H-SO-REAL$_H^{A,\mathcal{M}}(k)$	Game H-SO-IDEAL$_H^{A,\mathcal{M}}(k)$
$param \leftarrow_\$ A.\mathrm{pg}(1^k)$	$param \leftarrow_\$ A.\mathrm{pg}(1^k)$
$K \leftarrow_\$ \mathsf{HKg}(1^k)$	$K \leftarrow_\$ \mathsf{HKg}(1^k)$
$\mathbf{m}_1 \leftarrow_\$ \mathcal{M}(1^k, param)$	$\mathbf{m}_1 \leftarrow_\$ \mathcal{M}(1^k, param)$
For $i = 1$ to $|\mathbf{m}_1|$ do	For $i = 1$ to $|\mathbf{m}_1|$ do
$\quad \mathbf{h}[i] \leftarrow \mathsf{h}(K, \mathbf{m}_1[i])$	$\quad \mathbf{h}[i] \leftarrow \mathsf{h}(K, \mathbf{m}_1[i])$
$(state, I) \leftarrow_\$ A.\mathrm{cor}(K, \mathbf{h}, param)$	$(state, I) \leftarrow_\$ A.\mathrm{cor}(K, \mathbf{h}, param)$
$\omega \leftarrow_\$ A.\mathrm{g}(state, \mathbf{m}_1[I], param)$	$\omega \leftarrow_\$ A.\mathrm{g}(state, \mathbf{m}_1[I], param)$
Return $(\omega = A.\mathrm{f}(\mathbf{m}_1, param))$	$\mathbf{m}_0 \leftarrow_\$ \mathsf{Resamp}_{\mathcal{M}}(1^k, \mathbf{m}_1[I], I, param)$
	Return $(\omega = A.\mathrm{f}(\mathbf{m}_0, param))$

Fig. 2. Games to define the H-SO security.

Note that in this definition, d can be 0, which corresponds to a message sampler in which each message is independent of all other messages and has at least μ bits of min-entropy.

RESAMPLING. Following [3], let $\mathsf{Resamp}_{\mathcal{M}}(1^k, I, \mathbf{x}, param)$ be the algorithm that samples $r \leftarrow_\$ \mathsf{Coins}[k, \mathbf{m}, I, param]$ and returns $\mathcal{M}(1^k, param; r)$. (We note that Resamp may run in exponential time.) A *resampling algorithm* of $\mathcal{M}$ is an algorithm Rsmp such that $\mathsf{Rsmp}(1^k, I, \mathbf{x}, param)$ is identically distributed as $\mathsf{Resamp}_{\mathcal{M}}(1^k, I, \mathbf{x}, param)$. A message sampler $\mathcal{M}$ is *efficiently resamplable* if it admits a PT resampling algorithm.

H-SO SECURITY. Let $\mathsf{H} = (\mathsf{HKg}, \mathsf{h})$ be a hash function family with domain HDom and range HRng. To an adversary $A = (A.\mathrm{pg}, A.\mathrm{cor}, A.\mathrm{g}, A.\mathrm{f})$ and a message sampler $\mathcal{M}$, we associate the experiment in Fig. 2 for every $k \in \mathbb{N}$. We say that H is H-SO secure for a class $\mathscr{M}$ of efficiently resamplable message samplers and a class $\mathscr{A}$ of adversaries if for every $\mathcal{M} \in \mathscr{M}$ and any $A \in \mathscr{A}$,

$$\mathbf{Adv}_{\mathsf{H},A,\mathcal{M}}^{\text{h-so}}(k)$$
$$= \Pr\left[\text{H-SO-REAL}_{\mathsf{H}}^{A,\mathcal{M}}(k) \Rightarrow 1\right] - \Pr\left[\text{H-SO-IDEAL}_{\mathsf{H}}^{A,\mathcal{M}}(k) \Rightarrow 1\right]$$

is negligible in k.

DISCUSSION. We refer to the messages indexed by I as the "opened" messages. For every message $\mathbf{m}[i]$ that adversary A opens, we require that every message correlated to $\mathbf{m}[i]$ to also be opened.

We show that it is suffices to consider balanced H-SO adversaries where output of $A.\mathrm{f}$ is boolean. We call A δ-*balanced* boolean H-SO adversary if for all $b \in \{0, 1\}$,

$$\left| \Pr\left[t = b \ : \ t \leftarrow_\$ A.\mathrm{f}(m, param)\right] - \frac{1}{2} \right| \leq \delta.$$

for all $param$ and m output by $A.\mathrm{pg}$ and $\mathcal{M}$, respectively.

Theorem 2. Let $\mathsf{H} = (\mathsf{HKg}, \mathsf{h})$ be a hash function family with domain HDom and range HRng. Let A be a H-SO adversary against H with respect to message sampler $\mathcal{M}$. Then for any $0 \leq \delta < 1/2$, there is a δ-*balanced* boolean H-SO adversary B such that for all $k \in \mathbb{N}$

$$\mathbf{Adv}_{\mathsf{H},A,\mathcal{M}}^{\mathrm{h\text{-}so}}(k) \leq \left(\frac{2\sqrt{2}}{\delta} + \sqrt{2}\right)^2 \cdot \mathbf{Adv}_{\mathsf{H},B,\mathcal{M}}^{\mathrm{h\text{-}so}}(k).$$

where the running time of A is about that of B plus $\mathcal{O}(1/\delta)$.

We refer to Appendix A for the proof of Theorem 2. Next, we give a useful lemma that we later use in our proofs.

Lemma 3. Let X, Y be random variables where $\widetilde{\mathrm{H}}_\infty(X \mid Y) \geq \mu$. For any $0 \leq \delta < 1/2$, random variable Y is a δ-balanced boolean. Then, $\mathrm{H}_\infty(X \mid Y = b) \geq \mu - \log(\frac{1}{2} - \delta)$ for all $b \in \{0, 1\}$.

Proof. We know that $\Pr[Y = b] \geq 1/2 - \delta$, for all $b \in \{0, 1\}$. We also have that $\sum_b \Pr[Y = b] \max_x \Pr[X = x \mid Y = b] \leq 2^{-\mu}$. Therefore, we obtain that $\max_x \Pr[X = x \mid Y = b] \leq 2^{-\mu}(1/2 - \delta)$ for all $b \in \{0, 1\}$. Summing up, we get $\mathrm{H}_\infty(X \mid Y = b) \geq \mu - \log(\frac{1}{2} - \delta)$ for all $b \in \{0, 1\}$.   □

3.2 Achieving H-SO Security

We show in Theorem 4 that pair-wise independent hash functions are selective opening secure when the messages are independent and have high minentropy. Specifically, we give an upper-bound for the advantage of H-SO adversary attacking the pair-wise independent hash function. We first show that in the information theoretic setting, knowing the content of opened messages increases the upper-bound for advantage of adversary by at most factor of 2. This is because the messages are independent and knowing the opened messages does not increase the advantage of adversary on guessing the unopened messages. We point that for any vector of hash values and hash key, value I is uniquely defined (unbounded adversary can be assumed deterministic) and based on the independence of the messages, we could drop the probability of opened messages in the upper-bound for the advantage of adversary. Note that the adversary still may increase its advantage by choosing I adaptively without seeing the opened messages, we later prove this is not the case.

We show in Lemma 5 that for any hash key s in the set of "good hash keys", the probability of $H(s, X) = y$ is almost equally distributed over all hash value y. Therefore, we can show for any hash key s in the set of "good hash keys" and any vector of hash values, opening does not increases the upper-bound for advantage of adversary. Thus, it is only enough to bound the advantage of adversary without any opening.

Theorem 4. Let $\mathsf{H} = (\mathsf{HKg}, \mathsf{h})$ be a family of pair-wise independent hash function with domain HDom and range HRng. Let $\mathcal{M}$ be a $(\mu, 0)$-correlated, efficiently resamplable message sampler. Then for any computationally unbounded adversary A,

$$\mathbf{Adv}_{\mathsf{H},A,\mathcal{M}}^{\mathrm{h\text{-}so}}(k) \leq 2592v \sqrt[3]{2^{1-\mu}|\mathsf{HRng}(k)|^2}.$$

Proof. We need the following lemma whose proof we'll give later.

Lemma 5. Let $\mathsf{H} = (\mathsf{HKg}, \mathsf{h})$ be a pair-wise independent hash function with domain HDom and range HRng. Let X be a random variable over HDom such that $\mathrm{H}_\infty(X) \geq \eta$. Then, for all $y \in \mathsf{HRng}(k)$ and for any $\epsilon > 0$,

$$\left| \Pr\left[H(K, X) = y \right] - |\mathsf{HRng}(k)|^{-1} \right| \geq \epsilon |\mathsf{HRng}(k)|^{-1}.$$

for at most 2^{-u} fraction of $K \in [\mathsf{HKg}(1^k)]$, where $u = \eta - 2 \log |\mathsf{HRng}(k)| - 2 \log(1/\epsilon)$.

We begin by showing H is H-SO secure against any $\frac{1}{4}$-balanced boolean adversary B. Observe that for computationally unbounded adversary B, we can assume wlog that $B.\mathrm{cor}, B.\mathrm{g}$ and $B.\mathrm{f}$ are deterministic. Moreover, we can also assume that adversary $B.\mathrm{cor}$ pass $K, \mathbf{h}[\bar{I}]$ as state st to adversary $B.\mathrm{g}$. We denote by $\mathbf{Adv}_{\mathsf{H}, B, \mathcal{M}, s}^{\mathrm{h\text{-}so}}(k)$, advantage of B when $K = s$. For any fix key s we have

$$\Pr[\text{H-SO-REAL}_{\mathsf{H}, s}^{B}(k) \Rightarrow 1]$$

$$= \sum_{b=0}^{1} \sum_{I} \Pr[B.\mathrm{cor}(s, \mathbf{h}) \Rightarrow I \ \wedge \ B.\mathrm{g}(s, \mathbf{m}_1[I], \mathbf{h}[\bar{I}]) \Rightarrow b \ \wedge \ B.\mathrm{f}(\mathbf{m}_1) \Rightarrow b]$$

For any $\mathbf{y} \in (\mathsf{HRng}(k))^{\times v}$ and $s \in [\mathsf{HKg}(1^k)]$, we define $I_{s, \mathbf{y}}$ to be output of $B.\mathrm{cor}$ on input $s, \mathbf{y}$. We also define $M_{s, \mathbf{y}}^{b} = \{\mathbf{m}[I_{s, \mathbf{y}}] \mid B.\mathrm{g}(s, \mathbf{m}_1[I_{s, \mathbf{y}}], \mathbf{y}) \Rightarrow b\}$, for $b \in \{0, 1\}$. Thus,

$$\Pr[\text{H-SO-REAL}_{\mathsf{H}, s}^{B}(k) \Rightarrow 1]$$

$$= \sum_{b=0}^{1} \sum_{\mathbf{y}} \Pr[\mathbf{h} = \mathbf{y} \ \wedge \ \mathbf{m}_1[I_{s, \mathbf{y}}] \in M_{s, \mathbf{y}}^{b} \ \wedge \ B.\mathrm{f}(\mathbf{m}_1) \Rightarrow b]$$

The above probability is over the choice of $\mathbf{m}_1$. Similarly, we can define the probability of the experiment H-SO-IDEAL outputting 1. Therefore, we obtain

$$\mathbf{Adv}_{\mathsf{H}, B, \mathcal{M}, s}^{\mathrm{h\text{-}so}}(k) = \sum_{b=0}^{1} \sum_{\mathbf{y}} \Pr[\mathbf{h} = \mathbf{y} \ \wedge \ \mathbf{m}_1[I_{s, \mathbf{y}}] \in M_{s, \mathbf{y}}^{b} \ \wedge \ B.\mathrm{f}(\mathbf{m}_1) \Rightarrow b]$$

$$- \Pr[\mathbf{h} = \mathbf{y} \ \wedge \ \mathbf{m}_1[I_{s, \mathbf{y}}] \in M_{s, \mathbf{y}}^{b} \ \wedge \ B.\mathrm{f}(\mathbf{m}_0) \Rightarrow b]$$

Assume wlog that above difference is maximized when $b = 1$. For $d \in \{0, 1\}$, we define E_d as an event where $\mathbf{h}[I_{s, \mathbf{y}}] = \mathbf{y}[I_{s, \mathbf{y}}]$ and $\mathbf{m}_1[I_{s, \mathbf{y}}] \in M_{s, \mathbf{y}}^{1}$ and $B.\mathrm{f}(\mathbf{m}_d) = 1$. Note that the messages are independent and has μ bits of min-entropy. For convenience, we write I instead of $I_{s, \mathbf{y}}$. Then, we obtain

$$\mathbf{Adv}_{\mathsf{H}, B, \mathcal{M}, s}^{\mathrm{h\text{-}so}}(k) \leq 2 \cdot \sum_{\mathbf{y}} \Pr[E_1] \cdot \Pr[\mathbf{h}[\bar{I}] = \mathbf{y}[\bar{I}] \mid B.\mathrm{f}(\mathbf{m}_1) = 1]$$

$$- \Pr[E_0] \cdot \Pr[\mathbf{h}[\bar{I}] = \mathbf{y}[\bar{I}]]$$

Note that $\mathbf{m}_0$ and $\mathbf{m}_1$ have the same distribution. Then, we have $\Pr[E_0] = \Pr[E_1]$ and $\Pr[E_0] \leq \Pr[\mathbf{h}[I] = \mathbf{y}[I]]$. Therefore, we obtain

$$\mathbf{Adv}^{\text{h-so}}_{H,B,\mathcal{M},s}(k)$$
$$\leq 2 \cdot \sum_{\mathbf{y}} \Pr[\mathbf{h}[I] = \mathbf{y}[I]] \cdot \Big(\Pr[\mathbf{h}[\overline{I}] = \mathbf{y}[\overline{I}] \mid B.\mathrm{f}(\mathbf{m}_1) = 1] - \Pr[\mathbf{h}[\overline{I}] = \mathbf{y}[\overline{I}]] \Big)$$

We define random variable $\mathbf{X}[i] = (\mathbf{m}_1[i] \mid B.\mathrm{f}(\mathbf{m}_1) = 1)$, for all $i \in [v]$. From property (a) of Lemma 1 and Lemma 3, we obtain that $\mathrm{H}_\infty(\mathbf{X}[i]) \geq \mu - 3$. For all $i \in [v]$, we also have $\mathrm{H}_\infty(\mathbf{m}_1[i]) \geq \mu \geq \mu - 3$. Moreover, we know Lemma 5 holds for at most 2^{-u} fraction of $K \in [\mathsf{HKg}(1^k)]$, where $u = \mu - 3 - 2\log|\mathsf{HRng}(k)| - 2\log(1/\epsilon)$; we shall determine the value of ϵ later. Using union bound, for all $\mathbf{X}[i], \mathbf{m}[i]$, where $i \in [v]$ and for any $\epsilon > 0$, we obtain that for at least $1 - 2v2^{-u}$ fraction of K, we have $\big| \Pr\left[H(K, x[i]) = \mathbf{y}[i]\right] - |\mathsf{HRng}(k)|^{-1} \big| \leq \epsilon|\mathsf{HRng}(k)|^{-1}$, for all $i \in [v]$ and $x \in \{\mathbf{m}_1, \mathbf{X}\}$. Let S be the set of such K.

Now, we have for all $s \in S$ and $i \in [v]$, we obtain $(1 - \epsilon)|\mathsf{HRng}(k)|^{-1} \leq \Pr\left[\mathbf{h}[i] = \mathbf{y}[i]\right] \leq (1 + \epsilon)|\mathsf{HRng}(k)|^{-1}$. Let $|I_{s,\mathbf{y}}| = \ell$. Then,

$$\mathbf{Adv}^{\text{h-so}}_{H,B,\mathcal{M},s}(k) \leq 2 \cdot \sum_{\mathbf{y}} |\mathsf{HRng}(k)|^{-v}(1 + \epsilon)^\ell \Big((1 + \epsilon)^{v-\ell} - (1 - \epsilon)^{v-\ell} \Big)$$
$$\leq 2\Big((1 + \epsilon)^v - (1 - \epsilon)^v \Big)$$

We also have $(1 + \epsilon)^v = 1 + \sum_i \binom{v}{i}\epsilon^i \leq 1 + \sum_i \epsilon^i v^i$. For $\epsilon v < 1/2$, we obtain that $(1 + \epsilon)^v \leq 1 + 2\epsilon v$. Similarly, we obtain that $(1 - \epsilon)^v \geq 1 - 2\epsilon v$. Therefore, we have that $\mathbf{Adv}^{\text{h-so}}_{H,B,\mathcal{M},s}(k) \leq 8\epsilon v$. Then,

$$\mathbf{Adv}^{\text{h-so}}_{H,B,\mathcal{M}}(k) = \sum_{s \in S} \Pr\left[K = s\right] \cdot \mathbf{Adv}^{\text{h-so}}_{H,B,\mathcal{M},s}(k)$$
$$+ \sum_{s \in \overline{S}} \Pr\left[K = s\right] \cdot \mathbf{Adv}^{\text{h-so}}_{H,B,\mathcal{M},s}(k)$$
$$\leq \max_{s \in S} \mathbf{Adv}^{\text{h-so}}_{H,B,\mathcal{M},s}(k) + 2v2^{-u}.$$

Finally, by substituting $\epsilon = \sqrt[3]{2^{1-\mu}|\mathsf{HRng}(k)|^2}$, we obtain

$$\mathbf{Adv}^{\text{h-so}}_{H,B,\mathcal{M}}(k) \leq 16v \sqrt[3]{2^{1-\mu}|\mathsf{HRng}(k)|^2}.$$

Using Theorem 2, we obtain for any unbounded adversary A

$$\mathbf{Adv}^{\text{h-so}}_{H,A,\mathcal{M}}(k) \leq 2592v \sqrt[3]{2^{1-\mu}|\mathsf{HRng}(k)|^2}.$$

This completes the proof of Theorem 4.

PROOF OF LEMMA 5. We will need the following tail inequality for pair-wise independent distributions

Claim. Let $A_1, \cdots, A_n$ be pair-wise independent random variables in the interval $[0,1]$. Let $A = \sum_i A_i$ and $\mathbb{E}(A) = \mu$ and $\delta > 0$. Then,

$$\Pr\left[\,|A - \mu| > \delta\mu\,\right] \leq \frac{1}{\delta^2 \mu}.$$

PROOF OF CLAIM 3.2. From Chebychev's inequality, for any $\delta > 0$ we have

$$\Pr\left[\,|A - \mu| > \delta\mu\,\right] \leq \frac{\mathbf{Var}[A]}{\delta^2 \mu^2}.$$

Note that $A_1, \cdots, A_n$ are pair-wise independent random variables. Thus, we have $\mathbf{Var}[A] = \sum_i \mathbf{Var}[A_i]$. Moreover, we know that $\mathbf{Var}[A_i] \leq \mathbb{E}(A_i)$ for all $i \in [n]$, since the random variable A_i is in the interval $[0,1]$. Therefore, we have $\mathbf{Var}[A] \leq \mu$. This completes the proof of Claim 3.2.

We define $p_x = \Pr[X = x]$, for any $x \in \mathsf{HDom}(k)$. We consider the probability over the choice of key K. For every $x \in \mathsf{HDom}(k)$ and $y \in \mathsf{HRng}(k)$, we also define the following random variable

$$Z_{x,y} = \begin{cases} p_x & \text{if } H(K, x) = y \\ 0 & \text{otherwise} \end{cases}$$

We define random variable $A_{x,y} = Z_{x,y} 2^\eta$. Note that for every x, $H(K, x)$ is uniformly distributed, over the uniformly random choice of K. Therefore, we have $\mathbb{E}(Z_{x,y}) = p_x / |\mathsf{HRng}(k)|$, for every x, y. Let $Z_y = \sum_x Z_{x,y}$ and $A_y = \sum_x A_{x,y}$. Then, we have $\mathbb{E}(Z_y) = 1/|\mathsf{HRng}(k)|$ and $\mathbb{E}(A_y) = 2^\eta / |\mathsf{HRng}(k)|$. Moreover, for every x, y, we know $A_{x,y} \in [0,1]$ and for every y, the variables $A_{x,y}$ are pair-wise independent. Applying Claim 3.2, we obtain that for every y and $\delta > 0$

$$\Pr\left[\,\left|A_y - \frac{2^\eta}{|\mathsf{HRng}(k)|}\right| \geq \frac{\delta 2^\eta}{|\mathsf{HRng}(k)|}\,\right] \leq \frac{|\mathsf{HRng}(k)|}{\delta^2 2^\eta}.$$

Substituting Z_y for A_y and choosing $\delta = \epsilon$, we obtain that for every $\epsilon > 0$,

$$\Pr\left[\,\left|Z_y - \frac{1}{|\mathsf{HRng}(k)|}\right| \geq \frac{\epsilon}{|\mathsf{HRng}(k)|}\,\right] \leq \frac{|\mathsf{HRng}(k)|}{\epsilon^2 2^\eta}.$$

Using union bound, we obtain that with probability $|\mathsf{HRng}(k)|^2 / \epsilon^2 2^\eta = 2^{-u}$ over the choice of K that $|Z_y - 1/|\mathsf{HRng}(k)|| \geq \epsilon/|\mathsf{HRng}(k)|$, for all $y \in |\mathsf{HRng}(k)|$. This completes the proof of Lemma 5.   □

We show in Theorem 6 that the $2d$-wise independent hash functions are selective opening secure for (μ, d)-correlated message samplers.

Theorem 6. Let $\mathsf{H} = (\mathsf{HKg}, \mathsf{h})$ be a family of $2d$-wise independent hash function with domain HDom and range HRng. Let $\mathcal{M}$ be a (μ, d)-correlated, efficiently resamplable message sampler. Then for any computationally unbounded adversary A,

$$\mathbf{Adv}_{\mathsf{H},A,\mathcal{M}}^{\mathrm{h\text{-}so}}(k) \leq 2592v \sqrt[3]{2^{1-\mu} |\mathsf{HRng}(k)|^{2d}}.$$

Proof. We need the following lemma whose proof we'll give later.

Lemma 7. Let $H = (HKg, h)$ be a $2d$-wise independent hash function with domain $HDom$ and range $HRng$. Let $\mathbf{X} = (X_1, \cdots, X_t)$, where $t \leq d$ and X_i is a random variable over $HDom$ such that $H_\infty(X_i) \geq \eta$, for $i \in [t]$. Then, for all $\mathbf{y} = (y_1, \cdots, y_t)$, where $y_i \in HRng(k)$ and for any $\epsilon > 0$,

$$\left| \Pr[H(K, \mathbf{X}) = \mathbf{y}] - |HRng(k)|^{-t} \right| \geq \epsilon |HRng(k)|^{-t}.$$

for at most 2^{-w} fraction of $K \in [HKg(1^k)]$, where $w = \eta - 2t \log |HRng(k)| - 2\log(1/\epsilon)$.

We begin by showing H is H-SO secure against any $\frac{1}{4}$-balanced boolean adversary B. Observe that for computationally unbounded adversary B, we can assume wlog that $B.cor, B.g$ and $B.f$ are deterministic. Moreover, we can also assume that adversary $B.cor$ pass $K, \mathbf{h}[\bar{I}]$ as state st to adversary $B.g$. We denote by $\mathbf{Adv}^{\text{h-so}}_{H,B,\mathcal{M},s}(k)$, advantage of B when $K = s$. For any fix key s we have

$$\Pr[\text{H-SO-REAL}^B_{H,s}(k) \Rightarrow 1]$$

$$= \sum_{b=0}^{1} \sum_{I} \Pr[B.cor(s, \mathbf{h}) \Rightarrow I \ \wedge \ B.g(s, \mathbf{m}_1[I], \mathbf{h}[\bar{I}]) \Rightarrow b \ \wedge \ B.f(\mathbf{m}_1) \Rightarrow b]$$

For any $\mathbf{y} \in (HRng(k))^{\times v}$ and $s \in [HKg(1^k)]$, we define $I_{s,\mathbf{y}}$ to be output of $B.cor$ on input $s, \mathbf{y}$. We also define $M^b_{s,\mathbf{y}} = \{\mathbf{m}[I_{s,\mathbf{y}}] \mid B.g(s, \mathbf{m}_1[I_{s,\mathbf{y}}], \mathbf{y}) \Rightarrow b\}$, for $b \in \{0, 1\}$. Thus,

$$\Pr[\text{H-SO-REAL}^B_{H,s}(k) \Rightarrow 1]$$

$$= \sum_{b=0}^{1} \sum_{\mathbf{y}} \Pr[\mathbf{h} = \mathbf{y} \ \wedge \ \mathbf{m}_1[I_{s,\mathbf{y}}] \in M^b_{s,\mathbf{y}} \ \wedge \ B.f(\mathbf{m}_1) \Rightarrow b]$$

The above probability is over the choice of $\mathbf{m}_1$. Similarly, we can define the probability of the experiment H-SO-IDEAL outputting 1. Therefore, we obtain

$$\mathbf{Adv}^{\text{h-so}}_{H,B,\mathcal{M},s}(k) = \sum_{b=0}^{1} \sum_{\mathbf{y}} \Pr[\mathbf{h} = \mathbf{y} \ \wedge \ \mathbf{m}_1[I_{s,\mathbf{y}}] \in M^b_{s,\mathbf{y}} \ \wedge \ B.f(\mathbf{m}_1) \Rightarrow b]$$

$$- \Pr[\mathbf{h} = \mathbf{y} \ \wedge \ \mathbf{m}_1[I_{s,\mathbf{y}}] \in M^b_{s,\mathbf{y}} \ \wedge \ B.f(\mathbf{m}_0) \Rightarrow b]$$

Assume wlog that the above difference is maximized when $b = 1$. For $d \in \{0, 1\}$, we define E_d as an event where $\mathbf{h}[I_{s,\mathbf{y}}] = \mathbf{y}[I_{s,\mathbf{y}}]$ and $\mathbf{m}_1[I_{s,\mathbf{y}}] \in M^1_{s,\mathbf{y}}$ and $B.f(\mathbf{m}_d) = 1$. Note that the messages are independent and has μ bits of min-entropy. For convenience, we write I instead of $I_{s,\mathbf{y}}$. Then, we obtain

$$\mathbf{Adv}^{\text{h-so}}_{H,B,\mathcal{M},s}(k) \leq 2 \cdot \sum_{\mathbf{y}} \Pr[E_1] \cdot \Pr[\mathbf{h}[\bar{I}] = \mathbf{y}[\bar{I}] \mid B.f(\mathbf{m}_1) = 1]$$

$$- \Pr[E_0] \cdot \Pr[\mathbf{h}[\bar{I}] = \mathbf{y}[\bar{I}]]$$

Note that $\mathbf{m}_0$ and $\mathbf{m}_1$ have the same distribution. Then, we have $\Pr[E_0] = \Pr[E_1]$ and $\Pr[E_0] \leq \Pr[\mathbf{h}[I] = \mathbf{y}[I]]$. We define random variable $\mathbf{X}[i] = (\mathbf{m}_1[i] \mid B.\mathrm{f}(\mathbf{m}_1) = 1)$, for all $i \in [v]$. From property (a) of Lemma 1 and Lemma 3, we obtain that $\mathrm{H}_\infty(\mathbf{X}[i]) \geq \mu - 3$. For all $i \in [v]$, we also have $\mathrm{H}_\infty(\mathbf{m}_1[i]) \geq \mu \geq \mu - 3$

Moreover, we know Lemma 5 holds for at most 2^{-u} fraction of $K \in [\mathrm{HKg}(1^k)]$, where $u = \mu - 3 - 2d \log |\mathrm{HRng}(k)| - 2 \log(1/\epsilon)$; we shall determine the value of ϵ later. Partition $[v]$ to $L_1, \cdots, L_v$ such that $|L_k| \leq d$ and for all $i, j \in L_k$, messages $\mathbf{m}[i]$ and $\mathbf{m}[j]$ are correlated. Using union bound, for all $\mathbf{y}[L_i] \in (\mathrm{HRng}(k))^{\times |L_i|}$, where $i \in [v]$ and for any $\epsilon > 0$, we obtain that for at least $1 - 2v2^{-u}$ fraction of K, we have $\left| \Pr\left[H(K, x[L_i]) = \mathbf{y}[L_i] \right] - |\mathrm{HRng}(k)|^{-|L_i|} \right| \leq \epsilon |\mathrm{HRng}(k)|^{-|L_i|}$, for all $i \in [v]$ and $x \in \{\mathbf{m}_1, \mathbf{X}\}$. Let S be the set of such K.

Now, we have for all $s \in S$ and $i \in [v]$, we obtain $(1 - \epsilon)|\mathrm{HRng}(k)|^{-|L_i|} \leq \Pr\left[\mathbf{h}[L_i] = \mathbf{y}[L_i]\right] \leq (1 + \epsilon)|\mathrm{HRng}(k)|^{-|L_i|}$. Let $|I_{s,\mathbf{y}}| = \ell$. Then,

$$\mathbf{Adv}_{H,B,\mathcal{M},s}^{\text{h-so}}(k) \leq 2 \cdot \sum_{\mathbf{y}} |\mathrm{HRng}(k)|^{-v}(1 + \epsilon)^\ell \left((1 + \epsilon)^{v-\ell} - (1 - \epsilon)^{v-\ell}\right)$$

$$\leq 2\left((1 + \epsilon)^v - (1 - \epsilon)^v\right)$$

We also have $(1 + \epsilon)^v = 1 + \sum_i \binom{v}{i}\epsilon^i \leq 1 + \sum_i \epsilon^i v^i$. For $\epsilon v < 1/2$, we obtain that $(1 + \epsilon)^v \leq 1 + 2\epsilon v$. Similarly, we obtain that $(1 - \epsilon)^v \geq 1 - 2\epsilon v$. Therefore, we have that $\mathbf{Adv}_{H,B,\mathcal{M},s}^{\text{h-so}}(k) \leq 8\epsilon v$. Then,

$$\mathbf{Adv}_{H,B,\mathcal{M}}^{\text{h-so}}(k) = \sum_{s \in S} \Pr\left[K = s\right] \cdot \mathbf{Adv}_{H,B,\mathcal{M},s}^{\text{h-so}}(k)$$

$$+ \sum_{s \in \bar{S}} \Pr\left[K = s\right] \cdot \mathbf{Adv}_{H,B,\mathcal{M},s}^{\text{h-so}}(k)$$

$$\leq \max_{s \in S} \mathbf{Adv}_{H,B,\mathcal{M},s}^{\text{h-so}}(k) + 2v2^{-u}.$$

Finally, by substituting $\epsilon = \sqrt[3]{2^{1-\mu}|\mathrm{HRng}(k)|^2}$, we obtain

$$\mathbf{Adv}_{H,B,\mathcal{M}}^{\text{h-so}}(k) \leq 16v\sqrt[3]{2^{1-\mu}|\mathrm{HRng}(k)|^{2d}}.$$

Using Theorem 2, we obtain for any unbounded adversary A

$$\mathbf{Adv}_{H,A,\mathcal{M}}^{\text{h-so}}(k) \leq 2592v\sqrt[3]{2^{1-\mu}|\mathrm{HRng}(k)|^{2d}}.$$

This completes the proof of Theorem 6.

PROOF OF LEMMA 7. We define $p_\mathbf{x} = \Pr\left[\mathbf{X} = \mathbf{x}\right]$, for any $\mathbf{x} = (x_1, \cdots, x_t)$, where $x_i \in \mathrm{HDom}(k)$. We consider the probability over the choice of key K. For every $\mathbf{x}$ and $\mathbf{y}$, we also define the following random variable

$$Z_{\mathbf{x},\mathbf{y}} = \begin{cases} p_\mathbf{x} & \text{if } H(K, \mathbf{x}) = \mathbf{y} \\ 0 & \text{otherwise} \end{cases}$$

Let $A_{\mathbf{x},\mathbf{y}} = Z_{\mathbf{x},\mathbf{y}} 2^\eta$. Note that for all $i \in [t]$ and for every x_i, $H(K, x_i)$ is uniformly distributed, over the uniformly random choice of K. Moreover, H is t-wise independent. Therefore, we have $\mathbb{E}(Z_{\mathbf{x},\mathbf{y}}) = p_{\mathbf{x}}/|\mathsf{HRng}(k)|^t$, for every $\mathbf{x},\mathbf{y}$. Let $Z_{\mathbf{y}} = \sum_{\mathbf{x}} Z_{\mathbf{x},\mathbf{y}}$ and $A_{\mathbf{y}} = \sum_{\mathbf{x}} A_{\mathbf{x},\mathbf{y}}$. Then, we have $\mathbb{E}(Z_{\mathbf{y}}) = 1/|\mathsf{HRng}(k)|^t$ and $\mathbb{E}(A_{\mathbf{y}}) = 2^\eta/|\mathsf{HRng}(k)|^t$. Moreover, for every $\mathbf{x},\mathbf{y}$, we know $A_{\mathbf{x},\mathbf{y}} \in [0, 1]$ and for every $\mathbf{y}$, the variables $A_{\mathbf{x},\mathbf{y}}$ are pair-wise independent. Applying Claim 3.2, we obtain that for every $\mathbf{y}$ and $\delta > 0$

$$\Pr\left[\left| A_{\mathbf{y}} - \frac{2^\eta}{|\mathsf{HRng}(k)|^t} \right| \geq \frac{\delta 2^\eta}{|\mathsf{HRng}(k)|^t} \right] \leq \frac{|\mathsf{HRng}(k)|^t}{\delta^2 2^\eta}.$$

Substituting $Z_{\mathbf{y}}$ for $A_{\mathbf{y}}$ and choosing $\delta = \epsilon$, we obtain that for every $\epsilon > 0$,

$$\Pr\left[\left| A_{\mathbf{y}} - \frac{2^\eta}{|\mathsf{HRng}(k)|^t} \right| \geq \frac{\epsilon 2^\eta}{|\mathsf{HRng}(k)|^t} \right] \leq \frac{|\mathsf{HRng}(k)|^t}{\epsilon^2 2^\eta}.$$

Using union bound, we obtain that with probability $|\mathsf{HRng}(k)|^{2t}/\epsilon^2 2^\eta = 2^{-w}$ over the choice of K that $|Z_{\mathbf{y}} - |\mathsf{HRng}(k)|^{-t}| \geq \epsilon|\mathsf{HRng}(k)|^{-t}$, for all $\mathbf{y}$. Thus,

$$\left| \Pr\left[H(K, \mathbf{X}) = \mathbf{y} \right] - |\mathsf{HRng}(k)|^{-t} \right| \geq \epsilon|\mathsf{HRng}(k)|^{-t}.$$

with probability at most 2^{-w} over the choice of K. This completes the proof of Lemma 7.   □

4   Selective Opening Security for Deterministic Encryption

In this section, we give two different constructions of deterministic public key encryption and show that they achieve D-SO-CPA security. First, we show that lossy trapdoor functions that are $2t$-wise independent in the lossy mode are selective opening secure for t-correlated messages. However, it is an open problem to construct them for $t > 1$.

Hence, we give another construction of deterministic public key encryption using hash functions and lossy trapdoor permutation and show it is selective opening secure. A close variant of this scheme is shown to be D-SO-CPA secure in the NPROM [20]. Our scheme is efficient and only public-key primitive that it uses is a regular lossy trapdoor function, which has practical instantiations, e.g., both Rabin and RSA are regular lossy.

4.1   Achieving D-SO-CPA Security

We start by showing that $2t$-wise independent lossy trapdoor functions are selective opening secure. It was previously shown by Hoang et al. [20] that D-SO-CPA notion is achievable under the random oracle model. They leave it open to construct a D-SO-CPA secure scheme in the standard model. Here, we show that a

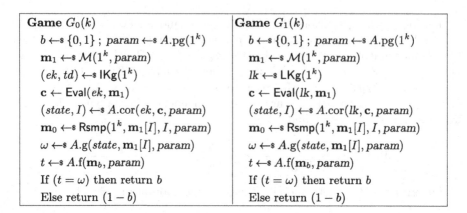

Fig. 3. Games G_0, G_1 of the proof of Theorem 8.

pair-wise independent lossy trapdoor function is D-SO-CPA secure for independent messages. We also show that a $2d$-wise independent lossy trapdoor function is D-SO-CPA secure for (μ, d)-correlated message samplers.

First, we show in Theorem 8 that a pair-wise independent lossy trapdoor functions is D-SO-CPA secure for $(\mu, 0)$-correlated message samplers.

Theorem 8. Let $\mathcal{M}$ be a $(\mu, 0)$-correlated, efficiently resamplable message sampler. Let LT be a lossy trapdoor function with domain LDom, range LRng and lossiness τ. Suppose LT is pair-wise independent. Then for any adversary A,

$$\mathbf{Adv}_{\mathsf{LT},A,\mathcal{M}}^{\mathrm{d\text{-}so\text{-}cpa}}(k) \leq 2 \cdot \mathbf{Adv}_{\mathsf{LT},B}^{\mathrm{ltdf}}(k) + 2592v\sqrt[3]{2^{1-\mu-2\tau}|\mathsf{LRng}(k)|^2}.$$

Proof. Consider games G_0, G_1 in Fig. 3. Then

$$\mathbf{Adv}_{\mathsf{LT},A,\mathcal{M}}^{\mathrm{d\text{-}so\text{-}cpa}}(k) = 2 \cdot \Pr\left[\,G_0(k) \Rightarrow 1\,\right] - 1.$$

We now explain the game chain. Game G_1 is identical to game G_0, except that instead of generating an injective key for the lossy trapdoor function, we generate a lossy one. Consider the following adversary B attacking the key indistinguishability of LT. It simulates game G_0, but uses its given key instead of generating a new one. It outputs 1 if the simulated game returns 1, and outputs 0 otherwise. Then

$$\Pr[G_0(k) \Rightarrow 1] - \Pr[G_1(k) \Rightarrow 1] \leq \mathbf{Adv}_{\mathsf{LT},B}^{\mathrm{ltdf}}(k).$$

Note that game G_1 is identical to games H-SO-REAL or H-SO-IDEAL, when $b = 1$ or $b = 0$, respectively. Then

$$\mathbf{Adv}_{\mathsf{LT},A,\mathcal{M}}^{\mathrm{h\text{-}so}}(k) = 2 \cdot \Pr\left[\,G_1(k) \Rightarrow 1\,\right] - 1.$$

Note that LT is pair-wise independent and τ-lossy. Then, size of the range of LT in the lossy mode is at most $2^{-\tau}|\mathsf{LRng}(k)|$. From Theorem 4

$$\mathbf{Adv}_{\mathsf{LT},A,\mathcal{M}}^{\mathrm{h\text{-}so}}(k) \leq 2592v\sqrt[3]{2^{1-\mu-2\tau}|\mathsf{LRng}(k)|^2}.$$

DE.Kg(1^k)	DE.Enc(pk, m)	DE.Dec(sk, c)
$(ek, td) \leftarrow\!\! _\$ \, \mathsf{IKg}(1^k)$	$(K_H, K_G, ek) \leftarrow pk$	$(K_H, K_G, td) \leftarrow sk$
$K_H \leftarrow\!\! _\$ \, \mathsf{HKg}(1^k)$	$r \leftarrow \mathsf{h}(K_H, m)$	$y \| r \leftarrow \mathsf{Inv}(td, c)$
$K_G \leftarrow\!\! _\$ \, \mathsf{GKg}(1^k)$	$y \leftarrow \mathsf{g}(K_G, r) \oplus m$	$m \leftarrow \mathsf{g}(K_G, r) \oplus y$
$pk \leftarrow (K_H, K_G, ek)$	$c \leftarrow \mathsf{Eval}(ek, y \| r)$	Return m
$sk \leftarrow (K_H, K_G, td)$	Return c	
Return (pk, sk)		

Fig. 4. D-PKE scheme DE[H, G, LT].

Summing up,

$$\mathbf{Adv}^{\text{d-so-cpa}}_{\mathsf{LT}, A, \mathcal{M}}(k) \leq 2 \cdot \mathbf{Adv}^{\text{ltdf}}_{\mathsf{LT}, B}(k) + 2592v \sqrt[3]{2^{1-\mu-2\tau} |\mathsf{LRng}(k)|^2}.$$

This completes the proof of Theorem 8.

Next, we show in Theorem 9 that a $2d$-wise independent lossy trapdoor functions is D-SO-CPA secure for (μ, d)-correlated message samplers.

Theorem 9. Let $\mathcal{M}$ be a (μ, d)-correlated, efficiently resamplable message sampler. Let LT be a lossy trapdoor function with domain LDom, range LRng and lossiness τ. Suppose LT is $2d$-wise independent. Then for any adversary A,

$$\mathbf{Adv}^{\text{d-so-cpa}}_{\mathsf{LT}, A, \mathcal{M}}(k) \leq 2 \cdot \mathbf{Adv}^{\text{ltdf}}_{\mathsf{LT}, B}(k) + 2592v \sqrt[3]{2^{1-\mu-2d\tau} |\mathsf{LRng}(k)|^{2d}}.$$

The proof of Theorem 9 is very similar to the proof of Theorem 8.

Although that $2t$-wise independent trapdoor functions are very efficient and secure against selective opening attack, it is an open problem to construct them for $t > 1$. Hence, we give a new construction of deterministic public key encryption that is selective opening secure. Our scheme DE[H, G, LT] is shown in Fig. 4, where LT is a lossy trapdoor function and H, G are hash functions. We begin by showing in Theorem 10 that DE is D-SO-CPA secure for independent messages when H, G are pair-wise independent hash functions and LT is a regular lossy trapdoor function.

Theorem 10. Let $\mathcal{M}$ be a $(\mu, 0)$-correlated, efficiently resamplable message sampler. Let $\mathsf{H} = (\mathsf{HKg}, \mathsf{h})$ with domain $\{0, 1\}^n$ and range $\{0, 1\}^\ell$ and $\mathsf{G} = (\mathsf{GKg}, \mathsf{g})$ with domain $\{0, 1\}^\ell$ and range $\{0, 1\}^n$ be hash function families. Suppose H and G are pair-wise independent. Let LT be a regular lossy trapdoor function with domain $\{0, 1\}^{n+\ell}$, range $\{0, 1\}^p$ and lossiness τ. Let DE[H, G, LT] be as above. Then for any adversary A,

$$\mathbf{Adv}^{\text{d-so-cpa}}_{\mathsf{DE}, A, \mathcal{M}}(k) \leq 2 \cdot \mathbf{Adv}^{\text{ltdf}}_{\mathsf{LT}, B}(k) + 2592v \sqrt[3]{2^{1-\mu-2\tau+2p}}.$$

Proof. We begin by showing the following lemma.

Lemma 11. Let $\mathsf{H} = (\mathsf{HKg}, \mathsf{h})$ with domain $\{0,1\}^n$ and range $\{0,1\}^\ell$ and $\mathsf{G} = (\mathsf{GKg}, \mathsf{g})$ with domain $\{0,1\}^\ell$ and range $\{0,1\}^n$ be hash function families. Suppose H and G are pair-wise independent. Let LT be a regular lossy trapdoor function with domain $\{0,1\}^{n+\ell}$, range $\{0,1\}^p$ and lossiness τ. Let X be a random variable over $\{0,1\}^n$ such that $\mathrm{H}_\infty(X) \geq \eta$. Then, for all $lk \in [\mathsf{LKg}(1^k)]$, all $c \in \mathsf{Img}(lk)$ and any $\epsilon > 0$,

$$\left| \Pr\left[\, \mathsf{DE.Enc}(pk, X) = c \,\right] - 2^{\tau-p} \right| \geq \epsilon 2^{\tau-p}.$$

for at most 2^{-u} fraction of public key pk, where $u = \eta + 2\tau - 2p - 2\log(1/\epsilon)$.

PROOF OF LEMMA 11. We define $p_x = \Pr\left[X = x\right]$, for any $x \in \{0,1\}^n$. We consider the probability over the choice of public key pk. fix the lossy key $lk \in [\mathsf{LKg}(1^k)]$, we consider the probability over the choice of K_H, K_G. For every $x \in \{0,1\}^n$ and $c \in \mathsf{Img}(lk)$, we also define the following random variable

$$Z_{x,c} = \begin{cases} p_x & \text{if } \mathsf{DE.Enc}(pk, x) = c \\ 0 & \text{otherwise} \end{cases}$$

Let $A_{x,c} = Z_{x,c} 2^n$. Note that that for every x, $\mathsf{h}(K_H, x)$ is uniformly distributed, over the uniformly random choice of K_H. Moreover, for every x and K_H, $\mathsf{g}(K_G, \mathsf{h}(K_H, x))$ is uniformly distributed, over the uniformly random choice of K_G. Since LT is a regular LTDF, we have $\mathbb{E}(Z_{x,c}) = p_x \cdot 2^{\tau-p}$, for every x, c. Let $Z_c = \sum_x Z_{x,c}$ and $A_c = \sum_x A_{x,c}$. Then, we have $\mathbb{E}(Z_c) = 2^{\tau-p}$ and $\mathbb{E}(A_c) = 2^{n+\tau-p}$. Moreover, for every x, c, we know $A_{x,c} \in [0,1]$ and for every c, the variables $A_{x,c}$ are pair-wise independent. Applying Claim 3.2, we obtain that for every c and $\delta > 0$

$$\Pr\left[\, \left| A_c - 2^{n+\tau-p} \right| \geq \delta \cdot 2^{n+\tau-p} \,\right] \leq \frac{2^{p-\eta-\tau}}{\delta^2}.$$

Substituting Z_c for A_c and choosing $\delta = \epsilon$, we obtain that for every $\epsilon > 0$,

$$\Pr\left[\, \left| Z_c - 2^{\tau-p} \right| \geq \epsilon \cdot 2^{\tau-p} \,\right] \leq \frac{2^{p-\eta-\tau}}{\epsilon^2}.$$

Using union bound, we obtain that $|Z_c - 2^{\tau-p}| \geq \epsilon \cdot 2^{\tau-p}$ with probability $2^{2p-\eta-2\tau}/\epsilon^2 = 2^{-u}$ over the choice of K_H, K_G, for all $lk \in [\mathsf{LKg}(1^k)]$, all $c \in \mathsf{Img}(lk)$. This completes the proof of Lemma 11. □

Consider games G_0, G_1 in Fig. 5. Then

$$\mathbf{Adv}_{\mathsf{DE}, A, \mathcal{M}}^{\text{d-so-cpa}}(k) = 2 \cdot \Pr\left[G_0(k) \Rightarrow 1\right] - 1.$$

We now explain the game chain. Game G_1 is identical to game G_0, except that instead of generating an injective key for the lossy trapdoor function, we

Game $G_0(k)$	Game $G_1(k)$
$b \leftarrow\!\!{\scriptstyle\$}\ \{0,1\}$; $param \leftarrow\!\!{\scriptstyle\$}\ A.\mathrm{pg}(1^k)$	$b \leftarrow\!\!{\scriptstyle\$}\ \{0,1\}$; $param \leftarrow\!\!{\scriptstyle\$}\ A.\mathrm{pg}(1^k)$
$\mathbf{m}_1 \leftarrow\!\!{\scriptstyle\$}\ \mathcal{M}(1^k, param)$	$\mathbf{m}_1 \leftarrow\!\!{\scriptstyle\$}\ \mathcal{M}(1^k, param)$
$(ek, td) \leftarrow\!\!{\scriptstyle\$}\ \mathsf{IKg}(1^k)$; $K_H \leftarrow\!\!{\scriptstyle\$}\ \mathsf{HKg}(1^k)$	$lk \leftarrow\!\!{\scriptstyle\$}\ \mathsf{LKg}(1^k)$; $K_H \leftarrow\!\!{\scriptstyle\$}\ \mathsf{HKg}(1^k)$
$K_G \leftarrow\!\!{\scriptstyle\$}\ \mathsf{GKg}(1^k)$; $pk \leftarrow (K_H, K_G, ek)$	$K_G \leftarrow\!\!{\scriptstyle\$}\ \mathsf{GKg}(1^k)$; $pk \leftarrow (K_H, K_G, lk)$
$\mathbf{c} \leftarrow \mathsf{DE.Enc}(pk, \mathbf{m}_1)$	$\mathbf{c} \leftarrow \mathsf{DE.Enc}(pk, \mathbf{m}_1)$
$(state, I) \leftarrow\!\!{\scriptstyle\$}\ A.\mathrm{cor}(pk, \mathbf{c}, param)$	$(state, I) \leftarrow\!\!{\scriptstyle\$}\ A.\mathrm{cor}(pk, \mathbf{c}, param)$
$\mathbf{m}_0 \leftarrow\!\!{\scriptstyle\$}\ \mathsf{Rsmp}(1^k, \mathbf{m}_1[I], I, param)$	$\mathbf{m}_0 \leftarrow\!\!{\scriptstyle\$}\ \mathsf{Rsmp}(1^k, \mathbf{m}_1[I], I, param)$
$\omega \leftarrow\!\!{\scriptstyle\$}\ A.\mathrm{g}(state, \mathbf{m}_1[I], param)$	$\omega \leftarrow\!\!{\scriptstyle\$}\ A.\mathrm{g}(state, \mathbf{m}_1[I], param)$
$t \leftarrow\!\!{\scriptstyle\$}\ A.\mathrm{f}(\mathbf{m}_b, param)$	$t \leftarrow\!\!{\scriptstyle\$}\ A.\mathrm{f}(\mathbf{m}_b, param)$
If $(t = \omega)$ then return b	If $(t = \omega)$ then return b
Else return $(1 - b)$	Else return $(1 - b)$

Fig. 5. Games G_0, G_1 of the proof of Theorem 10.

generate a lossy one. Consider the following adversary B attacking the key indistinguishability of LT. It simulates game G_0, but uses its given key instead of generating a new one. It outputs 1 if the simulated game returns 1, and outputs 0 otherwise. Then

$$\Pr[G_0(k) \Rightarrow 1] - \Pr[G_1(k) \Rightarrow 1] \leq \mathbf{Adv}^{\mathrm{ltdf}}_{\mathsf{LT}, B}(k).$$

Similar to proof of Theorem 4, using Lemma 11, we obtain that

$$\Pr\left[G_1(k) \Rightarrow 1\right] \leq 1296 v \sqrt[3]{2^{1-\mu-2\tau+2p}} + \frac{1}{2}.$$

Summing up,

$$\mathbf{Adv}^{\mathrm{d\text{-}so\text{-}cpa}}_{\mathsf{DE}, A, \mathcal{M}}(k) \leq 2 \cdot \mathbf{Adv}^{\mathrm{ltdf}}_{\mathsf{LT}, B}(k) + 2592 v \sqrt[3]{2^{1-\mu-2\tau+2p}}.$$

This completes the proof of Theorem 10.

We now extend our result to include correlated messages. We show that it is enough to use $2t$-wise independent hash functions to extend the security to t-correlated messages. Let $\mathsf{DE}[\mathsf{H}, \mathsf{G}, \mathsf{LT}]$ be PKE scheme shown in Fig. 4, where LT is a lossy trapdoor function and H, G are hash functions. We show in Theorem 12 that DE is D-SO-CPA secure for t-correlated messages when H, G are $2t$-wise independent hash functions and LT is a regular lossy trapdoor function.

Theorem 12. Let $\mathcal{M}$ be a (μ, d)-correlated, efficiently resamplable message sampler. Let $\mathsf{H} = (\mathsf{HKg}, \mathrm{h})$ with domain $\{0,1\}^n$ and range $\{0,1\}^\ell$ and $\mathsf{G} = (\mathsf{GKg}, \mathrm{g})$ with domain $\{0,1\}^\ell$ and range $\{0,1\}^n$ be hash function families. Suppose H and G are $2d$-wise independent. Let LT be a regular lossy trapdoor function with domain $\{0,1\}^{n+\ell}$, range $\{0,1\}^p$ and lossiness τ. Let $\mathsf{DE}[\mathsf{H}, \mathsf{G}, \mathsf{LT}]$ be as above. Then for any adversary A,

$$\mathbf{Adv}^{\mathrm{d\text{-}so\text{-}cpa}}_{\mathsf{DE}, A, \mathcal{M}}(k) \leq 2 \cdot \mathbf{Adv}^{\mathrm{ltdf}}_{\mathsf{LT}, B}(k) + 2592 v \sqrt[3]{2^{1-\mu+2d(-\tau+p)}}.$$

The proof of Theorem 12 is very similar to the proof of Theorem 10.

Game ONE-MORE-INV$_{\text{TDF}}^A(k)$	**Oracle** $\mathcal{C}(i)$
$j \leftarrow 0$; $(ek, td) \leftarrow\!\!\$ \, \text{Kg}(1^k)$	$j \leftarrow j + 1$
For $i = 1$ to v do	If $j \geq v$ then
$\quad \mathbf{x}[i] \leftarrow\!\!\$ \, \text{TDom}(k)$	$\quad$ Return $\bot$
$\quad \mathbf{y}[i] \leftarrow \text{Eval}(ek, \mathbf{x}[i])$	$\quad$ Return $\mathbf{x}[i]$
$\mathbf{x}' \leftarrow\!\!\$ \, A^{\mathcal{C}}(ek, \mathbf{y})$	
Return $(\mathbf{x} = \mathbf{x}')$	

Fig. 6. Games to define the One-More security.

5   Results for One-More-RSA Inversion Problem

In this section, we recall the definition of one-more-RSA inversion problem. This problem is a natural extension of the RSA problem to a setting where the adversary has access to a corruption oracle. Bellare *et al.* [4] first introduce this notion and show that assuming hardness of one-more-RSA inversion problem leads to a proof of security of Chaum's blind signature scheme in the random oracle model. Here we show that one-more inversion problem is hard for RSA with a large enough encryption exponent e. More generally, we show that one-more inversion problem is hard for any regular lossy trapdoor function.

5.1   Security Notion

Here we give a formal definition of one-more-RSA inversion problem. Our definition is more general and considers this problem for any trapdoor function. Intuitively, in the one-more inversion problem, the adversary gets a number of image points, and must output the inverses of image points, while it has access to the corruption oracle and can see the preimage of image points of its choice. We note that the number of corruption queries is less than the number of image points. We also note that a special case of the one-more inversion problem in which there is only one image point is exactly the problem underlying the notion of one-wayness.

ONE-MORE INVERSION PROBLEM. Let $\text{TDF} = (\text{Kg}, \text{Eval}, \text{Inv})$ be a trapdoor function with domain $\text{TDom}(\cdot)$ and range $\text{TRng}(\cdot)$. To an adversary A, we associate the experiment in Fig. 6 for every $k \in \mathbb{N}$. We say that TDF is one-more[v] secure for a class $\mathscr{A}$ of adversaries if for every any $A \in \mathscr{A}$,

$$\mathbf{Adv}_{\text{TDF}, A, v}^{\text{one-more}}(k) = \Pr\left[\text{ONE-MORE-INV}_{\text{TDF}}^{A,v}(k) \Rightarrow 1 \right]$$

is negligible in k.

5.2   Achieving One-More Security

We show in Theorem 13 that a regular lossy trapdoor function is one-more secure. We point out that, for large enough encryption exponent e, RSA is a regular lossy trapdoor function [24].

Game $G_0(k)$	Game $G_1(k)$	Oracle $\mathcal{C}(i)$ // G_0–G_2
$j \leftarrow 0$	$j \leftarrow 0$	$j \leftarrow j + 1$
$(ek, td) \leftarrow\!\!{\$}\ \mathsf{IKg}(1^k)$	$lk \leftarrow\!\!{\$}\ \mathsf{LKg}(1^k)$	If $j \geq v$ then
For $i = 1$ to v do	For $i = 1$ to v do	Return $\perp$
$\quad \mathbf{x}[i] \leftarrow\!\!{\$}\ \mathsf{LDom}(k)$	$\quad \mathbf{x}[i] \leftarrow\!\!{\$}\ \mathsf{LDom}(k)$	Return $\mathbf{x}[i]$
$\quad \mathbf{y}[i] \leftarrow \mathsf{Eval}(ek, \mathbf{x}[i])$	$\quad \mathbf{y}[i] \leftarrow \mathsf{Eval}(lk, \mathbf{x}[i])$	
$\mathbf{x}' \leftarrow\!\!{\$}\ A^{\mathcal{C}}(ek, \mathbf{y})$	$\mathbf{x}' \leftarrow\!\!{\$}\ A^{\mathcal{C}}(lk, \mathbf{y})$	
Return $(\mathbf{x} = \mathbf{x}')$	Return $(\mathbf{x} = \mathbf{x}')$	
Game $G_2(k)$	**Game $G_3(k)$**	**Oracle $\mathcal{C}(i)$ // G_3**
$j \leftarrow 0$	$j \leftarrow 0$; $I \leftarrow \perp$	$j \leftarrow j + 1$
$lk \leftarrow\!\!{\$}\ \mathsf{LKg}(1^k)$	$lk \leftarrow\!\!{\$}\ \mathsf{LKg}(1^k)$	$I \leftarrow I \cup \{i\}$
For $i = 1$ to v do	For $i = 1$ to v do	If $j \geq v$ then
$\quad \mathbf{y}[i] \leftarrow\!\!{\$}\ \mathsf{Img}(lk)$	$\quad \mathbf{y}[i] \leftarrow\!\!{\$}\ \mathsf{Img}(lk)$	Return $\perp$
$\quad \mathbf{x}[i] \leftarrow\!\!{\$}\ \mathsf{P}(lk, y)$	$\mathbf{x}' \leftarrow\!\!{\$}\ A^{\mathcal{C}}(lk, \mathbf{y})$	$\mathbf{x}[i] \leftarrow\!\!{\$}\ \mathsf{P}(lk, y)$
$\mathbf{x}' \leftarrow\!\!{\$}\ A^{\mathcal{C}}(lk, \mathbf{y})$	For $i \notin I$ do	Return $\mathbf{x}[i]$
Return $(\mathbf{x} = \mathbf{x}')$	$\quad \mathbf{x}[i] \leftarrow\!\!{\$}\ \mathsf{P}(lk, y)$	
	Return $(\mathbf{x} = \mathbf{x}')$	

Fig. 7. Games G_2, G_3 of the proof of Theorem 13.

Pass [29] showed that the one-more inversion problem for any certified, homomorphic trapdoor permutation cannot be reduced to a more "standard" assumption, meaning one that consists of a fixed number of rounds between challenger and adversary. As noted by Kakvi and Kiltz [23], RSA is not certified unless e is a prime larger than N so there is no contradiction.

Theorem 13. Let LT be a regular lossy trapdoor function with domain LDom, range LRng and lossiness τ. Then for any adversary A and any $v \in \mathbb{N}$,

$$\mathbf{Adv}_{\mathsf{LT},A,v}^{\text{one-more}}(k) \leq \mathbf{Adv}_{\mathsf{LT},B}^{\text{ltdf}}(k) + v \cdot 2^{-\tau}.$$

Proof. Consider games G_1–G_3 in Fig. 7. Then

$$\mathbf{Adv}_{\mathsf{LT},A,v}^{\text{one-more}}(k) = \Pr\left[G_0(k) \Rightarrow 1\right].$$

We now explain the game chain. Game G_1 is identical to game G_0, except that instead of generating an injective key for the lossy trapdoor function, we generate a lossy one. Consider the following adversary B attacking the key indistinguishability of LT. It simulates game G_0, but uses its given key instead of generating a new one. It outputs 1 if the simulated game returns 1, and outputs 0 otherwise. Then

$$\Pr[G_0(k) \Rightarrow 1] - \Pr[G_1(k) \Rightarrow 1] \leq \mathbf{Adv}_{\mathsf{LT},B}^{\text{ltdf}}(k).$$

Let $\mathsf{P}(lk, y) = \{x \mid \mathsf{Eval}(lk, x) = y\}$. In game G_2, we reorder the code of game G_1 producing vector $\mathbf{y}$. Note that LT is a regular lossy trapdoor function.

Then, distribution of vector $\mathbf{y}$ is uniformly random on $\mathsf{Img}(lk)$ in game G_1. Thus, vectors $\mathbf{x}$ and $\mathbf{y}$ have the same distribution in game G_1 and G_2. Hence, the change is conservative, meaning that $\Pr[G_1(k) \Rightarrow 1] = \Pr[G_2(k) \Rightarrow 1]$. Moreover, game G_3 is identical to game G_2. Thus, we have $\Pr[G_2(k) \Rightarrow 1] = \Pr[G_3(k) \Rightarrow 1]$.

Let $\mathbf{y}[\bar{I}]$ be the unopened images, where $|\bar{I}| \geq 1$. Note that in game G_3, for all $i \in \bar{I}$, $\mathbf{x}[i]$ is chosen uniformly at random after adversary A outputs $\mathbf{x}'$. Therefore, we obtain $\Pr[G_3(k) \Rightarrow 1] \leq |\bar{I}| \cdot 2^{-\tau}$. Summing up,

$$\mathbf{Adv}_{\mathsf{LT},A,v}^{\text{one-more}}(k) \leq \mathbf{Adv}_{\mathsf{LT},B}^{\mathsf{ltdf}}(k) + v \cdot 2^{-\tau}.$$

This completes the proof of Theorem 13.

Acknowledgments. We thank the PKC 2021 anonymous reviewers for helpful comments. We thank Jonathan Katz and Viet Tung Hoang for insightful discussions. Mohammad Zaheri was supported by NSF grant No. 1565387 and NSF grant No. 1149832.

A   Deferred Proofs

PROOF OF THEOREM 2. The proof is similar to the proof of Theorem 3.1 from [17]. The proof of Theorem 2 follows from the following claims. We begin by showing that it is suffices to consider H-SO adversaries where the output of $A.\mathsf{f}$ is boolean.

Claim. Let $\mathsf{H} = (\mathsf{HKg}, \mathsf{h})$ be a hash function family with domain HDom and range HRng. Let A be a H-SO adversary against H with respect to message sampler $\mathcal{M}$. Then, there is a boolean H-SO adversary B such that for all $k \in \mathbb{N}$

$$\mathbf{Adv}_{\mathsf{H},A,\mathcal{M}}^{\text{h-so}}(k) \leq 2 \cdot \mathbf{Adv}_{\mathsf{H},B,\mathcal{M}}^{\text{h-so}}(k).$$

where the running time of B is about that of A.

Proof. Consider adversary B in Fig. 8. We define E_A and E_B to be events where games H-SO-REAL$_{\mathsf{H}}^{A,\mathcal{M}}$ and H-SO-REAL$_{\mathsf{H}}^{B,\mathcal{M}}$ output 1, respectively. Hence,

$$\Pr[E_B] = \Pr[E_A] + \frac{1}{2}(1 - \Pr[E_A])$$

$$= \frac{1}{2}\Pr[E_A] + \frac{1}{2}.$$

We also define T_A and T_B to be the events where games H-SO-IDEAL$_{\mathsf{H}}^{A,\mathcal{M}}$ and H-SO-IDEAL$_{\mathsf{H}}^{B,\mathcal{M}}$ output 1, respectively. Similarly, we have $\Pr[T_B] = \Pr[T_A]/2 + 1/2$. Thus, we have $\mathbf{Adv}_{\mathsf{H},A,\mathcal{M}}^{\text{h-so}}(k) \leq 2 \cdot \mathbf{Adv}_{\mathsf{H},B,\mathcal{M}}^{\text{h-so}}(k)$. This completes the proof.

Next, we claim that it is suffices to consider balanced H-SO adversaries meaning the probability the partial information is 1 or 0 is approximately 1/2.

Algorithm $B.\mathrm{pg}(1^k)$	**Algorithm** $B.\mathrm{g}(st, \mathbf{m}[I], \mathrm{pars})$
$param \leftarrow\!\!{}_\$ A.\mathrm{pg}(1^k)$	$(r, param) \leftarrow pars$
$r \leftarrow\!\!{}_\$ \{0,1\}^{A.\mathrm{f.rl}(k)}$	$\omega \leftarrow\!\!{}_\$ A.\mathrm{g}(st, \mathbf{m}[I], param)$
$pars \leftarrow (r, param)$	Return $\langle r, \omega \rangle$
Return $pars$	**Algorithm** $B.\mathrm{f}(\mathbf{m}, pars)$
Algorithm $B.\mathrm{cor}(k, \mathbf{h}, pars)$	$(r, param) \leftarrow pars$
$(r, param) \leftarrow pars$	$t \leftarrow\!\!{}_\$ A.\mathrm{f}(\mathbf{m}, param)$
$(I, st) \leftarrow\!\!{}_\$ A.\mathrm{cor}(k, \mathbf{h}, param)$	Return $\langle r, t \rangle$
Return (I, st)	

Fig. 8. H-SO adversary B in the proof of Claim A.

Claim. Let $\mathsf{H} = (\mathsf{HKg}, \mathsf{h})$ be a hash function family with domain HDom and range HRng. Let B be a boolean H-SO adversary against H with respect to the message sampler $\mathcal{M}$. Then for any $0 \le \delta < 1/2$, there is a δ-*balanced* boolean H-SO adversary C such that for all $k \in \mathbb{N}$

$$\mathbf{Adv}^{\mathrm{h\text{-}so}}_{\mathsf{H},B,\mathcal{M}}(k) \le \left(\frac{2}{\delta}+1\right)^2 \cdot \mathbf{Adv}^{\mathrm{h\text{-}so}}_{\mathsf{H},C,\mathcal{M}}(k).$$

where the running time of C is about that of B plus $\mathcal{O}(1/\delta)$

Proof. For simplicity, we assume $1/\delta$ is an integer. Consider adversary C in Fig. 9. Note that C is δ-*balanced*, since for all $b \in \{0,1\}$

$$\left| \Pr\left[t = b \,:\, t \leftarrow\!\!{}_\$ C.\mathrm{f}(m, param) \right] - \frac{1}{2} \right| \le \frac{1}{2/\delta+1}.$$

We define E_B and E_C to be events where games H-SO-REAL$_\mathsf{H}^{B,\mathcal{M}}$ and H-SO-REAL$_\mathsf{H}^{C,\mathcal{M}}$ output 1, respectively. Let T be the event that $i, j = 2/\delta + 1$. Therefore we have

$$\Pr\left[E_C\right] = \Pr\left[E_C \mid T\right] \cdot \Pr\left[T\right] + \Pr\left[E_C \mid \overline{T}\right] \cdot \Pr\left[\overline{T}\right]$$

$$= \left(\frac{1}{2/\delta+1}\right)^2 \Pr\left[E_B\right] + \frac{1}{2}\Pr\left[\overline{T}\right].$$

We also define T_B and T_C to be the events where games H-SO-IDEAL$_\mathsf{H}^{B,\mathcal{M}}$ and H-SO-IDEAL$_\mathsf{H}^{C,\mathcal{M}}$ output 1, respectively. Similarly, we have

$$\Pr\left[T_C\right] = \left(\frac{1}{2/\delta+1}\right)^2 \Pr\left[T_B\right] + \frac{1}{2}\Pr\left[\overline{T}\right].$$

Summing up, we obtain that $\mathbf{Adv}^{\mathrm{h\text{-}so}}_{\mathsf{H},B,\mathcal{M}}(k) \le \left(\frac{2}{\delta}+1\right)^2 \cdot \mathbf{Adv}^{\mathrm{h\text{-}so}}_{\mathsf{H},C,\mathcal{M}}(k)$. This completes the proof of Claim A.

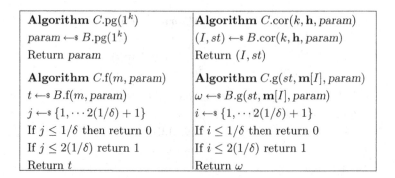

Fig. 9. H-SO adversary C in the proof of Claim A.

References

1. Bellare, M., Dowsley, R., Keelveedhi, S.: How secure is deterministic encryption? In: Katz, J. (ed.) PKC 2015. LNCS, vol. 9020, pp. 52–73. Springer, Heidelberg (2015). https://doi.org/10.1007/978-3-662-46447-2_3

2. Bellare, M., Dowsley, R., Waters, B., Yilek, S.: Standard security does not imply security against selective-opening. In: Pointcheval, D., Johansson, T. (eds.) EUROCRYPT 2012. LNCS, vol. 7237, pp. 645–662. Springer, Heidelberg (2012). https://doi.org/10.1007/978-3-642-29011-4_38

3. Bellare, M., Hofheinz, D., Yilek, S.: Possibility and impossibility results for encryption and commitment secure under selective opening. In: Joux, A. (ed.) EUROCRYPT 2009. LNCS, vol. 5479, pp. 1–35. Springer, Heidelberg (2009). https://doi.org/10.1007/978-3-642-01001-9_1

4. Bellare, M., Namprempre, C., Pointcheval, D., Semanko, M.: The one-more-RSA-inversion problems and the security of Chaum's blind signature scheme. J. Cryptol. **16**(3), 185–215 (2003)

5. Bellare, M., Rogaway, P.: Random oracles are practical: a paradigm for designing efficient protocols. In: Ashby, V. (ed.) ACM CCS 1993, Fairfax, Virginia, USA, 3–5 November 1993, pp. 62–73. ACM Press (1993)

6. Bendlin, R., Nielsen, J.B., Nordholt, P.S., Orlandi, C.: Lower and upper bounds for deniable public-key encryption. In: Lee, D.H., Wang, X. (eds.) ASIACRYPT 2011. LNCS, vol. 7073, pp. 125–142. Springer, Heidelberg (2011). https://doi.org/10.1007/978-3-642-25385-0_7

7. Böhl, F., Hofheinz, D., Kraschewski, D.: On definitions of selective opening security. In: Fischlin, M., Buchmann, J., Manulis, M. (eds.) PKC 2012. LNCS, vol. 7293, pp. 522–539. Springer, Heidelberg (2012). https://doi.org/10.1007/978-3-642-30057-8_31

8. Canetti, R.: Towards realizing random oracles: hash functions that hide all partial information. In: Kaliski, B.S. (ed.) CRYPTO 1997. LNCS, vol. 1294, pp. 455–469. Springer, Heidelberg (1997). https://doi.org/10.1007/BFb0052255

9. Canetti, R., Dwork, C., Naor, M., Ostrovsky, R.: Deniable encryption. In: Kaliski, B.S. (ed.) CRYPTO 1997. LNCS, vol. 1294, pp. 90–104. Springer, Heidelberg (1997). https://doi.org/10.1007/BFb0052229

10. Canetti, R., Feige, U., Goldreich, O., Naor, M.: Adaptively secure multi-party computation. In: 28th ACM STOC, Philadephia, PA, USA, 22–24 May 1996, pp. 639–648. ACM Press (1996)
11. Canetti, R., Halevi, S., Katz, J.: Adaptively-secure, non-interactive public-key encryption. In: Kilian, J. (ed.) TCC 2005. LNCS, vol. 3378, pp. 150–168. Springer, Heidelberg (2005). https://doi.org/10.1007/978-3-540-30576-7_9
12. Chaum, D.: Blind signatures for untraceable payments. In: Chaum, D., Rivest, R.L., Sherman, A.T. (eds.) CRYPTO 1982, pp. 199–203, Santa Barbara, CA, USA. Plenum Press, New York (1982)
13. Coron, J.-S.: Optimal security proofs for PSS and other signature schemes. In: Knudsen, L.R. (ed.) EUROCRYPT 2002. LNCS, vol. 2332, pp. 272–287. Springer, Heidelberg (2002). https://doi.org/10.1007/3-540-46035-7_18
14. Damgård, I., Nielsen, J.B.: Improved non-committing encryption schemes based on a general complexity assumption. In: Bellare, M. (ed.) CRYPTO 2000. LNCS, vol. 1880, pp. 432–450. Springer, Heidelberg (2000). https://doi.org/10.1007/3-540-44598-6_27
15. Dodis, Y., Reyzin, L., Smith, A.: Fuzzy extractors: how to generate strong keys from biometrics and other noisy data. In: Cachin, C., Camenisch, J.L. (eds.) EUROCRYPT 2004. LNCS, vol. 3027, pp. 523–540. Springer, Heidelberg (2004). https://doi.org/10.1007/978-3-540-24676-3_31
16. Dwork, C., Naor, M., Reingold, O., Stockmeyer, L.J.: Magic functions. J. ACM **50**(6), 852–921 (2003)
17. Fuller, B., O'Neill, A., Reyzin, L.: A unified approach to deterministic encryption: new constructions and a connection to computational entropy. In: Cramer, R. (ed.) TCC 2012. LNCS, vol. 7194, pp. 582–599. Springer, Heidelberg (2012). https://doi.org/10.1007/978-3-642-28914-9_33
18. Goyal, V., O'Neill, A., Rao, V.: Correlated-input secure hash functions. In: Ishai, Y. (ed.) TCC 2011. LNCS, vol. 6597, pp. 182–200. Springer, Heidelberg (2011). https://doi.org/10.1007/978-3-642-19571-6_12
19. Heuer, F., Kiltz, E., Pietrzak, K.: Standard security does imply security against selective opening for markov distributionss. Cryptology ePrint Archive, Report 2015/853 (2015). http://eprint.iacr.org/2015/853
20. Hoang, V.T., Katz, J., O'Neill, A., Zaheri, M.: Selective-opening security in the presence of randomness failures. In: Cheon, J.H., Takagi, T. (eds.) ASIACRYPT 2016. LNCS, vol. 10032, pp. 278–306. Springer, Heidelberg (2016). https://doi.org/10.1007/978-3-662-53890-6_10
21. Hofheinz, D., Rao, V., Wichs, D.: Standard security does not imply indistinguishability under selective opening. Cryptology ePrint Archive, Report 2015/792 (2015). http://eprint.iacr.org/2015/792
22. Hofheinz, D., Rupp, A.: Standard versus selective opening security: separation and equivalence results. In: Lindell, Y. (ed.) TCC 2014. LNCS, vol. 8349, pp. 591–615. Springer, Heidelberg (2014). https://doi.org/10.1007/978-3-642-54242-8_25
23. Kakvi, S.A., Kiltz, E.: Optimal security proofs for full domain hash, revisited. In: Pointcheval, D., Johansson, T. (eds.) EUROCRYPT 2012. LNCS, vol. 7237, pp. 537–553. Springer, Heidelberg (2012). https://doi.org/10.1007/978-3-642-29011-4_32
24. Kiltz, E., O'Neill, A., Smith, A.: Instantiability of RSA-OAEP under chosen-plaintext attack. In: Rabin, T. (ed.) CRYPTO 2010. LNCS, vol. 6223, pp. 295–313. Springer, Heidelberg (2010). https://doi.org/10.1007/978-3-642-14623-7_16

25. Nielsen, J.B.: Separating random oracle proofs from complexity theoretic proofs: the non-committing encryption case. In: Yung, M. (ed.) CRYPTO 2002. LNCS, vol. 2442, pp. 111–126. Springer, Heidelberg (2002). https://doi.org/10.1007/3-540-45708-9_8

26. Nielsen, J.B.: A threshold pseudorandom function construction and its applications. In: Yung, M. (ed.) CRYPTO 2002. LNCS, vol. 2442, pp. 401–416. Springer, Heidelberg (2002). https://doi.org/10.1007/3-540-45708-9_26

27. O'Neill, A., Peikert, C., Waters, B.: Bi-deniable public-key encryption. In: Rogaway, P. (ed.) CRYPTO 2011. LNCS, vol. 6841, pp. 525–542. Springer, Heidelberg (2011). https://doi.org/10.1007/978-3-642-22792-9_30

28. Pandey, O., Pass, R., Vaikuntanathan, V.: Adaptive one-way functions and applications. In: Wagner, D. (ed.) CRYPTO 2008. LNCS, vol. 5157, pp. 57–74. Springer, Heidelberg (2008). https://doi.org/10.1007/978-3-540-85174-5_4

29. Pass, R.: Limits of provable security from standard assumptions. In: Fortnow, L., Vadhan, S.P. (eds.) 43rd ACM STOC, San Jose, CA, USA, 6–8 June 2011, pp. 109–118. ACM Press (2011)

30. Peikert, C., Waters, B.: Lossy trapdoor functions and their applications. In: Ladner, R.E., Dwork, C. (eds.) 40th ACM STOC, Victoria, British Columbia, Canada, 17–20 May 2008, pp. 187–196. ACM Press (2008)

31. Sahai, A., Waters, B.: How to use indistinguishability obfuscation: deniable encryption, and more. In: Shmoys, D.B. (ed.) 46th ACM STOC, pp. 475–484, New York, NY, USA, 31 May–3 June 2014. ACM Press (2014)

Revisiting (R)CCA Security and Replay Protection

Christian Badertscher[1], Ueli Maurer[2], Christopher Portmann[2],
and Guilherme Rito[2(✉)]

[1] IOHK, Zurich, Switzerland
`christian.badertscher@iohk.io`
[2] ETH Zurich, Zurich, Switzerland
`{maurer,chportma,gteixeir}@inf.ethz.ch`

Abstract. This paper takes a fresh approach to systematically characterizing, comparing, and understanding CCA-type security definitions for public-key encryption (PKE), a topic with a long history. The justification for a concrete security definition X is relative to a benchmark application (e.g. confidential communication): Does the use of a PKE scheme satisfying X imply the security of the application? Because unnecessarily strong definitions may lead to unnecessarily inefficient schemes or unnecessarily strong computational assumptions, security definitions should be as weak as possible, i.e. as close as possible to (but above) the benchmark. Understanding the hierarchy of security definitions, partially ordered by the implication (i.e. at least as strong) relation, is hence important, as is placing the relevant applications as benchmark levels within the hierarchy.

CCA-2 security is apparently the strongest notion, but because it is arguably too strong, Canetti, Krawczyk, and Nielsen (Crypto 2003) proposed the relaxed notions of *Replayable CCA* security (RCCA) as perhaps the weakest meaningful definition, and they investigated the space between CCA and RCCA security by proposing two versions of *Detectable RCCA* (d-RCCA) security which are meant to ensure that replays of ciphertexts are either publicly or secretly detectable (and hence preventable).

The contributions of this paper are three-fold. First, following the work of Coretti, Maurer, and Tackmann (Asiacrypt 2013), we formalize the three benchmark applications of PKE that serve as the natural motivation for security notions, namely the construction of certain types of (possibly replay-protected) confidential channels (from an insecure and an authenticated communication channel). Second, we prove that RCCA does not achieve the confidentiality benchmark and, contrary to previous belief, that the proposed d-RCCA notions are not even relaxations of CCA-2 security. Third, we propose the natural security notions corresponding to the three benchmarks: an appropriately strengthened version of RCCA to ensure confidentiality, as well as two notions for capturing public and secret replay detectability.

C. Badertscher—Work done while author was at the University of Edinburgh, Scotland.

J. A. Garay (Ed.): PKC 2021, LNCS 12711, pp. 173–202, 2021.
https://doi.org/10.1007/978-3-030-75248-4_7

1   Introduction

When designing a cryptographic security notion, it is of central importance to keep in mind the purpose and applications it is developed for. For CCA-2 secure encryption schemes[1], the most important historical application is to enable confidential communication: assuming an insecure channel from Alice to Bob (over which ciphertexts are sent), and an authenticated channel from Bob to Alice (over which the public key can be transmitted authentically), the scheme should construct a confidential channel, i.e. an idealized object with the property that whatever Alice sends to Bob does not leak any information to an attacker (except possibly the length of the message), and where the only active capability of the attacker is to inject new messages (uncorrelated to Alice's inputs)[2]. Coretti, Maurer, and Tackmann [10] proved that indeed CCA-2 security is sufficient for this construction to be achieved, by having Bob generating a key-pair, sending the public key authentically to Alice, and by letting Alice encrypt all messages with respect to the obtained public key. It is also known that CCA-2 security is actually too strong for this task: a CCA-2 secure scheme can be easily modified, for example by appending a single bit to ciphertexts which is ignored by the decryption algorithm, to yield a scheme that is not CCA-2 secure but still allows to achieve a confidential channel.

To address the question what weaker security notion(s) would actually match more closely to the application of secure communication, Canetti, Krawczyk, and Nielsen [8] study relaxed CCA-2 security notions and their relationships; they formalize an entire spectrum: at the weakest end, they propose RCCA security, which for large message spaces (size super-polynomial in the security parameter) is known to achieve confidential channels [10]. This fact has bolstered RCCA security into becoming the default security notion in settings where CCA-2 is not achievable, such as in rerandomizable encryption schemes [14,22] and updatable encryption schemes [16]. Intuitively, a scheme can be RCCA secure even if it is easy to create from a known ciphertext another one that still decrypts to the same message. Inheriting from prior work on relaxing CCA-2 security, most notably [1,17,24], they further provide formalizations for intermediate notions between CCA-2 and RCCA. These so-called detectable notions of RCCA security further demand that modifications of an already known ciphertext can be efficiently detected—either with the help of the secret key (sd-RCCA) or the public key only (pd-RCCA) yielding two separate security notions. These notions of detectable RCCA security, and in particular pd-RCCA, are designed to capture an appealing property of CCA-2 security, namely that replays can be efficiently detected. This not only admits a more precise language to specify the types of replays a scheme admits, but furthermore is a useful property in applications like voting or access-control encryption, where a trusted third party must perform

---

[1] Note that throughout this work, if not otherwise stated, we refer to the indistinguishability-based versions of security notions.

[2] Hence, the confidential channel does not provide any authenticity to Bob.

the filtering without access to the secret key [3]. We elaborate on the former aspects later in Remark 1 at the end of Sect. 1.1.

It has however never been formally investigated whether the detectable notions are suitable to capture the security of the intended application of replay detection. Moreover, our analysis shows that these detectable RCCA notions (i.e. pd-RCCA and sd-RCCA) are actually not proper relaxations of CCA-2, in that they are not implied by CCA-2.

In this work, we fill this gap and provide a systematic treatment of these relaxations of CCA-2 security using the Constructive Cryptography framework by Maurer and Renner [18,19] and building upon the work of Coretti et al. [10]. We formalize the intuitive security goals that RCCA security and the detectable RCCA security notions aim to achieve, yielding what we call benchmarks to assess whether the existing security notions are adequate. We observe that none of the previous notions seems to allow a proof that they meet this level of security and therefore propose new security notions for detectable RCCA security (which can be regarded as the corrections of the existing ones), show which benchmarks they achieve, and prove that they are implied by CCA-2. In summary, this shows that the newly introduced notions are placed correctly in the spectrum between CCA-2 and RCCA and that they can be safely used in the intended applications.

1.1 Overview of Contributions

A Systematic Approach to RCCA and Replay Protection. Following the constructive paradigm, a construction consists of three elements: the assumed resources (such as an insecure communication channel), the constructed or ideal resource (such as a confidential channel), and the real-world protocol. A protocol is said to achieve the construction, if there is a simulator such that the real world (consisting of the protocol running with the assumed resources) is indistinguishable from the ideal system (consisting of the ideal resource and the simulator). This way, it is ensured that any attack on the real system can be translated into an attack to the ideal system, the latter being secure by definition.

Building upon the work of Coretti et al. [10], we present three benchmarks to approach the intended security of RCCA and replay protection:

- The construction of a confidential channel between Alice and Bob from an insecure communication channel (and an authenticated channel to distribute the public key). This is arguably the most natural goal of confidential (and non-malleable) communication. An encryption scheme should achieve this construction by having Bob generating the key-pair and sending the public key to Alice over the authenticated channel. Alice sends encryptions of the messages over the insecure channel to Bob, who can decrypt the ciphertexts and output the resulting messages. This benchmark is formalized in Sect. 3.1.
- The construction of a replay-protected confidential channel from (essentially) the same resources as above. A replay-protected confidential channel is a channel that only allows an attacker to deliver each message sent by Alice at most once to Bob. This construction captures the most basic form of replay

protection. An encryption scheme can be applied as above, except that Bob must make use of the secret key (and a memory resource to store received ciphertexts) to detect and filter out replays. This construction is formalized in Sect. 3.2.

- The construction of a replay-protected confidential channel from basically the same resources, but where the task of detecting replays is done by a third-party, say Charlie, that does not need to have access to Bob's secret key. Hence, an encryption scheme is employed as above, but the task of filtering and detecting replays can be outsourced to any party possessing the public key (having sufficient memory to store the received ciphertexts). This benchmark is formalized in Sect. 3.3.

We note that only the first benchmark is taken from existing literature [10] (which is an abstract version of the UC-formalization $\mathcal{F}_{\mathrm{RPKE}}$ defined in [8])[3] while the other benchmarks are new formulations and variants of the known goal of replay protection. The benefits of our benchmarks is that they yield a precise way to assess the guarantees provided by a security notion for an encryption scheme: does a scheme secure with respect to a certain notion achieve the above construction(s)?

New Intermediate Notions Between CCA-2 and RCCA. We propose three game-based security notions, each designed to suffice for achieving the intended benchmark. The abbreviations stand for confidential (cl), secret-key replay protection (srp), and public-key replay protection (prp):

- We first propose IND-cl-RCCA, a security notion which is sufficient to achieve confidential communication even for small message spaces, which we prove in Sect. 6.1. This is the weakest new notion we introduce and we prove that it achieves the first benchmark; cl-RCCA should then take the role of RCCA as the default security notion when one aims at the design of schemes that enable confidential communication (in particular when the message space size is small). Note that cl-RCCA is strictly stronger than RCCA since the latter does not achieve confidential communication for small message spaces (see Theorem 1).[4]
- The second security notion we introduce is IND-srp-RCCA and it achieves the second benchmark: realizing a replay protected confidential channel. The notion is hence designed to enable the implementation of a replay-protection mechanism by the receiver, who knows the secret decryption key. We also argue why the strengthening compared to cl-RCCA (and sd-RCCA) is needed to achieve replay-protection: from a conceptual perspective, implementing a replay-protector as part of the receiver requires the detection of replays without necessarily ever seeing the original ciphertext by the sender which is

---

[3] We note that all our results are independent of the specific details of the underlying composable framework; analogous results would be obtained when working in the UC framework [6].

[4] We note that NM-RCCA [8], which is stronger than IND-RCCA, does not seem to be sufficient to achieve the first benchmark either.

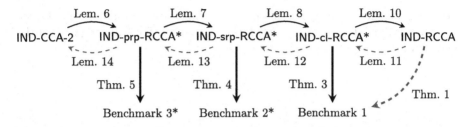

Fig. 1. New notions of security between CCA-2 and RCCA, and their relations to each other and to the benchmarks. Solid black arrows denote implications and dashed red arrows denote separations. The new security notions introduced in this paper are marked with *.

a security requirement that is not captured by cl-RCCA (nor sd-RCCA).[5] The notion and the construction proof appear in Sect. 6.2.
- We finally propose a security notion to capture the idea of publicly-detectable RCCA that we call IND-prp-RCCA. This notion is sufficient to achieve the third benchmark and therefore captures the outsourced replay-protection mechanism that was originally envisioned from pd-RCCA. This notion and the construction proof appear in Sect. 6.3.

We finally show that all these notions can be strictly separated: IND-RCCA security, the weakest notion considered in this work, is strictly weaker than IND-cl-RCCA. The latter is strictly weaker than IND-srp-RCCA, which is in turn strictly weaker than IND-prp-RCCA. Finally, IND-prp-RCCA is strictly weaker than IND-CCA-2 security. These results are proven in Sect. 7; Fig. 1 illustrates all these new notions, their relations to each other and to the benchmarks.

Technical Inconsistencies with Existing pd-RCCA and sd-RCCA Notions. Numerous weaker versions of CCA-2 security have been proposed [1,8,17,24] which are essentially equivalent versions of what is formalized in [8] as *publicly detectable* (pd)-RCCA and *secretly detectable* (sd)-RCCA. We show for the given formalizations that the notions are generally not implied by CCA-2 security (unless one would restrict, for example, explicitly to the case of deterministic decryption [1], or alternatively to the case of perfect correctness), which seems to be a rather unintended artifact of the concrete definition as we show in Sect. 5. While these shortcomings can be fixed, the existing notions do not appear to suffice to achieve the intended benchmarks for replay protection (see Sect. 6), leaving the state of affairs unclear, as depicted in Fig. 2. This justifies the need to propose new intermediate notions that provably avoid these shortcomings: on one hand, our notions are implied by CCA-2, and on the other hand, they deliver the desired level of security required by a replay protection mechanism. The security notions and results of this paper clean up the space between CCA-2 and RCCA security, yielding, as aforementioned, a clean hierarchy of security

---

[5] More concretely, the simulator in the construction proof of a confidential channel only requires the (much milder) detection of *honestly* generated ciphertext replays.

notions as depicted in Fig. 1: not only all notions are separated, but also we show that each of the notions we introduce is sufficient for achieving each of the benchmarks.

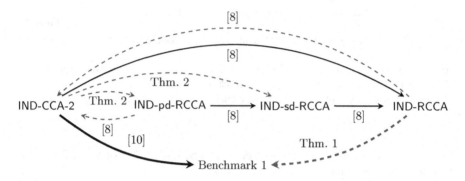

Fig. 2. Relations between the notions of security from [8]. The solid black arrows denote implications whilst the dashed red arrows denote separations.

Remark 1. Recall that the original motivation of introducing relaxed versions of CCA security stems from the observation that CCA is much stronger than the composable confidentiality requirement [8]. RCCA has the built-in assumption that generating replays of a (challenge) ciphertext is generally easy and therefore, in the security game the adversary is denied to decrypt a broad class of ciphertexts. Detectable RCCA as introduced in [8, Definition 7], develops a language to talk about the ability to detect specific kinds of replays and introduce a relation among ciphertexts accompanied by an efficient algorithm to evaluate it. Therefore, to capture detectable RCCA security, aside of the ordinary three algorithms of a PKE system, there is by definition an additional one to detect replays. While in this work we develop a composable understanding of what [8] calls the ability to detect replays, our IND-srp-RCCA and IND-prp-RCCA notions can equivalently be seen as ordinary PKE notions. Confidentiality then means that no adversary learns anything about the plaintext when the challenger denies decryption queries that the replay detection algorithm considers being replays of the challenge ciphertext.

1.2 Further Related Work

The investigation of relaxed, enhanced, and modified versions of CCA-2 security has a rich history and has found numerous applications in proxy-reencryption, updatable encryption, attribute based-encryption, rerandomizable encryption, or steganography [2,5,7,9,12–14,16,22,23].

The main relaxations of CCA-2, upon which the formalization of [8] builds, have been proposed in [24] as benign malleability and in [1] as generalized CCA-2 security, and also relate to loose ciphertext-unforgeability [17]. All these versions fall essentially into the formalization of public detectability discussed above, and all suffer from analogous technical issues, and hence in this work we focus on the formalization given in [8]. Three different flavours of RCCA have been introduced: IND-RCCA, UC-RCCA and NM-RCCA. In this work we focus on IND-RCCA. Our first benchmark is an abstract version of UC-RCCA. While the third flavour, NM-RCCA, is a strengthening of IND-RCCA (since it captures one additional attack vector), it does not seem to suffice to construct a confidential channel (or imply UC-RCCA for small message spaces) and is superseded in our treatment by IND-cl-RCCA that provably constructs the confidential channel for any message space.

A further relaxation of CCA-2 security, only loosely related to this work, is called detectable CCA-2 [15] and formalizes the detection of "dangerous" queries in CCA-2 (without considering replayable properties). This notion provides a rather weak level of security on its own (in that it does not imply RCCA) [15].

Another line of research has consisted in studying q-bounded security definitions [11] wherein a scheme is assumed to only be used to decrypt at most q messages. Cramer et al. [11] give a black-box construction of a IND-q-bounded-CCA-2 secure PKE scheme from any IND-CPA secure one. The proposed construction crucially relies on knowing the value q in advance as it is hardcoded in the scheme.

2 Preliminaries

2.1 Constructive Cryptography

The Constructive Cryptography (CC) framework [18,19] is a composable security framework which views cryptography as a resource theory: a protocol transforms the assumed resources into the constructed resources.[6] For example, if Alice and Bob have (access to) a shared secret key and an authentic channel, by running a one-time pad they construct a secure channel—this example is treated more formally further in this section.

In this view, encryption is the task of constructing channel resources. We thus start by defining various channels—used and constructed in this work—here below. Then we give the formal definition of a construction in CC.

INS. The weakest channel we consider is the (completely) insecure channel **INS**, where any message input by the sender goes straight to the adversary, and the adversary may insert any messages into the channel, which are then delivered to the receiver. This is drawn in the top left in Fig. 3.

AUT. In order to distribute the public keys used by PKE schemes, the players will also need an authentic channel **AUT**, which guarantees that anything

---

[6] Resources essentially correspond to (ideal) functionalities in UC [6], though in CC we additionally model the ability of players to communicate as having access to a channel resource.

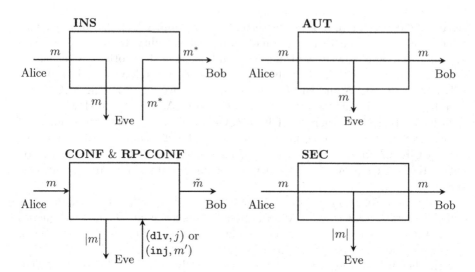

Fig. 3. A depiction of the channels used in this work. From top-left to bottom right: an insecure channel **INS**, an authentic channel **AUT**, a (replay protected) confidential channel (**RP-**)**CONF**, and a secure channel **SEC**.

received by the legitimate receiver was sent by the legitimate sender, but an adversary may also receive a copy of these messages. For simplicity, in our model we do not allow the adversary to either block an authentic channel or insert any replays. Such a channel is drawn in the top right of Fig. 3.

CONF. A confidential channel **CONF** only leaks the message length (denoted $|m|$) to the adversary, i.e. when the message m is input by the sender, the adversary receives $|m|$ at her interface. She can choose which message $j \leq i$ is delivered to the receiver, where i is the total number of messages input by the sender so far, or—since the channel is only confidential, but does not provide authenticity—the adversary may also inject a message of her own with $(\texttt{inj}, m')$, and m' is then delivered to the receiver. This is depicted in the bottom left of Fig. 3.

RP-CONF. The **CONF** channel described above allows the adversary to deliver multiple times the same message to the receiver by inserting multiple times $(\texttt{dlv}, j)$. We define a stronger channel, the replay protected confidential channel **RP-CONF**, which will only process each $(\texttt{dlv}, j)$ query at most once.

SEC. Finally, the secure channel **SEC** is both confidential and authentic, and is drawn in the bottom right of Fig. 3.

We will often consider channels that only transmit n messages, i.e. the sender may only input n messages. These channels will be denoted **NAME**$[n]$. The main properties of these channels are summarized in Fig. 4.

Formally, a *resource* (e.g. a channel) in an N-player setting is an interactive system with N interfaces, where each player may interact with the system at their

Channel Name	Symbol	Leak $l(m)$	Insert	Replays
Insecure Channel	**INS**	m	Yes	Yes
Authentic Channel	**AUT**	m	No	No
Confidential Channel	**CONF**	$|m|$	Yes	Yes
Replay Protected Confidential Channel	**RP-CONF**	$|m|$	Yes	No
Secure Channel	**SEC**	$|m|$	No	No

Fig. 4. A summary of the channel properties used in this work. *Leak* is the information about the message given to Eve, where $|m|$ denotes the length of the message. *Insert* denotes whether Eve is allowed to insert messages of her own into the channel. *Replay* denotes whether Eve can force a channel to deliver multiple times a message that was sent only once.

interface by receiving outputs and providing inputs. These may be mathematically modeled as random systems [20,21] and can be specified by pseudo-code or an informal description as the channels above. In this work we consider the 3 player setting, and the interfaces are labeled A, B, and E for Alice, Bob, and Eve.

If multiple resources $\mathbf{R}_1, \ldots, \mathbf{R}_\ell$ are accessible to players, we write $[\mathbf{R}_1, \ldots, \mathbf{R}_\ell]$ for the new resource resulting from having all resources accessible in parallel to the parties.

Operations run locally by some party (e.g. encrypting or decrypting a message) are modeled by interactive systems with two interface and are called *converters*. The inner interface connects to the available resources, whereas the outer interface is accessible to the corresponding party to provide inputs and receive outputs. The composition of the resource and the converter is a new resource. For example, let $\mathbf{R}$ be a resource, and let α be a converter which we connect at the A-interface of $\mathbf{R}$, then we write $\alpha^A \mathbf{R}$ for the new resource resulting from this connection. Formally, a converter is thus a map between resources.

To illustrate this, we draw the real system corresponding to a one-time pad encryption in Fig. 5. Here, the players have access to a secret key **KEY** and an authentic channel **AUT**. Alice runs the encryption converter $\mathsf{enc}_{\mathsf{otp}}$, which sends the ciphertext on the authentic channel. Bob runs the decryption converter $\mathsf{dec}_{\mathsf{otp}}$, which outputs the result of the decryption. The entire resource drawn on the left in Fig. 5 is denoted $\mathsf{enc}_{\mathsf{otp}}^A \mathsf{dec}_{\mathsf{otp}}^B [\mathbf{KEY}, \mathbf{AUT}]$, where the order of $\mathsf{enc}_{\mathsf{otp}}$ and $\mathsf{dec}_{\mathsf{otp}}$ does not matter since converters at different interfaces commute.

In order to argue that the protocol $\mathsf{otp} = (\mathsf{enc}_{\mathsf{otp}}, \mathsf{dec}_{\mathsf{otp}})$ constructs a secure channel **SEC** from a shared secret key **KEY** and an authentic channel **AUT**, we need to find a converter σ_{otp} (called a *simulator*) such that when this simulator is attached to the adversarial interface of the constructed resource **SEC** (resulting in $\sigma_{\mathsf{otp}}^E \mathbf{SEC}$), the real and ideal systems are indistinguishable. As illustrated in Fig. 5, a simulator σ_{otp} which outputs a random string of the right length is sufficient for proving that the one-time pad constructs a secure channel.

Distinguishability between two systems $\mathbf{R}$ and $\mathbf{S}$ is defined with respect to a distinguisher $\mathbf{D}$ which interacts with one of the systems, and has to output a

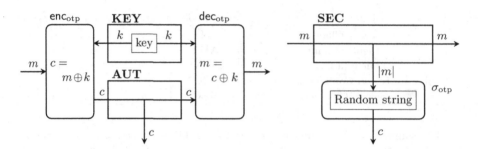

Fig. 5. The real and ideal systems for the one-time pad. Viewed as a black box, the real and ideal systems are indistinguishable.

bit corresponding to its guess. Let $\mathbf{D[R]}$ and $\mathbf{D[S]}$ denote the random variables corresponding to the output of $\mathbf{D}$ when interacting with $\mathbf{R}$ and $\mathbf{S}$, respectively. Then its advantage in distinguishing between the two is given by

$$\Delta^{\mathbf{D}}(\mathbf{R}, \mathbf{S}) := \Pr[\mathbf{D[R]} = 0] - \Pr[\mathbf{D[S]} = 0].$$

In the case of the one-time pad example with $\mathbf{R}$ denoting the real system and $\mathbf{S}$ the ideal system (drawn on the left and right in Fig. 5) we have that for all $\mathbf{D}$, $\Delta^{\mathbf{D}}(\mathbf{R}, \mathbf{S}) = 0$.

We now have all the elements needed to define a cryptographic construction in the three party setting.

Definition 1 (Asymptotic security [18,19]). *Let $\pi = \{(\pi_k^A, \pi_k^B)\}_{k \in \mathbb{N}}$ be an efficient family of converters, and let $\mathbf{R} = \{\mathbf{R}_k\}_{k \in \mathbb{N}}$ and $\mathbf{S} = \{\mathbf{S}_k\}_{k \in \mathbb{N}}$ be two efficient families of resources. We say that π asymptotically constructs $\mathbf{R}$ from $\mathbf{S}$ if there exists an efficient family of simulators $\sigma = \{\sigma_k\}_{k \in \mathbb{N}}$ such that for any efficient family of distinguishers $\mathbf{D} = \{\mathbf{D}_k\}_{k \in \mathbb{N}}$,*

$$\varepsilon(k) = \Delta^{\mathbf{D}_k}(\pi_k \mathbf{R}_k, \sigma_k \mathbf{S}_k)$$

is negligible. The construction is information-theoretically secure if the same holds for all (possibly inefficient) families of distinguishers.

For clarity we have made the security parameter k explicit in Definition 1, though in most of the technical part of this work we leave this parameter implicit to simplify the notation.

2.2 Public Key Encryption

We recap the basic definitions when a public-key encryption (PKE) system is considered correct and CCA/RCCA secure.

Definition 2. *A Public Key Encryption (PKE) scheme Π with message space $\mathcal{M} \subseteq \{0,1\}^*$, is a triple $\Pi = (G, E, D)$ of Probabilistic Polynomial-Time algorithms (PPTs) such that for any PPT adversary $\mathbf{A}$, the function $Corr(k)$ defined below is at most negligible in (the security parameter) k*

$$Corr(k) := \Pr \left[\begin{array}{c} (\mathrm{pk}, \mathrm{sk}) \leftarrow G\left(1^k\right) \\ m \leftarrow \mathbf{A}\left(1^k, \mathrm{pk}\right) \end{array} \middle| \quad D_{\mathrm{sk}}\left(E_{\mathrm{pk}}\left(m\right)\right) \neq m \quad \right]$$

We point out that the above condition is a succinct expression that captures the correctness of communication protocols in general and intuitively says that even under knowledge of the sampled public key of the system, no one can find (except with negligible probability) a message that would violate the correctness condition (where the error term can be understood as computational distance to a perfectly correct channel). Furthermore, the correctness requirement often holds w.r.t. all adversaries.

Definition 3. *A PKE scheme $\Pi = (G, E, D)$ is IND-CCA-2 secure if no PPT distinguisher $\mathbf{D}$ distinguishes the two game systems $\mathbf{G}_0^{\Pi\text{-IND-CCA-2}}$ and $\mathbf{G}_1^{\Pi\text{-IND-CCA-2}}$ (specified below) with non-negligible advantage (in the security parameter k) over random guessing (i.e. if $\Delta^{\mathbf{D}}\left(\mathbf{G}_0^{\Pi\text{-IND-CCA-2}}\right), \mathbf{G}_1^{\Pi\text{-IND-CCA-2}} \leq negl(k)$). For $b \in \{0,1\}$, game system $\mathbf{G}_b^{\Pi\text{-IND-CCA-2}}$ is as follows:*

Initialization: $\mathbf{G}_b^{\Pi\text{-IND-CCA-2}}$ *generates a key-pair* $(\mathrm{pk}, \mathrm{sk}) \leftarrow G\left(1^k\right)$, *and sends* pk *to* $\mathbf{D}$.

First decryption stage: *Whenever* $\mathbf{D}$ *queries* (ciphertext, c), *the game system* $\mathbf{G}_b^{\Pi\text{-IND-CCA-2}}$ *computes* $m = D_{\mathrm{sk}}\left(c\right)$ *and sends* m *to* $\mathbf{D}$.

Challenge stage: *When* $\mathbf{D}$ *queries* (test messages, m_0, m_1), *for* $m_0, m_1 \in \mathcal{M}$ *such that* $|m_0| = |m_1|$, $\mathbf{G}_b^{\Pi\text{-IND-CCA-2}}$ *computes* $c^* = E_{\mathrm{pk}}\left(m_b\right)$, *and sends* c^* *to* $\mathbf{D}$.[7]

Second decryption stage: *Whenever* $\mathbf{D}$ *queries* (ciphertext, c), *the game system* $\mathbf{G}_b^{\Pi\text{-IND-CCA-2}}$ *replies* test *if* $c = c^*$ *and replies* $m = D_{\mathrm{sk}}\left(c\right)$ *(i.e. the decryption of c) otherwise.*

For simplicity, throughout the paper we will omit the prefix Π from the notation of the game systems, unless needed for clarity.

Definition 4. *A PKE scheme $\Pi = (G, E, D)$ is IND-RCCA secure if it is secure according to the definition of IND-CCA-2 security (Definition 3), but where the IND-RCCA game systems differ from the IND-CCA-2 game systems in the second decryption stage, which now works as follows: In the following, let m_0, m_1 be the two challenge messages queried by distinguisher $\mathbf{D}$ during the Challenge stage:*

Second decryption stage: *When* $\mathbf{D}$ *queries* (ciphertext, c), *the game system computes* $m = D_{\mathrm{sk}}\left(c\right)$. *If* $m \in \{m_0, m_1\}$, *then the game system replies with the special response* test *to* $\mathbf{D}$, *and otherwise sends* m *to* $\mathbf{D}$.

---

[7] Unless explicitly stated, we assume that $\mathbf{D}$ can only perform a single challenge query.

2.3 Public Key Encryption with Replay Filtering

We now introduce two new types of PKE schemes, namely ones in which cipher-text replays can be efficiently detected by an algorithm F that is defined as part of the scheme. For the correctness condition of these schemes we require, in addition to the usual correctness condition of PKE schemes, that with high probability F cannot relate two fresh encryptions of any messages. This is an essential requirement such that F can be used for filtering out ciphertext replays, because the correctness condition guarantees that it will not filter out honestly generated ciphertexts (later in Sect. 6.2 we couple such schemes with the proper security notions).

Definition 5. *A PKE scheme with Secret (Replay) Filtering (PKESF) Π with message space $\mathcal{M} \subseteq \{0,1\}^*$, is a 4-tuple $\Pi = (G, E, D, F)$ of PPT algorithms such that for any PPT adversary $\mathbf{A}$, the function $Corr(k)$ defined below is at most negligible in (the security parameter) k*

$$Corr(k) := \Pr \left[\begin{array}{c} (\mathrm{pk}, \mathrm{sk}) \leftarrow G(1^k) \\ (m, m') \leftarrow \mathbf{A}(1^k, \mathrm{pk}) \end{array} \middle| \begin{array}{c} F(\mathrm{pk}, \mathrm{sk}, E_{\mathrm{pk}}(m), E_{\mathrm{pk}}(m')) = 1 \\ \vee \quad D_{\mathrm{sk}}(E_{\mathrm{pk}}(m)) \neq m \end{array} \right]$$

A PKE scheme with Public (Replay) Filtering (PKEPF) Π is just like a PKESF except that F now does not receive the secret key sk.

As one might note, from any correct and IND-CCA-2 secure PKE scheme $\Pi = (G, E, D)$, one can define a correct PKEPF scheme $\Pi' = (G, E, D, F)$ where $F(\mathrm{pk}, c, c') = 1$ if and only if $c = c'$; the correctness of Π' with respect to Definition 5 follows from the correctness and IND-CCA-2 security of Π.

2.4 Reductions

Most of the proofs in this work consist in showing reductions between various security definitions. Both the constructive statements introduced in Sect. 2.1 and game-based definitions such as IND-CCA-2 (Definition 3) can be viewed as distinguishing systems—the real world $\mathbf{W}_0$ from the ideal world $\mathbf{W}_1$ and game $\mathbf{G}_0$ from game $\mathbf{G}_1$, respectively. A reduction between two such definitions consists in proving that if a distinguisher $\mathbf{D}$ can succeed in one task, then a (related) distinguisher $\mathbf{D}'$ can succeed in the other. We only give explicit reductions with single blackbox access to $\mathbf{D}$ in this work, i.e. we define $\mathbf{D}' := \mathbf{DC}$, where $\mathbf{DC}$ denotes the composition of two systems $\mathbf{D}$ and $\mathbf{C}$. $\mathbf{C}$ is called the *reduction system* (or simply the *reduction*).

For example, if we wish to reduce the task of breaking a constructive definition (with real and ideal systems $\mathbf{W}_0 = \pi^{AB}\mathbf{R}$ and $\mathbf{W}_1 = \sigma^E \mathbf{S}$ for some simulator σ) to a game-based definition (with games $\mathbf{G}_0$ and $\mathbf{G}_1$), we will typically fix σ and find a system $\mathbf{C}$ such that $\mathbf{W}_0 = \mathbf{CG}_0$ and $\mathbf{W}_1 = \mathbf{CG}_1$. Then

$$\Delta^{\mathbf{D}}(\mathbf{W}_0, \mathbf{W}_1) = \Delta^{\mathbf{D}}(\mathbf{CG}_0, \mathbf{CG}_1) = \Delta^{\mathbf{DC}}(\mathbf{G}_0, \mathbf{G}_1),$$

i.e. given a distinguisher $\mathbf{D}$ that can distinguish $\mathbf{W}_0$ from $\mathbf{W}_1$ with non-negligible advantage, we get an explicit new distinguisher $\mathbf{DC}$ that can win the game

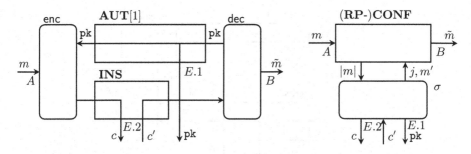

Fig. 6. Real and ideal systems for (replay protected) confidential channel construction. Capital letters $(A, B, E.1, E.2)$ represent interface labels and small letters $(m, \tilde{m}, c, c', j, \mathtt{pk})$ represent values that are in- or output.

with non-negligible advantage. Or, the contrapositive, if $\mathbf{G}_0$ and $\mathbf{G}_1$ are hard to distinguish, then in particular they are hard to distinguish for all distinguishers of the form $\mathbf{DC}$ (for any efficient $\mathbf{D}$ and fixed $\mathbf{C}$). This means that no efficient distinguish $\mathbf{D}$ can tell $\mathbf{W}_0$ from $\mathbf{W}_1$ for the given simulator σ.

3 Benchmarking Confidentiality

In this section we present three benchmark constructions to capture the security of confidential communication and replay protected confidential communication.

3.1 Benchmark 1: The CONF Channel

The first channel we want to construct is the confidential channel **CONF** introduced in Sect. 2.1. The ideal system thus simply consists of this channel and a simulator σ, as depicted on the right in Fig. 6, and is denoted $\sigma^E\mathbf{CONF}$.

In order to achieve this, Alice and Bob need an authentic channel for one message $\mathbf{AUT}[1]$ (from Bob to Alice), so that Bob can send his public key authentically to Alice. They also use a completely insecure channel **INS** to transmit the ciphertexts. Alice's converter enc encrypts any messages with the public key obtained from $\mathbf{AUT}[1]$, and sends the resulting ciphertext on **INS** (i.e. for a PKE $\Pi = (G, E, D)$, enc runs E). Bob's converter dec generates the key-pair $(\mathtt{pk}, \mathtt{sk})$, sends $\mathtt{pk}$ over $\mathbf{AUT}[1]$ to Alice, and decrypts any ciphertext received from **INS** using $\mathtt{sk}$ (i.e. dec runs G and D). The resulting message is output at Bob's outer interface B (to the environment/distinguisher). This real system is drawn on the left in Fig. 6), and is denoted $\mathsf{enc}^A\mathsf{dec}^B[\mathbf{AUT}[1], \mathbf{INS}]$.

As already mentioned, we will often parameterize channels by the number messages that can be input at Alice's interface. As an example, we will denote by $\mathbf{CONF}[n]$ the confidential channel where at most n messages can be input at Alice's interface.

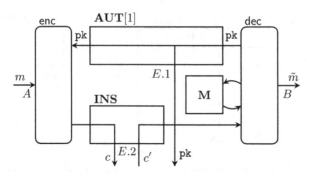

Fig. 7. Real system for constructing a replay protected confidential channel. Capital letters $(A, B, E.1, E.2)$ represent interface labels and small letters $(m, \tilde{m}, c, c', \mathtt{pk})$ represent values that are in- or output.

3.2 Benchmark 2: The RP-CONF Channel

As explained in Sect. 1.1, our second benchmark is the construction of a stronger channel, namely a replay protected confidential channel, i.e. one in which an adversary's input $(\mathtt{dlv}, j)$ may only be processed once for each j. The ideal system σ^E**RP-CONF** is thus similar to the one of Benchmark 1, only differing in the underlying ideal channel which now is the stronger **RP-CONF** channel.

The real system is similar to the real system from Benchmark 1 in that we want to construct **RP-CONF** from a single use authentic channel **AUT**[1] and an insecure channel **INS**. However, the replay detection algorithm requires memory to store the ciphertexts it has already processed. We model this memory use explicitly by providing a memory resource **M** to the decryption converter. This is drawn in Fig. 7. The real system is thus $\mathtt{enc}^A \mathtt{dec}^B[\mathbf{AUT}[1], \mathbf{INS}, \mathbf{M}]$.

If one uses a public key encryption scheme with replay filtering defined by an algorithm F (see Sect. 2.3), then Alice's converter enc runs the encryption algorithm as for a normal PKE, but Bob's converter additionally runs the filtering algorithm F before decrypting to detect (and filter out) replays.

3.3 Benchmark 3: The RP-CONF Channel with Outsourceable Replay Protection

In this section we again want to construct a replay protected confidential channel **RP-CONF**—but where the job of filtering out ciphertext replays is outsourced to a third party. The ideal system is thus identical to Benchmark 2, i.e. σ^E**RP-CONF**.

The real system now has three honest parties, Alice the sender, Bob the receiver, and Charlie the replay-filterer, where each runs its own converter enc, dec and rp, respectively. As before, a public key pk is generated by dec and sent on an authentic channel **AUT**[1]$_B$ to both Alice and Charlie—but Eve gets a copy as well—where the index B denotes the origin of the authenticated message. And as before, enc encrypts the message and sends it on an insecure channel **INS**,

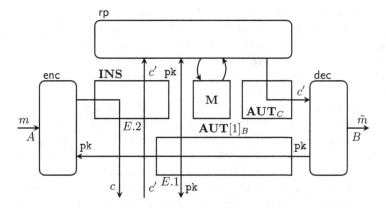

Fig. 8. Real system for constructing a replay protected confidential channel with outsourced replay filtering. As in previous figures, the sender Alice is on the left, the receiver Bob is on the right and the eavesdropper Eve is below. In this setting we have another party, Charlie, above in the picture, to whom replay detection is outsourced, and who runs the converter rp. Capital letters $(A, B, E.1, E.2)$ represent interface labels and small letters $(m, \tilde{m}, c, c', \mathrm{pk})$ represent values that are in- or output.

but this time Charlie is on the receiving end of **INS**. Charlie then runs rp, which decides if the message should be forwarded to Bob through $\mathbf{AUT}_C$ or if it gets filtered out—this channel needs to be authenticated so that Eve cannot change the messages or inject replays again.[8] To do this, rp needs access to the memory resource **M** so that it can store the previously forwarded (i.e. not filtered out) ciphertexts. Finally, dec decrypts the ciphertexts received. This is depicted in Fig. 8.

Note that in this setup, rp does not have access to the secret key and so it must detect replays with the public key only; since dec does not have access to the memory **M**, it can not perform the replay filtering itself. In the case where the players use a PKEPF $\Pi = (G, E, D, F)$, then enc runs E, dec runs G and D, and rp runs F.

4   IND-RCCA Is Not Sufficient for Benchmark 1

In this section we give a correct and IND-RCCA secure PKE scheme which does not achieve Benchmark 1 (see Sect. 3.1). As already mentioned, this separation result is in spirit with the separation proven in [8] between UC-RCCA and IND-RCCA for small message spaces.

Theorem 1. *There is a correct and* IND-RCCA *secure PKE scheme* Π' *for which there is an efficient distinguisher* **D** *such that for any simulator* σ,

$$\Delta^{\mathbf{D}}\left(\mathrm{enc}^A\mathrm{dec}^B[\mathbf{AUT}[1], \mathbf{INS}[1]], \sigma^E\mathbf{CONF}[1]\right) \geq \frac{1}{2}.$$

---

[8] Note that omitting Eve's reading interface in $\mathbf{AUT}_C$ is done here for simplicity and at no loss of generality.

At a high level, we construct an IND-RCCA secure PKE scheme Π' for the binary message space that is malleable, in that an adversary can tamper a ciphertext into another that decrypts to a related message. While such tampering attacks do not help an adversary winning the IND-RCCA game for Π'[9], we show that Benchmark 1 cannot be achieved using Π', as it still allows an attacker to tamper with what Alice sends.

Let $\Pi = (G, E, D)$ be a correct and IND-RCCA secure PKE scheme for the binary message $\mathcal{M} = \{0, 1\}$. From Π, we construct a PKE scheme $\Pi' = (G', E', D')$, which works just as Π, except that now, E' appends an extra bit 0 to the ciphertexts, and during decryption D' uses D internally to decrypt the input ciphertext (ignoring the last bit appended by E'), and then XORs the plaintext output by D with the extra bit that was appended to the ciphertext during encryption (unless D outputs $\perp$, in which case D' also outputs $\perp$). It is easy to see, on one hand, that if Π is correct and IND-RCCA secure, then so is Π'. On the other hand, it is also easy to come up with a distinguisher that can distinguish, for any simulator σ^E the real world system $\mathrm{enc}^A \mathrm{dec}^B [\mathbf{AUT}[1], \mathbf{INS}[1]]$ from the ideal world system $\sigma^E \mathbf{CONF}[1]$, where protocol $\pi = (\mathrm{enc}, \mathrm{dec})$ uses Π' as the underlying PKE scheme. A formal proof of Theorem 1 can be found in [4].

5   Technical Issues with pd-RCCA and sd-RCCA

In [8], Canetti et al. introduce pd-RCCA and sd-RCCA as supposedly relaxed versions of CCA-2 security. Although other supposedly relaxed versions of CCA-2, such as Benign Malleability [24] and generalized CCA-2 security [1], had been introduced before, these notions are subsumed by the definition of pd-RCCA and suffer from the same technical issues we uncover in this section. For this reason, we will focus only on the pd-RCCA and sd-RCCA security notions. We now recall the definition of IND-pd-RCCA and IND-sd-RCCA [8].

Definition 6. *Let $\Pi = (G, E, D)$ be an encryption scheme.*

1. *Say that a family of binary relations $\equiv_{\mathrm{pk}}$ (indexed by the public keys of Π) on ciphertext pairs is a* compatible *relation for Π if for all key-pairs $(\mathrm{pk}, \mathrm{sk})$ of Π:*
   (a) *For any two ciphertexts c, c', if $c \equiv_{\mathrm{pk}} c'$, then $D_{\mathrm{sk}}(c) = D_{\mathrm{sk}}(c')$, except with negligible probability over the random choices of D.*
   (b) *For any plaintext $m \in \mathcal{M}$, if c and c' are two ciphertexts obtained as independent encryptions of m (i.e. two applications of algorithm E on m using independent random bits), then $c \equiv_{\mathrm{pk}} c'$ only with negligible probability.*

---

[9] Note that, even if the adversary manages to maul the challenge ciphertext into one that decrypts to a different plaintext, it cannot leverage this attack into distinguishing the two game systems, because in the case of the binary message space the IND-RCCA game systems will not decrypt a ciphertext that decrypts to any of the two challenge plaintexts.

2. *We say that a relation family as above is* publicly computable *(resp.* secretly computable*) if for all key pairs* (pk, sk) *and ciphertext pairs* (c, c') *it can be determined whether* $c \equiv_{\text{pk}} c'$ *using a PPT algorithm taking inputs* (pk, c, c') *(resp.* $(\text{pk}, \text{sk}, c, c')$*).*

3. *We say that* Π *is* publicly-detectable Replayable-CCA *(IND-pd-RCCA) if there exists a compatible and publicly computable relation family* $\equiv_{\text{pk}}$ *such that* Π *is secure according to the standard definition of* IND-CCA-2 *(Definition 3), but where the game systems differ from the* IND-CCA-2 *game systems in the second decryption stage, which now works as follows: In the following, let* c^* *be the challenge ciphertext output by the game system:*

   Second decryption stage: *When* $\mathbf{D}$ *queries* $(\texttt{ciphertext}, c)$*, the game system replies* $\texttt{test}$ *if* $c^* \equiv_{\text{pk}} c$*, and otherwise computes* $m = D_{\text{sk}}(c)$ *and then sends* m *to* $\mathbf{D}$*.*

   Similarly, we say that Π *is* secretly-detectable Replayable-CCA *(IND-sd-RCCA) if the above holds for a secretly computable relation family* $\equiv_{\text{pk}}$*.*

Remark 2. Note that Condition 1b, which demands two fresh encryptions of any plaintext not to be detected as replays of one another, is equivalent to the additional correctness condition imposed for PKESF and PKEPF schemes (see Definition 5). As mentioned in [8], and as we will see later, the correctness of the replay filtering algorithm follows from the semantic security of the underlying PKE scheme.

It is claimed in [8] that IND-CCA-2 security implies IND-pd-RCCA security (with the equality relation serving as the compatible relation), which in turn implies IND-sd-RCCA security. However, as we now show, Definition 6 is not an actual relaxation of the IND-CCA-2 security notion. More concretely, we prove that IND-CCA-2 security does not entail IND-pd-RCCA nor even IND-sd-RCCA security, according to their definition.

Theorem 2. *If there is a correct and* IND-CCA-2 *secure PKE scheme, then there is a correct and* IND-CCA-2 *secure PKE scheme which is not* IND-pd-RCCA *nor* IND-sd-RCCA *secure.*

Throughout the rest of the section, let $\Pi = (G, E, D)$ be a correct and IND-CCA-2 secure PKE scheme. Without loss of generality, assume that all messages in Π's message space have the same length. We create a scheme $\Pi' = (G', E', D')$ (see Algorithm 1) that is a correct and IND-CCA-2 secure PKE scheme, but is not IND-pd-RCCA nor IND-sd-RCCA secure.

Lemma 1. *If* Π *is correct and* IND-CCA-2 *secure, then so is* Π'*.*

Proof. It is easy to see that if Π is correct and IND-CCA-2 secure then Π' is a correct PKE scheme. We now prove that Π' is IND-CCA-2 secure.

Let $\mathbf{D}$ be a distinguisher for the IND-CCA-2 game systems for Π'. We construct a distinguisher $\mathbf{D}'$, which internally uses $\mathbf{D}$, for the IND-CCA-2 game systems for Π such that

$$\Delta^{\mathbf{D}'}\left(\mathbf{G}_0^{\Pi\text{-IND-CCA-2}}, \mathbf{G}_1^{\Pi\text{-IND-CCA-2}}\right) = \Delta^{\mathbf{D}}\left(\mathbf{G}_0^{\Pi'\text{-IND-CCA-2}}, \mathbf{G}_1^{\Pi'\text{-IND-CCA-2}}\right). \quad (5.1)$$

Algorithm 1. The Π' scheme.

1: **procedure** $G'(1^n)$	10: **procedure** $D'_{sk':=(sk,c)}(c)$
2: $(pk, sk) \leftarrow G(1^n)$	11: **if** $sk'.c \neq c$ **then**
3: $\tilde{m} \leftarrow^{\$} \mathcal{M}$	12: **return** $D_{sk}(c)$
4: $c \leftarrow E_{pk}(\tilde{m})$	13: **else**
5: **return** $(pk', sk') \leftarrow (pk, (sk, c))$	14: $b \leftarrow^{\$} \{0, 1\}$
6: **end procedure**	15: **if** $b = 0$ **then**
	16: **return** $\perp$
7: **procedure** $E'_{pk':=pk}(m)$	17: **else**
8: **return** $E_{pk}(m)$	18: **return** $D_{sk}(c)$
9: **end procedure**	19: **end if**
	20: **end if**
	21: **end procedure**

$\mathbf{D}'$ works as follows: When $\mathbf{D}'$ receives pk from the game, it picks a plaintext $\tilde{m}$ uniformly at random from $\mathcal{M}$, generates a ciphertext $c = E_{pk}(\tilde{m})$, and forwards pk to $\mathbf{D}$. Before the challenge ciphertext is set, whenever $\mathbf{D}$ queries $(\texttt{ciphertext}, c')$, $\mathbf{D}'$ first checks if $c = c'$: if this is the case then $\mathbf{D}'$ flips a coin uniformly at random and (depending on the outcome of the coin) either returns $\perp$ as the result of the query, or forwards it to the IND-CCA-2 game. If $c \neq c'$ then $\mathbf{D}'$ simply forwards the query to the game. Upon receiving the result of the decryption query, $\mathbf{D}'$ forwards it to $\mathbf{D}$. When $\mathbf{D}$ issues the challenge query, $\mathbf{D}'$ forwards it to the game, and, upon receiving the challenge ciphertext c^* from the game, $\mathbf{D}'$ forwards it back to $\mathbf{D}$. After the challenge ciphertext is set, whenever $\mathbf{D}$ issues a decryption query $(\texttt{ciphertext}, c')$, $\mathbf{D}'$ behaves just as before, unless $c' = c^*$. In such case, $\mathbf{D}'$ simply forwards the decryption query to the IND-CCA-2 game and returns the result to $\mathbf{D}$. When $\mathbf{D}$ outputs a guess b, $\mathbf{D}'$ outputs the same guess and terminates. Clearly, (5.1) holds, and thus, if Π is IND-CCA-2 secure, then so is Π'. $\square$

We now show that a compatible relation for Π' cannot relate any freshly generated ciphertext to itself.

Lemma 2. *Let $\equiv_{pk}$ be any family of compatible relations for Π' (indexed by the public keys of Π'). Then, for each pk in the support of Π''s public keys, we have: for any fresh encryption c of some plaintext $m \in \mathcal{M}$ under pk, $c \not\equiv_{pk} c$.*

Proof. For each public key pk in the support of Π''s public keys, let $\equiv_{pk}$ be a compatible relation for Π' with respect to pk. For each ciphertext c that can be generated as a fresh encryption of some plaintext m by E' under pk, there is a key-pair (pk, sk) (for the same public key pk) such that $\Pr[D'_{sk}(c) \neq D'_{sk}(c)] \geq \frac{1}{2}$. Hence, by the compatibility condition of Definition 6, $c \not\equiv_{pk} c$. $\square$

Lemma 3. Π' *is not* IND-pd-RCCA *nor* IND-sd-RCCA *secure.*

Proof. By the definitions of IND-pd-RCCA and IND-sd-RCCA, the challenge ciphertext c^* is always a fresh encryption of some plaintext. By Lemma 2 it then follows $c^* \not\equiv_{\text{pk}} c^*$. As such, a distinguisher is allowed to simply ask for the decryption of the challenge c^* and thus distinguish the two game systems.   □

Lemmas 1 and 3 conclude the proof of Theorem 2.

A way to avoid this technical issue with the definitions of IND-pd-RCCA and IND-sd-RCCA is by restricting the class of schemes one considers. For instance, if one would require the decryption algorithm to be deterministic, then the equality relation between ciphertexts would be a compatible relation. Alternatively, one could require PKE schemes to have perfect correctness. In this case, the equality relation between ciphertexts that are in the support of the encryption algorithm (for some public key pk and message $m \in \mathcal{M}$) would be a compatible relation. It however appears as more natural to have security notions that do not depend on this fact (which is true for most if not all confidentiality notions). Furthermore, it might not always be feasible to have perfect correctness or detectability [3] and therefore, avoiding this dependence is crucial.

6   Relaxing Chosen Ciphertext Security

As discussed in Sect. 1, while IND-CCA-2 is generally a too strong security notion, IND-RCCA security is too weak, in that it is not sufficient to achieve the weaker Benchmark 1 for small message spaces. In this section we introduce three new security notions—which are provably between IND-CCA-2 and IND-RCCA, see Sect. 7—and prove that they are sufficient to achieve the three benchmarks introduced in Sect. 3.

6.1   Achieving Benchmark 1: Constructing the CONF Channel

A game-based security notion that captures the confidentiality of an encryption scheme against active adversaries is one which is sufficiently strong to achieve a confidential channel (as defined in Sect. 3.1). Yet, it must also be as weak as possible so that it does not exclude any schemes which provide confidentiality. To achieve this, we introduce the IND-cl-RCCA security notion, and its multi-challenge version $[n]$IND-cl-RCCA.

Definition 7. *We say that a PKE scheme $\Pi = (G, E, D)$ is IND-cl-RCCA secure if there exists an efficient algorithm v that takes as input a key-pair (pk, sk) and a pair of ciphertexts c, c' and outputs a boolean (corresponding to whether the ciphertexts seem related or not), such that no PPT distinguisher $\mathbf{D}$ distinguishes the game systems $\mathbf{G}_0^{\text{IND-cl-RCCA}}$ and $\mathbf{G}_1^{\text{IND-cl-RCCA}}$ (specified below) with non-negligible advantage (in the security parameter k) over random guessing. For $b \in \{0, 1\}$, game system $\mathbf{G}_b^{\text{IND-cl-RCCA}}$ is as follows:*

192   C. Badertscher et al.

Initialization: $\mathbf{G}_b^{\mathsf{IND\text{-}cl\text{-}RCCA}}$ *generates a key-pair* $(\mathrm{pk}, \mathrm{sk}) \leftarrow G\left(1^k\right)$, *and sends* pk *to* **D**.

First decryption stage: *Whenever* **D** *queries* $(\texttt{ciphertext}, c)$, *the game system* $\mathbf{G}_b^{\mathsf{IND\text{-}cl\text{-}RCCA}}$ *computes* $m = D_{\mathrm{sk}}(c)$ *and sends* m *to* **D**.

Challenge stage: *When* **D** *queries* $(\texttt{test messages}, m_0, m_1)$, *for* $m_0, m_1 \in \mathcal{M}$ *such that* $|m_0| = |m_1|$, $\mathbf{G}_b^{\mathsf{IND\text{-}cl\text{-}RCCA}}$ *computes* $c^* = E_{\mathrm{pk}}(m_b)$, *and sends* c^* *to* **D**.

Second decryption stage: *Whenever* **D** *queries* $(\texttt{ciphertext}, c)$, *the game system* $\mathbf{G}_b^{\mathsf{IND\text{-}cl\text{-}RCCA}}$ *calls* $v(\mathrm{pk}, \mathrm{sk}, c^*, c)$ *and decrypts* c, *obtaining a plaintext* $m = D_{\mathrm{sk}}(c)$. *If* v's *output is* 1 *and* $m = m_b$, *the game system replies* test *to* **D**, *and in all other cases the game replies with* m.

At a high level, the job of algorithm v is to disallow strategies that an adversary could take to win the security game, but would not help break confidentiality of the encryption. In the context of the IND-cl-RCCA game, v is used to disallow adversaries to pursue strategies in which they would ask for the decryption of a ciphertext that would decrypt to the challenge message (a so-called *replay*). Thus, the game can only refuse to answer a decryption query for a ciphertext c if both of the following two conditions are met: 1. according to v, c is a replay of the challenge ciphertext; and 2. c indeed decrypts to the same plaintext as the challenge ciphertext. Note that if one would relax the second condition to checking if c decrypts to one of the (two) challenge plaintexts, the resulting security notion would be equivalent to RCCA security; allowing the adversary to perform decryption queries of ciphertexts that do not decrypt to the same as the challenge ciphertext is the key for capturing the non-malleability feature of confidential channels.

IND-cl-RCCA security is sufficient for achieving Benchmark 1 for a single message (i.e. constructing an ideal **CONF**[1] channel)—this follows from Theorem 3 below. However, it is not clear whether it is also sufficient for achieving Benchmark 1 for multiple messages: since, in order to check if two ciphertexts are related, v requires the secret key, it becomes apparently unfeasible to detect relations between pairs of arbitrary ciphertexts, which is crucial for making a hybrid reduction from distinguishing $\mathrm{enc}^A \mathrm{dec}^B[\mathbf{AUT}[1], \mathbf{INS}[n]]$ from **CONF**[n] to distinguishing the two IND-cl-RCCA game systems. To achieve Benchmark 1 for multiple messages, we now present the multi-challenge version of IND-cl-RCCA security, which we denote by [n]IND-cl-RCCA security, where n is the maximum number of challenge queries that a distinguisher can make.

Definition 8. *We say that a PKE scheme* $\Pi = (G, E, D)$ *is* [n]IND-cl-RCCA *secure if it is secure according to Definition 7, but where, for* $b \in \{0, 1\}$, *the game system* $\mathbf{G}_b^{[n]\mathsf{IND\text{-}cl\text{-}RCCA}}$, *which now accepts* n *challenge queries, behaves as follows:*

Initialization: *First,* $\mathbf{G}_b^{[n]\mathsf{IND\text{-}cl\text{-}RCCA}}$ *creates and initializes a table* t *of plaintext-ciphertext pairs which is initially empty. Then,* $\mathbf{G}_b^{[n]\mathsf{IND\text{-}cl\text{-}RCCA}}$ *runs* $(\mathrm{pk}, \mathrm{sk}) \leftarrow G\left(1^k\right)$, *and sends* pk *to* **D**.

Decryption queries: *Whenever* **D** *queries* (ciphertext, c), *the game system calls, for each plaintext-ciphertext pair* $(m_{b,j}, c_j^*)$ *stored in* t, $v\left(\text{pk}, \text{sk}, c_j^*, c\right)$ *and decrypts* c, *obtaining a plaintext* $m = D_{\text{sk}}(c)$. *If for every plaintext-ciphertext pair stored in* t, *either* v's *output is* 0 *or* $m \neq m_{b,j}$, *then the game system replies with* m *to* **D**. *Otherwise, let* $(m_{b,l}, c_l^*)$ *be the plaintext-ciphertext pair stored in* t *with the smallest* l *such that both* $v\left(\text{pk}, \text{sk}, c_l^*, c\right) = 1$ *and* $m = m_{b,l}$. *Then,* $\mathbf{G}_b^{[n]\text{IND-cl-RCCA}}$ *replies* (test, l) *to* **D**.

i-th challenge query (for $i \leq n$): *Whenever the distinguisher* **D** *issues a challenge query* (test messages, $m_{0,i}, m_{1,i}$), *where* $m_{0,i}, m_{1,i} \in \mathcal{M}$ *such that* $|m_{0,i}| = |m_{1,i}|$, *the game system computes* $c_i^* = E_{\text{pk}}(m_{b,i})$, *stores* $(m_{b,i}, c_i^*)$ *in table* t, *and sends* c_i^* *to* **D**.

We now show that $[n]$IND-cl-RCCA security is sufficient for achieving Benchmark 1 when Alice is restricted to sending up to n messages. Thus, we need to prove that the construction is indistinguishable from the ideal $\mathbf{CONF}[n]$ channel up to the $[n]$IND-cl-RCCA security of the underlying PKE scheme.

Remark 3. Note that the above security notion stands in sharp contrast with the q-bounded security notions from [11], which bound to q the number of decryption queries an adversary can make. Even if a PKE scheme is only [1]IND-cl-RCCA secure—the weakest security notion introduced in this paper—the adversary is not restricted in the number of decryption queries it can issue to the game. Note that in order to achieve our benchmarks, no such restriction can be imposed, as it would be a restriction on the distinguisher (sending at most q ciphertexts at Eve's interface) which would impede general composability.

Let $\Pi = (G, E, D)$ be a correct and $[n]$IND-cl-RCCA secure PKE scheme, and let the protocol $\pi = (\text{enc}, \text{dec})$ be such that Alice's converter enc runs the encryption algorithm E to encrypt plaintexts, and Bob's converter dec runs the key-pair generation algorithm G to generate a public-secret key-pair and runs D to decrypt the received ciphertexts.

To prove that π constructs $\mathbf{CONF}[n]$ from $\mathbf{AUT}[1]$ and $\mathbf{INS}[n]$ (Definition 1), we show how to create, from any algorithm v that satisfies Definition 8, an efficient simulator σ which internally uses v such that any distinguisher **D** for $\text{enc}^A\text{dec}^B[\mathbf{AUT}[1], \mathbf{INS}[n]]$ and $\sigma^E\mathbf{CONF}[n]$ can be transformed into an equally good distinguisher for the $[n]$IND-cl-RCCA game systems. Then, from the $[n]$IND-cl-RCCA security of Π, it follows that there is such an algorithm v, implying that no efficient distinguisher **D** can distinguish between the real world $\text{enc}^A\text{dec}^B[\mathbf{AUT}[1], \mathbf{INS}[n]]$ and the ideal world $\sigma^E\mathbf{CONF}[\text{n}]$ with simulator σ attached. In turn, this implies that Benchmark 1 is achieved.

Theorem 3. *Let* v *be an algorithm that suits* $[n]$IND-cl-RCCA *(Definition 8). There exists an efficient simulator* σ *and an efficient reduction* **R** *such that for every distinguisher* **D**,

$$\Delta^{\mathbf{D}}\left(\text{enc}^A\text{dec}^B[\mathbf{AUT}[1], \mathbf{INS}[n]], \sigma^E\mathbf{CONF}[n]\right)$$

$$= \Delta^{\mathbf{DR}}\left(\mathbf{G}_0^{[n]\text{IND-cl-RCCA}}, \mathbf{G}_1^{[n]\text{IND-cl-RCCA}}\right).$$

Proof. Consider the following simulator σ for interface E of **CONF**$[n]$, which has two sub-interfaces denoted by $E.1$ and $E.2$ on the outside (since the real-world system also has two sub-interfaces at E): Initially, σ generates a key-pair $(\mathsf{pk}, \mathsf{sk})$ and outputs pk at $E.1$. When it receives the i-th input l_i at the inside interface in (which is connected to **CONF**$[n]$), σ generates an encryption $c \leftarrow E_{\mathsf{pk}}(\tilde{m})$ of a randomly chosen message $\tilde{m}$ of length l_i, records $(i, \tilde{m}, c)$ and outputs c at $E.2$. When c' is input at $E.2$, σ proceeds as follows: First, it decrypts c', obtaining some plaintext m'. If $(j, \tilde{m}, c)$ has been recorded for some j such that $\tilde{m} = m'$ and $v(\mathsf{pk}, \mathsf{sk}, c, c') = 1$, then σ outputs (dlv, j) at in (where j is the smallest index satisfying this condition). If no such triple has been recorded, σ outputs (inj, m') at in (unless $m' = \bot$).

Having defined the simulator σ, we now introduce a reduction system **R**, such that for any efficient distinguisher **D**

1. $\mathbf{RG}_0^{[n]\text{IND-cl-RCCA}} \equiv \mathsf{enc}^A \mathsf{dec}^B[\mathbf{AUT}[1], \mathbf{INS}[n]]$; and
2. $\mathbf{RG}_1^{[n]\text{IND-cl-RCCA}} \equiv \sigma^E \mathbf{CONF}[n]$.

Consider the following reduction system **R** (which processes at most n inputs at the outside A interface): Initially, **R** forwards the public key pk generated by the game system to the $E.1$ interface. When the j-th message m is input at the A interface of **R**: **R** chooses a message $\tilde{m}$ of length $|m|$ uniformly at random, and makes the challenge query $(\mathsf{test\ messages}, m, \tilde{m})$ to the game system, which replies with some ciphertext c. Then, **R** records $m_j^* = m$. Next, **R** outputs c at the outside $E.2$ interface. When (inj, c') is input at interface $E.2$, **R** behaves as follows. First, **R** makes a decryption query for c' to the game, obtaining some m'. If $m' = (\mathsf{test}, j)$, then **R** outputs m_j^* at interface B. If $m' = \bot$, **R** ignores the injection, and nothing happens. Else, **R** outputs m' at the B interface. It is easy to see that indeed $\mathbf{RG}_0^{[n]\text{IND-cl-RCCA}} \equiv \mathsf{enc}^A \mathsf{dec}^B[\mathbf{AUT}[1], \mathbf{INS}[n]]$ and $\mathbf{RG}_1^{[n]\text{IND-cl-RCCA}} \equiv \sigma^E \mathbf{CONF}[n]$. Using the above facts, it finally follows

$$\Delta^{\mathbf{D}}\left(\mathsf{enc}^A \mathsf{dec}^B[\mathbf{AUT}[1], \mathbf{INS}[n]], \sigma^E \mathbf{CONF}[n]\right)$$

$$= \Delta^{\mathbf{D}}\left(\mathbf{RG}_0^{[n]\text{IND-cl-RCCA}}, \mathbf{RG}_1^{[n]\text{IND-cl-RCCA}}\right)$$

$$= \Delta^{\mathbf{DR}}\left(\mathbf{G}_0^{[n]\text{IND-cl-RCCA}}, \mathbf{G}_1^{[n]\text{IND-cl-RCCA}}\right).$$

$\square$

6.2   Achieving Benchmark 2: Constructing the RP-CONF Channel

Another use of IND-CCA-2 security is for achieving replay protected confidential communication. As hinted by Benchmarks 2 and 3, replay protection comes in two flavours: 1. private detection and filtering of replays; and 2. public detection and filtering of replays. We begin by looking into the setting where Bob is the one responsible for filtering out ciphertext replays (Benchmark 2).

Before introducing a new security notion, we first look into why IND-cl-RCCA does not seem to suffice for constructing the **RP-CONF** channel. First, note

that, the **RP-CONF** channel construction (Benchmark 2) has to protect not
only against replays of ciphertexts sent by Alice, but also against replays of
ciphertexts injected by Eve. This is so since the receiving end (i.e. the dec converter) does not know where the ciphertexts have originated.[10] Hence, for each
ciphertext that the converter receives, it has to make sure that it is not a replay
of any previously received ciphertext, implying that the converter has to impede
all ciphertext replays. When one tries to make a reduction from distinguish-
ing the real world construction $\mathsf{enc}^A\mathsf{dec}^B[\mathbf{AUT}[1], \mathbf{INS}, \mathbf{M}]$ and the ideal world
channel **RP-CONF** to winning the IND-cl-RCCA game, two critical issues arise:

1. The algorithm v used by the game systems might not compute an *equivalence*
   relation: Consider the case where Alice inputs a message m into the channel
   which results in a ciphertext c being output at the E interface. Eve can
   create two distinct replays of the ciphertext c, say c' and c'', and input them
   into the E interface. While, from IND-cl-RCCA security, v should detect that
   ciphertext c is related to both c' and c'', it does not necessarily detect whether
   c' is related to c''. In such case, v cannot be used to detect ciphertext replays,
   as it would allow Eve to replay what Alice sends, by generating different
   replays of c and injecting them into the channel (without ever injecting c into
   the channel).
2. The reduction does not have access to the secret key generated by the game
   system: Even assuming that v computes an equivalence relation, it is not clear
   how one could reduce distinguishing the real and ideal worlds to distinguishing
   the two underlying IND-cl-RCCA game systems. Since any reduction system
   $\mathbf{R}$ that one would attach to the game systems does not have access to the
   secret key, it is not clear how $\mathbf{R}$ would be able to check if any arbitrary pair
   of ciphertexts c' and c'' are related according to v (i.e. $\mathbf{R}$ would be able to
   compute $v(\mathsf{pk}, \mathsf{sk}, c', c'')$ without knowing sk).

Interestingly these remarks also apply to the IND-sd-RCCA notion from [8], hinting at the fact that the IND-sd-RCCA security notion does not capture what it
was meant to capture. Another interesting remark is that, as for IND-cl-RCCA,
the single challenge and the multi challenge versions of IND-sd-RCCA security
do not seem to be necessarily equivalent.[11] With this, we now introduce IND-
srp-RCCA security, which captures the secret detectability of ciphertext replays.

Definition 9. *A PKE scheme $\Pi = (G, E, D)$ is* IND-srp-RCCA *secure if there
exists an efficient algorithm v that computes, for each key-pair $(\mathsf{pk}, \mathsf{sk})$, an equivalence relation over ciphertexts c, c' such that for every key-pair $(\mathsf{pk}, \mathsf{sk})$ in the
support of $G(1^k)$ and every pair of ciphertexts c, c', if $v(\mathsf{pk}, \mathsf{sk}, c, c') = 1$ then
$\delta(D_{\mathsf{sk}}(c), D_{\mathsf{sk}}(c')) \leq negl(k)$ (where the randomness is over the internal randomness of D), and if no efficient distinguisher $\mathbf{D}$ distinguishes the game systems
$\mathbf{G}_0^{\mathsf{IND}\text{-}\mathsf{srp}\text{-}\mathsf{RCCA}}$ and $\mathbf{G}_1^{\mathsf{IND}\text{-}\mathsf{srp}\text{-}\mathsf{RCCA}}$ (specified below) with non-negligible advantage*

---

[10] Note that, other than the assumption that the public key is authentically transmitted, we are only assuming an insecure channel between Alice and Bob.
[11] We leave the problem of proving whether these notions are equivalent or not as open.

(in the security parameter k) over random guessing. The IND-srp-RCCA *game systems work just as the* IND-CCA-2 *game systems, except that the* IND-srp-RCCA *game systems give distinguisher* **D** *oracle access to v throughout the entire game (so that* **D** *can check whether any two ciphertexts c, c' are related according to v with respect to the key-pair* pk, sk *generated by the game system), and also except for the second decryption stage, which now works as follows:*

Second decryption stage: *Whenever* **D** *queries* (ciphertext, *c*), *the game system replies* test *if* $v(\text{pk}, \text{sk}, c^*, c) = 1$ *and replies* $m = D_{\text{sk}}(c)$ *otherwise.*

Definition 9 addresses both of the issues we mentioned above by, on one hand giving the distinguisher oracle access to v, and on the other hand by requiring that v computes an equivalence relation. The requirement that for any key-pair pk, sk and any pair of ciphertexts c, c', if $v(\text{pk}, \text{sk}, c, c') = 1$ then $\delta(D_{\text{sk}}(c), D_{\text{sk}}(c')) \leq \text{negl}(k)$ is captures that the two ciphertexts c and c' can only be considered as replays of one another if they "carry essentially the same information".

The definition of IND-srp-RCCA security is written for a PKE scheme $\Pi = (G, E, D)$, but by taking the algorithm v required to exist by Definition 9 as a replay-filtering algorithm, we get a PKESF scheme $\Pi' = (G, E, D, v)$. Conversely, a PKESF scheme $\Pi = (G, E, D, F)$ is IND-srp-RCCA secure if the underlying PKE scheme $\Pi' = (G, E, D)$ is IND-srp-RCCA secure with respect to the filtering algorithm F of Π. Correctness of an IND-srp-RCCA secure PKESF Π' then follows from the correctness of the corresponding PKE $\Pi = (G, E, D)$.

It is instructive to see why IND-srp-RCCA security does indeed require the filtering algorithm v to be meaningful. Consider, e.g. a trivial filtering algorithm such as the one that always sets $v(\text{pk}, \text{sk}, c, c') = 0$. This algorithm will not satisfy the definition above. But more importantly, it turns out that the above definition implies that Benchmark 2 is satisfied (see Theorem 4 further below), and by definition, Benchmark 2 requires the filtering algorithm to be meaningful (as otherwise the real and ideal systems are trivially distinguishable).

Lemma 4. *Consider any correct PKE scheme* $\Pi = (G, E, D)$ *that is* IND-srp-RCCA *secure, and let v be an algorithm with respect to which Π is* IND-srp-RCCA *secure. Then,* $\Pi' = (G, E, D, v)$ *is a correct PKESF scheme.*

Proof. We show a slightly stronger statement. The event $D_{\text{sk}}(E_{\text{pk}}(m)) \neq m \vee v(\text{pk}, \text{sk}, E_{\text{pk}}(m), E_{\text{pk}}(m')) = 1$ can only occur if at least one of $D_{\text{sk}}(E_{\text{pk}}(m)) \neq m$ or $v(\text{pk}, \text{sk}, E_{\text{pk}}(m), E_{\text{pk}}(m')) = 1$ occurs (for any adversary producing such messages). From the correctness of Π, it follows that $D_{\text{sk}}(E_{\text{pk}}(m)) \neq m$ only occurs with negligible probability. Thus, it now only remains to show that $v(\text{pk}, \text{sk}, E_{\text{pk}}(m), E_{\text{pk}}(m')) = 1$ occurs with at most negligible probability too.

Letting $c = E_{\text{pk}}(m)$ and $c' = E_{\text{pk}}(m')$, from the correctness of Π we have that $\delta(m, D_{\text{sk}}(c)) \leq \text{negl}(k)$ and $\delta(m', D_{\text{sk}}(c')) \leq \text{negl}(k)$. From the definition of IND-srp-RCCA security we have that if $v(\text{pk}, \text{sk}, c, c') = 1$ then $\delta(D_{\text{sk}}(c), D_{\text{sk}}(c')) \leq \text{negl}(k)$. Combining these last 3 inequalities with the triangle inequality we find that $\delta(m, m') \leq \text{negl}(k)$. But note that m and m' are deterministic values (unlike $D_{sk}(c)$ and $D_{sk}(c')$ which are random variables over the distribution of the encryption and decryption randomness), hence we must have $\delta(m, m') = 0$ and $m = m'$. Putting this together, we have just shown that if $v\left(pk, sk, E_{pk}(m), E_{pk}(m')\right) = 1$ then $m = m'$.

Now, suppose that for some $m \in \mathcal{M}$ we have that with non-negligible probability $v\left(pk, sk, E_{pk}(m), E_{pk}(m)\right) = 1$ (i.e. v declares two fresh encryptions of the m as related). Then it is easy to create an efficient distinguisher $\mathbf{D}$ that has non-negligible advantage in distinguishing the two IND-srp-RCCA game systems of Π with respect to v: First, $\mathbf{D}$ makes a challenge query (test messages, $m, \bar{m}$) to the game system (where $m \neq \bar{m}$), and then $\mathbf{D}$ generates a fresh encryption $c = E_{pk}(m)$ of m, and asks for the decryption of c to the game system. If the game system replies test, then $\mathbf{D}$ outputs 0, and otherwise outputs 1. It is easy to see that $\mathbf{D}$'s advantage in distinguishing the two game systems is at least half of the probability that event $v\left(pk, sk, E_{pk}(m), E_{pk}(m)\right) = 1$ occurs, which by our assumption is non-negligible. Thus, $\mathbf{D}$ has non-negligible advantage in distinguishing the two game systems, contradicting that Π is IND-srp-RCCA secure with respect to v. From this contradiction, it follows that for any m, $v\left(pk, sk, E_{pk}(m), E_{pk}(m)\right) = 1$ can only occur with negligible probability. $\square$

The following result states that the IND-srp-RCCA security of a PKESF $\Pi = (G, E, D, F)$ suffices for constructing an **RP-CONF**$[n]$ channel, i.e. satisfying Benchmark 2. To prove this, one creates a simulator σ which internally uses F such that any distinguisher $\mathbf{D}$ for $\mathrm{enc}^A\mathrm{dec}^B[\mathbf{AUT}[1], \mathbf{INS}[n], \mathbf{M}]$ and $\sigma^E\mathbf{RP\text{-}CONF}[n]$ can be transformed into an equally good distinguisher for the IND-srp-RCCA game systems. A formal proof of Theorem 4 can be found in [4].

Theorem 4. *Let $\Pi = (G, E, D, F)$ be a correct PKESF scheme that is* IND-srp-RCCA *secure. There exists an efficient simulator σ and for any $n \in \mathbb{N}$ there exists an efficient reduction $\mathbf{R}$ such that for every distinguisher $\mathbf{D}$,*

$$\Delta^{\mathbf{D}}\left(\mathrm{enc}^A\mathrm{dec}^B[\mathbf{AUT}[1], \mathbf{INS}[n], \mathbf{M}], \sigma^E\mathbf{RP\text{-}CONF}[n]\right)$$

$$= n \cdot \Delta^{\mathbf{DR}}\left(\mathbf{G}_0^{\mathsf{IND\text{-}srp\text{-}RCCA}}, \mathbf{G}_1^{\mathsf{IND\text{-}srp\text{-}RCCA}}\right).$$

6.3 Achieving Benchmark 3: Constructing the RP-CONF Channel with Outsourceable Replay Protection

We now look into the setting where a third party who does not possess the secret-key is responsible for filtering out ciphertext replays (Benchmark 3). In this setting IND-srp-RCCA security seems too weak, as the algorithm v which the IND-srp-RCCA game systems use for detecting ciphertext replays (i.e. to check if two ciphertexts are replays of one another) have access to the secret-key. For this reason, we will now introduce the IND-prp-RCCA security notion, which is the analogous of IND-srp-RCCA security for public detection of ciphertext replays.

Definition 10. *A scheme $\Pi = (G, E, D)$ is* IND-prp-RCCA *secure if there is an efficient algorithm v that computes, for each public key* pk, *an equivalence relation over ciphertexts c, c' such that for every* pk *in the support of $G(1^k)$ and every pair of ciphertexts c, c', if $v(\text{pk}, c, c') = 1$ then $\delta(D_{\text{sk}}(c), D_{\text{sk}}(c')) \leq negl(k)$ (where the randomness is over the internal randomness of D and over the conditional distribution of the secret key* sk *for the given public key* pk *according to the key-pair distribution of $G(1^k)$), and if no efficient distinguisher $\mathbf{D}$ distinguishes the two* IND-prp-RCCA *game systems (described ahead) with non-negligible advantage (in the security parameter k) over random guessing. The* IND-prp-RCCA *game systems work just as the* IND-srp-RCCA *game systems, except that now the game system does not have to provide the distinguisher with oracle access to v, as the distinguisher can anyway check whether any two ciphertexts are related according to v by itself.*

Recall that IND-pd-RCCA security was introduced to capture efficient public detectability of ciphertext replays [8]. However, apart from the technical issues we already identified with its definition, it turns out to be crucial, like in the previous section, that the replay detection algorithm computes an equivalence relation over ciphertexts in order to meet the benchmark.

Just like for IND-srp-RCCA, Definition 10 is written for a PKE scheme $\Pi = (G, E, D)$, but by taking the algorithm v required to exist by Definition 10 as a replay-filtering algorithm, we get a PKEPF scheme $\Pi' = (G, E, D, v)$. Correctness of an IND-prp-RCCA secure PKEPF Π' then follows from the correctness of the corresponding PKE $\Pi = (G, E, D)$.

Lemma 5. *Consider any correct PKE scheme $\Pi = (G, E, D)$ that is* IND-prp-RCCA *secure, and let v be an algorithm with respect to which Π is* IND-prp-RCCA *secure. Then, $\Pi' = (G, E, D, v)$ is a correct PKEPF scheme.*

We omit the proof of Lemma 5 as it resembles the one of Lemma 4.

Theorem 5 states that the IND-prp-RCCA security of a PKEPF scheme $\Pi = (G, E, D, F)$ suffices for constructing an $\mathbf{RP\text{-}CONF}[n]$ channel even when the filtering is run by a third-party without access to the secret key, i.e. it satisfies Benchmark 3. To prove this, one would have to create a simulator σ which internally used F such that any distinguisher $\mathbf{D}$ for $\text{enc}^A\text{dec}^B\text{rp}^C[\mathbf{AUT}[1]_B, \mathbf{AUT}_C, \mathbf{INS}[n], \mathbf{M}]$ and $\sigma^E\mathbf{RP\text{-}CONF}[n]$ could be transformed into an equally good distinguisher for the IND-prp-RCCA game systems. This result can be obtained along the lines of Theorem 4, whose proof can be found in the full version of this paper [4].

Theorem 5. *Let $\Pi = (G, E, D, F)$ be a correct and* IND-prp-RCCA *secure PKEPF scheme. There exists an efficient simulator σ and for any $n \in \mathbb{N}$ there exists an efficient reduction $\mathbf{R}$ such that for every distinguisher $\mathbf{D}$,*

$$\Delta^{\mathbf{D}}\left(\text{enc}^A\text{dec}^B\text{rp}^C[\mathbf{AUT}[1]_B, \mathbf{AUT}_C, \mathbf{INS}[n], \mathbf{M}], \sigma^E\mathbf{RP\text{-}CONF}[n]\right)$$

$$= \Delta^{\mathbf{DR}}\left(\mathbf{G}_0^{\text{IND-prp-RCCA}}, \mathbf{G}_1^{\text{IND-prp-RCCA}}\right).$$

7 Relating the Security Games

In this section we prove all the implications and separations between the game-based security notions that are depicted in Fig. 1.

Lemma 6. IND-CCA-2 $\Rightarrow$ IND-prp-RCCA.

Proof. Define v so that $v\,(\text{pk}, c, c') = 1$ if and only if $c = c'$. Note that v satisfies IND-prp-RCCA security, since if $v\,(\text{pk}, c, c') = 1$ then $\delta\,(D_{\text{sk}}\,(c), D_{\text{sk}}\,(c')) = 0$. $\square$

Lemma 7. IND-prp-RCCA $\Rightarrow$ IND-srp-RCCA.

Proof. Any algorithm v that satisfies IND-prp-RCCA also satisfies IND-srp-RCCA security (where v ignores the secret key sk). $\square$

The proof of the following result can be found in [4].

Lemma 8. *Any correct and* IND-srp-RCCA *secure PKE scheme* Π *is* [n]IND-cl-RCCA *secure.*

Lemma 9. [n]IND-cl-RCCA $\Rightarrow$ [n − 1]IND-cl-RCCA.

Proof. Any distinguisher for the [n − 1]IND-cl-RCCA game systems is also a distinguisher for the [n]IND-cl-RCCA systems with the same advantage. $\square$

Lemma 10. [1]IND-cl-RCCA $\Rightarrow$ IND-RCCA.

Proof. From any distinguisher **D** for the IND-RCCA game systems we create a distinguisher **D'** for the [1]IND-cl-RCCA game systems: **D'** uses **D** internally forwarding every query between **D** and the [1]IND-cl-RCCA game, except for decryption queries, where it behaves as follows: If, after the challenge plaintexts m_0 and m_1 are set, **D** makes a decryption query of some ciphertext such that the [1]IND-cl-RCCA game replies with either m_0 or m_1, then **D'** sends test to **D**, and otherwise it sends what was output by the IND-RCCA game system. $\square$

Lemma 11. IND-RCCA $\not\Rightarrow$ [1]IND-cl-RCCA.

Proof. By Theorem 3, [1]IND-cl-RCCA security suffices for achieving Benchmark 1 for a single message. By Theorem 1, IND-RCCA does not suffice for achieving Benchmark 1 for a single message. $\square$

For the sake of simplicity, the two following results (Lemmata 12 and 13) assume the existence of an IND-CCA-2 secure PKE scheme. We note that both results can be generalized to only assume an [n]IND-cl-RCCA (IND-srp-RCCA, respectively) secure scheme at the price of having a less elegant proof.

Lemma 12. [n]IND-cl-RCCA $\not\Rightarrow$ IND-srp-RCCA.

Proof. From a IND-CCA-2 secure scheme $\Pi = (G, E, D)$, we create a scheme $\Pi' = (G', E', D')$ that is $[n]$IND-cl-RCCA secure but not IND-srp-RCCA secure. Π' works just as Π except that now during encryption E' appends a bit 0 to the ciphertexts generated by E, and during decryption, if the last bit of the ciphertext is 0 then D' ignores it and decrypts the ciphertext using D, and otherwise, with $\frac{1}{2}$ probability D' outputs $\perp$ and with the remaining $\frac{1}{2}$ probability D' ignores the last bit and decrypts the ciphertext using D.

Clearly, it is easy to create an algorithm v that suits $[n]$IND-cl-RCCA such that no distinguisher has non-negligible advantage in distinguishing the two $[n]$IND-cl-RCCA game systems for Π' with respect to v: for $b \in \{0, 1\}$, $v(\mathrm{pk}, \mathrm{sk}, c \,\|\, 0, c' \,\|\, b) = 1$ if and only if $c = c'$. On the other hand, any algorithm v' that suits IND-srp-RCCA cannot relate ciphertexts $c \,\|\, 0$ and $c \,\|\, 1$ since $\delta(D'_{\mathrm{sk}}(c \,\|\, 0), D'_{\mathrm{sk}}(c \,\|\, 1))$ is not negligible anymore. As such, a distinguisher can ask for the decryption of $c \,\|\, 1$ and use this to distinguish the game systems. $\square$

Lemma 13. IND-srp-RCCA $\not\Rightarrow$ IND-prp-RCCA.

Proof. From a IND-CCA-2 secure scheme $\Pi = (G, E, D)$, we create a scheme $\Pi' = (G', E', D')$ that is IND-srp-RCCA secure but not IND-prp-RCCA secure. Π' works just as Π except that now G' additionally picks a bit b uniformly at random and sets the key-pair to be $(\mathrm{pk}, (\mathrm{sk}, b))$, where $(\mathrm{pk}, \mathrm{sk})$ was the key-pair generated by G. More, during encryption E' uses E internally to generate a ciphertext c and outputs (c, c) as the ciphertext, and during decryption, on input (c_0, c_1), D' uses D internally to decrypt c_b (where b is the bit of the secret key that was sampled by G').

It is easy to create an algorithm v that suits IND-srp-RCCA such that no distinguisher has non-negligible advantage in distinguishing the two IND-srp-RCCA game systems for Π' with respect to v: for $b \in \{0, 1\}$, $v(\mathrm{pk}, \mathrm{sk}, (c_0, c_1), (c_0', c_1')) = 1$ if and only if $c_b = c_b'$, where b is again the bit of the secret key.

On the other hand, any algorithm v' that suits IND-prp-RCCA cannot relate ciphertext (c, c) with any of the following ciphertexts: (c, c_0'), (c, c_1'), (c_0', c) and (c_1', c), where c_0' and c_1' are fresh encryptions of 0 and 1 respectively. This is so since, otherwise, either one could use v' to break the semantic security of Π (contradicting that it is IND-CCA-2 secure), or v' would not be suitable for IND-prp-RCCA, as one of $\delta(D'_{\mathrm{sk}}(c, c), D'_{\mathrm{sk}}(c, c_0'))$, $\delta(D'_{\mathrm{sk}}(c, c), D'_{\mathrm{sk}}(c, c_1'))$, $\delta(D'_{\mathrm{sk}}(c, c), D'_{\mathrm{sk}}(c_0', c))$ and $\delta(D'_{\mathrm{sk}}(c, c), D'_{\mathrm{sk}}(c_1', c))$ is not negligible anymore. As such, a distinguisher can ask for the decryption of these four ciphertexts and use the outputs to distinguish the IND-prp-RCCA game systems. $\square$

Lemma 14. IND-prp-RCCA $\not\Rightarrow$ IND-CCA-2.

Proof. Consider an IND-prp-RCCA secure PKE scheme $\Pi = (G, E, D)$; we create a scheme $\Pi' = (G', E', D')$ that is IND-prp-RCCA secure but not IND-CCA-2 secure: Π' works exactly as Π except that E' appends a bit 0 to the ciphertexts generated by E, and during decryption D' ignores the last bit added by E' is ignored. Since Π is IND-prp-RCCA secure, so is Π'. However, Π' is not IND-CCA-2 secure. $\square$

References

1. An, J.H., Dodis, Y., Rabin, T.: On the security of joint signature and encryption. In: Knudsen, L.R. (ed.) EUROCRYPT 2002. LNCS, vol. 2332, pp. 83–107. Springer, Heidelberg (2002). https://doi.org/10.1007/3-540-46035-7_6
2. Backes, M., Cachin, C.: Public-key steganography with active attacks. In: Kilian, J. (ed.) TCC 2005. LNCS, vol. 3378, pp. 210–226. Springer, Heidelberg (2005). https://doi.org/10.1007/978-3-540-30576-7_12
3. Badertscher, C., Matt, C., Maurer, U.: Strengthening access control encryption. In: Takagi, T., Peyrin, T. (eds.) ASIACRYPT 2017, Part I. LNCS, vol. 10624, pp. 502–532. Springer, Cham (2017). https://doi.org/10.1007/978-3-319-70694-8_18
4. Badertscher, C., Maurer, U., Portmann, C., Rito, G.: Revisiting (r)cca security and replay protection. Cryptology ePrint Archive, Report 2020/177 (2020). https://eprint.iacr.org/2020/177
5. Bellare, M., Desai, A., Pointcheval, D., Rogaway, P.: Relations among notions of security for public-key encryption schemes. In: Krawczyk, H. (ed.) CRYPTO 1998. LNCS, vol. 1462, pp. 26–45. Springer, Heidelberg (1998). https://doi.org/10.1007/BFb0055718
6. Canetti, R.: Universally composable security: a new paradigm for cryptographic protocols. In: 42nd Annual Symposium on Foundations of Computer Science, pp. 136–145. IEEE Computer Society Press (2001). https://doi.org/10.1109/SFCS.2001.959888
7. Canetti, R., Hohenberger, S.: Chosen-ciphertext secure proxy re-encryption. Cryptology ePrint Archive, Report 2007/171 (2007). http://eprint.iacr.org/2007/171
8. Canetti, R., Krawczyk, H., Nielsen, J.B.: Relaxing chosen-ciphertext security. In: Boneh, D. (ed.) CRYPTO 2003. LNCS, vol. 2729, pp. 565–582. Springer, Heidelberg (2003). https://doi.org/10.1007/978-3-540-45146-4_33
9. Coretti, S., Dodis, Y., Tackmann, B., Venturi, D.: Self-destruct non-malleability. Cryptology ePrint Archive, Report 2014/866 (2014). http://eprint.iacr.org/2014/866
10. Coretti, S., Maurer, U., Tackmann, B.: Constructing confidential channels from authenticated channels—public-key encryption revisited. In: Sako, K., Sarkar, P. (eds.) ASIACRYPT 2013, Part I. LNCS, vol. 8269, pp. 134–153. Springer, Heidelberg (2013). https://doi.org/10.1007/978-3-642-42033-7_8
11. Cramer, R., et al.: Bounded CCA2-secure encryption. In: Kurosawa, K. (ed.) ASIACRYPT 2007. LNCS, vol. 4833, pp. 502–518. Springer, Heidelberg (2007). https://doi.org/10.1007/978-3-540-76900-2_31
12. Dachman-Soled, D., Fuchsbauer, G., Mohassel, P., O'Neill, A.: Enhanced chosen-ciphertext security and applications. In: Krawczyk, H. (ed.) PKC 2014. LNCS, vol. 8383, pp. 329–344. Springer, Heidelberg (2014). https://doi.org/10.1007/978-3-642-54631-0_19
13. Green, M., Hohenberger, S., Waters, B.: Outsourcing the decryption of ABE ciphertexts. In: USENIX Security 2011: 20th USENIX Security Symposium. USENIX Association (2011)
14. Groth, J.: Rerandomizable and replayable adaptive chosen ciphertext attack secure cryptosystems. In: Naor, M. (ed.) TCC 2004. LNCS, vol. 2951, pp. 152–170. Springer, Heidelberg (2004). https://doi.org/10.1007/978-3-540-24638-1_9
15. Hohenberger, S., Lewko, A., Waters, B.: Detecting dangerous queries: a new approach for chosen ciphertext security. In: Pointcheval, D., Johansson, T. (eds.) EUROCRYPT 2012. LNCS, vol. 7237, pp. 663–681. Springer, Heidelberg (2012). https://doi.org/10.1007/978-3-642-29011-4_39

16. Klooß, M., Lehmann, A., Rupp, A.: (R)CCA secure updatable encryption with integrity protection. In: Ishai, Y., Rijmen, V. (eds.) EUROCRYPT 2019, Part I. LNCS, vol. 11476, pp. 68–99. Springer, Cham (2019). https://doi.org/10.1007/978-3-030-17653-2_3

17. Krawczyk, H.: The order of encryption and authentication for protecting communications (or: how secure is SSL?). In: Kilian, J. (ed.) CRYPTO 2001. LNCS, vol. 2139, pp. 310–331. Springer, Heidelberg (2001). https://doi.org/10.1007/3-540-44647-8_19

18. Maurer, U.: Constructive cryptography – a new paradigm for security definitions and proofs. In: Mödersheim, S., Palamidessi, C. (eds.) TOSCA 2011. LNCS, vol. 6993, pp. 33–56. Springer, Heidelberg (2012). https://doi.org/10.1007/978-3-642-27375-9_3

19. Maurer, U., Renner, R.: Abstract cryptography. In: ICS 2011: 2nd Innovations in Computer Science, pp. 1–21. Tsinghua University Press (2011)

20. Maurer, U.M.: Indistinguishability of random systems. In: Knudsen, L.R. (ed.) EUROCRYPT 2002. LNCS, vol. 2332, pp. 110–132. Springer, Heidelberg (2002). https://doi.org/10.1007/3-540-46035-7_8

21. Maurer, U.M., Pietrzak, K., Renner, R.: Indistinguishability amplification. In: Menezes, A. (ed.) CRYPTO 2007. LNCS, vol. 4622, pp. 130–149. Springer, Heidelberg (2007). https://doi.org/10.1007/978-3-540-74143-5_8

22. Prabhakaran, M., Rosulek, M.: Rerandomizable RCCA encryption. In: Menezes, A. (ed.) CRYPTO 2007. LNCS, vol. 4622, pp. 517–534. Springer, Heidelberg (2007). https://doi.org/10.1007/978-3-540-74143-5_29

23. Prabhakaran, M., Rosulek, M.: Homomorphic encryption with CCA security. In: Aceto, L., Damgård, I., Goldberg, L.A., Halldórsson, M.M., Ingólfsdóttir, A., Walukiewicz, I. (eds.) ICALP 2008, Part II. LNCS, vol. 5126, pp. 667–678. Springer, Heidelberg (2008). https://doi.org/10.1007/978-3-540-70583-3_54

24. Shoup, V.: A proposal for an ISO standard for public key encryption. Cryptology ePrint Archive, Report 2001/112 (2001). http://eprint.iacr.org/2001/112

Cryptographic Protocols

Single-to-Multi-theorem Transformations for Non-interactive Statistical Zero-Knowledge

Marc Fischlin[✉] and Felix Rohrbach

Cryptoplexity, Technische Universität Darmstadt, Darmstadt, Germany
{marc.fischlin,felix.rohrbach}@cryptoplexity.de
http://www.cryptoplexity.de

Abstract. Non-interactive zero-knowledge proofs or arguments allow a prover to show validity of a statement without further interaction. For non-trivial statements such protocols require a setup assumption in form of a common random or reference string (CRS). Generally, the CRS can only be used for one statement (single-theorem zero-knowledge) such that a fresh CRS would need to be generated for each proof. Fortunately, Feige, Lapidot and Shamir (FOCS 1990) presented a transformation for any non-interactive zero-knowledge proof system that allows the CRS to be reused any polynomial number of times (multi-theorem zero-knowledge). This FLS transformation, however, is only known to work for either computational zero-knowledge or requires a structured, non-uniform common reference string.

In this paper we present FLS-like transformations that work for non-interactive statistical zero-knowledge arguments in the common *random* string model. They allow to go from single-theorem to multi-theorem zero-knowledge and also preserve soundness, for both properties in the adaptive and non-adaptive case. Our first transformation is based on the general assumption that one-way permutations exist, while our second transformation uses lattice-based assumptions. Additionally, we define different possible soundness notions for non-interactive arguments and discuss their relationships.

Keywords: Non-interactive arguments · Statistical zero-knowledge · Soundness · Transformation · One-way permutation · Lattices · Dual-mode commitments

1 Introduction

In a non-interactive proof for a language $\mathcal{L}$ the prover P shows validity of some theorem $x \in \mathcal{L}$ via a proof π based on a common string crs chosen by some external setup procedure. The common requirements are completeness—that the honest prover is able to convince the verifier V for true statements x—and soundness—that the verifier will not accept false statements $x \notin \mathcal{L}$ from

© International Association for Cryptologic Research 2021
J. A. Garay (Ed.): PKC 2021, LNCS 12711, pp. 205–234, 2021.
https://doi.org/10.1007/978-3-030-75248-4_8

malicious provers. Blum et al. [5] showed that such non-interactive proofs can also be zero-knowledge [22], saying that a simulator can create a proof π on behalf of P if it has the ability to place some trapdoor information in crs.

1.1 Flavors of Non-interactive Zero-Knowledge

Non-interactive zero-knowledge protocols come in many variations:

- If the prover is computationally unbounded then one speaks of a NIZK *proof system* whereas in *arguments* or *argument systems* the prover runs in polynomial time [8].
- Zero-knowledge may be *computational* (NICZK) or *statistical* (NISZK) or even *perfect* (NIPZK). Note that non-interactive statistical (or perfect) zero-knowledge for NP requires that the prover is computationally bounded, unless the polynomial hierarchy collapses [31].
- The common string crs may be uniformly distributed over all bit strings of a certain length, in which case one speaks of the *common random string* or, less frequently, of the *uniform reference string* model. In any other case the string may have more structure and one calls it a *common reference string* or, sometimes, also *public parameter* model. In this work, we will focus on the case where the crs is uniformly distributed.

Another important aspect is the question of when malicious parties choose their challenge statement x. Both zero-knowledge and soundness come in an adaptive and in a non-adaptive version. The adaptive versions say that the adversary may choose the statement x after having seen the common reference string. For zero-knowledge this means that the simulator must prepare crs independently of x and then find a valid proof π after learning a maliciously chosen $x \in \mathcal{L}$. Adaptive soundness says that the malicious prover P* first receives crs and then tries to find a false statement $x \notin \mathcal{L}$ with a convincing proof π.

Remarkably, for soundness one usually merely distinguishes between non-adaptive and adaptive notions. But there are also different ways how to capture the fact that a malicious prover P* needs to succeed for an invalid statement $x \notin \mathcal{L}$. Either one assumes that the prover only outputs invalid statements, thus excluding some adversaries, or one penalizes the prover and declares it to lose if it chooses some $x \in \mathcal{L}$.[1] The penalizing definition implies the exclusive one. We note that Arte and Bellare [3], in a concurrent work, have proposed a similar distinction between exclusive and penalizing soundness.

Both notions, exclusive and penalizing soundness, already appeared implicitly in the literature, e.g., the work by Blum et al. [7] gives both an adaptive and a non-adaptive soundness definition in the exclusive setting. Indeed, non-adaptive soundness in the literature is often cast in this style. In contrast, for adaptive soundness nowadays one often encounters the penalizing variant. It seems,

---

[1] We use here the terminology from [4] for the comparable scenario of admissible decryption queries in chosen-ciphertext security.

however, that the adaptive/exclusive version is already sufficient for many applications, e.g., to build universally composable NIZK protocols [26]. We discuss this in more detail in Sect. 3 when defining the different versions.

1.2 From Single-theorem to Multi-theorem Proofs

In this work we focus on another important property of NIZK, namely, if the crs can be used only once (*bounded* or *single-theorem*) or is applicable for many proofs (*unbounded* or *multi-theorem*). The latter is of course preferable, and indeed Feige et al. [17,18] show how to generally turn single-theorem NICZK proofs and arguments into multi-theorem zero-knowledge protocols. We call this the FLS-transformation.

The idea of the FLS-transformation is to augment the common random string by an extra uniformly distributed portion $\mathrm{crs}^{\mathrm{aux}}$ and let the prover for this NP-language show that "$x \in \mathcal{L}$ or $\mathrm{crs}^{\mathrm{aux}}$ is the output of a pseudorandom generator". This allows the simulator to create this part $\mathrm{crs}^{\mathrm{aux}}$ pseudorandomly and use the generator's seed as a witness for simulating the or-proof. If the original proof is zero-knowledge, then it is also witness indistinguishable [19], and then one cannot distinguish or-proofs generated by the genuine prover with the witness for x from proofs created by the simulator with the witness for $\mathrm{crs}^{\mathrm{aux}}$.

Soundness, on the other hand, is not affected because a random string $\mathrm{crs}^{\mathrm{aux}}$ is not pseudorandom, except with exponentially small probability. Hence, for invalid x the "or" of the statements $x \notin \mathcal{L}$ or "$\mathrm{crs}^{\mathrm{aux}}$ is pseudorandom" would not be satisfied either with overwhelming probability. This implies that a prover would still need to break soundness of the or-protocol.

The FLS-transformation, per se, is only known to work for non-interactive *computational* zero-knowledge. The reason is that the pseudorandom string $\mathrm{crs}^{\mathrm{aux}}$ of the zero-knowledge simulator is only computationally indistinguishable from a truly random string. There exists a folklore "dual version" of the FLS-transformation for non-interactive perfect (and therefore also statistical) zero-knowledge, where the crs contains a pseudorandom value by construction. But this transformation requires a structured, non-uniformly chosen crs, whereas we are interested in the setting of common *random* strings. For completeness, we provide a formal description of that folklore result along our terminology in the eprint version [20].

It is thus unclear if the FLS-transformation can be used equally smoothly for statistical zero-knowledge in the common random string model. For example, Peikert and Shiehian [32] recently presented a statistical zero-knowledge argument for NP based on LWE in the common random string model, which is only zero-knowledge for a single theorem. They therefore asked whether there is an FLS-like transformation to achieve multi-theorem zero-knowledge in the statistical case.

1.3 Known NISZK Constructions

There are only a few known constructions of NISZK and NIPZK protocols for the general class NP. Groth et al. [25,26] were the first to give a NIPZK argument for NP based on specific number-theoretic constructions over bilinear groups. Their protocol achieves multi-theorem adaptive zero-knowledge, but only non-adaptive/exclusive soundness (although this can be extended to some limited form of adaptive soundness, called adaptive culpable soundness). It is cast in the common reference string model.

Abe and Fehr [1] later showed how to achieve NIPZK arguments for NP under some form of the knowledge-of-exponent assumption. Their protocol achieves adaptive multi-theorem zero-knowledge and is adaptively sound (in the penalizing setting). This protocol is again in the common reference string model.

Sahai and Waters [34] show how to build NIPZK arguments for NP based on indistinguishability obfuscation and one-way functions. Their solution is adaptive multi-theorem zero-knowledge and non-adaptively/exclusively sound. It is designed in the common reference string model.

Peikert and Shiehian [32] constructed NISZK arguments for NP based on the LWE assumption. Their construction is based on the NIZK framework of Canetti et al. [9,10] as well as Holmgren and Lombardi [27] which, among others, constructs a non-adaptively/exclusively sound NISZK argument for NP in the common random string model. Their protocol is adaptively zero-knowledge for single theorems. The instantiation of Peikert and Shiehian [32] uses the LWE assumption to implement the primitives and inherits the characteristics of the solutions in [9,10,27].

An interesting observation, based on [11, Footnote 13], is that one should be able to show adaptive soundness for the constructions in [9] when using the exclusive notion. Noteworthy, Canetti et al. [11] merely claim non-adaptive soundness, because for the adaptive version they switch to the penalizing variant. They detail why this notion cannot be achieved with the current construction, and the point touches precisely the difference between penalizing and exclusive soundness. Reverting to adaptive/exclusive soundness, the construction may satisfy this weaker level. This gives the interesting twist that the solution by Peikert and Shiehian [32] may already be adaptively/exclusively sound, such that our transformation lifts it from single-theorem to multi-theorem (adaptive) zero-knowledge.

Libert et al. [29] recently showed how to build *designated-verifier* statistical zero-knowledge arguments based on the (kernel) k-linear assumption, and how this construction can also be turned into a public verifiable NISZK argument. Their public verifiable construction achieves multi-theorem zero-knowledge and non-adaptive/exclusive soundness in the common reference string model.

In another work, Libert et al. [28] achieve multi-theorem zero-knowledge in the common *random* string model. Their protocol provides non-adaptive/non-uniform soundness, i.e., where one quantifies over all inputs $x \notin \mathcal{L}$ and the crs is chosen as part of the experiment. We will later argue that in the non-adaptive case this notion is equivalent to non-adaptive/exclusive and to non-adaptive/penalizing soundness for non-uniform provers (Fig. 1).

1.4   Our Results

In this work we show multiple FLS-SZK-transformations which preserve statistical zero-knowledge. Moreover, they allow to preserve non-adaptive or adaptive zero-knowledge and also inherit the adaptive security of soundness (in the exclusive variant). In detail, we show:

- For statistical zero-knowledge we show how to transform any single-theorem zero-knowledge NISZK argument for NP-languages into one which is a multi-theorem zero-knowledge NISZK argument in the common random string model. This requires only the existence of one-way permutations[2].
- For perfect zero-knowledge we show that our transformation can be augmented to preserve perfect zero-knowledge. This, however, comes at the cost of having a zero-knowledge simulator which runs in expected polynomial-time.
- Finally, we show that we can build a transformation for statistical zero-knowledge from the Learning with Errors (LWE) assumption in the common

Work	Soundness	CRS uniform?	ZK	Required
FLS* [17,18]	adaptive/ penalizing	✓	computational	PRGs
folklore*	adaptive/ exclusive	✗	perfect	PRGs
Groth et al. [25,26]	non-adaptive/ exclusive	✗	perfect	bilinear groups
Abe and Fehr [1]	adaptive/ penalizing	✗	perfect	knowledge-of-exponent
Sahai and Waters [34]	non-adaptive/ exclusive	✗	perfect	iO
Libert et al. [29]	non-adaptive/ exclusive	✗	statistical	k-linear
Libert et al. [28]	non-adaptive/ non-uniform	✓	statistical	LWE
this work*	adaptive/ exclusive	✓	statistical	OWP or LWE
	adaptive/ exclusive	✓	perfect	OWP+ expected simulation

Fig. 1. Comparison of different multi-theorem NIZK schemes. The entries marked with * are actually transformations for the single-to-multi-theorem cases.

---

[2] Note that we define one-way permutations as one-way functions that are 1-1 and length-preserving, not as a family of such functions.

random string model. This transformation, in contrast to the construction by Libert et al. [28], even works for *adaptively* sound NISZK arguments. This fits in nicely with the recent construction of statistical zero-knowledge arguments based on LWE [32].

- Additionally, we define and discuss the different soundness properties for non-interactive arguments and analyze their relationship. In particular, we show that in the non-adaptive case, the notions of exclusive, penalizing, and non-uniform soundness are all equivalent when considering non-uniform provers.

Our techniques for the constructions based on general assumptions uses a "dual" version of the original FLS-transformation. That is, instead of building the or-language for crs^{aux} being pseudorandom, we use that crs^{aux} is *not* pseudorandom. Since this is in general a coNP-language we need to make sure that it is also in NP. We achieve this by using the Blum-Micali-Yao pseudorandom generator [6,35] based on one-way permutations and hardcore bits, which lies in NP ∩ coNP. Soundness for our dual FLS-transformation then follows since we can let the malicious prover run on a pseudorandom string crs^{aux} instead, since this is indistinguishable for the efficient prover in an argument. Then the or of the two statements, $x \in \mathcal{L}$ or crs^{aux} is not pseudorandom, is again not satisfied.

The construction based on LWE is inspired by a primitive called dual-mode commitment scheme, i.e., a commitment which can be either perfectly-binding or statistically-hiding, based on the choice of how to generate the public key. The public keys for both modes are computationally indistinguishable. We note that the usefulness of such dual-mode commitments for non-interactive zero-knowledge is well known, starting with the work by Groth et al. [25] where this technique was called parameter switching, to recent efforts like the construction of Libert et al. [29]. Most times, however, the solutions work over certain structures and yield arguments in the common reference string model.

Here, we use a construction of Gorbunov et al. [23] to build these dual-mode commitments where the (statistically-hiding) public key and a commitment can be chosen as uniform bit strings. As in the FLS-transformation we extend the CRS by a public key string pk and a random commitment string c and extend the language to "$x \in \mathcal{L}$ or c is a commitment to 1". For the simulator, we choose our public key to be statistically-hiding. In our construction, a statistically-hiding public key will be statistically close to a uniformly random string and indeed generate a commitment to the value 1.

However, for the soundness game we exchange the public key pk for a perfectly-binding one and change the commitment to 0, thereby forcing the malicious prover to prove x to be in $\mathcal{L}$. We emphasize that we only switch between these modes and merely require computational indistinguishability of the different types of public keys. In particular, we do not need to rely on the SIS assumption as considered in [23] but, as pointed out in [13], the LWE assumption suffices. Indeed, one could directly use Regev's LWE encryption scheme [33] which also supports a statistically-hiding, lossy mode.

1.5   Squeezing in into Possibility and Impossibility Results

There are some known impossibility results for statistical and perfect zero-knowledge arguments. Strictly speaking, these results do not infringe with our results here, since we show how to *transform* statistical zero-knowledge arguments (from single to multiple theorems) but do not give constructions. Still, one may wonder if the combination of our transformations with the impossibility results have any implications on potential constructions.

Abe and Fehr [1] were the first to show that NISZK arguments cannot be proven to be adaptively sound via so-called direct black-box reductions, unless the language is in P/poly. One property which such direct reductions has is that one can use an efficient alternative to the crs generator which in addition outputs the simulator's trapdoor information (property II.(b) in [1]). Our construction, however, bypasses this property because for the soundness proof it generates a bad crs which does not have a trapdoor. In this sense, our technique indicates that the notion of direct black-box reductions may be too restrictive.

Pass [30], using similar ideas and techniques as [1], shows that *adaptive* statistical and perfect zero-knowledge arguments with *adaptive* soundness cannot be based on hard primitives via black-box reductions. How does the result of Pass [30] match our results? First we remark that our NIPZK is indeed *adaptively* sound and *adaptively* zero-knowledge. But the simulator only runs in polynomial time averaged over its internal randomness. Such simulators escape the results in [30].

Yet, the most striking difference between the results in [1,30] and our transformations lies in the distinct notions of adaptive soundness. We show that our transformations preserve adaptive/exclusive soundness. Opposite to that, the impossibility results of [1,30] rely on the ability of the malicious prover to occasionally output theorems $x \in \mathcal{L}$. Put differently, they rule out the stronger form of adaptive/penalizing sound arguments, whereas we argue that adaptive/exclusive soundness is preserved. As remarked above, however, adaptive/exclusive sound arguments may still be sufficient for applications.

1.6   Concurrent Work

As mentioned earlier, Arte and Bellare [3] have touched upon the issue of different soundness notions in non-interactive proofs as well. Their starting point are dual-mode systems in which the common reference string can be generated in two modes, and in how far such systems allow for transference of security properties in the different modes. Our work instead focuses on the transformations for multi-theorem statistical zero-knowledge arguments.

Arte and Bellare define notions of penalizing and exclusive soundness, called SND-P and SND-E, with which our adaptive notions for soundness coincide (for efficient provers).[3] Remarkably, they show a separating example of their exclusive and penalizing soundness notion in the adaptive case, under the decisional

---

[3] Strictly speaking, their notion of exclusiveness allows for a negligible error which could be integrated in our notion as well.

Diffie-Hellman assumption. This example applies to our notions in the adaptive setting as well. We complement this result by showing that the notions are equivalent in the non-adaptive case, assuming non-uniform provers.

Another notably difference between the two works lies in the applications of the different soundness notions. Arte and Bellare discuss the example of the Bellare-Goldwasser signature scheme where penalizing soundness is required and exclusive soundness is insufficient. We argue along the implication of culpability that exclusive soundness may suffice in many settings.

2   Preliminaries

An NP-relation $\mathcal{R}$ consists of pairs (x, ω) of theorems and witnesses where the length of witness is polynomially bounded in the length of the theorem, and where one can efficiently decide membership. More formally, there exists a polynomial-time Turing machine $M_{\mathcal{R}}$ and a polynomial $p_{\mathcal{R}}$ such that

$$\mathcal{R} = \{(x, \omega) \mid |\omega| \leq p_{\mathcal{R}}(|x|) \wedge M_{\mathcal{R}}(x, \omega) = 1\}.$$

The induced language $\mathcal{L}_{\mathcal{R}}$ is given by

$$\mathcal{L}_{\mathcal{R}} = \{x \in \{0, 1\}^* \mid \exists \omega : (x, \omega) \in \mathcal{R}\}.$$

2.1   Non-interactive Arguments

A non-interactive argument or proof system for an NP-relation is now a protocol in which the setup algorithm Setup generates a common string crs which the prover P then uses to generate a proof π for the input (x, ω). The verifier V then checks this proof against crs and x only. There are some length restrictions, of course, namely that the length of the theorem x determines the length of the common string. In particular, we assume that there is a polynomial p_{Setup} such that crs $\in \{0, 1\}^{p_{\mathsf{Setup}}(n)}$ for any crs $\overset{\$}{\leftarrow}$ Setup(1^n). Let $\mathcal{R}(1^n) = \{(x, \omega) \in \mathcal{R} \mid |x| = n\}$ and $\mathcal{L}_{\mathcal{R}}(1^n) = \{x \in \mathcal{L}_{\mathcal{R}} \mid |x| = n\}$ denote the restriction of inputs of the relation and language with length $|x| = n$ such that the length of the common string for such inputs is given by $p_{\mathsf{Setup}}(n)$. Note that the verifier can easily check that $|x|$ matches the security parameter n such that we can assume that this is always the case.

We note that the string crs generated by Setup may be uniformly distributed, in which case we speak of a common random string. It may have a different distribution, in which case we call it a common reference string. In particular, we see a common random string as a special case of a common reference string.

The usual completeness notion of non-interactive arguments and proofs asks that the verifier V accepts genuine proofs π generated by the prover P for input $x \in \mathcal{L}_{\mathcal{R}}$. Soundness, on the hand, demands that the verifier does not accept false proofs generated by a malicious prover P* for inputs $x \notin \mathcal{L}_{\mathcal{R}}$. As explained in the introduction there are various possibilities to define soundness, which we will discuss in Sect. 3, and just use one example of the possible definitions here.

Definition 1 (Non-interactive Argument). *A non-interactive argument for an* NP-*relation* $\mathcal{R}$ *(in the common reference string model) is a triple of probabilistic polynomial-time algorithms* $\Pi = (\textsf{Setup}, P, V)$ *satisfying the completeness and soundness condition:*

(Perfect) Completeness: *For every* $n \in \mathbb{N}$, *every* $(x, \omega) \in \mathcal{R}(1^n)$, *every* $crs \xleftarrow{\$}$ $\textsf{Setup}(1^n)$, *every* $\pi \xleftarrow{\$} P(1^n, x, \omega, crs)$ *we have that* $V(1^n, x, \pi, crs) = 1$ *with probability* 1.

(Non-adaptive/Exclusive) Soundness: *For every (possibly malicious) probabilistic polynomial-time prover* P^* *outputting only* $x \notin \mathcal{L}_\mathcal{R}$ *there exists a negligible function* $\epsilon(n)$ *such that for every* $n \in \mathbb{N}$ *we have*

$$\Pr\left[V(1^n, x, \pi, crs) = 1\right] \leq \epsilon(|x|),$$

where the probability is over $(x, st) \xleftarrow{\$} P^*(1^n)$, $crs \xleftarrow{\$} \textsf{Setup}(1^n)$, *as well as* $\pi \xleftarrow{\$} P^*(1^n, st, crs)$, *and* V's *randomness.*

We say that the argument is in the common random *string model if* $\textsf{Setup}(n)$ *outputs uniformly distributed strings over* $\{0,1\}^{p_{\textsf{Setup}}(n)}$ *for every* $n \in \mathbb{N}$.

2.2 Zero-knowledge

We next define zero-knowledge with the usual notion of a simulator ZKSim. In the non-interactive setting this algorithm has the advantage to choose the common string crs to simulate proofs. In the bounded case the distinguisher only gets to see a single proof for a chosen theorem, where the proof is either genuine or fabricated by the simulator. We simultaneously define the single-theorem and multi-theorem case where the distinguisher learns one or many (genuine or simulated) proofs. We first define both cases in the adaptive setting where the distinguisher selects the theorems in dependence of the common string and of previous proofs and in the non-adaptive case where the distinguisher chooses the statement(s) in advance. We stress that we are interested in statistical zero-knowledge here such that the distinguisher is unbounded, except that it can only ask for polynomially many proofs. We also allow the simulator to run in *expected* polynomial time in specially marked cases.

Definition 2 (Statistical and Perfect Zero Knowledge). *Let* $\mathcal{R}$ *be an* NP-*relation and let* $\Pi = (\textsf{Setup}, P, V)$ *be a non-interactive argument for* $\mathcal{R}$. *The argument is zero-knowledge if it satisfies one of the following properties:*

Non-adaptive Multi-theorem Zero-knowledge: *For any unbounded algorithm* D *there exists a probabilistic algorithm* ZKSim, *the simulator, running in (expected) polynomial time, such that the advantage*

$$\textsf{Adv}^{naSZK}_{\Pi, \textsf{ZKSim}, D}(1^n) := \Pr\left[\textsf{Expt}^{naSZK}_{\Pi, \textsf{ZKSim}, D}(1^n) = 1\right] - \frac{1}{2}$$

is negligible for polynomially bounded q, *where experiment* $\textsf{Expt}^{naSZK}_{\Pi, \textsf{ZKSim}, D}(1^n)$ *is defined in Fig. 2. If the advantage of any such* D *is always 0 then the argument is called perfect zero-knowledge.*

$\mathsf{Expt}^{\mathrm{naSZK}}_{\Pi,\mathsf{ZKSim},\mathsf{D}}(1^n)$:

1 $b \xleftarrow{\$} \{0,1\}$
2 $(\mathsf{st_D}, x_1, \omega_1, \ldots, x_\mathsf{q}, \omega_\mathsf{q}) \xleftarrow{\$} \mathsf{D}(1^n)$
3 $\mathsf{crs}_0 \xleftarrow{\$} \mathsf{Setup}(1^n)$
4 $(\mathsf{crs}_1, \mathsf{st}_\mathsf{ZKSim}) \xleftarrow{\$} \mathsf{ZKSim}(1^n)$
5 for $i = 1..\mathsf{q}$ do
6   if $(x_i, \omega_i) \in \mathcal{R}$ then
7      $\pi_{i,0} \xleftarrow{\$} \mathsf{P}(1^n, x_i, \omega_i, \mathsf{crs}_0)$
8      $\pi_{i,1} \xleftarrow{\$} \mathsf{ZKSim}(1^n, \mathsf{st}_\mathsf{ZKSim}, x_i)$
9   else $\pi_{i,0} \leftarrow \pi_{i,1} \leftarrow \bot$
10 $d \xleftarrow{\$} \mathsf{D}(1^n, \mathsf{st_D}, \pi_{1,b}, \ldots, \pi_{\mathsf{q},b}, \mathsf{crs}_b)$
11 return $b = d$

$\mathsf{Expt}^{\mathrm{aSZK}}_{(\mathsf{Setup},\mathsf{P},\mathsf{V}),\mathsf{ZKSim},\mathsf{D}}(1^n)$:

1 $b \xleftarrow{\$} \{0,1\}$, $\mathsf{q} \leftarrow 0$, $\mathsf{st_D} \leftarrow \bot$
2 $\mathsf{crs}_0 \xleftarrow{\$} \mathsf{Setup}(1^n)$
3 $(\mathsf{crs}_1, \mathsf{st}_\mathsf{ZKSim}) \xleftarrow{\$} \mathsf{ZKSim}(1^n)$
4 repeat
5    $\mathsf{q} \leftarrow \mathsf{q} + 1$
6    $(\mathsf{st_D}, x, \omega) \xleftarrow{\$} \mathsf{D}(1^n, \mathsf{st_D}, \mathsf{crs}_b)$
7   if $(x, \omega) \in \mathcal{R}$ then
8      $\pi_0 \xleftarrow{\$} \mathsf{P}(1^n, x, \omega, \mathsf{crs}_0)$
9      $\pi_1 \xleftarrow{\$} \mathsf{ZKSim}(1^n, \mathsf{st}_\mathsf{ZKSim}, x)$
10   else $\pi_0 \leftarrow \pi_1 \leftarrow \bot$
11    $(\mathsf{st_D}, \mathsf{cont}, d) \xleftarrow{\$} \mathsf{D}(1^n, \mathsf{st_D}, \pi_b)$
12 until $\mathsf{cont} = \mathtt{false}$
13 return $b = d$

Fig. 2. Non-adaptive and adaptive statistical zero-knowledge experiments.

Adaptive Multi-theorem Zero Knowledge: *For any unbounded algorithm D there exists a probabilistic algorithm ZKSim, the simulator, running in (expected) polynomial time, such that the advantage*

$$\mathsf{Adv}^{aSZK}_{\Pi,\mathsf{ZKSim},\mathsf{D}}(1^n) := \Pr\left[\mathsf{Expt}^{aSZK}_{\Pi,\mathsf{ZKSim},\mathsf{D}}(1^n) = 1\right] - \frac{1}{2}$$

is negligible for polynomially bounded q, *where experiment* $\mathsf{Expt}^{aSZK}_{\Pi,\mathsf{ZKSim},\mathsf{D}}(1^n)$ *is defined in Fig. 2. If the advantage of any such D is always 0 then the argument is called perfect zero-knowledge.*

The argument is single-theorem zero-knowledge of the corresponding type if the property holds for $\mathsf{q} = 1$.

Definition 3 (Statistical Witness Indistinguishability). *Let $\mathcal{R}$ be an* NP-*relation. A non-interactive argument $\Pi = (\mathsf{Setup}, \mathsf{P}, \mathsf{V})$ for $\mathcal{R}$ is called statistical witness indistinguishable (NISWI) if it satisfies one of the following properties:*

Non-adaptive Multi-theorem Witness Indistinguishability: *For any unbounded algorithm D the advantage*

$$\mathsf{Adv}^{naSWI}_{\Pi,\mathsf{D}}(1^n) := \Pr\left[\mathsf{Expt}^{naSWI}_{\Pi,\mathsf{D}}(1^n) = 1\right] - \frac{1}{2}$$

is negligible for polynomially bounded q, *where the experiment* $\mathsf{Expt}^{naSWI}_{\Pi,\mathsf{D}}(1^n)$ *is defined in Fig. 3. If the advantage of any such D is always 0 then the argument is called perfect witness indistinguishable.*

$\underline{\textsf{Expt}_{\Pi,\textsf{D}}^{\textsf{naSWI}}(1^n)\text{:}}$

1 $b \xleftarrow{\$} \{0, 1\}$

2 $(\textsf{st}_\textsf{D}, (x_i, \omega_{i,0}, \omega_{i,1})_{i=1..\textsf{q}}) \xleftarrow{\$} \textsf{D}(1^n)$

3 $\textsf{crs} \xleftarrow{\$} \textsf{Setup}(1^n)$

4 for $i = 1..\textsf{q}$ do

5   if $(x_i, \omega_{i,0}) \in \mathcal{R} \wedge (x_i, \omega_{i,1}) \in \mathcal{R}$

6      $\pi_{i,0} \xleftarrow{\$} \textsf{P}(1^n, x_i, \omega_{i,0}, \textsf{crs})$

7      $\pi_{i,1} \xleftarrow{\$} \textsf{P}(1^n, x_i, \omega_{i,1}, \textsf{crs})$

8   else $\pi_{i,0} \leftarrow \pi_{i,1} \leftarrow \bot$

9 $d \xleftarrow{\$} \textsf{D}(1^n, \textsf{st}_\textsf{D}, \pi_{1,b}, \ldots, \pi_{\textsf{q},b}, \textsf{crs})$

10 return $b = d$

$\underline{\textsf{Expt}_{\Pi,\textsf{D}}^{\textsf{aSWI}}(1^n)\text{:}}$

1 $b \xleftarrow{\$} \{0, 1\}$, $\textsf{q} \leftarrow 0$, $\textsf{st}_\textsf{D} \leftarrow \bot$

2 $\textsf{crs} \xleftarrow{\$} \textsf{Setup}(1^n)$

3 repeat

4    $\textsf{q} \leftarrow \textsf{q} + 1$

5    $(\textsf{st}_\textsf{D}, x, \omega_0, \omega_1) \xleftarrow{\$} \textsf{D}(1^n, \textsf{st}_\textsf{D}, \textsf{crs}_b)$

6   if $(x, \omega_0) \in \mathcal{R} \wedge (x, \omega_1) \in \mathcal{R}$

7      $\pi_0 \xleftarrow{\$} \textsf{P}(1^n, x, \omega_0, \textsf{crs})$

8      $\pi_1 \xleftarrow{\$} \textsf{P}(1^n, x, \omega_1, \textsf{crs})$

9   else $\pi_0 \leftarrow \pi_1 \leftarrow \bot$

10    $(\textsf{st}_\textsf{D}, \textsf{cont}, d) \xleftarrow{\$} \textsf{D}(1^n, \textsf{st}_\textsf{D}, \pi_b)$

11 until $\textsf{cont} = \textbf{false}$

12 return $b = d$

Fig. 3. Non-adaptive and adaptive statistical witness indistinguishability experiments.

Adaptive Multi-theorem Witness Indistinguishability: *For any unbounded algorithm D the advantage*

$$\textsf{Adv}_{\Pi,D}^{aSWI}(1^n) := \Pr\left[\textsf{Expt}_{\Pi,D}^{aSWI}(1^n) = 1\right] - \frac{1}{2}$$

is negligible for polynomially bounded $\textsf{q}$*, where the experiment* $\textsf{Expt}_{\Pi,D}^{aSWI}(1^n)$ *is defined in Fig. 3. If the advantage of any such D is always* 0 *then the argument is called perfect witness indistinguishable.*

The argument is single-theorem witness indistinguishable of the corresponding type if the property holds for $\textsf{q} = 1$.

2.3   From Single-Theorem Zero-Knowledge to Multi-Theorem Witness Indistinguishability

We repeat here the well known fact that zero-knowledge implies witness indistinguishability, and that witness indistinguishability is closed under repetitions [19]. We state the results here for sake of completeness and according to our terminology in the statistical setting.

Lemma 1. *Any adaptive resp. non-adaptive single-theorem NISZK argument is also an adaptive resp. non-adaptive single-theorem NISWI argument.*

Proof (Sketch). We only argue the adaptive case; the non-adaptive case follows analogously. We can perform a game hop starting with the witness-indistinguishability experiment $\textsf{Expt}_{\Pi,D}^{aSWI}(1^n)$. In this hop we replace the CRS and both proofs π_0 and π_1 in each iteration by simulated ones, all created by the simulator ZKSim without knowledge of the witnesses ω_0 and ω_1 but using the same trapdoor. Note that we can view the proofs in the WI experiment as two sequentially requested proofs in the ZK experiment, such that the SZK property ensures that this hop is statistically indistinguishable. (In the non-adaptive case we would split each entry $(x_i, \omega_{i,0}, \omega_{i,1})$ in D's initial choice into two entries $(x_i, \omega_{i,0})$ and $(x, \omega_{i,1})$.)

But now both proofs π_0 and π_1 are created without the specific witness, and since the simulator does not update its state for giving proofs, the order in which the proofs are computed is irrelevant. In this case the bit b is perfectly hidden from the distinguisher such that the advantage in predicting b is 0.   □

Lemma 2. *Any adaptive resp. non-adaptive single-theorem NISWI argument is also an adaptive resp. non-adaptive multi-theorem NISWI argument.*

Proof (Sketch). We again only discuss the adaptive case since the non-adaptive case follows analogously. The proof follows by a hybrid argument. For this we reduce the multi-theorem distinguisher D to a bounded one D_1 which only makes one query. Let $Q(n)$ be a polynomial upper bound on the number of queries q which D makes. The bounded distinguisher D_1 initially picks an index $i \xleftarrow{\$} \{1, 2, \ldots, Q(n)\}$ and then internally runs in the first stage (Line 5) the distinguisher D up to the i-th query $(st_D, x, \omega_0, \omega_1)$. All requested proofs up to this step are computed internally by D_1 via P and the left witness, and returned to D. The i-th query is then computed externally, and D_1 then hands the proof back to D. In the final steps till halting, D_1 computes the remaining proofs for ω_1, and eventually returns D's decision bit d unchanged.

It can be shown that the advantage of the bounded distinguisher D_1 is at most a factor $Q(n)$ larger than the one of D. Since $Q(n)$ is polynomial, the difference is negligible.   □

3   Soundness of Non-interactive Arguments

Soundness of a non-interactive argument assures that a (computationally-bound) malicious prover is unable to convince the verifier of a false statement. Commonly, soundness is defined in two variants: Adaptive soundness, with allows the (possibly malicious) prover P^* to chose the statement to prove x before seeing the common random string crs, and non-adaptive soundness, in which the prover P^* has to decide on the statement x before the common random string crs is generated.

Remarkably, there is another dimension of definitional choice for soundness which often goes unnoticed in the literature. This dimension refers to the question how we measure success of the malicious prover. Clearly, the malicious prover should not make the verifier accept for a statement x not in the language. But there are two possibilities to capture the non-membership requirement. One is to disallow P^* to output $x \in \mathcal{L}$ at all. The other one is to declare P^* to lose if it picks $x \in \mathcal{L}$. Following the work of Bellare et al. [4] about the question how to deal with inadmissible decryption queries in CCA-secure encryption schemes, we call the former stipulation of P^* outputting only $x \notin \mathcal{L}$ *exclusive*, because it excludes certain adversaries. The latter is called *penalizing* as it punishes P^* if it chooses $x \in \mathcal{L}$.

3.1   Soundness Definitions

In total, we define five soundness notions: adaptive vs. non-adaptive, and exclusive vs. penalizing, as well as a non-uniform variant that only exists for the non-adaptive case. We typically speak of non-adaptive/exclusive and adaptive/penalizing soundness etc. to distinguish the different types. Figure 4 provides an overview. It is also easy to see that adaptive soundness implies non-adaptive soundness in both settings, and penalizing soundness implies exclusive soundness in any of the other dimensions. The latter is easy to see because any malicious prover P^* breaking exclusive soundness must output $x \notin \mathcal{L}$ such that this prover also satisfies the winning condition in the penalizing setting. In this chapter, we highlight the further connections between these definitions and their implications.

The difference between exclusive and penalizing soundness may appear to be insignificant. Indeed, for non-interactive *proofs* it is folklore to show that the weakest one of the five notions, non-adaptive/exclusive soundness, implies the strongest one, adaptive/penalizing soundness. See for instance [21]. This may explain why today's literature mostly distinguishes between the (exclusive) non-adaptive notion and the (penalizing) adaptive notion. An exception is the seminal paper by Blum et al. [7] which defines the adaptive version according to the exclusive dimension (without using our terminology here, of course). We emphasize, however, that the equivalence of all notions is not known to hold for non-interactive *arguments*.

Is a more fine-grained distinction between exclusive and penalizing soundness in arguments necessary? We argue that it is. Roughly, the difference is that in the exclusive case the malicious prover (and any other party) knows that its output is not in the language, in the penalizing case even the prover may itself be oblivious about this. This is an important ingredient in Pass' impossibility result to build adaptive sound and adaptive statistical zero-knowledge arguments based on black-box reductions [30]. The result crucially relies on the malicious prover choosing a (random or pseudorandom) statement for which it does not know the status. In other words, this impossibility results rules out the strongest form of adaptive/penalizing soundness.

We next argue that the weaker form of adaptive/exclusive soundness is very relevant. It is easy to see that this notion implies a slightly weaker notion of adaptive/*culpable* soundness [26]. This notion is similar to our definition of adaptive/exclusive soundness, but also requires the malicious prover to output an efficiently verifiable witness (denoted ω_{guilt} in [26]) that the statement x is *not* in the language $\mathcal{L}$. Our exclusive notion asks P^* to output $x \notin \mathcal{L}$. We prove the implication that adaptive/exclusive yields adaptive/culpable soundness formally in Sect. 3.3.

The noteworthy fact is that adaptive/culpable soundness suffices for many applications. One of the most important ones is the possibility to derive

| | non-adaptive | | adaptive |

$$\textit{non-adaptive} \qquad\qquad \textit{adaptive}$$

exclusive soundness:
1. // only P^* outputting $x \notin \mathcal{L}$
2. $(x, \mathrm{st}_{P^*}) \xleftarrow{\$} P^*(1^n)$
3. $\mathrm{crs} \xleftarrow{\$} \mathsf{Setup}(1^n)$
4. $\pi \xleftarrow{\$} P^*(1^n, \mathrm{crs}, \mathrm{st}_{P^*})$
5. **return** $\mathsf{V}(1^n, x, \pi, \mathrm{crs})$

exclusive soundness:
1. // only P^* outputting $x \notin \mathcal{L}$
2.
3. $\mathrm{crs} \xleftarrow{\$} \mathsf{Setup}(1^n)$
4. $(x, \pi) \xleftarrow{\$} P^*(1^n, \mathrm{crs})$
5. **return** $\mathsf{V}(1^n, x, \pi, \mathrm{crs})$

penalizing soundness:
1. $(x, \mathrm{st}_{P^*}) \xleftarrow{\$} P^*(1^n)$
2. $\mathrm{crs} \xleftarrow{\$} \mathsf{Setup}(1^n)$
3. $\pi \xleftarrow{\$} P^*(1^n, \mathrm{crs}, \mathrm{st}_{P^*})$
4. **return** $\mathsf{V}(1^n, x, \pi, \mathrm{crs}) \wedge x \notin \mathcal{L}$

penalizing soundness:
1.
2. $\mathrm{crs} \xleftarrow{\$} \mathsf{Setup}(1^n)$
3. $(x, \pi) \xleftarrow{\$} P^*(1^n, \mathrm{crs})$
4. **return** $\mathsf{V}(1^n, x, \pi, \mathrm{crs}) \wedge x \notin \mathcal{L}$

non-uniform soundness:
1. // for all $x \notin \mathcal{L}$
2. $\mathrm{crs} \xleftarrow{\$} \mathsf{Setup}(1^n)$
3. $\pi \xleftarrow{\$} P^*(1^n, \mathrm{crs}, x)$
4. **return** $\mathsf{V}(1^n, x, \pi, \mathrm{crs})$

Fig. 4. Different notions of soundness.

universally composable NIZK argument [26]. Other applications include correctness proofs for shuffles [14,15,24] or for e-voting [12]. Since adaptive/exclusive soundness implies adaptive/culpable soundness, any protocol satisfying the exclusive notion is also applicable in such settings.

We can now define arguments with the different soundness properties:

Definition 4 (Soundness of non-interactive Arguments). *A non-interactive argument for an NP-relation $\mathcal{R}$ (in the common reference string model) is a triple of probabilistic polynomial-time algorithms $\Pi = (\mathsf{Setup}, \mathsf{P}, \mathsf{V})$ satisfying the completeness as well as at least one of the soundness conditions:*

Non-adaptive/Exclusive Soundness: *For every (possibly malicious) probabilistic polynomial-time prover P^* outputting only $x \notin \mathcal{L}_{\mathcal{R}}$ there exists a negligible function $\epsilon(n)$ such that for every $n \in \mathbb{N}$ we have*

$$\Pr\left[\mathsf{V}(1^n, x, \pi, crs) = 1\right] \leq \epsilon(|x|),$$

where the probability is over $(x, st) \overset{\$}{\leftarrow} P^*(1^n)$, *crs* $\overset{\$}{\leftarrow}$ *Setup*(1^n), *as well as* $\pi \overset{\$}{\leftarrow} P^*(1^n, st, crs)$, *and V's randomness.*

Non-adaptive/Penalizing Soundness: *For every (possibly malicious) probabilistic polynomial-time prover* P^* *there exists a negligible function* $\epsilon(n)$ *such that for every* $n \in \mathbb{N}$ *we have*

$$\Pr\left[V(1^n, x, \pi, crs) = 1 \wedge x \notin \mathcal{L}_\mathcal{R}\right] \leq \epsilon(|x|),$$

where the probability is over $(x, st) \overset{\$}{\leftarrow} P^*(1^n)$, *crs* $\overset{\$}{\leftarrow}$ *Setup*(1^n), *as well as* $\pi \overset{\$}{\leftarrow} P^*(1^n, st, crs)$, *and V's randomness.*

Adaptive/Exclusive Soundness: *For every (possibly malicious) probabilistic polynomial-time prover* P^* *outputting only* $x \notin \mathcal{L}_\mathcal{R}$ *there exists a negligible function* $\epsilon(n)$ *such that for every* $n \in \mathbb{N}$ *we have*

$$\Pr\left[V(1^n, x, \pi, crs) = 1\right] \leq \epsilon(|x|),$$

where the probability is over crs $\overset{\$}{\leftarrow}$ *Setup*(1^n), $(x, \pi) \overset{\$}{\leftarrow} P^*(1^n, crs)$, *and V's randomness.*

Adaptive/Penalizing Soundness: *For every (possibly malicious) probabilistic polynomial-time prover* P^* *there exists a negligible function* $\epsilon(n)$ *such that for every* $n \in \mathbb{N}$ *we have*

$$\Pr\left[V(1^n, x, \pi, crs) = 1 \wedge x \notin \mathcal{L}_\mathcal{R}\right] \leq \epsilon(|x|),$$

where the probability is over crs $\overset{\$}{\leftarrow}$ *Setup*(1^n), $(x, \pi) \overset{\$}{\leftarrow} P^*(1^n, crs)$, *and V's randomness.*

Non-adaptive/Non-uniform Soundness: *For every (possibly malicious) probabilistic polynomial-time prover* P^* *there exists a negligible function* $\epsilon(n)$ *such that for every* $n \in \mathbb{N}$ *and every* $x \notin \mathcal{L}_\mathcal{R}$ *with* $|x| = n$, *we have*

$$\Pr\left[V(1^n, x, \pi, crs) = 1 \wedge x \notin \mathcal{L}_\mathcal{R}\right] \leq \epsilon(|x|),$$

where the probability is over crs $\overset{\$}{\leftarrow}$ *Setup*(1^n), *and* $\pi \overset{\$}{\leftarrow} P^*(1^n, x, crs)$, *and V's randomness.*

3.2   Equivalence of the Non-adaptive Soundness Notions

We now show that the non-adaptive soundness definitions are all equivalent if we allow the malicious provers to be non-uniform:

Theorem 1. *For non-uniform (malicious) provers, a non-interactive argument* $\Pi = ($*Setup, P, V*$)$ *has non-adaptive/exclusive soundness iff it has non-adaptive/-non-uniform soundness, and has non-adaptive/non-uniform soundness iff it has non-adaptive/penalizing soundness.*

Proof. Non-adaptive/exclusive soundness follows directly from non-adaptive/penalizing soundness, therefore we only show that non-adaptive/non-uniform soundness follows from non-adaptive/exclusive soundness and that non-adaptive/penalizing soundness follows from non-adaptive/non-uniform soundness.

We start by showing non-adaptive/non-uniform soundness follows from non-adaptive/exclusive soundness. Let $\Pi = (\mathsf{Setup}, \mathsf{P}, \mathsf{V})$ be the non-interactive argument in question. Assume that there exists a successful malicious prover $\mathsf{P}^*_{na/nu}$ against the non-adaptive/non-uniform soundness, i.e., for any negligible function $\epsilon(n)$ there exists an $x \notin \mathcal{L}$ such that

$$\Pr\left[V(\mathrm{crs}, x, \mathsf{P}^*_{na/nu}(\mathrm{crs}, x))\right] > \epsilon(|x|),$$

where the probability is over crs $\xleftarrow{\$} \mathsf{Setup}(1^n)$, as well as $\mathsf{P}^*_{na/nu}$'s and V's randomness. We can now construct a malicious prover $\mathsf{P}^*_{na/ex}$ against non-adaptive/exclusive soundness as follows: We define the first-stage algorithm $\mathsf{P}^*_{na/ex,1}(1^n)$ to choose $x \notin \mathcal{L}$ of length n non-uniformly, such that $\mathsf{P}^*_{na/nu}$'s success probability is maximized. The state st is left empty. Further, the second-stage algorithm $\mathsf{P}^*_{na/ex,2}$ merely calls $\mathsf{P}^*_{na/nu}$ internally, ignoring the state st. Then, the success probability of $\mathsf{P}^*_{na/ex}$ is at least as large as the one of $\mathsf{P}^*_{na/nu}$ and thus non-negligible.

Next, we show that non-adaptive/penalizing soundness follows from non-adaptive/non-uniform soundness. Assume that there exists a successful malicious prover $\mathsf{P}^*_{na/pn}$ against the non-adaptive/penalizing soundness, i.e., for any negligible function ϵ there exists an $n \in \mathbb{N}$ such that

$$\Pr[V(\mathrm{crs}, x, \pi) = 1 \wedge x \notin \mathcal{L})] > \epsilon(n),$$

where the probability is over $(x, \mathrm{st}) \xleftarrow{\$} \mathsf{P}^*_{na/pn,1}(1^n)$, crs $\xleftarrow{\$} \mathsf{Setup}(1^n)$, $\pi \xleftarrow{\$} \mathsf{P}^*_{na/pn,2}$ as well as V's internal randomness.

We can now construct a malicious prover $\mathsf{P}^*_{na/nu}$ against non-adaptive/non-uniform soundness as follows: For each input length n, we fix the pair $(\bar{x}, \bar{\mathrm{st}})$, $\bar{x} \in \{0,1\}^n, \bar{x} \notin \mathcal{L}$, on which $\mathsf{P}^*_{na/pn,2}$'s success probability is maximized (we bound the length of $\bar{\mathrm{st}}$ by $\mathsf{P}^*_{na/pn,1}$'s running time). Next we define $\mathsf{P}^*_{na/nu}$ as follows: On input x, $\mathsf{P}^*_{na/nu}$ checks whether x equals $\bar{x}$, and if that is the case, it internally calls $\mathsf{P}^*_{na/pn,2}(crs, \bar{x}, \bar{\mathrm{st}})$ to generate a proof. Otherwise, $\mathsf{P}^*_{na/nu}$ returns an empty proof. Note that we use the non-uniformity to save the sequence of $(\bar{x}, \bar{\mathrm{st}})$ for each input length. It is again easy to see that this prover is indeed a successful malicious prover against non-adaptive/non-uniform soundness.   □

For adaptive soundness, Arte and Bellare [3] showed that there exists a protocol that provides *adaptive/exclusive* soundness but not *adaptive/penalizing* soundness. This indicates that a NISZK protocol with *adaptive/exclusive* soundness might indeed be achievable, compared to one with *adaptive/penalizing* soundness, for which Pass [30] showed a black-box impossibility result.

3.3 Exclusive Soundness Implies Culpable Soundness

In this section we show that adaptive/exclusive soundness implies the notion of adaptive/culpable soundness of [26]. We first recall the definition of culpable soundness (according to our terminology). For an NP-relation $\mathcal{R}$ let $\mathcal{R}_{\text{guilt}}$ be an NP-relation for the complement of $\mathcal{L}_{\mathcal{R}}$, i.e., $x \notin \mathcal{L}_{\mathcal{R}}$ means that there is a polynomial size ω_{guilt} such that $(x, \omega_{\text{guilt}}) \in \mathcal{R}_{\text{guilt}}$. Note that the relation $\mathcal{R}_{\text{guilt}}$ is efficiently verifiable as an NP-relation (and $\mathcal{L}_{\mathcal{R}}$ is therefore in co-NP).

Definition 5 (Adaptive/Culpable Soundness). *A non-interactive argument (Setup, P, V) for an NP-relation $\mathcal{R}$ (in the common reference string model) has adaptive culpable soundness if for any PPT algorithm P^*_{culp} there exists a negligible function ϵ such that*

$$\Pr\left[V(1^n, x, \pi, crs) = 1 \wedge (x, \omega_{guilt}) \in \mathcal{R}_{guilt}\right] \leq \epsilon(n),$$

where the probability is over $crs \xleftarrow{\$} Setup(1^n)$, $(x, \pi, \omega_{guilt}) \xleftarrow{\$} P^*_{culp}(1^n, crs)$, and V's internal randomness.

Proposition 1. *A non-interactive argument (Setup, P, V) for an NP-relation $\mathcal{R}$ (in the common reference string model) which has a corresponding relation $\mathcal{R}_{guilt}$ and is adaptive/exclusive sound is also adaptive/culpable sound.*

Proof. Assume that we have a successful prover P^*_{culp} against culpable soundness. We construct a malicious prover P^*_{ex} against exclusive soundness as follows. P^*_{ex} receives as input crs and forwards this to P^*_{culp} which, then, outputs (x, π, ω_{guilt}). Our prover P^*_{ex} checks in polynomial time if $(x, \omega_{guilt}) \in \mathcal{R}_{guilt}$. If not it immediately outputs $\bot$, else it returns (x, π).

Note that since we interpret outputs $\bot$ as $\bot \notin \mathcal{L}_{\mathcal{R}}$ our prover P^*_{ex} only outputs values not in the language. It is thus an admissible attacker against exclusive soundness. Furthermore, P^*_{culp} can only win for $x \notin \mathcal{L}_{\mathcal{R}}$ such that only outputting (x, π) for those x cannot decrease the success probability. This yields that P^*_{ex} has the same success probability as P^*_{culp}. □

4 Constructions Based on General Assumptions

4.1 Multi-theorem NISZK Based on One-Way Permutations

Our approach uses the same idea as in [17] of having crs^{aux}, but we apply it in a dual way. That is, we use a language saying that crs^{aux} is *not* pseudorandom. Since this is in general a coNP-relation we use the Blum-Micali-Yao [6,35] generator for one-way permutations,

$$G(s) = f^{|s|}(s)\| \text{hb}(s)\| \text{hb}(f(s))\| \ldots \| \text{hb}(f^{|s|-1}(x)),$$

where s is the seed of length $|s| = n$, f is a one-way permutation, $f^i(s)$ the i-fold iteration of f for input s, and hb is a hardcore bit for f. Proving that a string

$\mathrm{crs}^{\mathrm{aux}}$ is *not* in the range of G is easy if one presents the unique seed s such that the first bits are equal to $f^{|s|}(s)$ and that the remaining bits are not the hardcore bits.

For our simulator we can thus generate a perfectly distributed common random string by picking s randomly, computing $G(s)$, and randomly flipping the hardcore bits:

$$\mathrm{crs}^{\mathrm{aux}} \leftarrow G(s) \oplus 0^{|s|} \| t$$

where each bit $t_i \xleftarrow{\$} \{0,1\}$ in $t = t_1 \| \ldots \| t_{|s|}$ is chosen uniformly and independently. Unless all t_i's are 0 —which happens with probability $2^{-|s|}$— this gives the simulator a witness for $\mathrm{crs}^{\mathrm{aux}}$ not being pseudorandom in form of s, t. If $t = 0^{|s|}$ the we let the simulator abort. This unlikely event of all t_i's being 0 causes our simulator to be statistical zero-knowledge instead of being perfect zero-knowledge.

For the malicious prover in the soundness game we will hand over a pseudorandom string $G(s)$ instead of a truly random one. For the bounded prover this is computationally indistinguishable. But then the prover does not have a witness for the or-part and would thus need to break soundness of the other protocol part for $x \notin \mathcal{L}_{\mathcal{R}}$. This step preserves any exclusive soundness notion but not penalizing soundness, because we need to be able to detect diverging success behavior of the prover in the two cases (which we may not necessarily be able to in the penalizing setting since we cannot check if x is in the language or not).

Below we formally define the augmented language $\mathcal{L}_{\mathcal{R}}^{\mathrm{or}}$ as

$$\mathcal{L}_{\mathcal{R}}^{\mathrm{or}} = \left\{ (x,y) \mid \exists \omega : (x,\omega) \in \mathcal{R} \vee \exists s, t \in \{0,1\}^{\lfloor |y|/2 \rfloor} : y = G(s) \oplus 0^{|s|} \| t, t \neq 0^{|s|} \right\}$$

and the corresponding relation $\mathcal{R}^{\mathrm{or}}$ accordingly. Note that this is an NP-relation such that, if we have any single-theorem statistical NIZK for general NP-relations, then we also have a multi-theorem statistical witness-indistinguishable argument for this relation $\mathcal{R}^{\mathrm{or}}$.

For pseudorandomness of G we consider for any probabilistic polynomial-time algorithm $\mathcal{D}$ the probability that $\mathcal{D}(1^n, y_{b'}) = b'$ where the probability is taken over $b' \xleftarrow{\$} \{0,1\}$, $y_0 \leftarrow G(s)$ for $s \xleftarrow{\$} \{0,1\}^n$, $y_1 \xleftarrow{\$} \{0,1\}^{2n}$. Let $\mathsf{Adv}_{G,\mathsf{D}}^{\mathrm{PRG}}(1^n) := \Pr\left[\mathcal{D}(1^n, y_{b'}) = b'\right] - \frac{1}{2}$ be $\mathcal{D}$'s advantage. We say that G is a pseudorandom generator if for any probabilistic polynomial-time algorithm $\mathcal{D}$ this advantage is negligible. Note that the Blum-Micali-Yao generator based on a one-way permutation f achieves this property.

Construction 2 (SZK-FLS-Transformation). *Let $\mathcal{R}$ be an* NP-*relation. Let f be a one-way permutation and $\Pi^{\mathrm{or}} = (\mathsf{Setup}^{\mathrm{or}}, \mathsf{P}^{\mathrm{or}}, \mathsf{V}^{\mathrm{or}})$ be a multi-theorem non-interactive statistical witness-indistinguishable argument for the* NP-*relation $\mathcal{R}^{\mathrm{or}}$. We construct a multi-theorem non-interactive statistical zero knowledge argument $\Pi = (\mathsf{Setup}, \mathsf{P}, \mathsf{V})$ for $\mathcal{R}$ as follows (see also Fig. 5):*

Setup(1^n)	P($1^n,x,\omega$,crs)	V($1^n,x,\pi$,crs)
$\mathrm{crs}^{\mathrm{or}} \overset{\$}{\leftarrow} \mathsf{Setup}^{\mathrm{or}}(1^n)$	$/\!/ \ \mathrm{crs} = \mathrm{crs}^{\mathrm{or}}\|\mathrm{crs}^{\mathrm{aux}}$	$/\!/ \ \mathrm{crs} = \mathrm{crs}^{\mathrm{or}}\|\mathrm{crs}^{\mathrm{aux}}$
$\mathrm{crs}^{\mathrm{aux}} \overset{\$}{\leftarrow} \{0,1\}^{2n}$	$\pi^{\mathrm{or}} \overset{\$}{\leftarrow} \mathsf{P}^{\mathrm{or}}((x,\mathrm{crs}^{\mathrm{aux}}),\omega,\mathrm{crs}^{\mathrm{or}})$	$d \overset{\$}{\leftarrow} \mathsf{V}^{\mathrm{or}}((x,\mathrm{crs}^{\mathrm{aux}}),\pi,\mathrm{crs}^{\mathrm{or}})$
$\mathrm{crs} \leftarrow \mathrm{crs}^{\mathrm{or}}\|\mathrm{crs}^{\mathrm{aux}}$	$\pi \leftarrow \pi^{\mathrm{or}}$	**return** d
return crs	**return** π	

Fig. 5. SZK-FLS-Transformation for multi-theorem NISZK argument (additional input 1^n omitted for P^{or} and V^{or} for space reasons).

CRS: *We define the sampling algorithm* $\mathsf{Setup}(1^n)$ *for the common random string* crs *for our construction as*

$$\mathsf{Setup}(1^n) = \mathsf{Setup}^{\mathrm{or}}(1^n)\|U_{2n},$$

where U_{2n} *is the uniform distribution on all $2n$-bit strings.*

Prover: *The prover* P, *receiving* 1^n, $\mathrm{crs} = \mathrm{crs}^{\mathrm{or}}\|\mathrm{crs}^{\mathrm{aux}}$, x *and* ω *(for* $\mathcal{R}$*) as input, uses* $(x,\mathrm{crs}^{\mathrm{aux}})$ *and* ω *for the augmented relation* $\mathcal{R}^{\mathrm{or}}$ *and computes a witness-indistinguishable proof* π^{or} *for this* NP-*relation using the string* $\mathrm{crs}^{\mathrm{or}}$.

Verifier: *The verifier* V *receives* 1^n, $\mathrm{crs} = \mathrm{crs}^{\mathrm{or}}\|\mathrm{crs}^{\mathrm{aux}}$, x, *and a proof* π^{or} *for* $\mathcal{R}^{\mathrm{or}}$. *The verifier accepts iff* $\mathsf{V}^{\mathrm{or}}(1^n,(x,\mathrm{crs}^{\mathrm{aux}}),\pi^{\mathrm{or}},\mathrm{crs}^{\mathrm{or}})$ *accepts.*

Theorem 3. *Let* $\mathcal{R}$ *be an* NP-*relation. Assuming that* $\Pi^{\mathrm{or}} = (\mathsf{Setup}^{\mathrm{or}},\mathsf{P}^{\mathrm{or}},\mathsf{V}^{\mathrm{or}})$ *is a non-interactive statistical single-theorem zero-knowledge argument for* $\mathcal{R}^{\mathrm{or}}$ *and that* f *is a one-way permutation, the non-interactive argument system* $\Pi = (\mathsf{Setup},\mathsf{P},\mathsf{V})$ *in Construction 2 is a multi-theorem statistical zero-knowledge argument. Furthermore, if the underlying protocol* Π^{or} *is (non-adaptively resp. adaptively) exclusively sound, then so is the derived protocol* Π; *if* Π^{or} *is adaptive resp. non-adaptive zero-knowledge, then so is* Π.

Proof. *(Perfect) Completeness:* Note that the verifier V accepts a genuine proof $\pi^{\mathrm{or}} \overset{\$}{\leftarrow} \mathsf{P}(1^n,x,\omega,\mathrm{crs})$ for original data $\mathrm{crs} = \mathrm{crs}^{\mathrm{or}}\|\mathrm{crs}^{\mathrm{aux}} \overset{\$}{\leftarrow} \mathsf{Setup}(1^n)$ and $x \in \mathcal{L}_{\mathcal{R}}$ if and only if V^{or} accepts π^{or} for $(x,\mathrm{crs}^{\mathrm{aux}})$ under $\mathrm{crs}^{\mathrm{or}}$. The latter is always true since $x \in \mathcal{L}_{\mathcal{R}}$ such that the pair $(x,\mathrm{crs}^{\mathrm{aux}})$ of the or-relation is also in $\mathcal{L}_{\mathcal{R}}^{\mathrm{or}}$, the output of P is given by the output of P^{or} for valid input, and the verifier V^{or} accepts genuine proofs of P^{or}.

Non-adaptive/Exclusive Soundness: Assume that Π^{or} is non-adaptively/exclusively sound. Our argument to show that Π, too, has this property is as follows. We will first substitute the "real" common random string by one in which the augmented component $\mathrm{crs}^{\mathrm{aux}}$ is always in the range of the pseudorandom generator G. This will be indistinguishable for the bounded prover P^* such that P^* outputs a valid proof with roughly equal probability for pseudorandom G. In this step we exploit the property of non-adaptive/exclusive soundness that

$x \notin \mathcal{L}_\mathcal{R}$ is chosen before crs. But then the or-language does not have a witness for either part, such that the malicious prover would have to break (non-adaptive) exclusive soundness of the protocol for $\mathcal{R}^{\mathrm{or}}$.

More formally, let crs be a CRS generated as described above and crs_G an artificial CRS generated as

$$\mathrm{crs}_G \leftarrow \mathsf{Setup}^{\mathrm{or}}(1^n)\|G(s),$$

where s is chosen uniformly from $\{0,1\}^n$. In a first game hop we argue that a successful malicious prover P^* for such a CRS is almost as successful as for a genuine one, that is,

$$\Pr\left[\mathsf{V}(1^n, x, \pi, \mathrm{crs}) = 1\right] \approx \Pr\left[\mathsf{V}(1^n, x, \pi, \mathrm{crs}_G) = 1\right]$$

are negligibly close, where the probability is over $(x, \mathrm{st}) \xleftarrow{\$} \mathsf{P}^*(1^n)$, $\mathrm{crs} \xleftarrow{\$} \mathsf{Setup}(1^n)$ and $\pi \xleftarrow{\$} \mathsf{P}^*(1^n, \mathrm{st}, \mathrm{crs})$ and V's randomness in the first case, and accordingly over $(x, \mathrm{st}) \xleftarrow{\$} \mathsf{P}^*(1^n)$, $\mathrm{crs}_G \xleftarrow{\$} \mathsf{Setup}^{\mathrm{or}}(1^n)\|G(s)$, $\pi \xleftarrow{\$} \mathsf{P}^*(1^n, \mathrm{st}, \mathrm{crs}_G)$ and V's randomness in the second case.

We show the indistinguishability by defining a distinguisher $\mathcal{D}$ against the pseudorandom generator G. For security parameter n the distinguisher receives a string $y \in \{0,1\}^{2n}$ as input, either picked uniformly at random, or being the output of the pseudorandom generator. The distinguisher then invokes the prover and verifier to decide:

$$
\begin{array}{l}
\underline{\mathcal{D}(1^n, y)} \\[2pt]
(x, \mathrm{st}) \xleftarrow{\$} \mathsf{P}^*(1^n) \\
\mathrm{crs}^{\mathrm{or}} \xleftarrow{\$} \mathsf{Setup}^{\mathrm{or}}(1^n) \\
\mathrm{crs} \leftarrow \mathrm{crs}^{\mathrm{or}}\|y \\
\pi \xleftarrow{\$} \mathsf{P}^*(1^n, \mathrm{st}, crs) \\
\textbf{return } \mathsf{V}(1^n, x, \pi, \mathrm{crs})
\end{array}
$$

We claim that the distinguishing advantage bounds the difference between the two games, where G_0 is the original soundness game (with output 1 indicating that P^* has won) and G_1 describes the game where we use the artificial string crs_G instead. Since the two games correspond syntactically to the cases that the distinguisher receives a random y resp. a pseudorandom y we get:

$$\Pr[\mathsf{G}_0(1^n) = 1] - \Pr[\mathsf{G}_1(1^n)] \le 2 \cdot \mathsf{Adv}^{\mathrm{PRG}}_{G,\mathsf{D}}(1^n).$$

Next we turn the malicious prover P^* in G_1 against non-adaptive/exclusive soundness against the unbounded scheme Π into one of the same type for the augmented scheme Π^{or}. Note that we are guaranteed that P^* always outputs $x \notin \mathcal{L}_\mathcal{R}$ by assumption. Our prover $\mathsf{P}^*_{\mathrm{or}}$ against Π^{or} works as follows:

$\mathsf{P}_{\mathrm{or}}^*(1^n)$	$\mathsf{P}_{\mathrm{or}}^*(1^n, \mathrm{st}_{\mathrm{or}}, \mathrm{crs}^{\mathrm{or}})$
$(x, \mathrm{st}) \xleftarrow{\$} \mathsf{P}^*(1^n)$	$/\!/ \; \mathrm{st}_{\mathrm{or}} = (\mathrm{st}, \mathrm{crs}^{\mathrm{aux}})$
$s \xleftarrow{\$} \{0,1\}^n$	$\mathrm{crs} \leftarrow \mathrm{crs}^{\mathrm{or}} \| \mathrm{crs}^{\mathrm{aux}}$
$\mathrm{crs}^{\mathrm{aux}} \leftarrow G(s)$	$\pi \xleftarrow{\$} \mathsf{P}^*(1^n, \mathrm{st}, \mathrm{crs})$
$\mathrm{st}_{\mathrm{or}} \leftarrow (\mathrm{st}, \mathrm{crs}^{\mathrm{aux}})$	**return** π
return $((x, \mathrm{crs}^{\mathrm{aux}}), \mathrm{st}_{\mathrm{or}})$	

We first observe that, if P^* always outputs $x \notin \mathcal{L}_{\mathcal{R}}$, then our prover $\mathsf{P}_{\mathrm{or}}^*$ always outputs $(x, \mathrm{crs}^{\mathrm{aux}}) \notin \mathcal{L}_{\mathcal{R}}^{\mathrm{or}}$. This holds as the string $\mathrm{crs}^{\mathrm{aux}}$ is pseudorandom such that neither condition of the or-language is satisfied. In addition, $\mathsf{P}_{\mathrm{or}}^*$ is efficient. Hence, $\mathsf{P}_{\mathrm{or}}^*$ is also an admissible attacker against non-adaptive/exclusive soundness, this time against $\mathcal{L}_{\mathcal{R}}^{\mathrm{or}}$.

We conclude that, by the soundness of Π^{or}, the success probability of prover $\mathsf{P}_{\mathrm{or}}^*$ must be negligible. But because $\mathsf{P}_{\mathrm{or}}^*$ has the same success probability as P^* in G_1 it follows that the winning probability of P^* in G_1 must also be negligible. Since this success probability is negligibly close to the one of P^* in G_0 by the pseudorandomness of G, we derive that P^* success probability against our derived protocol Π must be negligible.

Adaptive/Exclusive Soundness: The proof in the adaptive case follows exactly as in the non-adaptive case. Only this time P^* chooses $x \notin \mathcal{L}_{\mathcal{R}}$ after seeing crs. But both the distinguisher $\mathcal{D}$ against the pseudorandomness $\mathcal{D}$, as well as the prover $\mathsf{P}_{\mathrm{or}}^*$ against soundness, can assemble the common random string before P^* selects x. It follows as before that the probability of $\mathsf{P}_{\mathrm{or}}^*$ against adaptive/exclusive soundness of Π^{or} and thus the one of P^* against Π must be negligible.

Zero Knowledge: The simulator ZKSim works as follows: On input 1^n it first generates $\mathrm{crs} = \mathrm{crs}^{\mathrm{or}} \| \mathrm{crs}^{\mathrm{aux}}$, where $\mathrm{crs}^{\mathrm{or}} \xleftarrow{\$} \mathsf{Setup}^{\mathrm{or}}(1^n)$ and $\mathrm{crs}^{\mathrm{aux}}$ is sampled as

$$\mathrm{crs}^{\mathrm{aux}} \leftarrow G(s) \oplus 0^{|s|} \| t$$

for s, t chosen uniformly from $\{0,1\}^n$. Note that since f is a permutation this CRS has the same distribution as a truly random string. If $t = 0^{|s|}$ then the simulator immediately aborts. Else it outputs crs as the common random string and (s, t) as state $\mathrm{st}_{\mathsf{ZKSim}}$. When receiving a (valid) theorem $x \in \mathcal{L}_{\mathcal{R}}$ the simulator runs the prover P^{or} for $\mathcal{R}^{\mathrm{or}}$ on input $1^n, (x, \mathrm{crs}^{\mathrm{aux}}), \mathrm{crs}^{\mathrm{or}}$ and witness (s, t) to generate a proof π^{or}. The state remains unchanged.

By assumption, Π^{or} is single-theorem statistical zero knowledge (either adaptively or non-adaptively secure). Further, by Lemma 1 it is single-theorem statistical witness indistinguishable, and by Lemma 2 also multi-theorem statistical witness indistinguishable for the same level of adaptiveness. Therefore, whenever ZKSim is able to find a valid $t \neq 0^{|s|}$, the statistical distance between genuine proofs by P^{or} (for witness ω) and proofs by ZKSim resp. P^{or} (with witness (s, t)) is given by a negligible term $\epsilon(n)$ for any distinguisher requesting at most q proofs. As ZKSim fails to derive $t \neq 0^{|s|}$ with probability 2^{-n}, the overall statistical distance is therefore at most $\epsilon(n)+2^{-n}$ and thus negligible. Thus, $\Pi = (\mathsf{Setup}, \mathsf{P}, \mathsf{V})$ is multi-theorem statistical zero knowledge. We note that the protocol inherits the notion of zero-knowledge adaptiveness from Π^{or}.   □

We remark that the transformation also preserves adaptive/culpable soundness. For this notion the distinguisher against the pseudorandom generator in the soundness part can check efficiently if the prover's choice x is in the language or not with the help of the witness ω_{guilt} which the prover needs to output, too.

4.2   Adaptive Perfect Zero-Knowledge Under Expected Poly-Time

The construction in the previous section displays a small error in the simulation, even if we would start with a perfect zero-knowledge or witness-indistinguishable argument. The reason is that our simulator may not generate a valid pair (s, t) with $t \neq 0^{|s|}$. However, to preserve perfect zero-knowledge the simulator cannot simply discard such bad pairs, else outputs of the form $G(s)$ would not be hit (while a uniformly chosen string may actually be in the range of G).

The solution in the single-theorem case is to use the fact that the event of picking bad t's is very unlikely, namely, 2^{-n}. We will now decrease the probability further such that we can safely search for the actual witness ω for the x part in this rare case, without violating polynomial run time on the average. For this let $p_{\mathcal{R}}$ denote the polynomial which bounds the witness length of relation $\mathcal{R}$. Then we use a pseudorandom generator $G(s)$ as before, but we iterate the one-way permutation f for $p_{\mathcal{R}}(n)$ steps. Now the probability of picking some input $(s, t) \in \{0,1\}^n \times \{0,1\}^{p_{\mathcal{R}}(n)}$ with $t = 0^{p_{\mathcal{R}}(n)}$ is $2^{-p_{\mathcal{R}}(n)}$. Given that this happens we let the simulator (later, after having obtained the input x) search through all potential witnesses $w \in \{0,1\}^{\leq p_{\mathcal{R}}(n)}$ and each time check in polynomial time $q_{\mathcal{R}}(n)$ if $(x, w) \in \mathcal{R}$. The run time of the simulator for the exhaustive search is then bounded from above by $2 \cdot 2^{p_{\mathcal{R}}(n)} \cdot q_{\mathcal{R}}(n)$. But since this step is only executed with probability at most $2^{-p_{\mathcal{R}}(n)}$ the overall run time of the simulator remains polynomial in expectation.

If we assume that the original argument system Π^{or} is perfectly witness indistinguishable for non-adaptively chosen statements, then the derived protocol is perfectly zero-knowledge, with as simulator running in expected polynomial time and holding either a witness s, t for the auxiliary part or a witness for x to compute the proof. As in the statistical case, the protocol still preserves non-adaptive/exclusive or adaptive/exclusive soundness.

The next step is to extend the above idea to multiple theorems. If we have polynomial many statements $x_1, \ldots, x_q$ then we would have to search for all witnesses to simulate the proofs if $t = 0 \ldots 0$. But the time to search for all these witnesses by brute force is additive and requires at most $2q \cdot q_{\mathcal{R}}(n) \cdot 2^{p_{\mathcal{R}}(n)}$ many steps. Hence, the expected run time is still polynomial.

We finally remark that our simulator only attains the simple notion of expected polynomial where we average the number of steps over the randomness of the algorithm. It is not known if one can modify the simulator to achieve more robust notions, such as Levin's average-time complexity.

5 A Lattice-based Construction

The main drawbacks of the previous constructions based on general assumptions is that they are not directly applicable to lattice-based problems because they require a one-way permutation. In this section we therefore present a multi-theorem extension in the common random string using dual-mode commitments, based on the Learning-With-Errors (LWE) assumption.

5.1 Dual-mode Commitment Schemes Based on Lattices

A (non-interactive) commitment scheme consists of a probabilistic polynomial-time algorithm to generate a public key and another probabilistic polynomial-time algorithm which allows to commit to a message under a public key. The scheme can be statistically-hiding (and computationally-binding), or it can be perfectly-binding (and computationally-hiding). A dual-mode scheme has now two key generation algorithms, one for the statistically-hiding and one for the perfectly-binding case. Furthermore, the output of the two key generation algorithms is computationally indistinguishable. To preserve statistical zero-knowledge we make the additional assumption that the public key output in hiding mode is close to uniform:

Definition 6 (Dual-mode Commitment Scheme). *A non-interactive commitment scheme $\Gamma = (Gen_H, Gen_B, Com)$ is called a* dual-mode commitment scheme *if,*

Statistically-Hiding Mode: *The scheme (Gen_H, Com) is a statistically-hiding, computationally-binding commitment scheme. Furthermore, the output of Gen_H is statistically close to the uniform distribution.*

Perfectly-Binding Mode: *The scheme (Gen_B, Com) is a perfectly-binding, computationally-hiding commitment scheme.*

Indistinguishability of Modes: *The random variables Gen_H and Gen_B are computationally indistinguishable.*

Note that for a dual commitment scheme, it suffices to show that the scheme is statistically-hiding in the hiding mode, perfectly-binding in the binding mode, and that the modes are computationally indistinguishable. The complementary property of the corresponding mode (with computational guarantees) follows immediately.

For the dual-mode commitments, we will use (a stripped-off version of) the two homomorphic trapdoor functions defined by Gorbunov et al. [23]. As pointed out in [13], these two trapdoor functions give rise to a dual-mode commitment scheme. It has been shown in [13] that it can be used together with a non-interactive witness-indistinguishable proof system for bounded distance decoding to build non-interactive *designated-verifier* computational zero-knowledge arguments. We will describe this dual-mode commitment scheme now in detail and provide proof sketches based on the security proofs in [23].

The construction of the commitment scheme in [23] itself is based on the SIS problem [2], stating that for parameters $n, m = \text{poly}(n), q$ and β_{SIS} it is hard to find a short non-zero integer vector u (of length at most β_{SIS}) to a given random $n \times m$-matrix A over $\mathbb{Z}_q$ such that $Au = 0$. The noteworthy property is that there is also a method to generate an $n \times m$ matrix A over $\mathbb{Z}_q$ together with a trapdoor in a secure way. This is implemented by an algorithm TrapGen, taking $1^n, 1^m$ and q as input. Furthermore, there exists an algorithm $\text{Sam}(1^m, 1^m, q)$ which outputs a "small" matrix $U \in \mathbb{Z}_q^{m \times m}$. As discussed in [23] it holds that A generated by $\text{TrapGen}(1^n, 1^m, q)$ is statistically close to uniform, and that A and $A \cdot U$ (sampled according to Sam) are statistically close to A and a uniform matrix V'. The final ingredient is a fixed and easy to compute matrix $G \in \mathbb{Z}_q^{n \times m}$ for the given parameter which allows us to build the commitment scheme. We can then commit to a value $x \in \mathbb{Z}_q$ for matrix A by computing $A \cdot U + x \cdot G$. Note that since $A \cdot U$ is statistically close to a uniform matrix V' we obtain that x is statistically hidden.

We note that we do not take advantage of the trapdoor property here in our construction, but instead sample a uniform matrix A (in the hiding mode). Moreover, as pointed out in [13], the SIS assumption is not necessary either. The LWE assumption suffices for our purpose, since we only need that the mode switching is computationally indistinguishable. Indeed, the same could be already accomplished with Regev's encryption scheme [33] where one can alter to a lossy mode. We describe the dual-commitment scheme more formally in the following constructions:

Construction 4 (Hiding-mode Commitment Scheme).

Key Generation Gen$_H$: *We sample $A \in \mathbb{Z}_q^{n \times m}$ uniformly and set $pk \leftarrow A$.*
Commitment Com: *For input pk and $x \in \mathbb{Z}_q$, we sample $U \leftarrow \text{Sam}(1^m, 1^m, q)$ and return $\text{Com}(pk, x; U) = pk \cdot U + x \cdot G$. To open the commitment, we reveal x and U (or the randomness used to sample U).*

Proposition 2. *Construction 4 is a statistically hiding commitment scheme.*

Proof. As shown in [23], we have that the following two tuples are statistically close:

$$(pk, x, pk \cdot U + x \cdot G) \equiv_s (pk, x, V')$$

where $U \leftarrow \text{Sam}(1^m, 1^m, q)$ and $V' \leftarrow \mathbb{Z}_q^{n \times m}$, i.e., the commitment is statistically indistinguishable from a random matrix. This holds for public keys generated by TrapGen and, since that algorithm's output is close to uniform, also for the random matrix A.   □

Next we recall from [23] how we can switch to a perfectly-binding mode by assuming the hardness of LWE. This problem states that given a matrix A and $As + e$ for a small error vector e sampled from a distribution χ, recovering s is hard [33].

Construction 5 (Binding-mode Commitment Scheme).

Key Generation $\mathbf{Gen}_B$: *We sample $A' \leftarrow \mathbb{Z}_q^{(n-1) \times m}$ uniformly and $s' \xleftarrow{\$} \mathbb{Z}_q^{n-1}$ and set*

$$pk \leftarrow \begin{pmatrix} A' \\ s'A' + e \end{pmatrix},$$

where e is a short "noise vector" sampled from χ.

Commitment Com: *The commitment is identical to the one in Construction 4.*

Proposition 3. *Construction 5 is a perfectly binding commitment scheme.*

Proof. To show this construction is perfectly binding, it suffices to show that we can uniquely recover x using s. Indeed, if we know s', we can set $s = (-s', 1)$ and $z = (0, \ldots, 0, r)$ and calculate

$$s \left(pk \cdot U + x \cdot G \right) G^{-1}(z) = e \cdot U \cdot G^{-1}(z) + x \cdot \langle s, z \rangle = x \cdot r + e'.$$

Note that G^{-1} is a polynomial-time algorithm whose existence is guaranteed by Lemma 2.2 in [23]. For correctly chosen parameters r and e, this lets us recover x uniquely. Now, as s does not depend on x or U, if for two pairs (x, U) and (x', U')

$$pk \cdot U + x \cdot G = pk \cdot U' + x' \cdot G,$$

holds, then we have $x = x'$. $\qquad\square$

Proposition 4. *Assuming the $LWE(q, \chi)$-assumption holds, Constructions 4 and 5 together form a dual-mode commitment scheme.*

Proof. We start by showing that the public keys of both schemes are computationally indistinguishable. First, note that all but the last column of matrix A are generated uniformly random (or statistically close to that) for both public keys. Therefore, the problem is equivalent to distinguish between $A's + e$ and v' given A', where $v' \in \mathbb{Z}_q^n$ is a uniformly random vector and s and e are sampled as described in the scheme. However, this is exactly the decisional LWE problem. By our assumption, the two public keys are therefore indistinguishable.

We have not yet shown that Construction 4 is computationally binding and that Construction 5 is computationally hiding. However, we argue this follows directly from what we have shown already. Assume Construction 5 would not be computationally hiding, i.e., there exists an adversary that, given a public key pk, can distinguish between a commitment to x and x' with notable advantage. However, in this case, we can use this adversary to distinguish the public keys of the schemes, as Construction 4 is statistically hiding and no adversary with notable advantage can exist here.

Similarly, assume that Construction 4 is not computationally binding. Then, there exists an adversary that, given a public key pk, can generate a commitment c that opens to two values x and x' with non-negligible probability. However, as Construction 5 is perfectly binding, we can use such an adversary to distinguish between public keys of the two schemes. $\qquad\square$

5.2 SZK-FLS-Transformation Based on Lattices

We will now define our multi-theorem transformation based on the dual-mode commitment scheme in the previous section. As before, we will use the FLS-type transform, therefore we only need to define a sampling algorithm for the auxiliary CRS $\mathrm{crs}^{\mathrm{aux}}$ and an augmented or-relation $\mathcal{R}^{\mathrm{or}}$ for this string.

The sampling algorithm $\mathsf{Setup}^{\mathrm{aux}}$ to generate $\mathrm{crs}^{\mathrm{aux}}$ will just generate uniformly random values representing a public key pk and a commitment c:

$$\mathrm{crs}^{\mathrm{aux}} = (\mathrm{pk}, c) \leftarrow U_{nmq} \times U_{nmq}.$$

Note that a random public key corresponds to the hiding-mode public key.

Technically the public key and the commitment in $\mathrm{crs}^{\mathrm{aux}}$ are matrices over $\mathbb{Z}_q$, and not uniform strings as required by the common random string model. However, we can generate random elements in $\mathbb{Z}_q$ from uniform strings by interpreting a random string of length $|q| + n$ as an integer and mapping it to the residue mod q. The statistically distance to a uniform element from $\mathbb{Z}_q$ is then exponentially small. We stress that we can also go "backwards" with this technique. Given a random value $v \in \mathbb{Z}_q$ we can add a random multiple $i \cdot q$ to v for $i \xleftarrow{\$} \{0, 1, \ldots, 2^{n-1}\}$ to get an (almost) uniform $|q| + n$ bit string which would map to v again. Hence, from now on we switch between random matrices from $\mathbb{Z}_q$ and uniformly random string whenever convenient.

Our relation will now ask for a given public key pk of the commitment scheme and commitment c, both found in the common random string, if there is a matrix $U \leftarrow \mathsf{Sam}(1^m, 1^m, q)$ resp. randomness u such that $U = \mathsf{Sam}(1^m, 1^m, q; u)$, such that the commitment opens to 1:

$$((\mathrm{pk}, c), u) \in \mathcal{R}^{\mathrm{or}} :\Longleftrightarrow U = \mathsf{Sam}(1^m, 1^m, q; u) \wedge c = \mathsf{Com}(\mathrm{pk}, 1; U).$$

Given these two properties we can now use the same construction as for the one-way permutation, only that we use the relation above and the sampler $\mathsf{Setup}^{\mathrm{aux}}$ to generate $\mathrm{crs}^{\mathrm{aux}}$. In fact the construction is otherwise identical to the one in Fig. 5:

Construction 6 (SZK-FLS-Dual-Mode-Transformation). *Let $\mathcal{R}$ be an NP-relation. Further, let $\Gamma = (\mathsf{Gen}_H, \mathsf{Gen}_B, \mathsf{Com})$ be a non-interactive dual-mode commitment scheme and suppose that $\Pi^{or} = (\mathsf{Setup}^{or}, P^{or}, V^{or})$ be a multi-theorem non-interactive statistical witness-indistinguishable argument for the NP-relation $\mathcal{R}^{or}$. We construct a multi-theorem non-interactive statistical zero knowledge argument $\Pi = (\mathsf{Setup}, P, V)$ for $\mathcal{R}$ as in Fig. 5 with the following exception:*

CRS: *We define the sampling algorithm $\mathsf{Setup}(1^n)$ for the common random string crs for our construction as*

$$\mathsf{Setup}(1^n) = \mathsf{Setup}^{or}(1^n) \| \mathsf{Setup}^{aux}(1^n).$$

The prover algorithm P and verifier algorithm V are as before.

Theorem 7. *Let $\mathcal{R}$ be an* NP-*relation. Assuming that $\Pi^{or} = (\mathsf{Setup}^{or}, \mathsf{P}^{or}, \mathsf{V}^{or})$ is a non-interactive statistical single-theorem zero-knowledge argument for $\mathcal{R}^{or}$ and that $\Gamma = (\mathsf{Gen}_H, \mathsf{Gen}_B, \mathsf{Com})$ is a dual-mode non-interactive commitment scheme, the non-interactive argument $\Pi = (\mathsf{Setup}, \mathsf{P}, \mathsf{V})$ in Construction 6 is a multi-theorem statistical zero-knowledge argument. Furthermore, if the underlying protocol Π^{or} is (non-adaptively resp. adaptively) exclusively sound, then so is the derived protocol Π; if Π^{or} is adaptive resp. non-adaptive zero-knowledge, then so is Π.*

Proof. The proof is very close to the one of Theorem 3 such that we only sketch the main differences here.

(Perfect) Completeness: It follows as in the one-way permutation case that the honest verifier accepts proofs generated by P for $x \in \mathcal{L}_{\mathcal{R}}$.

Exclusive Soundness: To show exclusive soundness (in the non-adaptive or adaptive case) we first switch the auxiliary string to a randomly sampled binding key $\mathrm{pk} \stackrel{\$}{\leftarrow} \mathsf{Gen}_B(1^n)$ and a 0-commitment $\mathsf{Com}(\mathrm{pk}, 0; U)$, instead of using uniformly random values. Note that we can use two game hops to show that this is computationally indistinguishable from genuine common random strings. In the first hop we replace the random key component in $\mathrm{crs}^{\mathrm{aux}}$ by a key $\mathrm{pk} \stackrel{\$}{\leftarrow} \mathsf{Gen}_H(1^n)$, which is even statistically close. Then we replace the random commitment component in $\mathrm{crs}^{\mathrm{aux}}$ by a random commitment to 0, $\mathsf{Com}(\mathrm{pk}, 0; U)$. This is again statistically indistinguishable.

And finally we switch to a binding key $\mathrm{pk} \stackrel{\$}{\leftarrow} \mathsf{Gen}_B(1^n)$ and a 0-commitment under this key. This is computationally indistinguishable by the indistinguishability of the dual-mode key generation. (The additional 0-commitment can be computed easily given a hiding or binding key.) This is where we again use exclusive soundness to turn a malicious prover into a distinguisher against the dual-mode scheme, analogously to the distinguisher against the pseudorandomness of the generator in the one-way permutation case.

We now have an auxiliary string which contains a binding key and a 0-commitment, such that the or-part in the $\mathcal{R}^{or}$ cannot be satisfied. It follows now as before that soundness of the constructed protocol follows from the soundness of the original non-interactive argument.

Zero-Knowledge: For adaptive multi-theorem zero-knowledge we remark that the simulator ZKSim can create the key part in the auxiliary string as a hiding key $\mathrm{pk} \stackrel{\$}{\leftarrow} \mathsf{Gen}_H(1^n)$ and the commitment part as a 1-commitment under pk. Since the key pk and the 1-commitment are statistically close to a uniform strings, the simulator's string $\mathrm{crs}^{\mathrm{aux}}$ is statistically close to a uniform string. For this string $\mathrm{crs}^{\mathrm{aux}}$ the simulator can use the randomness of the commitment as a witness. The remaining steps in the proof are identical to the ones in the proof of Theorem 3. $\qquad\square$

6   Conclusion

We have shown how to apply the idea of the FLS transformation also for statistical zero-knowledge arguments. Let us highlight two important aspects of our transformations.

First, our transformations based on one-way permutations and on lattices work in the common *random* string model and does not require any structure of the CRS. Common *reference* strings have the inherent disadvantage that they have some structure and that one needs to trust the party which generates the string. A prominent example is the discussion about the trustworthiness of the Zcash reference string and follow-up suggestions to use common random strings instead, e.g., [16]. Of course, a party generating a common *random* string may also impose some trust assumption, as our lattice-based solution with the implicit trapdoor generation algorithm shows. But several measures to thwart attacks can be implemented much easier than for structured strings. This includes the computation of the string as the output of a hash function, or by xoring common random strings from several sources.

The other aspect we would like to emphasize that our transformations preserve adaptive security for both zero-knowledge and soundness. This does not conflict with black-box impossibility result for such statistical zero-knowledge arguments [1,30], because in the course of showing adaptive soundness we have, in passing, encountered a possibility to bypass the impossibility results. A key observation is that one may be able to achieve adaptive soundness and zero-knowledge if one switches to the notion of exclusive soundness. This adaptive/exclusive soundness implies adaptive/culpable soundness and thus suffices for many practical applications.

Acknowledgments. We thank the anonymous reviewers for valuable comments. Funded by the Deutsche Forschungsgemeinschaft (DFG, German Research Foundation) – SFB 1119 – 236615297.

References

1. Abe, M., Fehr, S.: Perfect NIZK with adaptive soundness. In: Vadhan, S.P. (ed.) TCC 2007. LNCS, vol. 4392, pp. 118–136. Springer, Heidelberg (2007). https://doi.org/10.1007/978-3-540-70936-7_7
2. Ajtai, M.: Generating hard instances of lattice problems (extended abstract). In: 28th ACM STOC, pp. 99–108. ACM Press, May 1996
3. Arte, V., Bellare, M.: Dual-Mode NIZKs: possibility and impossibility results for property transfer. In: Bhargavan, K., Oswald, E., Prabhakaran, M. (eds.) INDOCRYPT 2020. LNCS, vol. 12578, pp. 859–881. Springer, Cham (2020). https://doi.org/10.1007/978-3-030-65277-7_38
4. Bellare, M., Hofheinz, D., Kiltz, E.: Subtleties in the definition of IND-CCA: when and how should challenge decryption be disallowed? J. Cryptol. **28**(1), 29–48 (2015)
5. Blum, M., Feldman, P., Micali, S.: Non-interactive zero-knowledge and its applications (extended abstract). In: 20th ACM STOC. pp. 103–112. ACM Press, May 1988

6. Blum, M., Micali, S.: How to generate cryptographically strong sequences of pseudo-random bits. SIAM J. Comput. **13**(4), 850–864 (1984). https://doi.org/10.1137/0213053

7. Blum, M., Santis, A.D., Micali, S., Persiano, G.: Noninteractive zero-knowledge. SIAM J. Comput. **20**(6), 1084–1118 (1991). https://doi.org/10.1137/0220068

8. Brassard, G., Chaum, D., Crépeau, C.: Minimum disclosure proofs of knowledge. J. Comput. Syst. Sci. **37**(2), 156–189 (1988). https://doi.org/10.1016/0022-0000(88)90005-0

9. Canetti, R., et al.: Fiat-Shamir: from practice to theory. In: Charikar, M., Cohen, E. (eds.) 51st ACM STOC, pp. 1082–1090. ACM Press, June 2019

10. Canetti, R., Chen, Y., Reyzin, L., Rothblum, R.D.: Fiat-Shamir and correlation intractability from strong KDM-secure encryption. In: Nielsen, J.B., Rijmen, V. (eds.) EUROCRYPT 2018. LNCS, vol. 10820, pp. 91–122. Springer, Cham (2018). https://doi.org/10.1007/978-3-319-78381-9_4

11. Canetti, R., Lombardi, A., Wichs, D.: Fiat-Shamir: from practice to theory, Part II (NIZK and correlation intractability from circular-secure FHE). Cryptology ePrint Archive, Report 2018/1248 (2018). https://eprint.iacr.org/2018/1248

12. Chaidos, P., Groth, J.: Making sigma-protocols non-interactive without random oracles. In: Katz, J. (ed.) PKC 2015. LNCS, vol. 9020, pp. 650–670. Springer, Heidelberg (2015). https://doi.org/10.1007/978-3-662-46447-2_29

13. Couteau, G., Hofheinz, D.: Designated-verifier pseudorandom generators, and their applications. In: Ishai, Y., Rijmen, V. (eds.) EUROCRYPT 2019. LNCS, vol. 11477, pp. 562–592. Springer, Cham (2019). https://doi.org/10.1007/978-3-030-17656-3_20

14. Fauzi, P., Lipmaa, H.: Efficient culpably sound NIZK shuffle argument without random oracles. In: Sako, K. (ed.) CT-RSA 2016. LNCS, vol. 9610, pp. 200–216. Springer, Cham (2016). https://doi.org/10.1007/978-3-319-29485-8_12

15. Fauzi, P., Lipmaa, H., Siim, J., Zając, M.: An efficient pairing-based shuffle argument. In: Takagi, T., Peyrin, T. (eds.) ASIACRYPT 2017. LNCS, vol. 10625, pp. 97–127. Springer, Cham (2017). https://doi.org/10.1007/978-3-319-70697-9_4

16. Fauzi, P., Meiklejohn, S., Mercer, R., Orlandi, C.: Quisquis: a new design for anonymous cryptocurrencies. In: Galbraith, S.D., Moriai, S. (eds.) ASIACRYPT 2019. LNCS, vol. 11921, pp. 649–678. Springer, Cham (2019). https://doi.org/10.1007/978-3-030-34578-5_23

17. Feige, U., Lapidot, D., Shamir, A.: Multiple non-interactive zero knowledge proofs based on a single random string (extended abstract). In: 31st FOCS, pp. 308–317. IEEE Computer Society Press, October 1990

18. Feige, U., Lapidot, D., Shamir, A.: Multiple noninteractive zero knowledge proofs under general assumptions. SIAM J. Comput. **29**(1), 1–28 (1999). https://doi.org/10.1137/S0097539792230010

19. Feige, U., Shamir, A.: Witness indistinguishable and witness hiding protocols. In: 22nd ACM STOC, pp. 416–426. ACM Press, May 1990

20. Fischlin, M., Rohrbach, F.: Single-to-multi-theorem transformations for non-interactive statistical zero-knowledge. Cryptology ePrint Archive, Report 2020/1204 (2020). https://eprint.iacr.org/2020/1204

21. Goldreich, O.: Foundations of Cryptography, vol. 1. Cambridge University Press, Cambridge (2006)

22. Goldwasser, S., Micali, S., Rackoff, C.: The knowledge complexity of interactive proof systems. SIAM J. Comput. **18**(1), 186–208 (1989). https://doi.org/10.1137/0218012

23. Gorbunov, S., Vaikuntanathan, V., Wichs, D.: Leveled fully homomorphic signatures from standard lattices. In: Servedio, R.A., Rubinfeld, R. (eds.) 47th ACM STOC, pp. 469–477. ACM Press, June 2015

24. Groth, J., Lu, S.: A non-interactive shuffle with pairing based verifiability. In: Kurosawa, K. (ed.) ASIACRYPT 2007. LNCS, vol. 4833, pp. 51–67. Springer, Heidelberg (2007). https://doi.org/10.1007/978-3-540-76900-2_4

25. Groth, J., Ostrovsky, R., Sahai, A.: Perfect non-interactive zero knowledge for NP. In: Vaudenay, S. (ed.) EUROCRYPT 2006. LNCS, vol. 4004, pp. 339–358. Springer, Heidelberg (2006). https://doi.org/10.1007/11761679_21

26. Groth, J., Ostrovsky, R., Sahai, A.: New techniques for noninteractive zero-knowledge. J. ACM **59**(3), 111–1135 (2012). https://doi.org/10.1145/2220357.2220358

27. Holmgren, J., Lombardi, A.: Cryptographic hashing from strong one-way functions (or: One-way product functions and their applications). In: Thorup, M. (ed.) 59th FOCS, pp. 850–858. IEEE Computer Society Press, October 2018

28. Libert, B., Nguyen, K., Passelègue, A., Titiu, R.: Simulation-sound arguments for LWE and applications to KDM-CCA2 security. In: Moriai, S., Wang, H. (eds.) ASIACRYPT 2020. LNCS, vol. 12491, pp. 128–158. Springer, Cham (2020). https://doi.org/10.1007/978-3-030-64837-4_5

29. Libert, B., Passelègue, A., Wee, H., Wu, D.J.: New constructions of statistical NIZKs: dual-mode DV-NIZKs and more. In: Canteaut, A., Ishai, Y. (eds.) EUROCRYPT 2020. LNCS, vol. 12107, pp. 410–441. Springer, Cham (2020). https://doi.org/10.1007/978-3-030-45727-3_14

30. Pass, R.: Unprovable security of perfect NIZK and non-interactive non-malleable commitments. Comput. Complex. **25**(3), 607–666 (2016). https://doi.org/10.1007/s00037-016-0122-2

31. Pass, R., Shelat, A.: Unconditional characterizations of non-interactive zero-knowledge. In: Shoup, V. (ed.) CRYPTO 2005. LNCS, vol. 3621, pp. 118–134. Springer, Heidelberg (2005). https://doi.org/10.1007/11535218_8

32. Peikert, C., Shiehian, S.: Noninteractive zero knowledge for NP from (plain) learning with errors. In: Boldyreva, A., Micciancio, D. (eds.) CRYPTO 2019. LNCS, vol. 11692, pp. 89–114. Springer, Cham (2019). https://doi.org/10.1007/978-3-030-26948-7_4

33. Regev, O.: On lattices, learning with errors, random linear codes, and cryptography. In: Gabow, H.N., Fagin, R. (eds.) 37th ACM STOC. pp. 84–93. ACM Press, May 2005

34. Sahai, A., Waters, B.: How to use indistinguishability obfuscation: deniable encryption, and more. In: Shmoys, D.B. (ed.) 46th ACM STOC, pp. 475–484. ACM Press, May/June 2014

35. Yao, A.C.C.: Theory and applications of trapdoor functions (extended abstract). In: 23rd FOCS, pp. 80–91. IEEE Computer Society Press, November 1982

On the CCA Compatibility of Public-Key Infrastructure

Dakshita Khurana[1]($\boxtimes$) and Brent Waters[2]

[1] University of Illinois Urbana-Champaign, Champaign, USA
dakshita@illinois.edu
[2] University of Texas at Austin and NTT Research, Austin, USA
bwaters@cs.utexas.edu

Abstract. In this work, we put forth the notion of *compatibility* of any key generation or setup algorithm. We focus on the specific case of encryption, and say that a key generation algorithm KeyGen is X-compatible (for $X \in \{CPA, CCA1, CCA2\}$) if there exist encryption and decryption algorithms that together with KeyGen, result in an X-secure public-key encryption scheme.

We study the following question: Is every CPA-compatible key generation algorithm also CCA-compatible? We obtain the following answers:

- Every sub-exponentially CPA-compatible KeyGen algorithm is CCA1-compatible, assuming the existence of hinting PRGs and sub-exponentially secure keyless collision resistant hash functions.
- Every sub-exponentially CPA-compatible KeyGen algorithm is also CCA2-compatible, assuming the existence of non-interactive CCA2 secure commitments, in addition to sub-exponential security of the assumptions listed in the previous bullet.

Here, sub-exponentially CPA-compatible KeyGen refers to any key generation algorithm for which there exist encryption and decryption algorithms that result in a CPA-secure public-key encryption scheme *against sub-exponential adversaries*.

This gives a way to perform CCA secure encryption given any public key infrastructure that has been established with only (sub-exponential) CPA security in mind. The resulting CCA encryption makes black-box use of the CPA scheme and all other underlying primitives.

1 Introduction

Any public-key encryption scheme enables a receiver to recover the encrypted message only if they know a secret key corresponding to their public key. But what if the receiver only ever published a verification key for a digital signature scheme for which they possessed a signing key? Or published a hard puzzle for which they possessed a solution?

This question was one of the original motivations for the study of witness encryption. Garg et al. [14] showed that it is possible to encrypt a message so that it can only be opened by a recipient who knows an NP witness, assuming the

© International Association for Cryptologic Research 2021
J. A. Garay (Ed.): PKC 2021, LNCS 12711, pp. 235–260, 2021.
https://doi.org/10.1007/978-3-030-75248-4_9

existence of an appropriate witness encryption scheme. Put differently, assuming an appropriate witness encryption, almost any KeyGen algorithm that outputs a hard-to-invert string and a corresponding secret (such as a verification and signing key pair for a signature scheme) can be used to derive CPA-secure public key encryption.

In this work, we generalize this study. We put forth the notion of *compatibility* of any key generation or setup algorithm, while focusing on the specific case of encryption schemes. Here, recall that semantic security of (public key) encryption in [15] was only the first step towards formalizing security of encryption schemes. Semantic security, or equivalently indistinguishability-based security against chosen plaintext attacks (CPA) requires that encryptions of every pair of plaintexts appear indistinguishable to a computationally bounded attacker. Unfortunately, starting with the attacks of Bleichenbacher [4] against PKCS#1, it was quickly realized that systems that *only* satisfy CPA security often fail in practice. As a result, security against adaptive chosen ciphertext attacks (or, CCA security) has been accepted as the standard requirement from encryption schemes that need to withstand active attacks [8,11,26,29]. This guarantees security even against attackers that make oracle decryption queries to keys they do not have. If the adversary only has access to a decryption oracle *before* obtaining the challenge ciphertext, the resulting scheme is said to be CCA1 secure. On the other hand, if the adversary has access to the decryption oracle both before and after obtaining the challenge ciphertext, the resulting scheme is CCA2 secure.

We investigate whether arbitrary setup of KeyGen algorithms can be used to derive *CCA-secure* schemes. We will say that a key generation algorithm KeyGen is X-compatible (for $X \in \{CPA, CCA1, CCA2\}$) if there exist encryption and decryption algorithms that together with KeyGen, result in an X-secure public-key encryption scheme. As already discussed, the existence of (extractable) witness encryption suffices to prove CPA-compatibility for many non-trivial KeyGen algorithms. The focus of our work is to take a closer look at CCA-compatibility.

Specifically, we analyze what it takes for a KeyGen algorithm to be CCA-compatible. Our primary result stated informally, is the following:

> *It is always possible to get CCA secure encryption from any* KeyGen *procedure that gives rise to (sub-exponentially secure) CPA encryption.*

Combined with the CPA-compatibility of non-trivial KeyGen, this also implies CCA-compatibility of many non-trivial KeyGen algorithms.

This also means that we can always achieve CCA security using keys for cryptosystems that were originally deployed for CPA mode, without having to modify the public key. This would allow parties with access to public key infrastructures that have been established with only CPA security in mind, to use these infrastructures to perform CCA secure encryption instead. For instance, over the years, multiple encryption schemes have been developed that satisfy IND-CPA security alone. A recent example that gained some popularity is the messaging service telegram, that supplies end-to-end encryption using a new protocol employing AES, RSA, and Diffie-Hellman key exchange. Recently, [17] showed that this protocol is not IND-CCA secure. Our result ensures that (under reasonable cryptographic assumptions) careful participants can use the same underlying infrastructure to engage in encrypted communication without worrying about CCA2 attacks. Alternatively, suppose a user or an organization sets up what is supposed to be a CCA secure system, but the underlying computational assumption turned out to be false. For example, perhaps an attack on DDH was found in a specific group [7], and the scheme is somehow adjusted to recover CPA security. Then, the scheme can also be adjusted to recover CCA security (under our assumptions), with the same infrastructure as that used for CPA security. In these settings, while one could potentially ask users to switch to using a new key from the same system, changing an entire public key infrastructure would be far more cumbersome. We note that simple key encapsulation strategies would be insufficient: for example, sampling the key for a CCA secure encryption scheme and encapsulating it using a key for the original CCA-insecure infrastructure would not lead to the resulting ciphertext being CCA secure.

Preliminary Solutions in Idealized Models. In idealized models, there are known methods that implicitly allow one to obtain CCA security from any CPA-compatible KeyGen algorithm. For instance, in the Random Oracle model, the famous Fujisaki-Okamoto transform [12] converts any CPA secure encryption scheme to a CCA secure one, with the same KeyGen algorithm. We are interested in whether a similar effect can be achieved in the plain model.

A natural approach without a random oracle would be to leverage a common reference string (CRS) and implement the Naor-Yung methodology [11, 26] using simulation-sound NIZKs. We recall that the Naor-Yung (CCA secure) encryption of a message typically consists of two encryptions, under independent public keys, of the same message; and a simulation-sound NIZK proof that both ciphertexts encrypt the same message. If implemented naively, it appears that the KeyGen algorithm for the resulting CCA mode would have to output *two* independent public keys corresponding to the underlying CPA secure scheme. Even if we found a method to get rid of the second key, this still requires participants to place their trust in a central setup assumption to enable the (simulation-sound) NIZK. Given this state of affairs, we ask if it is possible to obtain CCA secure encryption by relying on the KeyGen algorithm of any CPA secure encryption scheme:

- in the plain model without assuming setup, CRS, or a random oracle,
- with black-box use of the CPA scheme (and additional primitives),
- and while making the weakest possible cryptographic assumptions.

Our Results. We take a novel approach to obtain a plain model solution that makes black-box use of the CPA scheme, and does not resort to NIZK (or NIWI) style assumptions. Specifically, we demonstrate CCA1-compatibility of any sub-exponentially CPA-compatible KeyGen algorithm while making black-box use of hinting PRGs and sub-exponential keyless collision resistant hash functions. We also demonstrate CCA2-compatibility of any sub-exponentially CPA-compatible KeyGen algorithm while additionally making black-box use of non-interactive CCA secure commitments. Such commitments were recently obtained [13] based on black-box use of subexponential one-way functions in BQP, and sub-exponential quantum-hard one-way functions, in addition to the assumptions listed above. Alternatively, these can be based on sub-exponential time-lock puzzles [13,24] in addition to the assumptions listed above. We informally summarize our results below.

Informal Theorem 1 *Every sub-exponentially* CPA-*compatible* KeyGen *algorithm against non-uniform adversaries is also* CCA1-*compatible against uniform adversaries, assuming the existence of hinting PRGs and sub-exponential keyless collision-resistant hash functions against uniform adversaries.*

Informal Theorem 2 *Every sub-exponentially* CPA-*compatible* KeyGen *algorithm against non-uniform adversaries is also* CCA2-*compatible against uniform adversaries, assuming the existence of sub-exponential hinting PRGs, sub-exponential keyless collision-resistant hash functions against uniform adversaries and sub-exponential non-interactive CCA secure commitments.*

2   Our Technique

2.1   Background: A Variant of Koppula-Waters [22]

Our starting point is a variant of the recent Koppula-Waters [22] approach to achieving CCA1 secure encryption based on CPA secure encryption and a new primitive they introduced, called a *hinting PRG*. A hinting PRG satisfies the following property: for a uniformly random short seed s, the matrix M obtained by first expanding $\mathrm{PRG}(s) = z_0 z_1 z_2 \ldots z_n$, sampling uniformly random $v_1 v_2 \ldots v_n$, and setting for all $i \in [n]$, $M_{s_i, i} = z_i$ and $M_{1-s_i, i} = v_i$, should be indistinguishable from a uniformly random matrix. Hinting PRGs are known based on CDH, LWE [22]. (One can also pursue a similar path using any circular secure symmetric key encryption [20] in lieu of the Hinting PRG.) Koppula and Waters [22] also require the CPA scheme to have two properties. First, the scheme should have perfect decryption correctness for most public/secret keys and second, any ciphertext should be decryptable given the encryption randomness.

Now, the KeyGen algorithm of the CCA1 scheme constructed by [20,22] executes the CPA KeyGen setup *twice* to obtain two independent public/secret key pairs, denoted by (pk_0, sk_0) and (pk_1, sk_1). Additionally, the CCA1 KeyGen algorithm samples and outputs the public parameters pp of an equivocal commitment scheme. To encrypt a message m, the encryption algorithm chooses a seed $s \leftarrow \{0,1\}^n$ and computes $H(s) = z_0 z_1 \ldots z_n$, where H is a hinting PRG. It uses z_0 to mask the message m; that is, it computes $c = m \oplus z_0$. The remaining ciphertext will contain n 'signals' that help the decryption algorithm to recover s bit by bit, which in turn will allow it to compute z_0 and hence unmask c.

The ith signal (for each $i \in [n]$) has three components $c_{0,i}, c_{1,i}, c_{2,i}$. If the ith bit of s is 0, then $c_{0,i}$ is an encryption of a random string y_i using the public key pk_0 and randomness z_i, and $c_{1,i}$ is an encryption of y_i using pk_1 (encrypted using true randomness). If the ith bit of s is 1, then $c_{0,i}$ is an encryption of y_i using public key pk_0 (encrypted using true randomness), $c_{1,i}$ is an encryption of y_i using public key pk_1 and randomness z_i. In both cases, $c_{2,i}$ is an equivocal commitment to s_i using randomness y_i. As a result, half the ciphertexts are encryptions with fresh randomness, while the remaining are encryptions with blocks of the hinting PRG output being used as randomness, and the positioning of the random/pseudorandom encryptions reveals the seed s.

The decryption algorithm first decrypts each $c_{0,i}$ (using secret key is sk_0) to obtain $y_1 y_2 \ldots y_n$. It then checks if $c_{2,i}$ is an equivocal commitment to 0 with randomness y_i. If so, it guesses that $s_i = 0$, else it guesses that $s_i = 1$. With this estimate for s, the decryption algorithm can compute $H(s) = z_0 z_1 \ldots z_n$ and then compute $c \oplus z_0$ to recover the message m. The decryption algorithm needs to enforce additional checks to prevent malicious decryption queries (made during the CCA1 experiment). In particular, the decryption algorithm needs to check that the guess for s is indeed correct. It conducts the following checks and outputs $z_0 \oplus c$ if they all pass.

- If the ith bit of s is guessed to be 0, then the decryption algorithm checks that $c_{0,i}$ is a valid ciphertext - it simply re-encrypts y_i using randomness z_i and checks if this equals $c_{0,i}$. Recall that the decryption procedure, before guessing the ith bit of s to be 0, also checks that $c_{2,i}$ is a commitment to 0 with randomness y_i.
- If the ith bit of s is guessed to be 1, then the decryption algorithm first recovers the message underlying ciphertext $c_{1,i}$. Note that $c_{1,i}$ should be encrypted using randomness z_i, hence using z_i, one can recover message $\widetilde{y}_i$ from $c_{1,i}$ (using the randomness recovery property of the PKE scheme). It then re-encrypts $\widetilde{y}_i$ and checks if it is equal to $c_{1,i}$, and also checks that $c_{2,i}$ is a commitment to 1 with randomness $\widetilde{y}_i$.

Inadequacies of this Transformation. At this point, we are far from having established CCA1 compatibility of arbitrary CPA infrastructure due the following reasons:

1. The transformation described so far crucially uses equivocal commitments, which require trusted setup or a common reference/random string, and this is something that we would like to avoid.
2. This transformation makes use of two public keys, and we are only guaranteed to get *a single key* from existing setup.

In fact, achieving CCA2 security is even more complex: in particular, the CCA2 setup in the transformation of [22] must also contain pairwise independent hash functions $h_1, h_2, \ldots, h_n$. These are used to prevent the adversary from mauling the challenge ciphertext into related ciphertexts and querying the decryption oracle on these ciphertexts.

In the coming section, we discuss how to achieve CCA1 compatibility by eliminating the two problems listed above. In the section after that, we discuss the more complex case of CCA2 compatibility.

2.2   Techniques for CCA1 Compatibility

To address the first item listed above, we rely on equivocal commitments without setup, that satisfy binding against uniform adversaries. The resulting CCA1 compatibility is also established against uniform PPT adversaries. We briefly recall how such equivocal commitments can be obtained based on keyless collision resistant hash functions against uniform adversaries [2,10,13,16]: the commit algorithm samples a uniformly random seed for a strong extractor, $g \leftarrow \{0,1\}^{\kappa}$ and a value v in the domain of a sufficiently compressing keyless collision resistant hash function. A commitment to a bit b is given by the string $H(v), (\mathsf{Ext}(g,v) \oplus b)$.

We use the resulting commitment scheme to generate $c_{2,i}$ values in the outline described above. Note that this commitment scheme cannot be efficiently equivocated by uniform adversaries, since that would lead to an efficient uniform algorithm that finds collisions in the hash function H. On the other hand, our proof of security will rely on the fact that most strings in the support of the commitment can be non-uniformly equivocated. Next, we discuss how to argue security when using these equivocal commitments in the transformation described above.

Arguing Security. To argue security, first observe that the equivocal commitment satisfies computational binding against PPT adversaries, which makes it infeasible for a CCA1 adversary to query the challenger on *ambiguous* ciphertexts that pass the decryption checks but potentially decrypt to different values under sk_0 and sk_1. This is because for such ciphertexts, for some $i \in [n]$, the component $c_{2,i}$ is both a commitment to 0 with randomness y_i recovered from $c_{0,i}$ and a commitment to 1 with randomness $\widetilde{y}_i$ recovered from $c_{1,i}$: clearly violating the binding property of the commitment scheme.

At the same time, the equivocality of the commitment enables the challenger to set for every $i \in [n]$, the values $c_{2,i}$ that are both commitments to 0 with randomness y_i and 1 with randomness $\widetilde{y}_i$. Next, via a careful hybrid argument that relies on perfect correctness of the encryption scheme, the binding property of the equivocal commitment and CPA security of the public key encryption scheme, the challenge ciphertext can be modified and made ambiguous: this means that in the challenge ciphertext for every $i \in [n]$, $c_{0,i}$ is an encryption of y_i, $c_{1,i}$ is a non-interactive commitment to $\widetilde{y}_i$, $c_{2,i}$ an equivocal commitment: i.e., a commitment to 0 with randomness y_i and to 1 with randomness $\widetilde{y}_i$.

At a very high level, this involves changing values encrypted under $c_{0,i}$ and $c_{1,i}$ by relying on CPA security of the encryption scheme. Values encrypted under $c_{1,i}$ can be modified relatively easily because only the secret key sk_0 is used to perform decryption queries. Arguing security when changing values encrypted under $c_{0,i}$ requires more care: in particular, such an argument is possible only if sk_0 is no longer used to answer the adversary's decryption queries. Therefore we first switch to using an alternative decryption strategy that relies on sk_1 instead of sk_0 to decrypt the adversary's ciphertexts. Unambiguity of the adversary's ciphertexts helps ensure that alternative decryption yields the same outputs as the original decryption strategy. When using alternate decryption, it becomes possible to change values encrypted under $c_{0,i}$ since sk_0 is no longer being used.

At the end of this argument, information about the hinting PRG seed s has *almost* been removed from the ciphertext, except that for all i where $s_i = 0$, $c_{s_i,i}$ is encrypted using randomness r_i which came from running the hinting PRG on s; whereas $c_{1-s_i,i}$ is encrypted using uniform randomness. These can all be replaced with uniformly random values by the property of the hinting PRG, thereby eliminating all information about s, and therefore m, from the ciphertext.

So far, the construction and security argument also relied on the use of *two* public/private key pairs. But as already pointed out, a CPA-compatible KeyGen algorithm will output a single public and private key. Next, we discuss how to eliminate the need for the second key.

Removing the Second Key via Non-interactive Commitments. Here, we begin by observing that the actual decryption algorithm only makes use of the secret key sk_0, and does not need the second secret key sk_1. It recovers messages underlying $c_{1,i}$ for all $i \in [n]$ where $s_i = 1$, using the *randomness* z_i that was supposedly used to create $c_{1,i}$.

As a result, the actual decryption algorithm does not need to *efficiently decrypt* $c_{1,i}$ and has no use for the secret key sk_1. Therefore, we eliminate the need for the second public key by setting the strings $c_{1,i}$ to be *non-interactive perfectly binding commitments* that do not require any public keys or public parameters, and where the committed message can be efficiently recovered given the randomness used to commit. Lombardi and Schaeffer [25] showed that such commitments can be obtained from any perfectly correct public-key encryption scheme. Specifically, we modify the encryption algorithm so that if $s_i = 0$, $c_{1,i}$ is a non-interactive commitment to 0^n using true randomness, and if $s_i = 1$, then $c_{1,i}$ is a non-interactive commitment to a random string x_i using randomness z_i. The remaining parts $\{c_{0,i}, c_{2,i}\}_{i \in [n]}$ will remain unmodified.

Now recall that the security argument outlined above points to an alternative decryption strategy that does actually use sk_1, instead of sk_0, to efficiently decrypt the adversary's ciphertexts. However, this alternative decryption algorithm is only used in a few hybrids in the proof of security, and when using non-interactive commitments, we allow these hybrids to *inefficiently* recover the values committed under $c_{1,i}$ by running an exponential time brute-force algorithm that checks all possible randomnees values that could potentially be used to build $c_{1,i}$.

In order to make the hybrid strategy still go through, we rely on complexity leveraging: we set security parameters so that all other primitives are secure against adversaries that can run in time large enough to execute the brute-force algorithm that recovers values committed under $c_{1,i}$ for $i \in [n]$. Specifically, we assume that the CPA encryption scheme to be upgraded has security parameter k and is 2^{k^e} secure for some constant $0 < e < 1$. We also assume that the keyless collision-resistant hash function responsible for the binding property of the equivocal commitments is 2^{k^ϵ}-secure for some constant $0 < \epsilon < 1$, and we set the security parameter for the non-interactive commitment to be $k^{\min(e,\epsilon)}$.

Additional Details of the Proof. We now provide additional details on the proof of CCA1 security of the resulting scheme. Recall that in the CCA1 security game, the adversary is allowed access to a decryption oracle before the challenge phase, where the adversary outputs m_0, m_1 and then obtains an encryption of m_b for b sampled uniformly at random.

We develop a sequence of hybrid experiments where the decryption oracle as well as the challenge ciphertext are modified in small increments, and where the first hybrid corresponds to providing the adversary access to the actual decryption oracle together with an encryption of m_b and the last one corresponds to providing the adversary access to the actual decryption oracle together with an encryption of uniform randomness.

The very next hybrid experiment is an exponential time hybrid that samples equivocal commitments $\{c_{2,i}\}_{i\in[n]}$ for the challenge ciphertext, together with randomness $\{y_{0,i}\}_{i\in[n]}$ and $\{y_{1,i}\}_{i\in[n]}$ that can be used to equivocally open these commitments to 0 and 1 respectively.

The third hybrid additionally modifies the components $c_{1,i}$ to "drown" out information about s via noise. In particular, while in the real game, the values $c_{1,i}$ are always commitments to $y_{s_i,i}$, in the challenge ciphertext these values are modified to become commitments to $y_{1,i}$, irrespective of what s_i is. On the other hand, the values $c_{0,i}$ remain encryptions of $y_{s_i,i}$, exactly as in the real experiment. In spite of the fact that equivocation takes exponential time, the proof of indistinguishability between this hybrid and the previous one does not need to rely on an exponential time reduction. Instead, we observe that the equivocal commitment strings $\{c_{2,i}\}_{i\in[n]}$ together with their openings can be fixed non-uniformly and independently of the strings $c_{1,i}$, and therefore these hybrids can be proven indistinguishable based on non-uniform hiding of the non-interactive commitment scheme. Since we must carefully manipulate the randomness used for $\{c_{1,i}\}_{i\in[n]}$ in both games, this hybrid requires a delicate argument.

The fourth hybrid modifies the decryption oracle so that instead of decrypting using the secret key of the public key encryption scheme, decryption is performed by running in time exponential in the security parameter of the commitment scheme (specifically, in time $2^{k^{\min(e,\epsilon)}}$) and performing a brute-force search for the randomness used to create the commitments $\{c_{1,i}\}_{i\in[n]}$. This hybrid is only indistinguishable from the previous one if an adversary cannot find ciphertexts that decrypt differently when using the secret key of the encryption scheme versus the brute-force algorithm discussed above. This hybrid requires a subtle argument that relies on the fact that no adversary can query the decryption oracle with "ambiguous" ciphertexts, in spite of being provided such ciphertexts in the challenge phase. Specifically, we crucially use the fact that the adversary does not observe any equivocations before obtaining the challenge ciphertext, and therefore cannot query the decryption oracle with any "ambiguous" ciphertexts (as this would lead to the adversary breaking binding of the equivocal commitment). This is the primary reason that we only obtain CCA1 security.

In the fifth hybrid, some of the challenge ciphertext values, that are independent of the message being encrypted, are chosen ahead of time. This maneuver helps us with the sixth hybrid, where in the challenge ciphertext, information about the PRG seed s is removed from the ciphertext components $\{c_{1,i}\}_{i\in[n]}$, making them all encryptions of $y_{0,i}$ instead of being encryptions of $y_{s_i,i}$. Again, since we must carefully manipulate the randomness used for $\{c_{0,i}\}_{i\in[n]}$ in both games, this hybrid requires a delicate argument.

In the seventh hybrid, we modify the decryption oracle again to go back to using the secret key of the public key encryption scheme to decrypt. Note that the only remaining information about s is in the *randomness* used to obtain $\{c_{i,0}, c_{i,1}\}_{i\in[n]}$ in the challenge ciphertext. In the seventh and eighth hybrids, we carefully re-order the randomness and rely on the security of the hinting PRG to switch to using uniform randomness everywhere. This eliminates all information about s and therefore about the message being encrypted in the challenge ciphertext.

2.3   Techniques for CCA2 Compatibility

We observe that the key barrier to proving CCA2 security in the hybrid arguments outlined above is the specific hybrid that *modifies the challenge ciphertext so it contains a commitment to both a 0 and a 1*. Given such a ciphertext, in a CCA2 game, an adversary could generate new strings that are a commitment to both a 0 and a 1, and use them to create ambiguous ciphertexts. Arguing that this cannot happen requires us to develop a much deeper technical toolkit.

Our first insight is that the requirement that an adversary, given an ambiguous ciphertext, be unable to generate *additional* ambiguous ciphertexts is reminiscent of *non-malleability*. As such, we will rely on non-interactive non-malleable (more precisely, CCA secure) commitments without setup. Up until recently, there were perceived strong barriers to obtaining non-malleable commitmens with less than 3 rounds of interaction [28]. But a sequence of recent works obtained two round [19,24] and even non-interactive [3,13,18,24] based on well-studied sub-exponential hardness assumptions. In particular, a recent work [13] obains black-box non-interactive non-malleable (and in fact CCA2 secure) commitments assuming kelyess collision resistant hash functions, against uniform adversaries.

Relying on CCA2 Secure Commitments. We now discuss modifications to the CCA1 transformation discussed in the previous section. Specifically, we will replace the non-interactive commitment (used to generate ciphertext components $\{c_{1,i}\}_{i\in[n]}$) in the construction outlined above, with a CCA2 secure commitment. Intuitively, using CCA2 secure commitments ensures that no matter how we change the $\{c_{1,i}\}_{i\in[n]}$ components in the challenge ciphertext, the corresponding $\{c_{1,i}\}_{i\in[n]}$ components in the adversary's decryption queries do not change (except in a computationally indistinguishable way). Proving that the resulting protocol is actually a CCA2 secure encryption scheme, is much trickier. We encounter several technical barriers in this process, which we discuss below.

Arguing Security. Recall that in the CCA2 security game, the adversary is allowed access to a decryption oracle both before and after the challenge phase, where the adversary outputs m_0, m_1 and then obtains an encryption of m_b for b sampled uniformly at random.

We will consider a sequence of hybrid experiments similar to the CCA1 setting, where the decryption oracle as well as the challenge ciphertext are modified in small increments. The first hybrid corresponds to providing the adversary access to the actual decryption oracle together with an encryption of m_b and the last one corresponds to providing the adversary access to the actual decryption oracle together with an encryption of uniform randomness.

The very next hybrid experiment, just like the CCA1 setting, is an exponential time hybrid that samples equivocal commitments $\{c_{2,i}\}_{i \in [n]}$ for the challenge ciphertext, together with randomness $\{y_{0,i}\}_{i \in [n]}$ and $\{y_{1,i}\}_{i \in [n]}$ that can be used to equivocally open these commitments to 0 and 1 respectively.

The third hybrid additionally modifies the components $c_{1,i}$ to "drown" out information about s via noise. In particular, while in the real game, the values $c_{1,i}$ are always commitments to $y_{s_i,i}$, in the challenge ciphertext these values are modified to become commitments to $y_{1,i}$, irrespective of what s_i is. On the other hand, the values $c_{0,i}$ remain encryptions of $y_{s_i,i}$, exactly as in the real experiment. At this point, the proof of indistinguishability of hybrids already significantly diverges from the CCA1 setting. Specifically, the proof of indistinguishability between this hybrid and the previous one, in the CCA1 setting, relied on nonuniform security of the non-interactive commitment – in order to perform the exponential time computation needed to equivocate the hash function. Here, we would ideally like to rely on CCA secure commitments which are potentially only secure against uniform adversaries (e.g., the black-box construction in [13] which is only secure against uniform adversaries). One option could be to assume that the CCA2 commitment is "hard" against adversaries running in time that is sufficient to compute openings of the equivocal commitment.

In the fourth hybrid, we would like to modify the decryption oracle so that instead of decrypting using the secret key of the public key encryption scheme, decryption is performed by running in time exponential in the security parameter of the commitment scheme (specifically, in time $2^{k^{\min(e,\epsilon)}}$) and performing a brute-force search for the randomness used to create the commitments $\{c_{1,i}\}_{i \in [n]}$. This hybrid is indistinguishable from the previous one only if an adversary cannot find ciphertexts that decrypt differently when using the secret key of the encryption scheme versus the brute-force algorithm discussed above: in other words if the adversary cannot query the oracle with "ambiguous" ciphertexts.

This is where the CCA2 setting diverges most significantly from the CCA1 setting. In the CCA1 setting, we could prove that the adversary does not make ambiguous decryption queries by relying on uniform binding of the equivocal commitment, but this is no longer true in the CCA2 setting. Specifically, we need to rule out an adversary that given ambiguous ciphertexts, creates new ones.

Therefore, in the proof, we will now have to rely on CCA2 commitments to maintain an invariant across all the hybrids discussed above. The invariant is as follows: except with negligible probability, the adversary does not make any oracle query for which there exists some $i \in [n]$ such that the components $(c_{0,i}, c_{1,i})$ encrypt/commit to two different openings of the string $c_{2,i}$.

To ensure that this invariant holds in the initial hybrid that corresponds to the real CCA2 experiment, we will use any adversary that breaks the invariant to contradict the binding property of the equivocal commitment. The corresponding reduction would have to *extract* two openings for the same equivocal commitment string, from a decryption query provided by the adversary. In particular, these openings will actually be the plaintexts underlying the ciphertext $c_{0,i}$ and the commitment string $c_{1,i}$. Extracting these two openings involves decrypting $c_{0,i}$ under sk_0, and brute-force breaking the CCA2 commitment string $c_{1,i}$. This use of brute force necessitates that the binding property of the equivocal commitment be hard to break even in time that is sufficient to break the CCA2 commitment.

But recall that arguing indistinguishability for the third hybrid actually required the exact opposite property: that the CCA2 commitment be hard to break even by adversaries running in time that is sufficient to compute openings of the equivocal commitment. It appears that we are at an impasse here, since we need the equivocal commitment and the CCA2 commitment to each take longer time to break than the other. One way to resolve this is to rely on a non-uniform reduction to argue indistinguishability between the second and third hybrids. But recall that the underlying black-box CCA commitments of [13] achieve only uniform security, at least when relying on on keyless collision resistant hash functions against uniform adversaries.

Fortunately for us, it turns out that [13] prove a much stronger property than uniform CCA security – they actually establish computation enabled CCA security. The computation enabled property allows the attacker to submit a randomized turing machine P at the beginning of the game. The challenger can run the program P and output the result for the attacker at the beginning of the game: crucially, the running time of P can be much larger than the uniform running time allowed to the adversary. This added property actually achieves a flavor of non-uniformity that helps our argument go through, by allowing us to perform special heavy computation at the beginning of the reduction between hybrids 2 and 3, while at the same time, allowing the binding property of the equivocal commitment to be hard to break even in time that is sufficient to break the CCA2 commitment.

Once we have these ingredients in place, we still need to ensure that the invariant continues to hold in all the other hybrids described above. This is tricky because checking the invariant involves decrypting $\{c_{0,i}\}_{i \in [n]}$ under sk_0, and also finding the messages committed via the CCA2 commitment strings $\{c_{1,i}\}_{i \in [n]}$, which may not necessarily be an efficient process. Recall that in the very next hybrid, we simply sample the commitment strings in an equivocal way – this hybrid is statistically indistinguishable from the previous one, and therefore the invariant also holds in this hybrid. In the hybrid after that, the commitment strings $c_{1,i}$ are modified in the challenge ciphertext to drown out information about s. Here, in order to prove that the invariant holds, we rely on CCA2 security of the commitment to find the messages committed via the CCA2 commitment strings $\{c_{1,i}\}_{i \in [n]}$ in all of the adversary's queries.

In the fourth hybrid, we change the way the adversary's queries are decrypted: here, we can prove (this time, by relying on the invariant) that the adversary does not make decryption queries that decrypt differently, except with negligible probability. In the next hybrid, we modify the decryption oracle again to go back to using the secret key sk_0 of the public key encryption scheme to decrypt. At this point, we are no longer able to argue that the invariant holds, but note that we only needed the invariant to argue that the way the adversary's queries are decrypted can be changed without affecting the adversary's advantage. Therefore, this point on, we will not make any changes to how the adversary's queries are decrypted, and so all we will need to do is argue indistinguishability of the subsequent hybrids. At this point, the only remaining information about s is in the *randomness* used to obtain $\{c_{i,0}, c_{i,1}\}_{i \in [n]}$ in the challenge ciphertext. In the next couple of hybrids, we carefully re-order the randomness and rely on the security of the hinting PRG to switch to using uniform randomness everywhere. All this while, we decrypt the adversary's oracle queries by breaking the CCA commitments (via brute-force). As a result, our reductions run in superpolynomial time, and we rely on sub-exponential hardness of the hinting PRG. This is different from the CCA1 setting where we could first go back to decrypting the adversary's oracle queries in polynomial time and then rely on polynomial hardness of the hinting PRG.

We provide some additional technical details about how we implement the invariant discussed in this overview. Specifically, we insert a hybrid after the first hybrid, where the experiment aborts (and the adversary wins) if he makes an oracle query that breaks the invariant: that is, if the adversary makes an oracle query for which there exists $i \in [n]$ such that the components $(c_{0,i}, c_{1,i})$ encrypt/commit to two different openings of the string $c_{2,i}$. This (inefficient) check is performed in all subsequent hybrids up until the fourth one, where we change the way the adversary's queries are decrypted. We perform careful reductions to argue indistinguishability of these hybrids while performing this inefficient check (as described above). After the fourth hybrid, we no longer need the invariant and we therefore remove this check before proceeding with subsequent hybrids. This concludes an overview of our construction and proof of security.

2.4 On Security Against Non-uniform Adversaries

Very recently, the security of keyless hash functions against adversaries with *non-uniform advice* has also been explored; in particular, [1,2,21] defined and constructed keyless collision-resistant hash functions that satisfy the following property: there exists a polynomial $p(\cdot)$ such that for any polynomial $s(\cdot)$, any PPT adversary with $s(\kappa)$ bits of non-uniform advice cannot find more than $p(s(\kappa))$ pairs of collisions. Subsequently, [3] used these hash functions and (sub-exponential) NIWIs to obtain one-message zero-knowledge without trusted setup and a weak form of soundness against provers with non-uniform advice.

We observe that relying on non-uniform secure primitives; more specifically substituting keyless collision-resistant hash functions against uniform adversaries with keyless collision-resistant hash functions against adversaries with non-uniform advice as described above, helps make our CCA constructions secure against non-uniform adversaries. In other words, we can make a stronger assumption on the underlying keyless hash function, to obtain stronger (non-uniform) security. The only difference would be the observation that an adversary with polynomial advice can only find polynomially many collisions, and therefore query the decryption oracle with only polynomially many ambiguous ciphertexts – the answers to which can be non-uniformly fixed and hardwired into the oracle.

2.5 On Setting Parameters for CCA Compatibility

For both the CCA1 and CCA2 transformations, our non-interactive commitment scheme used to create $\{c_{1,i}\}_{i\in[n]}$ needs to be easier to break "along some axis of hardness" than the PKE scheme so that there is a way to open it, while the PKE scheme is still hard. Our axis of choice in this paper, is basic computation time. As a result, our theorem statement requires the KeyGen algorithm to be sub-exponentially CPA compatible, i.e. to give rise to a sub-exponentially secure CPA encryption scheme. This could also potentially lead to issues if the original PKE scheme had parameters "on edge" of being broken: since we would need commitment scheme to be even easier to break in terms of computation time.

We point out that in these cases, there could be other different axes of hardness (e.g.,time-lock puzzles [3,24]) that could be exploited to achieve the same effect. As another example, following [18], one could show that any KeyGen that gives rise to *polynomially hard* PKE scheme secure against quantum adversaries can be combined with a commitment scheme that is quantum *in*-secure, to achieve CCA compatibility. As a result, there is still a way to open the commitments in BQP, while the CPA-secure PKE scheme is still hard. These approaches could improve the concrete parameters that one would need to use to instantiate these transformations, and the exact axis of hardness can be chosen depending upon the specifics of the application.

In the coming sections, we first discuss some key building blocks used by our transformations in Sect. 3, and define the notion of compatibility in Sect. 4. Next, we describe our CCA2 compatibility construction in Sect. 5, with analysis and proof of security deferred to the full version. We can use simpler assumptions and a simpler construction to achieve the weaker goal of CCA1 compatibility, as discussed above. This construction and analysis are deferred to the full version due to lack of space.

3 Preliminaries

In this section we will provide notions and security definitions for public key encryption, keyless collision resistant hash functions and non-interactive perfectly binding commitments. For public key encryption we will formulate a definition that can capture IND-CPA, IND-CCA1 and IND-CCA2 security. For all of our definitions we will be explicit to whether we are describing security against uniform or non-uniform adversaries as our results will be sensitive to this nuance.

We will use κ to denote the security parameter. We will denote by $\mathsf{negl}(\kappa)$ a function that is asymptotically smaller than the inverse of every polynomial in κ.

Public Key Encryption

A public key encryption scheme is specified by a triple of algorithms $(\mathsf{KeyGen}, \mathsf{Enc}, \mathsf{Dec})$, where $\mathsf{KeyGen}(1^\kappa; r_{\mathsf{KeyGen}}) \to (\mathsf{sk}, \mathsf{pk})$, $\mathsf{Enc}(\mathsf{pk}, \mathsf{msg}; r_{\mathsf{Enc}}) \to \mathsf{ct}$ and $\mathsf{Dec}(\mathsf{sk}, \mathsf{ct}) \to \mathsf{msg}$. These algorithms satisfy (perfect) correctness, and IND-CPA/CCA1/CCA2 security, which we will describe below. In addition, we require the following additional properties.

Security Parameter Retrievability. A PKE scheme is *security parameter retrievable* if there exists a polynomial time algorithm $\mathsf{RetrieveParam}$ that can extract the security parameter used to generate a public key. More formally $\forall \kappa, r_{\mathsf{KeyGen}}$ it must be that $\mathsf{RetrieveParam}(\mathsf{pk}) = \kappa$ where $(\mathsf{sk}, \mathsf{pk}) \leftarrow \mathsf{KeyGen}(1^\kappa; r_{\mathsf{KeyGen}})$.

Message Recovery from Randomness. We will additionally assume a message recovery from randomness property as given in [22]. Suppose that ct is an encryption of message msg under a (valid) public key $\mathsf{cpa.pk}$ and randomness r. Then the exists an algorithm $\mathsf{CPA.Recover}$ where $\mathsf{CPA.Recover}(\mathsf{cpa.pk}, \mathsf{ct}, r) = \mathsf{msg}$.

The encryption algorithm of any IND-CPA secure PKE scheme can be modified to include this property, as follows. Assume that messages are n bits long. Then one can use n additional random coins r' during encryption and append $\mathsf{msg} \oplus r'$ to the end of the ciphertext. The message can then be recovered from the random coins by a simple XOR operation with r'. Moreover, since the r' portion of the coins are not used elsewhere in encryption, IND-CPA security is preserved. This simple transformation only modifies the encryption algorithm and not the public key. Thus, from a compatibility perspective the setup algorithm remains the same. Therefore in our presentation we will assume that the public key encryption scheme has this property.

Security. We now describe security for public key encryption schemes. We will present a single game of (full) chosen ciphertext security and then derive IND-CCA-1 and IND-CPA security. We define the following security game between a challenger $\mathcal{C}$ and a *stateful* attacker $\mathcal{A}$.

1. C runs $\mathsf{KeyGen}(1^\kappa; r_{\mathsf{KeyGen}}) \rightarrow (\mathsf{sk}, \mathsf{pk})$ and gives pk to $\mathcal{A}$.
2. $\mathcal{A}$ then is allowed to make oracle queries to the function $\mathsf{Dec}(\mathsf{sk}, \cdot)$
3. $\mathcal{A}$ submits two messages $\mathsf{msg}_0, \mathsf{msg}_1 \in \mathcal{M} \times \mathcal{M}$ to C.
4. C chooses a coin $b \in \{0, 1\}$ and outputs $\mathsf{ct}^* \leftarrow \mathsf{Enc}(\mathsf{pk}, \mathsf{msg}_b; r_{\mathsf{Enc}})$ for random r_{Enc}.
5. $\mathcal{A}$ then is allowed to make oracle queries to the function $\mathsf{Dec}(\mathsf{sk}, \cdot)$ with the restriction that ct^* is not given as input to the oracle.
6. $\mathcal{A}$ outputs a bit b'.

We refer to the above security game as the IND-CCA2 security game. We define IND-CCA1 security as above, with the exception that the attacker is not allowed any decryption oracle queries in Step 5. We define the IND-CPA security game as above with the exception that the attacker is not allowed any decryption oracle queries in Step 2 and none in Step 5.

Definition 1 (Secure Public Key Encryption). *We will say that a public key encryption scheme is (IND-CCA2, IND-CCA1, IND-CPA) secure if for all non-uniform poly-time attackers $\mathcal{A}$ there exists a negligible function negl such that $\Pr[b' = b] \leq \frac{1}{2} + \mathsf{negl}(\kappa)$ in the (IND-CCA2, IND-CCA1, IND-CPA) security game.*

Definition 2 (Uniform Secure Public Key Encryption). *We will say that a public key encryption scheme is (IND-CCA2, IND-CCA1, IND-CPA) secure if for all poly-time uniform attackers $\mathcal{A}$ we have that there exists a negligible function negl such that $\Pr[b' = b] \leq \frac{1}{2} + \mathsf{negl}(\kappa)$ in the (IND-CCA2, IND-CCA1, IND-CPA) security game.*

In our construction we will also need to consider more fined-grained notions of security where we will specify a time function T that the attacker is allowed to run in. Typically, this will be used to specify security against an attacker that runs in time subexponential in the security parameter.

Definition 3 (Non-uniform T-secure Public Key Encryption). *We will say that a public key encryption scheme is T-(IND-CCA2, IND-CCA1, IND-CPA) secure if for every polynomial $p(\cdot)$, all non-uniform attackers $\mathcal{A}$ running in time at most $p(T(\kappa))$ and with at most $p(T(\kappa))$ bits of advice there exists a negligible function negl such that $\Pr[b' = b] \leq \frac{1}{2} + \mathsf{negl}(\kappa)$ in the (IND-CCA2, IND-CCA1, IND-CPA) security game.*

Definition 4 (Uniform T-secure Public Key Encryption). *We will say that a public key encryption scheme is T-(IND-CCA2, IND-CCA1, IND-CPA) secure if for every polynomial $p(\cdot)$ and all uniform attackers $\mathcal{A}$ running in time at most $p(T(\kappa))$ we have that there exists a negligible function negl such that $\Pr[b' = b] \leq \frac{1}{2} + \mathsf{negl}(\kappa)$ in the (IND-CCA2, IND-CCA1, IND-CPA) security game.*

Non-interactive Perfect Binding Commitments

Definition 5 (Non-interactive Perfectly Binding Commitments with Non-Uniform Security). *A non-interactive perfectly binding commitment is specified by a poly-time computable randomized algorithm* Com *that on input* $(1^\kappa, \mathsf{msg}; r)$ *outputs a commitment string* c *of length* $\ell(\kappa)$, *where* $\ell(\cdot)$ *is a polynomially bounded function, satisfying:*

- **Perfect Binding:** *For all* $c \in \{0,1\}^*$, κ, $\nexists(\mathsf{msg}_0, \mathsf{msg}_1, r_0, r_1)$ *such that* $\mathsf{msg}_0 \neq \mathsf{msg}_1$, *and* $c = \mathsf{Com}(1^\kappa, \mathsf{msg}_0; r_0)$ *and* $c = \mathsf{Com}(1^\kappa, \mathsf{msg}_1; r_1)$.
- **Computational Hiding:** *There exists a negligible function* $\mathsf{negl}(\cdot)$ *such that* $\forall \mathsf{msg}_0, \mathsf{msg}_1 \in \{0,1\}^*$ *s.t.* $|\mathsf{msg}_0| = |\mathsf{msg}_1|, \forall$ *non-uniform PPT* $\mathcal{A}$, $\Big| \Pr[\mathcal{A}$
$(\mathsf{Com}(1^\kappa, \mathsf{msg}_0, r)) = 1] - \Pr[\mathcal{A}(\mathsf{Com}(1^\kappa, \mathsf{msg}_1, r)) = 1] \Big| \leq \mathsf{negl}(\kappa)$ *where* $\mathcal{M}$ *denotes message space and the probability is over* r.

We will also assume a property of message recovery from randomness for our commitment scheme. Suppose that c is a commitment of message msg under randomness r. Then the exists an algorithm $\mathsf{Com.Recover}$ where $\mathsf{Com.Recover}(c, r) = \mathsf{msg}$. A similar argument to the one given above for public key encryption shows how one can derive a commitment scheme with the message recover from randomness property from any ordinary one. Finally, we will implicitly assume that any message m committed to using security parameter 1^κ can be retrieved with probability 1 by an algorithm running in time $2^\kappa q(\kappa)$ for some polynomial function q. We denote $\mathsf{Com.Dec}$ as the algorithm for doing this.

Equivocal Commitments without Setup

Equivocal commitments were proposed by DiCrescenzo, Ishai and Ostrovsky [9] as a bit commitment scheme with a trusted setup algorithm. During normal setup, the bit commitment scheme is statistically binding. However, there exists an alternative setup which produces public parameters along with a trapdoor, that produces commitments which can be opened to either 0 or 1. Moreover, the public parameters of the normal and alternative setup are computationally indistinguishable.

Here we will define a similar primitive, but without utilizing a trusted setup algorithm. In order for such a notion to be meaningful, we will require the commitment scheme to be computationally binding for any *uniform* T-time attacker, but there will exist an algorithm running in time $\mathsf{poly}(2^\kappa)$ that can be opened to 0 or 1. Moreover, such a commitment with one of the openings should be statistically indistinguishable from a commitment created in the standard manner. An equivocal commitment scheme without setup consists of 3 algorithms:

$\mathsf{Equiv.Com}(1^\kappa, b) \to (c, d)$ is a randomized PPT algorithm that on input a bit b and the 1^κ outputs a commitment c and decommitment d.

$\mathsf{Equiv.Decom}(c, d) \to \{0, 1, \bot\}$ is a deterministic polytime algorithm that takes in part of the commitment and it's opening and reveals the bit that it was committed to or $\bot$ to indicate failure.

Equiv.Equivocate$(1^\kappa) \to (c, d_0, d_1)$ is an (inefficient) randomized algorithm that in input 1^κ outputs decommitments to both 0 and 1.

An equivocal commitment is perfectly correct if $\forall b \in \{0, 1\}$

$$\Pr \begin{bmatrix} (c, d) \leftarrow \text{Equiv.Com}(1^\kappa, b) \\ b' \leftarrow \text{Equiv.Decom}(c, d) \\ b' = b \end{bmatrix} = 1$$

An equivocal commitment is efficient if Equiv.Com and Equiv.Decom run in poly(κ) time, and Equiv.Equivocate runs in time 2^κ.

An equivocal commitment without setup scheme (Equiv.Com, Equiv.Decom, Equiv.Equivocate) is said to be $T(\cdot)$ binding secure if for any *uniform* adversary $\mathcal{A}$ running in time $p(T(\kappa))$ for some polynomial p, there exists a negligible function negl$(\cdot)$ such that

$$\Pr\left[(c, d_0, d_1) \leftarrow \mathcal{A}(1^\kappa) : \text{Equiv.Decom}(c, d_0) = 0 \wedge \text{Equiv.Decom}(c, d_1) = 1\right] \leq \text{negl}(\kappa).$$

We sat that a scheme is equivocal if for all $b \in \{0, 1\}$ the statistical difference between the following two distributions is negligible in κ.

- $\mathcal{D}_0 = (c, d)$ where Equiv.Com$(1^\kappa, b) \to (c, d)$.
- $\mathcal{D}_1 = (c, d_b)$ where Equiv.Equivocate$(1^\kappa) \to (c, d_0, d_1)$.

We observe that our security definitions do not include an explicit hiding property of a committed bit. This property is actually implied by our equivocal property, and hiding will not be explicitly needed by our proof.

Hinting PRGs

We now provide the definition of hinting PRGs taken from [22]. Let $n(\cdot, \cdot)$ be a polynomial. A n-hinting PRG scheme consists of two PPT algorithms Setup, Eval with the following syntax.

Setup$(1^\kappa, 1^\ell)$: The setup algorithm takes as input the security parameter κ, and length parameter ℓ, and outputs public parameters pp and input length $n = n(\kappa, \ell)$.

Eval $(\text{pp}, s \in \{0, 1\}^n, i \in [n] \cup \{0\})$: The evaluation algorithm takes as input the public parameters pp, an n bit string s, an index $i \in [n] \cup \{0\}$ and outputs an ℓ bit string y.

Definition 6. *A hinting PRG scheme* (Setup, Eval) *is said to be secure if for any PPT adversary $\mathcal{A}$, polynomial $\ell(\cdot)$ there exists a negligible function negl$(\cdot)$ such that for all $\lambda \in \mathbb{N}$, the following holds:*

$$\left| \Pr\left[\beta \leftarrow A\left(\text{pp}, \left(y_0^\beta, \left\{ y_{i,b}^\beta \right\}_{i \in [n], b \in \{0,1\}} \right) \right) \right] - \frac{1}{2} \right| \leq \text{negl}(\lambda)$$

where the probability is over $(\text{pp}, n) \leftarrow \text{Setup}(1^\kappa, 1^{\ell(\lambda)}), s \leftarrow \{0, 1\}^n, \beta \leftarrow \{0, 1\}, y_0^0 \leftarrow \{0, 1\}^\ell, y_0^1 = \text{Eval}(\text{pp}, s, 0), y_{i,b}^0 \leftarrow \{0, 1\}^\ell \; \forall \; i \in [n], b \in \{0, 1\}, \text{ and } y_{i,s_i}^1 = \text{Eval}(\text{pp}, s, i), y_{i,\overline{s_i}}^1 \leftarrow \{0, 1\}^\ell \; \forall \; i \in [n].$

Computation Enabled CCA Commitments

We now define "computation enabled" CCA secure commitments [13]. Intuitively, these are tagged commitments where a commitment to message m under tag tag and randomness r is created as $\mathsf{CCA.Com}(\mathsf{tag}, m; r) \to \mathsf{Com}$. The scheme is statistically binding in that for all $\mathsf{tag}_0, \mathsf{tag}_1, r_0, r_1$ and $m_0 \neq m_1$ we have that $\mathsf{CCA.Com}(\mathsf{tag}_0, m_0; r_0) \neq \mathsf{CCA.Com}(\mathsf{tag}_1, m_1; r_1)$.

Our hiding property follows along the lines of chosen commitment security definitions [6] where an attacker gives a challenge tag tag^* along with messages m_0, m_1 and receives a challenge commitment Com^* to either m_0 or m_1 from the experiment. The attacker's job is to guess the message that was committed to with the aid of oracle access to an (inefficient) value function $\mathsf{CCACom.Val}$ where $\mathsf{CCACom.Val}(\mathsf{Com})$ will return m if $\mathsf{CCA.Com}(\mathsf{tag}, m; r) \to \mathsf{Com}$ for some r. The attacker is allowed oracle access to $\mathsf{CCACom.Val}(\cdot)$ for any $\mathsf{tag} \neq \mathsf{tag}^*$.

The computation enabled property allows the attacker to submit a randomized turing machine P at the beginning of the game. The challenger will run the program P and output the result for the attacker at the beginning of the game. This added property will be useful in our proof of security. In addition, we require a message recovery from randomness property, which allows one to open the commitment given all the randomness used to generate said commitment.

A computation enabled CCA secure commitment is parameterized by a tag space of size $N = N(\kappa)$ and tags in $[1, N]$. It consists of 3 algorithms:

$\mathsf{CCA.Com}(1^\kappa, \mathsf{tag}, m; r) \to \mathsf{Com}$ is a randomized PPT algorithm that takes as input the security parameter κ, a tag $\mathsf{tag} \in [N]$, a message $m \in \{0,1\}^*$ and outputs a commitment Com, including the tag $\mathsf{Com.tag}$. We denote the random coins explicitly as r.

$\mathsf{CCACom.Val}(\mathsf{Com}) \to m \cup \bot$ is a deterministic inefficient algorithm that takes in a commitment Com and outputs either a message $m \in \{0,1\}^*$ or a reject symbol $\bot$.

$\mathsf{CCACom.Recover}(\mathsf{Com}, r) \to m$ is a deterministic algorithm which takes a commitment Com and the randomness r used to generate Com and outputs the underlying message m.

We now define the correctness, efficiency properties, as well as the security properties of perfectly binding and message hiding.

A computation enabled CCA secure commitment scheme is perfectly correct if the following holds. $\forall m \in \{0,1\}^*$, $\mathsf{tag} \in [N]$ and r we have that

$$\mathsf{CCACom.Val}(\mathsf{CCA.Com}(1^\kappa, \mathsf{tag}, m; r)) = m.$$

A computation enabled CCA secure commitment scheme is efficient if $\mathsf{CCA.Com}, \mathsf{CCACom.Recover}$ run in time $\mathrm{poly}(|m|, \kappa)$, while $\mathsf{CCACom.Val}$ runs in time $\mathrm{poly}(|m|, 2^\kappa)$.

A computation enabled CCA secure commitment is perfectly binding if $\forall m_0, m_1 \in \{0,1\}^*$ s.t. $m_0 \neq m_1$ there does not exist $\mathsf{tag}_0, \mathsf{tag}_1, r_0, r_1$ such that $\mathsf{CCA.Com}(1^\kappa, \mathsf{tag}_0, m_0; r_0) = \mathsf{CCA.Com}(1^\kappa, \mathsf{tag}_1, m_1; r_1)$.

Remark 1. We remark that this is implied by correctness, as we know that if $\mathsf{CCA.Com}(1^\kappa, \mathsf{tag}_0, m_0; r_0) = \mathsf{CCA.Com}(1^\kappa, \mathsf{tag}_1, m_1; r_1)$, then

$$m_0 = \mathsf{CCACom.Val}(\mathsf{CCA.Com}(1^\kappa, \mathsf{tag}_0, m_0; r_0))$$
$$= \mathsf{CCACom.Val}(\mathsf{CCA.Com}(1^\kappa, \mathsf{tag}_1, m_1; r_1)) = m_1,$$

but $m_0 \neq m_1$, a contradiction.

We define our message hiding game between a challenger and an attacker. The game is parameterized by a security parameter κ.

1. The attacker sends a randomized and inputless Turing Machine algorithm P. The challenger runs the program on random coins and sends the output to the attacker. If the program takes more than 2^{2^κ} time to halt, the outputs halts the evaluation and outputs the empty string.[1]
2. The attacker sends a "challenge tag" $\mathsf{tag}^* \in [N]$.
3. The attacker makes repeated commitment queries Com. If $\mathsf{Com.tag} = \mathsf{tag}^*$ the challenger responds with $\bot$. Otherwise it responds as

$$\mathsf{CCACom.Val}(\mathsf{Com}).$$

4. For some w, the attacker sends two messages $m_0, m_1 \in \{0,1\}^w$.
5. The challenger flips a coin $b \in \{0,1\}$ and sends $\mathsf{Com}^* = \mathsf{CCA.Com}(\mathsf{tag}^*, m_b; r)$ for randomly chosen r.
6. The attacker again makes repeated queries of commitment Com. If $\mathsf{Com.tag} = \mathsf{tag}^*$ the challenger responds with $\bot$. Otherwise it sends

$$\mathsf{CCACom.Val}(\mathsf{Com}).$$

7. The attacker finally outputs a guess b'.

We define the attacker's advantage in the game to be $\Pr[b' = b] - \frac{1}{2}$ where the probability is over all the attacker and challenger's coins.

Definition 7. *An attack algorithm $\mathcal{A}$ is said to be e-conforming for some real value $e > 0$ if:*

1. *$\mathcal{A}$ is a (randomized) uniform algorithm.*
2. *$\mathcal{A}$ runs in polynomial time.*
3. *The program P output by $\mathcal{A}$ in Step 1 of the game terminates in time $p(2^{\kappa^e})$ and outputs at most $q(\kappa)$ bits for some polynomial functions p, q (For all possible random tapes given to the program P).*

Definition 8. *A computation enabled CCA secure commitment scheme given by algorithms $(\mathsf{CCA.Com}, \mathsf{CCACom.Val}, \mathsf{CCACom.Recover})$ is said to be e-computation enabled CCA secure if for any e-conforming adversary $\mathcal{A}$ there exists a negligible function $\mathsf{negl}(\cdot)$ such that the attacker's advantage in the game is $\mathsf{negl}(\kappa)$.*

---

[1] The choice of 2^{2^κ} is somewhat arbitrary as the condition is in place so that the game is well defined on all P.

Definition 9. *We say that our CCA secure commitment scheme can be recovered from randomness if the following holds. For all* $m \in \{0,1\}^*$, tag $\in [N]$, *and* r, CCACom.Recover(CCA.Com(1^κ, tag, $m; r$), r) = m.

Claim. Let (CCA.Com, CCACom.Val) be a set of algorithms which satisfy the correctness, efficiency, binding and Definition 8. Then there exists a set of algorithms (CCA'.Com, CCA'.Val, CCA'.Recover) which satisfy the same properties as well as Definition 9.

Proof. Consider the following transformation:

$$\text{RecoverRandom}(\text{NM} = (\text{CCA.Com}, \text{CCACom.Val})) \rightarrow \text{NM}' =$$

$$(\text{CCA}'.\text{Com}, \text{CCA}'.\text{Val}, \text{CCA}'.\text{Recover}) :$$

CCA'.Com(tag, $m; r = (r_0, r_1)$) : Let Com = CCA.Com(tag, r_0), and $c = r_1 \oplus m$.
    Output (Com, c).
CCA'.Val(Com' = (Com, c)) : Output CCACom.Val(Com).
CCA'.Recover(Com' = (Com, c), $r = (r_0, r_1)$) : Output $c \oplus r_1$.

We can see that correctness, efficiency and binding all hold if they do in the underlying scheme as they call the underlying CCA.Com, CCACom.Val once. To see that Definition 8 still holds, we can consider an attacker $\mathcal{A}$ against NM'. We can construct an attacker for NM by taking the challenge commitment Com, appending w uniformly random bits c' to it, and running $\mathcal{A}$ on (Com, c'). Let m be the underlying message in Com. Since c' is independent and uniformly random, so is $c' \oplus m$, meaning that (Com, c') produces a distribution of Com' identical to CCA'.Com. Finally, we can see that our transformation satisfies Definition 9 as $c \oplus r_1 = m \oplus r_1 \oplus r_1 = m$.

Connecting to Standard Security. We now connect our computation enabled definition of security to the standard notion of chosen commitment security. In particular, the standard notion of chosen commitment security is simply the computation enabled above, but removing the first step of submitting a program P. We prove two straightforward lemmas. The first showing that any computation enabled CCA secure commitment scheme is a standard secure one against uniform attackers. The second is that any non-uniformly secure standard scheme satisfies e-computation enabled security for any constant $e \geq 0$.

Definition 10. *A commitment* (CCA.Com, CCACom.Val, CCACom.Recover) *is said to be CCA secure against uniform/non-uniform attackers if for any polytime uniform/non-uniform adversary* $\mathcal{A}$ *there exists a negligible function* negl($\cdot$) *such that* $\mathcal{A}$'s *advantage in the above game with Step 1 removed is* negl(κ).

Claim. If (CCA.Com, CCACom.Val, CCACom.Recover) is an *e*-computation enabled CCA secure commitment scheme for some *e* as per Definition 8, then it is also a scheme that achieves standard CCA security against uniform poly-time attackers as per Definition 10.

Proof. This follows from the fact that any uniform attacker $\mathcal{A}$ in the standard security game with advantage $\epsilon(\kappa) = \epsilon$ immediately implies an *e*-conforming attacker $\mathcal{A}'$ with the same advantage where $\mathcal{A}'$ outputs a program P that immediately halts and then runs $\mathcal{A}$.

Claim. If (CCA.Com, CCACom.Val, CCACom.Recover) achieves standard CCA security against *non-uniform* poly-time attackers as per Definition 10, then it is an *e*-computation enabled CCA secure commitment scheme for any *e* as per Definition 8.

Proof. Suppose $\mathcal{A}$ is an *e*-conforming attacker for some *e* with some advantage $\epsilon = \epsilon(\kappa)$. Then our non-uniform attacker $\mathcal{A}'$ can fix the random coins of $\mathcal{A}$ and to maximize its probability of success. Since now $\mathcal{A}$ is deterministic save for randomness produced by the challenger in step 5, this deterministically fixes the P $\mathcal{A}$ sends, so $\mathcal{A}'$ can fix the coins of P to maximize success. Thus, $\mathcal{A}'$ can simulate $\mathcal{A}$ given the above aforementioned random coins of $\mathcal{A}$ and the output of P, both of which are poly-bounded by the fact that $\mathcal{A}$ is *e*-conforming. Since all non-challenger randomness was non-uniformly fixed to maximize success, $\mathcal{A}'$ has at least advantage ϵ as well. By our definition of standard security hiding, the advantage of $\mathcal{A}'$ must be negligible, so $\mathcal{A}$'s advantage must be as well.

Decryption in Exponential Time. We will implicitly assume that any message m committed to using security parameter 1^κ can be retrieved with probability 1 by an algorithm running in time $2^\kappa q(\kappa)$ for some polynomial function q. We denote CCACom.Dec as the algorithm for doing this.

4   Defining CCA Compatibility

In this section we provide formal definitions of what it means for a scheme to be CPA/CCA compatible. This will be a property of any KeyGen algorithm, and our main technical result will establish that CPA compatibility implies CCA compatibility (under appropriate hardness assumptions).

Definition 11 (CPA Compatibility). *An algorithm* KeyGen *is said to be non-uniform (resp., uniform) T-CPA-compatible for $T = T(\kappa)$ and message space $\mathcal{M}(\kappa)$, if there exist poly-time algorithms* Enc, Dec *such that* (KeyGen, Enc, Dec) *comprise a public key encryption scheme for message space $\mathcal{M}(\kappa)$, that satisfies $p(T)$-IND-CPA according to Definition 3 (resp., Definition 4), for every polynomial function $p(\cdot)$.*

Definition 12 (CCA1 Compatibility). *An algorithm* KeyGen *is said to be non-uniform (resp., uniform) T-CCA1-compatible for message space $\mathcal{M}(\kappa)$, if there exist poly-time algorithms* Enc, Dec *such that* (KeyGen, Enc, Dec) *comprise a public key encryption scheme for message space $\mathcal{M}(\kappa)$, that satisfies $p(T)$-IND-CCA1 according to Definition 3 (resp., Definition 4), for every polynomial function $p(\cdot)$.*

Definition 13 (CCA2 Compatibility). *An algorithm* KeyGen *is said to be non-uniform (resp., uniform) T-CCA2-compatible for message space $\mathcal{M}(\kappa)$, if there exist poly-time algorithms* Enc, Dec *such that* (KeyGen, Enc, Dec) *comprise a public key encryption scheme for message space $\mathcal{M}(\kappa)$, that satisfies $p(T)$-IND-CCA2 according to Definition 3 (resp., Definition 4), for every polynomial function $p(\cdot)$.*

Our main result is that any KeyGen that is non-uniform $T(\lambda)$-CPA-compatible where $T = 2^{\lambda^c}$ for any constant $c > 0$, is uniform λ-CCA1-compatible and uniform λ-CCA2-compatible, under appropriate computational hardness assumptions.

5   On CCA2 Compatibility

Our Construction

Let κ denote the security parameter, $0 < \delta < 1$ be a constant and $\kappa' = \kappa^\delta$. We now provide our construction of an IND-CCA2 secure encryption system that uses any $2^{\kappa'}$-CPA compatible KeyGen algorithm, according to Definition 11. Our construction relies on a hinting PRG, non-interactive computation enabled CCA commitments and subexponentially secure equivocal commitments.

Let (CPA.Enc, CPA.Dec) be the encryption and decryption algorithms of the non-uniform $2^{\kappa'}$-IND-CPA secure public key encryption scheme with randomness-recoverable ciphertexts and perfect decryption correctness, that is guaranteed to exist by Definition 11. We will also assume that the following exist:

- An equivocal commitment (Equiv.Com, Equiv.Decom, Equiv.Equivocate) that is $T = 2^{\kappa'}$ binding secure.
- A $2^{\kappa'}$-secure hinting PRG scheme HPRG = (HPRG.Setup, HPRG.Eval) against non-uniform adversaries.
- A non-interactive e-computation enabled CCA commitment scheme represented by algorithms (CCA.Com, CCACom.Val, CCACom.Recover), with security parameter κ' and with $e = 1/\delta$ (for the same δ), such that the commitment scheme can be broken in brute force in time $2^{\kappa'}$.
- An existentially unforgeable under chosen message attack (EUF-CMA) signature (Signature.Setup, Sign, Verify) with security parameter κ'.

We will now describe our CCA secure public key encryption scheme $\mathsf{PKE}_{\mathsf{CCA}}$ = (KeyGen, CCA.Enc, CCA.Dec) with message space $\{0,1\}^{\ell(\kappa)}$. For simplicity of notation, we will skip the dependence of ℓ on κ. We will also assume that the CPA scheme has message space $\{0,1\}^{\kappa+1}$ and uses $\ell(\kappa)$ bits of randomness for encryption.

KeyGen(1^κ): The KeyGen algorithm outputs a public key cca.pk.
CCA.Enc(cca.pk, $m \in \{0,1\}^\ell$): The encryption algorithm is as follows:

1. It runs RetrieveParam(cca.pk) $\to \kappa$ and then calculates $\kappa' = \kappa^\delta$.
2. It samples (HPRG.pp, 1^n) $\leftarrow$ HPRG.Setup($1^\lambda, 1^\ell$).
3. It then chooses $s \leftarrow \{0,1\}^n$.
4. For each $i \in [n]$, it chooses random $r_i \leftarrow \{0,1\}^\ell$ and sets $\widetilde{r}_i =$ HPRG.Eval(HPRG.pp, s, i).
5. For each $i \in [n]$, it chooses $v_i \leftarrow \{0,1\}^\kappa$. It sets $\sigma_i = $ Equiv.Com($1^\kappa, s_i; v_i$), and $y_i = s_i|v_i$.
6. It sets $c = $ HPRG.Eval(HPRG.pp, $s, 0$) $\oplus m$ and for each $i \in [n]$
   - If $s_i = 0$, $c_{0,i} = $ CPA.Enc(cpa.pk, $y_i; \widetilde{r}_i$), $c_{1,i} = $ CCA.Com($1^{\kappa'}, vk, y_i; r_i$).
   - If $s_i = 1$, $c_{0,i} = $ CPA.Enc(cpa.pk, $y_i; r_i$), $c_{1,i} = $ CCA.Com($1^{\kappa'}, vk, y_i; \widetilde{r}_i$).[2]
7. It sets $\alpha = \left(\mathsf{HPRG.pp}, 1^n, c, (c_{0,i}, c_{1,i}, \sigma_i)_{i \in [n]}\right)$.
8. It samples $(vk, sk) \leftarrow$ Signature.Setup($1^{\kappa'}$).
9. Finally, it computes $\tau = $ Sign(sk, α), and outputs (vk, α, τ) as the ciphertext.

PKE.Find(cca.pk, cca.sk, α)

Inputs: Public Key cca.pk = cpa.pk

Secret Key cca.sk = cpa.sk

Ciphertext $\alpha = \left(\mathsf{HPRG.pp}, 1^n, c, (c_{0,i}, c_{1,i}, \sigma_i)_{i \in [n]}\right)$

Output: $d \in \{0,1\}^n$

- Let $\kappa = $ RetrieveParam(cpa.pk).
- For each $i \in [n]$, do the following:
  1. Let $m_i = $ CPA.Dec(cpa.sk, $c_{0,i}$).
  2. If $m_i = 0|v_i$ and $\sigma_i = $ Equiv.Com($1^\kappa, 0; v_i$), set $d_i = 0$. Else set $d_i = 1$.
- Output $d = d_1 d_2 \ldots d_n$.

Fig. 1. Routine PKE.Find

---

[2] For ease of exposition we assume that ℓ coins are both used for encryption with security parameter κ as well as a commitment with security parameter κ'. In practice if one is less than then other the extraneous bits can be truncated.

$$\text{PKE.Check(cca.pk, cca.ct, } d)$$

Inputs: $\text{cca.pk} = \text{cpa.pk}, \text{cca.ct} = (vk, \alpha, \tau)$ where

$$\alpha = \left(\text{HPRG.pp}, 1^n, c, (c_{0,i}, c_{1,i}, \sigma_i)_{i \in [n]} \right), d \in \{0,1\}^n$$

Output: $\text{msg} \in \{0,1\}^\ell \cup \perp$

- Let $\kappa = \text{RetrieveParam(cpa.pk)}$. Compute $\kappa' = \kappa^e$.
- Let flag = true. For $i = 1$ to n, do the following:
  1. Let $\widetilde{r}_i = \text{HPRG.Eval(HPRG.pp}, d, i)$.
  2. If $d_i = 0$, let $m \leftarrow \text{CPA.Recover(cpa.pk}, c_{0,i}, \widetilde{r}_i)$. Parse $m = (s'|v')$ and perform the following checks. If any of the checks fail, set flag = false and exit loop.
     - $s' = 0$, $\text{CPA.Enc(cpa.pk}, m; \widetilde{r}_i) = c_{0,i}$.
     - $\sigma_i = \text{Equiv.Com}(1^\kappa, s'; v')$.
  3. If $d_i = 1$, let $m \leftarrow \text{CCACom.Recover}(1^{\kappa'}, c_{1,i}, \widetilde{r}_i)$. Parse $m = (s'|v')$ and perform the following checks. If any of the checks fail, set flag = false and exit loop.
     - $s' = 1$, $\text{CCA.Com}(1^{\kappa'}, vk, m; \widetilde{r}_i) = c_{1,i}$.
     - $\sigma_i = \text{Equiv.Com}(1^\kappa, s'; v')$.
- If flag = true, output $c \oplus \text{HPRG.Eval(HPRG.pp}, d, 0)$. Else $\perp$.

Fig. 2. Routine PKE.Check

$\text{CCA.Dec(cca.sk, cca.pk, cca.ct)}$: Parse ciphertext cca.ct as (vk, α, τ) where cca.sk $= \text{cpa.sk}$ and $\alpha = \left(\text{HPRG.pp}, 1^n, c, (c_{0,i}, c_{1,i}, \sigma_i)_{i \in [n]} \right)$. Output $\perp$ if $\text{Verify}(vk, \alpha, \tau) = 0$. Otherwise, set $d = \text{PKE.Find(cca.pk, cca.sk}, \alpha)$ (where PKE.Find is defined in Fig. 1), and output $\text{PKE.Check(cca.pk, cca.ct}, d)$ (where PKE.Check is defined in Figure 2).

References

1. Berman, I., Degwekar, A., Rothblum, R.D., Vasudevan, P.N.: Multi-collision resistant hash functions and their applications. In: Nielsen and Rijmen [27], pp. 133–161, https://doi.org/10.1007/978-3-319-78375-8_5
2. Bitansky, N., Kalai, Y.T., Paneth, O.: Multi-collision resistance: a paradigm for keyless hash functions. In: Diakonikolas, I., Kempe, D., Henzinger, M. (eds.) Proceedings of the 50th Annual ACM SIGACT STOC 2018, Los Angeles, CA, USA, June 25–29, 2018, pp. 671–684. ACM (2018). https://doi.org/10.1145/3188745.3188870
3. Bitansky, N., Lin, H.: One-message zero knowledge and non-malleable commitments. In: Beimel, A., Dziembowski, S. (eds.) TCC 2018. LNCS, vol. 11239, pp. 209–234. Springer, Cham (2018). https://doi.org/10.1007/978-3-030-03807-6_8

4. Bleichenbacher, D.: Chosen ciphertext attacks against protocols based on the RSA encryption standard PKCS #1. In: Krawczyk [23], pp. 1–12. https://doi.org/10.1007/BFb0055716

5. Boldyreva, A., Micciancio, D. (eds.): CRYPTO 2019. LNCS, vol. 11694. Springer, Cham (2019). https://doi.org/10.1007/978-3-030-26954-8

6. Canetti, R., Lin, H., Pass, R.: Adaptive hardness and composable security in the plain model from standard assumptions. In: Proceedings of the 51th Annual IEEE Symposium on Foundations of Computer Science. FOCS 2010, pp. 541–550 (2010)

7. Castryck, W., Sotáková, J., Vercauteren, F.: Breaking the decisional diffie-hellman problem for class group actions using genus theory. Cryptology ePrint Archive, Report 2020/151 (2020). https://eprint.iacr.org/2020/151

8. Cramer, R., Shoup, V.: A practical public key cryptosystem provably secure against adaptive chosen ciphertext attack. In: Krawczyk [23], pp. 13–25. https://doi.org/10.1007/BFb0055717

9. Crescenzo, G.D., Ishai, Y., Ostrovsky, R.: Non-interactive and non-malleable commitment. In: Proceedings of the Thirtieth Annual ACM STOC, Dallas, Texas, USA, 23–26 May 1998, pp. 141–150 (1998). https://doi.org/10.1145/276698.276722, http://doi.acm.org/10.1145/276698.276722

10. Damgård, I.B., Pedersen, T.P., Pfitzmann, B.: On the existence of statistically hiding bit commitment schemes and fail-stop signatures. In: Stinson, D.R. (ed.) CRYPTO 1993. LNCS, vol. 773, pp. 250–265. Springer, Heidelberg (1994). https://doi.org/10.1007/3-540-48329-2_22

11. Dolev, D., Dwork, C., Naor, M.: Nonmalleable cryptography. SIAM J. Comput. **30**(2), 391–437 (2000). https://doi.org/10.1137/S0097539795291562

12. Fujisaki, E., Okamoto, T.: Secure integration of asymmetric and symmetric encryption schemes. J. Cryptology **26**(1), 80–101 (2013). https://doi.org/10.1007/s00145-011-9114-1

13. Garg, R., Khurana, D., Lu, G., Waters, B.: Black-box non-interactive non-malleable commitments. Manuscript (2020)

14. Garg, S., Gentry, C., Sahai, A., Waters, B.: Witness encryption and its applications. In: Boneh, D., Roughgarden, T., Feigenbaum, J. (eds.) Symposium on Theory of Computing Conference, STOC 2013, Palo Alto, CA, USA, 1–4 June 2013.,pp. 467–476. ACM (2013). https://doi.org/10.1145/2488608.2488667

15. Goldwasser, S., Micali, S.: Probabilistic encryption. J. Comput. Syst. Sci. **28**(2), 270–299 (1984). https://doi.org/10.1016/0022-0000(84)90070-9

16. Halevi, S., Micali, S.: Practical and provably-secure commitment schemes from collision-free hashing. In: Koblitz, N. (ed.) CRYPTO 1996. LNCS, vol. 1109, pp. 201–215. Springer, Heidelberg (1996). https://doi.org/10.1007/3-540-68697-5_16

17. Jakobsen, J., Orlandi, C.: On the CCA (in)security of mtproto. In: Proc. of the 6th Workshop on Security and Privacy in Smartphones Mobile Devices, SPSM@CCS 2016, pp. 113–116 (2016). http://dl.acm.org/citation.cfm?id=2994468

18. Kalai, Y.T., Khurana, D.: Non-interactive non-malleability from quantum supremacy. In: Boldyreva and Micciancio [5], pp. 552–582. https://doi.org/10.1007/978-3-030-26954-8_18

19. Khurana, D., Sahai, A.: How to achieve non-malleability in one or two rounds. In: Umans [30], pp. 564–575. https://doi.org/10.1109/FOCS.2017.58

20. Kitagawa, F., Matsuda, T., Tanaka, K.: CCA security and trapdoor functions via key-dependent-message security. In: Boldyreva and Micciancio [5], pp. 33–64. https://doi.org/10.1007/978-3-030-26954-8_2

21. Komargodski, I., Naor, M., Yogev, E.: Collision resistant hashing for paranoids: dealing with multiple collisions. In: Nielsen and Rijmen [27], pp. 162–194. https://doi.org/10.1007/978-3-319-78375-8_6

22. Koppula, V., Waters, B.: Realizing chosen ciphertext security generically in attribute-based encryption and predicate encryption. In: Boldyreva, A., Micciancio, D. (eds.) CRYPTO 2019. LNCS, vol. 11693, pp. 671–700. Springer, Cham (2019). https://doi.org/10.1007/978-3-030-26951-7_23

23. Krawczyk, H. (ed.): CRYPTO 1998. LNCS, vol. 1462. Springer, Heidelberg (1998). https://doi.org/10.1007/BFb0055715

24. Lin, H., Pass, R., Soni, P.: Two-round and non-interactive concurrent non-malleable commitments from time-lock puzzles. In: Umans [3], pp. 576–587. https://doi.org/10.1109/FOCS.2017.59, https://ieeexplore.ieee.org/xpl/conhome/8100284/proceeding

25. Lombardi, A., Schaeffer, L.: A note on key agreement and non-interactive commitments. Cryptology ePrint Archive, Report 2019/279 (2019). https://eprint.iacr.org/2019/279

26. Naor, M., Yung, M.: Public-key cryptosystems provably secure against chosen ciphertext attacks. In: Ortiz, H. (ed.) Proceedings of the 22nd Annual ACM STOC, 1990, pp. 427–437. ACM (1990). https://doi.org/10.1145/100216.100273

27. Nielsen, J.B., Rijmen, V. (eds.): EUROCRYPT 2018. LNCS, vol. 10821. Springer, Cham (2018). https://doi.org/10.1007/978-3-319-78375-8

28. Pass, R.: Unprovable security of perfect NIZK and non-interactive non-malleable commitments. Comput. Complex. **25**(3), 607–666 (2016). https://doi.org/10.1007/s00037-016-0122-2

29. Rackoff, C., Simon, D.R.: Non-interactive zero-knowledge proof of knowledge and chosen ciphertext attack. In: Feigenbaum, J. (ed.) CRYPTO 1991. LNCS, vol. 576, pp. 433–444. Springer, Heidelberg (1992). https://doi.org/10.1007/3-540-46766-1_35

30. Umans, C. (ed.): 58th IEEE annual symposium on foundations of computer science, FOCS 2017, Berkeley, CA, USA, 15–17 October 2017. IEEE Computer Society (2017). https://ieeexplore.ieee.org/xpl/conhome/8100284/proceeding

Round-Optimal Verifiable Oblivious Pseudorandom Functions from Ideal Lattices

Martin R. Albrecht[1]([✉]), Alex Davidson[2,3], Amit Deo[1,4], and Nigel P. Smart[5,6]

[1] Information Security Group, Royal Holloway, University of London, London, UK
martin.albrecht@royalholloway.ac.uk
[2] Laboratório de Instrumentação e Física Experimental de Partículas,
Lisboa, Portugal
[3] Cloudflare, Lisbon, Portugal
[4] ENS de Lyon, Laboratoire LIP (U. Lyon, CNRS, ENSL, INRIA, UCBL),
Lyon, France
amit.deo@ens-lyon.fr
[5] COSIC-imec, KU Leuven, Leuven, Belgium
nigel.smart@kuleuven.be
[6] Department of Computer Science, University of Bristol, Bristol, UK

Abstract. Verifiable Oblivious Pseudorandom Functions (VOPRFs) are protocols that allow a client to learn verifiable pseudorandom function (PRF) evaluations on inputs of their choice. The PRF evaluations are computed by a server using their own secret key. The security of the protocol prevents both the server from learning anything about the client's input, and likewise the client from learning anything about the server's key. VOPRFs have many applications including password-based authentication, secret-sharing, anonymous authentication and efficient private set intersection. In this work, we construct the first round-optimal (online) VOPRF protocol that retains security from well-known subexponential lattice hardness assumptions. Our protocol requires constructions of non-interactive zero-knowledge arguments of knowledge (NIZKAoK). Using recent developments in the area of post-quantum zero-knowledge arguments of knowledge, we show that our VOPRF may be securely instantiated in the quantum random oracle model. We construct such arguments as extensions of prior work in the area of lattice-based zero-knowledge proof systems.

1 Introduction

A verifiable oblivious pseudorandom function (VOPRF) is an interactive protocol between two parties; a client and a server. Intuitively, this protocol allows a server to provide a client with an evaluation of a pseudorandom function (PRF) on an input x chosen by the client using the server's key k. Informally, the security of a VOPRF, from the server's perspective, guarantees that the client learns

---

The full version of this work is available as [1].

© International Association for Cryptologic Research 2021
J. A. Garay (Ed.): PKC 2021, LNCS 12711, pp. 261–289, 2021.
https://doi.org/10.1007/978-3-030-75248-4_10

nothing more than the PRF evaluated at x using k as the key where the server has committed to k in advance. Informally, security from the perspective of the client guarantees the conditions below:

1. the server learns nothing about the input x;
2. the client's output in the protocol is indeed the evaluation on input x and key k;

The fact that the client is ensured that its output corresponds to the key committed to by the server makes the protocol a *verifiable* oblivious PRF. If we were to remove this requirement, the protocol would be an *oblivious* pseudorandom function (OPRF). From a multi-party computation perspective, an OPRF can be seen as a protocol that securely achieves the functionality $g(x, k) = (F_k(x), \perp)$ where F_k is a PRF using key k and $\perp$ indicates that the server receives no output. Applications of (V)OPRFs include secure keyword search [24], private set intersection [32], secure data de-duplication [33], password-protected secret sharing [29,30], password-authenticated key exchange (PAKE) [31] and privacy-preserving lightweight authentication mechanisms [18].

A number of these applications have had recent and considerable real-world impact. The work of Jarecki et al. [31] constructs a PAKE protocol, known as OPAQUE, using an OPRF as a core primitive. The OPAQUE protocol is intended for integration with TLS 1.3 to enable password-based authentication, and it is currently in the process of being standardised [34] by the Crypto Forum Research Group (CFRG)[1] as part of the PAKE selection process [17]. In addition, the work of Davidson et al. [18] constructs a privacy-preserving authorisation mechanism (known as Privacy Pass) for anonymously bypassing Internet reverse Turing tests based entirely on the security of a VOPRF. The Privacy Pass protocol is currently used at scale by the web performance company Cloudflare [46], and there have also been recent efforts to standardise the protocol design [19]. Both Privacy Pass and OPAQUE use discrete-log (DL) based (V)OPRF constructions to produce notably performant protocols. Finally, there is a separate and ongoing effort being carried forward by the CFRG [20] focusing directly on standardising performant DL-based VOPRF constructions.

Unfortunately, and in spite of the practical value of VOPRFs, all of the available constructions in the literature to date (at the time of writing) are based on classical assumptions, such as decisional Diffie-Hellman (DDH) and RSA. As such, all current VOPRFs would be insecure when confronted with an adversary that can run quantum computations. Therefore, the design of a post-quantum secure VOPRF is required to ensure that the applications above remain secure in these future adversarial conditions.[2] In fact, for full post-quantum security, both the PRF and the VOPRF protocol itself must be secure in the quantum adversarial model. While PRF constructions with claimed post-quantum security are standard, it remains an open problem to translate these into secure VOPRF protocols.

---

[1] A subsidiary of the Internet Research Task Force (IRTF).

[2] Note that using post-quantum secure VOPRF primitives in either the OPAQUE or Privacy Pass examples above would immediately result in PQ-secure alternatives.

Constructions of PRFs arising from lattice-based cryptography originated from the work of Banerjee, Peikert and Rosen [6]. These constructions are post-quantum secure assuming the hardness of the learning with errors (LWE) problem against quantum adversaries [45]. To get around the fact that the LWE problem involves the addition of random small errors, carefully chosen rounding is used to obtain *deterministic* outputs for PRFs based on the LWE assumption [5,6,11]. These earlier works on LWE-based PRFs were followed by constructions of more advanced variants of PRFs [14,16,44]. Despite this, there is yet to be an OPRF protocol for any LWE-based PRF. The same is true for variants of these constructions based on the ring LWE (RLWE) problem [5].

Contributions. In this work, we instantiate a round-optimal[3] VOPRF whose security relies on subexponential hardness assumptions over lattices. Our construction assumes certain non-interactive zero-knowledge arguments of knowledge (NIZKAoKs). We use the protocol of Yang et al. [47] as an example instantiation of the required NIZKAoKs, to argue knowledge of inputs to the input-dependent part of PRF evaluations from the Banerjee and Peikert design [5] (henceforth BP14) in the ring setting. Alternatively, one can use Stern-like methods such as those in [36] and the recent protocol of Beullens [7]. These choices come with the advantage that results stating the validity of the Fiat-Shamir transform in the quantum random oracle model (QROM) [22,37] will apply.

We stress that our results show the *feasibility* of round-optimal VOPRF protocols based on lattice assumptions, rather than practicality. The performance of the VOPRF is negatively impacted by the required size of parameters (see Sect. 5.3). These parameters are necessary for instantiating our construction using reasonable underlying lattice assumptions – a consequence of using the BP14 PRF construction with our proof technique. Moreover, we require heavy zero-knowledge proof computations to ensure that neither participant deviates from the protocol. Some of these proofs may be removed by considering certain optimisations of our main protocol (see Sect. 3.2). Additionally, removing all zero-knowledge proofs and considering an honest-but-curious setting may result in a relatively efficient protocol (see Sect. 5.3).

Technical Overview. We design a VOPRF for a particular instantiation of the BP14 PRF in the ring setting. Specifically, for a particular *function* $\boldsymbol{a}^F$: $\{0,1\}^L \rightarrow R_q^{1 \times \ell}$ where $R_q := \mathbb{Z}_q[X]/\langle X^n + 1 \rangle$, we set out to design a VOPRF for the PRF

$$F_k(x) = \left\lceil \frac{p}{q} \cdot \boldsymbol{a}^F(x) \cdot k \right\rfloor$$

where the key $k \in R_q$ has small coefficients when represented in $\{-q/2, \ldots, q/2\}$, and $\lceil \cdot \rfloor$ represents rounding a rational to the nearest natural number. Our VOPRF protocol can be easily modified to handle other choices of $\boldsymbol{a}^F(x)$ (up to a change in parameter requirements). The security of this BP14 PRF construction can be reduced to the hardness of RLWE. Consider the PRF for 2-bit

---

[3] Meaning that only two messages are sent in the online (query) phase.

inputs: then $\boldsymbol{a}^F(x) = \boldsymbol{a}_1 \cdot G^{-1}(\boldsymbol{a}_2)$ where $\boldsymbol{a}_1, \boldsymbol{a}_2 \in R_q^{1 \times \ell}$ are uniform and public, $G = (1, 2, \ldots, 2^{\ell-1})$ and $G^{-1}(\boldsymbol{a}_2) \in R_2^{\ell \times \ell}$ is binary. Very informally, for small $\boldsymbol{e}, \boldsymbol{e}'' \in R_q^{1 \times \ell}$, uniform $\boldsymbol{e}' \in R_q^{1 \times \ell}/(R_q \cdot G)$ and q much larger than p, we can write

$$\left\lfloor \frac{p}{q} \cdot \boldsymbol{a}^F(x) \cdot k \right\rceil = \left\lfloor \frac{p}{q} \cdot k \cdot \boldsymbol{a}_1 \cdot G^{-1}(\boldsymbol{a}_2) \right\rceil = \left\lfloor \frac{p}{q} \cdot (k \cdot \boldsymbol{a}_1 + \boldsymbol{e}) \cdot G^{-1}(\boldsymbol{a}_2) \right\rceil$$

$$\approx_c \left\lfloor \frac{p}{q} \cdot (u) \cdot G^{-1}(\boldsymbol{a}_2) \right\rceil \quad \text{(RLWE)}$$

$$= \left\lfloor \frac{p}{q}(u'G + \boldsymbol{e}') \cdot G^{-1}(\boldsymbol{a}_2) \right\rceil = \left\lfloor \frac{p}{q}(u'\boldsymbol{a}_2 + \boldsymbol{e}'') + \frac{p}{q}\boldsymbol{e}' \cdot G^{-1}(\boldsymbol{a}_2) \right\rceil$$

$$\approx_c \left\lfloor \frac{p}{q} \cdot \boldsymbol{u}'' + \frac{p}{q} \cdot \boldsymbol{e}' \cdot G^{-1}(\boldsymbol{a}_2) \right\rceil \quad \text{(RLWE)}$$

$$= \left\lfloor \frac{p}{q} \cdot \tilde{\boldsymbol{u}} \right\rceil$$

where $\boldsymbol{u}, \boldsymbol{u}'', \tilde{\boldsymbol{u}}$ are uniform in $R_q^{1 \times \ell}$ and u' is uniform in R_q. The proof of pseudorandomness builds on these ideas.

To provide intuition for our VOPRF design, we describe the rough form of our protocol (without zero-knowledge proofs). Given a public uniform $\boldsymbol{a} \in R_q^{1 \times \ell}$, the high level overview is as follows:

1. The server publishes some commitment $\boldsymbol{c} := \boldsymbol{a} \cdot k + \boldsymbol{e}$ to a small key $k \in R_q$.
2. On input x, the client picks *small* $s \in R_q$, small $\boldsymbol{e}_1 \in R_q^{1 \times \ell}$ and sends $\boldsymbol{c}_x = \boldsymbol{a} \cdot s + \boldsymbol{e}_1 + \boldsymbol{a}^F(x)$.
3. On input small $k \in R_q$, the server sends $\boldsymbol{d}_x = \boldsymbol{c}_x \cdot k + \boldsymbol{e}'$ for small $\boldsymbol{e}' \in R_q^{1 \times \ell}$.
4. The client outputs $\boldsymbol{y} = \left\lfloor \frac{p}{q} \cdot (\boldsymbol{d}_x - \boldsymbol{c} \cdot s) \right\rceil$.

For server security, note that $\boldsymbol{d}_x = \boldsymbol{a} \cdot s \cdot k + \boldsymbol{a}^F(x) \cdot k + \boldsymbol{e}_1 \cdot k + \boldsymbol{e}'$. Suppose that we choose $\boldsymbol{e}'$ from a distribution that hides addition of terms $\boldsymbol{e}_1 \cdot k$, $\boldsymbol{e} \cdot s$ and $\boldsymbol{e}_x$ (where $\boldsymbol{e}_x$ is from some other narrow distribution). Then, from the perspective of the client, the server might as well have sent $\boldsymbol{d}_x = (\boldsymbol{a} \cdot k + \boldsymbol{e}) \cdot s + \boldsymbol{e}' + (\boldsymbol{a}^F(x) \cdot k + \boldsymbol{e}_x) = \boldsymbol{c} \cdot s + (\boldsymbol{a}^F(x) \cdot k + \boldsymbol{e}_x) + \boldsymbol{e}'$. Picking $\boldsymbol{e}_x$ from an appropriate distribution [5] makes the term in brackets i.e. $\boldsymbol{a}^F(x) \cdot k + \boldsymbol{e}_x$ computationally indistinguishable from uniform random under a RLWE assumption, even given the value of $\boldsymbol{c}$ which is also indistinguishable from random by a RLWE assumption. This implies that the message $\boldsymbol{d}_x$ leaks nothing about the server's key k.

For client security, we pick s from a valid RLWE secret distribution and a Gaussian $\boldsymbol{e}$. This implies that $\boldsymbol{c}_x = \boldsymbol{a} \cdot s + \boldsymbol{e} + \boldsymbol{a}^F(x)$ is indistinguishable from uniform by RLWE. Finally, we must show that the client does indeed recover $F_k(x)$ as its output $\boldsymbol{y}$. For correctness, we *would like to say* that

$$\left\lfloor \frac{p}{q} \cdot (\boldsymbol{d}_x - \boldsymbol{c} \cdot s) \right\rceil = \left\lfloor \frac{p}{q} \cdot \boldsymbol{a}^F(x) \cdot k + \frac{p}{q}(\boldsymbol{e}_1 \cdot k - \boldsymbol{e} \cdot s + \boldsymbol{e}') \right\rceil = \left\lfloor \frac{p}{q} \cdot \boldsymbol{a}^F(x) \cdot k \right\rceil.$$

Thus, we guarantee correctness if all coefficients of $\frac{p}{q} \cdot \boldsymbol{a}^F(x) \cdot k$ are at least $\left| \frac{p}{q}(\boldsymbol{e}_1 \cdot k - \boldsymbol{e} \cdot s + \boldsymbol{e}') \right|_\infty$ away from $\mathbb{Z} + \frac{1}{2}$. It turns out that this condition is satisfied with extremely high probability due to the 1-dimensional short integer solution (1D-SIS) assumption [15] regardless of the way an efficient server chooses its key. The form of $a^F(x)$ is crucial to the connection with the 1D-SIS problem. In particular, we rely on the fact that we can decompose $a^F(x)$ as $a'_1 \cdot a'_2$ where $a'_1 \in R_q^{1 \times \ell}$ is uniform random and $a'_2 \in R_q^{\ell \times \ell}$ has entries that are polynomials with *binary* coefficients.

Ultimately, the security of our VOPRF construction (with particular choices of NIZKAoK instantiations) holds in the QROM and relies on the hardness of sub-exponential RLWE and 1D-SIS which are both at least as hard as certain lattice problems. We discuss parameters in Sect. 5.3.

Related Work and Discussion. Subsequent to this work, Boneh et al. [10] constructed a post-quantum (V)OPRF with comparatively good efficiency from isogenies. Their construction also uses the random oracle model, but is also proven secure in the universal composability (UC) model unlike the construction in this work. A related primitive to a VOPRF is a verifiable random function (VRF). A VRF is a keyed pseudorandom function allowing an entity with the key to create publicly verifiable proofs of correct evaluation. Recently, Yang et al. [47] showed a lattice-based construction of a VRF using the definition of [42]. In fact, the proof systems of Yang et al. serve as a crucial foundation for one way of instantiating the proof systems used in our VOPRF. However, it should be noted that the Yang et al. construction (like ours) is not in the standard model due to the use of the Fiat-Shamir [23] transform.

While our work provides a first construction for a post-quantum VOPRF, it does not resolve this question completely. The reason VOPRFs enjoy popularity is their efficiency in the discrete logarithm setting. In contrast, our construction – while practically instantiable – is far less efficient. This relative inefficiency is partly due to our choice of relying on lattice-based constructions for our zero-knowledge proof systems, along with the super-polynomial factors required for the RLWE-based PRF and noise drowning. Improving these areas thus suggests ways to achieve concretely more efficient schemes. In fact, we do discuss attempts to optimise our main protocol with a view to reducing the impact of the zero-knowledge proofs. In particular, one can amortise the costs of the client zero-knowledge proof by sending queries in batches and sending one proof of a more complex statement. This saves a small additive term in the overall cost compared to sending the queries one at a time. Additionally, we discuss the use of a cut-and-choose approach to removing the server's zero-knowledge proof at the effective cost of extra repetitions of the protocol. Ultimately, this does not improve overall efficiency, but it does dramatically reduce the burden on the server. For more details, see Sect. 3.2. An alternative approach is to accept, for now, that VOPRFs are less appealing building blocks in a post-quantum world, and to revisit their applications to provide post-quantum alternatives on a per application basis.

One could alternatively instantiate VOPRFs using generic techniques for establishing Multi-Party Computation (MPC) protocols by treating a single execution of the VOPRF protocol, for a PRF like AES, as a single invocation of a classical two-party *actively secure* MPC protocol. But this does not give the round-optimality that we are after. See the full version of this work for a discussion about this.

Road Map. We begin with preliminaries in Sect. 2. Note that Definition 1 deviates from the usual MPC definition. In particular, we argue security against malicious clients when k is sampled from a key distribution for which the PRF is pseudorandom, rather than arguing security for arbitrary fixed k. Next is the VOPRF construction and discussion of optimisations (Sect. 3) followed by a high-level description of the zero-knowledge proof instantiations (Sect. 4). Finally, we give the security proof for our VOPRF protocol in Sect. 5.

2   Preliminaries

All algorithms will be considered to be randomised algorithms unless explicitly stated otherwise. A PPT algorithm is a randomised (i.e. probabilistic) algorithm with polynomial running time in the security parameter κ. We consider the probability distribution of outputs of algorithms as being over all possible choices of the internal coins of the algorithm. For a distribution $\mathcal{D}$, we denote the sampling of x according to distribution $\mathcal{D}$ by $x \leftarrow \mathcal{D}$. We write $x \leftarrow S$ for a finite set S to indicate sampling uniformly at random from S. We use the notation $\mathcal{D}_1 \approx_c \mathcal{D}_2$ to mean the distributions $\mathcal{D}_1$ and $\mathcal{D}_2$ are computationally indistinguishable and $\approx_s$ to denote statistical indistinguishability. We use the standard asymptotic notations. We let $\mathsf{negl}(\kappa)$ denote a negligible function (i.e. a function that is $\kappa^{-\omega(1)}$) and write $r_1 \gg r_2$ as short-hand for $r_1 \geq \kappa^{\omega(1)} \cdot r_2$. We say a distribution $\mathcal{D}$ is (B, δ)-bounded if $\Pr[\|x\| \geq B \mid x \leftarrow \mathcal{D}] < \delta$. If a distribution is (B, δ)-bounded for a negligible δ, then we say that distribution is simply B-bounded.

In this work we will use power of two cyclotomic rings. In particular, for some integer q, we will be considering polynomials in the power-of-two cyclotomic ring $R = \mathbb{Z}[X]/\langle X^n + 1 \rangle$ and $R_q := R/qR$ where n is a power-of-two. $R_{\leq c}$ is the set of elements of R where all coefficients have an absolute value at most c. We also use a rounding operation from $\mathbb{Z}_q$ to $\mathbb{Z}_{q'}$ where $q' < q$. For $x \in \mathbb{Z}_q$, this rounding operation is defined as

$$\lfloor x \rceil_{q'} := \lfloor (q'/q) \cdot x \rceil$$

where $\lfloor \cdot \rceil$ denotes rounding to the nearest integer (rounding down in the case of a tie). If q' divides q, we can lift rounded integers back up to $\mathbb{Z}_q$ by simply multiplying by q/q'. Note that lifting the result of a rounding takes an $x \in \mathbb{Z}_q$ to the nearest multiple of q/q'. Therefore, the difference between x and the result of this rounding then lifting is at most $q/(2 \cdot q')$. Polynomials and vectors are rounded component-wise. We write $\|\cdot\|$ for the Euclidean norm and $\|\cdot\|_\infty$ for the infinity norm. We define the norms of ring elements by considering the norms of their *coefficient* vectors. Vectors whose entries are ring elements will be denoted using bold characters and integer vectors will be indicated by an over-arrow e.g. $\boldsymbol{v}$ has ring entries and $\vec{w}$ has integer entries. Suppose $\boldsymbol{v} = (v_1, \ldots, v_n)$. A norm of $\boldsymbol{v}$ is the norm of the vector obtained by concatenating the coefficient vectors of $v_1, \ldots, v_n$.

Gaussian distributions. For any $\sigma > 0$, define the *Gaussian function* on $\mathbb{R}^n$ centred at $\boldsymbol{c} \in \mathbb{R}^n$ with parameter σ to be:

$$\rho_{\sigma,\boldsymbol{c}}(\boldsymbol{x}) = e^{-\pi \cdot \|\boldsymbol{x}-\boldsymbol{c}\|^2/\sigma^2}, \ \forall \boldsymbol{x} \in \mathbb{R}^n.$$

Define $\rho_\sigma(\mathbb{Z}) := \sum_{i \in \mathbb{Z}} \rho_\sigma(i)$. The *discrete Gaussian distribution over* $\mathbb{Z}$, denoted χ_σ assigns probability $\rho_\sigma(i)/\rho_\sigma(\mathbb{Z})$ to each $i \in \mathbb{Z}$ and probability 0 to each non-integer point. The *discrete Gaussian distribution over* R, denoted as $R(\chi_\sigma)$, is the distribution over R where each coefficient is distributed according to χ_σ. Using the results of [13, 25], χ_σ can be sampled in polynomial time. Moreover the Euclidean norm of a sample from $R(\chi_\sigma)$ can be bounded using an instantiation of Lemma 1.5 of [4]. We state this lemma next.

Lemma 1. *Let $\sigma > 0$ and $n = \mathsf{poly}(\kappa)$. Then*

$$\Pr\left[\|x\| \geq \sigma\sqrt{n} \mid x \leftarrow R(\chi_\sigma)\right] < \mathsf{negl}(\kappa).$$

In addition, following the same reasoning as in [21] we have the following "drowning/smudging" lemma.

Lemma 2. *Let $\sigma > 0$ and $y \in \mathbb{Z}$. The statistical distance between χ_σ and $\chi_\sigma + y$ is at most $|y|/\sigma$.*

2.1   Verifiable Oblivious Pseudorandom Functions

Recall that the main goal of our work is to build a verifiable oblivious pseudorandom function (VOPRF). A VOPRF is a protocol between two parties: a server $\mathbb{S}$ and a client $\mathbb{C}$, securely realising the ideal functionality in Fig. 1. The functionality consists of two phases, the initialisation phase and the query phase. The initialisation phase is divided into two steps: one run once by the server, and one run once by any client who wishes to utilise the VOPRF provided by the server. In the event that the functionality $\mathcal{F}_{\mathsf{VOPRF}}$ receives a valid input k from $\mathbb{S}$ during the initialisation phase, it stores the key for use during the query phase. This models a server ($\mathbb{S}$) in a real protocol committing to a PRF key k.

Next comes the query phase, where a client $\mathbb{C}$ sends some value x to $\mathcal{F}_{\mathsf{VOPRF}}$. Once this value x has been received, the server $\mathbb{S}$ either sends the functionality an instruction to abort or to deliver the value $y = F_k(x)$ to $\mathbb{C}$. Finally, the functionality carries out this instruction. Importantly, (assuming that no abort is triggered) the client has the guarantee that its output is indeed $F_k(x)$ i.e. the output of the client is *verifiably* correct when interacting with $\mathcal{F}_{\mathsf{VOPRF}}$.

We now describe the distributions that arise in the security requirement. We consider malicious adversaries throughout that behave arbitrarily and begin with the distributions of interest when a server has been corrupted. First, we consider a "real" world protocol Π between $\mathbb{C}(x)$ and $\mathbb{S}(k)$ along with an adversary $\mathcal{A}$. We denote $\mathsf{real}_{\Pi,\mathcal{A},\mathbb{S}}(x, k, 1^\kappa)$ to be the joint output distribution of $\mathcal{A}(k)$ (when corrupting $\mathbb{S}(k)$) and $\mathbb{C}(x)$ where $\mathbb{C}(x)$ behaves as specified by Π. In this setting, $\mathcal{A}$ interacts directly with $\mathbb{C}$. Now we introduce a simulator denoted Sim that lives

This is a two party functionality between a server $\mathbb{S}$ and a client $\mathbb{C}$. We assume there is a fixed PRF function defined by $F_k(x)$.

Init-S: On input of init from the server the functionality waits for an input k from party $\mathbb{S}$. If $\mathbb{S}$ returns **abort** then the functionality aborts. Otherwise, the functionality stores the value k if it is a *valid key*[†] and aborts if not.

Init-C: On input of init from a client, the functionality will return **abort** if the init procedure for the server has not successfully completed.

Query: On input of (query, x) from a client $\mathbb{C}$, if $x \neq \perp$ then the functionality waits for an input from party $\mathbb{S}$. If $\mathbb{S}$ returns **deliver** then the functionality sends $y = F_k(x)$ to party $\mathbb{C}$. If $\mathbb{S}$ returns **abort** then the functionality aborts.

Fig. 1. The Ideal Functionality $\mathcal{F}_{\mathsf{VOPRF}}$. [†]The notion of a valid key refers to whether the key conforms to a pre-determined distribution. See Definition 1 for more details on this requirement.

in the "ideal" world. Specifically, still assuming $\mathcal{A}$ corrupts a server, Sim interacts with $\mathcal{A}$ on one hand and with $\mathbb{C}(x)$ via $\mathcal{F}_{\mathsf{VOPRF}}$ on the other. In this setting, for any client/server input pair (x, k), we define $\mathsf{ideal}_{\mathcal{F}_{\mathsf{VOPRF}},\mathsf{Sim},\mathcal{A},\mathbb{S}}(x, k, 1^\kappa)$ to be the joint output distribution of $\mathcal{A}(k)$ and the honest client $\mathbb{C}(x)$ when $\mathcal{A}(k)$ interacts via Sim. Informally, one may interpret Sim as an attacker-in-the-middle between $\mathcal{A}$ and the outside world where Sim interacts with $\mathcal{F}_{\mathsf{VOPRF}}$ external to the view of $\mathcal{A}$. Security argues that whatever $\mathcal{A}$ can learn/affect in the real protocol can be emulated via Sim in the ideal setting.

Next, we describe the distributions of interest when a client has been corrupted by an adversary $\mathcal{A}$. We let $\mathcal{K}$ denote the key distribution under which PRF security of F holds. First, consider a "real" world case where $\mathcal{A}$ corrupts $\mathbb{C}(x)$ and directly interacts with honest $\mathbb{S}(k)$ which follows the specification of protocol Π. In this case, we use $\mathsf{real}_{\Pi,\mathcal{A},\mathbb{C}}(x, \mathcal{K}, 1^\kappa)$ to denote the joint output distribution of $\mathcal{A}(x)$ and $\mathbb{S}(k)$[4] where $k \leftarrow \mathcal{K}$. Now consider an alternative "ideal" world case where we introduce a simulator Sim interacting with $\mathcal{A}$ on one hand and with $\mathbb{S}(x)$ via $\mathcal{F}_{\mathsf{VOPRF}}$ on the other hand. Once again, one may wish to interpret the simulator as an attacker-in-the-middle interacting with $\mathcal{F}_{\mathsf{VOPRF}}$ external to the view of $\mathcal{A}$. In this alternative case, we denote the joint output distribution of $\mathcal{A}(x)$ and $\mathbb{S}(k)$ where $\mathcal{A}$ interacts via Sim and $k \leftarrow \mathcal{K}$ as $\mathsf{ideal}_{\mathcal{F}_{\mathsf{VOPRF}},\mathsf{Sim},\mathcal{A},\mathbb{C}}(x, \mathcal{K}, 1^\kappa)$.

Finally, for protocol Π, let $\mathsf{output}(\Pi, x, k)$ denote the output distribution of a *client* with input x running protocol Π with a server whose input key is k. Using the notation established above, we can present our definition of a VOPRF.

Definition 1. *A protocol Π is a verifiable oblivious pseudorandom function if all of the following hold:*

1. **Correctness:** *For every pair of inputs (x, k),*

$$\Pr[\mathsf{output}(\Pi, x, k) \neq F_k(x)] \leq \mathsf{negl}(\kappa).$$

---

[4] Note that the output of $\mathbb{S}(k)$ is $\perp$ in our construction.

2. **Malicious server security:** *For any PPT adversary $\mathcal{A}$ corrupting a server, there exists a PPT simulator* Sim *such that for every pair of inputs (x, k):*

$$\text{ideal}_{\mathcal{F}_{\text{VOPRF}}, \text{Sim}, \mathcal{A}, \mathbb{S}}(x, k, 1^{\kappa}) \approx_c \text{real}_{\Pi, \mathcal{A}, \mathbb{S}}(x, k, 1^{\kappa}).$$

3. **Average case malicious client security:** *For any PPT adversary $\mathcal{A}$ corrupting a client, there exists a PPT simulator* Sim *such that for all client inputs x:*
   - $\text{ideal}_{\mathcal{F}_{\text{VOPRF}}, \text{Sim}, \mathcal{A}, \mathbb{C}}(x, \mathcal{K}, 1^{\kappa}) \approx_c \text{real}_{\Pi, \mathcal{A}, \mathbb{C}}(x, \mathcal{K}, 1^{\kappa})$.
   - *If $\mathcal{A}$ correctly outputs $F_k(x)$ with all but negligible probability over the choice $k \leftarrow \mathcal{K}$ when interacting directly with $\mathbb{S}(k)$ using protocol Π, then $\mathcal{A}$ also outputs $F_k(x)$ with all but negligible probability when interacting via* Sim.

We now discuss this definition. Note that the correctness and malicious server security requirements are the standard ones used in MPC. Therefore, we restrict this discussion to the condition that we call average case malicious client security. The motivation for this non-standard property is that an honest server will always sample a key from distribution $\mathcal{K}$ as it wishes to provide *pseudorandom* function evaluations. In particular, PRF security holds with respect to this key distribution $\mathcal{K}$. Therefore, it makes sense to ask what a malicious client may learn/affect only in the case where $k \leftarrow \mathcal{K}$ which leads to the first point of our average case malicious client security requirement. The second point of the requirement captures the fact that adversaries may have access to an oracle that checks whether the PRF was evaluated correctly or not. Suppose that we give the adversary $\mathcal{A}$ access to an oracle which can check an input/output pair to the PRF is valid or not. Then $\mathcal{A}$ should not be able to distinguish whether it is interacting with a real server $\mathbb{S}$ or a simulation Sim. Note that our proof structure relies heavily on our alternative malicious client security definition. In particular, the definition above allows us to argue over the entropy of secret keys when making indistinguishability claims.

Alternative Definitions. Note that alternative security definitions exist for (V)OPRFs. In the UC security models that are favoured by Jarecki et al. [29, 30] the output of the PRF is wrapped in the output of a programmable random oracle evaluation. This is a fact that is utilised by the OPAQUE PAKE protocol [31] that allows arguing that the pseudorandom function evaluations are pseudorandom *even* to the server (the key-holder). Unfortunately, using a similar technique here is difficult as constructing programmable random oracles in the quantum random oracle model (QROM) is known to be difficult [9].

2.2 Computational Assumptions

Here we present the presumed quantum hard computational problems that will be used in our security proofs. Evidence that these problems are indeed quantum hard follows via reductions from standard lattice problems (see the full version of this work). These reductions from lattice problems will be used to asymptotically analyse secure parameter settings for our VOPRF. The first is the standard decisional RLWE problem [40].

Definition 2. (RLWE problem) *Let $q, m, n, \sigma > 0$ depend on κ (q, m, n are integers). The decision-RLWE problem (dRLWE$_{q,n,m,\sigma}$) is to distinguish between:*

$$(a_i, \ a_i \cdot s + e_i)_{i \in [m]} \in (R_q)^2 \quad and \quad (a_i, u_i)_{i \in [m]} \in (R_q)^2$$

for $a_i, u_i \leftarrow R_q; \ s, e_i \leftarrow R(\chi_\sigma)$.

We sometimes write dRLWE$_{q,n,\sigma}$, leaving the parameter m (representing the number of samples) implicit. The second problem is slightly less standard. It is the short integer solution problem in *dimension 1* (1D-SIS). The following formulation of the problem was used in [15] in conjunction with a lemma attesting to its hardness. See the full version of this work for more details.

Definition 3. (1D-SIS, [15, Definition 3.4]) *Let q, m, t depend on κ. The one-dimensional SIS problem, denoted 1D-SIS$_{q,m,t}$, is the following: Given a uniform $v \leftarrow \mathbb{Z}_q^m$, find non-zero $z \in \mathbb{Z}^m$ such that $\|z\|_\infty \leq t$ and $\langle v, z \rangle \in [-t, t] + q\mathbb{Z}$.*

2.3 Non-interactive Zero-Knowledge Arguments of Knowledge

The foundations of zero-knowledge (ZK) proof systems were established in a number of works [8,23,27,28]. At a high level, a ZK proof system for language $\mathcal{L}$ allows a prover $\mathbb{P}$ to convince a verifier $\mathbb{V}$ that some instance x is in $\mathcal{L}$, without revealing anything beyond this statement. Further, a ZK argument of knowledge (ZKAoK) system allows $\mathbb{P}$ to convince $\mathbb{V}$ that they hold a witness w attesting to the fact that x is in $\mathcal{L}$ (where the $\mathcal{L}$ is defined by a relation predicate $\mathsf{P}_\mathcal{L}(x, w)$).

Definition 4. (NIZKAoK) *Let $\mathbb{P}$ be a prover, let $\mathbb{V}$ be a verifier, let $\mathcal{L}$ be a language with accompanying relation predicate $\mathsf{P}_\mathcal{L}(\cdot, \cdot)$. Let $\mathcal{W}_\mathcal{L}(x)$ be a generic set of witnesses attesting to the fact that $x \in \mathcal{L}$, i.e. $\forall x \in \mathcal{L}$, and $w \in \mathcal{W}_\mathcal{L}(x)$ we have $\mathsf{P}_\mathcal{L}(x, w) = 1$. Let $\mathsf{nizk} = (\mathsf{Setup}, \mathbb{P}, \mathbb{V})$ be a tuple of algorithms defined as follows:*

- *$\mathsf{crs} \leftarrow \mathsf{nizk.Setup}(1^\kappa)$: outputs a common random string crs.*
- *$\pi \leftarrow \mathsf{nizk.\mathbb{P}}(\mathsf{crs}, x, w)$: on input crs, a word $x \in \mathcal{L}$ and a witness $w \in \mathcal{W}_\mathcal{L}(x)$; outputs a proof $\pi \in \{0,1\}^{\mathsf{poly}(\kappa)}$.*
- *$b \leftarrow \mathsf{nizk.\mathbb{V}}(\mathsf{crs}, x, \pi)$: on input crs, a word $x \in \mathcal{L}$ and a proof $\pi \in \{0,1\}^{\mathsf{poly}(\kappa)}$; outputs $b \in \{0,1\}$.*

Definition 5. (NIZKAoK Security) *We say that nizk is a non-interactive zero-knowledge argument of knowledge (NIZKAoK) for $\mathcal{L}$ if the following holds.*

1. (Completeness): *Consider $x \in \mathcal{L}$ and $w \in \mathcal{W}_\mathcal{L}(x)$, where $\mathsf{P}_\mathcal{L}(x, w) = 1$. Then:*

$$\Pr\left[1 \leftarrow \mathsf{nizk.\mathbb{V}}(\mathsf{crs}, x, \pi) \middle| {}^{\mathsf{crs} \leftarrow \mathsf{nizk.Setup}(1^\kappa)}_{\pi \leftarrow \mathsf{nizk.\mathbb{P}}(\mathsf{crs}, x, w)}\right] \geq 1 - \mathsf{negl}(\kappa).$$

2. (Computational knowledge extraction): *The proof system satisfies computational knowledge extraction with knowledge error $\bar{\kappa}$ if, for any PPT prover $\mathbb{P}^*$ with auxiliary information* aux, *the following holds. There exists a PPT algorithm* nizk.Extract *and a polynomial p such that, for any input x, then:*

$$\Pr\left[1 \leftarrow \mathsf{P}_{\mathcal{L}}(x, w') | w' \leftarrow \mathsf{nizk.Extract}(\mathbb{P}^*(\mathsf{crs}, x, \mathsf{aux}))\right] \geq \frac{\nu - \bar{\kappa}}{p(|x|)}$$

is satisfied, where ν is the probability that nizk.$\mathbb{V}(\mathsf{crs}, x, \mathbb{P}^*(\mathsf{crs}, x, \mathsf{aux}))$ *outputs 1.*

3. (Computational zero-knowledge): *There exists a simulated setup algorithm* nizk.SimSetup(1^κ) *outputting* $\mathsf{crs}_{\mathsf{Sim}}$ *and a trapdoor $\mathcal{T}$ along with a PPT algorithm* nizk.Sim$(\mathsf{crs}_{\mathsf{Sim}}, \mathcal{T}, x)$ *satisfying*

$$\left\{ \begin{smallmatrix} \mathsf{crs} \leftarrow \mathsf{nizk.Setup}(1^\kappa) \\ \pi \leftarrow \mathsf{nizk.P}(\mathsf{crs}, x, w) \end{smallmatrix} \right\} \approx_c \left\{ \pi_{\mathsf{Sim}} \leftarrow \mathsf{nizk.Sim}(\mathsf{crs}_{\mathsf{Sim}}, \mathcal{T}, x) \middle| (\mathsf{crs}_{\mathsf{Sim}}, \mathcal{T}) \leftarrow \mathsf{nizk.SimSetup}(1^\kappa) \right\}$$

$\forall x \in \mathcal{L}$ *and* $w \in \mathcal{W}_{\mathcal{L}}(x)$.

Interactive Proof Systems. An interactive proof system is one where the proving algorithm ($\mathbb{P}$) requires interaction with the verifier. Such an interaction could be an arbitrary protocol, with many message exchanges, but a typical (in the honest verifier case) scenario is a three-move protocol consisting of a commitment (from the prover), a uniformly chosen challenge (from the verifier) and then a response (from the prover). Such protocols are referred to as Σ-protocols. Fiat and Shamir [23] established a mechanism of switching a (constant-round) honest verifier zero-knowledge interactive proof of knowledge into a *non-interactive* zero-knowledge proof of knowledge in the random oracle model (ROM). In particular, the random challenge provided by the verifier is replaced with the output of a random oracle evaluation taking as input the statement x and the provers initial commitment. It was recently shown that the standard Fiat-Shamir transform is also secure in the *quantum* ROM (QROM) [22,37] assuming the underlying Σ-protocol satisfies certain properties.

2.4 Lattice PRF

We will use an instantiation of the lattice PRF from [5]. Below, we present relevant definitions/results, all of which are particular cases of definitions/results from [5]. We set $\ell = \lceil \log_2 q \rceil$ throughout. The construction from [5] makes use of *gadget matrices* that can be found in many previous works [5,15,26,43].

Gadgets G, G^{-1}. Define $G : R_q^{\ell \times \ell} \to R_q^{1 \times \ell}$ to be the linear operation corresponding to left multiplication by $(1, 2, \ldots, 2^{\ell-1})$. Further, define $G^{-1} : R_q^{1 \times \ell} \to R_q^{\ell \times \ell}$ to be the bit decomposition operation that essentially inverts G i.e. the ith column of $G^{-1}(a)$ is the bit decomposition of $a_i \in R_q$ into binary polynomials.

The instantiation of [5] that we will present our VOPRF with respect to is defined as $F_k(x) = \lfloor a_x \cdot k \rceil_p$ for $a_x \in R_q^{1 \times \ell}$ given below.

Definition 6. *Fix some* $a_0, a_1 \leftarrow R_q^{1 \times \ell}$. *For any* $x = (x_1, \ldots, x_L) \in \{0, 1\}^L$. *We define* $a_x \in R_q^{1 \times \ell}$ *as*

$$a_x := a_{x_1} \cdot G^{-1} \left(a_{x_2} \cdot G^{-1} \left(a_{x_3} \cdot G^{-1} \left(\ldots \left(a_{x_{L-1}} \cdot G^{-1} \left(a_{x_L} \right) \right) \right) \right) \right) \in R_q^{1 \times \ell}.$$

The pseudorandomness of this construction follows from the ring learning with errors (RLWE) assumption (with normal form secrets).

Theorem 1 ([5]). *Sample* $k \leftarrow R(\chi_\sigma)$. *If* $q \gg p \cdot \sigma \cdot \sqrt{L} \cdot n \cdot \ell$, *then the function* $F_k(x) = \lfloor a_x \cdot k \rceil_p$ *is a PRF under the* $\mathsf{dRLWE}_{q,n,\sigma}$ *assumption.*

When we eventually prove security of our VOPRF, it will be useful to define a special error distribution such that $a_x \cdot k + e$ remains indistinguishable from uniform (under RLWE) when e is sampled from this special error distribution. To this end, we introduce the distributions $\mathcal{E}_{a_0, a_1, x, \sigma}$ followed by a lemma that is implicit in the pseudorandomness proof of the PRF from [5].

Definition 7. *For* $a_0, a_1 \in R_q^{1 \times \ell}$, *define*

$$a_{x \backslash i} := G^{-1} \left(a_{x_{i+1}} \cdot G^{-1} \left(a_{x_{i+2}} \cdot G^{-1} \left(\cdots \left(a_{x_{L-1}} \cdot G^{-1} \left(a_{x_L} \right) \right) \cdots \right) \right) \right) \in R_q^{\ell \times \ell}.$$

Furthermore, let $\mathcal{E}_{a_0, a_1, x, \sigma}$ *be the distribution that is sampled by choosing* $e_i \leftarrow R(\chi_\sigma)^{1 \times \ell}$ *for* $i = 1, \ldots, L$ *and outputting*

$$e = \sum_{i=1}^{L-1} e_i \cdot a_{x \backslash i} + e_L.$$

Lemma 3 (Implicit in [5]). *If* $a_0, a_1 \leftarrow R_q^{1 \times \ell}, e \leftarrow \mathcal{E}_{a_0, a_1, x, \sigma}$ *and* $s \leftarrow R(\chi_\sigma)$, *then for any fixed* $x \in \{0, 1\}^L$,

$$(a_0, \ a_1, \ a_x \cdot s + e)$$

is indistinguishable from uniform random by the $\mathsf{dRLWE}_{q,n,\sigma}$ *assumption.*

In addition to introducing $\mathcal{E}_{a_0, a_1, x, \sigma}$, it will be useful to write down an upper bound on the infinity norm on errors drawn from this distribution. The following lemma follows from the fact that for $y \leftarrow \chi_\sigma$, $\|y\|_\infty \leq \sigma \sqrt{n}$ with all but negligible probability by Lemma 1. In fact, we could use the result that $\|y\|_\infty \leq \sigma n^{c'}$ with probability at least $1 - c \cdot \exp(-\pi n^{2c'})$ for any constant $c' > 0$ and some universal constant c to reduce the upper bound, but we choose not to for simplicity.

Lemma 4 (Bound on Errors). *Let* $x \in \{0, 1\}^L$, $\ell = \lceil \log_2 q \rceil$ *and* $n = \mathsf{poly}(\kappa)$. *Samples from* $\mathcal{E}_{a_0, a_1, x, \sigma}$ *have infinity norm at most* $L \cdot \ell \cdot \sigma \cdot n^{3/2}$ *with all but negligible probability.*

3   A VOPRF Construction from Lattices

In this section, we provide a construction emulating the DH blinding construction $H(x)^k = (H(x) \cdot g^r)^k/(g^k)^r$. In what follows, we will initially ignore the zero-knowledge proofs establishing that all computations are performed honestly. A detailed description of the protocol is in Fig. 2 but the main high-level idea follows.

Recall that we are working with power-of-two cyclotomic rings. Informally, suppose a *client* wants to obtain $a' \cdot k + e' \in R_q$ (where e' is relatively small) from a server holding a *short* k without revealing $a' \in R_q$. Further, suppose that the server has published an LWE instance $(a, c := a \cdot k + e)$ for truly uniformly a and small Gaussian e. One way to achieve our goal is to have the client compute $c_x := a \cdot s + e_1 + a'$ for Gaussian (s, e_1). Next the server responds by computing $d_x := c_x \cdot k + e''$ for relatively small e'' and the client finally outputs

$$
\begin{aligned}
d_x - c \cdot s &= (a \cdot s + e_1 + a') \cdot k + e'' - (a \cdot k + e) \cdot s \\
&= a' \cdot k + (e_1 \cdot k - e \cdot s + e'') \\
&\approx a' \cdot k.
\end{aligned}
$$

The above gives the intuition behind our actual protocol. Roughly, the idea is to replace a' with a_x from a BP14 evaluation. As mentioned above, a more detailed formulation of our construction is given in Fig. 2. In the protocol description, $\mathbb{P}_i$ and $\mathbb{V}_i$ denote prover and verifier algorithms for three different zero-knowledge argument systems indexed by $i \in \{0, 1, 2\}$.

3.1   Zero-Knowledge Argument of Knowledge Statements

The arguments of $\mathbb{P}_i$ algorithms fall into two groups separated by a colon. Arguments before a colon are intended as "secret" information pertaining to a witness for a statement. Arguments after a colon should be interpreted as "public" information specifying the statement that is being proved.

Client Proof. The client proof denoted $\mathbb{P}_1(x, s, e_1 : \mathsf{crs}_1, c_x, a, a_0, a_1)$ should prove knowledge of

- $x \in \{0, 1\}^L$
- $s \in R$ where $\|s\|_\infty \leq \sigma \cdot \sqrt{n}$
- $e_1 \in R^{1 \times \ell}$ where $\|e_1\|_\infty \leq \sigma \sqrt{n}$

such that $c_x = a \cdot s + e_1 + a_x \bmod q$.

CRS SetUp: To set up the CRS execute the following steps:
  - Pick $a_0, a_1 \leftarrow R_q^{1 \times \ell}$
  - Sample $a \leftarrow R_q^{1 \times \ell}$, sample $\overline{\mathsf{crs}}_0$ for proof system $\mathbb{P}_0$ and set $\mathsf{crs}_0 := (\overline{\mathsf{crs}}_0, a)$
  - Sample crs_1 and crs_2 for proof systems $\mathbb{P}_1$ and $\mathbb{P}_2$ respectively

Init: The initialisation procedure is executed by the server $\mathbb{S}$ and a client $\mathbb{C}$ both with initial input crs_0.
  - **Init-S:** The server $\mathbb{S}$ executes the following steps
    - $k \leftarrow R(\chi_\sigma), e \leftarrow R(\chi_\sigma)^{1 \times \ell}$.
    - $c \leftarrow a \cdot k + e \bmod q$.
    - $\pi_0 \leftarrow \mathbb{P}_0(k, e : \mathsf{crs}_0, c)$.

    and sends (c, π_0) to a client $\mathbb{C}$.
  - **Init-C:** On receipt of (c, π_0) a client executes
    - $b \leftarrow \mathbb{V}_0(\mathsf{crs}_0, c, \pi_0)$.
    - Output abort if $b = 0$, otherwise store c.

Query: This is a two round protocol between a client and the server, with a client going first.
  1. On input of $(x \in \{0, 1\}^L, \mathsf{crs}_1, \mathsf{crs}_2)$ a client $\mathbb{C}$ executes the following steps
     - $s \leftarrow R(\chi_\sigma), e_1 \leftarrow R(\chi_\sigma)^{1 \times \ell}$.
     - $a_x = a_{x_1} \cdot G^{-1} \left(\cdots \left(a_{x_{L-1}} \cdot G^{-1} \left(a_{x_L} \right) \right) \cdots \right) \bmod q$.
     - $c_x \leftarrow a \cdot s + e_1 + a_x \bmod q$.
     - $\pi_1 \leftarrow \mathbb{P}_1(x, s, e_1 : \mathsf{crs}_1, c_x, a, a_0, a_1)$.

     and sends (c_x, π_1) to the server $\mathbb{S}$.
  2. On receipt of (c_x, π_1) the server $\mathbb{S}$ executes the following steps
     - $b \leftarrow \mathbb{V}_1(\mathsf{crs}_1, c_x, a_0, a_1, \pi_1)$.
     - Output abort if $b = 0$
     - $e' \leftarrow R(\chi_{\sigma'})^{1 \times \ell}$.
     - $d_x = c_x \cdot k + e' \bmod q$.
     - $\pi_2 \leftarrow \mathbb{P}_2(k, e', e : \mathsf{crs}_2, c, d_x, c_x, a)$.

     and sends (d_x, π_2) to a client $\mathbb{C}$ while outputting $\perp$.
  3. On receipt of (d_x, π_2) a client $\mathbb{C}$ executes
     - $b \leftarrow \mathbb{V}_2(\mathsf{crs}_0, \mathsf{crs}_2, c, d_x, c_x, \pi_2)$.
     - Output abort if $b = 0$.
     - $y_x = \lfloor d_x - c \cdot s \rceil_p$.
     - Output y_x.

Fig. 2. VOPRF construction

Server Proofs. The server proof in the *initialisation phase* denoted $\mathbb{P}_0(k, e : \mathsf{crs}_0, c)$ has the purpose of proving knowledge of $k \in R, e \in R^{1 \times \ell}$ where $\|k\|_\infty$, $\|e\|_\infty \leq \sigma \cdot \sqrt{n}$ such that $c = a \cdot k + e \bmod q$ where crs_0 contains a.

The server proof in the *query phase* denoted by $\mathbb{P}_2(k, e', e : \mathsf{crs}_2, c, d_x, c_x, a)$ has the purpose of proving that there is some

  - $k \in R$ where $\|k\|_\infty \leq \sigma \cdot \sqrt{n}$
  - $e \in R^{1 \times \ell}$ where $\|e\|_\infty \leq \sigma \cdot \sqrt{n}$
  - $e' \in R^{1 \times \ell}$ where $\|e'\|_\infty \leq \sigma' \cdot \sqrt{n}$

such that

$$c = a \cdot k + e \bmod q,$$
$$d_x = c_x \cdot k + e' \bmod q. \tag{1}$$

It is important to note that both c and d_x each consist of ℓ ring elements. Therefore, the above system consists of a total of 2ℓ noisy products of public ring elements and k. Note that the well-definedness of normal form RLWE (where the secret is drawn from the error distribution) implies that the witnesses used by the prover in π_0 and π_2 share the same value k.

3.2   Optimisations

Removing $\mathbb{P}_0$ using Trapdoors. The main purpose of proof system 0 is to allow the security proof to extract k and forward it on to the functionality. On removing this proof, if the server does not commit to its key properly, it cannot carry out the zero-knowledge proof in the **Query** phase, leading to a protocol where no evaluations are given to clients. An alternative to the server's NIZKAoK in the **Init-S** phase, the proof could extract k via trapdoors. Using the methods of Micciancio and Peikert [41], one can sample a trapdoored $a \in R_q^m$ for $m = \mathcal{O}(\ell)$ that is indistinguishable from uniform where the trapdoor permits efficient inversion of the function $g_a(k, e) = a \cdot k + e$ for small e. Therefore, the malicious server security proof could extract k in the **Init-S** phase by using a trapdoored a along with the inversion algorithm. For clarity and simplicity, we do not incorporate these ideas directly into our protocol.

Truncating the PRF. Although the protocol in Fig. 2 is concerned with the evaluation of the full BP14 PRF, we may consider a truncated version of the PRF to improve efficiency. In particular, the BP14 PRF is evaluated as $F_k(x) := \lfloor a_x \cdot k \rceil_p \in R_p^{1 \times \ell}$ but we could easily truncate particular quantities in our protocol to consider the PRF $F'_k(x) := \lfloor a_x \cdot k \rceil_p$ where a_x is the ring element appearing in the first entry of a_x. The relevant values that are truncated from ℓ ring elements to a single ring element from our protocol are c, a_x, c_x, d_x, y_x. Ignoring the zero-knowledge elements of the protocol, this saves us a factor of ℓ. However, computation of the full a_x must still be performed by the client in order to calculate the truncated value. Additionally, the computation of a_x will still need to be considered by the client's zero-knowledge proof. As we will see in Sect. 4, the computation of a_x is the main source of inefficiency in the zero-knowledge proofs and our overall protocol. Therefore, we do not trivially save a factor of ℓ in computation time and zero-knowledge proof size by using a truncated BP14 PRF.

Batching Queries. We can save on the cost of zero-knowledge proof of the server in the **Query** phase by batching VOPRF queries. When the client sends a single value c_x, the server proves that c and c_x are computed with respect to the same k. If the client sends N individual queries, the server proves that c and c_{x_1} are with respect to the same k and then independently proves that c and c_{x_2} are with respect to the same k and so on. Instead, the server could simply prove that $c, c_{x_1}, \ldots, c_{x_N}$ are all with respect to the same k in one shot, saving an *additive* term of $\mathcal{O}(N \cdot \ell)$ in communication over N different VOPRF evaluations (although the overall complexity of the communication does not change asymptotically).

Cut-and-Choose. Another way in which we can improve efficiency (from the server's perspective) is to remove some of the zero-knowledge proofs using a cut-and-choose methodology. In particular, we can remove the need for the zero-knowledge proof from the server in the **Query** phase as follows. Firstly, in the **Init-S** phase, we make the server publish (for small k) the value $y := \lfloor a_{x'} \cdot k \rceil_p$ for some fixed x' in addition to the value $a \cdot k + e$ as well as a zero-knowledge proof attesting to the correct computation of these values for small k. The next change comes in the client message in the **Query** phase. Instead of sending a single pair (c_x, π_1), the client chooses a uniform subset X of $\{1, \ldots, N\}$ of size K. The client then sends N values $(c_{x_1}, \ldots, c_{x_N})$ where for all $j \in X$, $x_j = x'$ and for all $j' \notin X$, $x_{j'} = x$ for some x chosen by the client and a NIZKAoK attesting to this computation. The server then computes $d_{x_1}, \ldots, d_{x_N}$ as it does in Fig. 2 using $c_{x_1}, \ldots, c_{x_N}$ respectively. Next, the client processes each d_{x_i} individually to compute the values $y_{x_1} \ldots y_{x_N}$ as in the plain protocol. Finally, the client aborts if any of the following hold:

- there exists a $j^* \in X$ such that $y_{x_{j^*}} \neq y$
- $y_{x_{j'}}$ are not all equal for $j' \notin X$
- $y_{x_{j'}} = y$ for all $j' \notin X$ (see explanation below)

Otherwise, the client accepts $y_x = y_{x_{j'}}$ for any $j' \notin X$ as the evaluation at x. The client now must create N proofs for the most complex statements. On the other hand, the server does not need to create any proofs whatsoever in the online phase. The only way for the server to cheat now is to somehow guess the $N - K$ transcripts containing input x which can be done with probability at most $1/\binom{N}{K}$. Thus, the computational burden is mostly shifted to the client, which might be desirable in some settings.

On close inspection, there is a slight problem with the cut-and-choose optimisation described above. The issue is that a client might ask for an evaluation on input x such that $\lfloor a_x \cdot k \rceil_p = \lfloor a_{x'} \cdot k \rceil_p$ in which case the third condition causes an abort, even though the client obtained the correct evaluation. One way to get around this is to redefine the PRF slightly so that such collisions only occur with negligible probability. For example, for $L - 1$ bit inputs $x \in \{0,1\}^{L-1}$, suppose we use the alternative PRF $F'_k(x) := \lfloor a_{0\|x} \cdot k \rceil_p$. Since we can rewrite $a_{0\|x} \cdot k = a_0 \cdot Z_{x,k}$ where $Z_{x,k}$ has small entries as long as k is short. Then a collision in this PRF must lead to an equation $a_0 \cdot (Z_{x,k} - Z_{x',k}) = u \bmod q$ where $\|u\|_\infty \leq q/p$. Rearranging, this equation becomes $[1|a_0] \cdot \begin{bmatrix} u \\ (Z_{x,k} - Z_{x',k}) \end{bmatrix} = \mathbf{0} \bmod q$ which means that such a collision would imply a solution to a ring-SIS problem with respect to $[1|a]$ (in Hermite normal form). Therefore, for fixed x and any short k, it is unlikely that a collision in this alternative PRF will occur under some SIS assumption.

3.3 Correctness

Before proving correctness, we present a lemma that we will apply below. The proof of this lemma is in the full version of this work.

Lemma 5. *Fix any* $x \in \{0,1\}^L$. *Suppose there exists a PPT algorithm* $\mathcal{D}_x(a_0, a_1)$ *that outputs* $r \in R$ *such that* $\|r\|_\infty \leq B$ *and at least one coefficient of* $a_x \cdot r$ *is in the set* $(q/p) \cdot \mathbb{Z} + [-T, T]$ *with non-negligible probability (over a uniform choice of* $a_0, a_1 \leftarrow R_q^\ell$ *and its random coins). Then there exists an efficient algorithm solving* 1D-SIS$_{q/p,n\ell,\max\{n\ell B,T\}}$ *with non-negligible probability.*

Lemma 6 (Correctness). *Adopt the notation of Fig. 2, assuming an honest client and server. Define* $T := 2\sigma^2 n^2 + \sigma' \sqrt{n}$. *For any* $x \in \{0,1\}^L, k \in R_q$ *such that* $\|k\|_\infty \leq \sigma \cdot \sqrt{n}$, *we have that*

$$\Pr[\mathbf{y}_x \neq F_k(x)] \leq \mathsf{negl}(\kappa)$$

over the choice of PRF parameters $a_0, a_1 \leftarrow R_q^{1 \times \ell}$ *assuming the hardness of* 1D-SIS$_{q/p,n\ell,T}$.

Proof. Fix an arbitrary x. Assume there exists a k' such that $\|k'\| \leq \sigma \cdot \sqrt{n}$ where $\Pr[\mathbf{y}_x \neq F_{k'}(x)]$ is non-negligible over the choice of $a_0, a_1 \leftarrow R_q^{1 \times \ell}$. Expanding c and d_x from the protocol, we have that

$$\mathbf{y}_x = \lfloor a_x \cdot k' + e_1 \cdot k' + e' - e \cdot s \rceil_p.$$

Note that $e'' := e_1 \cdot k' - e \cdot s + e'$ has infinity norm less than T as defined in the lemma statement with all but negligible probability. It follows that there must be at least one coefficient of $a_x \cdot k'$ in the set $(q/p) \cdot \mathbb{Z} + [T, T]$ with non-negligible probability, otherwise $\mathbf{y}_x = \lfloor a_x \cdot k' \rceil_p =: F_{k'}(x)$. Applying Lemma 5 to the algorithm $\mathcal{D}_x(a_0, a_1)$ that ignores a_0, a_1 and simply outputs k' implies an efficient algorithm solving 1D-SIS$_{q/p,n\ell,\max\{n^{3/2}\ell\sigma,T\}}$.   □

The remainder of the security proof can be found in Sect. 5.

4   Lattice-Based NIZKAoK Instantiations

We now describe various instantiations of our zero-knowledge arguments of knowledge. Note that we use the Fiat-Shamir transform (on parallel repetitions) to obtain non-interactive proofs. We recall that the Fiat-Shamir transform has recently been shown to be secure in the QROM [22, 37] in certain settings. We place most of our attention on discussing how to instantiate Proof System 1, as the other proof systems may be derived straight-forwardly using a subset of the techniques arising in Proof System 1. For more precise details on how to instantiate Proof System 1 using the protocol of Yang et al. [47], see the full version of this work. Alternatively, one could use the same techniques as in [36] to represent the statement of interest in Proof System 1 as a permuted kernel problem and use the recent protocol of Beullens [7]. The advantage of doing so would be that the protocol of Beullens has been *shown* to be compatible with the aforementioned security results of the Fiat-Shamir transform in the QROM.

Note that the argument system of Yang et al. requires the modulus q to be a prime power. In contrast, 1D-SIS is known to be at least as hard as standard lattice problems when q has many large coprime factors [15]. In order to justify the use of a prime power modulus along with the use of the 1D-SIS assumption, we apply two minor lemmas given in the full version of this work. Alternatively, if one wished to use a highly composite modulus, then a Stern-based protocol such as in [35, 36] or the more efficient recent protocol of Beullens [7] may still be used. Nonetheless, all of the aforementioned argument systems involve rewriting PRF evaluations as a large system of linear equations. In our context, applying the argument system of Yang is slightly simpler. Additionally, a single execution of the protocol of Yang et al. achieves a soundness error of $2/(2\bar{p}+1)$ for some polynomial $\bar{p}$ much less than q. This is similar to the soundness error encountered in the Beullens protocol, but significantly improves on the soundness of Stern-based protocols. Therefore, roughly $\kappa/\log\bar{p}$ repetitions are required to reach a $2^{-\kappa}$ soundness error when using either of the protocol of Yang et al. or Beullens protocols.

Proof System 0: Small Secret RLWE Sample. Let $A \in \mathbb{Z}_q^{n\ell \times n}$ be the vertical concatenation of the negacyclic matrices associated to multiplication by the ring elements of $\boldsymbol{a} \in R_q^{1 \times \ell}$ respectively. Further, let $\vec{c} \in \mathbb{Z}_q^{n\ell}$ be the vertical concatenation of coefficient vectors of ring elements in $\boldsymbol{c} \in R_q^{1 \times \ell}$ respectively. The first proof aims to prove in zero knowledge, knowledge of a short solution $\vec{x} := (\vec{x}_1, \vec{x}_2)$, where $\|\vec{x}\|_\infty \leq \sigma \cdot \sqrt{n}$ to the system

$$\vec{c} = A \cdot \vec{x}_1 + \vec{x}_2 \bmod q.$$

This is an inhomogeneous SIS problem, so the zero-knowledge proof may be instantiated using either the protocol of Yang et al. or Beullens. Additionally, for this proof system, we may also use the protocol from [12]. All of these options avoid the so-called soundness gap seen in many lattice-based proof systems (e.g. [38, 39]) although the efficient protocol in [39] has been shown to be secure in the QROM when the Fiat-Shamir transform is applied [37]. Therefore, for simplicity and neatness we prefer to consider these systems when writing the security proof for our VOPRF although one may use the more efficient protocol of [39] in practice.

Proof System 1: Proofs of Masked Partial PRF Computation. This proof system aims to prove that for a known a and c, the prover knows short s and e along with a bit-string x such that $c = a \cdot s + e + a_x$ where a_x is part of the BP14 PRF evaluation. At a high level, we will run the protocol of Yang et al. [47] $\mathcal{O}(\kappa / \log \bar{p})$ times (for some $\bar{p} = \mathrm{poly}(\kappa)$) in parallel and apply the Fiat-Shamir heuristic. We focus on this instantiation for simplicity. We do not actually concretely present any ZKAoK protocol in this work, but we do highlight the reduction in the full version of this work showing that we may use the protocol of Yang et al. Similar methods (e.g. the decomposition-extension framework used by[36]) can be used to prove compatibility with the protocol of Beullens. Let P_n represent the power set of $\{1, \ldots, n\}^3$. The protocol of Yang et al. is a ZKAoK for the instance-witness set given by

$$\mathcal{R}^* = \left\{ ((\boldsymbol{A}, \vec{y}, \mathcal{M}), \vec{x}) \in \mathbb{Z}_q^{m \times n} \times \mathbb{Z}_q^m \times P_n \times \mathbb{Z}_q^n : {}^{\boldsymbol{A} \cdot \vec{x} = \vec{y} \bmod q \ \wedge}_{\forall (i,j,k) \in \mathcal{M}, x_i = x_j \cdot x_k \bmod q} \right\}.$$

Therefore, in order to show that we may use the protocol, we simply reduce our statement of interest to an instance $((\boldsymbol{A}', \vec{y}', \mathcal{M}'), \vec{w}') \in \mathcal{R}^*$. Then, the protocol of Yang et al. allows to argue knowledge of a witness $\vec{w}'$ such that $((\boldsymbol{A}', \vec{y}', \mathcal{M}'), \vec{w}') \in \mathcal{R}^*$. Details on reducing statements of the relevant form to instances in $\mathcal{R}^*$ are given in the full version of this work, but a high level overview follows.

First note that we can compute a_x recursively (similarly to [36]) by setting variables $B_i \in R_q^{\ell \times \ell}$ for $i = L - 1, \ldots, 0$ via $B_{L-1} = G^{-1}(a_{x_{L-1}})$, and $B_i = G^{-1}(a_{x_i} \cdot B_{i+1})$ for $i = L - 2, \ldots, 0$. Using this, we have $a_x = G \cdot B_0$. We can therefore use the system $G \cdot B_i = a_{x_i} \cdot B_{i-1}$ to facilitate computation of a_x along with the linear equation $c = a \cdot s + e_1 + G \cdot B_0$ to completely describe the statement being proved. However, the resulting system is over ring elements and is not linear in unknowns. To solve these issues, we simply replace ring multiplication by integer matrix-vector products and then linearise the resulting system (which places quadratic constraints amongst the entries of the solution). We also make use of binary decompositions to bound the infinity norms of valid solutions and ensure that necessary entries are in $\{0, 1\}$ via quadratic constraints[5].

Proof System 2: Proofs of Secret Equivalence. Recall that we wish to prove existence of a solution to Eq. (1). Note that d_x from the protocol in Sect. 3 are vectors holding ℓ ring elements. Therefore, Eq. (1) can be expressed as a system

$$\begin{aligned}
c_i &= a_i \cdot k + e_i & i &= 1, \ldots, \ell, \\
(d_x)_i &= (c_x)_i \cdot k + e_i' & i &= 1, \ldots, \ell,
\end{aligned}$$

where $\|e_i\|_\infty, \|k\|_\infty \leq \sigma \cdot \sqrt{n}$, $\|e_i'\|_\infty \leq \sigma' \cdot \sqrt{n}$. We can conceptualise the above as a large linear system $A' \cdot \vec{x} = \vec{c}$ where $\vec{x}$ is the concatenation of coefficient

---

[5] Using the fact that $x^2 = x \bmod q \iff x \in \{0, 1\}$ assuming q is a prime power.

vectors of $k, e_1, \ldots, e_\ell, e'_1, \ldots, e'_\ell$ and $\vec{c}$ is the concatenation of the coefficient vectors of $c_1, \ldots, c_\ell, (d_x)_1, \ldots, (d_x)_\ell$. Using this interpretation, we may instantiate this proof system using the same methods as in Proof System 0.

5   Security Proof

In this section, we show that the protocol in Fig. 2 is a VOPRF achieving security against malicious adversaries. In particular, corrupted clients and servers that attempt to subvert the protocol learn/affect only as much as in an ideal world, where they interact via the functionality $\mathcal{F}_{\mathsf{VOPRF}}$.

Theorem 2. (Security) *Assume $p|q$. The protocol in Fig. 2 is a secure VOPRF protocol (according to Definition 1) if the following conditions hold:*

- *$\forall i \in \{0, 1, 2\}, (\mathbb{P}_i, \mathbb{V}_i)$ is a NIZKAoK*
- *$\mathsf{dRLWE}_{q,n,\sigma}$ is hard,*
- *$\frac{q}{2p} \gg \sigma' \gg \max\{L \cdot \ell \cdot \sigma n^{3/2}, \sigma^2 n^2\},$*
- *$\mathsf{1D\text{-}SIS}_{q/(2p),n\cdot\ell,\max\{\ell\cdot\sigma n^{3/2}, 2\sigma^2 n^2 + \sigma'\sqrt{n}\}}$ is hard.*

Note that correctness of our protocol with respect to honest clients and servers is shown in Sect. 3.3. Therefore, what remains is to show average malicious client security and malicious server security.

Correctness of Non-aborting Malicious Protocol Runs. During the malicious client proof, it will be useful to call on the fact that a non-aborting protocol transcript enables computation of $F_k(x)$ with overwhelming probability:

Lemma 7. *Assume that $\mathsf{dRLWE}_{q,n,\sigma}$ is hard, σ and n are $\mathsf{poly}(\kappa)$, and $\frac{q}{2p} \gg \sigma' \gg \max\{L \cdot \ell \cdot \sigma n^{3/2}, \sigma^2 n^2\}$. For any $x \in \{0, 1\}^L$, consider a non-aborting run of the protocol in Fig. 2 between a (potentially malicious) efficient client $\mathbb{C}^*$ and honest server $\mathbb{S}$. Further, let s be the value that is extractable from the client's proof in the query phase. Then, the value of $\lfloor d_x - c \cdot s \rceil_p$ is equal to $\lfloor a_x \cdot k \rceil_p$ with all but negligible probability.*

Proof. We use the notation from Fig. 2. First note that for a *non-aborting* protocol run, any *efficient* client $\mathbb{C}^*$ must have produced c_x correctly using some $x \in \{0, 1\}^L, s, e_1$ where $\|s\|_\infty, \|e_1\|_\infty \leq \sigma \cdot \sqrt{n}$. Suppose that $e_x \leftarrow \mathcal{E}_{a_0, a_1, x, \sigma}$. We now use the fact that if $\sigma' \gg \max\{L \cdot \ell \cdot \sigma n^{3/2}, \sigma^2 n^2\}$, then $e' \leftarrow R(\chi_{\sigma'})^{1 \times \ell}$ and $(e_x - e_1 \cdot k - e \cdot s) + e'$ are statistically close which follows from Lemmas 4 and 2. Therefore, replacing e' by $(e_x - e_1 \cdot k - e \cdot s) + e'$ and noting that c_x must be well-formed due to the NIZKAoK, the client output equation in Fig. 2 can be written as

$$\left\lfloor \frac{p}{q}(d_x - c \cdot s) \right\rceil = \left\lfloor \frac{p}{q}(a_x \cdot k + e_x) + \frac{p}{q}e' \right\rceil$$

To complete the proof, we will use the fact that $\frac{p}{q}(a_x \cdot k + e_x)$ is computationally indistinguishable from uniform random over $\frac{p}{q}R_q^{1 \times \ell}$ when $e_x \leftarrow \mathcal{E}_{a_0, a_1, x, \sigma}$

assuming the hardness of $\mathsf{dRLWE}_{q,n,\sigma}$ (Lemma 3). This implies that every coefficient in $\frac{p}{q}(\boldsymbol{a}_x k + \boldsymbol{e}_x)$ is at least T away from $\mathbb{Z} + 1/2$ with all but negligible probability for any $T \ll 1$. Setting $T = \frac{p}{q}\left(\sigma' \cdot \sqrt{n} + L \cdot \ell \cdot \sigma n^{3/2}\right) \ll 1$ ensures that $T \leq \frac{p}{q} \cdot \|\boldsymbol{e}_x + \boldsymbol{e}'\|_\infty$ with all but negligible probability. It then follows that

$$\left\lfloor \frac{p}{q}\left(\boldsymbol{a}_x \cdot k + \boldsymbol{e}_x\right) + \frac{p}{q}\boldsymbol{e}' \right\rceil = \left\lfloor \frac{p}{q}\boldsymbol{a}_x \cdot k \right\rceil$$

as required. $\qquad\square$

5.1 Malicious Client Proof

Lemma 8 (Average-case malicious client security). *Assume that σ and n are $\mathsf{poly}(\kappa)$, and $p|q$, and let conditions (i) and (ii) be as follows:*

(i) $\mathsf{dRLWE}_{q,n,\sigma}$ is hard,
(ii) $\frac{q}{2p} \gg \sigma' \gg \max\{L \cdot \ell \cdot \sigma n^{3/2}, \sigma^2 n^2\}$.

If the above conditions hold and $(\mathbb{P}_1, \mathbb{V}_1)$ is a NIZKAoK, then the protocol in Fig. 2 has average-case security against malicious clients according to Definition 1.

Proof. We describe a simulation $\mathcal{S}$ that communicates with the functionality $\mathcal{F}_{\mathsf{VOPRF}}$ (environment) on one hand, and the malicious client $\mathbb{C}^*$ on the other. $\mathcal{S}$ carries out the following steps:

1. During **CRS SetUp**, publish honest $a, a_0, a_1, \mathsf{crs}_1$ and (dishonest) simulated versions of crs_0 and crs_2. Denote the simulated CRS elements crs'_0 and crs'_2.
2. Pass the init message onto $\mathcal{F}_{\mathsf{VOPRF}}$, then send $\mathbb{C}^*$ a uniform $\boldsymbol{c} \leftarrow R_q^{1\times\ell}$ with a simulated proof $\pi_{0,\mathsf{Sim}}$. Initialise an empty list received.
3. During the **Query** stage, for each message $(\boldsymbol{c}_x, \pi_1)$ from $\mathbb{C}^*$, do:
   (a) $b \leftarrow \mathbb{V}_1(\mathsf{crs}_1, \boldsymbol{c}_x, a, a_0, a_1, \pi_1)$. If $b = 0$ send abort to the functionality and abort the protocol with the malicious client. If $b = 1$ continue.
   (b) Extract the values $x, s, \boldsymbol{e}_1$ from π_1 using the ZKAoK extractor and send (query, x) to the functionality.
   (c) – If $\mathcal{F}_{\mathsf{VOPRF}}$ aborts:
          $\mathcal{S}$ aborts.
        – If $\mathcal{F}_{\mathsf{VOPRF}}$ returns $\boldsymbol{y} \in R_p^{1\times\ell}$ and $\forall \boldsymbol{y}^*, (x, \boldsymbol{y}^*) \notin$ received: (i.e. if this is the first time x is queried) uniformly sample

$$\boldsymbol{y}_q \leftarrow R_q^{1\times\ell} \cap \left(\frac{q}{p}\boldsymbol{y} + R_{\leq \frac{q}{2p}}^{1\times\ell}\right)$$

and do received.add$(x, \boldsymbol{y}_q)$.
        – If $\mathcal{F}_{\mathsf{VOPRF}}$ returns $\boldsymbol{y} \in R_p^\ell$ and $\exists \boldsymbol{y}^*$ s.t. $(x, \boldsymbol{y}^*) \in$ received: (i.e. x was previously queried) Then set $\boldsymbol{y}_q = \boldsymbol{y}^*$.

(d) Next pick $\bar{e}' \leftarrow \chi_{\sigma'}$ and set

$$\bar{d}_x = c \cdot s + \bar{e}' + y_q \bmod q.$$

Finally, produce a simulated proof $\pi_{2,\mathsf{Sim}}$ using crs_2' and send $(\bar{d}_x, \pi_{2,\mathsf{Sim}})$ to $\mathbb{C}^*$.

We now argue that $\mathbb{C}^*$ cannot decide whether it is interacting with $\mathcal{S}$ or with a genuine server. Firstly, recognise that $(\mathsf{crs}_0', \mathsf{crs}_2')$ is indistinguishable from honestly created $(\mathsf{crs}_0, \mathsf{crs}_2)$. Secondly, the malicious client cannot distinguish the simulator's uniform c sent during the **Init** phase from the real protocol by the $\mathsf{dRLWE}_{q,n,\sigma}$ assumption (condition (i)). This implies that both the **CRS SetUp** and **Init** phases that $\mathcal{S}$ performs are indistinguishable from the real protocol.

The most challenging step is arguing that the simulator's behaviour in the **Query** phase is indistinguishable from the real protocol from the malicious client's point of view. We will analyse the behaviour of the simulator assuming that no abort is triggered. We begin by arguing that the server message d_x in the real protocol with respect to any triple (x, s, e_1) can be replaced by a related message $c \cdot s + a_x \cdot k + e_x + e'''$ where $e_x \leftarrow \mathcal{E}_{a_0, a_1, x, \sigma}$ and $e''' \leftarrow R(\chi_{\sigma'})^{1 \times \ell}$ without detection by the following statistical argument. We have that the server response in the *real* protocol has d_x of the form

$$c \cdot s + e_1 \cdot k + a_x \cdot k + e' \tag{2}$$

where $e' \leftarrow R(\chi_{\sigma'})^{1 \times \ell}$. By Lemma 2, the message distribution in Eq. (2) is statistically indistinguishable from

$$a \cdot k \cdot s + e \cdot s + a_x \cdot k + e'' = c \cdot s + a_x \cdot k + e'' \tag{3}$$

where $e'' \leftarrow R(\chi_{\sigma'})^{1 \times \ell}$ due to the fact that $\sigma' \gg \sigma^2 n^2$. By a similar argument along with Lemma 4, the quantity given in Equation (3) is statistically close in distribution to

$$c \cdot s + e''' + (a_x \cdot k + e_x). \tag{4}$$

where $e_x \leftarrow \mathcal{E}_{a_0, a_1, x, \sigma}$ and $e''' \leftarrow R(\chi_{\sigma'})^{1 \times \ell}$. Next, using Lemma 3 and condition (i), we have that the bracketed term in Equation (4) is indistinguishable from random over $R_q^{1 \times \ell}$ by the hardness of $\mathsf{dRLWE}_{q,n,\sigma}$ (Lemma 3). In particular, from an efficient $\mathbb{C}^*$'s point of view, d_x cannot be distinguished from

$$c \cdot s + e''' + u_x$$

Note that on repeated queries, the errors sampled from $R(\chi_{\sigma'})^{1 \times \ell}$ are fresh. The fact that $\mathcal{S}$ samples y_q as a uniformly chosen element of a uniformly chosen interval implies the indistinguishability part of average-case malicious client security.

Next, we show that if the malicious client does indeed compute the correct value from the messages it receives from the honest server (in the real protocol), then it can do the same with the messages that it receives from the simulator.

In Lemma 7, we show that a malicious client which does not cause an abort can compute $\lfloor \boldsymbol{a}_x \cdot k \rceil_p$ from the messages it receives from the honest server with all but negligible probability. We now show that this is also the case with the messages it receives from $\mathcal{S}$. Consider $\boldsymbol{y}_q$ sampled by $\mathcal{S}$ and also the corresponding value $\bar{\boldsymbol{d}}_x$. In addition, define $\boldsymbol{e}_{\lfloor\rceil} := \boldsymbol{y}_q - (q/p) \cdot \boldsymbol{y} \in R^{1 \times \ell}_{\leq \frac{q}{2p}}$ so that $\boldsymbol{e}_{\lfloor\rceil}$ follows the uniform distribution over $R^{1 \times \ell}_{\leq \frac{q}{2p}}$. We have that

$$\left\lfloor \frac{p}{q} \left(\bar{\boldsymbol{d}}_x - \boldsymbol{c} \cdot s \right) \right\rceil = \left\lfloor \boldsymbol{y} + \frac{p}{q} \left(\boldsymbol{e}_{\lfloor\rceil} + \bar{\boldsymbol{e}}' \right) \right\rceil. \tag{5}$$

We also know that with all but negligible probability, $\|\bar{\boldsymbol{e}}'\|_\infty \leq \sigma'\sqrt{n}$, and that $\|\boldsymbol{e}_{\lfloor\rceil}\|_\infty$ is less than $q/(2p) - T$ with all but negligible probability as long as $T \ll (q/2p)$. Taking $T = \sigma'\sqrt{n}$, we get that with all but negligible probability,

$$\left\| \frac{p}{q} \left(\boldsymbol{e}_{\lfloor\rceil} + \bar{\boldsymbol{e}}' \right) \right\|_\infty \leq \frac{1}{2},$$

implying that the quantity in Equation (5) rounds correctly to $\boldsymbol{y}$ with all but negligible probability. Therefore, both the real protocol and simulator enable correct evaluation of the PRF.   □

5.2 Malicious Server Proof

Lemma 9. *Let conditions (i) and (ii) be as follows:*

(i) dRLWE$_{q,n,\sigma}$ *is hard,*
(ii) 1D-SIS$_{q/(2p),n\cdot\ell,\max\{\ell\cdot\sigma n^{3/2}, 2\sigma^2 n^2 + \sigma'\sqrt{n}\}}$ *is hard.*

If the above conditions hold and $(\mathbb{P}_0, \mathbb{V}_0)$ *and* $(\mathbb{P}_2, \mathbb{V}_2)$ *are both NIZKAoKs, then the protocol in Fig. 2 is secure in the presence of malicious servers.*

Proof. We construct a simulator $\mathcal{S}$ interacting with the malicious server $\mathbb{S}^*$ on one hand and with the functionality $\mathcal{F}_{\mathsf{VOPRF}}$ on the other. The simulator $\mathcal{S}$ behaves as follows:

1. During the CRS.SetUp phase, publish honest $\boldsymbol{a}, \boldsymbol{a}_0, \boldsymbol{a}_1, \mathsf{crs}_0, \mathsf{crs}_2$ and (dishonest) simulated crs'_1 to use with the proof systems.
2. During the **Init-C** phase, if $\mathbb{S}^*$ sends $\boldsymbol{c} \in R^{1 \times \ell}_q$ and an accepting proof π_0, then use the zero knowledge extractor to obtain a key k' from π_0 and forward this on to the functionality. If the message is not of the correct format, or the proof does not verify, then abort.
3. During the **Query** phase, select a uniform random value $\boldsymbol{u} \leftarrow R^{1 \times \ell}_q$, and using the ZK simulator, produce a simulated proof $\pi_{1,\mathsf{Sim}}$ using crs'_1. Send the message $(\boldsymbol{u}, \pi_{1,\mathsf{Sim}})$. Wait for a response of the form $(\bar{\boldsymbol{d}}_x, \tilde{\pi}_2)$ from $\mathbb{S}^*$. If the proof $\tilde{\pi}_2$ verifies, forward on deliver to $\mathcal{F}_{\mathsf{VOPRF}}$. Otherwise, forward abort to $\mathcal{F}_{\mathsf{VOPRF}}$.

We will show that the joint output of an honest client $\mathbb{C}$ and $\mathbb{S}^*$ in the real world (where they interact directly) and the ideal world (where they interact via $\mathcal{F}_{\mathsf{VOPRF}}$ and $\mathcal{S}$) are computationally indistinguishable. We begin by arguing that the malicious server $\mathbb{S}^*$ cannot distinguish whether it is interacting with a real client or $\mathcal{S}$, as described above. Firstly, replacing crs_1 by crs_1' is indistinguishable from the point of view of $\mathbb{S}^*$ by definition of a simulated CRS. Importantly, if $\mathbb{S}^*$ can produce valid proofs in the **Init** phase, the key k' obtained by the simulator is the *unique* ring element consistent with c (see the full version of this work for more details).

All that is left to consider is the **Query** phase. Note that in the real protocol, the client produces $\boldsymbol{c}_x$ which takes the form of a RLWE sample offset by some independent value. This implies that the value $\boldsymbol{c}_x$ is pseudorandom under the hardness of $\mathsf{dRLWE}_{q,n,\sigma}$. Therefore, the malicious server $\mathbb{S}^*$ cannot distinguish a real $\boldsymbol{c}_x$ from the pair $\boldsymbol{u}$ that $\mathcal{S}$ uses. By the properties of a ZK simulator, it follows that a real client message $(\boldsymbol{c}_x, \pi_1)$ and crs_1 is indistinguishable from $(\boldsymbol{u}, \pi_{1,\mathsf{Sim}})$ and crs_1'. Next, if the response from $\mathbb{S}^*$ has a valid proof, then $\mathcal{S}$ forwards on deliver. This means that the ideal functionality passes a PRF evaluation to the client using the server key k'. We now argue that this emulates the output on the client side when running the real protocol with malicious server $\mathbb{S}^*$.

The case where the proof verification fails is trivial since the client aborts in the real and ideal worlds. As a result, we focus on the case where the zero knowledge proof produced by $\mathbb{S}^*$ verifies correctly. Let $s \leftarrow R(\chi_\sigma)$ and $\boldsymbol{e}_1 \leftarrow R(\chi_\sigma)^{1 \times \ell}$ be sampled by the honest client. For this honest client interacting with malicious $\mathbb{S}^*$ in the real protocol, observe that

$$\frac{p}{q}\left(\boldsymbol{d}_x - \boldsymbol{c} \cdot s\right) = \frac{p}{q}\boldsymbol{a}_x \cdot k' + \frac{p}{q}(\boldsymbol{e}_1 \cdot k' - \boldsymbol{e} \cdot s + \boldsymbol{e}') \tag{6}$$

for $k', \boldsymbol{e}'$ chosen by $\mathbb{S}^*$ where $\|k'\|_\infty \leq \sigma \cdot \sqrt{n}$ and $\|\boldsymbol{e}'\|_\infty \leq \sigma' \cdot \sqrt{n}$. Therefore, rounding the quantity in Eq. (6) is guaranteed to result in the correct value if every coefficient of $\frac{p}{q} \cdot \boldsymbol{a}_x \cdot k'$ is further than

$$\left\| \frac{p}{q}(\boldsymbol{e}_1 \cdot k' - \boldsymbol{e} \cdot s + \boldsymbol{e}') \right\|_\infty$$

away from $\mathbb{Z} + 1/2$. In other words if $\mathbb{S}^*$ can force incorrect evaluation, it has found $k' \leq \sigma \cdot \sqrt{n}$ such that a coefficient of $\boldsymbol{a}_x \cdot k'$ is within a distance

$$\left\| \boldsymbol{e}_1 \cdot k' - \boldsymbol{e} \cdot s + \boldsymbol{e}' \right\|_\infty \leq 2\sigma^2 n^2 + \sigma' \sqrt{n}$$

of $\frac{q}{p}\mathbb{Z} + \frac{q}{2p} \subset \frac{q}{2p}\mathbb{Z}$. We now apply Lemma 5 with $2 \cdot p$, $T = 2\sigma^2 n^2 + \sigma'\sqrt{n}$ to show that $\mathbb{S}^*$ forcing incorrect evaluation with non-negligible probability violates the assumption that $\mathsf{1D\text{-}SIS}_{q/2p,n\cdot\ell,\max\{\ell\cdot\sigma n^{3/2},2\sigma^2 n^2+\sigma'\sqrt{n}\}}$ is hard. Therefore, condition (ii) enforces correct evaluation.   □

5.3   Setting Parameters

Let κ be the security parameter. Ignoring the NIZKAoK requirements for simplicity, Theorem 2 requires the following conditions:

- $\mathsf{dRLWE}_{q,n,\sigma}$ is hard,
- $\frac{q}{2p} \gg \sigma' \gg \max\{L \cdot \ell \cdot \sigma n^{3/2}, \sigma^2 n^2\}$,
- $\mathsf{1D\text{-}SIS}_{q/(2p),n\cdot\ell,\max\{\ell\cdot\sigma n^{3/2}, 2\sigma^2 n^2 + \sigma'\sqrt{n}\}}$ is hard.

We will be using the presumed hardness of SIVP_γ for approximation factors $\gamma = 2^{o(\sqrt{n})}$. The SIVP_γ lattice dimension associated to RLWE will be $n = \kappa^c$ (for some constant $c > 2$); the dimension associated to 1D-SIS hardness will be $n' = \kappa$. We first choose $L = \kappa, \sigma = \mathsf{poly}(n)$ and $\sigma' = \sigma^2 n^2 \cdot \kappa^{\omega(1)}$, and then set $q = p \cdot \prod_{i=1}^{n'} p_i$ by picking coprime $p, p_1, \ldots, p_{n'} = \sigma' \cdot \omega(\sqrt{nn' \log q \log n'})$. Having made these choices, we argue that each of the three conditions are satisfied. We argue RLWE hardness via SIVP for sub-exponential approximation factors $2^{\tilde{O}(n^{1/c})}$ (for $c > 2$), noting that $\sigma = \mathsf{poly}(n)$ and

$$
\begin{aligned}
q &= (\sigma')^{n'} \cdot \omega((n \cdot n' \cdot \log q \cdot \log n')^{n'/2}) \\
&= 2^{(2\log(n\sigma) + \omega(1)\log\kappa)\cdot n^{1/c}} \cdot \omega((n \cdot n' \cdot \log q \cdot \log n')^{n'/2}) \\
&= 2^{\omega(1)\cdot n^{1/c}\cdot\log n} \cdot \omega((n^{1+\frac{1}{c}} \cdot \log q \cdot \log n)^{n^{1/c}/2}) \\
&= 2^{\tilde{O}(n^{1/c})}.
\end{aligned}
$$

Now substituting in $\ell = \log q$ implies that the second condition can be satisfied. Finally for the 1D-SIS condition, we note that $q/p = \prod_{i=1}^{n'} p_i$ and

$$
\begin{aligned}
p_1 &= \sigma' \cdot \omega(\sqrt{n \cdot n' \log q \cdot \log n'}) \\
&= \sigma^2 n^2 \cdot \kappa^{\omega(1)} \cdot \omega(\sqrt{n \cdot n' \log q \cdot \log n'}) \\
&= (n')^{\omega(1)} \cdot \omega(\sqrt{n'^{1+c} \cdot \log q \cdot \log n'}).
\end{aligned}
$$

So we get hardness of our 1D-SIS instance via the presumed hardness of SIVP on n'-dimensional lattices for $(n')^{\omega(1)} \cdot \mathsf{poly}(n')$ approximation factors. We summarise the parameters of our construction in Table 1.

Table 1. Parameters of our VOPRF

Parameter	Description	Requirement	Asymptotic
n	Ring dimension	$n = \mathsf{poly}(\kappa)$	$\mathsf{poly}(\kappa)$
q	Original modulus	$q = p \cdot \sigma' \cdot \kappa^{\omega(1)}$	$\kappa^{\omega(1)}$
p	Rounding modulus	—	$\mathsf{poly}(\kappa)$
ℓ	$\log_2(q)$	—	$\omega(1)$
σ	Secret/error distribution	$q/\sigma = 2^{o(\sqrt{n})}$	$\mathsf{poly}(\kappa)$
σ'	Drowning distribution	$\sigma' = \sigma^2 n^2 \cdot \kappa^{\omega(1)}$	$\kappa^{\omega(1)}$
L	Bit-length of PRF input	—	—

To give a rough estimate for concrete bandwidth costs, we start by observing that we need q to be super-polynomial in κ for (a) PRF correctness and (b) noise drowning on the server side. We may pick $\log q \approx 256$ for $\kappa = 128$. Applying the "estimator" from [2] with the quantum cost model from [3] and noise standard deviation $\sigma = 3.2$ suggests that $n = 16,384$ provides security of $> 2^{128}$ operations (indeed, significantly more, suggesting room for fine tuning). Thus, a single RLWE sample takes about 0.5 MB. As specified in Sect. 3 our construction sends $2\,\ell$ such samples. However, an implementation could send only two such samples (see Sect. 3.2). Thus, each party would send about 1MB of RLWE sample material. Of course, a more careful analysis and optimisation – picking parameters, analysing bounds, applying rounding, perhaps removing the need for super-polynomial drowning – would reduce this magnitude.

In addition to this, each party must send material for the zero-knowledge proofs. In the full version of this work, we show that the statement associated to the client proof may be written as an instance of $\mathcal{R}^*$ consisting of *more than* $m' = n\ell^2(L-1)$ equations where the witness has a dimension of *more than* $n' = 4n\ell^2(L-1)$. Additionally, there are at least $|\mathcal{M}| := 4n\ell^2(L-1)$ constraints. This implies that the argument system of [47] requires the communication of at least $m' + 3n' + 4|\mathcal{M}| = 9n\ell^2(L-1)$ integers modulo q per repetition. Using the concrete parameters laid out above, we require $> 9 \cdot 16,384 \cdot 256^2 \cdot 127 > 2^{40}$ bits of communication per repetition. We remind the reader that choosing parameters of the ZKAoK of Yang appropriately would allow us to only repeat a small number of times and stress that this discussion gives a crude lower bound designed to give an intuition on the inefficiency of our scheme, rather than a formal analysis of the concrete cost of our scheme. We note that applying a SNARK or STARK would reduce the bandwidth requirement for proofs.

Acknowledgements. We thank Ward Beullens for helpful discussions and advice on replacing Stern-based ZKAoKs with more efficient alternatives.

The research of Albrecht was supported by EPSRC grants EP/S020330/1 and EP/S02087X/1, and by the European Union Horizon 2020 Research and Innovation Program Grant 780701; the research of Deo was partially supported by the EPSRC and the UK government as part of the Centre for Doctoral Training in Cyber Security at Royal Holloway, University of London (EP/K035584/1), the European Union Horizon 2020 Research and Innovation Program Grant 780701, and BPI-France in the context of the national project RISQ (P141580); the research of Smart was supported by CyberSecurity Research Flanders with reference number VR20192203, by ERC Advanced Grant ERC-2015-AdG-IMPaCT and by the FWO under an Odysseus project GOH9718N.

References

1. Albrecht, M.R., Davidson, A., Deo, A., Smart, N.P.: Round-optimal verifiable oblivious pseudorandom functions from ideal lattices. Cryptology ePrint Archive, Report 2019/1271 (2019). https://eprint.iacr.org/2019/1271
2. Albrecht, M.R., Player, R., Scott, S.: On the concrete hardness of learning with errors. J. Math. Cryptol. **9**(3), 169–203 (2015). http://www.degruyter.com/view/j/jmc.2015.9.issue-3/jmc-2015-0016/jmc-2015-0016.xml

3. Alkim, E., Ducas, L., Pöppelmann, T., Schwabe, P.: Post-quantum key exchange - a new hope. In: Holz, T., Savage, S. (eds.) USENIX Security 2016, pp. 327–343. USENIX Association (2016)
4. Banaszczyk, W.: New bounds in some transference theorems in the geometry of numbers. Mathematische Annalen **296**(1), (1993)
5. Banerjee, A., Peikert, C.: New and improved key-homomorphic pseudorandom functions. In: Garay, J.A., Gennaro, R. (eds.) CRYPTO 2014, Part I. LNCS, vol. 8616, pp. 353–370. Springer, Heidelberg (2014)
6. Banerjee, A., Peikert, C., Rosen, A.: Pseudorandom functions and lattices. In: Pointcheval, D., Johansson, T. (eds.) EUROCRYPT 2012. LNCS, vol. 7237, pp. 719–737. Springer, Heidelberg (2012)
7. Beullens, W.: Sigma protocols for MQ, PKP and SIS, and Fishy signature schemes. In: Canteaut, A., Ishai, Y. (eds.) EUROCRYPT 2020, Part III. LNCS, vol. 12107, pp. 183–211. Springer, Heidelberg (2020)
8. Blum, M., Feldman, P., Micali, S.: Non-interactive zero-knowledge and its applications (extended abstract). In: 20th ACM STOC, pp. 103–112. ACM Press (1988)
9. Boneh, D., Dagdelen, Ö., Fischlin, M., Lehmann, A., Schaffner, C., Zhandry, M.: Random oracles in a quantum world. In: Lee, D.H., Wang, X. (eds.) ASIACRYPT 2011. LNCS, vol. 7073, pp. 41–69. Springer, Heidelberg (2011)
10. Boneh, D., Kogan, D., Woo, K.: Oblivious pseudorandom functions from isogenies. In: Moriai, S., Wang, H. (eds.) ASIACRYPT 2020, Part II. LNCS, vol. 12492, pp. 520–550. Springer, Heidelberg (2020)
11. Boneh, D., Lewi, K., Montgomery, H.W., Raghunathan, A.: Key homomorphic PRFs and their applications. In: Canetti, R., Garay, J.A. (eds.) CRYPTO 2013, Part I. LNCS, vol. 8042, pp. 410–428. Springer, Heidelberg (2013)
12. Bootle, J., Lyubashevsky, V., Seiler, G.: Algebraic techniques for short(er) exact lattice-based zero-knowledge proofs. In: Boldyreva, A., Micciancio, D. (eds.) CRYPTO 2019, Part I. LNCS, vol. 11692, pp. 176–202. Springer, Heidelberg (2019)
13. Brakerski, Z., Langlois, A., Peikert, C., Regev, O., Stehlé, D.: Classical hardness of learning with errors. In: Boneh, D., Roughgarden, T., Feigenbaum, J. (eds.) 45th ACM STOC, pp. 575–584. ACM Press (2013)
14. Brakerski, Z., Tsabary, R., Vaikuntanathan, V., Wee, H.: Private constrained PRFs (and more) from LWE. In: Kalai, Y., Reyzin, L. (eds.) TCC 2017, Part I. LNCS, vol. 10677, pp. 264–302. Springer, Heidelberg (2017)
15. Brakerski, Z., Vaikuntanathan, V.: Constrained key-homomorphic PRFs from standard lattice assumptions - or: How to secretly embed a circuit in your PRF. In: Dodis, Y., Nielsen, J.B. (eds.) TCC 2015, Part II. LNCS, vol. 9015, pp. 1–30. Springer, Heidelberg (2015)
16. Canetti, R., Chen, Y.: Constraint-hiding constrained PRFs for NC^1 from LWE. In: Coron, J.S., Nielsen, J.B. (eds.) EUROCRYPT 2017, Part I. LNCS, vol. 10210, pp. 446–476. Springer, Heidelberg (Apr / May (2017)
17. CFRG: Cfrg pake selection process. Public GitHub repository (Summer 2019). https://github.com/cfrg/pake-selection. Accessed Jan 2020
18. Davidson, A., Goldberg, I., Sullivan, N., Tankersley, G., Valsorda, F.: Privacy pass: Bypassing internet challenges anonymously. PoPETs **2018**(3), 164–180 (2018)
19. Davidson, A., Sullivan, N.: The privacy pass protocol. Internet-Draft draft-privacy-pass-0, IETF Secretariat (November 2019). https://datatracker.ietf.org/doc/draft-privacy-pass/
20. Davidson, A., Sullivan, N., Wood, C.: Oblivious pseudorandom functions (OPRFs) using prime-order groups. Internet-Draft draft-irtf-cfrg-voprf-01, IETF Secretariat (July 2019). http://www.ietf.org/internet-drafts/draft-irtf-cfrg-voprf-01.txt

21. Dodis, Y., Goldwasser, S., Kalai, Y.T., Peikert, C., Vaikuntanathan, V.: Public-key encryption schemes with auxiliary inputs. In: Micciancio, D. (ed.) TCC 2010. LNCS, vol. 5978, pp. 361–381. Springer, Heidelberg (2010)

22. Don, J., Fehr, S., Majenz, C., Schaffner, C.: Security of the Fiat-Shamir transformation in the quantum random-oracle model. In: Boldyreva, A., Micciancio, D. (eds.) CRYPTO 2019, Part II. LNCS, vol. 11693, pp. 356–383. Springer, Heidelberg (2019)

23. Fiat, A., Shamir, A.: How to prove yourself: practical solutions to identification and signature problems. In: Odlyzko, A.M. (ed.) CRYPTO'86. LNCS, vol. 263, pp. 186–194. Springer, Heidelberg (1987)

24. Freedman, M.J., Ishai, Y., Pinkas, B., Reingold, O.: Keyword search and oblivious pseudorandom functions. In: Kilian, J. (ed.) TCC 2005. LNCS, vol. 3378, pp. 303–324. Springer, Heidelberg (2005)

25. Gentry, C., Peikert, C., Vaikuntanathan, V.: Trapdoors for hard lattices and new cryptographic constructions. In: Ladner, R.E., Dwork, C. (eds.) 40th ACM STOC, pp. 197–206. ACM Press (2008)

26. Gentry, C., Sahai, A., Waters, B.: Homomorphic encryption from learning with errors: Conceptually-simpler, asymptotically-faster, attribute-based. In: Canetti, R., Garay, J.A. (eds.) CRYPTO 2013, Part I. LNCS, vol. 8042, pp. 75–92. Springer, Heidelberg (2013)

27. Goldreich, O., Micali, S., Wigderson, A.: How to prove all NP-statements in zero-knowledge, and a methodology of cryptographic protocol design. In: Odlyzko, A.M. (ed.) CRYPTO'86. LNCS, vol. 263, pp. 171–185. Springer, Heidelberg (1987)

28. Goldwasser, S., Micali, S., Rackoff, C.: The knowledge complexity of interactive proof-systems (extended abstract). In: 17th ACM STOC, pp. 291–304. ACM Press (1985)

29. Jarecki, S., Kiayias, A., Krawczyk, H.: Round-optimal password-protected secret sharing and T-PAKE in the password-only model. In: Sarkar, P., Iwata, T. (eds.) ASIACRYPT 2014, Part II. LNCS, vol. 8874, pp. 233–253. Springer, Heidelberg (2014)

30. Jarecki, S., Kiayias, A., Krawczyk, H., Xu, J.: Highly-efficient and composable password-protected secret sharing (or: How to protect your bitcoin wallet online). In: EuroS&P, pp. 276–291. IEEE (2016)

31. Jarecki, S., Krawczyk, H., Xu, J.: OPAQUE: An asymmetric PAKE protocol secure against pre-computation attacks. In: Nielsen, J.B., Rijmen, V. (eds.) EUROCRYPT 2018, Part III. LNCS, vol. 10822, pp. 456–486. Springer, Heidelberg (2018)

32. Jarecki, S., Liu, X.: Efficient oblivious pseudorandom function with applications to adaptive OT and secure computation of set intersection. In: Reingold, O. (ed.) TCC 2009. LNCS, vol. 5444, pp. 577–594. Springer, Heidelberg (2009)

33. Keelveedhi, S., Bellare, M., Ristenpart, T.: Dupless: server-aided encryption for deduplicated storage. In: Presented as part of the 22nd USENIX Security Symposium (USENIX Security 13), pp. 179–194. USENIX, Washington, D.C. (2013)

34. Krawczyk, H.: The opaque asymmetric pake protocol. Internet-Draft draft-krawczyk-cfrg-opaque-02, IETF Secretariat (July 2019), http://www.ietf.org/internet-drafts/draft-krawczyk-cfrg-opaque-02.txt

35. Libert, B., Ling, S., Mouhartem, F., Nguyen, K., Wang, H.: Zero-knowledge arguments for matrix-vector relations and lattice-based group encryption. In: Cheon, J.H., Takagi, T. (eds.) ASIACRYPT 2016, Part II. LNCS, vol. 10032, pp. 101–131. Springer, Heidelberg (2016)

36. Libert, B., Ling, S., Nguyen, K., Wang, H.: Zero-knowledge arguments for lattice-based PRFs and applications to E-cash. In: Takagi, T., Peyrin, T. (eds.) ASI-ACRYPT 2017, Part III. LNCS, vol. 10626, pp. 304–335. Springer, Heidelberg (2017)

37. Liu, Q., Zhandry, M.: Revisiting post-quantum Fiat-Shamir. In: Boldyreva, A., Micciancio, D. (eds.) CRYPTO 2019, Part II. LNCS, vol. 11693, pp. 326–355. Springer, Heidelberg (2019)

38. Lyubashevsky, V.: Fiat-Shamir with aborts: applications to lattice and factoring-based signatures. In: Matsui, M. (ed.) ASIACRYPT 2009. LNCS, vol. 5912, pp. 598–616. Springer, Heidelberg (2009)

39. Lyubashevsky, V.: Lattice signatures without trapdoors. In: Pointcheval, D., Johansson, T. (eds.) EUROCRYPT 2012. LNCS, vol. 7237, pp. 738–755. Springer, Heidelberg (2012)

40. Lyubashevsky, V., Peikert, C., Regev, O.: On ideal lattices and learning with errors over rings. In: Gilbert, H. (ed.) EUROCRYPT 2010. LNCS, vol. 6110, pp. 1–23. Springer, Heidelberg (2010)

41. Micciancio, D., Peikert, C.: Trapdoors for lattices: Simpler, tighter, faster, smaller. In: Pointcheval, D., Johansson, T. (eds.) EUROCRYPT 2012. LNCS, vol. 7237, pp. 700–718. Springer, Heidelberg (2012)

42. Papadopoulos, D., Wessels, D., Huque, S., Naor, M., Včelák, J., Reyzin, L., Goldberg, S.: Making NSEC5 practical for DNSSEC. Cryptology ePrint Archive, Report 2017/099 (2017), http://eprint.iacr.org/2017/099

43. Peikert, C.: A decade of lattice cryptography. Cryptology ePrint Archive, Report 2015/939 (2015), http://eprint.iacr.org/2015/939

44. Peikert, C., Shiehian, S.: Privately constraining and programming PRFs, the LWE way. In: Abdalla, M., Dahab, R. (eds.) PKC 2018, Part II. LNCS, vol. 10770, pp. 675–701. Springer, Heidelberg (2018)

45. Regev, O.: On lattices, learning with errors, random linear codes, and cryptography. In: Gabow, H.N., Fagin, R. (eds.) 37th ACM STOC, pp. 84–93. ACM Press (May 2005)

46. Sullivan, N.: Cloudflare supports privacy pass. Cloudflare Blog (November 09 2017), https://blog.cloudflare.com/cloudflare-supports-privacy-pass/. Accessed Aug 2019

47. Yang, R., Au, M.H., Zhang, Z., Xu, Q., Yu, Z., Whyte, W.: Efficient lattice-based zero-knowledge arguments with standard soundness: construction and applications. In: Boldyreva, A., Micciancio, D. (eds.) CRYPTO 2019, Part I. LNCS, vol. 11692, pp. 147–175. Springer, Heidelberg (2019)

BETA: Biometric-Enabled Threshold Authentication

Shashank Agrawal[1], Saikrishna Badrinarayanan[2(✉)], Payman Mohassel[3],
Pratyay Mukherjee[2], and Sikhar Patranabis[2]

[1] Western Digital, Milpitas, CA, USA
shashank.agrawal@wdc.com
[2] Visa Research, Palo Alto, CA, USA
{sabadrin,pratmukh,sipatran}@visa.com
[3] Facebook, San Francisco, CA, USA

Abstract. In the past decades, user authentication has been dominated
by server-side password-based solutions that rely on "what users know".
This approach is susceptible to breaches and phishing attacks, and poses
usability challenges. As a result, the industry is gradually moving to
biometric-based client-side solutions that do not store any secret information on servers. This shift necessitates the safe storage of biometric
templates and private keys, which are used to generate tokens, on user
devices.

We propose a new generic framework called *Biometric Enabled
Threshold Authentication* (BETA) to protect sensitive client-side information like biometric templates and cryptographic keys. Towards this,
we formally introduce the notion of *Fuzzy Threshold Tokenizer* (FTT)
where an initiator can use a "close" biometric measurement to generate
an authentication token if at least t (the threshold) devices participate.
We require that the devices only talk to the initiator, and not to each
other, to capture the way user devices are connected in the real world. We
use the universal composability (UC) framework to model the security
properties of FTT, including the unforgeability of tokens and the privacy
of the biometric values (template and measurement), under a *malicious*
adversary. We construct *three* protocols that meet our definition.

Our first two protocols are general feasibility results that work for
any distance function, *any* threshold t and tolerate the *maximal* (i.e.
$t-1$) amount of corruption. They are based on *any* two round UC-
secure multi-party computation protocol in the standard model (with
a CRS) and threshold fully homomorphic encryption, respectively. We
show how to effectively use these primitives to build protocols in a constrained communication model with just four rounds of communication.

For the third protocol, we consider inner-product based distance metrics (cosine similarity, Euclidean distance, etc.) specifically, motivated by
the recent interest in its use for face recognition. We use Paillier encryption, efficient NIZKs for specific languages, and a simple garbled circuit
to build an efficient protocol for the common case of $n=3$ devices with
one compromised.

© International Association for Cryptologic Research 2021
J. A. Garay (Ed.): PKC 2021, LNCS 12711, pp. 290–318, 2021.
https://doi.org/10.1007/978-3-030-75248-4_11

1 Introduction

Traditionally, password-based authentication has been the dominant approach for authenticating users on the Internet, by relying on "what users know". However, this approach has its fair share of security and usability issues. It typically requires the servers to store a (salted) hash of all passwords, making them susceptible to offline dictionary attacks. Indeed, large-scale password breaches in the wild are extremely common [6,8]. Passwords also pose challenging usability problems. High entropy passwords are hard to remember by humans, while low entropy passwords provide little security, and research has shown that introducing complex restrictions on password choices can backfire [39, Sec A.3].

There are major ongoing efforts in the industry to address some of these issues. For example, "unique" biometric features such as finger-print [4], facial scans [1], and iris scans [9] are increasingly popular first or second factor authentication mechanisms for logging into devices and applications. Studies show that biometrics are much more user-friendly [2], particularly on mobile devices, as users do not have to remember or enter any secret information. At the same time, a (server-side) breach of biometric data is much more damaging because, unlike passwords, there is no easy way to change biometric information regularly.

Therefore, the industry is shifting away from transmitting or storing user secrets on the server-side. For example, biometric templates and measurements are stored and processed on the client devices where the matching also takes place. A successful match then unlocks a private signing key for a digital signature scheme which is used to generate a token on a fresh challenge. Instead of the user data, the token is transmitted to the server, who only stores a public verification key to verify the tokens. (Throughout the paper, we shall use the terms token and signature interchangeably.) Thus, a server breach does not lead to a loss of sensitive user data.

Most prominently, this is the approach taken by the FIDO Alliance [3], the world's largest industry-wide effort to enable an interoperable ecosystem of hardware-, mobile- and biometric-based authenticators that can be used by enterprises and service providers. This framework is also widely adopted by major Internet players and incorporated into all major browsers in the form of W3C standard Web Authentication API [10].

Hardware-Based Protection. With biometric data and private keys (for generating tokens) stored on client devices, a primary challenge is to securely protect them. As pointed out before, this is particularly crucial with biometrics since unlike passwords they are not replaceable. The most secure approach for doing so relies on hardware-based solutions such as secure enclaves [5] that provide physical separation between secrets and applications. However, secure hardware is not available on all devices, can be costly to support at scale, and provides very little programmability.

Software-Based Protection. Software-based solutions such as white-box cryptography are often based on ad-hoc techniques that are regularly broken [11].

The provably secure alternative, i.e. cryptographic obfuscation [13,37], is not yet practical for real-world use-cases.

A simple alternative approach is to apply "salt-and-hash" techniques, often used to protect passwords, to biometric templates before storing them on the client device. Here, naïve solutions fail because biometric matching is almost always a fuzzy match that checks whether the distance between two vectors is above a threshold or not.

Using Fuzzy Extractors. It is tempting to think that a better way to implement the hash-and-salt approach for biometric data is through a cryptographic primitive known as *fuzzy extractor* [21,33]. However, as also discussed by Dupont et al. [34], this approach only works for high-entropy biometric data and is susceptible to offline dictionary attacks.

Distributed Cryptography to the Rescue. Our work is motivated by the fact that most users own and carry *multiple devices* (laptop, smart-phone, smart-watch, etc.) and have other IoT devices around when authenticating (smart TV, smart-home appliances, etc.). We introduce a new framework for client-side biometric-based authentication that securely distributes both the biometric template as well as the secret signing key among multiple devices. These devices can collectively perform biometric matching and token generation without ever reconstructing the template or the signing key on any one device. We refer to this framework as *Biometric Enabled Threshold Authentication* (BETA for short) and study it at length in this paper.

Before diving deeper into the details, we note that while our primary motivation stems from a client-side authentication mechanism, our framework is quite *generic* and can be used in other settings. For example, it can also be used to protect biometric information on the *server-side* by distributing it among multiple servers who perform the matching and token generation (e.g., for a *single sign-on* authentication token) in a fully distributed manner.

1.1 Our Contributions

To concretely instantiate our framework BETA, we formally introduce the notion of *fuzzy threshold tokenizer* (FTT). We provide a universally composable (UC) security definition for FTT and design several protocols that realize it. We first briefly describe the notion of a Fuzzy Threshold Tokenizer.

Fuzzy Threshold Tokenizer. Consider a set of n parties/devices, a distribution $\mathcal{W}$ over vectors in $\mathbb{Z}_q^\ell$, a threshold t on the number of parties, a distance predicate Dist and an unforgeable threshold signature scheme TS. Initially, in a *global setup* phase, a user generates some public and secret parameters (in a trusted setting), and distributes them amongst the n devices she owns. Further, she also runs the setup of the scheme TS and secret shares the signing key amongst the devices. In an *enrollment* phase, user samples a biometric template

$\overrightarrow{\mathbf{w}} \in \mathbb{Z}_q^{\ell}$ according to $\mathcal{W}$ and securely shares it amongst all the devices. Any set of t devices can, together, completely reconstruct the biometric template $\overrightarrow{\mathbf{w}}$ and the signing key of the threshold signature scheme. Then, during an online *sign on session*, an initiating device P, with a candidate biometric measurement $\overrightarrow{\mathbf{u}}$ as input, can interact in a protocol with a set S of $(t-1)$ other devices. At the end of this, if $\overrightarrow{\mathbf{u}}$ is "close enough" to the template $\overrightarrow{\mathbf{w}}$ (with respect to distance predicate Dist), the initiating device P obtains a token (signature) on a message of its choice.

It is important to note that we do not allow the other participating $(t-1)$ devices to interact amongst themselves[1] and all communication goes through the initiating device P. This is a critical requirement on the communication model for FTT since in a typical usage scenario, one or two primary devices (e.g., a laptop or a smart-phone) play the role of the initiating device and all other devices are only paired/connected to the primary device. (These devices may not even be aware of the presence of other devices.) Indeed, this requirement makes the design of constant-round FTT protocols significantly more challenging. Further, in any round of communication, we only allow unidirectional exchange of messages, i.e., either P sends a message to some subset of the other $(t-1)$ devices or vice versa.

Security Definition. Consider a probabilistic polynomial time adversary $\mathcal{A}$ that corrupts a set T of devices where $|T| < t$. Informally, the security properties that we wish to capture in an FTT scheme are as follows:

(i) *Privacy of biometric template:* From any sign on session initiated by a corrupt device, $\mathcal{A}$ should not be able to learn any information about the biometric template $\overrightarrow{\mathbf{w}}$ apart from just the output of the predicate $\mathsf{Dist}(\overrightarrow{\mathbf{u}}, \overrightarrow{\mathbf{w}})$ for its choice of measurement $\overrightarrow{\mathbf{u}}$. If the sign on session was initiated by an honest device, $\mathcal{A}$ should learn no information about $\overrightarrow{\mathbf{w}}$. Crucially, we do not impose any restriction on the entropy of the distribution from which the template is picked.

(ii) *Privacy of biometric measurement:* For any sign on session initiated by an honest device, $\mathcal{A}$ should learn no information whatsoever about the measurement $\overrightarrow{\mathbf{u}}$.

(iii) *Token unforgeability*: $\mathcal{A}$ should not be able to compute a valid token (that verifies according to the threshold signature scheme TS) unless it initiated a sign on session on behalf of a corrupt party with a measurement $\overrightarrow{\mathbf{u}}$ such that $\mathsf{Dist}(\overrightarrow{\mathbf{u}}, \overrightarrow{\mathbf{w}}) = 1$. Furthermore, $\mathcal{A}$ should only be able to compute *exactly one* token from each such session.

Our *first contribution* is a formal modeling of the security requirements of a fuzzy threshold tokenizer via a real-ideal world security definition in the universal composability (UC) framework [26]. We refer the reader to Sect. 4 for the formal definition and a detailed discussion on its intricacies.

Our next contribution is a design of several protocols that realize this primitive.

---

[1] Note that corrupt parties can of course freely interact amongst themselves.

Protocol-1(π^{mpc}). Given any threshold signature scheme TS, for any distance measure Dist, any n, t, we construct a four round[2] UC-secure FTT protocol π^{mpc}. Our construction is based on any two-round (over a broadcast channel) UC-secure multi-party computation (MPC) protocol [15,38,45,48] in the CRS model that is secure against up to all but one corruption along with other basic primitives. π^{mpc} tolerates up to $(t-1)$ (which is maximal) malicious devices.

Protocol-2 (π^{tfhe}). Given any threshold signature scheme TS, for any distance measure Dist, any n, t, we construct a four round UC-secure FTT protocol π^{tfhe}. Our construction is based on any t out of n threshold fully homomorphic encryption scheme (TFHE) and other basic primitives. Like π^{mpc}, this protocol is secure against $(t-1)$ malicious devices.

The above two feasibility results are based on two incomparable primitives (two round MPC and threshold FHE). On the one hand, two-round MPC seems like a stronger notion than threshold FHE. But, on the other hand, two-round MPC is known from a variety of assumptions like LWE/DDH/Quadratic Residuosity, while threshold FHE is known only from LWE. Further, the two protocols have very different techniques which may be of independent interest.

Protocol-3 (π^{ip}). We design the third protocol π^{ip} specifically for the cosine similarity distance metric, which has recently been shown to be quite effective for face recognition (CosFace [55], SphereFace [43], FaceNet [53]). We pick a threshold of three for this protocol as people nowadays have at least three devices on them most of the time (typically, a laptop, a smart-phone and a smart-watch). π^{ip} is secure in the random oracle model as long as at most one of the devices is compromised. We use Paillier encryption, efficient NIZKs for specific languages, and a simple garbled circuit to build an efficient four-round protocol.

Efficiency analysis of π^{ip}. Finally, we perform a concrete efficiency analysis of our third protocol π^{ip}. We assume that biometric templates and measurements have ℓ features (or elements) and every feature can be represented with m bits. Let λ denote the computational security parameter and s denote the statistical security parameter. In the protocol π^{ip}, we use Paillier encryption scheme to encrypt each feature of the measurement and its product with the shares of the template. The initiator device proves that the ciphertexts are well-formed and the features are of the right length. For Paillier encryption, such proofs can be done efficiently using only $O(\ell m)$ group operations [30,31].

---

[2] Recall that by one communication round, we mean a unidirectional/non-simultaneous message exchange channel over a *peer-to-peer* network. That is, in each round either the initiator sends messages to some subset of the other participating devices or vice versa. In contrast, one round of communication over a *broadcast* channel means that messages are being sent *simultaneously* by multiple (potentially all) parties connected to the channel and all of them receive all the messages sent in that round. All our FTT protocols use peer-to-peer channels which is the default communication model in this paper.

The other devices use the homomorphic properties of Paillier encryption to compute ciphertexts for inner-product shares and some additional values. They are sent back to the initiator but with a MAC on them. Then the other devices generate a garbled circuit that takes the MAC information from them and the decrypted ciphertexts from the initiator to compute if the cosine value exceeds a certain threshold. The garbled circuit constructed here only does 5 multiplications on numbers of length $O(m + \log \ell + s)$. Oblivious transfers can be preprocessed in the setup phase between every pair of parties so that the online phase is quite efficient (only symmetric-key operations). Furthermore, since only one of the two helping devices can be corrupt, only one device needs to transfer the garbled circuit [44], further reducing the communication overhead. (We have skipped several important details of the protocol here, but they do not affect the complexity analysis. See Sect. 2.3 for a complete overview of the protocol.)

An alternate design appropach is to use the garbled circuit itself to compute the inner-product. However, there are two disadvantages of this approach. First, it does not scale efficiently with feature vector length. The number of multiplications to be done inside the garbled circuit would be linear in the number of features, or the size of the circuit would be roughly $O(m^2 \ell)$. This is an important concern because the number of features in a template can be very large (e.g., see Fig. 1 in the NISTIR draft on Ongoing Face Recognition Vendor Test (FRVT) [7]). Second, the devices would have to prove in zero knowledge that the bits fed as input to the circuit match the secret shares of the template given to them in the enrollment phase. This incurs additional computational overheads.

1.2   Related Work

Fuzzy identity based encryption, introduced by Sahai and Waters [52], allows decrypting a ciphertext encrypted with respect to some identity id if the decryptor possesses the secret key for an identity that almost matches id. However, unlike FTT, the decryptor is required to know both identities and which positions match. Recall that one of our main goals is to distribute the biometric template across all devices so that no one device ever learns it.

Function secret sharing, introduced by Boyle et al. [22], enables to share the computation of a function f amongst several users. Another interesting related primitive is homomorphic secret sharing [23]. However, both these notions don't quite fit in our context because of the limitations on our communication model and the specific security requirements against a malicious adversary.

Secure multiparty computation protocols in the private simultaneous messages model [14, 36, 41] consider a scenario where there is a client and a set of servers that wish to securely compute a function f on their joint inputs wherein the communication model only involves interaction between the client and each individual server. However, in that model, the adversary can either corrupt the client or a subset of servers but not both.

The work of Dupont et al. [34] construct a fuzzy password authenticated key exchange protocol where each of the two parties have a password with low entropy. At the end of the protocol, both parties learn the shared secret key only if the two passwords are "close enough" with respect to some distance measure. In our work, we consider the problem of generating signatures and also multiple parties. Another crucial difference is that in their work, both parties hold a copy of the password whereas in our case, the biometric template is distributed between parties and therefore is never exposed to any party. There is also a lot of work on distributed password authenticated key exchange [16] (and the references within) but their setting considers passwords (and so, equality matching) and not biometrics.

There has been a lot of work in developing privacy-preserving ways to compare biometric data [17,25,32] but it has mostly focused on computing specific distance measures (like Hamming distance) in the two-party setting where each party holds a vector. There has also been some privacy-preserving work in the same communication model as ours [19,29,42] but it has mainly focused on private aggregation of sensitive user data.

Open Problems. We leave it as an open problem to define weaker game-based security definitions for FTT and to design more efficient protocols that satisfy those. We also leave it open to design FTT protocols that tolerate adaptive corruptions and/or support dynamic addition/deletion of parties and rotation of signature keys.

2   Technical Overview

2.1   MPC Based Protocol

Emulating General Purpose MPC. Our starting point is the observation that suppose all the parties could freely communicate, then any UC-secure MPC protocol against a malicious adversary in the presence of a broadcast channel would intuitively be very useful in the design of an FTT scheme if we consider the following functionality: the initiator P^* has input $(\mathsf{msg}, S, \overrightarrow{\mathbf{u}})$, every party $P_i \in S$ has input (msg, S), their respective shares of the template $\overrightarrow{\mathbf{w}}$ and the signing key. The functionality outputs a signature on msg to party P^* if $\mathsf{Dist}(\overrightarrow{\mathbf{u}}, \overrightarrow{\mathbf{w}}) = 1$ and $|S| = t$. Recently, several works [15,24,38,45,49] have shown how to construct two round UC-secure MPC protocols in the CRS model in the presence of a broadcast channel from standard cryptographic assumptions. However, the issue with following this intuitive approach is that the communication model of our FTT primitive does not allow all parties to interact amongst each other - in particular, the parties in the set S can't directly talk to each other and all communication has to be routed through the initiator. Armed with this insight, our goal now is to emulate a two round MPC protocol π in our setting.

For simplicity, let us first consider $n = t = 3$. That is, there are three parties: P_1, P_2, P_3. Consider the case when P_1 is the initiator. Now, in the first round of our FTT scheme, P_1 sends msg to both parties. Then, in round 2, we have P_2 and P_3 send their round one messages of the MPC protocol π. In round 3 of our FTT scheme, P_1 sends its own round one message of the MPC protocol to both parties. Along with this, P_1 also sends P_2's round one message to P_3 and vice versa. So now, at the end of round 3 of our FTT scheme, all parties have exchanged their first round messages of protocol π.

Our next observation is that since we care only about P_1 getting output, in the underlying protocol π, only party P_1 needs to receive everyone else's messages in round 2. Therefore, in round 4 of our FTT scheme, P_2 and P_3 can compute their round two messages based on the transcript so far and just send them to P_1. This will enable P_1 to compute the output of protocol π.

Challenges. Unfortunately, the above scheme is insecure. Note that in order to rely on the security of protocol π, we crucially need that for any honest party P_i, every other honest party receives the same first round message on its behalf. Also, we require that all honest parties receive the same messages on behalf of the adversary. In our case, since the communication is being controlled and directed by P_1 instead of a broadcast channel, this need not be true if P_1 was corrupt and P_2, P_3 were honest. Specifically, one of the following two things could occur: (i) P_1 can forward an incorrect version of P_3's round one message of protocol π to P_2 and vice versa. (ii) P_1 could send different copies of its own round 1 message of protocol π to both P_2 and P_3.

Signatures to Solve Challenge 2. To solve the first problem, we simply enforce that P_3 sends a signed copy of its round 1 message of protocol π which is forwarded by P_1 to P_2. Then, P_2 accepts the message to be valid if the signature verifies. In the setup phase, we can distribute a signing key to P_3 and a verification key to everyone, including P_2. Similarly, we can ensure that P_2's actual round 1 message of protocol π was forwarded by P_1 to P_3.

Pseudorandom Functions to Solve Challenge 2. Tackling the second problem is a bit trickier. The idea is instead of enforcing that P_1 send the same round 1 message of protocol π to both parties, we will instead ensure that P_1 learns their round 2 messages of protocol π only if it did indeed send the same round 1 message of protocol π to both parties. We now describe how to implement this mechanism. Let us denote msg_2 to be P_1's round 1 message of protocol π sent to P_2 and msg_3 (possibly different from msg_2) to be P_1's round 1 message of protocol π sent to P_3. In the setup phase, we distribute two keys k_2, k_3 of a pseudorandom function (PRF) to both P_2, P_3. Now, in round 4 of our FTT scheme, P_3 does the following: instead of sending its round 2 message of protocol π as is, it encrypts this message using a secret key encryption scheme where the key is $\mathsf{PRF}(k_3, \mathsf{msg}_3)$. Then, in round 4, along with its actual message, P_2 also sends $\mathsf{PRF}(k_3, \mathsf{msg}_2)$ which would be the correct key used by P_3 to encrypt its round 2 message of protocol π only if $\mathsf{msg}_2 = \mathsf{msg}_3$. Similarly, we use the key k_2 to ensure that P_2's round 2 message of protocol π is revealed to P_1 only if $\mathsf{msg}_2 = \mathsf{msg}_3$.

The above approach naturally extends for arbitrary n, t. by sharing two PRF keys between every pair of parties. There, each party encrypts its round 2 message of protocol π with a secret key that is an XOR of all the PRF evaluations. There are additional subtle issues when we try to formally prove that the above protocol is UC-secure and we refer the reader to the full version [12] for more details about the proof.

2.2   Threshold FHE Based Protocol

The basic idea behind our second protocol is to use an FHE scheme to perform the distance predicate computation between the measurement $\overrightarrow{u}$ and the template $\overrightarrow{w}$. In particular, in the setup phase, we generate the public key pk of an FHE scheme and then in the enrollment phase, each party is given an encryption $ct_{\overrightarrow{w}}$ of the template. In the sign on phase, an initiator P^* can compute a ciphertext $ct_{\overrightarrow{u}}$ that encrypts the measurement and send it to all the parties in the set S which will allow them to each individually compute a ciphertext ct^* homomorphically that evaluates $Dist(\overrightarrow{u}, \overrightarrow{w})$. However, the first challenge is how to decrypt this ciphertext ct^*? In other words, who gets the secret key sk of the FHE scheme in the setup? If sk is given to all parties in S, then they can, of course, decrypt $ct_{\overrightarrow{u}}$ but that violates privacy of the measurement. On the other hand, if sk is given only to P^*, that allows P^* to decrypt $ct_{\overrightarrow{w}}$ violating privacy of the template.

Threshold FHE. Observe that this issue can be overcome if somehow the secret key is secret shared amongst all the parties in S in such a way that each of them, using their secret key share sk_i, can produce a partial decryption of ct^* that can then all be combined by P^* to decrypt ct^*. In fact, this is exactly the guarantee of threshold FHE. This brings us to the next issue that if only P^* learns whether $Dist(\overrightarrow{u}, \overrightarrow{w}) = 1$, how do the parties in S successfully transfer the threshold signature shares? (recall that the transfer should be conditioned upon Dist evaluating to 1) One natural option is, in the homomorphic evaluation of the ciphertext ct, apart from just checking whether $Dist(\overrightarrow{u}, \overrightarrow{w}) = 1$, perhaps the circuit could then also compute the partial signatures with respect to the threshold signature scheme if the check succeeds. However, the problem then is that, for threshold decryption, there must be a common ciphertext available to each party. In this case, however, each party would generate a partial signature using its own signing key share resulting in a different ciphertext and in turn preventing threshold decryption.

Partial Signatures. To overcome this obstacle, at the beginning of the sign-on phase, each party computes its partial signature σ_i and *information-theoretically* encrypts it via one-time pad with a uniformly sampled one-time key K_i. The parties then transfer the partial signatures in the same round in an encrypted manner without worrying about the result of the decryption. Now, to complete the construction, we develop a mechanism such that:

- Whenever the FHE decryption results in 1, P^* learns the set of one-time secret keys $\{K_i\}$ and hence reconstructs the set of partial signatures $\{\sigma_i\}$.

- Whenever the FHE decryption results in 0, P^* fails to learn any of the one-time secret keys, which in turn ensures that each of the partial signatures remains hidden from P^*.

To achieve that, we do the following: each party additionally broadcasts ct_{K_i}, which is an FHE encryption of its one-time secret key K_i, to every other party during the enrollment phase. Additionally, we use t copies of the FHE circuit being evaluated as follows: the ith circuit outputs K_i if $\mathsf{Dist}(\overrightarrow{\mathbf{u}}, \overrightarrow{\mathbf{w}}) = 1$ – that is, this circuit is homomorphically evaluated using the FHE ciphertexts $\mathsf{ct}_{\overrightarrow{\mathbf{u}}}, \mathsf{ct}_{\overrightarrow{\mathbf{w}}}, \mathsf{ct}_{K_i}$.[3] Now, at the end of the decryption, if $\mathsf{Dist}(\overrightarrow{\mathbf{u}}, \overrightarrow{\mathbf{w}})$ was indeed equal to 1, P^* learns the set of one-time keys $\{K_i\}$ via homomorphic evaluation and uses these to recover the corresponding partial signatures.

Consider the case where the adversary $\mathcal{A}$ initiates a session with a measurement $\overrightarrow{\mathbf{u}}$ such that $\mathsf{Dist}(\overrightarrow{\mathbf{u}}, \overrightarrow{\mathbf{w}}) = 0$. Our security proof formally establishes that the adversary $\mathcal{A}$ learns no information about each one-time key K_i of the honest parties and hence about the corresponding signature share. At a high level, we exploit the simulation and semantic security guarantees of the threshold FHE scheme to: (a) simulate the FHE partial decryptions to correctly output 0 and (b) to switch each ct_{K_i} to be an encryption of 0. At this point, we can switch each K_i to be a uniformly random string and hence "unrecoverable" to $\mathcal{A}$. We refer the reader to Sect. 6 for more details.

NIZKs. One key issue is that parties may not behave honestly - that is, in the first round, P^* might not run the FHE encryption algorithm honestly and similarly, in the second round, each party might not run the FHE partial decryption algorithm honestly which could lead to devastasting attacks. To solve this, we require each party to prove honest behavior using a non-interactive zero knowledge argument (NIZK). Finally, as in the previous section, to ensure that P^* sends the same message $\mathsf{ct}_{\overrightarrow{\mathbf{u}}}$ to all parties, we use a signature-based verification strategy, which adds two rounds resulting in a four round protocol.

2.3 Cosine Similarity: Single Corruption

In this section, we build a protocol for a specific distance measure[4] (Cosine Similarity). It is more efficient compared to our feasibility results. On the flip side, it tolerates only one corruption: that is, our protocol is UC-secure in the Random Oracle model against a malicious adversary that can corrupt only one party. For two vectors $\overrightarrow{\mathbf{u}}, \overrightarrow{\mathbf{w}}$, $\mathsf{CS.Dist}(\overrightarrow{\mathbf{u}}, \overrightarrow{\mathbf{w}}) = \frac{\langle \overrightarrow{\mathbf{u}}, \overrightarrow{\mathbf{w}} \rangle}{||\overrightarrow{\mathbf{u}}|| \cdot ||\overrightarrow{\mathbf{w}}||}$ where $||\overrightarrow{x}||$ denotes the L^2-norm of the vector. $\mathsf{Dist}(\overrightarrow{\mathbf{u}}, \overrightarrow{\mathbf{w}}) = 1$ if $\mathsf{CS.Dist}(\overrightarrow{\mathbf{u}}, \overrightarrow{\mathbf{w}}) \geq d$ where d is chosen by Dist. Without loss of generality, assume that distribution $\mathcal{W}$ samples

---

[3] Note that the creation and broadcasting of these ciphertexts can happen in parallel within a single round of communication between P^* and the other parties in the set S.

[4] Our construction can also be extended to work for the related Euclidean Distance function but we focus on Cosine Similarity in this section.

vectors $\overrightarrow{\mathbf{w}}$ with $\|\overrightarrow{\mathbf{w}}\| = 1$. Then, we check if $\langle \overrightarrow{\mathbf{u}}, \overrightarrow{\mathbf{w}} \rangle > (d \cdot \langle \overrightarrow{\mathbf{u}}, \overrightarrow{\mathbf{u}} \rangle)^2$ instead of CS.Dist($\overrightarrow{\mathbf{u}}, \overrightarrow{\mathbf{w}}$) $> d$. This syntactic change allows more flexibility.

Distributed Garbling. Our starting point is the following. Suppose we had $t = 2$. Then, we can just directly use Yao's [56] two party semi-honest secure computation protocol as a building block to construct a two round FTT scheme. In the enrollment phase, secret share $\overrightarrow{\mathbf{w}}$ into $\overrightarrow{\mathbf{w}}_1, \overrightarrow{\mathbf{w}}_2$ and give one part to each party. The initiator requests for labels via oblivious transfer (OT) corresponding to his share of $\overrightarrow{\mathbf{w}}$ and input $\overrightarrow{\mathbf{u}}$ while the garbled circuit, which has the other share of $\overrightarrow{\mathbf{w}}$ hardwired, reconstructs $\overrightarrow{\mathbf{w}}$, checks if $\langle \overrightarrow{\mathbf{u}}, \overrightarrow{\mathbf{w}} \rangle > (d \cdot \langle \overrightarrow{\mathbf{u}}, \overrightarrow{\mathbf{u}} \rangle)^2$ and if so, outputs a signature. This protocol is secure against a malicious initiator who only has to evaluate the garbled circuit, if we use an OT protocol that is malicious secure in the CRS model. However, to achieve malicious security against the garbler, we would need expensive zero knowledge arguments that prove correctness of the garbled circuit. Now, in order to build an efficient protocol that achieves security against a malicious garbler and to work with threshold $t = 3$, the idea is to distribute the garbling process between two parties.

Consider an initiator P_1 interacting with parties P_2, P_3. We repeat the below process for any initiator and any pair of parties that it must interact with. For ease of exposition, we just consider P_1, P_2, P_3 in this section. Both P_2 and P_3 generate one garbled circuit each using shared randomness generated during setup and the evaluator just checks if the two circuits are identical. Further, both P_2 and P_3 get the share $\overrightarrow{\mathbf{w}}_2$ and a share of the signing key in the enrollment and setup phase respectively. Note that since the adversary can corrupt at most one party, this check would guarantee that the evaluator can learn whether the garbled circuit was honestly generated. In order to ensure that the evaluator does not evaluate both garbled circuits on different inputs, we will also require the garbled circuits to check that P_1's OT receiver queries made to both parties was the same. The above approach is inspired from the three party secure computation protocol of Mohassel et al. [44].

However, the issue here is that P_1 needs a mechanism to prove in zero knowledge that it is indeed using the share $\overrightarrow{\mathbf{w}}_1$ received in the setup phase as input to the garbled circuit. Moreover, even without this issue, the protocol is computationally quite expensive. For cosine similarity, the garbled circuit will have to perform a lot of expensive operations - for vectors of length ℓ, we would have to perform $O(\ell)$ multiplications inside the garbled circuit. As mentioned in the introduction, because the number of features in a template (ℓ) can be very large for applications like face recognition, our goal is to improve the efficiency and scalability of the above protocol by performing only a constant number of multiplications inside the garbled circuit.

Additive Homomorphic Encryption. Our strategy to build an efficient protocol is to use additional rounds of communication to offload the heavy computation outside the garbled circuit and also along the way, solve the issue of the initiator using the right share $\overrightarrow{\mathbf{w}}_1$. In particular, if we can perform the inner product computation outside the garbled circuit in the first phase of the protocol, then the resulting garbled circuit in the second phase would have to perform only a constant number of operations. In order to do so, we leverage the tool of efficient additively homomorphic encryption schemes [35,47]. In our new protocol, in round 1, the initiator P_1 sends an encryption of $\vec{\mathbf{u}}$. P_1 can compute $\langle \vec{\mathbf{u}}, \vec{\mathbf{w}}_1 \rangle$ by itself. Both P_2 and P_3 respond with encryptions of $\langle \vec{\mathbf{u}}, \vec{\mathbf{w}}_2 \rangle$ computed homomorphically using the same shared randomness. P_1 can decrypt this to compute $\langle \vec{\mathbf{u}}, \vec{\mathbf{w}} \rangle$. The parties can then run the garbled circuit based protocol as above in rounds 3 and 4 of our FTT scheme: that is, P_1 requests for labels corresponding to $\langle \vec{\mathbf{u}}, \vec{\mathbf{w}} \rangle$ and $\langle \vec{\mathbf{u}}, \vec{\mathbf{u}} \rangle$ and the garbled circuit does the rest of the check as before. While this protocol is correct and efficient, there are still several issues.

Leaking Inner Product. The first problem is that the inner product $\langle \vec{\mathbf{u}}, \vec{\mathbf{w}} \rangle$ is currently leaked to the initiator P_1 thereby violating the privacy of the template $\vec{\mathbf{w}}$. To prevent this, we need to design a mechanism where no party learns the inner product entirely in the clear and yet the check happens inside the garbled circuit. A natural approach is for P_2 and P_3 to homomorphically compute an encryption of the result $\langle \vec{\mathbf{u}}, \vec{\mathbf{w}}_2 \rangle$ using a very efficient secret key encryption scheme. In our case, just a one time pad suffices. Now, P_1 only learns an encryption of this value and hence the inner product is hidden, while the garbled circuit, with the secret key hardwired into it, can easily decrypt the one-time pad.

Input Consistency. The second major challenge is to ensure that the input on which P_1 wishes to evaluate the garbled circuit is indeed the output of the decryption. If not, P_1 could request to evaluate the garbled circuit on suitably high inputs of his choice, thereby violating unforgeability! In order to prevent this attack, P_2 and P_3 homomorphically compute not just $x = \langle \vec{\mathbf{u}}, \vec{\mathbf{w}}_2 \rangle$ but also a message authentication code (mac) y on the value x using shared randomness generated in the setup phase. We use a simple one time mac that can be computed using linear operations and hence can be done using the additively homomorphic encryption scheme. Now, the garbled circuit also checks that the mac verifies correctly and from the security of the mac, P_1 can not change the input between the two stages. Also, we require P_1 to also send encryptions of $\langle \vec{\mathbf{u}}, \vec{\mathbf{u}} \rangle$ in round 1 so that P_2, P_3 can compute a mac on this as well, thereby preventing P_1 from cheating on this part of the computation too.

Ciphertext Well-Formedness. Another important issue to tackle is to ensure that P_1 does indeed send well-formed encryptions. To do so, we rely on efficient zero knowledge arguments from literature [30,31] when instantiating the additively homomorphic encryption scheme with the Paillier encryption scheme [47]. For technical reasons, we also need the homomorphic encryption scheme to be circuit-private. We refer the reader to the full version [12] for more details. Observe that in our final protocol, the garbled circuit does only a constant number of multiplications, which makes protocol computationally efficient and scalable.

Optimizations. To further improve the efficiency of our protocol, as done in Mohassel et al. [44], we will require only one of the two parties P_2, P_3 to actually send the garbled circuit. The other party can just send a hash of the garbled circuit and the initiator can check that the hash values are equal. We refer to Sect. 7 for more details on this and other optimizations.

3   Preliminaries

Let $\mathcal{P}_1, \ldots, \mathcal{P}_n$ denote the n parties and λ the security parameter. Recall that the L^2 norm of a vector $\overrightarrow{\mathbf{x}} = (\overrightarrow{\mathbf{x}}_1, \ldots, \overrightarrow{\mathbf{x}}_n)$ is defined as $||\overrightarrow{\mathbf{x}}|| = \sqrt{\overrightarrow{\mathbf{x}}_1^2 + \ldots + \overrightarrow{\mathbf{x}}_n^2}$. $\langle \overrightarrow{\mathbf{u}}, \overrightarrow{\mathbf{w}} \rangle$ denotes the inner product between two vectors $\overrightarrow{\mathbf{u}}, \overrightarrow{\mathbf{w}}$.

Definition 1. (Cosine Similarity). *For any two vectors* $\overrightarrow{\mathbf{u}}, \overrightarrow{\mathbf{w}} \in \mathbb{Z}_q^\ell$, *the Cosine Similarity between them is defined as follows:*

$$\mathsf{CS.Dist}(\overrightarrow{\mathbf{u}}, \overrightarrow{\mathbf{w}}) = \frac{\langle \overrightarrow{\mathbf{u}}, \overrightarrow{\mathbf{w}} \rangle}{||\overrightarrow{\mathbf{u}}|| \cdot ||\overrightarrow{\mathbf{w}}||}.$$

When using this distance measure, we say that $\mathsf{Dist}(\overrightarrow{\mathbf{u}}, \overrightarrow{\mathbf{w}}) = 1$ *if and only if* $\mathsf{CS.Dist}(\overrightarrow{\mathbf{u}}, \overrightarrow{\mathbf{w}}) \geq d$ *where d is a parameter specified by* $\mathsf{Dist}(\cdot)$.

3.1   Threshold Signature

Definition 2 (Threshold Signature [18]). *Let $n, t \in \mathbb{N}$. A threshold signature scheme* TS *is a tuple of four algorithms* (Gen, Sign, Comb, Ver) *that satisfy the correctness condition below.*

- Gen$(1^\lambda, n, t) \rightarrow (\mathsf{pp}, \mathsf{vk}, [\![\mathsf{sk}]\!]_n)$. *A randomized algorithm that takes n, t and the security parameter λ as input, and generates a verification-key* vk *and a shared signing-key* $[\![\mathsf{sk}]\!]_n$.
- Sign$(\mathsf{sk}_i, m) =: \sigma_i$. *A deterministic algorithm that takes a mesage m and signing key-share* sk_i *as input and outputs a partial signature* σ_i.
- Comb$(\{\sigma_i\}_{i \in S}) =: \sigma/\bot$. *A deterministic algorithm that takes a set of partial signatures* $\{\mathsf{sk}_i\}_{i \in S}$ *as input and outputs a signature σ or $\bot$ denoting failure.*
- Ver$(\mathsf{vk}, (m, \sigma)) =: 1/0$. *A deterministic algorithm that takes a verification key* vk *and a candidate message-signature pair (m, σ) as input, and outputs 1 for a valid signature and 0 otherwise.*

Correctness. *For all $\lambda \in \mathbb{N}$, any $t, n \in \mathbb{N}$ such that $t \leq n$, all $(\mathsf{pp}, \mathsf{vk}, [\![\mathsf{sk}]\!]_n)$ generated by* Gen$(1^\lambda, n, t)$, *any message m, and any set $S \subseteq [n]$ of size at least t, if $\sigma_i = $ Sign(sk_i, m) for $i \in S$, then* Ver$(\mathsf{vk}, (m, \mathsf{Comb}(\{\sigma_i\}_{i \in S}))) = 1$.

Definition 3 (Unforgeability). A threshold signatures scheme TS = (Gen, Sign, Comb, Ver) is unforgeable if for all $n, t \in \mathbb{N}$, $t \leq n$, and any PPT adversary $\mathcal{A}$, the following game outputs 1 with negligible probability (in security parameter).

- *Initialize.* Run $(\mathsf{pp}, \mathsf{vk}, [\![\mathbf{sk}]\!]_n) \leftarrow \mathsf{Gen}(1^\lambda, n, t)$. Give pp, vk to $\mathcal{A}$. Receive the set of corrupt parties $C \subset [n]$ of size at most $t - 1$ from $\mathcal{A}$. Then give $[\![\mathbf{sk}]\!]_C$ to $\mathcal{A}$. Define $\gamma := t - |C|$. Initiate a list $L := \emptyset$.
- *Signing queries.* On query (m, i) for $i \subseteq [n] \setminus C$ return $\sigma_i \leftarrow \mathsf{Sign}(\mathsf{sk}_i, m)$. Run this step as many times $\mathcal{A}$ desires.
- *Building the list.* If the number of signing query of the form (m, i) is at least γ, then insert m into the list L. (This captures that $\mathcal{A}$ has enough information to compute a signature on m.)
- *Output.* Eventually receive output $(m^\star, \sigma^\star)$ from $\mathcal{A}$. Return 1 if and only if $\mathsf{Ver}(\mathsf{vk}, (m^\star, \sigma^\star)) = 1$ and $m^\star \notin L$, and 0 otherwise.

4   Formalizing Fuzzy Threshold Tokenizer (FTT)

In this section we formally introduce the notion of *fuzzy threshold tokenizer* (FTT) and give a UC-secure definition. We first describe the algorithms/protocols in the primitive followed by the security definition in the next subsection.

Definition 4 (Fuzzy Threshold Tokenizer (FTT)). *Given a security parameter* $\lambda \in \mathbb{N}$*, a threshold signature scheme* $\mathsf{TS} = (\mathsf{TS.Gen}, \mathsf{TS.Sign}, \mathsf{TS.Combine}, \mathsf{TS.Verify})$*, biometric space parameters* $q, \ell \in \mathbb{N}$*, a distance predicate* $\mathsf{Dist} : \mathbb{Z}_q^\ell \times \mathbb{Z}_q^\ell \to \{0, 1\}$*,* $n \in \mathbb{N}$ *parties* $\mathcal{P}_1, \ldots, \mathcal{P}_n$ *and a threshold of parties* $t \in [n]$*, a FTT scheme/protocol consists of the following tuple* $(\mathsf{Setup}, \mathsf{Enrollment}, \mathsf{SignOn}, \mathsf{Ver})$ *of algorithms/protocols:*

- $\mathsf{Setup}(1^\lambda, n, t, \mathsf{TS}) \to (\mathsf{pp}_{\mathsf{setup}}, \{s_i, \mathsf{sk}_i^{\mathsf{TS}}\}_{i \in [n]}, \mathsf{vk})$ *: The* Setup *algorithm is run by a trusted authority. It first runs the key-generation of the threshold signature scheme,* $(\{\mathsf{sk}_i^{\mathsf{TS}}\}_{i \in [n]}, \mathsf{vk}) \leftarrow \mathsf{Gen}(1^\lambda, n, t)$*. It generates other public parameters* $\mathsf{pp}_{\mathsf{setup}}$ *and secret values* $s_1, \ldots, s_n$ *for each party respectively. It outputs* $(\mathsf{vk}, \mathsf{pp}_{\mathsf{setup}})$ *to every party and secrets* $(\mathsf{sk}_i^{\mathsf{TS}}, s_i)$ *to each party* $\mathcal{P}_i$*.* ($\mathsf{pp}_{\mathsf{setup}}$ *will be an implicit input in all the algorithms below.*)
- $\mathsf{Enrollment}(n, t, q, \ell, \mathsf{Dist}) \to (\{a_i\}_{i \in [n]})$ *: On input the parameters from any party, this algorithm is run by the trusted authority to choose a random sample* $\overrightarrow{\mathbf{w}} \leftarrow \mathcal{W}$*. Then, each party* $\mathcal{P}_i$ *receives some information* a_i*.*
- $\mathsf{SignOn}(\cdot)$ *:* SignOn *is a distributed protocol involving a party* P^* *along with a set* S *of parties. Party* $\mathcal{P}^*$ *has input a measurement* $\overrightarrow{\mathbf{u}}$*, message* msg *and its secret information* $(s_*, \mathsf{sk}_*^{\mathsf{TS}})$*. Each party* $P_i \in S$ *has input* $(s_i, \mathsf{sk}_i^{\mathsf{TS}})$*. At the end of the protocol,* P^* *obtains a (private) token* Token *(or* $\perp$*, denoting failure) as output. Each party* $\mathcal{P}_i \in S$ *gets output* (msg, i, S)*. The trusted authority is not involved in this protocol.*
- $\mathsf{Ver}(\mathsf{vk}, \mathsf{msg}, \mathsf{Token}) \to \{0, 1\}$ *:* Ver *is an algorithm which takes input verification key* vk*, message* msg *and token* Token*, runs the verification algorithm of the threshold signature scheme* $b := \mathsf{TS.Verify}(\mathsf{vk}, (\mathsf{msg}, \mathsf{Token}))$*, and outputs* $b \in \{0, 1\}$*. This can be run locally by any party or even any external entity.*

Communication Model. In the $\mathsf{SignOn}(\cdot)$ protocol, only party $\mathcal{P}^*$ can communicate directly with every party in the set S. We stress that the other parties in S can not interact directly with each other.

4.1   Security Definition

We formally define security via the universal composability (UC) framework [26]. Similar to the simplified UC framework [28] we assume existence of *a default authenticated channel* in the real world. This simplifies the definition of our ideal functionality and can be removed easily by composing with an ideal authenticated channel functionality (e.g. [27]).

Consider n parties $P_1, \ldots, P_n$. We consider a *fixed number of parties* in the system throughout the paper. That is, no new party can join the execution subsequently. Let π^{TS} be an FTT scheme parameterized by a threshold signature scheme TS. Consider an adversarial environment $\mathcal{Z}$. We consider a *static corruption* model where there are a fixed set of corrupt parties decided a priori.[5] Informally, it is required that for every adversary $\mathcal{A}$ that corrupts some subset of the parties and participates in the real execution of the protocol, there exist an ideal world adversary Sim, such that for all environments $\mathcal{Z}$, the view of the environment is same in both worlds. We describe it more formally below.

Real World. In the real execution, the FTT protocol π^{TS} is executed in the presence of an adversary $\mathcal{A}$. The adversary $\mathcal{A}$ takes as input the security parameter λ and corrupts a subset of parties. Initially, the Setup algorithm is implemented by a trusted authority. The honest parties follow the instructions of π^{TS}. That is, whenever they receive an "Enrollment" query from $\mathcal{Z}$, they will run the Enrollment phase of π^{TS}. Similarly, whenever they receive a "Sign on" query from $\mathcal{Z}$ with input $(\mathsf{msg}, \overrightarrow{\mathbf{u}}, S)$, they will initiate a $\mathsf{SignOn}(\cdot)$ protocol with the parties in set S and using input $(\mathsf{msg}, S, \mathsf{sk}_i^{\mathsf{TS}})$. If a $\mathsf{SignOn}(\cdot)$ protocol is initiated with them by any other party, they participate honestly using input $\mathsf{sk}_i^{\mathsf{TS}}$. $\mathcal{A}$ sends all messages of the protocol on behalf of the corrupt parties following any arbitrary polynomial-time strategy. We assume that parties are connected by point to point secure and authenticated channels.

Ideal World. The ideal world is defined by a trusted ideal functionality $\mathcal{F}_{\mathsf{FTT}}^{\mathsf{TS}}$ described in Fig. 1 that interacts with n (say) ideal dummy parties $\mathcal{P}_1, \ldots, \mathcal{P}_n$ and an ideal world adversary, a.k.a. the simulator Sim via secure (and authenticated) channels. The simulator can corrupt a subset of the parties and may fully control them. We discuss the ideal functionality in more detail later below.

The environment sets the inputs for all parties including the adversaries and obtain their outputs in both the worlds. However, the environment does *not* observe any internal interaction. For example, in the ideal world such interactions takes between the ideal functionality and another entity (a dummy party, or the simulator); in real world such interactions take place among the real parties. Finally, once the execution is over, the environment outputs a bit denoting either real or ideal world. For ideal functionality $\mathcal{F}$, adversary $\mathcal{A}$, simulator Sim, environment $\mathcal{Z}$ and a protocol π we formally denote the output of $\mathcal{Z}$ by random

---

[5] However, we allow the attacker to decide on the corrupt set adaptively after receiving the public values.

variable $\text{IDEAL}_{\mathcal{F},\text{Sim},\mathcal{Z}}$ in the ideal world and $\text{REAL}_{\pi,\mathcal{A},\mathcal{Z}}$ in the real world. We describe the ideal functionality for a FTT scheme in Fig. 1 and we elaborate on it in the next subsection.

Definition 5 (UC-Realizing FTT). *Let* TS *be a threshold signature scheme (Definition 3), $\mathcal{F}_{\text{FTT}}^{\text{TS}}$ be an ideal functionality as described in Fig. 1 and π^{TS} be a FTT scheme. π^{TS} UC-realizes $\mathcal{F}_{\text{FTT}}^{\text{TS}}$ if for any real world PPT adversary $\mathcal{A}$, there exists a PPT simulator* Sim *such that for all environments $\mathcal{Z}$,*

$$\text{IDEAL}_{\mathcal{F}_{\text{FTT}}^{\text{TS}},\text{Sim},\mathcal{Z}} \approx_c \text{REAL}_{\pi^{\text{TS}},\mathcal{A},\mathcal{Z}}$$

Intuitively, for any adversary there should be a simulator that can simulate its behavior such that no environment can distinguish between these two worlds. Also, our definition can also capture setup assumptions such as random oracles by considering a $\mathcal{G}$-hybrid model with an ideal functionality $\mathcal{G}$ for the setup.

Ideal Functionality $\mathcal{F}_{\text{FTT}}^{\text{TS}}$. The ideal functionality we consider is presented formally in Fig. 1. We provide an informal exposition here. Contrary to most of the UC ideal functionalities, our ideal functionality $\mathcal{F}_{\text{FTT}}^{\text{TS}}$ is parameterized with a threshold signature scheme TS = (TS.Gen, TS.Sign, TS.Combine, TS.Verify) (see discussion about this choice later in this section). The ideal functionality is parameterized with a distance predicate Dist, which takes two vectors, a template and a candidate measurement and returns 1 if and only if the two vectors are "close". Additionally, the functionality is parameterized with other standard parameters and a probability distribution over the biometric vectors.

The ideal functionality has an interface to handle queries from different parties. For a particular session, the first query it responds to "Setup" from Sim. In response, the functionality $\mathcal{F}_{\text{FTT}}^{\text{TS}}$ generates the key pairs of the given threshold signature scheme, gives the control for the corrupt parties to the simulator and marks this session "LIVE". Then, an "Enroll" query can be made by any party. $\mathcal{F}_{\text{FTT}}^{\text{TS}}$ chooses a template $\overrightarrow{w}$ at random from the distribution $\mathcal{W}$, stores it and marks the session as "ENROLLED".

For any "ENROLLED" session, $\mathcal{F}_{\text{FTT}}^{\text{TS}}$ can receive many "SignOn" queries (the previous two queries are allowed only once per session). This is ensured by not marking the session in response to any such query. The "SignOn" query from a party $\mathcal{P}_i$ contains a set S of parties (i.e. their identities), a message to be signed and a candidate measurement $\overrightarrow{u}$. If the set S contains any corrupt party, $\mathcal{F}_{\text{FTT}}^{\text{TS}}$ reaches out to the simulator for a response—this captures a corrupt party's power to deny a request.

Then, $\mathcal{F}_{\text{FTT}}^{\text{TS}}$ checks whether the measurement $\overrightarrow{u}$ is "close enough" by computing $b := \text{Dist}(\overrightarrow{u}, \overrightarrow{w})$. If b is 1, the size of the set $S = t$ and all parties in S send an agreement response, $\mathcal{F}_{\text{FTT}}^{\text{TS}}$ generates the partial signatures (tokens) on behalf of the parties in S and sends them *only to the initiator* $\mathcal{P}_i$; otherwise, it sends $\perp$ denoting failure to $\mathcal{P}_i$. Note that the signatures (or even the failure messages) are not sent to the simulator unless the initiator $\mathcal{P}_i$ is corrupt. This is crucial for our definition as it ensures that if a "SignOn" query is initiated by an honest party, then the simulator does not obtain *anything* directly, except

---

Ideal Functionality $\mathcal{F}_{\text{FTT}}^{\text{TS}}$

Given a threshold signature scheme (TS.Gen, TS.Sign, TS.Combine, TS.Verify), the functionality $\mathcal{F}_{\text{FTT}}^{\text{TS}}$ is parameterized by a security parameter $\lambda \in \mathbb{N}$, biometric space parameters $q, \ell \in \mathbb{N}$, a distance predicate $\text{Dist} : \mathbb{Z}_q^\ell \times \mathbb{Z}_q^\ell \rightarrow \{0, 1\}$, number of parties $n \in \mathbb{N}$ and a threshold of parties $t \in [n]$. It interacts with an ideal adversary (the simulator) Sim and n dummy parties $\mathcal{P}_1, \ldots, \mathcal{P}_n$ via the following queries.

- **On receiving a query of the form** ("Setup", sid, aux) **from** Sim, do as follows only if sid is unmarked:
  1. run $(\text{vk}, \{\text{sk}_i^{\text{TS}}\}_{i\in[n]}) \leftarrow \text{TS.Gen}(1^\lambda)$;
  2. send ("VerKey", sid, vk, aux) to Sim;
  3. receive ("Corrupt", sid, $C \subseteq [n]$) from Sim;
  4. send (sid, sk_i^{TS}) to each P_i for all $i \in [n]$.
  5. store the tuple (sid, vk, $\{\text{sk}_i^{\text{TS}}\}_{i\in[n]}$) and mark this session as "LIVE".

- **On receiving a query of the form** ("Enroll", sid) **from** $\mathcal{P}$, only if sid is marked "LIVE":
  1. choose $\overrightarrow{\mathbf{w}} \leftarrow \mathcal{W}$ and store the tuple (sid, $\overrightarrow{\mathbf{w}}$);
  2. send ("Enrolled", sid) to Sim and mark sid as "ENROLLED".

- **On receiving a query of the form** ("SignOn", sid, vk, msg, $\mathcal{P}$, $\overrightarrow{\mathbf{u}}$, $S \subseteq [n]$) **from** $\mathcal{P}$, if the session sid is not marked "ENROLLED", ignore this query. Else, retrieve the record (sid, pp, vk, $\{\text{sk}_i^{\text{TS}}\}_{i\in[n]}$) and let $\{\mathcal{P}_j\}_{j\in S}$ be the parties in the set. Send (msg, P_i, S) to each P_j for $j \in S$. Then, if $S \cap C \neq \emptyset$ (contains a corrupt party), send ("Signing Req", sid, msg, $\mathcal{P}$, S) to Sim. If Sim sends back ("Agreed", sid, msg, $\mathcal{P}$) then do as follows:
  1. **if** $\text{Dist}(\overrightarrow{\mathbf{u}}, \overrightarrow{\mathbf{w}}) = 1$, $|S| = t$ then: generate $\{\text{Token}_j \leftarrow \text{TS.Sign}(\text{sk}_j^{\text{TS}}, \text{msg})\}_{j\in S}$; and send (sid, msg, $\{\text{Token}_j\}_{j\in S}$) to $\mathcal{P}$.
  2. **otherwise**, return (sid, msg, $\perp$) to $\mathcal{P}$.

Fig. 1. The ideal functionality $\mathcal{F}_{\text{FTT}}^{\text{TS}}$.

when there is a corrupt party in S via which it knows such a query has been made and only learns the tuple $(m, \mathcal{P}_i, S)$ corresponding to the query. In fact, no one except the initiator learns whether "SignOn" was successful. Intuitively, a protocol realizing $\mathcal{F}_{\text{FTT}}^{\text{TS}}$ must guarantee that a corrupt party can *not* compute a valid sign-on token (signature) just by participating in a session started by an honest party. In our definition of $\mathcal{F}_{\text{FTT}}^{\text{TS}}$, such a token would be considered as a forgery. To the best of our knowledge, this feature has not been considered in prior works on threshold signatures.

We provide more discussions on our definition in the full version [12].

5   Any Distance Measure from MPC

In this section, we show how to construct a four round secure fuzzy threshold tokenizer using any two round malicious UC-secure MPC protocol in a broadcast channel as the main technical tool. Our tokenizer scheme satisfies Definition 1 for any n, t, for any distance measure. Formally, we show the following theorem:

Theorem 1. *Assuming unforgeable threshold signatures and a two round UC-secure MPC protocols in the CRS model in a broadcast channel, there exists a four round secure fuzzy threshold tokenizer protocol for any n, t and any distance predicate.*

Such two round MPC protocols can be built assuming DDH/LWE/QR/N^{th} Residuosity [15,38,45,49]. Threshold signatures can be built assuming LWE/Gap-DDH/RSA [18,20,54]. Instantiating this, we get the following corollary:

Corollary 1. *Assuming LWE, there exists a four round secure FTT protocol for any n, t and any distance predicate.*

We describe the construction below and defer the proof to the full version [12].

5.1   Construction

Notation. Let π be a two round UC-secure MPC protocol in the CRS model in the presence of a broadcast channel that is secure against a malicious adversary that can corrupt upto $(t-1)$ parties. Let π.Setup denote the algorithm used to generate the CRS. Let $(\pi.\mathsf{Round}_1, \pi.\mathsf{Round}_2)$ denote the algorithms used by any party to compute the messages in each of the two rounds and π.Out denote the algorithm to compute the final output. Let $(\mathsf{TS.Gen}, \mathsf{TS.Sign}, \mathsf{TS.Combine}, \mathsf{TS.Verify})$ be a threshold signature scheme, $(\mathsf{SKE.Enc}, \mathsf{SKE.Dec})$ be a secret key encryption scheme, $(\mathsf{Share}, \mathsf{Recon})$ be a (t, n) threshold secret sharing scheme and PRF be a pseudorandom function. We now describe the construction of our four round secure fuzzy threshold tokenizer protocol π^{Any} for any n and t.

Setup: The following algorithm is executed by a trusted authority:

- Generate $\mathsf{crs} \leftarrow \pi.\mathsf{Setup}(1^\lambda)$.
- For each $i \in [n]$, compute $(\mathsf{sk}_i, \mathsf{vk}_i) \leftarrow \mathsf{Gen}(1^\lambda)$.
- For every $i, j \in [n]$, compute $(\mathsf{k}_{i,j}^{\mathsf{PRF}}, \mathsf{k}_{j,i}^{\mathsf{PRF}})$ as uniformly random strings.
- Compute $(\mathsf{pp}^{\mathsf{TS}}, \mathsf{vk}^{\mathsf{TS}}, \mathsf{sk}_1^{\mathsf{TS}}, \dots, \mathsf{sk}_n^{\mathsf{TS}}) \leftarrow \mathsf{TS.Gen}(1^\lambda, n, t)$.
- For each $i \in [n]$, give $(\mathsf{crs}, \mathsf{pp}^{\mathsf{TS}}, \mathsf{vk}^{\mathsf{TS}}, \mathsf{sk}_i^{\mathsf{TS}}, \mathsf{sk}_i, \{\mathsf{vk}_j\}_{j\in[n]}, \{\mathsf{k}_{j,i}^{\mathsf{PRF}}, \mathsf{k}_{i,j}^{\mathsf{PRF}}\}_{j\in[n]})$ to party $\mathcal{P}_i$.

Enrollment: In this phase, any party $\mathcal{P}_i$ that wishes to enroll queries the trusted authority which then does the following:

- Sample a random vector $\overrightarrow{\mathbf{w}}$ from the distribution $\mathcal{W}$.
- Compute $(\overrightarrow{\mathbf{w}}_1, \dots, \overrightarrow{\mathbf{w}}_n) \leftarrow \mathsf{Share}(1^\lambda, \overrightarrow{\mathbf{w}}, n, t)$.
- For each $i \in [n]$, give $(\overrightarrow{\mathbf{w}}_i)$ to party $\mathcal{P}_i$.

SignOn Phase: In the SignOn phase, let's consider party $\mathcal{P}^*$ that uses input vector $\overrightarrow{\mathbf{u}}$, a message msg on which it wants a token. $\mathcal{P}^*$ interacts with the other parties in the below four round protocol.

Round 1: $(\mathcal{P}^* \rightarrow)^6$ Party $\mathcal{P}^*$ does the following:

1. Pick a set S consisting of t parties amongst $\mathcal{P}_1, \ldots, \mathcal{P}_n$. For simplicity, without loss of generality, we assume that $\mathcal{P}^*$ is also part of set S.
2. To each party $\mathcal{P}_i \in S$, send (msg, S).

Round 2: $(\rightarrow \mathcal{P}^*)$ Each Party $\mathcal{P}_i \in S$ (except $\mathcal{P}^*$) does the following:

1. Participate in an execution of protocol π with parties in set S using input $y_i = (\overrightarrow{\mathbf{w}}_i, \mathsf{sk}_i^{\mathsf{TS}})$ and randomness r_i to compute circuit $\mathcal{C}$ defined in Fig. 2. Compute first round message $\mathsf{msg}_{1,i} \leftarrow \pi.\mathsf{Round}_1(y_i; r_i)$.
2. Compute $\sigma_{1,i} = \mathsf{Sign}(\mathsf{sk}_i, \mathsf{msg}_{1,i})$.
3. Send $(\mathsf{msg}_{1,i}, \sigma_{1,i})$ to party $\mathcal{P}^*$.

Round 3: $(\mathcal{P}^* \rightarrow)$ Party $\mathcal{P}^*$ does the following:

1. Let $\mathsf{Trans}_{\mathsf{fuzzy\ threshold\ tokenizer}}$ denote the set of messages received in round 2.
2. Participate in an execution of protocol π with parties in set S using input $y_* = (\overrightarrow{\mathbf{w}}_*, \mathsf{sk}_*^{\mathsf{TS}}, \overrightarrow{\mathbf{u}}, \mathsf{msg})$ and randomness r_* to compute circuit $\mathcal{C}$ defined in Fig. 2. Compute first round message $\mathsf{msg}_{1,*} \leftarrow \pi.\mathsf{Round}_1(y_*; r_*)$.
3. To each party $\mathcal{P}_i \in S$, send $(\mathsf{Trans}_{\mathsf{fuzzy\ threshold\ tokenizer}}, \mathsf{msg}_{1,*})$.

Round 4: $(\rightarrow \mathcal{P}^*)$ Each Party $\mathcal{P}_i \in S$ (except $\mathcal{P}^*$) does the following:

1. Let $\mathsf{Trans}_{\mathsf{fuzzy\ threshold\ tokenizer}}$ consist of a set of messages of the form $(\mathsf{msg}_{1,j}, \sigma_{1,j}), \forall j \in S \setminus \mathcal{P}^*$. Output $\perp$ if $\mathsf{Verify}(\mathsf{vk}_j, \mathsf{msg}_{1,j}, \sigma_{1,j}) \neq 1$.
2. Let $\tau_1 = \{\mathsf{msg}_{1,j}\}_{j \in S}$ denote the transcript of protocol π after round 1. Compute second round message $\mathsf{msg}_{2,i} \leftarrow \pi.\mathsf{Round}_2(y_i, \tau_1; r_i)$.
3. Let $(\mathsf{Trans}_{\mathsf{fuzzy\ threshold\ tokenizer}}, \mathsf{msg}_{1,*})$ denote the message received from $\mathcal{P}^*$ in round 3. Compute $\mathsf{ek}_i = \oplus_{j \in S}\mathsf{PRF}(\mathsf{k}_{i,j}^{\mathsf{PRF}}, \mathsf{msg}_{1,*})$ and $\mathsf{ct}_i = \mathsf{SKE.Enc}(\mathsf{ek}_i, \mathsf{msg}_{2,i})$.
4. For each party $\mathcal{P}_j \in S$, compute $\mathsf{ek}_{j,i} = \mathsf{PRF}(\mathsf{k}_{j,i}^{\mathsf{PRF}}, \mathsf{msg}_{1,*})$.
5. Send $(\mathsf{ct}_i, \{\mathsf{ek}_{j,i}\}_{j \in S})$ to $\mathcal{P}^*$.

Output Computation: Every party $\mathcal{P}_j \in S$ outputs $(\mathsf{msg}, \mathcal{P}^*, S)$. Additionally, party $\mathcal{P}^*$ does the following to generate a token:

1. For each party $\mathcal{P}_j \in S$, compute $\mathsf{ek}_j = \oplus_{j \in S}\mathsf{ek}_{j,i}$, $\mathsf{msg}_{2,j} = \mathsf{SKE.Dec}(\mathsf{ek}_j, \mathsf{ct}_j)$.
2. Let τ_2 denote the transcript of protocol π after round 2. Compute the output of π: $\{\mathsf{Token}_i\}_{i \in S} \leftarrow \pi.\mathsf{Out}(y_*, \tau_2; r_*)$.
3. Reconstruct the signature as $\mathsf{Token} = \mathsf{TS.Combine}(\{\mathsf{Token}_i\}_{i \in S})$.
4. If $\mathsf{TS.Verify}(\mathsf{vk}^{\mathsf{TS}}, \mathsf{msg}, \mathsf{Token}) = 1$, then output $\{\mathsf{Token}_i\}_{i \in S}$. Else, output $\perp$.

Token Verification: Given a verification key $\mathsf{vk}^{\mathsf{TS}}$, message msg and a token $\{\mathsf{Token}_i\}_{i \in S}$, where $|S| = t$, the token verification algorithm does the following:

1. Compute $\mathsf{Token} \leftarrow \mathsf{TS.Combine}(\{\mathsf{Token}_i\}_{i \in S})$.
2. Output 1 if $\mathsf{TS.Verify}(\mathsf{vk}^{\mathsf{TS}}, \mathsf{msg}, \mathsf{Token}) = 1$. Else, output 0.

---

[6] The arrowhead denotes that in this round messages are outgoing from party $\mathcal{P}^*$.

Inputs:

- Party $\mathcal{P}_i \in S$ has input $(\vec{\mathbf{w}}_i, \mathsf{sk}_i^{\mathsf{TS}})$.
- Party $\mathcal{P}^* \in S$ additionally has input $(\vec{\mathbf{u}}, \mathsf{msg})$.

Computation:

- Compute $\vec{\mathbf{w}} = \mathsf{Recon}(\{\vec{\mathbf{w}}_i\}_{i \in S})$. Output $\perp$ to $\mathcal{P}^*$ if the reconstruction fails or if $\mathsf{Dist}(\vec{\mathbf{u}}, \vec{\mathbf{w}}) = 0$.
- Compute $\mathsf{Token}_i = \mathsf{TS.Sign}(\mathsf{sk}_i^{\mathsf{TS}}, \mathsf{msg})$. Output $\{\mathsf{Token}_i\}_{i \in S}$ to party $\mathcal{P}^*$.

Fig. 2. Circuit $\mathcal{C}$

6 Any Distance Measure Using Threshold FHE

In this section, we construct a FTT protocol for any distance measure using any fully homomorphic encryption (FHE) scheme with threshold decryption. Our token generation protocol satisfies the definition in Sect. 4 for any n, t, and works for any distance measure. Formally, we show the following theorem:

Theorem 2. *Assuming threshold fully-homomorphic encryption, non-interactive zero knowledge argument of knowledge (NIZK) and unforgeable threshold signatures, there exists a four round secure FTT protocol for any n, t and any distance predicate.*

Threshold FHE, NIZKs and unforgeable threshold signatures can be built assuming LWE [20,50]. Instantiating this, we get the following corollary:

Corollary 2. *Assuming LWE, there exists a four round secure FTT protocol for any n, t and any distance predicate.*

6.1 Construction

Notation. Let (TFHE.Gen, TFHE.Enc, TFHE.PartialDec, TFHE.Eval, TFHE. Combine) be a threshold FHE scheme and let (TS.Gen, TS.Sign, TS.Combine, TS.Verify) be a threshold signature scheme. Let (Prove, Verify) be a NIZK scheme and (Gen, Sign, Verify) be a strongly-unforgeable digital signature scheme and Commit be a non-interactive commitment scheme. We now describe the construction of our four round secure FTT protocol $\pi^{\mathsf{Any-TFHE}}$ for any n and k. We defer the proof to the full version [12].

Setup Phase: The following algorithm is executed by a trusted authority:

- Generate $(\mathsf{pk}^{\mathsf{TFHE}}, \mathsf{sk}_1^{\mathsf{TFHE}}, \ldots, \mathsf{sk}_N^{\mathsf{TFHE}}) \leftarrow \mathsf{TFHE.Gen}(1^\lambda, n, t)$ and $(\mathsf{pp}^{\mathsf{TS}}, \mathsf{vk}^{\mathsf{TS}}, \mathsf{sk}_1^{\mathsf{TS}}, \ldots, \mathsf{sk}_n^{\mathsf{TS}}) \leftarrow \mathsf{TS.Gen}(1^\lambda, n, t)$.
- For each $i \in [n]$, compute $\mathsf{com}_i \leftarrow \mathsf{Commit}(\mathsf{sk}_i^{\mathsf{TFHE}}; r_i^{\mathsf{com}})$ and $(\mathsf{sk}_i, \mathsf{vk}_i) \leftarrow \mathsf{Gen}(1^\lambda)$.
- For each $i \in [n]$, give the following to party $\mathcal{P}_i$: $(\mathsf{pk}^{\mathsf{TFHE}}, \mathsf{sk}_i^{\mathsf{TFHE}}, \mathsf{pp}^{\mathsf{TS}}, \mathsf{vk}^{\mathsf{TS}}, \mathsf{sk}_i^{\mathsf{TS}}, (\mathsf{vk}_1, \ldots, \mathsf{vk}_n), \mathsf{sk}_i, (\mathsf{com}_1, \ldots, \mathsf{com}_n), r_i^{\mathsf{com}})$.

Enrollment: In this phase, any party $\mathcal{P}_i$ that wishes to register a fresh template queries the trusted authority, which then executes the following algorithm:

- Sample a template $\vec{w}$ from the distribution $\mathcal{W}$ over $\{0,1\}^\ell$.
- Compute and give $\mathsf{ct}_{\vec{w}}$ to each party $\mathcal{P}_i$, where $\mathsf{ct}_{\vec{w}} = \mathsf{TFHE.Enc}(\mathsf{pk}^{\mathsf{TFHE}}, \vec{w})$.

SignOn Phase: In the SignOn phase, let's consider party $\mathcal{P}^*$ that uses input vector $\vec{u} \in \{0,1\}^\ell$ and a message msg on which it wants a token. $\mathcal{P}^*$ interacts with the other parties in the below four round protocol.

- **Round 1:** $(\mathcal{P}^* \to)^7$ Party $\mathcal{P}^*$ does the following:
    1. Compute ciphertext $\mathsf{ct}_{\vec{u}} = \mathsf{TFHE.Enc}(\mathsf{pk}^{\mathsf{TFHE}}, \vec{u}; r_{\vec{u}})$.
    2. Compute $\pi_{\vec{u}} \leftarrow \mathsf{Prove}(\mathsf{st}_{\vec{u}}, \mathsf{wit}_{\vec{u}})$ for $\mathsf{st}_{\vec{u}} = (\mathsf{ct}_{\vec{u}}, \mathsf{pk}^{\mathsf{TFHE}}) \in L_1$ using witness $\mathsf{wit}_{\vec{u}} = (\vec{u}, r_{\vec{u}})$ (language L_1 is defined in Fig. 3).
    3. Pick a set S consisting of t parties amongst $\mathcal{P}_1, \ldots, \mathcal{P}_n$. For simplicity, without loss of generality, we assume that $\mathcal{P}^*$ is also part of set S.
    4. To each party $\mathcal{P}_i \in S$, send $(\mathsf{ct}_{\vec{u}}, \pi_{\vec{u}})$.

Statement: The statement st is as follows: $\mathsf{st} = (\mathsf{ct}, \mathsf{pk})$.

Witness: The witness wit is as follows: $\mathsf{wit} = (x, r)$.

Relation: $R_1(\mathsf{st}, \mathsf{wit}) = 1$ if and only if $\mathsf{ct} = \mathsf{TFHE.Enc}(\mathsf{pk}, x; r)$.

Fig. 3. NP language L_1

- **Round 2:** $(\to \mathcal{P}^*)$ Each party $\mathcal{P}_i \in S$ (except $\mathcal{P}^*$) does the following:
    1. Abort and output $\perp$ if $\mathsf{Verify}(\pi_{\vec{u}}, \mathsf{st}_{\vec{u}}) \neq 1$ for language L_1 where the statement $\mathsf{st}_{\vec{u}} = (\mathsf{ct}_{\vec{u}}, \mathsf{pk}^{\mathsf{TFHE}})$.
    2. Sample a uniformly random one-time key $K_i \leftarrow \{0,1\}^\lambda$ and compute $\mathsf{ct}_{K_i} = \mathsf{TFHE.Enc}(\mathsf{pk}^{\mathsf{TFHE}}, K_i; r_{K_i})$.
    3. Compute $\pi_{K_i} \leftarrow \mathsf{Prove}(\mathsf{st}_{K_i}, \mathsf{wit}_{K_i})$ for $\mathsf{st}_{K_i} = (\mathsf{ct}_{K_i}, \mathsf{pk}^{\mathsf{TFHE}}) \in L_1$ using the witness $\mathsf{wit}_{K_i} = (K_i, r_{K_i})$ (language L_1 is defined in Fig. 3).
    4. Compute signatures $\sigma_{i,0} = \mathsf{Sign}(\mathsf{sk}_i, \mathsf{ct}_{\vec{u}})$ and $\sigma_{i,1} = \mathsf{Sign}(\mathsf{sk}_i, \mathsf{ct}_{K_i})$.
    5. Send the following to the party $\mathcal{P}^*$: $(\mathsf{ct}_{K_i}, \pi_{K_i}, \sigma_{i,0}, \sigma_{i,1})$.
- **Round 3:** $(\mathcal{P}^* \to)$ Party $\mathcal{P}^*$ checks if there exists some party $\mathcal{P}_i \in S$ such that $\mathsf{Verify}(\pi_{K_i}, \mathsf{st}_{K_i}) \neq 1$ for language L_1 where $\mathsf{st}_{K_i} = (\mathsf{ct}_{K_i}, \mathsf{pk}^{\mathsf{TFHE}})$. If yes, it outputs $\perp$ and aborts. Otherwise, it sends $\{(\mathsf{ct}_{K_i}, \pi_{K_i}, \sigma_{i,0}, \sigma_{i,1})\}_{\mathcal{P}_i \in S}$ to each party $\mathcal{P}_i \in S$.
- **Round 4:** $(\to \mathcal{P}^*)$ Each party $\mathcal{P}_i \in S$ (except $\mathcal{P}^*$) does the following:
    1. If there exists some party $\mathcal{P}_j \in S$ such that $\mathsf{Verify}(\pi_{K_j}, \mathsf{st}_{K_j}) \neq 1$ for language L_1 where $\mathsf{st}_{K_j} = (\mathsf{ct}_{K_j}, \mathsf{pk}^{\mathsf{TFHE}})$ (OR) $\mathsf{Verify}(\mathsf{vk}_j, \mathsf{ct}_{\vec{u}}, \sigma_{j,0}) \neq 1$ (OR) $\mathsf{Verify}(\mathsf{vk}_j, \mathsf{ct}_{K_j}, \sigma_{j,1}) \neq 1$, then output $\perp$ and abort.

---

[7] The arrowhead denotes that in this round messages are outgoing from party $\mathcal{P}^*$.

Inputs: A template $\vec{\mathbf{w}} \in \{0,1\}^\ell$, measurement $\vec{\mathbf{u}} \in \{0,1\}^\ell$ and string $K \in \{0,1\}^\lambda$.

Computation: If $\mathrm{Dist}(\vec{\mathbf{u}}, \vec{\mathbf{w}}) = 1$, output K. Else, output 0^λ.

Fig. 4. Circuit $\mathcal{C}$

Statement: The statement st is as follows: $\mathsf{st} = (\mathsf{ct}, \mu, \mathsf{com})$.

Witness: The witness wit is as follows: $\mathsf{wit} = (\mathsf{sk}^{\mathsf{TFHE}}, \mathsf{r})$.

Relation: $R_2(\mathsf{st}, \mathsf{wit}) = 1$ if and only if: (a) $\mathsf{TFHE.PartialDec}(\mathsf{sk}^{\mathsf{TFHE}}, \mathsf{ct}) = \mu$ *and* (b) $\mathsf{Commit}(\mathsf{sk}^{\mathsf{TFHE}}, \mathsf{r}) = \mathsf{com}$.

Fig. 5. NP language L_2

2. Otherwise, for each $\mathcal{P}_j \in S$, do the following:
   - Compute $\mathsf{ct}_{\mathcal{C},j} = \mathsf{TFHE.Eval}(\mathsf{pk}^{\mathsf{TFHE}}, \mathcal{C}_{\mathsf{Dist}}, \mathsf{ct}_{\vec{\mathbf{w}}}, \mathsf{ct}_{\vec{\mathbf{u}}}, \mathsf{ct}_{K_j})$ using circuit $\mathcal{C}$ (Fig. 4). Note that $\mathsf{ct}_{\mathcal{C},j}$ is either an encryption K_j or an encryption of 0^λ.
   - Compute a partial decryption: $\mu_{i,j} = \mathsf{TFHE.PartialDec}(\mathsf{sk}_i^{\mathsf{TFHE}}, \mathsf{ct}_{\mathcal{C},j})$.
   - Compute $\pi_{i,j} \leftarrow \mathsf{Prove}(\mathsf{st}_{i,j}, \mathsf{wit}_i)$ for $\mathsf{st}_{i,j} = (\mathsf{ct}_{\mathcal{C},j}, \mu_{i,j}, \mathsf{com}_i) \in L_2$ using $\mathsf{wit}_i = (\mathsf{sk}_i^{\mathsf{TFHE}}, \mathsf{r}_i^{\mathsf{com}})$ (language L_2 is defined in Fig. 5).
3. Compute partial signature $\mathsf{Token}_i = \mathsf{TS.Sign}(\mathsf{sk}_i^{\mathsf{TFHE}}, \mathsf{msg})$ and ciphertext $\mathsf{ct}_i = K_i \oplus \mathsf{Token}_i$.
4. Send $(\mathsf{ct}_i, \{(\pi_{i,j}, \mu_{i,j})\}_{\mathcal{P}_j \in S})$ to $\mathcal{P}^*$.

- **Output Computation:** Every party $\mathcal{P}_i \in S$ outputs $(\mathsf{msg}, \mathcal{P}^*, S)$. Additionally, party $\mathcal{P}^*$ does the following to generate a token:
  1. For each $\mathcal{P}_j \in S$, do the following:
     (a) For each $\mathcal{P}_i \in S$, abort if $\mathsf{Verify}(\pi_{i,j}, \mathsf{st}_{i,j}) \neq 1$ for language L_2 where $\mathsf{st}_{i,j} = (\mathsf{ct}_{\mathcal{C},j}, \mu_{i,j}, \mathsf{com}_i)$.
     (b) Set $K_j = \mathsf{TFHE.Combine}(\{\mu_{i,j}\}_{\mathcal{P}_i \in S})$. If $K_j = 0^\lambda$, output $\perp$.
     (c) Otherwise, recover partial signature $\mathsf{Token}_j = K_j \oplus \mathsf{ct}_j$.
  2. Reconstruct the signature as $\mathsf{Token} = \mathsf{TS.Combine}(\{\mathsf{Token}_i\}_{i \in S})$.
  3. If $\mathsf{TS.Verify}(\mathsf{vk}^{\mathsf{TS}}, \mathsf{msg}, \mathsf{Token}) = 1$, then output $\{\mathsf{Token}_i\}_{\mathcal{P}_i \in S}$. Else, output $\perp$.

Token Verification: Given a verification key $\mathsf{vk}^{\mathsf{TS}}$, message msg and a set of partial tokens $\{\mathsf{Token}_i\}_{\mathcal{P}_i \in S}$, the token verification algorithm outputs 1 if $\mathsf{TS.Verify}(\mathsf{vk}^{\mathsf{TS}}, \mathsf{msg}, \mathsf{Token}) = 1$, where $\mathsf{Token} = \mathsf{TS.Combine}(\{\mathsf{Token}_i\}_{\mathcal{P}_i \in S})$.

7 Cosine Similarity: Single Corruption

In this section, we construct an efficient four round secure FTT in the Random Oracle (RO) model for Euclidean Distance and Cosine Similarity. Our protocol satisfies Definition 1 for any n with threshold $t = 3$ and is secure against a malicious adversary that can corrupt any one party. The special case of $n = 3$ corresponds to the popularly studied three party honest majority setting. We first focus on the Cosine Similarity distance measure. In the full version, we explain how to extend our result for Euclidean Distance. Formally:

Theorem 3. *Assuming unforgeable threshold signatures, two message OT in the CRS model, circuit-private additively homomorphic encryption and NIZKs for NP languages L_1, L_2 defined below, there exists a four round secure fuzzy threshold tokenizer protocol for Cosine Similarity. The protocol works for any n, threshold $t = 3$ and is secure against a malicious adversary that can corrupt any one party.*

We describe the construction below and defer the proof to the full version [12].

Paillier Encryption Scheme. The Paillier encryption scheme [47] is an example of a circuit-private additively homomorphic encryption based on the Nth residuosity assumption. With respect to Paillier, we can also build NIZK arguments for languages L_1 and L_2 defined below, in the RO model. Formally:

Imported Theorem 1 ([31]). *Assuming the hardness of the Nth residuosity assumption, there exists a NIZK for language L_1, defined below, in the RO model.*

Imported Theorem 2 ([30]). *Assuming the hardness of the Nth residuosity assumption, there exists a NIZK for language L_2, defined below, in the RO model.*

The above NIZKs are very efficient and only require a constant number of group operations for both prover and verifier. Two message OT in the CRS model can be built assuming DDH/LWE/Quadratic Residuosity/N^{th} residuosity [40, 46, 51]. Threshold signatures can be built assuming LWE/Gap-DDH/RSA [18, 20, 54]. Instantiating the primitives used in Theorem 3, we get the following corollary:

Corollary 3. *Assuming the hardness of the Nth residuosity assumption and LWE, there exists a four round secure fuzzy threshold tokenizer protocol for Cosine Similarity in the RO model. The protocol works for any n, $t = 3$ and is secure against a malicious adversary that can corrupt any one party.*

NP Languages.
Let $(\mathsf{AHE.Setup}, \mathsf{AHE.Enc}, \mathsf{AHE.Add}, \mathsf{AHE.ConstMul}, \mathsf{AHE.Dec})$ be an additively homomorphic encryption scheme. Let $\mathsf{epk} \leftarrow \mathsf{AHE.Setup}(1^\lambda)$, $m = \mathsf{poly}(\lambda)$.
Language L_1:
Statement: $\mathsf{st} = (\mathsf{ct}, \mathsf{pk})$.   **Witness:** $\mathsf{wit} = (\mathsf{x}, \mathsf{r})$.

Relation: $R_1(st, wit) = 1$ if $ct = AHE.Enc(epk, x; r)$ AND $x \in \{0,1\}^m$

Language L_2:
Statement: $st = (ct_1, ct_2, ct_3, pk)$.   **Witness:** $wit = (x_2, r_2, r_3)$.
Relation: $R_2(st, wit) = 1$ if

$$ct_2 = AHE.Enc(epk, x_2; r_2) \text{ AND } ct_3 = AHE.ConstMul(pk, ct_1, x_2; r_3).$$

Construction. Let RO denote a random oracle, d be the threshold value for Cosine Similarity. Recall that we denote $Dist(\overrightarrow{u}, \overrightarrow{w}) = 1$ if $CS.Dist(\overrightarrow{u}, \overrightarrow{w}) \geq d$. Let (Share, Recon) be a $(2, n)$ threshold secret sharing scheme, $TS = (TS.Gen, TS.Sign, TS.Combine, TS.Verify)$ be a threshold signature scheme, (SKE.Enc, SKE.Dec) denote a secret key encryption scheme, PRF denote a pseudorandom function, (Garble, Eval) denote a garbling scheme for circuits, (Prove, Verify) be a NIZK system in the RO model, $AHE = (AHE.Setup, AHE.Enc, AHE.Add, AHE.ConstMul, AHE.Dec)$ be a circuit-private additively homomorphic encryption scheme and $OT = (OT.Setup, OT.Round_1, OT.Round_2, OT.Output)$ be a two message oblivious transfer protocol in the CRS model. We now describe the construction of our four round secure fuzzy threshold tokenizer protocol π^{CS} for Cosine Similarity.

Setup: The trusted authority does the following:

- Compute $(pp^{TS}, vk^{TS}, sk_1^{TS}, \ldots, sk_n^{TS}) \leftarrow TS.Gen(1^\lambda, n, k)$.
- For $i \in [n]$, generate $crs_i \leftarrow OT.Setup(1^\lambda)$ and pick a random PRF key k_i.
- For $i \in [n]$, give $(pp^{TS}, vk^{TS}, sk_i^{TS}, \{crs_j\}_{j \in [n]}, \{k_j\}_{j \in [n] \setminus i})$ to party $\mathcal{P}_i$.

Enrollment: In this phase, any party $\mathcal{P}_i$ that wishes to enroll, queries the trusted authority which then does the following:

- Sample a random vector $\overrightarrow{w}$ from the distribution $\mathcal{W}$. Without loss of generality, let's assume that the L2-norm of $\overrightarrow{w}$ is 1.
- For each $i \in [n]$, do the following:
  - Compute $(\overrightarrow{w}_i, \overrightarrow{v}_i) \leftarrow Share(1^\lambda, \overrightarrow{w}, n, 2)$.
  - Compute $(esk_i, epk_i) \leftarrow AHE.Setup(1^\lambda)$.
  - Let $\overrightarrow{w}_i = (w_{i,1}, \ldots, w_{i,\ell})$. $\forall j \in [\ell]$, compute $[\![w_{i,j}]\!] = AHE.Enc(epk_i, w_{i,j})$.
  - Give $(\overrightarrow{w}_i, sk_i, pk_i, \{[\![w_{i,j}]\!]\}_{j \in [\ell]})$ to party $\mathcal{P}_i$ and $(\overrightarrow{v}_i, pk_i, \{[\![w_{i,j}]\!]\}_{j \in [\ell]})$ to all the other parties.

SignOn Phase: In the SignOn phase, let's consider party $\mathcal{P}_i$ that uses an input vector $\overrightarrow{u} = (u_1, \ldots, u_\ell)$ and a message msg on which it wants a token. $\mathcal{P}_i$ picks two other parties $\mathcal{P}_j$ and $\mathcal{P}_k$ and interacts with them in the below protocol.

Round 1: $(\mathcal{P}_i \rightarrow)^8$ Party $\mathcal{P}_i$ does the following:

1. Let $S = (\mathcal{P}_j, \mathcal{P}_k)$ with $j < k$.
2. For each $j \in [\ell]$, compute the following:
   - $[\![u_j]\!] = \mathsf{AHE.Enc}(\mathsf{epk}_i, u_j; r_{1,j})$. $\pi_{1,j} \leftarrow \mathsf{Prove}(\mathsf{st}_{1,j}, \mathsf{wit}_{1,j})$ for $\mathsf{st}_{1,j} = ([\![u_j]\!], \mathsf{epk}_i) \in L_1$ using $\mathsf{wit}_{1,j} = (u_j, r_{1,j})$.
   - $[\![u_j^2]\!] = \mathsf{AHE.ConstMul}(\mathsf{epk}_i, [\![u_j]\!], u_j; r_{2,j})$. $\pi_{2,j} \leftarrow \mathsf{Prove}(\mathsf{st}_{2,j}, \mathsf{wit}_{2,j})$ for $\mathsf{st}_{2,j} = ([\![u_j]\!], [\![u_j]\!], [\![u_j^2]\!], \mathsf{epk}_i) \in L_2$ using $\mathsf{wit}_{2,j} = (u_j, r_{1,j}, r_{2,j})$.
   - $[\![w_{i,j} \cdot u_j]\!] = \mathsf{AHE.ConstMul}(\mathsf{epk}_i, [\![w_{i,j}]\!], u_j; r_{3,j})$. $\pi_{3,j} \leftarrow \mathsf{Prove}(\mathsf{st}_{3,j}, \mathsf{wit}_{3,j})$ for $\mathsf{st}_{3,j} = ([\![w_{i,j}]\!], [\![u_j]\!], [\![w_{i,j} \cdot u_j]\!], \mathsf{epk}_i) \in L_2$ using $\mathsf{wit}_{3,j} = (u_j, r_{1,j}, r_{3,j})$.
3. To both parties in S, send $\mathsf{msg}_1 = (S, \mathsf{msg}, \{[\![u_j]\!], [\![u_j^2]\!], [\![w_{i,j} \cdot u_j]\!], \pi_{1,j}, \pi_{2,j}, \pi_{3,j}\}_{j \in [\ell]})$.

Round 2: $(\rightarrow \mathcal{P}_i)$ Both parties $\mathcal{P}_j$ and $\mathcal{P}_k$ do the following:

1. Abort if any of the proofs $\{\pi_{1,j}, \pi_{2,j}, \pi_{3,j}\}_{j \in [\ell]}$ don't verify.
2. Generate randomness $(a, b, e, f, p, q, r_z) \leftarrow \mathsf{PRF}(k_i, \mathsf{msg}_1)$.
3. Using the algorithms of AHE, compute $[\![x_1]\!], [\![x_2]\!], [\![y_1]\!], [\![y_2]\!], [\![z_1]\!], [\![z_2]\!]$ as follows:
   - $x_1 = \langle \vec{u}, \vec{w}_i \rangle$, $y_1 = \langle \vec{u}, \vec{u} \rangle$, $z_1 = (\langle \vec{u}, \vec{v}_i \rangle + r_z)$.
   - $x_2 = (a \cdot x_1 + b)$, $y_2 = (e \cdot y_1 + f)$, $z_2 = (p \cdot z_1 + q)$
4. Send $([\![x_2]\!], [\![y_2]\!], [\![z_1]\!], [\![z_2]\!])$ to $\mathcal{P}_i$.

Round 3: $(\mathcal{P}_i \rightarrow)$ Party $\mathcal{P}_i$ does the following:

1. Abort if the tuples sent by both $\mathcal{P}_j$ and $\mathcal{P}_k$ in round 2 were not the same.
2. Compute $x_1 = \langle \vec{u}, \vec{w}_i \rangle$, $x_2 = \mathsf{AHE.Dec}(\mathsf{esk}_i, [\![x_2]\!])$.
3. Compute $y_1 = \langle \vec{u}, \vec{u} \rangle$, $y_2 = \mathsf{AHE.Dec}(\mathsf{esk}_i, [\![y_2]\!])$.
4. Compute $z_1 = \mathsf{AHE.Dec}(\mathsf{esk}_i, [\![z_1]\!])$, $z_2 = \mathsf{AHE.Dec}(\mathsf{esk}_i, [\![z_2]\!])$.
5. Generate and send $\mathsf{msg}_3 = \{\mathsf{ot}_{s,t}^{\mathsf{rec}} \leftarrow \mathsf{OT.Round}_1(\mathsf{crs}_i, s_t)\}_{s \in \{x,y,z\}, t \in \{1,2\}}$.

Round 4: $(\mathcal{P}_j \rightarrow \mathcal{P}_i)$ Party $\mathcal{P}_j$ does the following:

1. Compute $\tilde{\mathcal{C}} = \mathsf{Garble}(\mathcal{C})$ for the circuit $\mathcal{C}$ described in Fig. 6.
2. For each $s \in \{x, y, z\}, t \in \{0, 1\}$, let $\mathsf{lab}_{s,t}^0, \mathsf{lab}_{s,t}^1$ denote the labels of the garbled circuit $\tilde{\mathcal{C}}$ corresponding to input wires s_t. Generate $\mathsf{ot}_{s,t}^{\mathsf{sen}} = \mathsf{OT.Round}_2(\mathsf{crs}_i, \mathsf{lab}_{s,t}^0, \mathsf{lab}_{s,t}^1, \mathsf{ot}_{s,t}^{\mathsf{rec}})$. Let $\mathsf{ot}^{\mathsf{sen}} = \{\mathsf{ot}_{s,t}^{\mathsf{sen}}\}_{s \in \{x,y,z\}, t \in \{1,2\}}$
3. Compute $\mathsf{pad} = \mathsf{PRF}(k_i, \mathsf{msg}_3)$. Set $\mathsf{ct}_j = \mathsf{SKE.Enc}(\mathsf{pad}, \mathsf{TS.Sign}(\mathsf{sk}_j^{\mathsf{TS}}, \mathsf{msg}))$.
4. Send $(\tilde{\mathcal{C}}, \mathsf{ot}^{\mathsf{sen}}, \mathsf{ct}_j)$ to $\mathcal{P}_i$.

Round 4: $(\mathcal{P}_k \rightarrow \mathcal{P}_i)$ Party $\mathcal{P}_k$ does the following:

1. Compute $(\tilde{\mathcal{C}}, \mathsf{ot}^{\mathsf{sen}}, \mathsf{pad})$ exactly as done by $\mathcal{P}_j$.
2. Set $\mathsf{ct}_k = \mathsf{SKE.Enc}(\mathsf{pad}, \mathsf{TS.Sign}(\mathsf{sk}_k^{\mathsf{TS}}, \mathsf{msg}))$.
3. Send $(\mathsf{RO}(\tilde{\mathcal{C}}, \mathsf{ot}^{\mathsf{sen}}), \mathsf{ct}_k)$ to $\mathcal{P}_i$.

---

[8] The arrowhead denotes that in this round messages are outgoing from party $\mathcal{P}_i$.

Output Computation: Parties $\mathcal{P}_j, \mathcal{P}_k$ output $(\mathsf{msg}, \mathcal{P}_i, S)$. Party $\mathcal{P}_i$ does:

1. Let $(\widetilde{\mathcal{C}}, \mathsf{ot}^{\mathsf{sen}}, \mathsf{ct}_j)$ be the message received from $\mathcal{P}_j$ and $(\mathsf{msg}_4, \mathsf{ct}_k)$ be the message received from $\mathcal{P}_k$. Abort if $\mathsf{RO}(\widetilde{\mathcal{C}}, \mathsf{ot}^{\mathsf{sen}}) \neq \mathsf{msg}_4$.
2. For each $\mathsf{s} \in \{\mathsf{x}, \mathsf{y}, \mathsf{z}\}, \mathsf{t} \in \{0,1\}$, compute $\mathsf{lab}_{\mathsf{s},\mathsf{t}} = \mathsf{OT.Output}(\mathsf{ot}^{\mathsf{sen}}_{\mathsf{s},\mathsf{t}}, \mathsf{ot}^{\mathsf{rec}}_{\mathsf{s},\mathsf{t}}, \mathsf{r}^{\mathsf{ot}}_{\mathsf{s},\mathsf{t}})$. Let $\mathsf{lab} = \{\mathsf{lab}_{\mathsf{s},\mathsf{t}}\}_{\mathsf{s} \in \{\mathsf{x},\mathsf{y},\mathsf{z}\}, \mathsf{t} \in \{0,1\}}$. Compute $\mathsf{pad} = \mathsf{Eval}(\widetilde{\mathcal{C}}, \mathsf{lab})$.
3. Compute $\mathsf{Token}_j = \mathsf{SKE.Dec}(\mathsf{pad}, \mathsf{ct}_j)$, $\mathsf{Token}_k = \mathsf{SKE.Dec}(\mathsf{pad}, \mathsf{ct}_k)$, $\mathsf{Token}_i = \mathsf{TS.Sign}(\mathsf{sk}^{\mathsf{TS}}_i, \mathsf{msg})$, $\mathsf{Token} \leftarrow \mathsf{TS.Combine}(\{\mathsf{Token}_s\}_{s \in \{i,j,k\}})$.
4. Output $\{\mathsf{Token}_s\}_{s \in \{i,j,k\}}$ if $\mathsf{TS.Verify}(\mathsf{vk}^{\mathsf{TS}}, \mathsf{msg}, \mathsf{Token})$. Else, output $\perp$.

Inputs: $(\mathsf{x}_1, \mathsf{x}_2, \mathsf{y}_1, \mathsf{y}_2, \mathsf{z}_1, \mathsf{z}_2)$.   **Hardwired values:** $(\mathsf{a}, \mathsf{b}, \mathsf{e}, \mathsf{f}, \mathsf{p}, \mathsf{q}, \mathsf{r}_z, \mathsf{pad}, d^2)$.
Computation:

- Abort if $\mathsf{x}_2 \neq (\mathsf{a} \cdot \mathsf{x}_1 + \mathsf{b})$ (or) $\mathsf{y}_2 \neq (\mathsf{e} \cdot \mathsf{y}_1 + \mathsf{f})$ (or) $\mathsf{z}_2 \neq (\mathsf{p} \cdot \mathsf{z}_1 + \mathsf{q})$
- Compute $\mathsf{IP} = (\mathsf{z}_1 - \mathsf{r}_z) + \mathsf{x}_1$
- If $\mathsf{IP}^2 \geq (d^2 \cdot \mathsf{y}_1)$, output pad. Else, output $\perp$.

Fig. 6. Circuit $\mathcal{C}$ to be garbled.

Token Verification: Given a verification key $\mathsf{vk}^{\mathsf{TS}}$, message msg and token $(\mathsf{Token}_i, \mathsf{Token}_j, \mathsf{Token}_k)$, the token verification algorithm does the following:

1. Compute $\mathsf{Token} \leftarrow \mathsf{TS.Combine}(\{\mathsf{Token}_s\}_{s \in \{i,j,k\}})$.
2. Output 1 if $\mathsf{TS.Verify}(\mathsf{vk}^{\mathsf{TS}}, \mathsf{msg}, \mathsf{Token}) = 1$. Else, output 0.

References

1. About Face ID advanced technology. https://support.apple.com/en-us/HT208108. Accessed 07 Apr 2021
2. Advantages and disadvantages of biometrics. https://www.ukessays.com/dissertation/examples/information-systems/advantages-and-disadvantages-of-biometrics.php?vref=1. Accessed 07 Apr 2021
3. FIDO Alliance. https://fidoalliance.org/. Accessed 07 Apr 2021
4. Google Pixel Fingerprint. https://support.google.com/pixelphone/answer/6285273?hl=en. Accessed 07 Apr 2021
5. iOS Security – iOS 12, p. 8. https://www.apple.com/business/site/docs/iOS_Security_Guide.pdf. Accessed 07 Apr 2021
6. List of data breaches. https://en.wikipedia.org/wiki/List_of_data_breaches. Accessed 07 Apr 2021
7. NISTIR Draft on Ongoing Face Recognition Vendor Test Part 1: Verification. https://pages.nist.gov/frvt/reports/11/frvt_report_2020_01_21.pdf. Accessed 07 Apr 2021
8. Privacy Rights Clearinghouse - Data Breaches. https://www.privacyrights.org/data-breaches. Accessed 07 Apr 2021

9. Samsung Galaxy: Iris Scans for Security. https://www.samsung.com/global/galaxy/galaxy-s8/security/. Accessed 07 Apr 2021

10. Web Authentication: W3 Standard. https://www.w3.org/TR/2018/CR-webauthn-20180320/. Accessed 07 Apr 2021

11. White-Box Competition. https://whibox-contest.github.io/. Accessed 07 Apr 2021

12. Agrawal, S., Badrinarayanan, S., Mohassel, P., Mukherjee, P., Patranabis, S.: BETA: biometric enabled threshold authentication. IACR Cryptol. ePrint Arch. 2020, 679 (2020)

13. Barak, B., et al.: On the (Im)possibility of obfuscating programs. In: Kilian, J. (ed.) CRYPTO 2001. LNCS, vol. 2139, pp. 1–18. Springer, Heidelberg (2001). https://doi.org/10.1007/3-540-44647-8_1

14. Beimel, A., Ishai, Y., Kushilevitz, E.: Ad hoc PSM protocols: secure computation without coordination. In: Coron, J.-S., Nielsen, J.B. (eds.) EUROCRYPT 2017. LNCS, vol. 10212, pp. 580–608. Springer, Cham (2017). https://doi.org/10.1007/978-3-319-56617-7_20

15. Benhamouda, F., Lin, H.: k-round multiparty computation from k-round oblivious transfer via garbled interactive circuits. In: Nielsen, J.B., Rijmen, V. (eds.) EUROCRYPT 2018, Part II. LNCS, vol. 10821, pp. 500–532. Springer, Heidelberg (Apr / May (2018)

16. Blazy, O., Chevalier, C., Vergnaud, D.: Mitigating server breaches in password-based authentication: Secure and efficient solutions. In: CT-RSA (2016)

17. Blundo, C., De Cristofaro, E., Gasti, P.: EsPRESSo: efficient privacy-preserving evaluation of sample set similarity. In: Di Pietro, R., Herranz, J., Damiani, E., State, R. (eds.) DPM/SETOP -2012. LNCS, vol. 7731, pp. 89–103. Springer, Heidelberg (2013). https://doi.org/10.1007/978-3-642-35890-6_7

18. Boldyreva, A.: Threshold signatures, multisignatures and blind signatures based on the Gap-Diffie-Hellman-Group signature scheme. In: Desmedt, Y.G. (ed.) PKC 2003. LNCS, vol. 2567, pp. 31–46. Springer, Heidelberg (2003). https://doi.org/10.1007/3-540-36288-6_3

19. Bonawitz, K., et al.: Practical secure aggregation for privacy-preserving machine learning. In: Thuraisingham, B.M., Evans, D., Malkin, T., Xu, D. (eds.) ACM CCS 2017, pp. 1175–1191. ACM Press, October/November 2017

20. Boneh, D., Gennaro, R., Goldfeder, S., Jain, A., Kim, S., Rasmussen, P.M.R., Sahai, A.: Threshold cryptosystems from threshold fully homomorphic encryption. In: Shacham, H., Boldyreva, A. (eds.) CRYPTO 2018. LNCS, vol. 10991, pp. 565–596. Springer, Cham (2018). https://doi.org/10.1007/978-3-319-96884-1_19

21. Boyen, X.: Reusable cryptographic fuzzy extractors. In: Atluri, V., Pfitzmann, B., McDaniel, P. (eds.) ACM CCS 2004, pp. 82–91. ACM Press, October 2004

22. Boyle, E., Gilboa, N., Ishai, Y.: Function secret sharing. In: Oswald, E., Fischlin, M. (eds.) EUROCRYPT 2015. LNCS, vol. 9057, pp. 337–367. Springer, Heidelberg (2015). https://doi.org/10.1007/978-3-662-46803-6_12

23. Boyle, E., Gilboa, N., Ishai, Y., Lin, H., Tessaro, S.: Foundations of homomorphic secret sharing. In: Karlin, A.R. (ed.) ITCS 2018, vol. 94, pp. 21:1–21:21. LIPIcs, January 2018

24. Brakerski, Z., Perlman, R.: Lattice-based fully dynamic multi-key FHE with short ciphertexts. In: Robshaw, M., Katz, J. (eds.) CRYPTO 2016. LNCS, vol. 9814, pp. 190–213. Springer, Heidelberg (2016). https://doi.org/10.1007/978-3-662-53018-4_8

25. Bringer, J., Chabanne, H., Patey, A.: SHADE: secure HAmming DistancE computation from oblivious transfer. In: Adams, A.A., Brenner, M., Smith, M. (eds.) FC 2013. LNCS, vol. 7862, pp. 164–176. Springer, Heidelberg (2013). https://doi.org/10.1007/978-3-642-41320-9_11

26. Canetti, R.: Universally composable security: a new paradigm for cryptographic protocols. In: 42nd FOCS, pp. 136–145. IEEE Computer Society Press, October 2001

27. Canetti, R.: Universally Composable Signature, Certification, and Authentication. In: CSFW (2004)

28. Canetti, R., Cohen, A., Lindell, Y.: A simpler variant of universally composable security for standard multiparty computation. In: Gennaro, R., Robshaw, M. (eds.) CRYPTO 2015. LNCS, vol. 9216, pp. 3–22. Springer, Heidelberg (2015). https://doi.org/10.1007/978-3-662-48000-7_1

29. Chan, T.-H.H., Shi, E., Song, D.: Privacy-preserving stream aggregation with fault tolerance. In: Keromytis, A.D. (ed.) FC 2012. LNCS, vol. 7397, pp. 200–214. Springer, Heidelberg (2012). https://doi.org/10.1007/978-3-642-32946-3_15

30. Cramer, R., Damgård, I., Nielsen, J.B.: Multiparty computation from threshold homomorphic encryption. In: Pfitzmann, B. (ed.) EUROCRYPT 2001. LNCS, vol. 2045, pp. 280–300. Springer, Heidelberg (2001). https://doi.org/10.1007/3-540-44987-6_18

31. Damgård, I., Jurik, M.: A generalisation, a simplification and some applications of Paillier's probabilistic public-key system. In: Kim, K. (ed.) PKC 2001. LNCS, vol. 1992, pp. 119–136. Springer, Heidelberg (2001). https://doi.org/10.1007/3-540-44586-2_9

32. Dinh, T., Steinfeld, R., Bhattacharjee, N.: A lattice-based approach to privacy-preserving biometric authentication without relying on trusted third parties. In: Liu, J.K., Samarati, P. (eds.) ISPEC 2017. LNCS, vol. 10701, pp. 297–319. Springer, Cham (2017). https://doi.org/10.1007/978-3-319-72359-4_17

33. Dodis, Y., Reyzin, L., Smith, A.: Fuzzy extractors: how to generate strong keys from biometrics and other noisy data. In: Cachin, C., Camenisch, J.L. (eds.) EUROCRYPT 2004. LNCS, vol. 3027, pp. 523–540. Springer, Heidelberg (2004). https://doi.org/10.1007/978-3-540-24676-3_31

34. Dupont, P.-A., Hesse, J., Pointcheval, D., Reyzin, L., Yakoubov, S.: Fuzzy password-authenticated key exchange. In: Nielsen, J.B., Rijmen, V. (eds.) EUROCRYPT 2018. LNCS, vol. 10822, pp. 393–424. Springer, Cham (2018). https://doi.org/10.1007/978-3-319-78372-7_13

35. ElGamal, T.: A public key cryptosystem and a signature scheme based on discrete logarithms. In: Blakley, G.R., Chaum, D. (eds.) CRYPTO 1984. LNCS, vol. 196, pp. 10–18. Springer, Heidelberg (1985). https://doi.org/10.1007/3-540-39568-7_2

36. Feige, U., Kilian, J., Naor, M.: A minimal model for secure computation (extended abstract). In: 26th ACM STOC, pp. 554–563. ACM Press, May 1994

37. Garg, S., Gentry, C., Halevi, S., Raykova, M., Sahai, A., Waters, B.: Candidate indistinguishability obfuscation and functional encryption for all circuits. In: FOCS (2013)

38. Garg, S., Srinivasan, A.: Two-round multiparty secure computation from minimal assumptions. In: Nielsen, J.B., Rijmen, V. (eds.) EUROCRYPT 2018. LNCS, vol. 10821, pp. 468–499. Springer, Cham (2018). https://doi.org/10.1007/978-3-319-78375-8_16

39. Grassi, P.A., et al.: Nist special publication 800–63b: Digital identity guidelines: authentication and lifecycle management, June 2017. https://pages.nist.gov/800-63-3/sp800-63b.html

40. Halevi, S., Kalai, Y.T.: Smooth projective hashing and two-message oblivious transfer. J. Cryptol. **25**(1), 158–193 (2012)
41. Ishai, Y., Kushilevitz, E.: Private simultaneous messages protocols with applications. In: ISTCS 1997. Washington, DC, USA (1997)
42. Joye, M., Libert, B.: A scalable scheme for privacy-preserving aggregation of time-series data. In: Sadeghi, A.-R. (ed.) FC 2013. LNCS, vol. 7859, pp. 111–125. Springer, Heidelberg (2013). https://doi.org/10.1007/978-3-642-39884-1_10
43. Liu, W., Wen, Y., Yu, Z., Li, M., Raj, B., Song, L.: Sphereface: deep hypersphere embedding for face recognition. In: CVPR (2017)
44. Mohassel, P., Rosulek, M., Zhang, Y.: Fast and secure three-party computation: the garbled circuit approach. In: Ray, I., Li, N., Kruegel, C. (eds.) ACM CCS 2015. pp. 591–602. ACM Press, October 2015
45. Mukherjee, P., Wichs, D.: Two round multiparty computation via multi-key FHE. In: Fischlin, M., Coron, J.-S. (eds.) EUROCRYPT 2016. LNCS, vol. 9666, pp. 735–763. Springer, Heidelberg (2016). https://doi.org/10.1007/978-3-662-49896-5_26
46. Naor, M., Pinkas, B.: Efficient oblivious transfer protocols. In: Kosaraju, S.R. (ed.) 12th SODA, pp. 448–457. ACM-SIAM, January 2001
47. Paillier, P.: Public-key cryptosystems based on composite degree residuosity classes. In: Stern, J. (ed.) EUROCRYPT 1999. LNCS, vol. 1592, pp. 223–238. Springer, Heidelberg (1999). https://doi.org/10.1007/3-540-48910-X_16
48. Peikert, C., Shiehian, S.: Multi-key FHE from lwe, revisited. In: TCC (2016)
49. Peikert, C., Shiehian, S.: Multi-key FHE from LWE, revisited. In: Hirt, M., Smith, A.D. (eds.) TCC 2016-B, Part II. LNCS, vol. 9986, pp. 217–238. Springer, Heidelberg (Oct / Nov (2016)
50. Peikert, C., Shiehian, S.: Noninteractive zero knowledge for NP from (plain) learning with errors. In: Boldyreva, A., Micciancio, D. (eds.) CRYPTO 2019. LNCS, vol. 11692, pp. 89–114. Springer, Cham (2019). https://doi.org/10.1007/978-3-030-26948-7_4
51. Peikert, C., Vaikuntanathan, V., Waters, B.: A framework for efficient and composable oblivious transfer. In: Wagner, D. (ed.) CRYPTO 2008. LNCS, vol. 5157, pp. 554–571. Springer, Heidelberg (2008). https://doi.org/10.1007/978-3-540-85174-5_31
52. Sahai, A., Waters, B.: Fuzzy identity-based encryption. In: Cramer, R. (ed.) EUROCRYPT 2005. LNCS, vol. 3494, pp. 457–473. Springer, Heidelberg (2005). https://doi.org/10.1007/11426639_27
53. Schroff, F., Kalenichenko, D., Philbin, J.: FaceNet: a unified embedding for face recognition and clustering. In: CVPR (2015)
54. Shoup, V.: Practical threshold signatures. In: Preneel, B. (ed.) EUROCRYPT 2000. LNCS, vol. 1807, pp. 207–220. Springer, Heidelberg (2000). https://doi.org/10.1007/3-540-45539-6_15
55. Wang, H., et al.: Cosface: Large margin cosine loss for deep face recognition. In: CVPR (2018)
56. Yao, A.C.C.: How to generate and exchange secrets (extended abstract). In: 27th FOCS, pp. 162–167. IEEE Computer Society Press, October 1986

Masked Triples
Amortizing Multiplication Triples Across Conditionals

David Heath[(✉)], Vladimir Kolesnikov, and Stanislav Peceny

Georgia Institute of Technology, Atlanta, GA, USA
{heath.davidanthony,kolesnikov,stan.peceny}@gatech.edu

Abstract. A classic approach to MPC uses preprocessed *multiplication triples* to evaluate arbitrary Boolean circuits. If the target circuit features conditional branching, e.g. as the result of a IF program statement, then triples are wasted: one triple is consumed per AND gate, even if the output of the gate is entirely discarded by the circuit's conditional behavior.

In this work, we show that multiplication triples can be re-used across conditional branches. For a circuit with b branches, each having n AND gates, we need only a total of n triples, rather than the typically required $b \cdot n$. Because preprocessing triples is often the most expensive step in protocols that use them, this significantly improves performance.

Prior work similarly amortized *oblivious transfers* across branches in the classic GMW protocol (Heath et al., Asiacrypt 2020, [HKP20]). In addition to demonstrating conditional improvements are possible for a different class of protocols, we also concretely improve over [HKP20]: their maximum improvement is bounded by the *topology* of the circuit. Our protocol yields improvement independent of topology: we need triples proportional to the size of the program's longest execution path, regardless of the structure of the program branches.

We implemented our approach in C++. Our experiments show that we significantly improve over a "naïve" protocol and over prior work: for a circuit with 16 branches and in terms of total communication, we improved over naïve by 12× and over [HKP20] by an average of 2.6×.

Our protocol is secure against the semi-honest corruption of $p - 1$ parties.

Keywords: MPC · Conditional branching · Beaver triples

1 Introduction

Secure Multiparty Computation (MPC) enables untrusting parties to compute a function of their private inputs while revealing only the function output. In this work, we consider semi-honest MPC protocols that use the classic trick of Beaver to evaluate Boolean circuits by preprocessing 'multiplication triples' [Bea92].

In such protocols, XOR gates are 'free' (i.e., require no interaction), but each AND gate consumes a distinct multiplication triple. To generate these triples, the parties use a more expensive MPC protocol that can be run ahead of time in

© International Association for Cryptologic Research 2021
J. A. Garay (Ed.): PKC 2021, LNCS 12711, pp. 319–348, 2021.
https://doi.org/10.1007/978-3-030-75248-4_12

a preprocessing phase. The communication in this phase is proportional to the number of triples and is usually the performance bottleneck. Hence, if we reduce the number of required triples, then we significantly improve performance.

Because one triple is needed per AND gate, protocols waste significant work if the computed function has conditional behavior, e.g. as the result of an IF program statement. Each gate requires a distinct triple, even if the output of the gate is entirely discarded by the function's conditional behavior.

Our protocol re-uses multiplication triples across conditional branches. A single triple can support any number of AND gates, so long as the gates occur in mutually exclusive program branches. This re-use does require that the parties hold additional correlated randomness, but the parties can generate this randomness efficiently. Our approach greatly decreases total communication and hence improves performance.

1.1 High Level Intuition

Multiplication triples typically cannot be re-used (Sect. 2.5 reviews multiplication triples in detail): triples are essentially one-time-pads on cleartext values in the circuit: since no strict subset of parties knows the values in the triple, it is secure to use the triple to mask cleartext values. However, if we use the same triple for two different gates, then we violate security. We can work around this.

Consider two conditionally composed circuits C^0 and C^1, both with n AND gates. For sake of example, suppose C^0 is the active branch, but suppose the parties do not know and should not learn this fact. We re-use the same triples to evaluate gates in both C^0 and C^1 by carefully applying secret shared *masks* to the triples. For the inactive branch C^1, the parties mask the shares with XOR shares of *uniform* masks, randomizing the triples and preventing us from breaking the security of one-time-pad. By randomizing the triples, we violate the correctness of AND gates on the inactive branch, but this is of no concern: the output of each inactive AND gate is ultimately discarded. For the active branch C^0, the parties use the triples 'as is', meaning the active branch is evaluated normally. Of course, the parties should not know which branch is inactive, so from the perspective of the parties it should appear plausible that either branch could have used randomized triples. To achieve this, for the active branch the parties also XOR masks onto the triples, but in this case each mask is a sharing of zero: hence the XORing is a no-op.

The problem of amortizing triples across branches thus reduces to the problem of generating secret shared masks, both uniform and 'all-zero'. We present techniques for efficiently generating these masks, the most general of which is based on oblivious vector-scalar multiplication, achieved by a small number of 1-out-of-2 oblivious transfers. The crucial point is that the protocols for generating masks require far less communication than protocols for generating triples.[1] Thus, we decrease communication and improve performance.

---

[1] We emphasize communication improvement because multiplication triples are often constructed from communication-expensive *oblivious transfers* (OTs). Silent OT [BCG+19] is an exciting new primitive that largely removes the communication

1.2   Advantage Over [HKP20]

Recent work showed an improvement similar to ours: [HKP20] showed that oblivious transfers can be re-used across conditional branches in the classic GMW protocol (see Sect. 2.4 for a review).

However, [HKP20] has one significant disadvantage: their performance improvement depends on circuit topology. Efficient GMW implementations minimize latency by organizing circuits into *layers* of gates. The input wires into each layer are the outputs of previous layers only, and hence all gates in a particular layer can be executed simultaneously. This strategy yields latency proportional to the circuit's *multiplicative depth* instead of to the number of gates.

Due to this important optimization, [HKP20]'s performance improvement is limited by the 'relative alignment' of the layers across branches: two branches are highly aligned if each of their respective layers has a similar number of AND gates. Their protocol issues oblivious transfers that *simultaneously* run one gate per branch and hence cannot optimize gates that occur in different layers. The relative alignment of branches is dependent on the target application. [HKP20] suggests resorting to compiler technologies to extract more performance.

Our approach does not depend on topology. Instead, we depend only on the number of AND gates in each branch. The parties require enough triples to handle the maximum number of AND gates across the branches. It is difficult to analytically quantify our improvement over [HKP20] without a specific application in mind, but our experiments show that the improvement is significant. We ran both approaches across a variety of topologies, and on average we improved communication by 2.6× (see Sect. 8). In addition to concretely outperforming [HKP20], our approach also demonstrates that conditional improvement is possible for a different class of protocols (i.e. those based on triples), and hence is of independent interest.

1.3   Our Contributions

- **Efficient Re-use of Beaver Triples.** Our MPC protocol is secure against the semi-honest corruption of up to $p-1$ parties. The protocol re-uses triples across branches and requires a number of triples proportional only to the size of the longest execution path rather than to the size of the entire circuit.
- **Topology-Independent Improvement.** Unlike [HKP20], our improvement is independent of the topology of the conditional branches.
- **Implementation and evaluation.** We implemented our approach in C++ and report performance (see Sect. 8). For 2PC and a circuit with 16 branches, we improve communication over state-of-the-art [HKP20] on average by

---

overhead of OT. The trade off is increased computation: the classic OT extension of [IKNP03], which uses relatively little computation, is still preferable to Silent OT in most settings. This said, even if we were to use Silent OT, our improvement would be beneficial: we greatly reduce the needed number of OTs and hence would significantly reduce Silent OT computation overhead.

2.6× and over a standard triple-based protocol (i.e., without our conditional improvement) by 12×.

2   Preliminaries

2.1   Notation

- p denotes the number of parties.
- b denotes the number of branches.
- Subscript notation associates variables with parties. E.g., a_i is a variable held by party P_i.
- G denotes a pseudo-random generator (PRG).
- κ is the computational security parameter (e.g. 128).
- t denotes the 'taken' branch in a conditional, i.e. the branch that is active during the oblivious execution. $\bar{t}$ implies an inactive branch.
- Superscript notation associates variables with a particular branch. E.g., x^0 is associated with branch 0 while x^1 is associated with branch 1.
- $\in_\$$ denotes that the left hand side is uniformly drawn from the right hand set. E.g., $x \in_\$ \{0,1\}$ denotes that x is a uniform bit.
- $\triangleq$ denotes that the left hand side is defined to be the right hand side.
- We manipulate vectors and bitstrings (i.e., vectors of bits):
  - Variables denoting vectors are indicated with bold notation, e.g. $\boldsymbol{a}$. If we wish to explicitly write out a vector, we use parenthesized, comma-separated values, e.g. $(a, b, ..., y, z)$.
  - We index vectors with brackets and use 1-based indexing, e.g. $\boldsymbol{a}[1]$.
  - When clear from context, n denotes vector length.
  - When two bitstrings are known to have the same length, we use $\oplus$ to denote the bitwise XOR sum:

  $$\boldsymbol{a} \oplus \boldsymbol{b} = (\boldsymbol{a}[1], ..., \boldsymbol{a}[n]) \oplus (\boldsymbol{b}[1], ..., \boldsymbol{b}[n]) \triangleq (\boldsymbol{a}[1] \oplus \boldsymbol{b}[1], ..., \boldsymbol{a}[n] \oplus \boldsymbol{b}[n])$$

  - We indicate a bitwise vector scalar product by writing the scalar to the left of the vector:

  $$a\boldsymbol{b} = a(\boldsymbol{b}[1], ..., \boldsymbol{b}[n]) \triangleq (a(\boldsymbol{b}[1]), ..., a(\boldsymbol{b}[n]))$$

- We manipulate XOR secret shares. Section 2.2 presents our secret share notation and reviews basic properties.

2.2   XOR Secret Shares

Our main contribution is a Beaver-triple based construction for efficient conditional branching. Additionally, we review prior work that is based on the classic GMW protocol. Both techniques are based on XOR secret shares. Thus, we briefly establish notation for XOR shares and review their properties.

An XOR secret sharing held amongst p parties is a vector of bits $(x_1, ..., x_p)$ where each party P_i holds x_i. We refer to the full vector as a *sharing* and to the individual bits held by parties as *shares*. The semantic value of a sharing (i.e., the cleartext value that the sharing represents) is the XOR sum of its shares. If the semantic value of a sharing $(x_1, ..., x_p)$ is a bit x, i.e. $x_1 \oplus ... \oplus x_p = x$, then we use the shorthand $[\![x]\!]$ to denote the sharing:

$$[\![x]\!] \triangleq (x_1, ..., x_p) \qquad \text{such that } x_1 \oplus ... \oplus x_p = x$$

Typically, sharings are used in a context where no strict subset of parties knows the semantic value of the sharing. Nevertheless, parties can easily perform homomorphic linear operations over XOR sharings.

– Parties XOR two sharings by locally XORing their respective shares:

$$\begin{aligned}
[\![x]\!] \oplus [\![y]\!] &= (x_1, ..., x_p) \oplus (y_1, ..., y_p) && \text{Defn. sharing} \\
&= (x_1 \oplus y_1, ..., x_p \oplus y_p) && \text{Defn. vector XOR} \\
&= [\![x \oplus y]\!] && \text{XOR commutes, assoc., defn. sharing}
\end{aligned}$$

– Parties AND a sharing with a public constant by locally scaling each share.

$$\begin{aligned}
c[\![x]\!] &= c(x_1, ..., x_p) && \text{Defn. sharing} \\
&= (cx_1, ..., cx_p) && \text{Defn. vector scalar product} \\
&= [\![cx]\!] && \text{AND distributes over XOR , defn. sharing}
\end{aligned}$$

– Parties encode public constants as sharings by letting P_1 take the constant as his/her share and letting all other parties take 0 as his/her share.

$$[\![c]\!] = (c, 0, ..., 0) \qquad \text{0 identity, defn. sharing}$$

This allows the parties to XOR sharings with public constants.

A party can easily share her private bit x with the parties. She uniformly draws p bits, with the constraint that the p bits XOR to x. She then distributes $[\![x]\!]$ amongst the parties.

Parties can compute sharings of *uniform* values. To draw a uniform sharing, each party locally draws a uniform share. In our protocols, we overload $\in_\$$ notation to draw sharings: for example, $[\![x]\!] \in_\$ \{0,1\}$ indicates that each party P_i draws a uniform share x_i.

Finally, parties can *reconstruct* the semantic value of a sharing. To do so, each party broadcasts his/her share (or sends it to a specified output party). Upon receiving all shares, each party locally XORs the shares.

For security, we often require that each party's share be uniformly chosen. We point out where shares are uniform when relevant.

VS Functionality:

- INPUT: Parties $P_1, ..., P_p$ input a scalar $[\![s]\!]$ and a bitstring $[\![x]\!]$.
- OUTPUT: Parties output a uniform sharing $[\![sx]\!]$.

Fig. 1. The functionality defining VS gate semantics. VS gates allow parties to multiply a sharing of a bitstring by a sharing of a scalar.

2.3 Vector Scalar Multiplication

Next, we review how parties operate non-linearly over sharings. In contrast to typical approaches that consider AND gates, we instead consider more general *vector scalar multiplication* gates, which we call VS gates. We consider these more expressive gates because they are needed to review prior work [HKP20] and because we use VS gates in our constructions.

To begin, we extend the notion of sharings to vectors. Specifically, we define the sharing of a vector to be a vector of sharings:

$$[\![x]\!] = [\![(x[1], ..., x[n])]\!] \triangleq ([\![x[1]]\!], ..., [\![x[n]]\!])$$

Suppose we wish to scale a shared vector x by a shared bit s. That is, we wish to compute the scalar product $[\![sx]\!]$. Unlike linear operations, this vector scalar multiplication requires the parties to communicate.

[HKP20] showed that parties can use $p(p-1)$ oblivious transfers (OTs) to implement a VS gate. We review their VS protocol at a high level; Fig. 1 specifies the protocol functionality. For simplicity, we focus on $p = 2$ parties and length-2 vectors, but the approach generalizes to arbitrary p and n.

Suppose two parties P_1, P_2, holding sharings $[\![s]\!], [\![(a,b)]\!]$, wish to compute $[\![(sa, sb)]\!]$: semantically, they wish to scale the vector (a, b) by the bit s.

Observe the following equality over the desired semantic value:

$$(sa, sb) = s(a, b) \qquad\qquad\qquad \text{Distribute}$$
$$= (s_1 \oplus s_2)(a_1 \oplus a_2, b_1 \oplus b_2) \qquad\qquad \text{Defn. sharing}$$
$$= (s_1 a_1 \oplus s_1 a_2 \oplus s_2 a_1 \oplus s_2 a_2, s_1 b_1 \oplus s_1 b_2 \oplus s_2 b_1 \oplus s_2 b_2) \qquad \text{Distribute}$$
$$= s_1(a_1, b_1) \oplus s_1(a_2, b_2) \oplus s_2(a_1, b_1) \oplus s_2(a_2, b_2) \qquad\qquad \text{Group}$$

The first and fourth summands can be computed locally by the respective parties. Thus, we need only show how to compute $s_1(a_2, b_2)$ (the remaining third summand is computed symmetrically). To compute this vector AND, the parties perform a single 1-out-of-2 OT of length-2 secrets. Here, P_2 plays the OT sender and P_1 the receiver. P_2 draws two uniform bits $x, y \in_\$ \{0, 1\}$ and allows P_1 to choose between the following two secrets:

$$(x, y) \qquad (x \oplus a_2, y \oplus b_2)$$

P_1 chooses based on s_1 and hence receives $(x \oplus s_1 a_2, y \oplus s_1 b_2)$. P_2 uses the vector (x, y) as her share of this summand. Thus, the parties hold $[\![s_1(a_2, b_2)]\!]$.

Put together, the full vector multiplication $s(a,b)$ uses only two 1-out-of-2 OTs of length-2 secrets. VS gates generalize to arbitrary numbers of parties and vector lengths: a vector scaling of n elements between p parties requires $p(p-1)$ 1-out-of-2 OTs of length-n secrets.

VS gates are important for our constructions. We present a modification to the above protocol, used once per conditional branch, that is optimized for scalar multiplication of *long* vectors (see Sect. 6.2). This modification is similar to techniques in [KK13, ALSZ13] and reduces communication by up to half.

2.4   Efficient Conditionals from VS Gates: [HKP20] Review

[HKP20] was the first work to significantly reduce the cost of branching in the multi-party setting. Their MOTIF protocol extends the classic GMW protocol with VS gates in order to amortize oblivious transfers across conditional branches. We review how VS gates enable this amortization.

For simplicity, consider two branches computed by two parties. Since the two branches are conditionally composed, one branch is active and one is inactive.

MOTIF's key invariant, set up by the protocol's circuit gadgets, is that on each wire of the inactive branch the parties hold a sharing $[\![0]\!]$, whereas on the active branch they hold valid sharings. XOR gates immediately propagate this invariant: on the inactive branch, XOR gates output $[\![0]\!]$, while on the active branch XOR gates output valid sharings.[2]

Next, we review how VS gates make use of and propagate the invariant. Let $[\![a^0]\!]$, $[\![b^0]\!]$ be sharings held on wires in branch 0 and $[\![a^1]\!]$, $[\![b^1]\!]$ be sharings held on wires in branch 1. Suppose the parties wish to compute both $[\![a^0 b^0]\!]$ and $[\![a^1 b^1]\!]$. Despite the fact that the parties compute two AND gates, they need only two 1-out-of-2 OTs. Let t denote the active branch. Hence, $a^{\bar{t}}$ and $b^{\bar{t}}$ are both 0.

Observe the following equalities:

$$(a^t \oplus a^{\bar{t}})b^t = (a^t \oplus 0)b^t = a^t b^t$$
$$(a^t \oplus a^{\bar{t}})b^{\bar{t}} = (a^t \oplus 0)0 = 0$$

Thus computing both $[\![(a^t \oplus a^{\bar{t}})b^t]\!]$ and $[\![(a^t \oplus a^{\bar{t}})b^{\bar{t}}]\!]$, propagates the invariant: the active branch receives the correct sharing while the inactive branch receives $[\![0]\!]$. These products reduce to a vector-scalar product computable by a VS gate (see Fig. 1).

$$[\![(a^t \oplus a^{\bar{t}})(b^t, b^{\bar{t}})]\!]$$

Thus, MOTIF computes two AND gates for the price of one. This improvement generalizes to an arbitrary number of branches.

---

[2] MOTIF does not natively support NOT gates because they would break the invariant: NOT maps $[\![0]\!]$ to $[\![1]\!]$. NOT gates can be implemented by XOR gates together with a distinguished wire that holds $[\![1]\!]$ on the active branch and $[\![0]\!]$ on the inactive branch.

TripleGen Functionality:

- INPUT: Parties $P_1, ..., P_p$ provide no input.
- OUTPUT: Let $a, b \in_\$ \{0, 1\}$ be uniform bits. Parties output uniform sharings $[\![a]\!]$, $[\![b]\!]$, and $[\![ab]\!]$.

Fig. 2. The Beaver Triple preprocessing functionality, **TripleGen**.

Branch Layer Alignment. As discussed in Sect. 1.2, the MOTIF protocol is dependent on circuit topology. The less *aligned* the layers of the branches are (branches that are highly aligned have similar numbers of AND gates in each layer), the less the circuit benefits from MOTIF.

In the above example, the parties issued two OTs to implement the two AND gates simultaneously. The parties can only perform this optimization if *inputs for both gates are available*. If not, the parties cannot amortize the OTs. Hence, gates in different layers cannot share OTs in layer-by-layer evaluation.

In the p-party protocol, in each layer MOTIF eliminates all OTs except for the total of $p(p-1) \cdot \max(w^i)$ OTs, where w^i is the number of AND gates in the current layer of branch i. In contrast, our technique does not depend on the circuit's topology and is always proportional only to the circuit's longest execution path.

2.5 Semi-honest Triple-Based Protocol Review

In this work, we amortize Beaver triples across conditional branches. We thus review how triples enable non-linear operations over XOR sharings.

Suppose the parties hold sharings $[\![x]\!]$ and $[\![y]\!]$ and wish to compute a uniform sharing $[\![xy]\!]$. Suppose further that the parties have a Beaver triple: they have three uniform sharings $[\![a]\!], [\![b]\!], [\![ab]\!]$ where $a, b \in_\$ \{0, 1\}$ are uniform bits unknown to any strict subset of parties. First, the parties locally compute $[\![a \oplus x]\!]$ and $[\![b \oplus y]\!]$, then reconstruct the semantic values $a \oplus x$ and $b \oplus y$ by broadcasting shares. This is secure: $a \oplus x$ leaks nothing about x because a is uniform and secret (and similarly for y). The parties can now compute $[\![xy]\!]$ as follows:

$$(a \oplus x)(b \oplus y) \oplus (a \oplus x)[\![b]\!] \oplus (b \oplus y)[\![a]\!] \oplus [\![ab]\!] = [\![xy]\!]$$

This protocol is simple and efficient: the parties broadcast only two bits per AND gate. However, because the triple values a and b are used as one-time-pads on semantic values, one triple is typically needed per gate. Thus, the parties must preprocess many triples according to the functionality in Fig. 2. Computing this functionality is often the most expensive step in triple-based protocols. For example, triples might be achieved via the classic GMW protocol, requiring $p(p-1)$ OTs per triple. In this work, we show a technique that re-uses triples across conditional branches and hence decreases overall cost.

3   Related Work

We review related work, focusing on works that optimize secure evaluation of conditional branches or that use multiplication triples in the malicious model. MOTIF. The most closely related work is MOTIF [HKP20]. MOTIF amortizes oblivious transfers across conditional branches in the classic semi-honest GMW protocol [GMW87]. We reviewed this approach in detail in Sect. 2.4, explained why our approach outperforms MOTIF in Sect. 1.2, and present experimental comparisons between the two approaches in Sect. 8.

Stacked Garbling. Recent works demonstrated similar conditional improvements for the garbled circuit (GC) technique [Kol18, HK20b, HK20a]. [Kol18, HK20b] reduced communication in settings where one party knows which branch is active. [Kol18] is motivated by the use case where the GC generator knows the active branch, such as when evaluating one of several database queries. [HK20b] is motivated by zero knowledge proofs. [HK20a] superceded these prior works and for the first time showed that communication can be greatly improved even if *no party* knows which branch is active.

These works' "stacking" technique does not have an obvious analog for interactive multiparty protocols, so different techniques are needed, such as explored in [HKP20] and in this work. However, our approach follows the basic idea of *material re-use* introduced by Stacked Garbling: the expensive material is safely re-used in the (possibly incorrect) evaluation of inactive branches, whose output is obliviously discarded

Universal Circuits. We improve branching via cryptographic techniques. Another approach instead recompiles conditionals into a new form. Universal circuits (UCs) are programmable constructions that can evaluate any circuit up to a given size n. Branches can be compiled to one UC, potentially amortizing cost. At runtime, the UC can be programmed to compute the active branch.

Decades after Valiant's original work [Val76], UC enjoyed renewed interest due to its relevance to MPC, and UC constructions have steadily improved [KS08, LMS16, GKS17, AGKS19, KS16, ZYZL18]. Even with these improvements, representing conditional branches with UCs is often impractical. The state-of-the-art UC construction applied to a circuit with n gates still has factor $3 \log n$ overhead [LYZ+20]. Thus, UC-based conditional evaluation is often more expensive than simply evaluating the condition naïvely. UC-based branching is superceded by cryptographic techniques such as Stacked Garbling, MOTIF, and this work.

Maliciously Secure Triple-Based Protocols. We present an improved triple-based semi-honest protocol. Two exciting and related lines of work explore triple-based protocols in the malicious model. These two lines differ primarily in how they preprocess triples. One line generates triples using homomorphic encryption [BDOZ11, DPSZ12, DKL+13, KPR18] while another generates them using oblivious transfer [NNOB12, LOS14, FKOS15, KOS16, CDE+18]. To achieve malicious security, these methods rely on expensive primitives such as zero knowledge proofs and cut-and-choose. As a result, preprocessing is expensive.

Amortizing triples in these protocols would be an important improvement. While we make no claims in the malicious model, malicious improvements have historically been preceded by similar improvements in the semi-honest model. We leave investigating triple amortization in the malicious model as future work.

4   Technical Overview

As reviewed in Sect. 2.5, Beaver triples can efficiently and securely implement AND gates. In general, triples cannot be re-used, and hence a circuit with b branches each with n AND gates typically requires $n \cdot b$ triples.

As discussed in Sect. 1.1, our key observation is that triples *can* be re-used across conditional branches, as long as uniform XOR masks are *additionally* applied. These masks allow us to re-use the same triple to compute b gates across b branches. Thus b branches each with n gates require only n triples, improving the number of needed triples by factor b. Our technique does require the parties to hold additional shared per-branch masks, but these masks are computed cheaply.

This section presents our protocol, Π_{MT} (the 'masked triple protocol'), with detail sufficient to understand our contribution. Π_{MT} securely computes Boolean circuits among p parties, re-uses triples across conditional branches, and is secure against the semi-honest corruption of up to $p-1$ parties. Full formal algorithms, with accompanying proofs of correctness and security, are in Sect. 5.

4.1   Re-Using Beaver Triples

For simplicity, consider only two branches, C^0 and C^1 and, without loss of generality, let C^0 be the active branch. The parties re-use the same set of triples for both branches. For the inactive branch, the parties will mask the triples with sharings of uniform bits; on the active branch the parties will mask the triples with sharings of zeros.

Suppose the parties hold sharings $[\![x^0]\!], [\![y^0]\!]$ on branch 0 and $[\![x^1]\!], [\![y^1]\!]$ on branch 1. Suppose further that they wish to obliviously compute one of $[\![x^0y^0]\!]$ or $[\![x^1y^1]\!]$, depending on which branch is active. Let $[\![a]\!], [\![b]\!], [\![ab]\!]$ be a uniform preprocessed triple. On the active branch, the parties mask $[\![a]\!]$ and $[\![b]\!]$ with uniform sharings of 0:

$$[\![a]\!] \oplus [\![0]\!] = [\![a]\!] \qquad [\![b]\!] \oplus [\![0]\!] = [\![b]\!]$$

The parties use this masked triple to compute branch 0's AND gate normally: the parties compute and reconstruct $a \oplus x^0$ and $b \oplus y^0$, and then locally compute the correct product:

$$(a \oplus x^0)(b \oplus y^0) \oplus (a \oplus x^0)[\![b]\!] \oplus (b \oplus y^0)[\![a]\!] \oplus [\![ab]\!] = [\![x^0y^0]\!]$$

MaskGen Functionality:

- PARAMETERS: The size of output bitstrings n.
- INPUT: Parties $P_1, ..., P_p$ provide no private input.
- OUTPUT: Let $s \in_\$ \{0,1\}$ be a uniform bit. Let $r \in_\$ \{0,1\}^n$ be a uniform bitstring. Parties output $[\![s]\!]$ as well as the pair:

$$M^0, M^1 = \begin{cases} [\![0^n]\!], [\![r]\!] & \text{if } s = 0 \\ [\![r]\!], [\![0^n]\!] & \text{otherwise} \end{cases}$$

All output sharings are uniform.

Fig. 3. The MaskGen functionality provides parties with the pairs of masks needed to implement our optimization. The functionality computes two shared bitstrings. One bitstring is the all zero bitstring while the other is uniform. The two strings are swapped according to s, and the parties are given $[\![s]\!]$.

In contrast, on the inactive branch the parties mask their shares with uniform bits. Let $r, s \in_\$ \{0,1\}$ be two such bits and let the parties hold uniform sharings $[\![r]\!]$, $[\![s]\!]$. The parties compute:

$$[\![a]\!] \oplus [\![r]\!] = [\![a \oplus r]\!] \qquad [\![b]\!] \oplus [\![s]\!] = [\![b \oplus s]\!]$$

When the parties use this masked triple, they compute and reconstruct $a \oplus r \oplus x^1$ and $b \oplus s \oplus y^1$, and then locally compute the following expression:

$$(a \oplus r \oplus x^1)(b \oplus s \oplus y^1) \oplus (a \oplus r \oplus x^1)[\![b \oplus s]\!] \oplus (b \oplus s \oplus y^1)[\![a \oplus r]\!] \oplus [\![ab]\!]$$

The above expression does not correctly compute $[\![x^1 y^1]\!]$, but this is irrelevant since all computations performed in the inactive branch are ultimately discarded by the circuit's conditional behavior.

Now, consider the security of the above re-use. As discussed above, each party views the following reconstructed semantic values:

$$a \oplus x^0 \quad b \oplus y^0 \quad a \oplus r \oplus x^1 \quad b \oplus s \oplus y^1$$

Because a, b, r, s are all uniform, this view is simulated by four uniform bits. Thus, our approach is secure. See Sect. 5.3 for a formal proof.

Although we have shown that mask sharings allow triple amortization, we have not discussed how these sharings are computed. Figure 3 formalizes MaskGen, a preprocessing functionality that computes strings of masks M^0 and M^1 such that (1) the parties receive a uniform sharing $[\![s]\!]$ where $s \in_\$ \{0,1\}$, (2) M^s is a uniform sharing of all zeros, and (3) $M^{\bar{s}}$ is a uniform sharing of random bits. During the preprocessing phase, the parties use MaskGen to preprocess strings with size sufficient to mask each triple. We formalize and prove secure Π_{MT} in the MaskGen-hybrid (and TripleGen-hybrid) model. Instantiations of MaskGen are provided and proved secure in Sect. 6.

Entering a Conditional. MaskGen constructs two bitstrings that are ordered according to a uniform bit s (the parties hold a uniform sharing $[\![s]\!]$). To use our approach, the parties need to appropriately 'line up' the masks with the branches: the active branch should use the all zeros mask and the inactive branch should use the uniform mask. We assume the parties have explicit access to a sharing of the *branch condition*: the parties hold $[\![t]\!]$. Upon entering the conditional, the parties compute $[\![s \oplus t]\!]$ and then broadcast their shares to reconstruct $s \oplus t$. If $s \oplus t$ is 0, the parties do nothing. Otherwise, they locally swap their respective shares of the strings M^0 and M^1. After performing this conditional swap, the parties are assured that M^t is the all zeros mask and $M^{\bar{t}}$ is uniform. Note, $s \oplus t$ does not reveal the active branch t because s is uniform.

Exiting a Conditional. Exiting conditionals is performed using ordinary Boolean logic. Let $[\![x^0]\!]$, $[\![x^1]\!]$ be corresponding output sharings from the two branches. We leave the branch by multiplexing each such pair of outputs: we compute $[\![x^0 \oplus t(x^0 \oplus x^1)]\!] = [\![x^t]\!]$. Thus, multiplexing requires one AND gate per conditional output.

4.2 Nested Branches

We have presented a technique for handling conditionals with only two branches. To generalize to higher branching factors, we *nest* conditionals. At each conditional, we use MaskGen to generate fresh masks and then apply these masks to the (possibly already masked) triples. This trivially and securely allows us to handle arbitrary branching control flow.

As a brief argument of security, consider that each branch uses a distinct mask string from each of its parent conditionals. Further, if the branch is inactive (1) at least one mask string will be uniform and (2) the XOR sum of all uniform mask strings for the branch is *unique*. Thus, all AND gate broadcasts can be simulated by uniform bits. We argue this more formally in Sect. 5.3.

We note that instead of nesting, it is possible to generalize our approach to directly handle vectors of conditionals, e.g., corresponding to program switch statements. This direction is not necessarily preferable: for a circuit with b branches, both techniques amortize a triple across up to b gates, and the work required to generate masks is very similar. We present the nested formalization due to its generality and relative simplicity.

5 Π_{MT}: Formalization and Proofs

We now present Π_{MT} formally. Section 5.1 begins by defining circuit syntax, including circuits with explicit conditional branching. We then specify our protocol in Sect. 5.2 and prove it correct and secure in Sect. 5.3.

5.1   Circuit Formal Syntax

Conditional branching is central to our approach. Thus, traditional circuits that include only low-level gates are insufficient for our formalization. We instead use the syntax of [HK20a] which makes explicit conditional branching. We review and formally present their syntax.

Conventionally, a circuit is a list of Boolean gates together with specified input and output wires. We refer to this representation as a *netlist*. We do not modify the semantics of netlists and evaluate them using the standard triple-based technique (see Sect. 2.5).

We extend the space of circuits with notion of a *conditional*. A conditional is parameterized over two circuits, C^0 and C^1. By convention, the first bit of input to the conditional is the branch condition t. The semantics of a conditional is that branch C^t is given the remaining input to the overall conditional, and C^t's output is returned.

Finally, we require an extra notion that allows us to place conditionals 'in the middle' of the overall circuit. A *sequence* is parameterized over two circuits C' and C''. When executed, the sequence passes its input to C', feeds the output of C' as input to C'', then returns the output of C''.

More formally, the space of circuits $\mathcal{C}$ is defined inductively. Let C^0, C^1, C', C'' be arbitrary circuits. The space of circuits is defined as follows:

$$\mathcal{C} \triangleq Netlist(\cdot) \mid Cond(C^0, C^1) \mid Seq(C', C'')$$

That is, a circuit is either a (1) netlist, a (2) conditional, or a (3) sequence. By arbitrarily nesting conditionals and sequences, we may achieve complex branching control structure.

5.2 Π_{MT} Formalization

Figure 4 presents our protocol for handling circuits with conditional branching. Π_{MT} first delegates to $\mathtt{TripleGen}$, generating sufficient multiplication triples to handle the circuit, and then delegates to the sub-protocol $\mathtt{eval}$. $\mathtt{eval}$ recursively walks the structure of the circuit and securely achieves circuit semantics.

Π_{MT} formalizes the ideas stated in Sect. 4 in a natural manner. The most interesting case in $\mathtt{eval}$ is the handling of conditionals, where we (1) invoke the $\mathtt{MaskGen}$ oracle, (2) mask the available triples, and (3) recursively evaluate both branches. Although we for clarity write $\mathtt{MaskGen}$ inline, the actual $\mathtt{MaskGen}$ protocol does not depend on any circuit values, and thus can be moved to a preprocessing phase. After evaluating both branches, we discard the inactive branch outputs and propagate the active branch outputs via a *multiplexer*. The multiplexer is implemented simply as a netlist, and computes the following function for each corresponding pair of branch outputs $[\![x^0]\!], [\![x^1]\!]$:

$$[\![x^0 \oplus t(x^0 \oplus x^1)]\!] = [\![x^t]\!] \tag{1}$$

For simplicity, we abstract some algorithms and briefly describe them below. Other than Π_{Base}, which is discussed in Sect. 2.5, we do not write these algorithms in full, as they are simple.

Functionality:

- PARAMETERS: A circuit $C \in \mathcal{C}$.
- INPUT: Each party P_i inputs a private bitstring $\boldsymbol{inp}_i \in \{0,1\}^*$.
- OUTPUT: Each party P_i outputs $C(\boldsymbol{inp}_1, ..., \boldsymbol{inp}_p)$.

Semi-Honest Protocol:

$\Pi_{\text{MT}}(C, \boldsymbol{inp}_1, ..., \boldsymbol{inp}_p):$

$\quad [\![\boldsymbol{inp}]\!] \leftarrow \text{shareinput}(\boldsymbol{inp}_1, ..., \boldsymbol{inp}_p)$

$\quad [\![\boldsymbol{triples}]\!] \leftarrow \text{TripleGen}(\text{neededtriples}(C))$

$\quad [\![\boldsymbol{out}]\!] \leftarrow \text{eval}(C, [\![\boldsymbol{triples}]\!], [\![\boldsymbol{inp}]\!])$

$\quad \text{return reconstruct}([\![\boldsymbol{out}]\!])$

$\text{eval}(C, [\![\boldsymbol{triples}]\!], [\![\boldsymbol{inp}]\!]):$

$\quad \text{switch } C:$

$\quad\quad \text{case Sequence}(C', C''):$

$\quad\quad\quad \triangleright$ Parse $[\![\boldsymbol{triples}]\!]$ into parts of sufficient length for each circuit.

$\quad\quad\quad [\![\boldsymbol{triples'}]\!], [\![\boldsymbol{triples''}]\!] \leftarrow [\![\boldsymbol{triples}]\!]$

$\quad\quad\quad \text{return eval}(C'', [\![\boldsymbol{triples''}]\!], \text{eval}(C', [\![\boldsymbol{triples'}]\!], [\![\boldsymbol{inp}]\!]))$

$\quad\quad \text{case Cond}(C^0, C^1):$

$\quad\quad\quad \triangleright$ Parse $[\![\boldsymbol{triples}]\!]$ into triples for the conditional and for the multiplexer.

$\quad\quad\quad [\![\boldsymbol{triples}_{cond}]\!], [\![\boldsymbol{triples}_{mux}]\!] \leftarrow [\![\boldsymbol{triples}]\!]$

$\quad\quad\quad \triangleright$ Split the branch condition t from the other branch inputs.

$\quad\quad\quad \triangleright$ By convention, the first input wire is the condition bit.

$\quad\quad\quad [\![t]\!], [\![\boldsymbol{inp}_{cond}]\!] \leftarrow [\![\boldsymbol{inp}]\!]$

$\quad\quad\quad [\![M^0]\!], [\![M^1]\!], [\![s]\!] \leftarrow \text{MaskGen}(2 \cdot |[\![\boldsymbol{triples}_{cond}]\!]|)$

$\quad\quad\quad (s \oplus t) \leftarrow \text{reconstruct}([\![s]\!] \oplus [\![t]\!])$

$\quad\quad\quad (M^0, M^1) \leftarrow \text{if } (s \oplus t) \text{ then } (M^1, M^0) \text{ else } (M^0, M^1)$

$\quad\quad\quad [\![\boldsymbol{out}^0]\!] \leftarrow \text{eval}(C^0, \text{applymask}(M^0, [\![\boldsymbol{triples}_{cond}]\!]), [\![\boldsymbol{inp}_{cond}]\!])$

$\quad\quad\quad [\![\boldsymbol{out}^1]\!] \leftarrow \text{eval}(C^1, \text{applymask}(M^1, [\![\boldsymbol{triples}_{cond}]\!]), [\![\boldsymbol{inp}_{cond}]\!])$

$\quad\quad\quad \text{return mux}([\![t]\!], [\![\boldsymbol{out}^0]\!], [\![\boldsymbol{out}^1]\!], [\![\boldsymbol{triples}_{mux}]\!])$

$\quad\quad \text{case Netlist}(g_1, ..., g_k):$

$\quad\quad\quad \triangleright$ Evaluate with a standard triple-based protocol.

$\quad\quad\quad \text{return } \Pi_{\text{Base}}((g_1, ..., g_k), [\![\boldsymbol{triples}]\!], [\![\boldsymbol{inp}]\!])$

Fig. 4. Π_{MT} allows p parties to securely compute a circuit $C \in \mathcal{C}$. Π_{MT} delegates to a recursive sub-procecure eval.

- $\Pi_{\texttt{Base}}$ is the standard triple-based protocol as specified in Sect. 2.5. $\Pi_{\texttt{Base}}$ takes as input (1) a vector of gates $(g_1, ..., g_k)$, (2) a vector of (possibly masked) triples $[\![\boldsymbol{triples}]\!]$ and (3) the netlist input $[\![\boldsymbol{inp}]\!]$. $\Pi_{\texttt{Base}}$ returns a sharing of outputs $[\![\boldsymbol{out}]\!]$.
  We emphasize that while we do not, for simplicity, explicitly list $\Pi_{\texttt{Base}}$, the protocol *is not* a black-box functionality.[3]
- `neededtriples` computes the number of needed triples for the circuit C. This computed number is equal to the number of AND gates on the circuit's longest execution path.
- `shareinput` allows the parties to construct and distribute sharings of their respective private inputs.
- `reconstruct` allows parties to reconstruct a sharing via broadcast.
- `mux` computes the per-output multiplexer function (Eq. 1).
- `applymask` specifies how mask sharings are XORed onto triples. Specifically, for each uniformly shared triple $[\![a]\!]$, $[\![b]\!]$, $[\![c]\!]$, we draw two bits from the mask sharing and XOR one bit onto both $[\![a]\!]$ and $[\![b]\!]$.

5.3 Π_{MT} Proofs

Now that we have introduced Π_{MT}, we prove it both correct and secure in the `MaskGen`- and `TripleGen`-hybrid model. We instantiate `MaskGen` in Sect. 6.

In both proofs, we refer to the notion of a *valid* triple. A triple is valid if it is uniformly shared and of the following form: $[\![a]\!]$, $[\![b]\!]$, $[\![ab]\!]$. That is, the third term is a share of the product of the first two terms. An *invalid* triple is a triple $[\![a]\!]$, $[\![b]\!]$, $[\![c]\!]$ such that $c \neq ab$. Invalid triples arise in our protocol due to the application of extra masks to the first two entries in triples.

Theorem 1 (Π_{MT} correctness). *For all circuits $C \in \mathcal{C}$ and all private inputs $\boldsymbol{inp}_1, ..., \boldsymbol{inp}_p \in \{0, 1\}^*$:*

$$\Pi_{\mathsf{MT}}(C, \boldsymbol{inp}_1, ..., \boldsymbol{inp}_p) = C(\boldsymbol{inp}_1, ..., \boldsymbol{inp}_p)$$

Proof. By induction on the structure of C. The inductive invariant is as follows:

If the triples passed to `eval` are valid, then `eval` correctly implements the semantics of C.

We focus on conditionals; the correctness of netlists follows trivially from the standard triple-based protocol. The correctness of sequences is immediate.

Suppose C is a conditional $Cond(C^0, C^1)$. Further, suppose $[\![t]\!]$ is the branch condition. If the triples passed to the conditional are invalid, then the inductive invariant vacuously holds. Thus, we need only consider evaluation of a conditional on valid triples. The oracle call to `MaskGen` constructs two mask strings

---

[3] We cannot support $\Pi_{\texttt{Base}}$ as a black-box because it is possible to implement a protocol that securely handles netlists, but that is insecure when given *masked* triples. For example, the parties could out-of-band check the validity of triples and reveal all inputs if the triples are found invalid. Therefore, $\Pi_{\texttt{Base}}$ is a white-box protocol.

M^0, M^1 such that M^s is all-zero and $M^{\bar{s}}$ is uniform. By reconstructing $s \oplus t$ and accordingly locally swapping the two mask strings, the parties ensure M^t is the all-zero string. Thus, C^t is given valid triples (the valid triples are masked by sharings of zeros and hence remain valid) and, by induction, returns the correct semantic outputs. $C^{\bar{t}}$ will not return correct values, but these outputs are discarded by the multiplexer. Thus, conditionals support the inductive invariant.

The top level circuit is given valid triples via the oracle call to TripleGen. This fact, combined with the inductive invariant, implies that Π_{MT} is correct. □

Theorem 2 (Π_{MT} security). Π_{MT} *is secure against semi-honest corruption of up to $p-1$ parties in the* TripleGen*-hybrid and* MaskGen*-hybrid model.*

Proof. By construction of a simulator for one party, which we later generalize to simulate up to $p-1$ parties. Each broadcast received by a party can be simulated by a uniform bit.[4] We prove this simulation secure by induction on the structure of the circuit C. The inductive invariant is as follows:

Let $[\![a]\!], [\![b]\!], [\![c]\!]$ be a (possibly invalid) triple. For each triple, we refer to the semantic values a and b as the *one-time-pad* parts. eval uses both one-time-pad parts of each triple to mask at most one cleartext value.

For netlists, this is trivial: we use a distinct triple for each AND gate, and each one-time-pad part is used only to mask one of the gate inputs. Similarly, sequences satisfy the inductive invariant trivially: we provide different triples to both parts of the sequence.

Therefore we focus on conditionals. Consider a conditional $Cond(C^0, C^1)$. As a brief aside from proving that the inductive invariant holds, while the parties reconstruct $s \oplus t$, s is uniform, and hence this leaks nothing about t (i.e., $s \oplus t$ can be simulated by a uniform bit). Now, returning to the invariant: We first split the triples into sufficient numbers for the conditional body and for the multiplexer. The multiplexer is implemented by a netlist, and hence trivially satisfies our invariant. The conditional body is more complicated. Indeed, we use the same triples to evaluate both branches. However, our call to MaskGen together with the conditional swap ensures that $M^{\bar{t}}$ is a sharing of uniform bits. When we apply $M^{\bar{t}}$ to the triples, we re-randomize the one-time-pad parts of the triples. (Note, applying M^t (the all zeros mask) has no effect on the one-time-pad parts.) Thus, we provide independent one-time-pad parts to both C^0 and C^1, satisfying the inductive invariant.

Because each one-time-pad part is (1) uniform and (2) used to mask at most one cleartext value, and because each broadcast is masked by a one-time-pad part, each broadcast can be simulated by a uniform bit. Thus, we can simulate a single party's view.

---

[4] One caveat is that broadcasts used to reconstruct the circuit's outputs must XOR to the correct output value. The simulator must arrange the simulated output broadcasts such that they appropriately add up. This is typical in MPC proofs and is easy to set up.

The generalization from simulating one party to simulating up to $p-1$ is based on a simple observation about XOR secret shares: the view of $p-1$ parties holds no more information than the share of 1 party. The remaining broadcasts from the remaining, unsimulated parties can be simulated by uniform bits.

Π_{MT} is secure against semi-honest corruption of up to $p-1$ parties.   □

Some MPC techniques, e.g., computing multiplicative inverse [BIB89], rely on opening (randomized) intermediate values. This may not always be compatible with our optimization, since our randomization of the inactive branch may cause an invalid opened value, thereby revealing that it was in fact inactive.

6   Semi-Honest MaskGen Instantiations

In this section, we instantiate MaskGen (Fig. 3). We present three protocols, two formally and one informally, that follow two general approaches:

1. The first approach is generic in that it works for an arbitrary number of parties and is based on vector scalar multiplication (Sect. 2.3). Since our approach often uses long masks, we introduce a useful trick that improves vector scalar multiplication for long vectors.
2. In special cases, masks can be more efficiently derived starting from short seeds. We present two and three-party protocols which require communication proportional only to κ rather than to the mask length n.

6.1 p-Party Mask Generation

Our general mask generation technique, Π-MaskGen-VS (Fig. 5), allows p parties to preprocess length-n masks using only a single VS gate.

In this protocol, parties jointly sample a uniform sharing of a uniform bit $[\![s]\!]$ and a uniform bitstring $[\![r]\!]$. The parties compute $[\![sr]\!]$ via a VS gate, set the first mask to $[\![M^0]\!] = [\![sr]\!]$, and set the second mask to $[\![M^1]\!] = [\![sr]\!] \oplus [\![r]\!]$.

Π-MaskGen-VS is correct and secure.

Theorem 3. Π-MaskGen-VS *correctly implements* MaskGen.

Proof. s and r are uniform. Depending on s, the product sr is, of course, either all zeros or r. Thus, setting $[\![M^0]\!] = [\![sr]\!]$ and $[\![M^1]\!] = [\![sr]\!] \oplus [\![r]\!]$ places the all zeros mask in M^s.   □

Theorem 4. Π-MaskGen-VS *is secure against semi-honest corruption of up to* $p-1$ *parties in the* VS*-hybrid model.*

Proof. We communicate only once: when evaluating a single VS gate. Hence, the simulator is trivially constructed from the VS gate simulator.   □

Functionality:

 – Parties $P_1, \ldots, P_p$ compute MaskGen.

Semi-Honest Protocol:

       ▷ n is the output mask length.

      Π-MaskGen-VS(n) :

        ▷ Parties jointy sample r and s.

      $[\![r]\!] \in_\$ \{0,1\}^n$

      $[\![s]\!] \in_\$ \{0,1\}$

      $[\![sr]\!] \leftarrow [\![s]\!][\![r]\!]$ ▷ Computed via VS gate.

      $[\![M^0]\!] \leftarrow [\![sr]\!]$

      $[\![M^1]\!] \leftarrow [\![sr]\!] \oplus [\![r]\!]$

        ▷ M^s is all zeros, $M^{\bar{s}}$ is uniform.

      return $[\![s]\!]$, $[\![M^0]\!]$, $[\![M^1]\!]$

Fig. 5. Protocol Π-MaskGen-VS is our default method for generating masks, and is secure for an arbitrary number of parties.

Vector Scalar Multiplication for Long Vectors. We have shown that VS gates can efficiently compute pairs of masks. However, this requires us to evaluate VS gates over potentially long vectors: we compute VS gates over vectors with length proportional to the number of AND gates, which can be arbitrarily high.

As discussed in Sect. 2.3, we decompose vector scalar products into summands, some that are computed locally and others that are computed interactively. For each interactive summand, one party holds a bit a, one a vector b, and the two must jointly compute $[\![ab]\!]$. Let n be the length of b. To compute this product, the protocol presented by [HKP20] requires *two* messages of length n. In this section, we introduce a natural trick, Π-Half-VS-Long, that reduces this communication cost by half: only one message of length n need be sent, and the other can be derived from a pseudo-random seed. Both the functionality and the protocol are listed in Fig. 6. We explain the Π-Half-VS-Long trick in more detail in our proof of correctness. Our trick is similar to techniques in [KK13, ALSZ13]. Recall (from Sect. 2.3) that $p(p-1)$ interactive summands emerge from a single vector scalar multiplication. Thus, we can compose a full vector scalar multiplication protocol from $p(p-1)$ calls to Π-Half-VS-Long. We refer to this full protocol as Π-VS-Long.

Theorem 5. Π-Half-VS-Long, *and hence* Π-VS-Long, *is correct.*

Proof. The key observation is that P_1's input bit a determines one of two possible outcomes for the vector scalar multiplication. If $a = 0$, the output is a sharing of all zeros. In this case, P_1 and P_2's output shares must XOR to zeros. If $a = 1$, the output is a sharing of P_2's input vector b.

Functionality:

- INPUT: Party P_1 inputs a private bit a, P_2 inputs a private vector $\boldsymbol{b}$.
- OUTPUT: Parties output a uniform sharing $[\![ab]\!]$.

Semi-Honest Protocol:

$\Pi\text{-}\mathtt{Half}\text{-}\mathtt{VS}\text{-}\mathtt{Long}(a, \boldsymbol{b})$:

P_1 :	P_2 :
	$\boldsymbol{S} \in_\$ \{0,1\}^\kappa$
	▷ P_2 expands $\boldsymbol{S}$ to get his share of $\boldsymbol{ab}$.
	$(\boldsymbol{ab})_2 \leftarrow G(\boldsymbol{S})$
	$\boldsymbol{k} \in_\$ \{0,1\}^\kappa$
	▷ P_2 sends $G(\boldsymbol{k}) \oplus ((\boldsymbol{ab})_2 \oplus \boldsymbol{b})$ to P_1.
	$\boldsymbol{v} \leftarrow G(\boldsymbol{k}) \oplus ((\boldsymbol{ab})_2 \oplus \boldsymbol{b})$
$\boldsymbol{v} \leftarrow \mathtt{recv}(P_2)$	$\mathtt{send}(\boldsymbol{v}, P_1)$
▷ P_1 and P_2 run OT.	
▷ P_1 is the OT receiver.	▷ P_2 is the OT sender.
$\boldsymbol{w} \leftarrow \mathtt{OT}_{\mathtt{recv}}(a)$	$\mathtt{OT}_{\mathtt{send}}(\boldsymbol{S}, \boldsymbol{k})$
▷ $\boldsymbol{w} = a(\boldsymbol{S} \oplus \boldsymbol{k}) \oplus \boldsymbol{S}$.	
▷ If $a = 0$, $G(\boldsymbol{w}) = G(\boldsymbol{S}) = (\boldsymbol{ab})_2$.	
▷ If $a = 1$, $G(\boldsymbol{w}) \oplus \boldsymbol{v} = G(\boldsymbol{k}) \oplus \boldsymbol{v}$.	
$= (\boldsymbol{ab})_2 \oplus \boldsymbol{b}$.	
$(\boldsymbol{ab})_1 \leftarrow G(\boldsymbol{w}) \oplus a\boldsymbol{v}$	
$\mathtt{return}\ (\boldsymbol{ab})_1$	$\mathtt{return}\ (\boldsymbol{ab})_2$

Fig. 6. $\Pi\text{-}\mathtt{Half}\text{-}\mathtt{VS}\text{-}\mathtt{Long}$ can be used to evaluate the interactive subterms that emerge from computing a VS gate.

We achieve this functionality with a single 1-out-of-2 OT of length κ strings. P_1 acts as the OT receiver and uses as her choice bit a. If $a = 0$, P_1 receives the seed that P_2 used to generate her share. P_1 expands this seed and obtains the same share as P_2. If $a = 1$, P_1 receives a key that helps him to decrypt a ciphertext sent separately by P_2. The ciphertext holds a valid share of $\boldsymbol{b}$.

The correctness of $\Pi\text{-}\mathtt{VS}\text{-}\mathtt{Long}$ is immediate from the correctness of $\Pi\text{-}\mathtt{Half}\text{-}\mathtt{VS}\text{-}\mathtt{Long}$ and [HKP20]'s VS instantiation. $\qquad\square$

Next, we prove this faster vector scalar multiplication procedure secure. Ideally, we would modularly prove $\Pi\text{-}\mathtt{Half}\text{-}\mathtt{VS}\text{-}\mathtt{Long}$ and $\Pi\text{-}\mathtt{VS}\text{-}\mathtt{Long}$ secure by simulation. Unfortunately, this is not possible. Specifically, suppose that in $\Pi\text{-}\mathtt{Half}\text{-}\mathtt{VS}\text{-}\mathtt{Long}$ P_1 provides input $a = 0$. In this case, P_1 outputs the expansion of the pseudorandom seed $\boldsymbol{w}$ received by the OT oracle. Now we need to simulate $\boldsymbol{w}$ that matches the expansion $G(\boldsymbol{w})$ output by the protocol. Since G is assumed secure, this simulation is infeasible. Therefore, we forego modularity, and instead prove the security of our top level circuit protocol, Π_{MT}, but where we instantiate the MaskGen functionality based on Π-VS-Long. With our PRG-utilizing subprocedures 'inlined', we can prove the top-level protocol secure, since the expansions of PRG seeds no longer appear as protocol outputs and we can simulate the seeds simply by random strings.

Theorem 6. *Let* Π-MaskGen-VS' *be the protocol* Π-MaskGen-VS *(Fig. 5), with* VS *instantiated by* Π-VS-Long. *Let* Π'_{MT} *be the protocol* Π_{MT} *(Fig. 4), with* MaskGen *instantiated by* Π-MaskGen-VS'. Π'_{MT} *is secure against semi-honest corruption of up to* $p-1$ *parties in the* TripleGen-*hybrid and OT-hybrid model.*

Proof. By construction of a simulator.

The proof is similar to that of Theorem 2, so we elide most details. Because we explicitly instantiate MaskGen with Π-MaskGen-VS', we focus on the corresponding difference in the proof and explain how we simulate Π-MaskGen-VS' messages. Namely, we argue that all messages of Π-MaskGen-VS' are simulated by uniform bits.

Π-MaskGen-VS' invokes Π-VS-Long, which in turn makes $2(p-1)$ per-party calls to Π-Half-VS-Long. Each pair of parties P_i, P_j jointly call Π-Half-VS-Long twice, once where P_i is the receiver and once where P_i is the sender.

When P_i is the receiver, he receives two messages:

- First, P_i receives from P_j an encrypted share of $\boldsymbol{b}$: P_j chooses a PRG seed $\boldsymbol{k}$, expands $G(\boldsymbol{k})$, and then sends $G(\boldsymbol{k}) \oplus G(\boldsymbol{S}) \oplus \boldsymbol{b}$ to P_i. The simulator can simulate this received message by uniform bits because $\boldsymbol{k}$ and $\boldsymbol{S}$ are both uniform and because G is a secure PRG.
- Second, P_i receives a message from the OT oracle. Depending on its input bit a_i, P_i receives either the seed $\boldsymbol{k}$ or the seed $\boldsymbol{S}$ (which was used to generate $(a\boldsymbol{b})_2$). In either case, $\boldsymbol{k}$ and $\boldsymbol{S}$ are simulated by a uniform string. This does not conflict with the previously simulated message $G(\boldsymbol{k}) \oplus G(\boldsymbol{S}) \oplus \boldsymbol{b}$, since one of the seeds $\boldsymbol{k}$ or $\boldsymbol{S}$ remains hidden from P_i.

If P_i is the sender, no message is received; P_i's view is trivially simulated.

It is easy to see that the masks produced by Π-MaskGen-VS' are used exactly once in Π'_{MT}, and hence the inductive invariant of Theorem 2 is maintained.

Π'_{MT} is secure.   □

6.2   Efficient 2PC and 3PC Mask Generation

In this section, we present two efficient implementations of MaskGen, one for two parties, and one for three. At a high level, these methods are based on (1) distributing pseudo-random seeds and (2) expanding the seeds with a PRG into n-bit masks. The advantage of these seed-based methods is that they use communication proportional only to κ. This is a significant improvement over Π-MaskGen-VS, which uses communication proportional to the mask length n.

Functionality:

  – Parties P_1 and P_2 compute MaskGen.

Semi-Honest Protocol:

      Π-MaskGen-2P(n) :

        $[\![s]\!] \in_\$ \{0,1\}$; $[\![S]\!] \in_\$ \{0,1\}^\kappa$

        $[\![sS]\!] \leftarrow [\![s]\!][\![S]\!]$ ▷ Computed via VS gate.

        ▷ P_1, P_2 compute uniform shares of two seeds S^0, S^1.

        $[\![S^0]\!] \leftarrow [\![sS]\!]$; $[\![S^1]\!] \leftarrow [\![sS]\!] \oplus [\![S]\!]$

        ▷ P_1, P_2 expand their PRG seeds into n-bit masks.

        $[\![M^0]\!] \leftarrow$ Π-Expand-2P$([\![S^0]\!], n)$

        $[\![M^1]\!] \leftarrow$ Π-Expand-2P$([\![S^1]\!], n)$

        ▷ M^s is all zeros, $M^{\bar{s}}$ is uniform.

        return $[\![s]\!]$, $[\![M^0]\!]$, $[\![M^1]\!]$

        ▷ P_1 and P_2 expand their respective seeds into n-bit strings.

      Π-Expand-2P$((S_1, S_2), n)$:

        P_1 : return $G(S_1, n)$ P_2 : return $G(S_2, n)$

Fig. 7. Π-MaskGen-2P is an efficient two-party protocol for generating masks.

Two Party Improved Protocol. Figure 7 presents our protocol for two parties, Π_{MT}-2P. Here, the parties use vector scalar multiplication to distribute XOR sharings of two length-κ strings; one sharing encodes a uniform string and one encodes the all zeros string. The parties then interpret their respective shares as PRG seeds and apply G. Because of the nature of XOR sharings, this means that for the all zeros sharing, the parties generate the same pseudorandom expansion, so the resultant expansions are a sharings of all zeros. In contrast, the expansion of the random sharing leads to a larger pseudorandom sharing.

By using this protocol, the two parties can share arbitrarily long masks at the cost of only $O(\kappa)$ bits of communication.

Theorem 7. Π-MaskGen-2P *correctly implements* MaskGen.

Proof. By the correctness of VS gates and properties of XOR shares.

One of $[\![S^0]\!]$ and $[\![S^1]\!]$ is a sharing of zeros while the other is a sharing of a random bitstring. The position of the all-zeros sharing is determined by a uniform bit s. Consider one such sharing, and interpret both shares as PRG seeds. If the parties' two seeds are the same, then the expanded masks will also be the same, and will therefore XOR to zeros. If the parties' two seeds differ, then, by the properties of the PRG, the expanded masks will XOR to a uniform value.

Π-MaskGen-2P is correct.   □

We next prove Π-MaskGen-2P secure. Like Π-Half-VS-Long, we unfortunately cannot modularly prove this protocol secure by simulation: each party outputs the expansion of a PRG seed that appears in the party's view. We therefore instead prove that Π_{MT} is secure in the case where we instantiate MaskGen with Π-MaskGen-2P. This higher level approach works because the output of a PRG does not appear as final output, so the PRG seeds can be simulated.

Theorem 8 (Π_{MT}-2P Security). *Let Π_{MT}-2P be Π_{MT} (Fig. 4), where we instantiate MaskGen with Π-MaskGen-2P. Π_{MT}-2P is secure against semi-honest corruption of a single party in the TripleGen-hybrid and VS-hybrid model.*

Proof. The proof is nearly identical to that of Π_{MT} (Theorem 2); we therefore focus our discussion on the call to Π-MaskGen-2P.

In Π-MaskGen-2P, the parties jointly sample uniform sharings $[\![s]\!]$ and $[\![S]\!]$, and then compute $[\![sS]\!]$ via VS. VS outputs uniform sharings, and so the message each party receives from the VS oracle is simulated by uniform bits. The parties locally expand their shares to obtain masks $[\![M^0]\!]$ and $[\![M^1]\!]$. Because G is a secure PRG, $[\![M^s]\!]$ is a sharing of a *uniform string*.

Now, recall Theorem 2's inductive invariant: we must ensure that the top-level protocol uses the one-time-pad part of each multiplication triple at most once. Π_{MT}-2P XORs the current triples with both $[\![M^0]\!]$ and $[\![M^1]\!]$. Because $[\![M^s]\!]$ is a sharing of a uniform string, this appropriately rerandomizes the triples into the inactive branch, and hence we support the inductive invariant.

Π_{MT}-2P is secure against semi-honest corruption of a single party.   □

Three Party Informal MaskGen Protocol. The three party efficient MaskGen protocol is a relatively straightforward generalization of the two party protocol. However, the mask generation is notationally complex, so for simplicity we present informally. A similar technique was used in [BKKO20] to help to construct a two-private three-server distributed point function.

Unlike the two-party protocol, P_1, P_2, and P_3 each obtain two *pairs* of seeds. Each pair is used to generate one mask by (1) expanding both seeds with a PRG into an n-bit string and (2) XORing the two expanded outputs together. At a high level, we ensure that:

1. For the all zeros mask, each party holds the same seed as one other party. Thus, their PRG expansions XOR to zeros.
2. For the uniform mask, each party holds a seed distinct from all other parties. Thus, their PRG expansions XOR to a uniform mask.

The key difficulty is in making the two above scenarios indistinguishable from the perspective of any strict subset of parties. We contrast these two scenarios, showing that they appear indistinguishable.

In the first case, the parties are given seeds as follows:

$$P_1 : \boldsymbol{S}_1, \boldsymbol{S}_2 \qquad P_2 : \boldsymbol{S}_1, \boldsymbol{S}_3 \qquad P_3 : \boldsymbol{S}_2, \boldsymbol{S}_3$$

If we consider an adversary who corrupts any two parties, he will see that one seed is shared between them and the others appear uniform.

In the second case the parties are given seeds as follows:

$$P_1 : S_4, S_5 \qquad P_2 : S_4, S_6 \qquad P_3 : S_4, S_7$$

As in the first case, an adversary that corrupts two parties sees one seed in common; the others are uniform. Hence, the cases are indistinguishable for any one or two parties.

Thus, Π_{MT} instantiated with this three party MaskGen trick results in a secure and correct protocol. Seed distribution can easily be implemented by GMW extended with VS gates: the parties sample seven uniform seeds $S_1, ..., S_7 \in_\$ \{0, 1\}^\kappa$, swap them using a VS gate, and output each of them to the appropriate party.

7   Implementation

We implemented our approach in C++. Specifically, we implemented Π_{MT}, instantiating MaskGen with both Π-MaskGen-VS and Π-MaskGen-2P (we did not implement the three-party variant). We instantiated TripleGen with the natural approach based on random OT. For comparison, we also (1) implemented a standard triple-based protocol and (2) incorporated MOTIF's implementation into our repository. We discuss key aspects of our implementation in Sect. 7.1.

To the best of our knowledge, there is no comprehensive suite of MPC benchmark circuits, particularly for circuits that include conditional branches. Thus, we implemented a random circuit generator to produce benchmarks. In designing the circuit generator, our key goal was to capture the impact of branch alignment on MOTIF's performance such that we can highlight our improvement. The circuit generator samples circuits with a variety of branch alignments. We describe details of circuit generation in Sect. 7.2.

7.1   Key Implementation Aspects

Our implementation of Π_{MT} is straightforward, but we note some of its interesting aspects. We use the 1-out-of-2 OT protocol of [IKNP03] as implemented by EMP [WMK16] in order to generate both triples and masks. In Π_{MT} and standard triple-based protocol, we list AND gates in layers so that we can parallelize broadcasts for ANDs in the same circuit layer. MOTIF similarly parallelizes OTs for VS gates in the same layer. Thus, all three protocols use communication rounds proportional to the circuit's multiplicative depth.

7.2   Random Circuit Generation

Circuit generation consists of three main steps:

1. We parameterize circuits on the numbers of conditional branches, the number of circuit layers, the number of XOR and AND gates per branch, and the number of input/output wires to each branch. Each branch uses the same parameters.

2. We uniformly assign a number of gates to each branch's layers. We implement this functionality with a RANCOM algorithm [NW78], which is based on the balls-in-cells problem and is called separately for each branch.
3. We connect the gates layer by layer. Specifically, we maintain a pool of wires whose value has already been assigned (i.e., it is a branch input or the output of a gate). For each gate, we uniformly sample two inputs from the pool and choose a fresh output wire. Once a layer has been entirely connected, we add all of that layer's gate outputs to the pool.

The above strategy is relatively ad-hoc, and may not be representative of all applications. Again, we adopt the above approach (1) to show the impact of circuit alignment on our relative performance over MOTIF and (2) because no standard benchmark suite exists.

8   Performance Evaluation

We compare Π_{MT} to MOTIF and the standard triple-based protocol. We compare these protocols for various numbers of parties. All experiments were run on a commodity laptop running Ubuntu 20.04 with an Intel(R) Core(TM) i5-8350U CPU @ 1.70 GHz and 16 GB RAM. All parties were run on the same machine and network settings were configured with the tc command. We averaged each data point over 100 runs.

In each experiment, we generated random circuits as described in Sect. 7.2. We fixed the circuit parameters to 10 layers, 30,000 AND gates per branch and 30,000 XOR gates per branch. We set the number of branch input and output wires to 128. We generated a new circuit with these same parameters for each run of each experiment. We performed and report on three experiments:

1. We fixed the number of branches to two, fixed the number of parties to two, and explore variation in performance based on branch alignment (Sect. 8.1).
2. We fixed the number of parties to two, varied the number of branches, and explore corresponding communication and wall-clock runtime (Sect. 8.2 and Sect. 8.3).
3. We fixed the branching factor to 16, varied the number of parties, and explore corresponding communication.

Each experiment shows that our approach is preferred in almost every setting.

8.1   Branch Alignment

We first demonstrate MOTIF's dependence on circuit topology in the case of two branches. Figure 8 plots the distribution of the number of random OTs needed for two parties to evaluate each protocol. Across all 100 runs, Π_{MT} and the standard

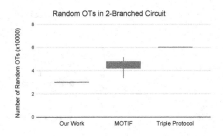

Fig. 8. Random OTs required to evaluate a circuit with two branches.

triple-based protocol always need the same number of OTs. On the other hand, MOTIF's performance differs depending on branch alignment. Because we sample alignments uniformly, this results in an increased number of consumed OTs.

Discussion. For two branches and on average, our approach required 1.5× fewer OTs than MOTIF and consistently required 2× fewer OTs than the standard triple-based protocol. Given that random OTs are the main communication bandwidth bottleneck, MOTIF is far from reducing communication by the optimal factor 2×. Π_{MT} never used more OTs than MOTIF. MOTIF's best run required 1.12× more OTs than Π_{MT} and 1.71× in the worst case.

8.2   Communication

We next report our 2PC communication improvement over both MOTIF and the standard triple-based protocol as a function of branching factor. We instantiated MaskGen with Π-MaskGen-2P.

Figure 9 plots both preprocessing communication and total communication. For further reference, Fig. 10 tabulates our communication improvement.

In our measurements, preprocessing constitutes both triple generation and mask generation. Each data point is averaged over 100 runs; the amount of communication may differ from run to run because each circuit has a randomly generated topology. In Π_{MT} the total communication is constant. In contrast, MOTIF communication differs significantly across runs due to the layering issue explained in Sect. 2.4.

Discussion. In this metric, Π_{MT} is preferred:

- **Preprocessing Communication.** On 16 branches, we improve communication by 2.96× over MOTIF and by 14.4× over the standard triple-based protocol. There are three reasons we did not achieve 16× improvement over standard triple-based protocol. First, both the standard triple-based approach and ours must perform the same number of *base OTs* to set up an OT extension matrix [IKNP03]. This adds a small amount of communication

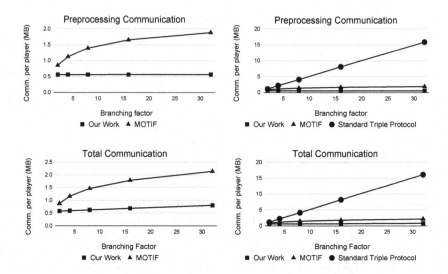

Fig. 9. 2PC comparison of Π_{MT} against `MOTIF` and a standard triple-based protocol. We plot the following metrics as functions of the *branching factor*: the preprocessing per-party communication (top), the total per-party communication (bottom).

# Branches	Π_{MT}(MB)	Π-MOTIF(MB)	Broadcast (MB)
2	0.57	0.86	1.11
4	0.58	1.16	2.19
8	0.61	1.46	4.10
16	0.67	1.79	8.19
32	0.80	2.14	16.09

Fig. 10. Per-party communication improvement for our 2PC random circuit experiment as a function of the branching factor.

(around 20KB) common to both approaches, which cuts slightly into our advantage. Second, we need one OT per each of $b - 1$ mask pairs. Third, entering and exiting conditionals have very small overhead differences.

- **Total Communication.** On 16 branches, our approach improves total communication by 2.6× over `MOTIF` and by 12× over the standard protocol. Our total communication improvement is lower than our preprocessing improvement because our evaluation phase communication is not improved. While improvement over the standard protocol is almost constant across runs, the improvement over `MOTIF` differs due to varying circuit topology: our improvement ranges from 2.16× to 2.93×.

8.3   Wall-Clock Time

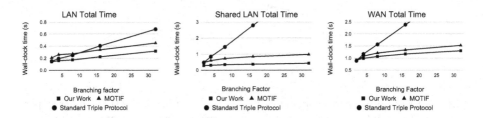

Fig. 11. 2PC comparison of Π_{MT} against MOTIF and a standard triple-based protocol. We plot the following metrics as functions of branching factor: wall-clock time on a LAN (left), the wall-clock time on a LAN where other processes share bandwidth (center), and the wall-clock time on a WAN (right).

We next present the wall-clock time improvements over MOTIF and the standard triple-based protocol. We consider three simulated network settings:

1. **LAN:** A simulated gigabit ethernet connection with 1Gbps bandwidth and 2ms round-trip latency.
2. **Shared LAN:** A simulated local area network connection where the protocol shares network bandwidth with a number of other processes. The connection features 50Mbps bandwidth and 2ms round-trip latency.
3. **WAN:** A simulated wide area network connection with 100Mbps bandwidth and 20ms round-trip latency.

Figure 11 plots total wall-clock time for each network setting.

Discussion. In these metrics, Π_{MT} is preferred:

- **LAN wall-clock time.** On a fast LAN, our approach's improvement is diminished compared to our communication improvement. On average and for 16 branches, we improve by 1.52× over MOTIF and by 1.81× over the standard protocol. A 1Gbps network is very fast, and our modest hardware struggles to keep up with available bandwidth.
- **Shared LAN wall-clock time.** On the more constrained shared LAN, our hardware easily keeps up with the communication channel, and we see corresponding improvement. On average and for 16 branches, we achieve 2.26× speedup over MOTIF and 7.43× speedup over the standard protocol.
- **WAN wall-clock time.** On this high-latency network our advantage is less pronounced. On average and for 16 branches, we achieve 1.14× speedup over MOTIF and 2.04× speedup over the standard protocol. This high-latency network highlights the weakness of multi-round protocols in such settings.

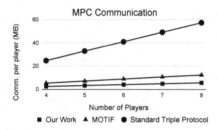

Fig. 12. Protocol per-party communication usage as a function of the number of parties. Like MOTIF and the standard protocol, we consume per-party communication linear in the number of parties.

8.4   Scaling to MPC

Our last experiment emphasizes our approach's scaling to the multiparty setting. This experiment uses the same circuit parameters as the former experiments, but we fix the number of branches to 16. We implemented Π-MaskGen-VS and ran the circuit among 4-8 parties. Figure 12 plots per-party communication as a function of the number of parties.

Discussion. Π_{MT} works well in the multiparty setting. Our optimization does not add additional costs as compared to MOTIF and standard triple-based protocol. Each technique consumes communication quadratic in the number of parties.

Acknowledgements. This work was supported in part by NSF award #1909769, by a Facebook research award, and by Georgia Tech's IISP cybersecurity seed funding (CSF) award.

References

[AGKS19] Alhassan, M.Y., Günther, D., Kiss, Á., Schneider, T.: Efficient and scalable universal circuits. Cryptology ePrint Archive, Report 2019/348 (2019). https://eprint.iacr.org/2019/348

[ALSZ13] Asharov, G., Lindell, Y., Schneider, T., Zohner, M.: More efficient oblivious transfer and extensions for faster secure computation. In: Sadeghi, A.-R., Gligor, V.D., Yung, M. (eds.) ACM CCS 2013, pp. 535–548. ACM Press, November 2013

[BCG+19] Boyle, E., Couteau, G., Gilboa, N., Ishai, Y., Kohl, L., Scholl, P.: Efficient pseudorandom correlation generators: silent OT extension and more. In: Boldyreva, A., Micciancio, D. (eds.) CRYPTO 2019. LNCS, vol. 11694, pp. 489–518. Springer, Cham (2019). https://doi.org/10.1007/978-3-030-26954-8_16

[BDOZ11] Bendlin, R., Damgård, I., Orlandi, C., Zakarias, S.: Semi-homomorphic encryption and multiparty computation. In: Paterson, K.G. (ed.) EUROCRYPT 2011. LNCS, vol. 6632, pp. 169–188. Springer, Heidelberg (2011). https://doi.org/10.1007/978-3-642-20465-4_11

[Bea92] Beaver, D.: Efficient multiparty protocols using circuit randomization. In: Feigenbaum, J. (ed.) CRYPTO 1991. LNCS, vol. 576, pp. 420–432. Springer, Heidelberg (1992). https://doi.org/10.1007/3-540-46766-1_34

[BIB89] Bar-Ilan, J., Beaver, D.: Non-cryptographic fault-tolerant computing in constant number of rounds of interaction. In: Rudnicki, P. (ed.) 8th ACM PODC, pp. 201–209. ACM, August 1989

[BKKO20] Bunn, P., Katz, J., Kushilevitz, E., Ostrovsky, R.: Efficient 3-party distributed ORAM. In: Galdi, C., Kolesnikov, V. (eds.) SCN 2020. LNCS, vol. 12238, pp. 215–232. Springer, Cham (2020). https://doi.org/10.1007/978-3-030-57990-6_11

[CDE+18] Cramer, R., Damgård, I., Escudero, D., Scholl, P., Xing, C.: SPD $\mathbb{Z}_{2^k}$: efficient MPC mod 2^k for dishonest majority. In: Shacham, H., Boldyreva, A. (eds.) CRYPTO 2018. LNCS, vol. 10992, pp. 769–798. Springer, Cham (2018). https://doi.org/10.1007/978-3-319-96881-0_26

[DKL+13] Damgård, I., Keller, M., Larraia, E., Pastro, V., Scholl, P., Smart, N.P.: Practical covertly secure MPC for dishonest majority – Or: breaking the SPDZ limits. In: Crampton, J., Jajodia, S., Mayes, K. (eds.) ESORICS 2013. LNCS, vol. 8134, pp. 1–18. Springer, Heidelberg (2013). https://doi.org/10.1007/978-3-642-40203-6_1

[DPSZ12] Damgård, I., Pastro, V., Smart, N., Zakarias, S.: Multiparty computation from somewhat homomorphic encryption. In: Safavi-Naini, R., Canetti, R. (eds.) CRYPTO 2012. LNCS, vol. 7417, pp. 643–662. Springer, Heidelberg (2012). https://doi.org/10.1007/978-3-642-32009-5_38

[FKOS15] Frederiksen, T.K., Keller, M., Orsini, E., Scholl, P.: A unified approach to MPC with preprocessing using OT. In: Iwata, T., Cheon, J.H. (eds.) ASIACRYPT 2015. LNCS, vol. 9452, pp. 711–735. Springer, Heidelberg (2015). https://doi.org/10.1007/978-3-662-48797-6_29

[GKS17] Günther, D., Kiss,Á., Schneider, T.: More efficient universal circuit constructions. Cryptology ePrint Archive, Report 2017/798 (2017). http://eprint.iacr.org/2017/798

[GMW87] Goldreich, O., Micali, S., Wigderson, A.: How to play any mental game or a completeness theorem for protocols with honest majority. In: Aho, A. (ed.) 19th ACM STOC, pages 218–229. ACM Press, May 1987

[HK20a] Heath, D., Kolesnikov, V.: Stacked garbling. In: Micciancio, D., Ristenpart, T. (eds.) CRYPTO 2020. LNCS, vol. 12171, pp. 763–792. Springer, Cham (2020). https://doi.org/10.1007/978-3-030-56880-1_27

[HK20b] Heath, D., Kolesnikov, V.: Stacked garbling for disjunctive zero-knowledge proofs. In: Canteaut, A., Ishai, Y. (eds.) EUROCRYPT 2020. LNCS, vol. 12107, pp. 569–598. Springer, Cham (2020). https://doi.org/10.1007/978-3-030-45727-3_19

[HKP20] Heath, D., Kolesnikov, V., Peceny, S.: MOTIF: (almost) free branching in GMW - via vector-scalar multiplication. In: Moriai, S., Wang, H. (eds.) ASIACRYPT 2020. Part III, volume 12493 of LNCS, pp. 3–30. Springer, Heidelberg (2020)

[IKNP03] Ishai, Y., Kilian, J., Nissim, K., Petrank, E.: Extending oblivious transfers efficiently. In: Boneh, D. (ed.) CRYPTO 2003. LNCS, vol. 2729, pp. 145–161. Springer, Heidelberg (2003). https://doi.org/10.1007/978-3-540-45146-4_9

[KK13]   Kolesnikov, V., Kumaresan, R.: Improved OT extension for transferring short secrets. In: Canetti, R., Garay, J.A. (eds.) CRYPTO 2013. LNCS, vol. 8043, pp. 54–70. Springer, Heidelberg (2013). https://doi.org/10.1007/978-3-642-40084-1_4

[Kol18]   Kolesnikov, V.: Free IF: how to omit inactive branches and implement S-universal garbled circuit (Almost) for free. In: Peyrin, T., Galbraith, S. (eds.) ASIACRYPT 2018. LNCS, vol. 11274, pp. 34–58. Springer, Cham (2018). https://doi.org/10.1007/978-3-030-03332-3_2

[KOS16]   Keller, M., Orsini, E., Scholl, P.: MASCOT: faster malicious arithmetic secure computation with oblivious transfer. In: Weippl, E.R., Katzenbeisser, S., Kruegel, C., Myers, A.C., Halevi, S. (eds.) ACM CCS 2016, pp. 830–842. ACM Press, October 2016

[KPR18]   Keller, M., Pastro, V., Rotaru, D.: Overdrive: making SPDZ great again. In: Nielsen, J.B., Rijmen, V. (eds.) EUROCRYPT 2018. LNCS, vol. 10822, pp. 158–189. Springer, Cham (2018). https://doi.org/10.1007/978-3-319-78372-7_6

[KS08]   Kolesnikov, V., Schneider, T.: A practical universal circuit construction and secure evaluation of private functions. In: Tsudik, G. (ed.) FC 2008. LNCS, vol. 5143, pp. 83–97. Springer, Heidelberg (2008). https://doi.org/10.1007/978-3-540-85230-8_7

[KS16]   Kiss, Á., Schneider, T.: Valiant's universal circuit is practical. In: Fischlin, M., Coron, J.-S. (eds.) EUROCRYPT 2016. LNCS, vol. 9665, pp. 699–728. Springer, Heidelberg (2016). https://doi.org/10.1007/978-3-662-49890-3_27

[LMS16]   Lipmaa, H., Mohassel, P., Sadeghian, S.: Valiant's universal circuit: Improvements, implementation, and applications. Cryptology ePrint Archive, Report 2016/017 (2016). http://eprint.iacr.org/2016/017

[LOS14]   Larraia, E., Orsini, E., Smart, N.P.: Dishonest majority multi-party computation for binary circuits. In: Garay, J.A., Gennaro, R. (eds.) CRYPTO 2014. LNCS, vol. 8617, pp. 495–512. Springer, Heidelberg (2014). https://doi.org/10.1007/978-3-662-44381-1_28

[LYZ+20] Liu, H., Yu, Y., Zhao, S., Zhang, J., Liu, W.: Pushing the limits of valiant's universal circuits: simpler, tighter and more compact. IACR Cryptology ePrint Archive 2020, 161 (2020)

[NNOB12] Nielsen, J.B., Nordholt, P.S., Orlandi, C., Burra, S.S.: A new approach to practical active-secure two-party computation. In: Safavi-Naini, R., Canetti, R. (eds.) CRYPTO 2012. LNCS, vol. 7417, pp. 681–700. Springer, Heidelberg (2012). https://doi.org/10.1007/978-3-642-32009-5_40

[NW78]   Nijenhuis, A., Wilf, H.S.: Combinatorial Algorithms For Computers and Calculators. AP Academic Press, New York (1978)

[Val76]   Valiant, L.G.: Universal circuits (preliminary report). In: STOC, pp. 196–203, New York, NY, USA, 1976. ACM Press

[WMK16]   Wang, X., Malozemoff, A.J., Katz, J.: MP-toolkit: Efficient MultiParty computation toolkit (2016). https://github.com/emp-toolkit

[ZYZL18] Zhao, S., Yu, Y., Zhang, J., Liu, H.: Valiant's universal circuits revisited: an overall improvement and a lower bound. Cryptology ePrint Archive, Report 2018/943 (2018). https://eprint.iacr.org/2018/943

Multi-party Threshold Private Set Intersection with Sublinear Communication

Saikrishna Badrinarayanan[1($\boxtimes$)], Peihan Miao[2], Srinivasan Raghuraman[1], and Peter Rindal[1]

[1] Visa Research, Palo Alto, USA
{sabadrin,srraghur,perindal}@visa.com
[2] University of Illinois at Chicago, Chicago, USA
peihan@uic.edu

Abstract. In multi-party threshold private set intersection (PSI), n parties each with a private set wish to compute the intersection of their sets if the intersection is sufficiently large. Previously, Ghosh and Simkin (CRYPTO 2019) studied this problem for the two-party case and demonstrated interesting lower and upper bounds on the communication complexity. In this work, we investigate the communication complexity of the multi-party setting ($n \geq 2$). We consider two functionalities for multi-party threshold PSI. In the first, parties learn the intersection if each of their sets and the intersection differ by at most T. In the second functionality, parties learn the intersection if the union of all their sets and the intersection differ by at most T.

For both functionalities, we show that any protocol must have communication complexity $\Omega(nT)$. We build protocols with a matching upper bound of $O(nT)$ communication complexity for both functionalities assuming threshold FHE. We also construct a computationally more efficient protocol for the second functionality with communication complexity $\tilde{O}(nT)$ under a weaker assumption of threshold additive homomorphic encryption. As a direct implication, we solve one of the open problems in the work of Ghosh and Simkin (CRYPTO 2019) by designing a two-party protocol with communication cost $\tilde{O}(T)$ from assumptions weaker than FHE.

As a consequence of our results, we achieve the first "regular" multi-party PSI protocol where the communication complexity only grows with the size of the set difference and does not depend on the size of the input sets.

1 Introduction

Private set intersection (PSI) protocols allow several mutually distrustful parties $P_1, P_2, \ldots, P_n$ each holding a private set $S_1, S_2, \ldots, S_n$ respectively to jointly compute the intersection $I = \bigcap_{i=1}^{n} S_i$ without revealing any other information. PSI has numerous privacy-preserving applications, e.g., DNA testing and pattern matching [TPKC07], remote diagnostics [BPSW07], botnet

© International Association for Cryptologic Research 2021
J. A. Garay (Ed.): PKC 2021, LNCS 12711, pp. 349–379, 2021.
https://doi.org/10.1007/978-3-030-75248-4_13

detection [NMH+10], online advertising [IKN+17, MPR+20]. Over the last years enormous progress has been made towards realizing this functionality efficiently [HFH99, FNP04, KS05, DCT10, DCW13, PSZ14, PSSZ15, KKRT16, OOS16, RR17, KMP+17, HV17, PSWW18, PRTY19, GN19, PRTY20, CM20]   in the two-party, multi-party, and server-aided settings with both semi-honest and malicious security.

Threshold PSI. In certain scenarios, the standard PSI functionality is not sufficient. In particular, the parties may only be willing to reveal the intersection if they have a *large* intersection. For example, in privacy-preserving data mining and machine learning [MZ17] where the data is vertically partitioned among multiple parties (that is, each party holds different features of the same object), the parties may want to learn the intersection of their datasets and start their collaboration only if their common dataset is sufficiently large. If their common dataset is too small, in which case they are not interested in collaboration, it is undesirable to let them learn the intersection. In privacy-preserving ride sharing [HOS17], multiple users only want to share a ride if large parts of their trajectories on a map intersect. In this case, the users may be interested in the intersection of their routes, but only when the intersection is large. This problem can be formalized as *threshold private set intersection*, where, roughly speaking, the parties only learn the intersection if their sets differ by at most T elements.

Many works [FNP04, HOS17, PSWW18, ZC18, GN19] achieve this functionality by first computing the cardinality of the intersection and then checking if this is sufficiently large. The communication complexity of these protocols scales at least linearly in the size of the smallest input set. Notice that Freedman et al. [FNP04] proved a lower bound of $\Omega(m)$ on the communication complexity of any private set intersection protocol, where m is the size of the smallest input set. This lower bound directly extends to protocols that only compute the cardinality of the intersection, which constitutes a fundamental barrier to the efficiency of the above protocols.

Recently, the beautiful work of Ghosh and Simkin [GS19a] revisited the communication complexity of *two-party* threshold PSI and demonstrated that the $\Omega(m)$ lower bound can be circumvented by performing a private intersection cardinality testing (i.e., testing whether the intersection is sufficiently large) instead of computing the actual cardinality. After passing the cardinality testing, their protocol allows each party to learn the set difference, where the communication complexity only grows with T, which could be sublinear in m. Specifically, [GS19a] proved a communication lower bound of $\Omega(T)$ for two-party threshold PSI and presented a protocol achieving a matching upper bound $O(T)$ based on fully homomorphic encryption (FHE). They also showed a computationally more efficient protocol with communication complexity of $\widetilde{O}(T^2)$ based on weaker assumptions, namely additively homomorphic encryption (AHE).

In this work, we investigate the communication complexity of *multi-party* threshold PSI. In particular, we ask the question of whether sublinear lower and upper bounds can also be achieved in the multi-party setting.

1.1   Our Contributions

We first identify and formalize the definition of multi-party threshold private set intersection. We put forth and study *two* functionalities that are in fact equivalent in the two-party case but are vastly different in the multi-party scenario. Assume there are n parties $P_1, P_2, \ldots, P_n$, and each party P_i holds a private set S_i of size m. The first functionality allows the parties to learn the intersection $I = \bigcap_{i=1}^{n} S_i$ only if $\forall i, |S_i \setminus I| \leq T$, or equivalently, $|I| \geq m - T$. In the second functionality, the parties can learn the intersection I only if $|(\bigcup_{i=1}^{n} S_i) \setminus I| \leq T$.

We briefly discuss the difference between the two functionalities. The first functionality focuses on whether the intersection is sufficiently large, hence we call it $\mathcal{F}_{\text{TPSI-int}}$. The second functionality focuses on whether the set difference is sufficiently small, thus we call it $\mathcal{F}_{\text{TPSI-diff}}$. In the two-party case, we have the guarantee that $|(\bigcup_{i=1}^{n} S_i) \setminus I| = 2 \cdot |S_i \setminus I|$, so we do *not* have to differentiate between these two functionalities. However, in the multi-party case, we only know that $2 \cdot |S_i \setminus I| \leq |(\bigcup_{i=1}^{n} S_i) \setminus I| \leq n \cdot |S_i \setminus I|$, hence the two functionalities could lead to very different outcomes. Which functionality to choose and what threshold to set in practice highly depend on the actual application.

Sublinear Communication. The core contribution of this work is demonstrating sublinear (in the set sizes) communication lower and upper bounds for both functionalities. We summarize our results in Table 1. For lower bound, we prove that both functionalities require at least $\Omega(nT)$ bits of communication. For upper bound, we present protocols for both functionalities achieving a matching upper bound of $O(nT)$ based on n-out-of-n threshold fully homomorphic encryption (TFHE) [BGG+18]. We also give a computationally more efficient protocol based on weaker assumptions, namely n-out-of-n threshold additively homomorphic encryption (TAHE) [Ben94, Pai99], with communication complexity of $\widetilde{O}(nT)$ that almost matches the lower bound.[1] All these protocols achieve semi-honest security where up to $(n-1)$ parties could be corrupted.

Table 1. Communication lower and upper bounds for multi-party threshold PSI.

Functionality	Communication lower bound	TFHE-based upper bound	TAHE-based upper bound
$\mathcal{F}_{\text{TPSI-int}}$	$\Omega(nT)$	$O(nT)$	Unknown
$\mathcal{F}_{\text{TPSI-diff}}$	$\Omega(nT)$	$O(nT)$	$\widetilde{O}(nT)$

Our Protocols. As summarized in Table 1, we present three protocols for upper bounds, one for $\mathcal{F}_{\text{TPSI-int}}$ and two for $\mathcal{F}_{\text{TPSI-diff}}$. At a high level, all three protocols compute their functionality in two phases. In the first phase, they perform

---

[1] $\widetilde{O}(\cdot)$ hides polylog factors. All the upper bounds omit a poly(λ) factor where λ is the security parameter.

a multi-party private intersection cardinality testing where the parties jointly decide whether their intersection is sufficiently large. In particular, for $\mathcal{F}_{\mathsf{TPSI\text{-}int}}$, the cardinality testing, which we call $\mathcal{F}_{\mathsf{CTest\text{-}int}}$, allows all the parties to learn whether $|I| \geq (m - T)$. For $\mathcal{F}_{\mathsf{TPSI\text{-}diff}}$, the cardinality testing, which we call $\mathcal{F}_{\mathsf{CTest\text{-}diff}}$, allows all the parties to learn whether $| (\bigcup_{i=1}^{n} S_i) \setminus I| \leq T$. The communication complexity of our protocols for $\mathcal{F}_{\mathsf{CTest\text{-}int}}$ and $\mathcal{F}_{\mathsf{CTest\text{-}diff}}$ is summarized in Table 2. In particular, for $\mathcal{F}_{\mathsf{CTest\text{-}int}}$, we present a protocol with communication complexity $O(nT)$ based on TFHE. For $\mathcal{F}_{\mathsf{CTest\text{-}diff}}$, we show a TFHE-based construction with communication complexity $O(nT)$ and a TAHE-based construction with communication complexity $\widetilde{O}(nT)$.

Table 2. Communication complexity of our protocols for multi-party private cardinality testing.

Functionality protocol	TFHE-based protocol	TAHE-based
$\mathcal{F}_{\mathsf{CTest\text{-}int}}$	$O(nT)$	Unknown
$\mathcal{F}_{\mathsf{CTest\text{-}diff}}$	$O(nT)$	$\widetilde{O}(nT)$

If the intersection is sufficiently large, namely it passes the cardinality testing, then the parties start the second phase of our protocols, which allows each party P_i to learn their set difference $S_i \setminus I$. We present a singe protocol for the second phase, which works for both $\mathcal{F}_{\mathsf{TPSI\text{-}int}}$ and $\mathcal{F}_{\mathsf{TPSI\text{-}diff}}$. The second-phase protocol is based on TAHE and has communication complexity of $O(nT)$. Thus, to construct a protocol for multi-party threshold PSI, we combine the first-phase protocols summarized in Table 2 with the second-phase one described above. Doing so, we achieve the communication upper bounds in Table 1.

This modular design enables our constructions to minimize the use of TFHE as it is not needed in the second phase. Moreover, it allows future work to focus on improving Table 2. In particular, to design a protocol for $\mathcal{F}_{\mathsf{TPSI\text{-}int}}$ from assumptions weaker than TFHE, future work could focus on building protocols for $\mathcal{F}_{\mathsf{CTest\text{-}int}}$ and directly plug in our second phase protocol after that.

Communication Topology. All our protocols are designed in the so-called *star network* topology, where a designated party communicates with every other party. An added benefit of this topology is that not all parties must be online at the same time. Our communication lower bounds are proved in *point-to-point* fully connected networks, which are a generalization of the star network.

For networks with broadcast channels, we prove another communication lower bound of $\Omega(T \log n + n)$ for $\mathcal{F}_{\mathsf{TPSI\text{-}int}}$ in the full version and leave further exploration in the broadcast model for future work.

1.2   Other Implications

Two-Party Threshold PSI. Recall that in the two-party case, both functionalities $\mathcal{F}_{\mathsf{TPSI\text{-}int}}$ and $\mathcal{F}_{\mathsf{TPSI\text{-}diff}}$ are identical. Ghosh and Simkin [GS19a] built a two-party threshold PSI protocol from AHE with communication complexity $\widetilde{O}(T^2)$. They left it as an open problem to build a two-party threshold PSI protocol with communication complexity $\widetilde{O}(T)$ from assumptions weaker than FHE. Observe that for the special case of $n = 2$, we can achieve a two-party threshold PSI protocol with communication complexity $\widetilde{O}(T)$ from AHE thereby solving this open problem (refer to Sect. 6 and Sect. 7 for more details).

Sublinear Communication PSI. Our multi-party threshold PSI protocols for both $\mathcal{F}_{\mathsf{TPSI\text{-}int}}$ and $\mathcal{F}_{\mathsf{TPSI\text{-}diff}}$ can also be used to achieve multi-party "regular" PSI[2] where the communication complexity only grows with the size of the set difference and independent of the input set sizes. In particular, if we run a sequence of multi-party threshold PSI protocols on $T = 2^0, 2^1, 2^2, \ldots$ until hitting the smallest $T = 2^k$ where the protocol outputs the intersection, then we can achieve multi-party PSI. The communication complexity of the resulting protocol is a factor $\log T$ times that of a single instance but still independent of the input set sizes. Therefore, when the intersection is very large, namely the set difference is significantly smaller than the set sizes, this new approach achieves the *first* multi-party PSI with sublinear (in the set sizes) communication complexity.

Compact MPC. It is an open problem to construct a *compact* MPC protocol in the plain model where the communication complexity does not grow with the output length of the function. Prior works [HW15, BFK+19] construct compact MPC for general functions in the presence of a trusted setup (CRS, random oracle) from strong computational assumptions such as obfuscation. Our multi-party threshold PSI protocols have communication complexity independent of the output size (the set intersection). To the best of our knowledge, ours are the *first* compact MPC protocols for any non-trivial function in the plain model. The only prior compact protocol in the plain model we are aware of is the two-party threshold PSI protocol [GS19a].

1.3   Concurrent and Independent Work

Concurrent to our work, a recent update to the full version of the paper by Ghosh and Simkin [GS19b] extends the two-party threshold PSI protocol to the multi-party setting and consider the functionality $\mathcal{F}_{\mathsf{TPSI\text{-}int}}$. They do not consider the functionality $\mathcal{F}_{\mathsf{TPSI\text{-}diff}}$ that we additionally consider in our work. For $\mathcal{F}_{\mathsf{TPSI\text{-}int}}$, [GS19b] also first constructs a TFHE-based protocol for the intersection cardinality testing $\mathcal{F}_{\mathsf{CTest\text{-}int}}$ with communication complexity $O(nT)$. Then in the second phase for computing the intersection, they use an MPC protocol to compute the evaluations of a random polynomial, where the communication complexity depends on how the MPC is instantiated, which is not discussed

Another concurrent work by Branco, Döttling, and Pu [BDP21] studies multi-party private intersection cardinality testing with the functionality $\mathcal{F}_{\mathsf{CTest\text{-}int}}$ and presents a TAHE-based protocol with communication complexity $\widetilde{O}(nT^2)$, which

---

[2] By "regular" PSI, we refer to the standard notion of PSI without threshold.

complements our Table 2. They also do not consider the other functionality $\mathcal{F}_{\text{CTest-diff}}$.

1.4 Roadmap

We describe some notations and definitions in Sect. 2, a technical overview in Sect. 3, and the lower bound in Sect. 4. We present the TFHE based protocols for $\mathcal{F}_{\text{CTest-int}}$ and $\mathcal{F}_{\text{CTest-diff}}$ in Sect. 5 and the TAHE based protocol for $\mathcal{F}_{\text{CTest-diff}}$ in Sect. 6. We present the second phase protocol to compute the actual intersection in Sect. 7.

2 Preliminaries

In this section, we introduce some notations and define the our ideal functionalities. See the full version for the remaining definitions.

2.1 Notations

We use λ to denote the security parameters. By $\mathsf{poly}(\lambda)$ we denote a polynomial function in λ. By $\mathsf{negl}(\lambda)$ we denote a negligible function, that is, a function f such that $f(\lambda) < 1/p(\lambda)$ holds for any polynomial $p(\cdot)$ and sufficiently large λ. We use $[\![x]\!]$ to denote an encryption of x. We use $\widetilde{O}(x)$ to ignore any polylog factor, namely $\widetilde{O}(x) = O(x \cdot \mathsf{polylog}(x))$.

2.2 Multi-party Threshold Private Set Intersection

Setting. Consider n parties $P_1, \ldots, P_n$ with input sets $S_1, \ldots, S_n$ respectively. Throughout the paper, we consider all the sets to be of equal size m. We assume that the set elements come from a field $\mathbb{F}_p$, where p is a $\Theta(\lambda)$-bit prime. Also, throughout the paper, we focus only on the point-to-point network channels. For the lower bounds, we consider a setting where every pair of parties has a point-to-point channel between them. For the upper bounds, we consider a more restrictive model – the star network, where only one central party has a point-to-point channel with every other party and the other parties cannot communicate with each other.

The goal of the parties is to run an MPC protocol Π at the end of which each party learns the intersection I of all the sets if certain conditions hold. In the definition of two-party threshold PSI, both parties P_1 and P_2 learn the intersection I if the size of their set difference is small, namely $|(S_1 \setminus S_2) \cup (S_2 \setminus S_1)| < 2T$. In the multi-party case, we consider two different functionalities, each of which might be better suited to different applications.

Functionalities. In the first definition, we consider functionality $\mathcal{F}_{\text{TPSI-int}}$, in which each party P_i learns the intersection I if the size of its own set minus the intersection is small, namely $|S_i \setminus I| \leq T$ for some threshold T. Recall that we consider all the sets to be of equal size, hence either all the parties learn the output or all of them don't. In the second definition, we consider a functionality $\mathcal{F}_{\mathsf{TPSI\text{-}diff}}$, where each party learns the intersection I if the size of the union of all the sets minus the intersection is small, namely $|(\bigcup_{i=1}^{n} S_i) \setminus I| \leq T$. The formal definitions of the two ideal functionalities are shown in Fig. 1 and Fig. 2.

Parameters: Parties $P_1, \ldots, P_n$. Each party has a set of m elements. Threshold $T \in \mathbb{N}$.

Inputs: Party P_i has an input set $S_i = \{a_1^i, \ldots, a_m^i\}$ where $a_j^i \in \mathbb{F}_p$ for all $j \in [m]$.

Output: Each party P_i receives $I = \bigcap_{i=1}^{n} S_i$ if and only if $|S_i \setminus I| \leq T$.

Fig. 1. Ideal functionality $\mathcal{F}_{\mathsf{TPSI\text{-}int}}$ for multi-party threshold PSI.

Parameters: Parties $P_1, \ldots, P_n$. Each party has a set of m elements. Threshold $T \in \mathbb{N}$.

Inputs: Party P_i has an input set $S_i = \{a_1^i, \ldots, a_m^i\}$ where $a_j^i \in \mathbb{F}_p$ for all $j \in [m]$.

Output: Each party P_i receives $I = \bigcap_{i=1}^{n} S_i$ if and only if $\left(\bigcup_{i=1}^{n} S_i \setminus I \right) \leq T$.

Fig. 2. Ideal functionality $\mathcal{F}_{\mathsf{TPSI\text{-}diff}}$ for multi-party threshold PSI.

2.3 Multi-party Private Intersection Cardinality Testing

An important building block in our multi-party threshold PSI protocols is a multi-party protocol for private intersection cardinality testing which we define below. Consider n parties $P_1, \ldots, P_n$ with input sets $S_1, \ldots, S_n$ respectively of equal size m. Their goal is to run an MPC protocol Π at the end of which each party learns whether the size of the intersection I of all the sets is sufficiently large. As before, we consider two functionalities. In the first functionality $\mathcal{F}_{\mathsf{CTest\text{-}int}}$, each party P_i learns whether $|S_i \setminus I| \leq T$. In the second functionality $\mathcal{F}_{\mathsf{CTest\text{-}diff}}$, each party learns whether $|(\bigcup_{i=1}^{n} S_i) \setminus I| \leq T$. The formal definitions of the two ideal functionalities are presented in Fig. 3 and Fig. 4.

Parameters: Parties $P_1, \ldots, P_n$. Each party has a set of m elements. Threshold $T \in \mathbb{N}$.

Inputs: Party P_i has an input set $S_i = \{a_1^i, \ldots, a_m^i\}$ where $a_j^i \in \mathbb{F}_p$ for all $j \in [m]$.

Output: Each party P_i receives similar if $|S_i \setminus I| \leq T$ and different otherwise where $I = \bigcap_{i=1}^{n} S_i$.

Fig. 3. Ideal functionality $\mathcal{F}_{\mathsf{CTest\text{-}int}}$ for multi-party intersection cardinality test.

Parameters: Parties $P_1, \ldots, P_n$. Each party has a set of m elements. Threshold $T \in \mathbb{N}$.

Inputs: Party P_i has an input set $S_i = \{a_1^i, \ldots, a_m^i\}$ where $a_j^i \in \mathbb{F}_p$ for all $j \in [m]$.

Output: Each party P_i receives similar if $\left| \left(\bigcup_{i=1}^n S_i \right) \setminus I \right| \leq T$ and different otherwise where $I = \bigcap_{i=1}^n S_i$.

Fig. 4. Ideal functionality $\mathcal{F}_{\mathsf{CTest\text{-}diff}}$ for multi-party intersection cardinality test.

3   Technical Overview

We now give an overview of the techniques used in our work. We denote P_1 as the designated party that can communicate with all the other parties.

3.1   TFHE-Based Protocol for $\mathcal{F}_{\mathsf{CTest\text{-}int}}$

In Sect. 5.1 we construct a protocol for $\mathcal{F}_{\mathsf{CTest\text{-}int}}$ from TFHE. Our starting point is the two-party protocol of [GS19a]. Recall that there are two parties Alice and Bob with sets $S_A = \{a_1, \ldots, a_m\}$ and $S_B = \{b_1, \ldots, b_m\}$ respectively. These sets define two polynomials $\mathsf{p}_A(\mathsf{x}) := \prod_{i=1}^m (\mathsf{x} - a_i)$ and $\mathsf{p}_B(\mathsf{x}) := \prod_{i=1}^m (\mathsf{x} - b_i)$. Let $I := S_A \cap S_B$ be the intersection. A key observation in [MTZ03, GS19a] is that $\mathsf{p}(\mathsf{x}) := \frac{\mathsf{p}_B(\mathsf{x})}{\mathsf{p}_A(\mathsf{x})} = \frac{\mathsf{p}_{B \setminus I}(\mathsf{x})}{\mathsf{p}_{A \setminus I}(\mathsf{x})}$. Both the numerator and denominator of p have degree $m - |I|$. If $m - |I| = |S_A \setminus I| \leq T$, then $\mathsf{p}(\mathsf{x})$ has degree at most $2T$ and can be recovered from $2T + 1$ evaluations by rational function interpolation.[3] Given $\mathsf{p}(\mathsf{x})$, the elements in $S_A \setminus I$ are simply the roots of the polynomial in the denominator.

Two-Party Protocol. At a high level, the two-party protocol [GS19a] works as follows. First, Alice and Bob evaluate their own polynomials on $2T + 1$ publicly known distinct points $\{\alpha_1, \ldots, \alpha_{2T+1}\}$ to obtain $\{\mathsf{p}_A(\alpha_1), \ldots, \mathsf{p}_A(\alpha_{2T+1})\}$ and $\{\mathsf{p}_B(\alpha_1), \ldots, \mathsf{p}_B(\alpha_{2T+1})\}$, respectively. Then, Alice generates a public-secret key pair for FHE and sends Bob the FHE public key, encrypted evaluations $\{[\![\mathsf{p}_A(\alpha_1)]\!], \ldots, [\![\mathsf{p}_A(\alpha_{2T+1})]\!]\}$, a uniformly random z and encrypted evaluation $[\![\mathsf{p}_A(z)]\!]$. Bob can homomorphically interpolate the rational function $[\![\mathsf{p}(\mathsf{x})]\!]$ from $\{[\![\mathsf{p}_A(\alpha_1)]\!], \ldots, [\![\mathsf{p}_A(\alpha_{2T+1})]\!]\}$ and $\{\mathsf{p}_B(\alpha_1), \ldots, \mathsf{p}_B(\alpha_{2T+1})\}$, and then homomorphically compute $[\![\mathsf{p}(z)]\!]$. Bob can also compute $\mathsf{p}_B(z)$ and homomorphically compute $\frac{\mathsf{p}_B(z)}{[\![\mathsf{p}_A(z)]\!]}$. We know that $\mathsf{p}(z) = \frac{\mathsf{p}_B(z)}{\mathsf{p}_A(z)}$ if and only if the degree of $\mathsf{p}(\mathsf{x})$ is $\leq 2T$. Therefore Bob homomorphically computes an encryption of the predicate $[\![b]\!] := \left([\![\mathsf{p}(z)]\!] \overset{?}{=} \frac{\mathsf{p}_B(z)}{[\![\mathsf{p}_A(z)]\!]} \right)$ and sends the encryption $[\![b]\!]$ back to Alice. Finally Alice decrypts and learns b.

---

[3] A rational function is a fraction of two polynomials. We refer to Minskey et al. [MTZ03] for details on rational function interpolation over a field. Also, we note that monic polynomials can be interpolated with $2T$ evaluation but we use $2T + 1$ for consistency with our other protocols.

Multi-party Protocol. For n parties, a natural idea is to consider

$$p(x) := \frac{p_2(x) + \cdots + p_n(x)}{p_1(x)} = \frac{p_{2\setminus I}(x) + \cdots + p_{n\setminus I}(x)}{p_{1\setminus I}(x)}, \tag{1}$$

where $p_i(x)$ encodes the set $S_i = \{a_1^i, \ldots, a_m^i\}$ as $p_i(x) := \prod_{j=1}^m (x - a_j^i)$. The n parties first jointly generate the TFHE keys. Each party P_i sends encrypted evaluations $\{[\![p_i(\alpha_1)]\!], \ldots, [\![p_i(\alpha_{2T+1})]\!], [\![p_i(z)]\!]\}$ to P_1. Now P_1 can interpolate $[\![p(x)]\!]$ from $2T + 1$ evaluations and compute an encryption $[\![b]\!] := \left([\![p(z)]\!] \stackrel{?}{=} \frac{[\![p_2(z)]\!] + \cdots + [\![p_n(z)]\!]}{p_1(z)} \right)$. Finally the parties jointly decrypt $[\![b]\!]$.

Unexpected Degree Reduction. This seemingly correct protocol has a subtle issue.[4] Intuitively, we want to argue that $p(x)$ in Eq. 1 has degree $\leq 2T$ if and only if $|S_1 \setminus I| \leq T$. However, this is not true because elements not in the intersection might be accidentally canceled out, which results in a lower degree than the intersection carnality would imply. As a concrete example, consider three sets with distinct elements $S_1 = \{a\}$, $S_2 = \{b\}$, $S_3 = \{c\}$, where $b + c = 2 \cdot a$. The intersection $I = \emptyset$. Ideally we hope the rational polynomial $p(x)$ has degree 1 in both the numerator and denominator because $|S_1 \setminus I| = 1$. However,

$$p(x) = \frac{(x - b) + (x - c)}{x - a} = \frac{2x - (b + c)}{x - a} = \frac{2x - 2a}{x - a} = 2.$$

Randomness to the Rescue. On first thought, this approach seems fundamentally flawed as additional roots can always be created if we add polynomials in the numerator. To solve this problem, we add a random multiplicative term $(x - r_i)$ to each polynomial p_i and set a new polynomial $p_i'(x) := p_i(x) \cdot (x - r_i)$ for a random r_i chosen by party P_i. Now, consider the rational polynomial

$$p'(x) := \frac{p_2'(x) + \cdots + p_n'(x)}{p_1'(x)} = \frac{p_{2\setminus I}'(x) + \cdots + p_{n\setminus I}'(x)}{p_{1\setminus I}'(x)}.$$

At a high level, the terms $(x - r_i)$ will randomize the roots of the numerator sufficiently to ensure that these roots are unlikely to coincide with the roots of the denominator.

3.2 TFHE-Based Protocol for $\mathcal{F}_{\text{CTest-diff}}$

In Sect. 5.2 we present an TFHE-based protocol for $\mathcal{F}_{\text{CTest-diff}}$. In summary, party P_1 tries to homomorphically interpolate

$$\tilde{p}_i(x) = \frac{p_i(x)}{p_1(x)} = \frac{p_{i\setminus 1}(x)}{p_{1\setminus i}(x)}$$

---

[4] In fact, this subtle issue was initially overlooked by [GS19b] in their recent update of the multi-party protocol. It has subsequently been fixed after we notified them.

from $(2T+1)$ evaluations and computes encrypted $D_{1,i} = S_1 \setminus S_i$ as well as $D_{i,1} = S_i \setminus S_1$ for every other party P_i. Note that if $|(\bigcup_{i=1}^{m} S_i) \setminus I| \leq T$, then $|S_i \setminus I| \leq T$ for all i and the degree of each $\widetilde{p}_i(x)$ is at most $2T$, hence P_1 can interpolate it using $(2T + 1)$ evaluations. Observe that $(\bigcup_{i=1}^{m} S_i) \setminus I = \bigcup_{i=2}^{m} (D_{1,i} \cup D_{i,1})$, because each element $a \in (\bigcup_{i=1}^{m} S_i) \setminus I$ must be one of the two cases: (1) $a \in S_1$ and $a \notin S_i$ for some i (i.e., $a \in D_{1,i}$), or (2) $a \notin S_1$ and $a \in S_i$ for some i (i.e., $a \in D_{i,1}$). Therefore, party P_1 can homomorphically compute an encryption of $(\bigcup_{i=1}^{m} S_i) \setminus I$ and an encryption of the predicate $b = \left(|(\bigcup_{i=1}^{m} S_i) \setminus I| \overset{?}{\leq} T \right)$.

Finally, as before, the n parties jointly decrypt $[\![b]\!]$ to learn the output.

3.3   TAHE-Based Protocol for $\mathcal{F}_{\text{CTest-diff}}$

Section 6 presents our protocol for $\mathcal{F}_{\text{CTest-diff}}$ based on TAHE. This protocol reduces the communication complexity for two-party from $\widetilde{O}(T^2)$ to $\widetilde{O}(T)$ as well as generalizes it to multi-party with communication $\widetilde{O}(Tn)$.

Two-Party Protocol. For two parties Alice and Bob with private sets S_A and S_B, if we encode their elements into two polynomials $p_A(x) = \sum_{i=1}^{m} x^{a_i}$ and $p_B(x) = \sum_{i=1}^{m} x^{b_i}$, then the number of monomials in the polynomial $p(x) := p_A(x) - p_B(x)$ is exactly $|(S_A \setminus S_B) \cup (S_B \setminus S_A)|$. Now the problem of cardinality testing (i.e., determining if $|(S_A \setminus S_B) \cup (S_B \setminus S_A)| \leq 2T$) has be reduced to determining whether the number of monomials in $p(x)$ is $\leq 2T$. Using the polynomial sparsity test of Grigorescu et al. [GJR10], we can further reduce the problem to determining whether the Hankel matrix below is singular or not:

$$ H = \begin{bmatrix} p(u^0) & p(u^1) & \cdots & p(u^{2T}) \\ p(u^1) & p(u^2) & \cdots & p(u^{2T+1}) \\ \vdots & \vdots & \ddots & \vdots \\ p(u^{2T}) & p(u^{2T+1}) & \cdots & p(u^{4T}) \end{bmatrix}, $$

where u is chosen uniformly at random. In the two-party protocol, Alice generates a public-secret key pair for AHE and sends Bob the public key, a uniformly random u along with encrypted Hankel matrix for p_A. Then Bob can homomorphically compute encrypted Hankel matrix for p. Now Alice holds the secret key and Bob holds an encryption of matrix H. They need to jointly perform a secure matrix singularity testing to determine if the matrix is singular, which can be done using the protocol of Kiltz et al. [KMWF07] with communication $\widetilde{O}(T^2)$.

Our Approach. Our key observation is that the protocol of Kiltz et al. [KMWF07] can be used to perform singularity testing for *arbitrary* matrices, while we are only interested in testing the singularity of Hankel matrices. Since a Hankel matrix only has linear (in its dimension) number of distinct entries, there is a more efficient way to test its singularity. In particular, the work of Brent et al. [BGY80] demonstrates an elegant connection between the problem of testing singularity of a Hankel matrix and the so-called "half-GCD" problem, which can be solved in quasi-linear time. Thus, testing singularity of the Hankel matrix H only takes $\widetilde{O}(T)$ computation. In our scenario, we can first let Alice and Bob learn an additive share of H, and then engage in a two-party computation (using AHE or Yao's garbled circuits) to jointly test if H is singular or not. The important point to note here is that both communication and computation are only quasi-linear in the dimension of H. This is already an improvement over the quadratic cost of protocol in [KMWF07] and solves the open problem posed by Ghosh and Simkin [GS19a].

Multi-party Protocol. In designing a multi-party protocol, our strategy is to first find a polynomial where the number of monomials equals the size of the set difference $|(\bigcup_{i=1}^{m} S_i) \setminus I|$. Furthermore, the polynomial should only involve linear operations among the parties, which allows the parties to obtain additive secret shares of the Hankel matrix for the polynomial. Then, the parties perform an MPC protocol to test singularity of the Hankel matrix.

3.4   Computing Set Intersection

In Sect. 7 we present a single construction that computes the concrete set intersection for both $\mathcal{F}_{\text{TPSI-int}}$ and $\mathcal{F}_{\text{TPSI-diff}}$ after the cardinality testing.

Two-Party Protocol. For two parties Alice and Bob, we use the first encoding method to encode the elements into two polynomials $p_A(x) = \prod_{i=1}^{m}(x - a_i)$ and $p_B(x) = \prod_{i=1}^{m}(x - b_i)$. After the cardinality testing, we already know that the rational polynomial $p(x) := \frac{p_B(x)}{p_A(x)} = \frac{p_{B \setminus I}(x)}{p_{A \setminus I}(x)}$ has degree at most $2T$. If Alice learns the evaluation of $p_B(\cdot)$ on $2T + 1$ distinct points $\{\alpha_1, \ldots, \alpha_{2T+1}\}$, then she can evaluate p_A on those points by herself and compute $\{p(\alpha_1), \ldots, p(\alpha_{2T+1})\}$. Using these evaluations of $p(\cdot)$, Alice can recover $p(x)$ by rational polynomial interpolation, and then learn the set difference $S_A \setminus I$ from the denominator of $p(x)$. However, $p(x)$ also allows Alice to learn $S_B \setminus I$, which breaks security. Instead of letting Alice learn the evaluations of $p_B(\cdot)$, the two-party protocol of [GS19a] enables Alice to learn the evaluations of a "noisy" polynomial $V(x) := p_A(x) \cdot R_1(x) + p_B(x) \cdot R_2(x)$, where R_1 and R_2 are uniformly random polynomials of degree T. Note that

$$p'(x) := \frac{V(x)}{p_A(x)} = \frac{p_{A \setminus I}(x) \cdot R_1(x) + p_{B \setminus I}(x) \cdot R_2(x)}{p_{A \setminus I}(x)}$$

has degree at most $3T$. Given $3T + 1$ evaluations of $V(\cdot)$, Alice can interpolate $p'(x)$ and figure out the denominator, but now the numerator is sufficiently random and does not leak any other information about S_B.

Multi-party Protocol. For n parties, we first encode each set $S_i = \{a_1^i, \ldots, a_m^i\}$ as a polynomial $p_i(x) := \prod_{j=1}^{m}(x - a_j^i)$, and then define

$$V(x) := p_1(x) \cdot R_1(x) + \cdots + p_n(x) \cdot R_n(x)$$
$$:= p_1(x) \cdot (R_{1,1}(x) + \cdots + R_{n,1}(x)) + \cdots + p_n(x) \cdot (R_{1,n}(x) + \cdots + R_{n,n}(x)),$$

where $(\mathsf{R}_{i,1}, \ldots, \mathsf{R}_{i,n})$ are random polynomials of degree T generated by party P_i. Different from the two-party protocol, it is crucial that each party P_i contributes a random term in every polynomial $\mathsf{R}_1, \ldots, \mathsf{R}_n$. For both functionalities $\mathcal{F}_{\mathsf{TPSI\text{-}int}}$ and $\mathcal{F}_{\mathsf{TPSI\text{-}diff}}$, if the protocol passes the cardinality testing, then

$$\mathsf{p}'(\mathsf{x}) := \frac{\mathsf{V}(\mathsf{x})}{\mathsf{p}_1(\mathsf{x})} = \frac{\mathsf{p}_{1\backslash I}(\mathsf{x}) \cdot \mathsf{R}_1(\mathsf{x}) + \cdots + \mathsf{p}_{n\backslash I}(\mathsf{x}) \cdot \mathsf{R}_n(\mathsf{x})}{\mathsf{p}_{1\backslash I}(\mathsf{x})}$$

has degree at most $3T$. If P_1 learns $3T + 1$ evaluations of $\mathsf{V}(\cdot)$, then it can interpolate $\mathsf{p}'(\mathsf{x})$ and recover $S_1 \setminus I$ from the denominator while the numerator does not leak any other information. Since $\mathsf{V}(\cdot)$ can be broken down to linear operations among the parties, it can be securely evaluated by TAHE.

Communication Blow-Up. However, this protocol requires $O(n^2)$ communication complexity per evaluation, and the total communication complexity is $O(n^2T)$ for $(3T + 1)$ evaluations. Observe that the bottleneck of the communication in this approach is that every party P_i needs to contribute n randomizing polynomials $(\mathsf{R}_{i,1}, \ldots, \mathsf{R}_{i,n})$. Through a careful analysis we demonstrate that it is sufficient for each party to only contribute two randomizing polynomials. The first is used to randomize their own polynomial while the second randomizes the polynomials from the other parties. Nevertheless, there is a subtle issue of unexpected degree reduction, similar to what we have seen in the TFHE-based protocol $\mathcal{F}_{\mathsf{CTest\text{-}int}}$. We follow the same approach as in the TFHE-based protocol by adding additional randomness in th polynomial, which reduces the communication complexity to $O(nT)$.

3.5   Lower Bounds

We briefly discuss the communication lower bound for multi-party threshold PSI. To prove lower bound in the point-to-point network, we perform a reduction from two-party threshold PSI (for which [GS19a] showed a lower bound of $\Omega(T)$) to multi-party threshold PSI. We first prove that the total "communication complexity of any party" is $\Omega(T)$ which denotes the sum of all the bits exchanged by that party (both sent and received). As a corollary, the total communication complexity of any multi-party threshold PSI protocol is $\Omega(nT)$. We refer to Sect. 4 for more details about the reduction.

To prove a lower bound in the broadcast model, we rely on the communication lower bound of the multi-party set disjointness problem shown by Braverman and Oshman [BO15]. We reduce the problem of multi-party set disjointness to multi-party threshold PSI $\mathcal{F}_{\mathsf{TPSI\text{-}int}}$ and prove a lower bound $\Omega(T \log n + n)$ for any multi-party threshold PSI protocol in the broadcast network. We refer to the full version for more details about the reduction.

4   Communication Lower Bound

In this section, we prove communication lower bounds for multi-party threshold PSI protocols in the point-to-point network model. Recall that we consider all parties to have sets of the same size m. We show that any secure protocol must have communication complexity at least $\Omega(n \cdot T)$ for both functionalities $\mathcal{F}_{\text{TPSI-int}}$ and $\mathcal{F}_{\text{TPSI-diff}}$. We prove the lower bound for $\mathcal{F}_{\text{TPSI-int}}$ and defer the proof for $\mathcal{F}_{\text{TPSI-diff}}$ to the full version. Before proving the lower bound, we first prove another related theorem below.

Theorem 1. *For any multi-party threshold PSI protocol for functionality $\mathcal{F}_{\text{TPSI-int}}$ that is secure against a semi-honest adversary that can corrupt up to $(n-1)$ parties, for every party P_i, the communication complexity of P_i is $\Omega(T)$.*[5]

Proof. Suppose this is not true. That is, suppose there exists a secure multi-party threshold PSI protocol Π for functionality $\mathcal{F}_{\text{TPSI-int}}$ in which for some party P_{i^*}, $\text{CC}(P_{i^*}) = o(T)$ where $\text{CC}(\cdot)$ denotes the communication complexity. We will now use this protocol Π as a subroutine to design a secure two-party threshold PSI protocol which has communication complexity $o(T)$.

Consider two parties Q_1 and Q_2 with input sets X_1 and X_2 (of same size m) who wish to run a secure two-party threshold PSI protocol for the following functionality: both parties learn the output if $|(X_1 \setminus X_2) \cup (X_2 \setminus X_1)| \leq 2 \cdot T$. We invoke the multi-party threshold PSI protocol Π with threshold T as follows: Q_1 emulates the role of party P_{i^*} with input set $S_{i^*} = X_1$ and Q_2 emulates the role of all the other $(n-1)$ parties with each of their input sets as X_2. From the definition of the functionality $\mathcal{F}_{\text{TPSI-int}}$, Q_1 learns the output at the end of the protocol if and only if $|X_1 \setminus I| \leq T$. Similarly, Q_2 learns the output at the end of the protocol if and only if $|X_2 \setminus I| \leq T$. Notice that since $|X_1| = |X_2|$ and $I = X_1 \cap X_2$, $|X_1 \setminus I| = |X_2 \setminus I|$. Thus, the parties learn the output if and only if $(|X_1 \setminus I|) + (|X_2 \setminus I|) \leq 2 \cdot T$, namely $|(X_1 \setminus X_2) \cup (X_2 \setminus X_1)| \leq 2 \cdot T$, which is the functionality of the two-party threshold PSI. Therefore, correctness is easy to observe. For security, notice that if Q_1 is corrupt, we can simulate it by considering only a corrupt P_{i^*} in the underlying protocol Π and if Q_2 is corrupt, we can simulate it by considering all parties except P_{i^*} to be corrupt in the underlying protocol Π.

Finally, notice that the communication complexity of the two-party protocol is exactly the same as $\text{CC}(P_{i^*})$ in the multi-party protocol Π, which is $o(T)$. However, recall from the work of Ghosh and Simkin [GS19a] that any two-party threshold PSI for this functionality has communication complexity lower bound $\Omega(T)$ leading to a contradiction. Thus, the assumption that there exists a secure multi-party PSI protocol Π in which for some party P_{i^*}, $\text{CC}(P_{i^*}) = o(T)$ is wrong and this completes the proof of the theorem.

It is easy to observe that as a corollary of the above theorem, in a setting with only point-to-point channels (which also includes the star network), the overall communication complexity of the protocol must be at least n times the minimum communication complexity that each party is involved in, giving the lower bound of $\Omega(n \cdot T)$. Formally,

---

[5] We define the communication complexity of a party P_i in any protocol execution as the complexity of all the communication that P_i is involved in. That is, the complexity of the messages both incoming to and outgoing from P_i.

Corollary 1. *For any multi-party threshold PSI protocol for functionality* $\mathcal{F}_{\mathsf{TPSI\text{-}int}}$ *that is secure against a semi-honest adversary that can corrupt up to* $(n-1)$ *parties, the communication complexity is* $\Omega(n \cdot T)$.

5   TFHE-Based Private Intersection Cardinality Testing

In this section, we present two protocols for private intersection cardinality testing, one for functionalities $\mathcal{F}_{\mathsf{CTest\text{-}int}}$ (described in Fig. 3) and the other for $\mathcal{F}_{\mathsf{CTest\text{-}diff}}$ (described in Fig. 4). Both protocols are based on n-out-of-n threshold fully homomorphic encryption with distributed setup. The former functionality states that the intersection must be of size at least $(m - T)$ where m is the size of each set. The latter functionality requires the difference between the union of all the sets and the intersection be of size at most T. Due to the possibility of elements appearing in a strict subset of the sets, these two functionalities are not equivalent.

5.1   Protocol for Functionality $\mathcal{F}_{\mathsf{CTest\text{-}int}}$

In this protocol, we compute the cardinality predicate b where $b = 1$ if and only if $\forall i, |S_i \setminus I| \leq T$. The communication complexity of this protocol involves sending $O(nT)$ TFHE ciphertexts and performing a single decryption of the result. We briefly describe the approach below.

Each party P_i first encodes their set S_i as a polynomial $\mathsf{p}_i(\mathsf{x}) := \prod_{a \in S_i} (\mathsf{x} - a) \in \mathbb{F}[\mathsf{x}]$. Each of these polynomials are then randomized as $\mathsf{p}_i'(\mathsf{x}) := \mathsf{p}_i(\mathsf{x}) \cdot (\mathsf{x} - r_i)$ where P_i uniformly samples $r_i \xleftarrow{\$} \mathbb{F}$. The central party also picks a random $z \xleftarrow{\$} \mathbb{F}$ which is sent to every other party. Each party P_i then computes $e_{i,j} := \mathsf{p}_i'(j)$ for $j \in [2T + 3]$ and $e_i' := \mathsf{p}_i'(z)$. P_i sends the ciphertexts $[\![e_{i,j}]\!] := \mathsf{TFHE.Enc}(\mathsf{pk}, e_{i,j})$ and $[\![e_i']\!] := \mathsf{TFHE.Enc}(\mathsf{pk}, e_i')$ to P_1. Party P_1 considers the rational polynomial

$$\mathsf{p}'(\mathsf{x}) = \frac{\mathsf{p}_2'(\mathsf{x}) + \cdots + \mathsf{p}_n'(\mathsf{x})}{\mathsf{p}_1'(\mathsf{x})}$$

and homomorphically computes $2T + 3$ encrypted evaluations

$$\left(j, [\![\frac{e_{2,j} + \cdots + e_{n,j}}{e_{1,j}}]\!] \right)$$

for $j = [2T + 3]$. Using these encrypted evaluations, P_1 homomorphically computes an encrypted rational polynomial $[\![\mathsf{p}^*(\mathsf{x})]\!]$ using rational polynomial interpolation. Note that $\mathsf{p}^*(\mathsf{x}) = \mathsf{p}'(\mathsf{x})$ if $\mathsf{p}'(\mathsf{x})$ has degree at most $2T + 2$. Furthermore, P_1 can homomorphically compute an encryption of the predicate $b := \left(\mathsf{p}^*(z) \stackrel{?}{=} \frac{e_2' + \cdots + e_n'}{e_1'} \right)$. Finally the parties jointly perform a threshold decryption of $[\![b]\!]$ and party P_1 learns the output which is sent to every other party. The full protocol is detailed in Fig. 5.

Parameters: Parties $P_1, \ldots, P_n$. Each party has a set of m elements. Threshold $T \in \mathbb{N}$. $\mathbb{F}$ is a finite field where $|\mathbb{F}| = \Omega(2^\lambda)$.

Inputs: Party P_i has an input set $S_i = \{a_1^i, \ldots, a_m^i\}$ where $a_j^i \in \mathbb{F}$ for all $j \in [m]$.

Output: Each party P_i receives similar if $|S_i \setminus I| \le T$ and different otherwise where $I = \bigcap_{i=1}^n S_i$.

Protocol:
1. Each party P_i generates $(\mathsf{pk}_i, \mathsf{sk}_i) \leftarrow \mathsf{TFHE.DistSetup}(1^\lambda, i)$ and sends pk_i to P_1. Then P_1 sends $\mathsf{pk} = (\mathsf{pk}_1 \| \ldots \| \mathsf{pk}_n)$ to all the other parties.
2. P_1 picks a random value $z \in \mathbb{F}$ and sends it to all the other parties.
3. Each party P_i does the following:
   (a) Define the polynomial $\mathsf{p}_i(x) := \prod_{a \in S_i} (x - a)$ and randomize it by $\mathsf{p}_i'(x) := \mathsf{p}_i(x) \cdot (x - r_i)$ where $r_i \overset{\$}{\leftarrow} \mathbb{F}$.
   (b) Compute $e_{i,j} := \mathsf{p}_i'(j)$ for $j \in [2T+3]$ and $e_i' := \mathsf{p}_i'(z)$.
   (c) Send encrypted evaluations $[\![e_{i,j}]\!] := \mathsf{TFHE.Enc}(\mathsf{pk}, e_{i,j})$ for all $j \in [2T+3]$ and $[\![e_i']\!] := \mathsf{TFHE.Enc}(\mathsf{pk}, e_i')$ to P_1.
4. P_1 does the following:
   (a) Use the algorithm $\mathsf{TFHE.Eval}$ to homomorphically compute an encryption $[\![\mathsf{p}^*(x)]\!]$ by rational polynomial interpolation from encrypted evaluations $\left(j, \left[\!\left[\frac{e_{2,j} + \cdots + e_{n,j}}{e_{1,j}} \right]\!\right] \right)$ for $j \in [2T+3]$.
   (b) Homomorphically compute the encrypted predicate $[\![b]\!]$ where $b = 1$ if $\mathsf{p}^*(z) = \frac{e_2' + \cdots + e_n'}{e_1'}$ and 0 otherwise.
5. P_1 sends $[\![b]\!]$ to all parties who respond with $[\![b : \mathsf{sk}_i]\!] := \mathsf{TFHE.PartialDec}(\mathsf{sk}_i, [\![b]\!])$. P_1 broadcasts $b := \mathsf{TFHE.Combine}(\mathsf{pk}, \{[\![b : \mathsf{sk}_i]\!]\}_{i \in [n]})$ and all parties output similar if $b = 1$ and different otherwise.

Fig. 5. Multi-party private intersection cardinality testing protocol $\Pi_{\mathsf{TFHE\text{-}CTest\text{-}int}}$ for $\mathcal{F}_{\mathsf{CTest\text{-}int}}$.

Theorem 2. *Assuming threshold FHE with distributed setup, protocol* $\Pi_{\mathsf{TFHE\text{-}CTest\text{-}int}}$ *(Fig. 5) securely realizes* $\mathcal{F}_{\mathsf{CTest\text{-}int}}$ *(Fig. 3).*

Proof. **Correctness.** We first prove the protocol is correct. By the correctness of the TFHE scheme, we only need to show that the computed predicate $b = 1$ if and only if $\forall i, |S_i \setminus I| \le T$. First consider the case where the protocol should output similar. Since

$$\mathsf{p}'(x) = \frac{\mathsf{p}_2'(x) + \cdots + \mathsf{p}_n'(x)}{\mathsf{p}_1'(x)} = \frac{\mathsf{p}_{2 \setminus I}(x) \cdot (x - r_2) + \cdots + \mathsf{p}_{n \setminus I}(x) \cdot (x - r_n)}{\mathsf{p}_{1 \setminus I}(x) \cdot (x - r_1)},$$

the degree of each term $\mathsf{p}_{i \setminus I}(x) \cdot (x - r_i)$ is at most $T+1$ and therefore the rational polynomial interpolation requires a total of $(2T+3)$ evaluation points. Therefore $\mathsf{p}^*(x) = \mathsf{p}'(x)$ and $\mathsf{p}^*(z) = \mathsf{p}'(z) = \frac{e_2' + \cdots + e_n'}{e_1'}$. Thus $b = 1$ as required.

Now consider the case where the protocol should output different, namely when $|I| < m - T$. Observe that $\gcd(\mathsf{p}_{1 \setminus I}, \cdots, \mathsf{p}_{n \setminus I}) = 1$ by construction and therefore

$$\gcd\left(\mathsf{p}_{2 \setminus I}'(x) + \cdots + \mathsf{p}_{n \setminus I}'(x), \mathsf{p}_{1 \setminus I}'(x) \right) = 1$$

except with negligible probability, where $p'_{i\backslash I}(x) := p_{i\backslash I}(x) \cdot (x - r_i)$. The algebraic proof is deferred to the full version.

Assuming gcd $\left(p'_{2\backslash I}(x) + \cdots + p'_{n\backslash I}(x), p'_{1\backslash I}(x) \right) = 1$, it then follows that the degree of the rational polynomial $p'(x)$ is the degree of $p'_{2\backslash I}(x) + \cdots + p'_{n\backslash I}(x)$ plus the degree of $p'_{1\backslash I}(x)$. The former must have a leading term with degree $(m - |I| + 1) > (T + 1)$. Similarly, the latter also has degree $(m - |I| + 1) > T + 1$. Hence the degree of $p'(x)$ is at least $2T + 4$. The probability of $b = 1$ is $\Pr_z[p'(z) = p^*(z)]$ where $p^*(x)$ is the polynomial interpolated by P_1 using $(2T + 3)$ evaluations. However, since the degree of $p'(x)$ is at least $2T + 4$, $\Pr_z[p'(z) = p^*(z)] \leq \mathsf{negl}(\lambda)$.

Communication Cost. Each party sends $(2T + 4)$ TFHE encryptions and one partial decryption to P_1 where each plaintext is a field element. P_1 sends one ciphertext to every other party. The size of each encryption and each partial decryption is $\mathsf{poly}(\lambda)$. Thus, the overall communication complexity is $O(n \cdot T \cdot \mathsf{poly}(\lambda))$ in a star network and the protocols runs in $O(1)$ rounds.

Security. Consider an environment $\mathcal{Z}$ who corrupts a set $\mathcal{S}^*$ of n^* parties where $n^* < n$. The simulator Sim has output $w \in \{\mathsf{similar}, \mathsf{different}\}$ from the ideal functionality. Sim sets a bit $b^* = 1$ if $w = \mathsf{similar}$ and $b^* = 0$ otherwise. Also, for each corrupt party P_i, Sim has as input the tuple (S_i, r_i) indicating the party's input and randomness for the protocol. The strategy of the simulator Sim for our protocol is described below.

1. Sim runs the distributed key generation algorithm TFHE.DistSetup$(1^\lambda, i)$ of the TFHE scheme honestly on behalf of each honest party P_i as in the real world. Note that Sim also knows $(\{\mathsf{sk}_i\}_{i \in \mathcal{S}^*})$ as it knows the randomness for the corrupt parties.
2. In Steps 2–4 of the protocol, Sim plays the role of the honest parties exactly as in the real world except that on behalf of every honest party P_i, whenever P_i has to send any ciphertext, compute $[\![0]\!] = \mathsf{TFHE.Enc}(0)$ using fresh randomness.
3. In Step 5, on behalf of each honest party P_i, instead of sending the value $[\![b : \mathsf{sk}_i]\!]$ by running the honest TFHE.PartialDec algorithm as in the real world, Sim computes the partial decryptions by running the simulator TFHE.Sim as follows: $\{[\![b : \mathsf{Sim}_i]\!]\}_{i \in [n] \backslash \mathcal{S}^*} \leftarrow \mathsf{TFHE.Sim}(C, b^*, [\![b]\!], \{\mathsf{sk}_i\}_{i \in \mathcal{S}^*})$ where the circuit C denotes the whole computation done by P_1 in the real world to evaluate bit b. On behalf of the honest party P_i the simulator sends $[\![b : \mathsf{Sim}_i]\!]$. This corresponds to the ideal world.

We now show that the above simulation strategy is successful against all environments $\mathcal{Z}$ that corrupt parties in a semi-honest manner. We will show this via a series of computationally indistinguishable hybrids where the first hybrid Hybrid_0 corresponds to the real world and the last hybrid Hybrid_2 corresponds to the ideal world.

- Hybrid_0 - **Real World:** In this hybrid, consider a simulator SimHyb that plays the role of the honest parties as in the real world.

- Hybrid$_1$ - **Simulate Partial Decryptions:** - In this hybrid, in Step 5, SimHyb simulates the partial decryptions generated by the honest parties as done in the ideal world. That is, the simulator calls $\{[\![b : \mathsf{Sim}_i]\!]\}_{i \in [n] \setminus S} \leftarrow$ TFHE.Sim$(C, b^*, [\![b]\!], \{\mathsf{sk}_i\}_{i \in S})$. On behalf of the honest party P_i the simulator sends $[\![b : \mathsf{Sim}_i]\!]$ instead of $[\![b : \mathsf{sk}_i]\!]$.
- Hybrid$_2$ - **Switch Encryptions:** In this hybrid, SimHyb now computes every ciphertext generated on behalf of any honest party as encryptions of 0 as done by Sim in the ideal world. This hybrid corresponds to the ideal world.

We show that every pair of consecutive hybrids is computationally indistinguishable in the full version.

5.2   Protocol for Functionality $\mathcal{F}_{\mathsf{CTest\text{-}diff}}$

This protocol will compute the cardinality predicate b where $b = 1$ if and only if $|(\bigcup_{i=1}^{n} S_i) \setminus I| \leq T$. The core idea behind the protocol is that P_1 (the star of the network) and P_i first run a protocol to compute an encryption (via TFHE) of their set differences $D_{1,i} = S_1 \setminus S_i$ and $D_{i,1} = S_i \setminus S_1$ with $O(T)$ communication complexity if $|S_1 \setminus S_i| \leq T$. Before we describe how this is achieved, notice that at this point, the protocol enables P_1 to reconstruct an encryption of $(\bigcup_{i=1}^{n} S_i) \setminus I = \bigcup_{i \in [n] \setminus \{1\}} (D_{1,i}^* \cup D_{i,1}^*)$ and a predicate b where $b = 1$ if and only if $|(\bigcup_{i=1}^{n} S_i) \setminus I| \leq T$. P_1 can then send this encryption to all parties to run threshold decryption.

We now describe in more detail how the encryption of $D_{1,i}$ and $D_{i,1}$ are computed. The idea follows from the two-party protocol of Ghosh and Simkin [GS19a]. Each party P_i encodes their set S_i as $\mathsf{p}_i(x) := \Pi_{a \in S_i}(x - a) \in \mathbb{F}[x]$. P_i then computes $e_{i,j} := \mathsf{p}_i(j)$ for $j \in [2T + 1]$ and $e_i' := \mathsf{p}_i(z)$ on a special random point $z \in \mathbb{F}$ (picked uniformly at random by P_1). Party P_i encrypts these values as $[\![e_{i,j}]\!], [\![e_i']\!]$ and sends them to P_1. Party P_1 considers the rational polynomial

$$\widetilde{\mathsf{p}}_i(x) = \frac{\mathsf{p}_i(x)}{\mathsf{p}_1(x)} = \frac{\mathsf{p}_{i \setminus 1}(x)}{\mathsf{p}_{1 \setminus i}(x)}$$

and homomorphically computes $2T + 1$ encrypted evaluations $\left(j, \left[\!\left[\frac{e_{i,j}}{e_{1,j}}\right]\!\right]\right)$ for $j = [2T + 1]$. Using these encrypted evaluations, P_1 homomorphically computes an encrypted rational polynomial $[\![\widetilde{\mathsf{p}}_i^*(x)]\!]$ using rational polynomial interpolation. P_1 then homomorphically reconstructs the roots of $\mathsf{p}_{i \setminus 1}(x)$ and $\mathsf{p}_{1 \setminus i}(x)$ from $\widetilde{\mathsf{p}}_i^*$ to obtain $[\![D_{i,1}^*]\!], [\![D_{1,i}^*]\!]$. Note that $\widetilde{\mathsf{p}}_i^*(x) = \widetilde{\mathsf{p}}_i(x)$ if $\widetilde{\mathsf{p}}_i(x)$ has degree at most $2T$, in which case $D_{i,1}^* = D_{i,1}$ and $D_{1,i}^* = D_{1,i}$.

In the final protocol, P_1 homomorphically computes encrypted predicates b_i where $b_i = 1$ iff $\widetilde{\mathsf{p}}_i^*(z) = \frac{e_i'}{e_1'}$ for each $i \in [n] \setminus \{1\}$ and encrypted predicate b' where $b' = 1$ iff $\left|\bigcup_{i \in [n] \setminus \{1\}} (D_{1,i}^* \cup D_{i,1}^*)\right| \leq T$. The output predicate b is homomorpically computed as $[\![b]\!] = [\![b' \cdot \prod_{i \in [n] \setminus \{1\}} b_i]\!]$ and jointly decrypted by all the parties. The protocol is formally described in Fig. 6.

Parameters: Parties $P_1, \ldots, P_n$. Each party has a set of m elements. Threshold $T \in \mathbb{N}$. $\mathbb{F}$ is a finite field where $|\mathbb{F}| = \Omega(2^\lambda)$.

Inputs: Party P_i has an input set $S_i = \{a_1^i, \ldots, a_m^i\}$ where $a_j^i \in \mathbb{F}$ for all $j \in [m]$.

Output: Each party P_i receives similar if $\left|\left(\bigcup_{i=1}^n S_i\right) \setminus I\right| \leq T$ and different otherwise where $I = \bigcap_{i=1}^n S_i$.

Protocol:
1. Each party P_i generates $(\mathsf{pk}_i, \mathsf{sk}_i) \leftarrow \mathsf{TFHE.DistSetup}(1^\lambda, i)$ and sends pk_i to P_1. Then P_1 sends $\mathsf{pk} = (\mathsf{pk}_1 \| \ldots \| \mathsf{pk}_n)$ to all the other parties.
2. P_1 picks a random value $z \in \mathbb{F}$ and sends it to all parties.
3. Each party P_i does the following:
    (a) Define the polynomial $\mathsf{p}_i(\mathsf{x}) := \prod_{a \in S_i} (\mathsf{x} - a)$.
    (b) Compute $e_{i,j} := \mathsf{p}_i(j)$ for $j \in [2T+1]$ and $e_i' := \mathsf{p}_i(z)$.
    (c) Send encrypted evaluations $[\![e_{i,j}]\!] := \mathsf{TFHE.Enc}(\mathsf{pk}, e_{i,j})$ for $j \in [2T+1]$ and $[\![e_i']\!] := \mathsf{TFHE.Enc}(\mathsf{pk}, e_i')$ to P_1.
4. P_1 does the following:
    (a) For each $i \in [n] \setminus \{1\}$, use the algorithm $\mathsf{TFHE.Eval}$ to homomorphically compute an encryption $[\![\widetilde{\mathsf{p}}_i^*(\mathsf{x})]\!]$ by rational polynomial interpolation from $2T+1$ encrypted evaluations $\left(j, \left[\!\!\left[\frac{e_{i,j}}{e_{1,j}}\right]\!\!\right]\right)$ for $j \in [2T+1]$.
    (b) For each $i \in [n] \setminus \{1\}$, homomorphically compute the encrypted predicate $[\![b_i]\!]$ where $b_i = 1$ if $\widetilde{\mathsf{p}}_i^*(z) = \frac{e_i'}{e_1'}$ and 0 otherwise.
    (c) For each $i \in [n] \setminus \{1\}$, homomorphically compute the encrypted roots $[\![D_{i,1}^*]\!]$, $[\![D_{1,i}^*]\!]$ of the numerator and denominator of $\widetilde{\mathsf{p}}_i^*(\mathsf{x})$, respectively.
    (d) Homomorphically compute the encrypted predicate $[\![b']\!]$ where $b' = 1$ if $\left|\bigcup_{i \in [n] \setminus \{1\}} (D_{1,i}^* \cup D_{i,1}^*)\right| \leq T$ and 0 otherwise.
5. P_1 sends $[\![b]\!] = \left[\!\!\left[b' \cdot \prod_{i \in [n] \setminus \{1\}} b_i\right]\!\!\right]$ to all parties who respond with $[\![b : \mathsf{sk}_i]\!] := \mathsf{TFHE.PartialDec}(\mathsf{sk}_i, [\![b]\!])$. P_1 broadcasts $b := \mathsf{TFHE.Combine}(\mathsf{pk}, \{[\![b : \mathsf{sk}_i]\!]\}_{i \in [n]})$ and all parties output similar if $b = 1$ and different otherwise.

Fig. 6. Multi-party private intersection cardinality testing protocol $\Pi_{\mathsf{TFHE\text{-}CTest\text{-}diff}}$ for $\mathcal{F}_{\mathsf{CTest\text{-}diff}}$

Theorem 3. *Assuming threshold FHE with distributed setup, protocol $\Pi_{\mathsf{TFHE\text{-}CTest\text{-}diff}}$ (Fig. 6) securely realizes $\mathcal{F}_{\mathsf{CTest\text{-}diff}}$ (Fig. 4).*

Proof. **Correctness.** We first prove the protocol is correct. By the correctness of the TFHE scheme, we only need to show that the computed predicate $b = 1$ if and only if $\left|\left(\bigcup_{i=1}^n S_i\right) \setminus I\right| \leq T$. First consider the case where the protocol should output similar. Since

$$\widetilde{\mathsf{p}}_i(\mathsf{x}) = \frac{\mathsf{p}_i(\mathsf{x})}{\mathsf{p}_1(\mathsf{x})} = \frac{\mathsf{p}_{i \setminus 1}(\mathsf{x})}{\mathsf{p}_{1 \setminus i}(\mathsf{x})},$$

both the numerator and denominator have degree at most T and therefore the rational polynomial interpolation requires at most $(2T+1)$ evaluation points. Hence $\widetilde{\mathsf{p}}_i^*(\mathsf{x}) = \widetilde{\mathsf{p}}_i(\mathsf{x})$ and $\widetilde{\mathsf{p}}_i^*(z) = \widetilde{\mathsf{p}}_i(z) = \frac{e_i'}{e_1'}$, thus $b_i = 1$. Since the roots of $\mathsf{p}_{i \setminus 1}$ is simply the set difference $D_{i,1} = S_i \setminus S_1$, we have $D_{i,1}^* = D_{i,1} = S_i \setminus S_1$.

Similarly $D_{1,i}^* = S_1 \setminus S_i$. Since $\left| \bigcup_{i \in [n] \setminus \{1\}} (D_{1,i}^* \cup D_{i,1}^*) \right| = |(\bigcup_{i=1}^n S_i) \setminus I| \leq T$, we have $b' = 1$. Hence the protocol will output $b = 1$.

Now consider the case where the protocol should output different, namely $|(\bigcup_{i=1}^n S_i) \setminus I| > T$. There are two possible cases. In the first case, $|S_i \setminus S_1| > T$ for some i. Then $\tilde{p}_i$ has degree at least $2T + 2$ but $\tilde{p}_i^*$ is interpolated from $2T + 1$ evaluation points, hence $b_i' = 0$ with all but negligible probability. In the second case, $|S_i \setminus S_1| \leq T$ for all $i \in [n] \setminus \{1\}$. Then $D_{i,1}^* = D_{i,1} = S_i \setminus S_1$, $D_{1,i}^* = S_1 \setminus S_i$, and $b_i = 1$ for all i. Since $|(\bigcup_{i=1}^n S_i) \setminus I| > T$, $b' = 0$. In both cases, we have $b = b' \cdot \prod_{i \in [n] \setminus \{1\}} b_i = 0$ with all but negligible probability.

Communication Cost. Each party sends $(2T + 2)$ TFHE encryptions and one partial decryption to P_1 where each plaintext is a field element. P_1 sends one ciphertext to every other party. The size of each encryption and each partial decryption is $\mathsf{poly}(\lambda)$. Thus, the overall communication complexity is $O(n \cdot T \cdot \mathsf{poly}(\lambda))$ in a star network and the protocols runs in $O(1)$ rounds.

Security. The proof of security is identical to the proof of Theorem 2. We defer the formal proof to the full version.

6   TAHE-Based Protocol for $\mathcal{F}_{\mathsf{CTest\text{-}diff}}$

In this section, we present a multi-party protocol for private intersection cardinality testing for functionality $\mathcal{F}_{\mathsf{CTest\text{-}diff}}$ based on threshold additive homomorphic encryption with distributed setup. That is, the parties learn whether their sets satisfy $|(\bigcup_{i=1}^n S_i) \setminus I| \leq T$. Our protocol works in the star network communication model where P_1 is the central party.

In our construction, we need a secure multi-party computation (MPC) protocol that tests the singularity of a specific Hankel matrix (defined later), which we discuss in Sect. 6.1. Using this, we present our complete protocol in Sect. 6.2.

6.1   Singularity Testing of Hankel Matrices

In Sect. 6.2, we will see that intersection cardinality testing can be reduced to determining whether the determinant of a specific matrix is 0 or not. The latter problem can be reduced to computing the so-called "Half-GCD" of two specific polynomials. In this section, we present a summary of the various results that go into these reductions and refer the reader to the cited works for further details.

Half-GCD Problem. Consider the ring of polynomials $\mathbb{F}[x]$. Note that since $\mathbb{F}[x]$ is a Euclidean domain, Euclid's GCD algorithm can be applied to polynomials as well. Consider $p_0, p_1 \in \mathbb{F}[x]$ with $d = \deg(p_0) > \deg(p_1) \geq 0$. The Euclidean algorithm can be viewed as a sequence of transformations of 2-vectors as below:

$$\begin{pmatrix} p_0 \\ p_1 \end{pmatrix} \xrightarrow{M_1} \begin{pmatrix} p_1 \\ p_2 \end{pmatrix} \xrightarrow{M_2} \cdots \xrightarrow{M_{h-1}} \begin{pmatrix} p_{h-1} \\ p_h \end{pmatrix} \xrightarrow{M_h} \begin{pmatrix} p_h \\ 0 \end{pmatrix} \qquad (2)$$

Here, $M_1, \ldots, M_h$ are 2×2 matrices, $p_2, \ldots, p_h \in \mathbb{F}[x]$. For vectors U, V and a matrix M, we write $U \xrightarrow{M} V$ to denote $U = MV$.

Equation 2 can be correctly interpreted if we define

$$M_i = \begin{pmatrix} q_i & 1 \\ 1 & 0 \end{pmatrix}.$$

We call such matrices *elementary matrices*, where q_i is a polynomial of positive degree. We also refer to q_i as the *partial quotient* in M_i. A *regular matrix* M is a product of zero or more elementary matrices, namely

$$M = M_1 M_2 \ldots M_k \qquad (k \geq 0)$$

where if $k = 0$, then M is defined to be the identity matrix of order 2.

We define the *half-GCD (HGCD)* problem for the polynomial ring $\mathbb{F}[x]$ as follows. Given $p_0, p_1 \in \mathbb{F}[x]$ with $d = \deg(p_0) > \deg(p_1) \geq 0$, compute a regular matrix

$$M = \texttt{HGCD}(p_0, p_1)$$

such that if

$$\begin{pmatrix} p_0 \\ p_1 \end{pmatrix} \xrightarrow{M} \begin{pmatrix} p_2 \\ p_3 \end{pmatrix},$$

then

$$\deg(p_2) \geq d/2 > \deg(p_3).$$

We now recall the result of Thull and Yap [TY90] on the computational complexity of HGCD.

Imported Theorem 4. *Consider the polynomial ring $\mathbb{F}[x]$ and the polynomials $p_0, p_1 \in \mathbb{F}[x]$ with $d = \deg(p_0) > \deg(p_1) \geq 0$. The computational complexity of the HGCD problem is $O(d \log^2 d)$.*

Singularity Testing of Hankel Matrices. Next, we proceed to outline the results that enable us to use the HGCD problem to test singularity of Hankel matrices. A Hankel matrix is a matrix in which each ascending skew-diagonal from left to right is constant. We will be working with square Hankel matrices. In particular, a $(k+1) \times (k+1)$ Hankel matrix takes the form

$$H = \begin{pmatrix} a_0 & a_1 & \cdots & a_k \\ a_1 & a_2 & \cdots & a_{k+1} \\ \vdots & \vdots & \vdots & \vdots \\ a_k & a_{k+1} & \cdots & a_{2k} \end{pmatrix}$$

where the $2k+1$ entries $a_0, a_1, \ldots, a_{2k}$ define H. Define the two polynomials

$$p_0(x) = x^{2k+1}$$
$$p_1(x) = a_0 + a_1 x + a_2 x^2 + \ldots + a_{2k} x^{2k}$$

where $p_0, p_1 \in \mathbb{F}[x]$. Let $M = \texttt{HGCD}(p_0, p_1)$ and

$$\begin{pmatrix} p_0 \\ p_1 \end{pmatrix} \xrightarrow{M} \begin{pmatrix} p_2 \\ p_3 \end{pmatrix}.$$

Then we have

$$\deg(p_2) \geq k + 1 > \deg(p_3).$$

We recall the setting and results of Brent, Gustavson and Yun [BGY80] that elegantly connect the singularity of H with the HGCD of $p_0(x)$ and $p_1(x)$.

Imported Theorem 5. *The Hankel matrix H is singular iff $\deg(p_3) < k$.*

Putting Imported Theorems 4 and 5 together, we have the following theorem.

Imported Theorem 6. *The computational complexity of testing singularity of a $(k+1) \times (k+1)$ Hankel matrix is $O(k \log^2 k)$.*

Multi-party Singularity Testing. Looking ahead, in our multi-party intersection cardinality testing protocol, we will need to test for the singularity of a Hankel matrix H which the parties have additive shares of, and the parties will run a secure multi-party computation (MPC) protocol to jointly test for the singularity of H. The ideal functionality $\mathcal{F}_{\mathsf{SingTest}}$ for the multi-party minimal polynomial computation is defined in Fig. 7. We will need an MPC protocol that realizes $\mathcal{F}_{\mathsf{SingTest}}$ with communication complexity at most $\widetilde{O}(k \cdot n \cdot \mathsf{poly}(\lambda))$. Any such protocol suffices, and we denote by Π_{SingTest} the MPC protocol realizing $\mathcal{F}_{\mathsf{SingTest}}$.

Parameters: Parties $P_1, \ldots, P_n$.

Inputs: Each party P_i inputs $2k + 1$ field elements $a_{0,i}, a_{1,i}, \ldots, a_{2k,i} \in \mathbb{F}$.

Output: Let

$$H_i = \begin{pmatrix} a_{0,i} & a_{1,i} & \cdots & a_{k,i} \\ a_{1,i} & a_{2,i} & \cdots & a_{k+1,i} \\ \vdots & \vdots & \vdots & \vdots \\ a_{k,i} & a_{k+1,i} & \cdots & a_{2k,i} \end{pmatrix}$$

be the Hankel matrix defined by the inputs of party P_i for $i = 1, \ldots, n$, and let

$$H = \sum_{i=1}^{n} H_i.$$

Determine if the Hankel matrix H is singular. Each party receives 0 if H is singular, and 1 otherwise.

Fig. 7. Ideal functionality $\mathcal{F}_{\mathsf{SingTest}}$ for multi-party singularity testing of a Hankel matrix.

Here we describe two such protocols with communication complexity $\widetilde{O}(k \cdot n \cdot \mathsf{poly}(\lambda))$ based on TAHE. In the first protocol, after the TAHE setup, each party

P_i sends $[\![H_i]\!]$ to P_1 and P_1 homomorphically computes $[\![H]\!]$. Afterwards P_1 can homomorphically evaluate a circuit C that computes a predicate $b \stackrel{?}{=} (\det(H) = 0)$, following the ideas from [FH96, CDN01]. Finally the parties jointly decrypt the encrypted output. Since the size and depth of C are both $O(k \log^2 k)$ by Imported Theorem 6, the total communication complexity of this protocol is $O(k \log^2 k \cdot n \cdot \mathsf{poly}(\lambda))$ and the round complexity is $O(k \log^2 k)$.

As a second protocol, the parties jointly compute another C' that takes H and a random PRF key r as input and outputs a Yao's garbled circuit [Yao86] that computes C. This approach is inspired by the work of Damgård et al. [DIK+08]. Since both H and r are additively shared among all the parties, this MPC can be done similarly as in the previous protocol, namely P_1 first obtains $[\![H]\!]$ and $[\![r]\!]$ and then homomorphically evaluates C'. Since the size C' is $\tilde{O}(k \cdot \mathsf{poly}(\lambda))$ and the depth of C' is constant assuming PRG is a circuit in NC^1 [AIK05], the total communication complexity of this protocol is $\tilde{O}(k \cdot n \cdot \mathsf{poly}(\lambda))$ and the round complexity is $O(1)$.

Two-Party Case. Notice that for two parties, $\mathcal{F}_{\mathsf{SingTest}}$ can be instantiated via Yao's garbled circuits with communication complexity $\tilde{O}(k \cdot \mathsf{poly}(\lambda))$.

6.2   Our Protocol

In this section we present our multi-party private intersection cardinality testing protocol. That is, the parties learn whether their sets satisfy $|(\bigcup_{i=1}^n S_i) \setminus I| \leq T$.

At a high level, our protocol first encodes each party P_i's set as a polynomial $\mathsf{p}_i(\mathsf{x}) = \sum_{j=1}^m \mathsf{x}^{a_j^i}$, and let $\mathsf{p}(\mathsf{x}) := (n-1)\mathsf{p}_1(\mathsf{x}) - \sum_{i=2}^n \mathsf{p}_i(\mathsf{x})$. Notice that a term x^a is cancelled out in the polynomial p if and only if the element a is in the set intersection I. Therefore, the number of monomials in p is exactly $|(\bigcup_{i=1}^n S_i) \setminus I|$.

To determine if the number of monomials in p is $\leq T$, we can apply the polynomial sparsity test of Grigorescu et al. [GJR10] similarly as in [GS19a]. In particular, pick a field $\mathbb{F}_q$, sample $u \stackrel{\$}{\leftarrow} \mathbb{F}_q$ uniformly at random, and compute the Hankel matrix

$$H = \begin{bmatrix} \mathsf{p}(u^0) & \mathsf{p}(u^1) & \cdots & \mathsf{p}(u^T) \\ \mathsf{p}(u^1) & \mathsf{p}(u^2) & \cdots & \mathsf{p}(u^{T+1}) \\ \vdots & \vdots & \ddots & \vdots \\ \mathsf{p}(u^T) & \mathsf{p}(u^{T+1}) & \cdots & \mathsf{p}(u^{2T}) \end{bmatrix}.$$

Determining if the number of monomials in p is $\leq T$ can be reduced to testing the singularity of H. In particular, we take the following theorem from [GJR10, Theorem 3] and [GS19a, Theorem 1].

Imported Theorem 7. *Let $q > T(T+1)(p-1)2^\kappa$ be a prime. If the number of monomials in p is $\leq T$, then $\Pr[\det(H) = 0] = 1$, and if the number of monomials in p is $> T$, then $\Pr[\det(H) = 0] \leq 2^{-\kappa}$,*

---

1. **Computing Shares of Hankel Matrix H.**
   (a) P_1 picks a uniform random $u \overset{\$}{\leftarrow} \mathbb{F}_q$ and sends to all other parties.
   (b) P_1 sets a polynomial $\mathsf{p}_1(\mathsf{x}) = \sum_{j=1}^{m}(n-1) \cdot \mathsf{x}^{a_j^1}$ in $\mathbb{F}_q[\mathsf{x}]$.
   (c) Each party P_i $(i = 2, 3, \ldots, n)$ sets a polynomial $\mathsf{p}_i(\mathsf{x}) = -\sum_{j=1}^{m} \mathsf{x}^{a_j^i}$ in $\mathbb{F}_q[\mathsf{x}]$.
   (d) Each party P_i $(i = 1, 2, 3, \ldots, n)$ computes the values $a_{j,i} = \mathsf{p}_i(u^j)$ for $j = 0, 1, \ldots, 2T$.

2. **Matrix Singularity Testing of H.** Parties invoke an instance of $\mathcal{F}_{\mathsf{SingTest}}$ where each party P_i inputs $a_{0,i}, \ldots, a_{2T,i}$ and obtains a bit b.

3. **Output.** Each party P_i outputs similar if $b = 0$ and different otherwise.

Fig. 8. Multi-party private intersection cardinality testing protocol $\Pi_{\mathsf{CTest\text{-}diff}}$.

In our multi-party private intersection cardinality testing protocol, the parties will first compute additive shares of H and then run a multi-party minimal polynomial computation protocol to jointly test the singularity of H. The protocol is presented in Fig. 8.

Theorem 8. *Let $q > T(T+1)(p-1)2^\kappa$ be a prime. Assuming threshold additive homomorphic encryption scheme with distributed setup, the protocol $\Pi_{\mathsf{CTest\text{-}diff}}$ (Fig. 8) securely realizes $\mathcal{F}_{\mathsf{CTest\text{-}diff}}$ in the $\mathcal{F}_{\mathsf{SingTest}}$-hybrid model.*

Proof. **Correctness.** By the correctness of $\mathcal{F}_{\mathsf{SingTest}}$, in Step 2 all the parties learn a bit b and $b = 0$ if and only if H is singular, where H is the Hankel matrix $H = \sum_{i=1}^{n} H_i$ and each Hankel matrix H_i is defined by the inputs of party P_i as

$$
H_i = \begin{pmatrix}
a_{0,i} & a_{1,i} & \cdots & a_{T,i} \\
a_{1,i} & a_{2,i} & \cdots & a_{T+1,i} \\
\vdots & \vdots & \ddots & \vdots \\
a_{T,i} & a_{T+1,i} & \cdots & a_{2T,i}
\end{pmatrix}
$$

for $i = 1, \ldots, n$. By Imported Theorem 7, $b = 0$ if and only if $|(\bigcup_{i=1}^{n} S_i) \setminus I| \leq T$ with all but negligible probability. Therefore the protocol is correct with all but negligible probability.

Communication Cost. The communication cost is the same as the protocol Π_{SingTest}. In particular, the round complexity is $O(1)$ in a star network and the total communication complexity is $\widetilde{O}(T \cdot n \cdot \mathsf{poly}(\lambda))$.

Security. We construct a PPT Sim which simulates the view of the corrupted parties. The simulator Sim gets the output $w \in \{\mathsf{similar}, \mathsf{different}\}$ from the ideal functionality. Sim sets a bit $b^* = 1$ if $w = \mathsf{similar}$ and $b^* = 0$ otherwise. Also, for each corrupt party P_i, Sim has as input the tuple (S_i, r_i) indicating the party's input and randomness for the protocol. The strategy of the simulator Sim for our protocol is described below.

1. Invoke the corrupted parties with their corresponding inputs and randomness.

2. Play the role of the honest parties as follows: Run the protocol honestly. Note that P_1 is the only party that ever sends a message, so this step in the simulation is trivial.
3. In Step 2, play the role of $\mathcal{F}_{\mathsf{SingTest}}$ and respond b^*.
4. Finally, output the view of the corrupted parties.

Next we argue that the view of the corrupted parties generated by Sim is computationally indistinguishable to their view in the real world from $\mathcal{Z}$'s point of view. The only difference between the real and ideal worlds is that in the ideal world, the output from $\mathcal{F}_{\mathsf{SingTest}}$ is replaced by 0 if $|(\bigcup_{i=1}^{n} S_i) \setminus I| \leq T$ and 1 otherwise. This is computationally indistinguishable from the real world because of the correctness of the protocol.

Corollary 2. *Assuming TAHE with distributed setup, protocol $\Pi_{\mathsf{CTest\text{-}diff}}$ (Fig. 8) securely realizes $\mathcal{F}_{\mathsf{CTest\text{-}diff}}$ in the star network communication model with communication complexity $\widetilde{O}(n \cdot T \cdot \mathsf{poly}(\lambda))$ and round complexity $O(1)$.*

7   Threshold PSI for $\mathcal{F}_{\mathsf{TPSI\text{-}diff}}$

Recall that in a multi-party threshold PSI protocol for functionality $\mathcal{F}_{\mathsf{TPSI\text{-}diff}}$ defined in Fig. 2, each party wishes to learn the intersection of all their sets if $|(\bigcup_{i=1}^{n} S_i) \setminus I| \leq T$, that is, if the size of the union of all their sets minus the intersection is less than the threshold T. In this section, we describe our multi-party threshold PSI protocol based on any protocol for multi-party private intersection cardinality testing. We rely on TAHE with distributed setup.

Theorem 9. *Assuming threshold additive homomorphic encryption with distributed setup, protocol $\Pi_{\mathsf{TPSI\text{-}diff}}$ (Fig. 9) securely realizes $\mathcal{F}_{\mathsf{TPSI\text{-}diff}}$ in the $\mathcal{F}_{\mathsf{CTest\text{-}diff}}$-hybrid model in the star network communication model. Our protocol is secure against a semi-honest adversary that can corrupt up to $(n-1)$ parties.*

The protocol runs in a constant number of rounds and the communication complexity is $O(n \cdot T \cdot \mathsf{poly}(\lambda))$ in the $\mathcal{F}_{\mathsf{CTest\text{-}diff}}$-hybrid model. We then instantiate the $\mathcal{F}_{\mathsf{CTest\text{-}diff}}$-hybrid with the two protocols from the previous sections: one based on TFHE from Sect. 5.2 that has round complexity $O(1)$ and $O(n \cdot T \cdot \mathsf{poly}(\lambda))$ communication complexity and the other based on TAHE from Sect. 6 that has round complexity $O(1)$ and communication complexity $\widetilde{O}(n \cdot T \cdot \mathsf{poly}(\lambda))$. Formally, we get the following corollaries:

Corollary 3. *Assuming TFHE (resp. TAHE) with distributed setup, protocol $\Pi_{\mathsf{TPSI\text{-}diff}}$ (Fig. 9) securely realizes $\mathcal{F}_{\mathsf{TPSI\text{-}diff}}$ in the star network communication model with communication complexity $O(n \cdot T \cdot \mathsf{poly}(\lambda))$ (resp. $\widetilde{O}(n \cdot T \cdot \mathsf{poly}(\lambda))$) and round complexity $O(1)$.*

Our threshold PSI protocol for functionality $\mathcal{F}_{\mathsf{TPSI\text{-}int}}$ is almost identical and we defer the details to the full version.

7.1 Protocol

Consider n parties $P_1, \ldots, P_n$ with input sets $S_1, \ldots, S_n$ of size m and a star network where the central party is P_1. The parties first run the private intersection cardinality testing protocols for functionality $\mathcal{F}_{\mathsf{CTest\text{-}diff}}$ from the previous sections and proceed if $|(\bigcup_{i=1}^{n} S_i) \setminus I| \leq T$. Then, each party P_i encodes its set as a polynomial $\mathsf{p}'_i(\mathrm{x}) = (\mathrm{x} - r_i) \cdot \prod_{j=1}^{m}(\mathrm{x} - a_j^i)$ where r_i is picked uniformly at random. The parties then compute $(3T + 4)$ evaluations of the following polynomial $\mathsf{V}(\cdot)$ on points $1, \ldots, (3T + 4)$ using threshold additive homomorphic encryption: $\mathsf{V}(\mathrm{x}) = \sum_{i=1}^{n} (\mathsf{p}'_i(\mathrm{x}) \cdot \mathsf{R}_i(\mathrm{x}))$ where each $\mathsf{R}_i(\cdot)$ is a uniformly random polynomial of degree T that is computed as an addition of n random polynomials - one generated by each party. Then, each party P_i interpolates the degree $(3T + 3)$ rational polynomial $\frac{\mathsf{V}(\cdot)}{\mathsf{p}'_i(\cdot)}$ using the $(3T + 4)$ evaluations. Finally, each party outputs the intersection as $S_i \setminus D_i$ where D_i denotes the roots of the above interpolated polynomial. Our protocol is formally described in Fig. 9.

Two-Party Case. For two parties Alice and Bob, we can rely on AHE alone, where Alice holds the secret key. In particular, define $\mathsf{V}(\mathrm{x}) := \mathsf{p}_A(\mathrm{x}) \cdot \left(\mathsf{R}_1^A(\mathrm{x}) + \mathsf{R}_1^B(\mathrm{x})\right) + \mathsf{p}_B(\mathrm{x}) \cdot \left(\mathsf{R}_2^A(\mathrm{x}) + \mathsf{R}_2^B(\mathrm{x})\right)$, where $(\mathsf{R}_1^A, \mathsf{R}_2^A)$ and $(\mathsf{R}_1^B, \mathsf{R}_2^B)$ are uniformly random polynomials of degree T generated by Alice and Bob, respectively. To obtain an evaluation of $\mathsf{V}(x)$, Alice first sends an encryption of $\mathsf{p}_A(x)$ and $\mathsf{R}_2^A(x)$ to Bob. Then Bob homomorphically computes an encryption of $r = \mathsf{p}_A(x) \cdot \mathsf{R}_1^B(x) + \mathsf{p}_B(x) \cdot \left(\mathsf{R}_2^A(x) + \mathsf{R}_2^B(x)\right)$ and sends it back. Alice can decrypt $[\![r]\!]$ and compute $\mathsf{V}(x) = \mathsf{p}_A(x) \cdot \mathsf{R}_1^A(x) + r$. The communication complexity is $O(T \cdot \mathsf{poly}(\lambda))$.

7.2 Security Proof

Correctness. If $|(\bigcup_{i=1}^{n} S_i) \setminus I| > T$, then the protocol terminates after the first step – private intersection cardinality testing. If, on the other hand, $|(\bigcup_{i=1}^{n} S_i) \setminus I| \leq T$, observe that polynomial $\mathsf{V}(\mathrm{x})$ can be rewritten as $\sum_{i=1}^{n} \mathsf{p}'_i(\mathrm{x}) \cdot U_i(\mathrm{x})$ where each U_i is a uniformly random polynomial of degree at most $T + 1$. Now, from the correctness of the TAHE scheme, each party P_i learns $3T + 4$ evaluations of the rational polynomial:

$$q_i(\mathrm{x}) = \frac{\mathsf{V}(\mathrm{x})}{\mathsf{p}'_i(\mathrm{x})} = \frac{\sum_{i=1}^{n} \mathsf{p}'_i(\mathrm{x}) \cdot U_i(\mathrm{x})}{\mathsf{p}'_i(\mathrm{x})} = \frac{\sum_{i=1}^{n} \mathsf{p}_{i \setminus I}(\mathrm{x}) \cdot (\mathrm{x} - r_i) \cdot U_i(\mathrm{x})}{\mathsf{p}_{i \setminus I}(\mathrm{x}) \cdot (\mathrm{x} - r_i)}.$$

Since $|S_i - I| \leq T$ for each $i \in [n]$, the numerator is a polynomial of degree at most $2T + 2$ and the denominator is a polynomial of degree at most $T + 1$. Further, since each U_i is uniformly random, we can show that the numerator is a random degree $2T + 2$ polynomial, and that the gcd of the polynomials in the numerator and denominator is 1 and hence no other terms will get canceled out. The algebraic proofs are deferred to the full version. Therefore, each party P_i can interpolate this rational polynomial using $3T + 4$ evaluation points and thereby learn the numerator and denominator. Finally, observe that for each party P_i,

Parameters: Parties $P_1, \ldots, P_n$. Each party has a set of m elements. Threshold $T \in \mathbb{N}$. $\mathbb{F}$ is a finite field where $|\mathbb{F}| = \Omega(2^\lambda)$.

Inputs: Party P_i has an input set $S_i = \{a_1^i, \ldots, a_m^i\}$ where $a_j^i \in \mathbb{F}$ for all $j \in [m]$.

Output: Each party P_i receives the set intersection $I = \bigcap_{i=1}^n S_i$ if and only if $|(\bigcup_{i=1}^n S_i) \setminus I| \le T$.

Protocol:

1. **Private Intersection Cardinality Testing.** The parties invoke $\mathcal{F}_{\mathsf{CTest\text{-}diff}}$ on inputs $S_1, \ldots, S_n$ and receive back $w \in \{\mathsf{similar}, \mathsf{different}\}$. If $w = \mathsf{different}$ then all parties output $\perp$.

2. **TAHE Key Generation.** Each party P_i generates $(\mathsf{pk}_i, \mathsf{sk}_i) \leftarrow$ TAHE.DistSetup$(1^\lambda, i)$ and sends pk_i to P_1. Then P_1 sends $\mathsf{pk} = (\mathsf{pk}_1 \| \ldots \| \mathsf{pk}_n)$ to all the other parties.

3. **Evaluations of Random Polynomial.** In this phase the parties will evaluate a polynomial

$$V(x) = \sum_{i=1}^n \left(p_i'(x) \cdot \left(R_1(x) + \ldots + R_{i-1}(x) + \widetilde{R}_i(x) + R_{i+1}(x) \ldots + R_n(x) \right) \right)$$

   for $x \in [3T+4]$ where the terms are defined as follows.
   (a) Each party P_i defines $p_i(x) = \prod_{j=1}^m (x - a_j^i)$ and $p_i'(x) = p_i(x) \cdot (x - r_i)$ where $r_i \xleftarrow{\$} \mathbb{F}$.
   (b) Each party P_i uniformly samples $R_i, \widetilde{R}_i \xleftarrow{\$} \mathbb{F}[x]$ of degree $T+1$, computes $R_i(x)$ for $x \in [3T+4]$ and sends encrypted $[\![R_i(x)]\!]$ to P_1.
   (c) For each $i \in [n], x \in [3T+4]$, party P_1 sends $[\![e_{i,x}]\!] = \left[\!\left[\sum_{j \in [n] \setminus \{i\}} R_j(x) \right]\!\right]$ to P_i.
   (d) For each $x \in [3T+4]$, each party P_i sends $[\![v_{i,x}]\!] = \left[\!\left[p_i'(x) \cdot \left(e_{i,x} + \widetilde{R}_i(x) \right) \right]\!\right]$ to P_1.
   (e) For each $x \in [3T+4]$, P_1 sends $[\![v_x]\!] = [\![\sum_{i=1}^n v_{i,x}]\!]$ to all P_i.
   (f) For each $x \in [3T+4]$, each party P_i sends $[\![v_x : \mathsf{sk}_i]\!] \leftarrow$ TAHE.PartialDec$(\mathsf{sk}_i, [\![v_x]\!])$ to P_1.
   (g) For each $x \in [3T+4]$, P_1 sends $V(x) =$ TAHE.Combine$(\mathsf{pk}, \{[\![v_x : \mathsf{sk}_i]\!]\}_{i \in [n]})$ to all P_i.

4. **Computing Set Intersection.** Each party P_i does the following:
   (a) Interpolate $q_i(x)$ to be the degree $3T+3$ rational polynomial such that $q_i(x) = \frac{V(x)}{p_i'(x)}$ for $x \in [3T+4]$ and the gcd of the numerator and denominator is 1. Let D_i be the roots of the denominator of $q_i(x)$.
   (b) Output the set intersection $I = S_i \setminus D_i$.

Fig. 9. Multi-party threshold PSI protocol $\Pi_{\mathsf{TPSI\text{-}diff}}$ for functionality $\mathcal{F}_{\mathsf{TPSI\text{-}diff}}$.

the roots of the denominator contains the set $S_i \setminus I$ and a random r_i, from which P_i can easily compute the intersection I.

Communication Cost. The first phase of the protocol, namely private intersection cardinality testing, has a communication complexity of $O(n \cdot T \cdot \mathsf{poly}(\lambda))$ when instantiated with the TFHE-based scheme in Sect. 5.2 and a communication complexity of $\widetilde{O}(n \cdot T \cdot \mathsf{poly}(\lambda))$ when instantiated with the TAHE-based scheme in Sect. 6.

We now analyze the communication cost for the second phase where the parties compute the concrete intersection. The TAHE key generation is independent of the set sizes and the threshold T and has a communication complexity of only $O(n \cdot \mathsf{poly}(\lambda))$. The bottleneck of the protocol is in Step 3, that is, evaluating the random polynomial. In Steps 3b, 3d, and 3f, every party sends $3T+4$ encryptions or partial decryptions to P_1 hence the cost for these steps is $O(n \cdot T \cdot \mathsf{poly}(\lambda))$. In Steps 3c, 3e, and 3g, P_1 sends $3T + 4$ ciphertexts or plaintexts to every other party so the cost of these steps is $O(n \cdot T \cdot \mathsf{poly}(\lambda))$. Finally, the last stage, namely computing the set intersection, does not involve any communication. Thus, the overall communication cost for computing the intersection is $O(n \cdot T \cdot \mathsf{poly}(\lambda))$.

Therefore, when the private intersection cardinality testing protocol is instantiated with the TFHE-based protocol, the overall communication complexity is $O(n \cdot T \cdot \mathsf{poly}(\lambda))$ and when instantiated with the TAHE-based scheme, the overall communication complexity is $\widetilde{O}(n \cdot T \cdot \mathsf{poly}(\lambda))$ for some apriori fixed polynomial $\mathsf{poly}(\cdot)$ and is independent of the size of each input set m.

Security. Consider an environment $\mathcal{Z}$ who corrupts a set $\mathcal{S}^*$ of n^* parties where $n^* < n$. The simulator Sim has the output of the functionality $\mathcal{F}_{\mathsf{TPSI\text{-}diff}}$, namely the intersection set I or $\perp$. Sim sets $w = \mathsf{similar}$ if the output is I and $w = \mathsf{different}$ if the output is $\perp$. In addition, Sim has the tuple (S_i, r_i) for each corrupt party P_i indicating the party's input and randomness for the protocol. The strategy of the simulator Sim for our multi-party threshold PSI protocol is described below.

(a) **Private Intersection Cardinality Testing:** Sim plays the role of the ideal functionality $\mathcal{F}_{\mathsf{CTest\text{-}diff}}$ and responds with w.

(b) **TAHE Key Generation:** Sim runs the distributed key generation algorithm $\mathsf{TAHE.DistSetup}(1^\lambda, i)$ of the TAHE scheme honestly on behalf of each honest party P_i as in the real world. Note that Sim also knows $(\{\mathsf{sk}_i\}_{i \in \mathcal{S}^*})$ as it knows the randomness for the corrupt parties.

(c) **Evaluations of Random Polynomial:** Sim does the following:

1. Encode the intersection set $I = \{b_1, \ldots, b_{|I|}\}$ as a polynomial as follows:
   $$\mathsf{p}_I(\mathsf{x}) = \Pi_{i=1}^{|I|}(\mathsf{x} - b_i).$$
2. Pick a random polynomial $U(\cdot)$ of degree $2T + 2$ and set the polynomial $V(\mathsf{x})$ as follows: $V(\mathsf{x}) = \mathsf{p}_I(\mathsf{x}) \cdot U(\mathsf{x})$.
3. In Steps 3b–3e, on behalf of every honest party P_i, whenever P_i has to send any ciphertext, send $[\![0]\!]$ using fresh randomness.
4. For each $x \in [3T + 4]$, let $[\![v_x]\!]$ denote the ciphertext that is sent to all the parties at the end of Step 3f.
5. In Step 3f, for each $j \in [3T + 4]$, on behalf of each honest party P_i, instead of computing $\{[\![v_x : \mathsf{sk}_i]\!]\}$ by running the honest $\mathsf{TAHE.PartialDec}$ algorithm as in the real world, Sim computes the partial decryptions by running the simulator $\mathsf{TAHE.Sim}$ as follows: $\{[\![v_x : \mathsf{sk}_i]\!]\} \leftarrow \mathsf{TAHE.Sim}(\mathsf{C}, V(x), [\![v_x]\!], \{\mathsf{sk}_i\}_{i \in \mathcal{S}^*})$, where C is the public linear circuit to compute $V(x)$ by P_1.
6. Finally, in Step 3g, if P_1 is honest, send the evaluations of polynomial $V(x)$ as in the real world description.

Hybrids. We now show that the above simulation strategy is successful against all environments $\mathcal{Z}$ that corrupt parties in a semi-honest manner. That is, the view of the corrupt parties along with the output of the honest parties is computationally indistinguishable in the real and ideal worlds. We will show this via a series of computationally indistinguishable hybrids where the first hybrid Hybrid_0 corresponds to the real world and the last hybrid Hybrid_4 corresponds to the ideal world.

- Hybrid_0 - **Real World:** In this hybrid, consider a simulator SimHyb that plays the role of the honest parties as in the real world.
- Hybrid_1 - **Private Intersection Cardinality Testing:** In this hybrid, SimHyb plays the role of the ideal functionality $\mathcal{F}_{\mathsf{CTest\text{-}diff}}$ and responds with similar if $|(\bigcup_{i=1}^{n} S_i) \setminus I| \leq T$ and different otherwise.
- Hybrid_2 - **Simulate Partial Decryptions:** In this hybrid, in the evaluations of random polynomial, SimHyb simulates the partial decryptions generated by the honest parties in Step 3f as done in the ideal world. That is, for each $j \in [3T + 4]$, SimHyb computes the partial decryptions as $\{[\![v_x : \mathsf{sk}_i]\!]\} \leftarrow \mathsf{TAHE.Sim}(C, \mathsf{V}(x), [\![v_x]\!], \{\mathsf{sk}_i\}_{i \in \mathcal{S}^*})$. Observe that the polynomial $\mathsf{V}(\cdot)$ is still computed as in the real world (and in Hybrid_2).
- Hybrid_3 - **Switch Polynomial Computation:** In this hybrid, the polynomial $\mathsf{V}(\cdot)$ is no longer computed as in the real world. Instead, SimHyb now picks a random polynomial $U(\cdot)$ of degree $2T + 2$ and sets the polynomial $\mathsf{V}(\cdot)$ as follows: $\mathsf{V}(\mathrm{x}) = \mathsf{p}_I(\mathrm{x}) \cdot U(\mathrm{x})$.
- Hybrid_4 - **Switch Encryptions:** In this hybrid, in the evaluations of random polynomial, SimHyb now computes every ciphertext generated on behalf of any honest party as encryptions of 0 as done by Sim in the ideal world. This hybrid corresponds to the ideal world.

We show that every pair of consecutive hybrids is computationally indistinguishable in the full version.

References

[AIK05]   Applebaum, B., Ishai, Y., Kushilevitz, E.: Computationally private randomizing polynomials and their applications. In: CCC (2005)

[BDP21]   Branco, P., Döttling, N., Pu, S.: Multiparty cardinality testing for threshold private set intersection. In: PKC (2021)

[Ben94]   Benaloh, J.: Dense probabilistic encryption May 1994

[BFK+19] Badrinarayanan, S., Fernando, R., Koppula, V., Sahai, A., Waters, B.: Output compression, MPC, and IO for turing machines. In: ASIACRYPT (2019)

[BGG+18] Boneh, D., Gennaro, R., Goldfeder, S., Jain, A., Kim, S., Rasmussen, P.M.R., Sahai, A.: Threshold cryptosystems from threshold fully homomorphic encryption. In: Shacham, H., Boldyreva, A. (eds.) CRYPTO 2018. LNCS, vol. 10991, pp. 565–596. Springer, Cham (2018). https://doi.org/10.1007/978-3-319-96884-1_19

[BGY80] Brent, R.P., Gustavson, F.G., Yun, D.Y.Y.: Fast solution of Toeplitz systems of equations and computation of padé approximants. J. Algorithms **1**(3), 259–295 (1980)

[BO15] Braverman, M., Oshman, R.: On information complexity in the broadcast model. In: PODC (2015)

[BPSW07] Brickell, J., Porter, D.E., Shmatikov, V., Witchel, E.: Privacy-preserving remote diagnostics. In: CCS (2007)

[CDN01] Cramer, R., Damgård, I., Nielsen, J.B.: Multiparty computation from threshold homomorphic encryption. In: Pfitzmann, B. (ed.) EUROCRYPT 2001. LNCS, vol. 2045, pp. 280–300. Springer, Heidelberg (2001). https://doi.org/10.1007/3-540-44987-6_18

[CM20] Chase, M., Miao, P.: Private set intersection in the internet setting from lightweight oblivious PRF. In: Micciancio, D., Ristenpart, T. (eds.) CRYPTO 2020. LNCS, vol. 12172, pp. 34–63. Springer, Cham (2020). https://doi.org/10.1007/978-3-030-56877-1_2

[DCT10] De Cristofaro, E., Tsudik, G.: Practical private set intersection protocols with linear complexity. In: FC (2010)

[DCW13] Dong, C., Chen, L., Wen, Z.: When private set intersection meets big data: an efficient and scalable protocol. In: CCS (2013)

[DIK+08] Damgård, I., Ishai, Y., Krøigaard, M., Nielsen, J.B., Smith, A.: Scalable multiparty computation with nearly optimal work and resilience. In: Wagner, D. (ed.) CRYPTO 2008. LNCS, vol. 5157, pp. 241–261. Springer, Heidelberg (2008). https://doi.org/10.1007/978-3-540-85174-5_14

[FH96] Franklin, M., Haber, S.: Joint encryption and message-efficient secure computation. J. Cryptol. **9**, 217–232 (1996)

[FNP04] Freedman, M.J., Nissim, K., Pinkas, B.: Efficient private matching and set intersection. In: Cachin, C., Camenisch, J.L. (eds.) EUROCRYPT 2004. LNCS, vol. 3027, pp. 1–19. Springer, Heidelberg (2004). https://doi.org/10.1007/978-3-540-24676-3_1

[GJR10] Grigorescu, E., Jung, K., Rubinfeld, R.: A local decision test for sparse polynomials. Inf. Process. Lett. **110**(20), 898–901 (2010)

[GN19] Ghosh, S., Nilges, T.: An algebraic approach to maliciously secure private set intersection. In: Ishai, Y., Rijmen, V. (eds.) EUROCRYPT 2019. LNCS, vol. 11478, pp. 154–185. Springer, Cham (2019). https://doi.org/10.1007/978-3-030-17659-4_6

[GS19a] Ghosh, S., Simkin, M.: The communication complexity of threshold private set intersection. In: Boldyreva, A., Micciancio, D. (eds.) CRYPTO 2019. LNCS, vol. 11693, pp. 3–29. Springer, Cham (2019). https://doi.org/10.1007/978-3-030-26951-7_1

[GS19b] Ghosh, S., Simkin, M.: The communication complexity of threshold private set intersection (2019). ia.cr/2019/175

[HFH99] Huberman, B.A., Franklin, M., Hogg, T.: Enhancing privacy and trust in electronic communities. In: Proceedings of the 1st ACM Conference on Electronic Commerce (1999)

[HOS17] Per, A., Hallgren, C.O., Sabelfeld, A.: Privacy-preserving ridesharing. In: CSF, Privatepool (2017)

[HV17] Hazay, C., Venkitasubramaniam, M.: Scalable multi-party private set-intersection. In: PKC (2017)

[HW15] Hubáček, P., Wichs, D.: On the communication complexity of secure function evaluation with long output. In: ITCS (2015)

[IKN+17]   Ion, M., et al.: Private intersection-sum protocol with applications to attributing aggregate ad conversions (2017). ia.cr/2017/738

[KKRT16]   Kolesnikov, V., Kumaresan, R., Rosulek, M., Trieu, N.: Efficient batched oblivious PRF with applications to private set intersection. In: CCS (2016)

[KMP+17]   Kolesnikov, V., Matania, N., Pinkas, B., Rosulek, M., Trieu, N.: Practical multi-party private set intersection from symmetric-key techniques. In: CCS (2017)

[KMWF07]   Kiltz, E., Mohassel, P., Weinreb, E., Franklin, M.: Secure linear algebra using linearly recurrent sequences. In: TCC (2007)

[KS05]   Kissner, L., Song, D.: Privacy-preserving set operations. In: Shoup, V. (ed.) CRYPTO 2005. LNCS, vol. 3621, pp. 241–257. Springer, Heidelberg (2005). https://doi.org/10.1007/11535218_15

[MPR+20]   Miao, P., Patel, S., Raykova, M., Seth, K., Yung, M.: Two-sided malicious security for private intersection-sum with cardinality. In: Micciancio, D., Ristenpart, T. (eds.) CRYPTO 2020. LNCS, vol. 12172, pp. 3–33. Springer, Cham (2020). https://doi.org/10.1007/978-3-030-56877-1_1

[MTZ03]   Minsky, Y., Trachtenberg, A., Zippel, R.: Set reconciliation with nearly optimal communication complexity. IEEE Trans. Inf. Theory **49**, 2213–2218 (2003)

[MZ17]   Mohassel, P., Zhang, Y.: SecureML: a system for scalable privacy-preserving machine learning. In: IEEE S and P (2017)

[NMH+10]   Nagaraja, S., Mittal, P., Hong, C.-Y., Caesar, M., Borisov, N.: BotGrep: finding P2P bots with structured graph analysis. In: USENIX security symposium (2010)

[OOS16]   Orrù, M., Orsini, E., Scholl, P.: Actively secure 1-out-of-n OT extension with application to private set intersection. In: CT-RSA (2016)

[Pai99]   Paillier, P.: Public-key cryptosystems based on composite degree residuosity classes. In: Stern, J. (ed.) EUROCRYPT 1999. LNCS, vol. 1592, pp. 223–238. Springer, Heidelberg (1999). https://doi.org/10.1007/3-540-48910-X_16

[PRTY19]   Pinkas, B., Rosulek, M., Trieu, N., Yanai, A.: SpOT-light: lightweight private set intersection from sparse OT extension. In: Boldyreva, A., Micciancio, D. (eds.) CRYPTO 2019. LNCS, vol. 11694, pp. 401–431. Springer, Cham (2019). https://doi.org/10.1007/978-3-030-26954-8_13

[PRTY20]   Pinkas, B., Rosulek, M., Trieu, N., Yanai, A.: PSI from PaXoS: fast, malicious private set intersection. In: Canteaut, A., Ishai, Y. (eds.) EUROCRYPT 2020. LNCS, vol. 12106, pp. 739–767. Springer, Cham (2020). https://doi.org/10.1007/978-3-030-45724-2_25

[PSSZ15]   Pinkas, B., Schneider, T., Segev, G., Zohner, M.: Phasing: private set intersection using permutation-based hashing. In USENIX (2015)

[PSWW18]   Pinkas, B., Schneider, T., Weinert, C., Wieder, U.: Efficient circuit-based PSI via cuckoo hashing. In: Nielsen, J.B., Rijmen, V. (eds.) EUROCRYPT 2018. LNCS, vol. 10822, pp. 125–157. Springer, Cham (2018). https://doi.org/10.1007/978-3-319-78372-7_5

[PSZ14]   Pinkas, B., Schneider, T., Zohner, M.: Faster private set intersection based on OT extension. In: USENIX (2014)

[RR17]   Rindal, P., Rosulek, M.: Malicious-secure private set intersection via dual execution. In: CCS (2017)

[TPKC07]   Troncoso-Pastoriza, J.R., Katzenbeisser, S., Celik, M.: Privacy preserving error resilient dna searching through oblivious automata. In: CCS (2007)

[TY90] Thull, K., Yap, C.: A unified approach to HGCD algorithms for polynomials and integers. Manuscript (1990)

[Yao86] Yao, A.C.-C.: How to generate and exchange secrets (extended abstract). In: FOCS (1986)

[ZC18] Zhao, Y., Chow, S.S.M.: Can you find the one for me? Privacy-preserving matchmaking via threshold PSI (2018). ia.cr/2018/184

On the (In)Security of the Diffie-Hellman Oblivious PRF with Multiplicative Blinding

Stanisław Jarecki[1]([✉]), Hugo Krawczyk[2], and Jiayu Xu[3]

[1] University of California, Irvine, Irvine, USA
stasio@ics.uci.edu
[2] Algorand Foundation, New York, USA
[3] George Mason University, Fairfax, USA
jiayux@uci.edu

Abstract. Oblivious Pseudorandom Function (OPRF) is a protocol between a client holding input x and a server holding key k for a PRF F. At the end, the client learns $F_k(x)$ and nothing else while the server learns nothing. OPRF's have found diverse applications as components of larger protocols, and the currently most efficient instantiation, with security proven in the UC model, is $F_k(x) = H_2(x, (H_1(x))^k)$ computed using so-called *exponential blinding*, i.e. the client sends $a = (H_1(x))^r$ for random r, the server responds $b = a^k$, which the client unblinds as $v = b^{1/r}$ to compute $F_k(x) = H_2(x, v)$.

However, this protocol requires two variable-base exponentiations on the client, while a more efficient *multiplicative blinding* scheme replaces one or both client exponentiations with fixed-base exponentiation, leading to the decrease of the client's computational cost by a factor between two to six, depending on pre-computation.

We analyze the security of the above OPRF with multiplicative blinding, showing surprising weaknesses that offer attack avenues which are not present using exponential blinding. We characterize the security of this OPRF implementation as a "Correlated OPRF" functionality, a relaxation of UC OPRF functionality used in prior work.

On the positive side, we show that the Correlated OPRF suffices for the security of OPAQUE, the asymmetric PAKE protocol, hence allowing OPAQUE the computational advantages of multiplicative blinding. Unfortunately, we also show examples of other OPRF applications which become insecure when using such blinding. The conclusion is that usage of multiplicative blinding for $F_k(x)$ defined as above, in settings where correct value g^k (needed for multiplicative blinding) is not authenticated, and OPRF inputs are of low entropy, must be carefully analyzed, or avoided all together. We complete the picture by showing a simple and safe alternative definition of function $F_k(x)$ which offers (full) UC OPRF security using either form of blinding.

© International Association for Cryptologic Research 2021
J. A. Garay (Ed.): PKC 2021, LNCS 12711, pp. 380–409, 2021.
https://doi.org/10.1007/978-3-030-75248-4_14

1   Introduction

An *Oblivious Pseudorandom Function* (OPRF) scheme consists of a Pseudorandom Function (PRF) F for which there exists a two-party protocol between a server S holding a PRF key k and a client C holding an input x through which C learns $F_k(x)$ and S learns nothing (in particular, nothing about the input x or the output $F_k(x)$). More generally, the security properties of the PRF, namely indistinguishability from a random function under polynomially many queries, must be preserved by the protocol. The OPRF notion was introduced explicitly in [8] but constructions, particularly those based on *blinded DH*, were studied earlier (e.g., [5,7,23]). OPRF has been formally defined under different models [8,10,11,18] with the last two works framing them in the Universally Composable (UC) framework [4]. The OPRF notion has found many applications, and recently such applications have been proposed for actual deployment in practice, including the Privacy Pass protocol [6] and the OPAQUE password-authenticated key exchange protocol [17]. This gave rise to standardization proposals for OPRFs [25] and the OPAQUE protocol [21,22,26], which further motivates understanding the costs and benefits of possible OPRF implementations.

Exponential vs. Multiplicative Blinding in Hashed Diffie-Hellman PRF.[1] In several of the above mentioned applications, the underlying PRF is instantiated with a *(Double) Hashed Diffie-Hellman* construction (2HashDH) [11], namely:

$$F_k(x) = H_2(x, (H_1(x))^k) \tag{1}$$

where hash functions H_1, H_2 are defined respectively as $H_1 : \{0,1\}^* \to \mathbb{G}\backslash\{1\}$ and $H_2 : \{0,1\}^* \times \mathbb{G} \to \{0,1\}^\tau$ for a multiplicative group $\mathbb{G}$ of prime order q, and the PRF key k is a random element in $\mathbb{Z}_q$, while τ is a security parameter. The protocol for the oblivious computation of 2HashDH used e.g. in [2,7,10,11] employs the so-called *exponential blinding* method, i.e. protocol Exp-2HashDH shown in Fig. 1: Client C sends to server S its input x blinded as $a = (H_1(x))^r$, for $r \leftarrow_R \mathbb{Z}_q$, and then unblinds the server's response $b = a^k$ as $v = b^{1/r}$ $[= (a^k)^{1/r} = (((H_1(x))^r)^k)^{1/r} = (H_1(x))^k]$ and outputs $H_2(x, v)$. It is easy to see that the client's input is perfectly hidden from the server because if $H_1(x) \neq 1$ then a is a random element in $\mathbb{G}$ independent from x.

An alternative *multiplicative blinding* technique, denoted Mult-2HashDH, is shown in Fig. 2. The protocol is an equivalent of Chaum's technique for blinding RSA signatures: Given generator g of group $\mathbb{G}$, the client blinds its input as $a = H_1(x) \cdot g^r$, and using the server's *public key* $z = g^k$ corresponding to the PRF key k, the client unblinds the server's response $b = a^k$ as $v = b \cdot z^{-r}$ $[= a^k \cdot (g^k)^{-r} = (H_1(x) \cdot g^r)^k \cdot g^{-kr} = (H_1(x))^k]$. It is easy to see that this blinding hides x with perfect security, as in the case of Exp-2HashDH.

Comparing the computational cost of the two techniques, we see that both require a single variable-base exponentiation for the server. However, for the

---

[1] In the context of additive groups, "multiplicative" would be replaced with "additive" and "exponential" with "scalar-multiplicative". A less confusing terminology could refer to these as fixed-base and var-base blindings, respectively.

Parameters: group $\mathbb{G}$ of order q, functions H_1, H_2 onto resp. $\mathbb{G} \setminus \{1\}$ and $\{0,1\}^{\ell}$

Client $\mathsf{C}(x)$ Server $\mathsf{S}(k)$

Pick $r \leftarrow_{\mathrm{R}} \mathbb{Z}_q$, set $a \leftarrow (H_1(x))^r$ $\xrightarrow{\quad a \quad}$

If $b \in \mathbb{G}$ output $y = H_2(x,v)$ for $\xleftarrow{\quad b \quad}$ If $a \in \mathbb{G}$ set $b \leftarrow a^k$
$v = b^{1/r}$ (otherwise abort)   (otherwise abort)

Fig. 1. Exp-2HashDH: Oblivious PRF using *Exponential* Blinding [11]

Parameters: as in Fig. 1, plus generator g of group $\mathbb{G}$

Client $\mathsf{C}(x)$ Server $\mathsf{S}(k, z = g^k)$

Pick $r \leftarrow_{\mathrm{R}} \mathbb{Z}_q$, set $a \leftarrow H_1(x) \cdot g^r$ $\xrightarrow{\quad a \quad}$

If $b, z \in \mathbb{G}$ output $y = H_2(x,v)$ for $\xleftarrow{\quad (b,z) \quad}$ If $a \in \mathbb{G}$ set $b \leftarrow a^k$
$v = b \cdot z^{-r}$ (otherwise abort)   (otherwise abort)

Fig. 2. Mult-2HashDH: Oblivious PRF using *Multiplicative* Blinding

client, Exp-2HashDH requires two variable-base exponentiations (for blinding and unblinding) while Mult-2HashDH involves a single *fixed-base* exponentiation for blinding and a variable-base exponentiation (to the base z) for unblinding.

In applications where the client stores z,[2] the latter exponentiation can use fixed-base optimization, reducing the client's total computation to two-fixed base exponentiations. Given that exponentiation with a fixed base is about 6–7 times faster than with a variable base (cf. [3,13]), Mult-2HashDH becomes at least 1.7 faster than Exp-2HashDH and 6x faster if z is stored at the client and treated as a fixed base. On the other hand, in cases where the client does not hold z, Mult-2HashDH requires the server to store z and send it with each execution of the OPRF protocol. This cost may not be significant in some cases but in constrained environments where bandwidth and/or storage is a costly resource (e.g., mobile and IoT scenarios) [9], Exp-2HashDH may be preferred. Fortunately, 2HashDH allows an application to choose the blinding mechanism that best fits its needs, possibly choosing one technique or the other depending on the network setting and client configuration.

These are good news for performance and implementation flexibility, but regarding security, things are not as straightforward, as we explain next.

---

[2] For example, in a password protocol such as OPAQUE [17], a user can cache values z corresponding to servers it accesses frequently, e.g., Google, Facebook, etc.

Is Multiplicative Blinding Secure? On the face of it, it would seem that exponential and multiplicative blindings are equivalent, functionally and security-wise, thus allowing for performance optimization and flexibility as discussed above. However, determining the security of Mult-2HashDH turns out to be non-trivial, showing unexpected attack avenues which are not present in Exp-2HashDH. In particular, while Exp-2HashDH has been proven to satisfy the UC OPRF notion from [11], protocol Mult-2HashDH is *not secure* under this same definition. The problem is, broadly speaking, that the dependency of the protocol on z implies that multiplicative blinding does not ensure full independence between OPRF instances indexed by different public keys.[3]

Let us elaborate. In protocol Exp-2HashDH, server's response b to the client's message $a \neq 1$ defines a unique key $k = \mathsf{DL}(a, b)$ for which C computes $y = F_k(x)$. (Since client's output is $y = H_2(x, v)$ for $v = b^{1/r}$ and $a = (H_1(x))^r$, it follows that $v = a^{k/r} = (H_1(x))^k$ and therefore $y = F_k(x)$ for $k = \mathsf{DL}(a, b)$.) In other words, server's response b commits the server to a single value k, hence to a unique function $F_k(x)$. This commitment to a unique function is central to the OPRF UC modeling from [11]. The same, however, does *not* hold for Mult-2HashDH where the server's response (b, z) to the client's message a gives the attacker an additional degree of freedom in manipulating C's output $y = H(x, b \cdot z^{-r})$. Specifically, response (b, z) given a determines pair (δ, z) where $\delta = b/a^k$ for $k = \mathsf{DL}(g, z)$, thus leading to the following function:

$$F_{(\delta, z)}(x) \triangleq H_2(x, \delta \cdot (h_x)^k) \quad \text{for} \quad z = g^k \text{ and } h_x = H_1(x) \tag{2}$$

which an honest C computes on its input x given S's response (b, z) in the Mult-2HashDH protocol. Indeed, if $a = h_x \cdot g^r$, $z = g^k$ and $\delta = b/a^k$ then

$$v = b \cdot z^{-r} = b \cdot (g^k)^{-r} = b \cdot (g^r)^{-k} = b \cdot (a/h_x)^{-k} = (b/a^k) \cdot (h_x)^k = \delta \cdot (h_x)^k$$

The important point is that value $\delta = b/a^k$ for $k = \mathsf{DL}(g, z)$ introduces a multiplicative shift in the value v computed by C. Moreover, an adversarial S can exploit this shift to create correlated responses that leak information on the client's input. In particular, for any choice of client input $\bar{x}$, an attacker S can find values $\delta_1, \delta_2, k_1, k_2$ such that

$$\delta_1 \cdot (h_{\bar{x}})^{k_1} = \delta_2 \cdot (h_{\bar{x}})^{k_2} \quad \text{for} \quad z_1 = g^{k_1}, z_2 = g^{k_2} \text{ and } h_{\bar{x}} = H_1(\bar{x}) \tag{3}$$

Using these values the attacker can respond to the first client's query a_1 with $(b_1, z_1) = (\delta_1 a_1^{k_1}, g^{k_1})$, and to a second query a_2 with $(\delta_2 a_2^{k_2}, g^{k_2})$, leading C to compute values v_1, v_2 that coincide if C's input is $x = \bar{x}$ and do not coincide if $x \neq \bar{x}$. In other words, $F_{(\delta_1, z_1)}(\bar{x}) = F_{(\delta_2, z_2)}(\bar{x})$, showing that in contrast to the family $\{F_k\}$ defined by Eq. (1), the function family $\{F_{(\delta, z)}\}$ defined by Eq. (2) is *not* a family of *independent* random functions in ROM.[4]

---

[3] The potential insecurity of multiplicative blinding as UC OPRF was pointed out in [17], which left its security analysis as an open question.

[4] Note that an honest server's response $(b, z) = (a^k, g^k)$ corresponds to $\delta = 1$ and the evaluated function $F_{(1, z)}$ is identical to the intended function F_k.

Potential Vulnerabilities. The core advantage a corrupt server may gain by exploiting the above correlations is the ability to test whether a given value of x has been input by the client in a previous interaction with the server. Our analysis of Mult-2HashDH shows that the server can test at most one such input per interaction. For OPAQUE, this property suffices to *prove the security of the protocol with Mult-2HashDH*. The intuitive reason is that in OPAQUE, a malicious server already has the ability to test guesses for the client's inputs (a password in the case of OPAQUE) with each interaction with the client, thus the above attack based on correlation does not add to the attacker's power. In contrast, in Sect. 7 we show examples of applications where the correlated nature of Mult-2HashDH opens attack avenues not available with exponential blinding. This demonstrates that the two OPRF implementations, Exp-2HashDH and Mult-2HashDH, are not equivalent vis-à-vis security, and replacing one with another within some application needs to be analyzed on a per-case basis, as we do here for OPAQUE.

Modeling Mult-2HashDH as Correlated OPRF. To analyze the security of applications that use Mult-2HashDH, we show that there are limits on the correlations which an adversary can create among the functions effectively evaluated in the Mult-2HashDH protocol. Specifically, each pair of functions can be correlated only as in Eq. (3) and *only on one* argument x. We prove this formally by introducing a relaxation of the UC OPRF functionality of [11] which we call *Correlated OPRF*. The purpose of this relaxation is to model the exact nature of function correlations which multiplicative blinding gives to a malicious server. We show that Mult-2HashDH realizes the Correlated OPRF functionality under the Gap$^+$-OMDH assumption in ROM, a mild strengthening of the Gap-OMDH assumption which sufficed for Exp-2HashDH to satisfy the UC OPRF functionality [11].

Security of OPAQUE under both Blindings. Based on the UC modeling of Mult-2HashDH as a Correlated OPRF, we prove the OPAQUE strong asymmetric PAKE protocol [17] secure using 2HashDH with multiplicative blinding. (*Strong* asymmetric PAKE is secure against pre-computation of password hashes before server compromise.) Specifically, we show that OPAQUE remains secure if the OPRF building block it uses is relaxed from the UC OPRF notion of [11] to the Correlated OPRF defined here. This means that the asymmetric PAKE standard being defined by the IETF on the basis of OPAQUE [21, 22, 26] can use the 2HashDH function and leave the choice of exponential or multiplicative blinding to individual implementations.

We believe that the same holds for another construction from [17], which shows that a composition of UC OPRF and any asymmetric PAKE results in a strong asymmetric PAKE. This transformation was proven secure using UC OPRF, implemented by Exp-2HashDH and we believe that this result can also be "upgraded" to the case of UC Correlated OPRF, i.e. using Mult-2HashDH, but we leave the formal verification of that claim to future work.

When is it Safe to Use Mult-2HashDH? In cases where the client has access to the value g^k in some authenticated/certified form, such as in applications requiring a Verifiable OPRF [10], e.g., Privacy Pass [6], one can use (1) with either blinding. For multiplicative blinding, one just uses the authenticated z in the unblinding. However, when z is received from the server in unauthenticated way, much care is needed, and security under multiplicative blinding needs to be proven on a per-application basis. Even then, small changes in applications and implementations may turn this mechanism insecure as evidenced by the case of using OPAQUE with a threshold OPRF which we show in Sect. 7 to be insecure if used with Mult-2HashDH. As a rule of thumb, *it seems prudent to advise not to use Mult-2HashDH in setting with unauthenticated g^k and where the input to the OPRF is taken from a low-entropy space.*

An Alternative OPRF Specification. Another fix is to replace function 2HashDH defined in Eq. (1) with the following simple modification, where $z = g^k$ is included under the hash, which is secure using *either* blinding:

$$F'_k(x) = H_2(x, z, H_1(x)^k) \text{ where } z = g^k \tag{4}$$

It can be shown that this scheme avoids the correlation attacks[5], and therefore can be proven secure with either blinding method as a realization of the UC OPRF functionality from [11]. The security holds even when the value z input into the hash by the client is the (unauthenticated) z received from the server.

However, while this scheme allows an implementation to choose (even at execution time) the blinding mechanism it prefers, it forces the transmission of z from server to client even in the case of exponential blinding, a drawback in constrained settings discussed above, e.g. [9]. In the case of OPAQUE, one can still use the simpler 2HashDH without transmitting z but with the subtleties and warnings surrounding security as demonstrated in this paper.[6]

2   Preliminaries

The Gap One-More Diffie-Hellman Assumptions. The security of protocol Mult-2HashDH as UC Correlated OPRF relies on the interactive Gap^+ *One-More Diffie-Hellman* (Gap$^+$-OMDH) assumption, a mild strengthening of the Gap-OMDH assumption used to realize UC OPRF [11] or *verifiable* UC OPRF [10]. Let $\mathbb{G}$ be a group of prime order q, and let g be an arbitrary generator of $\mathbb{G}$. Let $(\cdot)^k$ for $k \in \mathbb{Z}_q$ denote an oracle which returns $y = x^k$ on input $x \in \mathbb{G}$. Let CDH_g denote a CDH oracle which returns g^{xy} on input (g^x, g^y). Let DDH_g denote a DDH oracle which returns 1 on input (A, B, C) s.t. $C = \mathsf{CDH}_g(A, B)$, and 0

---

[5] The correlation between functions $F_{(\delta_1, z_1)}$ and $F_{(\delta_2, z_2)}$ would now require that $z_1 = z_2$, hence $k_1 = k_2$, in which case Eq. (3) holds only if $\delta_1 = \delta_2$, hence $(\delta_1, z_1) = (\delta_2, z_2)$.

[6] Another way for 2HashDH to realize UC OPRF with multiplicative blinding, is to add to Mult-2HashDH a zero-knowledge proof that (g, z, a, b) is a DDH tuple, but this would void the performance benefit of Mult-2HashDH.

otherwise. Let DDH_g^+ denote an oracle which returns 1 on input (A, B, A', B', C) s.t. $C = \mathsf{CDH}_g(A, B) \cdot \mathsf{CDH}_g(A', B')$, and 0 otherwise. The (N, Q)-Gap$^+$-OMDH assumption on group $\mathbb{G}$ states that for any polynomial-time algorithm $\mathcal{A}$,

$$\Pr_{k \leftarrow_R \mathbb{Z}_q, \; h_1, \ldots, h_N \leftarrow_R \mathbb{G}} \left[\mathcal{A}^{(\cdot)^k, \mathsf{DDH}_g^+}(g, g^k, h_1, \ldots, h_N) = (J, S) \right]$$

is negligible, where $J = (j_1, \ldots, j_{Q+1})$, $S = ((h_{j_1})^k, \ldots, (h_{j_{Q+1}})^k)$, Q is the number of $\mathcal{A}$'s $(\cdot)^k$ queries, and $j_1, \ldots, j_{Q+1}$ are *distinct* elements in $\{1, \ldots, N\}$.

In other words, Gap$^+$-OMDH models the following experiment: Let $\mathcal{A}$ have access to a DDH^+ oracle and an "exponentiation to k-th power" oracle for random k in $\mathbb{Z}_q$, and the number of queries to the latter is limited by Q. $\mathcal{A}$ is given N random elements in $\mathbb{G}$ as the challenge values, and since $\mathcal{A}$ is allowed to query the exponentiation oracle Q times, it is able to compute the k-th power of any Q of the N elements, but the assumption postulates that it is infeasible that $\mathcal{A}$ computes the k-th power of any $Q + 1$ of the N group elements, i.e. that it computes the k-th power of "one more" element.

The Gap-OMDH assumption is defined in the exact same way as Gap$^+$-OMDH, except $\mathcal{A}$ has access to oracle DDH_g instead of DDH_g^+. We believe that Gap$^+$-OMDH is a mild strengthening of Gap-OMDH because assuming OMDH in a group with a bilinear map implies both assumptions: Given an efficiently computable map $e : \mathbb{G} \times \mathbb{G} \to \mathbb{G}_T$ s.t. $e(g^a, g^b) = e(g, g)^{ab}$, one can implement DDH_g oracle, by checking if $e(A, B) = e(g, C)$, as well as DDH_g^+ oracle, by checking if $e(A, B) \cdot e(A', B') = e(g, C)$. In the full version [15] we show that the Gap$^+$-OMDH assumption holds in the generic group model, which extends similar argument given for Gap-OMDH in [12].

3   The Correlated OPRF Functionality $\mathcal{F}_{\mathsf{corOPRF}}$

As we explain in Sect. 1, we will model the type of PRF-correlations which protocol Mult-2HashDH allows with a correlated OPRF functionality, and here we define it as functionality $\mathcal{F}_{\mathsf{corOPRF}}$ shown in Fig. 3. In Sect. 4 we will argue that protocol Mult-2HashDH, i.e. the multiplicative blinding protocol together with the PRF defined in Eq. (1), realizes functionality $\mathcal{F}_{\mathsf{corOPRF}}$ under Gap-OMDH assumption in ROM.

Functionality $\mathcal{F}_{\mathsf{corOPRF}}$ is a relaxation of the OPRF functionality $\mathcal{F}_{\mathsf{OPRF}}$ of [17], which is an adaptive extension of the UC OPRF defined in [11]. To make this relation easier to see we mark in Fig. 3 all the code fragments which are novel with respect to functionality $\mathcal{F}_{\mathsf{OPRF}}$ of [17]. Below we will first explain the basic properties which $\mathcal{F}_{\mathsf{corOPRF}}$ shares with $\mathcal{F}_{\mathsf{OPRF}}$, and then we explain the crucial differences which make $\mathcal{F}_{\mathsf{corOPRF}}$ a relaxation of $\mathcal{F}_{\mathsf{OPRF}}$.

Correlated OPRF Model: Basic Logic. Functionality $\mathcal{F}_{\mathsf{corOPRF}}$ models OPRF in a similar way as $\mathcal{F}_{\mathsf{OPRF}}$ of [11,17]. First, when an honest server S initializes a PRF by picking a random key, this is modeled in the ideal world via call INIT from S, which initializes a random function $F_S : \{0,1\}^* \to \{0,1\}^\ell$.

<u>Public Parameters</u>: PRF output-length ℓ, polynomial in security parameter τ.
<u>Conventions</u>: $\forall i, x$ value $F_i(x)$ is initially undefined, and if undefined $F_i(x)$ is referenced then $\mathcal{F}_{\text{corOPRF}}$ sets $F_i(x) \leftarrow_R \{0,1\}^\ell$. Variable P ranges over all *honest* network entities and $\mathcal{A}^*$, and we assume *all corrupt entities are operated by* $\mathcal{A}^*$.

<u>Initialization</u>

– On (INIT, sid) from S, set tx $\leftarrow 0$, $\mathcal{N} \leftarrow [\text{S}]$, $\mathcal{E} \leftarrow \{\}$, $\mathcal{G} \leftarrow (\mathcal{N}, \mathcal{E})$.
  Ignore all subsequent INIT messages.
  Below "S" stands for the entity which sent the INIT message.

<u>Server Compromise</u>

– On (COMPROMISE, sid) from $\mathcal{A}^*$, declare server S as COMPROMISED.
  (If S is corrupted then it is declared COMPROMISED as well.)

<u>Offline Evaluation</u>

– On (OFFLINEEVAL, sid, i, x, L) from P do:
  (1) If P $= \mathcal{A}^*$ and $i \notin \mathcal{N}$ then append i to $\mathcal{N}$ and run CORRELATE(i, L);
  (2) Ignore this message if P $= \mathcal{A}^*$, S is not COMPROMISED, and $(i, \text{S}, x) \in \mathcal{E}$;
  (3) Send (OFFLINEEVAL, sid, $F_i(x)$) to P if (i) P $=$ S and $i =$ S or (ii) P $= \mathcal{A}^*$ and either $i \neq$ S or S is COMPROMISED.

<u>Online Evaluation</u>

– On (EVAL, sid, ssid, S$'$, x) from P, send (EVAL, sid, ssid, P, S$'$) to $\mathcal{A}^*$. On prfx from $\mathcal{A}^*$, reject it if prfx was used before. Else record $\langle$ssid, P, x, prfx, $0\rangle$ and send (Prefix, ssid, prfx) to P.

– On (SNDRCOMPLETE, sid, ssid$'$) from S, send (SNDRCOMPLETE, sid, ssid$'$, S) to $\mathcal{A}^*$. On prfx$'$ from $\mathcal{A}^*$ send (Prefix, ssid$'$, prfx$'$) to S. If there is a record $\langle$ssid, P, x, prfx, $0\rangle$ s.t. prfx$=$prfx$'$, change it to $\langle$ssid, P, x, prfx, $1\rangle$, else set tx++.

– On (RCVCOMPLETE, sid, ssid, P, i, L) from $\mathcal{A}^*$, retrieve $\langle$ssid, P, x, prfx, ok?$\rangle$ (ignore the message if there is no such record) and do:
  (1) If $i \notin \mathcal{N}$ then append i to $\mathcal{N}$ and run CORRELATE(i, L);
  (2) If S is not COMPROMISED and ok? $= 0$ do:
      If $i =$ S or $[(i, \text{S}, x) \in \mathcal{E}$ and P $= \mathcal{A}^*]$ do:
          If tx $= 0$ then ignore this message, else set tx$--$;
  (3) Send (EVAL, sid, ssid, $F_i(x)$) to P.

<u>CORRELATE(i, L)</u>:

– Reject if list L contains elements $(j, x), (j', x')$ s.t. $j = j'$ and $x \neq x'$.
  Else, for all $(j, x) \in L$ s.t. $j \in \mathcal{N}$, add (i, j, x) to $\mathcal{E}$ and set $F_i(x) \leftarrow F_j(x)$.

Fig. 3. The Correlated OPRF functionality $\mathcal{F}_{\text{corOPRF}}$. The (adaptive) OPRF functionality $\mathcal{F}_{\text{OPRF}}$ of [16] is formed by omitting all text in gray boxes .

Second, the real-world S can evaluate F_S off-line on any argument, which is modeled in the ideal world by call (OFFLINEEVAL, sid, i, x, L) from S with $i =$ S and $L =\perp$, which gives $F_S(x)$ to S. (The role of list L, which a malicious server can make non-empty, is discussed further below.) Third, in addition to the off-line evaluation, any client C can start an on-line OPRF protocol instance with S on local input x, which is modeled by call (EVAL, sid, ssid, S', x) from P $=$ C with S' $=$ S, where ssid stands for *sub-session ID*, a fresh identifier of this OPRF instance. If S honestly engages in this protocol, which is modeled by call (SNDRCOMPLETE, sid, ssid) from S, functionality $\mathcal{F}_{corOPRF}$ increments the server-specific ticket-counter tx, initially set to 0. If the real-world adversary allows an uninterrupted interaction between C and S, which is modeled by a call (RCVCOMPLETE, sid, ssid, C, i, L) with $i =$ S and $L =\perp$ from the ideal-world adversary $\mathcal{A}^*$, then $\mathcal{F}_{corOPRF}$ decrements counter tx and sends $F_S(x)$ to C.[7]

The man-in-the-middle adversary (our OPRF model does not rely on authenticated links) who interacts with client C, can make C output $F_i(x)$ for a different function $F_i \neq F_S$, using a call (RCVCOMPLETE, ssid, C, i, L) for $i \neq$ S, which models a real-world adversary acting like the server but on a wrong key $k_i \neq k$ in this interaction. To model a real-world adversary choosing different PRF keys in either offline or online evaluations, functionality $\mathcal{F}_{corOPRF}$ keeps a list of indexes $\mathcal{N}$ of independent random functions, and effectively associates each real-world key with a distinct index in $\mathcal{N}$, whereas the key of the honest server S is associated with a special symbol S.

Practical Implications. Note that RCVCOMPLETE computes function F_S on P's input x only if tx > 0, i.e. if the number of instances completed by S is greater than the number of instances completed by any client. This implies that if S engages in n OPRF instances this allows function F_S to be computed, by all other parties combined, on at most n arguments. However, the functionality does not establish strict binding between these server and client instances. Indeed, this *ticket-based* enforcement allows an OPRF functionality to be realized using homomorphic blinding without zero-knowledge proofs. Note that in protocol Exp-2HashDH of Fig. 1 the interaction between C and S can be "double blinded" by the network adversary, who can modify P's original message a as $a' = a^s$, and then modify S's response $b = a^k$ as $b' = b^{1/s}$. Such interaction produces the correct output on the client, but a' which S sees is a random group element, independent of a sent by C, which makes it impossible to identify the pair of C and S instances which the network adversary effectively pairs up.

Another feature which enables efficient $\mathcal{F}_{corOPRF}$ realization is that the argument x of client C engaging in an OPRF instance can be defined only *after* server S completes this instance. Note that in the ideal world C outputs $F_S(x)$ even if S completes an OPRF instance first, by sending message (SVRCOMPLETE, sid, ssid), and C only afterwards sends (EVAL, sid, ssid, S, x), fol-

---

[7] As in the adaptive version of UC OPRF $\mathcal{F}_{OPRF}$ [17], we allow server S to be adaptively compromised, via call COMPROMISE from $\mathcal{A}^*$, which models a leakage of the private state of S, including its PRF key and all its authentication tokens. One consequence of server compromise is that RCVCOMPLETE will no longer check that tx > 0.

lowed by RCVCOMPLETE from $\mathcal{A}^*$. Indeed, this "delayed input extraction" feature of $\mathcal{F}_{\mathsf{corOPRF}}$ enables protocol Exp-2HashDH to realize it in ROM, where the ideal-world adversary can extract argument x from the local computation of the real-world client, namely from H_2 query (x, v) for $v = (H_1(x))^k$, but that computation (and input-extraction) happens *after* S completes the protocol.

In some applications, notably OPAQUE [17], see Sect. 5, it is useful for OPRF to output a transcript, or its prefix, as a handle on OPRF instance in a higher-level protocol. Functionality $\mathcal{F}_{\mathsf{corOPRF}}$ allows each party to output a transcript prefix prfx, and if prfx output by S and C match then $\mathcal{F}_{\mathsf{corOPRF}}$ allows C session to compute the PRF output without using the tx counter. This does not affect the logic of tx-checking: Each run of SNDRCOMPLETE either increments tx or ok's some particular client OPRF instance, so either way the number of on-line OPRF evaluations is limited by the number of SNDRCOMPLETE instances.

Relaxation of the UC OPRF Model. The crucial difference between the Correlated OPRF functionality $\mathcal{F}_{\mathsf{corOPRF}}$ and the OPRF functionality $\mathcal{F}_{\mathsf{OPRF}}$ of [11] is that when any party evaluates function F_i for a *new* index $i \notin \mathcal{N}$, which corresponds to a real-world adversary evaluating the (O)PRF either offline or online on a new key, the adversary can supply a list L of *correlations* which the new function F_i will have with previously initialized functions F_j, $j \in \mathcal{N}$, potentially including the honest server function F_{S}. Such correlations were not allowed in $\mathcal{F}_{\mathsf{OPRF}}$, and indeed $\mathcal{F}_{\mathsf{corOPRF}}$ reduces to $\mathcal{F}_{\mathsf{OPRF}}$ if $\mathcal{A}^*$ sets L as an empty list in OFFLINEEVAL and RCVCOMPLETE messages. Argument L can specify a sequence of pairs (j, x) where $j \in \mathcal{N}$ is an index of a previously initialized function F_j, and the correlation consists of setting the value of the new function F_i on x as $F_j(x)$. After setting $F_i(x) \leftarrow F_j(x)$ for all $(j, x) \in L$, the values of F_i on *all other arguments* are set at random by $\mathcal{F}_{\mathsf{corOPRF}}$. Functionality $\mathcal{F}_{\mathsf{corOPRF}}$ keeps track of these correlations in a graph $\mathcal{G} = (\mathcal{N}, \mathcal{E})$, where $(i, j, x) \in \mathcal{E}$ if $F_i(x)$ is set to $F_j(x)$ in the above manner, i.e., an edge between i and j, labeled x, represents a correlation between functions F_i and F_j on argument x.

A crucial constraint on the correlation list L is that for each $j \in \mathcal{N}$ list L can contain only one entry of the form $(j, \cdot)$, i.e. two functions F_i, F_j can be correlated on *at most one* argument. Note that if the adversary correlates F_i with the honest server function F_{S} on argument x, and then evaluates $F_i(x)$ via the online OPRF instance, i.e. EVAL and RCVCOMPLETE where $\mathsf{P} = \mathcal{A}^*$, functionality $\mathcal{F}_{\mathsf{corOPRF}}$ treats this as an evaluation of F_{S} and decrements the ticket-counter tx. This restriction is necessary because otherwise the adversary could effectively compute F_{S} on more than n arguments even if an honest server S engages in only n OPRF instances: It could first correlate $n' > n$ adversarial functions $F_1, ..., F_{n'}$ with F_{S}, each function F_i on a different argument x_i, and each evaluation of $F_i(x_i)$ would reveal the value of F_{S} on all these arguments as well. However, our $\mathcal{F}_{\mathsf{corOPRF}}$ model allows $\mathcal{A}^*$ to let any *honest* party P compute $F_i(x)$ for F_i correlated with F_{S} without decrementing the ticket-counter tx. This is a weakness, e.g. if the higher-level application reveals these OPRF outputs to the attacker. A stronger version of $\mathcal{F}_{\mathsf{corOPRF}}$ would decrement tx even if $F_i(x) = F_{\mathsf{S}}(x)$ is computed by honest parties, but we used a weaker version for two reasons: First, it suffices for

OPAQUE security. Second, we can show that Mult-2HashDH realizes this weaker version under Gap^+-OMDH, and it is an open problem whether the same can shown for the stronger version of the functionality.

Necessity of the Relaxation. As noted in Sect. 1, Exp-2HashDH satisfies the UC OPRF notion of [11] because S's response b to C's message a defines key $k = \mathsf{DL}(a, b)$ s.t. C outputs $y = F_k(x)$ for function F_k defined in Eq. (1). However, in Mult-2HashDH, S's response (b, z) defines the function which C effectively computes as $F_{(\delta, z)}$ defined in Eq. (2). Moreover, different choices of (δ, z) do *not* define independent random functions. Indeed, an efficient attacker can easily pick (δ_1, z_1) and (δ_2, z_2) which satisfy Eq. (3) for any x, which implies that the two functions will be correlated by constraint $F_{(\delta_1, z_1)}(x) = F_{(\delta_2, z_2)}(x)$.

The consequences of such correlations can be illustrated by the following example. Assume that the higher-level application allows a malicious server to detect whether in two OPRF instances the client outputs the same two values or not. Let x_1 and x_2 be two client input candidates. If the server picks two indexes (δ_1, z_1) and (δ_2, z_2) s.t. $F_{(\delta_1, z_1)}(x_1) = F_{(\delta_2, z_2)}(x_1)$ and $F_{(\delta_1, z_1)}(x_2) \neq F_{(\delta_2, z_2)}(x_2)$ and inputs (δ_1, z_1) into the first OPRF instance and (δ_2, z_2) into the second one, then the client's outputs in these two executions will be the same if its input is x_1 and different if its input is x_2, and by the assumption on the application context the server will learn which one is the case. (In Sect. 7 we show examples of applications where this knowledge creates an attack avenue.)

The UC OPRF notion of [11] does not allow for this attack avenue because in that model each choice of a function index which server S can input into an OPRF instance defines an *independent* (pseudo)random function. However, no choice of two functions F_i, F_j for these two instances allows S to distinguish between C's input x_1 and x_2: If $F_i = F_j$ then C's output in the two instances will be the same for any x, and if $F_i \neq F_j$ then C's output in the two instances will be different, also for any x, except for a negligible probability that S finds two functions F_i, F_j among the polynomially-many random functions it can query offline s.t. $F_i(x) = F_j(x)$ for $x \in \{x_1, x_2\}$.

4   Security Analysis of Multiplicative DH-OPRF

Figure 2 in Sect. 1 shows the OPRF protocol Mult-2HashDH, which uses multiplicative blinding for oblivious evaluation of the (Double) Hashed Diffie-Hellman function defined in Eq. (1), i.e. $F_k(x) = H_2(x, (H_1(x))^k)$. Here, in Fig. 4, we render the same protocol as a realization of the Correlated OPRF functionality $\mathcal{F}_{\mathsf{corOPRF}}$ defined in Fig. 3. As we explain in Sect. 3, functionality $\mathcal{F}_{\mathsf{corOPRF}}$ reflects the correlations which a real-world adversary can introduce in the PRF functions the honest users compute in this protocol. Indeed, as we show in Theorem 1 below, under the *Gap One-More Diffie-Hellman* assumption protocol Mult-2HashDH securely realizes this functionality in ROM.

Theorem 1. *Protocol Mult-2HashDH realizes correlated OPRF functionality $\mathcal{F}_{\mathsf{corOPRF}}$ in the $\mathcal{F}_{\mathsf{RO}}$-hybrid world under the Gap-OMDH assumption.*

Setting: – Group $\mathbb{G}$ of prime order q with generator g.

  – Hash functions H_2, H_1 with ranges $\{0,1\}^\ell$ and $\mathbb{G}$, respectively.

Functions H_2, H_1 are specific to the OPRF instance initialized for a *unique* session id sid, and in practice they should be implemented by folding sid into their inputs.

Initialization: On input (INIT, sid), S picks $k \leftarrow_R \mathbb{Z}_q$ and records (sid, $k, z = g^k$).

Server Compromise: On (COMPROMISE, sid, S) from $\mathcal{A}$, reveal k to $\mathcal{A}$.

Offline Evaluation:
On (OFFLINEEVAL, sid, S, $x, \cdot$), S outputs (OFFLINEEVAL, sid, $F(k,x)$) where

$$F(k,x) \triangleq H_2(x, (H_1(x))^k))$$

Evaluation:

- On input (EVAL, sid, ssid, S, x), C picks $r \leftarrow_R \mathbb{Z}_q$, records (sid, ssid, r), sends (ssid, a) to S for $a = H_1(x) \cdot g^r$, and locally outputs (Prefix, ssid, a).

- On input (SNDRCOMPLETE, sid, ssid') and message (ssid, a) from C s.t. $a \in \mathbb{G}$, server S retrieves (sid, k, z), sends (ssid, b, z) to C for $b = a^k$, and locally outputs (Prefix, ssid', a). (Note that ssid and ssid' can be different.)

- On S's message (ssid, b, z) from S s.t. $b, z \in \mathbb{G}$ and C holds tuple (sid, ssid, r) for some r, party C outputs (EVAL, sid, ssid, y) for $y = H_2(x, b \cdot z^{-r})$.

Fig. 4. Protocol Mult-2HashDH of Fig. 2 as a realization of $\mathcal{F}_{\mathsf{corOPRF}}$.

Proof: We show that for any efficient environment $\mathcal{Z}$ and the real-world adversary $\mathcal{A}$ (more precisely, for $\mathcal{A}$ in the $\mathcal{F}_{\mathsf{RO}}$-hybrid world, i.e. the real world amended by random oracle hash functions), there exists an efficient simulator SIM, a.k.a. an "ideal-world adversary", s.t. the environment's view in the real world, where the honest parties implement the Mult-2HashDH protocol interacting with adversary $\mathcal{A}$, is indistinguishable from its view in the ideal world, where the honest parties are "dummy" entities which pass their inputs to (and outputs from) the ideal functionality $\mathcal{F}_{\mathsf{corOPRF}}$, and where the real-world adversary $\mathcal{A}$ is replaced by the simulator SIM (who locally interacts with $\mathcal{A}$). The construction of SIM is shown in Fig. 5. While the real-world adversary $\mathcal{A}$ works in a hybrid world with the random oracle modeled by functionality $\mathcal{F}_{\mathsf{RO}}$, for notation simplicity in Fig. 5 we short-circuit the $\mathcal{F}_{\mathsf{RO}}$ syntax and we assume that SIM implements oracles H_1, H_2. Without loss of generality, we assume that $\mathcal{A}$ is a "dummy" adversary who merely passes all messages between $\mathcal{Z}$ and SIM, hence we will treat $\mathcal{A}$ as just an interface of $\mathcal{Z}$. For brevity we also denote $\mathcal{F}_{\mathsf{corOPRF}}$ as $\mathcal{F}$, and we omit the (fixed) session identifier sid from all messages. Also, the simulator assumes that a unique party S for which this $\mathcal{F}$ instance is initialized is honest, and that its identity "S" encoded as a bitstring is different from any pair $(\delta, z) \in \mathbb{G}^2$.

Initialization: Pick $k \leftarrow_R \mathbb{Z}_q^*$ //SIM picks S's key//, set T_{H_1} as an empty table, set functions H_1, H_2 as undefined on all arguments, and set $\mathcal{N}_{\mathsf{SIM}} \leftarrow [\mathsf{S}]$ //$\mathcal{N}_{\mathsf{SIM}}$ is the list of identified function indices//.

Server Compromise: On (COMPROMISE, S) from $\mathcal{A}$, send (COMPROMISE, S) to $\mathcal{F}$ and reveal k to $\mathcal{A}$.

Hash query to H_1: On $\mathcal{A}$'s fresh query x to H_1, pick $u \leftarrow_R \mathbb{Z}_q \setminus \{0\}$, define $h_x \triangleq g^u$, set $H_1(x) \leftarrow h_x$, and add (x, u, h_x) to table T_{H_1}.
//T_{H_1} records $h_x = H_1(x)$ and the discrete-logarithm trapdoor $u = \mathsf{DL}(g, h_x)$//

Online Evaluation:

1. On (EVAL, ssid, C, S') from $\mathcal{F}$, pick $w \leftarrow_R \mathbb{Z}_q$, record (C, ssid, w), send (ssid, a) for $a \leftarrow g^w$ to $\mathcal{A}$, and send prfx $= a$ to $\mathcal{F}_{\mathsf{corOPRF}}$. (Abort if $\mathcal{F}_{\mathsf{corOPRF}}$ rejects it.)
2. On (SNDRCOMPLETE, ssid', S) from $\mathcal{F}$ and message (ssid, a') from $\mathcal{A}$ s.t. $a' \in \mathbb{G}$, send ssid and $(b', z^*) = ((a')^k, g^k)$ to $\mathcal{A}$ and prfx' $= a'$ to $\mathcal{F}_{\mathsf{corOPRF}}$.
3. On message (ssid, b, z) to C from $\mathcal{A}$ s.t. $b, z \in \mathbb{G}$, retrieve record (C, ssid, w) (ignore the message if there is no such record) and do:
   //C should output $F_{(\delta, z)}(x)$ for $\delta = b/a^{\mathsf{DL}(g, z)} = b/z^w$//
   (1) Set $\delta \leftarrow b/z^w$, $i \leftarrow (\delta, z)$, $L \leftarrow []$;
   (2) If $i = (1, g^k)$ //$\mathcal{A}$ lets C evaluate on F_{S}// then (re)set $i \leftarrow \mathsf{S}$;
   (3) If $i \notin \mathcal{N}_{\mathsf{SIM}}$ then for each $(x', u, h_{x'}) \in T_{H_1}$ and $(\delta', z') \in \mathcal{N}_{\mathsf{SIM}}$ do:
      If $\delta' \cdot (z')^u = \delta \cdot z^u$ then add (j, x') for $j = (\delta', z')$ to L;
      //correlation on x' between F_i and F_j for $j = (\delta', z')$//
      If $(h_{x'})^k = \delta \cdot z^u$ then add (S, x') to L; //correlation on x' with F_{S}//
   (4) Send (RCVCOMPLETE, ssid, C, i, L) to $\mathcal{F}$, and append i to $\mathcal{N}_{\mathsf{SIM}}$ if $i \notin \mathcal{N}_{\mathsf{SIM}}$.

Hash query to H_2: On $\mathcal{A}$'s fresh query (x, v) to H_2, do:

1. If $(x, u, h_x) \in T_{H_1}$ and $v = (h_x)^k$ //$\mathcal{A}$ evaluates $F_{\mathsf{S}}(x)$// then do:
   – If S is compromised, send (OFFLINEEVAL, S, $x, \perp$) to $\mathcal{F}$; on $\mathcal{F}$'s response (OFFLINEEVAL, y), set $H_2(x, v) \leftarrow y$;
   – Otherwise send (EVAL, ssid, S, x) and then (RCVCOMPLETE, ssid, SIM, S, $\perp$) to $\mathcal{F}$ for a fresh ssid; if $\mathcal{F}$ replies (EVAL, ssid, y) then set $H_2(x, v) \leftarrow y$, otherwise output HALT and abort.
2. If $(x, u, h_x) \in T_{H_1}$ and $v \neq (h_x)^k$ then for the first $(\delta, z) \in \mathcal{N}_{\mathsf{SIM}}$ s.t. $v = \delta \cdot z^u$ //$\mathcal{A}$ evaluates $F_{(\delta, z)}(x)$// send (OFFLINEEVAL, $i = (\delta, z), x, \perp$) to $\mathcal{F}$; on $\mathcal{F}$'s response (OFFLINEEVAL, y), set $H_2(x, v) \leftarrow y$.
3. If $H_2(x, v)$ remains undefined set $i = (v, 1)$ and: //$\mathcal{A}$ evaluates $F_{(v, 1)}(x)$//
   (1) If $i \notin \mathcal{N}_{\mathsf{SIM}}$ then for each $(x', u, h_{x'}) \in T_{H_1}$ and $(\delta', z') \in \mathcal{N}_{\mathsf{SIM}}$ do:
      If $\delta' \cdot (z')^u = v$ then add (j, x') for $j = (\delta', z')$ to L;
      If $(h_{x'})^k = v$ then add (S, x') to L;
   (2) Send (OFFLINEEVAL, i, x, L) to $\mathcal{F}$; on $\mathcal{F}$'s response (OFFLINEEVAL, y), set $H_2(x, v) \leftarrow y$, and append i to $\mathcal{N}_{\mathsf{SIM}}$ if $i \notin \mathcal{N}_{\mathsf{SIM}}$.

Fig. 5. Simulator SIM for Protocol Mult-2HashDH //with comments inline//

For a fixed environment $\mathcal{Z}$, let q_{H_1}, q_{H_2} be the number of $\mathcal{A}$'s queries to resp. H_1 and H_2 hash functions, and let q_C, q_S be the number of $\mathcal{Z}$'s invocations of resp. client and server OPRF instances, via resp. queries EVAL sent to some C and query SNDRCOMPLETE sent to S.

The Simulator. The simulator SIM, shown in Fig. 5, follows a similar simulation strategy to the one used to show that exponential blinding protocol realizes UC OPRF notions of [10,11,17]. At initialization, the simulator picks a random key k on behalf of server S. If SIM receives SNDRCOMPLETE from $\mathcal{F}$, i.e. server S wants to complete an OPRF instance, and SIM receives message a with matching ssid from adversary $\mathcal{A}$ playing a client, SIM replies as the real-world S would, i.e. with $(b, z) = (a^k, g^k)$. Responding to $\mathcal{A}$ playing a server is more complex. The simulator prepares for this by embeding discrete-logarithm trapdoors in H_1 outputs and in messages a formed on behalf of honest clients. Namely, for each x, SIM defines $H_1(x)$ as $h_x = g^u$ for random u, and it forms each message a on behalf of some honest client as $a = g^w$ for random w. The discrete-logarithm trapdoor $u = \mathsf{DL}(g, a)$ enables SIM to compute, given response (b, z) sent by $\mathcal{A}$ on behalf of some server, the function index $i = (\delta, z)$ for which a real-life honest client would effectively compute its output as $y = F_{(\delta,z)}(x)$ for $F_{(\delta,z)}$ defined as in Eq. (2). This is done by setting $\delta = b/z^w$ because then $\delta = b/a^k$ for $k = \mathsf{DL}(g, z)$. (See *Is multiplicative blinding secure?* in Sect. 1 for why the client effectively evaluates $F_{(\delta,z)}$ for $\delta = b/a^k$.) If $\mathcal{A}$ responds as the honest server S (or forwards S's response), SIM detects it because then $\delta = 1$, in which case SIM sets the function index to the "honest S function", $i \leftarrow$ S.

Finally, SIM checks if $i = (\delta, z)$ is in $\mathcal{N}_{\mathsf{SIM}}$, a sequence of function indices which SIM has previously identified, and if $i \notin \mathcal{N}_{\mathsf{SIM}}$, i.e. if it is a new function, SIM uses the trapdoors it embedded in H_1 outputs to detect if $F_i(x) = F_j(x)$ for any x queried to H_1 (without such query $\mathcal{A}$ cannot establish a correlation on x except for negligible probability) and any previously seen function index $j \in \mathcal{N}_{\mathsf{SIM}}$ or $j = $ S. The first condition holds if $\delta' \cdot (h_x)^{\mathsf{DL}(g,z')} = \delta \cdot (h_x)^{\mathsf{DL}(g,z)}$ for $i = (\delta, z)$ and $j = (\delta', z')$ while the second one holds if $(h_x)^k = \delta \cdot (h_x)^{\mathsf{DL}(g,z)}$. The simulator cannot compute $\mathsf{DL}(g, z)$ for an adversarial public key z, but the trapdoor in the hash function output $H_1(x) = h_x = g^u$ allows for computing $(h_x)^{\mathsf{DL}(g,z)}$ as z^u.

There is a further complication in the simulator's code, in responding to $\mathcal{A}$'s local H_2 queries (x, v). Such calls can represent either (I) an offline PRF evaluation on argument x of function $F_{(\delta,z)}$ s.t. $v = \delta \cdot (h_x)^{\mathsf{DL}(g,z)}$, where $(\delta, z) \in \mathcal{N}_{\mathsf{SIM}}$, or, if S is compromised (or corrupted), for $(\delta, z) = (1, g^k)$; or (II) in case $v = (h_x)^k$ and S is not compromised, they can represent a finalization of the computation of $F_S(x)$ by a malicious client in the online OPRF instance. Case (I) is treated similarly as the detection of the correlations explained above: SIM searches for index $i = (\delta, z)$ in $\mathcal{N}_{\mathsf{SIM}}$ s.t. $v = \delta \cdot (h_x)^{\mathsf{DL}(g,z)} = \delta \cdot z^u$ where $H_1(x) = h_x = g^u$, in which case this is interpreted as evaluation of F_i and SIM sets $H_2(x, v)$ to the value of $F_i(x)$ which the functionality defines in response to the offline evaluation call (OFFLINEEVAL, $i, x, \cdot$). If S is compromised then the simulator does this also for $i = $ S if $v = (h_x)^k$. However, in Case (II), i.e. if $v = (h_x)^k$

but S is not compromised, such query could come from $\mathcal{A}$'s post-processing of an online OPRF evaluation, hence SIM in this case sends (EVAL, ssid, S, x) and (RCVCOMPLETE, ssid, SIM, S, $\perp$) to $\mathcal{F}$. If $\mathcal{F}$ allows this call to evaluate successfully, i.e. if $\mathsf{tx} > 0$, then $\mathcal{F}$ return $y = F_S(x)$ and SIM defines $H_2(x, v) \leftarrow y$. Otherwise $\mathcal{F}$ will ignore this RCVCOMPLETE call, in which case SIM outputs HALT and aborts, which the environment will detect as a simulation failure. Indeed, this case corresponds to $\mathcal{A}$ evaluating function F_S on more arguments than the number of OPRF instances performed by S, i.e. the number of SNDRCOMPLETE calls from an ideal-world S to $\mathcal{F}$.

Finally, SIM must carefully handle $H_2(x, v)$ queries which are *not* recognized as evaluations of $F_i(x)$ for any $i \in \mathcal{N}_{\mathsf{SIM}} \cup \{\mathsf{S}\}$, because they can correspond to evaluating $F_{(\delta, z)}(x)$ for index (δ, z) which $\mathcal{A}$ will reveal in the future. SIM picks the simplest pair (δ, z) s.t. $\delta \cdot (h_x)^{\mathsf{DL}(g, z)} = v$, namely $(\delta, z) = (v, 1)$. If any future index $(\delta, z) \neq (v, 1)$ defined in a subsequent OPRF evaluation satisfies $\delta \cdot (h_x)^{\mathsf{DL}(g, z)} = v$, this will be detected by SIM as a correlation between $F_{(\delta, z)}$ and $F_{(v, 1)}$. Note that SIM must process $H_2(x, v)$ query as evaluation of $F_{(v, 1)}(x)$ even if $H_1(x)$ is undefined, because regardless of the value of $h_x = H_1(x)$ it will hold that $F_{(v, 1)}(x) = H_2(x, v)$, because $v \cdot (h_x)^{\mathsf{DL}(g, 1)} = v \cdot (h_x)^0 = v$. Indeed, an adversary can first query $H_2(x, v)$ for some (x, v), then compute $h_x = H_1(x)$, and then input (δ, z) into an OPRF instance for $\delta = v/(h_x)^{\mathsf{DL}(g, z)}$, which corresponds to oblivious evaluation of $F_{(\delta, z)}$, which is correlated with $F_{(v, 1)}$ on argument x.

Sequence of Games. Our proof uses the standard sequence of games method, starting from the interaction of $\mathcal{Z}$ (and "dummy" adversary $\mathcal{A}$) with the real-world protocol, and ending with the ideal world, in which $\mathcal{Z}$ instead interacts with the simulator SIM and functionality $\mathcal{F}$. We fix an arbitrary efficient environment $\mathcal{Z}$ which without loss of generality outputs a single bit, we use $\mathbf{G_i}$ to denote the event that $\mathcal{Z}$ outputs 1 when interacting with GAME i, and for each two adjacent games, GAME i and GAME $i + 1$, we argue that these games are indistinguishable to $\mathcal{Z}$, i.e. that there is a negligible difference between the probabilities of events $\mathbf{G_i}$ and $\mathbf{G_{i+1}}$, which implies that $\mathcal{Z}$'s advantage in distinguishing between the real world and the ideal world is also negligible. Let q_{H_1}, q_{H_2} be the total number of resp. H_1, H_2 queries made in the security game with $\mathcal{A}$ and $\mathcal{Z}$. Let q_C and q_S and q_S' be the number of resp. C and S sessions and S offline PRF evaluations started by $\mathcal{Z}$ via resp. the EVAL, SNDRCOMPLETE, and (OFFLINEEVAL, S, $\cdot$, $\cdot$) commands. Let $\epsilon_{\mathsf{OMDH}}(\mathbb{G}, N, Q)$ be the maximum advantage of any algorithm with computational resources comparable to $\mathcal{Z}$ against the (N, Q)-Gap$^+$-OMDH problem in $\mathbb{G}$.

GAME 1: (*Real world, except for discrete-logarithm trapdoors in H_1 outputs*) This is the real-world interaction, shown in Fig. 6, i.e. the interaction of environment $\mathcal{Z}$ and its subroutine $\mathcal{A}$ with honest entities C and S executing protocol Mult-2HashDH of Fig. 4. We assume that the interaction starts with server initialization, triggered by INIT command from $\mathcal{Z}$ to S. We denote the public key of server S as $z^* = g^k$. For visual clarity we omit the fixed sid tag and the variable ssid tags from all messages in Fig. 6. We assume that when functions H_1, H_2 are executed by C1, C2, and S2, these hash function calls are serviced as described in the lower-half of Fig. 6. Queries $H_2(x, v)$ are implemented as in the real world except that the game records tuples $(x, v, H_2(x, v))$ in table T_{H_2}. However, queries $H_1(x)$ are implemented with trapdoors embedded in values $h_x = H_1(x)$ by setting $h_x = g^{u_x}$ for random $u_x \leftarrow_{\mathrm{R}} \mathbb{Z}_q$ and recording (x, u_x, h_x) in table T_{H_1}.

GAME 2: (*Abort on hash H_1 collisions*) Abort if the security game ever encounters a collision in H_1, i.e. if for some argument x queried either by $\mathcal{A}$ or by the security game in oracles C1 and S2 (see Fig. 6), oracle H_1 picks u s.t. tuple (x', u, g^u) for some $x' \neq x$ is already in T_{H_1}. Clearly

$$|\Pr[\mathbf{G_2}] - \Pr[\mathbf{G_1}]| \leq \frac{(q_{\mathrm{H}_1})^2}{q}$$

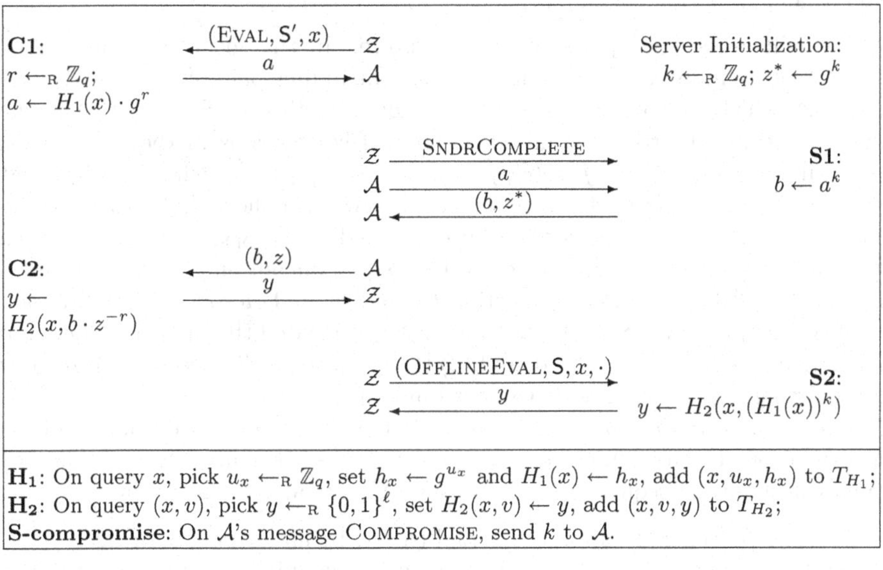
C1:
(EVAL, S′, x)
Z
Server Initialization:
r ←R Zq;
a
A
k ←R Zq; z* ← g^k
a ← H1(x) · g^r
Z
SNDRCOMPLETE
S1:
A
a
b ← a^k
A
(b, z*)
C2:
(b, z)
A
y ←
y
Z
H2(x, b · z^−r)
Z
(OFFLINEEVAL, S, x, ·)
S2:
Z
y
y ← H2(x, (H1(x))^k)
H1: On query x, pick ux ←R Zq, set hx ← g^ux and H1(x) ← hx, add (x, ux, hx) to TH1;
H2: On query (x, v), pick y ←R {0,1}^ℓ, set H2(x, v) ← y, add (x, v, y) to TH2;
S-compromise: On A's message COMPROMISE, send k to A.

Fig. 6. GAME 1: Interaction of $\mathcal{Z}/\mathcal{A}$ with Mult-2HashDH protocol.

GAME 3: (*Making* C*'s message input-oblivious*) We change how oracle C1 generates message a so that it is generated obliviously of input x. Namely, instead of computing $a = H_1(x) \cdot g^r = g^{u_x + r}$ for $r \leftarrow_{\mathrm{R}} \mathbb{Z}_q$, oracle C1 will now generate $a = g^w$ for $w \leftarrow_{\mathrm{R}} \mathbb{Z}_q$. The input x for this session ssid will be then passed to oracle C2, which (1) queries H_1 on x to retrieve (or create) tuple (x, u_x, g^{u_x}) from T_{H_1}, and (2) outputs $y = H_2(x, v)$ for $v = b \cdot z^{u_x - w}$. Note that for every x, and hence every u_x, value $w = (u_x + r) \bmod q$ is random in $\mathbb{Z}_q$ if r random in $\mathbb{Z}_q$, hence this modification does not change the distribution of values a output by C1. Moreover, if $w = (u_x + r) \bmod q$ then $z^{-r} = z^{u_x - w}$, thus C2's output is the same as in GAME 2, hence GAME 3 and GAME 2 are externally identical.

GAME 4: (*Defining adversarial functions*) We make a notational change in oracle C2, so that it outputs $y = H_2(x, v)$ for $v = \delta \cdot z^{u_x}$ where $\delta = b/z^w$. Since this is a merely notational difference, GAME 4 and GAME 3 are identical.

Note that this change makes oracles C1/C2 implement the following process: C1's message $a = g^w$ together with $\mathcal{A}$'s response (b, z) define (δ, z) s.t. $\delta = b/z^w$, which defines a function which C2 evaluates on $\mathcal{Z}$'s input x as $F_{(\delta, z)}$ for

$$F_{(\delta, z)}(x) \triangleq H_2(x, \delta \cdot z^{u_x}) \quad \text{where} \quad u_x \triangleq \mathsf{DL}(g, H_1(x)) \tag{5}$$

Note that Eq. (5) is equivalent to Eq. (2) where $F_{(\delta, z)}(x) = H_2(x, \delta \cdot (H_1(x))^k)$ for k s.t. $z = g^k$. For notational convenience we define also a "helper" function family $f_i : \{0, 1\}^* \to \mathbb{G}$ for $i \in \mathbb{G}^2$ s.t.

$$f_{(\delta, z)}(x) = \delta \cdot z^{u_x} \quad \text{where} \quad u_x \triangleq \mathsf{DL}(g, H_1(x)) \tag{6}$$

Note that $F_{(\delta, z)}(x) = H_2(x, f_{(\delta, z)}(x))$.

We will argue that pairs (δ, z) encountered in the security game can be thought of as indexes of random functions, including pair $(\delta, z) = (1, z^*)$ for $z^* = g^k$ which defines the "honest" random function of S, except that the adversary can "program" a limited number of correlations in these functions, by setting $i = (\delta, g^k)$ and $j = (\delta', g^{k'})$ s.t. $\delta'/\delta = (h_x)^{k-k'}$, which implies that $F_i(x) = F_j(x)$. In the next few game changes we will show that these correlations are constrained as prescribed by functionality $\mathcal{F}_{\mathsf{corOPRF}}$, i.e. that (1) each two functions can be "programmed" to have equal output only for a single argument, (2) that if an adversarial function F_i is correlated on some x with function F_S of the honest server S then evaluating $F_i(x)$ is treated the same as $F_\mathsf{S}(x)$, and in particular requires that $\mathsf{tx} > 0$, and (3) that otherwise all adversarial functions are indistinguishable from independent random functions.

GAME 5: (*Building correlation graph*) The security game will build a graph of correlations between functions $F_{(\delta, z)}$ occurring in the game. In particular the game will maintain sequence $\mathcal{N}_\mathsf{SIM}$ and sets $X_{H_1}, \mathcal{E}$, all initially empty:

1. Set X_{H_1} contains all inputs x queried to H_1, by either $\mathcal{A}$, C2, or S2.
2. Set $\mathcal{N}_\mathsf{SIM}$ contains all (δ, z) function indexes, including (1) the honest server function index $(1, z^*)$, (2) each (δ, z) defined by $\mathcal{A}$'s interaction with oracles C1/C2, as described in GAME 4, and (3) $(\delta, z) = (v, 1)$ for every direct query (x, v) of $\mathcal{A}$ to H_2.
3. Set $\mathcal{E}$ contains *labeled edges* between indexes in $\mathcal{N}_\mathsf{SIM}$, maintained as follows:
   (1) When function index $i = (\beta, z) \notin \mathcal{N}_\mathsf{SIM}$ is specified in C1/C2 then for each $j = (\delta', z')$ in $\mathcal{N}_\mathsf{SIM}$ and $x' \in X_{H_1}$, test if $f_j(x') = f_i(x')$, and if so then add (i, j, x'), i.e. an edge (i, j) with label x', to $\mathcal{E}$.
   (2) If H_2 is queried on new (x, v) by $\mathcal{A}$ or by oracles C2 or S2 for $(v, 1) \notin \mathcal{N}_\mathsf{SIM}$ then do step (1) above for $i = (v, 1)$. (Note that $f_{(v,1)}(x') = v$ for all x'.)

Since these are only notational changes GAME 5 and GAME 4 are identical.

GAME 6: (*Discarding double links*) We add an abort if there are two distinct values x, x' in X_{H_1} and two distinct function indexes $i = (\delta, z)$ and $j = (\delta', z')$ in

$\mathcal{N}_{\mathsf{SIM}}$ s.t. $f_i(x) = f_j(x)$ and $f_i(x') = f_j(x')$. These conditions imply respectively that $\delta'/\delta = (z/z')^{u_x}$ and $\delta'/\delta = (z/z')^{u_{x'}}$. Since H_1 collisions are discarded beginning in GAME 2, it follows that $u_{x'} \neq u_x$, which implies that $(\delta, z) = (\delta', z')$, i.e. this abort cannot happen. Consequently, GAME 6 and GAME 5 are identical.

GAME 7: (*Discarding future correlations*) We add an abort in H_1 processing if new query $x \notin X_{H_1}$ samples $h_x = H_1(x)$ s.t. there exists two distinct function indexes $i, j \in \mathcal{N}_{\mathsf{SIM}}$ s.t. $f_i(x) = f_j(x)$. Note that in this case there would be no edge (i, j, x) in $\mathcal{E}$, and that this is *the only* case in which $f_i(x) = f_j(x)$ but $(i, j, x) \notin \mathcal{E}$. However if query x to H_1 is made after defining i, j then $h_x = H_1(x)$ is independent of i, j, in which case $\Pr[f_i(x) = f_j(x)] = 1/q$, because this equation holds only for a single value h_x s.t. $u_x = \mathsf{DL}(g, h_x) = \mathsf{DL}((z_i/z_j), (\delta_j/\delta_i))$. If there are q_C instances of C2 and q_{H_2} queries to H_2 then there can be at most q_C indexes (δ, z) in $\mathcal{N}_{\mathsf{SIM}}$ s.t. $z \neq 1$ and at most q_{H_2} indexes (δ, z) s.t. $z = 1$. Since condition $f_i(x) = f_j(x)$ cannot be met if $i = (v, 1)$ and $j = (v', 1)$ for $v \neq v'$, each new query x to H_1 causes an abort only if u_x falls in the solution set of at most $q_C \cdot (q_{H_2} + q_C)$ equations, which implies that

$$|\Pr[\mathbf{G_7}] - \Pr[\mathbf{G_6}]| \leq \frac{q_{H_1} \cdot q_C \cdot (q_{H_2} + q_C)}{q}$$

- **Init:** Initialize RF R, pick $k \leftarrow_{\mathrm{R}} \mathbb{Z}_q$, set $\mathcal{N}_{\mathsf{SIM}} \leftarrow [(1, g^k)]$ and $X_{H_1} \leftarrow \{\}$.
- **H_1:** On input $x \notin X_{H_1}$, pick $u_x \leftarrow_{\mathrm{R}} \mathbb{Z}_q$, add x to X_{H_1}, output g^{u_x} to $\mathcal{A}$.
- **S1:** On input $a \in \mathbb{G}$, send $(b, z) = (a^k, g^k)$ to $\mathcal{A}$.
- **S2:** On input x, set $i \leftarrow (1, g^k)$ and send $R(i, x)$ to $\mathcal{A}$.
- **C1:** On input x, pick $w \leftarrow_{\mathrm{R}} \mathbb{Z}_q$, store (x, w), send $a = g^w$ to $\mathcal{A}$.
- **C2:** On input $(b, z) \in \mathbb{G}^2$, recover (x, w) stored by C1 and set $\delta \leftarrow b/z^w$. Assign $i \leftarrow (\delta, z)$. If $i \notin \mathcal{N}_{\mathsf{SIM}}$ then run PROCESS(i). Send $R(i, x)$ to $\mathcal{A}$.
- **H_2:** On new input (x, v) from $\mathcal{A}$ for $v \in \mathbb{G}$, set $i \leftarrow (v, 1)$. If $i \notin \mathcal{N}_{\mathsf{SIM}}$ then run PROCESS(i). Send $R(i, x)$ to $\mathcal{A}$.
- **S-Compromise:** On message (COMPROMISE, S) from $\mathcal{A}$, send k to $\mathcal{A}$.

- Subprocedure PROCESS(i): Parse i as $(\delta, z) \leftarrow i$. Define list L s.t.

$$L = \{ (j, x) \in \mathcal{N}_{\mathsf{SIM}} \times X_{H_1} \ \text{s.t.} \ j = (\delta', z') \ \text{and} \ \delta \cdot z^{u_x} = \delta' \cdot (z')^{u_x} \}$$

Abort it L contains $(j, x), (j, x')$ s.t. $x \neq x'$.
Otherwise append i to $\mathcal{N}_{\mathsf{SIM}}$, and for each (j, x) in L, reset $R(i, x) \leftarrow R(j, x)$.

Fig. 7. Interaction defined by GAME 9.

GAME 8: (*Implementing H_2 using correlated random functions*) We replace hash function H_2 using an oracle $\mathcal{R}$ that maintains a random function family, in which the adversary can "program" correlations as follows:

- When $\mathcal{R}$ starts it initializes a random function $R : \{0,1\}^* \times \{0,1\}^* \rightarrow \{0,1\}^{\ell}$ and an index sequence $\mathcal{I} \leftarrow [(1, z^*)]$;

- On query CORRELATE(i, L), $\mathcal{R}$ rejects if $i \notin \mathcal{I}$ or list L contains (j, x) and (j', x') s.t. $j = j'$ and $x \neq x'$. Otherwise it appends i to $\mathcal{I}$, and for each $(j, x) \in L$ it re-defines $R(i, x) \leftarrow R(j, x)$;
- On query EVAL(i, x), $\mathcal{R}$ replies $R(i, x)$ if $i \in \mathcal{I}$, else ignores this query.

We use oracle $\mathcal{R}$ to change the implementation of H_2 function called by oracles S2, C2, or the direct calls to H_2:

1. When $\mathcal{A}$ calls S2 on x: Assign $H_2(x, f_i(x)) \leftarrow \mathcal{R}.\text{EVAL}(i, x)$ for $i = (1, z^*)$.
2. When oracle C2 calls H_2 on $(x, f_i(x))$ for some $i = (\delta, z)$:
   (a) if $i \notin \mathcal{N}_{\mathsf{SIM}}$ then send CORRELATE(i, L) to $\mathcal{R}$ where L consists of all tuples (j, x') s.t. $f_i(x') = f_j(x')$ for some $j \in \mathcal{N}_{\mathsf{SIM}}$ and $x' \in X_{H_1}$;
   (b) set $H_2(x, f_i(x)) \leftarrow \mathcal{R}.\text{EVAL}(i, x)$.
3. When $\mathcal{A}$ calls H_2 on (x, v): Service it as in Step 2 but use $i = (v, 1)$.

To see the correspondence between GAME 8 and GAME 7, observe that starting from GAME 5 function H_2 is evaluated only on pairs of the form $(x, f_i(x))$ for some $i \in \mathcal{N}_{\mathsf{SIM}}$. Define $\mathcal{R}(i, x)$ as $H_2(x, f_i(x))$. Function $\mathcal{R}$ is not random even if H_2 is, because we have that $\mathcal{R}(i, x) = \mathcal{R}(j, x)$ for any i, j, x s.t. $f_i(x) = f_j(x)$. However, from GAME 7 this equation can hold, for any i, x s.t. H_2 is queried on $(x, f_i(x))$, only if i is a new index, $i = (\delta, z)$ or $i = (v, 1)$, appended to $\mathcal{N}_{\mathsf{SIM}}$ in a query to oracles resp. C1/C2 and H_2, for values j, x s.t. $j \in \mathcal{N}_{\mathsf{SIM}}$ and $x \in X_{H_1}$ at the time this query is made. Note that list L sent for a new function f_i to $\mathcal{R}$ in GAME 8 by oracles C1/C2 and H_2 consists exactly of all such pairs (j, x), hence it follows that GAME 8 and GAME 7 are identical.

   GAME 9: (*Walking back aborts in H_1*) We remove the aborts in H_1 introduced in GAME 2 and GAME 7, i.e. we no longer abort if (1) the same u_X was chosen before on some previous query to H_1, or (2) if there are two function indices $i = (z, \delta)$ and $j = (z', \delta')$ in $\mathcal{N}_{\mathsf{SIM}}$ s.t. $f_i(x) = f_j(x)$, i.e. $\delta \cdot z^{u_x} = \delta' \cdot (z')^{u_x}$. By the same arguments used above where these games are introduced, these two changes can be observed with probability at most $(q_{H_1}^2)/q$ and $(q_{H_1} \cdot q_C \cdot (q_{H_2} + q_C))/q$, respectively, which implies that

$$|\Pr[\mathbf{G_9}] - \Pr[\mathbf{G_8}]| \leq \frac{q_{H_1}^2 + q_{H_1} \cdot q_C \cdot (q_{H_2} + q_C)}{q}$$

Security Game Review. In Fig. 7 we put together all the changes made so far and review how the game oracles operate in GAME 9.

   GAME 10: (*Identifying existing functions in H_2 processing*) In GAME 9 a fresh query (x, v) to H_2 is answered as $R(i, x)$ for $i = (v, 1)$, and if $(v, 1) \notin \mathcal{N}_{\mathsf{SIM}}$ then function $R((v, 1), \cdot)$ is created and correlated with all previous functions $\{R(i, \cdot)\}_{i \in \mathcal{N}_{\mathsf{SIM}}}$ by the rule that $R((v, 1), x') \leftarrow R(i, x')$ for each $x' \in X_{H_1}$ and $i \in \mathcal{N}_{\mathsf{SIM}}$ s.t. $f_i(x') = v$. In GAME 10 we modify the code of oracle H_2 so that when it gets a fresh query (x, v) s.t. $x \in X_{H_1}$ it first checks if

$$v = f_i(x) \quad \text{for any index} \quad i \in \mathcal{N}_{\mathsf{SIM}} \tag{7}$$

(Note that if $x \in X_{H_1}$ the game can evaluate $f_{(\delta, z)}(x) = \delta \cdot z^{u_x}$ for any δ, z.) If $v = f_i(x)$ for some $i \in \mathcal{N}_{\mathsf{SIM}}$ then GAME 10 takes *the first* index i in $\mathcal{N}_{\mathsf{SIM}}$ s.t. $v = f_i(x)$ holds, replies $R(i, x)$, and does not create a new function $R((v, 1), \cdot)$ even if $(v, 1) \notin \mathcal{N}_{\mathsf{SIM}}$. (Note that this condition can hold for several indexes i in $\mathcal{N}_{\mathsf{SIM}}$, and indeed it will hold for all indexes of functions which are correlated on argument x. Note also that the index $i = (1, z^*)$ of the "honest server function" occurs as the first in $\mathcal{N}_{\mathsf{SIM}}$.) If $x \notin X_{H_1}$ or for all $i \in \mathcal{N}_{\mathsf{SIM}}$ $v \neq f_i(x)$ then the processing is as before, i.e. the game processes this query as a call to $R((v, 1), x)$. We show the modification done by GAME 10 in Fig. 8.

- **H$_2$**: On new input (x, v) from $\mathcal{A}$ for $v \in \mathbb{G}$:
  1. If $x \in X_{H_1}$ and $v = (g^k)^{u_x}$: Set $i \leftarrow (1, g^k)$, send $R(i, x)$ to $\mathcal{A}$
  2. If $x \in X_{H_1}$ and $v \neq (g^k)^{u_x}$, but $\exists\ (\delta, z) \in \mathcal{N}_{\mathsf{SIM}}$ s.t. $v = \delta \cdot z^{u_x}$ then set i to the *first* $(\delta, z) \in \mathcal{N}_{\mathsf{SIM}}$ for which it holds and send $R(i, x)$ to $\mathcal{A}$
  3. Else set $i \leftarrow (v, 1)$. If $i \notin \mathcal{N}_{\mathsf{SIM}}$ then run PROCESS(i). Send $R(i, x)$ to $\mathcal{A}$.

Fig. 8. GAME 10: modification in Fig. 7

Note that this modification doesn't change the value returned by $H_2(x, v)$: If condition (7) holds then either way $H_2(x, v) = R(i, x)$. The only other change this modification causes is that if (7) holds then function $R((v, 1), \cdot)$ is not created. However, this does not affect any future interactions with the random function R. Let X_{H_1} and $\mathcal{N}_{\mathsf{SIM}}$ are the values of these variables at the time $R((v, 1), \cdot)$ is created in GAME 9. Consider that at some subsequent step an evaluation call, either C2 or H_2, creates a new function $R(i, \cdot)$ s.t. $f_i(x) = f_{(v, 1)}(x)$ for some $x \in X'_{H_1}$ where X'_{H_1} and $\mathcal{N}'_{\mathsf{SIM}}$ denote the new values of these variables. Assume also that until this point there was no other opportunity to create $\mathcal{R}((v, 1), \cdot)$ in GAME 10, i.e. $i = (v, 1)$ was not used in oracle C2, and $H_2(x', v)$ was not queried on any x' s.t. $f_i(x') \neq v$ for some $i \in \mathcal{N}'_{\mathsf{SIM}}$. (This is the case when the modification of GAME 10 can affect the security experiment.) There are two cases to consider: (1) If $x \in X_{H_1}$ and $f_{(v, 1)}(x) = f_j(x)$ for some $j \in \mathcal{N}_{\mathsf{SIM}}$, then whether or not $R((v, 1), \cdot)$ is created in both games it holds that $R(i, x) = R(j, c)$; (2) If $x \notin X_{H_1}$, or $x \in X_{H_1}$ but $f_{(v, 1)}(x) \neq f_j(x)$ for any $j \in \mathcal{N}_{\mathsf{SIM}}$, then $R((v, 1), x)$ is uncorrelated with previous functions, but since $R((v, 1), x)$ is not used before, it does not matter if $R(i, x)$ is chosen at random or assigned as $R(i, x) \leftarrow R((v, 1), x)$. It follows that GAME 10 and GAME 9 are identical.

GAME 11: (*Ideal-world interaction*) In Fig. 9 we show the ideal-world game, denoted GAME 11, defined by the interaction of simulator SIM of Fig. 5 and functionality $\mathcal{F}_{\mathsf{corOPRF}}$ of Fig. 3. We use the same notation used for GAME 9 for the correlated random functions, i.e. we define $F_{\mathsf{S}}(x) = R((1, z^*), x)$ and for all $i \neq \mathsf{S}$ we define $F_i(x) = R(i, x)$. Also, we rename oracles which the game implements as in GAME 9: S1 implements $\mathcal{Z}$'s query SNDRCOMPLETE to S, S2 implements $\mathcal{Z}$'s query OFFLINEEVAL to S, C1 implements $\mathcal{Z}$'s query EVAL to C, and C2 responds to $\mathcal{A}$'s message (b, z) to C.

- **Init:** Initialize RF R, $k \leftarrow_R \mathbb{Z}_q^*$, $\mathcal{N}_{\mathsf{SIM}} \leftarrow [(1, g^k)]$, $X_{H_1} \leftarrow \{\}$, tx $\leftarrow 0$.
- **H_1:** On input $x \notin X_{H_1}$, pick $u_x \leftarrow_R \mathbb{Z}_q$, add x to X_{H_1}, output g^{u_x} to $\mathcal{A}$.
- **S1:** On input $a \in \mathbb{G}$, send $(b, z) = (a^k, g^k)$ to $\mathcal{A}$.
  If $\exists$ record $(x, w, a, 0)$ change it to $(x, w, a, 1)$, else tx++.
- **S2:** On input x, set $i \leftarrow (1, g^k)$ and send $R(i, x)$ to $\mathcal{A}$.
- **C1:** On input x, pick $w \leftarrow_R \mathbb{Z}_q$, store $(x, w, a, 0)$, send $a = g^w$ to $\mathcal{A}$.
- **C2:** On input $(b, z) \in \mathbb{G}^2$, recover $(x, w, a, \mathsf{ok}?)$ stored by C1 and set $\delta \leftarrow b/z^w$.
  Assign $i \leftarrow (\delta, z)$. If $i \notin \mathcal{N}_{\mathsf{SIM}}$ then run PROCESS(i). Send $R(i, x)$ to $\mathcal{A}$.
  If S not compromised, ok? = 0, and $i = (1, g^k)$ then do:
    If tx = 0 then *abort the game*, else set tx−−
- **H_2:** On new input (x, v) from $\mathcal{A}$ for $v \in \mathbb{G}$:
  1. If $x \in X_{H_1}$ and $v = (g^k)^{u_x}$: Set $i \leftarrow (1, g^k)$, send $R(i, x)$ to $\mathcal{A}$, and do:
       If S not compromised and tx = 0 then *abort the game*
       If S not compromised and tx > 0 then set tx−−
  2. If $x \in X_{H_1}$ and $v \neq (g^k)^{u_x}$, but $\exists (\delta, z) \in \mathcal{N}_{\mathsf{SIM}}$ s.t. $v = \delta \cdot z^{u_x}$ then set i to the *first* $(\delta, z) \in \mathcal{N}_{\mathsf{SIM}}$ for which it holds and send $R(i, x)$ to $\mathcal{A}$
  3. Else set $i \leftarrow (v, 1)$. If $i \notin \mathcal{N}_{\mathsf{SIM}}$ then run PROCESS(i). Send $R(i, x)$ to $\mathcal{A}$.
- **S-Compromise:** On message (COMPROMISE, S) from $\mathcal{A}$, send k to $\mathcal{A}$.

- Subprocedure PROCESS(i): Parse i as $(\delta, z) \leftarrow i$. Define list L s.t.

$$L = \{ (j, x) \in \mathcal{N}_{\mathsf{SIM}} \times X_{H_1} \ \text{s.t.} \ j = (\delta', z') \text{ and } \delta \cdot z^{u_x} = \delta' \cdot (z')^{u_x} \}$$

  Abort it L contains $(j, x), (j, x')$ s.t. $x \neq x'$.
  Otherwise append i to $\mathcal{N}_{\mathsf{SIM}}$, and for each (j, x) in L, reset $R(i, x) \leftarrow R(j, x)$.

Fig. 9. GAME 11: Interaction of $\mathcal{Z}/\mathcal{A}$ with the ideal-world execution

Figure 9 simplifies the ideal-world game by not accounting for function correlations using edge set $\mathcal{E}$, as done by $\mathcal{F}_{\mathsf{corOPRF}}$, and ignoring some of the conditional clauses in the code of simulator SIM. However, we argue that these overlooked clauses are never triggered. Assume that whenever sub-procedure PROCESS(i) programs a correlation $R(i, x) \leftarrow R(j, x)$ the game adds set (i, j, x) to $\mathcal{E}$. The conditional clauses missing from GAME 11 figure are in clauses (2) and (3) in H_2 processing. In clause (2), SIM ignores this call, and the game does not send $R(i, x)$ to $\mathcal{A}$, if S was not compromised and either $i = (1, g^k)$ or $(i, (1, g^k), x) \in \mathcal{E}$. However, condition $i = (1, g^k)$ implies that $v = (g^k)^{u_x}$, which is excluded by case (2). Likewise, condition $(i, (1, g^k), x) \in \mathcal{E}$ implies that $f_i(x) = f_{(1, g^k)}(x) = (g^k)^{u_x}$, which would trigger case (1) and is excluded in case (2). In clause (3) SIM would ignore this call and not send $R(i, x)$ to $\mathcal{A}$ under the same conditions, i.e. if S was not compromised and either $i = (1, g^k)$ or $(i, (1, g^k), x) \in \mathcal{E}$. Case $i = (v, 1) = (1, g^k)$ implies $k = 0$, which is excluded by sampling k in $\mathbb{Z}_q^* = \mathbb{Z}_q \setminus \{0\}$, and case $(i, (1, g^k), x) \in \mathcal{E}$ implies that $x \in X_{H_1}$ and $f_i(x) = f_{(1, g^k)}(x)$, which would trigger clause (1).

Finally, in Fig. 9 in two clauses when tx = 0, in C2 and H_2 case (1), we wrote that the game *aborts*. In the actual ideal-world game, the first case corresponds to functionality $\mathcal{F}_{\mathsf{corOPRF}}$ dropping the (RCVCOMPLETE, ..., C, ...) call from SIM, and not sending $R(i, x)$ to C, and thus to $\mathcal{Z}$. The second case corresponds to $\mathcal{F}_{\text{corOPRF}}$ not responding with $R(i, x)$ to SIM's call (RCVCOMPLETE, ..., SIM, ...), in which case SIM aborts. The difference is in the first case, but it is a syntactical difference because we can equate $\mathcal{Z}$'s not receiving any output from C in response to (RCVCOMPLETE, ..., C, ...), or any output from H_2 call, with the game returning an abort symbol.

The differences between GAME 10 and GAME 11, apart of the trivial difference of constraining key k s.t. $k \neq 0$ in GAME 11, consist of the following:

1. S1 either increments tx or changes ok? in some C1-record from 0 to 1.
2. C2 decrements tx if S not compromised, ok? $= 0$, $i = (1, g^k)$, and tx > 0.
3. C2 aborts the game if S not compromised, ok? $= 0$, $i = (1, g^k)$, and tx $= 0$.
4. H_2, clause 1, decrements tx if S not compromised, $i = (1, g^k)$, and tx > 0
5. H_2, clause 1, aborts the game if S not compromised, $i = (1, g^k)$, and tx $= 0$.

Let E be the event that game aborts either in C2 or H_2, denoted resp. E_{C2} and E_{H_2}. Note that unless event E happens GAME 10 and GAME 11 are identical (except for $1/q$ probability that $k = 0$ in GAME 10), and that event E can happen only if S is not compromised, thus the two games diverge only before S compromise. Note that E_{C2} requires that $i = (1, g^k)$, i.e. that $\mathcal{A}$ sends (b, z) to C2 s.t. $z = g^k$ and $b = z^w = g^{kw} = a^k$. Call such C2 query k-computed. Note that E_{H_2} requires that $i = (1, g^k)$, i.e. that $\mathcal{A}$ queries H_2 on (x, v) for $v = (h_x)^k$. Call such H_2 query k-computed as well. Since counter tx is decremented, or C-record $(x, w, a, 1)$ is "processed" only on such k-computed C2 and H_2 queries, and tx is incremented or record $(x, w, a, 1)$ is created with each query to S1, hence E happens only if $\mathcal{A}$ triggers more k-computed C2/H_2 queries than S1 queries.

Correlations Monitored only at Evaluation. Before we show that event E can happen with at most negligible probability, we need to change the way GAME 10 and GAME 11 build correlations in function R. Instead of setting them at the time a new function is added, in the modified games the correlations are checked only when a function is evaluated, i.e. the game keeps track of each referenced value of function R, i.e. each triple (δ', z', x') s.t. $R((\delta', z'), x')$ was queried eiter in S2, C2, or H_2. When the game queries a new point, $R(i, x)$ for $i = (\delta, z)$, the game looks for the first record (δ, z', x') on the list of queries s.t. $x' = x$ and $f_{(\delta', z')}(x) = f_{(\delta, z)}(x)$, i.e. $\delta'(z')^{u_x} = \delta(z)^{u_x}$. If so, the game first assigns $R(i, x) \leftarrow R(i', x)$ for $i = (\delta, z)$ and $i' = (\delta', z')$ and only then replies $R(i, x)$. It is easy to see that this is an equivalent process of keeping correlations because indeed the only information about these functions $R(i, \cdot)$ which the game reveals is through evaluated points, so it makes no difference if we postpone correlating values of $R(i, x)$ with $R(i', x)$ until $R(i, x)$ is actually queried.

We show a reduction to the Gap$^+$-OMDH assumption in the case E happens in GAME 10. Reduction $\mathcal{R}$ takes the Gap$^+$-OMDH challenge $(g, z^*, h_1, \ldots, h_N)$ where $N = (q_{H_1} + q_C)$, and responds to $\mathcal{A}$'s queries as follows:

1. Initialize $\mathcal{N}_{\mathsf{SIM}} \leftarrow [(1, z^*)]$ and $\mathcal{S} \leftarrow []$.
2. Embed OMDH challenges into H_1 and C1 outputs, i.e. assign each $H_1(x)$ output, and each value a sent by C1, to a unique OMDH challenge h_i.
3. On message a to S1, use oracle $(\cdot)^k$ to send back $b = a^k$ and $z = z^*$.
4. On query x to S2, set $(a, b, z) \leftarrow (1, 1, z^*)$, run $\mathrm{CORRELATE}((a, b, z), x)$, and output $R((a, b, z), x)$
5. On message (b, z) to C2, recovers C1 input x and output a, run $\mathrm{CORRELATE}((a, b, z), x)$, and output $R((a, b, z), x)$.
6. On query (x, v) to H_2, set $(a, b, z) \leftarrow (1, v, 1)$, run $\mathrm{CORRELATE}((a, b, z), x)$, and output $R((a, b, z), x)$.
7. If $\mathcal{A}$ queries S-Compromise, $\mathcal{R}$ aborts.
8. $\mathrm{CORRELATE}((a, b, z), x)$: Return if $(a, b, z, x) \in \mathcal{S}$. Otherwise, set $h_x \leftarrow H_1(x)$, and if $\exists \, (a', b', z', x)$ in $\mathcal{S}$ s.t.

$$b \cdot \mathsf{CDH}_g(z, h_x/a) = b' \cdot \mathsf{CDH}_g(z', h_x/a') \tag{8}$$

then set $R((a, b, z), x) \leftarrow R((a', b', z'), x)$. Otherwise add (a, b, z, x) to $\mathcal{S}$.

Observe that $\mathcal{R}$ can verify Eq. (8) using oracle DDH_g^+. Secondly, observe that $b \cdot \mathsf{CDH}_g(z, h_x/a)$ correctly evaluates $f_i(x)$ for the corresponding index i: In S2 we set $(a, b, z) = (1, 1, z^*)$, so $b \cdot \mathsf{CDH}_g(z, h_x/a) = \mathsf{CDH}_g(z^*, h_x) = (h_x)^k$ where $z^* = g^k$, as in GAME 10; In C2, in GAME 10 we compute $f_i(x) = f_{(\delta, z)}(x) = \delta \cdot (z)^{u_x} = \delta \cdot \mathsf{CDH}(z, h_x)$, but since $\delta = b/z^w = b \cdot \mathsf{CDH}(z, a^{-1})$ this implies that $f_i(x) = \delta \cdot \mathsf{CDH}_g(z, h_x/a)$; In H_2 we set $(a, b, z) = (1, v, 1)$, so $b \cdot \mathsf{CDH}_g(z, h_x/a) = v \cdot \mathsf{CDH}_g(1, h_x) = v$, also as in GAME 10.

Therefore $\mathcal{R}$ presents a view which is ideantical to GAME 10 as long as S-Compromise is not queried. Therefore event E occurs in the interaction with $\mathcal{R}$ with the same probability as in GAME 10. Let $Q = q_{\mathsf{S}}$ be the number of S1 queries, hence the number of $(\cdot)^k$ oracle accesses by $\mathcal{R}$. Event E implies that the number of k-computed C2 queries and k-computed H_2 queries is larger than Q, i.e. at least $Q+1$. Note that a k-computed H_2 query is a pair (x, v) s.t. $v = (h_x)^k$, so each such query computes $(h_i)^k = \mathsf{CDH}(h_i, z^*)$ on a unique OMDH challenge h_i. Likewise, a k-computed C2 query is a response $(b, z) = (a^k, g^k)$ to C1's message a, and since $\mathcal{R}$ embeds a unique OMDH challenge h_i into each a, such query also computes $a^k = \mathsf{CDH}(h_i, z^*)$ on a unique OMDH challenge h_i. Since $\mathcal{R}$ can use DDH_g^+ oracle to implement DDH, and test whether any H_2 or C2 query is k-computed, $\mathcal{R}$ will solve $Q + 1$ OMDH challenges if event E happens, which implies

$$|\Pr[\mathbf{G_{11}}] - \Pr[\mathbf{G_{10}}]| \leq \epsilon_{\mathrm{OMDH}}(\mathbb{G}, q_{\mathsf{H}_1}, q_{\mathsf{S}})$$

Summing up we conclude that the real-world and the ideal-world interactions are indistinguishable under the Gap-OMDH assumption.

5   Strong aPAKE Protocol Based on $\mathcal{F}_{\mathsf{corOPRF}}$

We show that the OPAQUE protocol of [17] remains secure as UC Strong aPAKE even if it is instantiated with the UC Correlated OPRF of Sect. 3 instead of UC

OPRF of [11]. This implies that one can safely modify the OPAQUE protocol by replacing the *exponential* blinding in the Hashed Diffie-Hellman OPRF with the *multiplicative* blinding (as done in [22]), thus shaving off either 1 variable-base exponentiation from the client, or 2 such exponentiations if the protocol is routinely performed with the same server.

Technically, we show that the OPAQUE compiler construction of [17], which shows that OPRF + AKE → saPAKE, can be used to construct UC saPAKE from any UC Correlated OPRF and any UC AKE which is adaptively secure and resilient to Key-Compromise Impersonation attack (AKE-KCI). We call this compiler OPAQUE+ and show it in Fig. 10. It is exactly the same as the OPAQUE compiler except that the OPRF functionality $\mathcal{F}_{\mathsf{OPRF}}$ used in [16] is replaced with the Correlated OPRF functionality $\mathcal{F}_{\mathsf{corOPRF}}$. We show that protocol OPAQUE+ realizes the UC saPAKE functionality.

The saPAKE and AKE-KCI Functionalities. Protocol OPAQUE+ and its analysis build on two functionalities from of [16]: The (strong) aPAKE functionality $\mathcal{F}_{\mathsf{saPAKE}}$ and the adaptively-secure UC AKE-KCI functionality $\mathcal{F}_{\mathsf{AKE-KCI}}$. We refer to that paper for their detailed description and rationale. We note that AKE-KCI protocol can be instantiated, for example, by the 3-message version of the HMQV protocol, called HMQV-C in [20], or the 3-message SIGMA protocol [19] underlying the design of TLS 1.3.

Security of OPAQUE+. We now state the security of OPAQUE+ in Theorem   2. As in [17], we assume that the adversary $\mathcal{A}$ always sends (COMPROMISE, sid) aimed at $\mathcal{F}_{\mathsf{corOPRF}}$ and (STEALPWDFILE, sid) aimed at S simultaneously, since in the real world when the attacker compromises the server, the corresponding OPRF session is always compromised simultaneously.

Theorem 2. *If protocol Π realizes functionality $\mathcal{F}_{\mathsf{AKE-KCI}}$, then protocol OPAQUE+ in Fig. 10 realizes the strong aPAKE functionality $\mathcal{F}_{\mathsf{saPAKE}}$ in the $(\mathcal{F}_{\mathsf{corOPRF}}, \mathcal{F}_{\mathsf{RO}})$-hybrid model.*

The security argument is very similar to that of OPAQUE in [17]; we briefly explain the differences. First of all, note that when the adversary acts as the client in Correlated OPRF, its power is exactly the same as the client in OPRF, hence for that case the security argument is the same in OPAQUE+ as in OPAQUE.

Secondly, an additional power which Correlated OPRF gives to the adversary is to make correlations between OPRF functions while acting as the server. Yet, this does not change the fact that for every function index i (no matter if $i = \mathsf{S}$ or i is an index created by the adversary) and every value $y \in \{0,1\}^\ell$, with overwhelming probability there is at most one argument x s.t. $y = F_i(x)$. In Correlated OPRF the adversary can find F_i with two arguments that form a collision in F_i if it finds (i_1, x_1) and (i_2, x_2) s.t. $F_{i_1}(x_1) = F_{i_2}(x_2)$ and then sets F_i to be correlated with F_{i_1} on x_1 and with F_{i_2} on x_2. In OPRF the adversary must look for such collisions within each function separately, but in either case the probability of a collision is upper-bounded by $q^2/2^\ell$ where q is the number of F evaluations on all indices. Hence the ciphertext c^* sent from the adversary

---

Public Components:

- KCI-secure AKE protocol Π with private/public keys denoted p_s, P_s, p_u, P_u;
- Random-key robust and equivocable authenticated encryption (AuthEnc, AuthDec) (see [17] for definitions of these properties);
- Functionality $\mathcal{F}_{\mathsf{corOPRF}}$ with output length parameter τ;

Password Registration

1. On input (STOREPWDFILE, sid, C, pw), S generates keys (p_s, P_s) and (p_c, P_c) and sends (INIT, sid) and (OFFLINEEVAL, sid, S, pw, $\perp$) to $\mathcal{F}_{\mathsf{corOPRF}}$. On $\mathcal{F}_{\mathsf{corOPRF}}$'s response (OFFLINEEVAL, sid, rw), S computes $c \leftarrow \mathsf{AuthEnc}_{\mathsf{rw}}(p_c, P_c, P_s)$ and records file[sid] $\leftarrow (p_s, P_s, P_c, c)$.

Server Compromise

1. On (STEALPWDFILE, sid) from $\mathcal{A}$, S retrieves file[sid] and sends it to $\mathcal{A}$.

Login

1. On (USRSESSION, sid, ssid, S, pw'), C sends (EVAL, sid, ssid, S, pw') to $\mathcal{F}_{\mathsf{corOPRF}}$ and records $\mathcal{F}_{\mathsf{corOPRF}}$'s response (Prefix, ssid, prfx).
2. On (SVRSESSION, sid, ssid), S retrieves file[sid] $= (p_s, P_s, P_c, c)$, sends c to C, sends (SNDRCOMPLETE, sid, ssid) to $\mathcal{F}_{\mathsf{corOPRF}}$, and given $\mathcal{F}_{\mathsf{corOPRF}}$'s response (Prefix, ssid, prfx') it runs Π on input (p_s, P_s, P_c) and $\mathsf{ssid}_\Pi = [\mathsf{ssid} \| \mathsf{prfx}']$.
3. On (EVAL, sid, ssid, rw') from $\mathcal{F}_{\mathsf{corOPRF}}$ and c from S, C computes $m \leftarrow \mathsf{AuthDec}_{\mathsf{rw}'}(c)$. If $m = (p'_c, P'_c, P'_s)$ then C retrieves (Prefix, ssid, prfx) and runs Π on input (p'_c, P'_c, P'_s) and $\mathsf{ssid}_\Pi = [\mathsf{ssid} \| \mathsf{prfx}]$; else C outputs (ABORT, sid, ssid) and halts.
4. Given Π's local output SK, each party outputs (sid, ssid, SK).

Fig. 10. OPAQUE+: Strong aPAKE in the $(\mathcal{F}_{\mathsf{corOPRF}}, \mathcal{F}_{\mathsf{RO}})$-Hybrid World

---

to an honest client together with index i^* of the random function F_{i^*} which the adversary makes that honest client compute on its password, together commit to a unique password guess pw* such that $\mathsf{AuthDec}_{\mathsf{rw}^*}(c^*) \neq \perp$ for $\mathsf{rw}^* = F_{i^*}(\mathsf{pw}^*)$.

Lastly, in the Correlated OPRF an adversarial function F_{i^*} is not guaranteed to be completely independent from the honest server's function F_k for every $i^* \neq$ S. Instead, the adversary can correlate F_{i^*} with F_k, although on only a single point x. This allows the adversary a potentially damaging behavior in which it forwards ciphertext $c^* = c$ from the honest server to the honest client and lets the honest client evaluate F_{i^*} on its password. In case both parties' passwords are equal to x the client will compute $F_{i^*}(x) = F_k(x)$, and thus the two parties will establish a key if their shared passwords are equal to x, and fail to establish a key otherwise. This "conditional password test" could not be done in protocol OPAQUE, and yet it is not an attack on saPAKE, because it requires the adversary to guess the password; therefore, the simulator can (1) use a TESTABORT command to check if the client and server's passwords match, and if so, it can then (2) use a TESTPWD command to check if the adversary's password guess is correct. If both checks pass, the simulator can compromise both client's and server's sessions, and make these two sessions connect with the same session key; if either check fails, the simulator can force the client to abort.

We present the full proof of Theorem 2 in the full version of this paper [15].

6 Concrete OPAQUE+ Instantiation Using HMQV

Figure 11 shows a concrete instantiation of protocol OPAQUE+ of Fig. 10, where the UC Correlated OPRF is instantiated with protocol Mult-2HashDH, and UC AKE is instantiated with HMQV [20]. Note that the protocol takes 3 flows (τ_s can be piggybacked with S's earlier message), and 2 fixed-base (fb) and 2 variable-base (vb) (multi-base) exp's for C and resp. 1fb and 2vb exp's for S.

7 Insecure Applications of Multiplicative Blinding

As we noted in the introduction, the correlations allowed by Mult-2HashDH can be exploited in some applications for the benefit of a corrupt server. We illustrate this ability with several examples.

Consider a setting where a client C with input x interacts using Mult-2HashDH with a server S with key k to compute $y = F_k(x) = H_2(x, (h_x)^k)$ where h_x denotes $H_1(x)$. C then uses y for some task; for concreteness, think of x as a password and y as a key that allows C to authenticate to some application. At some point S becomes corrupted and wants to check whether a given value x' equals the user's input x. Using correlations as described in the introduction, e.g., Eq. (3), S mounts the following attack: When C sends its blinded value $a = h_x g^r$, S chooses random k', sets $z = g^{k'}$ and $b = (h_{x'})^{k-k'} a^{k'}$, and sends (b, z) to C, who computes the unblinded value $v = b(z)^{-r}$ and outputs $y' = H_2(x, v)$. It can be checked that $v = (h_x)^k$ if and only if $x' = x$.[8] If S can observe whether C recovered the correct value $y' = y$, e.g. whether it successfully authenticated using the recoverd y', then S learns whether C's secret x equals S's guess x'.

The Correlated OPRF functionality, which Mult-2HashDH realizes, assures that server S cannot test more than one guess x' per interaction, and while in some applications, like the PAKE protocol OPAQUE, this ability doesn't affect the application, e.g. because the application itself allows the attacker such on-line guess-and-test avenue, in other cases this suffices to break the application. Below we show a few application examples which are all secure with Exp-2HashDH, but not with Mult-2HashDH. In all examples the application doesn't expose the client to on-line attacks, and using Exp-2HashDH ensures that the implementation does not either, but using Mult-2HashDH adds this exposure and breaks the application.

---

[8] Observe that $v = bz^{-r} = (h_{x'})^{k-k'}(h_x g^r)^{k'}(g^{k'})^{-r} = h_{x'}^k (h_{x'}/h_x)^{k'}$, hence $v = (h_x)^k$ iff $h_x = h_{x'}$. Using the terminology of Eq. (2), C computes $y' = F_{(\delta,z)}(x)$ for $F_{(\delta,z)}$ which is *correlated* with F_k on x', hence $y' = F_k(x)$ iff $x = x'$.

Public Parameters and Components

Group $\mathbb{G}$ of prime order q with generator g;

Random-key robust and equivocable authenticated encryption $(\mathsf{AuthEnc}, \mathsf{AuthDec})$ (see [17] for definitions of these properties);

Hash functions $H_1, H_3, H_5 : \{0,1\}^* \to \{0,1\}^\tau$, $H_2 : \{0,1\}^* \to \mathbb{G}$, $H_4 : \{0,1\}^* \to \mathbb{Z}_q$

Pseudorandom function (PRF) $f : \{0,1\}^* \to \{0,1\}^\tau$

S on $(\textsc{StorePwdFile}, \mathsf{sid}, \mathsf{pw})$

Pick $k, p_s, p_c \leftarrow_R \mathbb{Z}_q$, set $(z, P_s, P_c) \leftarrow (g^k, g^{p_s}, g^{p_c})$, $\mathsf{rw} \leftarrow F_k(\mathsf{pw})$, $c \leftarrow \mathsf{AuthEnc}_{\mathsf{rw}}(p_c, P_s)$; record $\mathsf{file}[\mathsf{sid}] \leftarrow \langle k, z, c, p_s, P_c \rangle$ and erase everything else

C on $(\textsc{UsrSession}, \mathsf{sid}, \mathsf{ssid}, S, \mathsf{pw})$	S on $(\textsc{SvrSession}, \mathsf{sid}, \mathsf{ssid})$
	retrieve $\langle k, z, c, p_s, P_c \rangle \leftarrow \mathsf{file}[\mathsf{sid}]$
$r, x_c \leftarrow_R \mathbb{Z}_q$	$x_s \leftarrow_R \mathbb{Z}_q$
$a \leftarrow H_2(\mathsf{pw}) \cdot g^r, X_c \leftarrow g^{x_c}$ $\xrightarrow{\quad a, X_c \quad}$	
$\mathsf{rw} \leftarrow H_1(\mathsf{pw}, b \cdot z^{-r})$ $\xleftarrow{\quad b, z, X_s, c \quad}$	$b \leftarrow a^k, X_s \leftarrow g^{x_s}$
parse $(p_c, P_s) \leftarrow \mathsf{AuthDec}_{\mathsf{rw}}(c)$	
(if this parsing fails C outputs ABORT)	

C and S set $\mathsf{ssid}' \leftarrow H_5(\mathsf{sid}, \mathsf{ssid}, a)$, $e_c \leftarrow H_4(X_c, S, \mathsf{ssid}')$, $e_s \leftarrow H_4(X_s, C, \mathsf{ssid}')$

$K \leftarrow H_3\left((X_s P_s^{e_s})^{x_c + e_c p_c}\right)$	$K \leftarrow H_3\left((X_c P_c^{e_c})^{x_s + e_s p_s}\right)$
$\xleftarrow{\quad \tau_s \quad}$	$\tau_s \leftarrow f_K(1, \mathsf{ssid}')$
if $\tau_s \neq f_K(1, \mathsf{ssid}')$: $(SK, \tau_c) \leftarrow (\perp, \perp)$	
else: $SK \leftarrow f_K(0, \mathsf{ssid}')$ and $\tau_c \leftarrow f_K(2, \mathsf{ssid}')$	
$\xrightarrow{\quad \tau_c \quad}$	if $\tau_c \neq f_K(2, \mathsf{ssid}')$: $SK \leftarrow \perp$
	else: $SK \leftarrow f_K(0, \mathsf{ssid}')$
output $(\mathsf{sid}, \mathsf{ssid}, SK)$	output $(\mathsf{sid}, \mathsf{ssid}, SK)$

Fig. 11. Protocol OPAQUE+ (Fig. 10) with Mult-2HashDH and HMQV

OPAQUE with Outsourced Envelope. Recall that OPAQUE [17] combines an OPRF with an authenticated key-exchange (AKE) protocol as follows: At registration, the server and the user choose private-public AKE key pairs. The user then runs an OPRF with the server where the user's input is a password pw and the server's input is an OPRF key k. The output of the OPRF, learned only by the user, is a random key $\mathsf{rw} = F_k(\mathsf{pw})$, and the user uses rw to authenticate-encrypt her AKE private key and the server's public key. The ciphertext c that results from this encryption is stored by the server, together with the OPRF key k, the user's public AKE key, and the server's AKE key pair. At login, the user runs the OPRF with the server on input pw, learns rw, uses rw to decrypt its own private key and the server's public key encrypted in c, and uses these keys to run the AKE with the server. Only a user in possession of the registered password can successfully run the AKE.

However, consider a modification where the user stores ciphertext c at some other location than server S, e.g. a laptop or another server. In this case a malicious S, who holds only OPRF key k and the AKE keys, cannot stage either online or offline attacks on the user's password: Without ciphertext c, S cannot test candidate values $rw = F_k(pw)$. However, this property is *not* ensured if OPRF is implemented with Mult-2HashDH. Indeed, using the strategy described above, a malicious S can test whether the user's password is equal to a chosen pw^*, by running login using function F_{k^*} which is correlated on argument pw^* with function F_k used in registration. If the user recovers its credentials and authenticates in that login, S learns that $pw = pw^*$. Crucially, this online attack opportunity for server S is not available using Exp-2HashDH.

Device-Enhanced PAKE. [14,24] presents a password protocol that uses an auxiliary device (typically a smartphone but can also be an online server) in the role of a password manager. When the user wishes to password-authenticate to a server S, it communicates with the device who holds key k for 2HashDH OPRF. The user's input to the OPRF is her password, and the OPRF result $rw = F_k(pw)$ is used as the "randomized" password with service S. Using Exp-2HashDH, a corrupt device learns nothing about the user's password, but it can test a guess for the user's password at the cost of one online interaction with S per guess. However, using Mult-2HashDH, the corrupt device can validate a guess without interacting with S, by watching if the user's interaction with S succeeded, thus resulting in weaker security guarantees.

Threshold OPRF (Including Threshold OPAQUE). A multi-server threshold implementation of Exp-2HashDH is presented in [12]. It ensures the security of the OPRF as long as no more than a threshold of servers are compromised. Such threshold OPRF can be used e.g. to construct Password-Protected Secret Sharing (PPSS) [1,11], which in turn can implement Threshold PAKE. It is straightforward to see that the above correlation attacks apply to these constructions if Exp-2HashDH is replaced with Mult-2HashDH. They allow a single corrupted server to choose correlated values with which it can verify guesses for the client's inputs. As an illustration, consider a 2-out-of-2 Threshold OPRF that computes h_x^k as $h_x^{k_1+k_2}$ using two servers S_1, S_2 with respective keys k_1, k_2. Such a scheme should ensure that nothing can be learned about the input x without compromising both servers. However, a corrupted S_2 can check whether C's input x equals any guess x' by mounting the above attack using ony key k_2. If C reconstructs the correct y, then $x = x'$. This attack also applies to OPAQUE with a multi-server threshold implementation of Mult-2HashDH.

All these examples show that in order to use Mult-2HashDH in an application where an authenticated g^k is not available to the client, a dedicated proof of security (as the one we develop here for OPAQUE) is essential. Even in that case, one can consider this as "fragile evidence", as eventual changes to the application may void the security proof. Thus a safer alternative is to use the scheme (4) presented in the introduction, which implements UC OPRF using both forms of blinding, and would be secure in all the above applications.

References

1. Bagherzandi, A., Jarecki, S., Saxena, N., Lu, Y.: Password-protected secret sharing. In: ACM Conference on Computer and Communications Security — CCS 2011. ACM (2011)

2. Boyen, X.: HPAKE: password authentication secure against cross-site user impersonation. In: Garay, J.A., Miyaji, A., Otsuka, A. (eds.) CANS 2009. LNCS, vol. 5888, pp. 279–298. Springer, Heidelberg (2009). https://doi.org/10.1007/978-3-642-10433-6_19

3. Brickell, E.F., Gordon, D.M., McCurley, K.S., Wilson, D.B.: Fast exponentiation with precomputation. In: Rueppel, R.A. (ed.) EUROCRYPT 1992. LNCS, vol. 658, pp. 200–207. Springer, Heidelberg (1993). https://doi.org/10.1007/3-540-47555-9_18

4. Canetti, R.: Universally composable security: a new paradigm for cryptographic protocols. In: IEEE Symposium on Foundations of Computer Science - FOCS 2001, pp. 136–145. IEEE (2001)

5. Chaum, D., Pedersen, T.P.: Wallet databases with observers. In: Brickell, E.F. (ed.) CRYPTO 1992. LNCS, vol. 740, pp. 89–105. Springer, Heidelberg (1993). https://doi.org/10.1007/3-540-48071-4_7

6. Davidson, A., Goldberg, I., Sullivan, N., Tankersley, G., Valsorda, F.: Privacy pass: bypassing internet challenges anonymously. In: Privacy Enhancing Technologies Symposium - PETS 2018, pp. 164–180. Sciendo (2019)

7. Ford, W., Kaliski, B.S.: Server-assisted generation of a strong secret from a password. In: IEEE 9th International Workshops on Enabling Technologies: Infrastructure for Collaborative Enterprises - WET ICE 2000, pp. 176–180. IEEE (2000)

8. Freedman, M.J., Ishai, Y., Pinkas, B., Reingold, O.: Keyword search and oblivious pseudorandom functions. In: Kilian, J. (ed.) TCC 2005. LNCS, vol. 3378, pp. 303–324. Springer, Heidelberg (2005). https://doi.org/10.1007/978-3-540-30576-7_17

9. Haase, B., Labrique, B.: AuCPace: efficient verifier-based PAKE protocol tailored for the IIoT. In: CHES (2019)

10. Jarecki, S., Kiayias, A., Krawczyk, H.: Round-optimal password-protected secret sharing and T-PAKE in the password-only model. In: Sarkar, P., Iwata, T. (eds.) ASIACRYPT 2014. LNCS, vol. 8874, pp. 233–253. Springer, Heidelberg (2014). https://doi.org/10.1007/978-3-662-45608-8_13

11. Jarecki, S., Kiayias, A., Krawczyk, H., Xu, J.: Highly-efficient and composable password-protected secret sharing (Or: how to protect your bitcoin wallet online). In: IEEE European Symposium on Security and Privacy - EuroS&P 2016, pp. 276–291. IEEE (2016)

12. Jarecki, S., Kiayias, A., Krawczyk, H., Xu, J.: TOPPSS: cost-minimal password-protected secret sharing based on threshold OPRF. In: Gollmann, D., Miyaji, A., Kikuchi, H. (eds.) ACNS 2017. LNCS, vol. 10355, pp. 39–58. Springer, Cham (2017). https://doi.org/10.1007/978-3-319-61204-1_3

13. Jarecki, S., Krawczyk, H., Resch, J.: Updatable oblivious key management for storage systems. In: ACM Conference on Computer and Communications Security — CCS 2019. ACM (2019)

14. Jarecki, S., Krawczyk, H., Shirvanian, M., Saxena, N.: Device-enhanced password protocols with optimal online-offline protection. In: Proceedings of the 11th ACM on Asia Conference on Computer and Communications Security, pp. 177–188. ACM (2016)

15. Jarecki, S., Krawczyk, H., Xu, J.: On the (In)Security of the Diffie-Hellman oblivious PRF with multiplicative blinding. IACR Cryptology ePrint Archive 2021:273
16. Jarecki, S., Krawczyk, H., Xu. J.: OPAQUE: an asymmetric PAKE protocol secure against pre-computation attacks. IACR Cryptology ePrint Archive 2018:163
17. Jarecki, S., Krawczyk, H., Xu, J.: OPAQUE: an asymmetric PAKE protocol secure against pre-computation attacks. In: Nielsen, J.B., Rijmen, V. (eds.) EUROCRYPT 2018. LNCS, vol. 10822, pp. 456–486. Springer, Cham (2018). https://doi.org/10.1007/978-3-319-78372-7_15
18. Jarecki, S., Liu, X.: Fast secure computation of set intersection. In: Garay, J.A., De Prisco, R. (eds.) SCN 2010. LNCS, vol. 6280, pp. 418–435. Springer, Heidelberg (2010). https://doi.org/10.1007/978-3-642-15317-4_26
19. Krawczyk, H.: SIGMA: The 'SIGn-and-MAc' approach to authenticated Diffie-Hellman and its use in the IKE protocols. In: Boneh, D. (ed.) CRYPTO 2003. LNCS, vol. 2729, pp. 400–425. Springer, Heidelberg (2003). https://doi.org/10.1007/978-3-540-45146-4_24
20. Krawczyk, H.: HMQV: a high-performance secure Diffie-Hellman protocol. In: Shoup, V. (ed.) CRYPTO 2005. LNCS, vol. 3621, pp. 546–566. Springer, Heidelberg (2005). https://doi.org/10.1007/11535218_33
21. Krawczyk, H., The OPAQUE asymmetric PAKE protocol, May 2020. https://tools.ietf.org/html/draft-krawczyk-cfrg-opaque
22. Krawczyk, H., Lewi, K., Wood, C.A.: The OPAQUE asymmetric PAKE protocol, November 2020. https://tools.ietf.org/html/draft-irtf-cfrg-opaque
23. Naor, M., Pinkas, B., Reingold, O.: Distributed pseudo-random functions and KDCs. In: Stern, J. (ed.) EUROCRYPT 1999. LNCS, vol. 1592, pp. 327–346. Springer, Heidelberg (1999). https://doi.org/10.1007/3-540-48910-X_23
24. Shirvanian, M., Saxena, N., Jarecki, S., Krawczyk, H.: Building and studying a password store that perfectly hides passwords from itself. IEEE Trans. Dependable Secure Comput. **16**, 5 (2019)
25. Sullivan, N.: Exported authenticators in TLS, May 2020. https://tools.ietf.org/html/draft-ietf-tls-exported-authenticator
26. Sullivan, N., Krawczyk, H., Friel, O., Barnes, R.: Usage of OPAQUE with TLS 1.3, March 2019. https://tools.ietf.org/html/draft-sullivan-tls-opaque

An Efficient and Generic Construction for Signal's Handshake (X3DH): Post-Quantum, State Leakage Secure, and Deniable

Keitaro Hashimoto[1,2]($\boxtimes$), Shuichi Katsumata[2], Kris Kwiatkowski[3], and Thomas Prest[3]

[1] Tokyo Institute of Technology, Tokyo, Japan
hashimoto.k.au@m.titech.ac.jp
[2] AIST, Tokyo, Japan
shuichi.katsumata@aist.go.jp
[3] PQShield, Oxford, UK
{kris.kwiatkowski,thomas.prest}@pqshield.com

Abstract. The Signal protocol is a secure instant messaging protocol that underlies the security of numerous applications such as WhatsApp, Skype, Facebook Messenger among many others. The Signal protocol consists of two sub-protocols known as the X3DH protocol and the double ratchet protocol, where the latter has recently gained much attention. For instance, Alwen, Coretti, and Dodis (Eurocrypt'19) provided a concrete security model along with a generic construction based on simple building blocks that are instantiable from versatile assumptions, including post-quantum ones. In contrast, as far as we are aware, works focusing on the X3DH protocol seem limited.

In this work, we cast the X3DH protocol as a specific type of authenticated key exchange (AKE) protocol, which we call a *Signal-conforming AKE* protocol, and formally define its security model based on the vast prior work on AKE protocols. We then provide the first efficient generic construction of a Signal-conforming AKE protocol based on standard cryptographic primitives such as key encapsulation mechanisms (KEM) and signature schemes. Specifically, this results in the first post-quantum secure replacement of the X3DH protocol on well-established assumptions. Similar to the X3DH protocol, our Signal-conforming AKE protocol offers a strong (or stronger) flavor of security, where the exchanged key remains secure even when all the non-trivial combinations of the long-term secrets and session-specific secrets are compromised. Moreover, our protocol has a weak flavor of deniability and we further show how to strengthen it using ring signatures. Finally, we provide a full-fledged, generic C implementation of our (weakly deniable) protocol. We instantiate it with several Round 3 candidates (finalists and alternates) to the NIST post-quantum standardization process and compare the resulting bandwidth and computation performances. Our implementation is publicly available.

© International Association for Cryptologic Research 2021
J. A. Garay (Ed.): PKC 2021, LNCS 12711, pp. 410–440, 2021.
https://doi.org/10.1007/978-3-030-75248-4_15

1   Introduction

Secure instant messaging (SIM) ensures privacy and security by making sure that only the person you are sending the message to can read the message, a.k.a. end-to-end encryption. With the ever-growing awareness against mass-surveillance of communications, people have become more privacy-aware and the demand for SIM has been steadily increasing. While there have been a range of SIM protocols, the Signal protocol [1] is widely regarded as the gold standard. Not only is it used by the Signal app[1], the Signal protocol is also used by WhatsApp, Skype, Facebook Messenger among many others, where the number of active users is well over 2 billions. One of the reasons for such popularity is due to the simplicity and the strong security properties it provides, such as forward secrecy and post-compromise secrecy, while simultaneously allowing for the same user experience as any (non-cryptographically secure) instant messaging app.

The Signal protocol consists of two sub-protocols: the X3DH protocol [45] and the double ratchet protocol [44]. The former protocol can be viewed as a type of key exchange protocol allowing two parties to exchange a secure initial session key. The latter protocol is executed after the X3DH protocol and it allows two parties to perform a secure back-and-forth message delivery. Below, we briefly recall the current affair of these two protocols.

The Double Ratchet Protocol. The first attempt at a full security analysis of the Signal protocol was made by Cohn-Gordon et al. [18,19]. They considered the Signal protocol as one large protocol and analyzed the security guarantees in its entirety. Since the double ratchet protocol was understood to be the root of the complexity, many subsequent works aimed at further abstracting and formalizing (and in some cases enhancing) the security of the double ratchet protocol by viewing it as a stand-alone protocol [2,9,26,36,37,49]. Under these works, our understanding of the double ratchet protocol has much matured. Notably, Alwen et al. [2] fully abstracted the complex Diffie-Hellman based double ratchet protocol used by Signal and provided a concrete security model along with a generic construction based on simple building blocks. Since these blocks are instantiable from versatile assumptions, including post-quantum ones, their work resulted in the first *post-quantum secure* double ratchet protocol. Here, we elucidate that all the aforementioned works analyze the double ratchet protocol as a stand-alone primitive, and hence, it is assumed that any two parties can securely share an initial session key, for instance, by executing a "secure" X3DH protocol.

The X3DH Protocol. In contrast, other than the white paper offered by Signal [45] and those indirectly considered by Cohn-Gordon et al. [18,19], works focusing on the X3DH protocol seems to be limited. As far as we are aware, there is one recent work that studies the formalization [14] and a few papers that study one of the appealing security properties, known as (off-line) *deniability*, claimed by the X3DH protocol [51–53].

---

[1] The name Signal is used to point to the app *and* the protocol.

Brendel et al. [14] abstract the X3DH protocol and provides the first generic construction based on a new primitive they call a *split key encapsulation mechanism* (KEM). However, so far, instantiations of split KEMs with strong security guarantees required for the X3DH protocol are limited to Diffie-Hellman style assumptions. In fact, the recent result of Guo et al. [33] implies that it would be difficult to construct them from one of the promising post-quantum candidates: lattice-based assumptions (and presumably coded-based assumptions). On the other hand, Vatandas et al. [53] study one of the security guarantees widely assumed for the X3DH protocol called (off-line) deniability [45, Section 4.4] and showed that a strong knowledge-type assumption would be necessary to formally prove it. Unger and Goldberg [51,52] construct several protocols that can be used as a drop-in replacement of the X3DH protocol that achieves a strong flavor of (on-line) deniability from standard assumptions, albeit by making a noticeable sacrifice in the security against key-compromise attacks: a type of attack that exploits leaked secret information of a party. For instance, while the X3DH protocol is secure against key-compromise impersonation (KCI) attacks [11],[2] the protocols of Unger and Goldberg are no longer secure against such attacks.[3]

Motivation. In summary, although we have a rough understanding of what the X3DH protocol offers [18,19,45], the current state of affairs is unsatisfactory for the following reasons, and making progress on these issues will be the focus of this work:

– It is difficult to formally understand the security guarantees offered by the X3DH protocol or to make a meaningful comparison among different protocols achieving the same functionality as the X3DH protocol without a clearly defined security model.
– The X3DH protocol is so far only instantiable from Diffie-Hellman style assumptions [14] and it is unclear whether such assumptions are inherent to the Signal protocol.
– Ideally, similarly to what Alwen et al. [2] did for the double ratchet protocol, we would like to abstract the X3DH protocol and have a generic construction based on simple building blocks that can be instantiated from versatile assumptions, including but not limited to post-quantum ones.
– No matter how secure the double ratchet protocol is, we cannot completely secure the Signal protocol if the initial X3DH protocol is the weakest link in the chain (e.g., insecure against state-leakage and only offering security against classical adversaries).

---

[2] Although [45, Section 4.6] states that the X3DH protocol is susceptible to KCI attacks, this is only because they consider the scenario where the *session-specific* secret is compromised. If we consider the standard KCI attack scenario where the long-term secret is the only information being compromised [11], then the X3DH protocol is secure. .

[3] Being vulnerable against KCI attacks seems to be intrinsic to on-line deniability [45, 51,52].

1.1   Our Contribution

In this work, we cast the X3DH protocol (see Fig. 1) as a specific type of authenticated key exchange (AKE) protocol, which we call a *Signal-conforming AKE* protocol, and define its security model based on the vast prior work on AKE protocols. We then provide an efficient generic construction of a Signal-conforming AKE protocol based on standard cryptographic primitives: an (IND-CCA secure) KEM, a signature scheme, and a pseudorandom function (PRF). Since all of these primitives can be based on well-established post-quantum assumptions, this results in the first post-quantum secure replacement of the X3DH protocol. Similarly to the X3DH protocol, our Signal-conforming AKE protocol offers a strong flavor of key-compromise security. Borrowing terminologies from AKE-related literature, our protocol is proven secure in the strong Canetti-Krawczyk (CK) type security models [15,30,39,42], where the exchanged session key remains secure even if all the non-trivial combinations of the long-term secrets and session-specific secrets of the parties are compromised. In fact, our protocol is more secure than the X3DH protocol since it is even secure against KCI-attacks where the parties' session-specific secrets are compromised (see Footnote 5).[4] We believe the level of security offered by our Signal-conforming AKE protocol aligns with the level of security guaranteed by the double ratchet protocol where (a specific notion of) security still holds even when such secrets are compromised. Moreover, while our Signal-conforming AKE already provides a weak form of deniability, we can strengthen its deniability by using a ring signature scheme instead of a signature scheme. Likewise to the X3DH protocol [53] although our construction seemingly offers (off-line) deniability, the formal proof relies on a strong knowledge-type assumption. However, relying on such assumptions seems unavoidable considering that all known deniable AKE protocols secure against key-compromise attacks, including the X3DH protocol, rely on them [24,53,57].

We implemented our (weakly deniable) Signal-conforming AKE protocol in C, building on the open source libraries PQClean and LibTomCrypt. Our implementation[5] is fully generic and can thus be instantiated with a wide range of KEMs and signature schemes. We instantiate it with several Round 3 candidates (finalists and alternates) to the NIST post-quantum standardization process, and compare the bandwidth and computation costs that result from these choices. Our protocol performs best with "balanced" schemes, for example most lattice-based schemes. The isogeny-based scheme SIKE offers good bandwidth performance, but entails a significant computation cost. Finally, schemes with large public keys (Classic McEliece, Rainbow, etc.) do not seem to be a good match for our protocol, since these keys are transferred at each run of the protocol.

---

[4] The X3DH can be made secure against leakge of session-specific secrets by using NAXOS trick [42], but it requires additional computation. Because it affects efficiency, we do not consider AKE protocols using NAXOS trick (e.g., [30,40,56]).

[5] It is available at the URL [41].

1.2   Technical Overview

We now briefly recall the X3DH protocol and abstract its required properties by viewing it through the lens of AKE protocols. We then provide an overview of how to construct a Signal-conforming AKE protocol from standard assumptions.

Recap on the X3DH Protocol. At a high level, the X3DH protocol allows for an asynchronous key exchange where two parties, say Alice and Bob, exchange a session key without having to be online at the same time. Even more, the party, say Bob, that wishes to send a secure message to Alice can do so without Alice even knowing Bob. For instance, imagine the scenario where you send a friend request and a message at the same time before being accepted as a friend. At first glance, it seems what we require is a non-interactive key exchange (NIKE) since Bob needs to exchange a key with Alice who is offline, while Alice does not yet know that Bob is trying to communicate with her. Unfortunately, solutions based on NIKEs are undesirable since they either provide weaker guarantees than standard (interactive) AKE or exhibit inefficient constructions [10,17,29,50].

The X3DH protocol circumvents this issue by considering an *untrusted server* (e.g., the Signal server) to sit in the middle between Alice and Bob to serve as a public bulletin board. That is, the parties can store and retrieve information from the server while the server is not assumed to act honestly. A simplified description of the X3DH protocol, which still satisfies our purpose, based on the classical Diffie-Hellman (DH) key exchange is provided in Fig. 1.[6] As the first step, Alice sends her DH component $g^x \in \mathbb{G}$ to the server[7] and then possibly goes offline. We point out that Alice does *not* need to know who she will be communicating with at this point. Bob, who may ad-hocly decide to communicate with Alice, then fetches Alice's first message from the server and uploads its DH component g^y to the server. As in a typical DH key exchange, Bob computes the session key k_B using the long-term secret exponent $b \in \mathbb{Z}_p$ and session-specific secret exponent $y \in \mathbb{Z}_p$. Since Bob can compute the session key k_B while Alice is offline, he can begin executing the subsequent double ratchet protocol without waiting for Alice to come online. Whenever Alice comes online, she can fetch whatever message Bob sent from the server.

Casting the X3DH Protocol as an AKE Protocol. It is not difficult to see that the X3DH protocol can be cast as a specific type of AKE protocol. In particular, we can think of the server as an adversary that tries to mount a man-in-the-middle (MIM) attack in a standard AKE protocol. Viewing the server as a malicious adversary, rather than some semi-honest entity, has two benefits: the parties do not need to put trust in the server since the protocol is supposed

---

[6] We assume Alice and Bob know each other's long-term key. In practice, this can be enforced by "out-of-bound" authentications (see [45, Section 4.1]).

[7] In the actual protocol, Alice also signs g^x sent to the server (i.e., *signed pre-keys*). We ignore this subtlety as it does not play a crucial role in the analysis of security. See Remark 4.2 for more detail. Also, we note that in practice, Bob may initiate the double ratchet protocol using k_B and send his message to Alice along with g^y to the server before Alice responds. .

Alice: $(\mathsf{lpk_A} = g^a, \mathsf{lsk_A} = a)$		Server		Bob: $(\mathsf{lpk_B} = g^b, \mathsf{lsk_B} = b)$
				Fetch (Alice, g^x)
$x \leftarrow\!\!\$\ \mathbb{Z}_p$				$y \leftarrow\!\!\$\ \mathbb{Z}_p$
Store x	$\xrightarrow{\ g^x\ }$	Store	$\xrightarrow{\ g^x\ }$	$\mathsf{k_B} := \mathsf{KDF}((g^x)^b,$
Upload g^x to server		(Alice, g^x)		$\quad (g^a)^y, (g^x)^y)$
-- go offline --				Upload g^y to server
				Erase y
-- come online --		Store		
Fetch $((\text{Alice}, \text{Bob}), g^y)$	$\xleftarrow{\ g^y\ }$	$((\text{Alice}, \text{Bob}),$	$\xleftarrow{\ g^y\ }$	
$\mathsf{k_A} := \mathsf{KDF}((g^b)^x, (g^y)^a, (g^y)^x)$		$g^y)$		

Fig. 1. Simplified description of the X3DH Protocol. Alice and Bob have the long-term key pairs $(\mathsf{lpk_A}, \mathsf{lsk_A})$ and $(\mathsf{lpk_B}, \mathsf{lsk_B})$, respectively. Alice and Bob agree on a session key $\mathsf{k_A} = \mathsf{k_B}$, where KDF denotes a key derivation function.

to be secure even against a malicious server, while the server or the company providing the app is relieved from having to "prove" that it is behaving honestly. One distinguishing feature required by the X3DH protocol when viewed as an AKE protocol is that it needs to be a two-round protocol where the initiator message is generated *independently* from the receiver. That is, Alice needs to be able to store her first message to the server without knowing who she will be communicating with. In this work, we define an AKE protocol with such functionality as a *Signal-conforming* AKE protocol.

Regarding the security model for a Signal-conforming AKE protocol, we base it on the vast prior works on AKE protocols. Specifically, we build on the recent formalization of [20,32] that study the tightness of efficient AKE protocols (including a slight variant of the X3DH protocol) and strengthen the model to also incorporate *state leakage* compromise; a model where an adversary can obtain session-specific information called *session-state*. Since the double ratchet protocol considers a very strong form of state leakage security, we believe it would be the most rational design choice to discuss the X3DH protocol in a security model that captures such leakage as well. Informally, we consider our Signal-conforming AKE protocol in the Canetti-Krawczyk (CK) type security model [15,30,39,42], which is a strengthening of the Bellare-Rogaway security model [7] considered by [20,32]. A detailed discussion and comparison between ours and the numerous other security models of AKE protocols are provided in Sect. 3.

Lack of Signal-Conforming AKE Protocol. The main feature of a Signal-conforming AKE protocol is that the initiator's message does *not* depend on the receiver. Although this seems like a very natural feature considering DH-type AKE protocols, it turns out that they are quite unique (see Brendel et al. [14] for some discussion). For instance, as far as we are aware, the only other assumption that allows for a clean analog of the X3DH protocol is based on the *gap* CSIDH assumption recently introduced by De Kock et al. [22] and Kawashima et al. [38]. Considering the community is still in the process of assessing the concrete parameter selection for *standard* CSIDH [13,48], it would be desirable to base the X3DH protocol on more well-established and versatile assumptions. On the other hand, when we turn our eyes to known generic construction of AKE protocols [30,31,34,54,55] that can be instantiated from versatile assumptions, including post-quantum ones, we observe that none of them is Signal-conforming. That is, they are all either non-2-round or the initiator's message depends on the public key of the receiver.

Our Construction. To this end, in this work, we provide a new practical generic construction of a Signal-conforming AKE protocol from an (IND-CCA secure) KEM and a signature scheme. We believe this may be of independent interest in other scenarios where we require an AKE protocol that has a flavor of "receiver obliviousness."[8] The construction is simple: The construction is simple: Let us assume Alice and Bob's long-term key consist of KEM key pairs (ek_A, dk_A) and (ek_B, dk_B) and signature key pairs (vk_A, sk_A) and (vk_B, sk_B), respectively. The Signal-conforming AKE protocol then starts by Alice (i.e., the initiator) generating a session-specific KEM key (ek_T, dk_T) and sending ek_T to Bob (i.e., the receiver).[9] Here, observe that Alice's message does not depend on who she will be communicating with. Bob then constructs two ciphertexts: one using Alice's long-term key $(K_A, C_A) \leftarrow$ KEM.Encap(ek_A) and another using the session-specific key $(K_T, C_T) \leftarrow$ KEM.Encap(ek_T). It then signs these ciphertext $M := (C_A, C_T)$ as $\sigma_B \leftarrow$ SIG.Sign(sk_B, M), where we include other session-specific components in M in the actual construction. Since sending σ_B in the clear may serve as public evidence that Bob communicated with Alice, Bob will hide this. To this end, he derives two keys, a session key k_{AKE} and a one-time pad key k_{OTP}, by running a key derivation function on input the random KEM keys (K_A, K_T). Bob then sends $(C_A, C_T, c := \sigma_B \oplus k_{OTP})$ to Alice and sets the session key as k_{AKE}. Once Alice receives the message from Bob, she decrypts the ciphertexts (C_A, C_T), derives the two keys (k_{AKE}, k_{OPT}), and checks if $\sigma := c \oplus k_{OTP}$ is a valid signature of Bob's. If so, she sets the session key as k_{AKE}. At a high level, Alice (explicitly) authenticates Bob through verifying Bob's signature and Bob (implicitly) authenticates Alice since Alice is the only party that can decrypt *both* ciphertexts (C_A, C_T). We turn this intuition into a formal proof and show that our scheme satisfies a strong flavor of security where the shared session key remains pseudorandom even to an adversary that can obtain any non-trivial combinations of the long-term private keys (i.e., dk_A, dk_B, sk_A, sk_B) and session-specific secret keys (i.e., dk_T). Notably, our protocol satisfies a stronger notion of security compared to the X3DH protocol since it prevents an adversary to

---

[8] This property has also been called as *post-specified peers* [16] in the context of Internet Key Exchange (IKE) protocols.

[9] As we briefly commented in Footnote 10, Alice can sign her message ek_T as in the X3DH protocol. This will only make our protocol more secure. See Remark 4.2 for more detail.

impersonate Alice even if her session-specific secret key is compromised [45, Section 4.6].

Finally, our Signal-conforming AKE protocol already satisfies a limited form of deniability where the publicly exchanged messages do not directly leak the participant of the protocol. However, if Alice at a later point gets compromised or turns malicious, she can publicize the signature σ_B sent from Bob to cryptographically prove that Bob was communicating with Alice. This is in contrast to the X3DH protocol that does not allow such a deniability attack. We, therefore, show that we can protect Bob from such attacks by replacing the signature scheme with a *ring* signature scheme. In particular, Alice now further sends a session-specific ring signature verification key vk_T, and Bob signs to the ring $\{\mathsf{vk}_T, \mathsf{vk}_B\}$. Effectively, when Alice outputs a signature from Bob $\sigma_{B,T}$, she cannot fully convince a third party whether it originates from Bob since she could have signed $\sigma_{B,T}$ using her signing key sk_T corresponding to vk_T. Although the intuition is clear, it turns out that turning this into a formal proof is quite difficult. Similar to all previous works on AKE protocols satisfying a strong flavor of key-compromise security [24,57] (including the X3DH protocol [53]), the proof of deniability must rely on a strong knowledge-type assumption. We leave it as future work to investigate the deniability of our Signal-conforming AKE protocols from more standard assumptions.

2 Preliminaries

The operator $\oplus$ denotes bit-wise "XOR", and $\|$ denotes string concatenation. For $n \in \mathbb{N}$, we write $[n]$ to denote the set $[n] := \{1, \ldots, n\}$. For $j \in [n]$, we write $[n\backslash j]$ to denote the set $[n\backslash j] := \{1, \ldots, n\} \setminus \{j\}$. We denote by $x \leftarrow_\$ S$ the sampling of an element x uniformly at random from a finite set S. PPT (resp. QPT) stands for probabilistic (resp. quantum) polynomial time. Due to page limitation, we refer standard definitions to the full version.

3 Security Model for Signal-Conforming AKE Protocols

In this section, we define a security model for a *Signal-conforming* authenticated key exchange (AKE) protocol; AKE protocols that can be used as a drop-in replacement of the X3DH protocol. We first provide in Sects. 3.1 to 3.3 a game-based security model building on the recent formalization of [20,32] targeting general AKE protocols. We then discuss in Sect. 3.4 the modifications needed to make it Signal-conforming. A detailed comparison and discussion between ours and other various security models for AKE protocols are provided in Sect. 3.5.

3.1 Execution Environment

We consider a system of μ parties $P_1, \ldots, P_\mu$. Each party P_i is represented by a set of ℓ oracles $\{\pi_i^1, \ldots, \pi_i^\ell\}$, where each oracle corresponds to a single execution of a protocol, and $\ell \in \mathbb{N}$ is the maximum number of protocol sessions per party. Each oracle is equipped with fixed randomness but is otherwise deterministic. Each oracle π_i^s has access to the long-term key pair $(\mathsf{lpk}_i, \mathsf{lsk}_i)$ of P_i and the public keys of all other parties, and maintains a list of the following local variables:

- rand_i^s is the randomness hard-wired to π_i^s;
- sid_i^s ("session identifier") stores the identity of the session as specified by the protocol;
- Pid_i^s ("peer id") stores the identity of the intended communication partner;
- $\Psi_i^s \in \{\bot, \mathtt{accept}, \mathtt{reject}\}$ indicates whether oracle π_i^s has successfully completed the protocol execution and "accepted" the resulting key;
- k_i^s stores the session key computed by π_i^s;
- state_i^s holds the (secret) session-state values and intermediary results required by the session;
- $\mathsf{role}_i^s \in \{\bot, \mathtt{init}, \mathtt{resp}\}$ indicates π_i^s's role during the protocol execution.

For each oracle π_i^s, these variables, except the randomness, are initialized to $\bot$. An AKE protocol is executed interactively between two oracles. An oracle that first sends a message is called an *initiator* ($\mathsf{role} = \mathtt{init}$) and a party that first receives a message is called a *responder* ($\mathsf{role} = \mathtt{resp}$). The computed session key is assigned to the variable k_i^s if and only if π_i^s reaches the $\mathtt{accept}$ state, that is, $\mathsf{k}_i^s \neq \bot \iff \Psi_i^s = \mathtt{accept}$.

Partnering. To exclude trivial attacks in the security model, we need to define a notion of "partnering" of two oracles. Intuitively, this dictates which oracles can be corrupted without trivializing the security game. We define the notion of partnering via session-identifiers following the work of [15,23]. Discussions on other possible choices of the definition for partnering is provide in Sect. 3.5.

Definition 3.1 (Partner Oracles). *For any $(i,j,s,t) \in [\mu]^2 \times [\ell]^2$ with $i \neq j$, we say that oracles π_i^s and π_j^t are partners if (1) $\mathsf{Pid}_i^s = j$ and $\mathsf{Pid}_j^t = i$; (2) $\mathsf{role}_i^s \neq \mathsf{role}_j^t$; and (3) $\mathsf{sid}_i^s = \mathsf{sid}_j^t$.*

For correctness, we require that two oracles executing the AKE protocol faithfully (i.e., without adversarial interaction) derive identical session-identifiers. We also require that two such oracles reach the $\mathtt{accept}$ state and derive identical session keys except with all but a negligible probability. We call a set $S \subseteq ([\mu] \times [\ell])^2$ to have a *valid pairing* if the following properties hold:

- For all $((i,s),(j,t)) \in S$, $i \leq j$.
- For all $(i,s) \in [\mu] \times [\ell]$, there exists a unique $(j,t) \in [\mu] \times [\ell]$ such that $i \neq j$ and either $((i,s),(j,t)) \in S$ or $((j,t),(i,s)) \in S$.

In other words, a set with a valid pairing S partners off each oracle π_i^s and π_j^t in a way that the pairing is unique and no oracle is left out without a pair. We define correctness of an AKE protocol as follows.

Definition 3.2 $((1 - \delta)$**-Correctness).** *An AKE protocol* Π_{AKE} *is* $(1 - \delta)$-*correct if for any set with a valid pairing* $S \subseteq ([\mu] \times [\ell])^2$, *when we execute the AKE protocol faithfully between all the oracle pairs included in* S, *it holds that*

$$(1 - \delta) \leq \Pr \begin{bmatrix} \pi_i^s \text{ and } \pi_j^t \text{ are partners } \wedge \Psi_i^s = \Psi_j^t = \mathsf{accept} \\ \wedge \mathsf{k}_i^s = \mathsf{k}_j^t \neq \perp \text{ for all } ((i,s),(j,t)) \in S \end{bmatrix},$$

where the probability is taken over the randomness used in the oracles.

3.2 Security Game

We define security of an AKE protocol via the following game, denoted by $G_{\Pi_{\mathsf{AKE}}}(\mu, \ell)$, played between an adversary $\mathcal{A}$ and a challenger $\mathcal{C}$. The security game is parameterized by two integers μ (the number of honest parties) and ℓ (the maximum number of protocol executions per party), and is run as follows:

Setup: $\mathcal{C}$ first chooses a secret bit $b \leftarrow_{\$} \{0, 1\}$. Then $\mathcal{C}$ generates the public parameter of Π_{AKE} and μ long-term key pair $\{(\mathsf{lpk}_i, \mathsf{lsk}_i) \mid i \in [\mu]\}$, and initializes the collection of oracles $\{\pi_i^s \mid i \in [\mu], s \in [\ell]\}$. $\mathcal{C}$ runs $\mathcal{A}$ providing the public parameter and all the long-term public keys $\{\mathsf{lpk}_i \mid i \in [\mu]\}$ as input.

Phase 1: $\mathcal{A}$ adaptively issues the following queries any number of times in an arbitrary order:
  - $\mathsf{Send}(i, s, m)$: This query allows $\mathcal{A}$ to send an arbitrary message m to oracle π_i^s. The oracle will respond according to the protocol specification and its current internal state. To start a new oracle, the message m takes a special form:
  $\langle \mathsf{START} : \mathsf{role}, j \rangle$; $\mathcal{C}$ initializes π_i^s in the role role, having party P_j as its peer, that is, $\mathcal{C}$ sets $\mathsf{Pid}_i^s := j$ and $\mathsf{role}_i^s := \mathsf{role}$. If π_i^s is an initiator (i.e., $\mathsf{role} = \mathtt{init}$), then $\mathcal{C}$ returns the first message of the protocol.[10]
  - $\mathsf{RevLTK}(i)$: For $i \in [\mu]$, this query allows $\mathcal{A}$ to learn the long-term secret key lsk_i of party P_i. After this query, P_i is said to be *corrupted*.
  - $\mathsf{RegisterLTK}(i, \mathsf{lpk}_i)$: For $i \in \mathbb{N} \setminus [\mu]$, this query allows $\mathcal{A}$ to register a new party P_i with public key lpk_i. We do not require that the adversary knows the corresponding secret key. After the query, the pair (i, lpk_i) is distributed to all other oracles. Parties registered by $\mathsf{RegisterLTK}$ are corrupted by definition.
  - $\mathsf{RevState}(i, s)$: This query allows $\mathcal{A}$ to learn the session-state state_i^s of oracle π_i^s. After this query, state_i^s is said to be *revealed*.
  - $\mathsf{RevSessKey}(i, s)$: This query allows $\mathcal{A}$ to learn the session key k_i^s of oracle π_i^s.

Test: Once $\mathcal{A}$ decides that Phase 1 is over, it issues the following special Test-query which returns a real or a random key depending on the secret bit b.
  - $\mathsf{Test}(i, s)$: If $(i, s) \notin [\mu] \times [\ell]$ or $\Psi_i^s \neq \mathsf{accept}$, $\mathcal{C}$ returns $\perp$. Else, $\mathcal{C}$ returns k_b, where $k_0 := \mathsf{k}_i^s$ and $k_1 \leftarrow_{\$} \mathcal{K}$ (where $\mathcal{K}$ is the session key space).

---

[10] Looking ahead, when the first message is independent of party P_j (i.e., $\mathcal{C}$ can first create the first message without knowledge of P_j and then set $\mathsf{Pid}_i^s := j$), we call the scheme *receiver oblivious*. See Sect. 3.4 for more details.

After this query, π_i^s is said to be *tested*.

Phase 2: $\mathcal{A}$ adaptively issues queries as in Phase 1.

Guess: Finally, $\mathcal{A}$ outputs a guess $b' \in \{0, 1\}$. At this point, the tested oracle must be *fresh*. Here, an oracle π_i^s with $\mathsf{Pid}_i^s = j$[11] is *fresh* if all the following conditions hold:

1. $\mathsf{RevSessKey}(i, s)$ has not been issued;
2. if π_i^s has a partner π_j^t for some $t \in [\ell]$, then $\mathsf{RevSessKey}(j, t)$ has not been issued;
3. P_i is not corrupted or state_i^s is not revealed;
4. if π_i^s has a partner π_j^t for some $t \in [\ell]$, then P_j is not corrupted or state_j^t is not revealed;
5. if π_i^s has no partner oracle, then P_j is not corrupted.

If the tested oracle is not fresh, $\mathcal{C}$ aborts the game and outputs a random bit b' on behalf of $\mathcal{A}$. Otherwise, we say $\mathcal{A}$ wins the game if $b = b'$.

The advantage of $\mathcal{A}$ in the security game $G_{\Pi_{\mathsf{AKE}}}(\mu, \ell)$ is defined as $\mathsf{Adv}_{\Pi_{\mathsf{AKE}}}^{\mathsf{AKE}}(\mathcal{A}) := \left| \Pr[b = b'] - \frac{1}{2} \right|$.

Definition 3.3 (Security of AKE Protocol). *An AKE protocol Π_{AKE} is secure if $\mathsf{Adv}_{\Pi_{\mathsf{AKE}}}^{\mathsf{AKE}}(\mathcal{A})$ is negligible for any QPT adversary $\mathcal{A}$.*

3.3 Security Properties

In this section, we explain the security properties captured by our security model. Comparison between other protocols is differed to Sect. 3.5.

The freshness clauses Items 1 and 2 imply that we only exclude the reveal of session keys for the tested oracle and its partner oracles. This captures *key independence*; if the revealed keys are different from the tested oracle's key, then such keys must not enable computing the session key. Note that key independence implies resilience to "no-match attacks" presented by Li and Schäge [43]. This is because revealed keys have no information on the tested oracle's key. Moreover, the two items capture *implicit authentication* between the involved parties. This is because an oracle π that computes the same session key as the tested oracle but disagrees on the peer would not be a partner of the tested oracle, and hence, an adversary can obtain the tested oracle's key by querying the session key computed by π. Specifically, our model captures resistance to *unknown key-share* (UKS) attacks [12]; a successful UKS attack is a specific type of attack that breaks implicit authentication where two parties compute the same session key but have different views on whom they are communicating with.

The freshness clauses Items 3 to 5 indicate that the game allows the adversary to reveal any subset of the four secret information—the long-term secret keys and the session-states of the two parties (where one party being the party defined by the tested oracle and the other its peer)—except for the combination where both the long-term secret key and session-state of one of the party is revealed. These clauses capture *weak forward secrecy* [39]: the adversary can obtain the

---

[11] Note that by definition, the peer id Pid_i^s of a tested oracle π_i^s is always defined.

long-term secret keys of both parties if it has been passive in the protocol run of the two oracles. Another property captured by our model is resistance to *key-compromise impersonation* (KCI) attacks [11]. Recall that KCI attacks are those where the adversary uses a party P_i's long-term secret key to impersonate other parties towards P_i. This is captured by our model because the adversary can learn the long-term secret key of a tested oracle without any restrictions. Most importantly, our model captures resistance to *state leakage* [15,30,39,42] where an adversary is allowed to obtain session-states of both parties. We point out that our security model is strictly stronger than the recent models [20,32] that do not allow the adversary to learn sessions-states. More discussion on state leakage is provided in Sect. 3.5.

3.4 Property for Signal-Conforming AKE: Receiver Obliviousness

In this work, we care for a specific type of (two-round) AKE protocol that is compatible with the X3DH protocol [45] used by the Signal protocol [1]. As explained in Sect. 1.2, the X3DH protocol can be viewed as a special type of AKE protocol where the Signal server acts as an (untrusted) bulletin board, where parties can store and retrieve information from. More specifically, the Signal server can be viewed as an adversary for an AKE protocol that controls the communication channel between the parties. When casting the X3DH protocol as an AKE protocol, one crucial property is that the first message of the initiator is generated *independently* of the communication partner. This is because, in secure messaging, parties are often *offline* during the key agreement so if the first message depended on the communication partner, then we must wait until they become online to complete the key agreement. Since we cannot send messages without agreeing on a session key, such an AKE protocol where the first message depends on the communication partner cannot be used as a substitute for the X3DH protocol.

We abstract this crucial yet implicit property achieved by the X3DH protocol as *receiver obliviousness*.[12]

Definition 3.4 (Receiver Obliviousness/Signal-Conforming). *An AKE protocol is* receiver oblivious *(or* Signal-conforming*) if it is two-rounds and the initiator can compute the first-message without knowledge of the peer id and long-term public key of the communication peer.*

Many Diffie-Hellman type AKE protocols (e.g., the X3DH protocol used in Signal and some CSIDH-based AKE protocols [22,38]) can be checked to be receiver oblivious. In contrast, known generic AKE protocols such as [30,31,34,54,55] are not receiver oblivious since the first message requires the knowledge of the receiver's long-term public key.

---

[12] This property has also been called as *post-specified peers* [16] in the context of Internet Key Exchange (IKE) protocols.

Initiator P_i		Responder P_j
$\mathsf{lpk}_i = (\mathsf{ek}_i, \mathsf{vk}_i), \mathsf{lsk}_i = (\mathsf{dk}_i, \mathsf{sk}_i)$		$\mathsf{lpk}_j = (\mathsf{ek}_j, \mathsf{vk}_j), \mathsf{lsk}_j = (\mathsf{dk}_j, \mathsf{sk}_j)$

$(\mathsf{ek}_T, \mathsf{dk}_T) \leftarrow \mathsf{wKEM.KeyGen}(\mathsf{pp}_{\mathsf{wKEM}})$

$\mathsf{state}_i := \mathsf{dk}_T$

$\qquad\qquad\qquad\qquad\qquad\qquad\qquad\qquad (K, C) \leftarrow \mathsf{KEM.Encap}(\mathsf{ek}_i)$

$K \leftarrow \mathsf{KEM.Decap}(\mathsf{dk}_i, C) \qquad\qquad\qquad\qquad (K_T, C_T) \leftarrow \mathsf{wKEM.Encap}(\mathsf{ek}_T)$

$K_T \leftarrow \mathsf{wKEM.Decap}(\mathsf{dk}_T, C_T) \qquad \mathsf{ek}_T \qquad K_1 \leftarrow \mathsf{Ext}_s(K); K_2 \leftarrow \mathsf{Ext}_s(K_T)$

$K_1 \leftarrow \mathsf{Ext}_s(K); K_2 \leftarrow \mathsf{Ext}_s(K_T) \qquad\xrightarrow{\hspace{1cm}}\qquad \mathsf{sid}_j := P_i\|P_j\|\mathsf{lpk}_i\|\mathsf{lpk}_j\|\mathsf{ek}_T\|C\|C_T$

$\mathsf{sid}_i := P_i\|P_j\|\mathsf{lpk}_i\|\mathsf{lpk}_j\|\mathsf{ek}_T\|C\|C_T \quad C, C_T, c \quad \mathsf{k}_j\|\tilde{k} \leftarrow \mathsf{F}_{K_1}(\mathsf{sid}_j) \oplus \mathsf{F}_{K_2}(\mathsf{sid}_j)$

$\mathsf{k}_i\|\tilde{k} \leftarrow \mathsf{F}_{K_1}(\mathsf{sid}_i) \oplus \mathsf{F}_{K_2}(\mathsf{sid}_i) \qquad \xleftarrow{\hspace{1cm}} \qquad \sigma \leftarrow \mathsf{SIG.Sign}(\mathsf{sk}_j, \mathsf{sid}_j)$

$\sigma \leftarrow c \oplus \tilde{k} \qquad\qquad\qquad\qquad\qquad\qquad\qquad c \leftarrow \sigma \oplus \tilde{k}$

$\qquad\qquad\qquad\qquad\qquad\qquad\qquad\qquad\qquad\quad$ Output the session key k_j

$\mathsf{SIG.Verify}(\mathsf{vk}_j, \mathsf{sid}_i, \sigma) \overset{?}{=} 1$

Output the session key k_i

Fig. 2. Our Signal-conforming AKE protocol $\Pi_{\mathsf{SC\text{-}AKE}}$.

3.5 Relation to Other Security Models

In the literature of AKE protocols, many security models have been proposed: the Bellare-Rogaway (BR) model [7], the Canetti-Krawczyk (CK) model [15], the CK+ model [30,39], the extended CK (eCK) model [42], and variants therein [3, 20,21,32,34,35]. Although many of these security models are built based on similar motivations, there are subtle differences. (A comparison between our model and the models listed above can be found in the full version.)

4   Generic Construction of Signal-Conforming AKE $\Pi_{\mathsf{SC\text{-}AKE}}$

In this section, we propose a Signal-conforming AKE protocol $\Pi_{\mathsf{SC\text{-}AKE}}$ that can be used as a drop-in replacement for the X3DH protocol. Unlike the X3DH protocol, our protocol can be instantiated from post-quantum assumptions, and moreover, it also provides stronger security against state leakage. The protocol description is presented in Fig. 2. Details follow.

Building Blocks. Our Signal-conforming AKE protocol $\Pi_{\mathsf{SC\text{-}AKE}}$ consists of the following building blocks.

- $\Pi_{\mathsf{KEM}} = (\mathsf{KEM.Setup}, \mathsf{KEM.KeyGen}, \mathsf{KEM.Encap}, \mathsf{KEM.Decap})$ is a KEM scheme that is IND-CCA secure and assume we have $(1 - \delta_{\mathsf{KEM}})$-correctness.[13]

---

[13] To prove the security of $\Pi_{\mathsf{SC\text{-}AKE}}$, we require Π_{KEM} and Π_{wKEM} to have high min-entropy of the encapsulation key and the ciphertext.

- $\Pi_{\mathsf{wKEM}} = (\mathsf{wKEM.Setup}, \mathsf{wKEM.KeyGen}, \mathsf{wKEM.Encap}, \mathsf{wKEM.Decap})$ is a KEM schemes that is IND-CPA secure (and not IND-CCA secure) and assume we have $(1 - \delta_{\mathsf{wKEM}})$-correctness.
- $\Pi_{\mathsf{SIG}} = (\mathsf{SIG.Setup}, \mathsf{SIG.KeyGen}, \mathsf{SIG.Sign}, \mathsf{SIG.Verify})$ is a signature scheme that is EUF-CMA secure and $(1 - \delta_{\mathsf{SIG}})$-correctness. We denote d as the bit length of the signature generated by SIG.Sign.
- $\mathsf{F} : \mathcal{FK} \times \{0,1\}^* \rightarrow \{0,1\}^{\kappa+d}$ is a pseudo-random function family with key space $\mathcal{FK}$.
- $\mathsf{Ext} : \mathcal{S} \times \mathcal{KS} \rightarrow \mathcal{FK}$ is a strong randomness extractor.

Public Parameters. All the parties in the system are provided with the following public parameters as input: $(s, \mathsf{pp}_{\mathsf{KEM}}, \mathsf{pp}_{\mathsf{wKEM}}, \mathsf{pp}_{\mathsf{SIG}})$. Here, s is a random seed chosen uniformly from $\mathcal{S}$, and pp_{X} for $\mathsf{X} \in \{\mathsf{KEM}, \mathsf{wKEM}, \mathsf{SIG}\}$ are public parameters generated by X.Setup.

Long-Term Public and Secret Keys. Each party P_i runs $(\mathsf{ek}_i, \mathsf{dk}_i) \leftarrow \mathsf{KEM.KeyGen}(\mathsf{pp}_{\mathsf{KEM}})$ and $(\mathsf{vk}_i, \mathsf{sk}_i) \leftarrow \mathsf{SIG.KeyGen}(\mathsf{pp}_{\mathsf{SIG}})$. Party P_i's long-term public key and secret key are set as $\mathsf{lpk}_i = (\mathsf{ek}_i, \mathsf{vk}_i)$ and $\mathsf{lsk}_i = (\mathsf{dk}_i, \mathsf{sk}_i)$, respectively.

Construction. A key exchange between an initiator P_i in the s-th session (i.e., π_i^s) and responder P_j in the t-th session (i.e., π_j^t) is executed as in Fig. 2. More formally, we have the following.

1. Party P_i sets $\mathsf{Pid}_i^s := j$ and $\mathsf{role}_i^s := \mathtt{init}$. P_i computes $(\mathsf{dk}_T, \mathsf{ek}_T) \leftarrow \mathsf{wKEM.KeyGen}(\mathsf{pp}_{\mathsf{wKEM}})$ and sends ek_T to party P_j. P_i stores the ephemeral decapsulation key dk_T as the session-state i.e., $\mathsf{state}_i^s := \mathsf{dk}_T$.[14]
2. Party P_j sets $\mathsf{Pid}_j^t := i$ and $\mathsf{role}_j^t := \mathtt{resp}$. Upon receiving ek_T, P_j first computes $(\mathsf{K}, \mathsf{C}) \leftarrow \mathsf{KEM.Encap}(\mathsf{ek}_i)$ and $(\mathsf{K}_T, \mathsf{C}_T) \leftarrow \mathsf{wKEM.Encap}(\mathsf{ek}_T)$. Then P_j derives two PRF keys $\mathsf{K}_1 \leftarrow \mathsf{Ext}_s(\mathsf{K})$, $\mathsf{K}_2 \leftarrow \mathsf{Ext}_s(\mathsf{K}_T)$. It then defines the session-identifier as $\mathsf{sid}_j^t := P_i\|P_j\|\mathsf{lpk}_i\|\mathsf{lpk}_j\|\mathsf{ek}_T\|\mathsf{C}\|\mathsf{C}_T$ and computes $\mathsf{k}_j\|\tilde{k} \leftarrow \mathsf{F}_{\mathsf{K}_1}(\mathsf{sid}_j) \oplus \mathsf{F}_{\mathsf{K}_2}(\mathsf{sid}_j)$, where $\mathsf{k}_j \in \{0,1\}^\kappa$ and $\tilde{k} \in \{0,1\}^d$, and sets the session key as $\mathsf{k}_j^t := \mathsf{k}_j$. P_j then signs $\sigma \leftarrow \mathsf{SIG.Sign}(\mathsf{sk}_j, \mathsf{sid}_j^t)$ and encrypts it as $\mathsf{c} \leftarrow \sigma \oplus \tilde{k}$. Finally, it sends $(\mathsf{C}, \mathsf{C}_T, \mathsf{c})$ to P_i and sets $\Psi_j := \mathtt{accept}$. Here, note that P_j does not require to store any session-state, i.e., $\mathsf{state}_j^t = \bot$.
3. Upon receiving $(\mathsf{C}, \mathsf{C}_T, \mathsf{c})$, P_i first decrypts $\mathsf{K} \leftarrow \mathsf{KEM.Decap}(\mathsf{dk}_i, \mathsf{C})$ and $\mathsf{K}_T \leftarrow \mathsf{wKEM.Decap}(\mathsf{dk}_T, \mathsf{C}_T)$, and derives two PRF keys $\mathsf{K}_1 \leftarrow \mathsf{Ext}_s(\mathsf{K})$ and $\mathsf{K}_2 \leftarrow \mathsf{Ext}_s(\mathsf{K}_T)$. It then sets the session-identifier as $\mathsf{sid}_i^s := P_i\|P_j\|\mathsf{lpk}_i\|\mathsf{lpk}_j\|\mathsf{ek}_T\|\mathsf{C}\|\mathsf{C}_T$ and computes $\mathsf{k}_i\|\tilde{k} \leftarrow \mathsf{F}_{\mathsf{K}_1}(\mathsf{sid}_i) \oplus \mathsf{F}_{\mathsf{K}_2}(\mathsf{sid}_i)$, where $\mathsf{k}_j \in \{0,1\}^\kappa$ and $\tilde{k} \in \{0,1\}^d$. P_i then decrypts $\sigma \leftarrow \mathsf{c} \oplus \tilde{k}$ and checks whether $\mathsf{SIG.Verify}(\mathsf{vk}_j, \mathsf{sid}_i^s, \sigma) = 1$ holds. If not, P_i sets $(\Psi_i, \mathsf{k}_i^s, \mathsf{state}_i) := (\mathtt{reject}, \bot, \bot)$ and stops. Otherwise, it sets $(\Psi_i, \mathsf{k}_i^s, \mathsf{state}_i) := (\mathtt{accept}, \mathsf{k}_i, \bot)$. Here, note that P_i deletes the session-state $\mathsf{state}_i^s = \mathsf{dk}_T$ at the end of the key exchange.

---

[14] Notice the protocol is receiver oblivious since the first message is computed independently of the receiver.

Remark 4.1 (A Note on Session-State). The session-state of the initiator P_i contains the ephemeral decryption key dk_T and P_i must store it until the peer responds. Any other information that is computed after receiving the message from the peer is immediately erased when the session key is established. In contrast, the responder P_j has no session-state because the responder directly computes the session key after receiving the initiator's message and does not have to store any session-specific information. That is, all states can be erased as soon as a session key is computed.

Remark 4.2 (Signed Prekeys). In the X3DH protocol, the initiator sends the first message with a signature attached called *signed prekey*. Informally, this allows Bob to *explicitly* authenticate Alice, while otherwise without the signature, Bob can only *implicitly* authenticate Alice. Moreover, this signature enhances the X3DH protocol to be *perfect* forward secret rather than being only *weak* forward secret, where the former allows the adversary to be active in the protocol run of the two oracles. Indeed, according to [45], the X3DH is considered to have perfect forward secrecy. We observe that adding such signature in our protocol has the same effect as long as the added signature is not included in the session-identifier. This is due to Li and Schäge [43, Appendix D], who showed that adding new messages to an already secure protocol cannot lower the security as long as the derived session keys and the session-identifiers remain the same as the original protocol. Here, note the latter implies that the partnering relation remains the same. Similarly, Cremers and Feltz [21] show that adding a signature to the exchanged messages can enhance weak forward secrecy to perfect forward secrecy for natural classes of AKE protocols.

Security. Correctness holds by a routine check. The following establishes the security or $\Pi_{\mathsf{SC\text{-}AKE}}$. We provide a proof overview and refer the full proof to the full version.

Theorem 4.1 (Security of $\Pi_{\mathsf{SC\text{-}AKE}}$). *Assume Π_{wKEM} is IND-CPA secure, Π_{KEM} is IND-CCA secure, Π_{SIG} is EUF-CMA secure, and F is secure PRF. Then $\Pi_{\mathsf{SC\text{-}AKE}}$ is secure AKE protocol with respect to Definition 3.3.*

Proof Sketch. Let $\mathcal{A}$ be an adversary that plays the security game $G_{\Pi_{\mathsf{SC\text{-}AKE}}}(\mu, \ell)$. We distinguish between all possible strategies that can be taken by $\mathcal{A}$. Specifically, $\mathcal{A}$'s strategy can be divided into the eight types of strategies listed in Table 1.

Here, each strategy is mutually independent and covers all possible (non-trivial) strategies. We point out that for our specific AKE construction we have $\mathsf{state}_{\mathsf{resp}} := \bot$ since the responder does not maintain any states (see Remark 4.1). Therefore, the Type-1 (resp. Type-3, Type-7) strategy is strictly stronger than the Type-2 (resp. Type-4, Type-8) strategy. Concretely, for our proof, we only need to consider the following four cases and to show that $\mathcal{A}$ has no advantage in each cases: (a) $\mathcal{A}$ uses the Type-1 strategy; (b) $\mathcal{A}$ uses the Type-3 strategy; (c) $\mathcal{A}$ uses the Type-5 or Type-6 strategy; (d) $\mathcal{A}$ uses the Type-7 strategy.

Table 1. The strategy taken by the adversary in the security game when the tested oracle is fresh. "Yes" means the tested oracle has some (possibly non-unique) partner oracles and "No" means it has none. "✓" means the secret-key/session-state is revealed to the adversary, "✗" means the secret-key/session-state is not revealed. "-" means the session-state is not defined.

Strategy	Role of tested oracle	Partner oracle	lsk_{init}	state_{init}	lsk_{resp}	state_{resp}
Type-1	init or resp	Yes	✓	✗	✓	✗
Type-2	init or resp	Yes	✓	✗	✗	✓
Type-3	init or resp	Yes	✗	✓	✓	✗
Type-4	init or resp	Yes	✗	✓	✗	✓
Type-5	init	No	✓	✗	✗	-
Type-6	init	No	✗	✓	✗	-
Type-7	resp	No	✗	-	✓	✗
Type-8	resp	No	✗	-	✗	✓

In cases (a), (b) and (d), the session key is informally protected by the security properties of KEM, PRF, and randomness extractor. In case (a), since the ephemeral decapsulation key dk_T is not revealed, K_T is indistinguishable from a random key due to the IND-CPA security of Π_{wKEM}. On the other hand, in case (b) and (d), since the initiator's decapsulation key dk_{init} is not revealed, K is indistinguishable from a random key due to the IND-CCA security of Π_{KEM}. Here, we require IND-CCA security because there are initiator oracles other than the tested oracle that uses dk_{init}, which the reduction algorithm needs to simulate. This is in contrast to case (a) where dk_T is only used by the tested oracle. Then, in all cases, since either K_T or K has sufficient high min-entropy from the view of the adversary, Ext on input K_T or K outputs a uniformly random PRF key. Finally, we can invoke the pseudo-randomness of the PRF and argue that the session key in the tested oracle is indistinguishable from a random key.

In case (c), the session key is informally protected by the security property of the signature scheme. More concretely, in case (c), the tested oracle is an initiator and the signing key sk_{resp} included in the long-term key of its peer is not revealed. Then, due to the EUF-CMA security of Π_{SIG}, $\mathcal{A}$ cannot forge the signature for the session-identifier of the tested oracle sid_{test}. In addition, since the tested oracle has no partner oracles, no responder oracle ever signs sid_{test}. Therefore, combining these two, we conclude that the tested oracle cannot be in the accept state unless $\mathcal{A}$ breaks the signature scheme. In other words, when $\mathcal{A}$ queries Test, the tested oracle always returns $\bot$. Thus the session key of the tested oracle is hidden from $\mathcal{A}$.

5 Instantiating Post-quantum Signal-Conforming AKE $\Pi_{\mathsf{SC\text{-}AKE}}$

In this section, we present the implementation details of our post-quantum Signal-conforming AKE protocol $\Pi_{\mathsf{SC\text{-}AKE}}$. We take existing implementations of post-quantum KEMs and signature schemes submitted for the NIST PQC standardization. To instantiate our Signal-conforming AKE we pair variants of KEMs and signature schemes corresponding to the same security level. We consider security levels 1, 3 and 5 as defined by NIST for the PQC standardization. With more than 30 variants of KEM and 13 variants of signature schemes, we can create at least 128 different instantiations of post-quantum Signal-conforming AKE protocols. The provided implementation simulates post-quantum, weakly deniable authenticated key exchange between two entities. We study the efficiency of our instantiations through two metrics—the total amount of data exchanged between parties and run-time performance. Our implementation is available at the URL [41].

5.1   Instantiation Details

Our implementation is instantiated with the following building blocks:

- s: (pseudo)-randomly generated 32 bytes of data calculated at session initialization phase,
- Ext_s: uses HMAC-SHA256 as a strong randomness extractor. As an input message we use a key K_T prepended with byte 0x02 which works as a domain separator (since we also use HMAC-SHA256 as a PRF). Security of using HMAC as a strong randomness extractor is studied in [28],
- PRF: uses HMAC-SHA256 as a PRF. The session-specific sid is used as an input message to HMAC, prepended with byte 0x01. An output from Ext_s is used as a key. Security of using HMAC as a PRF is studied in [4],
- b: depends on the security level of the underlying post-quantum KEM scheme, where $b \in \{128, 192, 256\}$,
- d: depends on the byte length of the signature generated by the post-quantum signature scheme Π_{SIG},
- Π_{KEM}, Π_{wKEM}, Π_{SIG}: to instantiate $\Pi_{\mathsf{SC\text{-}AKE}}$, implementation uses pairs of KEM and signature schemes. List of the schemes used can be found in the table (Table 2) below. We always use the same KEM scheme for Π_{KEM} and Π_{wKEM}.

Table 2. Considered KEM and signature schemes under NIST security level 1, 3, and 5.

NIST security level	KEM	Signature
1	SABER, CLASSIC-MCELIECE, KYBER, NTRU HQC, SIKE, FRODOKEM, BIKE	RAINBOW, FALCON, DILITHIUM SPHINCS, PICNIC
3	SABER, NTRU, CLASSIC-MCELIECE, KYBER, SIKE, HQC, BIKE, FRODOKEM	DILITHIUM, RAINBOW PICNIC, SPHINCS
5	SABER, CLASSIC-MCELIECE, NTRU, KYBER FRODOKEM, SIKE, HQC	FALCON, RAINBOW PICNIC, SPHINCS

At a high level, the implementation is split into 3 main parts. The initiator's ephemeral KEM key generation (`offer` function), the recipient's session key generation (`accept` function), and initiator's session key generation (`finalize` function). Additionally there is an initialization part which performs the generation and exchange of the long-term public keys as well as dynamic initialization of memory. To evaluate the computational cost of $\Pi_{\text{SC-AKE}}$, we instantiate it with concrete parameters as described above. The implementation runs 3 main functions in a loop for a fixed amount of time. We do not include the time spent in the initialization phase, hence the cost of key generation and memory initialization has no impact on the results.

Finally, we use an implementation of post-quantum algorithms that can be found in libOQS[15]. We also use LibTomCrypt[16] which provides an implementation of the building blocks HMAC, HKDF and SHA-256.

5.2   Efficiency Analysis

In this subsection, we provide an assessment of the costs related to running the concrete instantiation of $\Pi_{\text{SC-AKE}}$. We provide two metrics:

- Communication cost: the amount of data exchanged between two parties trying to establish a session key.
- Computational cost: number of CPU cycles spent in computation during session establishment by both parties.

The computational cost of the protocol depends on the performance of the cryptographic primitives used. More precisely, the most expensive operations are those done by the post-quantum schemes. $\Pi_{\text{SC-AKE}}$ performs 7 such operations during a session agreement: the initiator runs a KEM key generation, two KEM decapsulations and one signature verification, and the recipient performs two KEM encapsulations and one signing.

For benchmarking, we modeled a scenario in which two parties try to establish a session key. Alice generates and makes her long-term public key lpk_A and ephemeral KEM key ek_T publicly available. Bob retrieves the pair $(\text{lpk}_A, \text{ek}_T)$ and uses it to perform his part of the session establishment. Namely, Bob generates the triple (C, C_T, c) and sends it to Alice along with its long-term public key lpk_B. Upon receipt, Alice finalizes the process by computing the session key on her side. We note that in the case of the Signal protocol, both parties communicate with a server (e.g., the Signal server), and not directly. For simplicity, we abstract this fact out of our scenario. Further note that in the Signal protocol, the long-term public keys lpk must be fetched from the server as the parties do not store the keys lpk corresponding to those that they have not communicated with before[17]

Table 3 provides the results for Round 3 candidates of the NIST PQC standardization process.[18] The **CPU cycles** column is related to the computational

---

[15] https://github.com/open-quantum-safe/liboqs.

[16] https://github.com/libtom/libtomcrypt.

[17] The X3DH protocol assumes the parties authenticate the long-term public keys through some authenticated channel [45, Section 4.1].

[18] The results for all 128 instantiations can be found at the URL [41].

cost. It is the number of cycles needed on both the initiator and responder side to run the protocol for a given instantiation. We run benchmarking on the Intel Xeon E3-1220v3 @3.1 GhZ with Turbo Boost disabled. The last four columns relate to communication cost. They contain the byte size of the data exchanged during session key establishment. In particular, the lpk column contains the size of the long-term public key. The ek_T column contains the size of the ephemeral KEM key. The (C, C_T, c) column is the size of the triple generated by Bob. Here, the amount of data transferred from Alice to Bob is the sum of lpk and ek_T, while the amount of data transferred from Bob to Alice is the sum of lpk and C, C_T, c. Finally, the column **Total** contains the total size of data exchanged between Alice and Bob.

Table 3. Computational and communication cost of running $\Pi_{\text{SC-AKE}}$ instantiated with various post-quantum schemes.

Scheme	CPU cycles	lpk	ek_T	(C, C_T, c)	Total
NIST security level 1					
Dilithium2/Saber Light	2770622	1856	672	3516	7900
Dilithium2/Kyber512	3059898	1984	800	3516	8284
Falcon512/NTRU hps2048509	28830055	1596	699	2088	5979
SPHINCS-SHAKE256-128f-s/Saber Light	269464814	704	672	18448	20528
NIST security level 3					
Dilithium4/Saber	4204171	2752	992	5542	12038
Dilithium4/NTRU hps2048677	24513381	2690	930	5226	11536
SPHINCS-SHAKE256-192f-s/Kyber768	337783175	1232	1184	37840	41488
Dilithium4/SIKE p610	790625496	2222	462	4338	9244
NIST security level 5					
Falcon1024/Saber Fire	37423092	3105	1312	4274	11796
Falcon1024/Kyber1024	37875710	3361	1568	4466	12756
Falcon1024/SIKE p751	356918904	2357	564	2522	7800
SPHINCS-SHAKE256-256f-s/SIKE p751	1041010995	628	564	50408	52228

In a scenario as described above, instantiations with Falcon, Dilithium, Saber and Kyber schemes seem to be the most promising when it comes to computational cost. The communication cost can be minimized by using the SIKE scheme as Π_{KEM} and Π_{wKEM}, but this significantly increases the computational cost.

We note that the computational cost is far less absolute as it depends on the concrete implementation of the post-quantum schemes. Our implementation is biased by the fact that it uses unoptimized, portable C code. There are two reasons for such a choice. First, our goal was to show the expected results on a broad number of platforms. Second, the libOQS library that we used does not provide hardware-assisted optimizations for all schemes, hence enabling those optimizations only for some algorithms would provide biased results.

Our implementation is based on open-source libraries, which makes it possible to perform fine-tuning and further analysis. For example, one could imagine a scenario for IoT devices that knows in advance which devices it may communicate with. Then, the long term keys of the devices can be exchanged prior to the session key establishment. In such a scenario, schemes with larger public keys may become more attractive since transferring long-term public keys could be done ahead of time.

Note on Low Quality Network Links. We anticipate $\Pi_{\mathsf{SC\text{-}AKE}}$ to be used with handheld devices and areas with a poor quality network connection. In such cases, larger key, ciphertext and signature sizes generated may negatively impact the quality of the connection. Network packet loss is an additional factor which should be considered when choosing schemes for concrete instantiation.

Data on the network is exchanged in packets. The maximum transmission unit (MTU) defines the maximal size of a single packet, usually set to 1500 bytes. Ideally, the size of data sent between participants in a single pass is less than MTU. Network quality is characterized by a packet loss rate. When a packet is lost, the TCP protocol ensures that it is retransmitted, where each retransmission causes a delay. A typical data loss on a high-quality network link is below 1%, while data loss on a mobile network depends on the strength of the network signal.

Depending on the scheme used, increased packet loss may negatively impact session establishment time (see [47]). For example, a scheme instantiated with `Falcon512/NTRU hps2048509` requires exchange of $npacks = 7$ packets over the network, where instantiation with `SPHINCS-SHAKE256-128f-simple/Saber Light` requires 16. Assuming increased packet rate loss of 5%, the probability of losing a packet in the former case is $1 - (1 - rate)^{npacks} = 30\%$, where in the latter it is 56%. In the latter case, at the median, every other session key establishment will experience packet retransmission and hence a delay.

6   Adding Deniability to Our Signal-Conforming AKE $\Pi_{\mathsf{SC\text{-}AKE}}$

In this section, we provide a theory-oriented discussion on the deniability aspect of our Signal-conforming AKE protocol $\Pi_{\mathsf{SC\text{-}AKE}}$. In the following, we first informally show that $\Pi_{\mathsf{SC\text{-}AKE}}$ already has a very weak form of deniability that may be acceptable in some applications. We then show that we can slightly modify $\Pi_{\mathsf{SC\text{-}AKE}}$ to satisfy a more stronger notion of deniability. As it is common with all deniable AKE protocols secure against key-compromise attacks [24,53,57], we prove deniability by relying on strong knowledge-type assumptions , including a variant of the *plaintext-awareness* (PA) for the KEM scheme [5,6,8].

Weak Deniability of $\Pi_{\mathsf{SC\text{-}AKE}}$. Our Signal-conforming AKE protocol $\Pi_{\mathsf{SC\text{-}AKE}}$ already satisfies a weak notion of deniability, where the communication transcript does not leave a trace of the two parties if both parties honestly executed the AKE protocol. Namely, an adversary that is passively collecting the communication transcript cannot convince a third party that communication between two parties took place. Informally, this can be observed by checking that all the contents in the transcript can be simulated by the adversary on its own. We discuss a stronger notion of deniability next.

6.1   Definition of Deniability and Tool Preparation

We follow a simplified definition of deniability for AKE protocols introduced by Di Raimondo et al. [24]. Discussion on the simplification is provided in Remark 6.2. Let Π be an AKE protocol and KeyGen be the key generation algorithm. That is, for any integer $\mu = \mu(\kappa)$ representing the number of parties in the system, define $\mathsf{KeyGen}(1^\kappa, \mu) \to (\mathsf{pp}, \overrightarrow{\mathsf{lpk}}, \overrightarrow{\mathsf{lsk}})$, where pp is the public parameter used by the system and $\overrightarrow{\mathsf{lpk}} := \{\mathsf{lpk}_i \mid i \in [\mu]\}$ and $\overrightarrow{\mathsf{lsk}} := \{\mathsf{lsk}_i \mid i \in [\mu]\}$ are the corresponding long-term public and secret keys of the μ parties, respectively.

Let $\mathcal{M}$ denote an adversary that engages in an AKE protocol with μ-honest parties in the system with long-term public keys $\overrightarrow{\mathsf{lpk}}$, acting as either an initiator or a responder. $\mathcal{M}$ may run individual sessions against an honest party in a concurrent manner and may deviate from the AKE protocol in an arbitrary fashion. The goal of $\mathcal{M}$ is not to impersonate someone to an honest party P but to collect (cryptographic) evidence that an honest party P interacted with $\mathcal{M}$. Therefore, when $\mathcal{M}$ interacts with P, it can use a long-term public key $\mathsf{lpk}_\mathcal{M}$ that can be either associated to or not to $\mathcal{M}$'s identity (that may possibly be generated maliciously). We then define the *view* of the adversary $\mathcal{M}$ as the entire sets of input and output of $\mathcal{M}$ and the *session keys* computed in all the protocols in which $\mathcal{M}$ participated with an honest party. Here, we assume in case the session is not completed by $\mathcal{M}$, the session key is defined as $\bot$. We denote this view as $\mathsf{View}_\mathcal{M}(\mathsf{pp}, \overrightarrow{\mathsf{lpk}}, \overrightarrow{\mathsf{lsk}})$.

In order to define deniability, we consider a simulator SIM that simulates the view of honest parties (both initiator and responder) to the adversary $\mathcal{M}$ *without* knowledge of the corresponding long-term secret keys $\overrightarrow{\mathsf{lsk}}$ of the honest parties. Specifically, SIM takes as input all the input given to the adversary $\mathcal{M}$ (along with the description of $\mathcal{M}$) and simulates the view of $\mathcal{M}$ with the real AKE protocol Π. We denote this simulated view as $\mathsf{SIM}_\mathcal{M}(\mathsf{pp}, \overrightarrow{\mathsf{lpk}})$. Roughly, if the view simulated by $\mathsf{SIM}_\mathcal{M}$ is indistinguishable from those generated by $\mathsf{View}_\mathcal{M}$, then we say the AKE protocol is deniable since $\mathcal{M}$ could have run $\mathsf{SIM}_\mathcal{M}$ (which does not take any secret information as input) to generate its view in the real protocol. More formally, we have the following.

Definition 6.1 (Deniability). *We say an AKE protocol Π with key generation algorithm KeyGen is deniable, if for any integer $\mu = \mathrm{poly}(\kappa)$ and PPT adversary $\mathcal{M}$, there exist a PPT simulator $\mathsf{SIM}_\mathcal{M}$ such that the following two distributions are (computationally) indistinguishable for any PPT distinguisher $\mathcal{D}$:*

$$\mathcal{F}_{\mathsf{Real}} := \{\mathsf{pp}, \overrightarrow{\mathsf{lpk}}, \mathsf{View}_\mathcal{M}(\mathsf{pp}, \overrightarrow{\mathsf{lpk}}, \overrightarrow{\mathsf{lsk}}) : (\mathsf{pp}, \overrightarrow{\mathsf{lpk}}, \overrightarrow{\mathsf{lsk}}) \leftarrow \mathsf{KeyGen}(1^\kappa, \mu)\},$$

$$\mathcal{F}_{\mathsf{Sim}} := \{\mathsf{pp}, \overrightarrow{\mathsf{lpk}}, \mathsf{SIM}_\mathcal{M}(\mathsf{pp}, \overrightarrow{\mathsf{lpk}}) : (\mathsf{pp}, \overrightarrow{\mathsf{lpk}}, \overrightarrow{\mathsf{lsk}}) \leftarrow \mathsf{KeyGen}(1^\kappa, \mu)\}.$$

When $\mathcal{M}$ is semi-honest (i.e., it follows the prescribed protocol), we say Π is deniable against semi-honest adversaries. *When $\mathcal{M}$ is malicious (i.e., it takes any efficient strategy), we say Π is* deniable against malicious adversaries.

Remark 6.1 (Including Public Information and Session Keys). It is crucial that the two distributions $\mathcal{F}_{\mathsf{Real}}$ and $\mathcal{F}_{\mathsf{Sim}}$ include the public information $(\mathsf{pp}, \overrightarrow{\mathsf{lpk}})$. Otherwise, $\mathsf{SIM}_{\mathcal{M}}$ can simply create its own set of $(\mathsf{pp}', \overrightarrow{\mathsf{lpk}'}, \overrightarrow{\mathsf{lsk}'})$ and simulate the view to $\mathcal{M}$. However, this does not correctly capture deniability in the real-world since $\mathcal{M}$ would not be able to convince anybody with such a view using public information that it cooked up on its own. In addition, it is essential that the value of the session key is part of the output of $\mathsf{SIM}_{\mathcal{M}}$. This guarantees that the contents of the sessions authenticated by the session key can also be denied.

Remark 6.2 (Comparison between Prior Definition). Our definition is weaker than the deniability notion originally proposed by Di Raimondo et al. [24]. In their definition, an adversary $\mathcal{M}$ (and therefore the simulator $\mathsf{SIM}_{\mathcal{M}}$) is also provided as input some auxiliary information aux that can depend non-trivially on $(\mathsf{pp}, \overrightarrow{\mathsf{lpk}}, \overrightarrow{\mathsf{lsk}})$.[19] For instance, this allows to capture information that $\mathcal{M}$ may have obtained by eavesdropping conversations between honest parties (which is not modeled by $\mathsf{View}_{\mathcal{M}}$). Since our goal is to provide a minimal presentation on the deniability of our protocol, we only focus on the weaker definition where $\mathcal{M}$ does not obtain such auxiliary information. We leave it as future work to prove our protocol deniable in the sense of Di Raimondo et al. [24]. We also note that stronger forms of deniability are known and formalized in the universally composable (UC) model [25,51,52], however, AKE protocols satisfying such a strong deniability notion are known to achieve weaker security guarantees. For instance, as noted in [52], an AKE protocol cannot be on-line deniable while also being secure against KCI attacks.

Remark 6.3 (Extending to Malicious Quantum Adversaries). We only consider classical deniability above. Although we can show deniability for semi-honest quantum adversaries, we were not able to do so for malicious quantum adversaries. This is mainly due to the fact that to prove deniability against malicious classical adversaries, we require a strong knowledge type assumption (i.e., plaintext-awareness for KEM) that assumes an extractor can invoke the adversary multiple of times on the *same* randomness. We leave it as an interesting problem to formally define a set of tools that allow to show deniability even against malicious quantum adversaries.

Required Tools. To argue deniability in the following section we rely on the following tools: ring signature, plaintext-aware (PA-1) secure KEM scheme, and

---

[19] Although in [24, Definition 2], aux is defined as fixed information that $\mathcal{M}$ cannot adaptively choose, we observe that in their proof they implicitly assume that aux is sampled adaptively from some distribution dependent on $(\mathsf{pp}, \overrightarrow{\mathsf{lpk}}, \overrightarrow{\mathsf{lsk}})$. Such a definition of aux is necessary to invoke PA-2 security of the underlying encryption scheme.

a non-interactive zero-knowledge (NIZK) argument.[20] We use standard notions of ring signatures and NIZK arguments. On the other hand, we use a slightly stronger variant of PA-1 secure KEM schemes than those originally defined in [5,6,8]. Informally, a KEM scheme is PA-1 secure if for any adversary $\mathcal{M}$ that outputs a valid ciphertext C, there is an extractor $\mathsf{Ext}_{\mathcal{M}}$ that outputs the matching session key K. In our work, we require PA-1 security to hold even when $\mathcal{M}$ is given multiple public keys rather than a single public key [46]. We note that although Di Raimondo et al. [24] considered the standard notion of PA-1 security, we observe that their proof only works in the case where multiple public keys are considered. Finally, we further require the extractor $\mathsf{Ext}_{\mathcal{M}}$ to be efficiently computable given $\mathcal{M}$.

6.2 Deniable Signal-Conforming AKE $\Pi_{\mathsf{SC\text{-}DAKE}}$ Against Semi-Honest Adversaries

We first provide a Signal-conforming AKE protocol $\Pi_{\mathsf{SC\text{-}DAKE}}$ that is deniable against semi-honest adversaries. The construction of $\Pi_{\mathsf{SC\text{-}DAKE}}$ is a simple modification of $\Pi_{\mathsf{SC\text{-}AKE}}$ where a standard signature is replaced by a ring signature. In the subsequent section, we show how to modify $\Pi_{\mathsf{SC\text{-}DAKE}}$ to a protocol that is deniable against malicious adversaries by relying on further assumptions. The high-level idea presented in this section naturally extends to the malicious setting. An overview of $\Pi_{\mathsf{SC\text{-}DAKE}}$ and $\Pi'_{\mathsf{SC\text{-}DAKE}}$ is provided in Fig. 3.

Building Blocks. Our deniable Signal-conforming AKE protocol $\Pi_{\mathsf{SC\text{-}DAKE}}$ against semi-honest adversaries consists of the following building blocks.

- Π_{KEM} = (KEM.Setup, KEM.KeyGen, KEM.Encap, KEM.Decap) is a KEM scheme that is IND-CCA secure and assume we have $(1 - \delta_{\mathsf{KEM}})$-correctness.[21]
- Π_{wKEM} = (wKEM.Setup, wKEM.KeyGen, wKEM.Encap, wKEM.Decap) is a KEM schemes that is IND-CPA secure (and not IND-CCA secure) and assume we have $(1 - \delta_{\mathsf{wKEM}})$-correctness.
- Π_{RS} = (RS.Setup, RS.KeyGen, RS.Sign, RS.Verify) is a ring signature scheme that is anonymous and unforgeable and assume we have $(1 - \delta_{\mathsf{RS}})$-correctness. We denote d as the bit length of the signature generated by RS.Sign.
- $\mathsf{F} : \mathcal{FK} \times \{0,1\}^* \to \{0,1\}^{\kappa+d}$ is a pseudo-random function family with key space $\mathcal{FK}$.
- $\mathsf{Ext} : \mathcal{S} \times \mathcal{KS} \to \mathcal{FK}$ is a strong randomness extractor.

Public Parameters. All the parties in the system are provided the following public parameters as input: $(s, \mathsf{pp}_{\mathsf{KEM}}, \mathsf{pp}_{\mathsf{wKEM}}, \mathsf{pp}_{\mathsf{RS}})$. Here, s is a random seed chosen uniformly from $\mathcal{S}$, and pp_{X} for $\mathsf{X} \in \{\mathsf{KEM}, \mathsf{wKEM}, \mathsf{RS}\}$ are public parameters generated by X.Setup.

---

[20] Due to the page limitation, the formal definitions of these tools are provided in the full version.

[21] Similar to $\Pi_{\mathsf{SC\text{-}AKE}}$, to prove the security of $\Pi_{\mathsf{SC\text{-}DAKE}}$, we require Π_{KEM} and Π_{wKEM} to have high min-entropy of the encapsulation key and the ciphertext.

Common public parameters: $(s, pp_{KEM}, pp_{wKEM}, \boxed{PP_{RS}}, \boxed{crs})$

Initiator P_i	Responder P_j
$lpk_i = (ek_i, \boxed{vk_i}), lsk_i = (dk_i, \boxed{sk_i})$	$lpk_j = (ek_j, \boxed{vk_j}), lsk_j = (dk_j, \boxed{sk_j})$

$(ek_T, dk_T) \leftarrow wKEM.KeyGen(pp_{wKEM})$

$\boxed{(vk_T, sk_T) \leftarrow RS.KeyGen(pp_{RS}; rand_T)}$

$X_T \leftarrow (pp_{RS}, vk_T); W_T \leftarrow (sk_T, rand_T)$

$\pi_T \leftarrow NIZK.Prove(crs, X_T, W_T)$

$state_i := dk_T$

$X_T \leftarrow (pp_{RS}, vk_T)$

$NIZK.Verify(crs, X_T, \pi_T) \stackrel{?}{=} 1$

$(K, C) \leftarrow KEM.Encap(ek_i)$

$(K_T, C_T) \leftarrow wKEM.Encap(ek_T)$

$\xrightarrow{\quad ek_T, \boxed{vk_T}, \ulcorner \pi_T \urcorner \quad}$

$K \leftarrow KEM.Decap(dk_i, C)$

$K_T \leftarrow wKEM.Decap(dk_T, C_T)$

$K_1 \leftarrow Ext_s(K); K_2 \leftarrow Ext_s(K_T)$

$K_1 \leftarrow Ext_s(K); K_2 \leftarrow Ext_s(K_T)$

$sid_j := P_i \| P_j \| lpk_i \| lpk_j \| ek_T \| vk_T \| C \| C_T$

$sid_i := P_i \| P_j \| lpk_i \| lpk_j \| ek_T \| vk_T \| C \| C_T$

$k_j \| \tilde{k} \leftarrow F_{K_1}(sid_j) \oplus F_{K_2}(sid_j)$

$k_i \| \tilde{k} \leftarrow F_{K_1}(sid_i) \oplus F_{K_2}(sid_i)$

$\xleftarrow{\quad C, C_T, c \quad}$

$\boxed{\sigma \leftarrow RS.Sign(sk_j, sid_j, \{vk_T, vk_j\})}$

$\sigma \leftarrow c \oplus \tilde{k}$

$c \leftarrow \sigma \oplus \tilde{k}$

Output the session key k_j

$\boxed{RS.Verify(\{vk_T, vk_j\}, sid_i, \sigma) \stackrel{?}{=} 1}$

Output the session key k_i

Fig. 3. Deniable Signal-conforming AKE protocol $\Pi_{SC\text{-}DAKE}$ and $\Pi'_{SC\text{-}DAKE}$. The components that differ from the non-deniable protocol $\Pi_{SC\text{-}AKE}$ is indicated by a box. The protocol with (resp. without) the gray and dotted-box component satisfies deniability against malicious (resp. semi-honest) adversaries.

Long-Term Public and Secret Keys. Each party P_i runs $(ek_i, dk_i) \leftarrow KEM.KeyGen(pp_{KEM})$ and $(vk_i, sk_i) \leftarrow RS.KeyGen(pp_{RS})$. Party P_i's long-term public key and secret key are set as $lpk_i = (ek_i, vk_i)$ and $lsk_i = (dk_i, sk_i)$, respectively.

Construction. A key exchange between an initiator P_i in the s-th session (i.e., π_i^s) and responder P_j in the t-th session (i.e., π_j^t) is executed as in Fig. 2. More formally, we have the following.

1. Party P_i sets $Pid_i^s := j$ and $role_i^s := \texttt{init}$. P_i computes $(dk_T, ek_T) \leftarrow wKEM.KeyGen(pp_{wKEM})$ and $(vk_T, sk_T) \leftarrow RS.KeyGen(pp_{RS})$, and sends (ek_T, vk_T) to party P_j. P_i erases the signing key sk_T and stores the ephemeral decapsulation key dk_T as the session-state i.e., $state_i^s := dk_T$.[22]

2. Party P_j sets $Pid_j^t := i$ and $role_j^t := \texttt{resp}$. Upon receiving (ek_T, vk_T), P_j first computes $(K, C) \leftarrow KEM.Encap(ek_i)$ and $(K_T, C_T) \leftarrow wKEM.Encap(ek_T)$ and derives two PRF keys $K_1 \leftarrow Ext_s(K)$, $K_2 \leftarrow Ext_s(K_T)$. It then defines the session-identifier as $sid_j^t := P_i \| P_j \| lpk_i \| lpk_j \| ek_T \| vk_T \| C \| C_T$ and computes

---

[22] Notice the protocol is receiver oblivious since the first message is computed independently of the receiver.

$k_j \| \tilde{k} \leftarrow \mathsf{F}_{\mathsf{K}_1}(\mathsf{sid}_j) \oplus \mathsf{F}_{\mathsf{K}_2}(\mathsf{sid}_j)$, where $k_j \in \{0,1\}^\kappa$ and $\tilde{k} \in \{0,1\}^d$. P_j sets the session key as $\mathsf{k}_j^t := k_j$. P_j then signs $\sigma \leftarrow \mathsf{RS.Sign}(\mathsf{sk}_j, \mathsf{sid}_j^t, \{\mathsf{vk}_T, \mathsf{vk}_j\})$ and encrypts it as $\mathsf{c} \leftarrow \sigma \oplus \tilde{k}$. Finally, it sends $(\mathsf{C}, \mathsf{C}_T, \mathsf{c})$ to P_i and sets $\Psi_j := \mathtt{accept}$. Here, note that P_j does not require to store any session-state, i.e., $\mathsf{state}_j^t = \perp$.

3. Upon receiving $(\mathsf{C}, \mathsf{C}_T, \mathsf{c})$, P_i first decrypts $\mathsf{K} \leftarrow \mathsf{KEM.Decap}(\mathsf{dk}_i, \mathsf{C})$ and $\mathsf{K}_T \leftarrow \mathsf{wKEM.Decap}(\mathsf{dk}_T, \mathsf{C}_T)$, and derives two PRF keys $\mathsf{K}_1 \leftarrow \mathsf{Ext}_s(\mathsf{K})$ and $\mathsf{K}_2 \leftarrow \mathsf{Ext}_s(\mathsf{K}_T)$. It then sets the session-identifier as $\mathsf{sid}_i^s := P_i \| P_j \| \mathsf{lpk}_i \| \mathsf{lpk}_j \| \mathsf{ek}_T \| \mathsf{vk}_T \| \mathsf{C} \| \mathsf{C}_T$ and computes $k_i \| \tilde{k} \leftarrow \mathsf{F}_{\mathsf{K}_1}(\mathsf{sid}_i) \oplus \mathsf{F}_{\mathsf{K}_2}(\mathsf{sid}_i)$, where $k_i \in \{0,1\}^\kappa$ and $\tilde{k} \in \{0,1\}^d$. P_i then decrypts $\sigma \leftarrow \mathsf{c} \oplus \tilde{k}$ and checks whether $\mathsf{RS.Verify}(\{\mathsf{vk}_T, \mathsf{vk}_j\}, \mathsf{sid}_i^s, \sigma) = 1$ holds. If not, P_i sets $(\Psi_i, \mathsf{k}_i^s, \mathsf{state}_i) := (\mathtt{reject}, \perp, \perp)$ and stops. Otherwise, P_i sets $(\Psi_i, \mathsf{k}_i^s, \mathsf{state}_i) := (\mathtt{accept}, k_i, \perp)$. Here, note that P_i deletes the session-state $\mathsf{state}_i^s = \mathsf{dk}_T$ at the end of the key exchange.

Security. We first check that $\Pi_{\mathsf{SC\text{-}DAKE}}$ is correct and secure as a standard AKE protocol. Since the proof is similar in most parts to the non-deniable protocol $\Pi_{\mathsf{SC\text{-}AKE}}$, we defer the details to the full version. The main difference from the security proof of $\Pi_{\mathsf{SC\text{-}AKE}}$ is that we have to make sure that using a ring signature instead of a standard signature does not allow the adversary to mount a key-compromise impersonation (KCI) attack (see Sect. 3.3 for the explanation on KCI attacks).

The following guarantees deniability of our protocol $\Pi_{\mathsf{SC\text{-}DAKE}}$ against semi-honest adversaries.

Theorem 6.1 (Deniability of $\Pi_{\mathsf{SC\text{-}DAKE}}$ against Semi-Honest Adversaries). *Assume Π_{RS} is anonymous. Then, the Signal-conforming protocol $\Pi_{\mathsf{SC\text{-}DAKE}}$ is deniable against semi-honest adversaries.*

Proof. Let $\mathcal{M}$ be any PPT semi-honest adversary. We explain the behavior of the simulator $\mathsf{SIM}_\mathcal{M}$ by considering three cases: (a) $\mathcal{M}$ initializes an initiator P_i, (b) $\mathcal{M}$ queries the initiator P_i on message $(\mathsf{C}, \mathsf{C}_T, \mathsf{c})$, and (c) $\mathcal{M}$ queries the responder P_j on message $(\mathsf{ek}_T, \mathsf{vk}_T)$. In case (a), $\mathsf{SIM}_\mathcal{M}$ runs the honest initiator algorithm and returns $(\mathsf{ek}_T, \mathsf{vk}_T)$ as specified by the protocol. In case (b), since $\mathcal{M}$ is semi-honest, we are guaranteed that it runs the honest responder algorithm to generate $(\mathsf{C}, \mathsf{C}_T, \mathsf{c})$. In particular, since $\mathcal{M}$ is run on randomness sampled by $\mathsf{SIM}_\mathcal{M}$, $\mathsf{SIM}_\mathcal{M}$ gets to learn the key K that was generated along with C. Therefore, $\mathsf{SIM}_\mathcal{M}$ runs the real initiator algorithm except that it uses K extracted from $\mathcal{M}$ rather than computing $\mathsf{K} \leftarrow \mathsf{KEM.Decap}(\mathsf{dk}_i, \mathsf{C})$. Here, note that $\mathsf{SIM}_\mathcal{M}$ cannot run the latter since it does not know the corresponding dk_i held by an honest initiator party P_i. In case (c), similarly to case (b), $\mathsf{SIM}_\mathcal{M}$ learns dk_T and sk_T used by $\mathcal{M}$ to generate ek_T and vk_T. Therefore, $\mathsf{SIM}_\mathcal{M}$ runs the honest responder algorithm except that it runs $\sigma \leftarrow \mathsf{RS.Sign}(\mathsf{sk}_T, \mathsf{sid}_j, \{\mathsf{vk}_T, \mathsf{vk}_j\})$ instead of running $\sigma \leftarrow \mathsf{RS.Sign}(\mathsf{sk}_j, \mathsf{sid}_j, \{\mathsf{vk}_T, \mathsf{vk}_j\})$ as in the real protocol. Here, note that $\mathsf{SIM}_\mathcal{M}$ cannot run the latter since it does not know the corresponding sk_j held by an honest responder party P_j.

Let us analyze $\mathsf{SIM}_{\mathcal{M}}$. First, for case (a), the output by $\mathsf{SIM}_{\mathcal{M}}$ is distributed exactly as in the real transcript. Next, for case (b), the only difference between the real distribution and $\mathsf{SIM}_{\mathcal{M}}$'s output distribution (which is the derived session key k) is that $\mathsf{SIM}_{\mathcal{M}}$ uses the KEM key K output by KEM.Encap to compute the session key rather than using the KEM key decrypted using KEM.Decap with the initiator party P_i's decryption key dk_i. However, by $(1 - \delta_{\mathsf{KEM}})$-correctness of Π_{KEM}, these two KEM keys are identical with probability at least $(1 - \delta_{\mathsf{KEM}})$. Hence, the output distribution of $\mathsf{SIM}_{\mathcal{M}}$ and the real view are indistinguishable. Finally, for case (c), the only difference between the real distribution and $\mathsf{SIM}_{\mathcal{M}}$'s output distribution (which is the derived session key and the message sent $(\mathsf{C}, \mathsf{C}_T, \mathsf{c})$) is how the ring signature is generated. While the real protocol uses the signing key sk_j of the responder party P_j, the simulator $\mathsf{SIM}_{\mathcal{M}}$ uses sk_T. However, the signatures outputted by these two distributions are computationally indistinguishable assuming the anonymity of Π_{RS}. Hence, the output distribution of $\mathsf{SIM}_{\mathcal{M}}$ and the real view are indistinguishable.

Combining everything together, we conclude the proof.   □

6.3 Deniable Signal-Conforming AKE $\Pi'_{\mathsf{SC\text{-}DAKE}}$ Against Malicious Adversaries

We discuss security of our Signal-conforming AKE protocol $\Pi'_{\mathsf{SC\text{-}DAKE}}$ against malicious adversaries. As depicted in Fig. 3, to achieve deniability against malicious adversaries, we modify the protocol so that the initiator party adds a NIZK proof attesting to the fact that it constructed the verification key of the ring signature vk_T honestly. Formally, we require the following additional building blocks.

Building Blocks. Our deniable Signal-conforming AKE protocol $\Pi'_{\mathsf{SC\text{-}DAKE}}$ against malicious adversaries requires the following primitives in addition to those required by $\Pi_{\mathsf{SC\text{-}DAKE}}$ in the previous section.

- $\Pi_{\mathsf{KEM}} = (\mathsf{KEM.Setup}, \mathsf{KEM.KeyGen}, \mathsf{KEM.Encap}, \mathsf{KEM.Decap})$ is an IND-CCA secure KEM scheme as in the previous section that additionally satisfies $\mathsf{PA}_\mu\text{-}1$ security with an efficiently constructible extractor, where μ is the number of parties in the system.
- $\Pi_{\mathsf{NIZK}} = (\mathsf{NIZK.Setup}, \mathsf{NIZK.Prove}, \mathsf{NIZK.Verify})$ is a NIZK argument system for the relation $\mathcal{R}_{\mathsf{RS}}$ where $(\mathsf{X}, \mathsf{W}) \in \mathcal{R}_{\mathsf{RS}}$ if and only if the statement $\mathsf{X} = (\mathsf{pp}, \mathsf{vk})$ and witness $\mathsf{W} = (\mathsf{sk}, \mathsf{rand})$ satisfy $(\mathsf{vk}, \mathsf{sk}) = \mathsf{RS.KeyGen}(\mathsf{pp}; \mathsf{rand})$.

Additional Assumption. We require a knowledge-type assumption to prove deniability against malicious adversaries. Considering that all of the previous AKE protocols satisfying a strong form of security and deniability require such knowledge-type assumptions [24,53,57], this seems unavoidable. On the other hand, there are protocols achieving a strong form of deniability from standard assumptions [25,51,52], however, they make a significant compromise in the security such as being vulnerable to KCI attacks and state leakages.

The following knowledge assumption is defined similarly in spirit to those of Di Raimondo et al. [24] that assumed that for any adversary $\mathcal{M}$ that outputs a valid MAC, then there exists an extractor algorithm Ext that extracts the corresponding MAC key. Despite it being a strong knowledge-type assumption in the standard model, we believe it holds in the random oracle model if we further assume the NIZK comes with an *online* knowledge extractor[23] like those provide by Fischlin's NIZK [27]. We leave it to future works to investigate the credibility of the following assumption and those required to prove deniability of the X3DH protocol [53].

Assumption 6.2 (Key-Awareness Assumption for $\Pi'_{\text{SC-DAKE}}$). *We say that $\Pi'_{\text{SC-DAKE}}$ has the* key-awareness *property if for all PPT adversaries $\mathcal{M}$ interacting with a real protocol execution in the deniability game as in Definition 6.1, there exists a PPT extractor $\text{Ext}_{\mathcal{M}}$ such that for any choice of $(\text{pp}, \overrightarrow{\text{lpk}}, \overrightarrow{\text{lsk}}) \in \text{KeyGen}(1^\kappa, \mu)$, whenever $\mathcal{M}$ outputs a ring signature verification key vk and a NIZK proof π for the language $\mathcal{L}_{\text{RS}}$, then $\text{Ext}_{\mathcal{M}}$ taking input the same input as $\mathcal{M}$ (including its randomness) outputs a signing key sk such that $(\text{vk}, \text{sk}) \in \text{RS.KeyGen}(\text{pp}_{\text{RS}})$ for any $\text{pp}_{\text{RS}} \in \text{RS.Setup}(1^\kappa)$.*

With the added building blocks along with the key-awareness assumption, we prove the following theorem. The high-level approach is similar to the previous proof against semi-honest adversaries but the concrete proof requires is rather involved. The main technicality is when invoking the $\text{PA}_\mu\text{-}1$ security: if we do the reduction naively, the extractor needs the randomness used to sample the ring signature key pairs of the honest party but the simulator of the deniability game does not know such randomness. We circumvent this issue by hard-wiring the verification key of the ring signature of the adversary and considering $\text{PA}_\mu\text{-}1$ security against non-uniform adversary. The proof is presented in the full version.

Theorem 6.3 (Deniability of $\Pi'_{\text{SC-DAKE}}$ against Malicious Adversaries). *Assume Π_{KEM} is $\text{PA}_\mu\text{-}1$ secure with an efficiently constructible extractor, Π_{RS} is anonymous, Π_{NIZK} is sound,[24] and the key-awareness assumption in Assumption 6.2 holds. Then, the Signal-conforming protocol $\Pi'_{\text{SC-DAKE}}$ with μ parties is deniable against malicious adversaries.*

Finally, we show $\Pi'_{\text{SC-DAKE}}$ is correct and secure as a standard Signal-conforming AKE protocol in the full version.

Acknowledgement. The second author was supported by JST CREST Grant Number JPMJCR19F6. The third and fourth authors were supported by the Innovate UK Research Grant 104423 (PQ Cybersecurity).

---

[23] This guarantees that the witness from a proof can be extracted without rewinding the adversary.

[24] We note that this is redundant since it is implicitly implied by the key-awareness assumption. We only include it for clarity.

References

1. Signal protocol: Technical documentation. https://signal.org/docs/
2. Alwen, J., Coretti, S., Dodis, Y.: the double ratchet: security notions, proofs, and modularization for the signal protocol. In: Ishai, Y., Rijmen, V. (eds.) EURO-CRYPT 2019, Part I. LNCS, vol. 11476, pp. 129–158. Springer, Cham (2019). https://doi.org/10.1007/978-3-030-17653-2_5
3. Bader, C., Hofheinz, D., Jager, T., Kiltz, E., Li, Y.: Tightly-secure authenticated key exchange. In: Dodis, Y., Nielsen, J.B. (eds.) TCC 2015, Part I. LNCS, vol. 9014, pp. 629–658. Springer, Heidelberg (2015). https://doi.org/10.1007/978-3-662-46494-6_26
4. Bellare, M.: New proofs for NMAC and HMAC: security without collision-resistance. Cryptology ePrint Archive, Report 2006/043
5. Bellare, M., Desai, A., Pointcheval, D., Rogaway, P.: Relations among notions of security for public-key encryption schemes. In: Krawczyk, H. (ed.) CRYPTO 1998. LNCS, vol. 1462, pp. 26–45. Springer, Heidelberg (1998). https://doi.org/10.1007/BFb0055718
6. Bellare, M., Palacio, A.: Towards plaintext-aware public-key encryption without random oracles. In: Lee, P.J. (ed.) ASIACRYPT 2004. LNCS, vol. 3329, pp. 48–62. Springer, Heidelberg (2004). https://doi.org/10.1007/978-3-540-30539-2_4
7. Bellare, M., Rogaway, P.: Entity authentication and key distribution. In: Stinson, D.R. (ed.) CRYPTO 1993. LNCS, vol. 773, pp. 232–249. Springer, Heidelberg (1994). https://doi.org/10.1007/3-540-48329-2_21
8. Bellare, M., Rogaway, P.: Optimal asymmetric encryption. In: De Santis, A. (ed.) EUROCRYPT 1994. LNCS, vol. 950, pp. 92–111. Springer, Heidelberg (1995). https://doi.org/10.1007/BFb0053428
9. Bellare, M., Singh, A.C., Jaeger, J., Nyayapati, M., Stepanovs, I.: Ratcheted encryption and key exchange: the security of messaging. In: Katz, J., Shacham, H. (eds.) CRYPTO 2017, Part III. LNCS, vol. 10403, pp. 619–650. Springer, Cham (2017). https://doi.org/10.1007/978-3-319-63697-9_21
10. Bernstein, D.J.: Curve25519: new Diffie-Hellman speed records. In: Yung, M., Dodis, Y., Kiayias, A., Malkin, T. (eds.) PKC 2006. LNCS, vol. 3958, pp. 207–228. Springer, Heidelberg (2006). https://doi.org/10.1007/11745853_14
11. Blake-Wilson, S., Johnson, D., Menezes, A.: Key agreement protocols and their security analysis. In: Darnell, M. (ed.) Cryptography and Coding 1997. LNCS, vol. 1355, pp. 30–45. Springer, Heidelberg (1997). https://doi.org/10.1007/BFb0024447
12. Blake-Wilson, S., Menezes, A.: Unknown key-share attacks on the station-to-station (STS) protocol. In: Imai, H., Zheng, Y. (eds.) PKC 1999. LNCS, vol. 1560, pp. 154–170. Springer, Heidelberg (1999). https://doi.org/10.1007/3-540-49162-7_12
13. Bonnetain, X., Schrottenloher, A.: Quantum security analysis of CSIDH. In: Canteaut, A., Ishai, Y. (eds.) EUROCRYPT 2020, Part II. LNCS, vol. 12106, pp. 493–522. Springer, Cham (2020). https://doi.org/10.1007/978-3-030-45724-2_17
14. Brendel, J., Fischlin, M., Günther, F., Janson, C., Stebila, D.: Towards post-quantum security for signal's X3DH handshake. In: SAC 2020
15. Canetti, R., Krawczyk, H.: Analysis of key-exchange protocols and their use for building secure channels. In: Pfitzmann, B. (ed.) EUROCRYPT 2001. LNCS, vol. 2045, pp. 453–474. Springer, Heidelberg (2001). https://doi.org/10.1007/3-540-44987-6_28

16. Canetti, R., Krawczyk, H.: Security analysis of IKE's signature-based key-exchange protocol. In: Yung, M. (ed.) CRYPTO 2002. LNCS, vol. 2442, pp. 143–161. Springer, Heidelberg (2002). https://doi.org/10.1007/3-540-45708-9_10

17. Cash, D., Kiltz, E., Shoup, V.: The Twin Diffie-Hellman problem and applications. In: Smart, N. (ed.) EUROCRYPT 2008. LNCS, vol. 4965, pp. 127–145. Springer, Heidelberg (2008). https://doi.org/10.1007/978-3-540-78967-3_8

18. Cohn-Gordon, K., Cremers, C., Dowling, B., Garratt, L., Stebila, D.: A formal security analysis of the signal messaging protocol. In: IEEE European Symposium on Security and Privacy (EuroS&P), pp. 451–466

19. Cohn-Gordon, K., Cremers, C., Dowling, B., Garratt, L., Stebila, D.: A formal security analysis of the signal messaging protocol. J. Cryptol. 1–70

20. Cohn-Gordon, K., Cremers, C., Gjøsteen, K., Jacobsen, H., Jager, T.: Highly efficient key exchange protocols with optimal tightness. In: Boldyreva, A., Micciancio, D. (eds.) CRYPTO 2019, Part III. LNCS, vol. 11694, pp. 767–797. Springer, Cham (2019). https://doi.org/10.1007/978-3-030-26954-8_25

21. Cremers, C., Feltz, M.: Beyond eCK: perfect forward secrecy under actor compromise and ephemeral-key reveal. In: Foresti, S., Yung, M., Martinelli, F. (eds.) ESORICS 2012. LNCS, vol. 7459, pp. 734–751. Springer, Heidelberg (2012). https://doi.org/10.1007/978-3-642-33167-1_42

22. de Kock, B., Gjøsteen, K., Veroni, M.: Practical isogeny-based key-exchange with optimal tightness. In: SAC 2020

23. de Saint Guilhem, C.D., Fischlin, M., Warinschi, B.: Authentication in key-exchange: definitions, relations and composition. In: 2020 IEEE 33rd Computer Security Foundations Symposium (CSF), pp. 288–303

24. Di Raimondo, M., Gennaro, R., Krawczyk, H.: Deniable authentication and key exchange. In: ACM CCS, pp. 400–409 (2006)

25. Dodis, Y., Katz, J., Smith, A., Walfish, S.: Composability and on-line deniability of authentication. In: Reingold, O. (ed.) TCC 2009. LNCS, vol. 5444, pp. 146–162. Springer, Heidelberg (2009). https://doi.org/10.1007/978-3-642-00457-5_10

26. Durak, F.B., Vaudenay, S.: Bidirectional asynchronous ratcheted key agreement with linear complexity. In: Attrapadung, N., Yagi, T. (eds.) IWSEC 2019. LNCS, vol. 11689, pp. 343–362. Springer, Cham (2019). https://doi.org/10.1007/978-3-030-26834-3_20

27. Fischlin, M.: Communication-efficient non-interactive proofs of knowledge with online extractors. In: Shoup, V. (ed.) CRYPTO 2005. LNCS, vol. 3621, pp. 152–168. Springer, Heidelberg (2005). https://doi.org/10.1007/11535218_10

28. Fouque, P.-A., Pointcheval, D., Zimmer, S.: HMAC is a randomness extractor and applications to TLS. In: ASIACCS 2008, pp. 21–32

29. Freire, E.S.V., Hofheinz, D., Kiltz, E., Paterson, K.G.: Non-interactive key exchange. In: Kurosawa, K., Hanaoka, G. (eds.) PKC 2013. LNCS, vol. 7778, pp. 254–271. Springer, Heidelberg (2013). https://doi.org/10.1007/978-3-642-36362-7_17

30. Fujioka, A., Suzuki, K., Xagawa, K., Yoneyama, K.: Strongly secure authenticated key exchange from factoring, codes, and lattices. In: Fischlin, M., Buchmann, J., Manulis, M. (eds.) PKC 2012. LNCS, vol. 7293, pp. 467–484. Springer, Heidelberg (2012). https://doi.org/10.1007/978-3-642-30057-8_28

31. Fujioka, A., Suzuki, K., Xagawa, K., Yoneyama, K.: Practical and post-quantum authenticated key exchange from one-way secure key encapsulation mechanism. In: ASIACCS 2013, pp. 83–94

32. Gjøsteen, K., Jager, T.: Practical and tightly-secure digital signatures and authenticated key exchange. In: Shacham, H., Boldyreva, A. (eds.) CRYPTO 2018, Part II. LNCS, vol. 10992, pp. 95–125. Springer, Cham (2018). https://doi.org/10.1007/978-3-319-96881-0_4

33. Guo, S., Kamath, P., Rosen, A., Sotiraki, K.: Limits on the efficiency of (Ring) LWE based non-interactive key exchange. In: Kiayias, A., Kohlweiss, M., Wallden, P., Zikas, V. (eds.) PKC 2020, Part I. LNCS, vol. 12110, pp. 374–395. Springer, Cham (2020). https://doi.org/10.1007/978-3-030-45374-9_13

34. Hövelmanns, K., Kiltz, E., Schäge, S., Unruh, D.: Generic authenticated key exchange in the quantum random oracle model. In: Kiayias, A., Kohlweiss, M., Wallden, P., Zikas, V. (eds.) PKC 2020, Part II. LNCS, vol. 12111, pp. 389–422. Springer, Cham (2020). https://doi.org/10.1007/978-3-030-45388-6_14

35. Jager, T., Kiltz, E., Riepel, D., Schäge, S.: Tightly-secure authenticated key exchange, revisited. Cryptology ePrint Archive, Report 2020/1279

36. Jost, D., Maurer, U., Mularczyk, M.: Efficient ratcheting: almost-optimal guarantees for secure messaging. In: Ishai, Y., Rijmen, V. (eds.) EUROCRYPT 2019, Part I. LNCS, vol. 11476, pp. 159–188. Springer, Cham (2019). https://doi.org/10.1007/978-3-030-17653-2_6

37. Jost, D., Maurer, U., Mularczyk, M.: A unified and composable take on ratcheting. In: Hofheinz, D., Rosen, A. (eds.) TCC 2019, Part II. LNCS, vol. 11892, pp. 180–210. Springer, Cham (2019). https://doi.org/10.1007/978-3-030-36033-7_7

38. Kawashima, T., Takashima, K., Aikawa, Y., Takagi, T.: An efficient authenticated key exchange from random self-reducibility on CSIDH. In: Hong, D. (ed.) ICISC 2020. LNCS, vol. 12593, pp. 58–84. Springer, Cham (2021). https://doi.org/10.1007/978-3-030-68890-5_4

39. Krawczyk, H.: HMQV: a high-performance secure Diffie-Hellman protocol. In: Shoup, V. (ed.) CRYPTO 2005. LNCS, vol. 3621, pp. 546–566. Springer, Heidelberg (2005). https://doi.org/10.1007/11535218_33

40. Kurosawa, K., Furukawa, J.: 2-pass key exchange protocols from CPA-secure KEM. In: CT-RSA, pp. 385–401 (2014)

41. Kwiatkowski, K.: Signal-conforming AKE protocol implementation. https://github.com/post-quantum-cryptography/post-quantum-state-leakage-secure-ake

42. LaMacchia, B., Lauter, K., Mityagin, A.: Stronger security of authenticated key exchange. In: Susilo, W., Liu, J.K., Mu, Y. (eds.) ProvSec 2007. LNCS, vol. 4784, pp. 1–16. Springer, Heidelberg (2007). https://doi.org/10.1007/978-3-540-75670-5_1

43. Li, Y., Schäge, S.: No-match attacks and robust partnering definitions: defining trivial attacks for security protocols is not trivial. In: ACM CCS, pp. 1343–1360 (2017)

44. Marlinspike, M., Perrin, T.: The double ratchet algorithm. https://signal.org/docs/specifications/doubleratchet/

45. Marlinspike, M., Perrin, T.: The X3DH key agreement protocol. https://signal.org/docs/specifications/x3dh/

46. Myers, S., Sergi, M., Shelat: Blackbox construction of a more than non-malleable CCA1 encryption scheme from plaintext awareness. In: Visconti, I., De Prisco, R. (eds.) SCN 2012. LNCS, vol. 7485, pp. 149–165. Springer, Heidelberg (2012). https://doi.org/10.1007/978-3-642-32928-9_9

47. Paquin, C., Stebila, D., Tamvada, G.: Benchmarking post-quantum cryptography in TLS. Cryptology ePrint Archive, Report 2019/1447

48. Peikert, C.: He gives C-sieves on the CSIDH. In: Canteaut, A., Ishai, Y. (eds.) EUROCRYPT 2020, Part II. LNCS, vol. 12106, pp. 463–492. Springer, Cham (2020). https://doi.org/10.1007/978-3-030-45724-2_16

49. Poettering, B., Rösler, P.: Towards bidirectional ratcheted key exchange. In: Shacham, H., Boldyreva, A. (eds.) CRYPTO 2018, Part I. LNCS, vol. 10991, pp. 3–32. Springer, Cham (2018). https://doi.org/10.1007/978-3-319-96884-1_1

50. Pointcheval, D., Sanders, O.: Forward secure non-interactive key exchange. In: Abdalla, M., De Prisco, R. (eds.) SCN 2014. LNCS, vol. 8642, pp. 21–39. Springer, Cham (2014). https://doi.org/10.1007/978-3-319-10879-7_2

51. Unger, N., Goldberg, I.: Deniable key exchanges for secure messaging. In: ACM CCS, pp. 1211–1223 (2015)

52. Unger, N., Goldberg, I.: Improved strongly deniable authenticated key exchanges for secure messaging. PoPETs 1, 21–66 (2018)

53. Vatandas, N., Gennaro, R., Ithurburn, B., Krawczyk, H.: On the cryptographic deniability of the signal protocol. In: Conti, M., Zhou, J., Casalicchio, E., Spognardi, A. (eds.) ACNS 2020, Part II. LNCS, vol. 12147, pp. 188–209. Springer, Cham (2020). https://doi.org/10.1007/978-3-030-57878-7_10

54. Xue, H., Au, M.H., Yang, R., Liang, B., Jiang, H.: Compact authenticated key exchange in the quantum random oracle model. Cryptology ePrint Archive, Report 2020/1282

55. Xue, H., Lu, X., Li, B., Liang, B., He, J.: Understanding and constructing AKE via double-key key encapsulation mechanism. In: Peyrin, T., Galbraith, S. (eds.) ASIACRYPT 2018, Part II. LNCS, vol. 11273, pp. 158–189. Springer, Cham (2018). https://doi.org/10.1007/978-3-030-03329-3_6

56. Yang, Z., Chen, Y., Luo, S.: Two-message key exchange with strong security from ideal lattices. In: CT-RSA, pp. 98–115 (2018)

57. Yao, A.C., Zhao, Y.: Deniable internet key exchange. In: Zhou, J., Yung, M. (eds.) ACNS 2010. LNCS, vol. 6123, pp. 329–348. Springer, Heidelberg (2010). https://doi.org/10.1007/978-3-642-13708-2_20

Cryptographic Pseudorandom Generators Can Make Cryptosystems Problematic

Koji Nuida[1,2]([⊠]) [iD]

[1] Institute of Mathematics for Industry, Kyushu University, Fukuoka, Japan
nuida@imi.kyushu-u.ac.jp
[2] National Institute of Advanced Industrial Science and Technology (AIST),
Tokyo, Japan

Abstract. Randomness is an essential resource for cryptography. For practical randomness generation, the security notion of pseudorandom generators (PRGs) intends to automatically preserve (computational) security of cryptosystems when used in implementation. Nevertheless, some opposite case such as in computational randomness extractors (Barak et al., CRYPTO 2011) is known (but not yet systematically studied so far) where the security can be lost even by applying secure PRGs. The present paper aims at pushing ahead the observation and understanding about such a phenomenon; we reveal such situations at layers of primitives and protocols as well, not just of building blocks like randomness extractors. We present three typical types of such cases: (1) adversaries can legally see the seed of the PRGs (including the case of randomness extractors); (2) the set of "bad" randomness may be not efficiently recognizable; (3) the formulation of a desired property implicitly involves non-uniform distinguishers for PRGs. We point out that the semi-honest security of multiparty computation also belongs to Type 1, while the correctness with negligible decryption error probability for public key encryption belongs to Types 2 and 3. We construct examples for each type where a secure PRG (against uniform distinguishers only, for Type 3) does not preserve the security/correctness of the original scheme; and discuss some countermeasures to avoid such an issue.

Keywords: Pseudorandom generators · Public key encryption · Multiparty computation

1 Introduction

Randomness is an essential resource for cryptography. While theoretical design of cryptosystems usually relies on ideal randomness, it is practically expensive to generate a large amount of (almost) ideal randomness, therefore some efficient "approximation" of randomness is necessary. When computational security is sufficient, a standard way is to use cryptographically secure pseudorandom generators (PRGs) in implementation. Due to the way of defining the security of

J. A. Garay (Ed.): PKC 2021, LNCS 12711, pp. 441–468, 2021.
https://doi.org/10.1007/978-3-030-75248-4_16

PRGs (i.e., computational indistinguishability of the output from being uniformly random), it is widely expected in the area of cryptography that if the cryptosystem is secure assuming ideal randomness, and the PRG is also secure, then the cryptosystem implemented by the PRG instead of the ideal randomness will be secure as well. Indeed, usually no security caution is given when a cryptosystem is implemented by using a cryptographically secure PRG; such a use of PRG is even frequently recommended by professional cryptographers.

However, in fact there exists some situation where (computational) security of a cryptographic scheme is *not* preserved by implementation using a secure PRG. Namely, Barak et al. has shown in Sect. 4.1 of [3] the following. Let $\mathsf{Ext}(X; S)$ be a randomness extractor with source distribution X and random seeds chosen from S. We consider the situation that a random seed $s \leftarrow S$ is replaced by a PRG's output $\mathcal{R}(s_0)$ with shorter seed $s_0 \leftarrow S_0$. Roughly speaking, their result gives a pair of a secure extractor $\mathsf{Ext}(X; S)$ and a secure PRG $\mathcal{R}$ that yields an *insecure* extractor $\mathsf{Ext}(X; \mathcal{R}(S_0))$. A consequence is that the aforementioned standard methodology of implementing the randomness by secure PRGs does *not always* guarantee the security of the implemented scheme. (Some conditions to avoid such a loss of security are also discussed in their paper.) This fact should have impact for evaluating security of practically used cryptosystems where the use of cryptographic PRGs is recommended. Nevertheless, to the author's best knowledge, such a phenomenon caused by PRGs has not been systematically studied in the literature. The present paper aims at pushing ahead the observation and understanding about such a phenomenon for the case of other kinds of cryptographic schemes.

1.1 Our Contributions

In this paper, we look at the aforementioned possible phenomenon that some required property of (computationally secure) cryptographic schemes may be lost by applying PRGs even if the PRG itself is secure. We point out the following three types of typical situations where such a phenomenon may happen.

Type 1: The Seed of the PRG is Visible for Adversaries
This includes the known case of randomness extractors Ext mentioned above. Namely, its security is defined as $\mathsf{Ext}((X; S), S, Z) \overset{c}{\approx} (U, S, Z)$ under certain conditions for X and Z where $\overset{c}{\approx}$ denotes the computational indistinguishability and U denotes the uniform distribution on some set (see Definition 4 of [3] for details). The essence is that *the adversary in the security notion* (i.e., the distinguisher behind the notation $\overset{c}{\approx}$) *can also see the internal randomness S of* Ext. On the other hand, the security definition $\mathcal{R}(S_0) \overset{c}{\approx} U$ for a PRG $\mathcal{R}$ supposes that the seed (internal randomness) is not visible for the adversary. Intuitively, as the security of PRGs does not suppose the case where the internal randomness is visible for the adversary, the security of the PRG may be useless to preserve the security of the randomness extractor with visible seeds.

Here we point out that such a security notion with visible randomness in fact also appears in situations closer to real applications (rather than just building blocks like randomness extractors). Concretely, the standard security notion for *multiparty computation* (MPC) is also of this type (see Sect. 3.1 for details). Here we focus on two-party computation (2PC) among MPC for the sake of simplicity, and give the following result.

Theorem 1 (Informal). *Under a certain assumption, there is a pair of a 2PC protocol π and a secure PRG $\mathcal{R}$ with the following property: π is secure (in the semi-honest model) against a party $\mathcal{P}$ but the protocol becomes insecure against the party $\mathcal{P}$ when the internal randomness for $\mathcal{P}$ is generated by using $\mathcal{R}$.*

See Sect. 3 for details. Roughly summarizing, we construct two pairs $(\pi_1, \mathcal{R}_1)$ and $(\pi_2, \mathcal{R}_2)$ as in the statement; π_1 is artificially constructed but is very simple; while π_2 is complicated but is a practical protocol chosen from a paper by Asharov et al. in ACM CCS 2013 [1] (more precisely, Protocol 51 in Sect. 5.2 of its full version [2]). We note that possibilities for such connections between a party's randomness and the security against the same party have been suggested in some previous papers [17,22], but no concrete example of the connection was given in the literature before the present work. (We also note that the underlying assumption in the theorem is not a standard one, which is a main drawback of the result. Nevertheless, the assumption is at least not immediately falsifiable, which suggests that it would not be able to guarantee in general that a secure PRG preserves the security of MPC.)

It should be emphasized that there is no contradiction in the theorem where the semi-honest security is lost by applying a secure PRG, as the semi-honest model requests each party to follow the protocol *precisely, including the ideal randomness generation*. However, the possible gap between security of MPC with ideal randomness and with PRGs seems to be not recognized in the research area; our result here gives a caution for this point. In the author's opinion, the situation for (semi-honest) MPC with PRGs would have to be similar to cryptography in the random oracle model (ROM) where most of the cryptographers know the gap between ROM and the real (cf. Sect. 1.2 below) and they explicitly accept the rigorous imperfectness as a trade-off with practical efficiency.

We might expect that such a loss of security would not occur for "natural" cases, especially with "natural" PRGs, as the construction of PRG $\mathcal{R}$ in our theorem above is very artificial and impractical. But the meaning of "natural" here is not rigorous; it is worthy to establish some sufficient conditions for *provably* preventing such a loss of security. Towards this affirmative direction, in this paper we give the following result. Here we say (roughly) that a simulator $\mathcal{S}$ for a party $\mathcal{P}$ in a security proof of a 2PC protocol is *with raw randomness*, if $\mathcal{S}$ generates the simulated randomness for $\mathcal{P}$ by using a part of randomness for $\mathcal{S}$ "as is" (rather than adjusting according to the other part of the output of $\mathcal{S}$); see Definition 1 in Sect. 3.5 for the precise definition. We also recall that the *min-entropy* of a random variable X is defined by $H_\infty(X) = -\max_x \log_2 \Pr[X = x]$.

Theorem 2 (Informal). *Let π be a semi-honest 2PC protocol that is information-theoretically secure against a party $\mathcal{P}$ with raw randomness for simulator* *(see above for the terminology). Let $\mathcal{R}$ be a PRG and suppose that the difference of min-entropy of $\mathcal{R}$'s output distribution from that of ideal randomness is at most of logarithmic order (with respect to the security parameter). Then by generating the randomness for $\mathcal{P}$ with $\mathcal{R}$, the protocol π remains information-theoretically secure against semi-honest $\mathcal{P}$ with raw randomness for simulator.*

See Sect. 3.5 for details. We emphasize that if we remove the condition of "with raw randomness for simulator" (respectively, "information-theoretically secure") from the hypothesis, then the protocol-PRG pair $(\pi_1, \mathcal{R}_1)$ (respectively, $(\pi_2, \mathcal{R}_2)$) appeared in the proof of Theorem 1 gives a counterexample, therefore the condition is essential in the statement.

On the other hand, the current condition for PRG in the theorem (which implies that the PRG has only logarithmic stretch) looks very severe and it is important to weaken the condition. In particular, it is desirable for such a theorem to be based on some computational property of PRGs, rather than information-theoretic one such as min-entropy. Here we intuitively explain a difficulty behind the problem; let $\mathcal{S}$ and $\mathcal{S}_{\mathrm{PRG}}$ be simulators to be constructed in the security of an original protocol Π and its variant Π_{PRG} using a PRG $\mathcal{R}$, respectively. To show that the security of Π implies the security of Π_{PRG}, it suffices to show an implication from $\mathcal{S}$ to $\mathcal{S}_{\mathrm{PRG}}$, or equivalently, that if the output of $\mathcal{S}_{\mathrm{PRG}}$ can be distinguished by an algorithm D_{PRG} then the output of $\mathcal{S}$ will also be distinguished by some algorithm D. When constructing D from D_{PRG}, a straightforward strategy (using D_{PRG} in a black-box manner) would involve a process to convert a given input for D into an input for D_{PRG}. However, now an input for D involves randomness for Π (to be generated by $\mathcal{R}$ in the case of Π_{PRG}) and an input for D_{PRG} involves a seed for $\mathcal{R}$; hence, such a conversion as above might require a kind of "inversion" of $\mathcal{R}$ from its output to its seed, which would be difficult due to the security of $\mathcal{R}$. Our proof in this paper escapes successfully from such a difficulty in the reduction-based proof by utilizing the extremely high min-entropy for the PRG. It looks a challenging task to handle such a difficulty by basing on computational security of the PRG.

Type 2: The "Bad" Randomness may be not Efficiently Recognizable
Intuitively, when the security of some cryptosystem against a (polynomial-time) adversary (who cannot see the internal randomness) is concerned, it suffices for the PRG to fool this adversary only, therefore the usual security of the PRG can ensure that the security of the cryptosystem is preserved. In contrast, here we point out that the security of PRGs may be not sufficient to preserve the *correctness* of a cryptosystem; the security is of course important, but the correctness should be even more important. We focus only on the case of public key encryption (PKE); to point out the existence of such a phenomenon is a main purpose of the present work, and more exhaustive studies among other kinds of cryptographic schemes are future research topics.

When a PKE scheme has perfect (zero-error) correctness, the way of randomness generation does not affect the correctness at all. On the other hand, here we deal with PKE schemes with negligible but *non-zero* decryption error probability, and we want to generate the randomness for key generation by using a PRG. The issue we point out is the following: even if the ratio of "bad" randomness yielding a key with high error probability is negligible among the whole space, in general *the set of "bad" randomness may be not efficiently recognizable*[1]. If the set were efficiently recognizable, the security of a PRG would ensure that the probability of choosing "bad" randomness is only negligibly changed by the PRG, therefore the correctness would be preserved. But it is in general not true, therefore the probability of choosing "bad" randomness may increase non-negligibly even if the PRG is secure[2]:

Theorem 3 (Informal). *Under a certain assumption, there is a pair of a PKE scheme and a secure PRG with the following property: the probability of choosing "bad" randomness in the key generation is exponentially small when the ideal randomness is used but becomes 1 when the output of the PRG is used instead.*

See Sect. 4 for details. Such an issue of "bad" randomness may potentially occur also in other cryptosystems. Although the example in the theorem is artificially constructed and the author has not found any such example among the schemes proposed in the literature, the result still suggests that it might be important to check if the set of "bad" randomness is efficiently recognizable when designing a new cryptosystem; such an issue in correctness (rather than security) has not been noticed in the literature to the author's best knowledge.

We note that there is a general solution (at least for PKE) to avoid such an issue, which is a conversion method to make the scheme perfectly correct, proposed by Bitansky and Vaikuntanathan [5][3]. But the method has large overhead and is not very practical. The situation is similar also for the Type 3 below.

Type 3: Non-uniform Distinguishers are Implicitly Related
For example, the standard security notion for MPC (cf. Sect. 7.2 of [16]) is explicitly based on the indistinguishability of random variables against *non-uniform* distinguishers with advice $z = z_\lambda$ dependent solely on the security parameter λ. Then it is natural that the PRG should also be secure against non-uniform distinguishers. In contrast, here we point out that there are cases in cryptography where non-uniform security (not just the security against uniform distinguishers) is required for the PRG *but the relevance of non-uniformity is implicit*. Concretely, we again deal with the correctness with negligible errors for PKE, but here we focus on the encryption algorithm rather than key generation. To

---

[1] "Performing key generation (using the randomness), encryption, and decryption and then checking if the result is correct" is in general *not* an efficient procedure, as the corresponding "bad" plaintext to be encrypted may be not efficiently samplable.

[2] The issue remains even if the PRG is secure against non-uniform distinguishers with advice. Although the set of "bad" randomness is fixed for each security parameter, this set may be too complicated to be included in the advice of polynomial length.

[3] Such so-called "immunization" methods had also been studied before, e.g., [13,20, 23], but those methods remove the errors only partially. We note also that such methods did not concern the issue as in the paper and their motivations were different; e.g., preventing attacks that utilize decryption errors (e.g., [21]).

the author's best knowledge, such relevance of non-uniform security for PRGs to the *correctness*[4] of PKE has not been studied in the literature.

An intuitive explanation is as follows. In a usual definition for correctness, the decryption error probability has to be negligible for *any* plaintext. When falsifying the correctness (under the use of a PRG), the error probability will be non-negligible for *some* plaintext. The essence is that *such a "bad" plaintext* m_λ *at each security parameter* λ *is not necessarily found in polynomial time*, therefore a distinguisher for the PRG that utilizes the plaintexts m_λ should be non-uniform with advice m_λ. More precisely, we give the following result.

Theorem 4 (Informal). *Under a certain assumption (including the gap between uniform and non-uniform security for PRGs[5]), there is a pair of a PKE scheme and a (uniformly) secure PRG for which the decryption error probability is exponentially small when the ideal randomness is used in encryption but becomes non-negligible when the output of the PRG is used instead.*

See Sect. 5 for details. We note that any non-uniformly secure PRG used in the encryption algorithm preserves the correctness. But switching from uniform to non-uniform security may worsen the security parameter in practical implementations, due to some results on attacks by non-uniform algorithms, e.g., [4,7,26]. We also give a possible strategy of avoiding non-uniformly secure PRGs in ensuring the correctness after the use of a PRG; see Theorem 10 for details.

1.2   Related Work

One may feel some similarity of the results in this paper to a famous result by Canetti, Goldreich, and Halevi [6] showing that there is a scheme involving a (keyless) hash function that is provably secure when the hash function is modeled as a random oracle but becomes insecure for any concrete implementation of the hash function. In some sense, both of the present paper and theirs reveal gaps between cryptography based on idealized frameworks (ideal randomness/ROM) and that based on real objects (PRGs/hash functions). We emphasize, however, that there exists the following difference between the two results; the "real objects" in [6] (hash functions) themselves do not have provable security, while the present paper shows that even *provably secure* "real objects" (PRGs) can cause insecurity in implementation, which may have stronger impact. (On the other hand, a point of the present paper weaker than theirs is that our result here shows the existence of at least one "problematic" real object, while [6] shows that *any* such real object is "problematic".)

We also note another related result by Hirose [18] that for any (keyless) hash function under a certain model of construction that is secure when an ideal block cipher is used in the construction, there exists a block cipher that is provably

---

[4] For the *security* of PKE, the theory can be reasonably based on the uniform complexity treatment [14].

[5] The issue discussed here will disappear if there is no such gap.

secure but by which the resulting hash function becomes insecure. This result also focused on insecurity caused by provably secure building blocks, but our result in this paper covers wider situations, not just hash functions.

One may also feel that the topic of the present paper seems to be related to some other topics concerning non-ideal randomness in cryptography, such as cryptography based on so-called "imperfect randomness" (e.g., [10,12]) and the security issues caused by "backdoored PRGs" (e.g., [8,9]). But actually, the former topic above mainly deals with randomness that is significantly far from being ideal; in contrast, the present paper focuses on the use of randomness that is significantly close to ideal. On the other hand, the latter topic above studies the problem of the use of maliciously (and secretly) designed PRGs; while the main concern of the present paper originates from the practical impossibility of implementing the ideal randomness even if an engineer is honest and makes a best effort. Hence our problem setting is significantly different.

Finally, we mention about a previous work by Dodis et al. [11] which also studies situations where some internal states of a PRG are leaked to an adversary. An advantage of their result is that security notions for PRGs concerning such situations are established and precise constructions of PRGs satisfying their conditions are given. However, we emphasize that their security notion in fact considers only *partial* leakage of inputs to the PRG; in sequential updates of the internal state depending on newly supplied random seeds, an adversary obtains some intermediate states and then the PRG intends to quickly recover an unpredictable state with the help of subsequent *unknown* seeds. In contrast, Type 1 in our argument here considers more severe cases where the *entire* input (seed) to the PRG is known by an adversary; due to the difference of situations, the affirmative results in [11] would not (straightforwardly) resolve our problem.

2   Preliminaries

For a probabilistic algorithm $\mathcal{A}$, we may write $\mathcal{A}(x; r)$ instead of $\mathcal{A}(x)$ to emphasize the choice of randomness r. We adopt a convention that an advice $z = z_\lambda$ for a non-uniform algorithm $\mathcal{A} = \mathcal{A}^{(z_\lambda)}$ depends solely on the security parameter λ.[6] We let "polynomial-time" mean "polynomial-time with respect to λ". For a finite set S, let $\Delta(X, Y) = (1/2) \sum_{z \in S} |\Pr[z \leftarrow X] - \Pr[z \leftarrow Y]|$ be the statistical distance of random variables X and Y on S. Let $U[S]$ denote the uniform distribution on S. We write $x \leftarrow_R S$ to mean that x is sampled from S uniformly at random. We may identify a bit sequence with an integer via binary expressions of integers.

Let I_λ ($\lambda \geq 1$) be index sets. Let $X = (X_{\lambda,w})_{\lambda,w}$ and $Y = (Y_{\lambda,w})_{\lambda,w}$ be families of random variables indexed by $\lambda \geq 1$ and $w \in I_\lambda$. We say that X and Y are *uniformly* (respectively, *non-uniformly*) *indistinguishable*, denoted by $X \overset{\text{u.c}}{\approx} Y$ (respectively, $X \overset{\text{nu.c}}{\approx} Y$), if for any probabilistic polynomial-time

---

[6] By an appropriate padding to the input, our convention here can be made consistent with a standard convention where an advice depends solely on the input length.

(PPT) uniform (respectively, non-uniform) distinguisher $\mathcal{D}$, there is a negligible function $\varepsilon(\lambda) \in \lambda^{-\omega(1)}$ satisfying that the *advantage* $|\Pr[\mathcal{D}(1^\lambda, X_{\lambda,w}) = 1] - \Pr[\mathcal{D}(1^\lambda, Y_{\lambda,w}) = 1]|$ is at most $\varepsilon(\lambda)$ for any λ and $w \in I_\lambda$. We say that X and Y are *information-theoretically indistinguishable*, denoted by $X \overset{i}{\approx} Y$, if there is a negligible function $\varepsilon(\lambda)$ with $\Delta(X_{\lambda,w}, Y_{\lambda,w}) \le \varepsilon(\lambda)$ for any λ and $w \in I_\lambda$.

In this paper, we let a *pseudorandom generator* (*PRG*) $\mathcal{R}$ be a deterministic polynomial-time algorithm that takes security parameter 1^λ and a seed $s \in \{0,1\}^{\ell_{in}(\lambda)}$ as input and outputs an element of $\{0,1\}^{\ell_{out}(\lambda)}$, where $\ell_{in}(\lambda)$ and $\ell_{out}(\lambda)$ are some polynomially bounded and polynomial-time computable functions satisfying that $\lambda \le \ell_{in}(\lambda) < \ell_{out}(\lambda)$ and $\ell_{in}(\lambda)$ is a strictly increasing function[7]. We say that a PRG $\mathcal{R}$ is *uniformly* (respectively, *non-uniformly*) *secure*, if $\mathcal{R}(1^\lambda, U[\{0,1\}^{\ell_{in}(\lambda)}]) \overset{u.c}{\approx}$ (respectively, $\overset{nu.c}{\approx}$) $U[\{0,1\}^{\ell_{out}(\lambda)}]$.

3   Type 1: Schemes with Visible Seeds

In this section, we observe (as mentioned in Sect. 1.1) that the standard security notion for (semi-honest) two-party computation (2PC) is formalized in a way that the internal randomness is visible for adversaries; and consequently, the security of PRGs (where the seed is supposed to be not visible for adversaries) may be unable to in general preserve the security of a protocol when a PRG is applied. We state and prove Theorems 1 and 2 in a more precise manner.

3.1   Basic Definitions

Let π be a 2PC protocol with parties $\mathcal{P}_1$ and $\mathcal{P}_2$ to compute function values $\vec{f}(\vec{x}) = (f_1(\vec{x}), f_2(\vec{x}))$ from input pair $\vec{x} = (x_1, x_2)$. Let $\vec{r} = (r_1, r_2)$ be the pair of randomness for $\mathcal{P}_1$ and $\mathcal{P}_2$, $\vec{m}_i(1^\lambda, \vec{x}; \vec{r})$ ($i = 1, 2$) be the list of messages received by $\mathcal{P}_i$ during the protocol, and $\pi(1^\lambda, \vec{x}; \vec{r})$ denote the pair of outputs by $\mathcal{P}_1$ and $\mathcal{P}_2$ in π. Following the standard formulation (cf. Sect. 7.2 of [16]), we say that π is *secure against semi-honest* $\mathcal{P}_i$, if there is a PPT simulator $\mathcal{S}_i$ for which $\left(\mathcal{S}_i(1^\lambda, x_i, f_i(\vec{x})), \vec{f}(\vec{x})\right)_{\lambda, \vec{x}} \overset{nu.c}{\approx} \left(x_i, r_i, \vec{m}_i(1^\lambda, \vec{x}; \vec{r}), \pi(1^\lambda, \vec{x}; \vec{r})\right)_{\lambda, \vec{x}}$ (see Sect. 2 for the notation $\overset{nu.c}{\approx}$). We also say "information-theoretically secure", if the relation $\overset{i}{\approx}$ holds instead of $\overset{nu.c}{\approx}$.

An important observation is that the internal randomness r_i for party $\mathcal{P}_i$ is included in the input to the distinguisher behind the notation $\overset{nu.c}{\approx}$. This is practically reasonable, as a corrupted party will be able to see the party's internal randomness for the protocol which is stored in the party's own device.

For a 2PC protocol π, a PRG $\mathcal{R}$, and $i \in \{1, 2\}$, let $\pi \circ_i \mathcal{R}$ denote the modified version of π where, for internal randomness (r'_1, r'_2), party $\mathcal{P}_i$ executes the protocol π with randomness $r_i \leftarrow \mathcal{R}(1^\lambda, r'_i)$, while the other party $\mathcal{P}_{3-i}$ executes π by using randomness $r_{3-i} \leftarrow r'_{3-i}$ as is.

---

[7] One may think that the seed length of a PRG should satisfy $\ell_{in}(\lambda) = \lambda$; but our seemingly generalized style is just for the sake of technical ease and our argument can indeed be translated into the more strict style where $\ell_{in}(\lambda) = \lambda$ always holds.

Algorithm 1: First 2PC protocol π_1 for Theorem 1

Input : ($\mathcal{P}_1$) Blum integer N (as in the text); and randomness $r_1 \in \{0,1\}^{3\lambda}$
($\mathcal{P}_2$) λ-bit prime factors $p < q$ of N; and randomness $r_2 \in \{0,1\}^2$

Output: none

1 (By $\mathcal{P}_1$) $y \leftarrow r_1 \bmod N$ and send y to $\mathcal{P}_2$
2 (By $\mathcal{P}_2$) **if** $y \in \mathsf{QR}_{pq}$ **then**
3 $\quad$ uniformly sample one of the four square roots ξ of $y \in (\mathbb{Z}/pq\mathbb{Z})^\times$
4 $\quad$ send $\eta \leftarrow \xi$ to $\mathcal{P}_1$
5 **else**
6 $\quad$ send $\eta \leftarrow \bot$ to $\mathcal{P}_1$
7 **end**

3.2   First Protocol for Theorem 1

We define a 2PC protocol π_1 as in Algorithm 1.[8] For security parameter $\lambda \geq 5$, an input pair is given by $x_1 = N$ and $x_2 = (p, q)$ where $N = pq$ is a Blum integer with λ-bit primes $p < q$ (i.e., $p \equiv q \equiv 3 \pmod 4$). Let $\mathsf{QR}_N = \mathsf{QR}_{pq} \subseteq (\mathbb{Z}/N\mathbb{Z})^\times$ denote the set of quadratic residues modulo $N = pq$. Note that the computation by $\mathcal{P}_2$ is of polynomial time as $\mathcal{P}_2$ has the prime factors p, q of N. Here we focus only on the security against semi-honest $\mathcal{P}_1$, though π_1 is also secure against $\mathcal{P}_2$.

Proposition 1. π_1 *is information-theoretically secure against semi-honest* $\mathcal{P}_1$.

Proof. We consider the PPT simulator $\mathcal{S}$ as in Algorithm 2.[9] We write $\eta = \eta(y)$ in π_1. Moreover, for $y' \in \mathbb{Z}/N\mathbb{Z}$, let $g(y')$ denote the uniform random variable on the set $\{r' \in \{0,1\}^{3\lambda} \mid r' \bmod N = y'\}$ (see also Line 9 of Algorithm 2). Then we have $(r_1, \eta(y)) \overset{i}{\approx} (g(y), \eta(y))$ by the definition of g. Now, as N is a Blum integer, ± 1 and $\pm a$ in $\mathcal{S}$ are complete representatives for $(\mathbb{Z}/N\mathbb{Z})^\times / \mathsf{QR}_N$. Therefore $y' \overset{i}{\approx} U[(\mathbb{Z}/N\mathbb{Z})^\times]$ and $\eta^\dagger = \eta(y')$, while $y \overset{i}{\approx} U[(\mathbb{Z}/N\mathbb{Z})^\times]$ in π_1 as r_1 is λ-bit longer than $N = pq$. Hence $y \overset{i}{\approx} y'$ and $(g(y), \eta(y)) \overset{i}{\approx} (g(y'), \eta(y')) \overset{i}{\approx} (r_1^\dagger, \eta^\dagger)$. Summarizing, we have $(N, r_1, \eta) \overset{i}{\approx} (N, r_1^\dagger, \eta^\dagger) = \mathcal{S}(1^\lambda, N)$, which implies the claim. $\qquad\square$

3.3   First PRG for Theorem 1

We define a PRG for $\mathcal{P}_1$'s randomness in π_1. In order to describe the underlying assumption, first we introduce some terminology. We say that a deterministic

---

[8] Some reader may feel strange because the two parties' inputs in the protocol are very correlated and the protocol has no output. This is for the sake of simplifying the argument, and in fact our protocol can be converted into a more "natural" but complicated form. See Appendix A for the details.

[9] In fact, in order to let the internal randomness for $\mathcal{S}$ be a *bit sequence*, we have to, and indeed we can, approximate (with exponentially small deviation from the ideal) the procedures in Lines 1, 2 and 9 by PPT algorithms with random bit sequences.

Algorithm 2: Simulator $\mathcal{S}$ for $\mathcal{P}_1$ in protocol π_1

Input : 1^λ and $\mathcal{P}_1$'s local input N

Output: N, simulated randomness $r_1^\dagger$, and simulated message $\eta^\dagger$ from $\mathcal{P}_2$

1 $x' \leftarrow_R (\mathbb{Z}/N\mathbb{Z})^\times$

2 take some $a \in (\mathbb{Z}/N\mathbb{Z})^\times$ with Jacobi symbol $\left(\frac{a}{N}\right) = -1$

3 $a' \leftarrow_R \{\pm 1, \pm a\}$ and $y' \leftarrow (x')^2 \cdot a' \in (\mathbb{Z}/N\mathbb{Z})^\times$

4 **if** $y' = (x')^2$ **then**

5 $\quad$ | $\quad \eta^\dagger \leftarrow x'$

6 **else**

7 $\quad$ | $\quad \eta^\dagger \leftarrow \perp$

8 **end**

9 sample a value $r_1^\dagger \in \{0,1\}^{3\lambda}$ of the uniform random variable, denoted by $g(y')$, on the set of all $r' \in \{0,1\}^{3\lambda}$ with $r' \bmod N = y'$

10 **return** $(N, r_1^\dagger, \eta^\dagger)$

---

polynomial-time algorithm $\mathcal{B} = \mathcal{B}(1^\lambda)$ is a *Blum integer generator*, if its output $\mathcal{B}(1^\lambda)$ (with $\lambda \geq 5$) is a Blum integer with two λ-bit prime factors[10]. We say that $\mathcal{B}$ is *efficiently factorizable*, if there is a PPT *uniform* algorithm $\mathcal{F}$ satisfying that $\mathcal{F}(\mathcal{B}(1^\lambda))$ is a prime factor of $\mathcal{B}(1^\lambda)$ with probability $\Omega(1)$.[11] Then our assumption here is described as follows.

Assumption 1. *There exists a Blum integer generator $\mathcal{B}$ that is not efficiently factorizable; and there exists a non-uniformly secure PRG for any choices of $\ell_{in}(\lambda)$ and $\ell_{out}(\lambda)$ (satisfying the constraints in our definition of PRGs)[12].*

Now let $\ell_\mathcal{S}(\lambda)$ denote the bit length of the randomness for $\mathcal{S}$. We define $\mathcal{R}_1^*(1^\lambda, r^*)$ for $r^* \in \{0,1\}^{\ell_\mathcal{S}(\lambda)}$ to be the second component $r_1^\dagger$ of the output of $\mathcal{S}(1^\lambda, \mathcal{B}(1^\lambda); r^*)$. Then our PRG $\mathcal{R}_1 \colon \{0,1\}^{3\lambda-1} \to \{0,1\}^{3\lambda}$ is defined as follows: first it converts $r_1' \in \{0,1\}^{3\lambda-1}$ to $r^* \in \{0,1\}^{\ell_\mathcal{S}(\lambda)}$ by using a PRG $\mathcal{R}_1^\dagger$ as in Assumption 1 (with $\ell_{in}(\lambda) = 3\lambda - 1$ and $\ell_{out}(\lambda) = \ell_\mathcal{S}(\lambda)$), and then it outputs $\mathcal{R}_1^*(1^\lambda, r^*)$. The PRG satisfies the following:

Proposition 2. *The PRG $\mathcal{R}_1$ is non-uniformly secure.*

Proof. We have $r^* \stackrel{\text{nu.c}}{\approx} U[\{0,1\}^{\ell_\mathcal{S}(\lambda)}]$ by the security of $\mathcal{R}_1^\dagger$, therefore we have $\mathcal{R}_1(1^\lambda, r_1') = \mathcal{R}_1^*(1^\lambda, r^*) \stackrel{\text{nu.c}}{\approx} \mathcal{R}_1^*(1^\lambda, U[\{0,1\}^{\ell_\mathcal{S}(\lambda)}]) \stackrel{\text{i}}{\approx} U[\{0,1\}^{3\lambda}]$ by Proposition 1 (for $\stackrel{\text{i}}{\approx}$) and the fact that $\mathcal{R}_1^*$ is PPT (for $\stackrel{\text{nu.c}}{\approx}$). Hence the claim follows. $\square$

Now we give a precise version of Theorem 1 as follows:

---

[10] The reason of restricting $\mathcal{B}$ to be deterministic is that $\mathcal{B}$ will be used as a component of the desired PRG and hence may not have its own internal randomness.

[11] The factorization is trivially easy if $\mathcal{F}$ may be non-uniform, as $\mathcal{B}$ is deterministic.

[12] Such a PRG can be obtained from a PRG with 1-bit stretch by a standard technique based on hybrid argument (cf. Construction 3.3.2 and Theorem 3.3.3 of [15]).

Algorithm 3: Non-uniform distinguisher $\mathcal{D}$ for the simulator $\mathcal{S}$ for π_1

Input : 1^λ and $\mathcal{P}_1$'s view $(N, \widehat{r}_1, \widehat{\eta})$, either in real π_1 or simulated by $\mathcal{S}$
(also given prime factors $p_\lambda < q_\lambda$ of $N_\lambda \leftarrow \mathcal{B}(1^\lambda)$ as advice)

Output: $b \in \{0, 1\}$

1   *always return $b \leftarrow 0$ when $N \neq N_\lambda$; below we assume $N = N_\lambda$*

2   emulate the protocol π_1 with inputs N_λ and (p_λ, q_λ) where $\widehat{r}_1$ plays the role of
    randomness for $\mathcal{P}_1$, and get emulated $\mathcal{P}_2$'s message $\overline{\eta}$

3   return $b \leftarrow \chi[\widehat{\eta}, \overline{\eta} \in (\mathbb{Z}/N_\lambda\mathbb{Z})^\times$ and $(\widehat{\eta})^2 = (\overline{\eta})^2$ and $\overline{\eta} \notin \{\widehat{\eta}, -\widehat{\eta}\}]$

Theorem 5. *Under Assumption 1, the protocol π_1 is secure against semi-honest $\mathcal{P}_1$ and the PRG $\mathcal{R}_1$ is non-uniformly secure, but the protocol $\pi_1 \circ_1 \mathcal{R}_1$ is not secure against semi-honest $\mathcal{P}_1$.*

Before giving the proof, we first explain an intuitive idea towards the proof and an outline of the proof. We observe that if $\pi_1 \circ_1 \mathcal{R}_1$ were secure, then for $\mathcal{P}_1$'s input $N = \mathcal{B}(1^\lambda)$ in $\pi_1 \circ_1 \mathcal{R}_1$, $\mathcal{P}_1$ would be unable to obtain any information that cannot be deduced directly from N. In particular, as $\mathcal{B}$ is not efficiently factorizable by Assumption 1, $\mathcal{P}_1$ would be unable to obtain a prime factor of N. However, in fact a corrupted $\mathcal{P}_1$ can factorize N during the protocol $\pi_1 \circ_1 \mathcal{R}_1$ as follows: (1) Given randomness $r_1' \in \{0,1\}^{3\lambda-1}$, $\mathcal{P}_1$ generates $r^* \in \{0,1\}^{\ell_S(\lambda)}$ as above, and executes $\mathcal{S}(1^\lambda, N; r^*)$ and obtains $(N, r_1^\dagger, \eta^\dagger)$. (2) $\mathcal{P}_1$ executes the protocol π_1 with input N and randomness $r_1^\dagger$, and obtains $\mathcal{P}_2$'s message η (note that this is a correct execution of $\pi_1 \circ_1 \mathcal{R}_1$). (3) If $\eta^\dagger \neq \perp$ and $\eta \neq \pm\eta^\dagger \bmod N$, then $\mathcal{P}_1$ computes $p' \leftarrow \gcd(\eta^2 - (\eta^\dagger)^2, N)$ and outputs p'.

Now if $\eta^\dagger \neq \perp$ (which occurs with probability $1/4$), then $\eta^\dagger$ is a square root of $y' = r_1^\dagger \bmod N$. Hence by the construction of π_1, η is one of the four square roots of y', therefore $\eta \neq \pm\eta^\dagger$ occurs with probability $1/2$. In this case, we have $\eta^2 - (\eta^\dagger)^2 = (\eta - \eta^\dagger)(\eta + \eta^\dagger)$ and $\eta \pm \eta^\dagger \not\equiv 0 \pmod{N}$, therefore $\eta - \eta^\dagger$ is divisible by precisely one of the two prime factors of N, which is equal to p'. Hence $\mathcal{P}_1$ can factorize N with probability $\Omega(1)$, a contradiction. This shows the claim.

We start the proof of Theorem 5. Owing to Propositions 1 and 2, it suffices to show that $\pi_1 \circ_1 \mathcal{R}_1$ is not secure against $\mathcal{P}_1$. This follows from the contraposition of the following proposition and Assumption 1 on $\mathcal{B}$.

Proposition 3. *Suppose that the protocol $\pi_1 \circ_1 \mathcal{R}_1$ is secure against $\mathcal{P}_1$. Then there exists a PPT uniform algorithm $\mathcal{F}$ that outputs a prime factor of $\mathcal{B}(1^\lambda)$ with probability $\Omega(1)$.*

Proof. Let $\widetilde{S}$ denote a simulator for $\mathcal{P}_1$ in $\pi_1 \circ_1 \mathcal{R}_1$ implied by the hypothesis. First we consider a PPT non-uniform distinguisher $\mathcal{D}$ in Algorithm 3 for the simulator $\mathcal{S}$ for the protocol π_1, where we let $\chi[P] = 1$ if a condition P holds and $\chi[P] = 0$ otherwise.

When $(N_\lambda, \widehat{r}_1, \widehat{\eta})$ is a view in real π_1, $y \leftarrow \widehat{r}_1 \bmod N_\lambda$ is in QR_N with probability $\approx 1/4$ (where "$\approx$" means "the difference is negligible"). If it is the case, then $\widehat{\eta}$ is a square root of y modulo N_λ. Moreover, in the emulation in Line 2

Algorithm 4: Distinguisher $\widetilde{\mathcal{D}}$ for the simulator $\widetilde{\mathcal{S}}$ for $\pi_1 \circ_1 \mathcal{R}_1$

    Input : 1^λ and $\mathcal{P}_1$'s view $(N, \widetilde{s}, \widetilde{\eta})$, either in real $\pi_1 \circ_1 \mathcal{R}_1$ or simulated by $\widetilde{\mathcal{S}}$
    Output: $b \in \{0, 1\}$
  1 *always return* $b \leftarrow 0$ *when* $N \neq N_\lambda = \mathcal{B}(1^\lambda)$; *below we assume* $N = N_\lambda$
  2 $(N_\lambda, \widehat{r}_1, \widehat{\eta}) \leftarrow \mathcal{S}(1^\lambda, N_\lambda; \mathcal{R}_1^\dagger(1^\lambda, \widetilde{s}))$
  3 return $b \leftarrow \chi[\widehat{\eta}, \widetilde{\eta} \in (\mathbb{Z}/N_\lambda\mathbb{Z})^\times$ and $(\widehat{\eta})^2 = (\widetilde{\eta})^2$ and $\widetilde{\eta} \notin \{\widehat{\eta}, -\widehat{\eta}\}]$

---

using the *same* randomness $\widehat{r}_1$ for $\mathcal{P}_1$ and *fresh* randomness for $\mathcal{P}_2$, the emulated $\mathcal{P}_1$ sends the same y, while the emulated $\mathcal{P}_2$ replies a uniformly random square root $\widetilde{\eta}$ of y *independent of* $\widehat{\eta}$. Therefore, when $y \in \mathsf{QR}_N$, we have $b = 1$ with conditional probability $1/2$. Hence $\mathcal{D}$ outputs 1 with probability $\approx 1/8$. Now Proposition 1 implies that $\mathcal{D}$ also outputs 1 with probability $\approx 1/8$ when $(N_\lambda, \widehat{r}_1, \widehat{\eta}) \leftarrow \mathcal{S}(1^\lambda, N_\lambda; s_*)$ with ideally random s_*.

We regard the process "run $\mathcal{D}$ for input $(N_\lambda, \widehat{r}_1, \widehat{\eta}) \leftarrow \mathcal{S}(1^\lambda, N_\lambda; s_*)$" as a PPT non-uniform distinguisher with advice (p_λ, q_λ) against the non-uniformly secure PRG $\mathcal{R}_1^\dagger$. Then it follows that the probability of $b = 1$ is still at least $1/8 - \mathsf{negl}(\lambda) \in \Omega(1)$ when $s_* \leftarrow \mathcal{R}_1^\dagger(1^\lambda, s)$ and s is a uniformly random seed for $\mathcal{R}_1^\dagger$, where negl denotes some negligible function.

For the latter case $(N_\lambda, \widehat{r}_1, \widehat{\eta}) \leftarrow \mathcal{S}(1^\lambda, N_\lambda; s_*)$ with $s_* \leftarrow \mathcal{R}_1^\dagger(1^\lambda, s)$, the component $\widehat{r}_1$ coincides with the output of the PRG $\mathcal{R}_1$ with seed s, therefore the emulated protocol in Line 2 of $\mathcal{D}$ is nothing but the protocol $\pi_1 \circ_1 \mathcal{R}_1$ with randomness s for $\mathcal{P}_1$. Now we consider a PPT distinguisher $\widetilde{\mathcal{D}}$ in Algorithm 4 for simulator $\widetilde{\mathcal{S}}$.

By the argument above, when $(N_\lambda, \widetilde{s}, \widetilde{\eta})$ is a view in real $\pi_1 \circ_1 \mathcal{R}_1$ with input (p_λ, q_λ) for $\mathcal{P}_2$, the probability distribution of $\widetilde{\eta}$ conditioned on the given $(\widetilde{s}, \widehat{r}_1, \widehat{\eta})$ coincides with that of $\overline{\eta}$ in $\mathcal{D}$ for the same $(\widehat{r}_1, \widehat{\eta})$, therefore the probability that $\widetilde{\mathcal{D}}$ outputs $b = 1$ is also $\Omega(1)$ in this case. Now the hypothesis on the simulator $\widetilde{\mathcal{S}}$ implies that the probability of $b = 1$ is also $\Omega(1)$ even when $(N_\lambda, \widetilde{s}, \widetilde{\eta})$ is simulated by $\widetilde{\mathcal{S}}$. That is, by generating $(N_\lambda, \widetilde{s}, \widetilde{\eta}) \leftarrow \widetilde{\mathcal{S}}(1^\lambda, \mathcal{B}(1^\lambda))$ and $(N_\lambda, \widehat{r}_1, \widehat{\eta}) \leftarrow \mathcal{S}(1^\lambda, N_\lambda; \mathcal{R}_1^\dagger(1^\lambda, \widetilde{s}))$, the conditions $\widehat{\eta}, \widetilde{\eta} \in (\mathbb{Z}/N_\lambda\mathbb{Z})^\times$, $(\widehat{\eta})^2 = (\widetilde{\eta})^2$, and $\widetilde{\eta} \notin \{\widehat{\eta}, -\widehat{\eta}\}$ are satisfied with probability $\Omega(1)$; and if it is the case, then a prime factor of N_λ can be found by computing $\gcd(\widetilde{\eta} - \widehat{\eta}, N_\lambda)$. As the aforementioned process of generating $\widetilde{\eta}$ and $\widehat{\eta}$ from $\mathcal{B}(1^\lambda)$ is PPT and uniform, this yields the algorithm $\mathcal{F}$ as in the statement. Hence Proposition 3 holds. $\square$

3.4 Second Protocol and PRG for Theorem 1

We give another pair of a 2PC protocol π_2 and a PRG $\mathcal{R}_2$ for Theorem 1. An outline of the argument is as follows. The protocol π_2 is an oblivious transfer (OT) protocol proposed by Asharov et al. in ACM CCS 2013 [1], or more precisely, Protocol 51 in Sect. 5.2 of its full version [2]. The key idea of their OT protocol is to construct a function, denoted here by $\mathcal{H}$, that can sample a random element h of an underlying cyclic group $\mathbb{G} = \langle g \rangle$ in a way that the discrete logarithm of

h with respect to g is unknown even if the seed used for sampling h is known. Now the Receiver of the 1-out-of-2 OT protocol with input $\sigma \in \{0, 1\}$ generates $h \in \mathbb{G}$ by using $\mathcal{H}$ and g^α with random α, and sends (g^α, h) when $\sigma = 0$ and (h, g^α) when $\sigma = 1$ to the Sender. The Sender encrypts the two inputs in a way like the hashed ElGamal encryption where each of the two elements of $\mathbb{G}$ given from the Receiver is used as a public key, and sends the two ciphertexts (c_0, c_1) to the Receiver. Then the Receiver can decrypt c_σ and obtain the corresponding input of the Sender as the "secret key" α is known; while the other $c_{1-\sigma}$ cannot be decrypted (hence the other input remains secret) as the "secret key" corresponding to h is not known as mentioned above.

Then our construction of the PRG $\mathcal{R}_2$ is based on the following observation: there is a secure PRG $\mathcal{R}_2'$ that can "cancel" the effect of the function $\mathcal{H}$. Namely, when $h \in \mathbb{G}$ is sampled by $\mathcal{H}$ using an input generated by $\mathcal{R}_2'$ with seed s, now the discrete logarithm of h can be efficiently recovered from s. Then we construct a secure PRG $\mathcal{R}_2$ that involves $\mathcal{R}_2'$ to convert a part s of the seed (s, α) into $\mathcal{R}_2'(s)$. By using the output $(\mathcal{R}_2'(s), \alpha)$ of $\mathcal{R}_2$ in π_2 instead of the Receiver's original randomness, now the Receiver can also decrypt $c_{1-\sigma}$ and break the security, as the corresponding "secret key" can be recovered from s as mentioned above.

Now we move to a precise argument. First, we recall the construction of the OT protocol π_2 mentioned above. To make the argument precise, here we explicitly state that the internal randomness for the two parties are bit sequences, and the uniform samplings of objects in the protocol are performed approximately with exponentially small deviation. The input objects for the protocol (except the security parameter) can be classified into global parameters that can be reused for several protocol executions (such as the underlying cyclic group) and "actual" inputs for each individual protocol execution. For the global parameters, in this paper we put an assumption that a secure global parameter can be chosen efficiently and *deterministically* (see Assumption 2 below). This technical assumption would also have some practical meaning, as it may sometimes happen that an implementation of a protocol hard-wires such a reusable global parameter.

In order to specify our choice of global parameters, we quote the following description from the text in the second paragraph of Sect. 5.2 in [2] (where "[......]" indicates omission by the author of the present paper):

> [......] *We also assume that it is possible to sample a random element of the group, and the DDH assumption will remain hard even when the coins used to sample the element are given to the distinguisher (i.e., (g, h, g^a, h^a) is indistinguishable from (g, h, g^a, g^b) for random a, b, even given the coins used to sample h). [......] For finite fields, one can sample a random element $h \in \mathbb{Z}_p$ of order q by choosing a random $x \in_R \mathbb{Z}_p$ and computing $h = x^{(p-1)/q}$ until $h \neq 1$. [......]*

Accordingly, we use the subgroup of a given order q in the multiplicative group $(\mathbb{F}_p)^\times$ of a finite field $\mathbb{F}_p$ (denoted by $\mathbb{Z}_p$ in the quoted text) as the underlying group of the protocol, where p is a t-bit prime for some polynomially bounded $t \geq \lambda$ and q is a divisor of $p-1$. Then the aforementioned sampling method $\mathcal{H}$ for

---

Algorithm 5: The algorithm $\mathcal{H}$ to sample a subgroup element

---

Input : $x' \in \{0,1\}^{2t}$
Output: an element h in the order-q subgroup of $(\mathbb{F}_p)^\times$
1 $x \leftarrow x' \bmod p$
2 **if** $x \neq 0$ **then**
3 $\quad\mid\quad$ return $h \leftarrow x^{(p-1)/q} \bmod p$
4 **else**
5 $\quad\mid\quad$ return $h \leftarrow 1$
6 **end**

---

the group elements can be realized as in Algorithm 5, where slight modification is made in order to ensure that it always halts within finite (and polynomial) time. This algorithm has the following property.

Lemma 1. *The output $\mathcal{H}(x')$ for $x' \leftarrow_R \{0,1\}^{2t}$ is in the unique subgroup of order q in $(\mathbb{F}_p)^\times$ and its probability distribution is exponentially close to uniform over this subgroup.*

Proof. First, if $x = 0$ in the algorithm, then the output h is 1; while if $x \neq 0$, then $h = x^{(p-1)/q} \bmod p$ is an element of $(\mathbb{F}_p)^\times$ of order dividing q, as $(\mathbb{F}_p)^\times$ is a cyclic group of order $p-1$. This implies the former part of the statement. On the other hand, for the latter part of the statement, as the bit length of p is $t \geq \lambda$, the distribution of x is exponentially close to the uniform distribution over $(\mathbb{F}_p)^\times$. Therefore, we may assume without loss of generality that $x \leftarrow_R (\mathbb{F}_p)^\times$. Then $h = x^{(p-1)/q} \bmod p$ becomes a uniformly random element of the subgroup. This implies the latter part of the statement. Hence Lemma 1 holds. $\square$

Our assumption mentioned above, which is a (possibly nonstandard) variant of the decisional Diffie–Hellman (DDH) assumption, is the following:

Assumption 2. *There exists a deterministic polynomial-time algorithm to choose a t-bit prime p with $t \geq \lambda$, a divisor q of $p-1$, a generator g of the subgroup of order q in $(\mathbb{F}_p)^\times$, and a deterministic polynomial-time key derivation function $\mathsf{KDF}: \langle g \rangle \to \{0,1\}^L$ for some L, satisfying the following: the two distributions of*

$$(p,q,g,g^r \bmod p, x', \mathsf{KDF}(\mathcal{H}(x')^r \bmod p))$$

and

$$(p,q,g,g^r \bmod p, x', z)$$

with $r \leftarrow_R \{0,\ldots,q-1\}$, $x' \leftarrow_R \{0,1\}^{2t}$, $z \leftarrow_R \{0,1\}^L$ are non-uniformly indistinguishable.

Then the protocol π_2 is described in Algorithm 6; here the global parameters are chosen as in Assumption 2 (in particular, the choice of global parameters is deterministic given a security parameter 1^λ). The result in the original paper implies that π_2 is secure in the semi-honest model under Assumption 2.

The following is another precise version of Theorem 1 to be proved here.

Algorithm 6: The OT protocol in [2] (called π_2 here)

Input : (global parameters) t-bit prime p, divisor q of $p - 1$, $g \in (\mathbb{F}_p)^\times$ of
order q, and KDF: $\langle g \rangle \to \{0, 1\}^L$
($\mathcal{P}_1$ (Sender)) $(x^{\langle 0 \rangle}, x^{\langle 1 \rangle}) \in (\{0, 1\}^L)^2$; and randomness $r_1 \in \{0, 1\}^{2t}$
($\mathcal{P}_2$ (Receiver)) $\sigma \in \{0, 1\}$; and randomness $(r'_2, r''_2) \in (\{0, 1\}^{2t})^2$
Output: ($\mathcal{P}_1$) none
($\mathcal{P}_2$) $\bar{x} \in \{0, 1\}^L$ // To be equal to $x^{\langle \sigma \rangle}$

1 (By $\mathcal{P}_2$) $h \leftarrow \mathcal{H}(r'_2)$ and $\alpha \leftarrow r''_2 \bmod q$
2 (By $\mathcal{P}_2$) if $\sigma = 0$ then
3 $\quad\mid\quad (h^{(0)}, h^{(1)}) \leftarrow (g^\alpha \bmod p, h)$
4 else
5 $\quad\mid\quad (h^{(0)}, h^{(1)}) \leftarrow (h, g^\alpha \bmod p)$
6 end
7 (By $\mathcal{P}_2$) send $(h^{(0)}, h^{(1)})$ to $\mathcal{P}_1$
8 (By $\mathcal{P}_1$) $r \leftarrow r_1 \bmod q$ and $u \leftarrow g^r \bmod p$
9 (By $\mathcal{P}_1$) $(k^{(0)}, k^{(1)}) \leftarrow ((h^{(0)})^r \bmod p, (h^{(1)})^r \bmod p)$
10 (By $\mathcal{P}_1$) $(v^{(0)}, v^{(1)}) \leftarrow \left(x^{(0)} \oplus \mathsf{KDF}(k^{(0)}), x^{(1)} \oplus \mathsf{KDF}(k^{(1)}) \right)$
11 (By $\mathcal{P}_1$) send u, $v^{(0)}$, and $v^{(1)}$ to $\mathcal{P}_2$
12 (By $\mathcal{P}_2$) return $\bar{x} \leftarrow v^{(\sigma)} \oplus \mathsf{KDF}(u^\alpha \bmod p)$

Theorem 6. *Assume that there exists a non-uniformly secure PRG for any choices of $\ell_{\mathrm{in}}(\lambda)$ and $\ell_{\mathrm{out}}(\lambda)$ (satisfying the constraints in PRGs). Assume moreover that the parameters in the protocol π_2 satisfy that $(p - 1)/q$ is coprime to q, and that a generator g_0 of $(\mathbb{F}_p)^\times$ can also be chosen in deterministic polynomial time. Then there is a non-uniformly secure PRG $\mathcal{R}_2$ with 1-bit stretch $\ell_{\mathrm{out}}(\lambda) - \ell_{\mathrm{in}}(\lambda) = 1$ satisfying that $\pi_2 \circ_2 \mathcal{R}_2$ is not secure against $\mathcal{P}_2$.*

As mentioned above, the basic strategy for constructing $\mathcal{R}_2$ is to enable $\mathcal{P}_2$ to know the discrete logarithm of $h^{(1-\sigma)} \leftarrow \mathcal{H}(r'_2)$ from the seed for $\mathcal{R}_2$ generating the input r'_2 for $\mathcal{H}$. Then the party $\mathcal{P}_2$ using the PRG $\mathcal{R}_2$ will be able to also unmask $v^{(1-\sigma)}$ by using the seed for $\mathcal{R}_2$ and hence obtain the other $x^{(1-\sigma)}$ as well, violating the security of the OT.

To make the argument precise, we first recall the current assumptions described above: the global parameters p, q, g, and KDF, as well as a generator g_0 of $(\mathbb{F}_p)^\times$, can be *deterministically* chosen in polynomial time, and $(p - 1)/q$ is coprime to q. We construct a prototype algorithm $\mathcal{R}_2^*$ for our PRG as in Algorithm 7; our PRG $\mathcal{R}_2$ is then constructed as the composition $\mathcal{R}_2 = \mathcal{R}_2^* \circ \mathcal{R}_2^\dagger : \{0, 1\}^{4t-1} \to \{0, 1\}^{4t}$ where $\mathcal{R}_2^\dagger : \{0, 1\}^{4t-1} \to \{0, 1\}^{9t}$ is a non-uniformly secure PRG implied by the hypothesis of Theorem 6. Now we have the following result on the $\mathcal{R}_2^*$.

Proposition 4. *For $s = (s_1, s_2, s_3, s_4) \leftarrow_R \{0, 1\}^{9t}$, the output distribution of $\mathcal{R}_2^*(1^\lambda, s)$ is exponentially close to $U[\{0, 1\}^{2t} \times \{0, 1\}^{2t}]$, and the e and $r^\dagger$ computed in $\mathcal{R}_2^*$ satisfy that $\mathcal{H}(r^\dagger) = g^e \bmod p$.*

Algorithm 7: The prototype $\mathcal{R}_2^*$ of our PRG

   Input : 1^λ and seed
$$s = (s_1, s_2, s_3, s_4) \in \{0,1\}^{2t} \times \{0,1\}^{2t} \times \{0,1\}^{3t} \times \{0,1\}^{2t}$$
   Output: $(r_2', r_2'') \in \{0,1\}^{2t} \times \{0,1\}^{2t}$

 1 choose p, q, g, KDF, and g_0 deterministically as in the text
 2 compute the multiplicative inverse d of $(p-1)/q$ modulo q
 3 $e \leftarrow s_1 \bmod q$
 4 $h^\dagger \leftarrow g^e \bmod p$
 5 $e' \leftarrow s_2 \bmod (p-1)$
 6 $h^{\dagger\dagger} \leftarrow (h^\dagger)^d \cdot g_0{}^{qe'} \bmod p$
 7 $r^\dagger \leftarrow h^{\dagger\dagger} + (s_3 \bmod K) \cdot p$ where $K = \lfloor (2^{2t} - 1 - h^{\dagger\dagger})/p \rfloor + 1$
    // we have $0 \le r^\dagger \le 2^{2t} - 1$
 8 return $(r_2', r_2'') \leftarrow (r^\dagger, s_4)$ // identify $r^\dagger$ with a 2t-bit sequence

---

Proof. For the latter part of the statement, we have $r^\dagger \bmod p = h^{\dagger\dagger}$ and

$$(h^{\dagger\dagger})^{(p-1)/q} = (h^\dagger)^{d \cdot (p-1)/q} \cdot g_0{}^{qe' \cdot (p-1)/q} = h^\dagger \cdot g_0{}^{e'(p-1)} = h^\dagger = g^e \text{ in } (\mathbb{F}_p)^\times$$

as $h^\dagger \in \langle g \rangle$ and $d \cdot (p-1)/q \equiv 1 \pmod{q}$. Hence we have $\mathcal{H}(r^\dagger) = g^e \bmod p$ by the construction of $\mathcal{H}$, as desired.

For the former part of the statement, it suffices to show that the distribution of $r^\dagger$ is exponentially close to uniform over $\{0,1\}^{2t}$. Let $f \in \{0, \ldots, p-2\}$ be the discrete logarithm of g with respect to g_0. Then f is a multiple of $(p-1)/q$ as $g^q = 1$ in $\mathbb{F}_p$; we put $f = f'(p-1)/q$ with $1 \le f' \le q-1$. Now both f' and $(p-1)/q$ are coprime to q, so is f.

As s_1 and s_2 are of 2t-bit lengths and $t \ge \lambda$, the distributions of e and e' are exponentially close to uniform over $\{0, \ldots, q-1\}$ and $\{0, \ldots, p-2\}$, respectively. Hence we assume from now that $e \leftarrow_R \{0, \ldots, q-1\}$ and $e' \leftarrow_R \{0, \ldots, p-2\}$ without loss of generality.

We have $h^{\dagger\dagger} = g^{ed} \cdot g_0{}^{qe'} = g_0{}^{fed+qe'}$ in $\mathbb{F}_p$. Let $\beta = fed + qe' \bmod (p-1)$. Then we have $\beta \bmod q = e \cdot fd \bmod q \in \{0, \ldots, q-1\}$. As fd is coprime to q by the argument above, $\beta \bmod q$ is uniformly random (as well as e) and independent of e'. On the other hand, we have $\lfloor \beta/q \rfloor = e' + \lfloor fed/q \rfloor \bmod ((p-1)/q)$. As $e' \leftarrow_R \{0, \ldots, p-2\}$, it follows that the pair $(\beta \bmod q, \lfloor \beta/q \rfloor)$ is also uniformly random, so is β. Hence $h^{\dagger\dagger} = g_0{}^\beta$ is uniformly random over $(\mathbb{F}_p)^\times$.

Moreover, as s_3 has 3t-bit length and $t \ge \lambda$, it follows that, given an $h^{\dagger\dagger}$, the conditional distribution of $r^\dagger$ is exponentially close to uniform over the set $\{r_2' \in \{0,1\}^{2t} \mid r_2' \bmod p = h^{\dagger\dagger}\}$. This implies that, if the distribution of $r_2' \bmod p$ with $r_2' \leftarrow_R \{0,1\}^{2t}$ were identical to the uniform distribution of $h^{\dagger\dagger}$, then the distribution of $r^\dagger$ would be exponentially close to uniform over $\{0,1\}^{2t}$. In fact, as p has t-bit length and $t \ge \lambda$, the distribution of $r_2' \bmod p$ is exponentially close to uniform; therefore the distribution of $r^\dagger$ is indeed exponentially close to uniform, as desired. Hence the former part of the statement holds. This completes the proof of Proposition 4.   □

The former part of Proposition 4 and the non-uniform security of $\mathcal{R}_2^\dagger$ imply that our PRG $\mathcal{R}_2 = \mathcal{R}_2^* \circ \mathcal{R}_2^\dagger$ is also non-uniformly secure. Moreover, when party $\mathcal{P}_2$ in the protocol π_2 uses the PRG $\mathcal{R}_2$ with seed $\widetilde{s}$ to generate the internal randomness $(r_2', r_2'') = (r^\dagger, s_4) \leftarrow \mathcal{R}_2^*(1^\lambda, s)$ with $s \leftarrow \mathcal{R}_2^\dagger(1^\lambda, \widetilde{s})$, the element h is equal to $\mathcal{H}(r_2') = \mathcal{H}(r^\dagger) = g^e \bmod p$ and its discrete logarithm e can be recovered from the seed $\widetilde{s}$ for $\mathcal{R}_2$ by computing $s \leftarrow \mathcal{R}_2^\dagger(1^\lambda, \widetilde{s})$ and then computing e from s as in Line 3 of Algorithm 7. This enables $\mathcal{P}_2$ to obtain $x^{(1-\sigma)}$ as well as $x^{(\sigma)}$ as explained above, which means that now the protocol is not secure against $\mathcal{P}_2$. This completes the proof of Theorem 6.

3.5 Sufficient Conditions for Preserving the Security

To prevent the loss of security as in Theorem 1, here we give some sufficient conditions for a 2PC protocol π and a PRG $\mathcal{R}$ to ensure that $\pi \circ_i \mathcal{R}$ is also secure, as in Theorem 2 in Sect. 1.1. We introduce the following notion.

Definition 1. *We say that a simulator $\mathcal{S}_i$ for party $\mathcal{P}_i$ is with raw randomness, if the randomness for $\mathcal{S}_i$ is of the form (r_i, τ_i) where r_i is the same as the randomness for $\mathcal{P}_i$, and we have $\mathcal{S}_i(1^\lambda, x_i, f_i(\vec{x}); r_i, \tau_i) = \langle r_i, \mathcal{T}_{\mathcal{S}_i}(1^\lambda, x_i, f_i(\vec{x}), r_i; \tau_i)\rangle$ for a PPT algorithm $\mathcal{T}_{\mathcal{S}_i}$, where the notation $\langle r_i, V_i \rangle$ denotes the simulated view for $\mathcal{P}_i$ consisting of the randomness r_i and the remaining part V_i (here the components in $\langle r_i, V_i \rangle$ are appropriately reordered to keep consistency with the syntax in the definition of a party's view).*

Namely, such a simulator $\mathcal{S}_i$ generates the randomness part of $\mathcal{P}_i$'s view by just outputting a part r_i of $\mathcal{S}_i$'s own randomness, and then $\mathcal{S}_i$ generates the other parts of $\mathcal{P}_i$'s view by using the remaining part τ_i of the randomness (in a way specified by the algorithm $\mathcal{T}_{\mathcal{S}_i}$). For example, the simulator $\mathcal{S}$ in the proof of Proposition 1 for the security of protocol π_1 is *not* with raw randomness (as it generates the randomness part $r_1^\dagger$ according to the other part), while the simulator in the security proof of protocol π_2 above given in the original paper [2] is in fact with raw random tape. We give a precise version of Theorem 2.

Theorem 7. *Let π be a 2PC protocol that is information-theoretically secure against a party $\mathcal{P}$ in the semi-honest model where the corresponding simulator is with raw randomness (see above for the terminology). Let $\mathcal{R}$ be a PRG to generate the randomness for $\mathcal{P}$. Suppose moreover that $\ell_{\mathrm{out}}(\lambda) - H_\infty(\mathcal{R}(1^\lambda, *)) \in O(\log \lambda)$ with uniformly random seed for $\mathcal{R}$ where λ denotes the security parameter and $\ell_{\mathrm{out}}(\lambda)$ denotes the bit length of outputs of $\mathcal{R}$. Then, even by generating the randomness for $\mathcal{P}$ using $\mathcal{R}$, the protocol π remains information-theoretically secure against semi-honest $\mathcal{P}$ and the corresponding simulator is with raw randomness.*

Proof. Let $\mathcal{S}$ be the simulator with raw randomness in the hypothesis. By symmetry, we suppose $\mathcal{P} = \mathcal{P}_1$, and we give a simulator $\widetilde{\mathcal{S}}$ for $\mathcal{P}_1$ in the protocol $\pi \circ_1 \mathcal{R}$ as stated. Put $I = \{0,1\}^{\ell_{\mathrm{in}}(\lambda)}$ and $O = \{0,1\}^{\ell_{\mathrm{out}}(\lambda)}$.

Given 1^λ, $\vec{x} = (x_1, x_2)$, a local output o_1 of $\mathcal{P}_1$, and randomness $r_1 \in O$ for $\mathcal{P}_1$ in π, the simulated view for $\mathcal{P}_1$ in π is given by $\langle r_1, \mathcal{T}_{\mathcal{S}}(1^\lambda, x_1, o_1, r_1)\rangle$ (see

Definition 1 for the notations). On the other hand, let $V_{\text{real}}(1^\lambda, \vec{x}, r_1)$ denote the random variable of the view for $\mathcal{P}_1$ except the randomness r_1 in a real execution of π with input pair $\vec{x}$ and randomness r_1 for $\mathcal{P}_1$. Then the view for $\mathcal{P}_1$ in a real π is $\langle r_1, V_{\text{real}}(1^\lambda, \vec{x}, r_1) \rangle$. Now we define the simulator $\widetilde{S}$ in $\pi \circ_1 \mathcal{R}$ as follows:

– Given 1^λ and a local input/output pair (x_1, o_1) as input, $\widetilde{S}$ chooses $\widetilde{r}_1 \leftarrow_R I$, computes $r_1 \leftarrow \mathcal{R}(1^\lambda, \widetilde{r}_1)$, and outputs $\langle \widetilde{r}_1, \mathcal{T}_S(1^\lambda, x_1, o_1, r_1) \rangle$.

This $\widetilde{S}$ is with raw randomness by the construction.

Note that the view for $\mathcal{P}_1$ in real $\pi \circ_1 \mathcal{R}$ is given by $\langle \widetilde{r}_1, V_{\text{real}}(1^\lambda, \vec{x}, \mathcal{R}(1^\lambda, \widetilde{r}_1)) \rangle$. Now let Δ and $\widetilde{\Delta}$ denote the statistical distances between the real and simulated views for $\mathcal{P}_1$ in π and in $\pi \circ_1 \mathcal{R}$, respectively, for given 1^λ, $\vec{x} = (x_1, x_2)$, and o_1. Then we have the following (where notations 1^λ are omitted):

$$2\widetilde{\Delta} = \sum_{\widetilde{s}_1 \in I, V_1} |\Pr[\langle \widetilde{r}_1, \mathcal{T}_S(x_1, o_1, \mathcal{R}(\widetilde{r}_1)) \rangle = \langle \widetilde{s}_1, V_1 \rangle]$$

$$- \Pr[\langle \widetilde{r}_1, V_{\text{real}}(\vec{x}, \mathcal{R}(\widetilde{r}_1)) \rangle = \langle \widetilde{s}_1, V_1 \rangle]|$$

$$= \sum_{\widetilde{s}_1 \in I, V_1} \left| \frac{1}{|I|} \Pr[\mathcal{T}_S(x_1, o_1, \mathcal{R}(\widetilde{s}_1)) = V_1] - \frac{1}{|I|} \Pr[V_{\text{real}}(\vec{x}, \mathcal{R}(\widetilde{s}_1)) = V_1] \right|$$

$$= \frac{1}{|I|} \sum_{s_1 \in O, V_1} |I_{s_1}| \cdot |\Pr[\mathcal{T}_S(x_1, o_1, s_1) = V_1] - \Pr[V_{\text{real}}(\vec{x}, s_1) = V_1]|$$

where we write $I_{s_1} = \{\widetilde{s}_1 \in I \mid \mathcal{R}(\widetilde{s}_1) = s_1\}$. Now we have $|I_{s_1}|/|I| \leq 2^{-H_\infty(\mathcal{R})}$ for each s_1 (where $H_\infty(\mathcal{R}) = H_\infty(\mathcal{R}(1^\lambda, *))$) by the definition of min-entropy, therefore

$$2\widetilde{\Delta} \leq 2^{-H_\infty(\mathcal{R})} \sum_{s_1 \in O, V_1} |\Pr[\mathcal{T}_S(x_1, o_1, s_1) = V_1] - \Pr[V_{\text{real}}(\vec{x}, s_1) = V_1]| \ .$$

On the other hand, we have

$$2\Delta$$

$$= \sum_{s_1 \in O, V_1} |\Pr[\langle r_1, \mathcal{T}_S(x_1, o_1, r_1) \rangle = \langle s_1, V_1 \rangle] - \Pr[\langle r_1, V_{\text{real}}(\vec{x}, r_1) \rangle = \langle s_1, V_1 \rangle]|$$

$$= \sum_{s_1 \in O, V_1} \left| \frac{1}{|O|} \Pr[\mathcal{T}_S(x_1, o_1, s_1) = V_1] - \frac{1}{|O|} \Pr[V_{\text{real}}(\vec{x}, s_1) = V_1] \right|$$

$$= \frac{1}{|O|} \sum_{s_1 \in O, V_1} |\Pr[\mathcal{T}_S(x_1, o_1, s_1) = V_1] - \Pr[V_{\text{real}}(\vec{x}, s_1) = V_1]| \ .$$

Hence we have $\widetilde{\Delta} \leq 2^{-H_\infty(\mathcal{R})} \cdot |O| \cdot \Delta = 2^{\ell_{\text{out}}(\lambda) - H_\infty(\mathcal{R})} \cdot \Delta$. By the hypothesis, Δ is negligible due to the information-theoretic security of π, and $2^{\ell_{\text{out}}(\lambda) - H_\infty(\mathcal{R})} \in 2^{O(\log \lambda)}$ is polynomially bounded in λ. This implies that $\widetilde{\Delta}$ is also negligible, as desired. This completes the proof of Theorem 7.   □

4   Type 2: Non-recognizable "Bad" Randomness

In this and the next sections, we focus on the correctness for PKE schemes[13] with negligible but non-zero decryption error probability, and point out (as mentioned in Sect. 1.1) that the use of a secure PRG may violate the correctness.

First we introduce some terminology. A PKE scheme $\Pi = (\mathsf{Gen}, \mathsf{Enc}, \mathsf{Dec})$ consists of three PPT algorithms as follows; $\mathsf{Gen}(1^\lambda)$ outputs a pair $(\mathsf{pk}, \mathsf{sk})$ of a public key pk and a secret key sk; $\mathsf{Enc}_{\mathsf{pk}}(m)$ for a plaintext m outputs a ciphertext c; and $\mathsf{Dec}_{\mathsf{sk}}(c)$ deterministically outputs either a plaintext or a "decryption failure" symbol $\bot$. We say that a key pair $(\mathsf{pk}, \mathsf{sk})$ for a PKE scheme $\Pi = (\mathsf{Gen}, \mathsf{Enc}, \mathsf{Dec})$ is $\alpha(\lambda)$-correct, if

$$\Pr[\mathsf{Dec}_{\mathsf{sk}}(\mathsf{Enc}_{\mathsf{pk}}(m)) = m] \geq \alpha(\lambda) \text{ for any plaintext } m$$

where the probability is taken for the randomness in Enc. Here "perfectly correct" means 1-correct; we also say that Π is perfectly correct, if all key pairs are perfectly correct. On the other hand, we say that $(\mathsf{pk}, \mathsf{sk})$ is $\beta(\lambda)$-erroneous, if

$$\Pr[\mathsf{Dec}_{\mathsf{sk}}(\mathsf{Enc}_{\mathsf{pk}}(m)) \neq m] \geq \beta(\lambda) \text{ for at least one plaintext } m.$$

Here we show the following result, which is a precise version of Theorem 3:

Theorem 8. *Assume that there exist a perfectly correct PKE scheme Π^* for any (polynomially bounded) choice of plaintext length[14] and a (uniformly or non-uniformly) secure PRG $\mathcal{R}^*$ for any choices of $\ell_{\text{in}}^*(\lambda)$ and $\ell_{\text{out}}^*(\lambda)$ (satisfying the constraints in PRGs). Then there exists a pair of a PKE scheme $\Pi = (\mathsf{Gen}, \mathsf{Enc}, \mathsf{Dec})$ and a secure PRG $\mathcal{R}$ with the following two properties:*

- *The original Gen generates a not perfectly correct key pair with only exponentially small probability.*
- *When the PRG $\mathcal{R}$ is used in Gen, all key pairs generated by the resulting Gen are 1-erroneous.*

Proof. We assume that $\ell_{\text{out}}^*(\lambda) - \ell_{\text{in}}^*(\lambda) \geq \lambda$ for the PRG $\mathcal{R}^*$ and that the PKE scheme $\Pi^* = (\mathsf{Gen}^*, \mathsf{Enc}^*, \mathsf{Dec}^*)$ has plaintext space $\{0,1\}^{\ell_{\text{in}}^*(\lambda)}$ in the hypothesis of the theorem. We construct the PKE scheme Π in the theorem by modifying Π^* as follows:

- A public key pk for Π consists of a public key pk^* for Π^* and $r \leftarrow_R \{0,1\}^{\ell_{\text{out}}^*(\lambda)}$; $\mathsf{pk} = (\mathsf{pk}^*, r)$. The secret key $\mathsf{sk} = \mathsf{sk}^*$ is not changed.
- For a plaintext $m \in \{0,1\}^{\ell_{\text{in}}^*(\lambda)}$, the encryption algorithm Enc first checks if $\mathcal{R}^*(1^\lambda, m) = r$ or not. If $\mathcal{R}^*(1^\lambda, m) \neq r$, then encryption and decryption are performed in the same way as Π^*. If $\mathcal{R}^*(1^\lambda, m) = r$, then Enc outputs a broken ciphertext (say $\bot$) which always yields decryption error.

---

[13] As the security is not the central topic here, we just implicitly assume IND-CPA security for the PKE schemes in the following arguments.

[14] Again, such a PKE scheme can be obtained via a hybrid argument (cf. Sect. 5.2.5.3 of [16]) from a perfectly correct PKE scheme with 1-bit plaintexts.

As $\ell_{\mathrm{out}}^*(\lambda) - \ell_{\mathrm{in}}^*(\lambda) \geq \lambda$, the probability that the component r of pk is in the range of $\mathcal{R}^*$ is at most $2^{-\lambda}$. As the behavior of Π coincides with Π^* whenever r is not in the range of $\mathcal{R}^*$, the requirement for correctness of Π is satisfied.

We define the PRG $\mathcal{R}$ in a way that, it ideally samples the internal randomness r_{gen} for Gen^* and samples $r \in \{0,1\}^{\ell_{\mathrm{out}}^*(\lambda)}$ by $r \leftarrow \mathcal{R}^*(1^\lambda, s)$ with $s \leftarrow_R \{0,1\}^{\ell_{\mathrm{in}}^*(\lambda)}$; $(r_{\mathsf{gen}}, r) \leftarrow \mathcal{R}(1^\lambda, (r_{\mathsf{gen}}, s))$.[15] Then the modified key generation algorithm chooses the components pk^* and r of pk by using the two output components of $\mathcal{R}$, respectively. Note that the security of $\mathcal{R}^*$ implies the security of $\mathcal{R}$ straightforwardly. Now for any public key $\mathsf{pk} = (\mathsf{pk}^*, r)$ in Π generated by using $\mathcal{R}$ with seed (r_{gen}, s) as above, we have $r = \mathcal{R}^*(1^\lambda, s)$ by the construction, therefore decryption error will occur with probability 1 for plaintext $m = s$. Hence, now any key pair for Π is 1-erroneous, and the claim holds.   □

5   Type 3: Implicit Non-uniform Distinguishers

In this section, we continue to focus on the correctness for PKE schemes with negligible errors, but here we deal with the randomness in the encryption algorithm instead of the key generation studied in the previous section. We point out the implicit relation to non-uniform security of PRGs, and show the following result which is a precise version of Theorem 4.

Theorem 9. *Assume that there exist a perfectly correct PKE scheme Π^* for any (polynomially bounded) choice of plaintext length. Assume moreover that there exists a uniformly secure PRG $\mathcal{R}^*$ that is not non-uniformly secure, for any choices of $\ell_{\mathrm{in}}^*(\lambda)$ and $\ell_{\mathrm{out}}^*(\lambda)$ (satisfying the constraints in PRGs). Then there exist a PKE scheme $\Pi = (\mathsf{Gen}, \mathsf{Enc}, \mathsf{Dec})$ and a uniformly secure PRG $\mathcal{R}$ with the following two properties:*

- *All key pairs of Π are $(1 - \varepsilon(\lambda))$-correct for an exponentially small $\varepsilon(\lambda)$.*
- *When the PRG $\mathcal{R}$ is used in Enc of Π, all key pairs are $\beta(\lambda)$-erroneous with respect to the resulting Enc for a non-negligible $\beta(\lambda)$.*

We explain an outline of the proof. First, by the hypothesis on $\mathcal{R}^*$, there is a PPT non-uniform distinguisher $\mathcal{D}^*$ for $\mathcal{R}^*$ with non-negligible advantage. We assume that the PKE scheme $\Pi^* = (\mathsf{Gen}^*, \mathsf{Enc}^*, \mathsf{Dec}^*)$ in the hypothesis has plaintext space involving the advice for $\mathcal{D}^*$. The PKE scheme Π has the same key generation and decryption algorithms as Π^*.

The encryption algorithm Enc for Π is defined by modifying Enc^* as follows. For the internal randomness, two blocks called Block k ($k = 0, 1$) of polynomially many random bit sequences is added, each of which follows a probability distribution X_k. Originally, X_0 and X_1 are identical and uniform. Then, given a plaintext m, Enc first tries to distinguish the distributions X_0 and X_1 by using the polynomially many random samples provided in Blocks 0 and 1. Here Enc uses the distinguisher $\mathcal{D}^*$ with advice m. If $\mathcal{D}^*$ detects a significant bias between

---

[15] The technical constraint for $\mathcal{R}$ that the seed length should be a strictly increasing function of λ can be ensured by adjusting the seed length of $\mathcal{R}^*$.

the two blocks then Enc outputs a broken ciphertext (say $\perp$) that always yields decryption error; otherwise Enc encrypts m in the same way as Enc^*.

In the original Enc, X_0 and X_1 are identical, therefore (if the size of two blocks is sufficiently large) $\mathcal{D}^*$ detects a significant bias with only exponentially small probability whatever the plaintext (the advice for $\mathcal{D}^*$) is. This implies the first condition in the statement. On the other hand, we construct the PRG $\mathcal{R}$ in a way that $\mathcal{R}$ replaces the distribution X_0 with the output distribution of $\mathcal{R}^*$ while it keeps the distribution X_1 unchanged (the standard hybrid argument implies that $\mathcal{R}$ is uniformly secure as well as $\mathcal{R}^*$). When the $\mathcal{R}$ is applied to Enc (denoted by Enc'), $\mathcal{D}^*$ with the correct advice m can distinguish the output distribution X_0 of $\mathcal{R}^*$ from the uniform distribution X_1, therefore (if the size of two blocks is sufficiently large) the $\mathcal{D}^*$ inside Enc' detects a significant bias with non-negligible probability. As this case yields decryption error, the decryption error probability of Enc' for the plaintext m becomes non-negligible, implying the second condition in the statement. Hence the claim holds.

Now we move to a precise proof of the theorem.

Proof (Theorem 9). First, by the hypothesis on $\mathcal{R}^*$, there is a PPT non-uniform distinguisher $\mathcal{D}^*$ for $\mathcal{R}^*$ with non-negligible advantage; that is, there are an integer $k \geq 1$ and infinitely many λ's for which the advantage is larger than λ^{-k}. We focus on those λ's from now on. Let $Q(\lambda)$ be a polynomial bound for the length of advice which the PPT $\mathcal{D}^*$ can read. We assume that the PKE scheme $\Pi^* = (\mathsf{Gen}^*, \mathsf{Enc}^*, \mathsf{Dec}^*)$ in the hypothesis has plaintext space $\{0,1\}^{Q(\lambda)}$. The PKE scheme Π has the same key generation and decryption algorithms as Π^*.

The encryption algorithm Enc for Π is defined as in Algorithm 8, where we set $\rho(\lambda) = 16\lambda^{2k+1}$ and $\theta(\lambda) = 8\lambda^{k+1}$. Roughly summarizing, the internal randomness for Enc involves (besides the other components) uniformly random $\ell_{\mathrm{out}}^*(\lambda)$-bit sequences $r_{i,j}$ with $i \in \{0,1\}$ and $1 \leq j \leq \rho(\lambda)$. Before encrypting plaintext m, for each i, Enc runs $\mathcal{D}^*$ (with randomly fixed prefix m^* of m as advice) $\rho(\lambda)$ times independently for inputs $r_{i,1}, \ldots, r_{i,\rho(\lambda)}$ and counts the number μ_i of output bits being 1. If the numbers μ_0 and μ_1 differ at most $\theta(\lambda)$, then Enc encrypts m in the same way as Π^*. Otherwise, Enc outputs a broken ciphertext (say $\perp$) that always yields decryption error.

Intuitively, when the $r_{i,j}$'s are ideally random, all the corresponding output distributions of $\mathcal{D}^*$ are identical, therefore the difference of the numbers of 1's in "$i=0$ part" and "$i=1$ part" will be small with high probability, implying the required correctness for Π. Precisely, the opposite condition $|\mu_0 - \mu_1| > \theta(\lambda)$ implies that $|\mu_i - \rho(\lambda) \cdot p_1| > \theta(\lambda)/2$ for at least one $i \in \{0,1\}$, where p_1 denotes the probability that $\mathcal{D}^*$ outputs 1 for a uniformly random input from $\{0,1\}^{\ell_{\mathrm{out}}^*(\lambda)}$. By Hoeffding's Inequality (Lemma 2 below) with $n = \rho(\lambda) = 16\lambda^{2k+1}$ and $nt = \theta(\lambda)/2 = 4\lambda^{k+1}$ (hence $nt^2 = (nt)^2/n = \lambda$), the latter condition holds with probability at most $2 \cdot 2\exp(-2nt^2) = 4e^{-2\lambda}$. Hence the behavior of Π deviates from the correct Π^* with exponentially small probability, as desired.

Lemma 2 (Hoeffding's Inequality [19]). *Let $X_1, \ldots, X_n$ be independent random variables, each taking the value 1 with probability p and the value 0*

Algorithm 8: Encryption algorithm Enc for our PKE scheme Π

Input : 1^λ and plaintext $m \in \{0,1\}^{Q(\lambda)}$
(the internal randomness involves components $r_{i,j} \in \{0,1\}^{\ell^*_{\text{out}}(\lambda)}$
with $i \in \{0,1\}$ and $1 \le j \le \rho(\lambda)$, as well as the other components)
Output: (possibly broken) ciphertext c
1 choose a prefix m^* of m uniformly at random
2 **for** $i \leftarrow 0$ **to** 1 **do**
3 $\quad$ $\mu_i \leftarrow 0$
4 $\quad$ **for** $j \leftarrow 1$ **to** $\rho(\lambda)$ **do**
5 $\quad\quad$ **if** $\mathcal{D}^{*(m^*)}(1^\lambda, r_{i,j})$ *(with fresh randomness)* outputs 1 **then**
6 $\quad\quad\quad$ $\mu_i \leftarrow \mu_i + 1$
7 $\quad\quad$ **end**
8 $\quad$ **end**
9 **end**
10 **if** $|\mu_0 - \mu_1| \le \theta(\lambda)$ **then**
11 $\quad$ return $c \leftarrow \text{Enc}^*(m)$
12 **else**
13 $\quad$ return a broken ciphertext c (yielding decryption error)
14 **end**

---

with probability $1 - p$ for a common p. Then for any $t > 0$, we have

$$\Pr\left[\left|\frac{X_1 + \cdots + X_n}{n} - p\right| \ge t\right] \le 2\exp\left(-2nt^2\right).$$

On the other hand, the seed for our PRG $\mathcal{R}$ is the same as the internal randomness for Enc except that the components $r_{0,1}, \ldots, r_{0,\rho(\lambda)}$ are replaced with independent and uniformly random $s_1, \ldots, s_{\rho(\lambda)} \in \{0,1\}^{\ell^*_{\text{in}}(\lambda)}$. When $\mathcal{R}$ generates the internal randomness for Enc, each $r_{0,j}$ is chosen by $r_{0,j} \leftarrow \mathcal{R}^*(1^\lambda, s_j)$, while the other components, including the $r_{1,j}$'s, are ideally sampled. By a standard hybrid argument, the uniform security of $\mathcal{R}^*$ implies the uniform security of $\mathcal{R}$. (We note that, the technical constraint for the seed length to be a strictly increasing function of λ can be ensured by adding some dummy components to the seed.) Intuitively, as $\mathcal{D}^*$ can distinguish the PRG $\mathcal{R}^*$ from ideal randomness, now the difference of the numbers of 1's in the pseudorandom "$i = 0$ part" and the ideally random "$i = 1$ part" will be large with high probability, which yields a broken ciphertext with high probability as well.

To make the argument precise, let m^* be a prefix of some plaintext m that is the correct advice for $\mathcal{D}^*$ to distinguish $\mathcal{R}^*$. Let p_0 denotes the probability that $\mathcal{D}^*$ outputs 0 for an input $\mathcal{R}^*(1^\lambda, s)$ with $s \leftarrow_R \{0,1\}^{\ell^*_{\text{in}}(\lambda)}$, while p_1 is the same as above. Then the hypothesis on $\mathcal{D}^*$ implies that $|p_0 - p_1| > \lambda^{-k}$ and hence $|\rho(\lambda) \cdot p_0 - \rho(\lambda) \cdot p_1| > \rho(\lambda)\lambda^{-k} = 2\theta(\lambda)$ for this choice of m^*. Now the opposite condition $|\mu_0 - \mu_1| \le \theta(\lambda)$ implies that $|\mu_i - \rho(\lambda) \cdot p_i| > \theta(\lambda)/2$ for at least one $i \in \{0,1\}$. Hoeffding's Inequality with the same parameters n, t as above also implies that the latter condition holds with probability at most $4e^{-2\lambda}$. By taking into account the choice of m^* among the $Q(\lambda) + 1$ candidates, it follows that decryption error occurs for the m with probability at least

$$\beta(\lambda) = \frac{1 - 4e^{-2\lambda}}{Q(\lambda) + 1} \ .$$

We moreover set $\beta(\lambda) = 0$ for the remaining λ's not focused in the argument above; the resulting $\beta(\lambda)$ is still a non-negligible function. Hence all key pairs are $\beta(\lambda)$-erroneous when the PRG $\mathcal{R}$ is applied, as desired. This completes the proof of Theorem 9.   □

From now, given an individual correct PKE scheme $\Pi = (\mathsf{Gen}, \mathsf{Enc}, \mathsf{Dec})$, we provide a possible strategy to generically convert (depending on the Π) a uniformly secure PRG $\mathcal{R}$ into a uniformly secure PRG $\overline{\mathcal{R}}$ that preserves the correctness when applied to generate the randomness for Enc.

We introduce some notations. Let $(\mathsf{pk}, \mathsf{sk})$ be a key pair for Π with security parameter λ, let m be a plaintext, and let $r \in \{0, 1\}^{L(\lambda)}$ where $L(\lambda)$ is the length of randomness for Enc. We define a function $\mathcal{F}_{\lambda, \mathsf{pk}, \mathsf{sk}, m, r} \colon \{0, 1\}^{L(\lambda)} \to \{0, 1\}$ by

$$\mathcal{F}_{\lambda, \mathsf{pk}, \mathsf{sk}, m, r}(r^\dagger) = \begin{cases} 0 & \text{if } \mathsf{Dec}_\mathsf{sk}(\mathsf{Enc}_\mathsf{pk}(m; r \oplus r^\dagger)) = m \ , \\ 1 & \text{if } \mathsf{Dec}_\mathsf{sk}(\mathsf{Enc}_\mathsf{pk}(m; r \oplus r^\dagger)) \neq m \ . \end{cases}$$

We say that a PRG $\mathcal{R}^\dagger$ with output length $\ell_{\mathsf{out}}^\dagger(\lambda) = L(\lambda)$ $\eta(\lambda)$-*fools the function family* $\mathcal{F}$, if for any $\mathsf{ind} = (\lambda, \mathsf{pk}, \mathsf{sk}, m, r)$ as above, we have

$$\left| \Pr\left[\mathcal{F}_{\mathsf{ind}}(\mathcal{R}^\dagger(1^\lambda, U[\{0,1\}^{\ell_{\mathsf{in}}^\dagger(\lambda)}])) = 1 \right] - \Pr\left[\mathcal{F}_{\mathsf{ind}}(U[\{0,1\}^{L(\lambda)}]) = 1 \right] \right| \leq \eta(\lambda) \ .$$

Then we define the PRG[16] $\overline{\mathcal{R}}$ with seed $\overline{s} = (s, s^\dagger) \in \{0, 1\}^{\ell_{\mathsf{in}}(\lambda)} \times \{0, 1\}^{\ell_{\mathsf{in}}^\dagger(\lambda)}$ by

$$\overline{\mathcal{R}}(1^\lambda, \overline{s}) = \mathcal{R}(1^\lambda, s) \oplus \mathcal{R}^\dagger(1^\lambda, s^\dagger) \ .$$

Such an XOR-ing construction of a PRG combining two PRGs of different types has been studied in the literature in some different contexts; for example, this is similar to the "dual-mode PRG" in [25]. Now if $\mathcal{R}^\dagger$ is PPT, then the security $\mathcal{R}(1^\lambda, U[\{0,1\}^{\ell_{\mathsf{in}}(\lambda)}]) \overset{\mathsf{u.c}}{\approx} U[\{0,1\}^{L(\lambda)}]$ of $\mathcal{R}$ implies that

$$\overline{\mathcal{R}}(1^\lambda, U[\{0,1\}^{\overline{\ell}_{\mathsf{in}}(\lambda)}]) \overset{\mathsf{u.c}}{\approx} U[\{0,1\}^{L(\lambda)}] \oplus \mathcal{R}^\dagger(1^\lambda, U[\{0,1\}^{\ell_{\mathsf{in}}^\dagger(\lambda)}]) = U[\{0,1\}^{L(\lambda)}] \ ,$$

i.e., $\overline{R}$ is uniformly secure. Moreover, we have the following result.

Theorem 10. *Suppose that the PRG* $\mathcal{R}^\dagger$ *$\eta(\lambda)$-fools the function family $\mathcal{F}$ (see above for the terminology) and a key pair* $(\mathsf{pk}, \mathsf{sk})$ *of Π with security parameter λ is $\alpha(\lambda)$-correct. Then, when the randomness for* Enc *is generated by the PRG* $\overline{\mathcal{R}}$, *the key pair* $(\mathsf{pk}, \mathsf{sk})$ *becomes* $(\alpha(\lambda) - \eta(\lambda))$-*correct.*

---

[16] We assume that the PRG $\overline{\mathcal{R}}$ satisfies the constraint $\overline{\ell}_{\mathsf{in}}(\lambda) = \ell_{\mathsf{in}}(\lambda) + \ell_{\mathsf{in}}^\dagger(\lambda) < \overline{\ell}_{\mathsf{out}}(\lambda) = L(\lambda)$ for input/output lengths.

Proof. Let m be any plaintext. We have to evaluate the probability

$$\varepsilon = \Pr[\mathsf{Dec}_{\mathsf{sk}}(\mathsf{Enc}_{\mathsf{pk}}(m; \overline{\mathcal{R}}(1^\lambda, U[\{0,1\}^{\overline{\ell}_{\mathrm{in}}(\lambda)}]))) \neq m]$$

$$= \sum_s 2^{-\ell_{\mathrm{in}}(\lambda)} \Pr[\mathsf{Dec}_{\mathsf{sk}}(\mathsf{Enc}_{\mathsf{pk}}(m; \mathcal{R}(1^\lambda, s) \oplus \mathcal{R}^\dagger(1^\lambda, U[\{0,1\}^{\ell_{\mathrm{in}}^\dagger(\lambda)}]))) \neq m]$$

$$= \sum_s 2^{-\ell_{\mathrm{in}}(\lambda)} \Pr[\mathcal{F}_{\mathcal{R}(1^\lambda, s)}(\mathcal{R}^\dagger(1^\lambda, U[\{0,1\}^{\ell_{\mathrm{in}}^\dagger(\lambda)}])) = 1]$$

where s runs over $\{0,1\}^{\ell_{\mathrm{in}}(\lambda)}$ and we write $\mathcal{F}_r = \mathcal{F}_{\lambda, \mathsf{pk}, \mathsf{sk}, m, r}$. Now, as $\mathcal{R}^\dagger$ $\eta(\lambda)$-fools the function family $\mathcal{F}$ by the hypothesis, we have

$$\varepsilon \leq 2^{-\ell_{\mathrm{in}}(\lambda)} \sum_s \left(\Pr[\mathcal{F}_{\mathcal{R}(1^\lambda, s)}(U[\{0,1\}^{L(\lambda)}]) = 1] + \eta(\lambda) \right)$$

$$= \eta(\lambda) + 2^{-\ell_{\mathrm{in}}(\lambda)} \sum_s \Pr[\mathsf{Dec}_{\mathsf{sk}}(\mathsf{Enc}_{\mathsf{pk}}(m; \mathcal{R}(1^\lambda, s) \oplus U[\{0,1\}^{L(\lambda)}])) \neq m] \ .$$

As each $\mathcal{R}(1^\lambda, s) \oplus U[\{0,1\}^{L(\lambda)}]$ is identical to $U[\{0,1\}^{L(\lambda)}]$, it follows that

$$\varepsilon \leq \eta(\lambda) + \Pr[\mathsf{Dec}_{\mathsf{sk}}(\mathsf{Enc}_{\mathsf{pk}}(m)) \neq m] \leq \eta(\lambda) + (1 - \alpha(\lambda)) = 1 - (\alpha(\lambda) - \eta(\lambda))$$

by the hypothesis on $(\mathsf{pk}, \mathsf{sk})$. This implies the claim.   □

Theorem 10 reduces our task to develop a "special-purpose" PRG $\mathcal{R}^\dagger$ that fools the *explicitly restricted* function family $\mathcal{F}$. The complexity of each function in the family is almost the sum of complexity of Enc, Dec, and the given PRG $\mathcal{R}$, which will be fairly small when the PKE scheme Π and the PRG $\mathcal{R}$ are efficient. Developing a PRG fooling this function family might be a relatively easier task than developing a non-uniformly secure PRG, the latter having to fool *any* non-uniform distinguisher with *arbitrarily large* (polynomially bounded) *complexity*. To develop such a special-purpose PRG $\mathcal{R}^\dagger$, some techniques in the area of derandomization such as those in [24, 27] would be useful.

Acknowledgements. The author thanks all the members of a study group "Shin-Akarui-Angou-Benkyoukai", in particular Shota Yamada, Tadanori Teruya, Kazumasa Shinagawa, Takashi Yamakawa, Takahiro Matsuda, Yusuke Sakai, Keita Emura, and Goichiro Hanaoka, for fruitful discussions. This work was supported by JST PRESTO Grant Number JPMJPR14E8, by JST CREST Grant Number JPMJCR14D6, and by JST CREST Grant Number JPMJCR19F6.

A   A "Natural" Variant of Algorithm 1

Here we give a "natural" variant of 2PC protocol π_1 defined in Sect. 3.2 (Algorithm 1) where the inputs for two parties are not correlated and the parties have outputs in the protocol. The modified protocol is given in Algorithm 9. Here $\mathcal{F}_{\mathsf{EQ}}$ denotes an ideal functionality for two-party equality test, where the common output $\beta = 1$ (respectively, $\beta = 0$) means that the two inputs are equal (respectively, not equal).

Algorithm 9: A variant of protocol π_1

Input : ($\mathcal{P}_1$) a non-negative integer $N < 2^{2\lambda}$
    ($\mathcal{P}_2$) λ-bit integers p, q
Output: (common to $\mathcal{P}_1$ and $\mathcal{P}_2$) an integer $\iota \in \{0, 1, 2\}$
1 (By $\mathcal{P}_2$) **if** $p \geq q$, *or p or q is not a prime $\equiv 3$* (mod 4) **then**
2 | halt the protocol, where both parties output $\iota = 2$
3 **end**
4 (By $\mathcal{P}_1$ and $\mathcal{P}_2$) execute $\mathcal{F}_{\mathsf{EQ}}(N, pq)$ and obtain common output β
5 **if** $\beta = 0$ **then**
6 | halt the protocol, where both parties output $\iota = 1$
7 **end**
8 (By $\mathcal{P}_1$ and $\mathcal{P}_2$) execute the protocol π_1 with inputs N and (p, q)
9 halt the protocol, where both parties output $\iota = 0$

In the part of the protocol before executing π_1, the two parties check if their inputs satisfy the required conditions in the original protocol π_1. More precisely, first, the input (p, q) for $\mathcal{P}_2$ in π_1 should satisfy that $p < q$, p and q are primes, and $p \equiv q \equiv 3$ (mod 4). In the protocol here, $\mathcal{P}_2$ first checks if these conditions hold, and if it fails then the protocol halts at this step. Secondly, assuming the conditions for $\mathcal{P}_2$'s input, the input N for $\mathcal{P}_1$ should satisfy that $N = pq$. This condition is checked by using $\mathcal{F}_{\mathsf{EQ}}$, and if it fails then the protocol halts at this step. Once these conditions have been verified, the parties can execute the protocol π_1 with the correct input pair. By focusing on the input pairs satisfying the conditions in π_1, the protocol here inherits from π_1 the property that the security will be lost by applying a certain secure PRG to the randomness for $\mathcal{P}_1$.

For the security against $\mathcal{P}_1$, if the output is $\iota = 2$, then $\mathcal{P}_1$ receives no message and hence the security holds trivially. If $\iota = 1$, then $\mathcal{P}_1$ just participates in the execution of $\mathcal{F}_{\mathsf{EQ}}$ and obtains the output $\beta = 0$, therefore the security follows from the security of $\mathcal{F}_{\mathsf{EQ}}$. Finally, if $\iota = 0$, then $\mathcal{P}_1$ participates in the execution of $\mathcal{F}_{\mathsf{EQ}}$ with output being always $\beta = 1$ and also participates in π_1, therefore the security also follows from the security of $\mathcal{F}_{\mathsf{EQ}}$ and π_1.

For the sake of completeness, we describe in Algorithm 10 a well-known implementation of $\mathcal{F}_{\mathsf{EQ}}$ using the lifted-ElGamal cryptosystem. Here $\boxplus$ and $\boxdot$ denote the homomorphic addition and homomorphic scalar multiplication, respectively. We analyze the behavior of the protocol as follows:

- If $x_1 = x_2$, then the ciphertext c in the protocol is a random ciphertext of plaintext $r(x_2 - r_1) = 0$ (note that the randomness in c has also been perfectly rerandomized, as a random ciphertext $\mathsf{Enc}(0)$ was homomorphically added). Hence the protocol outputs the correct value $\beta = 1$, and now the message received by $\mathcal{P}_1$ is a random ciphertext $\mathsf{Enc}(0)$ as mentioned above, which can be perfectly simulated.
- If $x_1 \neq x_2$, then $x_2 - x_1 \in (\mathbb{F}_P)^\times$ by the property $P > 2^{2\lambda+1}$, while $r \leftarrow_R (\mathbb{F}_P)^\times$. Therefore the plaintext $r(x_2 - x_1)$ for c is also uniformly random over $(\mathbb{F}_P)^\times$ and hence the protocol outputs the correct value $\beta = 0$ (note

---

Algorithm 10: Implementation of the functionality $\mathcal{F}_{\mathsf{EQ}}$

Input : $(\mathcal{P}_i\ (i=1,2))$ a non-negative integer $x_i < 2^{2\lambda}$
Output: (common to $\mathcal{P}_1$ and $\mathcal{P}_2$) a bit β
1 (By $\mathcal{P}_1$) generate a key pair $(\mathsf{pk},\mathsf{sk})$ for the lifted-ElGamal cryptosystem
   $(\mathsf{Gen},\mathsf{Enc},\mathsf{Dec})$ with plaintext space $\mathbb{F}_P$ of prime order $P > 2^{2\lambda+1}$
2 (By $\mathcal{P}_1$) send pk and $\mathsf{Enc}(-x_1)$ to $\mathcal{P}_2$
3 (By $\mathcal{P}_2$) generate $r \boxdot (\mathsf{Enc}(x_2) \boxplus \mathsf{Enc}(-x_1)) \boxplus \mathsf{Enc}(0) = \mathsf{Enc}(r(x_2 - x_1))$ for
   $r \leftarrow_R (\mathbb{F}_P)^\times$, and send $c \leftarrow \mathsf{Enc}(r(x_2 - x_1))$ to $\mathcal{P}_1$
4 (By $\mathcal{P}_1$) **if** c *is a ciphertext of plaintext* 0 **then**
5 $\quad\big|\quad$ halt the protocol, where both parties output $\beta = 1$
6 **else**
7 $\quad\big|\quad$ halt the protocol, where both parties output $\beta = 0$
8 **end**

---

that, though $r(x_2 - x_1)$ can be large and the lifted-ElGamal cryptosystem enables to efficiently decrypt small plaintexts only, the protocol just checks if the ciphertext c has plaintext 0 or not, which is still efficiently checkable). Moreover, in this case, the received message c is a random ciphertext for a uniformly random non-zero plaintext, which can be perfectly simulated.

Hence the correctness and the security (against $\mathcal{P}_1$) of the implemented $\mathcal{F}_{\mathsf{EQ}}$ have been verified. In particular, the security against $\mathcal{P}_1$ is information-theoretic. Therefore, as well as the original protocol π_1, the variant of π_1 given here also has information-theoretic security against $\mathcal{P}_1$, as desired.

References

1. Asharov, G., Lindell, Y., Schneider, T., Zohner, M.: More efficient oblivious transfer and extensions for faster secure computation. In: 2013 ACM SIGSAC Conference on Computer and Communications Security, CCS 2013, Berlin, Germany, 4–8 November 2013, pp. 535–548 (2013)
2. Asharov, G., Lindell, Y., Schneider, T., Zohner, M.: More efficient oblivious transfer and extensions for faster secure computation. IACR Cryptology ePrint Archive 2013:552 (2013)
3. Barak, B., et al.: Leftover hash lemma, revisited. In: Rogaway, P. (ed.) CRYPTO 2011. LNCS, vol. 6841, pp. 1–20. Springer, Heidelberg (2011). https://doi.org/10.1007/978-3-642-22792-9_1
4. Bernstein, D.J., Lange, T.: Non-uniform cracks in the concrete: the power of free precomputation. In: Sako, K., Sarkar, P. (eds.) ASIACRYPT 2013. LNCS, vol. 8270, pp. 321–340. Springer, Heidelberg (2013). https://doi.org/10.1007/978-3-642-42045-0_17
5. Bitansky, N., Vaikuntanathan, V.: A note on perfect correctness by derandomization. In: Coron, J.-S., Nielsen, J.B. (eds.) EUROCRYPT 2017. LNCS, vol. 10211, pp. 592–606. Springer, Cham (2017). https://doi.org/10.1007/978-3-319-56614-6_20
6. Canetti, R., Goldreich, O., Halevi, S.: The random oracle methodology, revisited. J. ACM **51**(4), 557–594 (2004)

7. De, A., Trevisan, L., Tulsiani, M.: Time space tradeoffs for attacks against one-way functions and PRGs. In: Rabin, T. (ed.) CRYPTO 2010. LNCS, vol. 6223, pp. 649–665. Springer, Heidelberg (2010). https://doi.org/10.1007/978-3-642-14623-7_35

8. Degabriele, J.P., Paterson, K.G., Schuldt, J.C.N., Woodage, J.: Backdoors in pseudorandom number generators: possibility and impossibility results. In: Robshaw, M., Katz, J. (eds.) CRYPTO 2016. LNCS, vol. 9814, pp. 403–432. Springer, Heidelberg (2016). https://doi.org/10.1007/978-3-662-53018-4_15

9. Dodis, Y., Ganesh, C., Golovnev, A., Juels, A., Ristenpart, T.: A formal treatment of backdoored pseudorandom generators. In: Oswald, E., Fischlin, M. (eds.) EUROCRYPT 2015. LNCS, vol. 9056, pp. 101–126. Springer, Heidelberg (2015). https://doi.org/10.1007/978-3-662-46800-5_5

10. Dodis, Y., Ong, S.J., Prabhakaran, M., Sahai, A.: On the (im)possibility of cryptography with imperfect randomness. In: 45th Symposium on Foundations of Computer Science (FOCS 2004), Rome, Italy, 17–19 October 2004, Proceedings, pp. 196–205 (2004)

11. Dodis, Y., Pointcheval, D., Ruhault, S., Vergnaud, D., Wichs, D.: Security analysis of pseudo-random number generators with input: /dev/random is not robust. In: 2013 ACM SIGSAC Conference on Computer and Communications Security, CCS 2013, Berlin, Germany, 4–8 November 2013, pp. 647–658 (2013)

12. Dodis, Y., Yao, Y.: Privacy with imperfect randomness. In: Gennaro, R., Robshaw, M. (eds.) CRYPTO 2015. LNCS, vol. 9216, pp. 463–482. Springer, Heidelberg (2015). https://doi.org/10.1007/978-3-662-48000-7_23

13. Dwork, C., Naor, M., Reingold, O.: Immunizing encryption schemes from decryption errors. In: Cachin, C., Camenisch, J.L. (eds.) EUROCRYPT 2004. LNCS, vol. 3027, pp. 342–360. Springer, Heidelberg (2004). https://doi.org/10.1007/978-3-540-24676-3_21

14. Goldreich, O.: A uniform-complexity treatment of encryption and zero-knowledge. J. Cryptol. 6(1), 21–53 (1993). https://doi.org/10.1007/BF02620230

15. Goldreich, O.: The Foundations of Cryptography - volume 1, Basic Techniques. Cambridge University Press, New York (2001)

16. Goldreich, O.: The Foundations of Cryptography - Volume 2, Basic Applications. Cambridge University Press, New York (2004)

17. Hazay, C., Zarosim, H.: The feasibility of outsourced database search in the plain model. In: Zikas, V., De Prisco, R. (eds.) SCN 2016. LNCS, vol. 9841, pp. 313–332. Springer, Cham (2016). https://doi.org/10.1007/978-3-319-44618-9_17

18. Hirose, S.: Secure block ciphers are not sufficient for one-way hash functions in the Preneel-Govaerts-Vandewalle model. In: Nyberg, K., Heys, H. (eds.) SAC 2002. LNCS, vol. 2595, pp. 339–352. Springer, Heidelberg (2003). https://doi.org/10.1007/3-540-36492-7_22

19. Hoeffding, W.: Probability inequalities for sums of bounded random variables. J. Am. Stat. Assoc. 58(301), 13–30 (1963)

20. Holenstein, T., Renner, R.: One-way secret-key agreement and applications to circuit polarization and immunization of public-key encryption. In: Shoup, V. (ed.) CRYPTO 2005. LNCS, vol. 3621, pp. 478–493. Springer, Heidelberg (2005). https://doi.org/10.1007/11535218_29

21. Howgrave-Graham, N., et al.: The impact of decryption failures on the security of NTRU encryption. In: Boneh, D. (ed.) CRYPTO 2003. LNCS, vol. 2729, pp. 226–246. Springer, Heidelberg (2003). https://doi.org/10.1007/978-3-540-45146-4_14

22. Hub'avcek, P., Wichs, D.: On the communication complexity of secure function evaluation with long output. In: Proceedings of the 2015 Conference on Innovations in Theoretical Computer Science, ITCS 2015, Rehovot, Israel, 11–13 January 2015, pp. 163–172 (2015)

23. Lin, H., Tessaro, S.: Amplification of chosen-ciphertext security. In: Johansson, T., Nguyen, P.Q. (eds.) EUROCRYPT 2013. LNCS, vol. 7881, pp. 503–519. Springer, Heidelberg (2013). https://doi.org/10.1007/978-3-642-38348-9_30

24. Nisan, N., Wigderson, A.: Hardness vs randomness. J. Comput. Syst. Sci. **49**(2), 149–167 (1994)

25. Nuida, K.: How to use pseudorandom generators in unconditional security settings. In: Chow, S.S.M., Liu, J.K., Hui, L.C.K., Yiu, S.M. (eds.) ProvSec 2014. LNCS, vol. 8782, pp. 291–299. Springer, Cham (2014). https://doi.org/10.1007/978-3-319-12475-9_20

26. Pietrzak, K., Skorski, M.: Non-uniform attacks against pseudoentropy. In: 44th International Colloquium on Automata, Languages, and Programming, ICALP 2017, Warsaw, Poland, pp. 39:1–39:13 (2017)

27. Shaltiel, R., Umans, C.: Simple extractors for all min-entropies and a new pseudorandom generator. In: 42nd Annual Symposium on Foundations of Computer Science, FOCS 2001, Las Vegas, Nevada, USA, 14–17 October 2001, pp. 648–657 (2001)

Publicly Verifiable Zero Knowledge from (Collapsing) Blockchains

Alessandra Scafuro[1]([✉]), Luisa Siniscalchi[2], and Ivan Visconti[3]

[1] North Carolina State University, Raleigh, USA
ascafur@ncsu.edu
[2] Concordium Blockchain Research Center, Aarhus University, Aarhus, Denmark
lsiniscalchi@cs.au.dk
[3] DIEM, University of Salerno, Fisciano, Italy
visconti@unisa.it

Abstract. Publicly Verifiable Zero-Knowledge proofs are known to exist only from setup assumptions such as a trusted common reference string or a random oracle. Unfortunately, the former requires a trusted party while the latter does not exist.

Blockchains are distributed systems that already exist and provide certain security properties (under some honest majority assumption), hence, a natural recent research direction has been to use a blockchain as an alternative setup assumption.

In TCC 2017 Goyal and Goyal proposed a construction of a publicly verifiable zero-knowledge (pvZK) proof system for some proof-of-stake blockchains. The zero-knowledge property of their construction however relies on some additional and not fully specified assumptions about the current and future behavior of honest blockchain players.

In this paper we provide several contributions. First, we show that when using a blockchain to design a provably secure protocol, it is dangerous to rely on demanding additional requirements on behaviors of the blockchain players. We do so by showing an "attack of the clones" whereby a malicious verifier can use a smart contract to slyly (not through bribing) clone capabilities of honest stakeholders and use those to invalidate the zero-knowledge property of the proof system by Goyal and Goyal.

Second, we propose a new publicly verifiable zero-knowledge proof system that relies on non-interactive commitments and on an assumption on the min-entropy of some blocks appearing on the blockchain.

Third, motivated by the fact that blockchains are a recent innovation and their resilience in the long run is still controversial, we introduce the concept of collapsing blockchain, and we prove that the zero-knowledge property of our scheme holds even if the blockchain eventually becomes insecure and all blockchain players eventually become dishonest.

Keywords: Publicly verifiable zero knowledge · (Collapsing) blockchain

ⓒ International Association for Cryptologic Research 2021
J. A. Garay (Ed.): PKC 2021, LNCS 12711, pp. 469–498, 2021.
https://doi.org/10.1007/978-3-030-75248-4_17

1 Introduction

Following the success of Bitcoin many other cryptocurrencies based on blockchain technology have been proposed and, despite a few security issues, they are still expanding their networks with gigantic market capitalizations. What is so appealing in decentralized blockchains?

Public Verifiability. One of the most supported answers is the paradigm shift from trust in some entity to "public verifiability". This property allows every one to check that the system works consistently with the pre-specified rules of the game. This makes users willing to be involved in transactions recorded in a blockchain therefore investing their real-world money. In many blockchain applications both anonymity and public verifiability are required, calling for advanced cryptographic primitives such as publicly verifiable zero-knowledge proofs. For example, when the blockchain is used to record payments, confidential transactions are indeed implemented using publicly verifiable zero-knowledge proofs called zk-SNARKs [9,20].

Publicly Verifiable Zero-Knowledge Proofs. Known constructions of publicly verifiable zero-knowledge (pvZK) proofs are instantiated with *non-interactive* zero-knowledge proofs (NIZK) and, as such, require setup assumptions. Indeed, despite a significant effort of the research community, constructions of NIZK proofs either rely on the existence of a trusted common reference string (CRS) computed by a trusted entity or are based on heuristic assumptions (e.g., random oracles). Recent existing work has shown mechanisms to relax the trust assumptions required to generate the CRS [14] or to mitigate the effect of a malicious CRS [26,30]. While this line of work is very promising, it still requires the employment of third entities that help computing the CRS.

Publicly Verifiable Zero-Knowledge Proofs from a "Blockchain Assumption". Since its introduction in 2008 with Nakamoto's protocol [31], blockchain protocols have been scrutinized by many communities, and currently, we have a good understanding of the security properties they provide and the class of adversaries they withstand. In particular, several works from the cryptographic community provided a formalization of the Bitcoin security guarantees [19,32], a formalization of the ideal functionality it implements [5] as well as game-theoretic analysis [3]. Furthermore, new blockchain designs have been proposed, based on different assumptions on the collective power of the adversary. Some prominent examples that are also implemented in practice are Ouroboros [4] and Algorand [22].

Given that blockchains have been formally analyzed and are up and running in practice, a natural question to ask is whether we can use a blockchain as a setup assumption *to replace* trusted setups required for certain cryptographic tasks, particularly, for publicly verifiable zero-knowledge proof systems that are needed the most in blockchain applications.

This question was first investigated by Goyal and Goyal in [23], where they aimed to construct NIZK using as setup the existence of a proof-of-stake (PoS) blockchain. The security of the NIZK proof provided in [23] – that we will denote by GG-NIZK– however is analyzed in a threat model that does not faithfully match the threat model of PoS blockchains, since it considers only static adversaries and additionally requires that honest stakeholder never reveal their secret keys. Specifically, the zero-knowledge property of GG-NIZK is proved in the presence of a *static adversary* who decides in advance which stakeholder will corrupt in its entire attack. This does not match the widely accepted threat model for proof-of-stake blockchains where an adversary is allowed to corrupt stakeholders at any time, and the only restriction is that, at any point, the total amount of stake held by the adversary is a minority of the total stake of the system. Moreover, in the GG-NIZK security analysis, the zero-knowledge property holds under the additional assumption that honest stakeholders will never leak their stakeholder keys, not even when such keys become irrelevant for the blockchain protocol (for example, because there is zero stake associated to them).

It was observed in [34] that the assumption on stakeholder keys further limits the generality of GG-NIZK since it cannot be used in conjunction with *any* proof-of-stake (PoS) blockchain. In particular [34] observes that one could design a PoS blockchain where stakeholders are required to often refresh their stakeholder keys, by regularly publishing new public keys and voiding old keys by posting their secret keys on the blockchain. Such blockchain protocol, while being a potentially valid PoS blockchain protocol, cannot be used to instantiate GG-NIZK.

The full version of [23] has been recently updated [24] adding a section in the appendix where the authors confirm the security of their construction even in light of the counter-example of [34] by stressing that they expect honest stakeholders to delete keys when they lose significance.

In light of the observations of [34] and of the counter-argument of [24], a natural question to ask is whether such additional assumptions/expectations on the behavior of honest stakeholders required in [23,24] could be symptomatic of unexpected security flaws that would manifest when GG-NIZK is executed with a *real blockchain environment, even one that complies with all GG-NIZK assumptions/expectations.* In other words, assuming that the additional restrictions on the power of the adversary and the behavior of honest stakeholders are met, would GG-NIZK be actually secure when executed in the presence of a PoS blockchain that complies with them?

A negative answer to the above question would signify that constructing a publicly verifiable zero-knowledge proof that leverages any blockchain assumption is still an open question.

1.1   Our Contribution

In this paper we target the problem of constructing publicly verifiable zero-knowledge proofs leveraging a blockchain assumption and provide the following contributions.

A More Realistic Blockchain Threat Model. We consider a model where the blockchain can potentially be used to post and fulfill arbitrary smart contracts. Since all existent blockchain protocols either already support or aim to support smart contracts capabilities (e.g., Ethereum Casper, Cardano) and, since smart contracts are among the most appealing feature of blockchains, this model is arguably realistic. Within this model, an adversary can consequently also leverage her ability to publish smart contracts just like any party who uses the blockchain.

Within this threat model, we show that the zero-knowledge property of GG-NIZK is easily violated *even assuming that all restrictions required by the security analysis of GG-NIZK are satisfied*, that is, even assuming that the adversary can only perform static corruption and that honest stakeholders will never reveal their keys. Specifically, we present an adversarial strategy that leverages legitimate smart contracts to collect information that are useful to disturb the security of the external cryptographic protocols that use the blockchain as a building block. We name this type of attacks "attack of the clones" to highlight the adversary's aim to *clone* the capability of a honest player to perform computations using her secret key. However, the smart contract posted by the adversary is completely harmless for a honest stakeholder. Indeed, it does not ask the stakeholder to do anything that will make her lose her stake, or perform any operation against the consensus protocol. Yet, it allows the adversary to break the zero knowledge of the GG-NIZK proof. Our attack leverages a specific dangerous use of stakeholder identifiers in the GG-NIZK. The starting point is that the NIZK proof of [23] includes encryptions of shares of the witness under the public keys inferred by the identifiers of the stakeholders. To break the zero-knowledge property of the NIZK of [23] our attack is rather simple: after the NIZK proof π is received, the adversarial verifier posts a smart contract containing ciphertexts (these are the ciphertext contained in π) and a promised reward (e.g., money, raffle tickets for a vacation in Barbados, etc.) in exchange for decryptions.

Notice that an honest stakeholder participating in this smart contract remains fully honest, does not subtract any resource (unlike in bribing attacks against proof-of-work blockchains) from the participation to the consensus protocol and does not reveal her secret keys to anyone. She just plays with smart contracts as contemplated by the blockchain rules and uses her stake for some harmless entertainment. Indeed, the crux of this attack is that a stakeholder is not aware that an external cryptographic protocol is basing its zero-knowledge property on the assumption that stakeholders would not entertain in smart contracts that are harmless for the underlying blockchain protocol.

One might object that it is plausible that a PoS blockchain would simply forbid the execution of such "weird" smart contracts. However, it is not clear what a "weird" smart contract is, and whether the above smart contract could be redesigned in order to look innocent and harmless (furthermore, the well known DAO attack inflicted to Ethereum suggests that it is unclear whether we are able to identify and stop an harmful smart contract too much in advance).

Our attack is obviously a simple example and after-the-fact can possibly be mitigated, for instance by adding specific further restrictions on how the stakeholder should use her secret keys. However, the point of our attack is not prove that there is no blockchain for which GG-NIZK can be secure. Instead, we want to highlight the vulnerabilities arising when the long-term security of a cryptographic protocol relies on the behavior of blockchain players.

The main lesson of our attack is the following: when designing protocols that leverage a blockchain assumption, one has to consider a threat model where the adversary is allowed to perform the *same actions that are allowed on the blockchain* (e.g., run smart contracts[1]). Note that this should be true even when analyzing the consensus protocol itself. However, since this is out of the scope of this paper, we assume that the underlying blockchain consensus protocol is secure in the presence of smart contracts.

Another lesson to be drawn by our attack is that, when using the blockchain as an underlying assumption, one should take into account the unstable and evolving nature of blockchains. Unlike a common reference string, blockchains evolve over time –due to software updates for example, or governance decisions– stake is transferred among players, new smart contracts are installed etc. Last but not least one might take into account the possibility that a blockchain that todays is reliable tomorrow could collapse and could then be completely controlled by an adversary.

The above attack on the ZK of GG-NIZK leaves open the following natural question.

Can we design a pvZK proof leveraging the existence of blockchains, that makes no particular assumption on the underlying consensus mechanism neither on the way honest keys must be used (for instance, they can still be used in smart contracts)?

Publicly Verifiable Zero Knowledge from a Generic Blockchain in Our Threat Model. As a second contribution we provide a new protocol for pvZK that is secure in the blockchain threat model discussed above even in the presence of adaptive adversaries. To show this security guarantee, we will prove that once the proof (computed using our protocol) is published, it will preserve its security even if the blockchain collapses, that is, even if the adversary corrupts all the players of the blockchain (and gets all the secrets). We now proceed describing our protocol and our blockchain assumption.

A recent work by Choudhuri et al. [16] shows that using a blockchain as a black-box object that provides only a global ledger does not allow to overcome some impossibility results in the plain model and in particular it does not allow

---

[1] We note that this threat model was never considered before. [34] only made observations about additional limitations that GG-NIZK imposes on their underlying blockchain. Instead, in this work we are showing an attack that works for any PoS blockchain (even the ones that comply with GG-NIZK pre-requirement) allowing the execution of such smart contracts.

to construct NIZK proofs. We notice that their argument can be extended also to pvZK proofs (see Sect. 5 for more details). Therefore, in order to build a publicly verifiable zero-knowledge proof system from a blockchain, it seems that one needs to provide more power to the simulator besides black-box access to a global ledger. Thus, following [23] we will assume that the simulator has the power of controlling the honest players. However, unlike [23] we assume that the adversary can adaptively corrupt players and moreover we want our pvZK proof to remain zero knowledge even in case of blockchain failure, in the sense that in the future the adversary might take full control over the blockchain.

To leverage this simulation power while making no assumption on the consensus protocol underlying the blockchain (i.e., we do not assume that the blockchain is based on proof-of-work, proof-of-stake, etc.), we require that the blockchain satisfies a more nuanced notion of chain quality. Very informally (a formal definition is provided in Assumption 1) we assume the blockchain has the following mild structure. First, every block contains a distinguished field v. For concreteness, the reader can assume that this field is the same as the "coinbase" value of any Bitcoin block, and to ease the discussion, in the text that follows, we will call this field wallet. Our blockchain assumption, very roughly, is that there exists a parameter d, such that, for any sequence of d blocks, considering the new wallets[2] observed in the sequence, we have that a majority of those wallets has been generated by honest players using independent randomnesses. Essentially our blockchain assumption builds on top of the standard chain quality assumption, requiring that the adversary will be the "winning" node that decides the next block using a fresh wallet less often than honest players. Similar assumptions have been leveraged in the literature. For example [25,33] use the assumption that the majority of mined blocks are honest, to select a committee for secure computation. The difference between our blockchain assumption and the standard chain quality property is mainly that we additionally require that many of the honest blocks will additionally have an high-min entropy field. We discuss more extensively our blockchain assumption Sect. 3.1.

We will leverage this blockchain assumption and the simulator's control of the honest majority to build a pvZK proof as follows. The high-level idea is to follow the FLS approach [17] and prove the OR of two statements: either "x in L" or "Previously I have predicted the majority of fresh wallets appeared in the last d blocks". In particular our idea reminds the implementation of the FLS approach proposed by Barak [7] where the trapdoor theorem consists of some unpredictable information that becomes predictable during the straight-line simulation. The soundness of our construction will follow from similar arguments and will actually be simpler. The reason is that we implement the prediction step with perfectly binding commitments and thus, unlike Barak, we will not have to worry about a prover finding collisions in a collision-resistant hash function.

To implement this approach we need two ingredients: a non-interactive commitment scheme (that can be constructed from 1–1 one-way functions) and a

---

[2] Here we refer to wallets identifying the block leader cashing the reward and not to wallets involved in transactions.

publicly verifiable witness indistinguishable proof system pvWI. We use the pvWI proof system recently constructed in [34] which is the first pvWI proof system from a blockchain assumption. Our blockchain assumption implies the one of [34]. The pvWI proof system of [34] leverages the underlying blockchain assumption by providing an interactive prover and a non-interactive verification function. Concretely, the pvWI proof of [34] builds on a classic 3-round WI proof system where the first two rounds are played by the prover and blockchain: the prover posts the first round of the classic WI proof on the blockchain, then she waits for a few blocks extending the block containing the first message and from those extracts a challenge that corresponds to the second round of a classic 3-round WI proof. The third round of the classic WI proof is then sent to the actual verifier, who can use the blockchain to validate all 3 rounds, non-interactively. If the third round is posted on the blockchain then all verifiers can validate the proof. We need the following 3 properties from the pvWI proof: (1) *delayed-input* completeness, which means that the prover will use the theorem and the witness only for computing the last message of the protocol, which implies that all other messages of the pvWI proof are independent from the witness; (2) *WI in the presence of blockchain failure*, that is, (2.1) the WI property holds even when the prover is the only honest player and therefore the blockchain could be completely controlled by the adversary; (2.2) the WI property is preserved even when, *after* a pvWI proof is computed, the adversary could corrupt the prover; (3) unconditional soundness[3] in the presence of our blockchain assumption (i.e., Assumption 1). Since such properties were not explicitly claimed in [34] we show in the full version of this paper [35] that through minor updates to their protocol those 3 properties are satisfied. The reason why we need the above 3 special properties will be explained later when we will highlight the security proof.

With the above ingredients in hands, our pvZK proof system works as follows. First, the prover, using a non-interactive commitment scheme, commits to $u \cdot d$ strings $\mathsf{com}_1, \ldots, \mathsf{com}_{u \cdot d}$ (u is the blockchain parameters associated to our chain-quality assumption (Assumption 1), more details about u will be provided later) and posts the commitments on the blockchain. Note that the prover securely erases the decommitment information of $\mathsf{com}_1, \ldots, \mathsf{com}_{u \cdot d}$. Then, she waits until the blockchain is extended by a sequence of d blocks $\overline{B}_1, \ldots, \overline{B}_d$, that include n blocks $B_1, \ldots, B_n$ with fresh wallets (that is, with wallets that were not observed before). Let $v_1, \ldots, v_n$ be such fresh wallets observed on the blockchain. In the final step, the prover computes the pvWI proof, for the theorem:"$x \in \mathcal{L}$ or $(\mathsf{com}_1, \ldots, \mathsf{com}_{u \cdot d})$ are commitments of at least $n/2+1$ of the wallets $(v_1, \ldots, v_n)$".

The simulator $\mathsf{S}_{\mathsf{pvZK}}$ uses the same power of the simulator of [23] controlling the honest players in the simulated experiment (in particular, the simulator adds the blocks in the blockchain on behalf of honest players). Therefore $\mathsf{S}_{\mathsf{pvZK}}$ can predict the majority of the unpredictable new wallets associated with a sequence of d future blocks, and can use this knowledge as a trapdoor theorem when computing the messages of the pvWI proof. Notice that the simulator can not tightly predict the future wallets that will be permanently added to the

---

[3] See the paragraph below about the power of the adversary.

blockchain since there will be several other honest blocks to simulate that will circulate in the network, they might even appear in some forks but eventually will not be part of the blockchain. Since the simulator has no direct power to decide which branch of a fork will remain in the blockchain, we require way more than just d commitments. Indeed we consider the parameter u that measures the upper bound on the amount of valid blocks that honest players propose for each index of the sequence of blocks of the blockchain.

The pvZK that we construct preserves zero knowledge even in case of adaptive corruption during the protocol execution and in case the blockchain completely collapses and the adversary gets the state of all players. To achieve this strong form of zero knowledge, we use secure erasure so that differences in the committed values are not detected. Moreover we rely on the delayed-input pvWI so that the simulator can run the prover procedure of the pvWI except that a different witness is used in last message. Therefore before the last message is played, adaptive corruption is not harmful since the simulator played exactly like a prover of the pvWI. Assuming that the underlying pvWI is secure in case the blockchain collapses (fact that we prove), the proof remains zero-knowledge forever.

A crucial aspect of our construction is that the security of the prover is in the hands of the prover *only* and does not depend on the behavior of the stakeholders. To achieve adaptive security we rely on secure erasure. In contrast, even if the prover of GG-NIZK would erase its randomness, the proof would still suffer of our attack.

For the soundness proof, the main observation is that, as long as our blockchain assumption holds, even an unbounded malicious prover cannot break soundness since it cannot predict enough future wallets. This together with the perfect binding property of the commitment scheme and the unconditional soundness of the pvWI guarantees the soundness of our pvZK.

An additional property of our construction is that all messages except the last one can be computed even before knowing the statement to prove (i.e., it satisfies delayed-input completeness and adaptive-input zero knowledge and soundness).

Finally, we remark that even though messages of our pvZK proof can be very long, therefore exceeding some rule of the blockchain, one can anyway resort to techniques (and assumptions) like IPFS that allow to keep off-chain long message but still accessible by everyone and succinctly notarized on chain.

On the Computational Power of the Adversary and Rationality of Players. In a publicly verifiable proof assuming that an adversarial prover is PPT does not really say much about his limits with respect to the security of the blockchain. Indeed in case of proof-of-work blockchains the limitation of the adversary should be compared to the overall computational capabilities of the network rather than compared to a generic polynomial on input the security parameter. In our definition of soundness we will therefore consider an unbounded prover. When proving the security of our construction we will state explicitly our blockchain assumption and implicitly we will assume that the constraints on the adversary (see Sect. 3.2) required by the underlying blockchain are maintained.

We remark that this work following [23,24,34] considers either honest or corrupted players, without exploring the game-theoretic scenario where players are instead rational.

1.2 Related Work

The idea of using a blockchain as a trusted setup has been explored already (e.g., fair multi-party computation [12], extraction of week randomness [2]). In [11] a randomness beacon is obtained assuming players to be somehow rational (i.e., they assume that the adversary that will prefer to be honest cashing mining rewards rather than misbehaving compromising the beacon). In our work, as well as the one of [23], we consider zero-knowledge proofs with public verifiability sticking with the traditional setting where security holds against malicious players.

In [16] a blockchain is used as a global setup assumption to obtain concurrent self-composable secure computation protocol, which is impossible in the standard model. We stress that [16] does not provide public verifiability (for the interested reader we expand this discussion in Sect. 5). Recently in [10,25] a blockchain is used to maintain a secret via proactive secrete sharing. As mentioned above[25] requires some chain quality parameters ($\frac{n}{2} + 1, n$) which means that for any sequence of n blocks, the majority of them $\frac{n}{2} + 1$ are computed by honest parties. In [10] the adversary controls up to 25% of the stake. However using the technique discussed in [21] one could lift up this requirement to less than 50%.

In [6] the notion of Crowd verifiable zero-knowledge (CVZK) is introduced[4]. In CVZK a prover wants to convince a set of n verifiers of the validity of a certain statement. In more detail, a CVZK is a 3-round protocol where first the prover speaks, then n verifiers compute a private state and send as a second-round a string that may contain some entropy, finally, the prover finishes the proof π. The verification procedure takes as input π the corresponding statement and also the states of the n verifiers. Instead we consider a different notion requiring a zero-knowledge proof that is publicly verifiable (i.e., any verifier with no additional information could check the veracity of the statement). Moreover, the definition of CVZK does not require any setup at the price of allowing the simulator to run in super-polynomial time. Our goal is also to diminish the trust in the setups, however, instead of requiring super-polynomial time simulation, we exploit more realistic setups like the blockchains.

2 The Attack of the Clones to GG-NIZK [23]

A high-level overview of the NIZK presented in [23] was provided in the Introduction. In this section we describe an attack of clones with which a malicious

---

[4] Our results were publicly announced in [1] way before we have noticed CVZK, therefore the two works are independent.

verifier, using a smart contract, is able to break the zero-knowledge property of GG-NIZK without corrupting any player.

Our attack leverages the fact that, if a blockchain is used as setup assumption for a protocol Π, the security proof of Π must take into account the fact that a player of Π is also a legitimate player of the blockchain protocol. As such, legitimate blockchain activities – such as smart contracts – can be performed by her.

Before describing the attack, we provide a formal description of the GG-NIZK.

Notation for GG-NIZK

- Blockchain **B**: this is the latest version blockchain which might contain unconfirmed blocks.
- Stable Blockchain $\mathbf{B}'$: this is defined as $\mathbf{B}^{\lceil \ell_1}$, which is the blockchain **B** pruned of ℓ_1 blocks (that are possibly unconfirmed blocks).
- Parameter ℓ_2: number of last blocks taken into consideration in $\mathbf{B}'$.
- Stakeholders $\mathcal{M}$: set of public keys associated to the player that have added at least one block in the last ℓ_2 blocks of $\mathbf{B}'$. In [23], such public keys are crucially used for both encryption and signature.
- Chain quality parameters: ℓ_3, ℓ_4 used in the soundness proof.
- params:= $(1^{\ell_1}, 1^{\ell_2}, 1^{\ell_3}, 1^{\ell_4})$.

GG-NIZK: The Proof. A proof π for theorem x is computed as follows. Let w be the witness s.t. $(x, w) \in \mathcal{R}$.

1. Secret share the witness w using a weighted secret sharing scheme, using as weights the stake of the public keys appearing in $\mathcal{M}$. Do the same with the zero-string.
   Namely, produce the following two sets[5]:

   $$\{\mathsf{sh}_{1,i}\}_{i \in \mathcal{M}} = \mathsf{Share}(w, \{\mathsf{stake}_i\}_{i \in \mathcal{M}}, \beta \cdot \mathsf{stake}_{\mathsf{total}}, s_1)$$

   $$\{\mathsf{sh}_{2,i}\}_{i \in \mathcal{M}} = \mathsf{Share}(0, \{\mathsf{stake}_i\}_{i \in \mathcal{M}}, \beta \cdot \mathsf{stake}_{\mathsf{total}}, s_2)$$

2. Encrypt each weighted share using the public key of the corresponding player. Namely for all i such that $\mathsf{PK}_i \in \mathcal{M}$, sample random strings $r_{1,i}, r_{2,i}$ and compute: $\mathsf{ctx}_{1,i} = \mathsf{Enc}(\mathsf{PK}_i, \mathsf{sh}_{1,i}, r_{1,i})$ $\mathsf{ctx}_{2,i} = \mathsf{Enc}(\mathsf{PK}_i, \mathsf{sh}_{2,i}, r_{2,i})$.
3. Compute a non-interactive witness indistinguishable proof (NIWI) π_{niwi} for the theorem: (1) either the first set of ciphertexts are correct encryptions under the public keys in $\mathcal{M}$ of shares of the witness w or (2) (trapdoor witness) the second set of ciphertexts is a collection of correct encryptions under the public keys in $\mathcal{M}$ of shares of a valid fork of length $\ell_3 + \ell_4$.

---

[5] The role of s_1, s_2 and β is not relevant for our discussion and therefore they can be ignored.

Hence, a proof π for theorem $x \in L$ consists of the tuple:

$$\pi = (\mathbf{B}, \{\mathsf{ctx}_{1,i}, \mathsf{ctx}_{2,i}\}_{i \in \mathcal{M}}, \pi_{\mathsf{niwi}}, \mathsf{params})$$

Note that the proof π is not published on the blockchain and it is only sent to the verifier.

Security of GG-NIZK: Intuition. Zero knowledge follows from the assumption of honest majority of stake. Under such assumption, the simulator –controlling all honest players– is able to compute a valid fork that constitutes a valid trapdoor witness for the NIWI. Even if the trapdoor witness is encrypted in $(\mathsf{ctx}_{2,i})_{\mathsf{PK}_i \in \mathcal{M}}$, a malicious verifier cannot detect that the trapdoor witness was used, since it does not control enough secret keys (associated to the public keys in $\mathcal{M}$) that would allow for collection of enough shares.

Soundness is proved by witness extraction: the extractor controls a sufficient fraction of honest secret keys (associated to the public keys in $\mathcal{M}$) and this allows the decryption of enough ciphertexts, that leads to enough shares to reconstruct the witness.

Clearly by obtaining in the future (e.g., when those keys will correspond to a reduced amount of stake) the secrets of the involved stakeholders (through adaptive corruptions or by naturally receiving the keys from honest stakeholders) the adversary would be able to decrypt those ciphertexts therefore breaking the zero knowledge property and without violating the proof-of-stake assumption. This problem imposes the assumptions/limitations of the GG-NIZK discussed previously.

A Simple Smart Contract that Breaks the ZK Property of GG-NIZK. The zero-knowledge property of GG-NIZK crucially relies on the assumption that the malicious verifier – controlling only a minority of stake– does not have enough secret keys for the public keys in $\mathcal{M}$ to be able to decrypt enough ciphertexts and thus reconstruct the witness.

Our main observation is that in order to obtain decryptions of enough ciphertexts, a malicious verifier, does not necessarily need to *own* enough of the stake/secret keys of the honest players. Instead, the malicious verifier can upload a smart contract – that we called `DecryptionForBarbados`– where she promises a reward for a valid decryption of a certain ciphertext ctx under a certain public key PK. Notice that to run such smart contract the adversary does not need to corrupt the stakeholders, or get a stake transfer. So, the attack to works even if no-one is corrupted and even if no-stake is transferred. Obviously, when considering a blockchain with additional restrictions the our attack based on the above smart contract might not work, but still, the potential existence of other attacks should not be overlooked.

In more details, once the malicious verifier obtains $\pi = (\mathbf{B}, \{\mathsf{ctx}_{1,i}, \mathsf{ctx}_{2,i}\}_{i \in \mathcal{M}}, \pi_{\mathsf{niwi}}, \mathsf{params})$ from an honest prover she can publish a `DecryptionForBarbados` for some of (they could also be rerandomized if useful) the ciphertexts $\mathsf{ctx}_{1,i}$ for which she does not possess the secret key. The malicious verifier using `DecryptionForBarbados` is able to collect enough shares and reconstruct the witness that is encrypted in $\{\mathsf{ctx}_{1,i}, \mathsf{ctx}_{2,i}\}_{i \in \mathcal{M}}$, thus directly invalidating the ZK property of [23].

In Fig. 1 we give a more detailed description of `DecryptionForBarbados`. In order to keep the smart contract simple we assume that the decryption procedure of the underlying encryption scheme gives in output a pair (m, r) where r is the randomness used to encrypt and m is the message encrypted (see for instance [8]). For the same reason, we also assume that (m, r) are unique (for a public key PK).

Notation (borrowed from [27]).
- Ledger: the blockchain.
- Ledger[Pt_i] denotes the amount of money possessed by the secret key of party Pt_i.

`DecryptionForBarbados`

1. Init: Upon receiving (init, \$reward, ctx, PK_i) from a contractor $\mathcal{C}$:
   - Assert Ledger[$\mathcal{C}$] > \$reward.
   - Ledger[$\mathcal{C}$] := Ledger[$\mathcal{C}$] − \$reward.
   - Set state := INIT.
2. Claim: On input (claim, v) from a player Pt_i:
   - Parse $v = (m, r)$.
   - If $\mathsf{ctx} = \mathsf{Enc}_{\mathsf{PK}_i}(m, r)$ then set rewards Ledger[Pt] := Ledger[Pt] + \$reward.
   - Set state := CLAIMED.

Fig. 1. Description of `DecryptionForBarbados`.

Observations on the Smart Contract. We note that a player that uses her secret key to trigger `DecryptionForBarbados` in order to win the reward is not violating any assumption of the underlying PoS protocol or of GG-NIZK. Indeed, he is not exposing his secret key but simply providing a valid decryption of a certain ciphertext. Thus this is legitimate behavior of a honest player, she is simply executing an other application that runs on top of the blockchain.

Our smart contract is not a "bribing attack". Bribing assumes that one is paying somebody to do something wrong/break the rules. Instead in this context an honest player is still behaving honestly and he is not breaking any rule of the underlying PoS protocol.

We also note that since the proof π is not published on the blockchain (and is not required to be), honest players could be not aware that they are helping a malicious verifier to break the security of π.

3 Definitions

Preliminary. We denote the security parameter by λ and use "$||$" as concatenation operator (i.e., if a and b are two strings then by $a||b$ we denote the concatenation of a and b). We use the abbreviation PPT that stays for probabilistic polynomial time. We use $\mathsf{poly}(\cdot)$ to indicate a generic polynomial function. A *polynomial-time relation* $\mathcal{R}$ (or *polynomial relation*, in short) is a subset of $\{0,1\}^* \times \{0,1\}^*$ such that membership of (x,w) in $\mathcal{R}$ can be decided in time polynomial in $|x|$. For $(x,w) \in \mathcal{R}$, we call x the *instance* and w a *witness* for x. For a polynomial-time relation $\mathcal{R}$, we define the $\mathcal{NP}$-language $L_{\mathcal{R}}$ as $L_{\mathcal{R}} = \{x$ s.t. $\exists\ w : (x,w) \in \mathcal{R}\}$. Analogously, unless otherwise specified, for an $\mathcal{NP}$-language L we denote by $\mathcal{R}$ the corresponding polynomial-time relation (that is, $\mathcal{R}$ is such that $L = L_{\mathcal{R}}$). We will denote by $\mathcal{P}^{\mathsf{st}}$ a stateful algorithm $\mathcal{P}$ with state st. We will use the notation $r \in_R \{0,1\}^{\lambda}$ to indicate that r is sampled at random from $\{0,1\}^{\lambda}$. When we want to specify the randomness r used by an algorithm AI we use the following notation $\mathsf{AI}(\cdot; r)$.

3.1 Blockchain Protocols

In the next two sections we borrow the description of a blockchain protocol of [23,32], moreover we explicitly define the procedure executed by an honest player in order to add a block. A blockchain protocol Γ is parameterized by a validity predicate V that captures the semantics and rules of the blockchain. Γ consists of 4 polynomial-time algorithms (UpdateState, GetRecords, Broadcast, GenBlock) with the following syntax.

- UpdateState(1^{λ}, st): It takes as input the security parameter λ, state st and outputs the updated state st.
- GetRecords(1^{λ}, st): It takes as input the security parameter λ and state st. It outputs the longest ordered sequence of valid blocks **B** (or simply blockchain) contained in the state variable, where each block in the chain itself contains an unordered sequence of records messages.
- Broadcast(1^{λ}, m): It takes as input the security parameter λ and a message m, and broadcasts the message over the network to all nodes executing the blockchain protocol. It does not give any output.
- GenBlock(st, **B**, x): It takes as input a state st, a blockchain $\mathbf{B}^6$, $x \in \{0,1\}^*$ and outputs a candidate block B that contains a string v computed running a function f_{ID} that is defined as follows. The function $f_{\mathsf{ID}}(1^{\lambda}; r)$ takes as input the security parameter λ and running with $\mathsf{poly}(\lambda)$ bits of randomness r outputs a q bit string v, where $q = \mathsf{poly}(\lambda)$. Moreover every time that f_{ID} runs on input a freshly generated randomness it holds that $H_{\infty}(f_{\mathsf{ID}}(1^{\lambda}; \cdot)) \geq \lambda^7$. The generated block B could satisfy or not the validity predicate V. We will denote by B_v a block B that contains the string v computed using f_{ID}.

---

[6] In order to simplify the notation we make an abuse of notation and we explicitly add the blockchain as input of GenBlock even though the blockchain can be computed running GetRecords on input st.

[7] In the existing blockchains the value v could be an identifier of a wallet and f_{ID} is the randomized function that generates it.

Blockchain Notation. With the notation $\mathbf{B} \leq \mathbf{B}'$ we will denote that the blockchain $\mathbf{B}$ is a prefix of the blockchain $\mathbf{B}'$. We denote by $\mathbf{B}^{\lceil n}$ the chain resulting from "pruning" the last n blocks in $\mathbf{B}$. We will denote by Γ^{V} a blockchain protocol Γ that has validate predicate V. A blockchain $\mathbf{B}$ generated by the execution of Γ^{V} is the blockchain obtained by an honest player after calling GetRecords during an execution of Γ^{V}. An *honest execution of* GenBlock is an execution of GenBlock computed by an honest player. A blockchain protocol Γ can satisfy the property of chain-consistency, chain-growth and chain-quality defined in previous works [19,32]. In the rest of the paper we will denote by $\eta(\cdot)$ the chain consistency parameter of Γ^{V}.

Definition 1 (Block Trim Function). *Let B_v be a block generated using* GenBlock *that satisfies the validate predicate* V. *We define a block trim function as a deterministic function* trim *that on input B_v outputs v.*

Note that for two blocks B, B' that satisfy V and are generated by an honest execution of GenBlock it could happen that $\mathtt{trim}(B) = \mathtt{trim}(B')$. For instance this is the case when a honest player Pt runs GenBlock twice and both executions run f_{ID} on input the same randomness stored in the state of Pt.

Definition 2 (Good Execution of GenBlock). *Let $\overline{\mathbf{B}}$ be a blockchain generated by an execution of Γ^{V}. An execution of* GenBlock *is good w.r.t. a blockchain $\mathbf{B}$ if it holds that* GenBlock *runs on input $\overline{\mathbf{B}}$ s.t. $\mathbf{B} \leq \overline{\mathbf{B}}^{\lceil \eta(\lambda)}$, moreover* GenBlock *runs f_{ID} on input fresh randomness and outputs a block that satisfies the validity predicate* V.

Definition 3 (Pristine Block). *Let* trim *be the block trim function defined in Definition 1. Let $\mathbf{B}$ be a blockchain composed of k blocks generated by an execution of Γ^{V}. The j-th block B_j of $\mathbf{B}$ is* pristine *if for each B_i of $\mathbf{B}$ with $0 < i < j$ it holds that $v \neq v_i$ where $v = \mathtt{trim}(B_j)$ and $v_i = \mathtt{trim}(B_i)$.*

Assumption 1. *Let $\mathbf{B}$ be a blockchain generated during an execution of Γ^{V}. There exists $d = \mathsf{poly}(\lambda)$ and $u = \mathsf{poly}(\lambda)$ such that for any sequence of d consecutive blocks $B_{i+1}, \ldots, B_{i+d}$ added to $\mathbf{B}$ during the execution of Γ^{V}, let n be the number of pristine blocks in $B_{i+1}, \ldots, B_{i+d}$, it holds that:*

1. *At least $\lfloor n/2 + 1 \rfloor$ of the pristine blocks in the sequence $B_{i+1}, \ldots, B_{i+d}$ have been generated by honest players through good executions of* GenBlock *w.r.t. $\mathbf{B}$;*
2. *For each $j \in \{1, \ldots d\}$, the probability that honest players obtain through honest executions of* GenBlock *w.r.t. $\mathbf{B}$ $u' > u$ different blocks satisfying the validity predicate for the position $i + j$ in the blockchain is negligible in λ.*

We refer to d as the pristine parameter *and to u as the* attempts parameter.

Notice that n is a non-constant value that depends on the content of the specific d consecutive blocks taken into account. For the sake of simplifying the description of our construction we will assume wlog that n is also a pristine parameter.

On the Applicability of Our Assumption. It is well known that blockchains need an incentive mechanism and this is typically implemented by assigning a reward each time a block is added to the chain. This process is often implemented as a lottery and some coins are generated and assigned to the winner of the lottery that is also the player that generated the new block added to the chain. In order to get the coin assigned, the winner also includes an identifier of her wallet to the block. Such identifiers usually correspond to public keys of signature schemes and as such they have a significant amount of min-entropy. Therefore, whenever such identifier is selected by a honest blockchain player and has never circulated in the network, it represents an unpredictable string. More concretely one could think in the case of Bitcoin to the coinbase transaction, since sometimes the rewards is cashed on a new wallet.

Our blockchain assumption assumes that given a sufficiently long sequence of blocks, if we restrict to identifiers that appear for the first time on the chain, then a majority of them was unpredictable before the long sequence of blocks started. Obviously an adversary can sometimes be the winner and therefore can use an identifier that is "fresh" in the eyes of others but that she knew already before the long sequence of blocks started. Therefore our assumption requires the adversary to have limited resources so that she places in the chain less blocks than what honest players using fresh identifiers do.

For concreteness, one can consider the current modus operandi of Bitcoin blockchain. To avoid double spending it is in general recommended to wait for 6 more blocks after the block including the spending transaction, this is called confirmation time. The choice of 6 blocks for a confirmation time suggests that it is believed that it would be very unlikely that the adversary could have produced in the meanwhile 7 blocks that cancel the spending transaction. If for instance we quantify "very unlikely" with something less than 2^{-70} then as a consequence the adversary must have probability of being the winner (therefore deciding the next block) less than 2^{-10}. Following this example, if an honest block includes a "fresh" wallet with probability at least 2^{-9} (which is very reasonable), then our assumption clearly holds for a sufficiently large sequence of blocks (i.e., considering a sufficiently large d).

We have considered Bitcoin and the 6-block confirmation rule just because it is the most popular example of blockchain and thus it is a natural target to check the concreteness of our assumption. Indeed, also coinbase transaction is just an example of a field with min-entropy that could be find in the blockchain (see also the examples mentioned in [13]). One could consider, for instance, privacy-preserving blockchains (e.g., [18,28] for the case of PoS blockchains), observing that the cryptographic material used to ensure privacy might imply the presence of fields with high min-entropy in a block.

Our construction is a mere feasibility result aiming at showing that publicly verifiable zero knowledge is possible with generic[8] blockchains.

---

[8] In the sense of the underlying consensus mechanism.

3.2 Execution of Γ^V in an Environment

At a very high level, the execution of the protocol Γ^V proceeds in rounds that model time steps. Each participant in the protocol runs the UpdateState algorithm to keep track of the current (latest) blockchain state. This corresponds to listening on the broadcast network for messages from other nodes. The GetRecords algorithm is used to extract an ordered sequence of blocks encoded in the blockchain state variable. The Broadcast algorithm is used by a player when she wants to post a new message m on the blockchain. Note that the message m is accepted by the blockchain protocol only if it satisfies the validity predicate V given the current state, (i.e., the current sequence of blocks).

Following prior works [19,29,32], we define the protocol execution following the activation model of the Universal Composability framework of [15] (though like [23] we will not prove UC-security of our results). For any blockchain protocol Γ^V(UpdateState, GetRecords, Broadcast, GenBlock), the protocol execution is directed by the environment $\mathcal{Z}(1^\lambda)$. The environment $\mathcal{Z}$ activates the players as either honest or corrupt and is also responsible for providing inputs/records to all players in each round.

All the corrupt players are controlled by the adversary $\mathcal{A}$ that can corrupt players adaptively during the execution of Γ^V.

Specifically $\mathcal{A}$ can send a corruption request $\langle \text{corr}, \text{Pt}_i \rangle$ to player Pt_i at any point during the execution of Γ^V. The adversary is also responsible for the delivery of all network messages. Honest players start by executing UpdateState on input 1^λ with an empty state $\text{st} = \epsilon$.

- In round r, each honest player Pt_i potentially receives a message(s) m from $\mathcal{Z}$ and potentially receives incoming network messages (delivered by $\mathcal{A}$). It may then perform any computation, broadcast a message (using Broadcast algorithm) to all other players (which will be delivered by the adversary; see below) and update its state st_i. It could also attempt to "add" a new block to its chain: Pt_i will run the procedure GenBlock, and this execution of GenBlock could use fresh randomness for the function $f_{\text{ID}}(1^\lambda; \cdot)$ if requested by $\mathcal{Z}$.
- $\mathcal{A}$ is responsible for delivering all messages sent by players (honest or corrupted) to all other players. $\mathcal{A}$ cannot modify the content of messages broadcast by honest players, but it may delay or reorder the delivery of a message as long as it eventually delivers all messages within a certain time limit.
- At any point $\mathcal{Z}$ can communicate with adversary $\mathcal{A}$.

Constraints on the Adversary. In order to show that a blockchain enjoys some useful properties (e.g., chain consistency) prior works [19,32] restrict their analysis to compliant executions of Γ^V where some specific restrictions[9] are imposed to $\mathcal{Z}$ and $\mathcal{A}$. Those works showed that certain desirable security properties are respected except with negligible probability in any compliant execution. Obviously, when in our work we claim results assuming some properties of the blockchain, we are taking into account compliant executions of the underlying blockchain protocol only. The same is done by [23].

---

[9] For instance, they require that any broadcasted message is delivered in a maximum number of time steps.

3.3   Publicly Verifiable ZK Proof System from BlockchainS

Here we define delayed-input publicly verifiable zero knowledge w.r.t. blockchain failure over a blockchain protocol $\Gamma^V = ($UpdateState, GetRecords, Broadcast, GenBlock$)$. We will make use of the following notation.

The view of a blockchain player Pt consists of the messages received during an execution of Γ^V, along with its randomness and its inputs. Let $\text{Exec}^{\Gamma^V}(\mathcal{A}, \mathcal{H}, \mathcal{Z}, 1^\lambda)$ be the random variable denoting the joint view of all players in the execution Γ^V, with adversary $\mathcal{A}$ and set of honest players $\mathcal{H}$ in environment $\mathcal{Z}$, such a joint view fully determines the execution. Let $\Gamma_{\text{view}}^V(\mathcal{A}, \mathcal{H}, \mathcal{Z}, 1^\lambda)$ denote an execution of $\Gamma^V(\mathcal{A}, \mathcal{H}, \mathcal{Z}, 1^\lambda)$ producing view as joint view.

Definition 4 (Publicly Verifiable Proof System from Blockchain). *A pair of stateful* PPT *algorithms* $\Pi = (\mathcal{P}, \mathcal{V})$ *over a blockchain protocol* Γ^V *is a publicly verifiable proof system for the* $\mathcal{NP}$-*language* $\mathcal{L}$ *with witness relation* $\mathcal{R}$ *if it satisfies the following properties:*

Completeness. $\forall\ x, w\ s.t.\ (x, w) \in \mathcal{R},\ \forall$ PPT *adversary* $\mathcal{A}$ *any* PPT $\text{Pt}_j \in \mathcal{H}$ *where* $\mathcal{H}$ *is the set of honest parties, and for any environment* $\mathcal{Z}$, *assuming that* $\mathcal{P} \in \mathcal{H}$, *there exist negligible functions* $\nu_1(\cdot), \nu_2(\cdot)$ *such that:*

$$\Pr\left[\mathcal{V}(x, \pi, \mathbf{B}) = 1 \ \vdots \ \begin{array}{c} \text{view} \leftarrow \text{Exec}^{\Gamma^V}(\mathcal{A}, \mathcal{H}, \mathcal{Z}, 1^\lambda) \\ \pi \leftarrow \mathcal{P}^{\text{st}_\mathcal{P}}(x, w) \\ \mathbf{B} = \text{GetRecords}(1^\lambda, \text{st}_j) \end{array}\right] \geq 1 - \nu_1(|x|) - \nu_2(\lambda)$$

where $\text{st}_\mathcal{P}$ *denotes the state of* $\mathcal{P}$ *during the execution* $\Gamma_{\text{view}}^V(\mathcal{A}, \mathcal{H}, \mathcal{Z}, 1^\lambda)$. *The running time of* $\mathcal{P}$ *is polynomial in the size of the blockchain* $\mathbf{B} = \text{GetRecords}(1^\lambda, \text{st}_j)$ *where* st_j *is the state of* Pt_j *at the end of the execution* $\Gamma_{\text{view}}^V(\mathcal{A}, \mathcal{H}, \mathcal{Z}, 1^\lambda)$.[10]

Soundness. $\forall\ x \notin \mathcal{L},\ \forall$ *stateful adversary* $\mathcal{A}$ *and* PPT *honest player* $\text{Pt}_j \in \mathcal{H}$ *where* $\mathcal{H}$ *is the set of honest players and for any environment* $\mathcal{Z}$, *there exist negligible functions* $\nu_1(\cdot), \nu_2(\cdot)$ *such that:*

$$\Pr\left[\mathcal{V}(x, \pi, \mathbf{B}) = 1 \ \vdots \ \begin{array}{c} \text{view} \leftarrow \text{Exec}^{\Gamma^V}(\mathcal{A}, \mathcal{H}, \mathcal{Z}, 1^\lambda) \\ \pi, x \leftarrow \mathcal{A}^{\text{st}_\mathcal{A}} \\ \mathbf{B} = \text{GetRecords}(1^\lambda, \text{st}_j) \end{array}\right] \leq \nu_1(|x|) + \nu_2(\lambda)$$

where $\text{st}_\mathcal{A}$ *denotes the state of* $\mathcal{A}$ *during the execution* $\Gamma_{\text{view}}^V(\mathcal{A}, \mathcal{H}, \mathcal{Z}, 1^\lambda)$. *Furthermore* st_j *is the state of* Pt_j *at the end of the execution* $\Gamma^V{}_{\text{view}}(\mathcal{A}, \mathcal{H}, \mathcal{Z}, 1^\lambda)$. *The proof* π *might consist of multiple messages, i.e.,* $\pi = (\pi^1, \dots, \pi^m)$, *in this case, we will say that* Π *is an m-messages proof system. Moreover if* π *is composed of m-messages* $\pi = (\pi^1, \dots, \pi^m)$, $\mathcal{A}$ *is allowed to choose* x *just before computing the last message* π^m *of the proof* $\pi = (\pi^1, \dots, \pi^m)$.

---

[10] Note that the execution of $\Gamma_{\text{view}}^V(\mathcal{A}, \mathcal{H}, \mathcal{Z}, 1^\lambda)$ could continue even after π is provided by $\mathcal{P}$.

Definition 5 (Delayed-Input Completeness from Blockchain). *An m-messages proof system Π over a blockchain protocol Γ^{V} is **delayed-input**, if x, w are not involved before the computation of the last message π^m of the proof $\pi = (\pi^1, \ldots, \pi^m)$.*

Definition 6 (Witness Indistinguishability w.r.t. Blockchain Failure). *A publicly verifiable proof system $\Pi = (\mathcal{P}, \mathcal{V})$ over a blockchain protocol Γ^{V} for the $\mathcal{NP}$-language $\mathcal{L}$ with witness relation $\mathcal{R}$ is witness indistinguishable (WI) w.r.t. blockchain failure if it satisfies the following property:*

$\forall x, w_0, w_1$ such that $(x, w_0) \in \mathcal{R}$ and $(x, w_1) \in \mathcal{R}$, $\forall$ PPT adversary $\mathcal{A}$ and set of PPT honest players $\mathcal{H}$ and any PPT environment $\mathcal{Z}$, where $\mathcal{P} \in \mathcal{H}$ it holds that:

$$\left\{ \mathsf{view}_{\mathcal{A}} : \mathsf{view}_{\mathcal{A}} \leftarrow \mathsf{Exp}^0{}_{\mathcal{A}, \Pi, \Gamma^{\mathsf{V}}}(\lambda) \right\} \approx \left\{ \mathsf{view}_{\mathcal{A}} : \mathsf{view}_{\mathcal{A}} \leftarrow \mathsf{Exp}^1{}_{\mathcal{A}, \Pi, \Gamma^{\mathsf{V}}}(\lambda) \right\}$$

where $\mathsf{Exp}^b{}_{\mathcal{A}, \Pi, \Gamma^{\mathsf{V}}}(\lambda)$ is defined below, for $b \in \{0, 1\}$.

$\mathsf{Exp}^b{}_{\mathcal{A}, \Pi, \Gamma^{\mathsf{V}}}(\lambda, x, w_b)$:

- $\mathcal{P}$ *runs on input 1^λ.*
- *An execution of $\Gamma^{\mathsf{V}}(\mathcal{A}, \mathcal{Z}, \mathcal{H}, 1^\lambda)$ starts.*
  - $\mathcal{P}^{\mathsf{st}_\mathcal{P}}$ *outputs messages $\pi^1, \ldots, \pi^{m-1}$, where $\mathsf{st}_\mathcal{P}$ is the state of $\mathcal{P}$ in the execution $\Gamma^{\mathsf{V}}(\mathcal{A}, \mathcal{Z}, \mathcal{H}, 1^\lambda)$.*
  - *Upon receiving $(x, w_0) \in \mathcal{R}$, $(x, w_1) \in \mathcal{R}$ from $\mathcal{A}$.*
    - $\mathcal{P}^{\mathsf{st}_\mathcal{P}}$ *computes π^m on input π^{m-1}, x, w_b and outputs $\pi = (\pi^1, \ldots, \pi^m)$.*
  - $\mathcal{A}$ *can send a collapse request $\langle \mathsf{corr}, \mathsf{all} \rangle$ obtaining:*
    The state st_i from the honest player $\mathsf{Pt}_i \in \mathcal{H}$, for $i = 1, \ldots, |\mathcal{H}|$;
    The state $\mathsf{st}_\mathcal{P}$ from $\mathcal{P}$.
- *The execution of $\Gamma^{\mathsf{V}}(\mathcal{A}, \mathcal{Z}, \mathcal{H}, 1^\lambda)$ terminates and $\mathcal{A}$ outputs her view $\mathsf{view}_{\mathcal{A}}$ and this is the output of the experiment.*

Remark 1. The above definition does not assume that the blockchain satisfies the predicate V, even when $\mathcal{P}$ is the only honest player of Γ^{V}, and thus the blockchain could be completely controlled by the adversary. In this scenario we will say that $\Pi = (\mathcal{P}, \mathcal{V})$ enjoys WI w.r.t. blockchain failure over any blockchain protocol.

Definition 7 (Zero Knowledge w.r.t. Blockchain Failure). *A publicly verifiable proof system $\Pi = (\mathcal{P}, \mathcal{V})$ over a blockchain protocol Γ^{V} for the $\mathcal{NP}$-language $\mathcal{L}$ with witness relation $\mathcal{R}$ is Zero Knowledge (ZK) w.r.t. blockchain failure if there is a stateful PPT algorithm S such that $\forall\ x, w$ s.t. $(x, w) \in \mathcal{R}$, $\forall$ PPT adversary $\mathcal{A}$ and set of PPT honest players $\mathcal{H}$ and for any PPT environment $\mathcal{Z}$, where $\mathcal{P} \in \mathcal{H}$ it holds that:*

$$\left\{ \mathsf{view}_{\mathcal{A}} : \mathsf{view}_{\mathcal{A}} \leftarrow \mathsf{Exp}^0{}_{\mathcal{A}, \Pi, \Gamma^{\mathsf{V}}}(\lambda) \right\} \approx \left\{ \mathsf{view}_{\mathcal{A}} : \mathsf{view}_{\mathcal{A}} \leftarrow \mathsf{Exp}^1{}_{\mathcal{A}, \Pi, \mathsf{S}, \Gamma^{\mathsf{V}}}(\lambda) \right\}$$

where $\text{Exp}^0_{\mathcal{A},\Pi,\Gamma^{\vee}}(\lambda)$ *and* $\text{Exp}^1_{\mathcal{A},\Pi,\mathsf{S},\Gamma^{\vee}}(\lambda)$ *are defined below.*

$\text{Exp}^0_{\mathcal{A},\Pi,\Gamma^{\vee}}(\lambda)$:

- $\mathcal{P}$ *runs on input* 1^λ.
- *An execution of* $\Gamma^{\vee}(\mathcal{A},\mathcal{H},\mathcal{Z},1^\lambda)$ *starts.*

1. *At any point* $\mathcal{A}$ *can send a corruption request* $\langle \text{ZK}_{\text{corr}}(x,w)\rangle$ *(s.t.* $(x,w) \in \mathcal{R}$) *to* $\mathcal{P}$ *obtaining from* $\mathcal{P}$ *her state* $\text{st}_{\mathcal{P}}$.
2. $\mathcal{P}^{\text{st}_{\mathcal{P}}}$ *outputs messages* $\pi^1,\ldots,\pi^{m-1}$.
3. *If* $\mathcal{A}$ *did not compute Step 1* $\mathcal{P}$ *receives* $(x,w') \in \mathcal{R}$ *from* $\mathcal{A}$.
4. $\mathcal{P}^{\text{st}_{\mathcal{P}}}$ *outputs* $\pi = (\pi^1,\ldots,\pi^m)$.
5. *If* $\mathcal{A}$ *sends a collapse request* $\langle \text{corr}, \text{all}\rangle$ *obtains:*
   The state st_i *from honest player* $\text{Pt}_i \in \mathcal{H}$, *for* $i = 1,\ldots,|\mathcal{H}|$;
   The state $\text{st}_{\mathcal{P}}$ *from* $\mathcal{P}$, *if* $\mathcal{A}$ *did not compute Step 1.*

-*The execution of* $\Gamma^{\vee}(\mathcal{A},\mathcal{Z},\mathcal{H},1^\lambda)$ *terminates and* $\mathcal{A}$ *outputs her view* $\text{view}_{\mathcal{A}}$ *and this is the output of the experiment.*

$\text{Exp}^1_{\mathcal{A},\Pi,\mathsf{S},\Gamma^{\vee}}(\lambda)$:

- S *runs on input* 1^λ.
- *An execution of* $\Gamma^{\vee}(\mathcal{A},\mathsf{S},\mathcal{Z},1^\lambda)$ *starts.*

1. *At any point* $\mathcal{A}$ *can send a corruption request* $\langle \text{ZK}_{\text{corr}}(x,w)\rangle$ *(s.t.* $(x,w) \in \mathcal{R}$) *to* S *obtaining from* S *a state* $\text{st}_{\mathcal{P}}$.
2. S *outputs messages* $\pi^1,\ldots,\pi^{m-1}$.
3. *If* $\mathcal{A}$ *did not compute Step 1:* S *receives* $(x,w') \in \mathcal{R}$ *from* $\mathcal{A}$, S *ignores* w'.
4. S *outputs* $\pi = (\pi^1,\ldots,\pi^m)$.
5. *If* $\mathcal{A}$ *sends a collapse request* $\langle \text{corr}, \text{all}\rangle$ *obtains from* S:
   The state st_i *for each honest player* $\text{Pt}_i \in \mathcal{H}$, *for* $i = 1,\ldots,|\mathcal{H}|$;
   The state $\text{st}_{\mathcal{P}}$ *for the honest prover of* Π, *if* $\mathcal{A}$ *did not compute Step 1.*

-*The execution of* $\Gamma^{\vee}(\mathcal{A},\mathcal{Z},\mathcal{H},1^\lambda)$ *terminates and* $\mathcal{A}$ *outputs her view* $\text{view}_{\mathcal{A}}$ *and this is the output of the experiment.*

---

4   Publicly Verifiable ZK w.r.t. Blockchain Failure

We construct a delayed-input publicly verifiable zero-knowledge proof system w.r.t. blockchain failure $\Pi_{\text{pvZK}} = (\mathcal{P}_{\text{pvZK}}, \mathcal{V}_{\text{pvZK}})$ over any blockchain protocol $\Gamma^{\vee} = (\text{UpdateState}, \text{GetRecords}, \text{Broadcast}, \text{GenBlock})$ satisfying chain-consistency property, chain-growth property and Assumption 1. The parameters of Π_{pvZK} are reported in Table 1. We assume wlog that in a sequence of d blocks, n of them are pristine, where n is an even non-negative integer. Π_{pvZK} for the $\mathcal{NP}$-language $\mathcal{L}$ makes use of the following tools:

- The block trim function `trim` defined in Definition 1, that on input a block B outputs a q-bits long string v.

- A non-interactive statistically binding commitment scheme $\Pi_{\mathsf{Com}} = (\mathsf{Com}, \mathsf{VrfyOpen})$.
- A delayed-input publicly verifiable proof system $\Pi_{\mathsf{pvWI}} = (\mathcal{P}_{\mathsf{pvWI}}, \mathcal{V}_{\mathsf{pvWI}})$ over any blockchain protocol $\Gamma^{\mathsf{V}} = (\mathsf{UpdateState}, \mathsf{GetRecords}, \mathsf{Broadcast}, \mathsf{GenBlock})$ that satisfies chain-consistency property, chain-growth property and Assumption 1. Moreover Π_{pvWI} enjoys WI w.r.t. blockchain failure over any blockchain protocol. Π_{pvWI} is for $\mathcal{NP}$-language $\mathcal{L}_{\mathsf{pvWI}}$ which is associated to the relation $\mathcal{R}_{\mathsf{pvWI}} = \{((x, x_{\mathsf{com}}), w) : (x, w) \in \mathcal{R} \ \vee \ (x_{\mathsf{com}}, w) \in \mathcal{R}_{\mathsf{com}} \}$, where $\mathcal{R}$ is the relation associated to the $\mathcal{NP}$-language $\mathcal{L}$ and $\mathcal{R}_{\mathsf{com}}$ is the relation associated to the following $\mathcal{NP}$-language:

$$\mathcal{L}_{\mathsf{com}} = \left\{ \{\mathsf{com}_j\}_{j=1}^{u \cdot d}, \{v_i\}_{i=1}^{n} : \exists \, 1 \leq j_1 < \cdots < j_{n/2+1} \leq n, \ \{\mathsf{open}_{j_k}\}_{k=1}^{n/2+1} \right.$$
$$\left. \text{s.t. } \mathsf{VrfyOpen}(\mathsf{com}_{j_k}, \mathsf{open}_{j_k}, v_{j_k}) = 1 \ \forall k = 1, \ldots, n/2+1 \right\}$$

Loosely speaking the relation $\mathcal{R}_{\mathsf{com}}$ is satisfied if the message committed in com_{j_k} is v_{j_k} for at least $n/2 + 1$ distinct values of j_k. The instance length of $\mathcal{L}_{\mathsf{pvWI}}$ is ℓ and the size of the proof generated by $\mathcal{P}_{\mathsf{pvWI}}$ is of m messages.

Our delayed-input publicly verifiable zero-knowledge proof system w.r.t. blockchain failure $\Pi_{\mathsf{pvZK}} = (\mathcal{P}_{\mathsf{pvZK}}, \mathcal{V}_{\mathsf{pvZK}})$ is described in Fig. 2.

Table 1. Parameters of Π_{pvZK}.

Table of notation	
ℓ	Size of the theorem for $\mathcal{L}_{\mathsf{pvWI}}$
m	Number of messages of Π_{pvWI}
q	Output-length of the block trim function `trim`. See Definition 1
η	Chain consistency parameter of Γ^{V}
d, n	Pristine parameters of Γ^{V}. See Assumption 1
u	Attempts parameter of Γ^{V}. See Assumption 1

Theorem 1. *Let $\Gamma^{\mathsf{V}} = (\mathsf{UpdateState}, \mathsf{GetRecords}, \mathsf{Broadcast}, \mathsf{GenBlock})$ be any blockchain protocol that satisfies chain-consistency property, chain-growth property and Assumption 1. Let $\Pi_{\mathsf{Com}} = (\mathsf{Com}, \mathsf{VrfyOpen})$ be a non-interactive statistically binding commitment scheme. Let $\Pi_{\mathsf{pvWI}} = (\mathcal{P}_{\mathsf{pvWI}}, \mathcal{V}_{\mathsf{pvWI}})$ be a delayed-input publicly verifiable proof system over Γ^{V} for $\mathcal{NP}$-language $\mathcal{L}_{\mathsf{pvWI}}$. Moreover Π_{pvWI} enjoys WI w.r.t. blockchain failure over any blockchain protocol. Assuming secure erasure, $\Pi_{\mathsf{pvZK}} = (\mathcal{P}_{\mathsf{pvZK}}, \mathcal{V}_{\mathsf{pvZK}})$ (described in Fig. 2) is a delayed-input publicly verifiable zero-knowledge proof system w.r.t. blockchain failure over Γ^{V} for $\mathcal{NP}$.*

We note that a pvWI proof system that satisfies delayed-input completeness can be instantiated from OWPs using the work of [34]. In the full version [35] we

Publicly Verifiable ZK proof system w.r.t. blockchain failure $\Pi_{\mathsf{pvZK}} = (\mathcal{P}_{\mathsf{pvZK}}, \mathcal{V}_{\mathsf{pvZK}})$ Parameters are defined in Table 4.

Prover Procedure: $\mathcal{P}_{\mathsf{pvZK}}$. Input: instance x, witness w s.t. $(x, w) \in \mathcal{R}$.

— **First step.**

1. Compute $(\mathsf{com}_j, \mathsf{open}_j) \leftarrow \mathsf{Com}(0^q)$ and erase open_j for $j = 1, \ldots, d \cdot u$.
— **Blockchain Interaction.**
2. Set $\mathsf{st} = \epsilon$. Post $\mathsf{com}_1, \ldots, \mathsf{com}_{u \cdot d}$ on the blockchain by running $\mathsf{Broadcast}(1^\lambda, \mathsf{com}_1, \ldots, \mathsf{com}_{u \cdot d})$ and then monitor the blockchain by running $\mathsf{st} = \mathsf{UpdateState}(1^\lambda, \mathsf{st})$, $\mathbf{B} = \mathsf{GetRecords}(1^\lambda, \mathsf{st})$, until $\mathsf{com}_1, \ldots, \mathsf{com}_{u \cdot d}$ followed by d additional blocks $B_1, \ldots, B_d$ are posted on the blockchain $\mathbf{B}^{\lceil \eta}$ (i.e., we consider the blockchain $\mathbf{B}$ pruned of the last η blocks). Let $\overline{B_1}, \ldots, \overline{B_n}$ be the n pristine blocks in the sequence $B_1, \ldots, B_d$.
— **Second step.**
3. Compute $v_j = \mathsf{trim}(\overline{B_j})$ for $j = 1, \ldots, n$ and set $\mathsf{com} = \{\mathsf{com}_j\}_{j=1}^{u \cdot d}$, $\mathsf{val} = \{v_j\}_{j=1}^n$, $x_{\mathsf{com}} = (\mathsf{com}, \mathsf{val})$, $x_{\mathsf{pvWI}} = (x, x_{\mathsf{com}})$.
4. Obtain π_{pvWI}^1 with randomness r_1 executing $\mathcal{P}_{\mathsf{pvWI}}$ on input $1^\lambda, \ell$ and interacting with the blockchain if it is required by $\mathcal{P}_{\mathsf{pvWI}}$.
5. For $i = 2, \ldots, m - 1$:
   Obtain π_{pvWI}^i with randomness r_i executing $\mathcal{P}_{\mathsf{pvWI}}$ on input $\pi_{\mathsf{pvWI}}^{i-1}$ and interacting with the blockchain if it is required by $\mathcal{P}_{\mathsf{pvWI}}$.
6. Obtain π_{pvWI}^m executing $\mathcal{P}_{\mathsf{pvWI}}$ on input $\pi_{\mathsf{pvWI}}^{m-1}, x_{\mathsf{pvWI}}, w$ and interacting with the blockchain if it is required by $\mathcal{P}_{\mathsf{pvWI}}$.
7. Set $\pi_{\mathsf{pvWI}} = (\pi_{\mathsf{pvWI}}^1, \ldots, \pi_{\mathsf{pvWI}}^m)$ and $\pi = (x_{\mathsf{pvWI}}, \{\mathsf{com}_j\}_{j=1}^{u \cdot d}, \pi_{\mathsf{pvWI}})$ erase any randomness that $\mathcal{P}_{\mathsf{pvWI}}$ requests to erase and output π.

Verifier Procedure: $\mathcal{V}_{\mathsf{pvZK}}$. Input: x, $\pi = (x_{\mathsf{pvWI}}, \{\mathsf{com}_j\}_{j=1}^{u \cdot d}, \pi_{\mathsf{pvWI}})$, and a blockchain $\tilde{\mathbf{B}}$ s.t. $\mathbf{B}^{\lceil \eta} \leq \tilde{\mathbf{B}}$ works as follows.

— **Check Blockchain.** If the messages $\{\mathsf{com}_j\}_{j=1}^{u \cdot d}$ are not posted on the blockchain $\tilde{\mathbf{B}}^{\lceil \eta}$ then $\mathcal{V}_{\mathsf{pvZK}}$ outputs 0. Otherwise, let B^* be the block of the blockchain $\tilde{\mathbf{B}}^{\lceil \eta}$ where the messages $\{\mathsf{com}_j\}_{j=1}^{u \cdot d}$ are posted. Let $\overline{B_1}, \ldots, \overline{B_n}$ be the n pristine blocks of the blockchain $\tilde{\mathbf{B}}^{\lceil \eta}$ after B^*. $\mathcal{V}_{\mathsf{pvZK}}$ computes $v_j' = \mathsf{trim}(\overline{B_j})$ for $j = 1, \ldots, n$ and parses x_{pvWI} as instance x, commitments $\{\mathsf{com}_j\}_{j=1}^{u \cdot d}$, and strings $\{v_j\}_{j=1}^n$.

— **Check Proof.** Accept if all the following conditions are satisfied.
   - $v_j' = v_j$ for all $j \in \{1, \ldots, n\}$;
   - $\mathcal{V}_{\mathsf{pvWI}}(x_{\mathsf{pvWI}}, \pi_{\mathsf{pvWI}}, \tilde{\mathbf{B}}) = 1$.

Execution of Γ^V by honest player Pt_j:

Pt_j acts as described in Section 3.2, in particular, upon receiving a request of an execution of $\mathsf{GenBlock}$ using fresh randomness for the function $f_{\mathsf{ID}}(1^\lambda; \cdot)$ by $\mathcal{Z}$:
   Pt_j picks r at random from $\{0, 1\}^{\mathsf{poly}(\lambda)}$;
   Pt_j runs $\mathsf{GenBlock}$ and uses the randomness r to execute f_{ID}.
If $\mathcal{A}$ sends a collapse request $\langle \mathsf{corr}, \mathsf{all} \rangle$, $\mathcal{A}$ obtains $\mathsf{st}_{\mathsf{Pt}_i}$ from honest player Pt_i, for all $i = 1, \ldots, |\mathcal{H}|$, moreover $\mathcal{A}$ obtains the state $\mathsf{st}_{\mathcal{P}_{\mathsf{pvZK}}}$ of $\mathcal{P}_{\mathsf{pvZK}}$ (if $\mathcal{A}$ did not send a corruption request to $\mathcal{P}_{\mathsf{pvZK}}$ before).

Fig. 2. Description of $\Pi_{\mathsf{pvZK}} = (\mathcal{P}_{\mathsf{pvZK}}, \mathcal{V}_{\mathsf{pvZK}})$.

prove that Π_{pvWI} satisfies Definitions 4 and 6. Therefore we have the following corollary.

Corollary 1. *Let* $\Gamma^{\mathsf{V}} = (\mathsf{UpdateState}, \mathsf{GetRecords}, \mathsf{Broadcast}, \mathsf{GenBlock})$ *be a blockchain protocol that satisfies chain-consistency property, chain-growth property and Assumption 1. Assuming secure erasure, if one-way permutations exists, then* $\Pi_{\mathsf{pvZK}} = (\mathcal{P}_{\mathsf{pvZK}}, \mathcal{V}_{\mathsf{pvZK}})$ *is a delayed-input publicly verifiable zero-knowledge proof system w.r.t. blockchain failure over* Γ^{V} *for* $\mathcal{NP}$.

The proof of the Theorem 1 and the description of the simulator $\mathsf{S}_{\mathsf{pvZK}}$ for Π_{pvZK} can be found in the next subsections.

Note that the inputs of Π_{pvZK} (i.e., the statement x and the witness w) are used only in the last message of the protocol. Therefore the prover can *pre-process* all the other messages ahead of time (even without knowing the statement) and complete the last message whenever the statement becomes available.

4.1 Delayed-Input Completeness (Definition 5)

Let st and $\mathsf{st}_{\mathsf{Pt}_i}$ be respectively the states of $\mathcal{P}$ and of an honest player Pt_i after Step 7 of Π_{pvZK} (that is, after the proof has been computed). Since both $\mathcal{P}$ and $\mathcal{V}$ are running the protocol honestly, from the chain-consistency property follows that $\mathbf{B}^{\lceil \eta} \preceq \tilde{\mathbf{B}}$ (with overwhelming probability), where $\mathbf{B} = \mathsf{GetRecords}(\mathsf{st})$ and $\tilde{\mathbf{B}} = \mathsf{GetRecords}(\mathsf{st}_{\mathsf{Pt}_i})$. Therefore $\mathcal{V}$ performs all the blockchain checks on $\tilde{\mathbf{B}}$ successfully. After that $\mathcal{P}$ posts the commitments $\{\mathsf{com}_j\}_{j=1}^{u \cdot d}$ in the blockchain $\mathbf{B}$ we are guaranteed by the chain growth property of Γ^{V} and by Assumption 1 that new d blocks will be added to $\mathbf{B}$ and among them n will be pristine. Therefore $\mathcal{P}$ can construct the instance x_{com} (as defined in Step 3 of Fig. 2) in order to complete her execution running Π_{pvWI}.

Finally the completeness of Π_{pvZK} follows from the completeness of Π_{pvWI} and the correctness of Π_{Com}.

4.2 Soundness (Definition 4)

Claim 1. *If Assumption 1 holds for* Γ^{V} *then* Π_{pvZK} *is sound.*

Proof. Let $\mathcal{P}_{\mathsf{pvZK}}^{\star}$ be a successful adversary. Recall that $\mathcal{P}_{\mathsf{pvZK}}^{\star}$ is successful if it produces with non-negligible probability an accepting π of Π_{pvZK} w.r.t. $x \notin \mathcal{L}$, where x is adaptively chosen by $\mathcal{P}_{\mathsf{pvZK}}^{\star}$ before the last message of π.

Let B^* be the block in the blockchain $\mathbf{B}$ where the last commitment of the set of the commitments $\mathsf{com}_1, \ldots, \mathsf{com}_{u \cdot d}$ is posted by $\mathcal{P}_{\mathsf{pvZK}}^{\star}$, and let $B_1, \ldots, B_n$ be the n pristine blocks (in a sequence of d blocks) appeared in $\mathbf{B}$ after the block B^*.

From Assumption 1 it follows that in a sequence of n pristine blocks $B_1, \ldots, B_n$ at least $n/2 + 1$ are generated by honest players through good executions of $\mathsf{GenBlock}$ w.r.t. $\mathbf{B}$. Let $\overline{B}_1, \ldots, \overline{B}_{n/2+1}$ be the $n/2 + 1$ blocks generated by honest players through good executions of $\mathsf{GenBlock}$ w.r.t. $\mathbf{B}$ in the sequence of pristine blocks $B_1, \ldots, B_n$, and the value $\overline{v}_j$ be s.t. $\overline{v}_j = \mathtt{trim}(\overline{B}_j)$, for $j = 1, \ldots, n/2+1$. When $\mathcal{P}^\star_{\mathsf{pvZK}}$ posts $\mathsf{com}_1, \ldots, \mathsf{com}_{u \cdot d}$, it has no information about the values $\overline{v}_1, \ldots, \overline{v}_{n/2+1}$, because when $\mathcal{P}^\star_{\mathsf{pvZK}}$ posts $\mathsf{com}_1, \ldots, \mathsf{com}_{u \cdot d}$ each value $\overline{v}_j$ (for $j = 1, \ldots, n/2 + 1$) can be guessed with probability $2^{-\lambda}$ (since Assumption 1 holds and each $\overline{v}_j$ has at least λ bits of min-entropy). Moreover, since Π_{Com} is a perfectly binding commitment scheme, the committed message is uniquely identified in the commitment phase. Therefore the probability that $\mathcal{P}^\star_{\mathsf{pvZK}}$ correctly commits the values $\overline{v}_1, \ldots, \overline{v}_{n/2+1}$ is negligible. It follows that the values $\overline{v}_1, \ldots, \overline{v}_{n/2+1}$ are committed in $\mathsf{com}_1, \ldots, \mathsf{com}_{u \cdot d}$ only with negligible probability, therefore $x_{\mathsf{com}} \notin \mathcal{L}_{\mathsf{com}}$. Since by contradiction we are assuming that $\mathcal{P}^\star_{\mathsf{pvZK}}$ is successful w.r.t. $x \notin \mathcal{L}$, it follows that with non-negligible probability $x_{\mathsf{pvWI}} = (x_{\mathsf{com}}, x) \notin \mathcal{L}_{\mathsf{pvWI}}$. This contradicts the soundness property of Π_{pvWI}

4.3 Zero Knowledge w.r.t. Blockchain Failure (Definition 7)

Simulator $\mathsf{S}_{\mathsf{pvZK}}$. The simulator $\mathsf{S}_{\mathsf{pvZK}}$ is presented in Fig. 3, the red steps denote the steps of $\mathsf{S}_{\mathsf{pvZK}}$ that are different from the one of $\mathcal{P}_{\mathsf{pvZK}}$.

Zero Knowledge w.r.t. Blockchain Failure. Let $\mathcal{A}$ be the adversary as defined in Definitions 7. Intuitively, we want to prove that even if the blockchain collapses, the zero-knowledge property of Π_{pvZK} is still preserved.

In order to show that Π_{pvZK} satisfies zero knowledge w.r.t. blockchain failure we will consider the following hybrid experiments.

– Hybrid H_0. In hybrid experiment $H_0(\lambda)$ the simulator $\mathsf{S}'_{\mathsf{pvZK}}$ follows the honest prover procedure of $\mathcal{P}_{\mathsf{pvZK}}$.
– Hybrid H_1. Experiment $H_1(\lambda)$ is described as $H_0(\lambda)$ except that the simulator $\mathsf{S}'_{\mathsf{pvZK}}$ emulates the honest players in the execution of Γ^V, more precisely $\mathsf{S}'_{\mathsf{pvZK}}$ follows Step 3 and Steps 14 and 15 of Fig. 3.
  Note that after that the commitments are posted in the blockchain in $H_0(\lambda)$ when an honest player $\mathsf{Pt}_j \in \mathcal{H}$ receives a request from $\mathcal{Z}$ of an execution of $\mathsf{GenBlock}$ using fresh randomness for $f_{\mathsf{ID}}(1^\lambda; \cdot)$ Pt_j runs f_{ID} on input freshly generated randomness obtaining a freshly generated value v. It easy to see that in $H_1(\lambda)$ the value v is generated in the same way as $\mathsf{Pt}_j \in \mathcal{H}$ does in $H_0(\lambda)$ except that v is computed at the start of Π_{pvZK}. Since (1) the values $v_j \leftarrow f_{\mathsf{ID}}(1^\lambda; r_j)$ for $j = 1, \ldots, d \cdot u$ are identically distributed in the two hybrid experiments and (2) $\mathsf{S}'_{\mathsf{pvZK}}$ is behaving in the same way of the honest players in an execution of Γ^V, we have that $H_1 \equiv H_0$.
– Hybrid H_2. If a corruption of the form $\langle \mathsf{ZK}_{\mathsf{corr}}(x, w) \rangle$ occurs when Π_{pvZK} starts, $H_2(\lambda)$ corresponds to $H_1(\lambda)$, otherwise we consider a series of hybrid experiments $H_2^0(\lambda), \ldots, H_2^{u \cdot d}(\lambda)$ where $H_2^0(\lambda) = H_1(\lambda)$ and $H_2(\lambda) = H_2^{u \cdot d}(\lambda)$ and they are described as follows.
  Hybrid H_2^k with $k \in \{1, \ldots, u \cdot d\}$. The hybrid experiment $H_2^k(\lambda)$ is describe ad $H_2^{k-1}(\lambda)$ except that $\mathsf{S}'_{\mathsf{pvZK}}$ computes the k-th commitment following Steps 2–4 of Fig. 3. Indeed, $\mathsf{S}'_{\mathsf{pvZK}}$ computes $(\mathsf{com}_j, \mathsf{open}_j) \leftarrow \mathsf{Com}(v_j)$ for $j = 1, \ldots, k$ (where $v_j \leftarrow f_{\mathsf{ID}}(1^\lambda; r_j)$) and it computes $(\mathsf{com}_j, \mathsf{open}_j) \leftarrow \mathsf{Com}(0^q)$ for $j = k+1, \ldots, u \cdot d$.

Simulator Procedure: S_{pvZK}. Parameters are defined in Table 4.

— **First step.**

1. If a corruption request $\langle ZK_{corr}(x, w) \rangle$ is received, then execute the steps of $\mathcal{P}_{pvZK}$ on input x, w. Else continue with the following steps.
2. For $j = 1, \ldots, u \cdot d$:
3.   Pick r_j randomly in $\{0, 1\}^{poly(\lambda)}$ compute $v_j \leftarrow f_{ID}(1^\lambda; r_j)$ and set $R = R || r_j$.
4.   Compute $(com_j, open_j) \leftarrow Com(v_j)$.

— **Blockchain Interaction.**

5. Set $st = \epsilon$. Post $com_1, \ldots, com_{u \cdot d}$ on the blockchain by running $Broadcast(1^\lambda, com_1, \ldots, com_{u \cdot d})$ and then monitor the blockchain by running $st = UpdateState(1^\lambda, st)$, $\mathbf{B} = GetRecords(1^\lambda, st)$, until $com_1, \ldots, com_{u \cdot d}$ followed by d additional blocks $B_1, \ldots, B_d$ are posted on the blockchain $\mathbf{B}^{\lceil \eta}$. Let $\overline{B_1}, \ldots, \overline{B_n}$ be the n pristine blocks in the sequence $B_1, \ldots, B_d$.

— **Second step.**

6. Compute $v_j = trim(\overline{B_j})$ for $j = 1, \ldots, n$ and set $com = \{com_j\}_{j=1}^{u \cdot d}$, $val = \{v_j\}_{j=1}^n$, $x_{com} = (com, val)$, $\pi_{pvWI}^0 = (1^\lambda, \ell)$.
7. Let $B_{j_1}, \ldots, B_{j_k}$ be the pristine blocks generated by honest players in the sequence $B_1, \ldots, B_d$ set $w_{com} = open_{j_1}, \ldots, open_{j_k}$ (where $k \geq n/2 + 1$ by Assumption 1).
8. Obtain π_{pvWI}^1 with randomness r_1 executing $\mathcal{P}_{pvWI}$ on input $1^\lambda, \ell$ and interacting with the blockchain if it is required by $\mathcal{P}_{pvWI}$.
   If a corruption request $\langle ZK_{corr}(x, w) \rangle$ is received: erase the values $\{open_j\}_{j=1}^{u \cdot d}$ and output $st_{\mathcal{P}_{pvZK}} = r^1$ and π^1.
9. For $i = 2, \ldots, m - 1$:
       Obtain r^i, π_{pvWI}^i executing $\mathcal{P}_{pvWI}$ on input r^{i-1}, and π_{pvWI}^{i-1}
       interacting with the blockchain if it is required by $\mathcal{P}_{pvWI}$.
       If a corruption request $\langle ZK_{corr}(x, w) \rangle$ is received.
       Erase the values $\{open_j\}_{j=1}^{u \cdot d}$. Output $st_{\mathcal{P}_{pvZK}} = r' || r^i$ and $\pi^1, \ldots, \pi^i$.
10. If a corruption request $\langle ZK_{corr}(x, w) \rangle$ was not received, then:
11.   Upon receiving x from $\mathcal{A}$, set $x_{pvWI} = (x, x_{com})$
       Obtain π_{pvWI}^m executing $\mathcal{P}_{pvWI}$ with randomness on input $\pi_{pvWI}^{m-1}, x_{pvWI}, w_{com}$
       and interacting with the blockchain if it is required by $\mathcal{P}_{pvWI}$.
       Set $\pi_{pvWI} = (\pi_{pvWI}^1, \ldots, \pi_{pvWI}^m)$ and $\pi = (x_{pvWI}, \{com_j\}_{j=1}^n, \pi_{pvWI})$.
       Obtain $st_{\mathcal{P}_{pvWI}}$ from $\mathcal{P}_{pvWI}$ set $st_{\mathcal{P}_{pvZK}} = st_{pvWI}$ and erase $\{open\}_{i=1}^{u \cdot d}$. Output π.
12. If a corruption request $\langle ZK_{corr}(x, w) \rangle$ is received: output $st_{\mathcal{P}_{pvZK}}$.

— Execution of Γ^V simulating honest player Pt_j. Act on behalf of Pt_j as described in Section 3.2, in particular, upon receiving a request of an execution of GenBlock using fresh randomness for the function $f_{ID}(1^\lambda; \cdot)$:

13. Run $\mathbf{B} = GetRecords(1^\lambda, st_j)$, let np be number of pristine blocks posted after $com_1, \ldots, com_{u \cdot d}$ in the blockchain $\mathbf{B}^{\lceil \eta}$. Let K be the number of blocks added in the blockchain $\mathbf{B}^{\lceil \eta}$. Let nb be the number of honest executions of GenBlock already executed for the block B_{K+1}.
14. If $0 \leq np < n$: Parse R as $r_1, \ldots, r_{u \cdot d}$ and run an execution of GenBlock on behalf of honest player Pt_j with randomness r_{np+nb} to execute f_{ID}.
15. Else: Pick r at random from $\{0, 1\}^{poly(\lambda)}$ and GenBlock on behalf of honest player Pt_j with randomness r to execute f_{ID}.
16. If $\mathcal{A}$ sends a collapse request $\langle corr, all \rangle$ compute the following steps: Disclose state st_{Pt_i} of honest player Pt_i, for all $i = 1, \ldots, |\mathcal{H}|$. If a corruption request $\langle ZK_{corr}(x, w) \rangle$ did not occur obtain $st_{\mathcal{P}_{pvWI}}$ from $\mathcal{P}_{pvWI}$ set $st_{\mathcal{P}_{pvZK}} = st_{pvWI}$ and disclose $st_{\mathcal{P}_{pvZK}}$.

Fig. 3. Simulator S_{pvZK} of Π_{pvZK}.

Assuming secure erasure, from Claim 2 it holds that $H_2^{k-1} \approx H_2^k$ for all $k = 1, \ldots, u \cdot d$, therefore since H_1 corresponds to H_2^0 and H_2 corresponds to $H_2^{u \cdot d}$ we conclude that $H_1(\lambda) \approx H_2(\lambda)$.

- Hybrid H_3. If a corruption of the form $\langle \mathsf{ZK}_{\mathsf{corr}}(x, w) \rangle$ occurs during the computation of the first $m-1$ messages of Π_{pvWI}, we have that $H_2(\lambda)$ corresponds to $H_3(\lambda)$. Indeed due to the delayed-input property of Π_{pvWI}, $\mathsf{S}'_{\mathsf{pvZK}}$ computes the first $m-1$ messages of Π_{pvWI} as $\mathcal{P}_{\mathsf{pvZK}}$ does. Note that the decommitment information $\{\mathsf{open}_j\}_{j=1}^{u \cdot d}$ are securely erased by $\mathcal{P}_{\mathsf{pvZK}}$, therefore if $\mathsf{S}'_{\mathsf{pvZK}}$ receives a corruption request during the computation of the first $m-1$ messages of Π_{pvWI} she is able to exhibit randomness that is identically distributed to the one that $\mathcal{P}_{\mathsf{pvZK}}$ would have in her state.

  If a corruption of the form $\langle \mathsf{ZK}_{\mathsf{corr}}(x, w) \rangle$ does not occur during the computation of the first $m-1$ messages of Π_{pvWI}, then H_3 is defined as follow.

  The hybrid experiment $H_3(\lambda)$ is described exactly as $H_2(\lambda)$ except for the witness used to compute the last message π_{pvWI}^m generated using Π_{pvWI}, for which $\mathsf{S}'_{\mathsf{pvZK}}$ is acting as $\mathsf{S}_{\mathsf{pvZK}}$. In more details, for the computation of the message π_{pvWI}^m $\mathsf{S}'_{\mathsf{pvZK}}$ is behaving as described in Steps 11 of Fig. 3. Assuming secure erasure, since Π_{pvWI} satisfies WI w.r.t. blockchain failure it follows that $H_2(\lambda) \approx H_3(\lambda)$ (see Claim 3).

$H_0(\lambda)$ corresponds to the experiment where $\mathcal{P}_{\mathsf{pvZK}}$ is interacting with $\mathcal{A}$ and $H_3(\lambda)$ corresponds to the experiment where $\mathsf{S}_{\mathsf{pvZK}}$ is interacting with $\mathcal{A}$. Since $H_3(\lambda) \approx H_0(\lambda)$ it follows that $\mathcal{A}$ distinguishes the two experiments only with negligible probability.

Claim 2. *Assume that Π_{com} satisfies computationally hiding secure erasure, and the blockchain protocol Γ^{V} satisfies Assumption 1, then for every pair of messages $m_0, m_1 \in \{0,1\}^q$ it holds that $H_2^{k-1}(\lambda) \approx H_2^k(\lambda)$ for $k \in \{1, \ldots, u \cdot d\}$.*

Proof. Suppose by contradiction that the above claim does not hold, this implies that there exists an adversary $\mathcal{A}$ that is able to distinguish between $H_2^{k-1}(\lambda)$ and $H_2^k(\lambda)$. Note that $\mathcal{A}$ could wait until the protocol Π_{pvZK} ends and then can send a collapse request $\langle \mathsf{corr}, \mathsf{all} \rangle$. Using $\mathcal{A}$ it is possible to construct a malicious receiver $\mathcal{A}_{\mathsf{Com}}$ that breaks the hiding of Π_{Com} with non-negligible probability. Let $\mathcal{CH}$ be the challenger of the hiding game of Π_{Com}. $\mathcal{A}_{\mathsf{Com}}$ computes the following steps:

1. Compute v_k running $f_{\mathsf{ID}}(1^\lambda; r)$ where r is an uniformly chosen randomness and sends the messages $m_0 = 0^q$ and $m_1 = v_k$ to $\mathcal{CH}$.
2. Upon receiving $\tilde{\mathsf{com}}_k$ from $\mathcal{CH}$, $\mathcal{A}_{\mathsf{Com}}$ interacts with $\mathcal{A}$ computing all the messages of $\mathsf{S}'_{\mathsf{pvZK}}$ following the steps described in $H_2^k(\lambda)$ (and in $H_2^{k-1}(\lambda)$) except for the k-th commitment for which she uses $\tilde{\mathsf{com}}_k$.
3. Emulation of the state $\mathsf{st}_{\mathcal{P}_{\mathsf{pvZK}}}$ of $\mathcal{P}_{\mathsf{pvZK}}$ after π is compute: acts as $\mathsf{S}'_{\mathsf{pvZK}}$ in $H_2^k(\lambda)$ (and in $H_2^{k-1}(\lambda)$) and securely erase the decommitment information $\{\mathsf{open}_j\}_{j=1}^{u \cdot d}$ (except for $\tilde{\mathsf{open}}_k$ that was never available to $\mathcal{A}_{\mathsf{Com}}$), set the state $\mathsf{st}_{\mathcal{P}_{\mathsf{pvZK}}}$ as described $H_2^k(\lambda)$ (and in $H_2^{k-1}(\lambda)$) that is as described in Step 12 of Fig. 3.

4. execution of Γ^{V} :

    4.1. Emulate the honest players acting as the honest player of Γ^{V} (as described in Section $H_2^k(\lambda)$ (and in $H_2^{k-1}(\lambda)$)).

    4.2. After π of Π_{pvZK} is computed if $\mathcal{A}$ sends a collapse request $\langle \texttt{corr}, \texttt{all} \rangle$, disclose the states of all the honest players $\mathsf{st}_{\mathsf{Pt}_1}, \ldots, \mathsf{st}_{\mathsf{Pt}_{|\mathcal{H}|}}$ and $\mathsf{st}_{\mathcal{P}_{\mathsf{pvZK}}}$.

5. When $\mathcal{A}$ stops, $\mathcal{A}_{\mathsf{Com}}$ outputs the outcome of $\mathcal{A}$.

$\mathcal{A}_{\mathsf{Com}}$ emulates the states of all the honest players $\mathsf{st}_{\mathsf{Pt}_1}, \ldots, \mathsf{st}_{\mathsf{Pt}_{|\mathcal{H}|}}$ in a perfect manner, since $\mathcal{A}_{\mathsf{Com}}$ just acts as the honest players in the execution of Γ^{V}. Moreover, $\mathsf{st}_{\mathcal{P}_{\mathsf{pvZK}}}$ after π is computed in Step 3 of the above procedure, corresponds to the state of an honest $\mathcal{P}_{\mathsf{pvZK}}$ in $H_2^k(\lambda)$ (and in $H_2^{k-1}(\lambda)$). The proof is concluded observing that if $\mathcal{CH}$ uses the message m_0 to compute $\tilde{\mathsf{com}}_k$ then the reduction is distributed as H_2^{k-1} and as H_2^k otherwise.

Claim 3. *Assume that Π_{pvWI} satisfies WI w.r.t. blockchain failure as in Definition 6 over any blockchain protocol, secure erasure, and the blockchain protocol Γ^{V} satisfies Assumption 1, then for every $x_{\mathsf{pvWI}}, w_0, w_1$ s.t. $(x_{\mathsf{pvWI}}, w_0) \in \mathcal{R}_{\mathsf{pvWI}}$ and $(x_{\mathsf{pvWI}}, w_1) \in \mathcal{R}_{\mathsf{pvWI}}$ it holds that $H_2(\lambda) \approx H_3(\lambda)$.*

Proof. Suppose by contradiction that the above claim does not hold, this implies that there exists an adversary $\mathcal{A}$ that is able to distinguish between $H_2(\lambda)$ and $H_3(\lambda)$. Note that $\mathcal{A}$ could wait until the protocol Π_{pvZK} ends and then can send a collapse request $\langle \texttt{corr}, \texttt{all} \rangle$. Using $\mathcal{A}$ it is possible to construct a malicious verifier $\mathcal{A}_{\mathsf{pvWI}}$ that breaks the WI w.r.t. blockchain failure w.r.t. any blockchain protocol property of Π_{pvWI}. We remark that Π_{pvWI} enjoys WI w.r.t. blockchain failure w.r.t. any blockchain protocol (i.e., even w.r.t. a blockchain protocol where $\mathcal{P}_{\mathsf{pvWI}}$ is the only honest player of the blockchain protocol). Let $\mathcal{CH}$ be the challenger of the WI w.r.t. blockchain failure game of Π_{pvWI}. $\mathcal{A}_{\mathsf{pvWI}}$ computes the following steps.

1. $\mathcal{A}_{\mathsf{pvWI}}$ acts as described in $H_2(\lambda)$ and $H_3(\lambda)$ until Step 6 of Fig. 3. In particular, $\mathcal{A}_{\mathsf{pvWI}}$ computes the instance x_{com} and the witness w_{com} as explained, respectively, in Step 6 and in Steps 7, 14 and 15 of Fig. 3.

2. $\mathcal{A}_{\mathsf{pvWI}}$ interacts as a proxy between $\mathcal{CH}$ and $\mathcal{A}$ for the messages π_{pvWI}^1, $\ldots, \pi_{\mathsf{pvWI}}^{m-1}$, and interacting with the blockchain as a $\mathcal{P}_{\mathsf{pvWI}}$ would do upon request of $\mathcal{CH}$.

3. $\mathcal{A}$ chooses $(x, w) \in \mathcal{R}$ before the last message of Π_{pvZK} and therefore $\mathcal{A}_{\mathsf{pvWI}}$ (that is acting as $\mathcal{P}_{\mathsf{pvZK}}$) will obtain w s.t. $(x, w) \in \mathcal{R}$ and sends $x_{\mathsf{pvWI}} = (x, x_{\mathsf{com}}), w, w_{\mathsf{com}}$ to $\mathcal{CH}$ before the message π_{pvWI}^m. $\mathcal{A}_{\mathsf{pvWI}}$ completes the proof π of Π_{pvZK} using π_{pvWI}^m and interacting with the blockchain as a $\mathcal{P}_{\mathsf{pvWI}}$ would do upon request of $\mathcal{CH}$.

    3.1. Emulation of the state $\mathsf{st}_{\mathcal{P}_{\mathsf{pvZK}}}$ of $\mathcal{P}_{\mathsf{pvZK}}$ after π is computed:

        i. $\mathcal{A}_{\mathsf{pvWI}}$ sends a collapse request $\langle \texttt{corr}, \texttt{all} \rangle$ to $\mathcal{CH}$ obtaining $\mathsf{st}_{\mathcal{P}_{\mathsf{pvWI}}}$ from the challenger $\mathcal{CH}$.

        ii. $\mathcal{A}_{\mathsf{pvWI}}$ is acting as $\mathsf{S}'_{\mathsf{pvZK}}$ in $H_2(\lambda)$ (and in $H_3(\lambda)$) and securely erases the decommitment information $\{\mathsf{open}_j\}_{j=1}^{u \cdot d}$, set $\mathsf{st}_{\mathcal{P}_{\mathsf{pvZK}}} = \mathsf{st}_{\mathcal{P}_{\mathsf{pvWI}}}$.

4. execution of $\Gamma^{\vee}$:
   4.1. $\mathcal{A}_{\mathsf{pvWI}}$ emulates the honest players acting as the honest players of $\Gamma^{\vee}$ as described in $H_3(\lambda)$ (and in $H_2(\lambda)$).
   4.2. After π is computed if $\mathcal{A}$ sends a collapse request $\langle\mathtt{corr},\mathtt{all}\rangle$, $\mathcal{A}_{\mathsf{pvWI}}$ discloses the states of all the honest players $\mathsf{st}_{\mathsf{P}_{t_1}},\dots,\mathsf{st}_{\mathsf{P}_{t_{|\mathcal{H}|}}}$ and $\mathsf{st}_{\mathcal{P}_{\mathsf{pvZK}}}$.
5. When $\mathcal{A}$ stops, $\mathcal{A}_{\mathsf{pvWI}}$ outputs the outcome of $\mathcal{A}$.

We note that $\mathcal{A}_{\mathsf{pvWI}}$ simulates the states of all the honest players $\mathsf{st}_{\mathsf{P}_{t_1}},\dots,\mathsf{st}_{\mathsf{P}_{t_{|\mathcal{H}|}}}$ in a perfect way, this is because in the execution of $\Gamma^{\vee}$, $\mathcal{A}_{\mathsf{pvWI}}$ is behaving in the same way of the honest players of an execution of $\Gamma^{\vee}$ (as described in $H_3(\lambda)$ (and in $H_2(\lambda)$)). The proof is concluded observing that if $\mathcal{CH}$ uses the witness w to compute π^m_{pvWI} then the reduction is distributed as H_2, and as H_3 otherwise.

5   On Public Verifiability in [16]

A recent work [16] models the blockchain as a global ledger functionality $\mathcal{G}_{\mathtt{ledger}}$ available to all the participants of a cryptographic protocol. [16] constructs concurrent self-composable secure computation protocol for general functionalities in such global ledger model. The protocols constructed in [16] are not publicly verifiable, and therefore do not satisfy the main feature that we study and achieve in this work. Indeed the authors of [16] already notice in their work that non-interactive zero knowledge for NP is impossible in their model. We remark that actually the impossibility extends also to publicly verifiable zero knowledge for languages that are not in BPP and we give now a high-level intuition. First of all, note that in the model of [16], since the blockchain is modeled as a global ledger, the simulator S of the zero-knowledge property has the same power of the adversary while accessing $\mathcal{G}_{\mathtt{ledger}}$. Suppose now by contradiction that it is possible to construct a publicly verifiable zero-knowledge argument $\Pi = (\mathcal{P},\mathcal{V})$ for the $\mathcal{NP}$-language $\mathcal{L}$ in the $\mathcal{G}_{\mathtt{ledger}}$ model. This means that there exists a simulator S that having access to $\mathcal{G}_{\mathtt{ledger}}$ on input any instance $x \in \mathcal{L}$ outputs an accepting proof π w.r.t. x that is (computationally) indistinguishable from a proof generated by a honest prover $\mathcal{P}$. Let us now consider a malicious polynomial-time prover $\mathcal{P}^*$ that in the $\mathcal{G}_{\mathtt{ledger}}$-model wants to prove a false statement x^* to an honest verifier $\mathcal{V}$. We will show that $\mathcal{P}^*$ proves a false theorem with non-negligible probability, $\mathcal{P}^*$ works as follows. $\mathcal{P}^*$ internally runs S on input x^*. Moreover, each interaction that S wants to do with $\mathcal{G}_{\mathtt{ledger}}$ is emulated by $\mathcal{P}^*$ and this is possible since S and $\mathcal{P}^*$ are accessing $\mathcal{G}_{\mathtt{ledger}}$ in the same way. At the end of the execution, S outputs π^* w.r.t. x^*. $\mathcal{P}^*$ forwards π^* to $\mathcal{V}$. Note that we are guaranteed by the zero-knowledge property that π^* is accepting and the view of an honest verifier that receives π^* from $\mathcal{P}^*$ is (computationally) indistinguishable from the view that $\mathcal{V}$ has when she receives a proof from an honest prover. Finally we note that public verifiability guarantees that π^* can be accepted by any verifier non-interactively, The only caveat in the above reasoning can concern the fact that S might refuse to produce an accepting proof when $x \notin \mathcal{L}$. However this immediately shows that the language $\mathcal{L}$ is in BPP.

Acknowledgments. Research supported in part by NSF grants #1012798,#1764025, and in part by the European Union's Horizon 2020 research and innovation programme under grant agreement No 780477 (project PRIViLEDGE).

References

1. Pencil - workshop on privacy enhancing cryptography in ledgers (2019). https://priviledge-project.eu/pencil
2. Aggarwal, D., Obremski, M., Ribeiro, J., Siniscalchi, L., Visconti, I.: How to extract useful randomness from unreliable sources. In: Canteaut, A., Ishai, Y. (eds.) EUROCRYPT 2020. LNCS, vol. 12105, pp. 343–372. Springer, Cham (2020). https://doi.org/10.1007/978-3-030-45721-1_13
3. Badertscher, C., Garay, J., Maurer, U., Tschudi, D., Zikas, V.: But why does it work? A rational protocol design treatment of bitcoin. In: Nielsen, J.B., Rijmen, V. (eds.) EUROCRYPT 2018. LNCS, vol. 10821, pp. 34–65. Springer, Cham (2018). https://doi.org/10.1007/978-3-319-78375-8_2
4. Badertscher, C., Gazi, P., Kiayias, A., Russell, A., Zikas, V.: Ouroboros genesis: composable proof-of-stake blockchains with dynamic availability. In: Proceedings of the 2018 ACM SIGSAC Conference on Computer and Communications Security, CCS 2018, Toronto, ON, Canada, 15–19 October 2018, pp. 913–930 (2018)
5. Badertscher, C., Maurer, U., Tschudi, D., Zikas, V.: Bitcoin as a transaction ledger: a composable treatment. In: Katz, J., Shacham, H. (eds.) CRYPTO 2017. LNCS, vol. 10401, pp. 324–356. Springer, Cham (2017). https://doi.org/10.1007/978-3-319-63688-7_11
6. Baldimtsi, F., Kiayias, A., Zacharias, T., Zhang, B.: Crowd verifiable zero-knowledge and end-to-end verifiable multiparty computation. In: Moriai, S., Wang, H. (eds.) ASIACRYPT 2020. LNCS, vol. 12493, pp. 717–748. Springer, Cham (2020). https://doi.org/10.1007/978-3-030-64840-4_24
7. Barak, B.: How to go beyond the black-box simulation barrier. In: 42nd Annual Symposium on Foundations of Computer Science, FOCS 2001, , Las Vegas, Nevada, USA, 14–17 October 2001, pp. 106–115. IEEE Computer Society (2001)
8. Bellare, M., Rogaway, P.: Optimal asymmetric encryption. In: De Santis, A. (ed.) EUROCRYPT 1994. LNCS, vol. 950, pp. 92–111. Springer, Heidelberg (1995). https://doi.org/10.1007/BFb0053428
9. Ben-Sasson, E., Chiesa, A., Gabizon, A., Virza, M.: Quasi-linear size zero knowledge from linear-algebraic PCPs. In: Kushilevitz, E., Malkin, T. (eds.) TCC 2016. LNCS, vol. 9563, pp. 33–64. Springer, Heidelberg (2016). https://doi.org/10.1007/978-3-662-49099-0_2
10. Benhamouda, F., et al.: Can a public blockchain keep a secret? In: Pass, R., Pietrzak, K. (eds.) TCC 2020. LNCS, vol. 12550, pp. 260–290. Springer, Cham (2020). https://doi.org/10.1007/978-3-030-64375-1_10
11. Bentov, I., Gabizon, A., Zuckerman, D.: Bitcoin beacon. CoRR abs/1605.04559 (2016)
12. Bentov, I., Kumaresan, R.: How to use bitcoin to design fair protocols. IACR Crypto. ePrint Arch. **2014**, 129 (2014)
13. Bonneau, J., Clark, J., Goldfeder, S.: On bitcoin as a public randomness source. Cryptology ePrint Archive, Report 2015/1015 (2015). https://eprint.iacr.org/2015/1015

14. Bowe, S., Gabizon, A., Green, M.D.: A multi-party protocol for constructing the public parameters of the Pinocchio zk-SNARK. In: Zohar, A., et al. (eds.) FC 2018. LNCS, vol. 10958, pp. 64–77. Springer, Heidelberg (2019). https://doi.org/10.1007/978-3-662-58820-8_5

15. Canetti, R.: Universally composable security: a new paradigm for cryptographic protocols. In: 42nd Annual Symposium on Foundations of Computer Science, FOCS 2001, Las Vegas, Nevada, USA, 14–17 October 2001, pp. 136–145. IEEE Computer Society (2001)

16. Choudhuri, A.R., Goyal, V., Jain, A.: Founding secure computation on blockchains. In: Ishai, Y., Rijmen, V. (eds.) EUROCRYPT 2019. LNCS, vol. 11477, pp. 351–380. Springer, Cham (2019). https://doi.org/10.1007/978-3-030-17656-3_13

17. Feige, U., Lapidot, D., Shamir, A.: Multiple non-interactive zero knowledge proofs based on a single random string (extended abstract). In: 31st Annual Symposium on Foundations of Computer Science, St. Louis, Missouri, USA, 22–24 October 1990, vol. 1, pp. 308–317. IEEE Computer Society (1990)

18. Ganesh, C., Orlandi, C., Tschudi, D.: Proof-of-stake protocols for privacy-aware blockchains. In: Ishai, Y., Rijmen, V. (eds.) EUROCRYPT 2019. LNCS, vol. 11476, pp. 690–719. Springer, Cham (2019). https://doi.org/10.1007/978-3-030-17653-2_23

19. Garay, J., Kiayias, A., Leonardos, N.: The bitcoin backbone protocol: analysis and applications. In: Oswald, E., Fischlin, M. (eds.) EUROCRYPT 2015. LNCS, vol. 9057, pp. 281–310. Springer, Heidelberg (2015). https://doi.org/10.1007/978-3-662-46803-6_10

20. Gennaro, R., Gentry, C., Parno, B., Raykova, M.: Quadratic span programs and succinct NIZKs without PCPs. In: Johansson, T., Nguyen, P.Q. (eds.) EUROCRYPT 2013. LNCS, vol. 7881, pp. 626–645. Springer, Heidelberg (2013). https://doi.org/10.1007/978-3-642-38348-9_37

21. Gentry, C., Halevi, S., Magri, B., Nielsen, J.B., Yakoubov, S.: Random-index PIR with applications to large-scale secure MPC. Cryptology ePrint Archive, Report 2020/1248 (2020). https://eprint.iacr.org/2020/1248

22. Gilad, Y., Hemo, R., Micali, S., Vlachos, G., Zeldovich, N.: Algorand: scaling Byzantine agreements for cryptocurrencies. In: Proceedings of the 26th Symposium on Operating Systems Principles, Shanghai, China, 28–31 October 2017, pp. 51–68 (2017)

23. Goyal, R., Goyal, V.: Overcoming cryptographic impossibility results using blockchains. In: Kalai, Y., Reyzin, L. (eds.) TCC 2017. LNCS, vol. 10677, pp. 529–561. Springer, Cham (2017). https://doi.org/10.1007/978-3-319-70500-2_18

24. Goyal, R., Goyal, V.: Overcoming cryptographic impossibility results using blockchains. Cryptology ePrint Archive, Report 2017/935 (2017). https://eprint.iacr.org/2017/935

25. Goyal, V., Kothapalli, A., Masserova, E., Parno, B., Song, Y.: Storing and retrieving secrets on a blockchain. IACR Cryptol. ePrint Arch. **2020**, 504 (2020)

26. Groth, J., Kohlweiss, M., Maller, M., Meiklejohn, S., Miers, I.: Updatable and universal common reference strings with applications to zk-SNARKs. In: Shacham, H., Boldyreva, A. (eds.) CRYPTO 2018. LNCS, vol. 10993, pp. 698–728. Springer, Cham (2018). https://doi.org/10.1007/978-3-319-96878-0_24

27. Juels, A., Kosba, A.E., Shi, E.: The ring of gyges: investigating the future of criminal smart contracts. In: Proceedings of the 2016 ACM SIGSAC Conference on Computer and Communications Security, Vienna, Austria, 24–28 October 2016, pp. 283–295 (2016)

28. Kerber, T., Kiayias, A., Kohlweiss, M., Zikas, V.: Ouroboros crypsinous: privacy-preserving proof-of-stake. In: 2019 IEEE Symposium on Security and Privacy, SP 2019, San Francisco, CA, USA, 19–23 May 2019, pp. 157–174. IEEE (2019)

29. Kiayias, A., Panagiotakos, G.: Speed-security tradeoffs in blockchain protocols. IACR Cryptology ePrint Archive: Report 2015/1019 (2015). http://eprint.iacr.org/2015/1019

30. Maller, M., Bowe, S., Kohlweiss, M., Meiklejohn, S.: Sonic: zero-knowledge SNARKs from linear-size universal and updatable structured reference strings. In: Cavallaro, L., Kinder, J., Wang, X., Katz, J. (eds.) Proceedings of the 2019 ACM SIGSAC Conference on Computer and Communications Security, CCS 2019, London, UK, 11–15 November 2019, pp. 2111–2128. ACM (2019)

31. Nakamoto, S.: Bitcoin: a peer-to-peer electionic cash system (2008, unpublished)

32. Pass, R., Seeman, L., Shelat, A.: Analysis of the blockchain protocol in asynchronous networks. In: Coron, J.-S., Nielsen, J.B. (eds.) EUROCRYPT 2017. LNCS, vol. 10211, pp. 643–673. Springer, Cham (2017). https://doi.org/10.1007/978-3-319-56614-6_22

33. Pass, R., Shi, E.: The sleepy model of consensus. In: Takagi, T., Peyrin, T. (eds.) ASIACRYPT 2017. LNCS, vol. 10625, pp. 380–409. Springer, Cham (2017). https://doi.org/10.1007/978-3-319-70697-9_14

34. Scafuro, A., Siniscalchi, L., Visconti, I.: Publicly verifiable proofs from blockchains. In: Lin, D., Sako, K. (eds.) PKC 2019. LNCS, vol. 11442, pp. 374–401. Springer, Cham (2019). https://doi.org/10.1007/978-3-030-17253-4_13

35. Scafuro, A., Siniscalchi, L., Visconti, I.: Publicly verifiable zero knowledge from (collapsing) blockchains. Cryptology ePrint Archive, Report 2020/1435. https://eprint.iacr.org/2020/1435

Two-Server Distributed ORAM with Sublinear Computation and Constant Rounds

Ariel Hamlin[1(✉)] and Mayank Varia[2]

[1] Khoury College of Computer Sciences, Northeastern University, Boston, MA, USA
hamlin.a@northeastern.edu
[2] Boston University, Boston, MA, USA
varia@bu.edu

Abstract. Distributed ORAM (DORAM) is a multi-server variant of Oblivious RAM. Originally proposed to lower bandwidth, DORAM has recently been of great interest due to its applicability to secure computation in the RAM model, where circuit complexity and rounds of communication are equally important metrics of efficiency. All prior DORAM constructions either involve linear work per server (e.g., Floram) or logarithmic rounds of communication between servers (e.g., square root ORAM). In this work, we construct the first DORAM schemes in the 2-server, semi-honest setting that simultaneously achieve sublinear server computation and constant rounds of communication. We provide two constant-round constructions, one based on square root ORAM that has $O(\sqrt{N} \log N)$ local computation and another based on secure computation of a doubly efficient PIR that achieves local computation of $O(N^\epsilon)$ for any $\epsilon > 0$ but that allows the servers to distinguish between reads and writes. As a building block in the latter construction, we provide secure computation protocols for evaluation and interpolation of multivariate polynomials based on the Fast Fourier Transform, which may be of independent interest.

Keywords: Distributed oblivious RAM · Square root ORAM · Doubly efficient PIR · Secure multi-party computation · Fast fourier transform

1 Introduction

Oblivious RAM (ORAM) has been a vigorous area of study for the last three decades since it was introduced by Goldreich and Ostrovsky [17]. ORAM focuses on a client-server model where the server stores an outsourced database upon which the client wishes to execute a series of reads and writes. ORAM provides *privacy*, hiding the *contents* of the database, as well *obliviousness*, hiding the client's *access patterns*. In the traditional client-server model the client is assumed to be trusted. Recent efforts in the field have focused on lower bounds [35], optimal bandwidth [2,31], and various different settings [15,32].

Distributed ORAM (DORAM) is a variant of the basic client-server ORAM model in which there are *multiple* non-colluding servers. Data is duplicated across

J. A. Garay (Ed.): PKC 2021, LNCS 12711, pp. 499–527, 2021.
https://doi.org/10.1007/978-3-030-75248-4_18

the servers and the client interacts with both as part of an access. The client again remains the only trusted party. It was first introduced by Ostrovsky and Shoup [30], and later formally defined by Lu and Ostrovsky [26]. Lu and Ostrovsky were motivated by the desire to circumnavigate existing lower bounds in the single-server setting for bandwidth overhead, and their construction achieved $O(\log N)$ overhead by leveraging two non-communicating servers. Following their seminal paper there have been a number of works in the DORAM model that further reduce bandwidth [1,7], reduce blocksize [25], or achieve practical efficiency [37].

Another advantage of the multi-server model of DORAM is its natural application to secure computation over databases in the RAM model. Traditional secure computation relies on a circuit representation that is at least linear in the size of the data over which it computes. This is prohibitive for any sublinear computation run on a database, such as binary search. Lu and Ostrovsky observe in [26] that the application of DORAM in this case is highly advantageous. The parties in the secure computation can simply emulate the DORAM client for any database access. In particular, they present a generic transformation from a 2-server DORAM scheme to a 2-party secure computation. It should be noted that works applying ORAM to secure computation are not limited to the DORAM setting, but also include adaptations of single server schemes. For example, there has been significant work on adapting tree-based ORAM schemes [33,34] for secure computation. All of these DORAM constructions can be used in general-purpose secure computation like garbled RAM schemes [13,14,16,27], or in special-purpose protocols like dynamic searchable encryption schemes [21].

There are two main approaches to constructing ORAM for secure computation: the first is to apply a generic MPC compiler, such as Garbled Circuits, to a ORAM or DORAM client [18,19,33,34], and the second is to design a client specifically implemented by the two servers [5,11,23,36]. Even if we start with an ORAM with our desired asymptotics (i.e. square-root ORAM [17]) applying a generic MPC compilers results in a server computation cost at least linear in the database size if we are to maintain constant rounds. There are a number of works that focus directly on the second model, which offers greater flexibility since the servers are typically afforded much more storage space than the client.

However, in both approaches, the multi-server setting introduces a new set of challenges apart from those found in the single-server ORAM setting. Wang et al. [33] also observe that the traditional efforts to optimize bandwidth overhead are ineffective in a setting where there are other controlling factors, such as the size of the circuit representation of the ORAM client. This is the motivation behind their Circuit ORAM construction, which focuses on optimizing circuit size. Doerner and shelat [11] also show that in many cases, bandwidth is not the limiting factor but rather the latency between the two servers. This encouraged them to build a *constant round* DORAM for secure computation. Previous constructions had relied on recursive structures, which incurred a $O(\log N)$ rounds for each access, a prohibitive cost for latency dominated secure computation settings. Subsequent works in the constant round setting worked on improving on the $O(\sqrt{N})$ overhead of Floram, achieving $O(\log^3 N)$ overhead [23], or $O(\sqrt{N})$ in a black-box setting [5]. As with the original construction, these subsequent works require *linear* local computation for each server. While for small N, latency costs may still dominate, for sufficiently large N this linear work is prohibitive. This leaves us with the following question:

Can we construct a 2-server Distributed ORAM for secure computation that achieves both constant round and sublinear server work?

In this work, we answer the above question in the affirmative.

1.1 Our Contributions

We present the first DORAM constructions in the 2-server, semi-honest secure computation setting to achieve constant rounds *and* sublinear local computation on the servers.

- Our first sublinear DORAM construction achieves constant rounds and amortized local computation and bandwidth cost of $O(\sqrt{N} \log N)$ per access. It is based on square-root ORAM and has a modular build, allowing for subsequent improvements in the functionalities we rely on to be easily substituted.
- Our second sublinear DORAM construction is based on a secure computation of Doubly Efficient Private Information Retrieval (DEPIR) where the distinction between reads and writes is no longer hidden. In this setting, we achieve constant rounds with local computation and bandwidth of $O(N^\epsilon \cdot \text{poly}(\lambda))$ for any $\epsilon > 0$.

As an crucial building block toward the second construction, we present a secure two-party computation protocol for the Fast Fourier Transform (FFT) for multivariate polynomial evaluation and interpolation in quasilinear time and with only local computation; this may be of independent interest.

1.2 Technical Overview

In this section, we describe both of our DORAM constructions in more detail.

Sublinear DORAM. We start with describing the original square-root ORAM (introduced by Goldreich and Ostrovsky [17]) that our construction is based on. There is a single read-only array of size N, which we call the *store*, and a writable *stash* of $\sqrt{N}$ size. Elements in the store are (address, value) pairs; at initialization, the elements are permuted with a permutation known only to the client, and all elements are encrypted. To perform a read at a particular address, the client checks the stash using a linear scan; if not present then it reads the permuted element from the read-only store, and if present then it is retrieved from the stash and a random 'dummy' element is read from the store instead. The newly-read element is placed in the stash, in order to maintain the invariant that each element is read only *once* from the store. In the case of a write, a dummy is read from the store and the element is written in the stash.

After enough queries have been made to fill the stash, a duration that which we call an *epoch*, the elements from the stash are *reshuffled* back into the main store, with only the newest write at each location being kept.

While the basic square-root ORAM construction achieves constant rounds with sublinear communication and server computation, it is non-trivial to convert it to a two-party DORAM. There are two major issues incurred by shifting this to the two party case: (1) representing the permutation over the elements of the store and (2) merging the elements from the stash back into the store.

We first discuss how to represent the permutation that maps addresses to physical locations in the store. In [36], which is also based on square root ORAM, they choose to represent the permutation as a shared array in recursive ORAMs. This improves computation complexity but leads to $O(\log N)$ rounds of communication. To maintain constant rounds, we must instead find a compact representation of the permutation. We look for inspiration from the original square-root scheme. There, they generate a random 'tag' for each element in the store using a random oracle and then sort the elements according to the tag. A lookup then involves only a random oracle evaluation and a binary search across the sorted elements. However, because it is a single server scheme, they must use an oblivious sorting network in order to break the correlation between items in different epochs, which does not run efficiently in constant rounds. We leverage the fact that we have a two servers to break up the oblivious sort into its two components, 'oblivious' + 'sort'. To prevent the server from mapping items between epochs, we use a simple constant round functionality to obliviously permute elements that allows each server to permute the elements in turn. As long as one server is honest, the data is permuted obliviously. This allows us to generate the tags using an oblivious pseudorandom function (OPRF), rather than a random oracle, on the newly obliviously permuted elements and then sort the tags locally. Lookup again is just an OPRF evaluation on the address shares and then a local binary search on the store.

The second challenge arises during the reshuffling phase of the protocol. In the original square-root ORAM, elements are simply moved back into their original locations (updated elements in the store, dummies back in the stash) by executing another oblivious shuffle. To solve this in constant rounds, we again exploit the ability to obliviously permute elements by using our two server architecture. In order to do that though, we must ensure that the elements that we are permuting do not contain any duplicates. For example, if a read was executed on index i, there would be two copies of element i, one in the stash and one in the store. To solve this issue, we note that the elements that have been read in the store is public knowledge to both servers. As long as we maintain the invariant *if an element has been read (or written to), it is in the stash, and each element only occurs in the stash once*, we can simply concatenate elements in the stash with the *unread* elements in the store at the end of an epoch. Once we have concatenated the elements we can obliviously permute them to get our new store. The stash can then just be filled with new dummy elements.

A more detailed discussion of our construction can be found in Sect. 3.

DORAM with Unlimited Reads. Thanks to the modularity of our base scheme, the components are easily extensible. In the second half of this work, we improve the performance of the read-only data store while keeping the rest of the construction (the stash, our periodic shuffling technique at the end of each epoch, etc.) mostly intact.

The separation of our read-only store from a read-and-writable stash suggests an intriguing tradeoff: if we are willing to leak whether each operation is a read or a write operation, then it is beneficial to design an efficient read-only store that supports unlimited reads, and only pay for accessing the stash on (hopefully infrequent) write operations. This optimization allows us to increase the duration of each epoch, or in other words to amortize the cost of each shuffle over more reads. Concretely, in a scenario where the ratio of reads-to-writes is about N-to-1, then for any constant $\epsilon > 0$ we can construct a read-only store where whose amortized cost per query is just $O_\lambda(N^\epsilon)$. Here, the notation O_λ means that we suppress $\mathrm{poly}(\lambda)$ terms in order to focus on the dependency on the database size. By reducing the size of the stash to $O_\lambda(N^\epsilon)$, we can support write operations with this performance as well.

Our strategy to construct a unlimited-reads store might seem counterintuitive at first: we start from a doubly efficient PIR [4, 6] that supports unlimited reads and convert it into a two-server distributed data store. A *doubly efficient private information retrieval* (DEPIR) scheme is a client-server protocol for oblivious access to a public dataset that only requires sublinear computation for both the client and server operations and constant rounds of communication between the two. At first glance, it may seem that a 1-server DEPIR is a strictly stronger primitive than a 2-server DORAM, so we might expect to construct the latter generically as a secure computation of the former. However, this intuition isn't true because there are three properties that we aim to satisfy with DORAM, but that (even a doubly efficient) PIR does not:

- Support for writes,
- Hiding the contents of the database, in addition to access patterns, and
- Ensuring that the secure computation is constant rounds when the two parties collectively emulate the (sublinear but not constant time) client, in addition to the client-server communication.

The main observation underlying this approach is that the SK-DEPIR protocol of Canetti et al. [6] is highly amenable to secure computation as operations mostly involve linear algebra in a finite field that can be done purely locally, plus bitstring and set operations that are easy to handle in constant rounds. SK-DEPIR constructions are based on a locally decodable code (LDC) in the style of a Reed-Muller code, which encodes a dataset as a multivariate polynomial. As a result, the most challenging part of our multiparty computation protocol involves securely emulating the client's procedures to evaluate or interpolate a multivariate polynomial at $O(N)$ points. The naive methods for polynomial evaluation (via application of the Vandermonde matrix) or polynomial interpolation (via the Lagrange interpolation polynomial) involve multiplication of a public matrix by a secret-shared vector, which can be done non-interactively but requires $O(N^2)$ computation, which is too slow for our purposes.

Given a binary field $\mathbb{F} = GF(2^\ell)$ and a subspace $H^m \subset \mathbb{F}^m$, we construct secure computation protocols for evaluating or interpolating an m-variate polynomial $p \in \mathbb{F}[x_1, \ldots, x_m]$ on all points in H^m in time that is quasilinear (rather than quadratic) in $|H^m|$. This protocol may be of independent interest, and in our protocol it is needed to achieve our goal of sublinear computation for the overall DORAM scheme. We construct this secure computation scheme in two stages: first we construct a secure computation protocol for the Additive Fast Fourier Transform protocol of Gao and Mateer [12] for univariate polynomials over a binary field, and then we bootstrap this protocol to handle multivariate polynomials by using recursion on the number of variables in the polynomial as previously shown by Kedlaya and Umans [24]. All operations in this protocol reduce to linear combinations of secret variables, so the entire computation can be done locally by each party on their own boolean secret shares without the need for any communication.

1.3   Related Work

We focus on schemes that are directly designed for secure computation. A direct comparison of their local computation, bandwidth, and number of rounds can be seen in Table 1. The construction of Zahur et al. [36] is very similar to our basic construction, but instead of implementing the permutation by OPRF evaluation, they use Waksman networks and a recursive position map. This allows for sublinear server work but that the cost of non-constant rounds. Doerner et al. [11] uses function secret sharing to obtain a scheme with very good practical efficiency, but their need for linear server work limits scalability to large database lengths N. Gordon et al. [19] is in the more general DORAM model but uses PIR over tree-based ORAM. They are able to obtain $O(\log N)$ bandwidth but as with Doerner et al. they require linear local computation. Jarecki et al. focus on decreasing the round complexity and bandwidth of SC-DORAMs while still maintaining sublinear server computation. They are able to get the best combined set of parameters, but are still not able to achieve constant rounds of communication. Finally, Bunn et al. [5] achieve a 3-server DORAM scheme that achieves constant rounds and sublinear bandwidth, while providing a black-box construction. However, as with [11,19] they require linear server work.

2   Preliminaries

In this section, we provide several definitions and constructions of existing cryptographic primitives that we leverage in this work. We begin with a brief summary of our notation.

Given a bitstring $x \in \{0, 1\}^\ell$, a 2-of-2 boolean secret sharing $\langle x \rangle$ denotes the uniformly selection of two bitstrings x_1 for party 1 and x_2 for party 2 subject to the constraint that their boolean-xor $x_1 \oplus x_2 = x$. A binary field $\mathbb{F} = GF(2^\ell)$ is a

Table 1. Comparison of access in DORAM schemes for Secure Computation. Asterisks indicate schemes where the stash size is assumed to be $O(\log N)$ and $O(N^\epsilon)$, respectively, and the distinction between read and write is not hidden.

	No. Servers	Local Comp.	Bandwidth	Rounds
Zahur et al. [36]	2	$O\left(\sqrt{N}\log^3 N\right)$	$O\left(\sqrt{N}\log^3 N\right)$	$O(\log N)$
Floram [11]	2	$O(N)$	$O(\sqrt{N})$	$O(1)$
Florom* [11]	2	$O(N)$	$O(\log N)$	$O(1)$
Gordon et al. [19]	2	$O(N)$	$O(\log N)$	$O(1)$
Jarecki et al. [23]	3	$O(\log^3 N)$	$O(\log^3 N)$	$O(\log N)$
Bunn et al. [5]	3	$O(N)$	$O(\sqrt{N})$	$O(1)$
Sublinear DORAM	2	$O(\sqrt{N}\log N)$	$O(\sqrt{N}\log N)$	$O(1)$
Unlimited Reads DORAM*	2	$O_\lambda(N^\epsilon)$	$O_\lambda(N^\epsilon)$	$O(1)$

finite field of characteristic 2; there is a canonical bijection $\mathbb{F} \leftrightarrow \{0,1\}^\ell$ such that field addition corresponds to boolean-xor. Hence, we overload the notation $\langle f \rangle$ so that it applies to field elements $f \in \mathbb{F}$. This secret sharing scheme commutes with linear algebra in the field, i.e., $\langle cf + c'f' \rangle = c\langle f \rangle + c'\langle f' \rangle$ can be computed locally by each server from public constants $c, c' \in \mathbb{F}$. and secret shares $\langle f \rangle, \langle f' \rangle$.

We use the convention of 0-indexing, with $[N] = \{0, 1, \ldots, N-1\}$ as containing all whole numbers less than N. Additionally, $S \times S'$ denotes the Cartesian product of two sets. Bold letters v denote vectors, subscripts v_i indicate the ith element of a vector, and $(w_i)_{i \in [N]}$ constructs a vector from an ordered list of items $w_0, w_1, \ldots, w_{N-1}$. The notation $\|$ denotes concatenation of bitstrings, sets, or vectors into a single object of longer length containing the (ordered) union of all elements.

The notation $x \leftarrow \mathcal{D}$ indicates taking a sample from a probability distribution $\mathcal{D}$. By abuse of notation, $x \leftarrow S$ indicates sampling from the uniform distribution over set S; we sometimes use $x \xleftarrow{\$} S$ for emphasis. We use $\approx$ to indicate computational indistinguishability of two distributions; that is, $\mathcal{D} \approx \mathcal{D}'$ if no probabilistic polynomial time adversary $\mathcal{A}$ has a noticeable difference in output when given a sample from $\mathcal{D}$ or $\mathcal{D}'$.

2.1 Distributed Memory

First introduced by Bunn et al. [5], the ideal functionality $\mathcal{F}_{mem}$ in Fig. 1 captures the behavior achieved by a DORAM. The database is initialized on secret shares of the database, and subsequent accesses are also secret shared, as is their resulting output. This version of the definition deviates from the original in that the Init functionality returns shares of the database, and the access protocol takes in those same shares. This syntactic difference is included only to make

1. On input of $(\mathsf{Init}, \tilde{\mathsf{DB}})$, set $\mathsf{DB} = \tilde{\mathsf{DB}}$, return random additive shares of DB^s to party s.
2. On input additive shares of $(\mathsf{op}, \mathsf{elem}, \mathsf{DB})$ from two parties do:
    (a) if $\mathsf{op} = \mathsf{read}$ then set $o = \mathsf{DB}[\mathsf{addr}]$
    (b) if $\mathsf{op} = \mathsf{write}$ then set $o = \mathsf{DB}[\mathsf{addr}]$ and $\mathsf{DB}[\mathsf{addr}] = \mathsf{val}$
    (c) Let o^1, o^2 be random, additive shares of o, and DB^s be random additive shares of DB. Return (o^s, DB^s) to party s.

Fig. 1. Functionality $\mathcal{F}_{mem}$

our own proofs cleaner and does not fundamentally change the definition. While Bunn et al. provide a viable 3-server construction that meets this ideal functionality and provides the necessary performance; we leverage the construction of Doerner et al. [11] that requires only 2-servers. From their construction, we obtain Lemma 1.

Lemma 1. *There exists a protocol Π_{DORAM} that implements the functionality $\mathcal{F}_{mem}$ with the following complexity:*

- *Access of $\mathsf{op} = \mathsf{read}$ or $\mathsf{op} = \mathsf{write}$ results in $O(1)$ rounds of communication, $O(n)$ local server computation, and $O(\sqrt{n})$ communication bandwidth.*
- *Initializing the functionality results in $O(1)$ rounds of communication, $O(n)$ local server computation, and $O(n)$ communication bandwidth.*

2.2 Distributed Oblivious Pseudo-random Function

Distributed Oblivious Pseudo-random Function (DOPRF) achieves a distributed evaluation of a PRF between two parties. Typically one party hold the key, and the other the input, and only the second party learns the output. We require a variation of this ideal functionality, presented in Fig. 2, in which both the key and the input are additively secret shared between the two the two parties and both parties receive the output of the evaluation.

   We introduce a construction in Fig. 3 which meets our new ideal functionality that is effectively the semi-honest version of the DOPRF of Miao et al. [28], which itself is based on the work of Jarecki and Liu [22]. With only a small modification that allows the input and key to be secret-shared between the two servers. The construction leverages the Dodis-Yampolskiy pseudorandom function $F(k, x) = g^{1/(k+x)}$ [10], and it is secure under the q-Diffie Hellman inversion (q-DHI) assumption using a similar argument as in [28].

2.3 Constant-Round Equality Check

The functionality introduced in Fig. 4 allows for two parties to check if the element for which they both hold shares is present in a database for which they also

---

The functionality is assumed to be initialized with PRF f.

1. Upon receiving (x_1, k_1) from party 1 and (x_2, k_2) from party 2, compute $\sigma = f_{k_1 + k_2}(x_1 + x_2)$.
2. Returns σ to both party 1 and 2

Fig. 2. Functionality $\mathcal{F}_{DOPRF}$

Server 1 input: x_1, k_1	Common: $G, q = |G|, g \leftarrow G$	Server 2 input: x_2, k_2
choose key pair $(\mathsf{sk}, \mathsf{pk})$	$\xrightarrow{\mathsf{pk}, C = \mathsf{ENC}_{\mathsf{pk}}(k_1 + x_1)}$	choose $a \leftarrow [q], b \leftarrow [q2^\lambda]$
		let $\alpha = a(k_2 + x_2) + bq$
decrypt $\beta = \mathsf{DEC}_{\mathsf{sk}}(C^*)$	$\xleftarrow{C^*, h = g^a}$	let $C^* = \mathsf{ENC}_{\mathsf{pk}}(\alpha) \cdot C^a$
let $\gamma = \beta^{-1} \bmod q$		
$\quad = a(k + x)$		
output $\sigma = h^\gamma$	$\xrightarrow{\qquad \sigma \qquad}$	output σ

Fig. 3. DOPRF Protocol, using ElGamal encryption $(\mathsf{ENC}, \mathsf{DEC})$

hold shares. In particular it returns shares of a boolean b indicating the presence of a match, and if so the shares of that address. The database follows the invariant that there is only a single match within the database for the element. Both Damgard et al. and Nishide et al. [9,29] construct solutions that achieve the computation[1] with constant rounds.

2.4   Doubly Efficient Private Information Retrieval

First introduced by Canetti et al. and Boyle et al. [4,6], Doubly Efficent Private Information Retrieval (DEPIR) is a variant of PIR achieving sub-linear server work by allowing pre-processing of the database. The major building block DEPIR is locally decodably codes (LDCs). Specifically, an application of Reed-Muller Codes, which allows for *smooth* LDCs.

Definition 1 (Smooth LDC). *A s-smooth, k-query locally decodable code with message length* N*, codeword size* M*, with alphabet* Σ *is denoted by* $(s, k, N, M)_\Sigma$*-smooth LDC and consists of a tuple of PPT algorithms* $(\mathsf{Enc}, \mathsf{Query}, \mathsf{Dec})$ *with the following syntax:*

---

[1] The exact functionality including the indicator bit is not included in their constructions, but they can be easily be extended with an additional round of a conditional computations.

1. Upon receiving additive shares of $x \in \{0,1\}^B$ and $\mathsf{DB} \in \left(\{0,1\}^B\right)^N$ from both parties 1 and 2, computes $\mathsf{DB_{eq}} = \{x_i \overset{?}{=} x \mid x_i \in \mathsf{DB}\}$.
2. Let $\mathsf{b} = \bigvee_{x_i \in \mathsf{DB_{eq}}} x_i$ indicate if there was a match. If b is non-zero, let addr^s be random, additive shares of addr such that $\mathsf{DB_{eq}}[\mathsf{addr}] = 1$ otherwise, let addr^s be random shares of zero. Return $(\mathsf{b}^s, \mathsf{addr}^s)$ to party s.

Fig. 4. Functionality $\mathcal{F}_{EQ-DB}$

- Enc *takes a message* $m \in \Sigma^N$ *and outputs a codeword* $c \in \Sigma^M$
- Query *takes a index* $i \in [N]$ *and outputs a vector* $\boldsymbol{x} = (x_1, \ldots, x_k) \in [M]^N$
- Dec *takes in vector codeword symbols* $\boldsymbol{c} = (c_{x_1}, \ldots, c_{x_k}) \in \Sigma^N$ *and outputs a symbol* $y \in \Sigma$

And has the following properties:

- *Local Decodability:* *For all messages* $m \in \Sigma^L$ *and every index* $i \in [N]$:

$$\Pr[\mathsf{Dec}(\mathsf{Enc}(m)_{\boldsymbol{x}}) = m_i \; : \; \boldsymbol{x} \leftarrow \mathsf{Query}(i)] = 1$$

- *Smoothness:* *For all indices* $i \in [N]$, *a LDC is s-smooth if when sampling* $(x_1, \ldots, x_k) \leftarrow \mathsf{Query}(i)$, $(x_1, \ldots, x_k)$ *is uniformly distributed on* $[N]^s$ *for every distinct subset of size* s.

We now formally introduce DEPIR, in particular the secret key variant, called SK-DEPIR. Constructions rely on the *hidden permutation with noise* (HPN) assumption introduced by [6].[2] While it is a new assumption, the validity of the class of permuted puzzles assumptions has been explored by Boyle et al. [3].

Assumption 1 (Hidden permutation with noise). *Let* $m < t < r < u < |\mathbb{F}|$ *be functions of* λ *and* N *such that* $|\mathbb{F}|^m = \mathrm{poly}(\lambda)$ *and* $|\mathbb{F}|^t = \lambda^{\omega(1)}$. *Define the distribution* $\mathcal{D}(\pi, \mathsf{addr}, T)$ *that executes the* Query *protocol of* $\tilde{\Pi}_{store}$ *in the clear* (*without secret shares*) *to retrieve a set of vectors* $\tilde{Y} = (\tilde{\boldsymbol{y}}_i)_{i \in [u]}$ *and then outputs* $Z = (\pi(\tilde{\boldsymbol{y}}_i))_{i \in [u]}$, *when given a randomly-chosen permutation* $\pi : \mathbb{F}^m \twoheadrightarrow \mathbb{F}^m$, *integer* $\mathsf{addr} \in N$, *and set* $T \subset [u]$ *as input. The hidden permutation with noise assumption states that the distribution* $\mathcal{D}(\pi, \mathsf{addr}, T)$ *is computationally indistinguishable from the uniform distribution over* $(\mathbb{F}^m)^u$.

Definition 2 (Doubly Efficient PIR). *A Doubly Efficient PIR (DEPIR) for alphabet* Σ *consists of a tuple of PPT algorithms* (KeyGen, Process, Query, Resp, Dec) *with the following syntax:*

---

[2] A concurrent work by Boyle et al. [4] relies on an equivalent assumption called *Oblivious LDC*.

- KeyGen *takes the security parameter* 1^λ *and outputs the key* k
- Process *takes a key* k, *database* $\mathsf{DB} \in \Sigma^N$ *and outputs processed database* $\tilde{\mathsf{DB}}$
- Query *takes a key* k, *database index* $i \in [N]$ *and outputs a query* q *and temporary state* State
- Resp *takes a query* q, *processed database* $\tilde{\mathsf{DB}}$ *and outputs a server response* c
- Dec *takes a key* k, *server response* c, *temporary state* State *and outputs a database symbol* $y \in \Sigma$

And has the following properties:

- **Correctness:** *For all* $\mathsf{DB} \in \Sigma^N$ *and* $i \in [N]$:

$$
\Pr \left[\mathsf{Dec}(k, \mathsf{State}, c) = \mathsf{DB}_i \ : \
\begin{array}{l}
k \leftarrow \mathsf{KeyGen}\left(1^\lambda\right) \\
\tilde{\mathsf{DB}} \leftarrow \mathsf{Process}\left(k, \mathsf{DB}\right) \\
(q, \mathsf{State}) \leftarrow \mathsf{Query}\left(k, i\right) \\
c \leftarrow \mathsf{Resp}\left(\tilde{\mathsf{DB}}, q\right)
\end{array}
\right] = 1
$$

- **Double Efficiency:** *The runtime of* KeyGen *is* $\mathrm{poly}\left(\lambda\right)$, *the runtime of* Process *is* $\mathrm{poly}\left(N, \lambda\right)$, *and the runtime of* Query, Dec *is* $o\left(N\right) \cdot \mathrm{poly}\left(\lambda\right)$, *where* N *is the database size.*
- **Security:** *Any non-uniform PPT adversary* $\mathcal{A}$ *has only* $\mathrm{negl}\left(\lambda\right)$ *advantage in the following security game with a challenger* $\mathcal{C}$:
  1. $\mathcal{A}$ *sends to* $\mathcal{C}$ *a database* $\mathsf{DB} \in \Sigma^N$.
  2. $\mathcal{C}$ *picks a random bit* $b \leftarrow \{0, 1\}$, *and runs* $k \leftarrow \mathsf{KeyGen}\left(1^\lambda\right)$ *to obtain a key* k, *and then runs* $\tilde{\mathsf{DB}} \leftarrow \mathsf{Process}\left(k, \mathsf{DB}\right)$ *to obtain a processed database* $\tilde{\mathsf{DB}}$, *which it sends to* $\mathcal{A}$.
  3. $\mathcal{A}$ *selects two addresses* $i^0, i^1 \in [N]$, *and sends* (i^0, i^1) *to* $\mathcal{C}$.
  4. $\mathcal{C}$ *samples* $(q, \mathsf{State}) \leftarrow \mathsf{Query}(k, i^b)$, *and sends* 1 *to* $\mathcal{A}$.
  5. *Steps 3. and 4. are repeated an arbitrary (polynomial) number of times.*
  6. $\mathcal{A}$ *outputs a bit* b', *and his* **advantage** *in the game is defined to be* $\Pr[b = b'] - \frac{1}{2}$.

As shown in [4,6] we can achieve SK-DEPIR with sublinear or poly-log parameters. We will describe one such construction in Sect. 4.

Lemma 2. *There exists SK-DEPIR schemes with the following parameters, where* N *is the database size and* λ *is the security parameter:*

- **Sublinear SK-DEPIR:** *For any* $\epsilon > 0$, *the running time of* Process *can be* $N^{1+\epsilon} \cdot \mathrm{poly}(\lambda)$, *and the running time of* Query *and* Dec *can be* $N^\epsilon \cdot \mathrm{poly}(\lambda)$.
- **Polylog SK-DEPIR:** *The running time of* Process *can be* $\mathrm{poly}(\lambda, N)$, *and the running time of* Query *and* Dec *can be* $\mathrm{poly}(\lambda, \log N)$.

3   DORAM with Sublinear Computation

In this section we present our construction of $\mathcal{F}_{mem}$ that achieves sublinear server work and communication with constant rounds.

3.1   Construction

In this section, we describe how we bootstrap from a linear-work $\mathcal{F}_{mem}$ to a new protocol Π_{DORAM} that also instantiates $\mathcal{F}_{mem}$ but with sublinear work and constant rounds, as desired. The overall architecture of the scheme can be found in Fig. 5. We describe below our implementations of the store and stash.

We implement the stash as an another two-party DORAM (matching the $\mathcal{F}_{mem}$ functionality). We require a 2-party scheme with constant rounds, this can be instantiated by FLORAM [11] or Gordon et al. [19]. While they have linear server work for each access, because our stash is $t = \sqrt{N}$ records in size, this still results in sublinear server work within our protocol.

We implement the store in Fig. 9 as a permuted array of elements sorted by PRF evaluation on the address of the element. Neither server knows the underlying permutation because it is created using our oblivious permutation protocol shown in Fig. 8. We perform an $\mathcal{F}_{DOPRF}$ evaluation across the shares of the addresses, which allows us to look up records in constant rounds by computing the OPRF based on the address of the element being searched for, and then each party performs a local binary search on their own store to find the shares of the element.

At the start of an epoch, the stash contains all the dummy elements and the store contains all the elements of the database concatenated with t dummy elements. The elements in the store are all permuted and indexed as above. Note that we consider dummy to be addressed from 1 to t, so valid elements are indexed started at t. We also have (in the clear) a counter, starting at 1. The access logic is encapsulated within our access protocol in Fig. 7 and proceeds as follows. When we want to do a read, we check if the element is in the stash by calling $\mathcal{F}_{EQ-DB}$, which returns a secret shared boolean b indicating if the element is present, as well as the shares of the address to each party if it is present. We then use b as a selector bit in a shared conditional computation to see if we read the element (if the element is present in the stash) or the next dummy element (addressed at the counter) in the stash. Then we read an element from the store, using $\mathcal{F}_{store}$, again based on the selector bit. If the element is in the stash, we read the next dummy element at address counter, if it is not in the stash, we read the element itself. Finally, we write an element back to the stash, using $\mathcal{F}_{mem}$, either the dummy element we read (which is just overwriting the same element) if the element was in the stash, or the element read from the stash. The element is written back at the 'counter' location in the stash. The protocol then returns random additive shares of the element being read. If the operation is instead was a write the only variation in the above process is in the final step writing elements back to the stash, rather that writing to the 'counter' location automatically, if the element was previously in the stash, it is overwritten at that location.

At the end of an epoch (when the counter reaches t), the overarching Π_{DORAM} invokes $\Pi_{shuffle}$ in Fig. 10, which resets the state as mentioned above. In the original square-root ORAM scheme, removing duplicates required a costly oblivious sort operation, which is not constant round. By contrast, we achieve

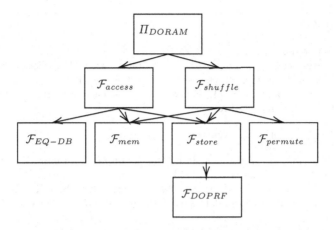

Fig. 5. The overall architecture of the ideal functionalities used in the Π_{DORAM} construction.

a constant-round reshuffling algorithm by leveraging the following invariant of $\mathcal{F}_{access}$: *if an element has been read (or written to) it is in the stash, and each element only occurs in the stash once*. This invariant allows us to simply note which elements in the store have been read during the epoch and eliminate them, knowing that their most recent copy is represented in the stash. This claim applies to dummy elements as well: during the shuffle operation, we only need to insert new dummy elements to replace those that have been overwritten in the stash by real writes. Once the unread elements and the current stash have been permuted obliviously by $\mathcal{F}_{permute}$, the stash is reinitialized with the dummy values and counter is reset to 1. We also note that we leverage $\mathcal{F}_{shuffle}$ when we first initialize the DORAM. We call $\mathcal{F}_{shuffle}$ on the original shares of the secret shared database, concatenated with the necessary dummy elements. The set of read elements is empty as is the stash, resulting in a permutation of the original database and dummies after $\mathcal{F}_{permute}$ is called.

Our oblivious permutation protocol in Fig. 8 does two things: it rerandomizes the shares held by each server and applies the same random permutation to each server's shares. Beginning with a vector of secret shares $\langle M \rangle$, server 2 begins $\Pi_{permute}$ by encrypting her own shares M^2 using an additively homomorphic encryption scheme and sending the result to server 1. Next, server 1 applies the same randomly-chosen permutation to her own shares M^1 as well as the ciphertexts from server 2, and she then rerandomizes each pair of shares by adding a random value to her own share and subtracting the same value (homomorphically) from server 2's share. She sends encrypted versions of both shares to server 2, who performs the same permute-and-rerandomize operation and sends the result to server 1 to complete the constant-round oblivious permutation.

On $(\mathsf{Init}, \langle \mathsf{DB} \rangle)$:

1. Server 1 computes $\mathsf{V} = \{(i, 0) \mid i \in [t]\}$
2. Each server calls $\mathcal{F}_{shuffle}$ on $(\mathsf{shuffle}, \mathsf{I}, \mathsf{State}))$ where $\mathsf{I} = \{\}$ and $\mathsf{State} = \{\mathsf{DB} \parallel \mathsf{V}, 0, \{\}\}$. Server s receives $(\mathsf{S}^s, \mathsf{M}^s, \mathsf{k}_s)$ as output.
3. Let $\mathsf{ctr} = 1$ and $\mathsf{I} = \{\}$. For Server s its current state is $\mathsf{State}^s = (\mathsf{ctr}, \mathsf{M}^s, \mathsf{S}^s, \mathsf{k}_s)$, returns State^s

On additive shares of $(\mathsf{op}, \mathsf{elem}, \mathsf{State})$:

1. If $\mathsf{ctr} = t$, call $\mathcal{F}_{shuffle}$ on $(\mathsf{shuffle}, \mathsf{I}, \mathsf{State})$ and update state for Server s with $(\mathsf{S}'^s, \mathsf{M}'^s, \mathsf{k}'^s)$. Set $\mathsf{ctr} = 1$ and $\mathsf{I} = \{\}$.
2. Call $\mathcal{F}_{access}$ on additive shares $(\mathsf{op}_i, \mathsf{elem}_i, \mathsf{State})$, recovering $(\mathsf{i}_\mathsf{M}, \langle \mathsf{elem} \rangle, \langle \mathsf{State} \rangle)$ and update state for Server s with S'^s. Set $\mathsf{I} = \mathsf{I} \cup \mathsf{i}_\mathsf{M}$ and $\mathsf{ctr} = \mathsf{ctr} + 1$
3. Return $(\mathsf{elem}^s, \mathsf{State}^s)$ to Server s.

Fig. 6. Π_{DORAM} Protocol

3.2 Complexity Analysis

Now consider the asymptotic complexity of our scheme. We first evaluate the complexity of the underlying protocols, and then compute the amortized complexity of the overall Π_{DORAM} protocol. The overall complexity when $t = \sqrt{N}$ is shown in Table 2.

- $\Pi_{permute}$: Each server must perform $O(N + t)$ encryption, decryption and other local operations. The entire encrypted store is sent, again resulting in $O(N + t)$ bandwidth. The protocol runs in 3 rounds, or $O(1)$.
- Π_{store}: Here we consider two separate costs, one for initialization, and one for performing an access. During initialization, local computation is dominated by the sorting across the OPRF outputs, $O((N + t)\log(N + t))$, and bandwidth by the OPRF computation itself, $O(N + t)$. We obtain constant rounds in initialization by executing all of the OPRF evaluations in parallel. On access, local computation is dominated by searching for the tag, $O(\log(N + t))$, and the only round of interaction and bandwidth is the OPRF evaluation.
- Π_{access}: Finding the element in the stash only takes local computation and bandwidth linear in the stash size and constant rounds. The two other operations of cost are accessing stash and the store, each of which take $O(t)$ and $O(\log(N+t))$ local computation and $O(\sqrt{t})$ and $O(1)$ bandwidth respectively. This leaves access dominated by finding the element in the stash, $O(t)$ local computation and bandwidth[3].
- $\Pi_{shuffle}$: Shuffle is dominated by the initialization of the store, inheriting the performance and bandwidth complexity directly from Π_{store}.

---

[3] For any value of $t < \log(N + t)$ then the cost of Π_{store} controls, but in our setting we consider a t greater than that.

1. On additive shares of $(\mathsf{op}, \mathsf{elem}_{in}, \mathsf{State})$, let $\mathsf{elem}_{in} = (\mathsf{addr}_{in}, \mathsf{val}_{in})$ and $\mathsf{State} = (\mathsf{ctr}, \mathsf{M}^s, \mathsf{k}_s, \mathsf{S}^s)$, where S is an array of elem.

2. Find element in stash or read next dummy address:
   (a) Compute additive shares of index i by calling $\mathcal{F}_{EQ-DB}$ in Figure 4 on additive shares of $(\mathsf{addr}_{in}, \mathsf{S})$, receiving random additive shares (b, i) as output.
   (b) Jointly compute random additive shares of i_S such that:

   $$\mathsf{i}_\mathsf{S} = \begin{cases} \mathsf{i} & \mathsf{b} = 1, \text{ element in stash.} \\ \mathsf{ctr} & \mathsf{b} = 0, \text{ element not in stash.} \end{cases}$$

   (c) Then recover elem_S by calling $\mathcal{F}_{mem}$ on secret shares of $(\mathsf{read}, (\mathsf{i}_\mathsf{S}, 0), \mathsf{S})$.

3. Look up either the next dummy element or the original element in the store:
   (a) Jointly compute random additive shares of addr_M:

   $$\mathsf{addr}_\mathsf{M} = \begin{cases} \mathsf{ctr} & \mathsf{b} = 1, \text{ element in stash.} \\ \mathsf{addr}_{in} & \mathsf{b} = 0, \text{ element not in stash.} \end{cases}$$

   (b) Call $\mathcal{F}_{store}$ on the additive shares of $(\mathsf{read}, \mathsf{addr}_\mathsf{M}, \mathsf{M}, \mathsf{k}_s)$, recovering $(\mathsf{i}_\mathsf{M}, \langle \mathsf{elem}_\mathsf{M} \rangle)$.

4. Write the read elem_M or input elem_{in} back to stash:
   (a) If $\mathsf{op} = \mathsf{read}$, jointly compute random additive shares of:

   $$(\mathsf{i}_\mathsf{W}, \mathsf{elem}_\mathsf{W}, \mathsf{elem}) = \begin{cases} (\mathsf{ctr}, \mathsf{elem}_\mathsf{M}, \mathsf{elem}_\mathsf{S}) & \mathsf{b} = 1, \text{ element in stash.} \\ (\mathsf{ctr}, \mathsf{elem}_\mathsf{M}, \mathsf{elem}_\mathsf{M}) & \mathsf{b} = 0, \text{ element not in stash.} \end{cases}$$

   (b) If $\mathsf{op} = \mathsf{write}$, jointly compute random additive shares of:

   $$(\mathsf{i}_\mathsf{W}, \mathsf{elem}_\mathsf{W}, \mathsf{elem}) = \begin{cases} (\mathsf{i}_\mathsf{S}, \mathsf{elem}_{in}, \mathsf{elem}_{in}) & \mathsf{b} = 1, \text{ element in stash.} \\ (\mathsf{ctr}, \mathsf{elem}_{in}, \mathsf{elem}_{in}) & \mathsf{b} = 0, \text{ element not in stash.} \end{cases}$$

   (c) Call $\mathcal{F}_{mem}$ on additive shares of $(\mathsf{write}, (\mathsf{i}_\mathsf{W}, \mathsf{elem}_\mathsf{W}), \mathsf{S})^a$.

5. Server s returns $(\mathsf{i}_\mathsf{M}, \langle \mathsf{elem} \rangle, \langle \mathsf{State} \rangle)$.

---

a Any functionality that returns an updated share of S or M is assumed to update the held state State, but is elided for notational simplicity.

Fig. 7. Π_{access} Protocol

We now consider the amortized complexity of the overall local computation of Π_{DORAM} during access. We consider the cost of shuffling averaged over an epoch of t accesses. The cost of accessing a single block, represented by Π_{access}, is $O(t)$. The cost of shuffle is $O((N + t) \log(N + t))$. We can consider the total cost of local computation during an epoch as:

$$D_{LC}(N, t) = t(t) + (N + t) \log(N + t)$$

On input (permute, $\langle M \rangle$):

1. Each server runs $\mathsf{pk}_s, \mathsf{sk}_s \leftarrow \mathsf{KeyGen}(1^\lambda)$ and sends pk_s to the other server.
2. For $s \in \{1,2\}$, and $s' = 3 - s$
   (a) Server s' encrypts their additive shares of the values $\mathsf{C}^{s'} = \{\mathsf{ENC}_{\mathsf{pk}_{s'}}(\mathsf{elem}_i^{s'}) \mid \mathsf{elem}_i^{s'} \in \mathsf{M}^{s'}\}$ and sends $\mathsf{C}^{s'}$ to Server s.
   (b) Server s chooses vector of random values $\{r_i \in \{0,1\}^B\}_{i \in [N]}$, and a random permutation π and updates locally $\{\mathsf{elem}_{\pi(i)}^s + r_i^s \mid \mathsf{elem}_i^s \in \mathsf{M}^s\}$. It then computes permutes and re-randomizes s' encrypted shares: $\mathsf{C}_r^{s'} = \{c_{\pi(i)^s}^{s'} \cdot \mathsf{ENC}_{\mathsf{pk}^{s'}}(-r_i^s) \mid c_i^{s'} \in \mathsf{C}^{s'}\}$ and sends $\mathsf{C}_r^{s'}$ to Server s'
   (c) Server s' decrypts $\mathsf{C}_r^{s'}$ to get $\mathsf{M}^{s'} = \{\mathsf{elem}_{\pi(i)}^s - r_i^s \mid i \in [N]\}$.
3. Return (M'^s) to Server s.

Fig. 8. $\Pi_{permute}$ Protocol

On input (Init, $\langle M \rangle$):

1. Choose the new random PRF keys for k_1 and k_2.
2. Server 1 and 2 call on $\mathcal{F}_{DOPRF}$ on inputs $(\mathsf{k}_1, \mathsf{addr}_i^1)$ and $(\mathsf{k}_2, \mathsf{addr}_i^2)$ respectively for all $(\mathsf{addr}_i, \mathsf{val}_i) \in \mathsf{M}$ in parallel. Let $\sigma_i = f_{\mathsf{k}_1 + \mathsf{k}_2}(\mathsf{addr}_i^1 + \mathsf{addr}_i^2)$, and $\Sigma = \{\sigma_i \mid i \in [N]\}$. Both servers sort $\mathsf{M}'^s = \{\sigma_i, \mathsf{elem}_i\}_{i \in [N]}$ in lexicographic order by σ.
3. Return $(\Sigma, \mathsf{M}'^s, \mathsf{k}_s)$

On input (read, $\langle \mathsf{addr}_i \rangle$, $\langle \mathsf{k} \rangle$, $\langle \mathsf{M} \rangle$):

1. Server 1 and Server 2 engage in $\mathcal{F}_{DOPRF}$ on inputs $(\mathsf{k}_1, \mathsf{addr}_i^1)$ and $(\mathsf{k}_2, \mathsf{addr}_i^2)$ respectively. Both servers obtain the output $\widetilde{\mathsf{addr}} = f_{\mathsf{k}_1 + \mathsf{k}_2}(\mathsf{addr}_i^1 + \mathsf{addr}_i^2)$
2. Each Server s performs a local binary search in M^s for $\widetilde{\mathsf{addr}}$ and recover its index i and additive shares of the element elem_i. Each server returns (i, elem_i^s).

Fig. 9. Π_{store} Protocol

On input (shuffle, State, I):

1. Let State $= (\mathsf{M}^s, \mathsf{k}_s, \mathsf{S}^s)$.
2. Let M_r^s be all unread elements in M^1 and M^2, i.e. $\mathsf{M}_r \notin \mathsf{I}$. Set $\mathsf{R}^s = \mathsf{M}_r^s \parallel \mathsf{S}^s$.
3. Let $\mathsf{V} = \{(i,0) \mid i \in [t]\}$ each server calls $\mathcal{F}_{mem}$ on additive shared input (Init, V). Server s receives S^s as output.
4. Servers 1 and 2 call $\mathcal{F}_{permute}$ on (permute, $\langle \mathsf{R} \rangle$). Server s receives (M'^s) as output, which in turn it calls $\mathcal{F}_{store}$ on (Init, M'^s) and receives $(\mathsf{M}^s, \mathsf{k}_s)$ as output.
5. Server s returns $(\mathsf{S}^s, \mathsf{M}^s, \mathsf{k}_s)$.

Fig. 10. $\Pi_{Shuffle}$ Protocol

Averaging over t-accesses we get:

$$D_{LC}(N, t) = t + \frac{N}{t} \log(N + t) + \log(N + t)$$

If we set $t = \sqrt{N}$ we get $D_{LC}(n) = O(\sqrt{N} \log N)$. For bandwidth, we do a similar computation and get $D_B(n) = O(\sqrt{N} \log N)$.

Table 2. A evaluation of each of the protocol's server computation, bandwidth and rounds of communication where $t = \sqrt{N}$. Note that the numbers for Π_{mem} are taken from Lemma 1 and Π_{DORAM} has been amortized where appropriate.

	Local Computation	Bandwidth	Rounds
$\Pi_{DORAM}(\text{Init})$	$O(N \log N)$	$O(N \log N)$	$O(1)$
$\Pi_{DORAM}(\text{op})$	$O(\sqrt{N} \log N)$	$O(\sqrt{N} \log N)$	$O(1)$
Π_{access}	$O(\sqrt{N})$	$O(\sqrt{N})$	$O(1)$
$\Pi_{shuffle}$	$O(N \log N)$	$O(N \log N)$	$O(1)$
$\Pi_{mem}(\text{Init})$	$O(\sqrt{N})$	$O(\sqrt{N})$	$O(1)$
$\Pi_{mem}(\text{read})$	$O(\sqrt{N})$	$O(\sqrt[4]{N})$	$O(1)$
$\Pi_{store}(\text{Init})$	$O(N \log N)$	$O(N)$	$O(1)$
$\Pi_{store}(\text{read})$	$O(\log N)$	$O(1)$	$O(1)$
$\Pi_{permute}$	$O(N)$	$O(N)$	$O(1)$

3.3 Security

In this section we provide the overall security statement and ideal functionalities. We refer the reader to the full paper [20] for the proof.

Notation and Valid Inputs. We define a set of notations and valid inputs for our various protocols used in the following proofs. We assume $\text{op} \in \{0,1\}$ where $\text{op} = 0$ represents a read operation and $\text{op} = 1$ is write. Valid elements are a tuple of an address and a value where $\text{addr} \in [N]$ and $\text{val} \in \{0,1\}^B$. The input database DB is made up of N valid elements. The store M is represented as key-value store, where the keys are the output of PRF f with key k and the values consist of valid elements. The stash S is an array of t valid elements. We define the set of valid inputs for an DORAM of N elements of block size B and t dummies as $\text{Dom}_{N,B,t}$.

Theorem 1. Π_{DORAM} *(Fig. 6) implements functionality* $\mathcal{F}_{mem}$ *and for each party there exists a PPT simulator for each Server* $s \in \{1,2\}$ Sim_D *such that:*

$$\left\langle \text{input}_{\mathcal{A}}, \text{output}^{\Pi_{D.}}, \text{view}_{\mathcal{A}}^{\Pi_{D.}} \right\rangle_{\text{input} \in \text{Dom}_{N,B,t}} \approx$$

$$\left\langle \text{input}_{\mathcal{A}}, \mathcal{F}_{mem}(\text{input}), \text{Sim}_D^s(\text{input}_{\mathcal{A}}, \mathcal{F}_{mem}(\text{input})_{\mathcal{A}}) \right\rangle_{\text{input} \in \text{Dom}_{N,B,t}}$$

where $\text{input} = \{(\text{Init}, \text{DB}), (\text{op}_i, \text{elem}_i, \text{ctr}, \text{M}, \text{S}, \text{k})\}$, *and* $\text{output} = \{(\text{ctr}, \text{M}, \text{S}, \text{k}), (\text{elem}, \text{ctr}, \text{M}, \text{S}, \text{k})\}$.

Proof (Theorem 1). See full paper [20] for proof.

On additive shares of $(\mathsf{op}, \mathsf{elem_{in}}, \mathsf{State})$ where $\mathsf{State} = (\mathsf{ctr}, \mathsf{M}, \mathsf{k}, \mathsf{S})$ and $\mathsf{elem_{in}} = (\mathsf{addr_{in}}, \mathsf{val_{in}})$ set $\mathsf{i_S}$, $\mathsf{addr_M}$, $\mathsf{i_W}$, $\mathsf{elem_W}$ and elem during the protocol according to the below table (as defined by op and if $\mathsf{addr_\in}$ is found in the stash):

op	$\mathsf{addr_{in}} \in \mathsf{S}$	$\mathsf{i_R}$	$\mathsf{addr_M}$	$\mathsf{i_W}$	$\mathsf{elem_W}$	elem
read	yes	$\mathsf{addr_{in}}$	ctr	ctr	$\mathsf{elem_M}$	$\mathsf{elem_S}$
read	no	ctr	$\mathsf{addr_{in}}$	ctr	$\mathsf{elem_M}$	$\mathsf{elem_M}$
write	yes	$\mathsf{addr_{in}}$	ctr	$\mathsf{addr_{in}}$	$\mathsf{elem_{in}}$	$\mathsf{elem_{in}}$
write	no	ctr	$\mathsf{addr_{in}}$	ctr	$\mathsf{elem_{in}}$	$\mathsf{elem_{in}}$

1. Recover $\mathsf{elem_S}$ by calling $\mathcal{F}_{mem}$ on secret shares of $(\mathsf{read}, (\mathsf{i_R}, 0), \mathsf{S})$.
2. Call $\mathcal{F}_{store}$ on the additive shares of $(\mathsf{read}, \mathsf{addr_M}, \mathsf{M}, \mathsf{k_s})$, recovering $(\mathsf{i_M}, \langle \mathsf{elem_M} \rangle)$.
3. Call $\mathcal{F}_{mem}$ on additive shares of $(\mathsf{write}, (\mathsf{i_W}, \mathsf{elem_W}), \mathsf{S})^a$.
4. Return $(\mathsf{i_M}, \langle \mathsf{elem} \rangle, \langle \mathsf{State} \rangle)$

---

^{a} Any functionality that returns an updated share of S or M is assumed to update the held state State, but is elided for notational simplicity.

Fig. 11. Functionality $\mathcal{F}_{access}$

On input of $(\mathsf{permute}, \langle \tilde{\mathsf{M}} \rangle)$:

1. Choose random permutation π and set $\mathsf{M} = \{ \tilde{\mathsf{M}}_{\pi(i)} \mid i \in [N] \}$.
2. Let M^s be a random additive share of M, and return M^s to Server s.

Fig. 12. Functionality $\mathcal{F}_{permute}$

1. On input of $(\mathsf{Init}, \langle \mathsf{M} \rangle)$: Choose PRF key k and for all $\mathsf{elem}_i \in \mathsf{M}$ compute $\sigma_i = f_k(\mathsf{addr}_i)$ and let $\Sigma = \{ \sigma_i \mid i \in [N] \}$. Set $\mathsf{M} = \{ (\sigma_i, \mathsf{elem}_i) \mid \mathsf{elem}_i \in \mathsf{M} \}$ and sort M in lexicographic order by σ. Let elem_i^s and k_s be random additive shares of elem_i and k respectively, and $\mathsf{M}^s = \{ (\sigma_i, \mathsf{elem}_i^s) \mid \mathsf{elem}_i \in \mathsf{M} \}$. Return $(\Sigma, \mathsf{M}^s, \mathsf{k}_s)$ to Server s.
2. On input additive shares of $(\mathsf{read}, \mathsf{addr}_i, \mathsf{k}, \mathsf{M})$ from two parties return additive shares of $\mathsf{M}[\mathsf{i_M}]$ where $\sigma_{\mathsf{i_M}} = f_k(\mathsf{addr}_i)$ and $\mathsf{i_M}$ to each server.

Fig. 13. Functionality $\mathcal{F}_{store}$

On input (shuffle, State, I):

1. Let State $= (M, k, S)$.
2. Let M_r be all unread elements in M, i.e. $M_r \notin I$. Set $R = M_r \parallel S$.
3. Let $V = \{(i, 0) \mid i \in [t]\}$ and call $\mathcal{F}_{mem}$ on additive shared input (Init, V), receiving S' as output.
4. Call $\mathcal{F}_{permute}$ on (permute, $\langle R \rangle$) receiving M' as output, which in turn is passed into $\mathcal{F}_{store}$ as (Init, M'). Finally, (M'', k') is received as output.
5. Server s returns random additive shares (S'^s, M''^s, k'^s).

Fig. 14. Functionality $\mathcal{F}_{shuffle}$

4 Sublinear DORAM with Unlimited Reads

In this section, we introduce an alternative DORAM construction $\tilde{\Pi}_{DORAM}$ that also implements the $\mathcal{F}_{mem}$ functionality with constant rounds, sublinear server work, and sublinear communication. This protocol differs from the construction in Sect. 3 in that it does not attempt to hide whether a query is a read or write operation, and in exchange it achieves better performance.

The construction in this section only needs to invoke the shuffle functionality $\mathcal{F}_{shuffle}$ after t write operations, independent of the number of read operations. In scenarios where writes are infrequent, the amortized cost per read can have a small $O_\lambda(N^\epsilon)$ dependency on the database size N for any constant $\epsilon > 0$. To build the new DORAM protocol $\tilde{\Pi}_{DORAM}$, we start from a SK-DEPIR that supports unlimited reads while hiding access patterns, and we emulate the server using secure 2-party computation (which hides the database contents as well).

We first describe how we instantiate the new version of store that relies on SK-DEPIR in Sect. 4.1, then show how to use the new $\mathcal{F}_{store}$ in the larger $\tilde{\Pi}_{DORAM}$ protocol in Sect. 4.2. Finally we show how to construct secure compuation of multivariate polynomial evaluation and interpolation using FFT in Sect. 4.3.

4.1 Instantiating $\mathcal{F}_{store}$ Using Secure Computation of SK-DEPIR

In this section, we show that a secure 2-party computation (2PC) of the Canetti et al. construction leads to an instantiation $\tilde{\Pi}_{store}$ of the $\mathcal{F}_{store}$ functionality. The construction we present in this section achieves sublinear communication with a constant number of rounds and quasilinear server work. To do so, we first construct a 2PC protocol for a locally decodable code, and then we construct $\tilde{\Pi}_{store}$ as a 2PC of a secret key doubly efficient private information retrieval (SK-DEPIR) protocol based on an LDC.

We focus on a block size $B = \ell$, so that each block can canonically be encoded as a field element in $\mathbb{F} = GF(2^\ell)$. Put another way, all references to the database size N are enumerated in terms of the number of blocks, but if one desires a lower block length like $B = 1$ then N should instead be interpreted in terms of the number of bits of the database.

Given a binary field $\mathbb{F}$, a subspace $H \subset \mathbb{F}$, and an integer m, let $N = |H|^m$ and $M = |\mathbb{F}|^m$. Let $(x_i)_{i \in [r]}$ be arbitrary, distinct non-zero constants. Finally, define the bijections $\iota : [N] \to H^m$ and $\delta : B \to \mathbb{F}$ via lexicographic ordering.

On input $(\mathsf{Enc}, \langle \mathsf{D} \rangle)$ for database $\mathsf{D} \in B^N$:

1. For all $i \in [N]$, compute shares of $c_i = \iota(i) \in H^m$ and $d_i = \delta(\mathsf{D}[i]) \in \mathbb{F}$.
2. Securely interpolate polynomial $\psi : \mathbb{F}^m \to \mathbb{F}$ of degree t from $\{(c_i, d_i)\}_{i \in [N]}$.
3. Securely evaluate $\mathsf{E} = (v, \psi(v))_{v \in \mathbb{F}^m}$, the truth table of ψ on $\mathbb{F}^m$. Output $\langle \mathsf{E} \rangle$.

On input $(\mathsf{Query}, \langle q \rangle)$ for an index $q \in [N]$:

1. Randomly choose a degree-t polynomial $\phi : \mathbb{F} \to \mathbb{F}^m$ such that $\phi(0) = \iota(q)$.
2. Securely evaluate $y_i = \phi(x_i)$ for all $i \in [r]$, and output shares $(\langle y_i \rangle)_{i \in [r]}$.

On input $(\mathsf{Dec}, (\langle a_i \rangle)_{i \in [r]})$:

1. Securely interpolate polynomial $\tilde{\phi} : \mathbb{F} \to \mathbb{F}$ of degree $r - 1$ with $\tilde{\phi}(x_i) = a_i$ $\forall i$.
2. Output shares $\langle \delta^{-1}(\tilde{\phi}(0)) \rangle$ of the block corresponding to field element $\phi(0)$.

Fig. 15. $\tilde{\Pi}_{ldc}$ protocol for secure 2-party computation of a Reed-Muller-style LDC

2PC for a Locally Decodable Code. First, we construct a secure 2-party computation protocol $\tilde{\Pi}_{ldc}$ of the locally decodable code used by Canetti et al. [6], which is a Reed-Muller-based polynomial code. We depict our construction in Fig. 15, in which the two parties maintain boolean secret shares of all input, intermediate, and output data from the LDC of Canetti et al.

Our 2PC protocol $\tilde{\Pi}_{ldc}$ operates over a binary field $\mathbb{F} = \mathbb{F}_2[z]/(\rho(z))$ of size $|\mathbb{F}| = 2^\ell$ defined using an irreducible polynomial ρ of degree ℓ. Elements of $\mathbb{F}$ can be represented using bitstrings of length ℓ in the canonical way, such that the addition of two elements corresponds to the boolean-xor of their bitstring values. Furthermore, we consider $H \subset \mathbb{F}$ to be the subspace of $\mathbb{F}$ of size $|H| = 2^h$ containing the span of basis elements $\mathcal{H} = \{z^{h-1}, z^{h-2}, \ldots, z, 1\}$; this corresponds to bitstrings that have $\ell - h$ leading 0s. Also, protocol $\tilde{\Pi}_{ldc}$ performs operations in the vector spaces H^m and $\mathbb{F}^m$ of sizes $N = |H|^m$ and $M = |\mathbb{F}|^m$, respectively.

We claim that this protocol can be securely evaluated efficiently and non-interactively. Throughout this section, we only consider boolean secret shares $\langle \cdot \rangle$, so that field addition and scalar multiplication can be performed locally by each server, without interaction. Hence, our claim amounts to the statement that all operations in $\tilde{\Pi}_{ldc}$ involve only linear algebra in the field along with concatenation/truncation of bitstrings, because all of these operations commute with boolean-xor.

Theorem 2. *Let $m < t < r < N < M$ be parameters of a Reed-Muller locally decodable code such that N and M are powers of 2. Then, protocol $\tilde{\Pi}_{ldc}$ in Fig. 15 is a secure two-party computation of an LDC with local decodability and smoothness. Furthermore, $\tilde{\Pi}_{ldc}$ requires no interaction between parties, and its computation cost is $O(M \log^2(M))$ for Enc and $O(r^2)$ for Query and Dec.*

On input (Init, $\langle M \rangle$), run the following steps of the SK-DEPIR:

1. KeyGen: Randomly choose a subset $T \subset [u]$ of size r.
2. Process: Run $\tilde{\Pi}_{ldc}$ on input (Enc, $\langle M \rangle$) to obtain shares of encoded database $\langle E \rangle$. Run u instances of $\Pi_{permute}$ on $\langle E \rangle$ to form permuted $\{\langle E^i \rangle\}_{i \in [u]}$. Run Π_{store} on input (Init, $\cup_{i \in [u], j \in [M]} (i \parallel j, \langle E^i[j] \rangle)$) to obtain $(\Sigma, \langle M \rangle, \langle k \rangle)$.
3. Output $(\Sigma, \langle M \rangle \cup \langle T \rangle, \langle k \rangle)$, the state from KeyGen and Process.

On input (read, $\langle addr \rangle, \langle k \rangle, \langle M \rangle \cup \langle T \rangle$), run the following steps of the SK-DEPIR:

1. Query: Run $\tilde{\Pi}_{ldc}$ on input (Query, $\langle addr \rangle$) to obtain shares of r elements $Y = ((\langle y_i \rangle))_{i \in [r]}$. Construct a longer vector $\tilde{Y} = (\langle \tilde{y}_i \rangle)_{i \in [u]}$ such that $\tilde{Y}|_T = Y$ and the remaining elements $\{\tilde{y}_i \mid i \in [u] \setminus T\}$ are chosen uniformly at random.
2. Resp: For $i \in [u]$, run Π_{store} on (read, $(i \parallel \langle \tilde{y}_i \rangle), \langle k \rangle, \langle M \rangle)$. Construct a list $L = (\langle elem^i \rangle)_{i \in [u]}$ of the shares of elements returned in response.
3. Dec: Truncate the list $\langle L|_T \rangle$ to responses of queries in Y. Run $\tilde{\Pi}_{ldc}$ on input (Dec, $\langle L|_T \rangle$) to obtain shares of a field element $\langle val \rangle$. Output $(\langle addr \rangle, \langle val \rangle)$.

Fig. 16. $\tilde{\Pi}_{store}$ protocol, based on secure 2PC of the SK-DEPIR scheme of Canetti et al., given any integers $m < t < r < u < N < M$ satisfying the HPN assumption.

Proof. Our 2PC protocol $\tilde{\Pi}_{ldc}$ contains methods for the servers to securely compute each of the 3 methods of an LDC on boolean secret-shared data. Ergo, the local decodability and smoothness of $\tilde{\Pi}_{ldc}$ follow immediately from the same properties of its non-secure-computation counterpart [6].

There are four types of operations used throughout $\tilde{\Pi}_{ldc}$, and we show below how to compute all of them non-interactively. The first two operations are used in Enc, and the last two in Query and Dec.

- Computing the lexicographic maps δ and ι: δ is the identity operation on bitstrings, and thanks to the specific basis we chose for H, computing $\iota(i)$ merely involves partitioning the bits of $i \in [N]$ into m strings of length h, padding with 0s in the $\ell - h$ leftmost bits. These string operations can can be performed independently in $O(N)$ time on each boolean secret share of i.
- Interpolation and evaluation of multivariate polynomial ψ: this task is challenging; we show in Sect. 4.3 a non-interactive secure 2-party protocol that performs these operations across all of $\mathbb{F}^m$ in time $O(M \log^2(M))$.
- Random sampling of multivariate polynomial ϕ: the parties already hold shares of the constant term $\phi_0 = \phi(0)$, and they can randomly choose all other t coefficients in $O(t)$ time.
- Evaluation of ϕ at r points and interpolation of $\tilde{\phi}$ from r points: since the evaluation points $(x_i)_{i \in [r]}$ are publicly known, the coefficients for polynomial evaluation and Lagrange interpolation can also be publicly (pre-)computed. Ergo, evaluating or interpolating a polynomial of degree $\leq r$ only involves linear algebra and takes $O(r^2)$ time.

Constructing $\tilde{\Pi}_{store}$ as a Secure Computation of SK-DEPIR. Next, we construct a new protocol $\tilde{\Pi}_{store}$ that also instantiates $\mathcal{F}_{store}$. It is a secure two-party computation of the client-server SK-DEPIR protocol of Canetti et al. [6] in which the two parties jointly emulate the server. In Fig. 16, we show simultaneously a secure computation of the SK-DEPIR protocol and how its methods (along with $\tilde{\Pi}_{ldc}$, $\Pi_{permute}$, and Π_{store}) combine to instantiate a new read-only storage protocol $\tilde{\Pi}_{store}$.

At a high level, the protocol $\tilde{\Pi}_{store}$ operates as follows. During initialization, the parties collectively construct the LDC encoding of the database, permute it u times, and store the concatenation of these u encoded databases $\mathsf{E}^0, \mathsf{E}^1, \ldots, \mathsf{E}^{u-1}$ in an instance of Π_{store}; the address corresponding to each element $\mathsf{E}^i[j]$ is the concatenation of the the instance number i and the location j within this instance. During a read operation, the parties look up $\tilde{\Pi}_{store}$ at one location within each permuted database E^i; r of these lookup operations retrieve data that can collectively be used to decode the desired value, and the remaining $u-r$ lookups are "decoy" lookups that provide security under the HPN assumption.

Lemma 2 shows two settings of parameters that satisfy the HPN assumption. Using these parameters, we show that $\tilde{\Pi}_{store}$ is an efficient and secure read-only data store.

Theorem 3. *Under the HPN assumption, the protocol $\tilde{\Pi}_{store}$ in Fig. 16 securely implements functionality $\mathcal{F}_{store}$ with constant rounds of communication. Furthermore, given any constant $\epsilon > 0$, there exist parameters m, t, u, and M such that the computation and communication cost of $\tilde{\Pi}_{store}$ is:*

- *$O_\lambda(N^{1+\epsilon})$ for* Init *and $O_\lambda(N^\epsilon)$ for* read, *or*
- *$O_\lambda(\mathrm{poly}(N))$ for* Init *and $O_\lambda(\log(N))$ for* read.

Proof. Our 2PC protocol $\tilde{\Pi}_{store}$ computes all methods of the Canetti et al. SK-DEPIR protocol over boolean secret-shared data, In particular, there exist constant-round secure computation protocols for all set operations in $\tilde{\Pi}_{store}$.

- Within KeyGen: to choose a subset $T \subset [u]$, form a set of r 1s and $(u-r)$ 0s, then permute this set using $\Pi_{permute}$. The result is a secret-shared indicator vector $\langle T \rangle$ of length u indicating which elements are in T.
- Within Query: form the set $\tilde{Y}$ by oversampling. Run the LDC Query operation on u values rather than r values (using an LDC protocol with u constants x_i) to compute $Y = (\langle y_i \rangle)_{i \in [u]}$, and let $\bar{Y} = (\langle \bar{y} \rangle)_{i \in [u]}$ be a secret-shared set of u random values. Compute $\tilde{Y}$ by multiplexing: in parallel, set each element $\langle \tilde{y}_i \rangle = \langle T[i] \wedge y_i \oplus (T[i] \oplus 1) \wedge \bar{y}_i \rangle$. (Since all values are boolean secret-shared, the bitwise-AND should be performed in 1 round between the $T[i]$ and each bit of y_i in turn, and similarly for the second term.)
- To truncate the list $\langle L \rangle|_T$ within Dec: first form a secret sharing of the index vector $\langle I \rangle$ that equals 0 at decoy values and where $I|_T = \{1, 2, \ldots, r\}$ at real values by bit composing $\langle T \rangle$ to an additive secret sharing $[[T]]$ [9,29], computing $[[I_i]] = [[T_i \cdot \sum_{j=0}^{i} T_j]] \; \forall i \in [u]$, and bit decomposing $[[I]]$ into a boolean secret sharing $\langle I \rangle$. Then, concatenate componentwise the elements of $\langle I \rangle$ and $\langle L \rangle$, permute this set using $\Pi_{permute}$, open all shares of indices I in parallel, and locally sort the values of $\langle L \rangle$ using the indices.

The computational cost of Query is $O(u^2)$ due to oversampling, and the cost of the set truncation within Dec is $O(u\log(u))$ as shown by Damgard et al. [9].

As a secure two-party computation of an existing SK-DEPIR scheme, $\tilde{\Pi}_{store}$ inherits the correctness property from Definition 2, which states that the read operation always returns the correct decoded database entry. Additionally, the use of $\Pi_{permute}$ within the protocol provides the random permutation π as required for use of the HPN assumption, so we also inherit the indistinguishability-style security property from Definition 2. Using these properties, it is straightforward to prove that $\tilde{\Pi}_{store}$ instantiates $\mathcal{F}_{store}$ using a similar sequence of hybrids as in the original proof; we omit the details for brevity.

The claims about computational costs follow from Lemma 2 plus the following two observations. First, the cost of Init is dominated by the cost of the SK-DEPIR Process method, since the $O(M)$ cost of $\Pi_{permute}$ and the $O(u\log(u))$ cost of the oblivious search in KeyGen are smaller than the parameters in Lemma 2. Second, the cost of read is dominated by the cost of the LDC Query and Dec since the call to Π_{store} within Resp costs $O(\log(u \cdot M))$ as per Table 2, which is $O_\lambda(\log(N))$ since $u < N$ and $M = O_\lambda(N)$.

4.2   The New DORAM Construction $\tilde{\Pi}_{DORAM}$

In this section, we show how to construct the new DORAM construction $\tilde{\Pi}_{DORAM}$ using this new instantiation $\tilde{\Pi}_{store}$ of the $\mathcal{F}_{store}$ functionality, which only needs to be shuffled and reconstructed after a specified bound t of write operations have been performed, irrespective of the number of read operations.

The updated $\tilde{\Pi}_{DORAM}$ protocol is shown in the full version. The protocol now initializes two versions of the store, one to keep track of which elements are written and leaks access patterns and the other, $\tilde{\Pi}_{access}$, that supports unlimited reads and does not leak access patterns. This first store is critical to maintain invariant used for reshuffling. In order to know what written elements that are found in the stash, we use this store to keep track of the items 'written' into the store. With the distinction between reads and writes no longer hidden, $\tilde{\Pi}_{DORAM}$ only increments the epoch counter when a write is performed. Reads do not count towards the contents of the stash.

The most significant change is within the access protocol, shown in the full version [20]. It now differentiates between read and write operations. For a read operation it calls $\tilde{\Pi}_{store}$ and does not write anything back to the stash. The write operation continues to be unchanged from the original protocol.

Reshuffling is shown in the full version [20]. When it comes to reshuffle after t writes, the protocol is similar except in one key difference. Though we now support two different stores, we perform the concatenation with elements in the stash *only* with the original store, not the augmented SK-DEPIR store. The latter does not keep track of the elements read (the indices i_M returned by $\tilde{\Pi}_{store}$ are simply random values and do not allow for the recovery of the elements). Instead we have to rely on the unread elements in the original store; namely the elements that were not written to as part of the store. The unread elements are identical to the elements found in the augmented store, so concatentation will

Table 3. A evaluation of each of the protocol's server computation, bandwidth and rounds of communication where stash size, $t = N^\epsilon$. Note that we assume N reads for every 1 write and $\tilde{\Pi}_{DORAM}$ has been amortized where appropriate.

	Local Computation	Bandwidth	Rounds
$\tilde{\Pi}_{DORAM}(\text{Init})$	$O_\lambda(N^{1+\epsilon}\log(N^{1+\epsilon}))$	$O_\lambda(N^{1+\epsilon}\log(N^{1+\epsilon}))$	$O(1)$
$\tilde{\Pi}_{DORAM}(\text{op})$	$O_\lambda(N^\epsilon)$	$O_\lambda(N^\epsilon)$	$O(1)$
$\tilde{\Pi}_{access}$	$O_\lambda(N^\epsilon)$	$O_\lambda(N^\epsilon)$	$O(1)$
$\tilde{\Pi}_{shuffle}$	$O_\lambda(N^{1+\epsilon}\log(N^{1+\epsilon}))$	$O_\lambda(N^{1+\epsilon}\log(N^{1+\epsilon}))$	$O(1)$
$\tilde{\Pi}_{store}(\text{Init})$	$O_\lambda(N^{1+\epsilon})$	$O_\lambda(N^{1+\epsilon})$	$O(1)$
$\tilde{\Pi}_{store}(\text{read})$	$O_\lambda(N^\epsilon)$	$O_\lambda(N^\epsilon)$	$O(1)$

result in the correct operation of $\tilde{\Pi}_{shuffle}$. The only other change is to instantiate these two stores, rather than the one store used within the original protocol.

We also consider the complexity of these new schemes in Table 3. Recall that we use O_λ to indicate complexities that only depend on N, ignoring any poly(λ) terms. The main difference between the complexity of our two schemes is the blowup incurred by the new implementation of $\tilde{\Pi}_{store}$. The LDC encoding incurs a $O_\lambda(N^{1+\epsilon})$ overhead for any choice of $\epsilon > 0$. This means any protocols that were original dominated by the computation or bandwidth of $\tilde{\Pi}_{store}$ initialization inherit this new cost. Recall in the original scheme the dominate cost of Π_{access} was the linear scan of the stash. In this setting, with the disparity of reads vs writes, we consider a smaller stash size. If we assume one write for every N reads and our smaller stash size, $\tilde{\Pi}_{DORAM}$ accesses amortize to be $O_\lambda(N^\epsilon)$.

4.3 2PC for Multivariate FFT over Binary Fields

The one remaining task in the specification of protocol $\tilde{\Pi}_{ldc}$ is to construct a secure computation of multivariate polynomial evaluation and interpolation. One effective, but slow, technique is to use Lagrange interpolation. For a univariate polynomial $p = \sum_i p \cdot x^i$, we can transform secret shares of a vector $\boldsymbol{p} = (p)$ of coefficients into shares of the vector $\hat{\boldsymbol{p}} = (p(i))$ of its evaluation at all points (or vice-versa) via multiplication by the Vandermonde matrix $\hat{\boldsymbol{p}} = A \cdot \boldsymbol{p}$, or its inverse $\boldsymbol{p} = A^{-1} \cdot \hat{\boldsymbol{p}}$, and shares of this matrix-vector multiplication can be computed locally by each party since the Vandermonde matrix A is public. However, the computational cost for matrix-vector multiplication is $\Omega(N^2)$.

The Fast Fourier Transform (FFT) [8] is a well-known algorithm for computing polynomial evaluation in quasilinear time, and the Inverse FFT similarly calculates polynomial interpolation efficiently. The fastest known FFT for binary fields is the additive FFT algorithm by Gao and Mateer [12]. As its name suggests, this algorithm solely involves linear operations. In this section, we design a secure computation protocol $\tilde{\Pi}_{mFFT}$ of FFT for multilinear polynomials over binary fields that can be performed locally (i.e., without interaction) with quasilinear computational cost. While this contribution may be of independent

---

Input: public integer h and basis $\mathcal{H} = \{v_0, v_1, \ldots, v_{h-1}\}$ of a subspace of $\mathbb{F}$ of size 2^h, plus shares $\langle \boldsymbol{p} \rangle$ of coefficients of a polynomial $p \in \mathbb{F}[x]$ of degree $2^h - 1$.

Output: shares $\langle \hat{\boldsymbol{p}} \rangle = \mathrm{FFT}(h, \mathcal{H}, \langle \boldsymbol{p} \rangle)$ of the evaluations of p on all points spanned by $\mathcal{H}$, in the ordering specified by $\mathcal{H}[i] = \sum_{j=0}^{h-1} i_j v_j$, where $i_j = $ the jth bit of i.

1. As the base case: if $h = 1$, then return $(\langle p(0) \rangle, \langle p(v_0) \rangle)$. For a degree-1 polynomial p, we compute $\langle p(0) \rangle = \langle p_0 \rangle$ and $\langle p(v_0) \rangle = \langle p_0 \rangle + v_0 \langle p_1 \rangle$.
2. Compute the new bases $\bar{\mathcal{H}} = \{\bar{v}_i\}$ and $\tilde{\mathcal{H}} = \{\tilde{v}_i\}$ of size $h - 1$ containing basis elements $\bar{v}_i = v_i \cdot v_{h-1}^{-1}$ and $\tilde{v}_i = \bar{v}_i^2 - \bar{v}_i$ for all $i \in [h-1]$.
3. Compute coefficients $\langle q_i \rangle = v_{h-1}^i \cdot \langle p_i \rangle$ of the polynomial $q = p(v_{h-1} \cdot x)$.
4. Execute the Taylor expansion algorithm $\mathrm{T}(h, \langle \boldsymbol{q} \rangle)$ in Fig. 18. Let $\langle \boldsymbol{f} \rangle$ and $\langle \boldsymbol{g} \rangle$ denote the shares of the resulting polynomials, each of degree $2^{h-1} - 1$.
5. Recursively compute $\langle \hat{\boldsymbol{f}} \rangle = \mathrm{FFT}(h-1, \tilde{\mathcal{H}}, \langle \boldsymbol{f} \rangle)$ and $\langle \hat{\boldsymbol{g}} \rangle = \mathrm{FFT}(h-1, \tilde{\mathcal{H}}, \langle \boldsymbol{g} \rangle)$.
6. Set $\langle \hat{p}_i \rangle = \langle \hat{f}_i \rangle + \bar{\mathcal{H}}[i] \cdot \langle \hat{g}_i \rangle$ and $\langle \hat{p}_{i+2^{h-1}} \rangle = \langle \hat{p}_i \rangle + \langle \hat{g}_i \rangle$ $\forall i \in [2^{h-1}]$. Return $\hat{\boldsymbol{p}}$.

Fig. 17. $\tilde{\Pi}_{1FFT}$ protocol for secure 2-party computation of the Additive Fast Fourier Transform of a univariate polynomial p in a binary field $\mathbb{F}$.

interest, in this work it completes the task from Sect. 4.1 of constructing a non-interactive $\tilde{\Pi}_{ldc}$ protocol with quasilinear (rather than quadratic) computation cost. For example, in the Enc protocol within $\tilde{\Pi}_{ldc}$, it allows for securely computing the coefficients of the polynomial $\psi : H^m \to \mathbb{F}$ in time $O(N \log^2 N)$ and securely evaluating the polynomial ψ at all locations in $\mathbb{F}^m$ in time $O(M \log^2 M)$.

We describe this protocol in two steps. First, we show how to securely evaluate FFT for univariate polynomials (building a secure computation of Taylor series expansion as a building block). Second, we bootstrap to a secure evaluation of FFT for multivariate polynomials. For brevity, we show these FFT protocols only in the forward (polynomial evaluation) direction. It is straightforward to validate that the same techniques apply to construct a secure computation protocol of inverse FFT (i.e., polynomial interpolation) in quasilinear time.

2PC Protocol $\tilde{\Pi}_{1FFT}$ for univariate FFT. In this section, we present a secure two-party computation protocol $\tilde{\Pi}_{1FFT}$. Let $H \subset \mathbb{F}$ be a subspace (possibly the entire field) of size $|H| = 2^h$ defined by a basis $\mathcal{H}$, and let $p = \sum_{i=0}^{2^h - 1} p_i \cdot x^i$ be a univariate polynomial of degree less than 2^h. This protocol begins with shares of the 2^h coefficients $\langle \boldsymbol{p} \rangle = (\langle p_i \rangle)_{i \in [2^h]}$ of the polynomial, and it returns the shares $\langle \hat{\boldsymbol{p}} \rangle = (\langle p(i) \rangle)_{i \in [2^h]}$ of its evaluation at all 2^h points in H.

The protocol $\tilde{\Pi}_{1FFT}$ is shown in Fig. 17, and it uses the Taylor series expansion algorithm in Fig. 18 as a building block. Each step of these algorithms only involves addition and scalar multiplication of secret-shared values, so the secure computation $\tilde{\Pi}_{1FFT}$ can be performed locally. These algorithms are precisely the secret-shared versions of their counterparts in Gao and Mateer [12].

We provide a high-level intuition of $\tilde{\Pi}_{1FFT}$ when considering the basis $\mathcal{H} = \{z^{h-1}, z^{h-2}, \ldots, z, 1\}$, in which case $q = p$; full details are given in [12]. The core idea of the Fast Fourier Transform is to reduce the evaluation of one polynomial q

---

Input: public integer h, shares of coefficients $\langle q \rangle$ of a polynomial of degree $2^h - 1$.

Output: $\langle f \rangle, \langle g \rangle = \mathrm{T}(h, \langle q \rangle)$ such that each vector is of length $\leq 2^{h-1}$ and they collectively form the Taylor series expansion $q(x) = \sum_{i=0}^{2^{h-1}} (f_i + g_i x) \cdot (x^2 - x)^i$.

1. As the base case: if $h = 1$ so $\deg(q) = 1$, return $\langle f_0 \rangle = \langle q_0 \rangle$ and $\langle g_0 \rangle = \langle q_1 \rangle$.
2. Partition the vector $\langle q \rangle$ into $\langle t^0 \rangle$ containing the first 2^{h-1} elements, $\langle t^1 \rangle$ containing the next 2^{h-2} elements, and $\langle t^2 \rangle$ containing the last 2^{h-2} elements.
3. Compute the vectors $\langle t \rangle = \langle t^1 \rangle + \langle t^2 \rangle$ of length 2^{h-2}, $\langle q^0 \rangle = \langle t^0 \rangle + (\mathbf{0} \parallel \langle t \rangle)$ of length 2^{h-1}, and $\langle q^1 \rangle = (\langle t \rangle \parallel \langle t^2 \rangle)$ of length 2^{h-1}. Here, $\mathbf{0}$ denotes the vector containing 2^{h-2} zero elements, and $\parallel$ denotes vector concatenation.
4. Recursively, find $\langle f^0 \rangle, \langle g^0 \rangle = \mathrm{T}(h - 1, \langle q^0 \rangle)$ and $\langle f^1 \rangle, \langle g^1 \rangle = \mathrm{T}(h - 1, \langle q^1 \rangle)$.
5. Return the concatenated vectors $\langle f \rangle = \langle f^0 \rangle \parallel \langle f^1 \rangle$ and $\langle g \rangle = \langle g^0 \rangle \parallel \langle g^1 \rangle$.

Fig. 18. Protocol for Taylor expansion of a polynomial $q(x) \in \mathbb{F}[x]$ at $x^2 - x$.

into the evaluation of two polynomials f and g of half the degree, plus quasilinear work to "stitch" the results together into an evaluation of q. Gao and Mateer [12] show how this can be done over binary fields, based on these observations:

- The Taylor expansion $q(x) = \sum_{i=0}^{2^{h-1}} (f_i + g_i x) \cdot (x^2 - x)^i$ leads to an equation $q(x) = f(x^2 - x) + x \cdot g(x^2 - x)$ involving polynomials $f(z) \triangleq \sum_{i=0}^{2^{h-1}} f_i \cdot z^i$ and $g(z) \triangleq \sum_{i=0}^{2^{h-1}} g \cdot z^i$ of lower degree $2^{h-1} - 1$.
- The function $x \mapsto x^2 - x$ is 2-to-1, and specifically it maps the 2^h-sized space spanned by $\mathcal{H}$ into the smaller 2^{h-1} space spanned by the basis $\tilde{\mathcal{H}}$.

Ergo, in order to evaluate the polynomial q at all points spanned by $\mathcal{H}$, it suffices to evaluate polynomials f and g at all points spanned by the smaller basis $\tilde{\mathcal{H}}$ and combine the results using the Taylor expansion $q(x) = f(x^2 - x) + x \cdot g(x^2 - x)$.

We provide a secure 2-party computation of Gao and Mateer's method of computing the Taylor expansion of q in Fig. 18, and we provide a 2PC of polynomial evaluation in Fig. 17. The only operations that involve secret-shared data are linear combinations and splitting/joining vectors, all of which can be performed locally. Note that step 2 of Fig. 17 involves more complicated algebra, but it only involves public (non-secret-shared) values, so it can be performed locally and pre-computed before parties receive their input shares.

2PC Protocol $\tilde{\Pi}_{mFFT}$ for Multivariate FFT. Recall that the locally decodable code used in $\tilde{\Pi}_{ldc}$ is based on Reed-Muller codes, and as a result it uses multivariate polynomials. Here, we show how to bootstrap from an FFT for univariate polynomials into one for multivariate polynomials. The full protocol is shown in Fig. 19, and it is based on a technique used by Kedlaya and Umans [24].

Protocol $\tilde{\Pi}_{mFFT}$ operates via recursion over many evaluations of univariate polynomials. Given an m-variate polynomial p of total degree $< 2^h - 1$ for which the parties have shares of all coefficients, we rewrite the polynomial by conditioning on the power of the first variable: $p(x_0, \ldots, x_{m-1}) = \sum_{i=0}^{2^h-1} x_0^i \cdot$

Input: shares of coefficients $\langle p \rangle$ of an m-variate polynomial p of total degree $2^h - 1$.

Output: shares $\langle \hat{p} \rangle$ of evaluations $p(\boldsymbol{x})$ at all points $\boldsymbol{x} \in H^m$.

1. As the base case: if $m = 1$, then run protocol $\tilde{\Pi}_{1FFT}$ as shown in Fig. 17.
2. By rearranging terms, write $p(\boldsymbol{x}) = \sum_{i=0}^{2^h - 1} x_0^i \cdot p_i(x_1, x_2, \ldots, x_{m-1})$. Observe that the parties collectively hold shares of the coefficients of each $\langle \boldsymbol{p_i} \rangle$.
3. Recursively, get shares $\langle \hat{\boldsymbol{p_i}} \rangle$ of evaluations of each p_i at all points in H^{m-1}.
4. For each vector $\boldsymbol{c} \in H^{m-1}$, compute shares of the evaluation of the univariate polynomial $\langle p(x_0, \boldsymbol{c}) \rangle = \sum_{i=0}^{2^h - 1} \langle p_i(\boldsymbol{c}) \rangle \cdot x_0^i$ on all points in H using $\tilde{\Pi}_{1FFT}$.

Fig. 19. $\tilde{\Pi}_{mFFT}$ protocol for secure 2-party evaluation of a multivariate polynomial $p(x_0, \ldots, x_{m-1})$ at all points in a subspace $H^m \in \mathbb{F}^m$.

$p_i(x_1, x_2, \ldots, x_{m-1})$. We can evaluate the $(m - 1)$-variate polynomials p_i recursively, and use the results to evaluate the univariate polynomial over x_0. Since each univariate polynomial evaluation takes time quasilinear in $|H|$, a simple recurrence relation shows that the entire evaluation is quasilinear in $|H|^m = N$. This completes the construction, and it is the necessary building block to complete the proof of Theorem 2 and achieve quasilinear server computation for our LDC protocol.

Acknowledgments. We gratefully acknowledge conversations with Daniel Wichs and Jack Doerner for their valuable insights. This material is based upon work supported by the National Science Foundation under Grants 1414119, 1718135, 1750795, and 1931714.

References

1. Abraham, I., Fletcher, C.W., Nayak, K., Pinkas, B., Ren, L.: Asymptotically tight bounds for composing ORAM with PIR. In: Fehr, S. (ed.) PKC 2017. LNCS, vol. 10174, pp. 91–120. Springer, Heidelberg (2017). https://doi.org/10.1007/978-3-662-54365-8_5
2. Asharov, G., Komargodski, I., Lin, W.-K., Nayak, K., Peserico, E., Shi, E.: OptORAMa: optimal oblivious RAM. In: Canteaut, A., Ishai, Y. (eds.) EUROCRYPT 2020. LNCS, vol. 12106, pp. 403–432. Springer, Cham (2020). https://doi.org/10.1007/978-3-030-45724-2_14
3. Boyle, E., Holmgren, J., Weiss, M.: Permuted puzzles and cryptographic hardness. In: Hofheinz, D., Rosen, A. (eds.) TCC 2019. LNCS, vol. 11892, pp. 465–493. Springer, Cham (2019). https://doi.org/10.1007/978-3-030-36033-7_18
4. Boyle, E., Ishai, Y., Pass, R., Wootters, M.: Can we access a database both locally and privately? In: Kalai, Y., Reyzin, L. (eds.) TCC 2017. LNCS, vol. 10678, pp. 662–693. Springer, Cham (2017). https://doi.org/10.1007/978-3-319-70503-3_22
5. Bunn, P., Katz, J., Kushilevitz, E., Ostrovsky, R.: Efficient 3-party distributed ORAM. In: Galdi, C., Kolesnikov, V. (eds.) SCN 2020. LNCS, vol. 12238, pp. 215–232. Springer, Cham (2020). https://doi.org/10.1007/978-3-030-57990-6_11

6. Canetti, R., Holmgren, J., Richelson, S.: Towards doubly efficient private information retrieval. In: Kalai, Y., Reyzin, L. (eds.) TCC 2017. LNCS, vol. 10678, pp. 694–726. Springer, Cham (2017). https://doi.org/10.1007/978-3-319-70503-3_23

7. Chan, T.-H.H., Katz, J., Nayak, K., Polychroniadou, A., Shi, E.: More is less: perfectly secure oblivious algorithms in the multi-server setting. In: Peyrin, T., Galbraith, S. (eds.) ASIACRYPT 2018. LNCS, vol. 11274, pp. 158–188. Springer, Cham (2018). https://doi.org/10.1007/978-3-030-03332-3_7

8. Cooley, J.W., Tukey, J.W.: An algorithm for the machine calculation of complex fourier series. Math. Comput. **19**(90), 297–301 (1965)

9. Damgård, I., Fitzi, M., Kiltz, E., Nielsen, J.B., Toft, T.: Unconditionally secure constant-rounds multi-party computation for equality, comparison, bits and exponentiation. In: Halevi, S., Rabin, T. (eds.) TCC 2006. LNCS, vol. 3876, pp. 285–304. Springer, Heidelberg (2006). https://doi.org/10.1007/11681878_15

10. Dodis, Y., Yampolskiy, A.: A verifiable random function with short proofs and keys. In: Vaudenay, S. (ed.) PKC 2005. LNCS, vol. 3386, pp. 416–431. Springer, Heidelberg (2005). https://doi.org/10.1007/978-3-540-30580-4_28

11. Doerner, J., Shelat, A.: Scaling ORAM for secure computation. In: ACM Conference on Computer and Communications Security, pp. 523–535. ACM (2017)

12. Gao, S., Mateer, T.D.: Additive fast fourier transforms over finite fields. IEEE Trans. Inf. Theory **56**(12), 6265–6272 (2010)

13. Garg, S., Lu, S., Ostrovsky, R.: Black-box garbled RAM. In: FOCS, pp. 210–229. IEEE Computer Society (2015)

14. Garg, S., Lu, S., Ostrovsky, R., Scafuro, A.: Garbled RAM from one-way functions. In: STOC, pp. 449–458. ACM (2015)

15. Garg, S., Mohassel, P., Papamanthou, C.: TWORAM: round-optimal oblivious RAM with applications to searchable encryption. IACR Cryptol. ePrint Arch. **2015**, 1010 (2015)

16. Gentry, C., Halevi, S., Lu, S., Ostrovsky, R., Raykova, M., Wichs, D.: Garbled RAM revisited. In: Nguyen, P.Q., Oswald, E. (eds.) EUROCRYPT 2014. LNCS, vol. 8441, pp. 405–422. Springer, Heidelberg (2014). https://doi.org/10.1007/978-3-642-55220-5_23

17. Goldreich, O., Ostrovsky, R.: Software protection and simulation on oblivious rams. J. ACM **43**(3), 431–473 (1996)

18. Gordon, S.D., Katz, J., Kolesnikov, V., Krell, F., Malkin, T., Raykova, M., Vahlis, Y.: Secure two-party computation in sublinear (amortized) time. In: ACM Conference on Computer and Communications Security, pp. 513–524. ACM (2012)

19. Gordon, S.D., Katz, J., Wang, X.: Simple and efficient two-server ORAM. In: Peyrin, T., Galbraith, S. (eds.) ASIACRYPT 2018. LNCS, vol. 11274, pp. 141–157. Springer, Cham (2018). https://doi.org/10.1007/978-3-030-03332-3_6

20. Hamlin, A., Varia, M.: Two-server distributed ORAM with sublinear computation and constant rounds. IACR Cryptol. ePrint Arch. **2020**, 1547 (2020)

21. Hoang, T., Yavuz, A.A., Durak, F.B., Guajardo, J.: Oblivious dynamic searchable encryption via distributed PIR and ORAM. IACR Cryptol. ePrint Arch. **2017**, 1158 (2017)

22. Jarecki, S., Liu, X.: Efficient oblivious pseudorandom function with applications to adaptive OT and secure computation of set intersection. In: Reingold, O. (ed.) TCC 2009. LNCS, vol. 5444, pp. 577–594. Springer, Heidelberg (2009). https://doi.org/10.1007/978-3-642-00457-5_34

23. Jarecki, S., Wei, B.: 3PC ORAM with low latency, low bandwidth, and fast batch retrieval. In: Preneel, B., Vercauteren, F. (eds.) ACNS 2018. LNCS, vol. 10892, pp. 360–378. Springer, Cham (2018). https://doi.org/10.1007/978-3-319-93387-0_19

24. Kedlaya, K.S., Umans, C.: Fast modular composition in any characteristic. In: FOCS, pp. 146–155. IEEE Computer Society (2008)
25. Kushilevitz, E., Mour, T.: Sub-logarithmic distributed oblivious RAM with small block size. In: Lin, D., Sako, K. (eds.) PKC 2019. LNCS, vol. 11442, pp. 3–33. Springer, Cham (2019). https://doi.org/10.1007/978-3-030-17253-4_1
26. Lu, S., Ostrovsky, R.: Distributed oblivious RAM for secure two-party computation. In: Sahai, A. (ed.) TCC 2013. LNCS, vol. 7785, pp. 377–396. Springer, Heidelberg (2013). https://doi.org/10.1007/978-3-642-36594-2_22
27. Lu, S., Ostrovsky, R.: How to garble RAM programs. In: EUROCRYPT. Lecture Notes in Computer Science, vol. 7881, pp. 719–734. Springer (2013)
28. Miao, P., Patel, S., Raykova, M., Seth, K., Yung, M.: Two-sided malicious security for private intersection-sum with cardinality. In: Micciancio, D., Ristenpart, T. (eds.) CRYPTO 2020. LNCS, vol. 12172, pp. 3–33. Springer, Cham (2020). https://doi.org/10.1007/978-3-030-56877-1_1
29. Nishide, T., Ohta, K.: Multiparty computation for interval, equality, and comparison without bit-decomposition protocol. In: Okamoto, T., Wang, X. (eds.) PKC 2007. LNCS, vol. 4450, pp. 343–360. Springer, Heidelberg (2007). https://doi.org/10.1007/978-3-540-71677-8_23
30. Ostrovsky, R., Shoup, V.: Private information storage (extended abstract). In: STOC, pp. 294–303. ACM (1997)
31. Patel, S., Persiano, G., Raykova, M., Yeo, K.: Panorama: Oblivious RAM with logarithmic overhead. In: FOCS, pp. 871–882. IEEE Computer Society (2018)
32. Roche, D.S., Aviv, A.J., Choi, S.G.: A practical oblivious map data structure with secure deletion and history independence. In: IEEE Symposium on Security and Privacy, pp. 178–197. IEEE Computer Society (2016)
33. Wang, X., Chan, T.H., Shi, E.: Circuit ORAM: on tightness of the goldreich-ostrovsky lower bound. In: ACM Conference on Computer and Communications Security, pp. 850–861. ACM (2015)
34. Wang, X.S., Huang, Y., Chan, T.H., Shelat, A., Shi, E.: SCORAM: oblivious RAM for secure computation. In: ACM Conference on Computer and Communications Security, pp. 191–202. ACM (2014)
35. Weiss, M., Wichs, D.: Is there an oblivious RAM lower bound for online reads? In: Beimel, A., Dziembowski, S. (eds.) TCC 2018. LNCS, vol. 11240, pp. 603–635. Springer, Cham (2018). https://doi.org/10.1007/978-3-030-03810-6_22
36. Zahur, S., Wang, X., Raykova, M., Gascón, A., Doerner, J., Evans, D., Katz, J.: Revisiting square-root ORAM: efficient random access in multi-party computation. In: IEEE Symposium on Security and Privacy, pp. 218–234. IEEE Computer Society (2016)
37. Zhang, J., Ma, Q., Zhang, W., Qiao, D.: MSKT-ORAM: a constant bandwidth ORAM without homomorphic encryption. IACR Cryptol. ePrint Arch. **2016**, 882 (2016)

Flexible and Efficient Verifiable Computation on Encrypted Data

Alexandre Bois[1]([✉]), Ignacio Cascudo[2], Dario Fiore[2], and Dongwoo Kim[3]

[1] CentraleSupelec, University of Paris-Saclay, Gif-sur-Yvette, France
alexandre.bois-verdiere@student.ecp.fr
[2] IMDEA Software Institute, Madrid, Spain
{ignacio.cascudo,dario.fiore}@imdea.org
[3] Western Digital Research, Milpitas, USA
Dongwoo.Kim@wdc.com

Abstract. We consider the problem of verifiable and private delegation of computation [Gennaro et al. CRYPTO'10] in which a client stores private data on an untrusted server and asks the server to compute functions over this data. In this scenario we aim to achieve three main properties: the server should not learn information on inputs and outputs of the computation (privacy), the server cannot return wrong results without being caught (integrity), and the client can verify the correctness of the outputs faster than running the computation (efficiency). A known paradigm to solve this problem is to use a (non-private) verifiable computation (VC) to prove correctness of a homomorphic encryption (HE) evaluation on the ciphertexts. Despite the research advances in obtaining efficient VC and HE, using these two primitives together in this paradigm is concretely expensive. Recent work [Fiore et al. CCS'14, PKC'20] addressed this problem by designing specialized VC solutions that however require the HE scheme to work with very specific parameters; notably HE ciphertexts must be over $\mathbb{Z}_q$ for a large prime q.

In this work we propose a new solution that allows a flexible choice of HE parameters, while staying modular (based on the paradigm combining VC and HE) and efficient (the VC and the HE schemes are both executed at their best efficiency). At the core of our new protocol are new homomorphic hash functions for Galois rings. As an additional contribution we extend our results to support non-deterministic computations on encrypted data and an additional privacy property by which verifiers do not learn information on the inputs of the computation.

1 Introduction

We address the problem of verifiable computation on encrypted data. This problem arises in situations where a client wants to compute some function over private data on an untrusted machine (a cloud server for example) and is concerned

---

A. Bois—Work done while at IMDEA Software Institute.
D. Kim—Work done while at IMDARC, Seoul National University, Korea.

© International Association for Cryptologic Research 2021
J. A. Garay (Ed.): PKC 2021, LNCS 12711, pp. 528–558, 2021.
https://doi.org/10.1007/978-3-030-75248-4_19

about three issues. The first one is *efficiency*: the client wants to take advantage of the machine's computing power and to do many fewer operations than those needed to execute the computation. The second one is *privacy*—the client wants to keep the data hidden to the server—and the third one is *integrity*—the client wants to ensure that the results provided by the untrusted machine are correct.

If the goal is to solve privacy (and efficiency), then fully homomorphic encryption (FHE) is the answer. With FHE the server can receive data encrypted and compute any function on it. The first FHE scheme was proposed in 2009 by Gentry [Gen09], and since then we have several families of more efficient schemes, e.g., [BV11, BGV12, FV12, CKKS17, GSW13, DM15, CGGI16, CGGI17].

If the goal is to solve integrity (and efficiency), then the problem is in the scope of verifiable computation (VC) [GGP10]. In a nutshell, with a VC protocol the server can produce a proof about the correctness of a computation, and this proof can be checked by the client faster than recomputing the function. As of today, there exist several solutions to this problem based on different approaches, such as doubly-efficient interactive proofs [GKR08], FHE and garbled circuits [GGP10], functional/attribute-based encryption [PRV12, GKP+13], and succinct (interactive and non-interactive) arguments for NP, e.g., [Kil92, GGPR13, AHIV17, WTs+18, BCR+19].

When it comes to solving *both privacy and integrity* (while retaining efficiency), there exist fewer solutions. Gennaro et al. [GGP10] proposed a VC scheme with privacy based on combining garbled circuits and FHE, and Goldwasser et al. [GKP+13] proposed a VC scheme with privacy of inputs (but not outputs) based on succinct single-key functional encryption. Unfortunately, the concrete efficiency of these two solutions is not satisfactory, e.g. [GGP10] require the full FHE power, and [GKP+13] needs attribute-based encryption for expressive predicates and works for functions with single-bit outputs.

A third approach is that of Fiore et al. [FGP14] who proposed a generic construction of VC with privacy, obtained by combining an FHE scheme and a VC scheme: the basic idea is to use VC to prove the correctness of the FHE evaluations on ciphertexts. Efficiency-wise this approach is promising as it tries to reconcile the best of the two lines of work that individually address privacy (FHE) and integrity (VC) and that have advanced significantly in terms of efficiency.

The Efficiency Challenges of Proving Correctness of FHE Evaluation. The instantiation of [FGP14] generic construction still faces two challenges related to efficiency:

1. When executing a function g, the VC scheme must prove *the FHE evaluation of g*, whose representation is typically much larger than g, as it acts over FHE ciphertexts.
2. The FHE ciphertext space may not match the message space natively supported by the VC scheme. Although in theory this is not an issue for general-purpose VCs, in practice it would require expensive conversions that can significantly affect the cost of generating the VC proof. For example, many succinct arguments work for arithmetic circuits over a field $\mathbb{Z}_p = \mathbb{Z}/p\mathbb{Z}$ where

p is a large prime (e.g., the order of bilinear groups), whereas the FHE ciphertext spaces may be polynomial rings $\mathbb{Z}_q[X]/(f)$, $f \in \mathbb{Z}_q[X]$, where q is not necessarily a prime of exponential size (in the security parameter).

Fiore et al. [FGP14] proposed a concrete instantiation of their generic construction that, though supporting only the evaluation of quadratic functions, addresses both the two challenges above as follows. First, they use the HE scheme from [BV11], where a ciphertext consists of two polynomials in $\mathbb{Z}_q[X]/(f)$, and "force it" to work with $q = p$, where p is the prime order of bilinear groups used by their VC scheme. Second, they reduce the dependency of their VC scheme on the size of the ciphertexts (i.e., the degree d_f of the polynomial f) via a technique called homomorphic hashing. When executing a function g on n inputs, a strawman solution would require the VC to prove g's homomorphic evaluation, of size more than $O(d_f \cdot |g|)$. By using homomorphic hashing, they can have proofs generated in time $O(d_f \cdot n + |g|)$. Essentially, the ciphertext size impacts the cost of proof generation only on the number of inputs, which is unavoidable.

Recently, [FNP20] extended the approach of [FGP14] to support public verifiability and the evaluation of more than quadratic functions (still of constant degree) via the use of specialized zkSNARKs for polynomial rings. However, the scheme of [FNP20] still requires to instantiate the [BV11] HE scheme with a specific q order of the bilinear groups used by the zkSNARK.

To summarize, existing solutions [FGP14, FNP20] manage to avoid expensive conversions and achieve efficient proof generation, but pay the price of imposing specific values to the parameters of the HE scheme. This choice has several drawbacks. One problem is the efficiency of the HE scheme: the size of the modulus q mainly depends on the complexity of the computations to be supported (for correctness) and there are many cases where it can be as small as 50–60 bits and not necessarily a prime. Forcing it to be a prime of, say, 256 bits (because of discrete log security in bilinear groups) not only makes it unreasonably larger but also requires, due to security of the RingLWE problem, to increase the size of the polynomial ring, i.e., the degree of f. Similarly, in cases where for HE correctness q would be larger than 256 bits, then one must instantiate the bilinear groups at a security level higher than necessary. So, all in all, the techniques of [FGP14, FNP20] do not allow flexible choices of HE parameters.

1.1   Our Contributions

In this paper we provide new VC schemes with privacy of inputs and outputs that solve the two aforementioned efficiency challenges while staying *modular* (based on VC and FHE used independently) and *flexible* (no need to tweak the HE parameters).

Our VC schemes support HE computations of constant multiplicative depth, offer public delegation and public verifiability, and are multi-function, i.e., one can encode inputs with a function-independent key and delegate the execution of multiple functions on these inputs (see [PRV12]). These features are similar to those of the recent work [FNP20].

In contrast to previous works [FGP14, FNP20], we can use the [BV11] some-what homomorphic encryption scheme (where ciphertexts are in $\mathbb{Z}_q[X]/(f)$) *instantiated with any choice of the ciphertext modulus q* (Table 1).[1] This flexibility enables better and faster instantiations of the HE component than in [FGP14, FNP20].

For instance, in applications where q can be of about 50 bits we can set $deg(f) = 2^{11}$, which makes ciphertexts 40× shorter than using a 250-bits prime q, which would require $deg(f) = 2^{14}$. Furthermore, the fact that our modulus q does not have to be prime may lead to use optimized circuits and thus to faster executions in practice (an example is the lowest-digit-removal polynomial in [CH18], that has a lower degree for a modulus p^e than for a close prime modulus).

Table 1. Comparison of efficient VC schemes with privacy of inputs/outputs based on homomorphic encryption.

Scheme	Delegation	Verification	Max degree	HE modulus q
[FGP14]	priv	priv	2	Prime $> 2^\lambda$
[FNP20]	pub	pub	const	Prime $> 2^\lambda$
Ours	pub	pub	const	Any

As a key technique to achieve flexibility and to gain efficiency by working on smaller spaces, we define and construct new, more general, homomorphic hash functions for Galois rings. Briefly speaking, these functions can compress a ciphertext element from a polynomial ring $\mathbb{Z}_q[X]/(f)$, where $q = p^e$ for a prime p and f is arbitrary, into a smaller Galois ring (i.e., a polynomial ring $\mathbb{Z}_q[X]/(h)$ such that h is monic and its reduction modulo p is irreducible in $\mathbb{Z}_p[X]$). Next, thanks to the homomorphic property, we can use any VC scheme for proving arithmetic circuits over $\mathbb{Z}_q[X]/(h)$. As a concrete example, we show how to use the efficient GKR protocol [GKR08] for this task. In terms of efficiency, $h \in \mathbb{Z}_q[X]$ is a polynomial whose degree governs the soundness of the proofs (we need that $1/p^{deg(h)}$ is negligible) and is concretely smaller than the degree of f, e.g., $deg(h)$ can be between $2^4\times$ (when $p = 2$) and $2^{11}\times$ (when $p = q$) smaller.

We stress that previous homomorphic hash functions from [FGP14, FNP20] only map from $\mathbb{Z}_q[X]/(f)$ to $\mathbb{Z}_q$ and need q be a large prime. So they would not allow flexible choices of parameters. Our constructions instead have no restriction on q and can fine-tune the output space according to the desired soundness.

At the core of our result is a technique to speed up the prover costs in verifiable computation over polynomial rings. Given that polynomial rings are common algebraic structures used in many lattice-based cryptographic schemes, our methods and analysis might be easily reusable in other contexts different

---

[1] Precisely, our basic scheme in Sect. 3 works for a q that is a prime power; in the full version of this paper we generalize it to any (possibly composite) integer q.

from FHE. As an example, in Sect. 3.2 we show how our technique can be used to obtain a verifiable computation scheme for parallel, single-instruction multiple-data (SIMD) computations where the proof generation costs are minimally dependent on the number of parallel inputs.

Extensions for Non-deterministic Computations and Context-Hiding.
As an additional contribution, we generalize the notion of private VC to support non-deterministic computations along with context-hiding.

In brief, supporting nondeterministic computations means to consider functions of the form $g(x, w)$ in which the untrusted worker receives an encryption of the input x, holds an additional input w and can produce an encoding of $g(x, w)$. In this case, the security property becomes analogous to the one we have in proof systems for NP, namely the untrusted worker can produce an encoding y that is accepted only if there exists a w such that $y = g(x, w)$. Nondeterminism is useful to handle more complex computations, such as ones that use random coins, non-arithmetic operations (e.g., bit-decompositions) or (secret) computation parameters. For instance, with this we can prove re-randomization of ciphertexts, or evaluate polynomials with coefficients provided by the server.

To provide privacy against verifiers, we consider the notion of context hiding of [FNP20], which guarantees that the verifier learns no information about the input x beyond what can be inferred from the output $y = g(x)$. In our work, we extend context-hiding to the non-deterministic setting to ensure that the verifier learns nothing about (x, w). This includes both verifiers that only receive computation's results, and those who generated the input and the corresponding ciphertext/encoding (in which case x is already known).

Next, we extend our flexible VC constructions to support non-deterministic computations and achieve context-hiding. In particular, we show a scheme that is based on proving correctness of [BV11] HE evaluations and in which we address the two efficiency challenges mentioned earlier using our homomorphic hashing technique, thanks to which we keep the cost of proof generation $O(d_f \cdot n + |g|)$. To achieve context-hiding, however, instead of a verifiable computation for arithmetic circuits over the Galois ring $\mathbb{Z}_q[X]/(h)$, we use a commit-and-prove succinct zero-knowledge argument for circuits over this Galois ring. The latter could be instantiated by using existing schemes for $\mathbb{Z}_p$ (recall p is the prime such that $q = p^e$). The design of efficient ZK arguments that can directly and efficiently handle Galois rings is an interesting open problem for future research.

1.2   Organization

In Sect. 2, we introduce notation and preliminary definitions. Section 3 presents our generic VC scheme on encrypted data. In Sect. 4, we discuss an instantiation of our VC scheme and present our homomorphic hash functions. In Sect. 5, we further develop our scheme to handle nondeterministic computations with context-hiding.

2   Preliminary Definitions

In this section, we recall notation and basic definitions. Some of them are recalled only informally; we refer to the full version for more formal definitions.

Notation. Let $\lambda \in \mathbb{N}$ be the security parameter. We say that a function F is *negligible* in λ and denote it by $\mathsf{negl}(\lambda)$ if $F(\lambda) = o(\lambda^{-c})$ for all $c > 0$. A probability is said to be *overwhelming* if it is $1 - \mathsf{negl}(\lambda)$. Let $\mathcal{D}$ be a probability distribution and S be a set. The notation $r \xleftarrow{\$} \mathcal{D}$ means that r is randomly sampled from the distribution $\mathcal{D}$, while $r \xleftarrow{\$} S$ means that r is sampled uniformly randomly from the set S. All adversaries $\mathcal{A}$ and entities (a prover $\mathcal{P}$ and a verifier $\mathcal{V}$) in this paper are probabilistic polynomial-time (PPT) Turing machines. In this paper, a ring is always a commutative ring with a multiplicative identity 1.

2.1   Verifiable Computation

We recall the definition of a verifiable computation (VC) scheme [GGP10]. We use the notion of Multi-Function VC scheme from [PRV12], with a slight modification to handle public delegatability and verifiability (we will simply call this a VC scheme in the rest of this work). A multi-function VC scheme allows the computation of several functions on a single input and satisfies an adaptive security notion where the adversary can see many input encodings before choosing the function (similarly as the definition of a Split Scheme in [FGP14]).

Definition 1 (Verifiable Computation). *A verifiable computation scheme* $\mathcal{VC}$ *consists of a tuple of algorithms* (Setup, KeyGen, ProbGen, Compute, Verify, Decode)*:*

Setup$(1^\lambda) \to (PK, SK)$: *produces the public and private parameters that do not depend on the functions to be evaluated.*

KeyGen$_{PK}(g) \to (PK_g, SK_g)$: *produces a keypair for evaluating a specific function* g.

ProbGen$_{PK}(x) \to (\sigma_x, \tau_x)$: *The problem generation algorithm uses the public key PK to encode the input x as a value σ_x that is given to the server to compute with, and a public value τ_x which is given to the verifier.*

Compute$_{PK_g}(\sigma_x) \to \sigma_y$: *Using a public key for a function g and the encoded input σ_x, the server computes an encoded version σ_y of the function's output $y = g(x)$.*

Verify$_{PK_g}(\tau_x, \sigma_y) \to acc$: *Using the public key for a function g, and a verification token τ_x for an input x, the verification algorithm converts the server's output σ_y into a bit acc. If $acc = 1$ we say the client accepts (which means that σ_y decodes to $y = g(x)$ – see below), otherwise if $acc = 0$ we say the client rejects.*

Decode$_{SK, SK_g}(\sigma_y) \to y$: *using the secret keys, this algorithm decodes an output encoding σ_y to some value y.*

Remark 1. In our definition we did not include PK among the inputs of Compute and Verify; this can be done without loss of generality as in any scheme one can include PK into PK_g. Also, note that ProbGen takes only PK (and not PK_g) as an input; this highlights the fact that inputs can be encoded independently of the functions g that will be executed on them. Finally, we could have included SK among the inputs of KeyGen; in this case, however, one would partially lose the public delegation property.

A VC scheme satisfies *correctness*, *security*, *privacy*, and *outsourceability* whose definition is as follows:

Correctness. For any function g and input x,

$$\Pr\left[\begin{array}{c} \mathsf{Verify}_{PK_g}(\tau_x, \sigma_y) = 1 \\ \wedge\ \mathsf{Decode}_{SK, SK_g}(\sigma_y) = g(x) \end{array}\middle|\begin{array}{c} (PK, SK) \leftarrow \mathsf{Setup}(1^\lambda) \\ (PK_g, SK_g) \leftarrow \mathsf{KeyGen}_{PK}(g) \\ (\sigma_x, \tau_x) \leftarrow \mathsf{ProbGen}_{PK}(x) \\ \sigma_y \leftarrow \mathsf{Compute}_{PK_g}(\sigma_x) \end{array}\right] = 1.$$

To define security and privacy, we first describe the following experiments:

Experiment $\mathbf{Exp}_{\mathcal{A}}^{Verif}[\mathcal{VC}, \lambda]$
  $(PK, SK) \leftarrow \mathsf{Setup}(1^\lambda)$;
  $(x, st) \leftarrow \mathcal{A}^{O_{\mathsf{KeyGen}}(\cdot)}(PK)$;
  $(\sigma_x, \tau_x) \leftarrow \mathsf{ProbGen}_{PK}(x)$;
  $(g, \hat{\sigma}_y) \leftarrow \mathcal{A}^{O_{\mathsf{KeyGen}}(\cdot)}(st, \sigma_x, \tau_x)$;
  $acc \leftarrow \mathsf{Verify}_{PK_g}(\tau_x, \hat{\sigma}_y)$;
  if $acc = 1$ and $\mathsf{Decode}_{SK, SK_g}(\hat{\sigma}_y) \neq g(x)$
      output 1;
  else output 0;

Experiment $\mathbf{Exp}_{\mathcal{A}}^{Priv}[\mathcal{VC}, g, \lambda]$
  $b \leftarrow \{0, 1\}$;
  $(PK, SK) \leftarrow \mathsf{Setup}(1^\lambda)$;
  $(x_0, x_1, st) \leftarrow \mathcal{A}^{O_{\mathsf{KeyGen}}(\cdot)}(PK)$;
  $(\sigma_b, \tau_b) \leftarrow \mathsf{ProbGen}_{PK}(x_b)$;
  $\hat{b} \leftarrow \mathcal{A}^{O_{\mathsf{KeyGen}}(\cdot)}(st, \sigma_b, \tau_b)$;
  if $b = \hat{b}$ output 1;
  else output 0;

In the experiments above, $O_{\mathsf{KeyGen}}(g)$ is an oracle that can be called only once, it runs $PK_g \leftarrow \mathsf{KeyGen}_{PK}(g)$ and returns PK_g. The one-time use of the oracle is done for simplicity. Indeed, consider an experiment in which the adversary is allowed to query this oracle multiple times: an adversary playing in such an experiment can be reduced to one playing in the experiment above in a straightforward way, as the KeyGen algorithm uses only a public key and thus can be easily simulated. Similarly, this is why it is enough to give to the adversary only one specific encoding using ProbGen.

Security. For any PPT adversary $\mathcal{A}$, $\Pr[\mathbf{Exp}_{\mathcal{A}}^{Verif}[\mathcal{VC}, \lambda] = 1] \leq \mathsf{negl}(\lambda)$. Note that this is an adaptive notion of security, as defined in [FGP14].

Privacy. For any PPT adversary $\mathcal{A}$ and for any function g,

$$\Pr[\mathbf{Exp}_{\mathcal{A}}^{Priv}[\mathcal{VC}, g, \lambda] = 1] \leq \frac{1}{2} + \mathsf{negl}(\lambda).$$

Remark 2. Our definition of verifiable computation has public verifiability (anyone can use Verify only with public keys and τ_x) and public delegatability (anyone can run ProbGen and KeyGen). This immediately implies the notion of privacy in the presence of verification queries given in [FGP14], namely the scheme stays private even if the adversary learns whether its results are accepted or not.

Outsourceability. For any x and any honestly produced σ_y, the time required for $\mathsf{ProbGen}_{PK}(x)$, $\mathsf{Verify}_{PK_g}(\tau_x, \sigma_y)$, and $\mathsf{Decode}_{SK, SK_g}(\sigma_y)$ is $o(T)$ where T is the time required to compute $g(x)$, i.e., it allows efficient problem generation and verification followed by decoding.

The VC constructions we present in this paper are first built as public-coin interactive protocols which can be made non-interactive using the Fiat-Shamir heuristic. Therefore, we also consider interactive versions of Compute and Verify. Also, our constructions work in a simpler model in which KeyGen only outputs a public key without SK_g.

2.2 Fully Homomorphic Encryption

We briefly recall the notion of *(public-key) fully homomorphic encryption scheme* (FHE), which is a tuple of algorithms (FHE.ParamGen, FHE.KeyGen, FHE.Enc, FHE.Dec, FHE.Eval) working as follows:

FHE.ParamGen(1^λ) : generates the public parameters (e.g., description of plaintext space $\mathcal{M}$, ciphertext space, key space, randomness distributions, etc.) which are assumed input to all subsequent algorithms.

FHE.KeyGen(1^λ) $\to$ (pk, evk, dk) : outputs a public encryption key pk, a public evaluation key evk, and a secret decryption key dk.

FHE.Enc$_{\mathsf{pk}}(m) \to c$: encrypts a message $m \in \mathcal{M}$, and outputs ciphertext c.

FHE.Dec$_{\mathsf{dk}}(c) \to m^*$: decrypts a ciphertext c into a plaintext $m^* \in \mathcal{M}$.

FHE.Eval$_{\mathsf{evk}}(g, c_1, \ldots, c_n) \to c^*$: Given the evaluation key evk, a circuit $g : \mathcal{M}^n \to \mathcal{M}$, and n ciphertexts $c_1, \ldots, c_n$, it computes an output ciphertext c^*.

An FHE scheme should satisfy the usual notion of *correctness* and *semantic security*. In addition, we say that FHE is *compact* if the ciphertext size is bounded by some fixed polynomial in the security parameter, and is independent of the size of the evaluated circuit or the number of inputs it takes. We refer to the full version for the formal definitions.

In our work, we mainly consider SHE (a.k.a. somewhat homomorphic encryption), a restricted FHE notion that guarantees above-mentioned properties only if the circuit g is of a bounded degree which is fixed a-priori in SHE.ParamGen.

2.3 Succinct Argument Systems

Let $\mathcal{R}$ be an NP relation. An argument system Π for $\mathcal{R}$ comprises three algorithms (Π.Setup, $\mathcal{P}, \mathcal{V}$) working as follows:

Π.Setup(1^λ) $\to$ crs : outputs a common reference string crs.

$\mathcal{P}(\mathsf{crs}, x, w)$: given a statement x and a witness w, the prover interacts with the verifier below.

$\mathcal{V}(\mathsf{crs}, x)$: given a statement x, the verifier outputs 0 (reject) or 1 (accept) after interacting with the prover.

We denote by $\langle \mathcal{P}(\mathsf{crs}, x, w), \mathcal{V}(\mathsf{crs}, x) \rangle_\Pi = b$, with $b \in \{0, 1\}$, an execution between $\mathcal{P}$ and $\mathcal{V}$ where b is $\mathcal{V}$'s output at the end of the interaction. If $\mathcal{V}$ uses public randomness only, Π is said *public-coin*. Π is said *succinct* if the protocol's communication is at most polylogarithmic in the witness size. An argument system Π satisfies the standard *completeness* and *soundness* properties (see full version for the formal definitions).

3   Our VC Scheme - Generic Solution

In this section, we present our generic VC scheme for private verifiable computation. The high-level idea is to apply a succinct argument system on the image of evaluation process ($\mathsf{SHE.Eval}_{\mathsf{evk}}(g, c_1, \ldots, c_t)$) of SHE under a homomorphic hash function.

3.1   Building Blocks and Assumptions

Our generic VC scheme consists of three building blocks: SHE, Homomorphic Hash Functions, and a Succinct Argument System for deterministic polynomial-time computations. We first describe the assumptions on each building block necessary for the construction of the generic VC scheme. It will be shown, in Sect. 4, that these assumptions can be met to provide an instantiation of the VC scheme.

Notation. Let $R = \mathbb{Z}[X]/(f)$ denote a quotient polynomial ring with $f \in \mathbb{Z}[X]$, a monic polynomial of degree d_f. For a positive integer t, $R_t := R/tR = \mathbb{Z}_t[X]/(f)$. We use q to denote a power of some prime p, i.e., $q = p^e$.

Somewhat Homomorphic Encryption. We assume that the ciphertext space of given SHE is $R_q^D = (\mathbb{Z}_q[X]/(f))^D$ where $q = p^e$ is a power of prime p, and D is a positive integer. We also assume that the evaluation algorithm $\mathsf{SHE.Eval}_{\mathsf{evk}}$ can be represented by an arithmetic circuit[2] over the ring R_q (or R_q^D).

Homomorphic Hash Functions. To gain efficiency in proving (and verification), we exploit a homomorphic hash function defined by a ring homomorphism $H : \mathbb{Z}_q[X]^D \to \mathcal{D}_H$ to a ring $\mathcal{D}_H$. Let $\mathcal{H}$ be a family of hash functions $\{H\}$ where each H is as described above and the uniform sampling of $H \in \mathcal{H}$ can be done with a public-coin process. We assume that $\mathcal{H}$, when the domain is restricted to a subset $\mathcal{D} \subset \mathbb{Z}_q[X]^D$, is ε-universal whose definition follows.

Definition 2 (ε-Universal Hash Functions). *A family $\mathcal{H}$ of hash functions is ε-universal if for all $c, c' \in \mathcal{D}$ such that $c \neq c'$, it holds that*

$$\Pr[H \xleftarrow{\$} \mathcal{H} : H(c) = H(c')] \leq \varepsilon.$$

---

[2] It is composed of gates performing addition or multiplication.

We additionally assume that the set $\mathcal{D}$ in the above definition is large enough so that all ciphertexts arising can be embedded into it.

Succinct Argument System. We assume a public-coin succinct argument system Π that works for the relations represented by a (polynomial-size) arithmetic circuit over the rings $\mathcal{D}_H$ for all $H \in \mathcal{H}$.

3.2   The Generic Scheme

We now give a description of the generic private VC scheme using the building blocks and notation from Sect. 3.1. Our scheme follows the VC syntax from Sect. 2.1, except for Compute and Verify that we describe as a public-coin interactive protocol for two main reasons. First, we make use of a succinct argument system that can be interactive. Second, for security reasons, a homomorphic hash function must be sampled uniformly at random, unpredictably by a prover, e.g., a verifier samples and notifies a homomorphic hash function *after* a prover claimed an output. Note that a non-interactive version of our VC can be obtained in the random oracle model by applying the Fiat-Shamir transform.

In our VC scheme, a verifier $\mathcal{V}$ encrypts the input $x = (x_1, x_2, \ldots, x_n)$ (with SHE) and sends the encrypted inputs $(c_i)_{i=1}^n = (\mathsf{SHE.Enc}(x_i))_{i=1}^n \in (R_q^D)^n = ((\mathbb{Z}_q[X]/(f))^D)^n$ to a prover $\mathcal{P}$. We remark that $\mathcal{P}$ performs the homomorphic evaluation $\mathsf{SHE.Eval}_{\mathsf{evk}}(g, c_1, \ldots, c_n)$ *without* reduction modulo f, and then proves this computation. Namely, $\mathcal{P}$ computes the function $\hat{g} : (R_q^D)^n \to \mathbb{Z}_q[X]^D$ (not R_q^D) that describes $\mathsf{SHE.Eval}_{\mathsf{evk}}(g, \cdot)$ without reduction modulo f. In other words, $\hat{g}$ is such that:

$$\hat{g}(c_1, ..., c_n) \mod f = \mathsf{SHE.Eval}_{\mathsf{evk}}(g, c_1, ..., c_n) \in R_q^D.$$

The VC scheme consists of a tuple of algorithms (Setup, KeyGen, ProbGen, Compute, Verify, Decode) as follows.

Setup(1^λ) $\to (PK, SK)$:
  - Run $(\mathsf{pk}, \mathsf{evk}, \mathsf{sk}) \leftarrow \mathsf{SHE.KeyGen}(1^\lambda)$ to generate keys for SHE.
  - Set $PK = (\mathsf{pk}, \mathsf{evk})$ and $SK = \mathsf{sk}$.
KeyGen$_{PK}(g) \to (PK_g, SK_g)$:
  - Run $\mathsf{crs} \leftarrow \Pi.\mathsf{Setup}(1^\lambda)$ to generate the common reference string of Π for the circuit $\hat{g} : (R_q^D)^n \to \mathbb{Z}_q[X]^D$ over the ciphertexts.
  - Set $PK_g = (PK, \hat{g}, \mathsf{crs})$ and $SK_g = \emptyset$.
ProbGen$_{PK}(x) \to (\sigma_x, \tau_x)$:
  - Parse x as $(x_1, x_2, \ldots, x_n)$.
  - Run $c_i \leftarrow \mathsf{SHE.Enc}_{\mathsf{pk}}(x_i)$ for $i \in \{1, 2, \ldots, n\}$ to get ciphertexts $c_x = (c_1, c_2, \ldots, c_n) \in (R_q^D)^n$.
  - Set $\sigma_x = \tau_x = c_x$.
$\langle \mathsf{Compute}_{PK_g}(\sigma_x), \mathsf{Verify}_{PK_g}(\tau_x) \rangle$: prover and verifier proceed as follows.
  - Compute computes $c_y = \hat{g}(c_x)$ and sends it to Verify.
  - Verify samples and sends a homomorphic hash function $H \xleftarrow{\$} \mathcal{H}$.

- Compute and Verify both compute $\gamma_1 = H(c_1), \ldots, \gamma_n = H(c_n), \gamma_y = H(c_y)$.
- Compute and Verify run the argument system $\langle \mathcal{P}(\text{crs}, \hat{g}, \gamma_1, \ldots, \gamma_n, \gamma_y), \mathcal{V}(\text{crs}, \hat{g}, \gamma_1, \ldots, \gamma_n, \gamma_y)\rangle_\Pi$ in the roles of prover and verifier respectively. This is for $\mathcal{P}$ to convince $\mathcal{V}$ that $\gamma_y = \hat{g}(\gamma_1, \ldots, \gamma_n)$ over the ring $\mathcal{D}_H$.
- Let σ_y include c_y and the transcript of the interactive argument.
- Let b be the bit returned by $\mathcal{V}$. Verify accepts if and only if $b = 1$.

Decode$_{SK}(\sigma_y) \to y$: Compute $y = \text{SHE.Dec}_{sk}(c_y \bmod f)$.

Notice that if Π is a k-round public-coin interactive protocol, then the VC protocol described above is a $(k + 1)$-round public-coin protocol. By applying Fiat-Shamir to such a protocol, we obtain a non-interactive VC scheme in which the random oracle is used to derive the homomorphic hash function H and all the random challenges of $\mathcal{V}$ in Π. Then, Compute can be described as a non-interactive algorithm that on input σ_x outputs $\sigma_y = (c_y, \pi)$ where π are all the messages of $\mathcal{P}$, while Verify(τ_x, σ_y) is the algorithm that returns the acceptance bit of the non-interactive verifier on the hashed inputs, i.e., $\mathcal{V}(PK_g, H(c_1), \ldots, H(c_n), H(c_y))$.

The application of Fiat-Shamir may incur a security loss, which mainly boils down to its application to the k-round Π protocol. As shown in [BCS16], if Π satisfies the notion of state-restoration soundness this loss is only polynomial in the number of rounds. Notably, Canetti et al. [CCH+18] proved that the GKR protocol (that we consider in Sect. 4 to instantiate Π) satisfies this property.

Remark 3 (On a variant using universal arguments). Note that, if Π is a preprocessing argument system with a *universal* CRS (i.e., following the notion in [CHM+20]), then one can modify our VC scheme as follows: Π.Setup can be executed in Setup (of VC scheme) and the universal CRS is included in PK, while KeyGen would only run the deterministic preprocessing crs$_g \leftarrow$ Preprocess(CRS, g). The main benefit of this variant is that only the Setup algorithm must be executed in a trusted manner.

The generic scheme satisfies the properties of VC scheme given that all the building blocks satisfy the required properties.

Theorem 1. *For given security parameter λ, if we exploit a correct, compact, and secure SHE scheme, an ε-universal family of hash functions with $\varepsilon = \text{negl}(\lambda)$, and a complete succinct argument system Π with soundness $\delta = \text{negl}(\lambda)$, then our VC scheme is correct, secure, private and outsourceable.*

Proof. We refer to the formal definition of VC scheme (Definition 1) in Sect. 2.1. Our VC scheme is an interactive version of the generic private VC scheme from [FGP14], with the difference that there is an interactive Verify algorithm that uses homomorphic hashing. Therefore, we get the result as in [FGP14], except for the security for which we give a detailed proof.

The correctness of our VC scheme follows from the correctness of SHE and the completeness of the argument system Π.

The privacy of our VC scheme follows from the semantic security of SHE: if $\mathcal{P}$ could break the privacy of VC, it can run the VC scheme by itself on a ciphertext SHE.Enc(x_b) from the semantic security game of SHE then guess b with non-negligible advantage.

The outsourceability follows from the compactness of SHE scheme and the succinctness of the argument system Π that has verifier complexity $o(S)$ where S is the size of the circuit $\hat{g}$ (see next Lemma for a detailed complexity analysis).

For the security, we consider a slightly different version of the security experiment $\mathbf{Exp}_{\mathcal{A}}^{Verif}[\mathcal{VC}, \lambda]$ in Sect. 2.1, adapted to handle the case of protocols in which Compute and Verify interact. Namely, instead of an adversary that directly provides the result σ_y, we consider an adversary $\mathcal{A}$ that interacts with the challenger acting as an honest verifier, and $\mathcal{A}$ wins if the challenger accepts but the transcript decodes to a wrong result.

Let x and g respectively be the input and function chosen by $\mathcal{A}$ in the game, c_x be the encryption of x sent to $\mathcal{A}$, $\hat{c}_y$ be the result claimed by $\mathcal{A}$ in the first round, and c_y be the true result. We note $y = g(x)$ (if $\hat{c}_y$ does not encrypt y then necessarily $\hat{c}_y \neq c_y$). We now study the Verify algorithm: a homomorphic hash function $H \in \mathcal{H}$ is randomly sampled, either by $\mathcal{V}$ or by a random oracle using $\mathcal{A}$'s inputs and outputs, so that $\mathcal{A}$ cannot know it before sending $\hat{c}_y$. Thus, if we denote by A the event $\{H(\hat{c}_y) = H(c_y)\}$ and if $\mathcal{H}$ is a ε-universal family then $\Pr[A|c_y \neq \hat{c}_y] \leq \varepsilon$. If $H(\hat{c}_y) \neq H(c_y)$ then the only way left for $\mathcal{A}$ to have $\mathcal{V}$ accept is to cheat when applying Π with the false result $H(\hat{c}_y)$. Let B denote the event $\{\Pi(\mathcal{V}, \mathcal{A}, H(c), H(\hat{c}_y), r) = 1\}$. If Π has soundness δ then $\Pr\left[B|\bar{A} \cap (c_y \neq \hat{c}_y)\right] \leq \delta$.

The output bit b of the security game satisfies:

$$\begin{aligned}
\Pr[b = 1] &= \Pr[(A \cup B) \cap (\text{SHE.Dec}(\hat{c}_y \bmod f) \neq y)] \\
&\leq \Pr[(A \cup B)|c_y \neq \hat{c}_y] \\
&\leq \Pr\left[B|\bar{A} \cap (c_y \neq \hat{c}_y)\right] + \Pr[A|c_y \neq \hat{c}_y] \\
&\leq \delta + \varepsilon
\end{aligned}$$

This proves the result when ε and δ are negl(λ). $\qquad\square$

The required computational (or communication) cost of our VC scheme can be easily derived from that of the argument system Π and the homomorphic hash functions $\mathcal{H}$.

Lemma 1. *Let $T_{\mathcal{P}}^{\Pi}, T_{\mathcal{V}}^{\Pi}$, and C^{Π} respectively denote the time complexity of $\mathcal{P}$, that of $\mathcal{V}$, and the communication cost in the argument system Π, which will be signified as, e.g., $T_{\mathcal{P}}^{\Pi}(g; R)$ when denoting the complexity of $\mathcal{P}$ (in Π) for a circuit g over a ring R. Then, for a circuit g with n inputs and 1 output, the time complexity of $\text{Compute}_{PK_g}(\sigma_x)$, that of $\text{Verify}_{PK_g}(\tau_x)$, and the communication cost in the execution of $\langle \text{Compute}_{PK_g}(\sigma_x), \text{Verify}_{PK_g}(\tau_x) \rangle$, in our VC scheme*

(Theorem 1) is as follows:

$$Time\ [\text{Compute}_{PK_g}(\sigma_x)] : T_{\hat{g}} + (n+1) \cdot T_{Hash} + T_{\mathcal{P}}^{\sqcap}(\hat{g}; \mathcal{D}_H)$$

$$Time\ [\text{Verify}_{PK_g}(\tau_x)] : (n+1) \cdot T_{Hash} + T_{\mathcal{V}}^{\sqcap}(\hat{g}; \mathcal{D}_H)$$

$$Comm\ [\langle \text{Compute}_{PK_g}(\sigma_x), \text{Verify}_{PK_g}(\tau_x)\rangle] : |\hat{g}(c)| + |H| + C^{\sqcap}(\hat{g}; \mathcal{D}_H)$$

where $\hat{g}$ is the circuit corresponding to g over the ciphertext, $\mathcal{D}_H$ is the range space (ring) of a hash function $H \in \mathcal{H}$, $T_{\hat{g}}$ and T_{Hash} are the times for computing $\hat{g}$ (without reduction modulo f) and for evaluating a homomorphic hash function, respectively, $|\hat{g}(c)|$ is the size of the output ciphertext (from $\mathcal{P}$), and $|H|$ is the size of a homomorphic hash function.

The proof of this lemma directly follows from the description of the VC scheme. We remark that the complexity mainly depends on the ring $\mathcal{D}_H$ which can be much smaller than the ciphertext space $R_q^D \subseteq \mathbb{Z}_q[X]^D$ (see Sect. 4.3). It makes our VC scheme show better efficiency (in both asymptotic and concrete cost) than a naive VC (over the ciphertext space) without our homomorphic hash functions (see Sect. 4.4 for detailed analysis).

Applications to VC for SIMD Computations. Besides the application to HE computations, the use of ε-universal family of homomorphic hash functions can have broader applications in improving prover efficiency in VC over polynomial rings, i.e., when proving and verifying the computations over a polynomial ring. By combining this observation with the "packing" techniques of HE [SV14] one can obtain a VC scheme for SIMD (single-instruction multiple-data) operations where the prover's costs are less dependent on the number of (parallel) inputs. A bit more in detail, with the packing techniques of [SV14] one can encode a vector $(v_i)_i$ of m elements of $\mathbb{Z}_t$ into a polynomial $p \in R_t$ (such that $d_f \geq m$) in such a way that the result of computing $\hat{g}((p_j)_j)$ over $R_t := \mathbb{Z}_t[X]/(f)$ can be decoded to the vector $(g((v_{j,i})_j))_i$ over $\mathbb{Z}_t$. By using a homomorphic hash from R_t to $\mathbb{Z}_t[X]/(h)$ we can obtain a prover time which depends on $|g| \cdot d_h + d_f$, as opposed to $|\hat{g}| \approx |g| \cdot d_f$.[3] We remark that $d_h \approx \log_t \lambda$ (when t is prime) while d_f can be as large as the number of parallel inputs.

4   Instantiating Our VC Scheme

In this section, we provide concrete instantiations of the building blocks for our generic scheme presented in the previous section. In particular, our novel contributions are the constructions of two homomorphic hash functions. We also give a detailed efficiency analysis with example parameters.

---

[3] We assume that the cost of basic operation over a ring ($\mathbb{Z}_t[X]/(h)$ or $\mathbb{Z}_t[X]/(f)$) depends on its degree (d_h or d_f) for simplicity.

4.1 SHE - The BV Homomorphic Encryption Scheme

As an instantiation of SHE, we exploit the BV scheme [BV11] which allows homomorphic evaluation of circuits of limited multiplicative depth. The advantage of the BV scheme for our purpose is that its homomorphic additions and multiplications over ciphertexts are composed of arithmetic operations over R_q^D only.[4] As a result, this scheme can be easily combined with the homomorphic hash functions (which will be described in the following subsection) defined in our generic VC scheme.

Parameters. Let q and t ($t < q$) be coprime integers, $f \in \mathbb{Z}[X]$ be a monic polynomial of degree d_f, and $R := \mathbb{Z}[X]/(f)$. The plaintext space is $R_t := \mathbb{Z}_t[X]/(f)$, and the ciphertext space is $R_q^D = (\mathbb{Z}_q[X]/(f))^D$ where $D(\geq 2)$ bounds the total degree of a multi-variate polynomial which can be evaluated on ciphertexts, i.e., products of at most $D - 2$ input ciphertexts are allowed.

Homomorphic Operations. A ciphertext $c = (c_0, c_1, \ldots, c_{D-1}) \in R_q^D$ is identified as a polynomial $c(Y) \in R_q[Y]$ of degree at most $D - 1$ as follows:

$$c(Y) = \sum_{i=0}^{D-1} c_i Y^i.$$

Then, addition and multiplication of two ciphertexts $c = \mathsf{Enc}(m), c' = \mathsf{Enc}(m')$ are defined, respectively, by the usual addition and multiplication in $R_q[Y]$:

- $c_{\mathrm{add}}(Y) := c(Y) + c'(Y)$, i.e., $c_{\mathrm{add}} := (c_0 + c_0', c_1 + c_1', \ldots, c_{D-1} + c_{D-1}')$.
- $c_{\mathrm{mult}}(Y) := c(Y) \cdot c'(Y)$, i.e., $c_{\mathrm{mult}} := (\hat{c}_0, \hat{c}_1, \ldots, \hat{c}_{D-1})$ where $\sum_{i \geq 0}^{D-1} \hat{c}_i Y^i = c(Y) \cdot c'(Y)$.

The *correctness* ($\mathsf{Dec}(c_{\mathrm{add}}) = m + m'$, $\mathsf{Dec}(c_{\mathrm{mult}}) = m \cdot m'$) is guaranteed only if the degree (in Y) of result ciphertext (c_{add} or c_{mult}) does not exceed $D - 1$. We remark that a fresh ciphertext is of degree 1 (in Y), i.e., $c_i = 0$ for all $i > 2$, and the correctness is guaranteed for the computation represented by a (multivariate) polynomial of total degree at most $D - 1$.

   We refer to the full version of this article for the description of other algorithms ($\mathsf{KeyGen}, \mathsf{Enc}, \mathsf{Dec}$) of BV scheme and the concrete conditions for the *correctness* and *security* of BV scheme.

4.2 Argument System - The GKR Protocol over Rings

The GKR protocol [GKR08] is a (public-coin) interactive proof system for arithmetic circuits over a finite field. In [CCKP19], Chen et al. showed that the protocol can be generalized to handle arithmetic circuits over a finite ring. We exploit this GKR protocol over rings [CCKP19] (with Fiat-Shamir) as our instantiation of argument system, since it can efficiently prove and verify arithmetic of

---

[4] This is not the case in other schemes, e.g., BGV [BGV12] or FV [FV12] schemes where multiplication of ciphertexts accompanies rounding or bitwise operations.

rings[5] which constitutes the range $\mathcal{D}_H$ ($\mathbb{Z}_q[X]/(h)$ or $(\mathbb{Z}_q[X]/(h))^D$) of our hash functions (Sect. 4.3).

One drawback of the GKR protocol is that the circuit (to be verified) should be log-space uniform and be layered in low depth for efficient verification. A line of work has shown that many computations of interest are in this form [CMT12, Tha13] or can be converted to this form [WTs+18]. Therefore, we (plausibly) assume that the given circuit is log-space uniform and that a succinct description of the circuit can be found during the preprocessing phase (e.g., $\mathsf{KeyGen}_{PK}(g)$ finds such description for g and puts it into PK_g). We remark that, in our instantiation, the circuit already has low depth to be supported by the BV scheme.

In this section, we recall the definition of Galois rings, the Schwartz-Zippel lemma for rings, and give a summary of the GKR protocol over rings. In the full version of this article we add a detailed description of the GKR protocol [GKR08, Tha13] and its generalization to rings [CCKP19]. In this section, rings are commutative rings with multiplicative identity 1.

Galois Rings. Galois rings play a central role in the GKR protocol over rings and in our instantiation of hash functions. Galois rings are a natural generalization of Galois fields $\mathsf{GF}(p^n) = \mathbb{Z}_p[X]/(f)$, and proofs of the following properties of Galois rings can be found in [Wan03].

Definition 3 (Galois ring). *A Galois ring is a ring of the form*

$$\mathbb{Z}_{p^e}[X]/(f)$$

where p is a prime number, e is a positive number, $f \in \mathbb{Z}_{p^e}[X]$ is a monic polynomial whose reduction modulo p is an irreducible polynomial in $\mathbb{Z}_p[X]$.

We remark that a Galois ring $\mathbb{Z}_{p^e}[X]/(f)$ has many more invertible elements than the base ring $\mathbb{Z}_{p^e}$:

Lemma 2 (Units of Galois ring). *In a Galois ring $R_q := \mathbb{Z}_{p^e}[X]/(f)$, the set of units of R_q is $R_q \backslash pR_q$, i.e., the elements which are not divisible by p. In fact, we have a ring isomorphism $R_q/pR_q \cong \mathbb{F}_{p^{d_f}}$ where d_f is the degree of f.*

Schwartz-Zippel Lemma for Rings. We now present the Schwartz-Zippel lemma for rings, specifically, we focus on the case of Galois rings which is closely related to our instantiation.

Definition 4 (Sampling set). *Let R be a finite ring and $A \subset R$. We call A a sampling set if*

$$\text{for all } x, y \in A \text{ such that } x \neq y, \quad x - y \text{ is invertible.}$$

---

[5] Usual argument systems deal mainly with arithmetic of a field, and it requires to represent arithmetic of a ring by that of a field, resulting in substantial inefficiency.

Lemma 3 (Schwartz-Zippel). *Let R be a finite ring, and let $A \subset R$ be a sampling set. Let $f : R^n \to R$ be an n-variate nonzero polynomial of total degree D. Then*

$$\Pr_{x \leftarrow A^n} [f(x) = 0] \leq \frac{D}{|A|}.$$

Examples of Sampling Set. In a ring $\mathbb{Z}_{p^e}$ with p prime, $A = \{0, 1, .., p-1\}$ is a maximal sampling set with cardinality p. In a Galois ring $\mathbb{Z}_{p^e}[X]/(f)$ where f is a monic polynomial of degree d_f, the set $\{a_0 + a_1 X + \cdots + a_{d_f-1} X^{d_f-1} \mid a_i \in A\}$ is a maximal sampling set with cardinality p^{d_f}.

In the following, we borrow the result of [CCKP19], the generalized GKR protocol on the circuit over Galois rings. The soundness of the protocol is guaranteed by the Schwartz-Zippel lemma (Lemma 3), thus it depends on the size of sampling set, e.g., p^{d_f} in the following.

Theorem 2 (GKR protocol over Galois rings [CCKP19]). *Let $R_q := \mathbb{Z}_{p^e}[X]/(f)$ be a Galois ring where f is of degree d_f. Let $C : R_q^n \to R_q$ be an arithmetic circuit over R_q taking n inputs and outputting 1 output. Let C be of size (the number of arithmetic gates contained) S and depth d. Then, there exists an interactive protocol (with public coins) for C with perfect completeness and soundness $\frac{7d\log S}{p^{d_f}}$, which requires the same number of operations (over R_q) for a prover and a verifier as the GKR protocol over a finite field (where the required operations are over a finite field).*

Efficiency of GKR Protocol. The latest refinement [XZZ+19] of the GKR protocol reduced the prover's cost to $O(S)$. Since their technique can also be adapted to the protocol over Galois rings (their technique only uses addition, multiplication, and bookkeeping which are all available in arbitrary rings), the complexity of our instantiation is also $(T_{\mathcal{P}}^{\sqcap}, T_{\mathcal{V}}^{\sqcap}, C^{\sqcap})^6 = (O(S), O(n + d\log S)^7, O(d\log S))$. We remark that the space complexity of a verifier $\mathcal{V}$ can be $O(\log S)$ only (without increasing other cost) and that the time complexity $O(d\log S)$ of $\mathcal{V}$ can be regarded as $o(S)$ since d is a small constant in the usual utilization of BV scheme.

4.3 Our Homomorphic Hash Functions Realizations

In this section, we present explicit constructions of two families of ε-universal homomorphic hash functions on some domain $\mathcal{D} \subset \mathbb{Z}_q[X]^D$ with $q = p^e$ for a prime p. Both of our hash function families, taking as input D polynomials of $\mathbb{Z}_q[X]$, are based on the map of modulo reduction by a polynomial $h \in \mathbb{Z}_q[X]$,

---

[6] We refer to Lemma 1 for this notation.

[7] Here, we assume that the wiring predicate [CMT12] of the circuit is computable in $O(\log S)$ complexity. Generally, if the circuit is log-space uniform, the cost of verifier has an additional $O(poly(\log S))$ term.

which is a natural generalization of the evaluation map $(f \in \mathbb{Z}_q[X] \to f(r) \in \mathbb{Z}_q)$ exploited in the previous works [FGP14,FNP20]. The range of our hash function families are $(\mathbb{Z}_q[X]/(h))^D$ or $\mathbb{Z}_q[X]/(h)$ where $h \in \mathbb{Z}_q[X]$ is a monic polynomial whose reduction modulo p is irreducible in $\mathbb{Z}_p[X]$, i.e., $\mathbb{Z}_q[X]/(h)$ is a Galois ring.

4.3.1 Homomorphic Hash Function - I. Single Hash

We first give the definition of our hash functions specifying the domain $\mathcal{D}$.

Definition 5 (Single Hash Function). *Let N, D be positive integers and $q = p^e$ for a prime p, and let $\mathcal{D} = \{(z_i)_{i=0}^{D-1} \in \mathbb{Z}_q[X]^D : deg_X(z_i) \leq N\}$. For a monic polynomial $h \in \mathbb{Z}_q[X]$, the hash function H_h on $\mathcal{D}$ is defined as follows.*

$$H_h : \mathcal{D} \subset \mathbb{Z}_q[X]^D \longrightarrow (\mathbb{Z}_q[X]/(h))^D$$
$$(z_i)_{i=0}^{D-1} \mapsto (z_i \,(\mathrm{mod}\, h))_{i=0}^{D-1}$$

where $z_i \,(\mathrm{mod}\, h)$ is the remainder of z_i when divided by h in $\mathbb{Z}_q[X]$.

We can gather these hash functions into a family of hash functions which satisfies the ϵ-universality as follows.

Theorem 3. *Let $N, D, d_{\mathcal{H}}$ be positive integers and $q = p^e$ for a prime p. On $\mathcal{D} = \{(z_i)_{i=0}^{D-1} \in \mathbb{Z}_q[X]^D : deg_X(z_i) \leq N\}$, the family of functions $\mathcal{H} := \{H_h : h \in \mathbb{Z}_q[X]$ is monic, degree-$d_{\mathcal{H}}$, and irreducible (in $\mathbb{Z}_p[x]$)$\}$ is homomorphic and ε-universal for $\varepsilon = \frac{2N}{p^{d_{\mathcal{H}}}}$.*

In other words, for all $z, z' \in \mathcal{D}$ such that $z \neq z'$,

$$\Pr[H(z) = H(z') : H \xleftarrow{\$} \mathcal{H}] \leq \frac{2N}{p^{d_{\mathcal{H}}}}.$$

Proof. The homomorphic property of hash functions $H_h \in \mathcal{H}$ follows from that of the modulo reduction by $h \in \mathbb{Z}_q[X]$. For the probability of a collision, let $\Delta \in \mathbb{Z}_q[X]$ be a non zero element among the components of $z - z'$. Then, Δ is a non zero polynomial of degree at most N, and $H_h(z) = H_h(z')$ implies that Δ has $h \in \mathbb{Z}_q[X]$ as a factor, which is equivalent to that Δ has h as a factor in $\mathbb{Z}_p[X]$ (after modulo reduction by p).[8] Therefore,

$$\Pr[H(z) = H(z') : H \xleftarrow{\$} \mathcal{H}] \leq \Pr[h \text{ divides } \Delta \text{ in } \mathbb{Z}_p[X] : h \xleftarrow{\$} A(d_{\mathcal{H}}, p)]$$
$$\leq \frac{N}{d_{\mathcal{H}}} \times \frac{1}{I(d_{\mathcal{H}}, p)} \leq \frac{2N}{p^{d_{\mathcal{H}}}},$$

where $A(n, p)$ (and $I(n, p)$) denote the set (resp., the number) of monic irreducible polynomials of degree n in $\mathbb{Z}_p[X]$; the second inequality follows from the fact that, in $\mathbb{Z}_p[X]$, a degree-N polynomial can have at most N/d irreducible factors of degree d; the third inequality follows from the lower bound of $I(n, p)$ in the following lemma. □

---

[8] More precisely, the argument follows if Δ is not zero when reduced modulo p. Otherwise, $\Delta = p^k \delta$ for some $k < e$ and a polynomial δ which is not zero when reduced modulo p, and δ has h as a factor in $\mathbb{Z}_p[X]$: $h|\Delta$ gives that, by division, $\delta(X) = h(X)Q(X) + p^{e-k}r(X)$ in $\mathbb{Z}_q[X]$ and h is a factor of δ in $\mathbb{Z}_p[X]$.

Lemma 4. *Let μ be the Möbius function,[9] p be a prime number, and $n \geq 1$ be an integer. Let $I(n,p)$ be the number of monic irreducible polynomials in $\mathbb{Z}_p[X]$ of degree n. Then,*

$$I(n,p) = \frac{1}{n} \sum_{d|n} \mu\left(\frac{n}{d}\right) p^d.$$

It also holds for all n that $I(n,p) \geq \frac{1}{n}(p^n - 2p^{\lfloor \frac{n}{2} \rfloor})$ and $I(n,p) \geq \frac{p^n}{2n}$. Moreover, if n is also a prime number, then $I(n,p) = \frac{1}{n}(p^n - p)$. Finally, asymptotically we have $I(n,p) \underset{n \to \infty}{\sim} \frac{p^n}{n}$.

Proof. (sketch) We refer to [VZGG13, Lemma 14.38] for details. Let $A(d,p)$ denote the set of monic irreducible polynomials of degree d in $\mathbb{Z}_p$. Then, from the fact that $X^{p^n} - X = \prod_{d|n} \prod_{\phi \in A(d,p)} \phi$, computing the degree of that product and using the Möbius inversion formula, we get the equation on $I(n,p)$. If n is prime, then this formula has only two summands, namely for $d = 1$, and $d = n$. From the definition of μ, we get $I(n,p) = \frac{1}{n}(p^n - p)$. The bounds $\frac{1}{n}p^n \geq I(n,p) \geq \frac{1}{n}(p^n - 2p^{\lfloor \frac{n}{2} \rfloor})$ are not difficult to prove for all n. This implies the asymptotic statement. For $p^n \geq 16$, the lower bound above directly implies $I(n,p) \geq \frac{p^n}{2n}$. For $n = 1$ clearly $I(1,p) = p \geq \frac{p}{2n}$. Finally for the remaining cases ($p^n = 4, 8, 9$) it can be checked that $I(n,p) \geq \frac{p^n}{2n}$ also holds.   □

Remark 4 (Setting ε). We can set ε of the homomorphic hash family negligibly small, e.g., $d_{\mathcal{H}} \approx \lambda \log_p 2$ gives that $\varepsilon \approx \frac{1}{2^\lambda}$. In case of our instantiation with BV, the degree N of polynomials in $\mathcal{D}$ is bounded by $(d_f - 1)(D - 1)$, and ε can be bounded by $\frac{2(d_f-1)(D-1)}{p^{d_{\mathcal{H}}}}$.

Remark 5 (Sampling h). For an efficient instantiation of above homomorphic hash functions, one has to efficiently sample (uniformly randomly) an h from the set $A(n,p)$ of monic irreducible polynomials in $\mathbb{Z}_p[X]$ of degree n. We explain how to do so in Sect. 4.3.3.

4.3.2   Homomorphic Hash Function - II. Double Hash

Recall that ciphertext additions and multiplications of BV scheme (Sect. 4.1) respectively correspond to the additions and multiplications of polynomials in $R_q[Y]$ and that, in our generic VC scheme (Sect. 3.2), those ciphertext operations are carried on $(\mathbb{Z}_q[X])[Y]$ (polynomials in Y having coefficients from $\mathbb{Z}_q[X]$) by postponing the modulo f operation. Then, we can define a homomorphic hash with much smaller range $\mathbb{Z}_q[X]/(h)$, instead of $(\mathbb{Z}_q[X]/(h))^D$ in the previous section.

Definition 6 (Double Hash Function). *Let N and D be positive integers, and let $\mathcal{D} = \{z \in \mathbb{Z}_q[X][Y] : deg_X(z) \leq N \text{ and } deg_Y(z) < D\}$. For a monic*

---

[9] For $n \in \mathbb{Z}^+$, the function is defined as follows: if n is square-free with k prime factors, $\mu(n) = (-1)^k$; if $n = 1, \mu(n) = 1$; otherwise, $\mu(n) = 0$.

polynomial $h \in \mathbb{Z}_q[X]$ and an element $r \in \mathbb{Z}_q[X]/(h)$, the hash function $H_{r,h}$ on $\mathcal{D}$ is defined as follows.

$$H_{r,h} : \mathcal{D} \subset \mathbb{Z}_q[X][Y] \longrightarrow (\mathbb{Z}_q[X]/(h))[Y] \longrightarrow \mathbb{Z}_q[X]/(h)$$
$$\sum_{i=1}^{D-1} z_i Y^i \mapsto \sum_{i=1}^{D-1} \bar{z}_i Y^i \mapsto \sum_{i=1}^{D-1} \bar{z}_i r^i$$

where $\bar{z}_i := z_i \pmod{h}$ is the remainder of z_i when divided by h in $\mathbb{Z}_q[X]$.

Note that $H_{r,h}$ is indeed the composition of H_h (Definition 5) and an evaluation map $(z(Y) \to z(r))$ on $(\mathbb{Z}_q[X])[Y]$. Similarly as the case of single hash functions (Sect. 4.3.1), we can gather this hash functions into a family of hash functions which satisfies the ϵ-universality as follows.

Theorem 4. *Let $N, D, d_{\mathcal{H}}$ be positive integers and $q = p^e$ for a prime p. On $\mathcal{D} = \{z \in \mathbb{Z}_q[X][Y] : deg_X(z) \leq N \text{ and } deg_Y(z) < D\}$, the family of functions $\mathcal{H} := \{H_{r,h} : h \in \mathbb{Z}_q[X] \text{ is monic, degree-}d_{\mathcal{H}}, \text{ and irreducible (in } \mathbb{Z}_p[x]), \text{ and } r \in \mathbb{Z}_q[X]/(h) \text{ is from the maximal sampling set (Definition 4) of } \mathbb{Z}_q[X]/(h)\}$ is homomorphic and ε-universal for $\varepsilon = \frac{2N+D-1}{p^{d_{\mathcal{H}}}}$.*

In other words, for all $z, z' \in \mathcal{D}$ such that $z \neq z'$,

$$\Pr[H(z) = H(z') : H \xleftarrow{\$} \mathcal{H}] \leq \frac{2N + D - 1}{p^{d_{\mathcal{H}}}}.$$

Proof. As we noted, $H_{r,h}$ is the composition of H_h (Definition 5) and an evaluation map $(z(Y) \to z(r))$ on $R'_q[Y]$ where $R'_q := \mathbb{Z}_q[X]/(h)$. Therefore, the homomorphic property of $H_{r,h} \in \mathcal{H}$ follows from that of the H_h (Theorem 3) and that of the evaluation map $(z(Y) \in R'_q[Y] \to z(r) \in R'_q)$. For the probability of a collision, let $\Delta := z - z' \in \mathbb{Z}_q[X][Y]$. Then, Δ is a non zero polynomial of degree at most N in X and of degree less than D in Y. In the following, let $A = A(d_{\mathcal{H}}, p)$ be the set of monic irreducible polynomials of degree n in $\mathbb{Z}_p[X]$, and let B be the maximal sampling set (Definition 4) of R'_q. Then,

$$\Pr[H(z) = H(z') : H \xleftarrow{\$} \mathcal{H}] \leq \Pr_{h \leftarrow A}[H_h(\Delta) = 0 \in R'_q[Y]]$$
$$+ \Pr_{r \leftarrow B}[H_h(\Delta)(r) = 0 | H_h(\Delta) \neq 0 \in R'_q[Y]]$$
$$\leq \frac{2N}{p^{d_{\mathcal{H}}}} + \frac{D-1}{p^{d_{\mathcal{H}}}},$$

where the second inequality follows from Theorem 3 and Lemma 3: on the right side, the first summand is the result of Theorem 3 while the second summand follows from the fact that the degree of $H_h(\Delta)$ in Y is less than D and that the size of the maximal sampling set B of R'_q is $p^{d_{\mathcal{H}}}$ since R'_q is a Galois ring (see examples following Lemma 3). □

We can also set ε of the double hash family negligibly small: in our instantiation with BV, since the degree N of polynomials in $\mathcal{D}$ is bounded by $(d_f - 1)(D - 1)$,

$$\varepsilon \leq \frac{2(d_f - 1)(D - 1) + D - 1}{p^{d_{\mathcal{H}}}}. \tag{1}$$

Remark 6 (Comparison to Single Hash). Utilizing double hashes instead of single hashes gives better efficiency. With double hash, each addition (resp. multiplication) gate on the ciphertext space $(\mathbb{Z}_q[X])^D = \mathbb{Z}_q[X][Y]$ maps to each addition (resp. multiplication) gate of $R'_q = \mathbb{Z}_q[X]/(h)$ while the single hash maps each of them to at most D additions (resp. D^2 multiplications and D additions) of R'_q. See Sect. 4.4.2 for detailed analysis.

Remark 7 (Sampling r). Recall that the Galois ring $\mathbb{Z}_q[X]/(h)$ can be identified as a set $\{\sum_{i=0}^{d_h-1} a_i X^i : a_i \in \{0,1,2,\ldots,q-1\}\}$ where d_h is the degree of h. Therefore, sampling (uniformly randomly) r from the maximal *sampling set* (Definition 4) of $\mathbb{Z}_q[X]/(h)$ is simple, since the set can be identified as a set $\{\sum_{i=0}^{d_h-1} a_i X^i : a_i \in \{0,1,2,\ldots,p-1\}\} \subseteq \mathbb{Z}_q[X]/(h)$.

4.3.3 Efficient, Public-Coin Sampling of h

We now turn our attention to an efficient sampling method of a monic irreducible polynomial h of degree d_h in $\mathbb{Z}_p[X]$ for our hash functions (Sect. 4.3). We first recall a method that is based on a textbook algorithm [Ben81, VZGG13]. It samples an irreducible polynomial by repeatedly sampling a random monic polynomial, and then checking if it is irreducible by verifying whether it is coprime with $X^{p^i} - X$ for every $i \leq d_h/2$. In our version, we slightly change this algorithm to make explicit the number of public random coins needed to make it fail with negligible probability.

Theorem 5 (Ben-Or's Generation of Irreducible Polynomials [Ben81]). *There exists an algorithm that, on input $2d_h(d_h - 1)\lambda$ random elements of $\mathbb{Z}_p$, returns a uniformly sampled monic irreducible polynomial of degree d_h in $\mathbb{Z}_p[X]$, takes expected number of $\tilde{O}(d_h^2 \log p)$ operations in $\mathbb{Z}_p$ ($\tilde{O}$ hides logarithmic factors in d_h), and fails with probability $\leq 2^{-\lambda}$.*

In the full version we include a description of the algorithm and the proof.

A drawback of the above algorithm is its rejection sampling nature, which in a public coin instantiation (especially when applying the Fiat-Shamir heuristic to our protocol) forces us to sample a significant number of random coins ($2d_h(d_h - 1)\lambda$ $\mathbb{Z}_p$-elements) to make the probability of failure negligible.

To avoid this, we propose an alternative sampling method that achieves a similar complexity and uses much less random coins, $2d_h$ $\mathbb{Z}_p$-elements. It is based on the following observation: Let $\mathbb{F}_{p^{d_h}} := \mathbb{Z}_p[X]/(\phi)$ be a finite field. Then, it suffices to sample an element of $\mathbb{F}_{p^{d_h}}$ which is not contained in any of the subfields $\mathbb{F}_{p^k}$ with $k | d_h$, since the minimal polynomial of such element is monic, irreducible, and of degree d_h in $\mathbb{Z}_p[X]$. It turns out that given a generator α of the multiplicative group $\mathbb{F}_{p^{d_h}}^\times$, these sampleable elements are exactly α^j where

$$j = \sum_{i=0}^{d_h-1} a_i p^i \text{ and } (a_0, a_1, \ldots, a_{d_h-1}) \notin \bigcup_{k|d_h, k \neq d_h} \mathsf{Bad}_k, \text{ where}^{10}$$

$$\mathsf{Bad}_k = \{(\vec{v}^{d_h/k}) \in \mathbb{Z}_p^{d_h} : \vec{v} \in \{0,\ldots,p-1\}^k\}.$$

---

[10] $\vec{v}^\ell$ denotes ℓ concatenations of $\vec{v}$.

Theorem 6 (Sampling Irreducible Polynomials). *The following algorithm, on input* $2d_h$ *random elements of* $\mathbb{Z}_p$, *returns a uniformly sampled monic irreducible polynomial of degree* d_h *in* $\mathbb{Z}_p[X]$, *takes* $O(d_h M(d_h) \log p)$ *operations in* $\mathbb{Z}_p$ *where* $M(d_h)$ *denotes the complexity of multiplying polynomials of degree* d_h *in* $\mathbb{Z}_p[X]$, *and fails with probability* $\leq 4p^{-(d_h-1)} \approx 2^{-\lambda}$.

[Algorithm]

- Input: A prime p and a degree $d_h \in \mathbb{Z}_{>0}$.
- Random coins: $\rho_0^{(1)}, \ldots, \rho_{d_h-1}^{(1)}, \rho_0^{(2)}, \ldots, \rho_{d_h-1}^{(2)} \in \mathbb{Z}_p$.
- Output: A monic irreducible polynomial of degree d_h in $\mathbb{Z}_p[X]$.
- Setup:
  - Fix a finite field $\mathbb{F}_{p^{d_h}} := \mathbb{Z}_p[X]/(\phi)$ with an irreducible polynomial $\phi \in \mathbb{Z}_p[X]$ of degree d_h.
  - Let α be a generator of the multiplicative group $\mathbb{F}_{p^{d_h}}^\times$, compute and store
    $$\alpha_i = \alpha^{p^i} \text{ for } i \in \{1, \ldots, d_h - 1\}.$$
- Procedure:
  1. If $(\rho_0^{(1)}, \ldots, \rho_{d_h-1}^{(1)}) \notin \bigcup_{k|d_h, k \neq d_h} \mathsf{Bad}_k$, set $\beta = \prod_{i=0}^{d_h-1} \alpha_i^{\rho_i^{(1)}}$, go to 4.
  2. Else if $(\rho_0^{(2)}, \ldots, \rho_{d_h-1}^{(2)}) \notin \bigcup_{k|d_h, k \neq d_h} \mathsf{Bad}_k$, set $\beta = \prod_{i=0}^{d_h-1} \alpha_i^{\rho_i^{(2)}}$, go to 4.
  3. Else, return `fail`.
  4. Find the minimal polynomial h of β, using the algorithm in [Sho99].
  5. Return h

See the full version of the paper for a proof of this result.

Remark 8. Using Fast Fourier Transform algorithms or the Schönhage-Strassen algorithm we can set $M(d_h) = \tilde{O}(d_h)$ and the complexity above becomes $\tilde{O}(d_h^2 \log p)$ (where $\tilde{O}$ hides logarithmic factors in d_h).

Remark 9. If d_h is prime, we only need the coins $\rho_i^{(1)}$ as step 1 succeeds with overwhelming probability since $|\bigcup_{k|d_h, k \neq d_h} \mathsf{Bad}_k| = |\mathsf{Bad}_1| = p \ll p^{d_h}$.

4.4   Efficiency Analysis

In this section, we analyze the efficiency of the generic VC scheme (Sect. 3.2) instantiated with the concrete building blocks described so far. As before, let $R_t := \mathbb{Z}_t[X]/(f)$, let $g : (R_t)^n \to R_t$ denote the (delegated) computation of degree less than D over the plaintext space R_t, and $\mathcal{P}$ computes (then proves) the function $\hat{g} : (R_q^D)^n \to \mathbb{Z}_q[X]^D$ (not R_q^D) that describes $\mathsf{SHE.Eval}_{\mathsf{evk}}(g, \cdot)$ without reduction modulo f.

4.4.1   Combining Instantiations

The aggregation of building blocks can be summarized as follows:

SHE - BVscheme: In the setup, take a polynomial f of (large enough) degree d_f and a ciphertext modulus q satisfying 2^λ security and correctness of computation of any multivariate polynomial of degree $< D$ for plaintext modulus t, which sets the ciphertext space $R_q^D = (\mathbb{Z}_q[X]/(f))^D$. See more details in the full version.

Homomorphic Hash: Note that the ciphertext space R_q^D can be identified as (a subset of) $\mathbb{Z}_q[X]^D$ or $\mathbb{Z}_q[X][Y]$.[11] We can use our single hash or double hash, whose domain and range are as follows.

* Single: $\{(z_i)_{i=0}^{D-1} \in \mathbb{Z}_q[X]^D : deg_X(z_i) \leq N\} \longrightarrow (\mathbb{Z}_q[X]/(h))^D$
* Double: $\{z \in \mathbb{Z}_q[X][Y] : deg_X(z) \leq N \text{ and } deg_Y(z) < D\} \longrightarrow \mathbb{Z}_q[X]/(h)$

In both cases, $N = (d_f - 1)(D - 1)$ as noted before (in Remark following Theorem 3, 4). Note, in the range of both hash functions, that $\mathbb{Z}_q[X]/(h)$ is a Galois ring.

Argument System - GKR protocol over $\mathbb{Z}_q[X]/(h)$: Since the image of computations under the hash functions are in the ring $\mathbb{Z}_q[X]/(h)$ which is a Galois ring, we can use the GKR protocol to prove and verify such computations.

Security: We remark that the polynomial $h \in \mathbb{Z}_q[X]$ (where $q = p^e$) should be chosen of degree $\log_p \lambda$ to guarantee $\approx \frac{1}{2^\lambda}$ universality (and $\approx \frac{1}{2^\lambda}$ soundness) in the hash functions (resp. in the GKR protocol), from which our scheme gets $\approx \frac{1}{2^\lambda}$ soundness (see Theorem 1, 2, 3, 4).

4.4.2 Complexity of the Instantiation

As expected from the complexity analysis (Lemma 1) in Sect. 3.2, the efficiency of the instantiation mainly depends on the range space (ring) of hash functions and the costs of the argument system on that space.

Theorem 7. *In the instantiation of our VC scheme with soundness $2^{-\lambda}$ and the BV scheme having $R_q := \mathbb{Z}_q[X]/(f)$ as a ciphertext ring, assume that a verifier delegates a function $g : R_t^n \to R_t$ of degree less than D, which is described by an arithmetic circuit C over R_t of size S and depth d. Then, the required complexity $(T_{\mathcal{P}}, T_{\mathcal{V}}, C_{\mathcal{C}})$[12] measured by the number of operations (or elements) of $\mathbb{Z}_q$ is as follows.*

(i) with Single hash:

$$(\tilde{O}((n + D^2)d_f + \lambda D^2 S), \ \tilde{O}((n + D^2)d_f + \lambda d \log (D^2 S)), \ O(D^2 d_f + \lambda d \log (D^2 S)))$$

(ii) with Double hash:

$$(\tilde{O}((n + D^2)d_f + \lambda S), \quad \tilde{O}((n + D^2)d_f + \lambda d \log S), \quad O(D^2 d_f + \lambda d \log S))$$

where d_f is the degree of $f \in \mathbb{Z}_q[X]$ and $\tilde{O}$ hides the logarithmic factors. In $T_{\mathcal{P}}$, we assume that the prover $\mathcal{P}$ already has the result of computation $\hat{g} : (R_q^D)^n \to \mathbb{Z}_q[X]^D$ over the ciphertexts.

---

[11] For this, we skip the modulo reduction by f at the (delegated) computation.

[12] Each signifies the time complexity of $\mathcal{P}$, that of $\mathcal{V}$, and the communication cost.

Proof. (sketch) It follows from the fact that the homomorphic image of computation $\hat{g} : (R_q^D)^n \to \mathbb{Z}_q[X]^D$ under the single or double hash function, respectively, is composed of $O(D^2S)$ operations or $O(S)$ operations over $\mathbb{Z}_q[X]/(h)$ (with $\deg h = O(\lambda)$), respectively. The output $\hat{g}(c_1, \ldots, c_n) \in \mathbb{Z}_q[X]^D \subset \mathbb{Z}_q[X][Y]$ is a polynomial of degree $O(D)$ in Y and of $O(Dd_f)$ in X, hence is composed of $O(D^2d_f)$ elements of $\mathbb{Z}_q$, and the cost of evaluating hash function (on n input and 1 output) is $\tilde{O}((n + D^2)d_f)$. See full version for the full proof.   □

Note that computing $\hat{g} : (R_q^D)^n \to \mathbb{Z}_q[X]^D$ over ciphertexts costs $\Omega(d_f D^2 S)$ operations over $\mathbb{Z}_q$, and is roughly $\times D$ costly than the original ciphertext computation SHE.Eval$_{\mathsf{evk}}(g, \cdot) : (R_q^D)^n \to R_q^D$ (with mod f) which costs $\Omega(d_f DS)$. However, this gap is not significant given that the degree D of computation is not large.

Remark 10 (Ciphertext Computation vs Proof Generation). Since $d_f = \Omega(\sqrt{\lambda}\log q)$ for the security of BV scheme (from the hardness of LWE), double hash makes the proof generation cost $T_{\mathcal{P}} = \tilde{O}((n + D^2)d_f + \lambda S)$ asymptotically *negligible* to the cost of computing $\hat{g}$ (while single hash does not). In other words, with our scheme, there is no significant additional overhead for $\mathcal{P}$ to prove the correctness of its computation, as will be also demonstrated with concrete example parameters in the following section.

Table 2. Example parameters for our VC scheme: λ_{BV} and λ_s respectively denote the bit security of BV scheme and our VC scheme.

Circuit				BV scheme			GKR and Hash	Security	
g	n	d	D	$\log t$	$\log q$	$\log d_f$	d_h	λ_{BV}	λ_s
Inn Prod.	2^8	2	3	8	54	11	136		128.4
Inn Prod.	2^8	2	3	16	73	12	136	≥ 128	128.4
Inn Prod.	2^{10}	2	3	16	73	12	136		128.2
Poly Eval.	2^{10}	2	4	2	62	11	136	117.5	128.1
Poly Eval.	2^{10}	4	6	2	110	12	137		128.8
Poly Eval.	2^{10}	4	6	16	187	13	137	≥ 128	128.7
Poly Eval.	2^{12}	16	18	16	685	15	138		128.6

4.4.3   Concrete Parameters and Examples

To demonstrate the efficiency of our VC, we give some explicit parameters for the example computation. For $R_t := \mathbb{Z}_t[X]/(f)$, assume that a verifier delegates a (multivariate) polynomial $g : R_t^u \to R_t$ of (total) degree D. We let g be one of the two examples given below:

- Inner Product of two input vectors of dimension n over R_t, i.e.,

$$g : \quad \begin{array}{ccc} R_t^n \times R_t^n & \longrightarrow & R_t \\ ((a_1, a_2, \ldots, a_n), (b_1, b_2, \ldots, b_n)) & \mapsto & \sum_{i=1}^n a_i b_i. \end{array}$$

- (Degree-d_F) Polynomial Evaluation on n parallel input points of R_t, i.e.,

$$g: \quad \begin{array}{c} R_t^n \times R_t^{d_F+1} \\ ((a_1, a_2, \ldots, a_n), (F_0, F_1, \ldots, F_{d_F})) \end{array} \quad \longrightarrow \quad \begin{array}{c} R_t^n \\ (\sum_{i=0}^{d_F} F_i a_1^i, \sum_{i=0}^{d_F} F_i a_2^i, \ldots, \sum_{i=0}^{d_F} F_i a_n^i). \end{array}$$

We refer to the full version for the detailed description of above computations and the derivation of parameters.

In Table 2, we present several parameters for our VC scheme with double hash for those computations varying n, the depth d (equivalent to the degree of the input polynomial in the second example) of the circuit $g : R_t^u \to R_t$, and the plaintext modulus t.

Efficiency Improvement. With Table 2, we can give more concrete analysis on the efficiency of our VC scheme. In a naive approach without our hashing, the prover should generate a proof on the computation over $R_q = \mathbb{Z}_q[X]/(f)$ where the degree d_f of f is 2^{11}–2^{15} in above examples. In contrast, in our scheme with hashing, the proof is generated on the computation over $\mathbb{Z}_q[X]/(h)$ where the degree d_h of h is only 136–139 ($\approx \lambda_s$ as expected). Therefore, we can expect roughly $\times \frac{d_f}{d_h} \approx \times 15$–235 improvement in the cost of proof generation and the size of proof. It also implies that the cost of proof generation is not significant compared to the ciphertext computation, since the former is done over the ring $\mathbb{Z}_q[X]/(h)$ which is much smaller than the ring $\mathbb{Z}_q[X]/(f)$ of ciphertext.

We remark that the size of d_h does not increase seriously though the target computation g has more inputs and depth, and aforementioned efficiency improvement also appears in other computation. In addition, the improvement can be more drastic if the ciphertext modulus q is a power of prime bigger than 2: if $q = p^e$ for a prime p, we can take $d_h = \frac{139}{\log p}$ in our examples, resulting in additional $\times \log p$ improvement.

5   Context-Hiding VC for Nondeterministic Computations

In this section, we generalize the notion of private VC to support nondeterministic computations and public verifiability with *context-hiding*. Next, we show how to extend our construction of Sect. 3 to achieve these properties.

In brief, supporting nondeterministic computations means to consider functions of the form $g(x, w)$ in which the untrusted worker receives an encoding σ_x of the input x (which may hide x), holds an additional input w and can produce an encoding σ_y that, if computed honestly, is supposed to decode to $g(x, w)$. This is useful to handle more complex computations, such as ones that use random coins, non-arithmetic operations (e.g., bit-decompositions) or (secret) computation parameters. For instance, with this we can prove correct re-randomization of ciphertexts, or to evaluate polynomials with coefficients provided by the server.

For security, we require a notion similar to the soundness of proof systems, namely that a dishonest prover holding σ_x cannot produce an output σ_y which decodes to a value y for which there exists no w such that $y = g(x, w)$.

On the other hand, context-hiding—introduced in [FNP20] for deterministic computations $g(x)$ only—is a property that guarantees that the verifier does not learn any information about (x, w) beyond what can be inferred from y. Finally, public verifiability allows the computation to be verifiable by anyone (possibly a party different from the one who provided the input).

In the next section we introduce our definitions of context-hiding VC for nondeterministic computations, and then in the following section we sketch a construction of this primitive (fully detailed in the full version).

5.1 Definition of VC for Nondeterministic Computation and Context-Hiding

We extend the notion of verifiable computation from Sect. 2.1 to support nondeterministic computations and context-hiding, as informally explained above.

Formally, a VC scheme for non-deterministic computations is a tuple of algorithms as defined in Sect. 2.1 with the following differences.

$\mathsf{Compute}_{PK_g}(\sigma_x, w) \to \sigma_y$: Using the public keys, the encoded input σ_x and an additional input w, the server computes an encoded version of the function's output $y = g(x, w)$.

The notion of correctness considers the additional input w:

Correctness. For any function g and input x and w,

$$
\Pr\left[
\begin{array}{c}
\mathsf{Verify}_{PK_g}(\tau_x, \sigma_y) = 1 \\
\wedge\ \mathsf{Decode}_{SK, SK_g}(\sigma_y) = g(x, w)
\end{array}
\;\middle|\;
\begin{array}{l}
(PK, SK) \leftarrow \mathsf{Setup}(1^\lambda) \\
(PK_g, SK_g) \leftarrow \mathsf{KeyGen}_{PK}(g) \\
(\sigma_x, \tau_x) \leftarrow \mathsf{ProbGen}_{PK}(x) \\
\sigma_y \leftarrow \mathsf{Compute}_{PK_g}(\sigma_x, w)
\end{array}
\right] = 1.
$$

Privacy and Security. The notion of privacy is the same as in the Definition 1. For security, we instead consider the following experiment where $O_{\mathsf{KeyGen}}(g)$ is an oracle that calls $\mathsf{KeyGen}_{PK,SK}(g)$ and returns PK_g as in Sect. 2.1 (the difference lies in the final if condition).

> Experiment $\mathbf{Exp}_{\mathcal{A}}^{Verif}[\mathcal{VC}, \lambda]$
> $(PK, SK) \leftarrow \mathsf{Setup}(1^\lambda);$
> $(x, st) \leftarrow \mathcal{A}^{O_{\mathsf{KeyGen}}(\cdot)}(PK);$
> $(\sigma_x, \tau_x) \leftarrow \mathsf{ProbGen}_{PK}(x);$
> $(g, \hat{\sigma}_y) \leftarrow \mathcal{A}^{O_{\mathsf{KeyGen}}(\cdot)}(st, \sigma_x, \tau_x);$
> $acc \leftarrow \mathsf{Verify}_{PK_g}(\tau_x, \hat{\sigma}_y);$
> if $acc = 1$ and $\nexists w : \mathsf{Decode}_{SK, SK_g}(\hat{\sigma}_y) = g(x, w)$ output 1;
> else output 0;

Context-Hiding. Note that, in the definition of a publicly verifiable VC scheme, anyone with PK_g and τ_x can run Verify on σ_y to verify the correctness of the computation. A party who has the secret keys SK_g, SK can additionally get the computation result y encoded in σ_y.

In some applications, however, one may want to be assured that σ_y reveals nothing beyond y. In particular, it should not leak information about the inputs (x, w). We formalize this property in the following context-hiding notion. More specifically, we are interested in modeling two cases:

(a) no information about (x, w) should be leaked to a party that has τ_x (for verification) and SK, SK_g (for decoding of σ_y) together with σ_y;
(b) no information about w should be leaked to a party that, in addition to the information above (i.e., SK, SK_g, τ_x) has σ_x.

To motivate the properties above, consider an application where Alice stores encrypted confidential data x on a server $\mathcal{P}$ and allows a user Bob to get the results of a classification algorithm (computed by $\mathcal{P}$ with its own secret parameters w) on her data. In this case, one can be interested that no information about Alice's data x and the server's parameters w are leaked to Bob from the encoding σ_y when he decodes the result, e.g., in the case of lattice-based encryption, the noise revealed during the decryption of ciphertexts exposes such information. Furthermore, there can be use cases where Alice and Bob are the same entity, in which case we want to keep w hidden even to the party that knows x and its encoding σ_x.

Definition 7 (Context Hiding). *A VC scheme is context-hiding if there exist simulator algorithms $S_\tau, S_1, S_2, S_{3,a}, S_{3,b}$ such that:*

1. *the keys (PK, SK) and (PK^*, SK^*) are statistically indistinguishable, where $(PK, SK) \leftarrow \mathsf{Setup}(1^\lambda)$ and $(PK^*, SK^*, td) \leftarrow S_1(1^\lambda)$;*
2. *for any g the keys (PK_g, SK_g) and (PK_g^*, SK_g^*) are statistically indistinguishable, where $(PK_g, SK_g) \leftarrow \mathsf{KeyGen}_{PK,SK}(g)$ and $(PK_g^*, SK_g^*, td_g) \leftarrow S_2(td, g)$;*
3. *for any simulated keys $(PK^*, SK^*, td) \leftarrow S_1(1^\lambda)$, $(PK_g^*, SK_g^*, td_g) \leftarrow S_2(td, g)$, any function g, any inputs (x, w), and any honestly generated input/output encodings $(\sigma_x, \tau_x) \leftarrow \mathsf{ProbGen}_{PK}(x)$, $\sigma_y \leftarrow \mathsf{Compute}_{PK_g}(\sigma_x, w)$, the following distributions are negligibly close:*
   (a) $(PK^*, SK^*, PK_g^*, SK_g^*, \tau_x, \sigma_y) \approx (PK^*, SK^*, PK_g^*, SK_g^*, \tau_x^*, \sigma_y^*)$
      where $\tau_x^* \leftarrow S_\tau(td)$ and $\sigma_y^* \leftarrow S_{3,a}(td_g, \tau_x^*, g(x, w))$;
   (b) $(PK^*, SK^*, PK_g^*, SK_g^*, \sigma_x, \tau_x, \sigma_y) \approx (PK^*, SK^*, PK_g^*, SK_g^*, \sigma_x, \tau_x, \sigma_y^*)$
      where $\sigma_y^* \leftarrow S_{3,b}(td_g, \tau_x, g(x, w))$.

In the following lemma we show that property (3.a) of Definition 7 can be reduced to a simpler requirement essentially saying that τ_x statistically hides x.

Lemma 5. *Let $\mathcal{VC}$ be a VC scheme for which there exist simulator algorithms $S_1, S_2, S_{3,b}$ such that properties 1,2,3.b of Definition 7 hold. Furthermore, assume there exists a simulator algorithm S_τ such that, for any $(PK^*, SK^*, td) \leftarrow S_1(1^\lambda)$, for any input x and $(\sigma_x, \tau_x) \leftarrow \mathsf{ProbGen}_{PK}(x)$, we have $S_\tau(td) \approx \tau_x$. Then $\mathcal{VC}$ satisfies Definition 7.*

Proof. We prove the lemma by constructing the simulator $S_{3,a}$ from $S_{3,b}$ and S_τ as follows. Let $S_{3,a}(td, \tau_x^*, y)$ be the algorithm that simply outputs $S_{3,b}(td, \tau_x^*, y)$. To see that property (3.a) of Definition 7 is satisfied: first, observe that property 3.*b* holds even when removing σ_x from the view; second, we can create an hybrid view in which we replace τ_x with a simulated one $\tau_x^* \leftarrow S_\tau(td)$. By the simulation property of S_τ this view is negligibly close to the previous one (i.e., that of property (3.b) without σ_x). Also, the latter view is identical to that in the right-hand side of property (3.a).   □

Note that, as introduced in [FNP20], context-hiding is a meaningful property even in the case of deterministic computations, i.e., for empty w, where it assures that the values τ_x and σ_y do not reveal additional information on the input x.

5.2   Overview of Our Construction

We give an informal description of our VC construction that supports non-deterministic computations and context-hiding. For space restrictions, a detailed description of the scheme and the necessary building blocks are in the full version.

Let $g : R_t^n \times R_t^m \to R_t$ denote the nondeterministic computation to be delegated, and let $x \in R_t^n$ and $w \in R_t^m$ be the inputs of the client $\mathcal{C}$ and the prover $\mathcal{P}$ respectively. Also, assume that $\mathcal{P}$ receives an encryption $c_x = \mathsf{SHE.Enc_{pk}}(x)$.

In order to compute an encryption of $g(x, w)$, $\mathcal{P}$ can first encode w in a ciphertext c_w,[13] and then perform the corresponding encrypted computation $\hat{g} : (R_q^D)^n \times (R_q^D)^m \to \mathbb{Z}_q[X]^D$ (without reduction modulo f)[14] to obtain $c_y = \hat{g}(c_x, c_w)$. Note that checking the validity of such c_y means to check that

$$\exists c_w \in \Omega : c_y = \hat{g}(c_x, c_w)$$

where Ω is a (sub)set of valid ciphertexts.

Computing c_y in this way would not be enough for context-hiding, as c_y (in particular its "noise") may contain information on (x, w). To solve this issue, we exploit the noise flooding technique: $\mathcal{P}$ adds to the result $\hat{g}(c_x, c_w)$ an encryption c_0 of 0 with large noise that statistically hides the noise in $\hat{g}(c_x, c_w)$. If we let $\Omega_0 \subset \{\mathsf{SHE.Enc_{pk}}(0)\}$ be a subset of encryptions of 0 with the appropriate noise level, then checking the validity of such computation means to check that

$$\exists c_w \in \Omega, c_0 \in \Omega_0 : c_y = \hat{g}(c_x, c_w) + c_0$$

For the sake of achieving context-hiding, the above statement must be verifiable without knowing c_x, as context-hiding asks for hiding x even against a party who has the decryption key SK and may thus figure out x from c_x. For this reason, we follow an approach similar to [FNP20]: the client creates a commitment com_x to c_x and gives to the verifier $\tau_x = \mathsf{com}_x$, while the prover proves that it knows (c_x, c_w, c_0) such that com_x opens to c_x, $c_w \in \Omega, c_0 \in \Omega_0$ and $c_y = \hat{g}(c_x, c_w) + c_0$.

---

[13] This operation can be deterministic, e.g., embedding w in the ciphertext space.
[14] Recall that $R_q := \mathbb{Z}_q[X]/(f)$ and $\hat{g}(c_x, c_w) \bmod f = \mathsf{FHE.Eval_{pk}}(g, (c_x, c_w))$.

Next, to avoid that the cost of generating the proof above depends on $O(|\hat{g}| \cdot d_f)$ we adapt the homomorphic hashing technique to this context. In our (interactive) protocol, the prover sends to the verifier the result c_y (as in Sect. 3) as well as commitments $(\mathsf{com}_w, \mathsf{com}_0)$ to (c_w, c_0) and proves knowledge of their opening; next the verifier picks a homomorphic hash function H; finally, the prover creates a proof that the openings (c_x, c_w, c_0) of $(\mathsf{com}_x, \mathsf{com}_w, \mathsf{com}_0)$ are such that:

$$H(c_y) = \hat{g}(H(c_x), H(c_w)) + H(c_0) \land c_w \in \Omega \land c_0 \in \Omega_0$$

Starting from this idea, we enhance it in two ways.

First, by using the commit-and-prove paradigm we split further the statement above into two statements linked by the same commitment. Namely, we let the prover commit to $(\gamma_x = H(c_x), \gamma_w = H(c_w), \gamma_0 = H(c_0))$ in $(\mathsf{com}'_x, \mathsf{com}'_w, \mathsf{com}'_0)$ and then prove the following two relations w.r.t. such commitment:

$$\mathcal{R}_H : \gamma_x = H(c_x) \land \gamma_w = H(c_w) \land \gamma_0 = H(c_0) \land c_w \in \Omega \land c_0 \in \Omega_0$$
$$\mathcal{R}_{\hat{g}} : H(c_y) = \hat{g}(\gamma_x, \gamma_w) + \gamma_0$$

With this splitting we can use two separate proof systems: one for $\mathcal{R}_{\hat{g}}$ which is the computation $\hat{g}(\cdot)$ (over the small ring $\mathcal{D}_H$), and one for $\mathcal{R}_H$ which is about correct hashing and the suitability of the committed ciphertexts c_w, c_0.

Second, by exploiting the structure of the BV HE scheme, we discuss how to encode the checks $c_w \in \Omega \land c_0 \in \Omega_0$ in an efficient manner. For $c_0 \in \Omega_0$, we assume that in the (trusted) key generation one generates a vector of ciphertexts $\vec{\omega}_0 = (\omega_{0,i})_{i=1}^z$ such that each of them is an encryption of 0. Then, c_0 can be generated as $\langle \vec{\beta}, \vec{\omega}_0 \rangle$ where $\vec{\beta} \in \{0,1\}^z$ is a random binary vector. This way proving $c_0 \in \Omega_0$ boils down to proving that $\exists \vec{\beta} \in \{0,1\}^z : c_0 = \langle \vec{\beta}, \vec{\omega}_0 \rangle$.

For $c_w \in \Omega$, we prove the embedding of the plaintext in the ciphertext space. Namely, parsing c_w as the vector of coefficients $(c_{w,1}, \ldots, c_{w,(D+1) \cdot d_f})$, we need to prove that $c_{w,i} \in (-t/2, t/2] \cap \mathbb{Z}$, for $i = 1$ to d_f, and $c_{w,i} = 0$ for all $i > d_f$.

The solution sketched above needs two commit-and-prove arguments, one for $\mathcal{R}_H$ and one for $\mathcal{R}_{\hat{g}}$. We also present a variant VC construction in which the relation $\mathcal{R}_{\hat{g}}$ can be proven using a *non-zero-knowledge* verifiable computation such as GKR. In this case, we reveal the values $(\gamma_x = H(c_x), \gamma_w = H(c_w), \gamma_0 = H(c_0))$ to the verifiers, yet we show how this can preserve context-hiding. Roughly, we prove that when c is a fresh ciphertext (and thus has enough entropy), its hash $H(c)$ does not reveal any information about it. To use this assumption we modify the VC construction so that c_w is freshly encrypted (instead of embedding a plaintext in a deterministic way), whereas for c_x we show that it can be hashed a bounded number of times without loosing information on it. This assumption can also be removed if the prover re-randomizes c_x and proves its correct re-randomization in $\mathcal{R}_H$.

Acknowledgements. Research leading to these results has been partially supported by the Spanish Government under projects SCUM (ref. RTI2018-102043-B-I00), CRYPTOEPIC (ref. EUR2019-103816), SECURITAS (ref. RED2018-102321-T) and SecuRing (ref. PID2019-110873RJ-I00), by the Madrid Regional Government under project BLOQUES (ref. S2018/TCS-4339), and by a research grant from Nomadic Labs and the Tezos Foundation. This work was also supported in part by the National Research Foundation of Korea (NRF) funded by the Korean Government (MSIT) under Grant NRF-2017R1A5A1015626.

References

AHIV17. Ames, S., Hazay, C., Ishai, Y., Venkitasubramaniam, M.: Ligero: lightweight sublinear arguments without a trusted setup. In: Thuraisingham, B.M., Evans, D., Malkin, T., Xu, D. (eds.) ACM CCS 2017, pp. 2087–2104. ACM Press, New York (2017)

BCR+19. Ben-Sasson, E., Chiesa, A., Riabzev, M., Spooner, N., Virza, M., Ward, N.P.: Aurora: transparent succinct arguments for R1CS. In: Ishai, Y., Rijmen, V. (eds.) EUROCRYPT 2019. LNCS, vol. 11476, pp. 103–128. Springer, Cham (2019). https://doi.org/10.1007/978-3-030-17653-2_4

BCS16. Ben-Sasson, E., Chiesa, A., Spooner, N.: Interactive oracle proofs. In: Hirt, M., Smith, A. (eds.) TCC 2016. LNCS, vol. 9986, pp. 31–60. Springer, Heidelberg (2016). https://doi.org/10.1007/978-3-662-53644-5_2

Ben81. Ben-Or, M.: Probabilistic algorithms in finite fields. In: 22nd FOCS, pp. 394–398. IEEE Computer Society Press (October 1981)

BGV12. Brakerski, Z., Gentry, C., Vaikuntanathan, V.: (Leveled) fully homomorphic encryption without bootstrapping. In: Goldwasser, S. (ed.) ITCS 2012, pp. 309–325. ACM (January 2012)

BV11. Brakerski, Z., Vaikuntanathan, V.: Fully homomorphic encryption from ring-LWE and security for key dependent messages. In: Rogaway, P. (ed.) CRYPTO 2011. LNCS, vol. 6841, pp. 505–524. Springer, Heidelberg (2011). https://doi.org/10.1007/978-3-642-22792-9_29

CCH+18. Canetti, R., Chen, Y., Holmgren, J., Lombardi, A., Rothblum, G.N., Rothblum, R.D.: Fiat-Shamir from simpler assumptions. Cryptology ePrint Archive, Report 2018/1004 (2018). https://eprint.iacr.org/2018/1004

CCKP19. Chen, S., Cheon, J.H., Kim, D., Park, D.: Verifiable computing for approximate computation. Cryptology ePrint Archive, Report 2019/762 (2019). https://eprint.iacr.org/2019/762

CGGI16. Chillotti, I., Gama, N., Georgieva, M., Izabachène, M.: Faster fully homomorphic encryption: bootstrapping in less than 0.1 seconds. In: Cheon, J.H., Takagi, T. (eds.) ASIACRYPT 2016. LNCS, vol. 10031, pp. 3–33. Springer, Heidelberg (2016). https://doi.org/10.1007/978-3-662-53887-6_1

CGGI17. Chillotti, I., Gama, N., Georgieva, M., Izabachène, M.: Faster packed homomorphic operations and efficient circuit bootstrapping for TFHE. In: Takagi, T., Peyrin, T. (eds.) ASIACRYPT 2017. LNCS, vol. 10624, pp. 377–408. Springer, Cham (2017). https://doi.org/10.1007/978-3-319-70694-8_14

CH18.   Chen, H., Han, K.: Homomorphic lower digits removal and improved FHE bootstrapping. In: Nielsen, J.B., Rijmen, V. (eds.) EUROCRYPT 2018. LNCS, vol. 10820, pp. 315–337. Springer, Cham (2018). https://doi.org/10.1007/978-3-319-78381-9_12

CHM+20. Chiesa, A., Hu, Y., Maller, M., Mishra, P., Vesely, N., Ward, N.: Marlin: preprocessing zkSNARKs with universal and updatable SRS. In: Canteaut, A., Ishai, Y. (eds.) EUROCRYPT 2020. LNCS, vol. 12105, pp. 738–768. Springer, Cham (2020). https://doi.org/10.1007/978-3-030-45721-1_26

CKKS17. Cheon, J.H., Kim, A., Kim, M., Song, Y.: Homomorphic encryption for arithmetic of approximate numbers. In: Takagi, T., Peyrin, T. (eds.) ASIACRYPT 2017. LNCS, vol. 10624, pp. 409–437. Springer, Cham (2017). https://doi.org/10.1007/978-3-319-70694-8_15

CMT12.   Cormode, G., Mitzenmacher, M., Thaler, J.: Practical verified computation with streaming interactive proofs. In: Goldwasser, S. (ed.) ITCS 2012, pp. 90–112. ACM (January 2012)

DM15.   Ducas, L., Micciancio, D.: FHEW: bootstrapping homomorphic encryption in less than a second. In: Oswald, E., Fischlin, M. (eds.) EUROCRYPT 2015. LNCS, vol. 9056, pp. 617–640. Springer, Heidelberg (2015). https://doi.org/10.1007/978-3-662-46800-5_24

FGP14.   Fiore, D., Gennaro, R., Pastro, V.: Efficiently verifiable computation on encrypted data. In: Ahn, G.-J., Yung, M., Li, N. (eds.) ACM CCS 2014, pp. 844–855. ACM Press (November 2014)

FNP20.   Fiore, D., Nitulescu, A., Pointcheval, D.: Boosting verifiable computation on encrypted data. In: Kiayias, A., Kohlweiss, M., Wallden, P., Zikas, V. (eds.) PKC 2020. LNCS, vol. 12111, pp. 124–154. Springer, Cham (2020). https://doi.org/10.1007/978-3-030-45388-6_5

FV12.   Fan, J., Vercauteren, F.: Somewhat practical fully homomorphic encryption. Cryptology ePrint Archive, Report 2012/144 (2012). http://eprint.iacr.org/2012/144

Gen09.   Gentry, C.: Fully homomorphic encryption using ideal lattices. In: Mitzenmacher, M. (ed.) 41st ACM STOC, pp. 169–178. ACM Press, New York (2009)

GGP10.   Gennaro, R., Gentry, C., Parno, B.: Non-interactive verifiable computing: outsourcing computation to untrusted workers. In: Rabin, T. (ed.) CRYPTO 2010. LNCS, vol. 6223, pp. 465–482. Springer, Heidelberg (2010). https://doi.org/10.1007/978-3-642-14623-7_25

GGPR13. Gennaro, R., Gentry, C., Parno, B., Raykova, M.: Quadratic span programs and succinct NIZKs without PCPs. In: Johansson, T., Nguyen, P.Q. (eds.) EUROCRYPT 2013. LNCS, vol. 7881, pp. 626–645. Springer, Heidelberg (2013). https://doi.org/10.1007/978-3-642-38348-9_37

GKP+13. Goldwasser, S., Kalai, Y.T., Popa, R.A., Vaikuntanathan, V., Zeldovich, N.: How to run turing machines on encrypted data. In: Canetti, R., Garay, J.A. (eds.) CRYPTO 2013. LNCS, vol. 8043, pp. 536–553. Springer, Heidelberg (2013). https://doi.org/10.1007/978-3-642-40084-1_30

GKR08.   Goldwasser, S., Kalai, Y.T., Rothblum, G.N.: Delegating computation: interactive proofs for muggles. In: Ladner, R.E., Dwork, C. (eds.) 40th ACM STOC, pp. 113–122. ACM Press (May 2008)

GSW13. Gentry, C., Sahai, A., Waters, B.: Homomorphic encryption from learning with errors: conceptually-simpler, asymptotically-faster, attribute-based. In: Canetti, R., Garay, J.A. (eds.) CRYPTO 2013. LNCS, vol. 8042, pp. 75–92. Springer, Heidelberg (2013). https://doi.org/10.1007/978-3-642-40041-4_5

Kil92. Kilian, J.: A note on efficient zero-knowledge proofs and arguments (extended abstract). In: 24th ACM STOC, pp. 723–732. ACM Press (May 1992)

PRV12. Parno, B., Raykova, M., Vaikuntanathan, V.: How to delegate and verify in public: verifiable computation from attribute-based encryption. In: Cramer, R. (ed.) TCC 2012. LNCS, vol. 7194, pp. 422–439. Springer, Heidelberg (2012). https://doi.org/10.1007/978-3-642-28914-9_24

Sho99. Shoup, V.: Efficient computation of minimal polynomials in algebraic extensions of finite fields. In: Proceedings of the 1999 International Symposium on Symbolic and Algebraic Computation, ISSAC 1999 (1999)

SV14. Smart, N.P., Vercauteren, F.: Fully homomorphic SIMD operations. Des. Codes Cryptogr. **71**(1), 57–81 (2014)

Tha13. Thaler, J.: Time-optimal interactive proofs for circuit evaluation. In: Canetti, R., Garay, J.A. (eds.) CRYPTO 2013. LNCS, vol. 8043, pp. 71–89. Springer, Heidelberg (2013). https://doi.org/10.1007/978-3-642-40084-1_5

VZGG13. Von Zur Gathen, J., Gerhard, J.: Modern Computer Algebra. Cambridge University Press, Cambridge (2013)

Wan03. Wan, Z.-X.: Lectures on Finite Fields and Galois Rings. World Scientific Publishing Company, Singapore (2003)

WTs+18. Wahby, R.S., Tzialla, I., Shelat, A., Thaler, J., Walfish, M.: Doubly-efficient zkSNARKs without trusted setup. In: 2018 IEEE Symposium on Security and Privacy, pp. 926–943. IEEE Computer Society Press (May 2018)

XZZ+19. Xie, T., Zhang, J., Zhang, Y., Papamanthou, C., Song, D.: Libra: succinct zero-knowledge proofs with optimal prover computation. In: Boldyreva, A., Micciancio, D. (eds.) CRYPTO 2019. LNCS, vol. 11694, pp. 733–764. Springer, Cham (2019). https://doi.org/10.1007/978-3-030-26954-8_24

Transferable E-Cash: A Cleaner Model and the First Practical Instantiation

Balthazar Bauer[1]([✉]), Georg Fuchsbauer[2], and Chen Qian[3]

[1] Inria, ENS, CNRS, PSL, Paris, France
balthazar.bauer@ens.fr
[2] TU Wien, Vienna, Austria
georg.fuchsbauer@tuwien.ac.at
[3] NTNU, Trondheim, Norway
chen.qian@ntnu.no

Abstract. Transferable e-cash is the most faithful digital analog of physical cash, as it allows users to transfer coins between them in isolation, that is, without interacting with a bank or a "ledger". Appropriate protection of user privacy and, at the same time, providing means to trace fraudulent behavior (double-spending of coins) have made instantiating the concept notoriously hard. Baldimtsi et al. (PKC'15) gave a first instantiation, but, as it relies on a powerful cryptographic primitive, the scheme is not practical. We also point out a flaw in their scheme.

In this paper we revisit the model for transferable e-cash and propose simpler yet stronger security definitions. We then provide the first concrete construction, based on bilinear groups, give rigorous proofs that it satisfies our model, and analyze its efficiency in detail.

1 Introduction

Contrary to so-called "crypto"-currencies like Bitcoin [Nak08], a central ambition of the predating cryptographic *e-cash* has been user anonymity. Introduced by Chaum [Cha83], the goal was to realize a digital analog of physical cash, which allows users to pay without revealing their identity; and there has been a long line of research since [CFN88, Bra93, CHL05, BCKL09, FHY13, CPST16, BPS19] (to name only a few). In e-cash, a bank issues electronic coins to users, who can then spend them with merchants, who in turn can deposit them at the bank to get their account credited. User privacy should be protected in that not even the bank can link the withdrawing of a coin to its spending.

The main difference to the physical world is that digital coins can easily be duplicated, and therefore a so-called "double-spending" of a coin must be prevented. This can be readily achieved when all actors are online and connected (as with cryptocurrencies), since every spending is broadcast and payees simply refuse a coin that has already been spent.

Even in "anonymous" cryptocurrencies like *Monero* [vS13], which now also uses *confidential transactions* [Max15], or systems based on the Zerocoin/-cash [MGGR13, BCG+14] protocol, like *Zcash* [Zec20], or on Mimblewimble

ⓒ International Association for Cryptologic Research 2021
J. A. Garay (Ed.): PKC 2021, LNCS 12711, pp. 559–590, 2021.
https://doi.org/10.1007/978-3-030-75248-4_20

[Poe16,FOS19], users must be connected when they accept a payment, in order to prevent double-spending.

When users are allowed to spend coins to other users (or merchants) without continuous connectivity, then double-spending cannot be prevented; however, starting with [CFN88], ingenious methods have been devised for revealing a double-spender's identity while guaranteeing the privacy of all honest users.

Transferable E-Cash. In all traditional e-cash schemes, including such "offline" e-cash, once a coin is spent (transferred) after withdrawal, it must be deposited at the bank by the payee. A more powerful concept, and much more faithful to physical e-cash, is *transferable e-cash*, which allows users to re-transfer obtained coins, while at the same time remaining offline. Note that cryptocurrencies are inherently online, and every transfer of a coin could be seen as depositing a coin (and marking it spent) and re-issuing a new one (in the ledger).

Transferable e-cash was first proposed by Okamoto and Ohta [OO89, OO91], but the constructions only guaranteed very weak forms of anonymity. It was then shown [CP93] that *unbounded* adversaries can recognize coins they owned earlier and that a coin must grow in size with every transfer (since information about potential double-spenders needs to be encoded in it).

While other schemes [Bla08, CGT08] only achieve unsatisfactory anonymity notions, Canard and Gouget [CG08] define a stronger notion (which we call *coin transparency*): it requires that a (polynomial-time) adversary cannot recognize a coin he has already owned when it is later given back to him. This is not achieved by physical cash, as banknotes can be marked by users (or the bank); however, if an e-cash scheme allowed a merchant to identify users by tracing the coins given out as change, then it would violate the central claim of e-cash, namely anonymous payments. (Anonymous cryptocurrencies also satisfy a notion analogous to coin transparency.) A limitation of this notion is that the bank (more specifically, the part dealing with deposits) must be honest, as it must be able to link occurrences of the same coin to detect double-spending.

Prior Schemes. The first scheme achieving coin transparency [CG08] was completely impractical, as at every transfer, the payer sends a proof of (a proof of (...(a proof of a coin)...)) that she received earlier. The first practical scheme was given by Fuchsbauer et al. [FPV09], but it makes unacceptable compromises elsewhere: when a double-spending is detected, all (even innocent) users up to the double-spender must give up their anonymity.

Blazy et al. [BCF+11] overcome this problem and propose a scheme that assumes a trusted party (called the "judge") that can trace all coins and users in the system and has to actively intervene to identify double-spenders. The scheme thus reneges on the promise that users remain anonymous as long as they follow the protocol. Moreover, their proof of anonymity was flawed, as shown by Baldimtsi et al. [BCFK15].

Despite all its problems, Blazy et al.'s [BCF+11] scheme, which elegantly combined randomizable non-interactive zero-knowledge (NIZK) proofs [BCC+09] and commuting signatures [Fuc11], serves as starting point for our construction. In their scheme a coin consists of a signature by the bank and at every transfer the spender adds her own signature (thereby committing to her spending). To achieve anonymity, these signatures are not given in the clear; instead, coins are NIZK proofs of knowledge of signatures. Since the proofs can be rerandomized (that is, from a proof, anyone can produce a new proof of the same statement that looks unrelated to the original proof), coins can change appearance after every transfer. Users will thus not recognize a coin when they see it again later, meaning the scheme satisfies coin transparency.

Baldimtsi et al. [BCFK15] give an instantiation that avoids the "judge" by using a double-spending-tracing mechanism from classical offline e-cash. They add "tags" to the coin that hide the identity of the owner of the coin, except when she spends the coin twice, then the bank can from two such tags compute the user's identity. Users must also include signatures in the coin during transfer, which represent irrefutable proof of double-spending.

The main drawback of their scheme is efficiency. They rely on the concept of *malleable signatures* [CKLM14], a generalization of digital signatures, where a signature on a message m can be transformed into a signature on a message $T(m)$ for any allowed transformation T. *Simulation unforgeability* requires that from a signature one can extract all transformations it has undergone (even when the adversary that created it has seen "simulated" signatures).

In their scheme [BCFK15] a coin is a malleable signature computed by the bank, which can be *transformed* by a user if she correctly encodes her identity in a double-spending tag, adds an encryption (under the bank's public key) to it and randomizes all encryptions of previous tags contained in the coin.

None of the previous schemes explicitly considers *denominations* of coins (and neither do we). This is because efficient ("compact") withdrawing and spending can be easily achieved if the bank associates different keys to different denominations (since giving *change* is readily supported in transferable e-cash). Note that, in contrast to cryptocurrencies, where every transaction is publicly posted, hiding the *amount* of a payment is meaningless in transferable e-cash.

Our Contribution: Security Model. We revisit the formal model for transferable e-cash, starting from [BCFK15], whose model was a refined version of earlier ones. We then exhibit attacks against users who follow the protocol, against which previous models did not protect:

- When a user receives a coin (that is, the protocol accepts the received coin), then previous models did not guarantee that this coin will be accepted by other (honest) users when transferred. An adversary could thus send a malformed coin to a user, which the latter accepts but can then not spend.
- There were also no guarantees against a malicious bank which at coin deposit refuses to credit the user's account (e.g., by claiming that the coin was invalid or had been double-spent). In our model, when the bank refuses a coin, it must accuse a user of double-spending and provide a proof for this.

We then simplify the anonymity definitions, which in earlier version had been cluttered with numerous oracles the adversary has access to, and for which the intuitive notion that they were formalizing was hard to grasp. While our definitions are simpler, they are stronger in that they imply previous definitions (except for the previous notion of "spend-then-receive (StR) anonymity", whose existing formalizations we argue are not relevant in practice).

We also show that the proof of "StR anonymity" (a notion similar to coin transparency) of the scheme from [BCFK15] is flawed and that it only satisfies a weakening of the notion (Sect. 3.2).

Our Contribution: Instantiation. Our main contribution is a transferable e-cash scheme, which we prove satisfies our security model, and which is more efficient than the only previous realization [BCFK15]. Unfortunately, the authors do not provide concrete numbers, as they use malleable signatures in a black-box way. Arguably, these signatures are the main source of inefficiency, due to their generality and the strong security notions in the spirit of *simulation-sound extractability*, requiring that a coin (i.e., a malleable signature) stores every transformation it has undergone.

In contrast, we give a direct construction from the following primitives: Groth-Sahai proofs [GS08], which are randomizable; structure-preserving signatures [AFG+10], which are compatible with GS proofs; and rerandomizable encryption satisfying RCCA-security [CKN03] (the corresponding variant of CCA security, see Fig. 6). While we use signature schemes from the literature [AGHO11,Fuc11], we construct a new RCCA-secure encryption scheme that is tailored to our scheme, basing it on prior work [LPQ17]. Finally, our scheme also uses the (efficient) double-spending tags used previously [BCFK15].

Due to the existence of an omnipotent "judge", no such tags were required by Blazy et al. [BCF+11]. Interestingly, although we do not assume any active trusted parties, we achieve a comparable efficiency, which is a result of realizing the full potential of the tags: previously [BCFK15], tags had only served to *encode* a user's identity; but, as we show, they can in addition be used to *commit* the user. This allows us, contrary to all previous instantiations, to completely forgo the inclusion of user signatures in the coins, which considerably reduces their size. For a more detailed (informal) overview of our scheme see Sect. 5.1.

In terms of efficiency, our coins grow by around 100 elements from a bilinear group per transfer (see table on p. 28). We view this as practical by current standards, especially in view of numbers for deployed schemes: e.g., the parameters for *Zcash* consist of several 100 000 bilinear-group elements [Zec20].

2   Definition of Transferable E-Cash

The syntax and security definitions we present in the following are refinements of earlier work [CG08,BCF+11,BCFK15].

2.1   Algorithms and Protocols

An e-cash scheme is set up by running ParamGen and the bank generating its key pair via BKeyGen. The bank maintains a list of users $\mathcal{UL}$ and a list of deposited coins $\mathcal{DCL}$. Users run the protocol Register with the bank to obtain their secret key, and their public keys are added to $\mathcal{UL}$. With her secret key a user can run Withdraw with the bank to obtain coins, which she can transfer to others via the protocol Spend.

Spend is also used when a user deposits a coin at the bank. After receiving a coin, the bank runs CheckDS (for "double-spending") on it and the previously deposited coins in $\mathcal{DCL}$, which determines whether to accept the coin. If so, it is added to $\mathcal{DCL}$; if not (in case of double-spending), CheckDS returns the public key of the accused user and a proof Π, which can be verified using VfyGuilt.

ParamGen(1^λ),on input the security parameter λ in unary, outputs public parameters par, which are an implicit input to all of the following algorithms.

BKeyGen() is run by the bank $\mathcal{B}$ and outputs its public key $pk_\mathcal{B}$ and its secret key $sk_\mathcal{B} = (sk_\mathcal{W}, sk_\mathcal{D}, sk_{\mathcal{CK}})$, where $sk_\mathcal{W}$ is used to issue coins in Withdraw and to register users in Register; $sk_\mathcal{D}$ is used as the receiver secret key when coins are deposited via Spend; and $sk_{\mathcal{CK}}$ is used for CheckDS.

Register$\langle \mathcal{B}(sk_\mathcal{W}), \mathcal{U}(pk_\mathcal{B}) \rangle$ is a protocol between the bank and a user. The user obtains a secret key sk and the bank gets pk, which it adds to $\mathcal{UL}$.

Withdraw$\langle \mathcal{B}(sk_\mathcal{W}), \mathcal{U}(sk_\mathcal{U}, pk_\mathcal{B}) \rangle$ is run between the bank and a user, who outputs a coin c (or $\perp$ in case of error), while the bank outputs ok (in which case it debits the user's account) or $\perp$.

Spend$\langle \mathcal{U}(c, sk, pk_\mathcal{B}), \mathcal{U}'(sk', pk_\mathcal{B}) \rangle$ is run between two users and lets $\mathcal{U}$ spend a coin c to $\mathcal{U}'$ (who could be the bank). $\mathcal{U}'$ outputs a coin c' (or $\perp$), while $\mathcal{U}$ outputs ok (or $\perp$).

CheckDS($sk_{\mathcal{CK}}, \mathcal{UL}, \mathcal{DCL}, c$), run by the bank, takes as input its checking key, the lists of registered users $\mathcal{UL}$ and of deposited coins $\mathcal{DCL}$ and a coin c. It outputs an updated list $\mathcal{DCL}$ (when the coin is accepted) or a user public key $pk_\mathcal{U}$ and an incrimination proof Π.

VfyGuilt($pk_\mathcal{U}, \Pi$) can be executed by anyone. It takes a user public key and an incrimination proof and returns 1 (acceptance of Π) or 0 (rejection).

Note that we define a transferable e-cash scheme as stateless, in that there is no state information shared between the algorithms. A withdrawn coin, whether it was the first or the n-th coin issued to a specific user, is always distributed the same. Moreover, a received coin will only depend on the spent coin (and not on other spent or received coins). Thus, the bank and the users need not store anything about past transactions for transfer; the coin itself must be sufficient.

In particular, the bank can separate withdrawing from depositing, in that CheckDS, used during deposit, need not be aware of the withdrawn coins.

2.2 Security Definitions

Global Variables. In our security games, we store all information about users and their keys in the user list $\mathcal{UL}$. Its entries are of the form (pk_i, sk_i, uds_i), where uds_i indicates how many times user $\mathcal{U}_i$ has double-spent.

In the coin list $\mathcal{CL}$, we keep information about the coins created in the system. For each withdrawn or spent coin c, we store a tuple $(owner, c, cds, origin)$, where *owner* stores the index i of the user who withdrew or received the coin (coins obtained by the adversary are not stored); *cds* counts how often this *specific instance* of the coin has been spent; *origin* is set to "$\mathcal{B}$" if the coin was issued by the honest bank and to "$\mathcal{A}$" if it originates from the adversary; if the coin was originally spent by the challenger itself, then *origin* indicates which original coin this transferred coin corresponds to.

Finally, we maintain a list of deposited coins $\mathcal{DCL}$.

Oracles. Our security games use oracles, which differ depending on whether the adversary impersonates a corrupt bank or users. If during the oracle execution an algorithm fails (i.e., it outputs $\perp$) then the oracle also stops. Otherwise the call to the oracle is considered *successful*; a successful deposit oracle call must also not detect any double-spending.

Registration and Corruption of Users. The adversary can instruct the creation of honest users and either play the role of the bank during registration, or passively observe registration. It can moreover "spy" on users, meaning it can learn the user's secret key. This will strengthen yet simplify our anonymity games compared to [BCFK15], where once the adversary had learned the secret key of a user (by "corrupting" her), the user could not be a challenge user in the anonymity games anymore (yielding *selfless anonymity*, while we achieve *full anonymity*).

BRegist() plays the bank side of Register and interacts with $\mathcal{A}$. If successful, it adds $(pk, \perp, uds = 0)$ to $\mathcal{UL}$ (where *uds* is the number of double-spends).

URegist() plays the user side of the Register protocol when the bank is controlled by the adversary. Upon successful execution, it adds $(pk, sk, 0)$ to $\mathcal{UL}$.

Regist() plays both parties in the Register protocol and adds $(pk, sk, 0)$ to $\mathcal{UL}$.

Spy(i), for $i \leq |\mathcal{UL}|$, returns user i's secret key sk_i.

Withdrawal Oracles. The adversary can either withdraw a coin from the bank, play the role of the bank, or passively observe a withdrawal.

BWith() plays the bank side of the Withdraw protocol. Coins withdrawn by $\mathcal{A}$ (and thus unknown to the experiment) are not added to the coin list $\mathcal{CL}$.

UWith(i) plays user i in Withdraw when the bank is controlled by the adversary. Upon obtaining a coin c, it adds $(owner = i, c, cds = 0, origin = \mathcal{A})$ to $\mathcal{CL}$.

With(i) simulates a Withdraw protocol execution playing both $\mathcal{B}$ and user i. It adds $(owner = i, c, cds = 0, origin = \mathcal{B})$ to $\mathcal{CL}$.

Spend and deposit oracles.

Spd(j) spends the coin from the j-th entry $(owner_j, c_j, cds_j, origin_j)$ in $\mathcal{CL}$ to $\mathcal{A}$, who could be impersonating a user, or the bank during a deposit. The oracle plays $\mathcal{U}$ in the Spend protocol with secret key sk_{owner_j}. It increments the coin spend counter cds_j by 1. If afterwards $cds_j > 1$ then the owner's double-spending counter uds_{owner_j} is incremented by 1.

Expt$_{\mathcal{A}}^{\text{sound}}$ (λ):

> $par \leftarrow \mathsf{ParamGen}(1^{\lambda}); \quad pk_{\mathcal{B}} \leftarrow \mathcal{A}(par)$
> $(b, i_1, i_2) \leftarrow \mathcal{A}^{\mathtt{URegist},\mathtt{Spy}}$
> If $b = 0$ then run $\mathtt{UWith}(i_1)$ with $\mathcal{A}$
> Else run $\mathtt{Rcv}(i_1)$ with $\mathcal{A}$
> If this outputs $\bot$ then return 0
> Run $\mathtt{S\&R}(1, i_2)$; if one party outputs $\bot$ then return 1 and 0 otherwise

Fig. 1. Game for *soundness* (protecting users from financial loss)

$\mathtt{Rcv}(i)$ makes honest user i receive a coin from $\mathcal{A}$. The oracle plays $\mathcal{U}'$ in the Spend protocol with user i's secret key. It adds a new entry $(owner = i, c, cds = 0, origin = \mathcal{A})$ to $\mathcal{CL}$.

$\mathtt{S\&R}(j, i)$ spends the j-th coin in $\mathcal{CL}$ to user i. It runs $(ok, c) \leftarrow \mathsf{Spend}\langle\mathcal{U}(c_j, sk_{owner_j}, pk_{\mathcal{B}}), \mathcal{U}'(sk_i, pk_{\mathcal{B}})\rangle$ and adds $(owner = i, c, cds = 0, origin = j)$ to $\mathcal{CL}$. It increments the coin spend counter cds_j by 1. If afterwards $cds_j > 1$, then uds_{owner_j} is incremented by 1.

$\mathtt{BDepo}()$ lets $\mathcal{A}$ deposit a coin. It runs $\mathcal{U}'$ in Spend using the bank's secret key $sk_{\mathcal{D}}$ with the adversary playing $\mathcal{U}$. If successful, it runs CheckDS on the received coin and either updates $\mathcal{DCL}$ or returns a pair (pk, Π).

$\mathtt{Depo}(j)$, the honest deposit oracle, runs Spend between the owner of the j-th coin in $\mathcal{CL}$ and an honest bank. If successful, it increments cds_j by 1; if afterwards $cds_j > 1$, it also increments uds_{owner_j}. It runs CheckDS on the received coin and either updates $\mathcal{DCL}$ or returns a pair (pk, Π).

(No "UDepo" is needed since Spd lets user deposit at an adversarial bank.)

2.3   Economic Properties

We distinguish two types of security properties of transferable e-cash schemes. Besides anonymity notions, economic properties ensure that neither the bank nor users will incur an economic loss when participating in the system.

The following property was not required in any previous formalization of transferable e-cash in the literature and is analogous the property *clearing* defined for classical e-cash [BPS19].

Soundness. If an honest user accepted a coin during a withdrawal or a transfer, then she is guaranteed that the coin will be accepted by others, either honest users when transferring, or the bank when depositing. The game is formalized in Fig. 1 where i_2 plays the role of the receiver of a spending or the bank. For convenience, we define probabilistic polynomial-time (PPT) adversaries $\mathcal{A}$ to be stateful in all our security games.

Definition 1 (Soundness). *A transferable e-cash system is* sound *if for any PPT $\mathcal{A}$, we have* $\mathbf{Adv}_{\mathcal{A}}^{\text{sound}}(\lambda) := \Pr[\mathbf{Expt}_{\mathcal{A}}^{\text{sound}}(\lambda) = 1]$ *is negligible in λ.*

Unforgeability. This notion covers both *unforgeability* and *user identification* from [BCFK15] (which were not consistent as we explain in Sect. 3.2). It protects the bank, ensuring that no (coalition of) users can spend more coins than the number of coins they withdrew. Unforgeability also guarantees that whenever a coin is deposited and refused by CheckDS, it returns the identity of a registered user, who is accused of double-spending. (*Exculpability*, below, ensures that no innocent user will be accused.) The game is given in Fig. 2 and lets the adversary impersonate all users.

$\mathbf{Expt}_{\mathcal{A}}^{\mathrm{unforg}}(\lambda)$:
    $par \leftarrow \mathsf{ParamGen}(1^\lambda);\ (sk_\mathcal{B}, pk_\mathcal{B}) \leftarrow \mathsf{BKeyGen}(par)$
    $\mathcal{A}^{\mathtt{BRegist},\mathtt{BWith},\mathtt{BDepo}}\ (par, pk_\mathcal{B})$
    If in a BDepo call, CheckDS does not return a coin list:
        Return 1 if any of the following hold:
            – CheckDS outputs $\perp$
            – CheckDS outputs (pk, Π) and VfyGuilt $(pk, \Pi) = 0$
            – CheckDS outputs (pk, Π) and $pk \notin \mathcal{UL}$
    Let q_W be the number of calls to BWith
    If $q_W < |\mathcal{DCL}|$, then return 1 and 0 otherwise

Fig. 2. Game for *unforgeability* (protecting the bank from financial loss)

Definition 2 (Unforgeability). *A transferable e-cash system is* unforgeable *if* $\mathbf{Adv}_{\mathcal{A}}^{\mathrm{unforg}}(\lambda) := \Pr[\mathbf{Expt}_{\mathcal{A}}^{\mathrm{unforg}}(\lambda) = 1]$ *is negligible in λ for any PPT $\mathcal{A}$.*

Exculpability. This notion, a.k.a. *non-frameability*, ensures that the bank, even when colluding with malicious users, cannot wrongly accuse an honest user of double-spending. Specifically, it guarantees that an adversarial bank cannot produce a double-spending proof Π^* that verifies for the public key of a user i^* that has never double-spent. The game is formalized as in Fig. 3.

$\mathbf{Expt}_{\mathcal{A}}^{\mathrm{excul}}(\lambda)$:
    $par \leftarrow \mathsf{ParamGen}(1^\lambda);\ pk_\mathcal{B} \leftarrow \mathcal{A}(par)$
    $(i^*, \Pi^*) \leftarrow \mathcal{A}^{\mathtt{URegist},\mathtt{Spy},\mathtt{UWith},\mathtt{Rcv},\mathtt{Spd},\mathtt{S\&R},\mathtt{UDepo}}\ (par)$
    Return 1 if **all** of the following hold (and 0 otherwise):
        – VfyGuilt$(pk_{i^*}, \Pi^*) = 1$
        – There was no call Spy(i^*)
        – $uds_{i^*} = 0$

Fig. 3. Game for *exculpability* (protecting honest users from accusation)

Definition 3 (Exculpability). *A transferable e-cash system is* exculpable *if* $\mathbf{Adv}_{\mathcal{A}}^{\mathrm{excul}}(\lambda) := \Pr[\mathbf{Expt}_{\mathcal{A}}^{\mathrm{excul}}(\lambda) = 1]$ *is negligible in λ for any PPT $\mathcal{A}$.*

2.4 Anonymity Properties

Instead of following previous anonymity notions [BCF+11, BCFK15], we introduce new ones which clearly distinguish between the adversary's capabilities; in particular, whether or not it is able to detect double-spending. When the adversary impersonates the bank, we consider two cases: user anonymity and coin anonymity (and explain why this distinction is necessary).

As transferred coins necessarily grow in size [CP93], we can only guarantee indistinguishability of *comparable* coins. We therefore define $\mathsf{comp}(c_1, c_2) = 1$ iff $\mathsf{size}\,(c_1) = \mathsf{size}\,(c_2)$, where $\mathsf{size}(c) = 1$ after c was withdrawn and it increases by 1 after each transfer.

Coin Anonymity. This notion is closest to (and implies) the anonymity notion of classical e-cash: an adversary, who also impersonates the bank, issues two coins to the challenger and when she later receives them (via a deposit in classical e-cash), she should not be able to associate them to their issuances. In transferable e-cash, we allow the adversary to determine two series of honest users via which the coins are respectively transferred before being given back to the adversary.

The experiment is specified on the left of Fig. 4: users $i_0^{(0)}$ and $i_0^{(1)}$ withdraw a coin from the adversarial bank, user $i_0^{(0)}$ passes it to $i_1^{(0)}$, who passes it to $i_2^{(0)}$, etc., In the end, the last users of the two chains spend the coins to the adversary, but the order in which this happens depends on a bit b that parametrizes the game, and which the adversary must decide.

Expt$_{\mathcal{A},b}^{\text{c-an}}(\lambda)$:
   $par \leftarrow \mathsf{ParamGen}(1^\lambda)$
   $pk_{\mathcal{B}} \leftarrow \mathcal{A}(par)$
   $i_0^{(0)} \leftarrow \mathcal{A}^{\text{URegist,Spy}};$ run $\mathsf{UWith}(i_0^{(0)})$ with $\mathcal{A}$
   $i_0^{(1)} \leftarrow \mathcal{A}^{\text{URegist,Spy}};$ run $\mathsf{UWith}(i_0^{(1)})$ with $\mathcal{A}$
   $\left((i_1^{(0)}, \ldots, i_{k_0}^{(0)}), (i_1^{(1)}, \ldots, i_{k_1}^{(1)})\right)$
                     $\leftarrow \mathcal{A}^{\text{URegist,Spy}}$
   If $k_0 \neq k_1$ then return 0
   For $j = 1, \ldots, k_0$:
      Run $\mathsf{S\&R}(2j - 1, i_j^{(0)})$
      Run $\mathsf{S\&R}(2j, i_j^{(1)})$
   Run $\mathsf{Spd}(2k_0 + 1 + b)$ with $\mathcal{A}$
   Run $\mathsf{Spd}(2k_0 + 2 - b)$ with $\mathcal{A}$
   $b^* \leftarrow \mathcal{A}$; return b^*

Expt$_{\mathcal{A},b}^{\text{u-an}}(\lambda)$:
   $par \leftarrow \mathsf{ParamGen}(1^\lambda)$
   $pk_{\mathcal{B}} \leftarrow \mathcal{A}\,(par)$
   $(i_0^{(0)}, i_0^{(1)}) \leftarrow \mathcal{A}^{\text{URegist,Spy}}$
   Run $\mathsf{Rcv}(i_b)$ with $\mathcal{A}$
   $\left((i_1^{(0)}, \ldots, i_{k_0}^{(0)}), (i_1^{(1)}, \ldots, i_{k_1}^{(1)})\right)$
                     $\leftarrow \mathcal{A}^{\text{URegist,Spy}}$
   If $k_0 \neq k_1$ then return 0
   For $j = 1, \ldots, k_0$:
      Run $\mathsf{S\&R}(j, i_j^{(b)})$
   Run $\mathsf{Spd}(k_0 + 1)$ with $\mathcal{A}$
   $b^* \leftarrow \mathcal{A}$; return b^*

Fig. 4. Games for *coin* and *user anonymity* (protecting users from a malicious bank)

User Anonymity. Coin anonymity required that users who transfer the coin are honest. If one of the users through which the coin passes colluded with the bank, there would be a trivial attack: after receiving the two challenge coins, the bank simulates the deposit of one of them and the deposit of the coin intercepted by the colluding user. If a double-spending is detected, it knows that the received coin corresponds to the sequence of users which the colluder was part of.

Since double-spending detection is an essential feature of e-cash, attacks of this kind are impossible to prevent. However, we still want to guarantee that, while the bank can trace coins, the involved *users* remain anonymous. We formalize this in the game on the right of Fig. 4, where, in contrast to coin anonymity, there is only one coin and the adversary must distinguish the sequence of users through which the coin passes before returning to her. In contrast to coin anonymity, we now allow the coin to already have some "history", rather than being freshly withdrawn.

Expt$_{A,b}^{c\text{-tr}}(\lambda)$:

$par \leftarrow \mathsf{ParamGen}(1^\lambda)$; $((sk_\mathcal{W}, sk_\mathcal{D}, sk_{C\mathcal{K}}), pk_\mathcal{B}) \leftarrow \mathsf{BKeyGen}(par)$
$\mathcal{DCL}' \leftarrow \emptyset$ // *lists the challenge coins*
$ctr \leftarrow 0$ // *counts how often a challenge coin was deposited*
$i^{(0)} \leftarrow A^{\mathsf{URegist}, \mathsf{BDepo}', \mathsf{Spy}}(par, pk_\mathcal{B}, sk_\mathcal{W}, sk_\mathcal{D})$
         // *BDepo' uses* $\mathsf{CheckDS}'(\cdot, \cdot, \cdot, \cdot, \mathcal{DCL}')$ *(see below) instead of* $\mathsf{CheckDS}$
Run $\mathsf{Rcv}(i^{(0)})$ with A; let c_0 be the received coin stored in $\mathcal{CL}[1]$
$x_0 \leftarrow \mathsf{CheckDS}(sk_{C\mathcal{K}}, \emptyset, \mathcal{CL}, c_0)$
If $x_0 = \perp$ then $ctr \leftarrow ctr + 1$ // c_0 *had been deposited*
$\mathcal{DCL}' \leftarrow \mathsf{CheckDS}(sk_{C\mathcal{K}}, \emptyset, \emptyset, c_0)$ // *add* c_0 *to list of challenge coins*
$i^{(1)} \leftarrow A^{\mathsf{URegist}, \mathsf{BDepo}, \mathsf{Spy}}$
Run $\mathsf{Rcv}(i^{(1)})$ with A; let c_1 be the received coin stored in $\mathcal{CL}[2]$
$x_1 \leftarrow \mathsf{CheckDS}(sk_{C\mathcal{K}}, \emptyset, \mathcal{CL}, c_1)$
If $x_1 = \perp$ then $ctr \leftarrow ctr + 1$ // c_1 *had been deposited*
If $\mathsf{comp}(c_0, c_1) \neq 1$ then abort
$x_2 \leftarrow \mathsf{CheckDS}(sk_{C\mathcal{K}}, \emptyset, \mathcal{DCL}', c_1)$ // *add* c_1 *to list of challenge coins*
If $x_2 \neq \perp$ then $\mathcal{DCL}' \leftarrow x_2$ // (c_1 *could be a double-spending of* c_0)
$((i_1^{(0)}, \ldots, i_{k_0}^{(0)}), (i_1^{(1)}, \ldots, i_{k_1}^{(1)})) \leftarrow A^{\mathsf{URegist}, \mathsf{BDepo}', \mathsf{Spy}}$
If $k_0 \neq k_1$ then abort
If $(k_b \neq 0)$ then run $\mathsf{S\&R}(b+1, i_1^{(b)})$ // *spend coin* c_b *to user* $i_1^{(b)}$...
For $j = 2, \ldots, k_0$:   // ... *the received coin is placed in* $\mathcal{CL}[3]$
         Run $\mathsf{S\&R}(j+1, i_j^{(b)})$ // *spend coins consecutively*
Run $\mathsf{Spd}(k_0 + 2)$ with A // *and transfer it back to* A
$b^* \leftarrow A^{\mathsf{BDepo}'}$; return b^*

$\mathsf{CheckDS}'(sk_{C\mathcal{K}}, \mathcal{UL}, \mathcal{DCL}, c, \mathcal{DCL}')$:   // *used by* BDepo'
$x \leftarrow \mathsf{CheckDS}(sk_{C\mathcal{K}}, \emptyset, \mathcal{DCL}', c)$
If $x = \perp$:   // *the deposited coin* c *is a double-spending of* c_0 *or* c_1
         $ctr \leftarrow ctr + 1$
         If $ctr > 1$ then abort
Output $\mathsf{CheckDS}(sk_{C\mathcal{K}}, \emptyset, \mathcal{DCL}, c)$

Fig. 5. Game for *coin transparency* (protecting users from malicious users)

Coin Transparency. This is arguably the strongest anonymity notion and it implies that a user that transfers a coin cannot recognize it if she receives it again. As the bank can necessarily trace coins (for double-spending detection), it is assumed to be honest for this notion. Actually, only the detection key $sk_{\mathcal{CK}}$ must remain hidden from the adversary, while $sk_{\mathcal{W}}$ and $sk_{\mathcal{D}}$ can be given.

The game formalizing this notion, specified in Fig. 5, is analogous to coin anonymity, except that the challenge coins are not freshly withdrawn; instead, the adversary spends two coins of its choice to users of its choice, both are passed through a sequence of users of the adversary's choice and one of them is returned to the adversary.

There is another trivial attack that we need to exclude: the adversary could deposit the coin that is returned to him and one, say the first, of the coins he initially transferred to an honest user. Now if the deposit does not succeed because of double-spending, the adversary knows that it was the first coin that was returned to him. Again, this attack is unavoidable due to the necessity of double-spending detection. It is a design choice that lies outside of our model to implement sufficient deterrence from double-spending, so that it would exceed the utility of breaking anonymity.

This is the reason why the game aborts if the adversary deposits twice a coin from the set of "challenge coins" (consisting of the two coins the adversary transfers and the one it receives). The variable ctr counts how often a coin from this set was deposited. Note also that because $\mathcal{A}$ has $sk_{\mathcal{W}}$, and can therefore create unregistered users, we do not consider $\mathcal{UL}$ in this game.

Definition 4 (Anonymity). *For* $x \in \{c - an, u - an, c - tr\}$ *a transferable e-cash scheme satisfies* x *if* $\mathbf{Adv}_{\mathcal{A}}^{x}(\lambda) := \Pr[\mathbf{Expt}_{\mathcal{A},1}^{x}(\lambda) = 1] - \Pr[\mathbf{Expt}_{\mathcal{A},0}^{x}(\lambda) = 1]$ *is negligible in* λ *for any PPT adversary* $\mathcal{A}$.

3   Comparison with Previous Work

3.1   Model Comparison

In order to justify our new model, we start with discussing a security vulnerability of the previous model [BCFK15].

No Soundness Guarantees. In none of the previous models was there a security notion that guaranteed that an honest user could successfully transfer a coin to another honest user or the bank, even if the coin was obtained regularly.

Fuzzy Definition of "Unsuccessful Deposit". Previous models defined a protocol called "Deposit", which we separated into an interactive (Spend) and a static part (CheckDS). In their definition of unforgeability, the authors [BCFK15] use the concept of "successful deposit", whose meaning is unclear, since an "unsuccessful deposit" could mean one of the following:

- The bank detects a double-spending and provides a proof accusing the cheater (who could be different from the depositer).

- The user did not follow the protocol (e.g., by sending a malformed coin), in which case we cannot expect a proof of guilt from the bank.
- The user followed the protocol but using a coin that was double-spent (either earlier or during deposit); however, the bank does not obtain a valid proof of guilt and outputs $\perp$.

Our interpretation of the definition in [BCFK15] is that it does not distinguish the second and the third case. This is an issue, as the second case cannot be avoided (and must be dealt with outside the model, e.g. by having users sign their messages). But the third case *should* be prevented so the bank does not lose money without being able to accuse the cheater. This is now guaranteed by our unforgeability notion in Definition 2.

Simplification of Anonymity Definitions. We believe that our notions are more intuitive and simpler (e.g. by reducing the number of oracles of previous work). Our notions imply prior notions from the literature: we can prove that the existence of an adversary in a game from a prior notion implies the existence of an adversary in one of our games. (The general idea is to simulate most of the oracles using the secret keys of the bank or users, which in our notions can be obtained via the Spy oracle.) In particular:

$$\text{c-an} \Rightarrow \text{OtR-fa} \qquad \text{and} \qquad \text{u-an} \Rightarrow \text{StR*-fa}$$

where OtR-fa is *observe-then-receive full anonymity* [CG08, BCF+11, BCFK15] and StR*-fa is a variant of *spend-then-receive full anonymity* from [BCFK15].

The notion StR-fa [CG08, BCF+11] is similar to our coin transparency c-tr, with the following differences: in StR-fa, when the adversary deposits a coin, the bank provides a guilt proof when it can; and it lets the adversary obtain user secret keys. Coin transparency would imply StR-fa if CheckDS replaced its argument $\mathcal{UL}$ by $\emptyset$. This change is justified since (in both StR-fa and c-tr) the adversary can create unregistered users (using $sk_{\mathcal{W}}$), and thus CheckDS could return $\perp$ because it cannot accuse anyone in $\mathcal{UL}$.

Finally, no prior scheme, including [BCFK15], achieves StR-fa, as shown next.

3.2 A Flaw in a Proof in BCFK15

The authors [BCFK15] claim that their scheme satisfies StR-fa as defined in [BCF+11] (after having discovered a flaw in the StR-fa proof of the scheme of that paper). To achieve this anonymity notion (the most difficult one, as they note), they use malleable signatures, which guarantee that whenever an adversary, after obtaining *simulated* signatures, outputs a valid message/signature pair (m, σ), it must have derived the pair from received signatures. Formally, there exists an extractor that can extract a transformation from σ that links m to the messages on which the adversary queried signatures.

In the game formalizing StR-fa [BCF+11] (analogously to $\textbf{Expt}^{\text{c-tr}}$ in Fig. 5) the adversary receives $sk_{\mathcal{W}}$, which formalizes the notion that the part of the bank that issues coins can be corrupt. In their scheme [BCFK15], $sk_\mathcal{W}$ contains the signing key for the malleable signatures. However, with this the adversary can easily compute a *fresh* signature, and thus no extractor can recover a transformation explaining the signed message. This shows that a scheme based on malleable signatures only satisfies a weaker notion of StR-fa/c-tr, where all parts of the bank must be honest.

In contrast, we prove that our scheme satisfies c-tr; it can therefore be seen as the first scheme to satisfy the "spirit" of StR-fa, as captured by c-tr.

4   Primitives Used in Our Construction

4.1   Bilinear Groups

The building blocks of our scheme will be defined over a (Type-3, i.e., "asymmetric") bilinear group, which is a tuple $Gr = (p, \mathbb{G}, \hat{\mathbb{G}}, \mathbb{G}_T, e, g, \hat{g})$, where $\mathbb{G}, \hat{\mathbb{G}}$ and $\mathbb{G}_T$ are groups of prime order p; $\langle g \rangle = \mathbb{G}$, $\langle \hat{g} \rangle = \hat{\mathbb{G}}$, and $e \colon \mathbb{G} \times \hat{\mathbb{G}} \to \mathbb{G}_T$ is a bilinear map (i.e., for all $a, b \in \mathbb{Z}_p$: $e(g^a, \hat{g}^b) = e(g, \hat{g})^{ab}$) so that $e(g, \hat{g})$ generates $\mathbb{G}_T$. We assume that the groups are discrete-log-hard and other computational assumptions, such as SXDH, defined in the full version [BFQ20], hold as well. We assume that there exists an algorithm GrGen that, on input the security parameter λ in unary, outputs the description of a bilinear group with $p \geq 2^{\lambda-1}$.

4.2   Randomizable Proofs of Knowledge and Signatures

Commit-and-Prove Proof Systems. As coins must be unforgeable, at their core lie digital signatures. To achieve anonymity, these must be hidden, which can be achieved via non-interactive zero-knowledge (NIZK) proofs of knowledge; if these proofs are *re-randomizable*, then they can not even be recognized by a past owner. We will use Groth-Sahai NIZK proofs [GS08], which are randomizable [FP09, BCC+09] and include commitments to the witnesses.

We let $\mathcal{V}$ be set of values that can be committed, $\mathcal{C}$ be the set of commitments, $\mathcal{R}$ the randomness space and $\mathcal{E}$ the set of equations (containing equality) whose satisfiability can be proved. We assume that $\mathcal{V}$ and $\mathcal{R}$ are groups. We will use an extractable commitment scheme, which consists of the following algorithms:

C.Setup(Gr) takes as input a description of a bilinear group and returns a commitment key ck, which implicitly defines the sets $\mathcal{V}, \mathcal{C}, \mathcal{R}$ and $\mathcal{E}$.

C.ExSetup(Gr) returns an extraction key xk in addition to a commitment key ck.

C.SmSetup(Gr) returns a commitment key ck and a simulation trapdoor td.

C.Cm(ck, v, ρ), on input a key ck, a value $v \in \mathcal{V}$ and randomness $\rho \in \mathcal{R}$, returns a commitment in $\mathcal{C}$.

C.ZCm(ck, ρ), used when simulating proofs, is defined as C.Cm($ck, 0_\mathcal{V}, \rho$).

C.RdCm(ck, c, ρ) randomizes a commitment c to a fresh c' using randomness ρ.

C.Extr(xk, c), on input extraction key xk and a commitment c, outputs a value in $\mathcal{V}$. (This is the only algorithm that might not be polynomial-time.)

We extend C.Cm to vectors in $\mathcal{V}^n$: for $M = (v_1, \ldots, v_n)$ and $\rho = (\rho_1, \ldots, \rho_n)$ we define $\mathsf{C.Cm}(ck, M, \rho) := \big(\mathsf{C.Cm}(ck, v_1, \rho_1), \ldots, \mathsf{C.Cm}(ck, v_n, \rho_n)\big)$ and likewise $\mathsf{C.Extr}(xk, (c_1, \ldots, c_n)) := \big(\mathsf{C.Extr}(xk, c_1), \ldots, \mathsf{C.Extr}(xk, c_n)\big)$.

We now define a NIZK proof system that proves that committed values satisfy given equations from $\mathcal{E}$. Given a proof for commitments, the proof can be adapted to a randomization (via C.RdCm) of the commitments using C.AdptPrf.

$\mathsf{C.Prv}(ck, E, (v_1, \rho_1), \ldots, (v_n, \rho_n))$, on input a key ck, a set of equations $E \subset \mathcal{E}$, values $(v_1, \ldots, v_n)$ and randomness $(\rho_1, \ldots, \rho_n)$, outputs a proof π.

$\mathsf{C.Verify}(ck, E, c_1, \ldots, c_n, \pi)$, on input a commitment key ck, a set of equations in $\mathcal{E}$, a commitment vector $(c_1, \ldots, c_n)$, and a proof π, outputs a bit b.

$\mathsf{C.AdptPrf}(ck, E, c_1, \rho_1, \ldots, c_n, \rho_n, \pi)$, on input a set of equations, commitments $(c_1, \ldots, c_n)$, randomness $(\rho_1, \ldots, \rho_n)$ and a proof π, outputs a proof π'.

$\mathsf{C.SmPrv}(td, E, \rho_1, \ldots, \rho_n)$, on input the simulation trapdoor, a set of equations E with n variables and randomness $(\rho_1, \ldots, \rho_n)$, outputs a proof π.

$\mathcal{M}$-Structure-Preserving Signatures. To prove knowledge of signatures, we require a scheme that is compatible with Groth-Sahai proofs [AFG+10].

$\mathsf{S.Setup}(Gr)$, on input the bilinear group description, outputs signature parameters par_S, defining a message space $\mathcal{M}$. We require $\mathcal{M} \subseteq \mathcal{V}^n$ for some n.

$\mathsf{S.KeyGen}(par_S)$, on input the parameters par_S, outputs a signing key and a verification key (sk, vk). We require that vk is composed of values in $\mathcal{V}$.

$\mathsf{S.Sign}(sk, M)$, on input a signing key sk and a message $M \in \mathcal{M}$, outputs a signature Σ. We require that Σ is composed of values in $\mathcal{V}$.

$\mathsf{S.Verify}(vk, M, \Sigma)$, on input a verification key vk, a message M and a signature Σ, outputs a bit b. We require that S.Verify proceeds by evaluating equations from $\mathcal{E}$ (which we denote by $E_{\mathsf{S.Verify}(\cdot, \cdot, \cdot)}$).

$\mathcal{M}$-Commuting Signatures. As in a previous construction of transferable e-cash [BCF+11], we will use commuting signatures [Fuc11], which let the signer, given a commitment to a message, produce a commitment to a signature on that message, together with a proof, via the following functionality:

$\mathsf{SigCm}(ck, sk, c)$, given a signing key sk and a commitment c of a message $M \in \mathcal{M}$, outputs a committed signature c_Σ and a proof π that the signature in c_Σ is valid on the value in c, i.e., the committed values satisfy $\mathsf{S.Verify}(vk, \cdot, \cdot)$.

$\mathsf{SmSigCm}(xk, vk, c, \Sigma)$, on input the extraction key xk, a verification key vk, a commitment c and a signature Σ, outputs a committed signature c_Σ and a proof π of validity for c_Σ and c (the key xk is needed to compute π for c).

Correctness and Soundness Properties. We require the following properties of commitments, proofs and signatures, when the setup algorithms are run on any output $Gr \leftarrow \mathsf{GrGen}(1^\lambda)$ for any $\lambda \in \mathbb{N}$:

Perfectly binding commitments: C.Setup and the first output of C.ExSetup are distributed equivalently. Let $(ck, xk) \leftarrow \mathsf{C.ExSetup}$; then for every $c \in \mathcal{C}$ there exists exactly one $v \in \mathcal{V}$ such that $c = \mathsf{C.Cm}(ck, v, \rho)$ for some $\rho \in \mathcal{R}$. Moreover, $\mathsf{C.Extr}(xk, c)$ extracts that value v.

$\mathcal{V}'$-*extractability:* Committed values from a subset $\mathcal{V}' \subset \mathcal{V}$ can be efficiently extracted (e.g., $\mathcal{V}' = \mathbb{G}_1 \cup \mathbb{G}_2$ [GS08]). Let $(ck, xk) \leftarrow$ C.ExSetup; then C.Extr$(xk, \cdot)$ is efficient for all $c =$ C.Cm(ck, v, ρ) for any $v \in \mathcal{V}'$ and $\rho \in \mathcal{R}$.

Proof completeness: Let $ck \leftarrow$ C.Setup; then for all $(v_1, \ldots, v_n) \in \mathcal{V}^n$ satisfying $E \subset \mathcal{E}$, and $(\rho_1, \ldots, \rho_n) \in \mathcal{R}^n$ and $\pi \leftarrow$ C.Prv$(ck, E, (v_1, \rho_1), \ldots, (v_n, \rho_n))$ we have C.Verify$(ck, E,$ C.Cm$(ck, v_1, \rho_1), \ldots,$ C.Cm$(ck, v_n, \rho_n), \pi) = 1$.

Proof (knowledge) soundness: Let $(ck, xk) \leftarrow$ C.ExSetup, $E \subset \mathcal{E}$, $(c_1, \ldots, c_n) \in \mathcal{C}^n$. If C.Verify$(ck, E, c_1, \ldots, c_n, \pi) = 1$ for some π, then letting $v_i :=$ C.Extr(xk, c_i), for all i, we have that $(v_1, \ldots, v_n)$ satisfy E.

Randomizability: Let $ck \leftarrow$ C.Setup and $E \subset \mathcal{E}$; for all $(v_1, \ldots, v_n) \in \mathcal{V}^n$ satisfying E, and $\rho_1, \rho_1', \ldots, \rho_n, \rho_n' \in \mathcal{R}$ the following are distributed equivalently:

$$\Big(\text{C.RdCm}(\text{C.Cm}(ck, v_1, \rho_1), \rho_1'), \ldots, \text{C.RdCm}(\text{C.Cm}(ck, v_n, \rho_n), \rho_n'),$$
$$\text{C.AdptPrf}\big(ck, E, \text{C.Cm}(ck, v_1, \rho_1), \rho_1', \ldots, \text{C.Cm}(ck, v_n, \rho_n), \rho_n',$$
$$\text{C.Prv}(ck, E, (v_1, \rho_1), \ldots, (v_n, \rho_n)))\Big) \text{ and}$$

$$\Big(\text{C.Cm}(ck, v_1, \rho_1 + \rho_1'), \ldots, \text{C.Cm}(ck, v_n, \rho_n + \rho_n'),$$
$$\text{C.Prv}(ck, E, (v_1, \rho_1 + \rho_1'), \ldots, (v_n, \rho_n + \rho_n')))\Big)$$

Signature correctness: Let $(sk, vk) \leftarrow$ S.KeyGen(S.Setup) and $M \in \mathcal{M}$; then we have S.Verify$(vk, M,$ S.Sign$(sk, M)) = 1$.

Correctness of signing committed messages: Let $(ck, xk) \leftarrow$ C.ExSetup and let $(sk, vk) \leftarrow$ S.KeyGen(S.Setup), and $M \in \mathcal{M}$; for $\rho, \rho' \xleftarrow{\$} \mathcal{R}$, the following three are distributed equivalently:

$$\big(\text{C.Cm}(ck, \text{S.Sign}(sk, M), \rho'),\ \text{C.Prv}\big(ck, E_{\text{S.Verify}(vk, \cdot, \cdot)}, (M, \rho), (\Sigma, \rho'))\big) \text{ and}$$
$$\text{SigCm}\big(ck, sk, \text{C.Cm}(ck, M, \rho)\big) \ \text{andSmSigCm}\big(xk, vk, \text{C.Cm}(ck, M, \rho), \text{S.Sign}(sk, M)\big)$$

The first equivalence also holds for $ck \leftarrow$ C.Setup, since it is distributed like ck output by C.ExSetup.

Security Properties

Mode indistinguishability: Let $Gr \leftarrow$ GrGen(1^λ); then the outputs of C.Setup(Gr) and the first output of C.SmSetup(Gr) are computationally indistinguishable.

Perfect zero-knowledge in hiding mode: Let $(ck, td) \leftarrow$ C.SmSetup(Gr), $E \subset \mathcal{E}$ and $v_1, \ldots, v_n \in \mathcal{V}$ such that $E(v_1, \ldots, v_n) = 1$. For $\rho_1, \ldots, \rho_n \xleftarrow{\$} \mathcal{R}$ the following are distributed equivalently:

$$\big(\text{C.Cm}(ck, v_1, \rho_1), \ldots, \text{C.Cm}(ck, v_n, \rho_n), \text{C.Prv}\big(ck, E, (v_1, \rho_1), \ldots, (v_n, \rho_n))\big)$$
$$\text{and } \big(\text{C.ZCm}(ck, \rho_1), \ldots, \text{C.ZCm}(ck, \rho_n), \text{C.SmPrv}\big(td, E, \rho_1, \ldots, \rho_n)\big)$$

Signature unforgeability (under chosen message attack): No PPT adversary that is given vk output by S.KeyGen and an oracle for adaptive signing queries on messages $M_1, M_2, \ldots$ of its choice can output a pair (M, Σ), such that S.Verify$(vk, M, \Sigma) = 1$ and $M \notin \{M_1, M_2, \ldots\}$.

4.3   Rerandomizable Encryption Schemes

In order to trace double-spenders, some information must be retrievable from the coin by the bank. For anonymity, we encrypt this information. Since coins must change appearance in order to achieve coin transparency (Definition 4), we use rerandomizable encryption. We will prove consistency of encrypted messages with values used elsewhere, and to produce such a proof, knowledge of *parts* of the randomness is required; we therefore make this an explicit input of some algorithms, which thus are still probabilistic.

A rerandomizable encryption scheme E consists of four algorithms:

E.KeyGen(Gr), on input the group description, outputs an encryption key ek and
    a corresponding decryption key dk.

E.Enc(ek, M, ν) is probabilistic and on input an encryption key ek, a message M
    and (partial) randomness ν outputs a ciphertext.

E.ReRand(ek, C, ν'), on input an encryption key, a ciphertext and (partial) ran-
    domness, outputs a new ciphertext.

E.Dec(dk, C), on input a decryption key and a ciphertext, outputs either a mes-
    sage or $\bot$ indicating an error.

To prove statements about encrypted messages, we add two functionalities: E.Verify lets one check that a ciphertext encrypts a given message M, for which it is also given partial randomness ν. This will allow us to prove that a commit-ment c_M and a ciphertext C contain the same message. For this, we require that the equations defining E.Verify are in the set $\mathcal{E}$ supported by C.Prv.

This lets us define an equality proof $\tilde{\pi} = (\pi, c_\nu)$, where c_ν is a commitment to the randomness ν, and π proves that the values in c_M and c_ν verify the equa-tions E.Verify$(ek, \cdot, \cdot, C)$. To support rerandomization of ciphertexts, we define a functionality E.AdptPrf, which adapts a proof (π, c_ν) to a rerandomization.

E.Verify(ek, M, ν, C), on input an encryption key, a message, randomness and a
    ciphertext, outputs a bit.

E.AdptPrf$(ck, ek, c_M, C, \tilde{\pi} = (\pi, c_\nu), \nu')$, a probabilistic algorithm which, on input
    keys, a commitment, a ciphertext, an equality proof (i.e., a proof and a
    commitment) and randomness, outputs a new equality proof (π', c_ν').

Correctness Properties. We require the scheme to satisfy the following correctness properties for all key pairs $(ek, dk) \leftarrow$ E.KeyGen(Gr) for $Gr \leftarrow$ GrGen(1^λ):

– For all $M \in \mathcal{M}$ and randomness ν we have: E.Enc$(ek, M, \nu) = C$ if and only
   if E.Verify$(ek, M, \nu, C) = 1$.
– For all $M \in \mathcal{M}$ and ν: E.Verify$(ek, M, \nu, C) = 1$ implies E.Dec$(dk, C) = M$.
   (These two notions imply the standard correctness notion.)
– For all $M \in \mathcal{M}$ and randomness ν, ν', if $C \leftarrow$ E.Enc(ek, M, ν) then the fol-
   lowing are equally distributed: E.ReRand(ek, C, ν') and E.Enc$(ek, M, \nu + \nu')$.

- For all $ck \leftarrow$ C.Setup, all $(ek, dk) \leftarrow$ E.KeyGen, $M \in \mathcal{M}$ and randomness $\nu, \nu', \rho_M, \rho_\nu$, if we let

$$c_M \leftarrow \mathsf{C.Cm}(ck, M, \rho_M) \quad C \leftarrow \mathsf{E.Enc}(ek, M, \nu)$$
$$c_\nu \leftarrow \mathsf{C.Cm}(ck, \nu, \rho_\nu) \quad \pi \leftarrow \mathsf{C.Prv}\big(ck, \mathsf{E.Verify}(ek, \cdot, \cdot, C), (M, \rho_M), (\nu, \rho_\nu)\big)$$

then the following are equivalently distributed (with $\rho_\nu' \xleftarrow{\$} \mathcal{R}$):

$$\mathsf{E.AdptPrf}\big(ck, ek, c_M, \mathsf{E.Enc}(ek, C, \nu), (\pi, c_\nu), \nu'\big) \quad \text{and}$$
$$\big(\mathsf{C.Prv}(ck, \mathsf{E.Verify}(ek, \cdot, \cdot, \mathsf{E.ReRand}(ek, C, \nu')), (M, \rho_M), (\nu + \nu', \rho_\nu + \rho_\nu')\big),$$
$$\mathsf{C.RdCm}(ck, c_\nu, \rho_\nu')\big)$$

Security Properties. We require two properties: the standard (strongest possible) variant of CCA security; a new notion that is easier to achieve.

Replayable-CCA (RCCA) Security. We use the definition by Canetti et al. [CKN03], formalized in Fig. 6.

$\mathbf{Expt}_{\mathcal{A},b}^{\mathrm{RCCA}}(\lambda)$:	$\mathsf{GDec}(C)$:	$\mathbf{Expt}_{\mathcal{A},b}^{\mathrm{IACR}}(\lambda)$:
$(ek, dk) \leftarrow \mathsf{E.KeyGen}(1^\lambda)$	$m \leftarrow \mathsf{E.Dec}(dk, C)$	$(ek, dk) \leftarrow \mathsf{KeyGen}(1^\lambda)$
$(m_0, m_1) \leftarrow \mathcal{A}^{\mathsf{E.Dec}(dk, \cdot)}(ek)$	If $m \notin \{m_0, m_1\}$	$(C_0, C_1) \leftarrow \mathcal{A}(ek)$
$C \leftarrow \mathsf{E.Enc}(ek, m_b)$	Return m	$C \leftarrow \mathsf{E.ReRand}(ek, C_b)$
$b' \leftarrow \mathcal{A}^{\mathsf{GDec}(\cdot)}(C)$	Else return $\mathbf{replay}$	$b' \leftarrow \mathcal{A}(ek, C)$
Return b'.		Return b'

Fig. 6. Security games for rerandomizable encryption schemes

Indistinguishability of Adversarially Chosen and Randomized Ciphertexts (IACR). An adversary that is given a public key, chooses two ciphertexts and is then given the randomization of one of them cannot, except with a negligible advantage, distinguish which one it was given. The game is formalized in Fig. 6.

Definition 5. *For* $\mathrm{x} \in \{\mathrm{RCCA}, \mathrm{IACR}\}$, *a rerandomizable encryption scheme is* x-*secure if* $\Pr[\mathbf{Expt}_{\mathcal{A},1}^{\mathrm{x}}(\lambda) = 1] - \Pr[\mathbf{Expt}_{\mathcal{A},0}^{\mathrm{x}}(\lambda) = 1]$ *is negligible in* λ *for any PPT* $\mathcal{A}$.

4.4 Double-Spending Tag Schemes

Our e-cash scheme follows earlier approaches [BCFK15], where the bank represents a coin in terms of its *serial number* $sn = sn_0 \| \ldots \| sn_k$, which grows with every transfer. In addition, a coin contains $tag = tag_1 \| \ldots \| tag_k$, which enables tracing of double-spenders. The part sn_i is chosen by a user when she receives the coin, while the tag tag_i is computed by the sender as a function of sn_{i-1}, sn_i and her secret key.

Baldimtsi et al. [BCFK15] show how to construct such tags so they perfectly hide user identities, except when a user computes two tags with the same sn_{i-1} but different values sn_i: then her identity can be computed from the two tags. Note that this precisely corresponds to double-spending the coin that ends in sn_{i-1} to two users that choose different values for sn_i when receiving it.

We use the tags from [BCFK15], which we first formally define, and then show that their full potential had not been leveraged yet: in particular, we realize that the tag can also be used as method for users to *authenticate* the coin transfer. In earlier works [BCF+11, BCFK15], at each transfer the spender computed a signature that was included in a coin and that committed the user to the spending (and made her accountable in case of double-spending). Our construction *does not require any user signatures* and thus gains in efficiency.

Furthermore, in [BCFK15] (there were no tags in [BCF+11]), the malleable signatures took care of ensuring well-formedness of the tags, while we give an explicit construction. To be compatible with Groth-Sahai proofs, we define structure-preserving proofs of well-formedness for serial numbers and tags.

Syntax. An $\mathcal{M}$-double-spending tag scheme T is composed of the following polynomial-time algorithms:

T.Setup(Gr), on input a group description, outputs the parameters par_T (which are an implicit input to all of the following).

T.KeyGen(), on (implicit) input the parameters, outputs a tag key pair (sk, pk).

T.SGen(sk, n), the serial-number generation function, on input a secret key and a nonce $n \in \mathcal{N}$ (the nonce space), outputs a serial-number component sn and a proof $sn - pf$ of well-formedness.

T.SGen$_{init}$(sk, n), a variant of T.SGen, outputs a message $M \in \mathcal{M}$ instead of a proof. (SGen$_{init}$ is used for the first SN component, which is signed by the bank using a signature scheme that requires messages to be in $\mathcal{M}$.)

T.SVfy($pk, sn, sn - pf$), on input a public key, a serial number and a proof verifies that sn is consistent with pk by outputting a bit b.

T.SVfy$_{init}$(pk, sn, M), on input a public key, a serial number and a message in $\mathcal{M}$, checks their consistency by outputting a bit b.

T.SVfy$_{all}$, depending on the type of the input, runs T.SVfy$_{init}$ or T.SVfy.

T.TGen(sk, n, sn), the double-spending tag generator, takes as input a secret key, a nonce $n \in \mathcal{N}$ and a serial number, and outputs a double-spending tag $tag \in \mathcal{T}$ (the set of the double-spending tags) and a tag proof $t - pf$.

T.TVfy($pk, sn, sn', tag, t - pf$), on input a public key, two serial numbers, a double-spending tag, and a proof, checks consistency of the tag w.r.t. the key and the serial numbers by outputting a bit b.

T.Detect($sn, sn', tag, tag', \mathcal{L}$), double-spending detection, takes two serial numbers sn and sn', two tags $tag, tag' \in \mathcal{T}$ and a list of public keys $\mathcal{L}$ and outputs a public key pk (of the accused user) and a proof Π.

T.VfyGuilt(pk, Π), incrimination-proof verification, takes as input a public key and a proof and outputs a bit b.

Expt$_{\mathcal{A},b}^{\text{tag-anon}}(\lambda)$:
  $Gr \leftarrow \text{GrGen}(1^\lambda)$
  $par_T \leftarrow \text{T.Setup}(Gr)$
  $k := 0$
  $(sk_0, sk_1) \leftarrow \mathcal{A}(par_T)$
  $b^* \leftarrow \mathcal{A}^{O_1(sk_b), O_2(sk_b, \cdot, \cdot)}$
  Return $(b = b^*)$

$O_1(sk)$:
  $n \xleftarrow{\$} \mathcal{N}; \, T[k] := n; \, k := k + 1$
  $(sn, sn\text{-}pf) \leftarrow \text{T.SGen}(sk, n)$
  Return sn.

$O_2(sk, sn', i)$:
  If $T[i] = \bot$, abort the oracle call
  $n := T[i]; \, T[i] := \bot$
  $(tag, t\text{-}pf) \leftarrow \text{T.TGen}(sk, n, sn')$
  Return tag

Fig. 7. Game for *tag anonymity* (with oracles also used in *exculpability*) for double-spending tag schemes

Correctness Properties. For a double-spending tag scheme T we require that for all $par_T \leftarrow \text{T.Setup}(Gr)$ the following hold:

Verifiability: For every $n, n' \in \mathcal{N}$, after computing
  – $(sk, pk) \leftarrow \text{T.KeyGen}; \ (sk', pk') \leftarrow \text{T.KeyGen}$
  – $(sn, X) \leftarrow \text{T.SGen}(sk, n)$ **or** $(sn, X) \leftarrow \text{T.SGen}_{\text{init}}(sk, n)$
  – $(sn', sn - pf') \leftarrow \text{T.SGen}(sk', n')$
  – $(tag, t - pf) \leftarrow \text{T.TGen}(sk, n, sn')$
we have $\text{T.SVfy}_{\text{all}}(pk, sn, X) = \text{T.TVfy}(pk, sn, sn', tag, t - pf) = 1$.

SN-identifiability: For all tag public keys pk_1 and pk_2, all serial numbers sn and all X_1 and X_2, which can be messages in $\mathcal{M}$ or SN proofs, if

$$\text{T.SVfy}_{\text{all}}(pk_1, sn, X_1) = \text{T.SVfy}_{\text{all}}(pk_2, sn, X_2) = 1$$

then $pk_1 = pk_2$.

Bootability: There do not exist an SN message M, serial numbers $sn_1 \neq sn_2$ and tag keys (not necessarily distinct) pk_1, pk_2 such that:

$$\text{T.SVfy}_{\text{init}}(pk_1, sn_1, M) = \text{T.SVfy}_{\text{init}}(pk_2, sn_2, M) = 1.$$

2-show extractability: Let pk_0, pk_1 and pk_2 be tag public keys, sn_0, sn_1 and sn_2 be serial numbers, X_0 be either an SN proof or a message in $\mathcal{M}$, and $sn - pf_1$ and $sn - pf_2$ be SN proofs. Let tag_1 and tag_2 be tags, and $t - pf_1$ and $t - pf_2$ be tag proofs, and let $\mathcal{L}$ be a set of tag public keys with $pk_0 \in \mathcal{L}$. If

$$\text{T.SVfy}_{\text{all}}(pk_0, sn_0, X_0) = 1$$
$$\text{T.SVfy}(pk_1, sn_1, sn - pf_1) = \text{T.SVfy}(pk_2, sn_2, sn - pf_2) = 1$$
$$\text{T.TVfy}(pk_1, sn_0, sn_1, tag_1, t - pf_1) = \text{T.TVfy}(pk_2, sn_0, sn_2, tag_2, t - pf_2) = 1$$

and $sn_1 \neq sn_2$ then $\mathsf{T.Detect}(sn_1, sn_2, tag_1, tag_2, \mathcal{L})$ extracts (pk_0, Π) efficiently and we have $\mathsf{T.VfyGuilt}(pk_0, \Pi) = 1$.

$\mathcal{N}$-*injectivity:* For any secret key sk, the function $\mathsf{T.SGen}(sk, \cdot)$ is injective.

Security Properties

Exculpability: This notion formalizes soundness of double-spending proofs, in that no honestly behaving user can be accused. Let $par_\mathsf{T} \leftarrow \mathsf{T.Setup}$ and $(sk, pk) \leftarrow \mathsf{T.KeyGen}(par_\mathsf{T})$. Then we require that for a PPT adversary $\mathcal{A}$ that is given pk and can obtain SNs and tags for receiver SNs of its choice, both produced with sk (but no two tags for the same sender SN), is computationally hard to return a proof Π with $\mathsf{T.VfyGuilt}(pk, \Pi) = 1$. Formally, $\mathcal{A}$ gets access to oracles $O_1(sk)$ and $O_2(sk, \cdot, \cdot)$ defined in Fig. 7.

Tag anonymity: Our anonymity notions for transferable e-cash should hold even against a malicious bank that gets to see the serial numbers and double-spending tags for deposited coins and the *secret keys* of the users. We require thus that as long as the nonce n is random and only used once, serial numbers and tags reveal nothing about the user-specific values, such as sk and pk, that were used to generate them. The game is given in Fig. 7.

Definition 6 (Tag anonymity). *A* *double-spending tag scheme is* anonymous *if* $\Pr[\mathbf{Expt}_{\mathcal{A},1}^{\mathrm{tag-anon}}(\lambda) = 1] - \Pr[\mathbf{Expt}_{\mathcal{A},0}^{\mathrm{tag-anon}}(\lambda) = 1]$ *is negligible in λ for any PPT $\mathcal{A}$.*

5   Our Transferable E-Cash Construction

5.1   Overview

The bank validates new users in the system and creates money, and digital signatures can be used for both purposes: when a new user joins, the bank signs her public key, which serves as proof of being registered; during a coin issuing, the bank signs a message M_{sn} that is associated to the initial serial-number (SN) component sn_0 of a coin (chosen by the user withdrawing the coin), and this signature makes the coin unforgeable.

After a coin has been transferred k times, its core consists of a list of SNs $sn_0, sn_1, \ldots, sn_k$, together with a list of tags $tag_1, \ldots, tag_k$ (for a freshly withdrawn coin, we have $k = 0$). When a user spends such a coin, the receiver generates a fresh SN component sn_{k+1}, for which the spender must generate a tag tag_{k+1}, which is also associated with her public key and the last serial number sn_k (which she generated when she received the coin.)

These tags allow the bank to identify the cheater in case of double-spending, while they preserve honest users' anonymity, also towards the bank. A coin moreover contains the users' public key w.r.t. which the tags were created, as well as certificates from the bank on them. To provide anonymity, all these components are not given in the clear, but as a zero-knowledge proof of knowledge. As we use a commit-and-prove proof system, a coin contains commitments to its serial number, its tags, the user public keys and their certificates and proofs that ensure all of them are consistent.

Recall that a coin also includes a signature by the bank on (a message related to) the initial SN component. To achieve anonymity towards the bank (*coin anonymity*), the bank must sign this message blindly, which is achieved by using the SigCm functionality: the user sends a commitment to the serial number, and the bank computes a committed signature on the committed value.

Finally, the bank needs to be able to *detect* whether a double-spending occurred and *identify* the user that committed it. One way would be to give the serial numbers and the tags (which protect the anonymity of honest users) in the clear. This would yield a scheme that satisfies *coin anonymity* and *user anonymity* (note that in these two notions the bank is adversarially controlled). In contrast, *coin transparency*, the most intricate anonymity notion, would not be achieved, since the owner of a coin could easily recognize it when she receives it again by looking at its serial number.

Coin transparency requires to hide the serial numbers (and the associated tags), and to use a randomizable proof system, since the appearance of a coin needs to change after every transfer. At the same time we need to provide the bank with access to them; we thus include encryptions, under the bank's public key, in the coin. And we add proofs of consistency of the encrypted values. Now all of this must interoperate with the randomization of the coin, which is why we require rerandomizable encryption. Moreover, this has to be tied into the machinery of updating the proofs, which is necessary every time the ciphertexts and the commitments contained in a coin are refreshed.

5.2   Technical Description

Primitives Used. The basis of our transferable e-cash scheme is a randomizable extractable NIZK commit-and-prove scheme C to which we add compatible schemes: an $\mathcal{M}$-structure-preserving signature scheme S that admits an $\mathcal{M}$-commuting signature add-on SigCm, as well as a (standard) $\mathcal{M}'$-structure-preserving signature scheme S' (all defined in Sect. 4.2).

Our scheme moreover uses rerandomizable encryption (Sect. 4.3): a scheme E, which only needs to be IACR-secure, and an RCCA-secure scheme E', which will only be used for a single ciphertext per coin. (One can instantiate E with more efficient schemes.) Finally, we use a double-spending tag scheme T (Sect. 4.4). We require E, E' and T to be compatible with the proof system C, that is, the equations for E.Verify and E'.Verify, as well as T.SVfy, T.SVfy$_{init}$ and T.TVfy, are all in the set $\mathcal{E}$ of equations supported by C.

Auxiliary Functions. To simplify the description of our scheme, we first define several auxiliary functions. We let Rand denote an algorithm that randomizes a given tuple of commitments and ciphertext, as well as proofs for them (and adapts the proofs to the randomizations) by internally running C.RdCm, E.ReRand, C.AdptPrf and E.AdptPrf with the same randomness.

Below, we define $\mathsf{C.Prv}_{\mathrm{sn,init}}$ that produces a proof that a committed initial serial number sn was correctly generated w.r.t. a committed key pk_T and a committed message M (given the randomness ρ_{pk}, ρ_{sn} and ρ_M used for the commitments). We also define $\mathsf{C.Verify}_{\mathrm{sn,init}}$ that verifies such proofs. $\mathsf{C.Prv}_{\mathrm{sn}}$ and $\mathsf{C.Verify}_{\mathrm{sn}}$ do the same for non-initial serial numbers (for which there are no messages, but which require a proof of well-formedness instead).

$\mathsf{C.Prv}_{\mathrm{sn,init}}(ck, pk_\mathsf{T}, sn, M, \rho_{pk}, \rho_{sn}, \rho_M)$:
-   Return $\pi \leftarrow \mathsf{C.Prv}\big(ck, \mathsf{T.SVfy}_{\mathrm{init}}(\cdot, \cdot, \cdot) = 1, (pk_\mathsf{T}, \rho_{pk}), (sn, \rho_{sn}), (M, \rho_M)\big)$

$\mathsf{C.Verify}_{\mathrm{sn,init}}(ck, c_{pk}, c_{sn}, c_M, \pi_{sn})$:
-   Return $\mathsf{C.Verify}(ck, \mathsf{T.SVfy}_{\mathrm{init}}(\cdot, \cdot, \cdot) = 1, c_{pk}, c_{sn}, c_M, \pi_{sn})$

$\mathsf{C.Prv}_{\mathrm{sn}}(ck, pk_\mathsf{T}, sn, sn-pf, \rho_{pk}, \rho_{sn}, \rho_{sn-pf})$:
-   $\pi \leftarrow \mathsf{C.Prv}\big(ck, \mathsf{T.SVfy}(\cdot, \cdot, \cdot) = 1, (pk_\mathsf{T}, \rho_{pk}), (sn, \rho_{sn}), (sn-pf, \rho_{sn-pf})\big)$
-   Return $(\pi, \mathsf{C.Cm}(ck, sn-pf, \rho_{sn-pf}))$

$\mathsf{C.Verify}_{\mathrm{sn}}(ck, c_{pk}, c_{sn}, \tilde{\pi}_{sn} = (\pi_{sn}, c_{sn-pf}))$:
-   Return $\mathsf{C.Verify}(ck, \mathsf{T.SVfy}(\cdot, \cdot, \cdot) = 1, c_{pk}, c_{sn}, c_{sn-pf}, \pi_{sn})$

$\mathsf{C.Prv}_{\mathrm{tag}}$ produces a proof that a committed tag was correctly generated w.r.t. committed serial numbers sn and sn'; and $\mathsf{C.Verify}_{\mathrm{tag}}$ verifies such proofs.

$\mathsf{C.Prv}_{\mathrm{tag}}(ck, pk_\mathsf{T}, sn, sn', tag, \rho_{pk}, \rho_{sn}, \rho'_{sn}, \rho_{tag}, t-pf, \rho_{t-pf})$
-   $\pi \leftarrow \mathsf{C.Prv}\big(ck, \mathsf{T.TVfy}(\cdot, \cdot, \cdot, \cdot, \cdot) = 1, (pk_\mathsf{T}, \rho_{pk}), (sn, \rho_{sn}), (sn', \rho'_{sn}),$
    $\qquad\qquad\qquad\qquad\qquad\qquad\qquad (tag, \rho_{tag}), (t-pf, \rho_{t-pf})\big)$
-   Return $(\pi, \mathsf{C.Cm}(ck, t-pf, \rho_{t-pf}))$

$\mathsf{C.Verify}_{\mathrm{tag}}(ck, c_{pk}, c_{sn}, c'_{sn}, c_{tag}, \pi_{tag} = (\pi, c_{t-pf}))$:
-   Return $\mathsf{C.Verify}(ck, \mathsf{T.TVfy}(\cdot, \cdot, \cdot, \cdot, \cdot) = 1, c_{pk}, c_{sn}, c'_{sn}, c_{tag}, c_{t-pf}, \pi)$

$\mathsf{C.E.Prv}_{\mathrm{enc}}$ produces a proof that a ciphertext $\tilde{c}$ of M and $\mathsf{C.Cm}(ck, M, \rho_M)$ contain the same message; $\mathsf{C.E.Verify}_{\mathrm{enc}}$ verifies such proofs. (Note that the output of $\mathsf{C.E.Prv}_{\mathrm{enc}}$ is the same π as in the input of $\mathsf{E.AdptPrf}$; moreover, since ρ_ν is not used outside of $\mathsf{C.E.Prv}_{\mathrm{enc}}$, it can be sampled locally.)

$\mathsf{C.E.Prv}_{\mathrm{enc}}(ck, ek, M, \rho_M, \nu_M, \tilde{c})$:
-   $\rho_\nu \xleftarrow{\$} \mathcal{R};\ \pi \leftarrow \mathsf{C.Prv}(ck, \mathsf{E.Verify}(ek, \cdot, \cdot, \tilde{c}) = 1, (M, \rho_M), (\nu_M, \rho_\nu))$
-   Return $(\pi, \mathsf{C.Cm}(ck, \nu_M, \rho_\nu))$

$\mathsf{C.E.Verify}_{\mathrm{enc}}(ck, ek, c_M, \tilde{c}_M, \tilde{\pi}_{\mathrm{eq}} = (\pi_{\mathrm{eq}}, c_\nu))$:
-   Return $\mathsf{C.Verify}(ck, \mathsf{E.Verify}(ek, \cdot, \cdot, \tilde{c}_M) = 1, c_M, c_\nu, \pi_{\mathrm{eq}})$

Components of the Coin. There are two types of components, the *initial* components $coin_{init}$, and the *standard* components $coin_{std}$. The first is of the form

$$coin_{init} = \left(c_{pk}^0, c_{cert}^0, \pi_{cert}^0, c_{sn}^0, \pi_{sn}^0, \varepsilon, \varepsilon, c_M, c_\sigma^0, \pi_\sigma^0, \tilde{c}_{sn}^0, \tilde{\pi}_{sn}^0, \varepsilon, \varepsilon\right), \qquad (1)$$

where the "c-values" are commitments to the withdrawer's key pk, her certificate $cert$, the initial serial number sn and the related message M, the bank's signature σ on M; and $\tilde{c}_{sn}$ is an encryption of sn. Moreover, π_{cert} and π_{sn} prove validity of $cert$ and sn, and $\tilde{\pi}_{sn}$ proves that c_{sn} and $\tilde{c}_{sn}$ contain the same value. We use "empty values" ε for padding so that both coin-component types have the same format. Validity of an initial component is verified w.r.t. an encryption key for E' and two signature verification keys for S and S':

$\mathsf{VER}_{init}\left(ek', vk, vk', coin_{init}\right)$: Return 1 iff the following hold: // $coin_{init}$ as in (1)

 - $\mathsf{C.Verify}\left(ck, \mathsf{S'.Verify}(vk', \cdot, \cdot) = 1, c_{pk}^0, c_{cert}^0, \pi_{cert}^0\right)$
 - $\mathsf{C.Verify}\left(ck, \mathsf{S.Verify}(vk, \cdot, \cdot) = 1, c_M, c_\sigma^0, \pi_\sigma^0\right)$
 - $\mathsf{C.Verify}_{sn,init}\left(ck, c_{pk}^0, c_{sn}^0, c_M, \pi_{sn}^0\right) \wedge \mathsf{C.E'.Verify}_{enc}\left(ck, ek', c_{sn}^0, \tilde{c}_{sn}^0, \tilde{\pi}_{sn}^0\right)$

Standard components of a coin are of the form

$$coin_{std} = \left(c_{pk}^i, c_{cert}^i, \pi_{cert}^i, c_{sn}^i, \pi_{sn}^i, c_{tag}^i, \pi_{tag}^i, \varepsilon, \varepsilon, \varepsilon, \tilde{c}_{sn}^i, \tilde{\pi}_{sn}^i, \tilde{c}_{tag}^i, \tilde{\pi}_{tag}^i\right), \qquad (2)$$

and instead of M and the bank's signature they contain a commitment c_{tag} and an encryption $\tilde{c}_{tag}$ of the tag produced by the spender (and a proof π_{tag} of validity and $\tilde{\pi}_{tag}$ proving that the values in c_{tag} and $\tilde{c}_{tag}$ are equal). A coin is verified by checking the validity and consistency of each two consecutive components. If the first is an initial component then the values $c_{tag}^{i-1}, \pi_{tag}^{i-1}, \tilde{c}_{tag}^{i-1}$ and $\tilde{\pi}_{tag}^{i-1}$ are ε; if it is a standard component then c_M, c_σ^{i-1} and π_σ^{i-1} are ε.

$\mathsf{VER}_{std}\left(ek, vk', \left(c_{pk}^{i-1}, c_{cert}^{i-1}, \pi_{cert}^{i-1}, c_{sn}^{i-1}, \pi_{sn}^{i-1}, c_{tag}^{i-1}, \pi_{tag}^{i-1}, c_M, c_\sigma^{i-1}, \pi_\sigma^{i-1}, \tilde{c}_{sn}^{i-1},\right.\right.$
$\left.\left.\tilde{\pi}_{sn}^{i-1}, \tilde{c}_{tag}^{i-1}, \tilde{\pi}_{tag}^{i-1}\right), coin_{std}\right)$: // $coin_{std}$ as in (2)
Return 1 iff the following hold:

 - $\mathsf{C.Verify}\left(ck, \mathsf{S'.Verify}(vk', \cdot, \cdot) = 1, c_{pk}^i, c_{cert}^i, \pi_{cert}^i\right)$
 - $\mathsf{C.Verify}_{sn}\left(ck, c_{pk}^i, c_{sn}^i, \pi_{sn}^i\right) \wedge \mathsf{C.Verify}_{tag}\left(ck, c_{pk}^{i-1}, c_{sn}^{i-1}, c_{sn}^i, c_{tag}^i, \pi_{tag}^i\right)$
 - $\mathsf{C.E.Verify}_{enc}\left(ck, ek, c_{sn}^i, \tilde{c}_{sn}^i, \tilde{\pi}_{sn}^i\right) \wedge \mathsf{C.E.Verify}_{enc}\left(ck, ek, c_{tag}^i, \tilde{c}_{tag}^i, \tilde{\pi}_{tag}^i\right)$

Our Scheme. We now formally define our transferable e-cash scheme.

<u>ParamGen(1^λ)</u>:

 - $Gr \leftarrow \mathsf{GrGen}(1^\lambda)$
 - $par_S \leftarrow \mathsf{S.Setup}(Gr)$; $par_{S'} \leftarrow \mathsf{S'.Setup}(Gr)$
 - $par_T \leftarrow \mathsf{T.Setup}(Gr)$; $ck \leftarrow \mathsf{C.Setup}(Gr)$
 - Return $par = (1^\lambda, Gr, par_S, par_{S'}, par_T, ck)$

Recall that *par*, parsed as above, is an implicit input to all other algorithms.

BKeyGen():

- $(sk, vk) \leftarrow \mathsf{S.KeyGen}(par_\mathsf{S})$; $(sk', vk') \leftarrow \mathsf{S'.KeyGen}(par_{\mathsf{S'}})$
- $(ek', dk') \leftarrow \mathsf{E'.KeyGen}(Gr)$; $(ek, dk) \leftarrow \mathsf{E.KeyGen}(Gr)$
- $(sk_\mathsf{T}, pk_\mathsf{T}) \leftarrow \mathsf{T.KeyGen}(par_\mathsf{T})$ // $(sk_\mathsf{T}, pk_\mathsf{T}, cert)$ *let the bank act...*
- $cert \leftarrow \mathsf{S'.Sign}(sk', pk_\mathsf{T})$ //   *dots as* $\mathcal{U'}$ *in* Spend *during*
  deposit
- Return $\big(sk_\mathcal{W} = (sk, sk'), sk_{\mathcal{CK}} = (dk', dk),$
$$sk_\mathcal{D} = (cert, pk_\mathsf{T}, sk_\mathsf{T}), pk_\mathcal{B} = (ek', ek, vk, vk')\big)$$

Register$\langle \mathcal{B}(sk_\mathcal{W} = (sk, sk')), \mathcal{U}(pk_\mathcal{B} = (ek', ek, vk, vk'))\rangle$:

$\mathcal{U}$: $(sk_\mathsf{T}, pk_\mathsf{T}) \leftarrow \mathsf{T.KeyGen}(par_\mathsf{T})$; send pk_T to $\mathcal{B}$

$\mathcal{B}$: $cert_\mathcal{U} \leftarrow \mathsf{S'.Sign}(sk', pk_\mathsf{T})$; send $cert_\mathcal{U}$ to $\mathcal{U}$; output pk_T

$\mathcal{U}$: If $\mathsf{S'.Verify}(vk', pk_\mathsf{T}, cert_\mathcal{U}) = 1$, output $sk_\mathcal{U} \leftarrow (cert_\mathcal{U}, pk_\mathsf{T}, sk_\mathsf{T})$; else $\bot$

Withdraw$\langle \mathcal{B}(sk_\mathcal{W} = (sk, sk'), pk_\mathcal{B} = (ek', ek, vk, vk')),$
$$\mathcal{U}(sk_\mathcal{U} = (cert_\mathcal{U}, pk_\mathsf{T}, sk_\mathsf{T}), pk_\mathcal{B})\rangle:$$

$\mathcal{U}$: - $n \xleftarrow{\$} \mathcal{N}$; $\rho_{pk}, \rho_{cert}, \rho_{sn}, \rho_M \xleftarrow{\$} \mathcal{R}$
- $(sn, M_{sn}) \leftarrow \mathsf{T.SGen}_{\mathsf{init}}(sk_\mathsf{T}, n)$
- $c_{pk} \leftarrow \mathsf{C.Cm}(ck, pk_\mathsf{T}, \rho_{pk})$
- $c_{cert} \leftarrow \mathsf{C.Cm}(ck, cert_\mathcal{U}, \rho_{cert})$
- $c_{sn} \leftarrow \mathsf{C.Cm}(ck, sn, \rho_{sn})$
- $c_M \leftarrow \mathsf{C.Cm}(ck, M_{sn}, \rho_M)$
- $\pi_{cert} \leftarrow \mathsf{C.Prv}(ck, \mathsf{S'.Verify}(vk', \cdot, \cdot) = 1, (pk_\mathsf{T}, \rho_{pk}), (cert_\mathcal{U}, \rho_{cert}))$
- $\pi_{sn} \leftarrow \mathsf{C.Prv}_{\mathsf{sn,init}}(ck, pk_\mathsf{T}, sn, M_{sn}, \rho_{pk}, \rho_{sn}, \rho_M)$
- Send $(c_{pk}, c_{cert}, \pi_{cert}, c_{sn}, c_M, \pi_{sn})$ to $\mathcal{B}$

$\mathcal{B}$: - if $\mathsf{C.Verify}(ck, \mathsf{S'.Verify}(vk', \cdot, \cdot) = 1, c_{pk}, c_{cert}, \pi_{cert}) = 0$ or
       $\mathsf{C.Verify}_{\mathsf{sn,init}}(ck, c_{pk}, c_{sn}, c_M, \pi_{sn}) = 0$ then abort and output $\bot$
- $(c_\sigma, \pi_\sigma) \leftarrow \mathsf{SigCm}(ck, sk, c_M)$; send (c_σ, π_σ) to $\mathcal{U'}$; return ok

$\mathcal{U}$: - if $\mathsf{C.Verify}(ck, \mathsf{S.Verify}(vk, \cdot, \cdot) = 1, c_M, c_\sigma, \pi_\sigma) = 0$ then abort and output
   $\bot$
- $\nu_{sn} \xleftarrow{\$} \mathcal{R}$; $\tilde{c}_{sn} \leftarrow \mathsf{E'.Enc}(ek', sn, \nu_{sn})$
- $\tilde{\pi}_{sn} \leftarrow \mathsf{C.E'.Prv}_{\mathsf{enc}}(ck, ek', sn, \rho_{sn}, \nu_{sn}, \tilde{c}_{sn})$
- $\rho'_{pk}, \rho'_{cert}, \rho'_{sn}, \rho'_M, \rho'_\sigma, \nu'_{sn}, \rho'_{\tilde{\pi}, sn} \xleftarrow{\$} \mathcal{R}$
                      // *since* $\tilde{\pi}_{sn}$ *contains a commitment,*
                      we also sample randomness for it
- $c^0 \leftarrow \mathsf{Rand}\big((c_{pk}, c_{cert}, \pi_{cert}, c_{sn}, \pi_{sn}, c_M, c_\sigma, \pi_\sigma, \tilde{c}_{sn}, \tilde{\pi}_{sn}),$
$$(\rho'_{pk}, \rho'_{cert}, \rho'_{sn}, \rho'_M, \rho'_\sigma, \nu'_{sn}, \rho'_{\tilde{\pi}, sn})\big)$$
- Output $\big(c^0, n, sn, \rho_{sn} + \rho'_{sn}, \rho_{pk} + \rho'_{pk}\big)$

$\underline{\mathsf{Spend}}\langle \mathcal{U}(c, sk_{\mathcal{U}} = (cert, pk_{\mathsf{T}}, sk_{\mathsf{T}}), pk_{\mathcal{B}} = (ek', ek, vk, vk')),$
$$\mathcal{U}'(sk'_{\mathcal{U}} = (cert', pk'_{\mathsf{T}}, sk'_{\mathsf{T}}), pk_{\mathcal{B}})\rangle:$$

$\mathcal{U}':$ $- \ n' \xleftarrow{\$} \mathcal{N} \ ; \rho'_{pk}, \rho'_{cert}, \rho'_{sn}, \rho'_{sn-pf}, \nu'_{sn} \xleftarrow{\$} \mathcal{R}$

      $- \ (sn', sn - pf') \leftarrow \mathsf{T.SGen}(par_{\mathsf{T}}, sk'_{\mathsf{T}}, n')$

      $- \ c'_{pk} \leftarrow \mathsf{C.Cm}(ck, pk'_{\mathsf{T}}, \rho'_{pk}) \ ; c'_{cert} \leftarrow \mathsf{C.Cm}(ck, cert', \rho'_{cert})$

      $- \ c'_{sn} \leftarrow \mathsf{C.Cm}(ck, sn', \rho'_{sn}) \ ; c'_{sn-pf} \leftarrow \mathsf{C.Cm}(ck, sn - pf', \rho'_{sn-pf})$

      $- \ \tilde{c}'_{sn} \leftarrow \mathsf{E.Enc}(ek, sn', \nu'_{sn})$

      $- \ \pi'_{cert} \leftarrow \mathsf{C.Prv}(ck, \mathsf{S.Verify}(vk', \cdot, \cdot) = 1, (pk'_{\mathsf{T}}, \rho'_{pk}), (cert', \rho'_{cert}))$

      $- \ \pi'_{sn} \leftarrow \mathsf{C.Prv_{sn}}(ck, pk'_{\mathsf{T}}, sn', sn - pf, \rho'_{pk}, \rho'_{sn}, \rho'_{sn-pf})$

      $- \ \tilde{\pi}'_{sn} \leftarrow \mathsf{C.E.Prv_{enc}}(ck, ek, sn', \rho'_{sn}, \nu'_{sn}, \tilde{c}'_{sn})$

      $- \ \text{Send } (sn', \rho'_{sn}) \text{ to } \mathcal{U}$

$\mathcal{U}:$ $- \ \text{Parse } c \text{ as } \big(c^0, \big(c^j = (c^j_{pk}, c^j_{cert}, \pi^j_{cert}, c^j_{sn}, \pi^j_{sn}, c^j_{tag}, \pi^j_{tag},$
$$\tilde{c}^j_{sn}, \tilde{c}^j_{tag}, \tilde{\pi}^j_{sn}, \tilde{\pi}^j_{tag})\big)^i_{j=1}, n, sn, \rho_{sn}, \rho_{pk}\big) \ \ // i \ could \ be \ 0$$

      $- \ \rho_{tag}, \nu_{tag}, \rho_{t-pf} \xleftarrow{\$} \mathcal{R}$

      $- \ (tag, t - pf) \leftarrow \mathsf{T.TGen}(par_{\mathsf{T}}, sk_{\mathsf{T}}, n, sn')$

      $- \ c_{tag} \leftarrow \mathsf{C.Cm}(ck, tag, \rho_{tag}) \ ; \tilde{c}_{tag} \leftarrow \mathsf{E.Enc}(ek, tag, \nu_{tag})$

      $- \ \pi_{tag} \leftarrow \mathsf{C.Prv_{tag}}(ck, pk_{\mathsf{T}}, sn, sn', tag, t - pf, \rho_{pk}, \rho_{sn}, \rho'_{sn}, \rho_{tag}, \rho_{t-pf})$

      $- \ \tilde{\pi}_{tag} \leftarrow \mathsf{C.E.Prv_{enc}}(ck, ek, tag, \rho_{tag}, \nu_{tag}, \tilde{c}_{tag})$

      $- \ \text{Send } c' = \big(c^0, (c^j)^i_{j=1}, c_{tag}, \pi_{tag}, \tilde{c}_{tag}, \tilde{\pi}_{tag}\big) \text{ to } \mathcal{U}' \ ; \text{output } ok$

$\mathcal{U}':$ $- \ \text{If any of the following occur then abort and output } \perp:$

      $- \ \mathsf{VER_{init}}(ek', vk, vk', c^0) = 0$

      $- \ \mathsf{VER_{std}}(ek, vk, vk', c^{j-1}, c^j) = 0, \text{ for some } j = 1, \ldots, i$

      $- \ \mathsf{C.Verify_{tag}}(ck, c^i_{pk}, c^i_{sn}, c'_{sn}, c_{tag}, \pi_{tag}) = 0$

      $- \ \mathsf{C.E.Verify_{enc}}(ck, ek, c_{tag}, \tilde{c}_{tag}, \tilde{\pi}_{tag}) = 0$

      $- \ \text{pick uniform random } \rho''$

      $- \ c'' \leftarrow \mathsf{Rand}\big(((c^j)^i_{j=0}, c'_{pk}, c'_{cert}, \pi'_{cert}, c'_{sn}, \pi'_{sn}, c_{tag}, \pi_{tag}, \tilde{c}'_{sn}, \tilde{\pi}'_{sn}, \tilde{c}_{tag},$
$$\tilde{\pi}'_{tag}), \vec{\rho''}\big)$$

      $- \ \text{Output } \big(c'', n', sn', \rho'_{sn} + (\vec{\rho''})_{sn'}, \rho'_{pk} + (\vec{\rho''})_{pk'}\big)$

$\underline{\mathsf{CheckDS}}\big(sk_{\mathcal{CK}} = (dk', dk), \mathcal{DCL}, \mathcal{UL}, c\big):$

  $- \ \text{Parse } c \text{ as } \big(c^0 = (c^0_{pk}, c^0_{cert}, \pi^0_{cert}, c^0_{sn}, \pi^0_{sn}, c^0_M, c_\sigma, \pi_\sigma, \tilde{c}^0_{sn}, \tilde{\pi}^0_{sn}),$
$$(c^j = (c^j_{pk}, c^j_{cert}, \pi^j_{cert}, c^j_{sn}, \pi^j_{sn}, c^j_{tag}, \pi^j_{tag}, \tilde{c}^j_{sn}, \tilde{\pi}^j_{sn}, \tilde{c}^j_{tag}, \tilde{\pi}^j_{tag}))^i_{j=1}, n, sn,$$
$$\rho_{sn}, \rho_{pk}\big)$$

  $- \ \vec{sn} \leftarrow \big(\mathsf{E'.Dec}(dk', \tilde{c}^0_{sn}), \mathsf{E.Dec}(dk, \tilde{c}^1_{sn}), \ldots, \mathsf{E.Dec}(dk, \tilde{c}^i_{sn})\big)$

  $- \ \vec{tag} \leftarrow \big(\mathsf{E.Dec}(dk, \tilde{c}^1_{tag}), \ldots, \mathsf{E.Dec}(dk, \tilde{c}^i_{tag})\big)$

  $- \ \text{If for all } (\vec{sn'}, \vec{tag'}) \in \mathcal{DCL} : sn_0 \neq sn'_0$ // initial SN of checked coin...
      then return $\mathcal{DCL} \| (\vec{sn}, \vec{tag})$

                                    // ...different from those of deposited coins

  $- \ \text{Else let } j \text{ be minimal so that } sn_j \neq sn'_j$ // double-spent at j-th transfer

  $- \ (pk_{\mathsf{T}}, \Pi) \leftarrow \mathsf{T.Detect}\big(sn_j, sn'_j, tag_j, tag'_j, \mathcal{UL}\big)$

  $- \ \text{Return } (pk_{\mathsf{T}}, \Pi)$

$\underline{\mathsf{VfyGuilt}}(pk_{\mathsf{T}}, \Pi): \ \text{Return } \mathsf{T.VfyGuilt}(pk_{\mathsf{T}}, \Pi).$

5.3   Security Analysis

Theorem 7. *Our transferable e-cash scheme is perfectly* **sound**.

Because a user verifies the validity of all components of a coin before accepting it, perfect soundness of our scheme is a direct consequence of the correctness properties of S, S' and C, as well as perfect soundness of C and verifiability of T.

Detailed proofs of the following theorems are given in the full version [BFQ20]

Theorem 8. *Let $\mathcal{N}$ be the nonce space and $\mathcal{S}$ be the space of signatures of scheme S. Let $\mathcal{A}$ be an adversary that wins the* **unforgeability** *game with advantage ϵ and makes at most d calls to* BDepo. *Suppose that* C *is perfectly sound and $(\mathcal{M} \cup \mathcal{S})$-extractable. Then there exist adversaries against the unforgeability of the signature schemes S and S' with advantages ϵ_{sig} and ϵ'_{sig}, resp., such that*

$$\epsilon \leq \epsilon_{\text{sig}} + \epsilon'_{\text{sig}} + d^2/|\mathcal{N}|.$$

Assume that during the adversary's deposits the bank never picks the same final nonce twice. (The probability that there is a collision is at most $d^2/|\mathcal{N}|$.) In this case, there are two ways for the adversary to win:
(1) CheckDS outputs $\perp$, or an invalid proof, or an unregistered user: Suppose that, during a BDepo call for a coin c, CheckDS does not return a coin list. Recall that, by assumption, the final part (chosen by the bank at deposit) of the serial number of c is fresh. Since CheckDS runs T.Detect, by soundness of C and two-extractability of T, this will output a pair (pk, Π), such that VfyGuilt$(pk, \Pi) = 1$. Since a coin contains a commitment to a certificate for the used tag key (and proofs of validity), we can, again by soundness of C, extract an S'-signature on pk. Now if pk is not in $\mathcal{UL}$, then it was never signed by the bank, and $\mathcal{A}$ has thus broken unforgeability of S'.
(2) $q_W < |\mathcal{DCL}|$: If the adversary creates a valid coin that has not been withdrawn, then by soundness of C, we can extract a signature by the bank on a new initial serial number and therefore break unforgeability of S.

Theorem 9. *Let $\mathcal{A}$ be an adversary that wins* **exculpability** *game with advantage ϵ and makes u calls to the oracle* URegist. *Then there exist adversaries against mode-indistinguishability of* C *and tag-exculpability of* T *with advantages $\epsilon_{\text{m-ind}}$ and $\epsilon_{\text{t-exc}}$, resp., such that*

$$\epsilon \leq \epsilon_{\text{m-ind}} + u \cdot \epsilon_{\text{t-exc}}.$$

An incrimination proof in our e-cash scheme is simply an incrimination proof of the tag scheme T. Thus, if the reduction correctly guesses the user u that will be wrongfully incriminated by $\mathcal{A}$ (which it can with probability $1/u$), then we can construct an adversary against exculpability of T. The term $\epsilon_{\text{m-ind}}$ comes from the fact that we first need to switch C to hiding mode, so we can simulate π_{sn} and π_{tag} for the target user, since the oracles O_1 and O_2 in the game for tag exculpability (see Fig. 7) do not return $sn - pf$ and $t - pf$.

Theorem 10. *Let $\mathcal{A}$ be an adversary that wins the* **coin anonymity** *game* (c-an) *with advantage ϵ and let k be an upper-bound on the number of users transferring the challenge coins. Then there exist adversaries against mode-indistinguishability of* C *and tag-anonymity of* T *with advantages $\epsilon_{\text{m-ind}}$ and $\epsilon_{\text{t-an}}$, resp., such that*

$$\epsilon \ \leq \ 2\left(\epsilon_{\text{m-ind}} + (k+1)\,\epsilon_{\text{t-an}}\right).$$

Theorem 11. *Let $\mathcal{A}$ be an adversary that wins the* **user anonymity** *game* (u-an) *with advantage ϵ and let k be a bound on the number of users transferring the challenge coin. Then there exist adversaries against mode-indistinguishability of* C *and tag-anonymity of* T *with advantages $\epsilon_{\text{m-ind}}$ and $\epsilon_{\text{t-an}}$, resp., such that*

$$\epsilon \ \leq \ 2\,\epsilon_{\text{m-ind}} + (k+1)\,\epsilon_{\text{t-an}}.$$

In the proof of both theorems, we first define a hybrid game in which the commitment key is switched to hiding mode (hence the loss $\epsilon_{\text{m-ind}}$, which occurs twice for $b = 0$ and $b = 1$). All commitments are then perfectly hiding (and proofs reveal nothing either) and the only information contained in a coin are the serial numbers and tags. They are encrypted, but the adversary, impersonating the bank, can decrypt them.

We then argue that, by tag anonymity of T, the adversary cannot link a user to a pair (sn, tag), even when it knows the users' secret keys. We define a sequence of $k + 1$ hybrid games (as k transfers involve $k + 1$ users); going through the user vector output by the adversary, we can switch, one by one, all users from the first two the second vector. Each switch can be detected by the adversary with probability at most $\epsilon_{\text{t-an}}$. Note that the additional factor 2 for $\epsilon_{\text{t-an}}$ in game c-an is due to the fact that there are two coins for which we switch users, whereas there is only one in game u-an.

Theorem 12. *Let $\mathcal{A}$ be an adversary that wins the* **coin-transparency** *game* $(c - tr)$ *with advantage ϵ, let ℓ be the size of the two challenge coins, and k be an upper-bound on the number of users transferring the challenge coins. Then there exist adversaries against mode-indistinguishability of* C, *tag-anonymity of* T, *IACR-security of* E *and RCCA-security of* E' *with advantages $\epsilon_{\text{m-ind}}$, $\epsilon_{\text{t-an}}$, ϵ_{iacr} and ϵ_{rcca}, resp., such that*

$$\epsilon \ \leq \ 2\,\epsilon_{\text{m-ind}} + (k+1)\,\epsilon_{\text{t-an}} + (2\,\ell + 1)\,\epsilon_{\text{iacr}} + \epsilon_{\text{rcca}}.$$

The crucial difference to the previous anonymity theorems is that the bank is honest (which makes this strong notion possible). We therefore must rely on the security of the encryptions, for which the reduction thus does not know the decryption key. At the same time, the reduction must be able to detect double-spendings, when the adversary deposits coins. Since we use RCCA encryption, the reduction can do so by using its own decryption oracle.

As for c-an and u-an, the reduction first makes all commitments perfectly hiding and proofs perfectly simulatable (which loses $\epsilon_{\text{m-ind}}$ twice). Since all ciphertexts in the challenge coin given to the adversary are randomized, the

reduction can replace all of them, except the initial one, by IACR-security of
E. (Note that in the game these ciphertexts never need to be decrypted.) The
factor 2ℓ is due to the fact that there are at most ℓ encryptions of SN/tag *pairs*.
Finally, replacing the initial ciphertext (the one that enables detection of double-
spending) can be done by a reduction to RCCA-security of E′: the oracle Depo′
can be simulated by using the reduction's own oracles Dec and GDec (depending
on whether Depo′ is called before or after the reduction receives the challenge
ciphertext) in the RCCA-security game. Note that, when during a simulation
of CheckDS, oracle GDec outputs `replay`, the reduction knows that a challenge
coin was deposited, and uses this information to increase *ctr*.

6   Instantiation of the Building Blocks and Efficiency

The instantiations we use are all proven secure in the standard model under
non-interactive hardness assumptions.

Commitments and Proofs. The commit-and-prove system C will be instantiated with the SXDH-based instantiation of Groth-Sahai proofs [GS08].

Theorem 13 ([GS08]). *The Groth-Sahai proof system, allowing to commit val-
ues from* $\mathcal{V} := \mathbb{Z}_p \cup \mathbb{G} \cup \hat{\mathbb{G}}$ *is perfectly complete, perfectly sound and randomizable; it is* $(\mathbb{G} \cup \hat{\mathbb{G}})$*-extractable, mode-indistinguishable assuming SXDH, and
perfectly hiding in hiding mode.*

We note that moreover, all our proofs can be made zero-knowledge [GS08], and
thus simulatable, because all pairing-product equations we use are homogeneous
(i.e., the right-hand term is the neutral element). We have (efficient) extractability, as we only need to efficiently extract group elements from commitments (and
no scalars) in our reductions. (Note that for information-theoretic arguments
concerning soundness, Extr can also be inefficient.)

Signature Schemes. For efficiency and type-compatibility reasons, we use two
different signature schemes. The first one, S, must support the functionality
SigCm, which imposes a specific format of messages. The second scheme, S′, is
less restrictive, which allows for more efficient instantiations. While all our other
components rely on standard assumptions, we instantiate S with a scheme that
relies on a non-interactive q-type assumption defined in [AFG+10].

Theorem 14. *The signature scheme from [AFG+10, Sect. 4] with message
space* $\mathcal{M} := \{(g^m, \hat{g}^m) \mid m \in \mathbb{Z}_p\}$ *is (strongly) unforgeable assuming q-ADHSDH
and AWFCDH (see [BFQ20]), and it supports the* SigCm *functionality [Fuc11].*

Theorem 15. *The signature scheme from [AGHO11, Sect. 5] is structure-
preserving with message space* $\mathcal{M}' := \hat{\mathbb{G}}$ *and (strongly) unforgeable assuming
SXDH.*

Randomizable Encryption Schemes. To instantiate the RCCA-secure scheme E' we follow the approach by Libert et al. [LPQ17]. Their construction is only for one group element, but by adapting the scheme, it can support encryption of a vector in $\mathbb{G}^n$ for arbitrary n. In our e-cash scheme, we need to encrypt a vector in $\mathbb{G}^2$, and since it is not clear whether more recent efficient schemes like [FFHR19] can be adapted to this, we give an explicit construction, which we detail in the full version [BFQ20].

Recall that the RCCA-secure scheme E' is only used to encrypt the initial part of the serial number; using a less efficient scheme thus has a minor impact on the efficiency of our scheme. From all other ciphertexts contained in a coin (which are under scheme E) we only require IACR security, which standard ElGamal encryption satisfies under DDH(!). Thus, we instantiate E with ElGamal vector encryption. (Note that our instantiation of E' is also built on top of ElGamal). We prove the following in the full version [BFQ20].

Theorem 16. *Assuming SXDH, our randomizable encryption scheme [BFQ20] is RCCA-secure and ElGamal vector encryption is IACR-secure.*

Double-Spending Tags. We will use a scheme that builds on the one given in [BCFK15]. We have optimized the size of the tags and made explicit all the functionalities not given previously. We defer this to the full version [BFQ20].

Efficiency Analysis

We conclude by summarizing the sizes of objects in our scheme in the table below and refer to the full version [BFQ20] for the details of our analysis.

For a group $G \in \{\mathbb{G}, \hat{\mathbb{G}}, \mathbb{Z}_p\}$, let $|G|$ denote the size of an element of G. Let c_{btsrap} denote the coin output by $\mathcal{U}$ at the end of the Withdraw protocol (which corresponds to c_{init} plus secret values, like n, ρ_{sn}, etc., to be used when transferring the coin), and let c_{std} denote one (non-initial) component of the coin. After k transfers the size of a coin is $|c_{\text{btsrap}}| + k|c_{\text{std}}|$.

$|sk_{\mathcal{B}}|$	$9|\mathbb{Z}_p| + 2|\mathbb{G}| + 2|\hat{\mathbb{G}}|$	$|\Pi_{\text{guilt}}|$	$2|\mathbb{G}|$
$|pk_{\mathcal{B}}|$	$15|\mathbb{G}| + 8|\hat{\mathbb{G}}|$	$|c_{\text{btstrap}}|$	$6|\mathbb{Z}_p| + 147|\mathbb{G}| + 125|\hat{\mathbb{G}}|$
$|sk_{\mathcal{U}}|$	$|\mathbb{Z}_p| + 2|\mathbb{G}| + 2|\hat{\mathbb{G}}|$	$|c_{\text{std}}|$	$54|\mathbb{G}| + 50|\hat{\mathbb{G}}|$
$|pk_{\mathcal{U}}|$	$|\hat{\mathbb{G}}|$	$|(\vec{sn}, \vec{tag})|$	$(4t + 2)|\mathbb{G}|$

Acknowledgements. The first two authors were supported by the French ANR EfTrEC project (ANR-16-CE39-0002). This work is funded in part by the MSR–Inria Joint Centre. The second author is supported by the Vienna Science and Technology Fund (WWTF) through project VRG18-002.

References

AFG+10. Abe, M., Fuchsbauer, G., Groth, J., Haralambiev, K., Ohkubo, M.: Structure-preserving signatures and commitments to group elements. In: Rabin, T. (ed.) CRYPTO 2010. LNCS, vol. 6223, pp. 209–236. Springer, Heidelberg (2010). https://doi.org/10.1007/978-3-642-14623-7_12

AGHO11. Abe, M., Groth, J., Haralambiev, K., Ohkubo, M.: Optimal structure-preserving signatures in asymmetric bilinear groups. In: Rogaway, P. (ed.) CRYPTO 2011. LNCS, vol. 6841, pp. 649–666. Springer, Heidelberg (2011). https://doi.org/10.1007/978-3-642-22792-9_37

BCC+09. Belenkiy, M., Camenisch, J., Chase, M., Kohlweiss, M., Lysyanskaya, A., Shacham, H.: Randomizable proofs and delegatable anonymous credentials. In: Halevi, S. (ed.) CRYPTO 2009. LNCS, vol. 5677, pp. 108–125. Springer, Heidelberg (2009). https://doi.org/10.1007/978-3-642-03356-8_7

BCF+11. Blazy, O., Canard, S., Fuchsbauer, G., Gouget, A., Sibert, H., Traoré, J.: Achieving optimal anonymity in transferable e-cash with a judge. In: Nitaj, A., Pointcheval, D. (eds.) AFRICACRYPT 2011. LNCS, vol. 6737, pp. 206–223. Springer, Heidelberg (2011). https://doi.org/10.1007/978-3-642-21969-6_13

BCFK15. Baldimtsi, F., Chase, M., Fuchsbauer, G., Kohlweiss, M.: Anonymous transferable e-cash. In: Katz, J. (ed.) PKC 2015. LNCS, vol. 9020, pp. 101–124. Springer, Heidelberg (2015). https://doi.org/10.1007/978-3-662-46447-2_5

BCG+14. Eli, B.-S., et al.: Zerocash: decentralized anonymous payments from Bitcoin. In: IEEE S&P 2014 (2014)

BCKL09. Belenkiy, M., Chase, M., Kohlweiss, M., Lysyanskaya, A.: Compact e-cash and simulatable VRFs revisited. In: Shacham, H., Waters, B. (eds.) Pairing 2009. LNCS, vol. 5671, pp. 114–131. Springer, Heidelberg (2009). https://doi.org/10.1007/978-3-642-03298-1_9

BFQ20. Bauer, B., Fuchsbauer, G., Qian, C.: Transferable e-cash: a cleaner model and the first practical instantiation. Cryptology ePrint Archive, Report 2020/1400 (2020)

Bla08. Blanton, M.: Improved conditional e-payments. In: Bellovin, S.M., Gennaro, R., Keromytis, A., Yung, M. (eds.) ACNS 2008. LNCS, vol. 5037, pp. 188–206. Springer, Heidelberg (2008). https://doi.org/10.1007/978-3-540-68914-0_12

BPS19. Bourse, F., Pointcheval, D., Sanders, O.: Divisible e-cash from constrained pseudo-random functions. In: Galbraith, S.D., Moriai, S. (eds.) ASIACRYPT 2019. LNCS, vol. 11921, pp. 679–708. Springer, Cham (2019). https://doi.org/10.1007/978-3-030-34578-5_24

Bra93. Brands, S.: Untraceable off-line cash in wallet with observers. In: Stinson, D.R. (ed.) CRYPTO 1993. LNCS, vol. 773, pp. 302–318. Springer, Heidelberg (1994). https://doi.org/10.1007/3-540-48329-2_26

CFN88. Chaum, D., Fiat, A., Naor, M.: Untraceable electronic cash. In: Goldwasser, S. (ed.) CRYPTO 1988. LNCS, vol. 403, pp. 319–327. Springer, New York (1990). https://doi.org/10.1007/0-387-34799-2_25

CG08. Canard, S., Gouget, A.: Anonymity in transferable e-cash. In: Bellovin, S.M., Gennaro, R., Keromytis, A., Yung, M. (eds.) ACNS 2008. LNCS, vol. 5037, pp. 207–223. Springer, Heidelberg (2008). https://doi.org/10.1007/978-3-540-68914-0_13

CGT08. Canard, S., Gouget, A., Traoré, J.: Improvement of efficiency in (unconditional) anonymous transferable e-cash. In: Tsudik, G. (ed.) FC 2008. LNCS, vol. 5143, pp. 202–214. Springer, Heidelberg (2008). https://doi.org/10.1007/978-3-540-85230-8_19

Cha83. Chaum, D.: Blind signature system. In: Chaum, D. (ed.) Advances in Cryptology. Springer, Boston (1984). https://doi.org/10.1007/978-1-4684-4730-9_14

CHL05. Camenisch, J., Hohenberger, S., Lysyanskaya, A.: Compact e-cash. In: Cramer, R. (ed.) EUROCRYPT 2005. LNCS, vol. 3494, pp. 302–321. Springer, Heidelberg (2005). https://doi.org/10.1007/11426639_18

CKLM14. Chase, M., Kohlweiss, M., Lysyanskaya, A., Meiklejohn, S.: Malleable signatures: new definitions and delegatable anonymous credentials. In: IEEE CSF 2014 (2004)

CKN03. Canetti, R., Krawczyk, H., Nielsen, J.B.: Relaxing chosen-ciphertext security. In: Boneh, D. (ed.) CRYPTO 2003. LNCS, vol. 2729, pp. 565–582. Springer, Heidelberg (2003). https://doi.org/10.1007/978-3-540-45146-4_33

CP93. Chaum, D., Pedersen, T.P.: Transferred cash grows in size. In: Rueppel, R.A. (ed.) EUROCRYPT 1992. LNCS, vol. 658, pp. 390–407. Springer, Heidelberg (1993). https://doi.org/10.1007/3-540-47555-9_32

CPST16. Canard, S., Pointcheval, D., Sanders, O., Traoré, J.: Divisible e-cash made practical. IET Inf. Secur. 10(6), 332–347 (2016)

FFHR19. Faonio, A., Fiore, D., Herranz, J., Ràfols, C.: Structure-preserving and re-randomizable RCCA-secure public key encryption and its applications. In: Galbraith, S.D., Moriai, S. (eds.) ASIACRYPT 2019. LNCS, vol. 11923, pp. 159–190. Springer, Cham (2019). https://doi.org/10.1007/978-3-030-34618-8_6

FHY13. Fan, C.-I., Huang, V.S.-M., Yu, Y.-C.: User efficient recoverable off-line e-cash scheme with fast anonymity revoking. Math. Comput. Model. 58(1–2), 227–237 (2013)

FOS19. Fuchsbauer, G., Orrù, M., Seurin, Y.: Aggregate cash systems: a cryptographic investigation of Mimblewimble. In: Ishai, Y., Rijmen, V. (eds.) EUROCRYPT 2019. LNCS, vol. 11476, pp. 657–689. Springer, Cham (2019). https://doi.org/10.1007/978-3-030-17653-2_22

FP09. Fuchsbauer, G., Pointcheval, D.: Proofs on encrypted values in bilinear groups and an application to anonymity of signatures. In: Shacham, H., Waters, B. (eds.) Pairing 2009. LNCS, vol. 5671, pp. 132–149. Springer, Heidelberg (2009). https://doi.org/10.1007/978-3-642-03298-1_10

FPV09. Fuchsbauer, G., Pointcheval, D., Vergnaud, D.: Transferable constant-size fair e-cash. In: Garay, J.A., Miyaji, A., Otsuka, A. (eds.) CANS 2009. LNCS, vol. 5888, pp. 226–247. Springer, Heidelberg (2009). https://doi.org/10.1007/978-3-642-10433-6_15

Fuc11. Fuchsbauer, G.: Commuting signatures and verifiable encryption. In: Paterson, K.G. (ed.) EUROCRYPT 2011. LNCS, vol. 6632, pp. 224–245. Springer, Heidelberg (2011). https://doi.org/10.1007/978-3-642-20465-4_14

GS08. Groth, J., Sahai, A.: Efficient non-interactive proof systems for bilinear groups. In: Smart, N. (ed.) EUROCRYPT 2008. LNCS, vol. 4965, pp. 415–432. Springer, Heidelberg (2008). https://doi.org/10.1007/978-3-540-78967-3_24

LPQ17. Libert, B., Peters, T., Qian, C.: Structure-preserving chosen-ciphertext security with shorter verifiable ciphertexts. In: Fehr, S. (ed.) PKC 2017. LNCS, vol. 10174, pp. 247–276. Springer, Heidelberg (2017). https://doi.org/10.1007/978-3-662-54365-8_11

Max15. Maxwell, G.: Confidential transactions (2015). https://people.xiph.org/~greg/confidential_values.txt

MGGR13. Miers, I., Garman, C., Green, M., Rubin, A.D.: Zerocoin: anonymous distributed e-cash from Bitcoin. In: IEEE S&P 2013 (2013)

Nak08. Nakamoto, S.: Bitcoin: a peer-to-peer electronic cash (2008). bitcoin.org/bitcoin.pdf

OO89. Okamoto, T., Ohta, K.: Disposable zero-knowledge authentications and their applications to untraceable electronic cash. In: Brassard, G. (ed.) CRYPTO 1989. LNCS, vol. 435, pp. 481–496. Springer, New York (1990). https://doi.org/10.1007/0-387-34805-0_43

OO91. Okamoto, T., Ohta, K.: Universal electronic cash. In: Feigenbaum, J. (ed.) CRYPTO 1991. LNCS, vol. 576, pp. 324–337. Springer, Heidelberg (1992). https://doi.org/10.1007/3-540-46766-1_27

Poe16. Poelstra, A.: Mimblewimble (2016). https://download.wpsoftware.net/bitcoin/wizardry/mimblewimble.pdf

vS13. van Saberhagen, N.: Cryptonote v 2.0 (2013). https://cryptonote.org/whitepaper.pdf

Zec20. Zcash Protocol Specification (15 January 2020). https://zips.z.cash/protocol/protocol.pdf

Private Set Operations from Oblivious Switching

Gayathri Garimella[1]($\boxtimes$), Payman Mohassel[2], Mike Rosulek[1], Saeed Sadeghian[3], and Jaspal Singh[1]

[1] Oregon State University, Corvallis, USA
garimelg@oregonstate.edu
[2] Facebook, Madison, USA
[3] Security Compass, Toronto, Canada

Abstract. Private set intersection reveals the intersection of two private sets, but many real-world applications require the parties to learn only *partial information* about the intersection. In this paper we introduce a new approach for computing arbitrary functions of the intersection, provided that it is safe to also reveal the cardinality of the intersection. In the most general case, our new protocol provides the participants with secret shares of the intersection, which can be fed into any generic 2PC protocol. Certain computations on the intersection can also be done even more directly and efficiently, avoiding this secret-sharing step. These cases include computing *only* the cardinality of intersection, or the "cardinality-sum" application proposed in Ion *et al.* (ePrint 2017). Compared to the state-of-the-art protocol for computing on intersection (Pinkas et al., Eurocrypt 2019), our protocol has about $2.5 - 3\times$ less communication, and has faster running time on slower (50 Mbps) networks.

Our new techniques can also be used to privately compute the *union* of two sets as easily as computing the intersection. Our protocol concretely improves the leading private set union protocol (Kolesnikov et al., Asiacrypt 2020) by a factor of $2-2.5\times$, depending on the network speed. We then show how private set union can be used in a simple way to realize the "Private-ID" functionality suggested by Buddhavarapu et al. (ePrint 2020). Our protocol is significantly faster than the prior Private-ID protocol, especially on fast networks.

All of our protocols are in the two-party setting and are secure against semi-honest adversaries.

1 Introduction

In 2-party private set intersection (PSI), Alice's input is a set of items X, Bob's input is a set Y, and the output (given to one or both of them) is the **entire**

Authors from Oregon State University - Partially supported by NSF award 1617197 and a Facebook research award.

J. A. Garay (Ed.): PKC 2021, LNCS 12711, pp. 591–617, 2021.
https://doi.org/10.1007/978-3-030-75248-4_21

contents of the intersection $X \cap Y$. PSI protocols have become incredibly efficient over the last decade.

The fastest PSI protocols generally follow the rough approach of Pinkas et al. [PSZ14], which was the first special-purpose PSI protocols to be based on efficient OT (oblivious transfer) extension. Since then, the techniques have been considerably refined and improved for both semi-honest [PSSZ15, KKRT16, PRTY19, CM20] and malicious [DCW13, RR17a, RR17b, PRTY20] security. An entirely different approach to PSI requires public-key operations (e.g., key agreement or partially homomorphic encryption) linear in the size of the sets [Mea86, HFH99, FNP04, CT10, CT12, FHNP16]. Our focus in this work is on faster OT-extension-based PSI techniques.

Computing on the Intersection. Many real-world applications are closely related to PSI but in fact require only **partial/aggregate information about the intersection** to be revealed. In a notable real-world deployment of secure computation, Google is known to compute the cardinality of the intersection and the sum of values in the intersection [IKN+19, MPR+20]. More generally, we consider **private computing on set intersection (PCSI)**: the problem of securely computing $g(X \cap Y)$ for a (mostly) generic choice of function g.

There are several techniques for computing set intersections within generic 2PC, so that the intersection can be easily fed into another function. Huang, Katz and Evans [HEK12] gave an efficient sort-compare-shuffle circuit for use in either GMW or Yao's protocol. Further combinatorial improvements to intersection circuits were proposed in [PSSZ15, PSWW18]. The current state of the art for PCSI is due to [PSTY19], using a special-purpose preprocessing phase before using general-purpose 2PC to perform the necessary comparisons.

Why the Performance Gap? Plain PSI and PCSI are clearly closely related problems, and yet the state-of-the-art protocols for these problems have significantly different efficiency. Semi-honest PCSI – even in the simplest possible cases, like cardinality of intersection – is concretely about $20\times$ slower and requires over $30\times$ more communication than semi-honest PSI. Why is this the case?

All PSI and PCSI protocols use various combinatorial techniques to reduce the problem to a series of private equality tests. A private equality test (PEqT) takes a private string from each party and reveals (only) whether the strings are identical.

In the case of PSI, each party is allowed to learn whether each of their input items is in the intersection or not. This fact leads PSI protocols to use efficient, special-purpose PEqT subprotocols, which reveal the output of the equality test directly to at least one of the parties. This approach doesn't immediately work for PCSI, since in that case the participants should not learn whether a particular item is in the intersection or not. Instead, the outcome of the PEqTs should remain "inside the secure computation," prompting PCSI protocols to implement PEqTs simply as circuits within a general-purpose 2PC protocol.

These divergent choices of PEqTs lead to the differences in performance between PSI and PCSI. A general-purpose PEqT on ℓ-bit strings is a boolean circuit with ℓ non-free gates, leading to $O(\ell)$ cryptographic operations and $O(\ell\kappa)$ bits of communication. The state-of-the-art for special-purpose PEqTs [KKRT16] has cost that is *independent* of ℓ: only $O(\kappa)$ bits of communication and $O(1)$ symmetric-key cryptographic operations per equality test.

One exception to this general rule is due to Ciampi and Orlandi [CO18]. They provide a special-purpose PEqT (actually a generalization where one party has m items and the other has 1) that produces outputs in "encrypted form" that can be subsequently fed into a generic 2PC. However, their approach still requires $\Theta(\kappa\ell)$ bits of communication per comparison. While their concrete constants are smaller than a circuit-based comparison, their approach is not an asymptotic improvement.

Other Related Work. Another body of work studies the special case of computing the *cardinality* of intersection [HFH99, VC05, CZ09, CGT12, EFG+15, BA12, KS05, DD15]. It is not clear how to extend such results for computing more general functions of the intersection. The work of [BA12, EFG+15, MRR19] is in the multi-party setting ($n \geq 3$ parties) with an honest majority based on secret-sharing. As a result, no cryptographic operations are needed but the techniques are not applicable to the two-party setting.

1.1   Our Contribution

We describe a new approach for semi-honest PCSI, which leaks the cardinality $|X \cap Y|$. Hence, our protocol works to compute $g(X \cap Y)$ for any g that leaks the cardinality $|X \cap Y|$. This class of g includes many applications of interest, discussed below.

The main idea is to obliviously permute all of the strings that will be used in the PEqTs, so that one party does not know which items are tested in which PEqT instance. We can then use the more efficient special-purpose PEqTs, giving output directly to the party who is oblivious to the permutation. This reveals only the cardinality of the intersection (*i.e.*, how many PEqTs give output TRUE).

Obliviously permuting n items incurs a $\log n$ overhead. However, in return for this extra cost we are able to replace general-purpose PEqTs with special-purpose PEqTs, saving a factor of ℓ (for strings of length ℓ). In almost all situations, $\log n \ll \ell$ and the tradeoff is an asymptotic as well as concrete improvement over the state of the art.

Extensions and Applications. Our protocol supports any symmetric function $g(X \cap Y)$ that leaks $|X \cap Y|$. Useful such functions include:

- Computing the intersection; *i.e.*, PSI (although our protocol is not competitive with the most efficient PSI-only protocols).
- Computing *only* the cardinality of the intersection.
- Computing secret shares of the items in the intersection.
- The "intersection-sum" functionality proposed in [IKN+19], in which Alice has a set of keys $\{x_1, \ldots, x_n\}$ and Bob has a set of key-value pairs

$\{(y_1, v_1), \ldots, (y_n, v_n)\}$. Both parties learn the cardinality of $\{x_1, \ldots, x_n\} \cap \{y_1, \ldots, y_n\}$ as well as the sum of values $\sum_{i: y_i \in \{x_1, \ldots, x_n\}} v_i$. Although not strictly an instance of PCSI as we have defined it, our protocol is easily modified to realize this functionality.

For all of these cases except the plain-PSI case, our protocol gives the most concretely efficient solution to date.

We also show how to use our main techniques to also securely compute the **union** of the input sets. Our private set union protocol is concretely more efficient than the state-of-the-art protocol of [KRTW19].

Finally, we show how our techniques can be used to realize the "private ID" functionality proposed in [BKM+20]. In this functionality, both parties learn pseudorandom universal identifiers for the values in the union of their sets, as well as the identifiers corresponding to their own items. This functionality allows parties to locally sort their data sets according to these universal identifiers, and feed them into any general-purpose 2PC protocol for simplified processing. Our construction is the first instantiation of Private ID using OT-based techniques that are dominated by symmetric-key crypto operations.

We have implemented our protocols and give a full comparison to existing protocols.

2   Preliminaries

Security Model. We use the standard notion of security in the presence of semi-honest adversaries. Let π be a protocol for computing the function $f(x_1, x_2)$, where party P_i has input x_i. We define security in the following way.

For each party P, let $\text{VIEW}_P(1^\kappa, x_1, x_2)$ denote the view of party P during an honest execution of π on inputs x_1 and x_2. The view consists of P's input, random tape, and all messages exchanged as part of the π protocol.

Definition 1. *2-party protocol π securely realizes f in the presence of semi-honest adversaries if there exists a simulator Sim such that, for all inputs x_1, x_2 and all $i \in \{1, 2\}$:*

$$Sim(1^\kappa, i, x_i, f(x_1, x_2)) \cong_\kappa \text{VIEW}_{P_i}(1^\kappa, x_1, x_2)$$

where $\cong_\kappa$ denotes computational indistinguishability with respect to security parameter κ.

Essentially, a protocol is secure if the view of a party leaks no more information than $f(x_1, x_2)$.

3   Protocol Building Blocks

3.1   Oblivious Transfer

Oblivious Transfer (OT) is a fundamental cryptographic protocol widely used in secure computation, and initially introduced in [Rab05]. It allows a sender with two inputs m_0, m_1 and a receiver with a bit b to engage in a protocol where the receiver learns m_b, and neither party learns any additional information. A single OT requires public-key operations and hence is expensive. But a powerful technique called OT extension [IKNP03, KK13, ALSZ13] allows one to perform n OTs by only performing $O(\kappa)$ public-key operations (where κ is a computational security parameter) and $O(n)$ fast symmetric-key operations, allowing for faster and more scalable implementation when invoking many OTs. In Fig. 1 we formally define the ideal functionality for OT that provides n parallel instances of OT.

3.2   Oblivious Switching Network

An oblivious switching network works as follows. One party chooses a permutation π on n items, and the other party chooses a vector $\boldsymbol{x}$. The parties learn additive secret shares of $\pi(\boldsymbol{x})$ (i.e., $\boldsymbol{x}$ permuted according to π). The formal description of the functionality is given in Fig. 2.

Mohassel and Sadeghian [MS13] introduced oblivious switching and described a semi-honest oblivious switching protocol that is based on oblivious transfers. Briefly, the protocol works by considering a *universal switching network* (i.e., Waksman or Beneš network), which consists of $O(n \log n)$ 2-input, 2-output switches. The receiver chooses programming of the switches (whether to swap the order of the inputs or not) based on their permutation π. The sender chooses a random one-time pad for each wire of the network, and the invariant is that the receiver will learn the value on each wire but masked with the one-time pad of that wire. The parties use oblivious transfer to allow the receiver to select whether to learn the XOR of masks of input b and output b, or to learn the XOR of masks of input b and output $1 - b$. These XOR values suffice to preserve the invariant across the switches. At the output layer of the switching network, the sender holds a vector of one-time pads, and the receiver holds the permuted values masked by these one-time pads. We give more details in the full-version of our paper.

The total cost of the switching network is $O(n \log n)$ oblivious transfers, one for every switch in the switching network. Each OT is on a pair of 2ℓ-bit strings (two masks).

We described the ideal functionality to allow the input vector $\boldsymbol{x}$ to be longer than the output (secret-shared) vectors, which leads to π being an *injective function* rather than a permutation. This can be accomplished by simply permuting the input vector so that the desired items are "in the front", and then both parties truncating their vector of shares by the appropriate amount. In the full version of our paper we describe an optimization for injective functions that slightly improves over permuting-then-discarding.

3.3   Batch Oblivious PRF

Kolesnikov et al. [KKRT16] describe an efficient protocol for **batched oblivious PRF** (OPRF) based on OT extension. The protocol provides a batch of oblivious

---

Parameters: number of OTs n; payload length ℓ.

On input $(m_{1,0}, m_{1,1}), \ldots, (m_{n,0}, m_{n,1})$ from the sender, where each $m_{i,b} \in \{0,1\}^\ell$, and input $b \in \{0,1\}^n$ from the receiver:
1. Give output $(m_{1,b_1}, m_{2,b_2}, \ldots, m_{n,b_n})$ to the receiver.

Fig. 1. Ideal functionality $\mathcal{F}_{\mathsf{ot}}$ for n oblivious transfers.

Parameters: input length n_{in}; output length $n_{\mathsf{out}} \leq n_{\mathsf{in}}$; item length ℓ.

On input an injective function $\pi : [n_{\mathsf{out}}] \to [n_{\mathsf{in}}]$ from the receiver, and vector $x \in (\{0,1\}^\ell)^{n_{\mathsf{in}}}$ from the sender:
1. Choose uniform vector $a \leftarrow (\{0,1\}^\ell)^{n_{\mathsf{out}}}$.
2. Define the vector $b \in (\{0,1\}^\ell)^{n_{\mathsf{out}}}$ via $b_i = a_i \oplus x_{\pi(i)}$.
3. Give output a to the sender and b to the receiver.

Fig. 2. Ideal functionality $\mathcal{F}_{\mathsf{osn}}$ for oblivious switching network.

Parameters: batch size n; suitable PRF PRF.

On input vector $x \in (\{0,1\}^*)^n$ from the receiver:
1. For each $i \in [n]$, choose uniform PRF key k_i.
2. For each $i \in [n]$, define $f_i = \mathsf{PRF}(k_i, x_i)$.
3. Give vector k to the sender and vector f to the receiver.

Fig. 3. Ideal functionality $\mathcal{F}_{\mathsf{bOPRF}}$ for batch oblivious PRF.

Parameters: Number n of string-pairs to compare.

On input $x \in (\{0,1\}^*)^n$ from the sender, and $y \in (\{0,1\}^*)^n$ from the receiver:
1. Define the vector $e \in \{0,1\}^n$, where $e_i = 1$ if $x_i = y_i$ and $e_i = 0$ otherwise.
2. Give e to the receiver.

Fig. 4. Ideal functionality $\mathcal{F}_{\mathsf{bEQ}}$ for batch string equality testing.

PRF instances in the following way. In the ith instance, the receiver has an input x_i; the sender learns a PRF seed k_i and the receiver learns $\mathsf{PRF}(k_i, x_i)$. Note that the receiver learns the output of the PRF on only one value per key, and the sender does not learn which output the receiver learned. The batch OPRF functionality is described formally in Fig. 3.

The KKRT batch OPRF protocol is based on OT extension and extremely fast. Each OPRF instance requires roughly only 4.5κ total bits of communication between the parties, and a few calls to a hash function. On a fast network, a million OPRF instances can be generated in just a few seconds.

Technically speaking, the KKRT protocol realizes OPRF instances where the keys k_i are related in some sense. However, the PRF that it instantiates has all the expected security properties, even in the presence of such related keys. For the sake of simplicity, we ignore this issue in our notation. For more details, see [KKRT16].

3.4 Private Equality Tests

A private equality test (PEqT) allows two parties to determine whether their two input strings are equal (while leaking nothing else about the inputs).

An oblivious PRF can be used to realize a secure equality test in a simple way. Suppose Alice has input x and Bob has input y, and they would like to learn whether $x = y$. Alice acts as OPRF receiver with input x and learns $\mathsf{PRF}(k, x)$. Bob learns PRF seed k and sends the value $\mathsf{PRF}(k, y)$. If $x \neq y$ then the PRF property ensures that Bob's message looks random to Alice; otherwise the message is the PRF output that Alice already knows.

Using the batch OPRF protocol of [KKRT16], the parties can realize a large batch of equality tests in a natural way. The functionality $\mathcal{F}_{\mathsf{bEQ}}$ of Fig. 4 formalizes this batch equality testing. We take advantage of the fact that its output can be given to just one party.

3.5 Reducing PSI to $O(n)$ Comparisons

The leading protocol for PCSI is due to Pinkas et al. [PSTY19]. One of their main contributions is to show how to *interactively* reduce a PSI computation to $O(n)$ comparisons, using only a linear amount of communication.

The main idea behind the PSTY19 preprocessing is for Alice to use hash functions h_1, h_2, h_3 to assign her items to m bins via Cuckoo hashing, so that each bin has at most one item. Bob assigns each of his items y to all of the bins $h_1(y), h_2(y), h_3(y)$. The parties use the batch OPRF functionality $\mathcal{F}_{\mathsf{bOPRF}}$, with Alice acting as receiver. If she has placed item x in bin j, then she will receive output $\mathsf{PRF}(k_j, x)$, while Bob learns each k_j.

Now, Bob chooses a random value s_j for each bin j. The goal is to arrange that if Alice and Bob have a matching item in the jth bin, then Alice will somehow learn that bin's s_j value. Suppose for example that one of Bob's items in bin #1 is y^*. Then Bob needs to somehow communicate to Alice "if you have y^* in bin #1, then XOR your PRF output with $\mathsf{PRF}(k_1, y^*) \oplus s_1$". But he needs to do so without revealing y^* and the rest of his input items. He can do this by interpolating a polynomial P with the following property: if Bob has item y in bin j, then $P(y\|j) = \mathsf{PRF}(k_j, y) \oplus s_j$. Using the pseudorandomness of PRF and the randomness of the s_j values, it is possible to show that P is indistinguishable from a uniformly random polynomial, and hence it hides Bob's y-values.

Alice therefore can take her $\mathsf{PRF}(k_j, x)$ values and XOR with $P(y\|j)$. In the case that Bob also had this item x, then he would have assigned it to bin j (and to other bins as well), so Alice's result is s_j. If Bob did not have this x, then it is possible to show that Alice's result matches s_j with negligible probability (assuming the polynomial is over a sufficiently large field).

Overall, Alice obtains a vector of values (call them $t_1, \ldots, t_m$) where $t_j = s_j$ if and only if Alice's item in the jth bin is in the intersection. Hence we have reduced the problem of intersection to the problem of $m = O(n)$ string equality tests. These pairs of strings must be compared privately, since comparing them in the clear leaks information to both parties.

More Details. We write Cuckoo hashing with the following notation:

$$\mathcal{C} \leftarrow \mathsf{Cuckoo}^m_{h_1,h_2,h_3}(X)$$

This expression means to hash the items of X into m bins using Cuckoo hashing on hash functions $h_1, h_2, h_3 : \{0,1\}^* \rightarrow [m]$. The output is $\mathcal{C} = (C_1, \ldots, C_m)$, where for each $x \in X$ there is some $i \in \{1,2,3\}$ such that $C_{h_i(x)} = x\|i$.[1] Some positions of $\mathcal{C}$ will not matter, corresponding to empty bins.

Using this notation, the PSTY19 preprocessing is as follows:

---

1. Alice does $\mathcal{A} \leftarrow \mathsf{Cuckoo}^m_{h_1,h_2,h_3}(X)$.
2. The parties call $\mathcal{F}_{\mathsf{bOPRF}}$, where Alice is receiver with input $\mathcal{A}$ and Bob is sender. Bob receives output $(k_1, \ldots, k_m)$ and Alice receives output $(f_1, \ldots, f_m)$. For each $x \in X$ assigned to bin j by hash function i, we have $f_j = \mathsf{PRF}(k_j, x\|i)$.
3. For each $j \in [m]$, Bob choose a random s_j. He then interpolates a polynomial P of degree $< 3n$ such that for every $y \in Y$ and $i \in \{1,2,3\}$:

$$P(y\|i) = s_{h_i(y)} \oplus \mathsf{PRF}(k_{h_i(y)}, y\|i)$$

He sends P to Alice.
4. Alice computes a vector $(t_1, \ldots, t_m)$ where $t_j = P(\mathcal{A}_j) \oplus f_j$.

Mega-Bin Optimization. The PSTY19 approach requires parties to interpolate and evaluate a polynomial of degree $3n$, where n can be very large (e.g., $n = 2^{20}$). The fastest algorithms for interpolating such a polynomial (and evaluating it on n points) runs in $O(n \log^2 n)$ time. The cost of such polynomial operations can be prohibitive, so the authors of PSTY19 propose an alternative way to encode the same information.

Call a mapping "$y\|i \mapsto s_{h_i(y)} \oplus \mathsf{PRF}(k_{h_i(y)}, y\|i)$" a **hint**. Bob must convey $3n$ such hints to Alice in the protocol. One way to do this is to make $n' = n/\log n$ so-called *mega-bins* and assign each hint into a mega-bin using a hash function— i.e., assign the hint for $y\|i$ to the mega-bin indexed $H(y\|i)$ for a public random function $H : \{0,1\}^* \rightarrow [n']$. With these parameters, all mega-bins hold fewer than $O(\log n)$ items, with overwhelming probability. Bob adds dummy hints to each mega-bin so that all mega-bins contain the worst-case $O(\log n)$ number of hints (since the number of "real" hints per mega-bin leaks information about his input set). In each mega-bin, Bob interpolates a polynomial over the hints in that bin, and sends all the polynomials to Alice. For each $x\|i$ held by Alice, she can find the corresponding hint (if it exists) in the polynomial for the corresponding mega-bin.

---

[1] Appending the index of the hash function is helpful for dealing with edge cases like $h_1(x) = h_2(x)$, which happen with non-negligible probability.

The total communication cost is a degree-$O(\log n)$ polynomial for each of $n/\log n$ mega-bins; in other words, a constant-factor increase over sending a single degree-$3n$ polynomial. However, the total computation cost is an interpolation of a degree-$O(\log n)$ polynomial in each mega-bin, a total cost of $O\big((n/\log n)(\log n)(\log\log n)^2\big) = O(n(\log\log n)^2)$. In practice, the mega-bins are small enough that the asymptotically inferior quadratic polynomial interpolation algorithm is preferable, but this still leads to $O(n\log n)$ computational cost overall.

For simplicity, we describe our protocol in terms of the simpler single-polynomial solution, while our implementations use the mega-bins optimization.

4   Protocol Overviews and Details

In this section we give the details of our protocols for PCSI and related problems.

4.1   Our Protocol Core: Permuted Characteristic

All of our protocols build on the same core, which roughly consists of: (1) the PSTY19 preprocessing, reducing the intersection computation to $O(n)$ string equality tests; (2) an oblivious shuffle; (3) special-purpose equality tests.

We formalize this "protocol core" in terms of a **permuted characteristic** functionality $\mathcal{F}_{\text{pc}}$ defined in Fig. 5. Roughly speaking, the sender Alice learns a permutation π of her items, and the receiver Bob learns a vector e, where $e_i = 1$ if Alice's $\pi(i)$'th item is in Bob's set. In other words, e is the characteristic vector of Alice's (permuted) set with respect to the intersection.

Our protocol for permuted characteristic is given formally in Fig. 6.

Lemma 1. *The protocol in Fig. 6 securely realizes $\mathcal{F}_{pc}$ against semi-honest adversaries.*

Proof. Alice's view consists of her input, private randomness $\widetilde{\pi}$, outputs from $\mathcal{F}_{\text{bOPRF}}$ and $\mathcal{F}_{\text{osn}}$, and protocol message P from Bob. The simulator for a corrupt Alice runs the protocol honestly with the following changes:

- In step 2, it simulates uniform outputs f_j from $\mathcal{F}_{\text{bOPRF}}$.
- In step 4, it simulates a uniform polynomial P from Bob.
- In step 6, it chooses $\widetilde{\pi}$ so that $x_{\pi(i)} = A_{\widetilde{\pi}(i)}$, where π is the ideal output from $\mathcal{F}_{\text{pc}}$.

We show that this simulation is correct via the sequence of hybrids:

- *Hybrid 0.* The real interaction, in which Bob runs honestly with his input set Y.
- *Hybrid 1* The only change is that all terms of the form $\text{PRF}(k_j, \cdot)$ are replaced with uniform values, including Alice's outputs from the $\mathcal{F}_{\text{bOPRF}}$ functionality in step 2. This change is indistinguishable by the pseudorandomness of PRF.

Parameters: Number of items n for the sender and receiver.

On input $X = \{x_1, \ldots, x_n\} \subseteq \{0,1\}^*$ from the sender and $Y = \{y_1, \ldots, y_n\} \subseteq \{0,1\}^*$ from the receiver, with $|X| = |Y| = n$:

1. Choose a random permutation π over $[n]$.
2. Define the vector $e \in \{0,1\}^n$, where $e_i = 1$ if $x_{\pi(i)} \in Y$ and $e_i = 0$ otherwise.
3. Give the vector π to the sender and give e to the receiver.

Fig. 5. Permuted characteristic functionality $\mathcal{F}_{\mathsf{pc}}$.

Parameters: Size n of input sets. Cuckoo hashing parameters: hash functions h_1, h_2, h_3 and number of bins m.

Inputs: $X = \{x_1, \ldots, x_n\} \subseteq \{0,1\}^*$ from Alice; $Y = \{y_1, \ldots, y_n\} \subseteq \{0,1\}^*$ from Bob.

Protocol:

1. **(PSTY19 preprocessing)** Alice does $\mathcal{A} \leftarrow \mathsf{Cuckoo}^m_{h_1, h_2, h_3}(X)$.
2. The parties call $\mathcal{F}_{\mathsf{bOPRF}}$, where Alice is receiver with input $\mathcal{A}$ and Bob is sender. Bob receives output $(k_1, \ldots, k_m)$ and Alice receives output $(f_1, \ldots, f_m)$. Alice's output is such that, for each $x \in X$ assigned to bin j by hash function i, we have $f_j = \mathsf{PRF}(k_j, x\|i)$.
3. For each $j \in [m]$, Bob choose a random s_j.
4. Bob interpolates a polynomial P of degree $< 3n$ such that for every $y \in Y$ and $i \in \{1, 2, 3\}$, we have
$$P(y\|i) = s_{h_i(y)} \oplus \mathsf{PRF}(k_{h_i(y)}, y\|i)$$
   He sends P to Alice.
5. Alice computes a vector $(t_1, \ldots, t_m)$ where $t_j = P(\mathcal{A}_j) \oplus f_j$.
6. **(Oblivious shuffle)** Recall that Alice places her n items into m bins, with each item placed exactly once. Alice chooses a random injective function $\tilde{\pi} : [n] \to [m]$ such that $\tilde{\pi}(1), \ldots, \tilde{\pi}(n)$ are the non-empty bins of $\mathcal{A}$.
7. The parties invoke $\mathcal{F}_{\mathsf{osn}}$, where Alice acts as receiver with input $\tilde{\pi}$ and Bob acts as sender with input s. Alice receives output a and Bob receives output b, where $a_i \oplus b_i = s_{\tilde{\pi}(i)}$.
8. Alice locally computes vector a' as $a'_i = a_i \oplus t_{\tilde{\pi}(i)}$, so that a'_i and b_i are secret shares of $s_{\tilde{\pi}(i)} \oplus t_{\tilde{\pi}(i)}$. i.e; , $a'_i = b_i$ whenever $s_{\tilde{\pi}(i)} = t_{\tilde{\pi}(i)}$.
9. **(Equality tests)** The parties invoke $\mathcal{F}_{\mathsf{bEQ}}$, where Alice is sender with input a' and Bob is receiver with input b. Bob receives output e.
10. Recall that each Cuckoo bin $\mathcal{A}_{\tilde{\pi}(i)}$ holds some item $x_j \in X$. Define the permutation π on $[n]$ so that $x_{\pi(i)} = \mathcal{A}_{\tilde{\pi}(i)}$. Alice gives output π and Bob gives output e.

Fig. 6. Permuted characteristic protocol.

- *Hybrid 2* The only change is that in step 4 the polynomial P is chosen uniformly at random. Previously, P was interpolated through points of the form $s_{h_i(y)} \oplus \mathsf{PRF}(k_{h_i(y)}, y\|i)$. If Alice didn't have item y or didn't place item y according to hash function i, then the PRF-output term has been replaced by a random term that is independent of her view, so this output of P is uniform. For all other outputs of P (corresponding to Alice's placement of intersection items), the corresponding s_j values are uniform, making those P-outputs uniform as well. Overall, P is being interpolated to give only uniform outputs; hence P itself is distributed uniformly among polynomials of degree $<3n$. Hence this change in hybrids has no effect on Alice's view.
- *Hybrid 3* In the previous hybrid, Alice first chooses injective function $\tilde{\pi}$ and then uses it to compute permutation π. This induces a uniform distribution on π, so the same distribution can be obtained by first choosing uniform π and then computing the corresponding $\tilde{\pi}$.

The final hybrid corresponds to the simulator as described above.

Bob's view consists of his input, private randomness $\{s_j\}_j$, outputs from $\mathcal{F}_{\mathsf{bOPRF}}$, $\mathcal{F}_{\mathsf{osn}}$, $\mathcal{F}_{\mathsf{bEQ}}$. Clearly the outputs k_i from $\mathcal{F}_{\mathsf{bOPRF}}$ are distributed independently of the honest party's inputs. By definition, the output b from $\mathcal{F}_{\mathsf{osn}}$ is uniformly distributed, as a secret-share. This leaves only the output e of $\mathcal{F}_{\mathsf{bEQ}}$. It is a simple matter to check that e is distributed exactly as the ideal output of $\mathcal{F}_{\mathsf{pc}}$. Namely, it is a uniform bit-vector with exactly $|X \cap Y|$ ones. Hence, all of Bob's view can be trivially simulated given the ideal output e from $\mathcal{F}_{\mathsf{pc}}$.

4.2   Intersection and Union

Our protocol core (permuted characteristic) $\mathcal{F}_{\mathsf{pc}}$ can be used to realize plain **private set intersection (PSI)** and **private set union (PSU)** in a simple way. After $\mathcal{F}_{\mathsf{pc}}$, say Alice holds a permutation of her input set, and Bob holds the characteristic vector e. If the characteristic vector is 0 in position i, this means that Alice's ith item is in $X\backslash Y$. If the characteristic vector is 1 in position i, then Alice's ith item is in $X \cap Y$.

For PSI, the parties can use $n = |X|$ oblivious transfers to allow Bob to learn the items in $X \cap Y$. If $e_i = 1$, Bob will choose to learn Alice's ith item; otherwise he will choose to learn nothing.

Observe that PSU is equivalent to letting Bob learn $X\backslash Y$: Given the ideal PSU output $X \cup Y$ and Bob's input Y, he can indeed compute $X\backslash Y = (X \cup Y)\backslash Y$. Conversely, given $X\backslash Y$ and Bob's input Y, he can compute the PSU output $X \cup Y = (X\backslash Y) \cup Y$. With that in mind, Bob can easily compute $X\backslash Y$ by simply inverting his logic in the previous paragraph. If $e_i = 0$, Bob will choose to learn (via OT) Alice's ith item; otherwise he will choose to learn nothing.

The formal details of these PSI/PSU protocols are given in Fig. 7. We remark that this approach for PSI is not competitive with the state-of-the-art special-purpose protocols for PSI. In particular, an oblivious shuffle is unnecessary for PSI. We include this PSI protocol merely for illustrative purposes. However, as we shall see, our approach for PSU is indeed competitive with the state of the art, and is useful as a stepping stone to another interesting application.

Parameters: Size of sets n.

On input $X = \{x_1, \ldots, x_n\} \subseteq \{0,1\}^*$ from the sender and $Y = \{y_1, \ldots, y_n\} \subseteq \{0,1\}^*$ from the receiver:

1. **[for intersection:]** give $X \cap Y$ to the receiver
2. **[for union:]** give $X \cup Y$ to the receiver

Fig. 7. Ideal functionalities for intersection/union ($\mathcal{F}_{\mathsf{psi}}/\mathcal{F}_{\mathsf{psu}}$).

Parameters: Size of sets n.

Inputs: $X = \{x_1, \ldots, x_n\}$ for the sender; $Y = \{y_1, \ldots, y_n\}$ for the receiver.

Protocol:

1. Parties invoke $\mathcal{F}_{\mathsf{pc}}$ with inputs X, Y Sender obtains a permutation π. Receiver obtains characteristic vector e.
2. Parties invoke n instances of OT via $\mathcal{F}_{\mathsf{ot}}$. The receiver uses e as the choice bits.
3. **[For intersection:]**
   (a) The sender uses input $(\perp, x_{\pi(i)})$ as input to the ith OT.
   (b) The receiver learns $\{x_{\pi(i)} \mid e_i = 1\} = X \cap Y$, which he outputs.
4. **[For union:]**
   (a) The sender uses input $(x_{\pi(i)}, \perp)$ as input to the ith OT.
   (b) The receiver learns $\{x_{\pi(i)} \mid e_i = 0\} = X \setminus Y$, he outputs $\{X \setminus Y\} \cup Y$.

Fig. 8. Protocols for intersection and union.

Lemma 2. *The PSI and PSU protocols of Fig. 8 securely realize $\mathcal{F}_{\mathsf{psi}}$ and $\mathcal{F}_{\mathsf{psu}}$, respectively, (Fig. 7) against semi-honest adversaries.*

Proof (Proof sketch) We focus on the security proof for PSI, as the proof for PSU is analagous. Security against a corrupt sender is trivial, since their view consists of only the output π from $\mathcal{F}_{\mathsf{pc}}$. For a corrupt receiver, their view consists of the vector e and OT outputs. If $x_{\pi(i)} \in Y$, then $e_i = 1$ and the ith OT output is $x_{\pi(i)}$. Otherwise, $e_i = 0$ and the ith OT outputs is $\perp$. Furthermore, π is uniform, and therefore this distribution can be simulated given only ideal output $X \cap Y$: Sample a uniform binary vector e containing $|X \cap Y|$ 1s. Then choose a uniform assignment of elements of $X \cap Y$ to OT instances i for which $e_i = 1$.

Our protocols give output only to one party (the receiver). In the semi-honest setting, the receiver can simply report the output to the sender in order to provide output to both parties.

4.3   PCSI: Computing on the Intersection

We now discuss PCSI: computing a function of the intersection. Our approach inherently leaks the cardinality, and we formalize this in the ideal functionality

$\mathcal{F}_{\mathsf{pcsi+card}}$ of Fig. 9, which outputs the cardinality of the intersection along with a function g of the intersection.

Parameters: Size of sets n. Function g.

On input $X \subseteq \{0,1\}^*$ from the sender and $Y \subseteq \{0,1\}^*$ from the receiver:

1. Give $\left(|X \cap Y|, \ g(X \cap Y) \right)$ to the receiver.

Fig. 9. Ideal functionality for computing cardinality and an arbitrary function of the intersection $\mathcal{F}^g_{\mathsf{pcsi+card}}$.

Perhaps the most common instance of PCSI is to compute *only* the cardinality (*i.e.*, g is empty). This special case can be obtained trivially by our $\mathcal{F}_{\mathsf{pc}}$ protocol core:

Proposition 1. *If the parties run $\mathcal{F}_{\mathsf{pc}}$ on their inputs and the receiver outputs the hamming weight of e, then the resulting protocol securely realizes $\mathcal{F}^g_{\mathsf{pcsi+card}}$ for $g = \bot$, against semi-honest adversaries.*

Proof (Proof sketch). Security against corrupt sender is trivial since the sender's view consists only of a uniformly distributed permutation (*i.e.*, independent of anyone's inputs). Regarding a corrupt receiver: since π is uniformly chosen among permutations, the vector e is distributed as a uniform vector of length n with exactly $|X \cap Y|$ ones. This distribution can therefore be simulated given only the ideal output $|X \cap Y|$.

Note also that if the sizes of X and Y are public, then computing $|X \cap Y|$ is equivalent to computing $|X \cup Y|$, via the standard inclusion-exclusion formula.

Cardinality-Sum. If the function g is simple enough, then $\mathcal{F}^g_{\mathsf{pcsi+card}}$ can be realized in a very simple way from $\mathcal{F}_{\mathsf{pc}}$. We illustrate with an example, which does not exactly fit into the definition of $\mathcal{F}_{\mathsf{pcsi+card}}$ since one party has a set of key-value pairs. Our example involves the **cardinality-sum** functionality proposed by Ion et al. [IKN+19]. The functionality is described formally in Fig. 10. It reveals the intersection of the cardinality as well as the sum of all *values* whose *keys* are in the intersection.

In Fig. 11 we describe a simple protocol realizing the cardinality-sum functionality. Similar to how we achieve PSI & PSU from $\mathcal{F}_{\mathsf{pc}}$, this protocol uses oblivious transfers to let the receiver learn things, based on the characteristic vector. In this case, instead of learning the sender's items in the clear, the receiver learns either an additive secret share of 0 or a secret share of that item's associated value. Then the receiver can compute the sum by locally adding the shares.

Lemma 3. *The protocol of Fig. 11 securely realizes ideal functionality $\mathcal{F}_{\mathsf{card+sum}}$ (Fig. 10), against semi-honest adversaries.*

Parameters: Size of sets n. Group $\mathbb{G}$.

On input $X = \{(x_1, v_1), \ldots, (x_n, v_n)\}$ from the sender, where each $v_i \in \mathbb{G}$, and input $Y \subseteq \{0,1\}^*$ from the receiver:

1. Give output (c, s) to the receiver, where:

$$c = \left| \{x_1, \ldots, x_n\} \cap Y \right| \qquad\qquad s = \sum_{x_i \in Y} v_i$$

Fig. 10. Ideal functionality $\mathcal{F}_{\mathsf{card+sum}}$ for cardinality-sum.

Parameters: Size of sets n. Group $\mathbb{G}$.

Inputs: $X = \{(x_1, v_1), \ldots, (x_n, v_n)\}$ for the sender, where $v_i \in \mathbb{G}$; $Y \subseteq \{0,1\}^*$ for the receiver.

Protocol:

1. Parties invoke $\mathcal{F}_{\mathsf{pc}}$ with inputs $\{x_1, \ldots, x_n\}$ and Y. The Sender obtains a permutation π. Receiver obtains characteristic vector e.
2. The sender chooses a random vector $(r_1, \ldots, r_n) \leftarrow \mathbb{G}^n$ such that $\sum_i r_i = 0$.
3. Parties invoke n instances of OT via $\mathcal{F}_{\mathsf{ot}}$. The receiver uses e as their choice bits. The sender uses input $(r_i, r_i + v_{\pi(i)})$ as input to the ith OT. The receiver gets output $\hat{v}_i$ from the ith OT.
4. The receiver outputs $\left(\sum_i e_i, \ \sum_i \hat{v}_i \right)$.

Fig. 11. Protocol for cardinality-sum.

Proof (Proof sketch). Security against a corrupt sender is immediate. Relative to the cardinality protocol, the only addition to a corrupt receiver's view are the outputs of the OTs. View these outputs as the vector $r + q$, where r is uniform subject to having sum 0; and $q_i = v_i$ if $x_i \in Y$ and $q_i = 0$ otherwise. Since the r_i's are a perfect additive secret share of 0, the distribution of $r + q$ depends only on $\sum_i q_i$, which is the ideal output s.

General Case. More generally, suppose the sender has a set of key-value pairs (x_i, v_i), and the receiver has a set of keys Y. The parties can use parallel oblivious transfers to secret share a vector q, where:

$$q_i = \begin{cases} v_i & x_i \in Y \\ \tilde{v} & x_i \notin Y \end{cases}$$

where $\tilde{v}$ is some dummy/default value. In the case of cardinality-sum, $\tilde{v} = 0$.

With secret shares of such a vector, the parties can compute a function g that takes in a vector of inputs and ignores the dummy/default values in the input. In the case of cardinality-sum, g was simple addition and no interaction was required to compute it.

4.4   Secret-Shared Intersection

In some settings, it is more convenient for the parties to obtain secret shares of the items of the intersection, so that it can be fed into a generic 2PC.

To illustrate the challenges here, let's first consider a very natural approach that *doesn't* work. The parties run $\mathcal{F}_{pc}$, so that Bob learns the indices of Alice's intersection items, permuted according to the secret permutation π. Whereas with PSI/PSU, Bob used OT to selectively learn the items of the intersection (or set-difference), we might be tempted to have Bob now learn secret-shares of the items in the intersection.

To see why this isn't so straight forward, imagine that each party has 1 million items, and there are 10 in the intersection. Bob could indeed use OT to learn secret shares of those 10 items. But now it is time to run the 2PC to compute g on those 10 items. Alice prepared 1M additive shares, and she doesn't know which 10 of them should be given to g! Bob knows which ones are the right ones, but he can't tell Alice because she knows the secret permutation π—this would reveal the entire contents of the intersection to Alice!

We address this challenge by simply doing another oblivious switching network. Alice holds a secret permutation of her items. Bob knows which indices in this permutation correspond to items in the intersection. He chooses an injective function ρ whose range covers exactly those intersection items. They use an oblivious switching network, so that both parties learn additive shares of only those items referenced by ρ.

Details of this protocol are given in Fig. 13. Bear in mind that the input to g is necessarily given as an ordered vector. Most applications of PCSI will involve a function g that is symmetric, meaning that g is insensitive to the order of its inputs. However, note that the values that are fed into g are randomly permuted, from both parties' perspective (Bob didn't know π and Alice didn't know ρ). Hence, our protocol is meaningful even if g is sensitive to the order of its input items. In that case, we still achieve the most natural security, where the items of the intersection are randomly shuffled before being given as input to g.

Lemma 4. *The protocol of Fig. 13 securely realizes* $\mathcal{F}_{ss\text{-}int}$ *(Fig. 12), against semi-honest adversaries.*

Proof. Beyond the output of $\mathcal{F}_{pc}$, the only thing added to parties' views in Fig. 13 is the cardinality c and the secret shares output by $\mathcal{F}_{osn}$. The former can be inferred by the ideal output of $\mathcal{F}_{ss\text{-}int}$, and the latter coincides with the ideal output itself.

4.5   Private ID

Buddhavarapu *et al.* [BKM+20] proposed a useful functionality that they called **private-ID**. In this functionality, both parties provide a set of items. The functionality assigns to each item a truly random identifier (where identical items receive the same identifier). It then reveals to each party the identifiers corresponding to their own items, and also the entire set of *all* identifiers (*i.e.*, the identifiers of the union of their input sets).

Parameters: Size of sets n.

On input $X \subseteq \{0,1\}^*$ from Alice and $Y \subseteq \{0,1\}^*$ from Bob:

1. Let $z_1, \ldots, z_k$ be a random permutation of $X \cap Y$
2. Choose $\boldsymbol{a}$ uniformly at random. Define $\boldsymbol{b}$ via $b_i = a_i \oplus z_i$. I.e., $\boldsymbol{a}$ and $\boldsymbol{b}$ are secret shares of $(z_1, \ldots, z_k)$.
3. Give $\boldsymbol{a}$ to Alice and $\boldsymbol{b}$ to Bob.

Fig. 12. Ideal functionality for computing secret shares of the intersection $\mathcal{F}_{\text{ss-int}}$.

Parameters: Size of sets n.

Inputs: $X, Y \subseteq \{0,1\}^*$ for the sender and receiver, respectively.

Protocol:

1. Parties invoke $\mathcal{F}_{\text{pc}}$ with inputs $\{x_1, \ldots, x_n\}$ and Y Sender obtains a permutation π. Receiver obtains characteristic vector $\boldsymbol{e}$.
2. Let c be the Hamming weight of $\boldsymbol{e}$. The receiver announces c to the sender.
3. The receiver chooses a random injective function $\rho : [c] \to [n]$ such that $e_{\rho(i)} = 1$ for all i.
4. The parties invoke $\mathcal{F}_{\text{osn}}$ where the sender provides input $\{x_{\pi(1)}, \ldots, x_{\pi(n)}\}$ and the receiver provides input ρ. The result is that the parties hold secret shares of $(x_{\pi(\rho(1))}, \ldots, x_{\pi(\rho(c))})$.

Fig. 13. Protocol for secret-shared intersection.

The advantage of Private ID is that both parties can sort their private data relative to the global set of identifiers. They can then proceed item-by-item, doing any desired private computation, being assured that identical items are aligned.

Parameters: Number of items n for the sender and receiver; length of identifiers ℓ.

On input $X = \{x_1, \ldots, x_n\} \subseteq \{0,1\}^*$ from Alice and $Y = \{y_1, \ldots, y_n\} \subseteq \{0,1\}^*$ from Bob, with $|X| = |Y| = n$:

1. For every $z \in X \cup Y$, choose a random identifier $R(z) \leftarrow \{0,1\}^\ell$.
2. Define $R^* = \{R(z) \mid z \in X \cup Y\}$.
3. Give output $(R^*, R(x_1), \ldots, R(x_n))$ to Alice.
4. Give output $(R^*, R(y_1), \ldots, R(y_n))$ to Bob.

Fig. 14. Private ID functionality $\mathcal{F}_{\text{priv-ID}}$.

Parameters: Size n of input sets. Cuckoo hashing parameters: hash functions h_1, h_2, h_3 and number of bins m. An auxiliary PRF PRF'.

Inputs: $X = \{x_1, \ldots, x_n\} \subseteq \{0,1\}^*$ from Alice; $Y = \{y_1, \ldots, y_n\} \subseteq \{0,1\}^*$ from Bob.

Protocol:

1. **(Sloppy PRF Bob → Alice)** Alice does $\mathcal{A} \leftarrow \mathsf{Cuckoo}^m_{h_1,h_2,h_3}(X)$.
2. The parties call $\mathcal{F}_{\mathsf{bOPRF}}$, where Alice is receiver with input $\mathcal{A}$ and Bob is sender. Bob receives output $(k_1^B, \ldots, k_m^B)$ and Alice receives output $(f_1^A, \ldots, f_m^A)$. Alice's output is such that, for each $x \in X$ assigned to bin j by hash function i, we have $f_j = \mathsf{PRF}(k_j^B, x\|i)$.
3. Bob chooses a random PRF seed s^B. He interpolates a polynomial P^A of degree $< 3n$ such that for every $y \in Y$ and $i \in \{1,2,3\}$, we have

$$P^B(y\|i) = \mathsf{PRF}'(s^B, y) \oplus \mathsf{PRF}(k^B_{h_i(y)}, y\|i)$$

   He sends P^B to Alice.
4. For each item x that Alice assigned to a bin with hash function i, Alice defines

$$R^A(x) = P^B(x\|i) \oplus f^A_{h_i(x)} \oplus \mathsf{PRF}'(s^A, x)$$

5. **(Sloppy PRF Alice → Bob)** Bob does $\mathcal{B} \leftarrow \mathsf{Cuckoo}^m_{h_1,h_2,h_3}(Y)$.
6. The parties call $\mathcal{F}_{\mathsf{bOPRF}}$, where Bob is receiver with input $\mathcal{B}$ and Alice is sender. Alice receives output $(k_1^A, \ldots, k_m^A)$ and Bob receives output $(f_1^B, \ldots, f_m^B)$. Bob's output is such that, for each $y \in Y$ assigned to bin j by hash function i, we have $f_j^B = \mathsf{PRF}(k_j^A, x\|i)$.
7. Alice chooses a random PRF seed s^A. She interpolates a polynomial P^A of degree $< 3n$ such that for every $x \in X$ and $i \in \{1,2,3\}$, we have

$$P^A(x\|i) = \mathsf{PRF}'(s^A, x) \oplus \mathsf{PRF}(k^A_{h_i(x)}, x\|i)$$

   She sends P^A to Bob.
8. For each item y that Bob assigned to a bin with hash function i, Bob defines

$$R^B(y) = P^A(y\|i) \oplus f^B_{h_i(y)} \oplus \mathsf{PRF}'(s^B, y)$$

9. **(Union)** The parties invoke $\mathcal{F}_{\mathsf{psu}}$, with inputs $\{R^A(x) \mid x \in X\}$ for Alice and $\{R^B(y) \mid y \in Y\}$ for Bob. They obtain output U and output the following:

$$(U, \langle R^A(x_i) \mid i \in [n]\rangle) \text{ (Alice)}$$

$$(U, \langle R^B(y_i) \mid i \in [n]\rangle) \text{ (Bob)}$$

Fig. 15. Private-ID protocol.

Our Approach. Our approach for private-ID builds on oblivious PRF and private set union. Roughly speaking, suppose the parties run an oblivious PRF twice: first, so that Alice learns k_A and Bob learns $\mathsf{PRF}(k_A, y_i)$ for each of his items y_i; and second so that Bob learns k_B and Alice learns $\mathsf{PRF}(k_B, x_i)$ for each of her items x_i. We will define the random identifier of an item x as

$$R(x) \stackrel{\text{def}}{=} \mathsf{PRF}(k_A, x) \oplus \mathsf{PRF}(k_B, x).$$

Note that after running the relevant OPRF protocols, both parties can compute $R(x)$ for their own items. To complete the private-ID protocol, they must simply perform a private set *union* on their sets $R(X)$ and $R(Y)$.

This approach indeed leads to a fine private-ID protocol. In the full-version of our paper we present and prove secure an optimization we observe that a full-fledged OPRF is not needed and a so-called "**sloppy** OPRF" would suffice.

In particular, if Bob has an item y^* that is *not* held by Alice, then it doesn't matter whether Bob learns the "correct" value $\mathsf{PRF}(k_A, y^*)$. Suppose that Bob instead learns some other value z^* instead. Then Bob will consider $z^* \oplus \mathsf{PRF}(k_B, y^*)$ to be the identifier of this item. Since Alice doesn't know k_B, this identifier looks random to Alice, which is the only property we need from private-ID for an item that is held by Bob and not Alice.

Hence we instantiate this general OPRF-based approach, but with a more efficient "**sloppy** OPRF" protocol. In a sloppy OPRF, Alice provides a set X; Bob provides a set Y; Alice learns k_A and Bob learns a list of output values $z_1, \ldots, z_n$. For every $y_i \in Y$, if $y_i \in X$, then $z_i = \mathsf{PRF}(k_A, y_i)$, but for other z_i values there is no correctness guarantee.

We achieve a sloppy OPRF using the OPPRF idea that is also used in the PSTY19 pre-processing. Namely, Bob hashes his items into bins with Cuckoo hashing. They perform a batch-OPRF, where Bob will learn $\mathsf{PRF}(k_{h_i(y)}, y\|i)$ if he placed item y according to hash function h_i. Alice chooses a random seed s for a different PRF PRF' and sends a polynomial P that satisfies $P(x\|i) = \mathsf{PRF}'(s, x) \oplus \mathsf{PRF}(k_{h_i(y)}, y\|i)$ for all $x \in X$ and all $i \in \{1, 2, 3\}$. Bob will compute his final output as $P(y\|i) \oplus \mathsf{PRF}(k_{h_i(y)}, y\|i)$, which will equal $\mathsf{PRF}'(s, y)$ in the case that Alice held the item y.

Lemma 5. *The protocol in Fig. 15 securely realizes the $\mathcal{F}_{\mathsf{priv\text{-}ID}}$ functionality Fig. 14 in the presence of semi-honest adversaries.*

Proof. The protocol is symmetric with respect to the parties' roles, so we focus on the case of a corrupt Alice.

Claim. In step 8, when Bob computes R^B, it satisfies the property that if $y \in X \cap Y$ then $R^B(y) = \mathsf{PRF}'(s^A, y) \oplus \mathsf{PRF}'(s^B, y)$.

Proof. Suppose Bob placed item y into bin $h_i(y)$ according to hash function i. Then Bob computed $R^B(y)$ as $R^B(y) = P^A(y\|i) \oplus \mathsf{PRF}(k^B_{h_i(y)}, y\|i) \oplus \mathsf{PRF}'(s^B, y)$. Since $y \in X$ also, the polynomial P^A satisfies $P^A(y\|i) = \mathsf{PRF}(k^B_{h_i(y)}, y\|i) \oplus \mathsf{PRF}'(s^A, y)$. Substituting, we see that indeed $R^B(y) = \mathsf{PRF}'(s^A, y) \oplus \mathsf{PRF}'(s^B, x)$. This implies in particular that $R^A(y) = R^B(y)$ for $y \in X \cap Y$.

The simulator for corrupt Alice receives ideal output $(R^*, R(x_1), \ldots, R(x_n))$ and simulates Alice's view as follows:

- in step 2, uniform output f_j^A from $\mathcal{F}_{\mathsf{bOPRF}}$.
- in step 4, a polynomial P^B satisfying $P^B(x\|i) = f_{h_i(x)}^A \oplus R(x) \oplus \mathsf{PRF}'(s^A, x)$ for every item $x \in X$ placed according to hash function i, and uniform otherwise.
- in step 6, uniform keys k_j^A from $\mathcal{F}_{\mathsf{bOPRF}}$.
- in step 9, output $U = R^*$ from $\mathcal{F}_{\mathsf{psu}}$.

We show the correctness of this simulation via a sequence of hybrids:

- *Hybrid 0:* The real protocol interaction.
- *Hybrid 1:* Replace all terms of the form $\mathsf{PRF}'(s^B, y)$ with random; this change is indistinguishable from the pseudorandomness property.
- *Hybrid 2:* Replace all terms of the form $\mathsf{PRF}(k_j, x\|i)$ with random (including outputs f_j^A given to Alice); this change is indistinguishable from the security of $\mathcal{F}_{\mathsf{bOPRF}}$ and the pseudorandomness of PRF.

  Previously P^B was interpolated as $P^B(y\|i) = \mathsf{PRF}'(s^B, y) \oplus \mathsf{PRF}(k_{h_i(y)}^B, y\|i)$. Now, if Alice did not have item y and placed it according to hash function i, then the $\mathsf{PRF}(k_{h_i(y)}^B, y\|i)$ term is now uniform and independent of her view, making this output of P^B random. For $y\|i$ corresponding to Alice's item placement, the y's are distinct, and the $\mathsf{PRF}'(s^B, y)$ in those terms are now uniform, making this output of P^B random. In short, P^B is now a uniform polynomial.

  Note also that $R^B(y)$ is uniform for $y \in Y\backslash X$, because of the fresh random $\mathsf{PRF}'(s^B, y)$ term in its definition.
- *Hybrid 3:* Instead of computing $R^A(x)$ as in step 4, where one of the terms $P^B(x\|i)$ is a uniform value, we instead compute $R^A(x)$ randomly and then interpolate P^B to go through the correct value (and be otherwise uniform), i.e.,

$$P^B(x\|i) = R^A(x) \oplus f_{h_i(x)}^A \oplus \mathsf{PRF}'(s^A, x)$$

This change has no effect on Alice's view distribution. Note that in this hybrid, every $R^A(x)$ is random, and every $R^B(y)$ is random subject to $R^B(y) = R^A(y)$ in the case that $y \in X \cap Y$.

This final hybrid corresponds to the final simulation, after some slight rearranging. First, a random $R(z)$ is chosen for every $z \in X \cap Y$. Then the polynomial P^B is interpolated according to $\{R(x) \mid x \in X\}$, via the expression in the simulator description. Finally, the output of $\mathcal{F}_{\mathsf{psu}}$ is $\{R(z) \mid z \in X \cap Y\}$.

5   Comparing Communication Costs

In this section we compare our new approach to existing protocols. The focus in this section is on quantitative differences and communication complexity. In Sect. 6 we report on the running time of the implemented protocols.

5.1 PSU

The state of the art PSU protocol is due to Kolesnikov et al. [KRTW19]. In that protocol, each party's n items are hashed into $m = O(n/\log n)$ bins. The expected number of items per bin is n/m, but the worst-case load among the bins is larger by a constant factor. In order to hide the true number of items per bin, each party must add dummy items up to this worst-case maximum.

Within each bin, the parties perform a subprotocol with linear number of OPRFs, linear number of OTs, and quadratic communication. Specifically, the additional communication for β items in a bin is $\beta^2\sigma$, where $\sigma = \lambda + 2\log n$ and λ is the statistical security parameter.

Let c be the constant factor expansion within a bin to accommodate the dummy items (i.e., n/m expected items in a bin, padded to cn/m including dummies). For usual set sizes, the constant is 3.2–3.6. Then the total communication cost for the protocol is:

$$cn \cdot \mathsf{bOPRF} + cn \cdot \mathsf{OT} + (c^2 n \log n)\sigma$$

Here bOPRF and OT refer to the communication costs for a single bOPRF and OT, respectively.

Our protocol requires the following: $1.27n$ OPRFs, sending one degree-$3n$ polynomial (for the PSTY19 preprocessing), roughly $1.27n \log n$ OTs (for the switching network), and then n additional OTs (to selectively transfer the union). Note the constant bounding the size of the Beneš network is indeed 1. The total communication cost is therefore:

$$1.27n \cdot \mathsf{bOPRF} + 3n\sigma + (1.27n \log n + n) \cdot \mathsf{OT}$$

In comparings the protocols, the dominant term is the one containing $O(n \log n)$. Our protocol is superior if $1.27\mathsf{OT} < c^2\sigma$. Indeed, the cost of an OT is $\kappa + 2\ell$ (where ℓ is the length of the item being transferred), which in our implementation is $128 + 2 \cdot 60 = 248$. Hence $1.27\mathsf{OT} \approx 315$. In [KRTW19], $c^2\sigma$ is at least $10 \cdot 80 = 800$.

These pen-and-paper calculations match what we find empirically in Table 2 where our communication cost is half that of Kolesnikov et al. [KRTW19]. Our protocol is a significant constant factor better.

5.2 PCSI

For general-purpose PCSI, the leading protocol is due to Pinkas et al. [PSTY19] (PSTY19). Recall that our protocol builds on the first several steps of their protocol, which we call the PSTY19 preprocessing. We focus on the difference between the two approaches, after performing the common preprocessing. In [PSTY19], the authors report that the cost of preprocessing is roughly 4% of the total protocol cost; hence the differences we discuss in this section are reflective of the overall cost difference in the protocols.

In [PSTY19], the pre-processing is followed up with $1.27n$ private equality tests, which are performed inside generic MPC (*e.g.*, garbled circuits). To compare ℓ-bit items, the cost of such a private equality test is $2\ell\kappa$ using the state-of-the-art garbled circuit construction [ZRE15]. Hence the total communication cost is $2.54\ell\kappa n$.

In our protocol, the pre-processing is followed up by an oblivious switching network of roughly $1.27n \log n$ nodes, each requiring OT on strings of length 2ℓ. The cost of each OT is $\kappa + 4\ell$ bits, and our total communication cost is $1.27(n \log n)(\kappa + 4\ell)$.

Focusing on the asymptotically dominant term, our implementation is superior if the costs per items satisfy $1.27(\log n)(\kappa+4\ell) < 2.54\ell\kappa$. In our implementations, $\ell = 60$ and $\kappa = 128$. Hence our cost per item is $1.27 \cdot 368 \cdot \log n = 467 \log n$ and theirs is $2.54 \cdot 60 \cdot 128 \approx 19500$. We can see that for all reasonable values of n, our cost will be significantly less than their cost (the break-even point for these particular parameters is an unrealistic $n = 2^{41}$).

5.3 Cardinality-Sum, Private ID

For cardinality-sum, private-ID, and secret-shared intersection, our approach is the first based on efficient symmetric-key operations. The prior protocols of [IKN+19, MPR+20, BKM+20] are all based on public-key techniques (Diffie-Hellman and partially homomorphic encryption). As such, their protocols will have superior communication cost but significantly higher computation costs, due to their use of public-key operations linear in the size of the input sets.

6 Performance

In this section we discuss details of our implementation and report our performance in computing the following set operations: (1) **card**: cardinality of the intersection (permuted characteristic); (2) **psu**: union of the sets/**psi**: intersection of the sets; (3) **priv-ID**: computing a universal identifier for every item in the union; (4) **card-sum** sum of the associated values for every item in the intersection. We compare our work with the current fastest known protocol implementation for each functionality. To the best of our knowledge, there is no known implementation to compare our **card-sum** protocol and we leave it out of our comparison. Our run times for **card-sum** is almost equal to that of **psu**.

6.1 Experimental Setup

We ran all our protocols on a single Intel Xeon processor at 2.30 GHz with 256 GB RAM. We execute the protocol on a single thread and emulate the two network connections using Linux tc command. For the LAN setting, we set the network latency to 0.02 ms and bandwidth of 10 Gbps and for the WAN setting the latency is set to 80 ms and bandwidth 50 Mbps. We also use a tc sub-command to compute the communication complexity for all the protocols evaluated in the performance section. We stress that we used the same methodology and environment to compute all the reported costs in this section.

6.2   Implementation Details

For concrete analysis we set the computational security parameter $\kappa = 128$ and the statistical security parameter $\sigma = 40$. Our protocols are written in C++ and we use the following libraries in our implementation.

- *PSTY19 pre-processing phase.* We re-use the implementation by the authors of the paper [PSTY19]. Found: https://github.com/encryptogroup/OPPRF-PSI.git
- *Private equality tests.* We use the batch-OPRF construction of [KKRT16] implemented in libOTe library to compute the string equality tests. Found: https://github.com/osu-crypto/libOTe.git
- *Oblivious transfers and switching.* We generate many instances of oblivious transfer using the implementation of IKNP OT extension [IKNP03] from libOTe. Found: https://github.com/osu-crypto/libOTe.git
  Recent advances in OT extension [BCG+19b, BCG+19a] provide better asymptotic performance, but we found the existing implementations to improve over IKNP only in the multi-threaded case, while we measure only single-threaded performance. We developed our own implementation of Beneš network programming/evaluation. We used the code base in https://github.com/elf11/benes_network_implementation as a starting point. We emphasize that we made many corrections, implemented the functions to evaluate the network, augment it to an oblivious switching network. Further, we implemented the generalized OSN that can process any choice of input size n as opposed input sizes that are powers of 2.
- Additionally, we rely use the cryptoTools library as the general framework to compute hash functions, PRNG calls, creating channels, sending 128-bit blocks and so on. Found: https://github.com/ladnir/cryptoTools.git

In Table 1 we present a breakdown run time of each step in our permuted characteristic protocol. Unsurprisingly, the oblivious switching network is the most expensive step in the WAN setting, as its communication scales as $O(n \log n)$, while all other steps are linear.

6.3   Comparison Running Times

Now, we compare the run time of our protocol with the state-of-the-art for each of the functionalities. We analyse how our work compares to the previous best protocol and highlight the settings in which we beat their performance. For a fair comparison, we compiled and ran the comparison protocols and our protocol in the same hardware environment. We report the numbers for 3 input sizes $n = \{2^{12}, 2^{16}, 2^{20}\}$ all executed over a single thread. We choose our LAN

Table 1. Run time (in seconds) of our protocol core to compute the permuted characteristic (with breakdown for each step) for input set sizes $n = \{2^{12}, 2^{16}, 2^{20}\}$ executed over a single thread for the LAN and WAN configurations.

	LAN (s)			WAN (s)		
	2^{12}	2^{16}	2^{20}	2^{12}	2^{16}	2^{20}
Protocol steps						
PSTY19	0.70	2.97	43.47	1.03	6.27	67.53
OSN	0.39	2.39	32.44	2.72	12.19	186.68
PEqT	0.49	1.00	8.50	3.36	6.38	28.68
Protocol core	1.58	6.36	84.41	7.11	24.84	282.89

setting to have latency set to 0.02 ms and a bandwidth of 10 Gbps and our WAN setting to have latency set to 80 ms and bandwidth of 50 Mbps. For our protocol, we report the average run time over 5 iterations.

Private Set Union. From Table 2, we can see that the empirical communication cost of our protocol is roughly half the cost of [KRTW19]. This is consistent with our back-of-the-envelope estimates from Sect. 5. We highlight that our improvement over [KRTW19] increases with the size of the input set. This is because the run time is dominated by $O(n \log n)$ term and this becomes more significant with increased input sizes.

Table 2. Communication (in MB) and run time (in seconds) of private set union protocol for input set sizes $n = \{2^{12}, 2^{16}, 2^{20}\}$ executed over a single thread for LAN and WAN configurations.

PSU	LAN (s)			WAN (s)			Comm (MB)		
	2^{12}	2^{16}	2^{20}	2^{12}	2^{16}	2^{20}	2^{12}	2^{16}	2^{20}
[KRTW19]	1.42	12.77	243.03	4.76	46.56	823.01	7.74	131.4	2476
Our protocol	1.87	8.54	114.42	9.56	28.80	319.87	3.85	67.38	1155

Cardinality of Intersection. From Table 3 we can observe that the communication cost of our protocol is roughly a third of the cost of [PSTY19]. This contributes to our improved run time in the WAN setting. In the LAN setting, our cardinality protocol is comparable but does not beat the numbers of [PSTY19]. This can be attributed to the time-intensive programming of the switching network in the OSN step of our protocol.

Table 3. Communication (in MB) and run time (in seconds) of cardinality of intersection protocol for input set sizes $n = \{2^{12}, 2^{16}, 2^{20}\}$ executed over a single thread for LAN and WAN configurations.

Card	LAN (s)			WAN (s)			Comm (MB)		
	2^{12}	2^{16}	2^{20}	2^{12}	2^{16}	2^{20}	2^{12}	2^{16}	2^{20}
[PSTY19]	1.230	5.07	65.12	7.90	38.79	530.15	10.53	166.18	2656
Our protocol	1.60	6.56	84.882	8.40	24.57	284.62	2.93	55.49	1030

Private-ID. The implementation in Table 4 relies on techniques from public-key cryptography which explains their significantly lower communication costs. In comparison, our OT-based implementation that largely relies on symmetric-key operations has better performance. This is more noticeable with larger input sets, where the number of public-key operations increases linearly for [BKM+20]. It's consistent with this reasoning to see that our improvement in run times in more noticeable in the LAN setting. Unlike our Private-ID protocol, the run time of the protocol in [BKM+20] is a function of the intersection size. We sampled inputs where roughly half the elements were present in the intersection, for our experiments with both protocols. [BKM+20] implemented their protocol in Rust programming language with specific libraries that are tailored to be more efficient with elliptic curve operations speeding up their run time despite using public-key operations.

Table 4. Communication (in MB) and run time (in seconds) of the private-ID protocol for input set sizes $n = \{2^{12}, 2^{16}, 2^{20}\}$ executed over a single thread for LAN and WAN configurations.

priv-ID	LAN (s)			WAN (s)			Comm (MB)		
	2^{12}	2^{16}	2^{20}	2^{12}	2^{16}	2^{20}	2^{12}	2^{16}	2^{20}
[BKM+20]	2.76	34.70	394.60	6.63	40.49	426.11	0.99	14.85	224.26
Our protocol	2.75	9.70	118.14	12.74	34.09	346.32	4.43	76.57	1293

References

ALSZ13. Asharov, G., Lindell, Y., Schneider, T., Zohner, M.: More efficient oblivious transfer and extensions for faster secure computation. In: Sadeghi, A.-R., Gligor, V.D., Yung, M. (eds.) ACM CCS 2013, pp. 535–548. ACM Press (November 2013)

BA12. Blanton, M., Aguiar, E.: Private and oblivious set and multiset operations. In: Youm, H.Y., Won, Y. (eds.) ASIACCS 12, pp. 40–41. ACM Press (May 2012)

BCG+19a. Boyle, E., et al.: Efficient two-round OT extension and silent non-interactive secure computation. In: Cavallaro, L., Kinder, J., Wang, X.F., Katz, J. (eds.) ACM CCS 2019, pp. 291–308. ACM Press (November 2019)

BCG+19b. Boyle, E., Couteau, G., Gilboa, N., Ishai, Y., Kohl, L., Scholl, P.: Efficient pseudorandom correlation generators: silent OT extension and more. In: Boldyreva, A., Micciancio, D. (eds.) CRYPTO 2019. LNCS, vol. 11694, pp. 489–518. Springer, Cham (2019). https://doi.org/10.1007/978-3-030-26954-8_16

BKM+20. Buddhavarapu, P., Knox, A., Mohassel, P., Sengupta, S., Taubeneck, E., Vlaskin, V.: Private matching for compute. Cryptology ePrint Archive, Report 2020/599 (2020). https://eprint.iacr.org/2020/599

CGT12. De Cristofaro, E., Gasti, P., Tsudik, G.: Fast and private computation of cardinality of set intersection and union. In: Pieprzyk, J., Sadeghi, A.-R., Manulis, M. (eds.) CANS 2012. LNCS, vol. 7712, pp. 218–231. Springer, Heidelberg (2012). https://doi.org/10.1007/978-3-642-35404-5_17

CM20. Chase, M., Miao, P.: Private set intersection in the Internet setting from lightweight oblivious PRF. In: Micciancio, D., Ristenpart, T. (eds.) CRYPTO 2020. LNCS, vol. 12172, pp. 34–63. Springer, Cham (2020). https://doi.org/10.1007/978-3-030-56877-1_2

CO18. Ciampi, M., Orlandi, C.: Combining private set-intersection with secure two-party computation. In: Catalano, D., De Prisco, R. (eds.) SCN 2018. LNCS, vol. 11035, pp. 464–482. Springer, Cham (2018). https://doi.org/10.1007/978-3-319-98113-0_25

CT10. De Cristofaro, E., Tsudik, G.: Practical private set intersection protocols with linear complexity. In: Sion, R. (ed.) FC 2010. LNCS, vol. 6052, pp. 143–159. Springer, Heidelberg (2010). https://doi.org/10.1007/978-3-642-14577-3_13

CT12. De Cristofaro, E., Tsudik, G.: Experimenting with fast private set intersection. In: Katzenbeisser, S., Weippl, E., Camp, L.J., Volkamer, M., Reiter, M., Zhang, X. (eds.) Trust 2012. LNCS, vol. 7344, pp. 55–73. Springer, Heidelberg (2012). https://doi.org/10.1007/978-3-642-30921-2_4

CZ09. Camenisch, J., Zaverucha, G.M.: Private intersection of certified sets. In: Dingledine, R., Golle, P. (eds.) FC 2009. LNCS, vol. 5628, pp. 108–127. Springer, Heidelberg (2009). https://doi.org/10.1007/978-3-642-03549-4_7

DCW13. Dong, C., Chen, L., Wen, Z.: When private set intersection meets big data: an efficient and scalable protocol. In: Sadeghi, A.-R., Gligor, V.D., Yung, M. (eds.) ACM CCS 2013, pp. 789–800. ACM Press (November 2013)

DD15. Debnath, S.K., Dutta, R.: Secure and efficient private set intersection cardinality using bloom filter. In: Lopez, J., Mitchell, C.J. (eds.) ISC 2015. LNCS, vol. 9290, pp. 209–226. Springer, Cham (2015). https://doi.org/10.1007/978-3-319-23318-5_12

EFG+15. Egert, R., Fischlin, M., Gens, D., Jacob, S., Senker, M., Tillmanns, J.: Privately computing set-union and set-intersection cardinality via bloom filters. In: Foo, E., Stebila, D. (eds.) ACISP 2015. LNCS, vol. 9144, pp. 413–430. Springer, Cham (2015). https://doi.org/10.1007/978-3-319-19962-7_24

FHNP16. Freedman, M.J., Hazay, C., Nissim, K., Pinkas, B.: Efficient set intersection with simulation-based security. J. Cryptol. **29**(1), 115–155 (2016)

FNP04. Freedman, M.J., Nissim, K., Pinkas, B.: Efficient private matching and set intersection. In: Cachin, C., Camenisch, J.L. (eds.) EUROCRYPT 2004. LNCS, vol. 3027, pp. 1–19. Springer, Heidelberg (2004). https://doi.org/10.1007/978-3-540-24676-3_1

HEK12. Huang, Y., Evans, D., Katz, J.: Private set intersection: are garbled circuits better than custom protocols? In: 19th Annual Network and Distributed System Security Symposium, NDSS 2012, San Diego, California, USA, February 5–8, 2012 (2012)

HFH99. Huberman, B.A., Franklin, M., Hogg, T.: Enhancing privacy and trust in electronic communities. In: EC, pp. 78–86 (1999)

IKN+19. Ion, M., et al.: On deploying secure computing commercially: private intersection-sum protocols and their business applications. Cryptology ePrint Archive, Report 2019/723 (2019). https://eprint.iacr.org/2019/723

IKNP03. Ishai, Y., Kilian, J., Nissim, K., Petrank, E.: Extending oblivious transfers efficiently. In: Boneh, D. (ed.) CRYPTO 2003. LNCS, vol. 2729, pp. 145–161. Springer, Heidelberg (2003). https://doi.org/10.1007/978-3-540-45146-4_9

KK13. Kolesnikov, V., Kumaresan, R.: Improved OT extension for transferring short secrets. In: Canetti, R., Garay, J.A. (eds.) CRYPTO 2013. LNCS, vol. 8043, pp. 54–70. Springer, Heidelberg (2013). https://doi.org/10.1007/978-3-642-40084-1_4

KKRT16. Kolesnikov, V., Kumaresan, R., Rosulek, M., Trieu, N.: Efficient batched oblivious PRF with applications to private set intersection. In: Weippl, E.R., Katzenbeisser, S., Kruegel, C., Myers, A.C., Halevi, S. (eds.) ACM CCS 2016, pp. 818–829. ACM Press (October 2016)

KRTW19. Kolesnikov, V., Rosulek, M., Trieu, N., Wang, X.: Scalable private set union from symmetric-key techniques. In: Galbraith, S.D., Moriai, S. (eds.) ASIACRYPT 2019. LNCS, vol. 11922, pp. 636–666. Springer, Cham (2019). https://doi.org/10.1007/978-3-030-34621-8_23

KS05. Kissner, L., Song, D.: Privacy-preserving set operations. In: Shoup, V. (ed.) CRYPTO 2005. LNCS, vol. 3621, pp. 241–257. Springer, Heidelberg (2005). https://doi.org/10.1007/11535218_15

Mea86. Meadows, C.A.: A more efficient cryptographic matchmaking protocol for use in the absence of a continuously available third party. In: Proceedings of the 1986 IEEE Symposium on Security and Privacy, Oakland, California, USA, April 7–9, 1986, pp. 134–137 (1986)

MPR+20. Miao, P., Patel, S., Raykova, M., Seth, K., Yung, M.: Two-sided malicious security for private intersection-sum with cardinality. In: Micciancio, D., Ristenpart, T. (eds.) CRYPTO 2020. LNCS, vol. 12172, pp. 3–33. Springer, Cham (2020). https://doi.org/10.1007/978-3-030-56877-1_1

MRR19. Mohassel, P., Rindal, P., Rosulek, M.: Fast database joins for secret shared data. Cryptology ePrint Archive, Report 2019/518 (2019). https://eprint.iacr.org/2019/518

MS13. Mohassel, P., Sadeghian, S.: How to hide circuits in MPC an efficient framework for private function evaluation. In: Johansson, T., Nguyen, P.Q. (eds.) EUROCRYPT 2013. LNCS, vol. 7881, pp. 557–574. Springer, Heidelberg (2013). https://doi.org/10.1007/978-3-642-38348-9_33

PRTY19. Pinkas, B., Rosulek, M., Trieu, N., Yanai, A.: SpOT-light: lightweight private set intersection from sparse OT extension. In: Boldyreva, A., Micciancio, D. (eds.) CRYPTO 2019. LNCS, vol. 11694, pp. 401–431. Springer, Cham (2019). https://doi.org/10.1007/978-3-030-26954-8_13

PRTY20. Pinkas, B., Rosulek, M., Trieu, N., Yanai, A.: PSI from PaXoS: fast, malicious private set intersection. In: Canteaut, A., Ishai, Y. (eds.) EUROCRYPT 2020. LNCS, vol. 12106, pp. 739–767. Springer, Cham (2020). https://doi.org/10.1007/978-3-030-45724-2_25

PSSZ15. Pinkas, B., Schneider, T., Segev, G., Zohner, M.: Phasing: private set intersection using permutation-based hashing. In: 24th USENIX Security Symposium, USENIX Security 15, pp. 515–530 (2015)

PSTY19. Pinkas, B., Schneider, T., Tkachenko, O., Yanai, A.: Efficient circuit-based PSI with linear communication. In: Ishai, Y., Rijmen, V. (eds.) EUROCRYPT 2019. LNCS, vol. 11478, pp. 122–153. Springer, Cham (2019). https://doi.org/10.1007/978-3-030-17659-4_5

PSWW18. Pinkas, B., Schneider, T., Weinert, C., Wieder, U.: Efficient circuit-based PSI via Cuckoo hashing. In: Nielsen, J.B., Rijmen, V. (eds.) EUROCRYPT 2018. LNCS, vol. 10822, pp. 125–157. Springer, Cham (2018). https://doi.org/10.1007/978-3-319-78372-7_5

PSZ14. Pinkas, B., Schneider, T., Zohner, M.: Faster private set intersection based on OT extension. In: 23rd USENIX Security Symposium, USENIX Security 14, pp. 797–812 (2014)

Rab05. Rabin, M.O.: How to exchange secrets with oblivious transfer. Cryptology ePrint Archive, Report 2005/187 (2005). http://eprint.iacr.org/2005/187

RR17a. Rindal, P., Rosulek, M.: Improved private set intersection against malicious adversaries. In: Coron, J.-S., Nielsen, J.B. (eds.) EUROCRYPT 2017. LNCS, vol. 10210, pp. 235–259. Springer, Cham (2017). https://doi.org/10.1007/978-3-319-56620-7_9

RR17b. Rindal, P., Rosulek, M.: Malicious-secure private set intersection via dual execution. In: Thuraisingham, B.M., Evans, D., Malkin, T., Xu, D. (eds.) ACM CCS 2017, pp. 1229–1242. ACM Press (October/November 2017)

VC05. Vaidya, J., Clifton, C.: Secure set intersection cardinality with application to association rule mining. J. Comput. Secur. **13**(4), 593–622 (2005)

ZRE15. Zahur, S., Rosulek, M., Evans, D.: Two halves make a whole. In: Oswald, E., Fischlin, M. (eds.) EUROCRYPT 2015. LNCS, vol. 9057, pp. 220–250. Springer, Heidelberg (2015). https://doi.org/10.1007/978-3-662-46803-6_8

On Publicly-Accountable Zero-Knowledge and Small Shuffle Arguments

Nils Fleischhacker[1]([✉]) and Mark Simkin[2]

[1] Ruhr University Bochum, Bochum, Germany
mail@nilsfleischhacker.de
[2] Aarhus University, Aarhus, Denmark
simkin@cs.au.dk

Abstract. Constructing interactive zero-knowledge arguments from simple assumptions with small communication complexity and good computational efficiency is an important, but difficult problem. In this work, we study interactive arguments with noticeable soundness error in their full generality and for the specific purpose of constructing concretely efficient shuffle arguments.

To counterbalance the effects of a larger soundness error, we show how to transform such three-move arguments into publicly-accountable ones which allow the verifier to convince third parties of detected misbehavior by a cheating prover. This may be particularly interesting for applications where a malicious prover has to balance the profits it can make from cheating successfully and the losses it suffers from being caught.

We construct interactive, public-coin, zero-knowledge arguments with noticeable soundness error for proving that a target vector of commitments is a pseudorandom permutation of a source vector. Our arguments do not rely on any trusted setup and only require the existence of collision-resistant hash functions. The communication complexity of our arguments is *independent* of the length of the shuffled vector. For a soundness error of $2^{-5} = 1/32$, the communication cost is 153 bytes without and 992 bytes with public accountability, meaning that our arguments are shorter than shuffle arguments realized using Bulletproofs (IEEE S&P 2018) and even competitive in size with SNARKs, despite only relying on simple assumptions.

1 Introduction

Zero-knowledge arguments allow a prover to convince a verifier of the truth of a statement without leaking any additional information. Such arguments are a fundamental building block, ubiquitous in cryptography, with various applications in both theory and practice.

The quality of an argument system can be measured in several different ways. One of the most important quality measures is the size of the argument,

---

N. Fleischhacker—Funded by the Deutsche Forschungsgemeinschaft (DFG, German Research Foundation) under Germany's Excellence Strategy - EXC 2092 CASA - 390781972.

M. Simkin—Supported by a DFF Sapere Aude Grant 9064-00068B.

J. A. Garay (Ed.): PKC 2021, LNCS 12711, pp. 618–648, 2021.
https://doi.org/10.1007/978-3-030-75248-4_22

i.e. how many bits the prover needs to exchange with the verifier to convince them of the validity of the statement. Minimizing this measure is important for real-world applications, where the statements itself may be over several gigabytes large and where communicating large amounts of data over a wide area network can quickly turn into the main efficiency bottleneck. Another important measure is the computational efficiency of both prover and verifier. We would like our argument to incur as little computational overhead on both parties as possible. Finally, we would also like our arguments to rely on simple and well-studied assumptions. Arguments that rely on highly structured or even non-falsifiable assumptions may be prone to cryptanalysis, those that rely on more popular number-theoretic assumptions, like the discrete logarithm or the factoring assumption, can be broken by quantum computers, and arguments that require a common reference string need to rely on a trusted third party that has to generate this string.

One particularly popular class of zero-knowledge arguments are those that enable a prover to convince a verifier that two vectors of commitments or encryptions contain the same multiset of plaintext messages without revealing the messages themselves or the permutation between the two vectors. Shuffle arguments are used in applications like e-voting protocols [42], anonymous communication systems [18,38], decentralized online poker [10], cryptocurrencies [20,22], and others.

The idea of shuffle arguments originates in the work of Chaum on mixnets [18] and the first constructions were presented by Sako and Kilian [45] and Abe [1–3]. These, as well as early subsequent works [25,30,34,42], all had argument sizes, which were linear in the size ℓ of the permuted vector. The first sublinear shuffle argument, with an argument size of $\mathcal{O}\left(\ell^{2/3}\right)$, was presented by Groth and Ishai [33]. Following this work, Groth and Bayer [9,31] presented arguments with an argument size of $\mathcal{O}\left(\sqrt{\ell}\right)$ and recently Bünz et al. [17] showed how to obtain arguments, based on the discrete logarithm assumption, of size $\mathcal{O}\left(\log \ell\right)$ via sorting circuits. A different line of works construct so called SNARKs [37,40], which are constant-sized arguments for arbitrary statements. Unfortunately, SNARKs inherently rely on strong non-falsifiable assumptions [26], require a trusted setup, and are computationally expensive for the prover. Zero-knowledge arguments based on the MPC-in-the-head technique [5,35] do not require any trusted setup, base their security solely on the existence of collision-resistant hash functions, but have a proof size of $\mathcal{O}\left(\sqrt{\ell}\right)$. Interactive proofs based on probabilistically checkable proofs [37] only rely on collision-resistant hash functions, have proofs of size $\mathcal{O}\left(\log \ell\right)$, but are prohibitively expensive from a computational perspective.

Given this state of the art, it is evident that constructing small shuffle arguments, and more generally arbitrary arguments, from simple assumptions with good computational efficiency is a challenging, but important task. In this work, we ask:

Can we construct shuffle arguments of size $o(\log \ell)$ with good computational efficiency from simple assumptions that satisfy a relaxed, but still meaningful security notion?

Answering this question is of practical importance. In certain real-world scenarios, arguments that satisfy the strongest possible security notion can simply be too inefficient. In these cases more efficient arguments that satisfy a weaker security notion may provide an important trade-off between efficiency and security.

1.1 Our Contribution

In this work, we study interactive arguments with noticeable soundness errors, i.e. arguments that allow a cheating prover to convince a verifier of a false statement with some noticeable probability. Such arguments can still be useful in scenarios, where a malicious prover has to balance the profit that it can make from successfully cheating and the loss it has, when cheating is detected. Consider for instance a decentralized online poker game, where a malicious prover wins \$1 for every incorrect shuffle argument that is accepted by the verifier, but loses a \$100 security deposit if cheating is detected. In such a scenario, a soundness error as large as $1/2$ may be acceptable, since even then cheating is not profitable for a rationally behaving prover.

We study arguments with noticeable soundness error both in their full generality and for specific purpose of constructing concretely efficient shuffle arguments for pseudorandom shuffles. Concretely, we make the following contributions:

Publicly-Accountable Zero-Knowledge Arguments. To realize the idea of punishing cheating provers, we need to take care of two things. First, we need to ensure that a verifier, upon detecting a cheating attempt, obtains a publicly verifiable certificate that can be used to convince a third party auditor of the prover's malicious behavior. Secondly, we need to ensure that an honest prover cannot be falsely accused. We introduce the notion of *publicly-accountable zero-knowledge arguments* that formally model the two requirements above.

In the full version of this work, we show how to transform *any* three-move, honest-verifier zero-knowledge argument with a soundness error that is at least inversely polynomial in the security parameter into a publicly-accountable argument with only slightly larger communication complexity. This is achieved via two steps. We prove that those honest-verifier zero-knowledge arguments already satisfy full zero-knowledge and then show how such zero-knowledge arguments can be transformed into their publicly-accountable counterparts with the help of symmetric private information retrieval. In this version of the work we show how to make the shuffle arguments described below publicly accountable in a concretely efficient manner.

It is interesting to note that in contrast to sequential repetition, which is commonly used to make the soundness error negligible at the cost of a multiplicative factor that is linear in the security parameter, our transformation only incurs a small additive factor in terms of round and bandwidth complexity.

Shuffle Arguments for Pseudorandom Shuffles. Next, we focus on constructing efficient three-move (public-coin) honest-verifier zero-knowledge shuffle arguments with inversely polynomial soundness error. For this purpose, we make one additional observation that allows us to further simplify the problem we aim to solve. When looking at the majority of applications, where shuffle arguments are actually used, the concrete permutation between the input and the output vector is chosen at random. Most often, the goal is to simply hide the relation between entries in the input and the output vector, but the concrete permutation itself is irrelevant as long as it is sufficiently random. In e-voting, for example, users send their encrypted votes to an untrusted shuffling authority, which shuffles them to hide the voting preference of any specific user. In anonymous communication systems, users send messages through one or more shuffling authorities to some recipients and shuffling of the ciphertexts ensures that no outside observer can see which sender communicates with which recipient. Thus, we focus on shuffle arguments for pseudorandom shuffles instead of arbitrary shuffles.

We introduce the notion of *zero-knowledge arguments for partially fixed statements* and present conceptually simple interactive shuffling arguments satisfying this notion. The main idea behind our new notion is to consider statements that are only partially fixed, i.e. that consist of a fixed and a non-fixed part. The fixed part is known to both prover and verifier, whereas the non-fixed part is chosen by the prover. At the end of an interaction between prover and verifier, the verifier learns the full statement and is convinced of its correctness. For the specific case of shuffling, the fixed part is the initial vector of commitments and the non-fixed part is a permutation thereof. Our notion aims to capture the fact that we only care about the initial vector being permuted, but not about the concrete permutation that is used. Rather than requiring that zero-knowledge holds for all statements, we require that zero-knowledge holds for all partially fixed statements with a uniformly random non-fixed part. Our notion is, in spirit, similar to distributional zero-knowledge [19,27], but focuses on a particular distribution over the statements.

For this notion, we present the first computationally efficient shuffle arguments for pseudorandom permutations, whose argument size is *independent* of the length of the vector that is being permuted. More specifically, we present public-coin, three-move arguments in the standalone model based on simple assumptions, such as collision-resistant hash functions.[1] The soundness error in our constructions can be set arbitrarily small as long as it remains inversely

---

[1] Naturally, our arguments are only useful for vectors of rerandomizable commitments/encryptions, which may require specific number-theoretic assumptions. The arguments itself, however, only rely on simple assumptions.

polynomial in the security parameter. The computational overhead of our construction grows with smaller soundness errors. We show how an arbitrary number of shuffle arguments can be batched without any additional communication cost.

We evaluate the practical efficiency of our constructions by providing concrete argument sizes when instantiated in the standard model. Our evaluation shows that, for a soundness error of 2^{-5}, the instantiation of our shuffle argument has a communication cost of 153 bytes without and 992 bytes with public accountability,

This is on the same order of magnitude as SNARKs such as [32] at 144 bytes and smaller than Bulletproofs even when the permuted vector of commitments[2] is reasonably short. The size of our argument is independent of the specific number of commitments being shuffled. The computational cost of shuffling an ℓ-length vector with soundness error $1/t$ is dominated by computing $t \cdot \ell$ rerandomizations of the shuffled commitments for both prover and verifier. In practice for Pedersen and similar commitments, the cost for the verifier can be reduced to roughly 2ℓ rerandomization at the cost of roughly doubling the communication complexity. A detailed description of this modification can be found in the full version of this paper.

Since the non-fixed part of the partially fixed shuffle statement is chosen randomly in each execution, it follows that the fully fixed statement will be different in each execution with high probability. For this reason, we cannot reduce the soundness error via sequential repetition. Due to the non-negligible soundness error, we can also not use the Fiat-Shamir transform [23] for making them non-interactive.

1.2   Comparison to SNARKs

In terms of size, our shuffle arguments are similar to SNARKs. Our underlying assumptions, however, are significantly weaker. We do not rely on non-falsifiable assumptions or a trusted setup. In exchange, we have a noticeable soundness error. As such, for the specific case of shuffle arguments, our work shows that the need for a trusted setup and non-falsifiable assumptions can be overcome in a practically efficient manner in applications that can tolerate a small, but noticeable soundness error.

1.3   Relation to Secure Computation with Covert Security

Our concept of publicly-accountable zero-knowledge arguments is strongly related to general two- and multiparty computation protocols with covert security and public verifiability [6,7]. A protocol is said to be secure against covert adversaries and publicly verifiable, if an actively misbehaving party in the protocol execution is caught with some constant probability and the honest parties are

---

[2] For the sake of concreteness, we focus on commitments in this work. However, our arguments are also applicable to other primitives such as rerandomizable encryption schemes.

guaranteed to obtain a certificate that can be shown to third parties to incriminate the misbehaving party. Applying a generic secure computation compiler, like the one of Damgård, Orlandi, and Simkin [21], to transform zero-knowledge arguments into publicly-accountable ones can potentially work, but would result in arguments whose size has an exponentially worse dependence on the soundness error.

1.4   Technical Overview

In the following, we present the main ideas behind our public-coin, zero-knowledge shuffle argument and outline how it can be made publicly accountable. In the full version, we show how arbitrary public-coin arguments with a polynomially large challenge space can be made publicly accountable.

The Shuffle Argument. Initially, both prover and verifier are given an initial vector of commitments V. The goal of the prover is to choose some vector V' and convince the verifier that there exists some permutation π, such that $V' = \pi(V)$. To be precise, the permutation π here does two things. It first rerandomizes and then permutes all commitments in V. The high-level idea behind our construction is to let the prover choose a permutation π, which can be represented as a sequence of t pseudorandom permutations $\pi_1, \ldots, \pi_t$ in a space-efficient manner. The prover first computes V' by sequentially applying each permutation π_i for $1 \leq i \leq t$ and then sends a hash of the intermediate vectors V_i and V' to the verifier, who picks $t - 1$ permutations that shall be opened. The prover sends descriptions of these $t - 1$ permutations to the verifier. Skipping over some details, the verifier now uses V to check every permutation π_j with $j < i$ and V' to check every permutation π_j with $j > i$ by recomputing the intermediate vectors. Since π_i remains hidden from the verifier, it cannot learn the overall permutation π. A malicious prover can only convince the verifier of a false statement if it chose all π_j with $i \neq j$ as correct and π_i as an incorrect permutation. Thus the probability of a prover cheating successfully is $1/t$. An interesting open question is whether our approach can be modified to get a better dependence between t and the resulting soundness error.

If done naively, then the size of the argument described above is $\mathcal{O}\left(t \cdot \log(\ell!)\right)$, since the prover has to send each permutation π_j for $1 \leq j \leq t$ separately. This can easily be brought down to $\mathcal{O}(t)$ by sending only short random seeds which can be expanded into a pseudorandom permutation using a regular pseudorandom generator. To further reduce the size of our argument, we use a puncturable pseudorandom functions (PPRF), which behaves like a regular PRF but has an additional algorithm Puncture that allows the holder of a secret key k to compute a key $k\{x\}$, which can be used to evaluate the PPRF on every point $x' \neq x$. Importantly, for a PPRF it holds that the key $k\{x\}$ does not reveal anything about its evaluation at the point x. Assuming that we have a PPRF $\mathcal{F}$ whose range is the set of all possible permutations, we can now succinctly represent π_j as the evaluation $\mathcal{F}(k, j)$ for $1 \leq j \leq t$. When the verifier asks to open all but

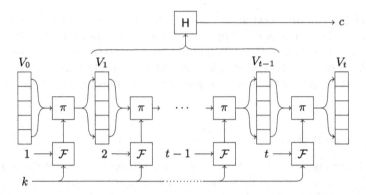

Fig. 1. The prover chooses the permutation and rerandomization by sampling a key k for a puncturable PRF. It then derives individual permutations and rerandomization factors for each stage by feeding the stage index through the PRF. The final result of performing the individual permutations forms the final shuffling and thus the prover-chosen part of the statement. The prover then hashes all of the intermediate permutations. The puncturable key k will allow the prover to partially open the computation of the intermediate permutations.

the i-th permutation, we return the punctured key $k\{i\}$ to the verifier. Using this approach, the size of the argument now mainly depends on the size of the punctured key and not directly on t. Using a PPRF based on the GGM construction [28], this brings down the size of the argument to $\mathcal{O}(\log t)$. Using a recent construction of PPRFs due to Aviram, Gellert, and Jager [8] we can make the size of our arguments even completely independent of t in the random oracle model. However, due to the large constants in Aviram et al.'s construction, this approach is only of theoretical interest. A visual illustration of our construction can be found in Fig. 1.

Making the Argument Publicly Accountable. To make the shuffle argument publicly-accountable, we need to ensure that a cheating prover produces some form of self-incriminating evidence whenever it fails to cheat. Since we want this evidence to be publicly verifiable, we need to assume that there exists a public signature key pk that is associated with the prover, who holds the corresponding signing key sk.

Ideally, we would like the prover to sign the transcript of all exchanged messages at the end of each execution and send this signature to the verifier. If the prover were to always do this, then we would be done, since the verifier would obtain a signature incriminating the prover, whenever it attempts to cheat, but is caught; assuming the prover always sends some last message, even if it can not respond correctly. Obviously this does not work, since the prover can simply abort the execution without signing anything, when it receives a challenge that it does not like. Our idea is to let the verifier receive the prover's last message corresponding to the verifier's challenge, without revealing the challenge to the prover. On a high-level, we achieve this through the use of symmetric private information retrieval, which enables a receiver holding an index $i \in \{1, \dots, t\}$ to obtain a value x_i from the sender's input vector $X = (x_1, \dots, x_t)$ in a manner that does not reveal i to the sender and does not reveal any x_j for $j \neq i$ to the receiver.

For the specific case of our shuffle arguments, the senders inputs will be a sequence of punctured keys and the receiver will retrieve one of them. We observe that in this instance the symmetric PIR can in fact be replaced by a very efficient oblivious key puncturing protocol implicit in the work of Boyle et al. [14].

2   Preliminaries

We denote by $\lambda \in \mathbb{N}$ the security parameter that is implicitly given as input to all algorithms in unary representation 1^λ. We denote by $\{0,1\}^\ell$ the set of all bit-strings of length ℓ. For a finite set S, we denote the action of sampling x uniformly at random from S by $x \leftarrow S$, and we denote the cardinality of S by $|S|$. An algorithm is efficient or PPT if it runs in time polynomial in the security parameter. If $\mathcal{A}$ is randomized then by $y := \mathcal{A}(x; r)$ we denote that $\mathcal{A}$ is run on input x and with random coins r and produces output y. If no randomness is specified, then it is assumed that $\mathcal{A}$ is run with freshly sampled uniform random coins. We write this as $y \leftarrow \mathcal{A}(x)$. A function $\mathsf{negl}(\lambda)$ is negligible if for every positive polynomial $\mathsf{poly}(\lambda)$ there exists an $N \in \mathbb{N}$ such that for all $\lambda > N$, $\mathsf{negl}(\lambda) \leq \frac{1}{\mathsf{poly}(\lambda)}$.

For two interactive Turing machines A and B we denote by $\langle A(a), B(b) \rangle$ the execution of the protocol between A and B an inputs a and b. We denote by $(t, s) \leftarrow \langle A(a), B(b) \rangle$ the outputs of A and B after the protocol execution respectively. In protocols where A does not receive an output, we write $s \leftarrow \langle A(a), B(b) \rangle$ to denote the output of B. We further denote by $\mathcal{T} := \langle A(a), B(b) \rangle$ the transcript resulting from the interaction.

2.1   Puncturable Pseudorandom Functions

Puncturable pseudorandom functions (PPRFs) can be constructed from one-way functions, where the key-length is $\mathcal{O}(\log |D|)$ and D is the input domain of the PRF [12,15,36]. Subsequent works have shown how to construct PPRFs with short keys from the strong RSA [8] and lattice-based assumptions [16].

Definition 1 (Puncturable PRFs). *The tuple $(\mathcal{F}, \mathsf{Puncture})$ of PPT algorithms is a secure puncturable pseudorandom function with key length $\kappa(\lambda)$, input length $i(\lambda)$, and range $O(\lambda)$ if the following conditions hold:*

Functionality: *For every $\lambda \in \mathbb{N}$, $k \in \{0,1\}^{\kappa(\lambda)}$, $x, x' \in \{0,1\}^{i(\lambda)}$ with $x \neq x'$, and $k' \leftarrow \mathsf{Puncture}(k, x)$ it holds that $\mathcal{F}(k, x') = \mathcal{F}(k', x')$.*

Pseudorandomness: *For any* PPT *adversary* $\mathcal{A}$ *it holds that*

$$\left| \begin{array}{l} \Pr[x \leftarrow \mathcal{A}(1^\lambda) : \mathcal{A}(\mathsf{Puncture}(k,x), \mathcal{F}(k,x)) = 1] \\ - \Pr[x \leftarrow \mathcal{A}(1^\lambda); y \leftarrow O(\lambda) : \mathcal{A}(\mathsf{Puncture}(k,x), y) = 1] \end{array} \right| \leq \mathsf{negl}(\lambda).$$

For our shuffle arguments (for vectors of length ℓ) we require a PPRF with range $\mathsf{Perm}_\ell \times \mathcal{R}^\ell$ where $\mathcal{R}$ is the randomness space of a perfectly and inversely rerandomizable commitment scheme and Perm_ℓ is the set of all $\ell!$ permutations over $\{0, \ldots, \ell-1\}$. To obtain a PPRF over this range, one can simply use a PPRF that outputs bit strings, potentially stretching the output using a pseudorandom generator, and combine it with a shuffling algorithm like the Fisher-Yates shuffle [24] by using the stretched output of the PPRF as the random tape of the shuffling algorithm.

2.2 Oblivious Key Puncturing

We formalize the notion of an oblivious key puncturing protocol (OPP) between a receiver R, who has a secret index i, and a sender S, who has a secret PRF key k. At the end of the protocol execution, the receiver should learn the key punctured at i, while the sender should learn nothing. An oblivious key puncturing protocol is effectively a special case of a symmetric PIR, where the sender's inputs are all possible punctured keys.

Definition 2 (Oblivious Key Puncturing). *Let* $(\mathcal{F}, \mathsf{Puncture})$ *be a secure puncturable PRF with key length* $\kappa(\lambda)$, *input length* $i(\lambda)$, *and range* $O(\lambda)$. *A pair of* PPT *algorithms* (S, R) *along with a setup algorithm* Setup *that outputs a* crs *is a secure receiver-extractable, oblivious key puncturing protocol for* $(\mathcal{F}, \mathsf{Puncture})$, *if the following conditions hold:*

Completeness: *For any* $k \in \{0,1\}^{\kappa(\lambda)}$ *and* $i \in \{0,1\}^{i(\lambda)}$, *it holds that*

$$\Pr\left[\begin{array}{c} \mathsf{crs} \leftarrow \mathsf{Setup}(1^\lambda); k' \leftarrow \mathsf{Puncture}(k,i); \\ k'' \leftarrow \langle \mathsf{S}(\mathsf{crs}, k), \mathsf{R}(\mathsf{crs}, i) \rangle \end{array} : k' = k'' \right] = 1.$$

Receiver Privacy: *For any* $i, i' \in \{0,1\}^{i(\lambda)}$ *and any malicious* PPT *sender* S^*, *it holds that*

$$\left| \begin{array}{l} \Pr[\mathsf{crs} \leftarrow \mathsf{Setup}(1^\lambda); b \leftarrow \langle \mathsf{S}^*(\mathsf{crs}), \mathsf{R}(\mathsf{crs}, i) \rangle : b = 1] \\ - \Pr[\mathsf{crs} \leftarrow \mathsf{Setup}(1^\lambda); b \leftarrow \langle \mathsf{S}^*(\mathsf{crs}), \mathsf{R}(\mathsf{crs}, i') \rangle : b = 1] \end{array} \right| \leq \mathsf{negl}(\lambda),$$

where the probabilities are taken over the random coins of Setup, S^* *and* R.

Sender Simulation: *There exists a* PPT *simulator* $\mathsf{Sim} = (\mathsf{Sim}_0, \mathsf{Sim}_1)$ *such such that for any key* $k \in \{0,1\}^{\kappa(\lambda)}$ *and any malicious* PPT *receiver* R^* *it holds that*

$$\left| \begin{array}{l} \Pr[\mathsf{crs} \leftarrow \mathsf{Setup}(1^\lambda); b \leftarrow \langle \mathsf{S}(\mathsf{crs}, k), \mathsf{R}^*(\mathsf{crs}, 1^\lambda) \rangle : b = 1] \\ \\ - \Pr\left[\begin{array}{c} (\mathsf{crs}, \mathsf{td}) \leftarrow \mathsf{Sim}_0(1^\lambda); \\ b \leftarrow \langle \mathsf{Sim}_1^{\mathsf{Puncture}(k, \cdot)}(\mathsf{crs}, \mathsf{td}), \mathsf{R}^*(\mathsf{crs}, 1^\lambda) \rangle \end{array} : b = 1 \right] \end{array} \right| \leq \mathsf{negl}(\lambda),$$

where Sim_1 *can query its oracle at most once and the probability is taken over the random coins of the involved parties.*

Remark 1. Protocols that need a (non-empty) CRS, require a trusted setup. For those protocols, using standard techniques, the trusted setup can be avoided at the cost of a constant number of additional rounds of communication.

It turns out that for the PPRF based on one-way functions [12,15,36], highly efficient instantiations of such an oblivious key puncturing protocol already exist implicitly in [14][3]. For a PPRF with domain D, the communication and computational complexity of their protocol is effectively that of $\log|D|$ invocations of an actively secure 1-out-of-2 oblivious transfer.

2.3 Commitments

Shuffle proofs are generally only of interest for rerandomizable commitment schemes. Our construction of shuffle proofs requires more than just perfect rerandomizability. Specifically we require that rerandomization can also be performed in reverse.

Definition 3 (Perfectly and Inversely Rerandomizable Commitments). *Let* $\mathcal{C} = (\mathsf{Setup}, \mathsf{Com})$ *be a commitment scheme with message space* $\mathcal{M}$ *and randomness space* $\mathcal{R}$. $\mathcal{C}$ *is perfectly and inversely rerandomizable, if there exist* PPT *algorithms* $\mathsf{Rerand}, \mathsf{Rerand}^{-1}$ *such that the following conditions hold:*

Perfect Rerandomization: *For every* $\mathsf{ck} \leftarrow \mathsf{Setup}(1^\lambda)$, $m \in \mathcal{M}$, *and* $c \leftarrow \mathsf{Com}(\mathsf{ck}, m)$ *it holds that for a uniformly chosen* $r \leftarrow \mathcal{R}$, $\mathsf{Rerand}(\mathsf{ck}, c, r)$ *and* $\mathsf{Com}(\mathsf{ck}, c; r)$ *are distributed identically.*

Inverse Rerandomization: *For every* $\mathsf{ck} \leftarrow \mathsf{Setup}(1^\lambda)$, $m \in \mathcal{M}$, $r \in \mathcal{R}$, *and* $c \leftarrow \mathsf{Com}(\mathsf{ck}, m)$ *it holds that* $\mathsf{Rerand}^{-1}(\mathsf{ck}, \mathsf{Rerand}(\mathsf{ck}, c, r), r) = c$.

One example of a popular commitment scheme satisfying the properties described above is the Pedersen commitment scheme [43]. Note that since we assume perfect rerandomizability, it is guaranteed that for any ck, c, r_1, and r_2, there exists an r_3 such that $\mathsf{Rerand}(\mathsf{ck}, \mathsf{Rerand}(\mathsf{ck}, c, r_1), r_2) = \mathsf{Rerand}(\mathsf{ck}, c, r_3)$.

3 Zero-Knowledge Argument for Partially Fixed Statements

In a regular proof or argument system, the full statement is fixed a priori and given to both the prover and verifier which then run an interactive protocol between them. In contrast in an arguments for partially fixed statements only a part x of the statement is fixed and the *prover gets to sample the rest of the*

---

[3] The authors prove (in Theorem 7 in [14]) that their construction satisfies a weaker notion than the one we defined here, but it can be easily seen that their construction satisfies our notion as well, when instantiated with an actively secure oblivious transfer.

statement y together with auxiliary information aux that will allow the prover to efficiently prove that $(x, y) \in \mathcal{L}$. Note, that aux is not necessarily just a regular witness for (x, y). In fact, in our shuffle proof, a regular witness for the statement would merely be the permutation and rerandomization factors. However, the auxiliary information used by our prover is a highly compact representation of a decomposition of both the permutation and rerandomization. This also implies that a prover in such a system is not necessarily capable of proving all $(x, y) \in \mathcal{L}$, but merely a, potentially small, subset. However, the definition of zero-knowledge will imply that the full statement (x, y) chosen by the prover is indistinguishable from a uniform choice of $(x, y) \in \mathcal{L}$ conditioned on x. To formally define such argument systems, we first define partially fixable languages, as those languages where y can be efficiently uniformly sampled conditioned on x.

Definition 4 (Partially Fixable Languages). *Let X, Y be sets. Let $\mathcal{L} \subseteq X \times Y$ be an NP language consisting of pairs $(x, y) \in X \times Y$ with the corresponding NP-relation $\mathcal{R}$. For any $x \in X$ we denote by $\mathcal{L}_x$ the language $\mathcal{L}_x = \{(x, y') \mid y' \in Y \wedge (x, y') \in \mathcal{L}\}$. $\mathcal{L}$ is called partially fixable if for all $x \in X$ such that $\mathcal{L}_x \neq \emptyset$ it is possible to uniformly sample from $\mathcal{L}_x$ in expected polynomial time.*

We can now define argument systems for such languages.

Definition 5 (Arguments for Partially Fixed Statements). *Let $\mathcal{L} \subseteq X \times Y$ be a partially fixable language with the corresponding NP-relation $\mathcal{R}$. A probabilistic polynomial time two-stage prover $\mathsf{P} = (\mathsf{P}_0, \mathsf{P}_1)$ and a probabilistic polynomial time verifier V are said to be an interactive argument for partially fixed statements of $\mathcal{L}$ with soundness error ϵ if the following conditions hold:*

Completeness: *For any $x \in X$ with $\mathcal{L}_x \neq \emptyset$ it holds that*

$$\Pr[(y, \mathsf{aux}) \leftarrow \mathsf{P}_0(x); b \leftarrow \langle \mathsf{P}_1(x, y, \mathsf{aux}), \mathsf{V}(x, y) \rangle : (x, y) \in \mathcal{L} \wedge b = 1] = 1.$$

Soundness: *For any malicious probabilistic polynomial time prover P^* and any $(x, y) \notin \mathcal{L}$ it holds that*

$$\Pr[b \leftarrow \langle \mathsf{P}^*(1^\lambda), \mathsf{V}(x, y) \rangle : b = 1] \le \epsilon + \mathsf{negl}(\lambda).$$

We are only interested in arguments that are zero knowledge. We define two flavors of zero-knowledge.

Definition 6 (Zero-Knowledge Arguments for Partially Fixed Statements). *Let (P, V) be an interactive argument for partially fixed statements of $\mathcal{L}$. The argument is said to be zero knowledge if there exists an expected polynomial time simulator Sim, such that for any (potentially malicious) polynomial time verifier V^*, all probabilistic polynomial time distinguishers $\mathcal{D}$, and all $x \in X$ with $\mathcal{L}_x \neq \emptyset$ it holds that*

$$\left| \begin{aligned} &\Pr[(y, \mathsf{aux}) \leftarrow \mathsf{P}_0(x); s \leftarrow \langle \mathsf{P}_1(x, y, \mathsf{aux}), \mathsf{V}^*(x, y) \rangle : \mathcal{D}(x, y, s) = 1] \\ &- \Pr[(x, y) \leftarrow \mathcal{L}_x; s \leftarrow \mathsf{Sim}^{\mathsf{V}^*(x, y)}(x, y) : \mathcal{D}(x, y, s) = 1] \end{aligned} \right| \le \mathsf{negl}(\lambda)$$

where Sim has the power of rewinding V^*.

Definition 7 (Honest Verifier Zero-Knowledge). *Let* (P, V) *be an interactive argument for partially fixed statements of* $\mathcal{L}$. *The argument is said to be* honest verifier *zero knowledge if there exists an expected polynomial time simulator* Sim, *such that for all probabilistic polynomial time distinguishers* $\mathcal{D}$, *and all* $x \in X$ *with* $\mathcal{L}_x \neq \emptyset$ *it holds that*

$$\left| \begin{array}{l} \Pr[(y, \mathcal{T}) \leftarrow \text{SIMU}(x) : \mathcal{D}(x, y, \mathcal{T}) = 1] \\ - \Pr[(y, \mathcal{T}) \leftarrow \text{REAL}(x) : \mathcal{D}(x, y, \mathcal{T}) = 1] \end{array} \right| \leq \mathsf{negl}(\lambda),$$

where REAL *and* SIMU *are defined as follows*

REAL(x)	SIMU(x)
$(y, \mathsf{aux}) \leftarrow \mathsf{P}_0(x)$	$(x, y) \leftarrow \mathcal{L}_x$
$\mathcal{T} := \langle \mathsf{P}_1(x, y, \mathsf{aux}), \mathsf{V}(x, y) \rangle$	$\mathcal{T} \leftarrow \mathsf{Sim}(x, y)$
return $(y, \mathcal{T})$	**return** $(y, \mathcal{T})$

We note several important differences compared to regular argument systems. When defining an argument systems where the prover can choose part of the statement completeness can no longer be defined by simply quantifying over all valid statements. Instead, completeness explicitly specifies that the honest prover will always choose valid statements. Further, in the definition of zero-knowledge, it is not necessarily clear how y should be chosen in the simulated case. The definition above requires that y is chosen uniformly at random from $\mathcal{L}_x$ in this case as opposed to also being chosen by the prover. This has an important implication. Namely it implicitly requires the honest prover to choose y in a way that is computationally indistinguishable from uniform, since otherwise there exists a trivial distinguisher. Lastly we note that these definitions coincide with the standard zero-knowledge argument definitions, when $|\mathcal{L}_x| = 1$.

4   On Three-Move Public-Coin HVZK Arguments and Zero-Knowledge

In the following, we show that any three-move public-coin[4] argument with a polynomially large challenge space that satisfies (computational) HVZK is also (computationally) zero-knowledge against malicious verifiers. A corollary of this result is that our shuffle argument from Sect. 5, which we will prove to be HVZK, is automatically fully zero-knowledge.

Theorem 1. *Let* (P, V) *be some three-move public-coin honest verifier zero-knowledge argument for language* $\mathcal{L} \subseteq X \times Y$ *and let* $\mathcal{C}$ *be the associated challenge space. If* $|\mathcal{C}| \leq \mathsf{poly}(\lambda)$ *then* (P, V) *is also zero-knowledge against malicious verifiers.*

---

[4] We call a three-move argument system public-coin if the second message is a uniformly random bit-string.

Proof. Let V^* be an arbitrary malicious polynomial time verifier. Let Sim' be the *honest verifier* zero-knowledge simulator for the 3-move public-coin argument as specified in Definition 7. To prove the theorem, we specify a zero-knowledge simulator Sim that takes as input a statement (x, y), has blackbox access to V^*, and produces an output that is computationally indistinguishable from the output of V^* in a real protocol execution.

At first sight, the proof of the theorem statement may seem trivial. Intuitively, Sim picks a random challenge d, runs the simulator Sim' to obtain a transcript (e, d, z), feeds the first message e to V^* and if the verifier outputs a challenge d^* with $d^* = d$, then we are done and otherwise we simply restart this whole process until we guess the verifier's challenge correctly. Unfortunately, this approach only works if we have an argument that satisfies *perfect* HVZK and it turns out that this naive simulator is not guaranteed to run in expected polynomial time if our argument system is only computationally HVZK.

To make sure that our simulator V^* does indeed run in expected polynomial time, we closely follow a proof strategy due to Goldreich and Kahan [29].[5] We specify the zero-knowledge simulator Sim in Fig. 2.

$\text{Sim}^{V^*(x,y)}(x, y)$	$\text{EstimateDelta}(x, y)$
1 : $\quad (e, d, z) \leftarrow \text{Sim}'(x, y)$	$k := 0, m := 0$
2 : $\quad d^* \leftarrow V^*(e)$	**while** $k < 12\lambda$
3 : $\quad$ **if** $d^* = $ abort	$\quad m := m + 1$
4 : $\quad\quad$ **return** abort	$\quad$ **rewind** V^*
5 : $\quad \widetilde{\delta} \leftarrow \text{EstimateDelta}(x, y)$	$\quad (e, d, z) \leftarrow \text{Sim}'(x, y)$
6 : $\quad$ **for** $0 \le i < \min\left(4|\mathcal{C}|\lambda\widetilde{\delta}^{-1}, 2^\lambda\right)$	$\quad$ **if** $V^*(e) \neq$ abort
7 : $\quad\quad$ **rewind** V^*	$\quad\quad k = k + 1$
8 : $\quad\quad (e, d, z) \leftarrow \text{Sim}'(x, y)$	**return** k/m
9 : $\quad\quad d^* \leftarrow V^*(e)$	
10 : $\quad\quad$ **if** $d = d^*$	
11 : $\quad\quad\quad$ **return** $V^*(z)$	
12 : **return** fail	

Fig. 2. Zero-knowledge simulator for any three-move public coin honest verifier zero knowledge argument with a polynomially large challenge space.

We first observe in Lemma 2 that for any verifier V^* the probability of aborting after seeing a simulated first message output by Sim' does not differ significantly from the probability of aborting after seeing a real first protocol message.

---

[5] See [39] for a very nice and detailed discussion of this proof strategy.

Lemma 2. *For any polynomial time algorithm* V^* *and any* $x \in X$, *such that* $\mathcal{L}_x \neq \emptyset$ *it holds that*

$$
\left| \begin{array}{l} \Pr\left[(y, e, d, z) \leftarrow \text{SIMU}(x) : V^*(x, y, e) = \text{abort}\right] \\ - \Pr\left[(y, e, d, z) \leftarrow \text{REAL}(x) : V^*(x, y, e) = \text{abort}\right] \end{array} \right| \leq \text{negl}(\lambda)
$$

Proof. Let V^* be an arbitrary malicious polynomial time verifier. Consider the following distinguisher $\mathcal{D}$ against the *honest verifier* zero-knowledge property of the argument: Upon receiving (x, y) and (e, d, z) as input, the distinguisher $\mathcal{D}$ invokes V^* with fresh random coins and input (x, y, e). If V^* aborts then $\mathcal{D}$ outputs 1. Otherwise it outputs 0. We observe that $\mathcal{D}$'s distinguishing advantage against the honest verifier zero-knowledge property of the argument corresponds exactly to the difference in the abort probabilities of V^*. Since the argument is honest verifier zero-knowledge, $\mathcal{D}$'s distinguishing advantage must be negligible and Lemma 2 thus follows.   □

Furthermore, we use an observation made previously by Goldreich and Kahan [29].

Lemma 3 ([29]). *For any algorithm* V^*, *let* $\delta = \delta(\lambda)$ *be the probability that it does* not *abort upon seeing a simulated first message. With probability at least* $1 - 2^{-\lambda}$, *the estimate* $\tilde{\delta}$ *in line 5 of* Sim *in Fig. 2 is within a constant factor of* δ.

Using these two observations we will now analyze the probability that one iteration of Sim's main loop is successful. I.e. we will show that the probability that for a precomputed transcript (e, d, z), V^* upon receiving input e will return d^* with $d = d^*$ with probability at least $\delta / |\mathcal{C}| - \text{negl}(\lambda)$.

Lemma 4. *Let* (P, V) *be a three-move public-coin honest verifier zero-knowledge argument for language* $\mathcal{L} \subseteq X \times Y$ *and let* $\mathcal{C}$ *be the associated challenge space with* $|\mathcal{C}| \leq \text{poly}(\lambda)$. *Let further* V^* *be any polynomial time verifier. For any* $x \in X$, *such that* $\mathcal{L}_x \neq \emptyset$ *it then holds that*

$$
\Pr\left[(y, e, d, z) \leftarrow \text{SIMU}(x) : V^*(x, y, e) = d\right] \geq \frac{\delta}{|\mathcal{C}|} - \text{negl}(\lambda).
$$

Proof. Let V^* be an arbitrary polynomial time verifier. Now consider the following distinguisher $\mathcal{D}$ against the honest verifier zero-knowledge property of the argument. The distinguisher $\mathcal{D}$ receives as input (x, y) and (e, d, z). It initializes V^*, provides it with (x, y, e), and receives back d^*. If $d^* = \text{abort}$, then $\mathcal{D}$ flips a random coin b and return that as its guess. Otherwise, $\mathcal{D}$ outputs 1 if $d = d^*$ and 0 if $d \neq d^*$. Let $\delta + \gamma$ be the probability that V^* aborts after seeing a first real message, where $|\gamma| = \text{negl}(\lambda)$ by Lemma 2. By the honest verifier zero-knowledge property of the argument it must then hold that

$$
\text{negl}(\lambda) \geq \left| \begin{array}{l} \Pr[(y, e, d, z) \leftarrow \text{SIMU}(x) : \mathcal{D}(x, y, e, d, z) = 1] \\ - \Pr[(y, e, d, z) \leftarrow \text{REAL}(x) : \mathcal{D}(x, y, e, d, z) = 1] \end{array} \right|
$$

$$
\begin{aligned}
&\left|\begin{aligned}
&\Pr\left[(y,e,d,z) \leftarrow \text{SIMU}(x) : \mathcal{D}(x,y,e,d,z) = 1 \mid \mathsf{V}^*(x,y,e) \neq \mathsf{abort}\right]\\
&\cdot \Pr\left[(y,e,d,z) \leftarrow \text{SIMU}(x) : \mathsf{V}^*(x,y,e) \neq \mathsf{abort}\right]\\
&+ \Pr\left[(y,e,d,z) \leftarrow \text{SIMU}(x) : \mathcal{D}(x,y,e,d,z) = 1 \mid \mathsf{V}^*(x,y,e) = \mathsf{abort}\right]\\
&\cdot \underbrace{\Pr\left[(y,e,d,z) \leftarrow \text{SIMU}(x) : \mathsf{V}^*(x,y,e) = \mathsf{abort}\right]}_{=1-\delta}
\end{aligned}\right|\\[4pt]
=&\left|\begin{aligned}
&- \Pr\left[(y,e,d,z) \leftarrow \text{REAL}(x) : \mathcal{D}(x,y,e,d,z) = 1 \mid \mathsf{V}^*(x,y,e) = \mathsf{abort}\right]\\
&\cdot \underbrace{\Pr\left[(y,e,d,z) \leftarrow \text{REAL}(x) : \mathsf{V}^*(x,y,e) = \mathsf{abort}\right]}_{=1-\delta-\gamma}\\
&- \Pr\left[(y,e,d,z) \leftarrow \text{REAL}(x) : \mathcal{D}(x,y,e,d,z) = 1 \mid \mathsf{V}^*(x,y,e) \neq \mathsf{abort}\right]\\
&\cdot \underbrace{\Pr\left[(y,e,d,z) \leftarrow \text{REAL}(x) : \mathsf{V}^*(x,y,e) \neq \mathsf{abort}\right]}_{=\delta+\gamma}
\end{aligned}\right|\\[4pt]
=&\left|\begin{aligned}
&\Pr\left[(y,e,d,z) \leftarrow \text{SIMU}(x) : \mathsf{V}^*(x,y,e) = d \mid \mathsf{V}^*(x,y,e) \neq \mathsf{abort}\right]\\
&\cdot \Pr\left[(y,e,d,z) \leftarrow \text{SIMU}(x) : \mathsf{V}^*(x,y,e) \neq \mathsf{abort}\right]\\
&+ \underbrace{\Pr\left[b \leftarrow \{0,1\} : b = 1\right]}_{=1/2} \cdot (1-\delta) - \underbrace{\Pr\left[b \leftarrow \{0,1\} : b = 1\right]}_{=1/2} \cdot (1-\delta-\gamma)\\
&\overbrace{}^{=1/|\mathcal{C}|}\\
&-\Pr\left[(y,e,d,z) \leftarrow \text{REAL}(x) : \mathsf{V}^*(x,y,e) = d \mid \mathsf{V}^*(x,y,e) \neq \mathsf{abort}\right]\\
&\cdot (\delta + \gamma)
\end{aligned}\right|\\[4pt]
=&\left|\begin{aligned}
&\Pr\left[(y,e,d,z) \leftarrow \text{SIMU}(x) : \mathsf{V}^*(x,y,e) = d \mid \mathsf{V}^*(x,y,e) \neq \mathsf{abort}\right]\\
&\cdot \Pr\left[(y,e,d,z) \leftarrow \text{SIMU}(x) : \mathsf{V}^*(x,y,e) \neq \mathsf{abort}\right] + \frac{\gamma}{2} - \frac{\delta+\gamma}{|\mathcal{C}|}
\end{aligned}\right|\\[4pt]
=&\left|\begin{aligned}
&\Pr\left[(y,e,d,z) \leftarrow \text{SIMU}(x) : \mathsf{V}^*(x,y,e) = d \mid \mathsf{V}^*(x,y,e) \neq \mathsf{abort}\right]\\
&\cdot \Pr\left[(y,e,d,z) \leftarrow \text{SIMU}(x) : \mathsf{V}^*(x,y,e) \neq \mathsf{abort}\right] - \frac{\delta}{|\mathcal{C}|} + \frac{(|\mathcal{C}|-2)\gamma}{2\,|\mathcal{C}|}
\end{aligned}\right|\\[4pt]
=&\left|\begin{aligned}
&\Pr\left[(y,e,d,z) \leftarrow \text{SIMU}(x) : \mathsf{V}^*(x,y,e) = d \mid \mathsf{V}^*(x,y,e) \neq \mathsf{abort}\right]\\
&\cdot \Pr\left[(y,e,d,z) \leftarrow \text{SIMU}(x) : \mathsf{V}^*(x,y,e) \neq \mathsf{abort}\right] - \frac{\delta}{|\mathcal{C}|} + \mathsf{negl}(\lambda)
\end{aligned}\right| \cdot \quad (1)
\end{aligned}
$$

We can now consider the two cases of the value between the absolute value bars in Eq. 1 being positive, or negative. If it's positive, then it holds that

$$
\frac{\delta}{|\mathcal{C}|} - \mathsf{negl}(\lambda) \leq \Pr\left[(y,e,d,z) \leftarrow \text{SIMU}(x) : \mathsf{V}^*(x,y,e) = d \mid \mathsf{V}^*(x,y,e) \neq \mathsf{abort}\right]
$$
$$
\cdot \Pr\left[(y,e,d,z) \leftarrow \text{SIMU}(x) : \mathsf{V}^*(x,y,e) \neq \mathsf{abort}\right]. \qquad (2)
$$

If it's negative, then it must hold that

$$
\mathsf{negl}(\lambda) \geq - \Pr\left[(y,e,d,z) \leftarrow \text{SIMU}(x) : \mathsf{V}^*(x,y,e) = d \mid \mathsf{V}^*(x,y,e) \neq \mathsf{abort}\right]
$$
$$
\cdot \Pr\left[(y,e,d,z) \leftarrow \text{SIMU}(x) : \mathsf{V}^*(x,y,e) \neq \mathsf{abort}\right] + \frac{\delta}{|\mathcal{C}|} - \mathsf{negl}(\lambda)
$$

and thereby that

$$\frac{\delta}{|\mathcal{C}|} - \mathsf{negl}(\lambda) \leq \Pr\left[(y, e, d, z) \leftarrow \mathrm{SIMU}(x) : \mathsf{V}^*(x, y, e) = d \mid \mathsf{V}^*(x, y, e) \neq \mathsf{abort}\right]$$
$$\cdot \Pr\left[(y, e, d, z) \leftarrow \mathrm{SIMU}(x) : \mathsf{V}^*(x, y, e) \neq \mathsf{abort}\right]. \tag{3}$$

Combining the two cases, i.e., Eqs. 2 and 3 we can use the law of total probability to conclude that

$$\Pr\left[(y, e, d, z) \leftarrow \mathrm{SIMU}(x) : \mathsf{V}^*(x, y, e) = d\right] \geq \frac{\delta}{|\mathcal{C}|} - \mathsf{negl}(\lambda).$$

as claimed.   □

We now want to use Lemma 4 to argue that the output of the simulator is indistinguishable from the output of V^* in a real execution. For this, consider the following. By Lemma 4, there exists a negligible function ϵ, such that

$$\Pr\left[(y, e, d, z) \leftarrow \mathrm{SIMU}(x) : \mathsf{V}^*(x, y, e) = d\right] \geq \frac{\delta}{|\mathcal{C}|} - \epsilon(\lambda).$$

For each security parameter $\lambda \in \mathbb{N}$ we can consider two cases:

Case i. If it holds that $\delta(\lambda) > 2|\mathcal{C}|\epsilon(\lambda)$, then we have $\epsilon(\lambda) < \delta/(2|\mathcal{C}|)$ and it therefore holds that

$$\Pr\left[(y, e, d, z) \leftarrow \mathrm{SIMU}(x) : \mathsf{V}^*(x, y, e) = d\right] \geq \frac{\delta}{|\mathcal{C}|} - \epsilon(\lambda) > \frac{\delta}{2|\mathcal{C}|}.$$

It follows that in expectation the simulator needs at most $2|\mathcal{C}|/\delta$ rewinding attempts to obtain one non-aborting and correctly guessed execution. Via markov-inequality it follows that the probability of not having seen a single non-aborting correctly guessed execution after $4\lambda|\mathcal{C}|/\delta$ rewindings is negligible.

Lastly observe that by Lemma 3 the estimate $\tilde{\delta}$ is within a constant factor of δ with probability $1 - 2^{-\lambda}$. Therefore, the simulator will output a valid transcript with a probability of $1 - \mathsf{negl}(\lambda)$, ensuring that the output of the simulator is indistinguishable from the output of V^* in a real execution with overwhelming probability.

Case ii. If it holds that $\delta(\lambda) \leq 2|\mathcal{C}|\epsilon(\lambda)$, then δ is smaller than a negligible function for this λ. Assume that in this case the rewinding strategy *always fails*. Then a real execution of V^* results in abort with probability at least $1 - (\delta - \mathsf{negl}(\lambda))$ by Lemma 2, while Sim outputs abort with probability $1 - \delta$. That means the statistical distance between the two output distributions is at most $\delta + \mathsf{negl}(\lambda)$ which is an overall negligible function. Combining the two cases, we can conclude that the distinguishing advantage against Sim is upper bounded by a negligible function for each $\lambda \in \mathbb{N}$ and thus is overall computationally indistinguishable from the output of V^* in a real execution.

It remains to bound the expected runtime of Sim. Again, by Lemma 3, the estimate $\tilde{\delta}$ is within a constant factor of δ with probability $1-2^{-\lambda}$. But whenever the estimate is *wrong*, the runtime of the main loop is still bounded by the worst case running time of 2^λ with the simulator outputting fail. We thus have an upper bound on the expected runtime of

$$\overbrace{\mathsf{poly}(\lambda)}^{\text{lines 1-4}} + \delta \left(\overbrace{\mathsf{poly}(\lambda) + \frac{12\lambda}{\tilde{\delta}}\mathsf{poly}(\lambda)}^{\mathsf{EstimateDelta}} + \overbrace{\left((1-2^{-\lambda})\frac{4\lambda\,|\mathcal{C}|}{\tilde{\delta}} + 2^{-\lambda}2^\lambda \right) \cdot \mathsf{poly}(\lambda)}^{\text{lines 6-12}} \right)$$

$$\leq \mathsf{poly}(\lambda) + (12\lambda + \mathcal{O}(1) \cdot 4\lambda\,|\mathcal{C}| + \delta\mathsf{poly}(\lambda)) \cdot \mathsf{poly}(\lambda) \leq \mathsf{poly}(\lambda).$$

$\square$

5   An Efficient Shuffle Argument

Let $\mathcal{C} = (\mathsf{Setup}, \mathsf{Com}, \mathsf{Rerand})$ be a perfectly and inversely rerandomizable commitment scheme with message space $\mathcal{M}$ and randomness space $\mathcal{R}$. To define shuffle arguments for $\mathcal{C}$, we first need to define partially fixable language of valid shuffles relative to a rerandomizable commitment scheme. To this end, we first define π as an algorithm that takes a vector of $\mathcal{C}$ commitments V, a permutation $p \in \mathsf{Perm}_\ell$, and randomnesses $r_0, \ldots, r_{\ell-1} \in \mathcal{R}^\ell$ as input, permutes the elements of V and randomizes each commitment. The algorithm π as well as it's inverse is described in Fig. 3. We can now define the partially fixable language of valid shuffles relative to π as follows.

Definition 8 (Valid Shuffle). *Let $\mathcal{C}$ be a perfectly rerandomizable commitment scheme with commitment space $\mathcal{C}$. The language $\mathsf{Shuffle}_\ell \subseteq \mathcal{C}^\ell \times \mathcal{C}^\ell$ of valid shuffles of vectors of length ℓ is defined as*

$$\mathsf{Shuffle}_\ell = \left\{ (V, V') \in \mathcal{C}^\ell \times \mathcal{C}^\ell \mid \exists (p, \vec{r}) \in \mathsf{Perm}_\ell \times \mathcal{R}^\ell. \ V' = \pi(V, p, \vec{r}) \right\}$$

Shuffles are transitive as stated by the following lemma.

Lemma 5. *If $(V, V') \in \mathsf{Shuffle}_\ell$ and $(V', V'') \in \mathsf{Shuffle}_\ell$, then $(V, V'') \in \mathsf{Shuffle}_\ell$.*

Proof. Since permutations are closed under composition and since, by assumption on the commitment scheme, it holds that for any $r_1, r_2 \in \mathcal{R}$, there exists an $r_3 \in \mathcal{R}$ such that $\mathsf{Rerand}(\mathsf{ck}, \mathsf{Rerand}(\mathsf{ck}, c, r_1), r_2) = \mathsf{Rerand}(\mathsf{ck}, c, r_3)$, the lemma immediately follows. $\square$

$\pi(V, p, r_0, \ldots, r_{\ell-1})$
for $0 \leq i < \ell$
$\quad V'[p(i)] := \mathsf{Rerand}(\mathsf{ck}, V[i], r_{p(i)})$
return V'

$\pi^{-1}(V', p, r_0, \ldots, r_{\ell-1})$
for $0 \leq i < \ell$
$\quad V[i] := \mathsf{Rerand}^{-1}(\mathsf{ck}, V'[p(i)], r_i)$
return V'

Fig. 3. The algorithms for rerandomizing and permuting a vector of ciphertexts, as well as its inverse.

Definition 9 (Shuffle Argument). *An interactive arguments for partially fixed statements of* $\mathsf{Shuffle}_\ell$ *relative to any perfectly rerandomizable commitment scheme* $\mathcal{C}$ *is called a shuffle argument for* $\mathcal{C}$.

Now, let $(\mathcal{F}, \mathsf{Puncture})$ be a puncturable pseudorandom function with key length $k(\lambda)$, input length $i(\lambda)$, and range $\mathsf{Perm}_\ell \times \mathcal{R}^\ell$. Let H be a collision resistant hash function. In Fig. 4 we then describe a simple three-move shuffle argument. We will first prove that this protocol is a zero knowledge shuffle argument as stated in the following theorem.

$\mathsf{P}_0(V_0)$	$\mathsf{V}_1(V_0', V_t', c)$	$\mathsf{V}_2(k')$
$k \leftarrow \{0,1\}^{k(\lambda)}$	$d \leftarrow \{1,\ldots,t\}$	**for** $1 \le i < d$
for $1 \le i \le t$	**return** d	$\quad V_i' := \pi(V_{i-1}', \mathcal{F}(k', i))$
$\quad V_i := \pi(V_{i-1}, \mathcal{F}(k,i))$		**for** $t > i \ge d$
$c := \mathsf{H}(V_1,\ldots,V_{t-1})$	$\mathsf{P}_2(d)$	$\quad V_i' := \pi^{-1}(V_{i+1}', \mathcal{F}(k', i+1))$
return $(V_t, (c, k))$	**if** $d \in \{1,\ldots,t\}$	**if** $\mathsf{H}(V_1',\ldots,V_{t-1}') = c$
	$\quad k' \leftarrow \mathsf{Puncture}(k,d)$	$\quad$ **return** 1
$\mathsf{P}_1(V_0, (c,k))$	$\quad$ **return** k'	**else return** 0
return c	**else**	
	$\quad$ **return** $\bot$	

Fig. 4. An algorithmic description of the shuffle argument.

Theorem 6. *Let* $\mathcal{C} = (\mathsf{Setup}, \mathsf{Com}, \mathsf{Rerand})$ *be a perfectly and inversely rerandomizable commitment scheme with message space* $\mathcal{M}$ *and randomness space* $\mathcal{R}$. *Let* $(\mathcal{F}, \mathsf{Puncture})$ *be a puncturable pseudorandom function with key length* $k(\lambda)$, *input length* $i(\lambda)$, *and range* $\mathsf{Perm}_\ell \times \mathcal{R}^\ell$. *Let* H *be a collision resistant hash function. Then the argument system* $\langle \mathsf{P} = (\mathsf{P}_0, \mathsf{P}_1, \mathsf{P}_2), \mathsf{V} = (\mathsf{V}_1, \mathsf{V}_2)\rangle$ *described in Fig. 4 is a zero-knowledge shuffle argument with soundness error* $1/t$ *for* $\mathcal{C}$.

Theorem 6 follows from Lemmas 7 and 10 as well as Corollary 12, which we prove in the following.

Lemma 7. *Let* $\mathcal{C}$, $(\mathcal{F}, \mathsf{Puncture})$, *and* H *be as in Theorem 6. Then the argument system described in Fig. 4 is complete.*

Proof. We need to show that it always holds that $(V_0, V_t') \in \mathsf{Shuffle}_\ell$ and that, in an interaction with the honest prover, the verifier always accepts and outputs 1.

Claim 8. *For any* $V_0 \in \mathcal{C}^\ell$ *and any* $(V_t, (c, k)) \leftarrow \mathsf{P}_0(V_0)$ *it holds that* $(V_0, V_t') \in \mathsf{Shuffle}_\ell$.

The prover computes each V_i as $V_i := \pi(V_{i-1}, \mathcal{F}(k,i))$, where $\mathcal{F}(k,i)$ outputs the description of a permutation and ℓ random values in $\mathcal{R}$. It then follows from the definition of π in Fig. 3 and the perfect rerandomizability of $\mathcal{C}$, that for $0 < i \le t$, $(V_{i-1}, V_i) \in \mathsf{Shuffle}_\ell$. Using Lemma 5 we can then conclude by induction, that $(V_0, V_t) \in \mathsf{Shuffle}_\ell$.

Claim 9. *For any $V_0 \in \mathcal{C}^\ell$ and any $(V_t, (c,k)) \leftarrow \mathsf{P}_0(V_0)$ any honest execution of $\langle \mathsf{P}(V_0, V_t, (c,k)), \mathsf{V}(V_0, V_t) \rangle$ will always output 1.*

We note that V_2 uses k' to recompute all V_i' for $1 \le i < t$. For $1 \le i < d$, this happens by computing $V_i' := \pi(V_{i-1}', \mathcal{F}(k',i)) = \pi(V_{i-1}', \mathcal{F}(k,i))$, where the last equality holds by the functionality requirement of the puncturable PRF, since $i \ne d$. As it always holds that $V_0' = V_0$, it follows by induction over i, that $V_i' = V_i$ for $1 \le i < d$.

For $d \le i < t$, the verifier computes $V_i' := \pi^{-1}(V_{i+1}', \mathcal{F}(k',i+1))$. It always holds that $V_t = V_t'$ and the prover computes $V_t := \pi(V_{t-1}, \mathcal{F}(k,t))$. This gives us $V_{t-1}' = \pi^{-1}(\pi(V_{t-1}, \mathcal{F}(k,t)), \mathcal{F}(k,t))$, since $t \ne d$. By the definition of π and π^{-1} we thus have that for $0 \le j < \ell$ it holds that

$$V_{t-1}'[j] = \mathsf{Rerand}^{-1}(\mathsf{Rerand}(V'[j], r_j), r_j) = V_{t-1}[j]$$

for some value of r_j. The last equality follows from the inverse rerandomizability of $\mathcal{C}$. Therefore, it follows that $V_{t-1}' = V_{t-1}$ and by induction that $V_i' = V_i$ for $d \le i < t$.

We thus have that with probability 1, $(V_1', \ldots, V_{t-1}') = (V_1, \ldots, V_{t-1})$ and therefore $\mathsf{H}(V_1', \ldots, V_{t-1}') = c$. It thus follows that V_2 outputs 1.

Combining the two claims Lemma 7 immediately follows. □

Lemma 10. *Let $\mathcal{C}$, $(\mathcal{F}, \mathsf{Puncture})$, and H be as in Theorem 6. Then the argument system described in Fig. 4 is sound with soundness error $1/t$.*

Proof. Let $(V_0^*, V_t^*) \notin \mathsf{Shuffle}_\ell$ and let P^* be an arbitrary probabilistic polynomial time prover. We will show, that

$$\Pr[b \leftarrow \langle \mathsf{P}^*(1^\lambda), \mathsf{V}(x,y) \rangle : b = 1] \le 1/t + \mathsf{negl}(\lambda).$$

We will assume without loss of generality, that P^* actually sends a first message c and that c is fixed.[6]

Let $d_0, d_1 \in \{1, \ldots, t\}$ be two arbitrary distinct challenges and let $k_0' \leftarrow \mathsf{P}^*(d_0)$ and $k_1' \leftarrow \mathsf{P}^*(d_1)$ be the corresponding responses. Consider, that the verifier works by recomputing $\mathbf{V}_b = (V_1^b, \ldots, V_{t-1}^b)$ and checking that it hashes to c. The verifier computes V_i^b as $V_i^b = \pi(V_{i-1}^b, \mathcal{F}(k_b', i))$ for $i < d_b$ and as $\pi^{-1}(V_{i+1}^b, \mathcal{F}(k_b', i+1))$ for $i \ge d_b$.

By definition of π and π^{-1}, this implies for $i < d_0$ that $(V_{i-1}^0, V_i^0) \in \mathsf{Shuffle}_\ell$ and for $i \ge d_0$ that $(V_i^0, V_{i+1}^0) \in \mathsf{Shuffle}_\ell$. By Lemma 5 we can thus conclude that

$$(V_0, V_{d_0-1}^0) \in \mathsf{Shuffle}_\ell \quad \text{and} \quad (V_{d_0}^0, V_t) \in \mathsf{Shuffle}_\ell. \tag{4}$$

---

[6] This is without loss of generality, since we can fix the prover's random coins to those that lead to the highest success probability.

Since $d_1 \neq d_0$, we have by the same reasoning, that

$$(V_{d_0-1}^1, V_{d_0}^1) \in \mathsf{Shuffle}_\ell. \tag{5}$$

If it were true, that $(V_{d_0-1}^0, V_{d_0}^0) = (V_{d_0-1}^1, V_{d_0}^1)$ then it would follow from Eqs. 4 and 5 by Lemma 5 that $(V_0, V_t) \in \mathsf{Shuffle}_\ell$ which would contradict the initial assumption. Therefore, it must hold that $(V_{d_0-1}^0, V_{d_0}^0) \neq (V_{d_0-1}^1, V_{d_0}^1)$ and $\mathbf{V}_0 \neq \mathbf{V}_1$. This would mean, however, that we could break collision resistance of H by presenting $\mathbf{V}_0, \mathbf{V}_1$ with probability

$$\Pr[(k_0', r_0) \leftarrow \mathsf{P}^*(d_0) : \mathsf{V}_2(k_0') = 1] \cdot \Pr[(k_1', r_1) \leftarrow \mathsf{P}^*(d_1) : \mathsf{V}_2(k_1') = 1].$$

Since the hash function is collision resistant, it follows that the above probability can be bounded by a negligible function. Thus, at least one of the two probabilities must be itself negligible. Since we have shown the above for all pairs of distinct challenges, this means that there can exist at most one challenge $d \in \{1, \dots, t\}$ such that $\Pr[(k', r) \leftarrow \mathsf{P}^*(d) : \mathsf{V}_2(k') = 1]$ is non-negligible. It thus ultimately follows that

$$\Pr[b \leftarrow \langle \mathsf{P}^*(1^\lambda), \mathsf{V}(x, y) \rangle : b = 1]$$

$$= \sum_{d=1}^{t} \Pr[\mathsf{V}_1(c) = d] \cdot \Pr[k' \leftarrow \mathsf{P}^*(d) : \mathsf{V}_2(k') = 1]$$

$$= \frac{1}{t} \cdot \sum_{d=1}^{t} \Pr[k' \leftarrow \mathsf{P}^*(d) : \mathsf{V}_2(k') = 1]$$

$$\leq \frac{1}{t} \cdot (1 + (t-1) \cdot \mathsf{negl}(\lambda)) \leq \frac{1}{t} + \mathsf{negl}(\lambda)$$

as claimed.

Lemma 11. *Let $\mathcal{C}$, $(\mathcal{F}, \mathsf{Puncture})$, and H be as in Theorem 6. Then the argument system described in Fig. 4 is honest verifier zero-knowledge.*

Before we prove Lemma 11, we first state the following simple corollary which follows immediately from by combining Lemma 11 with Theorem 1.

Corollary 12. *Let $\mathcal{C}$, $(\mathcal{F}, \mathsf{Puncture})$, and H be as in Theorem 6. Then the argument system described in Fig. 4 is zero-knowledge.*

Proof (Lemma 11). By Definition 7 we need to show that there exists a simulator Sim, such that

$$\left| \begin{array}{l} \Pr[(V_t, \mathcal{T}) \leftarrow \mathrm{SIMU}(V_0) : \mathcal{D}(V_0, V_t, \mathcal{T}) = 1] \\ - \Pr[(V_t, \mathcal{T}) \leftarrow \mathrm{REAL}(V_0) : \mathcal{D}(V_0, V_t, \mathcal{T}) = 1] \end{array} \right| \leq \mathsf{negl}(\lambda). \tag{6}$$

We specify the honest-verifier zero-knowledge simulator in Fig. 5 and use a series of game hops specified in Figs. 6 and 7 to prove that the above equation holds.

$$\boxed{\begin{array}{l} \mathsf{Sim}(V_0, V_t) \\ \hline d \leftarrow \{1, \ldots, t\} \\ k \leftarrow \{0, 1\}^{k(\lambda)} \\ \textbf{for } 1 \leq i < d \\ \quad V_i := \pi(V_{i-1}, \mathcal{F}(k, i)) \\ \textbf{for } t > i \geq d \\ \quad V_i := \pi^{-1}(V_{i+1}, \mathcal{F}(k, i+1)) \\ c := \mathsf{H}(V_1, \ldots, V_{t-1}) \\ k' \leftarrow \mathsf{Puncture}(k, d) \\ \textbf{return } (c; d; k') \end{array}}$$

Fig. 5. Honest-verifier zero knowledge simulator for the three-move protocol specified in Fig. 4

$$\boxed{\begin{array}{l} Game_1(V_0) \\ \hline d \leftarrow \{1, \ldots, t\} \\ k \leftarrow \{0, 1\}^{k(\lambda)} \\ \textbf{for } 1 \leq i < d \\ \quad V_i := \pi(V_{i-1}, \mathcal{F}(k, i)) \\ p \leftarrow \mathsf{Perm}_\ell, \vec{r} \leftarrow \mathcal{R}^\ell \\ V_t := \pi(V_0, p, \vec{r}) \\ \textbf{for } t > i \geq d \\ \quad V_i := \pi^{-1}(V_{i+1}, \mathcal{F}(k, i+1)) \\ c := \mathsf{H}(V_1, \ldots, V_{t-1}) \\ k' \leftarrow \mathsf{Puncture}(k, d) \\ b \leftarrow \mathcal{D}(V_0, V_t, (c; d; k')) \\ \textbf{return } b \end{array}}$$

Fig. 6. Game 1 for the proof of honest verifier zero-knowledge.

We first observe that

$$\Pr[(V_t, \mathcal{T}) \leftarrow \mathrm{SIMU}(V_0) : \mathcal{D}(V_0, V_t, \mathcal{T}) = 1] = \Pr[Game_1(V_0) = 1] \quad (7)$$

This is easily verified. V_t is chosen uniformly at random from all valid shufflings in both cases. Further, c, d and k' are all computed in exactly the same way. Similarly, we observe that

$$\Pr[(V_t, \mathcal{T}) \leftarrow \mathrm{REAL}(V_0) : \mathcal{D}(V_0, V_t, \mathcal{T}) = 1] = \Pr[Game_4(V_0)] \quad (8)$$

This is also easily verified. $Game_4$ computes V_t and (c, k) in exactly the same way as P_0, lets the honest verifier $\mathsf{V}_1(V_0, V_t, c)$ choose d and finally computes k' in exactly the same manner as P_2. What remains is to bound the differences between each pair of consecutive games.

Hop from $Game_1$ to $Game_2$. The changes between the two games are purely syntactic. In $Game_1$ the final shuffling V_t is sampled uniformly at random from all valid shuffles of V_0. In $Game_2$ the final shuffling V_t is computed as the composition of several intermediate *valid* shuffles. The shuffling at position d is chosen uniformly at random and *independently* from all other shuffles. Since all previous shuffles are valid, this makes V_d a uniformly random shuffling of V_0. Further, since all following shuffles are valid and the shuffling of V_d was independent, this makes V_t a uniformly random shuffling of V_0. Therefore V_t is distributed identically in both games. By the perfect and inverse rerandomizability of $\mathcal{C}$, it

$Game_2(V_0)$	$Game_3(V_0)$	$Game_4(V_0)$
$d \leftarrow \{1, \ldots, t\}$	$d \leftarrow \{1, \ldots, t\}$	
$k \leftarrow \{0,1\}^{k(\lambda)}$	$k \leftarrow \{0,1\}^{k(\lambda)}$	$k \leftarrow \{0,1\}^{k(\lambda)}$
for $1 \leq i < d$	**for** $1 \leq i \leq t$	**for** $1 \leq i \leq t$
$\quad V_i := \pi(V_{i-1}, \mathcal{F}(k, i))$	$\quad V_i := \pi(V_{i-1}, \mathcal{F}(k, i))$	$\quad V_i := \pi(V_{i-1}, \mathcal{F}(k, i))$
$p \leftarrow \mathrm{Perm}_\ell, \vec{r} \leftarrow \mathcal{R}^\ell$		
$V_d := \pi(V_{d-1}, p, \vec{r})$		
for $d < i \leq t$		
$\quad V_i := \pi(V_{i-1}, \mathcal{F}(k, i))$		
$c := \mathsf{H}(V_1, \ldots, V_{t-1})$	$c := \mathsf{H}(V_1, \ldots, V_{t-1})$	$c := \mathsf{H}(V_1, \ldots, V_{t-1})$
		$d \leftarrow \mathsf{V}_1(V_0, V_t, c)$
$k' \leftarrow \mathrm{Puncture}(k, d)$	$k' \leftarrow \mathrm{Puncture}(k, d)$	$k' \leftarrow \mathrm{Puncture}(k, d)$
$b \leftarrow \mathcal{D}(V_0, V_t, (c; d; k'))$	$b \leftarrow \mathcal{D}(V_0, V_t, (c; d; k'))$	$b \leftarrow \mathcal{D}(V_0, V_t, (c; d; k'))$
return b	**return** b	**return** b

Fig. 7. Game 2 through 4 for the proof of honest verifier zero-knowledge.

makes no difference, whether the V_i for $d < i < t$ are computed in the "forward" direction from V_{i-1} or in the "backwards" direction from V_{i+1}. Therefore the two games are perfectly equivalent, and it holds that

$$\Pr[Game_1(V_0) = 1] = \Pr[Game_2(V_0) = 1]. \tag{9}$$

Hop from $Game_2$ to $Game_3$. Note that the only difference between the two games is in the computation of V_d, which is computed as a uniformly random shuffle in $Game_2$ and as a *pseudorandom* shuffle in $Game_3$. This means we can bound the difference between the two games using a reduction to the pseudorandomness of the puncturable pseudorandom function. Specifically we use $\mathcal{D}$ as a distinguisher against $\mathcal{F}$ by requesting a key punctured on d and after receiving k' and $y = (p, \vec{r})$, computing V_i with key k' as in $Game_2$ except that we compute V_d using $y = (p, \vec{r})$. It is easy to see, that if y is uniformly random, then we perfectly simulate $Game_2$, whereas if $y = \mathcal{F}(k, d)$ we perfectly simulate $Game_3$. By the security of $\mathcal{F}$ it must therefore hold that

$$|\Pr[Game_2(V_0) = 1] - \Pr[Game_3(V_0) = 1]| \leq \mathsf{negl}(\lambda) \tag{10}$$

Hop from $Game_3$ to $Game_4$. The changes between the two games are again merely syntactic. In particular, the games behave identically, except that $Game_3$ chooses d uniformly at random from $\{1, \ldots, t\}$ whereas $Game_4$ lets the verifier choose $d \leftarrow \mathsf{V}_0(V_0, V_t, c)$. However, by definition of V_0 these two sampling strategies are identical and it holds that

$$\Pr[Game_3(V_0) = 1] = \Pr[Game_4(V_0) = 1]. \tag{11}$$

Finally, combining Eqs. 9 through 11, we get

$$|\Pr[Game_1(V_0) = 1] - \Pr Game_4(V_0) = 1| \leq \mathsf{negl}(\lambda), \qquad (12)$$

which combined with Eq. 7 and Eq. 8 gives us Eq. 6 thus concluding the proof.   □

In the full version of this paper, we additionally show how to modify the constrution to achieve straightline simulation in strict polynomial time in the CRS model. We also show how the amortized efficiency of the construction can be improved through batching and how the verifier's computational overhead can be optimized at the cost of a slightly worse communication complexity.

6   Public Accountability

If a public-key infrastructure (PKI), which associates the prover with a public key pk, is available, then we can discourage malicious provers from attempting to cheat by ensuring that the verifier obtains a publicly verifiable certificate that attests any failed cheating attempt by the prover. In the context of blockchains, such a certificate could for example be used to punish the prover through financial penalties.

In the following definition, we define this property by requiring the existence of a judge algorithm that can verify valid certificates and cannot be fooled by invalid certificates that falsely accuse an honest prover of misbehavior. For the sake of readability, we implicitly assume that the verifier has access to the prover's public key amd the prover has access to their own public and secret keys.

Definition 10 (Publicly-Accountable Zero-Knowledge Arguments). *Let $\mathcal{L} \subseteq X \times Y$ be a partially fixable language. Let (P, V) be an interactive zero-knowledge argument for $\mathcal{L}$ with soundness error ϵ in the PKI model. We say that the argument system is publicly accountable, if there exists a PPT algorithm Setup and a deterministic polynomial time judge algorithm J, such that the following conditions hold:*

Accountability: *Fix any $(x, y) \notin \mathcal{L}$ and let P^* be a malicious probabilistic polynomial time prover with*

$$\Pr[\mathsf{crs} \leftarrow \mathsf{Setup}(1^\lambda); b \leftarrow \langle \mathsf{P}^*(\mathsf{crs}), \mathsf{V}(\mathsf{crs}, x, y) \rangle : b = 1] \geq \delta\epsilon,$$

where the probability is taken over the random coins of the prover and the verifier and $0 < \delta \leq 1$. Then it holds that

$$\Pr[\mathsf{crs} \leftarrow \mathsf{Setup}(1^\lambda); \mathsf{cert} \leftarrow \langle \mathsf{P}^*(\mathsf{crs}), \mathsf{V}(\mathsf{crs}, x, y) \rangle : \mathsf{J}(\mathsf{crs}, \mathsf{pk}, \mathsf{cert}) = 1]$$
$$\geq \delta(1 - \epsilon) - \mathsf{negl}(\lambda),$$

where the probability is taken over the random coins of the prover and the verifier.

Defamation-Freeness: *For any $x \in X$ with $\mathcal{L}_x \neq \emptyset$, for any honest prover P and malicious probabilistic polynomial time verifier V*, it holds that*

$$\Pr \left[\begin{array}{c} \mathsf{crs} \leftarrow \mathsf{Setup}(1^\lambda); \\ (y, \mathsf{aux}) \leftarrow \mathsf{P}_0(\mathsf{crs}, x); \\ \mathsf{cert} \leftarrow \langle \mathsf{P}_1(x, y, \mathsf{aux}), \mathsf{V}^*(\mathsf{crs}, x, y) \rangle \end{array} : \mathsf{J}(\mathsf{pk}, \mathsf{cert}) = 1 \right] \leq \mathsf{negl}(\lambda).$$

We show that the three move zero-knowledge shuffle argument (P, V) described in Fig. 4 in Sect. 5 can be transformed into a publicly-accountable zero-knowledge argument.

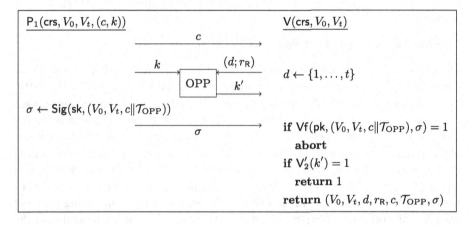

Fig. 8. The publicly-accountable transformation of the three-move shuffle argument. Here r_R refers to the random tape V uses to execute R in the OPP. $\mathcal{T}_\mathsf{OPP}$ refers to the full transcript resulting from the OPP execution.

Theorem 13. *Let $\langle \mathsf{P}', \mathsf{V}' \rangle$ be the three-move zero-knowledge shuffle argument described in Fig. 4 in Sect. 5. Let (S, R) be a secure receiver-extractable, oblivious key puncturing protocol for the puncturable PRF used in $\langle \mathsf{P}', \mathsf{V}' \rangle$. Let $(\mathsf{Gen}, \mathsf{Sig}, \mathsf{Vf})$ be an existentially unforgeable signature scheme. Then the protocol $\langle \mathsf{P}, \mathsf{V} \rangle$ with $\mathsf{P} = (\mathsf{P}'_0, \mathsf{P}_1)$, with P_1 and V as specified in Fig. 8 is a publicly-accountable zero-knowledge argument with soundness error $1/t$.*

Proof. We now show that this construction is indeed a publicly-accountable zero-knowledge argument.

Lemma 14. *The argument system (P, V) is complete.*

Proof. This directly follows from the completeness of the underlying argument system $(\mathsf{P}', \mathsf{V}')$, the completeness of the oblivious key puncturing protocol, and the correctness of the signature scheme. $\qquad\square$

Lemma 15. *The argument system (P, V) is sound with soundness error $1/t$.*

Proof. Let $(V_0, V_t) \notin \mathsf{Shuffle}_\ell$ and let P^* be an arbitrary malicious probabilistic polynomial time prover against (P, V). We use P^* to construct a probabilistic polynomial time prover $\widetilde{\mathsf{P}}$ against the original three move argument system $(\mathsf{P}', \mathsf{V}')$ as follows. $\widetilde{\mathsf{P}}$ initializes P^* with uniform random coins. Without loss of generality assume that P^* outputs a first message c, which $\widetilde{\mathsf{P}}$ forwards to the verifier. The verifier outputs a challenge d. $\widetilde{\mathsf{P}}$, acting on behalf of a simulated verifier towards P^*, engages in an execution of the oblivious puncturing protocol as the receiver, where d is the choice index. Let k' be the output that $\widetilde{\mathsf{P}}$ receives from P^* in this execution. $\widetilde{\mathsf{P}}$ forwards k' to the verifier. It is straightforward to see that $\widetilde{\mathsf{P}}$'s success probability is at least as large as the success probability of P^*. Since by Theorem 6 $\widetilde{\mathsf{P}}$'s success probability is bounded by $1/t + \mathsf{negl}(\lambda)$ the lemma follows. □

Lemma 16. *The argument system* (P, V) *is zero-knowledge.*

Proof. Let V^* be an arbitrary verifier to which we have blackbox access. Let $(\mathsf{Sim}_0, \mathsf{Sim}_1)$ be the simulator from the sender simulation property of the OPP. We construct a verifier $\widetilde{\mathsf{V}}'$ for the underlying argument system, which makes blackbox use of V^* and works as follows. First we let $\widetilde{\mathsf{V}}'$ sample a signature key pair $(\mathsf{sk}, \mathsf{pk})$ and whenever V^* asks the (simulated) PKI for the verification key of the prover, our verifier will return pk. Then $\widetilde{\mathsf{V}}'$ generates a simulated common reference string for the OPP as $(\mathsf{crs}, \mathsf{td}) \leftarrow \mathsf{Sim}_0(1^\lambda)$ and initializes $\mathsf{V}^*(\mathsf{crs}, 1^\lambda)$. Upon receiving a first prover message c, verifier $\widetilde{\mathsf{V}}'$ forwards the message to V^*. Then, $\widetilde{\mathsf{V}}'$ uses $\mathsf{Sim}_1(\mathsf{crs}, \mathsf{td})$ to execute the oblivious key puncturing protocol with V^*. If and when Sim_1 makes its single query d to its puncturing oracle, $\widetilde{\mathsf{V}}'$ simulates the oracle by outputting d as its challenge message and returning the response k' as the answer. Finally, $\widetilde{\mathsf{V}}'$ outputs whatever V^* outputs. Due to the sender simulation property of the OPP, the view of V^* when simulated by $\widetilde{\mathsf{V}}'$ is computationally indistinguishable from a real execution. Therefore the output of $\widetilde{\mathsf{V}}'$ is computationally indistinguishable from the output of V^* in a real execution of the publically accountable protocol. Since, $\widetilde{\mathsf{V}}'$ is a verifier for the underlying three-move argument and by Corollary 12 that argument is zero-knowledge, there exists a zero-knowledge simulator Sim' that can simulate this output given only blackbox access to $\widetilde{\mathsf{V}}'$. We can, thus, define the zero-knowledge simulator Sim with blackbox access to V^* simply as Sim' with blackbox access to $\widetilde{\mathsf{V}}'$. □

Lemma 17. *The argument system* (P, V) *satisfies accountability.*

Proof. The judge algorithm J is specified in Fig. 9. Let $(V_0, V_t) \notin \mathsf{Shuffle}_\ell$, let P^* be an arbitrary malicious PPT prover. Let $\mathsf{noAbort}(\vec{r})$ be the event that P^* does not abort and sends a valid signature when the parties run on random tapes $\vec{r} = (r_\mathsf{P}, r_\mathsf{V})$. Let $d(\vec{r})$ be the function that returns the verifier's challenge. Without loss of generality, we assume that for any fixed first message of the prover, there exists a set of verifier challenges $D(\vec{r})$, which the prover successfully answers in such a way that the verifier accepts.

$$\boxed{\begin{array}{l} \mathsf{J}(\mathsf{crs}, \mathsf{pk}, \mathsf{cert} = (V_0, V_t, d, r_\mathsf{R}, c, \mathcal{T}, \sigma)) \\ \hline \textbf{if } \mathsf{Vf}(\mathsf{pk}, (V_0, V_t, c\|\mathcal{T}), \sigma) = 0 \\ \quad \textbf{return } 0 \\ \quad k' := \mathsf{TCheck}(\mathsf{crs}, \mathcal{T}, d, r_\mathsf{R}) \\ \textbf{if } k' = \bot \\ \quad \textbf{return } 0 \\ \quad b := \mathsf{V}'_2(k') \\ \textbf{return } b \oplus 1 \end{array}}$$

Fig. 9. The judge algorithm J for the publicly-accountable transformation of a three-move zero-knowledge argument. Here TCheck refers to an algorithm that given a CRS, an OPP transcript $\mathcal{T}$, an input d and a random tape r_R outputs R's output, if the transcript is consistent with d and r_R and $\bot$ otherwise.

From the receiver privacy of the OPP, it follows that

$$\left| \Pr[\mathsf{noAbort}(\vec{r}) \mid d(\vec{r}) \in D(\vec{r})] - \Pr[\mathsf{noAbort}(\vec{r}) \mid d(\vec{r}) \notin D(\vec{r})] \right| \leq \mathsf{negl}(\lambda),$$

where the probability is taken over the random coins $\vec{r}$ of the parties. We observe that

$$\Pr[\mathsf{cert} \leftarrow \langle \mathsf{P}^*(1^\lambda; r_\mathsf{P}), \mathsf{V}(x, y; r_\mathsf{V}) \rangle : \mathsf{J}(\mathsf{pk}, \mathsf{cert}) = 1 \mid (V_0, V_t) \notin \mathsf{Shuffle}_\ell]$$
$$\geq \Pr[\mathsf{noAbort}(\vec{r}) \mid d(\vec{r}) \notin D(\vec{r})] \cdot \Pr[d(\vec{r}) \notin D(\vec{r})]$$
$$\geq (\Pr[\mathsf{noAbort}(\vec{r}) \mid d(\vec{r}) \in D(\vec{r})] - \mathsf{negl}(\lambda)) \cdot \Pr[d(\vec{r}) \notin D(\vec{r})]$$
$$\geq (\delta - \mathsf{negl}(\lambda)) \cdot (1 - \epsilon - \mathsf{negl}(\lambda))$$
$$\geq \delta(1 - \epsilon) - \mathsf{negl}(\lambda)$$

$\square$

Lemma 18. *The argument system* (P, V) *is defamation-free.*

Proof. Let $(V_0, V_t, d, r_\mathsf{R}, c, \mathcal{T}, \sigma))$ be the certificate presented by V*. We observe, that the existential unforgeability of the signature scheme implies that except with negligible probability, c and $\mathcal{T}$ must have originated from an interaction with the honest prover on input (V_0, V_t). The completeness of the OPP implies that TCheck will either output $\bot$, in which case J will output 0, or the correct response k' to the challenge d. It follows that (c, d, k') is the view of V' in an honest execution of the three-move shuffle argument. If $(V_0, V_t) \in \mathsf{Shuffle}_\ell$, the completeness of the argument implies that have $\mathsf{V}'_2(k') = 1$ and J will output 0. The lemma directly follows from the above observations. $\square$

The theorem statement follows from Lemmas 15, 16, 17, and 18. $\square$

7 Instantiation and Comparison

To evaluate the practical usefulness of the shuffle argument from Sect. 5 and its publicly accountable counterpart from Sect. 6, we explore how to instantiate

Table 1. Transcript size of shuffle arguments for vectors of length 100,000. The reported numbers for our constructions correspond to the instantiations described in Sect. 7 and are independent of the vector length and the type of commitment being shuffled. The numbers for Bayer-Groth [9] are taken from their paper for an instantiation in a q order subgroup of $\mathbb{Z}_p^*$ with $|q| = 160$ and $|p| = 1024$ shuffling ElGamal ciphertexts. For Bulletproofs [17], we consider an instantiation in ristretto255 [48] for shuffling Pedersen commitments. For the Groth SNARK [32] we consider an instantiation with curve BLS12-381 [13] and observe that the numbers are independent of the kind of commitments being shuffled and the vector length.

Scheme	Assumptions	Trusted setup	Soundness	Communication cost (byte)
This Work	CRHF, PRG	None	2^{-2}	81
			2^{-5}	153
			$2^{-\gamma}$	$32 + \lceil \gamma \cdot 24\frac{1}{8} \rceil$
This Work (with accountability)	CRHF, PRG, DDH	CRS	2^{-2}	416
			2^{-5}	992
			$2^{-\gamma}$	$32 + \gamma \cdot 192$
This Work (with accountability)	CRHF, PRG, RLWE	CRS	2^{-2}	$0.44 \cdot 2^{20}$
			2^{-5}	$1.1 \cdot 2^{20}$
			$2^{-\gamma}$	$32 + \gamma \cdot 0.215 \cdot 2^{20}$
Bayer-Groth [9]	Discrete logarithm	CRS	$\mathrm{negl}(\lambda)$	$700,000$
Bulletproofs [17]	Discrete logarithm	CRS	$\mathrm{negl}(\lambda)$	$1,600$
SNARKs [32]	Generic bilinear group	SRS	$\mathrm{negl}(\lambda)$	144

them in practice. We are particularly interested in the concrete communication complexities of such instantiations, since this is where our constructions shine. Towards this goal, we need to pick specific instantiations of the underlying building blocks, such as the collision-resistant hash function and the PPRF with its oblivious puncturing protocol. We aim for a security level of roughly 128 bits.

The Hash Function. The collision resistant hash function can in practice be instantiated using any of SHA-256 [46], SHA3-256, or SHAKE256 [47] with 256 bit output length. Any of these instantiations leads to hashes of size $|c| = 256$ bits.

The Puncturable PRF. The PPRF can be instantiated using the construction of Goldreich, Goldwasser and Micali (GGM) [28]. This construction relies on an internal length-doubling pseudorandom generator which can be instantiated using a secure stream cipher, such as AES [4] in CTR mode or ChaCha20 [11]. Taking the losses introduced by both the security proof of GGM as well as the proof of zero-knowledge into account, we require a PRG with $128 + \lceil 2 \log t + \log \log t \rceil$ bits of security to achieve our security goal of 128 bits. For reasonable values of t, using AES-192 in CTR mode would thus suffice. Simply instantiating GGM like this yields a PPRF with range $\{0,1\}^{192}$. As explained in Sect. 2, to construct a PPRF with range $\mathsf{Perm}_\ell \times \mathcal{R}^\ell$, the output can be stretched using a PRG and combined with the Fisher-Yates shuffle [24] by using the stretched output as the random tape of the shuffling algorithm. The necessary PRG can again be instantiated using, e.g., AES-192 in CTR mode or ChaCha20. Overall, the size of a punctured key with the AES-192 instantiation is $|k'| = \lceil \log t \rceil \cdot 192$ bits.

The Oblivious Puncturing Protocol. Using the PPRF construction of GGM mentioned above, we can use the oblivious puncturing protocol described in [14], which itself relies on $\lceil \log t \rceil$ many oblivious transfers with active security. These can be instantiated with the 2-round UC secure protocol of Peikert, Vaikunanthan, and Waters [44] over ristretto255 [48] by relying on the DDH assumption. From a computational point of view, the parties need to perform $10 \lceil \log t \rceil$ exponentiations, $6 \lceil \log t \rceil$ multiplications, and $2t$ evaluations of a PRG for one oblivious puncturing. Using our instantiation, the OPP runs in two rounds and thus the overall protocol runs in three, since the signature σ can be sent in parallel with the second message of the OPP from the prover to the verifier.

To obtain post-quantum security, we can instantiate the oblivious transfer with the protocol of Micciancio and Sorrell [41], which relies on the ring learning with errors assumption.

Acknowledgments. The authors would like to thank the anonymous PKC reviewer for pointing out the efficient OPP instantiation implicit in [14] as a practical replacement for general purpose PIR. The authors would also like to thank Ivan Damgård for the insightful discussions about the Goldreich and Kahan proof technique as well as Diego F. Aranha and Cathie Yun for information about practical instantiations of SNARKs and Bulletproofs respectively.

References

1. Abe, M.: Universally verifiable mix-net with verification work independent of the number of mix-servers. In: Nyberg, K. (ed.) EUROCRYPT 1998. LNCS, vol. 1403, pp. 437–447. Springer, Heidelberg (1998). https://doi.org/10.1007/BFb0054144
2. Abe, M.: Mix-networks on permutation networks. In: Lam, K.-Y., Okamoto, E., Xing, C. (eds.) ASIACRYPT 1999. LNCS, vol. 1716, pp. 258–273. Springer, Heidelberg (1999). https://doi.org/10.1007/978-3-540-48000-6_21
3. Abe, M., Hoshino, F.: Remarks on mix-network based on permutation networks. In: Kim, K. (ed.) PKC 2001. LNCS, vol. 1992, pp. 317–324. Springer, Heidelberg (2001). https://doi.org/10.1007/3-540-44586-2_23
4. Advanced Encryption Standard (AES). National Institute of Standards and Technology (NIST), FIPS PUB 197, U.S. Department of Commerce, November 2001
5. Ames, S., Hazay, C., Ishai, Y., Venkitasubramaniam, M.: Ligero: lightweight sublinear arguments without a trusted setup. In: ACM CCS 2017, pp. 2087–2104 (2017)
6. Asharov, G., Orlandi, C.: Calling out cheaters: covert security with public verifiability. In: Wang, X., Sako, K. (eds.) ASIACRYPT 2012. LNCS, vol. 7658, pp. 681–698. Springer, Heidelberg (2012). https://doi.org/10.1007/978-3-642-34961-4_41

7. Aumann, Y., Lindell, Y.: Security against covert adversaries: efficient protocols for realistic adversaries. In: Vadhan, S.P. (ed.) TCC 2007. LNCS, vol. 4392, pp. 137–156. Springer, Heidelberg (2007). https://doi.org/10.1007/978-3-540-70936-7_8

8. Aviram, N., Gellert, K., Jager, T.: Session resumption protocols and efficient forward security for TLS 1.3 0-RTT. In: Ishai, Y., Rijmen, V. (eds.) EUROCRYPT 2019. LNCS, vol. 11477, pp. 117–150. Springer, Cham (2019). https://doi.org/10.1007/978-3-030-17656-3_5

9. Bayer, S., Groth, J.: Efficient zero-knowledge argument for correctness of a shuffle. In: Pointcheval, D., Johansson, T. (eds.) EUROCRYPT 2012. LNCS, vol. 7237, pp. 263–280. Springer, Heidelberg (2012). https://doi.org/10.1007/978-3-642-29011-4_17

10. Bentov, I., Kumaresan, R., Miller, A.: Instantaneous decentralized poker. In: Takagi, T., Peyrin, T. (eds.) ASIACRYPT 2017. LNCS, vol. 10625, pp. 410–440. Springer, Cham (2017). https://doi.org/10.1007/978-3-319-70697-9_15

11. Bernstein, D.J.: Chacha, a variant of salsa20. In: Workshop Record of SASC, vol. 8, pp. 3–5 (2008)

12. Boneh, D., Waters, B.: Constrained pseudorandom functions and their applications. In: Sako, K., Sarkar, P. (eds.) ASIACRYPT 2013. LNCS, vol. 8270, pp. 280–300. Springer, Heidelberg (2013). https://doi.org/10.1007/978-3-642-42045-0_15

13. Bowe, S.: BLS12-381: New zk-SNARK Elliptic Curve Construction, March 2017. https://electriccoin.co/blog/new-snark-curve/

14. Boyle, E., et al.: Efficient two-round OT extension and silent non-interactive secure computation. In: ACM CCS 2019, pp. 291–308 (2019)

15. Boyle, E., Goldwasser, S., Ivan, I.: Functional signatures and pseudorandom functions. In: Krawczyk, H. (ed.) PKC 2014. LNCS, vol. 8383, pp. 501–519. Springer, Heidelberg (2014). https://doi.org/10.1007/978-3-642-54631-0_29

16. Brakerski, Z., Vaikuntanathan, V.: Constrained key-homomorphic PRFS from standard lattice assumptions. In: Dodis, Y., Nielsen, J.B. (eds.) TCC 2015. LNCS, vol. 9015, pp. 1–30. Springer, Heidelberg (2015). https://doi.org/10.1007/978-3-662-46497-7_1

17. Bünz, B., Bootle, J., Boneh, D., Poelstra, A., Wuille, P., Maxwell, G.: Bulletproofs: short proofs for confidential transactions and more. In: 2018 IEEE Symposium on Security and Privacy, pp. 315–334 (2018)

18. Chaum, D.: Untraceable electronic mail, return addresses, and digital pseudonyms. Commun. ACM 24(2), 84–88 (1981)

19. Chung, K.-M., Lui, E., Pass, R.: From weak to strong zero-knowledge and applications. In: Dodis, Y., Nielsen, J.B. (eds.) TCC 2015. LNCS, vol. 9014, pp. 66–92. Springer, Heidelberg (2015). https://doi.org/10.1007/978-3-662-46494-6_4

20. Dagher, G.G., Bünz, B., Bonneau, J., Clark, J., Boneh, D.: Provisions: Privacy-preserving proofs of solvency for bitcoin exchanges. In: ACM CCS 2015, pp. 720–731 (2015)

21. Damgård, I., Orlandi, C., Simkin, M.: Black-box transformations from passive to covert security with public verifiability. In: Micciancio, D., Ristenpart, T. (eds.) CRYPTO 2020. LNCS, vol. 12171, pp. 647–676. Springer, Cham (2020). https://doi.org/10.1007/978-3-030-56880-1_23

22. Fauzi, P., Meiklejohn, S., Mercer, R., Orlandi, C.: Quisquis: a new design for anonymous cryptocurrencies. In: Galbraith, S.D., Moriai, S. (eds.) ASIACRYPT 2019. LNCS, vol. 11921, pp. 649–678. Springer, Cham (2019). https://doi.org/10.1007/978-3-030-34578-5_23

23. Fiat, A., Shamir, A.: How to prove yourself: practical solutions to identification and signature problems. In: Odlyzko, A.M. (ed.) CRYPTO 1986. LNCS, vol. 263, pp. 186–194. Springer, Heidelberg (1987). https://doi.org/10.1007/3-540-47721-7_12

24. Fisher, R.A., Yates, F.: Statistical Tables for Biological, Agricultural and Medical Research, 3rd edn. Oliver and Boyd, Edinburgh (1949)

25. Furukawa, J., Sako, K.: An efficient scheme for proving a shuffle. In: Kilian, J. (ed.) CRYPTO 2001. LNCS, vol. 2139, pp. 368–387. Springer, Heidelberg (2001). https://doi.org/10.1007/3-540-44647-8_22

26. Gentry, C., Wichs, D.: Separating succinct non-interactive arguments from all falsifiable assumptions. In: 43rd ACM STOC, pp. 99–108 (2011)

27. Goldreich, O.: A uniform-complexity treatment of encryption and zero-knowledge. J. Cryptol. **6**(1), 21–53 (1993). https://doi.org/10.1007/BF02620230

28. Goldreich, O., Goldwasser, S., Micali, S.: How to construct random functions (extended abstract). In: 25th FOCS, pp. 464–479 (1984)

29. Goldreich, O., Kahan, A.: How to construct constant-round zero-knowledge proof systems for NP. J. Cryptol. **9**(3), 167–189 (1996). https://doi.org/10.1007/BF00208001

30. Groth, J.: A verifiable secret shuffle of homomorphic encryptions. In: Desmedt, Y.G. (ed.) PKC 2003. LNCS, vol. 2567, pp. 145–160. Springer, Heidelberg (2003). https://doi.org/10.1007/3-540-36288-6_11

31. Groth, J.: Linear algebra with sub-linear zero-knowledge arguments. In: Halevi, S. (ed.) CRYPTO 2009. LNCS, vol. 5677, pp. 192–208. Springer, Heidelberg (2009). https://doi.org/10.1007/978-3-642-03356-8_12

32. Groth, J.: On the size of pairing-based non-interactive arguments. In: Fischlin, M., Coron, J.-S. (eds.) EUROCRYPT 2016. LNCS, vol. 9666, pp. 305–326. Springer, Heidelberg (2016). https://doi.org/10.1007/978-3-662-49896-5_11

33. Groth, J., Ishai, Y.: Sub-linear zero-knowledge argument for correctness of a shuffle. In: Smart, N. (ed.) EUROCRYPT 2008. LNCS, vol. 4965, pp. 379–396. Springer, Heidelberg (2008). https://doi.org/10.1007/978-3-540-78967-3_22

34. Groth, J., Lu, S.: Verifiable shuffle of large size ciphertexts. In: Okamoto, T., Wang, X. (eds.) PKC 2007. LNCS, vol. 4450, pp. 377–392. Springer, Heidelberg (2007). https://doi.org/10.1007/978-3-540-71677-8_25

35. Ishai, Y., Kushilevitz, E., Ostrovsky, R., Sahai, A.: Zero-knowledge from secure multiparty computation. In: 39th ACM STOC, pp. 21–30 (2007)

36. Kiayias, A., Papadopoulos, S., Triandopoulos, N., Zacharias, T.: Delegatable pseudorandom functions and applications. In: ACM CCS 2013, pp. 669–684 (2013)

37. Kilian, J.: A note on efficient zero-knowledge proofs and arguments (extended abstract). In: 24th ACM STOC, pp. 723–732 (1992)

38. Kwon, A., Lazar, D., Devadas, S., Ford, B.: Riffle: an efficient communication system with strong anonymity. PoPETs **2016**(2), 115–134 (2016)

39. Lindell, Y.: How to simulate it - A tutorial on the simulation proof technique. Cryptology ePrint Archive, Report 2016/046 (2016). http://eprint.iacr.org/2016/046

40. Micali, S.: CS proofs (extended abstracts). In: 35th FOCS, pp. 436–453 (1994)

41. Micciancio, D., Sorrell, J.: Simpler statistically sender private oblivious transfer from ideals of cyclotomic integers. In: Moriai, S., Wang, H. (eds.) ASIACRYPT 2020. LNCS, vol. 12492, pp. 381–407. Springer, Cham (2020). https://doi.org/10.1007/978-3-030-64834-3_13

42. Neff, C.A.: A verifiable secret shuffle and its application to e-voting. In: ACM CCS 2001, pp. 116–125 (2001)

43. Pedersen, T.P.: Non-interactive and information-theoretic secure verifiable secret sharing. In: Feigenbaum, J. (ed.) CRYPTO 1991. LNCS, vol. 576, pp. 129–140. Springer, Heidelberg (1992). https://doi.org/10.1007/3-540-46766-1_9

44. Peikert, C., Vaikuntanathan, V., Waters, B.: A framework for efficient and composable oblivious transfer. In: Wagner, D. (ed.) CRYPTO 2008. LNCS, vol. 5157, pp. 554–571. Springer, Heidelberg (2008). https://doi.org/10.1007/978-3-540-85174-5_31

45. Sako, K., Kilian, J.: Receipt-free mix-type voting scheme. In: Guillou, L.C., Quisquater, J.-J. (eds.) EUROCRYPT 1995. LNCS, vol. 921, pp. 393–403. Springer, Heidelberg (1995). https://doi.org/10.1007/3-540-49264-X_32

46. Secure Hash Standard (SHS). National Institute of Standards and Technology, NIST FIPS PUB 180–4, U.S. Department of Commerce, August 2015

47. SHA-3 Standard: Permutation-Based Hash and Extendable-Output Functions. National Institute of Standards and Technology, NIST FIPS PUB 202, U.S. Department of Commerce, Aug 2015

48. de Valence, H., Grigg, J., Tankersley, G., Valsorda, F., Isis Lovecruft, M.H.: The ristretto255 and decaf448 groups. IETF CFRG Internet Draft (2020)

Beyond Security and Efficiency: On-Demand Ratcheting with Security Awareness

Andrea Caforio[1]([✉]), F. Betül Durak[2], and Serge Vaudenay[1]

[1] Ecole Polytechnique Fédérale de Lausanne (EPFL), Lausanne, Switzerland
andrea.caforio@epfl.ch
[2] Robert Bosch LLC - Research and Technology Center, Pittsburgh, PA, USA

Abstract. Secure asynchronous two-party communication applies ratcheting to strengthen privacy, in the presence of internal state exposures. Security with ratcheting is provided in two forms: forward security and post-compromise security. There have been several such secure protocols proposed in the last few years. However, they come with a high cost.

In this paper, we propose two generic constructions with favorable properties. Concretely, our first construction achieves *security awareness*. It allows users to detect non-persistent active attacks, to determine which messages are not safe given a potential leakage pattern, and to acknowledge for deliveries.

In our second construction, we define a hybrid system formed by combining two protocols: typically, a weakly secure "light" protocol and a strongly secure "heavy" protocol. The design goals of our hybrid construction are, first, to let the sender decide which one to use in order to obtain an efficient protocol with *ratchet on demand*; and second, to restore the communication between honest participants in the case of a message loss or an active attack.

We can apply our generic constructions to *any* existing protocol.

1 Introduction

In recent messaging applications, protocols are secured with end-to-end encryption to enable secure communication services for their users. Besides security, there are many other characteristics of communication systems. The nature of two-party protocols is that it is *asynchronous*: the messages should be transmitted regardless of the counterpart being online; the protocols do not have any control over the time that participants send messages; and, the participants change their roles as a *sender* or a *receiver* arbitrarily.

Many deployed systems are built with some sort of security guarantees. However, they often struggle with security vulnerabilities due to the internal state compromises that occur through *exposures* of participants. In order to prevent the attacker from decrypting past communication after an exposure, a state

J. A. Garay (Ed.): PKC 2021, LNCS 12711, pp. 649–677, 2021.
https://doi.org/10.1007/978-3-030-75248-4_23

update procedure is applied. Ideally, such updates are done through one-way functions which delete the old states and generate new ones. This guarantees *forward secrecy*. Additionally, to further prevent the attacker from decrypting future communication, *ratcheting* is used. This adds some source of randomness in every state update to obtain what is called *future secrecy*, or *backward secrecy*, or *post-compromise security*, or even *self-healing*.

Formal definitions of ratcheting security given have been recently studied, by Bellare et al. [2], followed by many others subsequent studies [1,7–10]. Some of these schemes are key-exchange protocols while others are secure messaging. Since secure ratcheted messaging boils down to secure key exchange, we consider these works as equivalent.

Previous Work. Early ratcheting protocols were suggested in Off-the-Record (OTR) and then Signal [3,11]. The security of Signal was studied by Cohn-Gordon et al. [5]. Unger et al. [12] surveyed many ratcheting techniques. Alwen et al. [1] formalized the concept of "double ratcheting" from Signal.

Cohn-Gordon et al. [6] proposed a ratcheted protocol at CSF 2016 but requiring synchronized roles. Bellare et al. [2] proposed another protocol at CRYPTO 2017, but unidirectional and without forward secrecy. Poettering and Rösler (PR) [10] designed a protocol with "*optimal*" security (in the sense that we know no better security so far), but using a random oracle, and heavy algorithms such as hierarchical identity-based encryption (HIBE). Yet, their protocol does not guarantee security against compromised random coins. Jaeger and Stepanovs (JS) [8] proposed a similar protocol with security against compromised random coins: with random coin leakage *before* usage. Their protocol also requires HIBE and a random oracle.

Durak and Vaudenay (DV) [7] proposed a protocol with slightly lower security[1] but relying on neither HIBE nor random oracles. They rely on a public-key cryptosystem, a digital signature scheme, a one-time symmetric encryption scheme, and a collision-resistant hash function. They further show that a uni-directional scheme with post-compromise security implies public-key cryptography, which obviates any hope of having a fully secure protocol solely based on symmetric cryptography. At EUROCRYPT 2019, Jost, Maurer, and Mularczyk (JMM) [9] proposed concurrently and independently a protocol with security between optimal security and the security of the DV protocol.[2] They achieve it even with random coin leakage *after* usage. Contrarily to other protocols achieving security with corrupted random coins, in their protocol, random coin leakage does not necessarily imply revealing part of the state of the participant. In the same conference, Alwen, Coretti, and Dodis [1] proposed two other ratcheting protocols denoted as ACD and ACD-PK with security against adversarially *chosen* random coins and *immediate decryption*. Namely, messages can be decrypted even though some previous messages have not been received yet. The ACD-PK protocol offers a good level of security, although having immediate decryption

---

[1] More precisely, the security is called "*sub-optimal*" [7].

[2] They call this security level "*near-optimal*" [9].

may lower it a bit as it will be discussed shortly. On the other hand, during a phase when the direction of communication does not change, the ACD protocol is fully based on symmetric cryptography, hence has lower security (in particular, no post-compromise security in this period). However, it is much more efficient. Following the authors of ACD, we consider Signal and ACD as equivalent.

We summarize these results in Table 1. The first four rows are based on DV [7, Table 1]. The other rows of the table will be discussed shortly.

Recently, Yan and Vaudenay [13] proposed Encrypt-then-Hash (EtH), a simple, natural, and extremely efficient ratchet protocol based on symmetric cryptography only, which provides forward secrecy but not post-compromise security. In short, it replaces the encryption key by its hash after every encryption or decryption, and needs one key for each direction of communication.

We are mostly interested in the DV model [7]. It gives a simple description of the KIND security and FORGE security. The former deals with key indistinguishability where the generated keys are indistinguishable from random strings and the latter states that update messages for ratcheted key exchange are unforgeable. Additionally, they present the notion of RECOVER-security which guarantees that participants can no longer accept messages from their counterpart after they receive a forged message. Even though FORGE security avoids nontrivial forgeries, there are still (unavoidable) trivial forgeries. They occur when the state of a participant is exposed and the adversary decides to impersonate him. With RECOVER security, when an adversary impersonates someone (say Bob), the impersonated participant is out and can no longer communicate with the counterpart (say Alice). It does not mean to bother participants but rather work for their benefit. Indeed, this security notion guarantees that the attack is eventually detected by Bob if he is still alive. If the protocol has a way to resume secure communication based on an explicit action from the users, this property is particularly appealing.

What makes the DV model simple is that all technicalities are hidden in a *cleanness* notion which eliminates trivial attack strategies. The adversary can only win when the attack scenario trace is "clean". This model makes it easy to consider several cleanness notions, specifically for hybrid protocols. The difficulty is perhaps to provide an exhaustive list of criteria for attacks to be clean.

Our Contributions. We start with formally and explicitly defining a notion of *security awareness* in which the users detect active attacks by realizing they can no longer communicate; users can be confident that nothing in the protocol can compromise the confidentiality of an acknowledged message if it did not leak before; and users can deduce from an incoming message which of the messages they sent have been delivered when the incoming message was formed.

More concretely, we elaborate on the RECOVER security to offer optimal security awareness. We start by defining a new notion called s-RECOVER. We make sure that not only is a receiver of a forgery no longer able to receive genuine messages via r-RECOVER-security but he can no longer send a message to his counterpart either via s-RECOVER-security. The r-RECOVER security is equal to RECOVER security of the DV protocol. Both r-RECOVER and s-RECOVER notions imply that reception of a genuine message offers a strong guarantee of having no forgery in the past: after an active attack ended, participants realize they can no longer communicate. Our security-awareness notion makes also explicit that the receiver of a message can deduce (in absence of a forgery) which of his messages have been seen by his counterpart (which we call an *acknowledgment extractor*). Hence, each sent message implicitly carries an acknowledgment for all received messages. Finally, what we want from the history of receive/send messages and exposures of a participant is the ability to deduce which message remains private (or "clean"). We call it a *cleanness extractor*.

Then, we give another *generic* construction to compose "any" two protocols with different security levels to allow a sender to select which security level to use. By composing a strongly secure protocol (such as PR, JS, JMM, DV) with a lighter and weakly secure one (such as EtH [13], which is solely based on symmetric cryptography), we obtain the notion of *ratchet on-demand*. When the ratcheting becomes infrequent, we obtain the excellent software performances of EtH as we will show in our implementation results. Hybrid constructions already exist, like Signal/ACD. However, they offer no control on the choice of the protocol to be used. Instead, they ratchet if (and only if) the direction of communication alternates.

We find that there would be an advantage to offer more fine grained flexibility. The decision to ratchet or not could of course be made by the end user or rather be triggered by the application at an upper layer, based on a security policy. For instance, it could make sense to ratchet on a smartphone for every new message following bringing back the app to foreground, or to ratchet no more than once an hour.

Another interesting outcome of our hybrid system is that we can form our hybrid system with *two identical* protocols: an upper one and a lower one. The lower protocol is used to communicate the messages and the upper protocol is used to control the lower protocol: to setup or to reset it. With this hybrid structure with identical protocols, we can repair broken communication in the case of a message loss or active attacks. As far as we observe, the complexity of the hybrid system is the same as the complexity of the underlying protocol. Since our security-aware property breaks communication in the case of an active attack, this repairing construction is a nice additional tool.

Last but not least, we implemented the many existing protocols: PR, JS, DV, JMM, ACD, ACD-PK, together with EtH. We observe that EtH is the fastest one. This is not surprising for all protocols which heavily use public-key cryptography, but it is surprising for ACD. Our goal is to offer a high level of security with the performances of EtH. We reach it with on-demand ratcheting when the participant demands healing scarcely.

Finally, we conclude that security awareness can be added on top of an existing protocol (even a hybrid one) in a generic way to strengthen security. We propose this generic strengthening (called chain) of protocol to obtain r-RECOVER and s-RECOVER security on the top of any protocol. As an example, we apply it on the ratchet-on-demand hybrid protocol composed with DV and EtH and obtain our final protocol.

We provide a comparison of all the protocols with r-RECOVER-security, s-RECOVER-security, acknowledgment extractor and cleanness extractor in Table 1. Note that this table is made to help both the authors and the readers to have a fair understanding of what specified properties each protocol has or not. We stress that "any" protocol could form a hybrid system to provide ratchet-on-demand and repairing a broken communication in the case of message loss or active attacks. The protocol which is shown in the last column is the case where we chose to use DV and EtH to construct our hybrid system.

Table 1. Comparison of Several Protocols with our protocol chain(hybrid(ARCAD$_{DV}$, EtH)) from Corollary 29 in Sect. 3.3: security level; worst case complexity for exchanging n messages; types of coin-leakage security; plain model (i.e. no random oracle); PKC or less (i.e. no HIBE). DV and ARCAD$_{DV}$ have identical characteristics. ARCAD$_{DV}$ is based on DV and described in Appendix B. The terms "optimal", "near-optimal", and "sub-optimal" from Durak-Vaudenay [7] are mentioned on p. 2. "Pragmatic" degrades a bit security to offer on-demand ratcheting. "id-optimal" is optimal among protocols with immediate decryption.

	PR [10]	JS [8]	JMM [9]	DV [7]	ACD-PK [1]	Ours
Security	Optimal	Optimal	Near-optimal	Sub-optimal	Id-optimal	Pragmatic
Worst case complexity	$O(n^2)$	$O(n^2)$	$O(n^2)$	$O(n)$	$O(n)$	$O(n)$
Coins leakage resilience	No	Pre-send	Post-send	No	Chosen coins	No
Plain model (no ROM)	No	No	No	Yes	Yes	Yes
PKC or less	No	No	Yes	Yes	Yes	Yes
Immediate decryption	No	No	No	No	Yes	No
r-RECOVER security	No	Yes	No	Yes	No	Yes
s-RECOVER security	No	Yes	No	No	No	Yes
ack. extractor	Yes	Yes	Yes	Yes	No	Yes
Cleanness extractor	Yes	Yes	Yes	Yes	Yes	Yes
Category	BARK	ARCAD	ARCAD	BARK	ARCAD	ARCAD

To summarize, our contributions are:

- we formally define the notion of security awareness, construct a generic protocol strengthening called chain, and prove its security;
- we define the notion of on-demand ratcheting, construct a generic hybrid protocol called hybrid, define and prove its security;
- we implement PR, JS, DV, JMM, ACD, ACD-PK, and EtH protocols in order to clearly compare their performances.

Notation. We have two participants named Alice (A) and Bob (B). Whenever we talk about either one of the participants, we represent it as P, then $\overline{P}$ refers to P's counterpart. We have two roles send and rec for sender and receiver respectively. We define $\overline{\text{send}}$ = rec and $\overline{\text{rec}}$ = send. When the communication is unidirectional, the participants are called the *sender* S and the *receiver* R.

Structure of the Paper. In Sect. 2, we revisit the preliminary notions from Durak-Vaudenay [7] and Alwen-Coretti-Dodis [1]. They all are essential to be able to follow our results. In Sect. 3, we define a new notion named security awareness and build a protocol with regard to the notion. In Sect. 4, we define a new protocol called on-demand ratcheting with better performance than state-of the-art. Finally, in Appendix A, we present our implementation results with the figures comparing various protocols. Appendix B presents $\mathsf{ARCAD_{DV}}$: the DV protocol in a simplified form and in the frame of ARCAD.

2   Preliminaries

2.1   ARCAD Definition and Security

In this section, we recall the DV model [7] and we slightly adapt it to define asynchronous ratcheted communication with additional data denoted as ARCAD. That is, we consider message encryption instead of key agreement (BARK: bidirectional asynchronous ratcheted key agreement). The difference between BARK and ARCAD is the same as the difference between KEM and cryptosystems: pt is input to Send instead of output of Send. Additionally, we treat associated data ad to authenticate. Like DV [7][3], we adopt asymptotic security rather than exact security, for more readability. Adversaries and algorithms are probabilistic polynomially bounded (PPT) in terms of a parameter λ.

As we slightly change our direction from key exchange to encryption, we feel that it is essential to redefine the set of definitions from BARK for ARCAD. In this section, some of the definitions are marked with the reference [7]. It means that these definitions are unchanged except for possible necessary notation changes. The other definitions are straightforward adaptations to fit ARCAD. We try not to overload this section by redefining already existing terminology, hence, we let less essential definitions in the full version [4].

Definition 1 (ARCAD). *An* asynchronous ratcheted communication with additional data (ARCAD) *consists of the following PPT algorithms:*

- $\mathsf{Setup}(1^\lambda) \xrightarrow{\$} \mathsf{pp}$: *This defines the common public parameters* pp.
- $\mathsf{Gen}(1^\lambda, \mathsf{pp}) \xrightarrow{\$} (\mathsf{sk}, \mathsf{pk})$: *This generates the secret key* sk *and the public key* pk *of a participant.*
- $\mathsf{Init}(1^\lambda, \mathsf{pp}, \mathsf{sk_P}, \mathsf{pk_{\overline{P}}}, \mathsf{P}) \to \mathsf{st_P}$: *This sets up the initial state* $\mathsf{st_P}$ *of* P *given his secret key, and the public key of his counterpart.*
- $\mathsf{Send}(\mathsf{st_P}, \mathsf{ad}, \mathsf{pt}) \xrightarrow{\$} (\mathsf{st'_P}, \mathsf{ct})$: *it takes as input a plaintext* pt *and some associated data* ad *and produces a ciphertext* ct *along with an updated state* $\mathsf{st'_P}$.
- $\mathsf{Receive}(\mathsf{st_P}, \mathsf{ad}, \mathsf{ct}) \to (\mathsf{acc}, \mathsf{st'_P}, \mathsf{pt})$: *it takes as input a ciphertext* ct *and some associated data* ad *and produces a plaintext* pt *with an updated state* $\mathsf{st'_P}$ *together with a flag* acc.[4]

---

[3] Proceedings version.

[4] In our work, we assume that acc = false implies that $\mathsf{st'_P} = \mathsf{st_P}$ and pt = $\bot$, i.e. the state is not updated when the reception fails. Other authors assume that $\mathsf{st'_P} = \mathsf{pt} = \bot$, i.e. no further reception can be done.

An additional Initall$(1^\lambda, pp) \rightarrow (st_A, st_B, z)$ *algorithm, which returns the initial states of* A *and* B *as well as public information* z, *is defined as follows:*

Initall$(1^\lambda, pp)$:

1: Gen$(1^\lambda, pp) \rightarrow (sk_A, pk_A)$

2: Gen$(1^\lambda, pp) \rightarrow (sk_B, pk_B)$

3: $st_A \leftarrow$ Init$(1^\lambda, pp, sk_A, pk_B, A)$

4: $st_B \leftarrow$ Init$(1^\lambda, pp, sk_B, pk_A, B)$

5: $z \leftarrow (pp, pk_A, pk_B)$

6: *return* (st_A, st_B, z)

Initall is defined for convenience as an initialization procedure for all games. None of our security games actually cares about how Initall is made from Gen and Init. This is nice because there is little to change to define a notion of "symmetric-cryptography-based ARCAD" with a slight abuse of definition: we only need to define Initall. This approach was already adopted for EtH [13] which was proven as a "secure ARCAD" in this way.

For all global variables v in the game such as received$_{ct}^P$, st_P, or ct_P (which appear in Fig. 1 and Fig. 2, for instance), we denote the value of v at time t by $v(t)$. The notion of *time* is participant-specific. It refers to the number of elementary operations he has done. We assume neither synchronization nor central clock. Time for two different participants can only be compared when they are run non-concurrently by an adversary in a game.

Definition 2 (Correctness of ARCAD). *Consider the correctness game given on Fig. 1.*[5] *We say that an ARCAD protocol is* correct *if for all sequence* sched *of tuples of the form* (P, "send", ad, pt) *or* (P, "rec"), *the game never returns 1. Namely,*

- *at each stage, for each* P, received$_{pt}^P$ *is prefix of* sent$_{pt}^{\overline{P}}$[6];
- *each* RATCH(P, "rec") *call returns* acc = true.

We note that RATCH(P, "rec", ad, ct) ignores messages when decryption fails. For this reason, when we say that a participant P "receives" a message, we may implicitly mean that the message was accepted. More precisely, it means that decryption succeeded and RATCH returned acc = true.

In addition to the RATCH oracle (in Fig. 1) which is used to ratchet (either to send or to receive), we define several other oracles (in Fig. 2): EXP$_{st}$ to obtain the state of a participant; EXP$_{pt}$ to obtain the last received message pt; CHALLENGE to send either the plaintext or a random string. All those oracles are used without change throughout all security notions in this paper.

Definition 3 (Matching status [7]). *We say that* P *is in a* matching status *at time* t *for* P *if*

---

[5] We use the programming technique of "function overloading" to define the RATCH oracle: there are two definitions depending on whether the second input is "rec" or "send".

[6] By saying that received$_{pt}^P$ is prefix of sent$_{pt}^{\overline{P}}$, we mean that sent$_{pt}^{\overline{P}}$ is the concatenation of received$_{pt}^P$ with a (possible empty) list of (ad, pt) pairs.

Oracle RATCH(P, "rec", ad, ct)	Game Correctness(sched)
1: ct_P ← ct	1: set all sent_* and received_* to ∅
2: ad_P ← ad	2: Setup(1^λ) $\xrightarrow{\$}$ pp
3: (acc, st'_P, pt_P) ← Receive(st_P, ad_P, ct_P)	3: Initall(1^λ, pp) $\xrightarrow{\$}$ (st_A, st_B, z)
4: if acc then	4: initialize two FIFO lists incoming_A, incoming_B ← ∅
5: st_P ← st'_P	5: i ← 0
6: append (ad_P, pt_P) to received_pt^P	6: loop
7: append (ad_P, ct_P) to received_ct^P	7: i ← i + 1
8: end if	8: if sched_i of form (P, "rec") then
9: return acc	9: if incoming_P is empty then return 0
	10: pull (ad, ct) from incoming_P
Oracle RATCH(P, "send", ad, pt)	11: acc ← RATCH(P, "rec", ad, ct)
10: pt_P ← pt	12: if acc = false then return 1
11: ad_P ← ad	13: else
12: (st'_P, ct_P) ← Send(st_P, ad_P, pt_P)	14: parse sched_i = (P, "send", ad, pt)
13: st_P ← st'_P	15: ct ← RATCH(P, "send", ad, pt)
14: append (ad_P, pt_P) to sent_pt^P	16: push (ad, ct) to incoming_P̄
15: append (ad_P, ct_P) to sent_ct^P	17: end if
16: return ct_P	18: if received_pt^A not prefix of sent_pt^B then return 1
	19: if received_pt^B not prefix of sent_pt^A then return 1
	20: end loop

Fig. 1. The Correctness Game of ARCAD Protocol.

1. *at any moment of the game before time* t *for* P, received$_{ct}^P$ *is a prefix of* sent$_{ct}^{\overline{P}}$ — *this defines the time* $\overline{t}$ *for* $\overline{P}$ *when* $\overline{P}$ *sent the last message in* received$_{ct}^P$(t);
2. *at any moment of the game before time* $\overline{t}$ *for* $\overline{P}$, received$_{ct}^{\overline{P}}$ *is a prefix of* sent$_{ct}^P$.

We further say that time t *for* P *originates from time* $\overline{t}$ *for* $\overline{P}$.

Intuitively, P is in a matching status at a given time if his state is not influenced by an active attack (i.e. message injection/modification/erasure/replay).

Definition 4 (Forgery). *Given a participant* P *in a game, we say that* (ad, ct) ∈ received$_{ct}^P$ *is a forgery if at the moment of the game just before* P *received* (ad, ct), P *was in a matching status, but no longer after receiving* (ad, ct).

Definition 5 (Trivial forgery). *Let* (ad, ct) *be a forgery received by* P. *At the time* t *just before the* RATCH(P, "rec", ad, ct) *call,* P *was in a matching status. We assume that time* t *for* P *originates from time* $\overline{t}$ *for* $\overline{P}$. *If there is an* EXP$_{st}(\overline{P})$ *call between time* $\overline{t}$ *for* $\overline{P}$ *and the next* RATCH($\overline{P}$, "send", ., .) *call (or just after time* $\overline{t}$ *is there is no further* RATCH($\overline{P}$, "send", ., .) *call), we say that* (ad, ct) *is a trivial forgery.*

We give a brief description of the DV security notions [7] as follows.
FORGE-security: It makes sure that there is no forgery, except trivial ones.

r-RECOVER-security[7]: If an adversary manages to forge (trivially or not) a message to one of the participants, then this participant can no longer accept genuine messages from his counterpart.

PREDICT-security: The adversary cannot guess the value ct which will be output from the Send algorithm.

KIND-security: We omit this security notion which is specific to key exchange. Instead, we consider **IND-CCA-security** in a real-or-random style.

We define the ratcheting security with IND-CCA notion. Before defining it, we like to introduce a predicate called C_{clean} as IND-CCA is relative to this predicate. The purpose of C_{clean} is to discard trivial attacks. Somehow, the technicality of the security notion is hidden in this cleanness notion. An "optimal" cleanness predicate discards only trivial attacks but other predicates may discard more and allow to have more efficient protocols [7].

More precisely, for "clean" cases, a security property must be guaranteed. A "trivial" attack (i.e. an attack that no protocol can avoid) implies a non-clean case. If the cleanness notion is tight, this is an equivalence.

In the full version [4] we recall the most useful cleanness predicates. In short, $C_{leak} \wedge C_{trivial\ forge}^{A,B}$ corresponds to the DV-cleanness notion for post-compromise security ("sub-optimal") and C_{sym} is the weaker cleanness notion for forward secrecy only which is adapted to symmetric cryptographic schemes.

Game $\mathsf{IND\text{-}CCA}_{b,C_{clean}}^{\mathcal{A}}(1^\lambda)$

1: $\mathsf{Setup}(1^\lambda) \xrightarrow{\$} \mathsf{pp}$
2: $\mathsf{InitAll}(1^\lambda, \mathsf{pp}) \xrightarrow{\$} (\mathsf{st}_A, \mathsf{st}_B, z)$
3: set all sent_*^* and $\mathsf{received}_*^*$ variables to $\emptyset$
4: set t_{test} to $\perp$
5: $b' \leftarrow \mathcal{A}^{\mathsf{RATCH}, \mathsf{EXP}_{st}, \mathsf{EXP}_{pt}, \mathsf{CHALLENGE}}(z)$
6: if $\neg C_{clean}$ then return $\perp$
7: return b'

Oracle $\mathsf{EXP}_{st}(P)$
1: return st_P

Oracle $\mathsf{CHALLENGE}(P, \mathsf{ad}, \mathsf{pt})$
1: if $\mathsf{t}_{test} \neq \perp$ then return $\perp$
2: if $b = 0$ then
3:     replace pt by a random string of same length
4: end if
5: $\mathsf{ct} \leftarrow \mathsf{RATCH}(P, \text{"send"}, \mathsf{ad}, \mathsf{pt})$
6: $(t, P, \mathsf{ad}, \mathsf{pt}, \mathsf{ct})_{test} \leftarrow (\mathsf{time}_P, P, \mathsf{ad}, \mathsf{pt}, \mathsf{ct})$
7: return ct

Oracle $\mathsf{EXP}_{pt}(P)$
1: return pt_P

Fig. 2. IND-CCA Game. (Oracle RATCH is defined in Fig. 1)

Definition 6 (C_{clean}-IND-CCA security). *Let C_{clean} be a cleanness predicate. We consider the $\mathsf{IND\text{-}CCA}_{b,C_{clean}}^{\mathcal{A}}$ game of Fig. 2. We say that the ARCAD is C_{clean}-IND-CCA-secure if for any PPT adversary, the advantage*

$$\mathsf{Adv}(\mathcal{A}) = \left| \Pr\left[\mathsf{IND\text{-}CCA}_{0,C_{clean}}^{\mathcal{A}}(1^\lambda) \to 1\right] - \Pr\left[\mathsf{IND\text{-}CCA}_{1,C_{clean}}^{\mathcal{A}}(1^\lambda) \to 1\right] \right|$$

of $\mathcal{A}$ in $\mathsf{IND\text{-}CCA}_{b,C_{clean}}^{\mathcal{A}}$ security game is negligible.

---

[7] It is called RECOVER-security in DV [7]. We call it r-RECOVER because we will enrich it with an s-RECOVER notion in Sect. 3.1.

Game FORGE$_{C_{clean}}^{A}(1^\lambda)$	Game r-RECOVER$^A(1^\lambda)$
1: Setup$(1^\lambda) \overset{\$}{\to}$ pp	1: win $\leftarrow 0$
2: Initall$(1^\lambda, pp) \overset{\$}{\to} (st_A, st_B, z)$	2: Setup$(1^\lambda) \overset{\$}{\to}$ pp
3: $(P, ad, ct) \leftarrow A^{RATCH,EXP_{st},EXP_{pt}}(z)$	3: Initall$(1^\lambda, pp) \overset{\$}{\to} (st_A, st_B, z)$
4: RATCH$(P, \text{"rec"}, ad, ct) \to acc$	4: set all sent$_*^*$ and received$_*^*$ variables to $\emptyset$
5: if $acc = $ false then return 0	5: $P \leftarrow A^{RATCH,EXP_{st},EXP_{pt}}(z)$
6: if $\neg C_{clean}$ then return 0	6: if we can parse received$_{ct}^P = (seq_1, (ad, ct), seq_2)$
7: if (ad, ct) is not a forgery (Def. 4) for P then	and sent$_{ct}^{\overline{P}} = (seq_3, (ad, ct), seq_4)$ with $seq_1 \neq$
return 0	seq_3 (where (ad, ct) is a single message and
8: return 1	all seq_i are finite sequences of single messages)
	then win $\leftarrow 1$
	7: return win

Game PREDICT$^A(1^\lambda)$	4: RATCH$(P, \text{"send"}, ad, pt) \to ct$
1: Setup$(1^\lambda) \overset{\$}{\to}$ pp	5: if $(ad, ct) \in$ received$_{ct}^P$ then return
2: Initall$(1^\lambda, pp) \overset{\$}{\to} (st_A, st_B, z)$	1
3: $(P, ad, pt) \leftarrow A^{RATCH,EXP_{st},EXP_{pt}}(z)$	6: return 0

Fig. 3. FORGE, r-RECOVER, and PREDICT Games. (Oracles RATCH, EXP$_{st}$, EXP$_{pt}$ are defined in Fig. 1 and Fig. 2.)

Definition 7 (C$_{clean}$-FORGE security). *Given a cleanness predicate* C$_{clean}$, *consider* FORGE$_{C_{clean}}^{A}$ *game in Fig. 3 associated to the adversary* A. *Let the advantage of* A *be the probability that the game outputs 1. We say that* ARCAD *is* C$_{clean}$*-FORGE-secure if, for any PPT adversary, the advantage is negligible.*

In this definition, we added the notion of cleanness which determines if an attack is trivial or not. The original notion of FORGE security [7] is equivalent to using the following C$_{trivial}$ predicate C$_{clean}$:

C$_{trivial}$: the last (ad, ct) message is not a trivial forgery (following Definitions 5).

The purpose of this update in the definition is to allow us to easily define a weaker form of FORGE-security for symmetric protocols and in Sect. 3.3.

Definition 8 (r-RECOVER security [7]). *Consider the* r-RECOVER^A *game in Fig. 3 associated to the adversary* A. *Let the advantage of* A *in succeeding in the game be* $\Pr(\text{win} = 1)$. *We say that the* ARCAD *is* r-RECOVER-secure, *if for any PPT adversary, the advantage is negligible.*

Definition 9 (PREDICT security [7]). *Consider* PREDICT$^A(1^\lambda)$ *game in Fig. 3 associated to the adversary* A. *Let the advantage of* A *in succeeding in the game be the probability that 1 is returned. We say that the* ARCAD *is* PREDICT-secure, *if for any PPT adversary, the advantage is negligible.*

PREDICT-security is useful to reduce the notion of matching status to the two conditions that received$_{ct}^P$ is a prefix of sent$_{ct}^{\overline{P}}$ at time t for P and received$_{ct}^{\overline{P}}$ is a prefix of sent$_{ct}^P$ at time $\overline{t}$ for $\overline{P}$.

2.2 The Epoch Notion in Secure Communication

We define the epochs in an equivalent way to the work done by Alwen et al. [1].[8] Epochs are useful to designate the sequence of messages, as both participants may not see exactly the same. We will use epoch numbers in the design of our hybrid scheme for on-demand ratcheting in Sect. 4.1.

Epochs are a set of consecutive messages going in the same direction. An epoch is identified by an integer counter e. Each message is assigned one epoch counter e_m. Hence, the epochs are non-intersecting. For convenience, each participant P keeps the epoch value e_{send}^P of the last sent message and the epoch value e_{rec}^P of the last received message. They are used to assign an epoch to a message to be sent.

Definition 10 (Epoch). *Epochs are non-intersecting sets of messages which are defined by an integer. During the game, we let e_{rec}^P (resp. e_{send}^P) be the epoch of the last received (resp. sent) message by P. At the very beginning of the protocol, we define e_{send}^P and e_{rec}^P specifically. For the participant A, $e_{rec}^A = -1$ and $e_{send}^A = 0$. For the participant B, $e_{send}^B = -1$ and $e_{rec}^B = 0$. The procedure to assign an epoch e_m to a new sent message follows the rule described next:*
If $e_{rec}^P < e_{send}^P$, then the message is put in the epoch $e_m = e_{send}^P$. Otherwise, it is put in epoch $e_m = e_{rec}^P + 1$.

Let $e_P = \max\{e_{rec}^P, e_{send}^P\}$. Let $b_A = 0$ and $b_B = 1$. We have

$$e_{send}^P = \begin{cases} e_P & \text{if } e_P \bmod 2 = b_P \\ e_P - 1 & \text{otherwise} \end{cases} \qquad e_{rec}^P = \begin{cases} e_P & \text{if } e_P \bmod 2 \neq b_P \\ e_P - 1 & \text{otherwise} \end{cases}$$

Therefore, it is equivalent to maintain (e_{rec}^P, e_{send}^P) or e_P. The procedure to manage e_P and e_m is described by Alwen et al. [1].

We will use a counter c for each epoch e. We will use the order on (e, c) pairs defined by

$$(e, c) < (e', c') \iff (e < e' \vee (e = e' \wedge c < c'))$$

3 Security Awareness

3.1 s-RECOVER Security

We gave the DV r-RECOVER security definition [7] in Definition 8. It is an important notion to capture that P cannot accept a genuine ct from $\overline{P}$ after P receives a forgery. However, r-RECOVER-security does not capture the fact that when it is $\overline{P}$ who receives a forgery, P could still accept messages which come from $\overline{P}$. We strengthen r-RECOVER security with another definition called s-RECOVER.

---

[8] The notion of epoch appeared in Poettering-Rösler [10] before.

Definition 11 (s-RECOVER security). *In the* s-RECOVER^A *game in Fig. 4 with the adversary* A, *we let the advantage of* A *in succeeding in the game be* $\Pr(\text{win} = 1)$. *We say that the* ARCAD *is* s-RECOVER-*secure, if for any PPT adversary, the advantage is negligible.*

```
Game s-RECOVER^A (1^λ)
 1: win ← 0
 2: Setup(1^λ) $→ pp
 3: Initall(1^λ, pp) $→ (st_A, st_B, z)
 4: set all sent* and received* variables to ∅
 5: P ← A^{RATCH,EXP_st,EXP_pt} (z)
 6: if received_ct^P is a prefix of sent_ct^P̄ then
 7:     set t̄ to the time when P̄ sent the last message in received_ct^P
 8:     if received_ct^P(t̄) is not a prefix of sent_ct^P̄ then win ← 1
 9: end if
10: return win
```

Fig. 4. s-RECOVER Security Game. (RATCH and EXP oracles are defined in Fig. 1 and Fig. 2.)

Ideally, what we want from the protocol is that participants can detect forgeries by realizing that they are no longer able to communicate to each other. We cannot prevent impersonation to happen after a state exposure but we want to make sure that the normal exchange between the participants is cut. Hence, if a participant eventually receives a genuine message (e.g. because it was authenticated after meeting in person), he should feel safe that no forgeries happened. Contrarily, detecting a communication cut requires an action from the participants, such as restoring communication using a super hybrid structure, as we will suggest in Sect. 4.1.

We directly obtain the following useful result:[9]

Lemma 12. *If an* ARCAD *is* r-RECOVER, s-RECOVER, *and* PREDICT *secure, whenever* P *receives a genuine message from* P̄ *(i.e., an* (ad, ct) *pair sent by* P̄ *is accepted by* P), P *is in a matching status (following Definition 3), except with negligible probability.*

Our notion of RECOVER-security and forgery is quite strong in the sense that it focuses on the ciphertext. Some protocols such as JMM [9] focus on the plaintext. In JMM, ct includes some encrypted data and some signature but only the encrypted data is hashed. Hence, an adversary can replace the signature by another signature after exposure of the signing key. It can be seen as not so important because it must sign the same content. However, the signature has a

---

[9] The proof is provided in the full version [4].

key update and the adversary can make the receiver update to any verifying key to desynchronize, then re-synchronize at will. Consequently, *the* JMM *protocol does not offer* RECOVER *security* as we defined it. Contrarily, PR [10] hashes (ad, ct) but does not use it in the next ad or to compute the next ct. Thus, PR *has no* RECOVER *security* either.[10] One may think that it is easy to fix this by hashing all messages but this is not as simple. We propose in Sect. 3.3 the chain transformation which can fix any protocol, thanks to Lemma 18.

3.2   Security Awareness

To have a security-awareness notion, we want r-RECOVER, s-RECOVER, and PREDICT security[11], we want to have an acknowledgment extractor (to be aware of message delivery), and we want to have a cleanness extractor (to be aware of the cleanness of every message, if not subject to trivial exposure). The last two notions are defined below. This means that on the one hand, impersonations are eventually discovered, and on the other hand, by assuming that no impersonation occurs and assuming that exposures are known, a participant P knows exactly which messages are safe, at least after one round-trip occurred.

Definition 13 (Security-awareness). *A protocol is* C_{clean}-*security-aware if*

- *it is* r-RECOVER, s-RECOVER, *and* PREDICT-*secure;*
- *there is an acknowledgment extractor (Definition 15);*
- *there is a cleanness extractor for* C_{clean} *(Definition 16).*

To make participants aware of the security status of any (challenge) message, they need to know the history of exposures, they need to be able to reconstruct the history of RATCH calls from their own view, and they need to be able to evaluate the C_{clean} predicate. Thankfully, the C_{clean} predicates that we consider only depend on these histories. We first formally define the notion of transcript.

Definition 14 (Transcript). *In a game, for a participant* P, *we define the transcript of* P *as the chronological sequence* T_P *of all* (oracle, extra) *pairs involving* P *where each pair represents an oracle call to* oracle *with* P *as input (i.e. either* RATCH(P, "rec", ., .), RATCH(P, "send", ., .), $EXP_{pt}(P)$, $EXP_{st}(P)$, *or* CHALLENGE(P)), *except the unsuccessful* RATCH *calls which are omitted. For each pair with a* RATCH *or* CHALLENGE *oracle,* extra *specifies the role ("send" or "rec") and the message* (ad, ct) *of the oracle call. For other pairs,* extra $= \perp$.

---

[10] More precisely, in PR, if A is exposed then issues a message ct, the adversary can actually forge a ciphertext ct′ transporting the same pk and vfk and deliver it to B in a way which makes B accept. If A issues a new message ct″, delivering ct″ to B will pass the signature verification. The decryption following-up may fail, except if the kuKEM encryption scheme taking care of encryption does not check consistency, which is the case in the proposed one [10, Fig. 3, eprint version]. Therefore, ct″ may be accepted by B so PR is not r-RECOVER secure. The same holds for s-RECOVER security.

[11] We want it to be able to apply Lemma 12 and be aware of matching status.

The partial transcript *of* P *up to time* t *is the prefix* $T_P(t)$ *of* T_P *of all oracle calls until time* t. *The* RATCH-transcript *of* P *is the list* T_P^{RATCH} *of all extra elements in* T_P *which are not* $\perp$ *(i.e. it only includes* RATCH/CHALLENGE *calls). Similarly, the* partial RATCH-transcript *of* P *up to time* t *is the list* $T_P^{RATCH}(t)$ *of extra elements in* $T_P(t)$ *which are not* $\perp$.

Next, we formalize that a participant can be aware of which of his messages were received by his counterpart.

Definition 15 (Acknowledgment extractor). *We consider a game* Γ *where the transcript* T_P *is formed for a participant* P. *Given a message* (ad, ct) *successfully received by* P *at time* t *and which was sent by* $\overline{P}$ *at time* $\overline{t}$, *we let* (ad', ct') *be the last message successfully received by* $\overline{P}$ *before time* $\overline{t}$. *(If there is no such message, we set it to* $\perp$.)*

An acknowledgment extractor *is an efficient function* f *such that* $f(T_P^{RATCH}(t)) = (ad', ct')$ *for any time* t *when* P *is in a matching status (Definition 3).*

Given this extractor, P can iteratively reconstruct the entire flow of messages, and which messages crossed each other during transmission.

We formalize awareness of a participant for the safety of each message.

Definition 16 (Cleanness extractor). *We consider a game* Γ *where the transcript* T_P *is formed for a participant* P. *Let* t *be a time for* P *and* $\overline{t}$ *be a time for* $\overline{P}$. *Let* $T_P(t)$ *and* $T_{\overline{P}}(\overline{t})$ *be the partial transcripts at those time. We say that there is a* cleanness extractor *for* C_{clean} *if there is an efficient function* g *such that* $g(T_P(t), T_{\overline{P}}(\overline{t}))$ *has the following properties: if there is one* CHALLENGE *in the* $T_P(t)$ *transcript and, either* P *received* (ad_{test}, ct_{test}) *or there is a round trip* $P \to \overline{P} \to P$ *starting with* P *sending* (ad_{test}, ct_{test}) *to* $\overline{P}$, *then* $g(T_P(t), T_{\overline{P}}(\overline{t})) = C_{clean}(\Gamma)$. *Otherwise,* $g(T_P(t), T_{\overline{P}}(\overline{t})) = \perp$.

The function g is able to predict whether the game is "clean" for any challenge message. The case with an incomplete round trip $P \to \overline{P} \to P$ starting with P sending (ad_{test}, ct_{test}) to $\overline{P}$ is when the tested message was sent but somehow never acknowledged for the reception. If the message never arrived, we cannot say for sure if the game is clean because the counterpart may later either receive it and make the game clean or have a state exposure and make the game not clean. In other cases, the cleanness can be determined for sure.

3.3   Strongly Secure ARCAD with Security Awareness

In this section, we take a secure ARCAD (it could be $ARCAD_{DV}$, in the full version [4], or the hybrid one defined in Sect. 4) which we denote by $ARCAD_0$ and we transform it into another secure ARCAD which we denote by $ARCAD_1 = chain(ARCAD_0)$, that is *security aware*. We achieve security awareness by keeping some hashes in the states of participants. The intuitive way to build it is to make chains of hash of ciphertexts (like a blockchain) which will be sent and received and to associate each message to the digest of the chain. This enables a participant P to acknowledge its counterpart about received messages whenever P sends a new message.

We define a tuple (Hsent, Hreceived, snt_noack, rec_toack) and store it in the state of a participant. Hsent is the hash of all sent ciphertexts. It is computed by the sender and delivered to the counterpart along with ct. It is updated with hashing key hk and the old Hsent every time a new Send operation is called. Likewise, Hreceived is the hash of all received ciphertexts. It is computed with hk and the last stored Hreceived by the receiver upon receiving a message. It is updated every time a new Receive operation is run.

Using Hsent and Hreceived alone is sufficient for r-RECOVER security but not for s-RECOVER security.

rec_toack is a counter of received messages which need to be reported when the next Send operation is run. For each Send operation, the protocol attaches to ct the last Hreceived to acknowledge for received messages and reset rec_toack to 0. rec_toack is incremented by each Receive.

snt_noack is a *list of the hashes* of sent ciphertexts which are waiting for an acknowledgment. Basically, it is initialized to an empty array in the beginning and whenever a new Hsent is computed, it is accumulated in this array. The purpose of such a list is to keep track of the sent messages for which the sender expects an acknowledgment. More precisely, when the participant P keeps its list of sent ciphertexts in snt_noack, the counterpart $\overline{P}$ keeps a counter rec_toack telling that an acknowledgment is needed. Remember that $\overline{P}$ sends Hreceived back to the participant P to acknowledge him about received messages. As soon as $\overline{P}$ acknowledges, P deletes the hash of the acknowledged ciphertexts from snt_noack.

The principle of our construction is that if an adversary starts to impersonate a participant after exposure, there is a fork in the list of message chains which is viewed by both participants and those chains can never merge again without making a collision.

We give our security aware protocol on Fig. 5. The security of the protocol is proved with the following lemmas.

Theorem 17. *If* ARCAD$_0$ *is correct, then* chain(ARCAD$_0$) *is correct.*

The proof is straightforward.

Lemma 18. *If* H *is collision-resistant,* chain(ARCAD$_0$) *is* RECOVER-*secure (for both* s-RECOVER *and* r-RECOVER *security).*

Proof. All (ad, ct) messages seen by one participant P in one direction (send or receive) are chained by hashing. Hence, if received$_{ct}^{P}$ = (seq$_1$, (ad, ct), seq$_2$), the (ad, ct) message includes (in the second field of ct) the hash h of seq$_1$. If sent$_{ct}^{\overline{P}}$ = (seq$_3$, (ad, ct), seq$_4$), the (ad, ct) message includes the hash h of seq$_3$. If H is collision-resistant, then seq$_1$ $\neq$ seq$_3$ with negligible probability. Hence, we have r-RECOVER security.

Additionally, all genuine (ad, ct) messages include (in the third field of ct) the hash ack of messages which are received by the counterpart. This list must

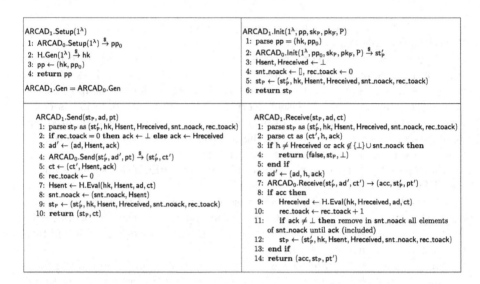

Fig. 5. Our Security-Aware $\mathsf{ARCAD}_1 = \mathsf{chain}(\mathsf{ARCAD}_0)$ Protocol.

be approved by P, thus it must match the list of hashes of messages that P sent. Hence, if $\mathsf{received}^P_{ct}$ is prefix of $\mathsf{sent}^{\overline{P}}_{ct}$ and $\overline{t}$ is the time when $\overline{P}$ sent the last message in $\mathsf{received}^P_{ct}$, then this message includes the hash of $\mathsf{received}^{\overline{P}}_{ct}(\overline{t})$ which must be a hash of a prefix of sent^P_{ct}. Thus, unless there is a collision in the hash function, $\mathsf{received}^{\overline{P}}_{ct}(\overline{t})$ is a prefix of sent^P_{ct} and we have s-RECOVER security. □

Lemma 19. $\mathsf{chain}(\mathsf{ARCAD}_0)$ *has an acknowledgment extractor.*

Proof. Let $(\mathsf{ad}, \mathsf{ct})$ be a message sent by $\overline{P}$ to P in a matching status. Let $(\mathsf{ad}', \mathsf{ct}')$ be the last message received by $\overline{P}$ before sending $(\mathsf{ad}, \mathsf{ct})$. Due to the protocol, ct includes the value of Hreceived after receiving $(\mathsf{ad}', \mathsf{ct}')$. Since this message is from P, P recognizes this hash Hreceived = Hsent from snt_noack. Both $(\mathsf{ad}', \mathsf{ct}')$ and this hash can be computed from $T_P^{\mathsf{RATCH}}(t)$. Hence, $\mathsf{chain}(\mathsf{ARCAD}_0)$ has an extractor. □

Lemma 20. $\mathsf{chain}(\mathsf{ARCAD}_0)$ *has a cleanness extractor for the following predicates:*

$$C_{\mathsf{leak}}, C^{P_{\mathsf{test}}}_{\mathsf{trivialforge}}, C^{A,B}_{\mathsf{trivialforge}}, C^{P_{\mathsf{test}}}_{\mathsf{forge}}, C^{A,B}_{\mathsf{forge}}, C_{\mathsf{ratchet}}, C_{\mathsf{noexp}}$$

Hence, there is an extractor for all cleanness predicates which we considered.[12]

The following result is trivial.

Lemma 21. *If* ARCAD_0 *is PREDICT-secure, then* $\mathsf{chain}(\mathsf{ARCAD}_0)$ *is PREDICT-secure.*

Consequently, if ARCAD_0 is PREDICT-secure, $\mathsf{chain}(\mathsf{ARCAD}_0)$ is security-aware.

---

[12] The proof is given in the full version [4].

4 On-Demand Ratcheting

In this section, we define a bidirectional secure communication messaging protocol with *hybrid on-demand* ratcheting. The aim is to design such a protocol to integrate two ratcheting protocols with different security levels: a strongly secure protocol using public-key cryptography and a weaker but much more efficient protocol with symmetric key primitives. The core of the protocol is to use the weak protocol with frequent exchanges and to use the strong one on demand by the sending participant. Hence, we build a more efficient protocol with on-demand ratcheting. Yet, it comes with a security drawback. Even though the security for the former is to provide post-compromise security, we secure part of the communication only with the forward secure protocol.

The sender uses a flag to tell which level of security the communication will have and apply ratcheting with public-key cryptography or the lighter primitives such as the EtH protocol [13]. The flag is set in the ad input and it is denoted as ad.flag. We call the strong protocol as $\mathsf{ARCAD_{main}}$ and the weak one as $\mathsf{ARCAD_{sub}}$. Ideally, the time to set the flag for specific security can be decided during the deployment of the application using the protocol. This choice may also be left to the users who can decide based on the confidentiality-level of their communication. The more often the protocol turns the flag on, the more secure is the hybrid on-demand protocol. If we do it for every message exchange, then we obtain $\mathsf{ARCAD_{main}}$ without $\mathsf{ARCAD_{sub}}$. If we do it for no message exchange, then we obtain $\mathsf{ARCAD_{sub}}$.

4.1 Our Hybrid On-Demand ARCAD Protocol

We give our on-demand ARCAD protocol on Fig. 6. It uses two sub-protocols called $\mathsf{ARCAD_{main}}$ and $\mathsf{ARCAD_{sub}}$. The former is to represent a strong-but-slow protocol such as $\mathsf{ARCAD_{DV}}$ (Fig. 11). The latter is typically a weaker-but-faster protocol like EtH [13]. The use of one or the other is based on a flag that can be turned on and off in ad (it is checked with ad.flag operation in the protocol). To have the flag on lets the protocol run $\mathsf{ARCAD_{main}}$ while setting the flag off means to run $\mathsf{ARCAD_{sub}}$. Assuming that $\mathsf{ARCAD_{main}}$ is ratcheting (i.e. post-compromise secure) and $\mathsf{ARCAD_{sub}}$ is not, this defines on-demand ratcheting. We denote our hybrid protocol as $\mathsf{hybridARCAD} = \mathsf{hybrid}(\mathsf{ARCAD_{main}}, \mathsf{ARCAD_{sub}})$.

We use as a reference the (e, c) number of messages in the $\mathsf{ARCAD_{main}}$ thread. Every $\mathsf{ARCAD_{main}}$ message creates a new $\mathsf{ARCAD_{sub}}$ send/receive state pair. The sending participant keeps the generated send state in a $\mathsf{sub}[e, c]$ register under the (e, c) number of the message and sends the generated receive state together with his message. The very first message which a participant sees (either in sending or receiving) forces the flag to indicate $\mathsf{ARCAD_{main}}$ as we have no initial $\mathsf{ARCAD_{sub}}$ state. The (e, c) number if authenticated and also explicitly added in the ciphertext. The receiving participant checks that (e, c) increases and uses the $\mathsf{sub}[e, c]$ register state to receive the message.

Theorem 22. *If the protocols* $\mathsf{ARCAD_{main}}$ *and* $\mathsf{ARCAD_{sub}}$ *are both correct, then the protocol* $\mathsf{hybrid}(\mathsf{ARCAD_{main}}, \mathsf{ARCAD_{sub}})$ *is correct.*

The proof is provided in the full version [4].

4.2   Application: Super-Scheme to (Re)set a Protocol

Our hybrid construction finds another application than on-demand ratcheting: defense against message loss or active attacks. Indeed, by using $\mathsf{ARCAD_{main}} = \mathsf{ARCAD_{sub}}$, we can set ad.flag to restore an $\mathsf{ARCAD_{sub}}$ communication which was broken due to a message loss. Normal communication works in the $\mathsf{ARCAD_{sub}}$ session, hence with a flag down. However, we may use $\mathsf{ARCAD_{main}}$ to start a new $\mathsf{ARCAD_{sub}}$ session. If $\mathsf{ARCAD_{sub}}$ gets broken due to a message loss or an active attack on it, $\mathsf{ARCAD_{main}}$ can be used to restart a new $\mathsf{ARCAD_{sub}}$ session. We cannot resume if the $\mathsf{ARCAD_{main}}$ session is broken. However, we can also make nested hybrid protocols with more than two levels of protocols inside for safety. It may increase the state sizes but the performance should be nearly the same. Then, only persistent message drop attacks would succeed to make a denial of service.

4.3   Security Definitions

We modify the predicates and the notion of FORGE-security from Sect. 2. In our hybrid protocol, each message $(\mathsf{ad}, \mathsf{ct})$ has a clearly defined (e, c) pair. A ct which is input or output from RATCH comes with an ad which has a clearly defined ad.flag bit.

Sub-games. Given a game Γ for the hybridARCAD scheme with an adversary $\mathcal{A}$, we define a game $\mathsf{main}(\Gamma)$ for $\mathsf{ARCAD_{main}}$ with an adversary $\mathcal{A}'$ which simulates everything but the $\mathsf{ARCAD_{main}}$ calls in Γ. Namely, $\mathcal{A}'$ simulates the enrichment of the states and all $\mathsf{ARCAD_{sub}}$ management together with $\mathcal{A}$.

Given a game Γ_{main} for $\mathsf{ARCAD_{main}}$ using no CHALLENGE oracle and an (e, c) pair, we denote by $\mathsf{main}_{e,c}(\Gamma_{\mathsf{main}})$ the variant of Γ_{main} in which the RATCH Send call making the message $(\mathsf{ad}, \mathsf{ct})$ with pair (e, c) is replaced by a CHALLENGE query with $b = 1$. This perfectly simulates Γ_{main} and produces the same value, and we can evaluate a predicate $\mathsf{C_{clean}}$ relative to this challenge message. We define $\mathsf{C_{clean}^{e,c}}(\Gamma_{\mathsf{main}}) = \mathsf{C_{clean}}(\mathsf{main}_{e,c}(\Gamma_{\mathsf{main}}))$. Intuitively, $\mathsf{C_{clean}^{e,c}}(\Gamma_{\mathsf{main}})$ means that the message of pair (e, c) was safely encrypted and should be considered as private because no trivial attack leaks it.

We also define $\mathsf{sub}_{e,c}(\Gamma)$ and $\mathsf{sub}'_{e,c}(\Gamma)$. We let P be the sending participant of the $\mathsf{ARCAD_{main}}$ message of pair (e, c). In $\mathsf{sub}'_{e,c}(\Gamma)$, the adversary $\mathcal{A}'$ simulates everything but the $\mathsf{ARCAD_{sub}}$ calls involving messages with pair (e, c). The initial states of P and $\overline{\mathsf{P}}$ are also set by the game $\mathsf{sub}'_{e,c}(\Gamma)$. However, it makes an $\mathsf{EXP_{st}}(\overline{\mathsf{P}})$ call at the beginning of the protocol to get the initial state $\mathsf{st_R}$ for $\mathsf{ARCAD_{sub}}$. With this state, $\mathcal{A}'$ can simulate the encryption of $\mathsf{st_R}$ with $\mathsf{ARCAD_{main}}$ and all the rest. Clearly, the simulation is perfect but it adds an initial $\mathsf{EXP_{st}}(\overline{\mathsf{P}})$ call.

The $\mathsf{sub}_{e,c}(\Gamma)$ game is a variant of $\mathsf{sub}'_{e,c}(\Gamma)$ without the additional $\mathsf{EXP_{st}}(\overline{\mathsf{P}})$. To simulate the encryption of $\mathsf{st_R}$, $\mathcal{A}'$ encrypts a random string instead. When it

hybridARCAD.Setup(1^λ)
1: $pp_{main} \leftarrow ARCAD_{main}.Setup(1^\lambda)$
2: $pp_{sub} \leftarrow ARCAD_{sub}.Setup(1^\lambda)$
3: **return** (pp_{main}, pp_{sub})

hybridARCAD.Gen(1^λ, pp_{main}, pp_{sub})
4: **return** $ARCAD_{main}.Gen(1^\lambda, pp_{main})$

hybridARCAD.Init(1^λ, (pp_{main}, pp_{sub}), sk_P, $pk_{\overline{P}}$, P)
1: $ARCAD_{main}.Init(1^\lambda, pp_{main}, sk_P, pk_{\overline{P}}, P) \rightarrow st_{main}$
2: initialize array $st_{sub}[]$ to empty
3: **if** $P = A$ **then** $(e_{send}, e_{rec}) \leftarrow (0, -1)$
4: **else** $(e_{send}, e_{rec}) \leftarrow (-1, 0)$
5: **end if**
6: initialize array ctr with $ctr[0] = -1$
7: $st_P \leftarrow (\lambda, pp_{sub}, st_{main}, st_{sub}[], e_{send}, e_{rec}, ctr[])$
8: **return** st_P

---

hybridARCAD.Send(st_P, ad, pt)
1: parse st_P as $(\lambda, pp_{sub}, st_{main}, st_{sub}[], e_{send}, e_{rec}, ctr[])$
2: $e \leftarrow max(e_{send}, e_{rec})$; $c \leftarrow ctr[e]$ ▷ current epoch
3: **if** ad.flag or $c = -1$ **then**
4:     **if** $e_{send} < e_{rec}$ **then** $e \leftarrow e_{rec} + 1$; $c \leftarrow 0$
5:     **else** $e \leftarrow e_{send}$; $c \leftarrow ctr[e] + 1$
6:     **end if**
7:     $ARCAD_{sub}.Initall(1^\lambda, pp_{sub}) \xrightarrow{\$} (st_S, st_R, z)$ ▷ create a new sub-state.
8:     $st_{sub}[e, c] \leftarrow st_S$
9:     $pt' \leftarrow (st_R, pt)$; $ad' \leftarrow (ad, 1, e, c)$
10:    $ARCAD_{main}.Send(st_{main}, ad', pt') \xrightarrow{\$} (st_{main}, ct')$ ▷ send using the main state.
11:    $ct \leftarrow (ct', e, c)$
12:    $e_{send} \leftarrow e$; $ctr[e_{send}] \leftarrow c$
13: **else**
14:    $ad' \leftarrow (ad, 0, e, c)$
15:    $ARCAD_{sub}.Send(st_{sub}[e, c], ad', pt) \xrightarrow{\$} (st_{sub}[e, c], ct')$ ▷ send using the sub-state.
16:    $ct \leftarrow (ct', e, c)$
17: **end if**
18: clean-up: erase $st_{sub}[e, c]$ for all (e, c) such that $(e, c) < (e_{send}, ctr[e_{send}])$ and $(e, c) < (e_{rec}, ctr[e_{rec}])$
19: clean-up: erase $ctr[e]$ for all e such that $e < e_{send}$ and $e < e_{rec}$
20: $st_P \leftarrow (\lambda, pp_{sub}, st_{main}, st_{sub}[], e_{send}, e_{rec}, ctr[])$
21: **return** (st_P, ct)

hybridARCAD.Receive(st_P, ad, ct)
22: parse st_P as $(\lambda, pp_{sub}, st_{main}, st_{sub}[], e_{send}, e_{rec}, ctr[])$
23: parse ct as (ct', e, c)
24: **if** $(e, c) < (e_{rec}, ctr[e_{rec}])$ **then return** $(false, st_P, \bot)$ ▷ (e, c) must increase
25: **if** ad.flag or $(e = 0$ and $ctr[0] = -1)$ **then**
26:    $ad' \leftarrow (ad, 1, e, c)$
27:    $ARCAD_{main}.Receive(st_{main}, ad', ct') \rightarrow (acc, st_{main}, pt')$
28:    parse pt' as (st_R, pt)
29:    **if** acc **then**
30:      $st_{sub}[e, c] \leftarrow st_R$
31:      $e_{rec} \leftarrow e$; $ctr[e] \leftarrow c$
32:    **end if**
33: **else**
34:    $ad' \leftarrow (ad, 0, e, c)$
35:    **if** $st_{sub}[e, c]$ undefined **then return** $(false, st_P, \bot)$
36:    $ARCAD_{sub}.Receive(st_{sub}[e, c], ad', ct') \rightarrow (acc, st_{sub}[e, c], pt)$
37: **end if**
38: clean-up: erase $st_{sub}[e, c]$ for all (e, c) such that $(e, c) < (e_{send}, ctr[e_{send}])$ and $(e, c) < (e_{rec}, ctr[e_{rec}])$
39: clean-up: erase $ctr[e]$ for all e such that $e < e_{send}$ and $e < e_{rec}$
40: $st_P \leftarrow (\lambda, pp_{sub}, st_{main}, st_{sub}[], e_{send}, e_{rec}, ctr[])$
41: **return** (acc, st_P, pt)

Fig. 6. On-Demand hybridARCAD = hybrid($ARCAD_{main}$, $ARCAD_{sub}$) Protocol.

comes to decrypt the obtained ciphertext, the random plaintext is ignored and the RATCH calls with $\mathsf{st_R}$ are simulated with the RATCH calls for the $\mathsf{ARCAD_{sub}}$ game. The simulation is no longer perfect but it does not add an $\mathsf{EXP_{st}}(\overline{\mathsf{P}})$ call.

Hybrid Cleanness. We assume two cleanness predicates $\mathsf{C_{clean}}$ and $\mathsf{C_{main}}$ (which could be the same) for $\mathsf{ARCAD_{main}}$ and one cleanness predicate $\mathsf{C_{sub}}$ for $\mathsf{ARCAD_{sub}}$. We define a hybrid predicate $\mathsf{C}^{\mathsf{C_{clean}}}_{\mathsf{C_{main},C_{sub}}}$ as follows. By abuse of notation, we write $\mathsf{C^{clean}_{main,sub}}$ instead, for more readability. Let Γ be a game played by an adversary $\mathcal{A}$ against $\mathsf{hybridARCAD}$.

We let $(\mathsf{ad,ct})$ be the challenge message $(\mathsf{ad_{test},ct_{test}})$ if it exists. Otherwise, $(\mathsf{ad,ct})$ is the last message in Γ. We let $(\mathsf{e,c})$ be the number of $(\mathsf{ad,ct})$. We let

$$\mathsf{C^{clean}_{main,sub}}(\Gamma) = \begin{cases} \text{if } (\mathsf{ad,ct}) \text{ belongs to } \mathsf{ARCAD_{main}} : \mathsf{C_{main}}(\mathsf{main}(\Gamma)) \\ \text{else}: \begin{cases} \text{if } \mathsf{C^{e,c}_{clean}}(\mathsf{main}(\Gamma)): & \mathsf{C_{sub}}(\mathsf{sub}_{e,c}(\Gamma)) \\ \text{else}: & \mathsf{C_{sub}}(\mathsf{sub}'_{e,c}(\Gamma)) \end{cases} \end{cases}$$

This means that if the challenge holds on an $\mathsf{ARCAD_{main}}$ message, we only care for $\mathsf{main}(\Gamma)$ to be $\mathsf{C_{main}}$-clean. Otherwise, either the $\mathsf{ARCAD_{main}}$ message initiating the relevant $\mathsf{ARCAD_{sub}}$ session is $\mathsf{C_{clean}}$ or not. If it is clean, we can replace it and consider $\mathsf{C_{sub}}$-cleanness for $\mathsf{sub}_{e,c}(\Gamma)$. Otherwise, the initial $\mathsf{ARCAD_{sub}}$ state $\mathsf{st_R}$ trivially leaked (or was exposed, equivalently) and we consider $\mathsf{C_{sub}}$-cleanness for $\mathsf{sub}'_{e,c}(\Gamma)$. The role of $\mathsf{C_{clean}}$ is to control which of the two games to use. $\mathsf{C_{clean}}$ must be a privacy cleanness notion for main. Contrarily, $\mathsf{C_{main}}$ and $\mathsf{C_{sub}}$ could be either privacy or authenticity notions.

Note that $\mathsf{C_{sub}}(\mathsf{sub}'_{e,c}(\Gamma)) = \mathsf{false}$ for $\mathsf{C_{sub}} = \mathsf{C_{noexp}}$, due to the $\mathsf{EXP_{st}}$ call.

We easily obtain the following result.

Lemma 23. *If* $\mathsf{ARCAD_{main}}$ *is* $\mathsf{C_{main}}$-*IND-CCA-secure and* $\mathsf{ARCAD_{sub}}$ *is* $\mathsf{C_{sub}}$-*IND-CCA-secure, then* $\mathsf{hybridARCAD}$ *is* $\mathsf{C_{clean}}$-*IND-CCA with* $\mathsf{C_{clean}} = \mathsf{C^{main}_{main,sub}}$.

Proof (sketch).[13] Let us assume that Γ is clean in the sense of $\mathsf{C_{clean}}$.

Let $(\mathsf{ad,ct})$ be the challenge (or last) message. If $(\mathsf{ad,ct})$ belongs to $\mathsf{ARCAD_{main}}$, then $\mathsf{main}(\Gamma)$ is $\mathsf{C_{main}}$-clean. The outcome of $\mathsf{main}(\Gamma)$ and Γ is the same. Due to the $\mathsf{C_{main}}$-IND-CCA security of $\mathsf{ARCAD_{main}}$, the advantage in Γ is negligible. Let us now assume that $(\mathsf{ad,ct})$ belongs to $\mathsf{ARCAD_{sub}}$.

$\mathsf{C^{e,c}_{C_{main}}}$ indicates if the $\mathsf{ARCAD_{main}}$ message of pair $(\mathsf{e,c})$ can be replaced by the encryption of something random to produce the same result, except with negligible probability. In this case, $\mathsf{sub}_{e,c}(\Gamma)$ produces the same outcome as Γ and $\mathsf{C_{clean}}$ implies that it must be $\mathsf{C_{sub}}$-clean. Due to the $\mathsf{C_{sub}}$-IND-CCA security of $\mathsf{ARCAD_{sub}}$, the advantage in Γ is negligible.

Similarly, if $\mathsf{C^{e,c}_{C_{main}}}(\Gamma)$ does not hold, $\mathsf{C_{clean}}$ implies that $\mathsf{sub}'_{e,c}(\Gamma)$ is clean. It produces the same outcome as Γ. Due to the $\mathsf{C_{sub}}$-IND-CCA security of $\mathsf{ARCAD_{sub}}$, the advantage in Γ is negligible.   □

---

[13] More details are provided in the full version [4].

In the FORGE game, we replace the $C_{trivial}$ predicate. Typically, by taking C_{main} as the predicate that tests if the last (ad, ct) message is a trivial forgery and by taking C_{sub} as the predicate that additionally tests if no EXP_{st} occurred, the $C_{main,sub}^{clean}$ predicate defines a new FORGE notion for $hybrid(ARCAD_{DV}, EtH)$. More generally, if $ARCAD_{main}$ is C_{main}-FORGE-secure and $ARCAD_{sub}$ is C_{sub}-FORGE-secure, we would like to have $C_{C_{main}^{clean}, C_{sub}}$-FORGE-security.

Game $FORGE_{C_{clean}}^{*,\mathcal{A}}(1^\lambda)$

1: $Setup(1^\lambda) \xrightarrow{\$} pp$
2: $InitAll(1^\lambda, pp) \xrightarrow{\$} (st_A, st_B, z)$
3: $(P, ad, ct) \leftarrow \mathcal{A}^{RATCH, EXP_{st}, EXP_{pt}}(z)$
4: **if** one participant (or both) is NOT in a matching status **then return** 0
5: $RATCH(P, \text{"rec"}, ad, ct) \rightarrow acc$
6: **if** $acc = false$ **then return** 0
7: **if** $\neg C_{clean}$ **then return** 0
8: **if** we can parse $received_{ct}^P = (seq_1, (ad, ct))$ and $sent_{ct}^{\bar{P}} = (seq_1, seq_2, (ad, ct), seq_3)$ **then return** 0
9: **return** 1

Fig. 7. Relaxed FORGE Security.

We almost have the reduction but there is something missing. Namely, a forgery for hybridARCAD in Γ may not be a forgery for neither $ARCAD_{main}$ in $main(\Gamma)$ nor $ARCAD_{sub}$ in $sub_{e,c}(\Gamma)$. This happens if the adversary in Γ drops the delivery of the last messages in a sub scheme. We relax FORGE-security using the FORGE* game in Fig. 7. Only Steps 4 and 8 are new. Our chain strengthening in Sect. 3 can later make the protocols fully FORGE-secure. We easily prove the following result.

Lemma 24. *If $ARCAD_{main}$ is C_{clean}-IND-CCA-secure and C_{main}-FORGE*-secure and if $ARCAD_{sub}$ is C_{sub}-FORGE*-secure, then hybridARCAD is C_{hybrid}-FORGE*, where $C_{hybrid} = C_{main,sub}^{clean}$.*

Proof (sketch).[14] If (ad, ct) belongs to $ARCAD_{main}$ and $\Gamma = FORGE^*$ succeeds to return 1, then $C_{main}(main(\Gamma))$ holds and $main(\Gamma)$ succeeds to return 1 as well. Similarly, if (ad, ct) belongs to $ARCAD_{sub}$ and Γ returns 1, then, depending on $C_{clean}^{e,c}(\Gamma)$, either $C_{sub}(sub_{e,c}(\Gamma))$ or $C_{sub}(sub_{e,c}'(\Gamma))$ holds, and either game succeeds to return 1 (thanks to IND-CCA security in the latter case). Applying FORGE* security of those protocols, this occurs with negligible probability. □

What FORGE* security does not guarantee is that some forgeries in a sub-scheme may occur in the far future, due to state exposure. Fortunately, our protocol mitigates this problem by making sure that old sub-protocols become obsolete. Indeed, our protocol makes sure that sent messages always have an increasing sequence of (e, c) pairs, and the same for received messages. Hence, we

---

[14] More details are provided in the full version [4].

cannot have a forgery with an old (e, c) pair. Another problem which is explicit in Step 8 of the game is that the adversary may prevent P from receiving a sequence seq_2 sent from $\overline{P}$ (namely in a sub-protocol). In Sect. 3, making the protocol r-RECOVER-secure fixes both problems. (See Lemma 26.) Hence, we will obtain FORGE-security.

4.4 Security-Aware Hybrid Construction

In this section, we apply our results from Sect. 3.3 to our hybrid constructions.

Lemma 25. *Let* $C_{clean} \in \{C_{trivial}, C_{noexp}\}$ *and* $ARCAD_1 = chain(ARCAD_0)$. *If* $ARCAD_0$ *is* C_{clean}-*FORGE-secure (resp.* C_{clean}-*FORGE*-secure), then* $ARCAD_1$ *is* C_{clean}-*FORGE-secure (resp.* C_{clean}-*FORGE*-secure).*

Proof. We reduce an adversary playing the FORGE game with $ARCAD_1$ to an adversary playing the FORGE game with $ARCAD_0$ by simulating the hashings. $ARCAD_1$ is an extension of $ARCAD_0$ such that an $ARCAD_1$ message $(ad, (ct', h, ack))$ is equivalent to an $ARCAD_0$ message $((ad, h, ack), ct')$. It is just reordering (ad, ct). Hence, a forgery for $ARCAD_1$ must be a forgery for $ARCAD_0$. FORGE*-security works the same.   □

Lemma 26. *Given* $ARCAD_{main}$ *and* $ARCAD_{sub}$, *let*

$$ARCAD_0 = hybrid(ARCAD_{main}, ARCAD_{sub}) \ , \ ARCAD_1 = chain(ARCAD_0)$$

If $ARCAD_{main}$ *is* C_{clean}-*IND-CCA-secure and* C_{main}-*FORGE*-secure and* $ARCAD_{sub}$ *is* C_{sub}-*FORGE*-secure, then* $ARCAD_1$ *is* $C_{main,sub}^{clean}$-*FORGE*-secure. If* H *is additionally collision-resistant, then* $ARCAD_1$ *is* $C_{main,sub}^{clean}$-*FORGE-secure.*

Proof. Due to Lemma 24, $C_{main,sub}^{clean}$-FORGE*-security works like in the previous result. To extend to $C_{main,sub}^{clean}$-FORGE-security, we just observe that $ARCAD_1$ is r-RECOVER-secure due to Lemma 18. We thus deduce $seq_2 = \bot$ from having $receive_{ct}^P = (seq_1, (ad, ct))$ and $sent_{ct}^{\overline{P}} = (seq_1, seq_2, (ad, ct), seq_3)$. Hence, we have a full forgery, except with negligible probability.   □

Lemma 27. *Let* $C_{clean} = C_{leak}$, $C_{ratchet}$, C_{noexp}, *or* C_{tforge}^S *(t = trivial or* $\bot$}, $S = P_{test}$ *or* $\{A, B\}$*), If* $ARCAD_0$ *is* C_{clean}-*IND-CCA-secure, then* $ARCAD_1$ *is* C_{clean}-*IND-CCA-secure.*

Proof. We reduce an adversary playing the IND-CCA game with $ARCAD_1$ to an adversary playing the IND-CCA game with $ARCAD_0$ by simulating the hashings. We easily see that the cleanness is the same and that the simulation is perfect.   □

We easily extend this result to hybrid constructions. We conclude with our final result.

Theorem 28. *Given* $\mathsf{ARCAD_{main}}$ *and* $\mathsf{ARCAD_{sub}}$, *let*

$$\mathsf{ARCAD_0} = \mathsf{hybrid}(\mathsf{ARCAD_{main}}, \mathsf{ARCAD_{sub}}) \ , \ \mathsf{ARCAD_1} = \mathsf{chain}(\mathsf{ARCAD_0})$$

We assume that 1. H *is collision-resistant; 2.* $\mathsf{ARCAD_{main}}$ *is* $\mathsf{C_{clean}}$*-IND-CCA-secure and* $\mathsf{C_{main}}$*-FORGE*-secure; 3.* $\mathsf{ARCAD_{sub}}$ *is* $\mathsf{C_{sub}}$*-FORGE*-secure and* $\mathsf{C'_{clean}}$*-IND-CCA-secure. Then,* $\mathsf{ARCAD_1}$ *is 1.* r*-RECOVER-secure, 2.* s*-RECOVER-secure, 3.* $\mathsf{C^{clean}_{main,sub}}$*-FORGE-secure, 4.* $\mathsf{C^{clean}_{clean,clean'}}$*-IND-CCA-secure, 5. with acknowledgement extractor.*

Corollary 29. *Let* $\mathsf{ARCAD_1} = \mathsf{chain}(\mathsf{hybrid}(\mathsf{ARCAD_{DV}}, \mathsf{EtH}))$ *(where* $\mathsf{ARCAD_{DV}}$ *is defined on Fig. 11) and let* $\mathsf{C_{clean}} = \mathsf{C_{leak}} \wedge \mathsf{C^{A,B}_{forge}}$. *With the assumptions from Theorem 30 and the* EtH *result [13, Th.2], if* H *is collision-resistant,* $\mathsf{ARCAD_1}$ *is* $\mathsf{C^{clean}_{trivial,noexp}}$*-FORGE-secure,* $\mathsf{C^{clean}_{clean,sym}}$*-IND-CCA-secure, and with security-awareness.*

In particular, when a sender deduces an acknowledgment for his message $\mathfrak{m}$ from a received message $\mathfrak{m}'$, if he can make sure that $\mathfrak{m}'$ is genuine and that no trivial exposure for $\mathfrak{m}$ happened, then he can be sure that his message $\mathfrak{m}$ is private, no matter what happened before or what will happen next.

5   Conclusion

We revisited the DV security model. We proposed an hybrid construction which would mostly use EtH and occasionally a stronger protocol, upon the choice of the sender, thus achieving on-demand ratcheting. Finally, we proposed the notion of security awareness to enable participants to have a better idea on the safety of their communication. We achieved what we think is the optimal awareness. Concretely, a participant is aware of which of his messages arrived to his counterpart when he sent the last received one. We make sure that any forgery (possibly due to exposure) would fork the chain of messages which is seen by both participants and result in making them unable to continue communication. We also make sure that assuming that the exposure history is known, participants can deduce which messages leaked.

A   Implementations/Comparisons with Existing Protocols

We compare the performances of $\mathsf{ARCAD_{DV}}$ and EtH to other ratcheted messaging and key agreement protocols that have surfaced since 2018. In particular, we implemented five other schemes from the literature[15]. Namely, the bidirectional asynchronous key-agreement protocol BRKE by PR [10], the similar secure messaging protocol by JS [8], the secure messaging protocol by JMM [9] and a modularized version of two protocols by ACD [1].In ACD [1], the given protocols

---

[15] Our code is available at https://github.com/qantik/ratcheted.

are both with symmetric key cryptography ACD and public-key cryptography ACD-PK. We did not implement the DV protocol [7], as ARCAD$_{DV}$ is a slightly modified version of DV, hence has identical performances.

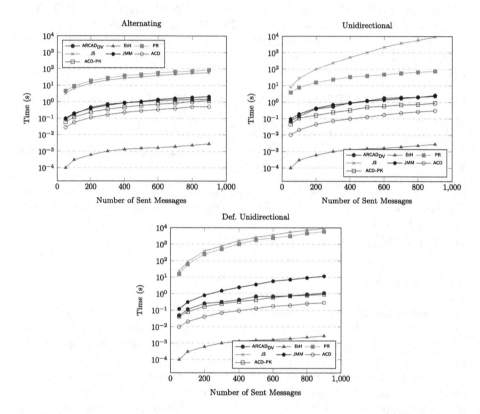

Fig. 8. Runtime Benchmarks The protocol in [10] is represented with PR; [8] with JS; [9] with JMM; and [1] with ACD and ACD-PK. ACD-PK is the public-key version with stronger security.

All the protocols were implemented in Go[16] and measured with its built-in benchmarking suite[17] on a regular fifth generation Intel Core i5 processor. In order to mitigate potential overheads garbage collection has been disabled for all runs. Go is comparable in speed to C/C++ though further performance gains are within reach when the protocols are re-implemented in the latter two. Additionally, some protocols deploy primitives for which no standard implementations exist, which is, for example, the case for the HIBE constructions used in the PR and JS protocols, making custom implementations necessary that can certainly be improved upon. For the deployed primitives, when we needed an

---

[16] https://golang.org/.
[17] https://golang.org/pkg/testing/.

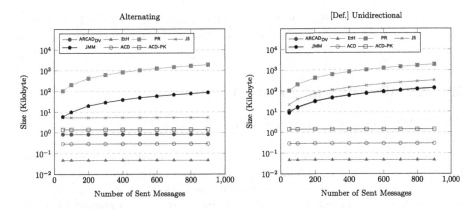

Fig. 9. State Size Benchmarks Due to the equivalent state sizes in unidirectional and deferred unidirectional traffic, one figure is omitted

AEAD scheme, we used AES-GCM. For public key cryptosystem, we used the elliptic curve version of ElGamal (ECIES); for the signature scheme, we used ECDSA. And, finally for the PRF-PRNG in [1] protocol, we used HKDF with SHA-256. Lastly, the protocols themselves may offer some room for performance tweaks.

The benchmarks can be categorized into two types as depicted in Fig. 8–9.

(a) Runtime designates the total required time to exchange n messages, ignoring potential latency that normally occurs in a network.

(b) State size shows the maximal size of a user state throughout the exchange of n messages.

A state is all the data that is kept in memory by a user. Each type itself is run on three canonical ways traffic can be shaped when two participants are communicating. In alternating traffic the parties are synchronized, i.e. take turns sending messages. In unidirectional traffic one participant first sends $\frac{n}{2}$ messages which are received by the partner who then sends the other half. Finally, in deferred unidirectional traffic both participants send $\frac{n}{2}$ messages before they start receiving. ACD-PK adds some public-key primitives to the double ratchet by ACD [1] to plug some post-compromise security gaps. These two variations serve as baselines to see how the metrics of a protocol can change when some of its internals are replaced or extended. Also note that due to the equivalent state sizes in unidirectional and deferred unidirectional traffic one figure is omitted.

As we can see, overall, the fastest protocol is EtH, followed by the two ACD protocols, then ARCAD$_{DV}$, then the JMM protocol, and lastly the strongest protocols PR and JS. ARCAD$_{DV}$ and JMM may be comparable except for deferred unidirectional communication.

The smallest state size is obtained with EtH. ARCAD$_{DV}$ performs well in terms of state size.

Clearly, hybrid(ARCAD_DV, EtH) has performances which are weighted averages of the ones of ARCAD_DV and EtH, depending on the frequency of on-demand ratcheting.

B ARCAD_DV Formal Protocol

With slight modifications, we transform the DV protocol [7] into an ARCAD that we call ARCAD_DV.

ARCAD_DV is based on a hash function H[18], a one-time symmetric cipher Sym[19], a digital signature scheme DSS[20], and a public-key cryptosystem PKC[21].

ARCAD_DV, just as DV, consists of many modules which are built on top of each other. The "smallest" module is a "naive" signcryption scheme SC which can be of the form

$$\text{SC.Enc}(\overbrace{\text{sk}_\text{S}, \text{pk}_\text{R}}^{\text{st}_\text{S}}, \text{ad}, \text{pt}) = \text{PKC.Enc}(\text{pk}_\text{R}, (\text{pt}, \text{DSS.Sign}(\text{sk}_\text{S}, (\text{ad}, \text{pt}))))$$

$$\text{SC.Dec}(\underbrace{\text{sk}_\text{R}, \text{pk}_\text{S}}_{\text{st}_\text{R}}, \text{ad}, \text{ct}) = \begin{bmatrix} (\text{pt}, \sigma) \leftarrow \text{PKC.Dec}(\text{sk}_\text{R}, \text{ct}) \; ; \\ \text{DSS.Verify}(\text{pk}_\text{S}, (\text{ad}, \text{pt}), \sigma) \; ? \; \text{pt} \; : \; \perp \end{bmatrix}$$

SC extends to a multiple-state (and multiple-key) encryption called onion. It handles the the case where the states get accumulated during a sequential send or receive operation during the communication. It generates a secret key to encrypt a plaintext. This secret key is, then, secret shared and encrypted under different states so that if a state is exposed, its shares would still remain confidential. onion leads to a unidirectional scheme called uni where participants have fixed roles as either senders or receivers. The underlying idea of unidirectional communication is to let the sender generate the next send/receive states for the future exchange during the current send operation and transmit the next receive state to the receiver. These future states are shown as st'_S and st'_R in the second row of Fig. 10. After each uni.Send and uni.Rec operations, the states are completely flushed to ensure security.

Finally, unidirectional communication allow us to construct the bidirectional ARCAD_DV as shown in the last row of Fig. 10. Since the communication become bidirectional, the participant P also keeps states for receiving. More specifically, the sender generates a pair of fresh states and transmits the send state to the counterpart so that s/he can use it to send a reply to back to the sender with this states.

ARCAD_DV is depicted on Fig. 11.

---

[18] H uses a common key hk generated by H.Gen and an algorithm H.Eval.

[19] Sym uses a key of length Sym.kl, encrypts over the domain Sym.$\mathcal{D}$ with algorithm Sym.Enc and decrypts with Sym.Dec.

[20] DSS uses a key generation DSS.Gen, a signing algorithm DSS.Sign, and a verification algorithm DSS.Verify.

[21] PKC uses a key generation PKC.Gen, an encryption algorithm PKC.Enc, and a decryption algorithm PKC.Dec.

Note that we removed some parts of the protocol which ensure r-RECOVER security. This is because the generic transformation in Sect. 3 which we apply on ARCAD$_{DV}$ will restore it in a stronger and generic way.

We recall the security results.

Theorem 30 (Security of ARCAD$_{DV}$ [7]). *ARCAD$_{DV}$ is correct. If* Sym.kl$(\lambda) = \Omega(\lambda)$, H *is collision-resistant,* DSS *is* SEF-OTCMA, PKC *is* IND-CCA-*secure, and* Sym *is* IND-OTCCA-*secure, then* ARCAD$_{DV}$ *is* C$_{trivial}$-FORGE-*secure,* $(C_{leak} \wedge C_{forge}^{A,B})$-IND-CCA-*secure and* PREDICT-*secure.*[22],[23]

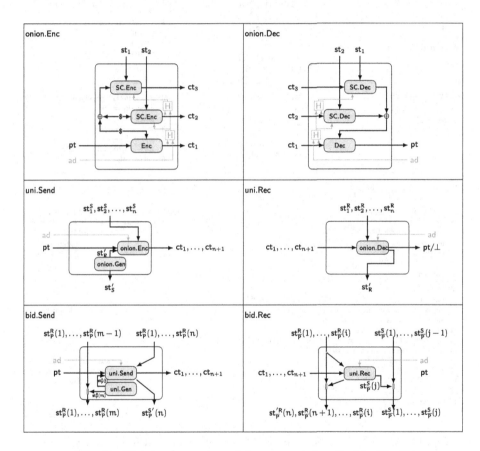

Fig. 10. High-level overview of the protocol described in Fig. 11

---

[22] SEF-OTCMA is the strong existential one-time chosen message attack. IND-OTCCA is the real-or-random indistinguishability under one-time chosen plaintext and chosen ciphertext attack. Their definitions are given in [7].

[23] Following Durak-Vaudenay [7], for a C$_{trivial}$-FORGE-secure scheme, $(C_{leak} \wedge C_{forge}^{A,B})$-IND-CCA security is equivalent to $(C_{leak} \wedge C_{trivial\ forge}^{A,B})$-IND-CCA security, which corresponds to the "sub-optimal" security in Table 1.

onion.Enc(1^λ, hk, $st_S^1, \ldots, st_S^n$, ad, pt)	onion.Dec(hk, $st_R^1, \ldots, st_R^n$, ad, $\vec{ct}$)
1: pick $k_1, \ldots, k_n$ in $\{0,1\}^{\mathsf{Sym}.kl(\lambda)}$	1: if $|\vec{ct}| \neq n+1$ then return $\perp$
2: $k \leftarrow k_1 \oplus \cdots \oplus k_n$	2: parse $\vec{ct} = (ct_1, \ldots, ct_{n+1})$
3: $ct_{n+1} \leftarrow$ Sym.Enc(k, pt)	3: $ad_{n+1} \leftarrow$ ad
4: $ad_{n+1} \leftarrow$ ad	4: for $i = n$ down to 1 do
5: for $i = n$ down to 1 do	5: $ad_i \leftarrow$ H.Eval(hk, ad_{i+1}, n, ct_{i+1})
6: $ad_i \leftarrow$ H.Eval(hk, ad_{i+1}, n, ct_{i+1})	6: SC.Dec(st_R^i, ad_i, ct_i) $\rightarrow k_i$
7: $ct_i \leftarrow$ SC.Enc(st_S^i, ad_i, k_i)	7: if $k_i = \perp$ then return $\perp$
8: end for	8: end for
9: return $(ct_1, \ldots, ct_{n+1})$	9: $k \leftarrow k_1 \oplus \cdots \oplus k_n$
	10: pt $\leftarrow$ Sym.Dec(k, ct_{n+1})
	11: return pt

uni.Init(1^λ)	uni.Send(1^λ, hk, $\vec{st}_S$, ad, pt)	uni.Receive(hk, $\vec{st}_R$, ad, $\vec{ct}$)
1: SC.Gen$_S$(1^λ) $\xrightarrow{\$}$ (sk_S, pk_S)	1: SC.Gen$_S$(1^λ) $\xrightarrow{\$}$ (sk'_S, pk'_S)	1: onion.Dec(hk, $\vec{st}_R$, ad, $\vec{ct}$) $\rightarrow$ pt'
2: SC.Gen$_R$(1^λ) $\xrightarrow{\$}$ (sk_R, pk_R)	2: SC.Gen$_R$(1^λ) $\xrightarrow{\$}$ (sk'_R, pk'_R)	2: if pt' $= \perp$ then
3: $st_S \leftarrow$ (sk_S, pk_R)	3: $st'_S \leftarrow$ (sk'_S, pk'_R)	3: return (false, $\perp$, $\perp$)
4: $st_R \leftarrow$ (sk_R, pk_S)	4: $st'_R \leftarrow$ (sk'_R, pk'_S)	4: end if
5: return (st_S, st_R)	5: pt' $\leftarrow$ (st'_R, pt)	5: parse pt' $=$ (st'_R, pt)
	6: onion.Enc(1^λ, hk, $\vec{st}_S$, ad, pt') $\rightarrow \vec{ct}$	6: return (true, st'_R, pt)
	7: return (st'_S, $\vec{ct}$)	

ARCAD$_{DV}$.Setup(1^λ)	ARCAD$_{DV}$.Gen(1^λ, hk)	ARCAD$_{DV}$.Init(1^λ, pp, sk_P, $pk_{\bar{P}}$, P)
1: H.Gen(1^λ) $\xrightarrow{\$}$ hk	1: SC.Gen$_S$(1^λ) $\xrightarrow{\$}$ (sk_S, pk_S)	1: parse $sk_P = (sk_S, sk_R)$
2: return hk	2: SC.Gen$_R$(1^λ) $\xrightarrow{\$}$ (sk_R, pk_R)	2: parse $pk_{\bar{P}} = (pk_S, pk_R)$
	3: sk $\leftarrow$ (sk_S, sk_R)	3: $st_P^{send} \leftarrow$ (sk_S, pk_R)
	4: pk $\leftarrow$ (pk_S, pk_R)	4: $st_P^{rec} \leftarrow$ (sk_R, pk_S)
	5: return (sk, pk)	5: $st_P \leftarrow$ (λ, hk, (st_P^{send}), (st_P^{rec}))
		6: return st_P

ARCAD$_{DV}$.Send(st_P, ad, pt)
1: parse $st_P = (\lambda, hk, (st_P^{send,1}, \ldots, st_P^{send,u}), (st_P^{rec,1}, \ldots, st_P^{rec,v}))$
2: uni.Init(1^λ) $\xrightarrow{\$}$ (st_{Snew}, $st_P^{rec,v+1}$)   ▷ append a new receive state to the st_P^{rec} list
3: pt' $\leftarrow$ (st_{Snew}, pt)   ▷ then, st_{Snew} is erased to avoid leaking
4: take the smallest i s.t. $st_P^{send,i} \neq \perp$ ▷ $i = u - n$ if we had n Receive since the last Send
5: uni.Send(1^λ, hk, $st_P^{send,i}, \ldots, st_P^{send,u}$, ad, pt') $\xrightarrow{\$}$ ($st_P^{send,u}$, ct)   ▷ update $st_P^{send,u}$
6: $st_P^{send,i}, \ldots, st_P^{send,u-1} \leftarrow \perp$ ▷ flush the send state list: only $st_P^{send,u}$ remains
7: $st'_P \leftarrow (\lambda, hk, (st_P^{send,1}, \ldots, st_P^{send,u}), (st_P^{rec,1}, \ldots, st_P^{rec,v+1}))$
8: return (st'_P, ct)

ARCAD$_{DV}$.Receive(st_P, ad, ct)
9: parse $st_P = (\lambda, hk, (st_P^{send,1}, \ldots, st_P^{send,u}), (st_P^{rec,1}, \ldots, st_P^{rec,v}))$
10: set $n+1$ to the number of components in ct   ▷ the onion has n layers
11: set i to the smallest index such that $st_P^{rec,i} \neq \perp$
12: if $i + n - 1 > v$ then return (false, st_P, $\perp$)
13: uni.Receive(hk, $st_P^{rec,i}, \ldots, st_P^{rec,i+n-1}$, ad, ct) $\rightarrow$ (acc, $st'_P{}^{rec,i+n-1}$, pt')
14: if acc $=$ false then return (false, st_P, $\perp$)
15: parse pt' $=$ ($st_P^{send,u+1}$, pt)   ▷ a new send state is added in the list
16: $st_P^{rec,i}, \ldots, st_P^{rec,i+n-2} \leftarrow \perp$ ▷ update stage 1: $n-1$ entries of st_P^{rec} were erased
17: $st_P^{rec,i+n-1} \leftarrow st_P^{rec,i+n-1}$ ▷ update stage 2: update $st_P^{rec,i+n-1}$
18: $st'_P \leftarrow (\lambda, hk, (st_P^{send,1}, \ldots, st_P^{send,u+1}), (st_P^{rec,1}, \ldots, st_P^{rec,v}))$
19: return (acc, st'_P, pt)

Fig. 11. ARCAD$_{DV}$ Protocol Adapted from DV [7] without RECOVER-Security.

References

1. Alwen, J., Coretti, S., Dodis, Y.: The double ratchet: security notions, proofs, and modularization for the signal protocol. In: Ishai, Y., Rijmen, V. (eds.) EURO-CRYPT 2019. LNCS, vol. 11476, pp. 129–158. Springer, Cham (2019). https://doi.org/10.1007/978-3-030-17653-2_5

2. Bellare, M., Singh, A.C., Jaeger, J., Nyayapati, M., Stepanovs, I.: Ratcheted encryption and key exchange: the security of messaging. In: Katz, J., Shacham, H. (eds.) CRYPTO 2017. LNCS, vol. 10403, pp. 619–650. Springer, Cham (2017). https://doi.org/10.1007/978-3-319-63697-9_21

3. Borisov, N., Goldberg, I., Brewer, E.: Off-the-record communication, or, why not to use PGP. In: Proceedings of the 2004 ACM Workshop on Privacy in the Electronic Society, WPES 2004, New York, NY, USA, pp. 77–84. ACM (2004)

4. Caforio, A., Betül Durak, F., Vaudenay, S.: On-demand ratcheting with security awareness. IACR Eprint 2019/965. https://eprint.iacr.org/2019/965.pdf

5. Cohn-Gordon, K., Cremers, C., Dowling, B., Garratt, L., Stebila, D.: A formal security analysis of the signal messaging protocol. In: 2017 IEEE European Symposium on Security and Privacy (EuroS&P), pp. 451–466, April 2017

6. Cohn-Gordon, K., Cremers, C., Garratt, L.: On post-compromise security. In: 2016 IEEE 29th Computer Security Foundations Symposium (CSF), pp. 164–178, June 2016

7. Durak, F.B., Vaudenay, S.: Bidirectional asynchronous ratcheted key agreement with linear complexity. In: Attrapadung, N., Yagi, T. (eds.) IWSEC 2019. LNCS, vol. 11689, pp. 343–362. Springer, Cham (2019). https://doi.org/10.1007/978-3-030-26834-3_20

8. Jaeger, J., Stepanovs, I.: Optimal channel security against fine-grained state compromise: the safety of messaging. In: Shacham, H., Boldyreva, A. (eds.) CRYPTO 2018. LNCS, vol. 10991, pp. 33–62. Springer, Cham (2018). https://doi.org/10.1007/978-3-319-96884-1_2

9. Jost, D., Maurer, U., Mularczyk, M.: Efficient ratcheting: almost-optimal guarantees for secure messaging. In: Ishai, Y., Rijmen, V. (eds.) EUROCRYPT 2019. LNCS, vol. 11476, pp. 159–188. Springer, Cham (2019). https://doi.org/10.1007/978-3-030-17653-2_6

10. Poettering, B., Rösler, P.: Towards bidirectional ratcheted key exchange. In: Shacham, H., Boldyreva, A. (eds.) CRYPTO 2018. LNCS, vol. 10991, pp. 3–32. Springer, Cham (2018). https://doi.org/10.1007/978-3-319-96884-1_1

11. Open Whisper Systems. Signal protocol library for Java/Android. GitHub repository (2017). https://github.com/WhisperSystems/libsignal-protocol-java

12. Unger, N., et al.: SoK: secure messaging. In: 2015 IEEE Symposium on Security and Privacy, pp. 232–249, May 2015

13. Yan, H., Vaudenay, S.: Symmetric asynchronous ratcheted communication with associated data. In: Aoki, K., Kanaoka, A. (eds.) IWSEC 2020. LNCS, vol. 12231, pp. 184–204. Springer, Cham (2020). https://doi.org/10.1007/978-3-030-58208-1_11

Group Encryption: Full Dynamicity, Message Filtering and Code-Based Instantiation

Khoa Nguyen[1], Reihaneh Safavi-Naini[2], Willy Susilo[3], Huaxiong Wang[1], Yanhong Xu[2(✉)], and Neng Zeng[4(✉)]

[1] School of Physical and Mathematical Sciences, Nanyang Technological University, Singapore, Singapore

[2] Department of Computer Science, University of Calgary, Calgary, Canada
yanhong.xu1@ucalgary.ca

[3] Institute of Cybersecurity and Cryptology, School of Computing and Information Technology, University of Wollongong, Wollongong, NSW, Australia

[4] Information Systems Technology and Design, Singapore University of Technology and Design, Singapore, Singapore
zeng_neng@sutd.edu.sg

Abstract. Group encryption (GE), introduced by Kiayias, Tsiounis and Yung (Asiacrypt'07), is the encryption analogue of group signatures. It allows to send verifiably encrypted messages satisfying certain requirements to certified members of a group, while keeping the anonymity of the receivers. Similar to the tracing mechanism in group signatures, the receiver of any ciphertext can be identified by an opening authority - should the needs arise. The primitive of GE is motivated by a number of interesting privacy-preserving applications, including the filtering of encrypted emails sent to certified members of an organization.

This paper aims to improve the state-of-affairs of GE systems. Our first contribution is the formalization of fully dynamic group encryption (FDGE) - a GE system simultaneously supporting dynamic user enrolments and user revocations. The latter functionality for GE has not been considered so far. As a second contribution, we realize the message filtering feature for GE based on a list of t-bit keywords and 2 commonly used policies: "permissive" - accept the message if it contains at least one of the keywords as a substring; "prohibitive" - accept the message if all of its t-bit substrings are at Hamming distance at least d from all keywords, for $d \geq 1$. This feature so far has not been substantially addressed in existing instantiations of GE based on DCR, DDH, pairing-based and lattice-based assumptions. Our third contribution is the first instantiation of GE under code-based assumptions. The scheme is more efficient than the lattice-based construction of Libert et al. (Asiacrypt'16) - which, prior to our work, is the only known instantiation of GE under post-quantum assumptions. Our scheme supports the 2 suggested policies for message filtering, and in the random oracle model, it satisfies the stringent security notions for FDGE that we put forward.

© International Association for Cryptologic Research 2021
J. A. Garay (Ed.): PKC 2021, LNCS 12711, pp. 678–708, 2021.
https://doi.org/10.1007/978-3-030-75248-4_24

1   Introduction

The study of group encryption - the encryption analogue of group signatures [17] - was initiated by Kiayias, Tsiounis and Yung (KTY) [29] in 2007. While group signatures allow the signers to hide their identities within a set of certified senders, group encryption protects the anonymity of the decryptors within a set of legitimate receivers. To keep users accountable for their actions, signatures/ciphertexts can be de-anonymized in cases of disputes, using a secret key possessed by an opening authority.

In a group encryption scheme, the sender of a ciphertext can generate publicly verifiable proofs that: (i) The ciphertext is well-formed and can be decrypted by some registered group member; (ii) The opening authority can identify the intended receiver should the needs arise; (iii) The plaintext satisfies certain requirements, such as being a witness for some public relation.

Group encryption (GE) schemes are motivated by a number of appealing privacy-preserving applications. A natural application is for encrypted email filtering, where GE allows a firewall to accept only those incoming emails that are intended for some certified organization user. If accepted, the encrypted messages are guaranteed to satisfy some prescribed requirements, such as the absence of spammy/unethical keywords or the presence of keywords that are of the organization's interests.

As pointed out in [29] and subsequent work [1,15,32,36], GE can also find interesting applications in the contexts of anonymous trusted third parties, oblivious retriever storage systems or asynchronous transfers of encrypted datasets. For instance, it allows to archive on remote servers encrypted datasets intended for some anonymous client who paid a subscription to the storage provider. Furthermore, the recipient can be identified by a judge if a misbehaving server is found guilty of hosting suspicious transaction records or any other illegal content.

From the theoretical point of view, one can build a secure GE scheme based on anonymous CCA2-secure public key encryption schemes, digital signatures, commitments and zero-knowledge proofs. The designs of GE are typically more sophisticated than for group signatures, due to the need of proving well-formedness of ciphertexts encrypted via hidden-but-certified users' public keys. In particular, as noted by Kiayias et al. [29], GE implies hierarchical group signatures [50] - a proper generalization of group signatures [4,5].

In their pioneering work, Kiayias et al. instantiated GE based on the Decisional Composite Residuosity (DCR) and the Decisional Diffie Hellman (DDH) assumptions. The zero-knowledge proof of ciphertext well-formedness in their scheme is interactive, but can be made non-interactive in the random oracle model using the Fiat-Shamir transformation [21]. Cathalo et al. [15] subsequently proposed a non-interactive realization based on pairings in the standard model. El Aimani and Joye [1] then suggested various efficiency improvements for pairing-based GE. The first construction of GE from lattice assumptions was later presented by Libert et al. [32].

Libert et al. [36] enriched the KTY model of GE by introducing a refined tracing mechanism inspired by that of traceable signatures [28]. In this setting, the opening authority can release a user-specific trapdoor that enables public tracing of ciphertexts sent to that specific users without violating other users' privacy. Izabachène et al. [26] suggested mediated traceable anonymous encryption - a related primitive that addresses the problem of eliminating subliminal channels.

CURRENT LIMITATIONS OF GE. To date, GE has been much less well-studied than group signatures [17], even though they are functionally dual to each other. The group signature primitive has a longer history of development, and serves as a primary case study for privacy-preserving authentication systems. Meanwhile, GE was introduced close to the rises of powerful encryption systems such as attribute-based [25], functional [8] and fully-homomorphic [22] encryption, and has not gained much traction. Nevertheless, given its compelling features and the nice applications it can potentially offer, we argue that GE deserves more attention from the community. In this work, we thus aim to contribute to the development of GE. To start with, we identify several limitations of existing GE systems.

First, the problem of user revocation, which is a prominent issue in multi-user cryptosystems, has not been formally addressed. The KTY model [29], while allowing dynamic enrolments of new users to the group, does not provide any mechanism to prevent revoked users (e.g., those who were expelled for misbehaviours, stopped subscribing to the services or retired from the organizations) from decrypting new ciphertexts intended for them (unless the whole system is re-initiated). We next observe that, although it was not discussed by authors of [36], their refined tracing method might pave the way for a mechanism akin to verifier-local revocation [9], in which verifiers test incoming ciphertexts using the trapdoors corresponding to *all* revoked users. Beside incurring complexity linear in the number of revoked users, such a mechanism is known to only provide a weak notion of anonymity (called selfless-anonymity) for non-revoked users. A formal treatment of fully dynamic GE (i.e., which supports both dynamic enrolments and revocations of users) with strong security requirements is therefore highly desirable.

The second limitation is about the usefulness of existing GE schemes in the context of email filtering - which is arguably the most natural application of the primitive. Recall that such filtering functionality is supposed to be done by defining a relation $R = \{(x, w)\}$ and accepting only messages w such that $(x, w) \in R$, for a publicly given x. However, in all known instantiations of GE, the relations for messages are defined according to the computationally hard problems used in other system components. More precisely, the KTY scheme [29] employs the discrete-log relation, i.e., it only accepts w if $g^w = h$ for given (g, h). Subsequent works follow this pattern: pairing-based relations are used in [1,15,36] and a Short-Integer-Solution relation is used in [32] for message filtering. While such treatment does comply the definitions of GE, it seems too limited to be useful for filtering spams. Designing GE schemes with expressive policies that capture real-life spam filtering methods is hence an interesting open question.

Third, regarding the diversity of concrete computational assumptions used in building GE, among all existing schemes, the only one that is not known to be vulnerable against quantum computers [48] is the lattice-based construction from [32]. This raises the question of realizing GE based on alternative quantum-resistant assumptions, e.g., those from codes, multivariates and isogenies. In terms of privacy-preserving cryptographic protocols, other post-quantum candidates are much less developed compared to lattice-based constructions, and it would be tempting to catch up in the scope of GE.

OUR CONTRIBUTIONS AND TECHNIQUES. This work addresses all the 3 limitations of existing GE that we discussed above. Our first contribution is a formal model for fully dynamic group encryption (FDGE), with carefully defined syntax and robust security notions. Our model empowers the KTY model with the user revocation functionality and paves the way for new instantiations of GE in which enrolling new users and revoking existing users can be done simultaneously and efficiently. As a second contribution, we suggest to realize message filtering for GE not based on computationally hard problems, but a list of keywords and how these keywords match with substrings of the encrypted messages. To this end, we define 2 policies for accepting "good" messages and rejecting "bad" ones, that capture the spirit of the String Matching problem and the Approximate String Matching problem that are widely used in contemporary spam filtering techniques. Our third contribution is the first code-based GE scheme that follows our FDGE model and that supports both of the 2 message filtering policies we propose. We provide more technical details in the following.

Group Encryption with Full Dynamicity. We formalize the primitive of FDGE as the encryption analogue of fully dynamic group signatures [10]. Beyond the usual joining algorithm of the KTY model [29], FDGE makes it possible to update the group periodically to reflect user revocations. Our model is defined in a way such that it captures the 2 most commonly used approaches for handling user revocations in group signatures, based on revocation lists [13] and accumulators [14]. As noted in [10], there is an attack inherently to group signature schemes following the revocation-list-based approach. When translated into the GE context, such attack would permit group users to decrypt ciphertexts sent to them even before they join the group. Our FDGE model does not allow such attack, and we view this as a preventative measure in case a revocation-list-based revocable GE will be proposed in the future.

Regarding security requirements, we define the notions of message secrecy, anonymity, and soundness that are inline with and carefully extended from the KTY model [29]. We consider adversaries with strong capabilities, including the ability to corrupt the group manager (GM) and/or the opening authority (OA) to a large extent. Specifically, not only do we permit full corruption[1] of the GM and/or OA when defining message secrecy and anonymity, but we also tolerate maliciously generated keys for the fully corrupted authorities. In terms

---

[1] Full corruption means that the adversary entirely controls the authority - who may no longer follow its program.

of soundness, only partial corruption[2] of OA is allowed. Note that the assumption on partially corrupted OA is minimal, since otherwise a fully corrupted OA could simply refuse to open ciphertexts.

Message Filtering. Spamming and spam filtering are complicated areas, and currently there is no single filtering solution that can address all the clever tricks of spammers. In the present work, we do not attempt to invent such a solution. Our goal is to equip GE schemes with some basic, yet commonly used policies for filtering. More precisely, we suggest to employ a public list $S = \{s_1, \ldots, s_k\}$ of k binary keywords, each of which has bit-length t, to test against length t substrings of the encrypted message $\mathbf{w} \in \{0,1\}^p$. This list can be regularly updated by the GM, depending on the interests and needs of the organization. The keywords s_i could either be "good" ones that all legitimate messages are expected to contain, or be "bad" ones that should be far - in terms of Hamming distance - from all substrings of $\mathbf{w}$. Respectively, we consider the following 2 policies.

1. **"Permissive":** $\mathbf{w}$ is a legitimate message if and only if there exists $i \in [1, k]$ such that s_i is a substring of $\mathbf{w}$. This policy captures the String Matching problem and can be applied when the current interests of the group are reflected by the keywords s_i's, and all messages that do not contain any of these keywords are rejected.
2. **"Prohibitive":** $\mathbf{w}$ is a legitimate message if and only if for every length-t substring $\mathbf{y}$ of $\mathbf{w}$ and every $s_i \in S$, their Hamming distance is at least d. This policy is related to the Approximate String Matching problem. Here, the keywords s_i's could correspond to topics that are unethical, illegal, adultery, or simply out of the group's interests. The requirement on minimum Hamming distance d is to address spammers who might slightly alter s_i so that it passes the filtering while still being somewhat readable.

Having defined the policies, our next step is to derive methods for proving in zero-knowledge that the secret message $\mathbf{w}$ satisfies each of the policies, which will be used by the message sender when proving the well-formedness of the ciphertext. Let us discuss the high-level ideas.

Regarding the permissive policy, our observation is that if we form matrix $\mathbf{W} \in \{0,1\}^{t \times (p-t+1)}$ whose columns are length-t substrings of $\mathbf{w}$, and matrix $\mathbf{S} \in \{0,1\}^{t \times k}$ whose columns are the keywords s_i, then $\mathbf{w}$ is legitimate if and only if there exist weight-1 vectors $\mathbf{g} \in \{0,1\}^{p-t+1}$ and $\mathbf{h} \in \{0,1\}^k$ such that $\mathbf{W} \cdot \mathbf{g} = \mathbf{S} \cdot \mathbf{h}$. Then, to handle this relation, we employ Stern's permuting technique [49] to prove knowledge of such $\mathbf{g}, \mathbf{h}$ and we adapt Libert et al.'s technique [32] for proving the well-formedness of the quadratic term $\mathbf{W} \cdot \mathbf{g}$.

As for the prohibitive policy, we consider all the $(p-t+1) \cdot k$ sums $\mathbf{z}_{i,j} \in \{0,1\}^t$ over $\mathbb{Z}_2$ of substrings of $\mathbf{w}$ and keywords in S. Then, $\mathbf{w}$ is legitimate if and only if all these sums have Hamming weight at least d. To prove these statements, we perform the following extension trick, inspired by [37].

---

[2] Partial corruption means that the adversary only knows the secret key of the authority who still follows its prescribed program.

We append $(t - d)$ coordinates to $\mathbf{z}_{i,j} \in \{0,1\}^t$ to get $\mathbf{z}_{i,j}^* \in \{0,1\}^{2t-d}$ with Hamming weight exactly t. Such an extension is always possible if $\mathbf{z}_{i,j}$ has weight at least d. Furthermore, the converse also holds: if $\mathbf{z}_{i,j}^*$ has weight t, then the original $\mathbf{z}_{i,j}$ must have weight at least $t - (t - d) = d$. At this point, it suffices to use Stern's permuting technique [49] for proving knowledge of fixed-weight binary vectors.

The techniques sketched above can be smoothly integrated into our code-based instantiation of FDGE.

Code-Based Instantiation. To design a scheme satisfying our model of FDGE, we would need: (1) An anonymous CCA2-secure public-key encryption to encrypt messages under a group user's public key and to encrypt the user's public key under the OA's public key; (2) A secure digital signature to certify public keys of group members; and (3) Zero-knowledge proofs compatible with the encryption and signature layers, as well as with the message filtering layer.

In the code-based setting, the first ingredient can be obtained from the randomized McEliece encryption scheme [46] that satisfies CPA-security and the Naor-Yung transformation [44]. The second ingredient seems not readily available, as code-based signatures for which there are efficient zero-knowledge proofs of knowledge of message/signature pairs are not known to date. To tackle this issue, we adapt the strategy of Ling et al. in their construction of lattice-based fully dynamic group signatures [38]. This amounts to replacing the signature scheme by an accumulator scheme [6] equipped with zero-knowledge arguments of membership. We hence can make use of the code-based realization of Merkle-tree acummulators recently proposed by Nguyen et al. [45].

The main idea is to use Merkle-tree accumulators to certify users' public key. Let $N = 2^\ell$ be the maximum expected number of group users. Let $\mathsf{pk} = (\mathbf{G}_0, \mathbf{G}_1)$ be a user public key, where $\mathbf{G}_0, \mathbf{G}_1$ are 2 McEliece encryption matrices (recall that we employ the Naor-Yung double encryption technique). Then pk is hashed to a vector $\mathbf{d} \neq \mathbf{0}$, which is placed at the tree leaf corresponding to the identity $j \in \{0,1\}^\ell$ of the user in the group. A tree root is then computed based on all the 2^ℓ leaves. The user's certificate, which is made available to message senders, consists of pk, j and hash values in the path from her leaf to the root.

When sending a message $\mathbf{w}$ satisfying "permissive" or "prohibitive" policy to user j, the sender uses pk to encrypt $\mathbf{w}$ as $\mathbf{c}_w$, and uses the OA's public key to encrypt j as $\mathbf{c}_{\mathsf{oa}}$, so that OA can recover j if necessary. As for well-formedness of ciphertext, sender proves in zero-knowledge that:

1. $\mathbf{w}$ satisfies the given policy. This can be done using the discussed techniques.
2. $\mathbf{c}_{\mathsf{oa}}$ is an honestly computed ciphertext of j. This part is quite straightforward to realize via techniques for Stern's protocol.
3. $\mathbf{c}_w$ is a correct ciphertext of the $\mathbf{w}$ from (1.), computed under some hidden public key pk, whose hash value $\mathbf{d} \neq \mathbf{0}$ is at the tree leaf corresponding to the j from (2.). This is indeed the most sophisticated portion of our scheme. It requires to demonstrate: (i) membership of $\mathbf{d}$ in the tree and $\mathbf{d} \neq \mathbf{0}$ is the

hash of value of pk; (ii) $\mathbf{c}_w$ has the form $\mathbf{c}_w = \mathsf{pk} \cdot \begin{bmatrix} \mathbf{r} \\ \mathbf{w} \end{bmatrix} + \mathbf{e}$, where $(\mathbf{r}, \mathbf{e})$ is the encryption randomness.

While statement (i) can be handled using the techniques from [37,45], (ii) would require to prove an Learning-Parity-with-Noise-like relation with hidden-but-certified matrix pk. We then tackle this problem by adapting the techniques for Learning-with-Errors relations [47] from [32] into the binary setting.

Having discussed the main technical ingredients of the scheme, let us now explain how user revocations and dynamic user enrolments can be done in a simple manner based on Merkle trees. The ideas, first suggested in [38], are as follows. At the setup phase, all leaves in the tree are set as $\mathbf{0}$. When a new user joins the group, as mentioned, $\mathbf{0}$ is changed to $\mathbf{d} \neq \mathbf{0}$. If the user is later revoked from the group, the value is set back to $\mathbf{0}$. For each change, the GM can efficiently update the tree by re-computing the path in time $\mathcal{O}(\log N)$. Note that in the zero-knowledge layer above, the sender in part proves that $\mathbf{d}$ is non-zero - which is interpreted as "the sender is indeed an active group user".

Putting everything together, we obtain the first construction of code-based (fully dynamic) GE. In the random oracle model, we prove that the scheme satisfies all the stringent security notions of FDGE, namely, message secrecy, anonymity and soundness, based on the security of the code-based technical ingredients we employ.

The scheme, however, should only be viewed as a proof-of-concept, as it is not practical - due to the involvement of heavy zero-knowledge arguments. However, in comparison with [32] the only known GE scheme from post-quantum assumptions, ours is more efficient. The main reason is that ours uses a Merkle tree - which can be viewed as a weak form of signatures, while theirs relies on a standard-model lattice-based signature scheme, whose supported zero-knowledge arguments incurred an overhead factor of $\log^2 q$, where $q > 2^{30}$. We estimate that, for 128 bits of security, our argument size is about 2 orders of magnitude smaller than theirs. In other words, our scheme is more efficient than [32], but is still not practical. We leave the problem of obtaining practically usable FDGE schemes from post-quantum assumptions as an interesting open question.

OTHER RELATED WORK.   Enabling efficient user revocations in advanced privacy-preserving cryptographic constructions is generally a challenging problem, since one has to ensure that revoked users are no longer able to act as active users, and the workloads of other parties (managers, non-revoked users, verifiers) do not significantly increase in the meantime. In the context of group signatures, several different approaches have been suggested [9,13,14] to address this problem, and efficient pairing-based constructions supporting both dynamic joining and efficient revocation were given in [34,35,43]. Bootle et al. [10] pointed out a few shortcomings of previous models, and put forward robust security notions for fully dynamic group signatures. Here, we adapt the [10] model to provide the first formal treatment of user revocation in the context of GE.

The major tools for building those privacy-preserving constructions are zero-knowledge (ZK) proof [24] and argument [12,23] systems that allow to prove the truth of a statement while revealing no additional information. Almost all known zero-knowledge proof/argument systems used in code-based cryptography follow Stern's framework [49]. Variants of Stern's protocol have been employed to design privacy-preserving constructions, such as proofs of plaintext knowledge [42], linear-size ring signatures [11,18,40,41], linear-size and sublinear-size group signatures [2,20], proofs of valid openings for commitments and proofs for general relations [27]. Recently, Nguyen et al. [45] proposed a number of new code-based privacy-preserving protocols, including accumulators, range proofs, logarithmic-size ring signatures and group signatures. However, prior to our work, no construction of code-based GE was known.

ORGANIZATION. The rest of the paper is organized as follows. In Sect. 2, we recall the background on Stern-like protocols and previous techniques for designing zero-knowledge protocols in Stern's framework. In Sect. 3, we present our ZK argument for a quadratic relation. This is crucial for proving the permissive relation in Sect. 4 - where we also present the strategies for proving the prohibitive relation. Section 5 introduces the model and security requirements of FDGE. Next, we present our code-based instantiation of FDGE in Sect. 6. Due to space limit, several supporting materials are deferred to the full version of the paper [51].

2   Preliminaries

NOTATIONS. Let $a, b \in \mathbb{Z}$. Denote $[a, b]$ as the set $\{a, \dots, b\}$. We simply write $[b]$ when $a = 1$. Let $\oplus$ denote the bit-wise addition operation modulo 2. If S is a finite set, then $x \xleftarrow{\$} S$ means that x is chosen uniformly at random from S. Throughout this paper, all vectors are column vectors. When concatenating vectors $\mathbf{x} \in \{0,1\}^m$ and $\mathbf{y} \in \{0,1\}^k$, for simplicity, we use the notation $(\mathbf{x}\|\mathbf{y}) \in \{0,1\}^{m+k}$ instead of $(\mathbf{x}^\top\|\mathbf{y}^\top)^\top$. The Hamming weight of vector $\mathbf{x} \in \{0,1\}^m$ is denoted by $wt(\mathbf{x})$. The Hamming distance between vectors $\mathbf{x}, \mathbf{y} \in \{0,1\}^m$ is denoted by $d_H(\mathbf{x}, \mathbf{y})$, and is equal to $wt(\mathbf{x} \oplus \mathbf{y})$. Denote by $\mathsf{B}(n, \omega)$ the set of all binary vectors of length n with Hamming weight ω, and by S_n the symmetric group of all permutations of n elements.

2.1   Stern-Like Protocols

The statistical zero-knowledge arguments of knowledge presented in this work are Stern-like [49] protocols. In particular, they are Σ-protocols in the generalized sense defined in [7,27] (where 3 valid transcripts are needed for extraction, instead of just 2). The basic protocol consists of 3 moves: commitment, challenge, response. If a statistically hiding and computationally binding string commitment is employed in the first move, then one obtains a statistical zero-knowledge argument of knowledge (ZKAoK) with perfect completeness, constant soundness error 2/3. In many applications, the protocol is repeated a sufficient number of times to make the soundness error negligibly small. For instance, to achieve soundness error 2^{-80}, it suffices to repeat the basic protocol 137 times.

An abstraction of Stern's protocols. We recall an abstraction, adapted from [31], which captures the sufficient conditions to run a Stern-like protocol. Looking ahead, this abstraction will be helpful for us in presenting our ZK argument systems: we will reduce the relations we need to prove to instances of the abstract protocol, using our specific techniques. Let K, L be positive integers, where $L \geq K$, and let VALID be a subset of $\{0,1\}^L$. Suppose that $\mathcal{S}$ is a finite set such that one can associate every $\phi \in \mathcal{S}$ with a permutation Γ_ϕ of L elements, satisfying the following conditions:

$$\begin{cases} \mathbf{w} \in \mathsf{VALID} \iff \Gamma_\phi(\mathbf{w}) \in \mathsf{VALID}, \\ \text{If } \mathbf{w} \in \mathsf{VALID} \text{ and } \phi \text{ is uniform in } \mathcal{S}, \text{ then } \Gamma_\phi(\mathbf{w}) \text{ is uniform in } \mathsf{VALID}. \end{cases} \quad (1)$$

We aim to construct a statistical ZKAoK for the following abstract relation:

$$\mathrm{R}_{\mathrm{abstract}} = \left\{ ((\mathbf{M}, \mathbf{v}); \mathbf{w}) \in \mathbb{Z}_2^{K \times L} \times \mathbb{Z}_2^K \times \mathsf{VALID} : \mathbf{M} \cdot \mathbf{w} = \mathbf{v} \right\}.$$

The conditions in (1) play a crucial role in proving in ZK that $\mathbf{w} \in \mathsf{VALID}$: To do so, the prover samples $\phi \xleftarrow{\$} \mathcal{S}$ and lets the verifier check that $\Gamma_\phi(\mathbf{w}) \in \mathsf{VALID}$, while the latter cannot learn any additional information about $\mathbf{w}$ thanks to the randomness of ϕ. Furthermore, to prove in ZK that the linear equation holds, the prover samples a masking vector $\mathbf{r}_w \xleftarrow{\$} \mathbb{Z}_2^L$, and convinces the verifier instead that $\mathbf{M} \cdot (\mathbf{w} \oplus \mathbf{r}_w) = \mathbf{M} \cdot \mathbf{r}_w \oplus \mathbf{v}$.

The interaction between prover $\mathcal{P}$ and verifier $\mathcal{V}$ can be found in [31] or the full version of the paper. The resulting protocol is a statistical ZKAoK with perfect completeness, soundness error $2/3$, and communication cost $\mathcal{O}(L)$.

2.2   Previous Extension and Permutation Techniques

In this section, we first recall the permutation technique that is designed to prove knowledge of a binary vector of fixed hamming weight, which originates from Stern [49].

Technique for Handling Binary Vector with Fixed Hamming Weight. For any $\mathbf{e} \in \mathsf{B}(n, \omega)$ and $\sigma \in \mathsf{S}_n$, it is easy to see that the following equivalence holds [3].

$$\mathbf{e} \in \mathsf{B}(n, \omega) \iff \sigma(\mathbf{e}) \in \mathsf{B}(n, \omega), \quad (2)$$

To show that the vector $\mathbf{e}$ has hamming weight ω, the prover samples a uniformly random permutation $\sigma \in \mathsf{S}_n$ and shows the verifier that $\sigma(\mathbf{e}) \in \mathsf{B}(n, \omega)$. Due to the above equivalence (2), the verifier should be convinced that $\mathbf{e} \in \mathsf{B}(n, \omega)$. Furthermore, $\sigma(\mathbf{e})$ reveal no information about $\mathbf{e}$ due to the uniformity of σ.

The above technique was later developed to prove various forms of secret vectors. We now review the extension and permutation techniques for proving the knowledge of arbitrary binary vectors, which were presented in [33].

---

[3] Note that for $\mathbf{e} = [e_1 | \cdots | e_m]^\top$, $\sigma(\mathbf{e})$ is defined as $\sigma(e_i) = e_{\sigma(i)}$ for $i \in [n]$.

Let $\oplus$ denote the bit-wise addition operation modulo 2. For any bit $b \in \{0,1\}$, denote by $\bar{b}$ the bit $b = b \oplus 1$. Note that, for any $b, d \in \{0,1\}$, we have $\overline{b \oplus d} = b \oplus d \oplus 1 = \bar{b} \oplus d$.

Techniques for Handling Arbitrary Binary Vectors. To prove the knowledge of a binary vector $\mathbf{x} \in \{0,1\}^n$, define the extension process and permutation as follows.

- For a binary vector $\mathbf{x} = [\, x_1 \mid \ldots \mid x_n \,]^\top \in \{0,1\}^n$, where $n \in \mathbb{Z}^+$, denote by $\mathsf{Encode}(\mathbf{x})$ the vector $[\, \bar{x}_1 \mid x_1 \mid \ldots \mid \bar{x}_n \mid x_n \,]^\top \in \{0,1\}^{2n}$.
- Let $\mathbf{I}_n^* \in \mathbb{Z}_2^{n \times 2n}$ be an extension of the identity matrix $\mathbf{I}_n$, obtained by inserting a zero-column $\mathbf{0}^n$ right before each column of $\mathbf{I}_n$. We have for $\mathbf{x} \in \{0,1\}^n$,

$$\mathbf{x} = \mathbf{I}_n^* \cdot \mathsf{Encode}(\mathbf{x}). \tag{3}$$

- For $\mathbf{b} = [\, b_1 \mid \ldots \mid b_n \,]^\top \in \{0,1\}^n$, define the permutation $F_{\mathbf{b}}$ that transforms vector $\mathbf{z} = [\, z_{1,0} \mid z_{1,1} \mid \ldots \mid z_{n,0} \mid z_{n,1} \,]^\top \in \{0,1\}^{2n}$ into:

$$F_{\mathbf{b}}(\mathbf{z}) = [\, z_{1,b_1} \mid z_{1,\bar{b}_1} \mid \ldots \mid z_{n,b_n} \mid z_{n,\bar{b}_n} \,]^\top.$$

Note that, for any $\mathbf{b}, \mathbf{x} \in \{0,1\}^n$, we have:

$$\mathbf{z} = \mathsf{Encode}(\mathbf{x}) \iff F_{\mathbf{b}}(\mathbf{z}) = \mathsf{Encode}(\mathbf{x} \oplus \mathbf{b}). \tag{4}$$

The above equivalence (4) is useful in the Stern's framework [49] for proving knowledge of binary witness-vectors. Towards the goal, one encodes $\mathbf{x}$ to $\mathbf{z} = \mathsf{Encode}(\mathbf{x})$, samples a random binary vector $\mathbf{b}$ and permutes $\mathbf{z}$ using $F_{\mathbf{b}}$. Then one demonstrates to the verifier that the permuted vector $F_{\mathbf{b}}(\mathbf{z})$ is of the correct form $\mathsf{Encode}(\mathbf{x} \oplus \mathbf{b})$. Due to (4), the verifier should be convinced that $\mathbf{z}$ is well formed, which further implies the knowledge of a binary vector $\mathbf{x}$. Meanwhile, vector $\mathbf{b}$ serves as a "one-time pad" that perfects hides $\mathbf{x}$. In addition, if we have to show that $\mathbf{x}$ appears somewhere else, we can use the same $\mathbf{b}$ at those places.

3   Zero-Knowledge Arguments for Quadratic Relations

In this section, we present our ZKAoK for quadratic relations. More concretely, our arguments demonstrate that a given value $\mathbf{c}$ is an honest evaluation of the form $\mathbf{A} \cdot \mathbf{r} \oplus \mathbf{e}$, where $\mathbf{A}, \mathbf{r}, \mathbf{e}$ are all secret and may satisfy other constraints. In the following, we present our ZKAoK for a variant of LPN relation, where we consider secret $\mathbf{A} \in \mathbb{Z}_2^{n \times m}, \mathbf{r} \in \mathsf{B}(m, t_r), \mathbf{e} \in \mathsf{B}(n, t)$. Looking ahead, this protocol is crucial in Sect. 4.2 that proves a message satisfies the permissive relation.

3.1   Proving a Variant of LPN Relation with Hidden Matrix

Let n, m, t, t_r be positive integers, $\mathbf{A} \in \mathbb{Z}_2^{n \times m}, \mathbf{r} \in \mathsf{B}(m, t_r), \mathbf{e} \in \mathsf{B}(n, t), \mathbf{c} \in \mathbb{Z}_2^n$. We now present our ZKAoK that allows $\mathcal{P}$ to prove its knowledge of $\mathbf{A}, \mathbf{r}, \mathbf{e}$ such that $\mathbf{c} = \mathbf{A} \cdot \mathbf{r} \oplus \mathbf{e}$. The associated relation is defined as follows:

$$R_{\mathrm{VLPN}} = \left\{ \left(\mathbf{c}; (\mathbf{A}, \mathbf{r}, \mathbf{e}) \right) \in \mathbb{Z}_2^n \times \left(\mathbb{Z}_2^{n \times m} \times \mathsf{B}(m, t_r) \times \mathsf{B}(n, t) \right) : \mathbf{c} = \mathbf{A} \cdot \mathbf{r} \oplus \mathbf{e} \right\}.$$

To prove $\mathbf{r}$ has fixed hamming, we introduce the following Hadamard product extension and extended matrix-vector product expansion and their corresponding permutations.

Hadamard Product Extension. Let vectors $\mathbf{a} \in \{0,1\}^m$, $\mathbf{r} \in B(m, t_r)$ and $\mathbf{c} = [a_1 \cdot r_1 | a_2 \cdot r_2 | \cdots | a_m \cdot r_m]^\top$. The goal is to prove the well-formedness of $\mathbf{c}$, i.e., $\mathbf{c}$ is a Hadamard product of two binary vectors, one of which has fixed hamming weight t_r. We therefore introduce the following extension and permutation.

- Define extension of $c_i = a_i \cdot r_i$ as $\mathsf{ext}'(c_i) \triangleq \mathsf{ext}'(a_i, r_i) = [\overline{a_i} \cdot r_i | a_i \cdot r_i]^\top \in \{0,1\}^2$. Let $\mathbf{h}' = [0|1]$, then we obtain $c_i = \mathbf{h}' \cdot \mathsf{ext}'(c_i)$.
- Define the extension of $\mathbf{c}$ to be vector of the form

$$\mathsf{ext}'(\mathbf{a}, \mathbf{r}) = [\overline{a_1} \cdot r_1 | a_1 \cdot r_1 | \overline{a_2} \cdot r_2 | a_2 \cdot r_2 | \cdots | \overline{a_m} \cdot r_m | a_m \cdot r_m]^\top \in \{0,1\}^{2m}.$$

- For any $\mathbf{b} = [b_1 | b_2 | \cdots | b_m]^\top \in \{0,1\}^m$, $\sigma \in S_m$, define permutation $\Psi_{\mathbf{b},\sigma}$ that transforms a vector

$$\mathbf{z} = [\, z_1^{(0)} \mid z_1^{(1)} \mid z_2^{(0)} \mid z_2^{(1)} \mid \cdots \mid z_m^{(0)} \mid z_m^{(1)} \,]^\top \in \mathbb{Z}^{2m}$$

to a vector

$$\Psi_{\mathbf{b},\sigma}(\mathbf{z}) = [\, z_{\sigma(1)}^{(b_{\sigma(1)})} \mid z_{\sigma(1)}^{(\overline{b_{\sigma(1)}})} \mid z_{\sigma(2)}^{(b_{\sigma(2)})} \mid z_{\sigma(2)}^{(\overline{b_{\sigma(2)}})} \mid \cdots \mid z_{\sigma(m)}^{(b_{\sigma(m)})} \mid z_{\sigma(m)}^{(\overline{b_{\sigma(m)}})} \,]^\top.$$

- For any $\mathbf{a}, \mathbf{b} \in \{0,1\}^m$, $\mathbf{r} \in B(m, t_r)$, $\sigma \in S_m$, it is verifiable that the following equivalence holds.

$$\mathbf{z} = \mathsf{ext}'(\mathbf{a}, \mathbf{r}) \iff \Psi_{\mathbf{b},\sigma}(\mathbf{z}) = \mathsf{ext}'\big(\sigma(\mathbf{a} \oplus \mathbf{b}), \sigma(\mathbf{r})\big). \tag{5}$$

Example. Let $m = 4$, $t_r = 2$, $\mathbf{a} = [1|1|0|1]^\top$, $\mathbf{b} = [0|1|0|1]^\top$, $\mathbf{r} = [1|0|0|1]^\top$, $\sigma(i) = i + 1$ for $i \in [3]$ and $\sigma(4) = 1$. We have $\mathbf{d} = \sigma(\mathbf{a} \oplus \mathbf{b}) = [0|0|0|1]^\top$, $\mathbf{e} = \sigma(\mathbf{r}) = [0|0|1|1]^\top$, and

$$
\begin{aligned}
\mathbf{z} = \mathsf{ext}'(\mathbf{a}, \mathbf{r}) &= [\, z_1^{(0)} \mid z_1^{(1)} \mid z_2^{(0)} \mid z_2^{(1)} \mid z_3^{(0)} \mid z_3^{(1)} \mid z_4^{(0)} \mid z_4^{(1)} \,]^\top \\
&= [\ 0\ \mid\ 1\ \mid\ 0\ \mid\ 0\ \mid\ 0\ \mid\ 0\ \mid\ 0\ \mid\ 1\ ]^\top; \\
\Psi_{\mathbf{b},\sigma}(\mathbf{z}) &= [\, z_2^{(b_2)} \mid z_2^{(\overline{b_2})} \mid z_3^{(b_3)} \mid z_3^{(\overline{b_3})} \mid z_4^{(b_4)} \mid z_4^{(\overline{b_4})} \mid z_1^{(b_1)} \mid z_1^{(\overline{b_1})} \,]^\top \\
&= [\, z_2^{(1)} \mid z_2^{(0)} \mid z_3^{(0)} \mid z_3^{(1)} \mid z_4^{(1)} \mid z_4^{(0)} \mid z_1^{(0)} \mid z_1^{(1)} \,]^\top \\
&= [\ 0\ \mid\ 0\ \mid\ 0\ \mid\ 0\ \mid\ 1\ \mid\ 0\ \mid\ 0\ \mid\ 1\ ]^\top; \\
\mathsf{ext}'(\mathbf{d}, \mathbf{e}) &= [\, \overline{d_1} \cdot e_1 \mid d_1 \cdot e_1 \mid \overline{d_2} \cdot e_2 \mid d_2 \cdot e_2 \mid \overline{d_3} \cdot e_3 \mid d_3 \cdot e_3 \mid \overline{d_4} \cdot e_4 \mid d_4 \cdot e_4 \,] \\
&= [\ 0\ \mid\ 0\ \mid\ 0\ \mid\ 0\ \mid\ 1\ \mid\ 0\ \mid\ 0\ \mid\ 1\ ]^\top.
\end{aligned}
$$

Extended Matrix-Vector Product Expansion. Let vectors $\mathbf{a}, \mathbf{r}$ be of the form $\mathbf{a} = [a_{1,1} | \cdots | a_{1,n} | \cdots | a_{m,1} | \cdots | a_{m,n}]^\top \in \mathbb{Z}_2^{mn}$ and $\mathbf{r} = [r_1 | \cdots | r_m]^\top \in B(m, t_r)$, and $\mathbf{c} \in \mathbb{Z}_2^{mn}$ be of the form

$$\mathbf{c} = [a_{1,1} \cdot r_1 | \cdots | a_{1,n} \cdot r_1 | a_{2,1} \cdot r_2 | \cdots | a_{2,n} \cdot r_2 | \cdots | a_{m,1} \cdot r_m | \cdots | a_{m,n} \cdot r_m]^\top.$$

We now present the techniques to show the well-formedness of $\mathbf{c}$.

Define extension of $\mathbf{c}$ to be a vector $\mathsf{expand}'(\mathbf{a}, \mathbf{r}) \in \mathbb{Z}_2^{2mn}$ of the form:

$$
\begin{aligned}
\mathsf{expand}'(\mathbf{a}, \mathbf{r}) = \big[\ \ & \overline{a_{1,1}} \cdot r_1 \,|\, a_{1,1} \cdot r_1 \,|\, \overline{a_{1,2}} \cdot r_1 \,|\, a_{1,2} \cdot r_1 \,|\cdots|\, \overline{a_{1,n}} \cdot r_1 \,|\, a_{1,n} \cdot r_1 \,| \\
& \overline{a_{2,1}} \cdot r_2 \,|\, a_{2,1} \cdot r_2 \,|\, \overline{a_{2,2}} \cdot r_2 \,|\, a_{2,2} \cdot r_2 \,|\cdots|\, \overline{a_{2,n}} \cdot r_2 \,|\, a_{2,n} \cdot r_2 \,|\cdots| \\
& \overline{a_{m,1}} \cdot r_m \,|\, a_{m,1} \cdot r_m \,|\, \overline{a_{m,2}} \cdot r_m \,|\, a_{m,2} \cdot r_m \,|\cdots|\, \overline{a_{m,n}} \cdot r_m \,|\, a_{m,n} \cdot r_m \big]^{\top}
\end{aligned}
$$

Now for $\mathbf{b} = [\, b_{1,1} \,|\cdots|\, b_{1,n} \,|\, b_{2,1} \,|\cdots|\, b_{2,n} \,|\cdots|\, b_{m,1} \,|\cdots|\, b_{m,n} \,]^{\top} \in \mathbb{Z}_2^{mn}$ and $\sigma \in \mathsf{S}_m$, we define $\Psi'_{\mathbf{b},\sigma}$ that transform vector $\mathbf{z} \in \{0,1\}^{2mn}$ of the following form

$$
\begin{aligned}
\mathbf{z} = \big[\ \ & z_{1,1}^{(0)} \,|\, z_{1,1}^{(1)} \,|\, z_{1,2}^{(0)} \,|\, z_{1,2}^{(1)} \,|\, \cdots \,|\, z_{1,n}^{(0)} \,|\, z_{1,n}^{(1)} \,| \\
& z_{2,1}^{(0)} \,|\, z_{2,1}^{(1)} \,|\, z_{2,2}^{(0)} \,|\, z_{2,2}^{(1)} \,|\, \cdots \,|\, z_{2,n}^{(0)} \,|\, z_{2,n}^{(1)} \,|\, \cdots \,| \\
& z_{m,1}^{(0)} \,|\, z_{m,1}^{(1)} \,|\, z_{m,2}^{(0)} \,|\, z_{m,2}^{(1)} \,|\, \cdots \,|\, z_{m,n}^{(0)} \,|\, z_{m,n}^{(1)} \,\big]
\end{aligned}
$$

to vector $\Psi'_{\mathbf{b},\sigma}$ of the following form

$$
\begin{aligned}
\Psi'_{\mathbf{b},\sigma}(\mathbf{z}) = \big[\ \ & y_{1,1}^{(0)} \,|\, y_{1,1}^{(1)} \,|\, y_{1,2}^{(0)} \,|\, y_{1,2}^{(1)} \,|\, \cdots \,|\, y_{1,n}^{(0)} \,|\, y_{1,n}^{(1)} \,| \\
& y_{2,1}^{(0)} \,|\, y_{2,1}^{(1)} \,|\, y_{2,2}^{(0)} \,|\, y_{2,2}^{(1)} \,|\, \cdots \,|\, y_{2,n}^{(0)} \,|\, y_{2,n}^{(1)} \,|\, \cdots \,| \\
& y_{m,1}^{(0)} \,|\, y_{m,1}^{(1)} \,|\, y_{m,2}^{(0)} \,|\, y_{m,2}^{(1)} \,|\, \cdots \,|\, y_{m,n}^{(0)} \,|\, y_{m,n}^{(1)} \,\big]
\end{aligned}
$$

such that $y_{i,j}^{(0)} = z_{\sigma(i),j}^{(b_{\sigma(i),j})}$ and $y_{i,j}^{(1)} = z_{\sigma(i),j}^{(\overline{b_{\sigma(i),j}})}$ for $i \in [n], j \in [m]$. For ease of notation, given $\mathbf{f} = (\mathbf{f}_1 \| \cdots \| \mathbf{f}_m) \in \{0,1\}^{mn}$, where each $\mathbf{f}_i \in \{0,1\}^n$, and $\sigma \in \mathsf{S}_m$, define

$$
\sigma^{(n)}(\mathbf{f}) = (\, \mathbf{f}_{\sigma(1)} \| \cdots \| \mathbf{f}_{\sigma(m)} \,).
$$

Precisely, $\sigma^{(n)}$ permutes the blocks of $\mathbf{f}$ using σ. The following equivalence then immediately follows from (5) for $\mathbf{a}, \mathbf{b} \in \{0,1\}^{mn}$, $\mathbf{r} \in \mathsf{B}(m, t_r)$, $\sigma_r \in \mathsf{S}_m$.

$$
\mathbf{z} = \mathsf{expand}'(\mathbf{a}, \mathbf{r}) \iff \Psi'_{\mathbf{b},\sigma_r}(\mathbf{z}) = \mathsf{expand}'\big(\sigma_r^{(n)}(\mathbf{a} \oplus \mathbf{b}), \sigma_r(\mathbf{r})\big). \tag{6}
$$

The Zero-Knowledge Argument. We now transform the relation R_{VLPN} to an instance of R_{abstract} such that the equivalences in (1) hold. Write $\mathbf{A} = [\, \mathbf{a}_1 \,|\cdots|\, \mathbf{a}_m \,] \in \mathbb{Z}_2^{n \times m}$ and $\mathbf{r} = [\, r_1 \,|\cdots|\, r_m \,]^{\top} \in \mathbb{Z}_2^m$, then we have

$$\mathbf{A} \cdot \mathbf{r} = \sum_{i=1}^{m} \mathbf{a}_i \cdot r_i = \sum_{i=1}^{m} [\, a_{i,1} \cdot r_i \,|\, a_{i,2} \cdot r_i \,|\, \cdots \,|\, a_{i,n} \cdot r_i \,]^{\top}$$

$$= \sum_{i=1}^{m} \big[\, \mathbf{h}' \cdot \mathsf{ext}'(a_{i,1}, r_i) \,|\, \mathbf{h}' \cdot \mathsf{ext}'(a_{i,2}, r_i) \,|\, \cdots \,|\, \mathbf{h}' \cdot \mathsf{ext}'(a_{i,n}, r_i) \,\big]^{\top}$$

$$= \sum_{i=1}^{m} \mathbf{H}'_{n,1}\big(\, \mathsf{ext}'(a_{i,1}, r_i) \,\|\, \mathsf{ext}'(a_{i,2}, r_i) \,\|\, \cdots \,\|\, \mathsf{ext}'(a_{i,n}, r_i) \,\big)$$

$$= \sum_{i=1}^{m} \mathbf{H}'_{n,1} \cdot \mathbf{z}_i$$

$$= \underbrace{[\mathbf{H}'_{n,1}| \cdots |\mathbf{H}'_{n,1}]}_{m \text{ times}} \cdot (\, \mathbf{z}_1 \,\|\, \cdots \,\|\, \mathbf{z}_m \,),$$

where $\mathbf{H}'_{n,1} = \begin{pmatrix} \mathbf{h}' & & & \\ & \mathbf{h}' & & \\ & & \ddots & \\ & & & \mathbf{h}' \end{pmatrix} \in \mathbb{Z}_2^{n \times 2n}$ and $\mathbf{z}_i = (\mathsf{ext}'(a_{i,1}, r_i)\| \cdots \|\mathsf{ext}'(a_{i,n},$

$r_i)) \in \mathbb{Z}_2^{2n}$. Denote $\mathbf{H}'_{n,m} = \underbrace{[\mathbf{H}'_{n,1}| \cdots |\mathbf{H}'_{n,1}]}_{m \text{ times}} \in \mathbb{Z}_2^{n \times 2mn}$, $\mathbf{z} = (\mathbf{z}_1\| \cdots \|\mathbf{z}_m) \in$
$\mathbb{Z}_2^{2mn}$, and $\mathbf{a} = [a_{1,1}| \cdots |a_{1,n}|a_{2,1}| \cdots |a_{2,n}| \cdots |a_{m,1}| \cdots |a_{m,n}]^{\top} \in \mathbb{Z}_2^{mn}$. Then $\mathbf{z}$
is indeed the extended expansion vector of $\mathbf{a}$ and $\mathbf{r}$, i.e., $\mathbf{z} = \mathsf{expand}'(\mathbf{a}, \mathbf{r})$. If no
ambiguity caused, we write $\mathbf{z} = \mathsf{expand}'(\mathbf{A}, \mathbf{r})$. Hence, we obtain the following:

$$\mathbf{c} = \mathbf{A} \cdot \mathbf{r} \oplus \mathbf{e} \iff \mathbf{c} = \mathbf{H}'_{n,m} \cdot \mathsf{expand}'(\mathbf{A}, \mathbf{r}) \oplus \mathbf{e}. \tag{7}$$

Denote $\mathbf{M}_{\mathrm{VLPN}} = [\mathbf{H}'_{n,m}|\mathbf{I}_n] \in \mathbb{Z}_2^{n \times L_{\mathrm{VLPN}}}$ and $\mathbf{w}_{\mathrm{VLPN}} = (\mathsf{expand}'(\mathbf{A}, \mathbf{r})\|\mathbf{e}) \in$
$\mathbb{Z}_2^{L_{\mathrm{VLPN}}}$ with $L_{\mathrm{VLPN}} = 2mn + n$. Hence $\mathbf{c} \overset{\triangle}{=} \mathbf{v}_{\mathrm{VLPN}} = \mathbf{M}_{\mathrm{VLPN}} \cdot \mathbf{w}_{\mathrm{VLPN}} \bmod 2$.

Now we are ready to specify the set $\mathsf{VALID}_{\mathrm{VLPN}}$ that contains of secret vector
$\mathbf{w}_{\mathrm{VLPN}}$, the set $\mathcal{S}_{\mathrm{VLPN}}$, and permutations $\{\Gamma_\phi : \phi \in \mathcal{S}_{\mathrm{VLPN}}\}$ such that the
equivalences in (1) hold. To this end, let $\mathsf{VALID}_{\mathrm{VLPN}}$ contain all vectors $\widehat{\mathbf{w}}_{\mathrm{VLPN}} =$
$(\widehat{\mathbf{z}}\|\widehat{\mathbf{e}}) \in \mathbb{Z}_2^{2mn+n}$ satisfying the following constraints:

- There exists $\widehat{\mathbf{a}} \in \mathbb{Z}_2^{nm}$ and $\widehat{\mathbf{r}} \in \mathsf{B}(m, t_r)$ such that $\widehat{\mathbf{z}} = \mathsf{expand}'(\widehat{\mathbf{a}}, \widehat{\mathbf{r}})$.
- $\widehat{\mathbf{e}} \in \mathsf{B}(n, t)$.

It is easy to that the secret vector $\mathbf{w}_{\mathrm{VLPN}}$ belongs to $\mathsf{VALID}_{\mathrm{VLPN}}$. Let $\mathcal{S}_{\mathrm{VLPN}} =$
$\{0,1\}^{mn} \times \mathsf{S}_m \times \mathsf{S}_n$. Then for each $\phi = (\mathbf{b}, \sigma_r, \sigma_e) \in \mathcal{S}_{\mathrm{VLPN}}$, define the
permutation Γ_ϕ that transforms vector of the form $\widehat{\mathbf{w}}_{\mathrm{VLPN}} = (\widehat{\mathbf{z}}\|\widehat{\mathbf{e}})$ with
$\widehat{\mathbf{z}} \in \mathbb{Z}_2^{2mn}, \widehat{\mathbf{e}} \in \mathbb{Z}_2^n$ to vector $\Gamma_\phi(\widehat{\mathbf{w}}_{\mathrm{VLPN}}) = (\Psi'_{\mathbf{b},\sigma_r}(\widehat{\mathbf{z}})\|\sigma_e(\widehat{\mathbf{e}}))$.

Based on the equivalence observed in (6) and (2), it can be checked that
the conditions in (1) are satisfied and we have successfully reduced the consider

relation R_{VLPN} to an instance of R_{abstract}. Now $\mathcal{P}$ and $\mathcal{V}$ can run the Stern-like protocol for the reduced statement R_{VLPN} (see the full version). The resulting protocol is a statistical ZKAoK with perfect completeness, soundness error $2/3$, and communication cost $\mathcal{O}(L_{\mathrm{VLPN}}) = \mathcal{O}(mn) = \mathcal{O}(\lambda^2)$ bits.

4   Message Filtering in Zero-Knowledge

In this section, we first specify the 2 policies we use for filtering messages encrypted in the code-based FDGE scheme of Sect. 6. Then we discuss our main ideas for proving in ZK that the underlying messages satisfy the given policies.

4.1   Formulation

Let $p, t, d \in \mathbb{Z}^+$ such that $p > t > d$. A string $\mathbf{y} = [y_1 | \cdots | y_t]^\top \in \{0, 1\}^t$ is called a substring of string $\mathbf{w} = [w_1 | \cdots | w_p]^\top \in \{0, 1\}^p$, denoted as $\mathbf{y} \sqsubset \mathbf{w}$, if there exists an integer $i \in [1, p-t+1]$ such that $y_j = w_{i+j-1}$ for all $j \in [1, t]$. The Hamming distance between $\mathbf{x}, \mathbf{y} \in \{0, 1\}^t$, denoted by $d_H(\mathbf{x}, \mathbf{y})$, is the number of coordinates at which $\mathbf{x}$ and $\mathbf{y}$ differ. In other words, $d_H(\mathbf{x}, \mathbf{y}) = wt(\mathbf{x} \oplus \mathbf{y})$.

Let $\mathbf{w} \in \{0, 1\}^p$ be an encrypted message and let $S = \{\mathbf{s}_1, \ldots, \mathbf{s}_k\}$ be a given list of $k \geq 1$ keywords, where $\mathbf{s}_i \in \{0, 1\}^t$, for all $i \in [1, k]$. We will realize 2 commonly used policies of message filtering.

1. **"Permissive"**: $\mathbf{w}$ is a legitimate message if and only if there exists $i \in [1, k]$ such that $\mathbf{s}_i$ is a substring of $\mathbf{w}$. The induced relation R_{permit} is defined as

$$R_{\mathrm{permit}} = \{((\mathbf{s}_1, \ldots, \mathbf{s}_k), \mathbf{w}) \in (\{0, 1\}^t)^k \times \{0, 1\}^p : \exists i \in [1, k] \text{ s.t. } \mathbf{s}_i \sqsubset \mathbf{w}\}. \quad (8)$$

2. **"Prohibitive"**: $\mathbf{w}$ is a legitimate message if and only if for every length-t substring $\mathbf{y}$ of $\mathbf{w}$ and every $\mathbf{s}_i \in S$, their Hamming distance is at least d. The corresponding relation R_{prohibit} is defined as

$$R_{\mathrm{prohibit}} = \{((\mathbf{s}_1, \ldots, \mathbf{s}_k), \mathbf{w}) \in (\{0, 1\}^t)^k \times \{0, 1\}^p :$$
$$d_H(\mathbf{s}_i, \mathbf{y}) \geq d, \forall i \in [1, k], \forall \mathbf{y} \sqsubset \mathbf{w}\}. \quad (9)$$

In the following, we will discuss our strategies for proving that message $\mathbf{w}$ satisfies each of the above policies.

4.2   Zero-Knowledge for the Permissive and Prohibitive Relations

Let $\mathbf{w} = [w_1 | \cdots | w_p]^\top$, and for each $i \in [p-t+1]$, let $\mathbf{w}_{[i]} = [w_i | \cdots | w_{i+t-1}]^\top$ be its i-th substring of length t. Our ideas for proving that $((\mathbf{s}_1, \ldots, \mathbf{s}_k), \mathbf{w}) \in R_{\mathrm{permit}}$ in ZK are as follows. First, we form matrices

$$\mathbf{W} = [\mathbf{w}_{[1]} | \cdots | \mathbf{w}_{[p-t+1]}] = \begin{bmatrix} w_1 & w_2 & \cdots & w_{p-t+1} \\ w_2 & w_3 & \cdots & w_{p-t+2} \\ \vdots & \vdots & \vdots & \vdots \\ w_t & w_{t+1} & \cdots & w_p \end{bmatrix} \in \{0, 1\}^{t \times (p-t+1)},$$

$\mathbf{S} = [\mathbf{s}_1 \mid \cdots \mid \mathbf{s}_k] \in \{0,1\}^{t \times k}$, and denote $\mathsf{permit}(\mathbf{w}) = (\mathbf{w}_{[1]} \| \cdots \| \mathbf{w}_{[p-t+1]}) \in \{0,1\}^{t(p-t+1)}$. We note that $((\mathbf{s}_1, \ldots, \mathbf{s}_k), \mathbf{w}) \in R_{\mathrm{permit}}$ if and only if there exist a column $\mathbf{w}_{[i]}$ of $\mathbf{W}$ and a column $\mathbf{s}_j$ of $\mathbf{S}$ such that $\mathbf{w}_{[i]} = \mathbf{s}_j$. Then, we observe that the task of the prover $\mathcal{P}$ is equivalent to proving the existence of $\mathbf{W}, \mathbf{g}, \mathbf{h}$ such that

$$\mathbf{W} \cdot \mathbf{g} = \mathbf{S} \cdot \mathbf{h} \quad \wedge \quad \mathbf{g} \in \mathsf{B}(p-t+1, 1) \quad \wedge \quad \mathbf{h} \in \mathsf{B}(k, 1).$$

To this end, we employ techniques for proving linear relation and quadratic relation (specifically the variant of LPN relation), as well as, for fix-weight relations in the framework of Stern's protocols. In the process, we prove the well-formedness of $\mathbf{W}$. Details are in the full version of this paper. The resulting protocol has communication cost $\mathcal{O}(t \cdot (p-t) + k)$ and is a sub-protocol in our FDGE construction of Sect. 6, where we additionally prove that $\mathbf{w}$ is the same as the plaintext encrypted in a given McEliece ciphertext.

On the other hand, to prove that $((\mathbf{s}_1, \ldots, \mathbf{s}_k), \mathbf{w}) \in R_{\mathrm{prohibit}}$, we consider $(p-t+1) \cdot k$ pairs $(\mathbf{w}_{[i]}, \mathbf{s}_j)$ and aim to prove that all the sums $\mathbf{z}_{i,j} = \mathbf{w}_{[i]} \oplus \mathbf{s}_j \in \{0,1\}^t$ have Hamming weight at least d. In other words, we reduce the problem to $(p-t+1) \cdot k$ sub-problems, for each of which, we needs to prove that $\mathbf{z}_{i,j}$ contains at least d coordinates equal to 1. To this end, we perform the following extension trick, adapted from [37].

We append $(t-d)$ coordinates to $\mathbf{z}_{i,j} \in \{0,1\}^t$ to get $\mathbf{z}_{i,j}^* \in \{0,1\}^{2t-d}$ such that $wt(\mathbf{z}_{i,j}^*) = t$, i.e., $\mathbf{z}_{i,j}^* \in \mathsf{B}(2t-d, t)$. We note that such an extension is always possible if $wt(\mathbf{z}_{i,j}) \geq d$. Furthermore, the converse also holds: if $\mathbf{z}_{i,j}^* \in \mathsf{B}(2t-d, t)$, then the original $\mathbf{z}_{i,j}$ must have weight at least $t - (t-d) = d$. Details are in the full version of this paper. As a result, we obtain a ZK protocol for R_{prohibit} with communication cost $\mathcal{O}(t \cdot (p-t+1) \cdot k)$. Similarly to the case of R_{permit}, this protocol can serve as a sub-protocol in our FDGE construction of Sect. 6, allowing us to realize the "prohibitive" filtering policy.

5   Fully Dynamic Group Encryption: Model and Security Requirements

In this section, we first present the model of fully dynamic group encryption FDGE that offers both dynamic join and revocation, which is developed from the one proposed by Kiayias et al. [29]. Our model is analogous to the fully dynamic group signature one proposed by Bootle et al. [10]. In a FDGE scheme, the parties involved are the sender, the verifier, the group manager GM who manages the group of receivers, and the opening authority OA who is capable of identifying the recipients of ciphertexts. $\mathcal{R}$ is a public relation for which a FDGE should be verifiable. Receivers can join and leave the group at the choice of the GM. We assume that the GM will publish group information info_τ at the beginning of each time epoch τ. The information depicts changes to the group such as the existing group members or the revoked members at current epoch τ. It is required that anyone can verify the authenticity and well-formedness of the group information. In addition, by comparing the current group information with the previous one, it is possible to recover the list of members revoked from the group at the current epoch. We also assume that the epoch maintains the order in which the group information was published, i.e., info_{τ_1} precedes info_{τ_2} if $\tau_1 < \tau_2$.

Compared to [29], our model enables the GM to remove some users from the group through a group updating algorithm GUpdate. Another difference is that we avoid interaction by employing a non-interactive zero-knowledge (NIZK) proof, which has already been considered by Cathalo, Libert and Yung [15]. As highlighted by the authors, non-interaction is highly desirable as the sender, who might be required to repeat the proof with many verifiers, needs to maintain a state and remember all the random coins used to generate the ciphertext.

Formally, a FDGE that is verifiable for a public relation $\mathcal{R}$ consists of the following polynomial-time algorithms.

$\mathsf{Setup}_{\mathsf{init}}(1^\lambda)$ The algorithm takes as input the security parameter 1^λ and outputs a set of public parameters pp.

$\mathsf{Setup}_{\mathsf{OA}}(\mathsf{pp})$ This algorithm is run by the opening authority OA. It takes as input pp and outputs a key pair $(\mathsf{pk}_{\mathsf{OA}}, \mathsf{sk}_{\mathsf{OA}})$.

$\mathsf{Setup}_{\mathsf{GM}}(\mathsf{pp})$ This algorithm is run by the group manger GM. It takes as input the public parameters pp and outputs a key pair $(\mathsf{pk}_{\mathsf{GM}}, \mathsf{sk}_{\mathsf{GM}})$. Meanwhile, GM initializes the group information info and a public registration directory **reg**.

$\mathsf{G}_\mathcal{R}(1^\lambda)$ This randomized algorithm takes as input the security parameter λ and outputs public and secret parameters $(\mathsf{pk}_\mathcal{R}, \mathsf{sk}_\mathcal{R})$ for the relation $\mathcal{R}$. Note that $\mathsf{sk}_\mathcal{R}$ is an empty string if a publicly samplable relation $\mathcal{R}$ is considered.

$\mathsf{Sample}_\mathcal{R}(\mathsf{pk}_\mathcal{R}, \mathsf{sk}_\mathcal{R})$ This probabilistic algorithm takes $(\mathsf{pk}_\mathcal{R}, \mathsf{sk}_\mathcal{R})$ as input and outputs a statement and witness pair (x, w).

$\mathcal{R}(\mathsf{pk}_\mathcal{R}, x, w)$ The polynomial-time testing algorithm takes as input $(\mathsf{pk}_\mathcal{R}, x, w)$ and returns 1 if and only if (x, w) is in the relation based on the public parameter $\mathsf{pk}_\mathcal{R}$.

$\langle \mathsf{Join}, \mathsf{Issue}(\mathsf{sk}_{\mathsf{GM}}) \rangle (\mathsf{pk}_{\mathsf{GM}}, \mathsf{info}_{\tau_{\mathsf{current}}})$ This is an interactive protocol securely run between a user and the GM. Both the Join and Issue algorithms takes as inputs $\mathsf{pk}_{\mathsf{GM}}$ and $\mathsf{info}_{\tau_{\mathsf{current}}}$ at current time epoch τ_{current} while the the latter algorithm takes $\mathsf{sk}_{\mathsf{GM}}$ as an additional input. Upon successful completion, the algorithm Join outputs a user key pair $(\mathsf{pk}, \mathsf{sk})$ while Issue adds a new record in the directory **reg**. Note that GM may update group information and that **reg** may store information like user identifier or user public key that may be used by GM and OA for later updating and opening.

$\mathsf{GUpdate}(\mathsf{sk}_{\mathsf{GM}}, \mathcal{S}, \mathsf{info}_{\tau_{\mathsf{current}}}, \mathbf{reg})$ This algorithm is run by the GM who will advance the epoch and update the group information. Given the secret key $\mathsf{sk}_{\mathsf{GM}}$, a set $\mathcal{S}$ of active users to be deleted from the group, current group information $\mathsf{info}_{\tau_{\mathsf{current}}}$, and the directory **reg**, the GM computes new group information $\mathsf{info}_{\tau_{\mathsf{new}}}$ and may update the directory **reg** as well. If there is no change to the group information or $\mathcal{S}$ contains inactive users (who has never joined the group yet or who has been revoked from the group), this algorithm aborts.

$\mathsf{Enc}(\mathsf{pk}_{\mathsf{GM}}, \mathsf{pk}_{\mathsf{OA}}, \mathsf{info}_\tau, w, \mathsf{pk}, L)$ This randomized encryption algorithm is run by the sender who wishes to encrypt a witness w for its chosen user pk. It returns a ciphertext ψ with a certain label L. As in [29], L is a public string bound to the ciphertext that may contain some transaction related data or be empty. If pk is not an active user at current time epoch τ or $\mathcal{R}(\mathsf{pk}_\mathcal{R}, x, w) = 0$, this algorithm aborts. Let coins_ψ be the random coins used to generate ψ.

$\mathcal{P}(\mathsf{pp}, \mathsf{pk}_{\mathsf{GM}}, \mathsf{pk}_{\mathsf{OA}}, \mathsf{info}_\tau, \mathsf{pk}_\mathcal{R}, x, \psi, L, w, \mathsf{pk}, \mathsf{coins}_\psi)$ This randomized proof algorithm is run by the sender who acts as a prover and demonstrates the honest computation of ciphertext ψ. Given all the inputs, it outputs a proof π_ψ. The proof ensures that there exists a certified and active group member at time τ, who is able to decrypt ψ and obtain w' such that $\mathcal{R}(\mathsf{pk}_\mathcal{R}, x, w') = 1$, and whose public key is encrypted under $\mathsf{pk}_{\mathsf{OA}}$ and can be later revealed using the OA's secret key $\mathsf{sk}_{\mathsf{OA}}$.

$\mathcal{V}((\mathsf{pp}, \mathsf{pk}_{\mathsf{GM}}, \mathsf{pk}_{\mathsf{OA}}, \mathsf{info}_\tau, \mathsf{pk}_\mathcal{R}, x, \psi, L), \pi_\psi)$ This verification algorithm is run by any verifier who on input the tuple $(\mathsf{pp}, \mathsf{pk}_{\mathsf{GM}}, \mathsf{pk}_{\mathsf{OA}}, \mathsf{info}_\tau, \mathsf{pk}_\mathcal{R}, x, \psi, L)$ and a corresponding proof π_ψ outputs bit 1 or 0. If the output is 1, we say the proof π_ψ is valid.

$\mathsf{Dec}(\mathsf{info}_\tau, \mathsf{sk}, \psi, L)$ This decryption algorithm is run by the user in possession of the secret key sk. Given all the inputs, it outputs w' such that $\mathcal{R}(\mathsf{pk}_\mathcal{R}, x, w') = 1$ or $\bot$ otherwise.

$\mathsf{Open}(\mathsf{info}_\tau, \mathsf{sk}_{\mathsf{OA}}, \psi, L)$ This opening algorithm is run by the OA who holds the key $\mathsf{sk}_{\mathsf{OA}}$. Given the inputs, it returns an *active* user public key pk or $\bot$ to indicate opening failure.

To ease the notations, we additionally use the following algorithms in the security experiments.

$\mathsf{IsActive}(\mathsf{info}_\tau, \mathsf{pk})$ This algorithm returns 1 if user pk is an active user at time τ and 0 otherwise.

CORRECTNESS. Informally, correctness of a GE scheme requires that an honest proof of correct encryption is always valid, that the designated receiver can always recover the encrypted message, and that the GM is capable of identifying the receiver. We model this requirement in the experiment $\mathbf{Expt}_\mathcal{A}^{\mathsf{corr}}(1^\lambda)$. Below, we first define some oracles that are accessible to the adversary.

$\mathsf{AddU}(\mathsf{sk}_{\mathsf{GM}})$ This oracle adds an honest user to the group at current time τ_{current}. It simulates the interactive protocol $\langle\mathsf{Join}, \mathsf{Issue}(\mathsf{sk}_{\mathsf{GM}})\rangle(\mathsf{pk}_{\mathsf{GM}}, \mathsf{info}_{\tau_{\mathrm{current}}})$ and maintains an honest user list HUL. Let the output of Join be $(\mathsf{pk}, \mathsf{sk})$. It then adds pk to HUL.

$\mathsf{GUp}(\cdot)$ This oracle allows the adversary to remove a set of active users from the group at current time epoch τ_{current}. When a set $\mathcal{S}$ is queried, it advances the time epoch to τ_{new} and updates the group information to $\mathsf{info}_{\tau_{\mathrm{new}}}$ by executing the algorithm $\mathsf{GUpdate}(\mathsf{sk_{GM}}, \mathcal{S}, \mathsf{info}_{\tau_{current}}, \mathbf{reg})$. As the algorithm GUpdate, it may update the **reg**.

Definition 1. *Define* $\mathbf{Adv}_{\mathcal{A}}^{corr}(1^\lambda) = \Pr[\mathbf{Expt}_{\mathcal{A}}^{corr}(1^\lambda) = 1]$ *as the advantage of an adversary $\mathcal{A}$ against correctness in the experiment* $\mathbf{Expt}_{\mathcal{A}}^{corr}(1^\lambda)$. *A FDGE is correct if, for any PPT adversary $\mathcal{A}$, the advantage of $\mathcal{A}$ is negligible in λ.*

Experiment $\mathbf{Expt}_{\mathcal{A}}^{corr}(1^\lambda)$
   $\mathsf{pp} \leftarrow \mathsf{Setup_{init}}(1^\lambda)$; $(\mathsf{pk_{OA}}, \mathsf{sk_{OA}}) \leftarrow \mathsf{Setup_{OA}}(\mathsf{pp})$; $(\mathsf{pk_{GM}}, \mathsf{sk_{GM}}) \leftarrow \mathsf{Setup_{GM}}(\mathsf{pp})$.
   $(\mathsf{pk_{\mathcal{R}}}, \mathsf{sk_{\mathcal{R}}}) \leftarrow \mathsf{G_{\mathcal{R}}}(1^\lambda)$; $\mathsf{HUL} \leftarrow \emptyset$.
   $(\mathsf{pk}, \tau, x, w, L) \leftarrow \mathcal{A}^{\mathsf{AddU, GUp}}(\mathsf{pp}, \mathsf{pk_{OA}}, \mathsf{pk_{GM}}, \mathsf{pk_{\mathcal{R}}})$.
   If $\mathsf{pk} \notin \mathsf{HUL}$ or $\mathsf{info}_\tau = \perp$ or $\mathsf{IsActive}(\mathsf{info}_\tau, \mathsf{pk}) = 0$
                         or $\mathcal{R}(\mathsf{pk_{\mathcal{R}}}, x, w) = 0$, return 0.
   $\psi \leftarrow \mathsf{Enc}(\mathsf{pk_{GM}}, \mathsf{pk_{OA}}, \mathsf{info}_\tau, w, \mathsf{pk}, L)$.
   $\pi_\psi \leftarrow \mathcal{P}(\mathsf{pp}, \mathsf{pk_{GM}}, \mathsf{pk_{OA}}, \mathsf{info}_\tau, \mathsf{pk_{\mathcal{R}}}, x, \psi, L, w, \mathsf{pk}, \mathsf{coins}_\psi)$.
   $w' \leftarrow \mathsf{Dec}(\mathsf{info}_\tau, \mathsf{sk}, \psi, L)$; $\mathsf{pk}' \leftarrow \mathsf{Open}(\mathsf{info}_\tau, \mathsf{sk_{OA}}, \psi, L)$.
   If $\mathcal{V}((\mathsf{pp}, \mathsf{pk_{GM}}, \mathsf{pk_{OA}}, \mathsf{info}_\tau, \mathsf{pk_{\mathcal{R}}}, x, \psi, L), \pi_\psi) = 0$ or $w' \neq w$
                         or $\mathsf{pk}' \neq \mathsf{pk}$, return 1 otherwise return 0.

5.1   Formulation of the Security Requirements

We now present three security requirements: message secrecy, anonymity, and soundness for FDGE, which are carefully adapted from the dynamic case. We formulate those requirements through experiments that are run between a challenger and an adversary. As mentioned earlier, the adversary is empowered with attack capability to the maximum extent possible. Specifically, in the definition of message secrecy and anonymity, it fully corrupts GM and/or OA and generates keys arbitrarily on behalf of them. Regarding soundness, only partial corruption of the OA whose key is still honestly generated is allowed. Details of the security requirements are described below.

MESSAGE SECRECY. This security notion protects the appointed receiver from a malicious adversary who tries to extract the information about the encrypted message. It requires that the adversary cannot distinguish a ciphertext that is an encryption of a real witness or encryption of a randomly chosen one even though it could fully corrupt the GM, the OA, and all group members except one that is chosen as the receiver. We model this requirement using $\mathbf{Expt}_{\mathcal{A}}^{sec-b}(1^\lambda)$ for $b \in \{0, 1\}$. In the following, we define some oracles that will be used in the experiment.

USER() This oracle simulates the algorithm Join, when interacted with adversary $\mathcal{A}$ who plays the role of GM, to introduce an honest user to the group at current time $\tau_{current}$. it maintains an honest user list HUL. Let the output of this oracle be $(\mathsf{pk}, \mathsf{sk})$ and add pk to HUL.

RevealU($\cdot$) This oracle allows the adversary to learn an honest user secret key. It maintains a bad user list BUL. When a user public key pk is queried, it returns the corresponding secret key sk and adds pk to BUL if pk $\notin$ BUL, and aborts otherwise.

$\mathsf{CH}_{\mathsf{ror}}^b(\tau, \mathsf{pk}, w, L)$ This is a real-or-random challenge oracle which is only called once. It returns $(\psi, \mathsf{coins}_\psi)$ such that $\psi \leftarrow \mathsf{Enc}(\mathsf{pk}_{\mathsf{GM}}, \mathsf{pk}_{\mathsf{OA}}, \mathsf{info}_\tau, w, \mathsf{pk}, L)$ if $b = 1$, whereas if $b = 0$ $\psi \leftarrow \mathsf{Enc}(\mathsf{pk}_{\mathsf{GM}}, \mathsf{pk}_{\mathsf{OA}}, \mathsf{info}_\tau, w', \mathsf{pk}, L)$ where w' is sampled uniformly from the space of all possible plaintexts. In both cases, coins_ψ are the random coins used for the computation of the challenged ciphertext ψ.

$\mathsf{DEC}(\mathsf{sk}, \cdot)$ This is an oracle for the decryption function Dec. When (ψ, τ, L) is queried to this oracle, it returns the output of $\mathsf{Dec}(\mathsf{info}_\tau, \mathsf{sk}, \psi, L)$. When a tuple $(\mathsf{pk}, \psi, \tau, L)$ should be rejected by this oracle, we write $\mathsf{DEC}^{\neg(\psi, \tau, L,)}(\cdot)$.

$\mathsf{PROVE}_{\mathcal{P}, \mathcal{P}'}^b(\mathsf{pk}, \tau, \mathsf{pk}_{\mathcal{R}}, x, w, L, \psi, \mathsf{coins}_\psi)$ This oracle can be invoked a polynomial number times. It generates proofs of validity of the challenged ciphertext. If $b = 1$, let $\pi_\psi \leftarrow \mathcal{P}(\mathsf{pp}, \mathsf{pk}_{\mathsf{GM}}, \mathsf{pk}_{\mathsf{OA}}, \mathsf{info}_\tau, \mathsf{pk}_{\mathcal{R}}, x, \psi, L, w, \mathsf{pk}, \mathsf{coins}_\psi)$ and return the output π_ψ. If $b = 0$, it runs a simulator $\mathcal{P}'$ that takes the same inputs as $\mathcal{P}$ except (w, coins_ψ) and returns whatever $\mathcal{P}'$ outputs.

In the experiment $\mathbf{Expt}_{\mathcal{A}}^{\mathsf{sec}-b}(1^\lambda)$, the adversary $\mathcal{A}$ fully controls the GM and the OA, and enrolls honest users to the group by interacting with the oracle USER. It is entitled to corrupt at most all but one honest users by querying the RevealU oracle and to update the group information, insofar as info and $\mathbf{reg}$ are well-formed. At some point, the adversary chooses a targeted receiver pk^* and has access to the DEC oracle with respect to pk^*. It then specifies a certain epoch τ^*, a label L^* together with the relation $\mathsf{pk}_{\mathcal{R}}^*$ and the statement witness pair (x^*, w^*). Afterwards, the challenger encrypts the witness w^* if $b = 1$ or a random message if $b = 0$ to the receiver pk^*, and sends the resultant ciphertext ψ^* to $\mathcal{A}$. After receiving it, $\mathcal{A}$ is allowed to query the PROVE oracle for proofs of its validity and still has access to the DEC oracle with respect to pk^* with the natural restriction that (ψ^*, τ^*, L^*) is forbidden. Finally, $\mathcal{A}$ is asked to guess the challenger's choice.

Definition 2. *Let the advantage of an adversary $\mathcal{A}$ against message secrecy be* $\mathbf{Adv}_{\mathcal{A}}^{\mathsf{sec}-b}(1^\lambda) = |\Pr[\mathbf{Expt}_{\mathcal{A}}^{\mathsf{sec}-1}(1^\lambda) = 1] - \Pr[\mathbf{Expt}_{\mathcal{A}}^{\mathsf{sec}-0}(1^\lambda) = 1]|$. *A FDGE satisfies message secrecy if, for any PPT adversary $\mathcal{A}$, the advantage of $\mathcal{A}$ is negligible in λ.*

Experiment $\mathbf{Expt}_{\mathcal{A}}^{\mathsf{sec}-b}(1^\lambda)$

$\quad \mathsf{pp} \leftarrow \mathsf{Setup}_{\mathsf{init}}(1^\lambda); (\mathsf{aux}, \mathsf{pk}_{\mathsf{GM}}, \mathsf{pk}_{\mathsf{OA}}) \leftarrow \mathcal{A}(\mathsf{pp}); \mathsf{HUL} \leftarrow \emptyset, \mathsf{BUL} \leftarrow \emptyset.$

$\quad$ Throughout the experiment, if info or $\mathbf{reg}$ is not well-formed, return 0.

$\quad (\mathsf{pk}^*, \mathsf{aux}) \leftarrow \mathcal{A}^{\mathsf{USER}, \mathsf{RevealU}}(\mathsf{aux}); \text{ if } \mathsf{pk}^* \notin \mathsf{HUL} \setminus \mathsf{BUL}, \text{ return } 0.$

$\quad$ Let sk^* be the corresponding secret key of pk^*.

$\quad (\tau^*, \mathsf{pk}_{\mathcal{R}}^*, x^*, w^*, L^*) \leftarrow \mathcal{A}^{\mathsf{DEC}(\mathsf{sk}^*, \cdot)}(\mathsf{aux}).$

$\quad$ If $\mathsf{IsActive}(\mathsf{info}_{\tau^*}, \mathsf{pk}^*) = 0$ or $\mathcal{R}(\mathsf{pk}_{\mathcal{R}}^*, x^*, w^*) = 0$ return 0.

$\quad (\psi^*, \mathsf{coins}_{\psi^*}) \leftarrow \mathsf{CH}_{\mathsf{ror}}^b(\tau^*, \mathsf{pk}^*, w^*, L^*).$

Let $\eth^* = (\mathsf{pk}^*, \tau^*, \mathsf{pk}_{\mathcal{R}}^*, x^*, w^*, L^*, \psi^*, \mathsf{coins}_{\psi^*})$.

$b' \leftarrow \mathcal{A}^{\mathsf{PRVOE}_{\mathcal{P}, \mathcal{P}'}^{b}(\eth^*), \mathsf{DEC}^{\neg(\psi^*, \tau^*, L^*)}(\mathsf{sk}^*, \cdot)}(\mathsf{aux}, \psi^*)$.

Return b'.

ANONYMITY. This notion aims to prevent the adversary from learning information about the identity of the receiver of a ciphertext. It requires that an adversary without possession of the secret key of OA is not capable of distinguishing which one of two group members of its choice is the recipient of a ciphertext. Note that the adversary is forbidden from corrupting these two challenged members since they know whether a ciphertext is intended for them by simply decrypting it. We model this requirement in $\mathbf{Expt}_{\mathcal{A}}^{\mathsf{anon}-b}(1^\lambda)$ for $b \in \{0, 1\}$, which will utilize the following challenge oracle $\mathsf{CH}_{\mathsf{anon}}^{b}$ and opening oracle OPEN.

$\mathsf{CH}_{\mathsf{anon}}^{b}(\tau, \mathsf{pk}_0, \mathsf{pk}_1, w, L)$ This is a challenge oracle that can be called only once. It returns $(\psi, \mathsf{coins}_{\psi})$ such that $\psi \leftarrow \mathsf{Enc}(\mathsf{pk}_{\mathsf{GM}}, \mathsf{pk}_{\mathsf{OA}}, \mathsf{info}_\tau, w, \mathsf{pk}_b, L)$.

$\mathsf{OPEN}(\mathsf{sk}_{\mathsf{OA}}, \cdot)$ This is an oracle for the opening algorithm Open. When decryption of a tuple (ψ, τ, L) is requested, it returns $\mathsf{Open}(\mathsf{info}_\tau, \mathsf{sk}_{\mathsf{OA}}, \psi, L)$. When a tuple (ψ, τ, L) is forbidden, we write $\mathsf{OPEN}^{\neg(\psi, \tau, L)}(\mathsf{sk}_{\mathsf{OA}}, \cdot)$.

In the experiment, the adversary $\mathcal{A}$ can fully corrupt the GM. By interacting with the oracles $\mathsf{USER}, \mathsf{RevealU}$, it can also introduce honest users to the group and learn up to all but two secret keys at a later point. As in the $\mathbf{Expt}_{\mathcal{A}}^{\mathsf{sec}-b}(1^\lambda)$, $\mathcal{A}$ is allowed to update the group at its will, provided that the group information info and **reg** are well-formed. Moreover, $\mathcal{A}$ has access to the $\mathsf{OPEN}(\mathsf{sk}_{\mathsf{OA}}, \cdot)$ oracle. At some point, $\mathcal{A}$ specifies two targeted receivers $\mathsf{pk}_0^*, \mathsf{pk}_1^*$ and is granted access to the DEC oracle with respect to both recipients. Next, it outputs a specific epoch τ^* and $(\mathsf{pk}_{\mathcal{R}}^*, x^*, w^*)$ to the challenger, who will encrypt the witness to receiver pk_b^*. Thereafter, the challenger sends the challenge ciphertext ψ^* to $\mathcal{A}$. The latter is further allowed to query the proof of validity of ψ^* and accessible to oracles $\mathsf{DEC}(\mathsf{sk}_0^*, \cdot), \mathsf{DEC}(\mathsf{sk}_1^*, \cdot), \mathsf{OPEN}(\mathsf{sk}_{\mathsf{OA}}, \cdot)$ with the constraint that the tuple (ψ^*, τ^*, L^*) is not queried to any of the oracles. Lastly, $\mathcal{A}$ is asked to guess which one of the two users is the challenger's choice.

Definition 3. *Define the advantage of an adversary $\mathcal{A}$ against anonymity as* $\mathbf{Adv}_{\mathcal{A}}^{\mathsf{anon}}(1^\lambda) = |\Pr[\mathbf{Expt}_{\mathcal{A}}^{\mathsf{anon}-1}(1^\lambda) = 1] - \Pr[\mathbf{Expt}_{\mathcal{A}}^{\mathsf{anon}-0}(1^\lambda) = 1]|$. *A FDGE satisfies anonymity if, for any PPT adversary $\mathcal{A}$, the advantage of $\mathcal{A}$ is negligible in λ.*

Experiment $\mathbf{Expt}_{\mathcal{A}}^{\mathsf{anon}-b}(1^\lambda)$

$\mathsf{pp} \leftarrow \mathsf{Setup}_{\mathsf{init}}(1^\lambda); (\mathsf{pk}_{\mathsf{OA}}, \mathsf{sk}_{\mathsf{OA}}) \leftarrow \mathsf{Setup}_{\mathsf{OA}}(\mathsf{pp}); (\mathsf{aux}, \mathsf{pk}_{\mathsf{GM}}) \leftarrow \mathcal{A}(\mathsf{pp}, \mathsf{pk}_{\mathsf{OA}})$.

$\mathsf{HUL} \leftarrow \emptyset, \mathsf{BUL} \leftarrow \emptyset$.

Throughout the experiment, if info or **reg** is not well-formed, return 0.

$(\mathsf{pk}_0^*, \mathsf{pk}_1^*, \mathsf{aux}) \leftarrow \mathcal{A}^{\mathsf{USER}, \mathsf{RevealU}, \mathsf{OPEN}(\mathsf{sk}_{\mathsf{OA}}, \cdot)}(\mathsf{aux})$.

If $\mathsf{pk}_0^* \notin \mathsf{HUL} \setminus \mathsf{BUL}$ or $\mathsf{pk}_1^* \notin \mathsf{HUL} \setminus \mathsf{BUL}$, return 0.

Let sk_0^* and sk_1^* be the secret keys of pk_0^* and pk_1^*, respectively.

$(\tau^*, \mathsf{pk}_{\mathcal{R}}^*, x^*, w^*, L^*, \mathsf{aux}) \leftarrow \mathcal{A}^{\mathsf{DEC}(\mathsf{sk}_0^*, \cdot), \mathsf{DEC}(\mathsf{sk}_1^*, \cdot), \mathsf{OPEN}(\mathsf{sk}_{\mathsf{OA}}, \cdot)}(\mathsf{aux})$.

If $\mathsf{IsActive}(\mathsf{info}_{\tau^*}, \mathsf{pk}_0^*) = 0$ or $\mathsf{IsActive}(\mathsf{info}_{\tau^*}, \mathsf{pk}_1^*) = 0$ or

$$\mathcal{R}(\mathsf{pk}_{\mathcal{R}}^*, x^*, w^*) = 0 \text{ return } 0.$$

$(\psi^*, \mathsf{coins}_{\psi^*}) \leftarrow \mathsf{CH}_{\mathsf{anon}}^b(\tau^*, \mathsf{pk}_0^*, \mathsf{pk}_1^*, w^*, L^*).$

Let $\eth^* = (\mathsf{pp}, \mathsf{pk}_{\mathsf{GM}}, \mathsf{pk}_{\mathsf{OA}}, \mathsf{info}_{\tau^*}, \mathsf{pk}_{\mathcal{R}}^*, x^*, \psi^*, L^*, w^*, \mathsf{pk}_b^*, \mathsf{coins}_{\psi^*}).$

Let $t^* = (\psi^*, \tau^*, L^*).$

$b' \leftarrow \mathcal{A}^{\mathcal{P}(\eth^*), \mathsf{DEC}^{\neg t^*}(\mathsf{sk}_0^*, \cdot), \mathsf{DEC}^{\neg t^*}(\mathsf{sk}_1^*, \cdot), \mathsf{OPEN}^{\neg t^*}(\mathsf{sk}_{\mathsf{OA}}, \cdot)}(\mathsf{aux}, \psi^*).$

Return b'.

SOUNDNESS. This notion requires that the adversary cannot generate a ciphertext with a valid proof associated with time epoch τ such that (1) the opening of the ciphertext is a public key that does not belong to any active group member at time τ, (2) the revealed public key is not in the language $\mathcal{L}_{\mathsf{pk}}^{\mathsf{pp}}$ of valid public keys, (3) the ciphertext is not in the space $\mathcal{L}_{\mathsf{ciphertext}}^{(\mathsf{pk}_{\mathsf{GM}}, \mathsf{pk}_{\mathsf{OA}}, \tau, \mathsf{pk}_{\mathcal{R}}, x, L, \mathsf{pk})}$ of valid ciphertexts. Note that $\mathcal{L}_{\mathsf{pk}}^{\mathsf{pp}} = \{\mathsf{pk} : \exists \mathsf{sk} \text{ such that } (\mathsf{pk}, \mathsf{sk}) \text{ is a valid user key pair}\}$ and that

$$\mathcal{L}_{\mathsf{ciphertext}}^{(\mathsf{pk}_{\mathsf{GM}}, \mathsf{pk}_{\mathsf{OA}}, \tau, \mathsf{pk}_{\mathcal{R}}, x, L, \mathsf{pk})} = \{\psi : \exists\, w \text{ such that } \psi = \mathsf{Enc}(\mathsf{pk}_{\mathsf{GM}}, \mathsf{pk}_{\mathsf{OA}}, \mathsf{info}_\tau, w, \mathsf{pk}, L),$$
$$\mathcal{R}(\mathsf{pk}_{\mathcal{R}}, x, w) = 1, \text{ and } \mathsf{IsActive}(\mathsf{info}_\tau, \mathsf{pk}) = 1\}.$$

We model this requirement in the experiment $\mathbf{Expt}_{\mathcal{A}}^{\mathsf{sound}}(1^\lambda)$. The adversary is given the secret key of OA and is permitted to adaptively register users to the group through oracle queries $\mathsf{REG}(\mathsf{sk}_{\mathsf{GM}})$, as defined below. In addition, it can remove some users from the group by querying the oracle $\mathsf{GUp}(\cdot)$.

$\mathsf{REG}(\mathsf{sk}_{\mathsf{GM}})$ This oracle simulates the GM and runs the algorithm Issue. When queried by adversary $\mathcal{A}$ who plays the role of a user, it interacts with $\mathcal{A}$ and if successful registers an adversarially controlled user to the group at current time τ_{current}. As the algorithm Issue, it maintains a public directory **reg** and may update the group information as well.

Definition 4. *Define* $\mathbf{Adv}_{\mathcal{A}}^{\mathsf{sound}}(1^\lambda) = \Pr[\mathbf{Expt}_{\mathcal{A}}^{\mathsf{sound}}(1^\lambda) = 1]$ *as the advantage of an adversary $\mathcal{A}$ against soundness in the experiment* $\mathbf{Expt}_{\mathcal{A}}^{\mathsf{sound}}(1^\lambda)$. *A FDGE satisfies soundness if, for any PPT adversary $\mathcal{A}$, the advantage of $\mathcal{A}$ is negligible in λ.*

Experiment $\mathbf{Expt}_{\mathcal{A}}^{\mathsf{sound}}(1^\lambda)$

$\mathsf{pp} \leftarrow \mathsf{Setup}_{\mathsf{init}}(1^\lambda);\ (\mathsf{pk}_{\mathsf{OA}}, \mathsf{sk}_{\mathsf{OA}}) \leftarrow \mathsf{Setup}_{\mathsf{OA}}(\mathsf{pp});\ (\mathsf{pk}_{\mathsf{GM}}, \mathsf{sk}_{\mathsf{GM}}) \leftarrow$
$\mathsf{Setup}_{\mathsf{GM}}(\mathsf{pp}).$

$(\tau, \mathsf{pk}_{\mathcal{R}}, x, \psi, L, \pi_\psi, \mathsf{aux}) \leftarrow \mathcal{A}^{\mathsf{REG}, \mathsf{GUp}}(\mathsf{pp}, \mathsf{pk}_{\mathsf{GM}}, \mathsf{pk}_{\mathsf{OA}}, \mathsf{sk}_{\mathsf{OA}}).$

If $\mathcal{V}((\mathsf{pp}, \mathsf{pk}_{\mathsf{GM}}, \mathsf{pk}_{\mathsf{OA}}, \mathsf{info}_\tau, \mathsf{pk}_{\mathcal{R}}, x, \psi, L), \pi_\psi) = 0$, return 0.

$\mathsf{pk} \leftarrow \mathsf{Open}(\mathsf{info}_\tau, \mathsf{sk}_{\mathsf{OA}}, \psi, L).$

If $\mathsf{IsActive}(\mathsf{info}_\tau, \mathsf{pk}) = 0$ or $\mathsf{pk} \notin \mathcal{L}_{\mathsf{pk}}^{\mathsf{pp}}$ or $\psi \notin \mathcal{L}_{\mathsf{ciphertext}}^{(\mathsf{pk}_{\mathsf{GM}}, \mathsf{pk}_{\mathsf{OA}}, \mathsf{pk}_{\mathcal{R}}, x, L, \mathsf{pk})}$,
return 1 else return 0.

6 A Code-Based Fully Dynamic Group Encryption Scheme

To build a code-based FDGE scheme, we require a key-private CCA2-secure encryption scheme [3], a digital signature scheme, and a zero-knowledge proof (argument) of knowledge protocol. In this paper, we work with the ZKAoK within Stern's framework [49]. In terms of the encryption scheme, we choose to work with the McEliece cryptosystem [39], specifically the randomized variant from [46]. The latter indeed has pseudorandom ciphertexts, which implies key-private CPA-security. To further achieve CCA2-security, we apply the Naor-Yung double encryption technique [44]. Note that there are other CCA2-secure variants of McEliece scheme like [16,19,30]. However, they either do not operate well in the Stern's framework or are completely impractical. Regarding the digital signature, we employ the Merkle-tree accumulator suggested in [45]. Precisely, when a user requests to join the group, it first generates its encryption key pair $(\mathsf{pk}, \mathsf{sk})$, and sends pk and its non-zero hash value $\mathbf{d}$ to GM. The latter, if accepts, then computes the Merkle tree root, where the leaf nodes are the hash values of all users. The witness for $\mathbf{d}$ is the proof of user's membership. To achieve dynamicity, following [38], we use an updating algorithm akin to [38] to set up the system so that (1) the value of the leaf node associated with a user who has not joined or who has been removed from the group is $\mathbf{0}$ (2) while it is updated to $\mathbf{d}$ when this user joins the group. When a sender encrypts messages to a user at some epoch, it has to show that the user's *non-zero* hash value is accumulated in the tree in this epoch. This mechanism effectively distinguish active users who are valid recipients of ciphertexts from those who are not.

As in the KTY model [29], we also require that user encryption keys are valid (i.e., in the language $\mathcal{L}_{\mathsf{pk}}^{\mathsf{pp}}$). One possible solution would be requiring a proof of knowledge of the McEliece decryption key when a user joins the group. This is however quite complicated and inefficient. Instead, GM encrypts random messages under the user's encryption key and asks the user to output the correct messages. By choosing the parameters properly, the running time of guessing correctly the messages if the user does not know the underlying decryption key is exponential. This then enforces validity of user encryption keys.

6.1 Description of the Scheme

Our scheme allows encryption witness $\mathbf{w} \in \{0,1\}^p$ that satisfies the permissive relation R_{permit} and/or the prohibitive relation R_{prohibit}. For simplicity, we present R_{permit} in the following construction. The details are described below.

$\mathsf{Setup}_{\mathsf{init}}(1^\lambda)$ On input the security parameter 1^λ, this algorithm proceeds as follows.

- Specify an integer $\ell = \ell(\lambda)$ that determines the maximum expected number $N = 2^\ell$ of potential users.

- Choose $n = \mathcal{O}(\lambda)$, $c = \mathcal{O}(1)$ such that c divides n, and set $m = 2^c \cdot \frac{2n}{c}$. Choose an integer $t_m < m$.

- Choose $t_1 = t_1(\lambda)$, $k_1 = k_1(\lambda)$ and $t_2 = t_2(\lambda)$, $k_2 = k_2(\lambda)$ such that (n, k_1, t_1), (n, k_2, t_2) are two sets of parameters for the McEliece encryption scheme.

- Sample a random matrix $\mathbf{B} \xleftarrow{\$} \mathbb{Z}_2^{n \times m}$ that specifies a hash function $h_{\mathbf{B}}$ that will be used build Merkle tree (see the full version of this paper, as well as [45]).

- Pick a statistical hiding and computationally binding commitment scheme $\mathsf{COM} : \{0,1\}^* \to \{0,1\}^n$ like the one in [45, Section 3.1]. This will serve as a building block for the ZK argument systems.

- Let $\mathcal{H}_{\mathsf{FS}} : \{0,1\}^* \to \{1,2,3\}^\kappa$, where $\kappa = \omega(\log \lambda)$, be a hash function that will be modeled as a random oracle in the Fiat-Shamir transforms [21].

Output public parameters

$$\mathsf{pp} = \{N, \ell, n, c, m, t_m, t_1, k_1, p, t_2, k_2, v, \mathbf{B}, \mathsf{COM}, \kappa, \mathcal{H}_{\mathsf{FS}}\}.$$

$\mathsf{Setup}_{\mathsf{OA}}(\mathsf{pp})$ This algorithm is run by the OA. Given the input pp, it triggers the McEliece key generation algorithm $\mathsf{KeyGen}_{\mathsf{ME}}(n, k_1, t_1)$ (see the full version) twice to obtain encryption key pairs $(\mathbf{G}_{\mathsf{oa},0}, \mathsf{sk}_{\mathsf{ME}}^{(\mathsf{oa},0)})$ and $(\mathbf{G}_{\mathsf{oa},1}, \mathsf{sk}_{\mathsf{ME}}^{(\mathsf{oa},1)})$. Set $\mathsf{pk}_{\mathsf{OA}} = (\mathbf{G}_{\mathsf{oa},0}, \mathbf{G}_{\mathsf{oa},1})$ and $\mathsf{sk}_{\mathsf{OA}} = (\mathsf{sk}_{\mathsf{ME}}^{(\mathsf{oa},0)}, \mathsf{sk}_{\mathsf{ME}}^{(\mathsf{oa},1)})$.

$\mathsf{Setup}_{\mathsf{GM}}(\mathsf{pp})$ This algorithm is run by the GM. It samples $\mathsf{sk}_{\mathsf{GM}} \xleftarrow{\$} \mathsf{B}(m, t_m)$, then computes $\mathsf{pk}_{\mathsf{GM}} = \mathbf{B} \cdot \mathsf{sk}_{\mathsf{GM}} \bmod 2$, and outputs $(\mathsf{pk}_{\mathsf{GM}}, \mathsf{sk}_{\mathsf{GM}})$. It also initializes the following.

- Let the registration table be $\mathbf{reg} := (\mathbf{reg}[0], \mathbf{reg}[1], \ldots, \mathbf{reg}[N-1])$, where for each $i \in [0, N-1]$: $\mathbf{reg}[i][1] = \mathbf{0}^n$, $\mathbf{reg}[i][2] = -1$, and $\mathbf{reg}[i][3] = -1$. Here, $\mathbf{reg}[i][1]$ denotes the hash value of the public encryption key of a registered user while $\mathbf{reg}[i][2], \mathbf{reg}[i][3]$ represent the epoch at which the user joins and leaves the group, respectively.

- Construct a Merkle tree $\mathcal{T}$ on top of $\mathbf{reg}[0][1], \ldots, \mathbf{reg}[N-1][1]$. (Note that $\mathcal{T}$ is an all-zero tree at this stage, when a new user joins the group, it will affect the Merkle tree.)

- Initialize a counter of registered users $j := 0$.

Then, GM outputs its public key $\mathsf{pk}_{\mathsf{GM}}$ and announces $\mathbf{reg}$ and the initial group information $\mathsf{info} = \emptyset$ while keeping $\mathcal{T}$ and j for himself. We remark that $\mathbf{reg}$ and info are visible to everyone but only editable by a party who knows $\mathsf{sk}_{\mathsf{GM}}$. In addition, anyone is able to verify the well-formedness of $\mathbf{reg}$ and info.

$\langle \mathsf{G}_{\mathcal{R}}, \mathsf{Sample}_{\mathcal{R}} \rangle$ The algorithm $\mathsf{G}_{\mathcal{R}}(1^\lambda, \mathsf{pp})$ proceeds by sampling parameters t, k for the relation R_{permit} (8). Let $(\mathsf{pk}_{\mathcal{R}}, \mathsf{sk}_{\mathcal{R}}) = ((p, t, k), \epsilon)$. Given $\mathsf{pk}_{\mathcal{R}}$, the algorithm $\mathsf{Sample}_{\mathcal{R}}$ outputs a set of keywords $S = \{s_1, \ldots, s_k\}$, $\mathbf{w} \in \mathbb{Z}_2^p$ such that $(S, \mathbf{w}) \in R_{\mathsf{permit}}$.

$\langle$Join, Issue$\rangle$. This is an interactive protocol securely run between a user and the GM. If a user requests to join the group at epoch τ, he will follow steps below.

1. The user first generates its encryption key pair. It runs McEliece key generation $\mathsf{KeyGen}_{\mathsf{ME}}(n, k_2, t_2)$ twice, obtaining $(\mathbf{G}_0, \mathsf{sk}_{\mathsf{ME}}^{(0)})$ and $(\mathbf{G}_1, \mathsf{sk}_{\mathsf{ME}}^{(1)})$. Set encryption key $\mathsf{pk}' = (\mathbf{G}_0, \mathbf{G}_1)$ and secret key $\mathsf{sk} = (\mathsf{sk}_{\mathsf{ME}}^{(0)}, \mathsf{sk}_{\mathsf{ME}}^{(1)})$.

2. It then computes the hash of its encryption key pk'. For $b \in \{0, 1\}$, write $\mathbf{G}_b = [\mathbf{g}_{k_2 b} | \cdots | \mathbf{g}_{k_2 b + k_2 - 1}]$. Let $D = \{\mathbf{g}_0, \mathbf{g}_1, \ldots, \mathbf{g}_{2k_2 - 1}\}$. It then runs the accumulation algorithm $\mathsf{Accu}_{\mathbf{B}}(D)$ (see the full version) to build a (sub)-Merkle tree based on D and the hash function $h_{\mathbf{B}}$, obtaining an accumulated hash value $\mathbf{d} \in \mathbb{Z}_2^n$. We call $\mathbf{d}$ the hash of pk'. If there is no ambiguity, we sometimes write $\mathsf{Accu}_{\mathbf{B}}(\mathsf{pk}')$ instead of $\mathsf{Accu}_{\mathbf{B}}(D)$.

3. If $\mathbf{d} = \mathbf{0}^n$, the user repeats Step 1 and 2. Otherwise, he sends $(\mathsf{pk}', \mathbf{d})$ to the GM.

Upon receiving the tuple $(\mathsf{pk}', \mathbf{d})$ from the user, the GM first computes the ranks r_1, r_2 of $\mathbf{G}_0, \mathbf{G}_1$, respectively, and $\mathbf{d}' = \mathsf{Accu}_{\mathbf{B}}(\mathsf{pk}')$. If $r_1 \neq k_2$ or $r_2 \neq k_2$ or $\mathbf{d}' \neq \mathbf{d}$ or $\mathbf{d}' = \mathbf{0}^n$, GM rejects. Otherwise, the two parties proceed as follows.

1. First, GM encrypts two random messages by running the deterministic McEliece encryption algorithm using the key pk'. It first samples $\mathbf{m}_0, \mathbf{m}_1 \xleftarrow{\$} \mathbb{Z}_2^{k_2}$ and $\mathbf{e}_0, \mathbf{e}_1 \xleftarrow{\$} \mathsf{B}(n, t_2)$, then computes $\mathbf{y}_0 = \mathbf{G}_0 \cdot \mathbf{m}_0 \oplus \mathbf{e}_0, \mathbf{y}_1 = \mathbf{G}_1 \cdot \mathbf{m}_1 \oplus \mathbf{e}_1$, and sends $\mathbf{y}_0, \mathbf{y}_1$ to the user.

2. Upon receiving the ciphertexts, user runs the deterministic McEliece decryption algorithm, obtaining $\mathbf{m}_0', \mathbf{m}_1'$. The user then sends $\mathbf{m}_0', \mathbf{m}_1'$ to the GM.

3. If $\mathbf{m}_0' \neq \mathbf{m}_0$ or $\mathbf{m}_1' \neq \mathbf{m}_1$, GM rejects. Otherwise GM issues an identifier to the user as $\mathsf{uid} = \mathsf{bin}(j) \in \{0, 1\}^\ell$. The user then sets his public key as $\mathsf{pk} = (\mathsf{pk}', \mathsf{bin}(j))$. From now on, we write $\mathsf{pk}_j' = (\mathbf{G}_{j,0}, \mathbf{G}_{j,1}), \mathsf{sk}_j = (\mathsf{sk}_{\mathsf{ME}}^{(j,0)}, \mathsf{sk}_{\mathsf{ME}}^{(j,1)})$ to distinguish keys of different users.

4. GM also performs the following updates:
   - Update $\mathcal{T}$ by running the algorithm $\mathsf{TUpdate}_{\mathbf{B}}(\mathsf{bin}(j), \mathbf{d})$.
   - Register the user to table $\mathbf{reg}$ as $\mathbf{reg}[j][1] := \mathbf{d}$; $\mathbf{reg}[j][2] := \tau$.
   - Increase the counter $j := j + 1$.

$\mathsf{GUpdate}(\mathsf{sk}_{\mathsf{GM}}, \mathcal{S}, \mathsf{info}_{\tau_{\mathrm{current}}}, \mathbf{reg})$ This algorithm is run by GM to update the group information while also advancing the epoch to τ_{new}. It works as follows.

1. Let the set $\mathcal{S}$ contain all the identifiers of registered users to be revoked. If $\mathcal{S} = \emptyset$, then go to Step 2.

   Otherwise, $\mathcal{S} = \{i_1, \ldots, i_r\}$, for some $i_1, \ldots, i_r \in [0, N - 1]$. Then, for all $t \in [r]$, GM runs $\mathsf{TUpdate}_{\mathbf{B}}(\mathsf{bin}(i_t), \mathbf{0}^n)$ to update the tree $\mathcal{T}$. Meanwhile, GM updates $\mathbf{reg}[j][3] = \tau_{\mathrm{new}}$.

2. At this point, each of the zero leaves in the tree $\mathcal{T}$ corresponds to either a revoked user or a potential user who has not yet registered. In other words, only active users in the new epoch τ_{new} have non-zero hashes of their encryption keys, denoted by $\{\mathbf{d}_j\}_j$, accumulated in the root $\mathbf{u}_{\tau_{\text{new}}}$ of the updated tree.

For each j, let $w^{(j)} \in \{0,1\}^\ell \times (\{0,1\}^n)^\ell$ be the witness for the fact that $\mathbf{d}_j$ is accumulated in $\mathbf{u}_{\tau_{\text{new}}}$. Then GM publishes the group information of the new epoch as:

$$\text{info}_{\tau_{\text{new}}} = \left(\mathbf{u}_{\tau_{\text{new}}}, \{w^{(j)}\}_j\right).$$

We remark that even though $\text{info}_{\tau_{\text{new}}}$ can be as large as $\mathcal{O}(\lambda \cdot 2^\ell \cdot \ell)$, it is not necessary for the sender or verifier to download them all. In deed, the sender when running the $\mathcal{P}$ algorithm only needs to download the respective witness $w^{(j)}$ of size $\mathcal{O}(\lambda \cdot \ell)$ bits. Meanwhile, the verifier who runs the $\mathcal{V}$ algorithm only needs to download $\mathbf{u}_{\tau_{\text{new}}}$ of size $\mathcal{O}(\lambda)$ bits. It is also worth noting that one is able to verify the well-formedness of registration table **reg** from group information $\text{info}_{\tau_{\text{current}}}$ and $\text{info}_{\tau_{\text{new}}}$[4], and vice versa[5].

$\text{Enc}(\text{pk}_{\text{GM}}, \text{pk}_{\text{OA}}, \text{info}_\tau, \mathbf{w}, \text{pk}, L)$ $\text{pk}_{\text{OA}} = (\mathbf{G}_{\text{oa},0}, \mathbf{G}_{\text{oa},1})$, $\text{pk} = (\text{pk}'_j, \text{bin}(j))$ for some $j \in [0, N-1]$ and let $L \in \{0,1\}^*$. This algorithm is run by a sender who wishes to send a message $\mathbf{w} \in \mathbb{Z}_2^p$ such that $(S, \mathbf{w}) \in R_{\text{permit}}$ to a chosen user j with encryption key pk'_j. If user j is an active user at current epoch τ, the sender downloads the corresponding witness $w^{(j)} = (\text{bin}(j), (\mathbf{w}_\ell, \cdots, \mathbf{w}_1))$ from info_τ and performs the following steps.

1. It first encrypts the message $\mathbf{w}$ under the encryption key pk'_j.
   - Parse $\text{pk}'_j = (\mathbf{G}_{j,0}, \mathbf{G}_{j,1})$.
   - Sample randomnesses $\mathbf{r}_{w,0}, \mathbf{r}_{w,1} \xleftarrow{\$} \mathbb{Z}_2^{k_2-p}$ and noises $\mathbf{e}_{w,0}, \mathbf{e}_{w,1} \xleftarrow{\$} B(n, t_2)$.
   - For $b \in \{0,1\}$, compute

$$\mathbf{c}_{w,b} = \mathbf{G}_{j,b} \cdot \begin{pmatrix} \mathbf{r}_{w,b} \\ \mathbf{w} \end{pmatrix} \oplus \mathbf{e}_{w,b} \in \mathbb{Z}_2^n. \tag{10}$$

Let $\mathbf{c}_w = (\mathbf{c}_{w,0}, \mathbf{c}_{w,1}) \in \mathbb{Z}_2^n \times \mathbb{Z}_2^n$.

2. Next, it encrypts the user's identity j under the key $\text{pk}_{\text{OA}} = (\mathbf{G}_{\text{oa},0}, \mathbf{G}_{\text{oa},1})$.
   - Let $\text{bin}(j) = [j_1| \dots |j_\ell]^\top \in \{0,1\}^\ell$.
   - Sample randomnesses $\mathbf{r}_{\text{oa},0}, \mathbf{r}_{\text{oa},1} \xleftarrow{\$} \mathbb{Z}_2^{k_1-\ell}$ and noises $\mathbf{e}_{\text{oa},0}, \mathbf{e}_{\text{oa},1} \xleftarrow{\$} B(n, t_1)$.
   - For $b \in \{0,1\}$, compute

$$\mathbf{c}_{\text{oa},b} = \mathbf{G}_{\text{oa},b} \cdot \begin{pmatrix} \mathbf{r}_{\text{oa},b} \\ \text{bin}(j) \end{pmatrix} \oplus \mathbf{e}_{\text{oa},b} \in \mathbb{Z}_2^n. \tag{11}$$

---

[4] For instance, if $w^{(j)}$ does not appear in $\text{info}_{\tau_{\text{current}}}$ but $\text{info}_{\tau_{\text{new}}}$ then $\mathbf{reg}[j][2] = \tau_{\text{new}}$. On the other hand, if $w^{(j)}$ appears in $\text{info}_{\tau_{\text{current}}}$ but not in $\text{info}_{\tau_{\text{new}}}$ then $\mathbf{reg}[j][3] = \tau_{\text{new}}$.

[5] It is easy to figure out all active users at specific time τ from **reg**, and thus enables verification of well-formedness of info_τ.

Let $\mathbf{c}_{oa} = (\mathbf{c}_{oa,0}, \mathbf{c}_{oa,1}) \in \mathbb{Z}_2^n \times \mathbb{Z}_2^n$.

3. It then generates a proof showing that $\mathbf{c}_{w,0}, \mathbf{c}_{w,1}$ both encrypt $\mathbf{w}$ and that $\mathbf{c}_{oa,0}, \mathbf{c}_{oa,1}$ both encrypt $\mathrm{bin}(j)$. The proof employs a Stern-like interactive ZK protocol on public input $(\mathbf{G}_{oa,0}, \mathbf{G}_{oa,1}, \mathbf{c}_w, \mathbf{c}_{oa}, L)$ and secret input $(\mathbf{G}_{j,0}, \mathbf{G}_{j,1}, \mathbf{w}, \mathrm{bin}(j), \mathbf{r}_{w,0}, \mathbf{r}_{w,1}, \mathbf{e}_{w,0}, \mathbf{e}_{w,1}, \mathbf{r}_{oa,0}, \mathbf{r}_{oa,1}, \mathbf{e}_{oa,0}, \mathbf{e}_{oa,1})$, described in detail in the full version. The interactive protocol is repeated κ times to achieve negligible soundness error and made non-interactive via Fiat-Shamir transform [21]. The resulting proof is a triple of form $\pi_{ct} = (\{\mathsf{CMT}_{ct,i}\}_{i=1}^{\kappa}, \mathsf{Ch}_{ct}, \{\mathsf{RSP}_{ct,i}\}_{i=1}^{\kappa})$ such that

$$\mathsf{Ch}_{ct} = \mathcal{H}_{\mathsf{FS}}(\{\mathsf{CMT}_{ct,i}\}_{i=1}^{\kappa}, \mathbf{G}_{oa,0}, \mathbf{G}_{oa,1}, \mathbf{c}_w, \mathbf{c}_{oa}, L).$$

Output the ciphertext $\psi = (\mathbf{c}_{w,0}, \mathbf{c}_{w,1}, \mathbf{c}_{oa,0}, \mathbf{c}_{oa,1}, \pi_{ct})$ and coins

$$\mathsf{coins}_{\psi} = (\mathbf{r}_{w,0}, \mathbf{r}_{w,1}, \mathbf{e}_{w,0}, \mathbf{e}_{w,1}, \mathbf{r}_{oa,0}, \mathbf{r}_{oa,1}, \mathbf{e}_{oa,0}, \mathbf{e}_{oa,1}). \tag{12}$$

$\mathcal{P}(\mathsf{pp}, \mathsf{pk}_{\mathsf{GM}}, \mathsf{pk}_{\mathsf{OA}}, \mathsf{info}_{\tau}, S, \psi, L, \mathbf{w}, \mathsf{pk}, \mathsf{coins}_{\psi})$ Let coins_{ψ} be of the form (12) and $\psi = (\mathbf{c}_{w,0}, \mathbf{c}_{w,1}, \mathbf{c}_{oa,0}, \mathbf{c}_{oa,1}, \pi_{ct})$. This algorithm is implemented by the sender above who has encrypted a message $\mathbf{w}$ to a user j at time epoch τ. The sender extracts $\mathbf{B}$ from pp. In addition to the witness $w^{(j)}$, he downloads $\mathbf{u}_{\tau}$ as well from info_{τ}. The goal of the sender is to convince the verifier in zero-knowledge that the following conditions hold.

1. The secret message $\mathbf{w} \in \mathbb{Z}_2^p$ is such that $(S, \mathbf{w}) \in R_{\mathrm{permit}}$.
2. The user encryption key pk_j' is correctly hashed to a non-zero value $\mathbf{d}_j$. In other words, $\mathsf{Accu}_{\mathbf{B}}(\mathsf{pk}_j') = \mathbf{d}_j$ and $\mathbf{d}_j \neq \mathbf{0}^n$.
3. The non-zero hash value $\mathbf{d}_j$ is honestly accumulated to value $\mathbf{u}_{\tau}$ at epoch τ, i.e., the equation $\mathsf{Verify}_{\mathbf{B}}(\mathbf{u}_{\tau}, \mathbf{d}_j, w^{(j)}) = 1$ holds.
4. $(\mathbf{c}_{w,0}, \mathbf{c}_{w,1}), (\mathbf{c}_{oa,0}, \mathbf{c}_{oa,1})$ are honest encryptions of $\mathbf{w}$ and $\mathrm{bin}(j)$, respectively. In other words, for $b \in \{0, 1\}$, Eqs. (10) and (11) hold.
5. The randomnesses $\mathbf{r}_{w,0}, \mathbf{r}_{w,1}, \mathbf{r}_{oa,0}, \mathbf{r}_{oa,1}$ are binary vectors while noises $\mathbf{e}_{w,0}, \mathbf{e}_{w,1}$ and $\mathbf{e}_{oa,0}, \mathbf{e}_{oa,1}$ are in the sets $\mathsf{B}(n, t_2)$ and $\mathsf{B}(n, t_1)$, respectively.

The proof employs a Stern-like interactive ZK protocol on public input $(\mathbf{B}, \mathsf{pk}_{\mathsf{OA}}, \mathbf{u}_{\tau}, S, \psi, L)$ and secret input $(\mathbf{w}, \mathsf{pk}, \mathsf{coins}_{\psi}, w^{(j)})$, provided in the full version. To achieve negligible soundness error, the protocol is repeated κ times. Then the Fiat-Shamir heuristic [21] is applied. The resulting proof is a triple $\pi_{\psi} = (\{\mathsf{CMT}_i\}_{i=1}^{\kappa}, \mathsf{Ch}, \{\mathsf{RSP}_i\}_{i=1}^{\kappa})$ where

$$\mathsf{Ch} = \mathcal{H}_{\mathsf{FS}}(\{\mathsf{CMT}_i\}_{i=1}^{\kappa}, \mathbf{B}, \mathsf{pk}_{\mathsf{OA}}, \mathbf{u}_{\tau}, S, \psi, L) \in \{1, 2, 3\}^{\kappa}.$$

$\mathcal{V}((\mathsf{pp}, \mathsf{pk}_{\mathsf{GM}}, \mathsf{pk}_{\mathsf{OA}}, \mathsf{info}_{\tau}, S, \psi, L), \pi_{\psi})$ This algorithm verifies the legitimacy of the ciphertext label pair (ψ, L) with respect to epoch τ and the set of keywords S by checking the validity of the proof π_{ψ}. It proceeds as follows.

1. Download $\mathbf{u}_{\tau}$ from info_{τ}.

2. Parse $\pi_\psi = (\{\mathsf{CMT}_i\}_{i=1}^\kappa, \mathsf{Ch}, \{\mathsf{RSP}_i\}_{i=1}^\kappa)$.

3. If $\mathsf{Ch} = [\mathsf{ch}_1|\cdots|\mathsf{ch}_\kappa]^\top \neq \mathcal{H}_{\mathsf{FS}}(\{\mathsf{CMT}_i\}_{i=1}^\kappa, \mathbf{B}, \mathsf{pk}_{\mathsf{OA}}, \mathbf{u}_\tau, S, \psi, L)$, return 0.

4. For $i \in [1, \kappa]$, verify the validity of RSP_i with respect to the commitment CMT_i and the challenge ch_i. If any of the verifications does not hold, return 0. Else return 1.

$\mathsf{Dec}(\mathsf{info}_\tau, \mathsf{sk}, \psi, L)$ This algorithm is run by a user j with secret key sk. Parse $\mathsf{sk} = (\mathsf{sk}_{\mathsf{ME}}^{(j,0)}, \mathsf{sk}_{\mathsf{ME}}^{(j,1)})$. It performs the following steps.

1. Parse $\psi = (\mathbf{c}_{w,0}, \mathbf{c}_{w,1}, \mathbf{c}_{\mathsf{oa},0}, \mathbf{c}_{\mathsf{oa},1}, \pi_{ct})$. It verifies the validity of π_{ct} as follows.

   - Let $\pi_{ct} = (\{\mathsf{CMT}_{ct,i}\}_{i=1}^\kappa, \mathsf{Ch}_{ct}, \{\mathsf{RSP}_{ct,i}\}_{i=1}^\kappa)$.
   - If $\mathsf{Ch}_{ct} \neq \mathcal{H}_{\mathsf{FS}}(\{\mathsf{CMT}_{ct,i}\}_{i=1}^\kappa, \mathbf{G}_{\mathsf{oa},0}, \mathbf{G}_{\mathsf{oa},1}, \mathbf{c}_{w,0}, \mathbf{c}_{w,1}, \mathbf{c}_{\mathsf{oa},0}, \mathbf{c}_{\mathsf{oa},1}, L)$, return $\bot$. Otherwise, let $\mathsf{Ch}_{ct} = [\mathsf{ch}_{ct,1}|\cdots|\mathsf{ch}_{ct,\kappa}]^\top$.
   - For $i \in [1, \kappa]$, verify the validity of $\mathsf{RSP}_{ct,i}$ with respect to the commitment $\mathsf{CMT}_{ct,i}$ and the challenge $\mathsf{ch}_{ct,i}$. If any of the verifications does not hold, return $\bot$.

2. If the above step does not return 0, it then runs the McElice decryption algorithm $\mathsf{Dec}_{\mathsf{ME}}(\mathsf{sk}_{\mathsf{ME}}^{(j,0)}, \mathbf{c}_{w,0})$ (see the full version), obtaining $\mathbf{w}'$.

3. If $(S, \mathbf{w}') \in R_{\mathrm{permit}}$, return $\mathbf{w}'$. Otherwise, return $\bot$.

$\mathsf{Open}(\mathsf{info}_\tau, \mathsf{sk}_{\mathsf{OA}}, \psi, L)$ This algorithm is run by the OA who possesses the key $\mathsf{sk}_{\mathsf{OA}} = (\mathsf{sk}_{\mathsf{ME}}^{(\mathsf{oa},0)}, \mathsf{sk}_{\mathsf{ME}}^{(\mathsf{oa},1)})$. It proceeds as follows.

1. Parse $\psi = (\mathbf{c}_{w,0}, \mathbf{c}_{w,1}, \mathbf{c}_{\mathsf{oa},0}, \mathbf{c}_{\mathsf{oa},1}, \pi_{ct})$. It verifies π_{ct} as in the algorithm Dec. It π_{ct} is invalid, it returns $\bot$.

2. Otherwise, it runs the decryption algorithm $\mathsf{Dec}_{\mathsf{ME}}(\mathsf{sk}_{\mathsf{ME}}^{(\mathsf{oa},0)}, \mathbf{c}_{\mathsf{oa},0})$, obtaining $[j_1'|\cdots|j_\ell']^\top$.

3. If info_τ does not include a witness containing the string $[j_1'|\cdots|j_\ell']^\top$, then return $\bot$.

4. Let $j' \in [0, N-1]$ be the integer that has binary representation $[j_1'|\cdots|j_\ell']^\top$. Output j'.

6.2   Asymptotic Efficiency, Correctness, and Security

Efficiency. We now analyze the efficiency of our construction with respect to the security parameter λ.

- The public key and secret key of GM have bit size $\mathcal{O}(\lambda)$.
- The public key and secret key of OA and each user have bit size $\mathcal{O}(\lambda^2)$.
- At each epoch, the sender who runs the $\mathcal{P}$ algorithm needs to download data of bit size $\mathcal{O}(\lambda \cdot \ell)$ while the verifier who runs the $\mathcal{V}$ algorithm needs to download data of bit size $\mathcal{O}(\lambda)$.
- The size of ciphertext ψ is $\mathcal{O}(\lambda^2)$ and size of proof π_ψ is $\omega(\log \lambda) \cdot \mathcal{O}(\lambda^2 + \ell \cdot \lambda)$.

Correctness. The above FDGE scheme is correct with all but negligible probability. It relies on the following three facts: (a) the correctness of the underlying McEliece encryption scheme and (b) the perfect completeness of the zero-knowledge argument used in the Enc algorithm and (c) the perfect completeness of the zero-knowledge argument used in the $\mathcal{P}$ algorithm. Therefore, in $\mathbf{Expt}_{\mathcal{A}}^{\mathsf{corr}}(1^\lambda)$ defined in Sect. 5, the $\mathcal{V}$ algorithm will output 1 by fact (c), and the Dec and Open algorithms will output $\mathbf{w}' = \mathbf{w}$ and $\mathsf{pk}' = \mathsf{pk}$, respectively, by fact (a) and (b).

Security. In Theorem 1, we prove the given FDGE satisfies the proposed security requirements in Sect. 5.1.

Theorem 1. *Assume the zero-knowledge argument used in the* Enc *algorithm is simulation-sound and zero-knowledge, the zero-knowledge argument used in the* $\mathcal{P}$ *algorithm is sound and zero-knowledge, the randomized McEliece encryption schemes have pseudorandom ciphertexts, and the hash function* h_B *is collision resistant. Then, in the random oracle model, the above* FDGE *scheme satisfies message secrecy, anonymity, and soundness.*

Due to space limit, details of the proof are provided in the full version.

Acknowledgements. Khoa Nguyen and Huaxiong Wang were supported by Singapore Ministry of Education under Research Grant MOE2019-T2-2-083 and by A*STAR, Singapore under research grant SERC A19E3b0099. Reihaneh Safavi-Naini and Yanhong Xu were in part supported by Natural Sciences and Engineering Research Council of Canada Discovery Grant Program and Alberta Innovates Strategic Chair in Information Security Research Program. Neng Zeng was supported by the Singapore Ministry of Education under MOE AcRF Tier 2 grant (MOE2018-T2-1-111).

References

1. El Aimani, L., Joye, M.: Toward practical group encryption. In: Jacobson, M., Locasto, M., Mohassel, P., Safavi-Naini, R. (eds.) ACNS 2013. LNCS, vol. 7954, pp. 237–252. Springer, Heidelberg (2013). https://doi.org/10.1007/978-3-642-38980-1_15

2. Alamélou, Q., Blazy, O., Cauchie, S., Gaborit, P.: A code-based group signature scheme. Designs Codes Cryptogr. 469–493 (2016). https://doi.org/10.1007/s10623-016-0276-6

3. Bellare, M., Boldyreva, A., Desai, A., Pointcheval, D.: Key-privacy in public-key encryption. In: Boyd, C. (ed.) ASIACRYPT 2001. LNCS, vol. 2248, pp. 566–582. Springer, Heidelberg (2001). https://doi.org/10.1007/3-540-45682-1_33

4. Bellare, M., Micciancio, D., Warinschi, B.: Foundations of group signatures: formal definitions, simplified requirements, and a construction based on general assumptions. In: Biham, E. (ed.) EUROCRYPT 2003. LNCS, vol. 2656, pp. 614–629. Springer, Heidelberg (2003). https://doi.org/10.1007/3-540-39200-9_38

5. Bellare, M., Shi, H., Zhang, C.: Foundations of group signatures: the case of dynamic groups. In: Menezes, A. (ed.) CT-RSA 2005. LNCS, vol. 3376, pp. 136–153. Springer, Heidelberg (2005). https://doi.org/10.1007/978-3-540-30574-3_11

6. Benaloh, J., de Mare, M.: One-way accumulators: a decentralized alternative to digital signatures. In: Helleseth, T. (ed.) EUROCRYPT 1993. LNCS, vol. 765, pp. 274–285. Springer, Heidelberg (1994). https://doi.org/10.1007/3-540-48285-7_24

7. Benhamouda, F., Camenisch, J., Krenn, S., Lyubashevsky, V., Neven, G.: Better zero-knowledge proofs for lattice encryption and their application to group signatures. In: Sarkar, P., Iwata, T. (eds.) ASIACRYPT 2014. LNCS, vol. 8873, pp. 551–572. Springer, Heidelberg (2014). https://doi.org/10.1007/978-3-662-45611-8_29

8. Boneh, D., Sahai, A., Waters, B.: Functional encryption: a new vision for public-key cryptography. Commun. ACM **55**(11), 56–64 (2012)

9. Boneh, D., Shacham, H.: Group signatures with verifier-local revocation. In: CCS 2004, pp. 168–177. ACM (2004)

10. Bootle, J., Cerulli, A., Chaidos, P., Ghadafi, E., Groth, J.: Foundations of fully dynamic group signatures. In: Manulis, M., Sadeghi, A.-R., Schneider, S. (eds.) ACNS 2016. LNCS, vol. 9696, pp. 117–136. Springer, Cham (2016). https://doi.org/10.1007/978-3-319-39555-5_7

11. Branco, P., Mateus, P.: A code-based linkable ring signature scheme. In: Baek, J., Susilo, W., Kim, J. (eds.) ProvSec 2018. LNCS, vol. 11192, pp. 203–219. Springer, Cham (2018). https://doi.org/10.1007/978-3-030-01446-9_12

12. Brassard, G., Chaum, D., Crépeau, C.: Minimum disclosure proofs of knowledge. J. Comput. Syst. Sci. **37**(2), 156–189 (1988)

13. Bresson, E., Stern, J.: Efficient revocation in group signatures. In: Kim, K. (ed.) PKC 2001. LNCS, vol. 1992, pp. 190–206. Springer, Heidelberg (2001). https://doi.org/10.1007/3-540-44586-2_15

14. Camenisch, J., Lysyanskaya, A.: Dynamic accumulators and application to efficient revocation of anonymous credentials. In: Yung, M. (ed.) CRYPTO 2002. LNCS, vol. 2442, pp. 61–76. Springer, Heidelberg (2002). https://doi.org/10.1007/3-540-45708-9_5

15. Cathalo, J., Libert, B., Yung, M.: Group encryption: non-interactive realization in the standard model. In: Matsui, M. (ed.) ASIACRYPT 2009. LNCS, vol. 5912, pp. 179–196. Springer, Heidelberg (2009). https://doi.org/10.1007/978-3-642-10366-7_11

16. Cayrel, P.-L., Hoffmann, G., Persichetti, E.: Efficient implementation of a CCA2-secure variant of McEliece using generalized Srivastava codes. In: Fischlin, M., Buchmann, J., Manulis, M. (eds.) PKC 2012. LNCS, vol. 7293, pp. 138–155. Springer, Heidelberg (2012). https://doi.org/10.1007/978-3-642-30057-8_9

17. Chaum, D., van Heyst, E.: Group signatures. In: Davies, D.W. (ed.) EUROCRYPT 1991. LNCS, vol. 547, pp. 257–265. Springer, Heidelberg (1991). https://doi.org/10.1007/3-540-46416-6_22

18. Dallot, L., Vergnaud, D.: Provably secure code-based threshold ring signatures. In: Parker, M.G. (ed.) IMACC 2009. LNCS, vol. 5921, pp. 222–235. Springer, Heidelberg (2009). https://doi.org/10.1007/978-3-642-10868-6_13

19. Döttling, N., Dowsley, R., Müller-Quade, J., Nascimento, A.C.A.: A CCA2 secure variant of the McEliece cryptosystem. IEEE Trans. Inf. Theory **58**(10), 6672–6680 (2012)

20. Ezerman, M.F., Lee, H.T., Ling, S., Nguyen, K., Wang, H.: A provably secure group signature scheme from code-based assumptions. In: Iwata, T., Cheon, J.H. (eds.) ASIACRYPT 2015. LNCS, vol. 9452, pp. 260–285. Springer, Heidelberg (2015). https://doi.org/10.1007/978-3-662-48797-6_12

21. Fiat, A., Shamir, A.: How to prove yourself: practical solutions to identification and signature problems. In: Odlyzko, A.M. (ed.) CRYPTO 1986. LNCS, vol. 263, pp. 186–194. Springer, Heidelberg (1987). https://doi.org/10.1007/3-540-47721-7_12

22. Gentry, C.: Fully homomorphic encryption using ideal lattices. In: STOC 2009, pp. 169–178. ACM (2009)

23. Goldreich, O., Micali, S., Wigderson, A.: How to prove all NP statements in zero-knowledge and a methodology of cryptographic protocol design (extended abstract). In: Odlyzko, A.M. (ed.) CRYPTO 1986. LNCS, vol. 263, pp. 171–185. Springer, Heidelberg (1987). https://doi.org/10.1007/3-540-47721-7_11

24. Goldwasser, S., Micali, S., Rackoff, C.: The knowledge complexity of interactive proof systems. SIAM J. Comput. 18(1), 186–208 (1989)

25. Goyal, V., Pandey, O., Sahai, A., Waters, B.: Attribute-based encryption for fine-grained access control of encrypted data. In: CCS 2006, pp. 89–98. ACM (2006)

26. Izabachène, M., Pointcheval, D., Vergnaud, D.: Mediated traceable anonymous encryption. In: Abdalla, M., Barreto, P.S.L.M. (eds.) LATINCRYPT 2010. LNCS, vol. 6212, pp. 40–60. Springer, Heidelberg (2010). https://doi.org/10.1007/978-3-642-14712-8_3

27. Jain, A., Krenn, S., Pietrzak, K., Tentes, A.: Commitments and efficient zero-knowledge proofs from learning parity with noise. In: Wang, X., Sako, K. (eds.) ASIACRYPT 2012. LNCS, vol. 7658, pp. 663–680. Springer, Heidelberg (2012). https://doi.org/10.1007/978-3-642-34961-4_40

28. Kiayias, A., Tsiounis, Y., Yung, M.: Traceable signatures. In: Cachin, C., Camenisch, J.L. (eds.) EUROCRYPT 2004. LNCS, vol. 3027, pp. 571–589. Springer, Heidelberg (2004). https://doi.org/10.1007/978-3-540-24676-3_34

29. Kiayias, A., Tsiounis, Y., Yung, M.: Group encryption. In: Kurosawa, K. (ed.) ASIACRYPT 2007. LNCS, vol. 4833, pp. 181–199. Springer, Heidelberg (2007). https://doi.org/10.1007/978-3-540-76900-2_11

30. Kobara, K., Imai, H.: Semantically secure McEliece public-key cryptosystems-conversions for McEliece PKC. In: Kim, K. (ed.) PKC 2001. LNCS, vol. 1992, pp. 19–35. Springer, Heidelberg (2001). https://doi.org/10.1007/3-540-44586-2_2

31. Libert, B., Ling, S., Mouhartem, F., Nguyen, K., Wang, H.: Signature schemes with efficient protocols and dynamic group signatures from lattice assumptions. In: Cheon, J.H., Takagi, T. (eds.) ASIACRYPT 2016. LNCS, vol. 10032, pp. 373–403. Springer, Heidelberg (2016). https://doi.org/10.1007/978-3-662-53890-6_13

32. Libert, B., Ling, S., Mouhartem, F., Nguyen, K., Wang, H.: Zero-knowledge arguments for matrix-vector relations and lattice-based group encryption. Theor. Comput. Sci. 759, 72–97 (2019)

33. Libert, B., Ling, S., Nguyen, K., Wang, H.: Zero-knowledge arguments for lattice-based accumulators: logarithmic-size ring signatures and group signatures without trapdoors. In: Fischlin, M., Coron, J.-S. (eds.) EUROCRYPT 2016. LNCS, vol. 9666, pp. 1–31. Springer, Heidelberg (2016). https://doi.org/10.1007/978-3-662-49896-5_1

34. Libert, B., Peters, T., Yung, M.: Group signatures with almost-for-free revocation. In: Safavi-Naini, R., Canetti, R. (eds.) CRYPTO 2012. LNCS, vol. 7417, pp. 571–589. Springer, Heidelberg (2012). https://doi.org/10.1007/978-3-642-32009-5_34

35. Libert, B., Peters, T., Yung, M.: Scalable group signatures with revocation. In: Pointcheval, D., Johansson, T. (eds.) EUROCRYPT 2012. LNCS, vol. 7237, pp. 609–627. Springer, Heidelberg (2012). https://doi.org/10.1007/978-3-642-29011-4_36

36. Libert, B., Yung, M., Joye, M., Peters, T.: Traceable group encryption. In: Krawczyk, H. (ed.) PKC 2014. LNCS, vol. 8383, pp. 592–610. Springer, Heidelberg (2014). https://doi.org/10.1007/978-3-642-54631-0_34

37. Ling, S., Nguyen, K., Stehlé, D., Wang, H.: Improved zero-knowledge proofs of knowledge for the ISIS problem, and applications. In: Kurosawa, K., Hanaoka, G. (eds.) PKC 2013. LNCS, vol. 7778, pp. 107–124. Springer, Heidelberg (2013). https://doi.org/10.1007/978-3-642-36362-7_8

38. Ling, S., Nguyen, K., Wang, H., Xu, Y.: Lattice-based group signatures: achieving full dynamicity (and deniability) with ease. Theor. Comput. Sci. **783**, 71–94 (2019)

39. McEliece, R.J.: A public-key cryptosystem based on algebraic coding theory. Coding Thv. **4244**, 114–116 (1978)

40. Aguilar Melchor, C., Cayrel, P.-L., Gaborit, P.: A new efficient threshold ring signature scheme based on coding theory. In: Buchmann, J., Ding, J. (eds.) PQCrypto 2008. LNCS, vol. 5299, pp. 1–16. Springer, Heidelberg (2008). https://doi.org/10.1007/978-3-540-88403-3_1

41. Melchor, C.A., Cayrel, P., Gaborit, P., Laguillaumie, F.: A new efficient threshold ring signature scheme based on coding theory. IEEE Trans. Inf. Theory **57**(7), 4833–4842 (2011)

42. Morozov, K., Takagi, T.: Zero-knowledge protocols for the McEliece encryption. In: Susilo, W., Mu, Y., Seberry, J. (eds.) ACISP 2012. LNCS, vol. 7372, pp. 180–193. Springer, Heidelberg (2012). https://doi.org/10.1007/978-3-642-31448-3_14

43. Nakanishi, T., Fujii, H., Hira, Y., Funabiki, N.: Revocable group signature schemes with constant costs for signing and verifying. In: Jarecki, S., Tsudik, G. (eds.) PKC 2009. LNCS, vol. 5443, pp. 463–480. Springer, Heidelberg (2009). https://doi.org/10.1007/978-3-642-00468-1_26

44. Naor, M., Yung, M.: Public-key cryptosystems provably secure against chosen ciphertext attacks. In: STOC 1990, pp. 427–437. ACM (1990)

45. Nguyen, K., Tang, H., Wang, H., Zeng, N.: New code-based privacy-preserving cryptographic constructions. In: Galbraith, S.D., Moriai, S. (eds.) ASIACRYPT 2019. LNCS, vol. 11922, pp. 25–55. Springer, Cham (2019). https://doi.org/10.1007/978-3-030-34621-8_2

46. Nojima, R., Imai, H., Kobara, K., Morozov, K.: Semantic security for the MCeliece cryptosystem without random oracles. Des. Codes Cryptogr. **49**(1–3), 289–305 (2008)

47. Regev, O.: On lattices, learning with errors, random linear codes, and cryptography. J. ACM, **56**(6), 34:1–34:40 (2009)

48. Shor, P.W.: Polynomial-time algorithms for prime factorization and discrete logarithms on a quantum computer. SIAM J. Comput. **26**(5), 1484–1509 (1997)

49. Stern, J.: A new paradigm for public key identification. IEEE Trans. Inf. Theory **42**(6), 1757–1768 (1996)

50. Trolin, M., Wikström, D.: Hierarchical group signatures. In: Caires, L., Italiano, G.F., Monteiro, L., Palamidessi, C., Yung, M. (eds.) ICALP 2005. LNCS, vol. 3580, pp. 446–458. Springer, Heidelberg (2005). https://doi.org/10.1007/11523468_37

51. Nguyen, K., Safavi-Naini, R., Susilo, W., Wang, H., Xu, Y., Zeng, N.: Group Encryption: Full Dynamicity, Message Filtering and Code-Based Instantiation. Cryptology ePrint Archive, Report 2021/226 (2021). https://eprint.iacr.org/2021/226

Steel: Composable Hardware-Based Stateful and Randomised Functional Encryption

Pramod Bhatotia[1,2], Markulf Kohlweiss[1], Lorenzo Martinico[1(✉)],
and Yiannis Tselekounis[1]

[1] School of Informatics, University of Edinburgh, Edinburgh, Scotland
{mkohlwei,lorenzo.martinico}@ed.ac.uk, tselekounis@sians.org
[2] Department of Informatics, TU Munich, Munich, Germany
pramod.bhatotia@in.tum.de

Abstract. Trusted execution environments (TEEs) enable secure execution of programs on untrusted hosts and cryptographically attest the correctness of outputs. As these are complex systems, it is essential to formally capture the exact security achieved by protocols employing TEEs, and ultimately, prove their security under composition, as TEEs are typically employed in multiple protocols, simultaneously.

Our contribution is twofold. On the one hand, we show that under existing definitions of attested execution setup, we can realise cryptographic functionalities that are unrealisable in the standard model. On the other hand, we extend the adversarial model to capture a broader class of *realistic adversaries*, we demonstrate weaknesses of existing security definitions this class, and we propose stronger ones.

Specifically, we first define a generalization of *Functional Encryption* that captures *Stateful and Randomised* functionalities (FESR). Then, assuming the ideal functionality for attested execution of Pass et al. (Eurocrypt '2017), we construct the associated protocol, Steel, and we prove that Steel UC-realises FESR in the *universal composition with global subroutines* model by Badertscher et al. (TCC '2020). Our work is also a validation of the compositionality of the Iron protocol by Fisch et al. (CCS '2017), capturing (non-stateful) hardware-based functional encryption.

As the existing functionality for attested execution of Pass et al. is too strong for real world use, we propose a weaker functionality that allows the adversary to conduct *rollback and forking attacks*. We demonstrate that Steel (realising stateful functionalities), contrary to the stateless variant corresponding to Iron, is not secure in this setting and discuss possible mitigation techniques.

1 Introduction

Due to the rise of cloud computing, most people living in countries with active digital economies can expect a significant amount of information about them to be stored on cloud platforms. Cloud computing offers economies of scale for computational resources with ease of management, elasticity, and fault tolerance driving

© International Association for Cryptologic Research 2021
J. A. Garay (Ed.): PKC 2021, LNCS 12711, pp. 709–736, 2021.
https://doi.org/10.1007/978-3-030-75248-4_25

further centralization. While cloud computing is ubiquitously employed for building modern online service, it also poses security and privacy risks. Cloud storage and computation are outside the control of the data owner and users currently have no mechanism to verify whether the third-party operator, even with good intentions, can handle their data with confidentiality and integrity guarantees.

Hardware-Based Solutions. To overcome these limitations, trusted execution environments (TEEs), such as Intel SGX [27], ARM Trustzone [45], RISC-V Keystone [29,38], AMD-SEV [33] provide an appealing way to build secure systems. TEEs provide a hardware-protected secure memory region called a *secure enclave* whose residing code and data are isolated from any layers in the software stack including the operating system and/or the hypervisor. In addition, TEEs offer remote attestation for proving their trustworthiness to third-parties. In particular, the remote attestation enables a remote party to verify that an enclave has a specific identity and is indeed running on a genuine TEE hardware platform. Given they promise a hardware-assisted secure abstraction, TEEs are now commercially offered by major cloud computing providers including Microsoft Azure [47], Google Cloud [46], and Alibaba Cloud [5].

Modeling Challenges. While TEEs provide a promising building block, it is not straightforward to design secure applications on top of TEEs. In particular applications face the following three challenges: (1) Most practical applications require combining trusted and untrusted components for improved performance and a low trusted computing base; (2) TEEs are designed to protect only the volatile, in-memory, "stateless" computations and data. Unfortunately, this abstraction is insufficient for most practical applications, which rely on stateful computation on untrusted storage mediums (SSDs, disks). Ensuring security for such untrusted storage mediums is challenging because TEEs are prone to rollback attacks; and lastly, (3) TEE hardware designs are prone to numerous side channel attacks exploiting memory access patterns, cache timing channels, etc. These side channel attacks have the potential to completely compromise the confidentiality, integrity, and authenticity (remote attestation) of enclaves.

Therefore, it is important to carefully model the security achieved by the protocols of such systems as well as the assumptions in the cryptography and the hardware, and the trust afforded in protocol participants. Ideally such modelling must be compositional to facilitate the construction of larger systems based on smaller hardware and cryptography components. Given a sufficiently expressive model of TEEs, they can be used as a powerful setup assumption to realise many protocols.

The model of Pass, Shi, and Tramer (PST) [44] takes an initial step towards modelling protocols employing TEEs. The PST model provides a compositional functionality for attested execution and shows how to instantiate various primitives impossible in the standard model, as well as some limitations of TEEs. The PST model was first weakened in [52], which provides a compelling example of how an excessively weak enclave, susceptible to side channel attacks that break confidentiality (but not integrity and authenticity), can still be used as setup for useful cryptographic primitives. Both models, however, live at two opposite extremes, and thus fail to capture realistic instantiations of real world trusted execution.

Functional Encryption and Limitations. One of the core primitives that enables privacy preserving computation and storage is *Functional Encryption* (FE), introduced by [16]. FE is a generalisation of Attribute/Identify Based Encryption [48,49], that enables authorized entities to compute over encrypted data, and learn the results in the clear. In particular, parties possessing the so-called functional key, sk_f, for the function f, can compute $f(x)$, where x is the plaintext, by applying the decryption algorithm on sk_f and an encryption of x. Access to the functional key is regulated by a trusted third party. While out of scope for our work, identifying such a party is an interesting question that requires establishing metrics for the trustworthiness of entities we might want to be able to decrypt functions, and the kind of functions that should be authorised for a given level of trust. An obvious option for the role of trusted authority would be that of a data protection authority, who can investigate the data protection practices of organisations and levy fines in case these are violated. Another approach could be decentralising this role, by allowing the functional key to be generated collectively by a number of data owners [1,23].

FE is a very powerful primitive but in practice highly non-trivial to construct. Motivated by the inefficiency of existing instantiations of FE for arbitrary functions, the work of [28] introduces Iron, which is a practically efficient protocol that realises FE based on Intel's SGX. In [28] the authors formally prove security of the proposed protocol, however their proof is in the standalone setting. In a related work, Matt and Maurer [41] show (building on [3]) that composable functional encryption (CFE) is impossible to achieve in the standard model, but achievable in the random oracle model. For another important variant of the primitive, namely, *randomized functional encryption*, existing constructions [2,30,37], are limited in the sense that they require a new functional key for each invocation of the function, i.e., decryptions with the same functional key always return the same output. Finally, existing notions of FE only capture *stateless* functionalities, which we believe further restricts the usefulness and applicability of the primitive. For instance, imagine a financial institution that sets its global lending rate based on the total liquidity of its members. Financial statements can be sent, encrypted, by each member, with each of these transactions updating the global view for the decryptor, who can then compute the function's result in real time.

Given the above limitations, in this work we leverage the power of hardware assisted computation to construct FE for a *broader class of functionalities* under the strongest notion of *composable security*.

1.1   Our Contributions

We consider a generalization of FE to arbitrary *stateful and probabilistic functionalities* (FESR), that subsumes multi-client FE [23] and enables cryptographic computations in a natural way, due to the availability of internal randomness. Our contributions are as follows:

- We formally define functional encryption for stateful and randomized functionalities (FESR), in the Universal Composition (UC) setting [28].
- We construct the protocol Steel and prove that it realizes FESR in the newly introduced Universal Composition with Global Subroutines (UCGS) model [9]. Our main building blocks are: (1) the functional encryption scheme of [28] and (2) the global attestation functionality of PST. Our treatment lifts the PST model to the UCGS setting, and by easily adapting our proofs one can also establish the UCGS-security of [28].
- Finally, we introduce a weaker functionality for attested execution in the UCGS model to allow rollback and forking attacks, and use it to demonstrate that Steel does not protect against these. Finally, we sketch possible mitigation techniques.

1.2   Technical Overview

Attested Execution via the Global Attestation Functionality G_{att} of PST [44]. Our UC protocols assume access to the *global attestation functionality*, G_{att}, that captures the core abstraction provided by a broad class of attested execution processors, such as Intel SGX [27]. It models multiple hardware-protected memory regions of a TEE, called *secure enclaves*. Each enclave contains trusted code and data. In combination with a call-gate mechanism to control entry and exit into the trusted execution environment, this guarantees that this memory can only be accessed by the enclave it belongs to, i.e., the enclave memory is protected from concurrent enclaves and other (privileged) code on the platform. TEE processing environments guarantee the authenticity, the integrity and the confidentiality of their executing code, data and runtime states, e.g. CPU registers, memory and others.

G_{att} is parametrised by a signature scheme and a registry that captures all the platforms that are equipped with an attested execution processor. At a high level, G_{att} allows parties to register programs and ask for evaluations over arbitrary inputs, while also receiving signatures that ensure correctness of the computation. Since the manufacturer's signing key pair can be used in multiple protocols simultaneously, G_{att} is defined as a *global functionality* that uses the same key pair across sessions.

Universal Composition with Global Subroutines [10]. In our work we model global information using the newly introduced UCGS framework, which resolves inconsistencies in GUC [19], an earlier work that aims to model executions in the presence of global functionalities. UCGS handles such executions via a *management* protocol, that combines the target protocol and one or more instances of the global functionality, and creates an embedding within the standard UC framework. In our work, G_{att} (cf. Sect. 2.2) is modeled as a global functionality in the UCGS framework (updating the original PST formulation in GUC).

Setting, Adversarial Model and Security. Our treatment considers three types of parties namely, encryptors, denoted by A, decryptors, denoted by B, as well as a single party that corresponds to the trusted authority, denoted by C. The adversary is allowed to corrupt parties in B and request for evaluations of functions of it's choice over messages encrypted by parties in A. We then require *correctness* of the computation, meaning that the state for each function has not been tampered with by the adversary, as well as *confidentiality* of the encrypted message, which ensures that the adversary learns only the output of the computation (and any information implied by it) and nothing more. Our treatment covers both stateful and randomized functionalities.

Steel: UCGS-secure FE for Stateful and Randomized Functionalities. Steel is executed by the sets of parties discussed above, where besides encryptors, all other parties receive access to G_{att}, abstracting an execution in the presence of secure hardware enclaves. Our protocol is based on Iron [28], so we briefly revisit the main protocol operations: (1) **Setup**, executed by the trusted party C, installs a *key management enclave* (KME), running a program to generate *public-key encryption* and *digital signature*, key pairs. The public keys are published, while the equivalent secrets are kept encrypted in storage (using SGX's terminology, the memory is sealed). Each of the decryptors installs a *decryption enclave* (DE), and attests its authenticity to the KME to receive the secret key for the encryption scheme over a secure channel. (2) **KeyGen**, on input function F, calls KME, where the latter produces a signature on the measurement of an instantiated enclave that computes F. (3) When **Encrypt** is called by an encryptor, it uses the published public encryption key to encrypt a message and sends the ciphertext to the intended recipients. (4) **Decrypt** is executed by a decrypting party seeking to compute some function F on a ciphertext. This operation instantiates a matching function enclave (or resume an existing one), whose role is that of computing the functional decryption, if an authorised functional key is provided.

Steel consists of the above operations, with the appropriate modifications to enable stateful functionalities. In addition, Steel provides some simplifications over the Iron protocol. In particular, we repurpose attestation's signature capabilities to supplant the need for a separate signature scheme to generate functional keys, and thus minimise the trusted computing base. In practice, a functional key for a function F can be produced by just letting the key generation process return F; as part of G_{att}'s execution, this produces an attestation signature σ over F, which becomes the functional key sk_F for that function, provided the generating enclave id is also made public (a requirement for verification, due to the signature syntax of attestation in G_{att}).

The statefulness of functional encryption is simply enabled by adding a state array to each functional enclave. The array is also stored locally by the corresponding decryption enclave, and is updated for every decryption of a given function. Similar to [44], a curious artefact in the protocol's modeling is the addition of a "backdoor" that programs the output of the function evaluation subroutine, such that, if a specific argument is set on the input, the function evaluation returns the value of that argument. The reason for this addition is to enable simulation of signatures over function evaluations that have already been computed using the ideal functionality. We note that this addition does not impact correctness, as the state array is not modified if the backdoor is used, nor confidentiality, since the output of this subroutine is never passed to any other party besides the caller B. Finally, a further addition is that our protocol requires the addition of a proof of plaintext knowledge on top of the underlying encryption scheme. The Steel protocol definition is presented in Sect. 4.

Security of Steel. Our protocol uses an existentially unforgeable under chosen message attacks (EU-CMA) signature scheme, Σ, a CCA-secure public-key encryption scheme, PKE, and a non-interactive zero knowledge scheme, N. Informally, Σ provides the guarantees required for realizing attested computation (as discussed above), PKE is used to protect the communication between enclaves, and for protecting the encryptors' inputs. For the latter usage, it is possible to reduce the security requirement to CPA-security as we additionally compute a simulation-extractable NIZK proof of well-formedness of the ciphertext that guarantees non-malleability.

Our proof is via a sequence of hybrids in which we prove that the real world protocol execution w.r.t. Steel is indistinguishable from the ideal execution, in the presence of an ideal functionality that captures FE for stateful and randomized functionalities. The goal is to prove that the decryptor learns nothing more than an authorized function of the private input plaintext, thus our hybrids gradually fake all relevant information accessed by the adversary. In the first hybrid,[1] all signature verifications w.r.t. the attestation key are replaced by an idealized verification process, that only accepts message/signature pairs that have been computed honestly (i.e., we omit verification via Σ). Indistinguishability is proven via reduction to the EU-CMA security of Σ. Next we fake all ciphertexts exchanged between enclaves that carry the decryption key for the target ciphertext, over which the function is evaluated (those hybrids require reductions to the CCA security of PKE).[2] The next hybrid substitutes ZK proofs over the target plaintexts with simulated ones, and indistinguishability with the previous one reduces to the zero knowledge property of N. Then, for maliciously generated ciphertexts under PKE – which might result via tampering with honestly generated encryptors' ciphertexts – instead of using the decryption operation of PKE, our simulator recovers the corresponding plaintext using the extractability property of N. Finally, we fake all ciphertexts of PKE, that encrypt the inputs to the functions (this reduces to CPA security). Note that, in [28], the adversary outputs the target message, which is then being encrypted and used as a parameter to the ideal world functionality that is accessed by the simulator in a black box way. In this work, we consider a stronger setting in which the adversary directly outputs ciphertexts of it's choice. While in the classic setting for Functional Encryption (where Iron lives) simulation security is easily achieved by asking

---

[1] Here we omit some standard UC-related hybrids.

[2] Here CCA security is a requirement as the adversary is allowed to tamper with honestly generated ciphertexts.

the adversarial enclave to produce an evaluation for the challenge ciphertext, in FESR the simulator is required to conduct all decryptions through the ideal functionality, so that the decryptor's state for that function can be updated. We address the above challenge by using the extractability property of NIZKs: for maliciously generated ciphertexts our simulator extracts the original plaintext and ask the ideal FESR functionality for it's evaluation. Simulation-extractable NIZK can be efficiently instantiated, e.g., using zk-SNARKs [12]. Security of our protocol is formally proven in Sect. 5. The simulator therein provided could be easily adapted to show that the Iron protocol UCGS-realises Functional Encryption, by replacing the NIZK operations for maliciously generated ciphertexts with a decryption from the enclave, as described above.

Rollback and Forking Attacks. Modeling attested execution via G_{att} facilitates composable protocol design, however, such a functionality cannot be easily realized since real world adversaries can perform highly non-trivial *rollback* and *forking* attacks against hardware components. In Sect. 6, we define a weaker functionality for attested execution, called $G_{att}^{rollback}$, that aims to capture rollback and forking attacks. To achieve this, we replace the enclave storage array in G_{att} with a tree data structure. While the honest party only ever accesses the last leaf of the tree (equivalent to a linked list), a corrupt party is able to provide an arbitrary path within the tree. This allows them to rollback the enclave, by re-executing a previous (non-leaf) state, and to support multiple forks of the program by interactively selecting different sibling branches. We give an example FESR function where we can show that correctness does not hold if $G_{att}^{rollback}$ is used instead of G_{att} within Steel, and discuss how countermeasures from the rollback protection literature can be adopted to address these attacks, with a consideration on efficiency.

1.3   Related Work

Hardware is frequently used to improve performance or circumvent impossibility results, e.g. [4,26,42]. As a relevant example, Chung et al. [25] show how to use of stateless hardware tokens to implement functional encryption.

The use of attestation has been widely adopted in the design of computer systems to bootstrap security [43]. In addition to formalising attested execution, Pass, Shi and Tramer (PST) [44] show that two-party computation is realisable in UC only if both parties have access to attested execution, and fair two-party computation is also possible if additionally both secure processors have access to a trusted clock. The PST model is the first work to formalise attested execution in the UC framework. The compositional aspect of UC allows for the reused of the model in several successive works [22,24,52,54]. Other attempts at providing a formal model for attested execution include the game-based models of Barbosa et al. [15], Bahmani et al. [13], Fisch et al. [28]. The latter model arises from the need to evaluate the security of Iron, a hardware-based realisation of functional encryption, which was later extended to verifiable functional encryption in Suzuki et al. [51].

Rollback attacks (also known as reset attacks in the cryptographic literature) are a common attack vectors against third-party untrusted computing infrastructure. An attacker who is in control of the underlying infrastructure can at times simply restart the system to restore a previous system state. Yilek [55] presents a general attack that is applicable to both virtual machine and enclave executions: it shows that an adversary capable of executing multiple rollback attacks on IND-CCA or IND-CPA secure encryption schemes might learn information about encrypted messages by running the encryption algorithm on multiple messages with the same randomness. In the absence of true hardware-based randomness that cannot be rolled back, these kinds of attacks can be mitigated using hedged encryption, a type of key-wrap scheme [32], such that for each encryption round, the original random coin and the plaintext are passed through a pseudorandom function to generate the randomness for the ciphertext.

The area of rollback attacks on TEEs is well studied. Platforms like SGX [21], TPMs [39], etc. provide trusted monotonic counters, from which it is possible to bootstrap rollback-resilient storage. However, trusted counters are too slow for most practical applications. Furthermore, they wear out after a short period of time. As their lifetime is limited, they are unreliable for applications that require frequent updates [40]. Moreover, an adversary that is aware of this vulnerability can attack protocols that rely exclusively on counters, by instantiating a malicious enclave on the same platform that artificially damages the counters.

To overcome the limitation of SGX counters, ROTE [40] uses a consensus protocol to build a distributed trusted counter service, with performance necessarily reduced through several rounds of network communication. In the same spirit, Ariadne [50] is an optimized (local) synchronous technique to increment the counter by a single bit flip for deterministic enclaves.

Speicher [14] and Palaemon [31] proposed an asynchronous trusted counter interface, which provide a systematic trade-off between performance and rollback protection, addressing some limitations of synchronous counters. The asynchronous counter is backed up by a synchronous counter interface with a period of vulnerability, where an adversary can rollback the state of a TEE-equipped storage server in a system until the last stable synchronous point. To protect against such attacks, these systems rely on the clients to keep the changes in their local cache until the counter stabilizes to the next synchronisation point.

Lightweight Collective Memory (Brandenburger et al. [17]) is a proposed framework that claims to achieve fork-linearizability: each honest client that communicates with a TEE (on an untrusted server that might be rolled back) can detect if the server is being inconsistent in their responses to any of the protocol clients (i.e. if they introduce any forks or non-linearity in their responses). Finally, [35,36,53], protect hardware memory against active attacks, while [6,34], protect cryptographic hardware against tampering and Trojan injection attacks, respectively.

2   Preliminaries

2.1   UC Background

Universal Composability (UC), introduced by Canetti [18], is a security framework that enables the security analysis of cryptographic protocols. It supports the setting where multiple instances of the *same*, or *different protocols*, can be executed concurrently. Many extensions and variants of the framework have been proposed over the years; our treatment is based on the recently released Universal Composability with Global Subroutines framework (UCGS) [10] and the 2020 version of UC [18]. We briefly summarise the aspects of UC and UCGS necessary to understand our work.

Universal Composability. Consider two systems of PPT interactive Turing machine instances $(\pi, \mathcal{A}, \mathcal{Z})$ and $(\phi, \mathcal{S}, \mathcal{Z})$, where $\mathcal{Z}$ is the initial instance, and $\pi, \mathcal{A}$ (and respectively $\phi, \mathcal{S}$) have comparable runtime balanced by the inputs of $\mathcal{Z}$. We say that the two systems are indistinguishable if $\mathcal{Z}$ making calls to $\pi, \mathcal{A}$ (resp. $\phi, \mathcal{S}$) cannot distinguish which system it is located in. The two systems are commonly referred to as the *real* and *ideal world* (respectively). $\mathcal{Z}$ can make calls to instances within the protocol by assuming the (external) identity of arbitrary instances (as defined by the control function). Depending on the protocol settings, it might be necessary to restrict the external identities available to the environment. A ξ-identity-bounded environment is limited to assume external identities as specified by ξ, a polynomial time boolean predicate on the current system configuration.

We now recall a few definitions. Please consult [10,18] or our full version for the formal definitions of terms such as *balanced, respecting, exposing, compliant.*

Definition 1 (UC emulation [18]). *Given two PPT protocols π, ϕ and some predicate ξ, we say that π UC-emulates ϕ with respect to ξ-identity bound environments (or π ξ-UC-emulates ϕ) if for any balanced ξ-identity-bounded environment and any PPT adversary, there exists a PPT simulator $\mathcal{S}$ such that the systems $(\phi, \mathcal{S}, \mathcal{Z})$ and $(\pi, \mathcal{A}, \mathcal{Z})$ are indistinguishable.*

Given a protocol π which UC-emulates a protocol ϕ, and a third protocol ρ, which calls ϕ as a subroutine, we can construct a protocol where all calls to ϕ are replaced with calls to π, denoted as $\rho^{\phi \to \pi}$.

Theorem 1 (Universal Composition [18]). *Given PPT protocols π, ϕ, ρ and predicate ξ, if π, ϕ are both subroutine respecting and subroutine exposing , ρ is (π, ϕ, ξ)-compliant and π ξ-UC-emulates ϕ, then protocol $\rho^{\phi \to \pi}$ UC-emulates ρ*

By the composition theorem, any protocol that leverages subroutine ϕ in its execution can now be instantiated using protocol π.

UCGS. As the name suggests, generalised UC (GUC) [19] is an important generalization of the UC model. It accounts for the existence of a shared subroutine γ, such that both ρ and its subroutine π (regardless of how many instances of π are called by ρ) can have γ as a subroutine. The presence of the *global subroutine* allows proving protocols that rely on some powerful functionality that needs to be globally accessible, such as a public key infrastructure (PKI) [20], a global clock [8], or trusted hardware [44].

Unfortunately GUC has inconsistencies and has not been updated from the 2007 to the 2020 version of UC.[3] Universal Composability with Global Subroutines [10] aims to rectify these issues by embedding UC emulation in the presence of a global protocol within the standard UC framework.

To achieve this, a protocol π with access to subroutine γ is replaced by a new structured protocol $\mu = M[\pi, \gamma]$, known as *management* protocol; μ allows multiplexing a single instance of π and γ into however many are required by ρ, by transforming the session and party identifiers. μ is a subroutine exposing protocol, and is given access to an execution graph directory instance, which tracks existing machines within the protocol, and the list of subroutine calls (implemented as a structured protocol). The execution graph directory can be queried by all instances within the extended session of μ, and is used to redirect the outputs of π and γ to the correct machine.

Below we revisit the UC emulation with global subroutines definition from [10].

Definition 2 (UC Emulation with Global Subroutines [10]). *Given protocols π, ϕ, and γ, π ξ-UC emulates ϕ in the presence of γ if $M[\pi, \gamma]$ ξ-UC emulates $M[\phi, \gamma]$*

Now we state the main UCGS theorem.

Theorem 2 (Universal Composition with Global Subroutines [10]). *Given subroutine-exposing protocols π, ϕ, ρ, and γ, if γ is a ϕ-regular setup and subroutine respecting, ϕ, π are γ-subroutine respecting, ρ is (π, ϕ, ξ)-compliant and $(\pi, M[x, \gamma], \xi)$-compliant for $x \in \{\phi, \pi\}$, then if π ξ-UC-emulates ϕ in the presence of γ, the protocol $\rho^{\phi \to \pi}$ UC-emulates ρ in the presence of γ.*

2.2   The G_{att} Functionality

We now reproduce the G_{att} global functionality defined in the PST model [44]. The functionality is parameterised with a signature scheme and a registry to capture all platforms with a TEE. The below functionality diverges from the original one in that we let vk be a global variable, accessible by enclave programs as G_{att}.vk. This allows us to use G_{att} for protocols where the enclave program does not trust the caller to its procedures to pass genuine inputs, making it necessary to conduct the verification of attestation from within the enclave.

---

[3] In a nutshell the inconsistency arises from a discrepancy in the proof that emulation for a single-challenge session version, called EUC (used to prove protocols secure), implies UC-emulation for the multi-challenge GUC notion (used to prove the composition theorem).

Functionality $G_{att}[\Sigma, reg, \lambda]$

State variables	Description
vk	Master verification key, available to enclave programs
msk	Master secret key, protected by the hardware
$\mathcal{T} \leftarrow \emptyset$	Table for installed programs

On message INITIALIZE *from a party P:*

   let $(spk, ssk) \leftarrow \Sigma.Gen(1^{\lambda}), vk \leftarrow spk, msk \leftarrow ssk$

On message GETPK *from a party P:*

   return vk

On message (INSTALL, idx, prog) *from a party P where P.pid $\in$ reg:*

   if P is honest **then**
      assert idx = P.sid
   generate nonce eid $\in \{0,1\}^{\lambda}$, **store** $\mathcal{T}[eid, P] = (idx, prog, \emptyset)$
   send eid to P

On message (RESUME, eid, input) *from a party P where P.pid $\in$ reg:*

   let $(idx, prog, mem) \leftarrow \mathcal{T}[eid, P]$, abort if not found
   let $(output, mem') \leftarrow prog(input, mem)$, **store** $\mathcal{T}[eid, P] = (idx, prog, mem')$
   let $\sigma \leftarrow \Sigma.Sign(msk, (idx, eid, prog, output))$ and **send** $(output, \sigma)$ **to** P

The G_{att} functionality is a generalisation over other TEE formalisations, such as the one in [28], which tries to closely model some SGX implementation details. For instance, their hardware primitive distinguishes between local and remote attestation by exposing two sets of functions to produce and verify *reports* (for local attestation) and *quotes* (for remote attestation). Both data structure include enclave metadata, a tag that can uniquely identify the running program, input and output to the computation and some authentication primitive based on the former (MAC for local reports, signature for remote quotes). The G_{att} primitive, intended as an abstraction over different vendor implementations, removes much of this detail: both local and remote attestation consist in verifying the output of a *resume* call to some enclave through a public verification key, available both to machines with and without enclave capabilities. The output of computations is similarly the (anonymous) id of the enclave, the UC session id, some unique encode for the code computed by the enclave (which could be its source code, or its hash), and the output of the computation. Unlike in the Iron model, input does not have to be included in the attested return value, but if security requires parties to verify input, the function ca return it as part of its output. On enclave installation, its memory contents are initialised by the specification of its code; this initial memory state is represented by symbol $\emptyset$.

3 Functional Encryption for Stateful and Randomized Functionalities

In this section we define the ideal functionality of functional encryption for *stateful* and *randomized functionalities* (FESR).

FESR *syntax.*

- *(Setup)*: given security parameter 1^λ as input, KeyGen outputs master keypair mpk, msk
- *(Key generation)*: Setup takes msk, $F \in \mathsf{F}$ and returns functional key $\mathsf{sk_F}$
- *(Encryption)*: given string $\mathsf{x} \in \mathcal{X}$ and mpk, Enc returns ciphertext ct or an error
- *(Decryption)*: on evaluation over some ciphertext ct and functional key $\mathsf{sk_F}$, Dec returns $\mathsf{y} \in \mathcal{Y}$

While the above definition matches with that of classical functional encryption, we inject non-determinism and statefulness (respectively) by adding two additional inputs to functions in the allowed function class

$$\mathsf{F} : \mathcal{X} \times \mathcal{S} \times \mathcal{R} \to \mathcal{Y} \times \mathcal{S}$$

where $\mathcal{S} = \{0,1\}^{s(\lambda)}, \mathcal{R} = \{0,1\}^{r(\lambda)}$ for polynomials $s(\cdot)$ and $r(\cdot)$.

3.1 Properties of FESR

Matt and Maurer [41] shows that the notion of functional encryption is equivalent, up to assumed resources, to that of an access control (AC) repository, where some parties A are allowed to upload data, and other parties B are allowed to retrieve some function on that data, if they have received authorisation (granted by a party C). A party B does not learn anything else about the stored data, besides the function they are authorised to compute (and length leakage $\mathsf{F_0}$).

To allow stateful and randomized functions, we extend the function class with support for private state and randomness as above. Whenever B accesses a function on the data from the repository, the repository draws fresh randomness, evaluates the function on the old state. The function updates the state and evaluates to a value. Intuitively, this ideal world AC repository models both confidentiality and correctness:

Confidentiality. Confidentiality holds as B does not learn anything about the data besides the evaluations of these stateful randomized functions.

Correctness. A stateful functionality defines a stateful automaton, a set of states $\mathcal{S}$, the initial state $\emptyset \in \mathcal{S}$, a probabilistic transition function $\delta : \mathcal{X} \times \mathcal{S} \to \mathcal{Y} \times \mathcal{S}$. For every transition, a new input is sampled from $\mathcal{R}$ and given to F along with the input, to determine the next state. The transition function determines, for a given input and the current state, the probability Pr_δ that the automaton will find itself in a certain next state, as well as an output value. Correctness requires that all consecutive outputs must always be justified by some input and a state reachable via δ from $\emptyset$.

Correctness holds for the ideal world AC repository as B can make exactly those state transitions by accessing a function on the data from the repository.

3.2 UC Functionality

Our treatment considers the existence of several parties of type A (encryptors), B (decryptors), and a singular trusted authority C. The latter is allowed to run the KeyGen, Setup algorithms; parties of type A run Enc, and those of type B run Dec. The set of all decryptors (resp. encryptors) is denoted by **B** (resp. **A**). When the functionality receives a message from such a party, their UC extended id is used to distinguish who the sender is and store or retrieve the appropriate data. For simplicity, in our ideal functionality we refer to all parties by their type, with the implied assumption that it might refer to multiple distinct UC parties. For the sake of conciseness, we also omit including the sid parameter as an argument to every message.

The functionality reproduces the four algorithms that comprise functional encryption. During KeyGen, a record $\mathcal{P}$ is initialised for all t instances of B, to record the authorised functions for each instance, and its state. The Setup call marks a certain B as authorised to decrypt function F, and initialises its state to $\emptyset$. The Enc call allows a party A, B, to provide some input x, and receive a unique identifying handle h. This handle can then be provided, along with some F, to a decryption party to obtain an evaluation of F on the message stored therein. Performing the computation will also result in updating the state stored in $\mathcal{P}$.

Functionality FESR[sid, F, A, B, C]

The functionality is parameterized by the randomized function class **F** such that for each $F \in \mathbf{F} : \mathcal{X} \times \mathcal{S} \times \mathcal{R} \rightarrow \mathcal{Y} \times \mathcal{S}$, over state space $\mathcal{S}$ and randomness space $\mathcal{R}$, and by three distinct types of party identities A, B, C interacting with the functionality via dummy parties (that identify a particular role). For each decryptor/function pair, a state value is recorded.

State variables	Description
F_0	Leakage function returning the length of the message
setup[·] ← false	Table recording which parties were initialized.
$\mathcal{M}[\cdot] \leftarrow \perp$	Table storing the plaintext for each message handler
$\mathcal{P}[\cdot] \leftarrow \perp$	Table of authorized functions and their states for all decryption parties

On message (SETUP, P) *from party* C, *for* $P \in \{\mathsf{A}, \mathsf{B}\}$:
  setup[P] ← true
  send (SETUP, P) **to** $\mathcal{A}$
On message (SETUP, P) *from* $\mathcal{A}$, *for* $P \in \{\mathsf{A}, \mathsf{B}\}$:
  setup[P] ← true

$\mathcal{P}[P, F_0] \leftarrow \emptyset$
send SETUP to P

On message (ENCRYPT, x) *from party* $P \in \{A, B\}$:
  if setup$[P]$ = true $\wedge$ x $\in \mathcal{X}$ then
    compute h $\leftarrow$ getHandle
    $\mathcal{M}[h] \leftarrow$ x
    send (ENCRYPTED, h) to P

On message (KEYGEN, F, B) *from party* C:
  if F $\in$ F$^+$ $\wedge$ setup$[B]$ = true then
    send (KEYGEN, F, B) to $\mathcal{A}$ and receive ACK
    $\mathcal{P}[B, F] \leftarrow \emptyset$
    send (ASSIGNED, F) to B

On message (DECRYPT, h, F) *from party* B:
  x $\leftarrow \mathcal{M}[h]$
  if C is honest then
    if $\mathcal{P}[B, F] \neq \perp \wedge$ x $\in \mathcal{X}$ then
      r $\leftarrow \mathcal{R}$
      s $\leftarrow \mathcal{P}[B, F]$
      $(y, s) \leftarrow F(x, s, r)$
      $\mathcal{P}[B, F] \leftarrow s'$
      return (DECRYPTED, y)
  else
    send (DECRYPT, h, F, x) to $\mathcal{A}$ and receive (DECRYPTED, y)
    return (DECRYPTED, y)

The functionality is defined for possible corruptions of parties in **B**, **A**. If C is corrupted, we can no longer guarantee the evaluation to be correct, since C might authorize the adversary to compute any function in F. In this scenario, we allow the adversary to learn the original message value x and to provide an arbitrary evaluation y.

Note that, our definition is along the lines of [11,41], however, as opposed to [11], in which A and/or C might also get corrupted, in this work we primarily focus on the security guarantees provided by FE, which is confidentiality of the encrypted message against malicious decryptors, B. Yet, it provides security against malicious encryptors, A, thus it satisfies *input consistency*, which was originally introduced by [11]. In addition, our definition is the first one that captures stateful and randomized functionalities, where the latter refers to the standard notion of randomized functionalities in which each invocation of the function uses independent randomness. Therefore, our protocol achieves a stronger notion of randomized FE than [2,30,37], which require a new functional key for each invocation of the function, i.e., decryptions with the same functional key always return the same output.

Both correctness and confidentiality clearly hold for the ideal functionality by inspection of the 4 lines r $\leftarrow \mathcal{R}$, s $\leftarrow \mathcal{P}[B, F]$, $(y, s') \leftarrow F(x, s, r)$, and $\mathcal{P}[B, F] \leftarrow s'$.

4   A UC-Formulation of **Steel**

In this section we present **Steel** in the UCGS setting. As we already state above, our treatment involves three roles: the *key generation* party C, the *decryption* parties **B**, and the *encryption* parties **A**. Among them, only the encryptor does not need to have access to an enclave. Like the FESR functionality, the protocol fulfills confidentiality and correctness in the face of an adversarial B. We do not give any guarantees of security for corrupted A, C; although we remark informally that, as long as its enclave is secure, a corrupted C has little chances of learning the secret key. Besides the evaluation of any function in F it authorises itself to decrypt, it can also fake or extract from proofs of ciphertext validity π by authorizing a fake reference string crs. Before formally presenting our protocol we highlight important assumptions and conventions:

- For simplicity of presentation, we assume a single instance each for A, B
- all communication between parties (α, β) occurs over secure channels $\mathcal{SC}_\alpha^\beta, \mathcal{SC}_\beta^\alpha$
- Functional keys are (attestation) signatures by an enclave prog_{KME} on input (keygen, F) for some function F; it is easy, given a list of keys, to retrieve the one which authorises decryptions of F
- keyword **fetch** retrieves a stored variable from memory and aborts if the value is not found
- on keyword **assert** , the program checks that an expression is true, and proceeds to the next line, aborting otherwise
- all variables within an enclave are erased after use, unless saved to encrypted memory through the **store** keyword

Protocol **Steel** is parameterised by a function family $F : \mathcal{X} \times \mathcal{S} \times \mathcal{R} \to \mathcal{Y} \times \mathcal{S}$, UC parties A, B, C, a CCA secure public key encryption scheme PKE, a EU-CMA secure signature scheme Σ, a Robust non-interactive zero-knowledge scheme N, and security parameter λ.

Protocol Steel[F, A, B, C, PKE, Σ, N, λ]

State variables	Description
$\text{mpk} \leftarrow \perp$	Local copy of master public key for participants
$\text{prog}_{\{\text{KME,DE,FE}\}} \leftarrow \dots$	Source code of enclaves as defined below
$\mathcal{K}[\cdot] \leftarrow \emptyset$	Table of function keys at B

Key Generation Authority C:

On message (SETUP, P)*:*

  if mpk $= \perp$ **then**
    $\text{eid}_{\text{KME}} \leftarrow G_{\text{att}}.\text{install}(\text{C.sid}, \text{prog}_{\text{KME}})$
    send GET **to** $\mathcal{CRS}$ **and receive** (CRS, crs)
    $(\text{mpk}, \cdot) \leftarrow G_{\text{att}}.\text{resume}(\text{eid}_{\text{KME}}, (\text{init}, \text{crs}, \text{C.sid}))$
  if $P = $ A **then**
    send (SETUP, mpk) **to** $\mathcal{SC}_{\text{A}}$
  else if $P = $ B **then**
    send (SETUP, mpk, eid_{KME}) **to** $\mathcal{SC}_{\text{B}}$ **and receive** (PROVISION, σ, eid_{DE}, pk_{KD})
    $(\text{ct}_{\text{key}}, \sigma_{\text{sk}}) \leftarrow G_{\text{att}}.\text{resume}(\text{eid}_{\text{KME}}, (\text{provision}, (\sigma, \text{eid}_{\text{DE}}, \text{pk}_{KD}, \text{eid}_{\text{KME}})))$
    send (PROVISION, $\text{ct}_{\text{key}}, \sigma_{\text{sk}}$) **to** $\mathcal{SC}_{\text{B}}$

On message (KEYGEN, F, B):

> **assert** $F \in \mathbf{F} \wedge \mathsf{mpk} \neq \perp$
> $((\mathsf{keygen}, F), \sigma) \leftarrow G_{\mathsf{att}}.\mathsf{resume}(\mathsf{eid}_{\mathsf{KME}}, (\mathsf{keygen}, F))$
> $\mathsf{sk}_F \leftarrow \sigma;$ **send** $(\text{KEYGEN}, (F, \mathsf{sk}_F))$ **to** $\mathcal{SC}_B$

Encryption Party A:

On message $(\text{SETUP}, \mathsf{mpk})$ *from* $\mathcal{SC}^{\mathsf{C}}$:

> **send** GET **to** $\mathcal{CRS}$ and **receive** $(\text{CRS}, \mathsf{crs})$
> **store** $\mathsf{mpk}, \mathsf{crs};$ **return** SETUP

On message $(\text{ENCRYPT}, m)$:

> **assert** $\mathsf{mpk} \neq \perp \wedge m \in \mathcal{X}$
> $\mathsf{ct} \xleftarrow{\text{r}} \mathsf{PKE.Enc}(\mathsf{mpk}, m)$
> $\pi \leftarrow \mathcal{P}((\mathsf{mpk}, \mathsf{ct}), (m, r), \mathsf{crs}), \mathsf{ct}_{\mathsf{msg}} \leftarrow (\mathsf{ct}, \pi)$
> **send** $(\text{WRITE}, \mathsf{ct}_{\mathsf{msg}})$ **to** $\mathcal{REP}$ and **receive** h
> **return** $(\text{ENCRYPTED}, h)$

Decryption Party B:

On message $(\text{SETUP}, \mathsf{mpk}, \mathsf{eid}_{\mathsf{KME}})$ *from* $\mathcal{SC}^{\mathsf{C}}$:

> **store** $\mathsf{mpk};$ $\mathsf{eid}_{\mathsf{DE}} \leftarrow G_{\mathsf{att}}.\mathsf{install}(B.\mathsf{sid}, \mathsf{prog}_{\mathsf{DE}})$
> **send** GET **to** $\mathcal{CRS}$ and **receive** $(\text{CRS}, \mathsf{crs})$
> $((\mathsf{pk}_{KD}, \cdot, \cdot), \sigma) \leftarrow G_{\mathsf{att}}.\mathsf{resume}(\mathsf{eid}_{\mathsf{DE}}, \mathsf{init\text{-}setup}, \mathsf{eid}_{\mathsf{KME}}, \mathsf{crs}, B.\mathsf{sid})$
> **send** $(\text{PROVISION}, \sigma, \mathsf{eid}_{\mathsf{DE}}, \mathsf{pk}_{KD})$ **to** $\mathcal{SC}_{\mathsf{C}}$ and **receive** $(\text{PROVISION}, \mathsf{ct}_{\mathsf{key}}, \sigma_{\mathsf{KME}})$
> $G_{\mathsf{att}}.\mathsf{resume}(\mathsf{eid}_{\mathsf{DE}}, (\mathsf{complete\text{-}setup}, \mathsf{ct}_{\mathsf{key}}, \sigma_{\mathsf{KME}}))$
> **return** SETUP

On message $(\text{KEYGEN}, (F, \mathsf{sk}_F))$ *from* $\mathcal{SC}^{\mathsf{C}}$:

> $\mathsf{eid}_F \leftarrow G_{\mathsf{att}}.\mathsf{install}(B.\mathsf{sid}, \mathsf{prog}_{\mathsf{FE}}[F])$
> $(\mathsf{pk}_{\mathsf{FD}}, \sigma_F) \leftarrow G_{\mathsf{att}}.\mathsf{resume}(\mathsf{eid}_F, (\mathsf{init}, \mathsf{mpk}, B.\mathsf{sid}))$
> $\mathcal{K}[F] \leftarrow (\sigma_F, \mathsf{eid}_F, \mathsf{pk}_{\mathsf{FD}}, \mathsf{sk}_F)$
> **return** $(\text{ASSIGNED}, F)$

On message $(\text{DECRYPT}, F, h)$:

> **assert** $\mathcal{K}[F] \neq \perp$
> **send** (READ, h) **to** $\mathcal{REP}$ and **receive** $\mathsf{ct}_{\mathsf{msg}}$
> $(\sigma_F, \mathsf{eid}_F, \mathsf{pk}_{\mathsf{FD}}, \mathsf{sk}_F) \leftarrow \mathcal{K}[F]$
> $((\mathsf{ct}_{\mathsf{key}}, \mathsf{crs}), \sigma_{\mathsf{DE}}) \leftarrow G_{\mathsf{att}}.\mathsf{resume}(\mathsf{eid}_{\mathsf{DE}}, (\mathsf{provision}, \sigma_F, \mathsf{eid}_F, \mathsf{pk}_{\mathsf{FD}}, \mathsf{sk}_F, F))$
> $((\mathsf{computed}, y), \cdot) \leftarrow G_{\mathsf{att}}.\mathsf{resume}(\mathsf{eid}_F, (\mathsf{run}, \sigma_{\mathsf{DE}}, \mathsf{eid}_{\mathsf{DE}}, \mathsf{ct}_{\mathsf{key}}, \mathsf{ct}_{\mathsf{msg}}, \mathsf{crs}, \perp))$
> **return** $(\text{DECRYPTED}, y)$

$\underline{\mathsf{prog}_{\mathsf{KME}}}$:

on input $(\mathsf{init}, \mathsf{crs}, \mathsf{idx})$:

> **assert** $\mathsf{pk} = \perp; (\mathsf{pk}, \mathsf{sk}) \leftarrow \mathsf{PKE.PGen}()$
> **store** $\mathsf{sk}, \mathsf{crs}, \mathsf{idx};$ **return** pk

on input $(\mathsf{provision}, (\sigma_{\mathsf{DE}}, \mathsf{eid}_{\mathsf{DE}}, \mathsf{pk}_{KD}, \mathsf{eid}_{\mathsf{KME}}))$:

> $\mathsf{vk}_{\mathsf{att}} \leftarrow G_{\mathsf{att}}.\mathsf{vk};$ **fetch** $\mathsf{crs}, \mathsf{idx}$
> **assert** $\Sigma.\mathsf{Vrfy}(\mathsf{vk}_{\mathsf{att}}, (\mathsf{idx}, \mathsf{eid}_{\mathsf{DE}}, \mathsf{prog}_{\mathsf{DE}}, (\mathsf{pk}_{KD}, \mathsf{eid}_{\mathsf{KME}}, \mathsf{crs}), \sigma_{\mathsf{DE}})$
> $\mathsf{ct}_{\mathsf{key}} \leftarrow \mathsf{PKE.Enc}(\mathsf{pk}_{KD}, \mathsf{sk})$
> **return** $\mathsf{ct}_{\mathsf{key}}$

on input (keygen, F):

> **return** (keygen, F)

```
prog_DE:                                          prog_FE[F]:
on input (init-setup, eid_KME, crs, idx):        on input (init, mpk, idx):
   assert pk_KD ≠ ⊥                                  assert pk_FD = ⊥
   (pk_KD, sk_KD) ← PKE.Gen()                        (pk_FD, sk_FD) = PKE.Gen(1^λ)
   store sk_KD, eid_KME, crs, idx                    mem ← ∅; store sk_FD, mem, mpk, idx
   return pk_KD, eid_KME, crs                        return pk_FD
on input (complete-setup, ct_key, σ_KME):        on input (run, σ_DE, eid_DE, ct_key, ct_msg, crs, y'):
   vk_att ← G_att.vk                                 if y' ≠ ⊥
   fetch eid_KME, sk_KD, idx                            return (computed, y')
   m ← (idx, eid_KME, prog_KME, ct_key)             vk_att ← G_att.vk; (ct, π) ← ct_msg
   assert Σ.Vrfy(vk_att, m, σ_KME)                   fetch sk_FD, mem, mpk, idx
   sk ← PKE.Dec(sk_KD, ct_key)                       m ← (idx, eid_DE, prog_DE, ct_key, crs)
   store sk, vk_att                                  assert Σ.Vrfy(vk_att, m, σ_DE)
on input (provision, σ, eid, pk_FD, sk_F, F):       sk = PKE.Dec(sk_FD, ct_key)
   fetch eid_KME, vk_att, sk, idx                    assert N.V((mpk, ct), π, crs)
   m_1 ← (idx, eid_KME, prog_KME, (keygen, F))       x = PKE.Dec(sk, ct)
   m_2 ← (idx, eid, prog_FE[F], pk_FD)               out, mem' ← F(x, mem)
   assert Σ.Vrfy(vk_att, m_1, sk_F) and             store mem ← mem'
   Σ.Vrfy(vk_att, m_2, σ)                            return (computed, out)
   return PKE.Enc(pk_FD, sk), crs
```

As we mention in the Introduction, our modeling considers a "backdoor" in the prog_FE.run subroutine, such that, if the last argument is set, the subroutine just returns the value of that argument, along with a label declaring computation. The addition of the label *computed* is necessary, otherwise the backdoor would allow producing an attested value for the public key generated in subroutine prog_FE.init.

As a further addition we strengthen the encryption scheme with a plaintext proof of knowledge (PPoK). For public key pk, ciphertext ct, plaintext m, ciphertext randomness r, the relation $R = \{(pk, ct), (m, r) | ct = PKE.Enc(mpk, m; r)\}$ defines the language L_R of correctly computed ciphertexts. As a chosen-plaintext secure PKE scheme becomes CCA secure when extended with a simulation-extractable PPoK this is a natural strengthening of the CCA security requirement of Iron. However, it enables the simulator to extract valid plaintexts from all adversarial ciphertexts. In our security proof the simulator will submit these plaintexts to FESR on behalf of the corrupt B to keep the decryption states of the real and ideal world synchronized.

5   UC-Security of Steel

We now prove the security of Steel in the UCGS framework. To make the PST model compatible with the UCGS model, we first define the identity bound ξ.

The Identity Bound ξ on the Environment. Our restrictions are similar to [44], namely we assume that the environment can access G_{att} in the following ways: (1) Acting as a corrupt party, and (2) acting as an honest party but only for non-challenge protocol instances.

We now prove our main theorem.

Theorem 3 Steel *(Sect. 4) UC-realizes the* FESR *functionality (Sect. 3) in the presence of the global functionality* G_{att} *and local functionalities* $\mathcal{CRS}, \mathcal{REP}, \mathcal{SC}$, *with respect to the identity bound* ξ *defined above.*

We present a simulator algorithm such that, for all probabilistic adversaries running in polynomial time with the ability of corrupting B. Following [41], our proof considers static corruption of a single party B, we did, however, not encounter any road-blocks to adaptive corruption of multiple decryptors besides increased proof notational complexity. The environment is unable to distinguish between an execution of the Steel protocol in the real world, and the protocol consisting of $\mathcal{S}_{\mathrm{FESR}}$, dummy parties A, C and ideal functionality FESR. Both protocols have access to the shared global subroutines of G_{att}. While hybrid functionalities $\mathcal{REP}, \mathcal{SC}, \mathcal{CRS}$ (for their definition, see the full version) are only available in the real world and need to be reproduced by the simulator, we use $\mathcal{SC}$ in the simulator to denote simulated channels, either between the simulator and corrupted parties (for corrupt parties), or between the simulator and itself (for honest parties).

Given protocols Steel, FESR, and G_{att}, Steel ξ-UC emulates FESR in the presence of G_{att} if $M[\text{Steel}, G_{\mathrm{att}}]$ ξ-UC emulates $M[\text{FESR}, G_{\mathrm{att}}]$ (see Definition 2). We focus or exposition on the messages exchanged between the environment and the machine instances executing Steel, FESR, and G_{att}, since the machine M is simply routing messages; i.e., whenever $\mathcal{Z}$ wants to interact with the protocol, M simply forwards the message to the corresponding party; the same holds for G_{att}.

The simulator operates in the ideal world, where we have the environment $\mathcal{Z}$ sending message to dummy protocol parties which forward their inputs to the ideal functionality FESR. $\mathcal{S}_{\mathrm{FESR}}$ is activated either by an incoming message from a corrupted party or the adversary, or when FESR sends a message to the ideal world adversary. As $\mathcal{A}$ is a dummy adversary which normally forwards all queries between the corrupt party and the environment, $\mathcal{S}_{\mathrm{FESR}}$ gets to see all messages $\mathcal{Z}$ sends to $\mathcal{A}$. The simulator is allowed to send messages to the FESR and G_{att} functionalities impersonating corrupt parties. In the current setting, the only party that can be corrupted such that FESR still gives non trivial guarantees is party B. Thus, whenever the real world adversary or the ideal world simulator call G_{att}.install and G_{att}.resume for the challenge protocol instance, they must do so using an extended identity of B.

Simulator $\mathcal{S}_{\mathrm{FESR}}[\mathsf{PKE}, \Sigma, \mathsf{N}, \lambda, \mathsf{F}]$

State variables	Description
$\mathcal{H}[\cdot] \leftarrow \emptyset$	Table of ciphertext and handles in public repository
$\mathcal{K} \leftarrow []$	List of $\mathsf{prog}_{\mathsf{FE}}[\mathsf{F}]$ enclaves and their $\mathsf{eid}_{\mathsf{F}}$
$\mathcal{G} \leftarrow \{\}$	Collects all messages sent to G_{att} and its response
$\mathcal{B} \leftarrow \{\}$	Collects all messages signed by G_{att}
$(\mathsf{crs}, \tau) \leftarrow \mathsf{N}.\mathcal{S}_1$	Simulated reference string and trapdoor

For Key Generation Authority C:

On message (SETUP, P) *from FESR:*

  if mpk $= \bot$ **then**
    $\mathsf{eid_{KME}} \leftarrow G_{\mathsf{att}}.\mathsf{install}(\mathsf{C.sid}, \mathsf{prog_{KME}})$
    $(\mathsf{mpk}, \cdot) \leftarrow G_{\mathsf{att}}.\mathsf{resume}(\mathsf{eid_{KME}}, \mathsf{init})$
  if $P = \mathsf{A}$ **then**
    send (SETUP, mpk) **to** $\mathcal{SC}_{\mathsf{A}}$
  else if $P = \mathsf{B}$ **then**
    send (SETUP, mpk, $\mathsf{eid_{KME}}$) **to** $\mathcal{SC}_{\mathsf{B}}$ **and receive** (PROVISION, σ, $\mathsf{eid_{DE}}$, pk_{KD})
    assert (C.sid, $\mathsf{eid_{DE}}$, $\mathsf{prog_{DE}}$, pk_{KD}) $\in \mathcal{B}[\sigma]$
    $(\mathsf{ct_{key}}, \sigma_{\mathsf{sk}}) \leftarrow G_{\mathsf{att}}.\mathsf{resume}(\mathsf{eid_{KME}}, (\mathsf{provision}, (\sigma, \mathsf{eid_{DE}}, \mathsf{pk}_{KD}, \mathsf{eid_{KME}}, \mathsf{crs}))))$
    send (PROVISION, $\mathsf{ct_{key}}$, σ_{sk}) **to** $\mathcal{SC}_{\mathsf{B}}$

On message (KEYGEN, F, B) *from FESR:*

  assert $\mathsf{F} \in \mathbf{F} \wedge \mathsf{mpk} \neq \bot$
  $((\mathsf{keygen}, \mathsf{F}), \sigma) \leftarrow G_{\mathsf{att}}.\mathsf{resume}(\mathsf{eid_{KME}}, (\mathsf{keygen}, \mathsf{F}))$
  $\mathsf{sk_F} \leftarrow \sigma$
  send (KEYGEN, (F, $\mathsf{sk_F}$)) **to** $\mathcal{SC}_{\mathsf{B}}$

For Decryption Party B:

On message GET *from party* B *to* $\mathcal{CRS}$:

  send (CRS, crs) **to** B

On message (READ, h) *from party* B *to* $\mathcal{REP}$:

  send (DECRYPT, $\mathsf{F_0}$, h) **to** FESR on behalf of B **and receive** $|\mathsf{m}|$
  assert $|\mathsf{m}| \neq \bot$
  $\mathsf{ct} \leftarrow \mathsf{PKE.Enc}(\mathsf{mpk}, 0^{|\mathsf{m}|})$
  $\pi \leftarrow \mathsf{N}.\mathcal{S}_2(\mathsf{crs}, \tau, (\mathsf{mpk}, \mathsf{ct}))$
  $\mathsf{ct_{msg}} \leftarrow (\mathsf{ct}, \pi)$; $\mathcal{H}[\mathsf{ct_{msg}}] \leftarrow h$
  send (READ, $\mathsf{ct_{msg}}$) **to** B

On message (INSTALL, idx, prog) *from party* B *to* G_{att}:

  $\mathsf{eid} \leftarrow G_{\mathsf{att}}.\mathsf{install}(\mathsf{idx}, \mathsf{prog})$
  $\mathcal{G}[\mathsf{eid}].\mathsf{install} \leftarrow (\mathsf{idx}, \mathsf{prog})$
  // $\mathcal{G}[\mathsf{eid}].install[1]$ is the program's code
  forward eid **to** B

On message (RESUME, eid, input) *from party* B *to* G_{att}:

  // The G_{att} registry does not allow B to access $\mathsf{eid_{KME}}$ in real world
  assert $\mathcal{G}[\mathsf{eid}] \neq \bot \wedge \mathsf{eid} \neq \mathsf{eid_{KME}}$
  if $\mathcal{G}[\mathsf{eid}].\mathsf{install}[1] \neq \mathsf{prog_{FE}}[\cdot] \vee \mathsf{input}[-1] \neq \bot$ **then**
    $(\mathsf{output}, \sigma) \leftarrow G_{\mathsf{att}}.\mathsf{resume}(\mathsf{eid}, \mathsf{input})$
    $\mathcal{G}[\mathsf{eid}].\mathsf{resume} \leftarrow \mathcal{G}[\mathsf{eid}].\mathsf{resume} \| (\sigma, \mathsf{input}, \mathsf{output}))$
    $\mathcal{B}[\sigma] \leftarrow (\mathcal{G}[\mathsf{eid}].\mathsf{install}[0], \mathsf{eid}, \mathcal{G}[\mathsf{eid}].\mathsf{install}[1], \mathsf{output})$
    if $\mathcal{G}[\mathsf{eid}].\mathsf{install}[1] = \mathsf{prog_{DE}} \wedge \mathsf{input}[0] = \mathsf{provision}$ **then**
      $(\mathsf{provision}, \sigma, \mathsf{eid}, \mathsf{pk_{FD}}, \mathsf{sk_F}, \mathsf{F}) \leftarrow \mathsf{input}$
      fetch $(\cdot, (\mathsf{init\text{-}setup}, \mathsf{eid_{KME}}, \mathsf{crs}), \cdot) \in \mathcal{G}[\mathsf{eid}].\mathsf{resume}$
      assert $(\mathsf{idx}, \mathsf{eid_{KME}}, \mathsf{prog_{KME}}, (\mathsf{keygen}, \mathsf{F})) \in \mathcal{B}[\mathsf{sk_F}]$
      assert $(\mathsf{idx}, \mathsf{eid_{DE}}, \mathsf{prog_{DE}}, \mathsf{ct_{key}}, \mathsf{crs}) \in \mathcal{B}[\sigma_{\mathsf{DE}}]$
    forward $(\mathsf{output}, \sigma)$ **to** B
  else

idx, prog$_{FE}$[F] ← $\mathcal{G}$[eid].install
(run, σ_{DE}, eid$_{DE}$, ct$_{key}$, ct$_{msg}$, crs, $\bot$) ← input
assert (σ_F, (init), (pk$_{FD}$)) ∈ $\mathcal{G}$[eid].resume
assert (idx, eid, prog$_{FE}$[F], pk$_{FD}$) ∈ $\mathcal{B}$[σ_F]
assert (idx, eid$_{DE}$, prog$_{DE}$, ct$_{key}$, crs) ∈ $\mathcal{B}$[σ_{DE}]
// If the ciphertext was not computed honestly and saved to $\mathcal{H}$
if $\mathcal{H}$[ct$_{msg}$] = $\bot$ **then**
    (ct, π) ← ct$_{msg}$
    (m, r) ← N.$\mathcal{E}$(τ, (mpk, ct), π)
    if m = $\bot$ **then send** (DECRYPT, F, $\bot$) **to** B **and abort**

    send (ENCRYPT, m) **to** FESR on behalf of B **and receive** h
    $\mathcal{H}$[ct$_{msg}$] ← h
h ← $\mathcal{H}$[ct$_{msg}$]
send (DECRYPT, F, h) **to** FESR on behalf of B **and receive** y
((computed, y), σ) ← G_{att}.resume(eid$_F$, (run, $\bot$, $\bot$, $\bot$, $\bot$, $\bot$, y))
$\mathcal{G}$[eid].resume ← $\mathcal{G}$[eid].resume $\|$ (σ, input, (computed, y)))
$\mathcal{B}$[σ] ← ($\mathcal{G}$[eid].install[0], eid, $\mathcal{G}$[eid].install[1], (computed, y))
forward ((computed, y), σ) **to** B

Designing the Simulation. The ideal functionality FESR and protocol Steel
share the same interface consisting of messages SETUP, KEYGEN, ENCRYPT,
DECRYPT. During Steel's SETUP, the protocol generates public parameters when
first run, and provisions the encrypted secret key to the enclaves of B. As neither
of these operations are executed by the ideal functionality, we need to simulate
them, generating and distributing keys outside of party C.

As in Steel, we distribute the public encryption key on behalf of C to any
newly registered B and A over secure channels. Once B has received this message,
it will try to obtain the (encrypted) decryption key for the global PKE scheme
from party C and its provision subroutine of prog$_{KME}$. Since C is a dummy party
in the ideal world, it would not respond to this request, so we let $\mathcal{S}_{FESR}$ respond.
In Steel key parameters are generated within the key management enclave, and
communication of the encrypted secret key to the decryption enclave produces
an attestation signature. Thus, the simulator, which can access G_{att} impersonating B, is required to install an enclave. Because of the property of anonymous
attestation, the environment cannot distinguish whether the new enclave was
installed on B or C. If the environment tries to resume the program running
under eid$_{KME}$ through B, this is intercepted and dropped by the simulator.

Before sending the encrypted secret key, the simulator verifies that B's public
key was correctly produced by an attested decryption enclave, and was initialised
with the correct parameters. If an honest enclave has been instantiated and we
can verify that it uses pk$_{KD}$, eid$_{KME}$, crs, we can safely send the encrypted sk to
the corrupted party as no one can retrieve the decryption key from outside the
enclave.

On message (KEYGEN, F, B) from the functionality after a call to KEYGEN,
$\mathcal{S}_{FESR}$ simply produces a functional key by running the appropriate prog$_{KME}$ pro-

cedure through G_{att}. Similarly, on receiving (READ, h) for $\mathcal{REP}$, $\mathcal{S}_{\text{FESR}}$ produces an encryption of a canonical message (a string of zeros) and simulates the response.

When the request to compute the functional decryption of the corresponding ciphertext is sent to $\text{prog}_{\text{FE}}[F]$, we verify that the party B has adhered to the Steel protocol execution, aborting if any of the required enclave installation or execution steps have been omitted, or if any of the requests were made with dishonest parameters generated outside the enclave execution (we can verify this through the attestation of enclave execution). If the ciphertext was not obtained through a request to $\mathcal{REP}$, we use the NIZK extractor to learn the plaintext m and submit a message (ENCRYPT, m) to FESR on behalf of the corrupt B. This guarantees that the state of FESR is in sync with the state of $\text{prog}_{\text{FE}}[F]$ in the real world.

If all such checks succeed, and the provided functional key is valid, $\mathcal{S}_{\text{FESR}}$ fetches the decryption from the ideal functionality. While the Steel protocol ignores the value of the attested execution of run, we can expect the adversary to check its result for authenticity. Therefore, it is necessary to pass the result of our decryption y through the backdoor we constructed in $\text{prog}_{\text{FE}}[F]$. This will produce an authentic attestation signature on y, which will pass any verification check convincingly (as discussed in the previous section, the backdoor does not otherwise impact the security of the protocol).

The full proof of security is available in the full version; for an overview, refer to Sect. 1.2.

6   Rollback and Forking Attacks

While the Attested Execution functionality modelled by G_{att} is a meaningful first step for modeling attested execution, it is easy to argue that it is not realisable (in a UC-emulation sense) by any of the existing Trusted Execution Environment platforms to date. In a follow-up paper, Tramer et al. [52] weaken the original G_{att} model to allow complete leakage of the memory state. This is perhaps an excessively strong model, as the use of side channel attacks might only allow a portion of the memory or randomness to be learned by the adversary. Additionally, there are many other classes of attacks that can not be expressed by this model. We now extend the G_{att} functionality to model *rollback* and *forking attacks* against an enclave.

6.1 $G_{\text{att}}^{\text{rollback}}$ Functionality

Our model of rollback and forking attacks is drawn from the formulation expressed in Matetic et al. [40], but with PST's improved modelling of attestation, which does not assume perfectly secure authenticated reads/writes between the attester and the enclave.

Matetic et al. model rollback by distinguishing between enclaves and enclave instances. Enclave instances have a distinct memory state, while sharing the same code. As with G_{att}, where the outside world has to call subroutines individually, the environment is not allowed to interact directly with a program once it is instantiated, except for pausing, resuming, or deleting enclave instances. Additionally, their model provides functions to store encrypted memory outside the enclave (*Seal*) and load memory back (*Unseal*).

In a typical rollback attack, an attacker crashes an enclave, erasing its volatile memory. As the enclave instance is restarted, it attempts to restart from the current state snapshot. By replacing this with a stale snapshot, the attacker is able to rewind the enclave state.

In a forking attack an attacker manages to run two instances of the same enclave concurrently, such that, once the state of one instance is changed by an external operation, querying the other instance will result in an outdated state. This relies on both enclaves producing signature that at the minimum attest the same program. On a system where attestation uniquely identifies each copy of the enclave, a forking attack can still be launched by an attacker conducting multiple rollback attacks and feeding different stale snapshots to a single enclave copy [17].

Our new functionality $G_{\mathsf{att}}^{\mathsf{rollback}}$ employs this idea to model the effect of both rollback and forking attacks. We replace the internal mem variable of G_{att} with a tree data structure. The honest caller to the functionality will always continue execution from the memory state of an existing leaf of the tree while an adversary can specify an arbitrary node of the tree (through a unique node identifier), to which the state of the enclave gets reset. The output mem' will then be appended as a new child branch to the tree. To model a rollback attack, the adversary specifies the parent node for the next call to resume (or any ancestor node to execute a second rollback). To model a forking attack, the adversary can interactively choose nodes in different branches of the tree. The functionality is parameterised with a signature scheme and a registry to capture all platforms with a TEE, like in the original formulation.

Functionality $G_{\mathsf{att}}[\Sigma, \mathsf{reg}, \lambda]$

State variables	Description
vk	Master verification key, available to enclave programs
msk	Master secret key, protected by the hardware
$\mathcal{T} \leftarrow \emptyset$	Table for installed programs

On message INITIALIZE *from a party P:*
   let $(\mathsf{spk}, \mathsf{ssk}) \leftarrow \Sigma.\mathsf{Gen}(1^\lambda), \mathsf{vk} \leftarrow \mathsf{spk}, \mathsf{msk} \leftarrow \mathsf{ssk}$
On message GETPK *from a party P:*
   return vk
On message (INSTALL, idx, prog) *from a party P where P.pid $\in$ reg:*
   if P is honest **then**
      assert idx $= P.\mathsf{sid}$
   generate nonce eid $\in \{0,1\}^\lambda$, **store** $\mathcal{T}[\mathsf{eid}, P] = (\mathsf{idx}, \mathsf{prog}, \mathsf{root}, \mathsf{Tree}(\emptyset))$
   send eid to P
On message (RESUME, eid, input, node) *from a party P where P.pid $\in$ reg:*

```
let (idx, prog, lastnode, tree) ← T[eid, P], abort if not found
if P is honest then
    let node ← lastnode
let mem ← access(tree, node)
let (output, mem') ← prog(input, mem)
let tree', child ← insertChild(tree, node, mem')
let update T[eid, P] = (idx, prog, child, tree')
let σ ← Σ.Sign(msk, (idx, eid, prog, output)) and send (output, σ) to P
```

The proposed rollback model is perhaps somewhat reductive, as it only allows "discrete" rollback operations, where memory states are quantised by program subroutines. It is conceivable that real world attackers would have a finer-grained rollback model, where they can interrupt the subroutine's execution, and resume from an arbitrary instruction.

Attack on Stateful Functional Encryption. Although our protocol uses probabilistic primitives, we deem the generic reset attack presented in [55] unrealistic for TEE platforms such as SGX, where an enclave is allowed direct access to a hardware-based source of randomness [7].

On the other hand, it easy to find a protocol-specific rollback attack on Steel. While F's state remains secret to a corrupt B interacting with $G_{att}^{rollback}$ (the memory is still sealed when stored), an adversary can make enclave calls produce results that would be impossible in the simpler model. As an example, take the following function from F that allows setting a key and sampling the output of a PRF function F for a single message:

```
function PRF-WRAPPER(x, mem)
    if mem = ∅ then
        K ← x
        Store mem ← K
        return ACK
    else if mem = 1⃗ then
        return ⊥
    else
        Store mem ← 1⃗
        return F_K(x)
```

An adversary who has completed initialisation of its decryption enclave with enclave id eid_{DE}, obtained a functional key sk through the execution of keygen on eid_{KME}, and initialised a functional enclave for PRF-WRAPPER with enclave id eid_F, public key pk_{FD} and attestation $σ$, executes the current operations for three ciphertexts $ct_K, ct_x, ct_{x'}$, encrypting a key K and plaintexts x, x':

1: $((ct_{key}, crs), σ_{DE}) ← G_{att}.resume(eid_{DE}, (provision, σ, eid, pk_{FD}, sk))$
2: $((computed, ACK), ·) ← G_{att}^{rollback}.resume(eid_F, (run, vk_{att}, σ_{DE}, eid_{DE}, ct_{key}, ct_k, crs, ⊥), node)$
3: // node is the node id for a leaf for eid_F's mem tree
4: $((computed, y), ·) ← G_{att}^{rollback}.resume(eid_F, (run, vk_{att}, σ_{DE}, eid_{DE}, ct_{key}, ct_x, crs, ⊥), node')$

5: // node$'$ is the node id for a leaf for eid$_F$'s mem tree
6: ((computed, y$'$), ·) ← $G_{att}^{rollback}$.resume(eid$_F$, (run, vk$_{att}$, σ_{DE}, eid$_{DE}$, ct$_{key}$, ct$_{x'}$, crs, ⊥), node$'$)
7: // node$'$ is the same node id as in the previous call (and thus to the parent of the current leaf in mem)

As a result of this execution trace, the adversary violates correctness by inserting an illegal transition (with input ϵ) in the stateful automaton for PRF-WRAPPER, from state access(tree, node$'$.$child$) = $\vec{1}$ back to access(tree, node$'$) = $[K]$, and then back to state $\vec{1}$ with input x$'$. The adversary can then obtain the illegal set of values y ← $F_K(x)$ and y$'$ ← $F_K(x')$, whereas in the ideal world after obtaining y, the only possible output for the function would be ⊥ (the only legal transition from state $\vec{1}$ leads back to itself). The simulator is unable to address this attack, as the memory state is internal to the ideal functionality, and the key will always be erased after the second call.

One might think that the simulator could respond by sampling a value from the uniform distribution and feed it through the enclave's backdoor; however, the environment can reveal the key k and messages x, x$'$ to the adversary, or conversely the adversary could reveal the uniform value to the environment. Thus the environment can trivially distinguish between the honest PRF output and the uniform distribution, and thus between the real and ideal world. Note that this communication between environment and adversary is necessary for universal composition as this leakage of k, x, x$'$ could happen as part of a wider protocol employing functional encryption.

Mitigation Techniques. In Sect. 1.3, we showed that rollback resilience for trusted execution environments is an active area of research, with many competing protocols. However, most solutions inevitably entail a performance trade-off.

Due to the modular nature of Steel, it is possible to minimise the performance impact. Observe that party B instantiates a single DE and multiple FE. We can reduce the performance penalty by making only DE rollback resilient. We guarantee correctness despite rollbacks of FE, by encoding a counter alongside the function state for each F. On a decryption request, the prog$_{FE}$ enclave is required to check in with the prog$_{DE}$ enclave to retrieve the decryption key as part of the provision call. To enable rollback resilience, we include the counter stored by prog$_{FE}$ as an additional parameter of this call. prog$_{DE}$ compares the counter received for the current evaluation of F with the one received during the last evaluation, and authorises the transfer of the secret key only if greater. Before evaluating the function, prog$_{FE}$ increases and stores its local counter.

To achieve rollback resilience for the prog$_{DE}$ enclave, we can rely on existing techniques in the literature, such as augmenting the enclave with asynchronous monotonic counters [14], or using protocols like LCM [17] or ROTE [40]. Formalising how these protocols can be combined with the $G_{att}^{rollback}$ functionality to achieve the fully secure G_{att} is left for future work.

We also note that Stateless functional encryption as implemented in IRON is resilient to rollback and forking because there is little state held between computation. Since we assume C is honest, the only programs liable to be attacked are DE and FE[F].

DE stores PKE Parameters after init setup, and the decrypted master secret key after complete setup. The adversary could try to gain some advantage by creating multiple PKE pairs before authenticating with the authority, but will never has access to the raw sk unless combining it with a leakage attack. Denial of Service is possible by creating concurrent enclaves (either DE or FE) with different PKs, and passing encrypted ciphertexts to the "wrong" copy which would be unable to decrypt (but it's not clear what the advantage of using rollback attacks would be, as the adversary could always conduct a DoS attack by denying the necessary resources to the enclave).

Acknowledgements. This research was partially supported by the National Cyber Security Centre, the UK Research Institute in Secure Hardware and Embedded Systems (RISE), and the European Union's Horizon 2020 Research and Innovation Programme under grant agreement 780108 (FENTEC).

References

1. Abdalla, M., Benhamouda, F., Kohlweiss, M., Waldner, H.: Decentralizing inner-product functional encryption. In: Lin, D., Sako, K. (eds.) PKC 2019. LNCS, vol. 11443, pp. 128–157. Springer, Cham (2019). https://doi.org/10.1007/978-3-030-17259-6_5

2. Agrawal, S., Wu, D.J.: Functional encryption: deterministic to randomized functions from simple assumptions. In: Coron, J.-S., Nielsen, J.B. (eds.) EUROCRYPT 2017. LNCS, vol. 10211, pp. 30–61. Springer, Cham (2017). https://doi.org/10.1007/978-3-319-56614-6_2

3. Agrawal, S., Gorbunov, S., Vaikuntanathan, V., Wee, H.: Functional encryption: new perspectives and lower bounds. In: Canetti, R., Garay, J.A. (eds.) CRYPTO 2013. LNCS, vol. 8043, pp. 500–518. Springer, Heidelberg (2013). https://doi.org/10.1007/978-3-642-40084-1_28

4. Ahmad, A., Joe, B., Xiao, Y., Zhang, Y., Shin, I., Lee, B.: OBFUSCURO: a commodity obfuscation engine on intel SGX. In: 26th Annual Network and Distributed System Security Symposium, NDSS 2019, San Diego, California, USA, February 24–27, 2019. The Internet Society (2019). ISBN 1-891562-55-X. https://www.ndss-symposium.org/ndss-paper/obfuscuro-a-commodity-obfuscation-engine-on-intel-sgx/

5. Cloud, A.: TEE-based confidential computing. https://www.alibabacloud.com/help/doc-detail/164536.htm (2020)

6. Ateniese, G., Kiayias, A., Magri, B., Tselekounis, Y., Venturi, D.: Secure outsourcing of cryptographic circuits manufacturing. In: Baek, J., Susilo, W., Kim, J. (eds.) ProvSec 2018. LNCS, vol. 11192, pp. 75–93. Springer, Cham (2018). https://doi.org/10.1007/978-3-030-01446-9_5

7. Aumasson, J., Merino, L.: SGX secure enclaves in practice: security and crypto review. Black Hat **2016**, 10 (2016)

8. Badertscher, C., Maurer, U., Tschudi, D., Zikas, V.: Bitcoin as a transaction ledger: a composable treatment. In: Katz, J., Shacham, H. (eds.) CRYPTO 2017. LNCS, vol. 10401, pp. 324–356. Springer, Cham (2017). https://doi.org/10.1007/978-3-319-63688-7_11

9. Badertscher, C., Canetti, R., Hesse, J., Tackmann, B., Zikas, V.: Universal composition with global subroutines: capturing global setup within plain UC. In: Pass, R., Pietrzak, K. (eds.) TCC 2020. LNCS, vol. 12552, pp. 1–30. Springer, Cham (2020). https://doi.org/10.1007/978-3-030-64381-2_1

10. Badertscher, C., Canetti, R., Hesse, J., Tackmann, B., Zikas, V.: Universal composition with global subroutines: capturing global setup within plain UC. In: Pass, R., Pietrzak, K. (eds.) TCC 2020. LNCS, vol. 12552, pp. 1–30. Springer, Cham (2020). https://doi.org/10.1007/978-3-030-64381-2_1

11. Badertscher, C., Kiayias, A., Kohlweiss, M., Waldner, H.: Consistency for functional encryption. Cryptology ePrint Archive, Report 2020/137 (2020). https://eprint.iacr.org/2020/137

12. Baghery, K., Kohlweiss, M., Siim, J., Volkhov, M.: Another look at extraction and randomization of groth's zk-SNARK. Cryptology ePrint Archive, Report 2020/811 (2020). https://eprint.iacr.org/2020/811

13. Bahmani, R., et al.: Secure multiparty computation from SGX. In: Kiayias, A. (ed.) FC 2017. LNCS, vol. 10322, pp. 477–497. Springer, Cham (2017). https://doi.org/10.1007/978-3-319-70972-7_27

14. Bailleu, M., Thalheim, J., Bhatotia, P., Fetzer, C., Honda, M., Vaswani, K.: SPEICHER: securing lsm-based key-value stores using shielded execution. In: Merchant, A., Weatherspoon, H. (eds.) 17th USENIX Conference on File and Storage Technologies, FAST 2019, Boston, MA, February 25–28, 2019, pages 173–190. USENIX Association (2019). URL https://www.usenix.org/conference/fast19/presentation/bailleu

15. Barbosa, M., Portela, B., Scerri, G., Warinschi, B.: Foundations of hardware-based attested computation and application to SGX. Cryptology ePrint Archive, Report 2016/014 (2016). http://eprint.iacr.org/2016/014

16. Boneh, D., Sahai, A., Waters, B.: Functional encryption: definitions and challenges. In: Ishai, Y. (ed.) TCC 2011. LNCS, vol. 6597, pp. 253–273. Springer, Heidelberg (2011). https://doi.org/10.1007/978-3-642-19571-6_16

17. Brandenburger, M., Cachin, C., Lorenz, M., Kapitza, R.: Rollback and forking detection for trusted execution environments using lightweight collective memory. CoRR (2017). URL http://arxiv.org/abs/1701.00981v2

18. Canetti, R.: Universally composable security: a new paradigm for cryptographic protocols. Cryptology ePrint Archive, Report 2000/067 (2000). http://eprint.iacr.org/2000/067

19. Canetti, R., Dodis, Y., Pass, R., Walfish, S.: Universally composable security with global setup. In: Vadhan, S.P. (ed.) TCC 2007. LNCS, vol. 4392, pp. 61–85. Springer, Heidelberg (2007). https://doi.org/10.1007/978-3-540-70936-7_4

20. Canetti, R., Shahaf, D., Vald, M.: Universally composable authentication and key-exchange with global PKI. In: Cheng, C.-M., Chung, K.-M., Persiano, G., Yang, B.-Y. (eds.) PKC 2016. LNCS, vol. 9615, pp. 265–296. Springer, Heidelberg (2016). https://doi.org/10.1007/978-3-662-49387-8_11

21. Cen, S., Zhang, B.: Trusted time and monotonic counters with intel software guard extensions platform services (2017). https://software.intel.com/sites/default/files/managed/1b/a2/Intel-SGX-Platform-Services.pdf

22. Cheng, R., et al.: Ekiden: a platform for confidentiality-preserving, trustworthy, and performant smart contract execution. CoRR, abs/1804.05141 (2018). URL http://arxiv.org/abs/1804.05141

23. Chotard, J., Dufour Sans, E., Gay, R., Phan, D.H., Pointcheval, D.: Decentralized multi-client functional encryption for inner product. In: Peyrin, T., Galbraith, S. (eds.) ASIACRYPT 2018. LNCS, vol. 11273, pp. 703–732. Springer, Cham (2018). https://doi.org/10.1007/978-3-030-03329-3_24

24. Choudhuri, A.R., Green, M., Jain, A., Kaptchuk, G., Miers, I.: Fairness in an unfair world: fair multiparty computation from public bulletin boards. In: Thuraisingham, B.M., Evans, D., Malkin, T., Xu, D. (eds.) ACM CCS, Dallas, TX, USA, Oct. 31 - Nov. 2, 2017. pp. 719–728. ACM (2017)

25. Chung, K.-M., Katz, J., Zhou, H.-S.: Functional encryption from (small) hardware tokens. In: Sako, K., Sarkar, P. (eds.) ASIACRYPT 2013. LNCS, vol. 8270, pp. 120–139. Springer, Heidelberg (2013). https://doi.org/10.1007/978-3-642-42045-0_7

26. Ciampi, M., Lu, Y., Zikas, V.: Collusion-preserving computation without a mediator. Cryptology ePrint Archive, Report 2020/497 (2020). https://eprint.iacr.org/2020/497

27. Costan, V., Devadas, S.: Intel SGX explained. Cryptology ePrint Archive, Report 2016/086 (2016). http://eprint.iacr.org/2016/086

28. Fisch, B., Vinayagamurthy, D., Boneh, D., Gorbunov, S.: IRON: functional encryption using intel SGX. In: Thuraisingham, B.M., Evans, D., Malkin, T., Xu, D. (eds.) ACM CCS, Dallas, TX, USA, Oct. 31 - Nov. 2, 2017, pp. 765–782. ACM (2017)

29. Garlati, C., Pinto, S.: A clean slate approach to Linux security RISC-V enclaves (2020)

30. Goyal, V., Jain, A., Koppula, V., Sahai, A.: Functional encryption for randomized functionalities. In: Dodis, Y., Nielsen, J.B. (eds.) TCC 2015. LNCS, vol. 9015, pp. 325–351. Springer, Heidelberg (2015). https://doi.org/10.1007/978-3-662-46497-7_13

31. Gregor, F., et al.: Trust management as a service: enabling trusted execution in the face of byzantine stakeholders. CoRR, abs/2003.14099 (2020). URL https://arxiv.org/abs/2003.14099

32. Hoang, V.T., Reyhanitabar, R., Rogaway, P., Vizár, D.: Online authenticated-encryption and its nonce-reuse misuse-resistance. In: Gennaro, R., Robshaw, M. (eds.) CRYPTO 2015. LNCS, vol. 9215, pp. 493–517. Springer, Heidelberg (2015). https://doi.org/10.1007/978-3-662-47989-6_24

33. Kaplan, D., Powell, J., Woller, T.: AMD memory encryption. White paper (2016)

34. Kiayias, A., Tselekounis, Y.: Tamper resilient circuits: the adversary at the gates. In: Sako, K., Sarkar, P. (eds.) ASIACRYPT 2013. LNCS, vol. 8270, pp. 161–180. Springer, Heidelberg (2013). https://doi.org/10.1007/978-3-642-42045-0_9

35. Kiayias, A., Liu, F.H., Tselekounis, Y.: Practical non-malleable codes from l-more extractable hash functions. In: Weippl, E.R., Katzenbeisser, S., Kruegel, C., Myers, A.C., Halevi, S. (eds.) ACM CCS, Vienna, Austria, Oct. 24–28, 2016. pp. 1317–1328. ACM (2016)

36. Kiayias, A., Liu, F.-H., Tselekounis, Y.: Non-malleable codes for partial functions with manipulation detection. In: Shacham, H., Boldyreva, A. (eds.) CRYPTO 2018. LNCS, vol. 10993, pp. 577–607. Springer, Cham (2018). https://doi.org/10.1007/978-3-319-96878-0_20

37. Komargodski, I., Segev, G., Yogev, E.: Functional encryption for randomized functionalities in the private-key setting from minimal assumptions. J. Cryptol. 31(1), 60–100 (2017). https://doi.org/10.1007/s00145-016-9250-8

38. Lee, D., Kohlbrenner, D., Shinde, S., Asanović, K., Song, D.: Keystone: an open framework for architecting trusted execution environments. In: Proceedings of the Fifteenth European Conference on Computer Systems, pp. 1–16 (2020)

39. Levin, D., Douceur, J.R., Lorch, J.R., Moscibroda, T.: Trinc: small trusted hardware for large distributed systems. NSDI **9**, 1–14 (2009)
40. Matetic, S., et al.: ROTE: rollback protection for trusted execution. Cryptology ePrint Archive, Report 2017/048 (2017). http://eprint.iacr.org/2017/048
41. Matt, C., Maurer, U.: A definitional framework for functional encryption. In: Fournet, C., Hicks, M. (eds.) CSF 2015Computer Security Foundations Symposium, Verona, Italy, jul 13–17, pp. 217–231 IEEE (2015)
42. Nayak, K., et al.: HOP: hardware makes obfuscation practical. In: NDSS 2017, San Diego, CA, USA, Feb. 26 - Mar. 1, The Internet Society (2017)
43. Parno, B., McCune, J.M., Perrig, A.: Bootstrapping trust in commodity computers. In: 2010 IEEE Symposium on Security and Privacy, Berkeley/Oakland, CA, USA, May 16–19, pp. 414–429. IEEE Computer Society Press (2010)
44. Pass, R., Shi, E., Tramèr, F.: Formal abstractions for attested execution secure processors. In: Coron, J.-S., Nielsen, J.B. (eds.) EUROCRYPT 2017. LNCS, vol. 10210, pp. 260–289. Springer, Cham (2017). https://doi.org/10.1007/978-3-319-56620-7_10
45. Pinto, S., Santos, N.: Demystifying arm trustzone: a comprehensive survey. ACM Comput. Surv. **51**, 1–36 (2019)
46. Porter, N., Golanand, G., Lugani, S.: Introducing google cloud confidential computing with confidential VMs. (2020)
47. Russinovich, M.: Introducing azure confidential computing (2017)
48. Sahai, A., Waters, B.: Fuzzy identity-based encryption. In: Cramer, R. (ed.) EUROCRYPT 2005. LNCS, vol. 3494, pp. 457–473. Springer, Heidelberg (2005). https://doi.org/10.1007/11426639_27
49. Shamir, A.: Identity-based cryptosystems and signature schemes. In: Blakley, G.R., Chaum, D. (eds.) CRYPTO 1984. LNCS, vol. 196, pp. 47–53. Springer, Heidelberg (1985). https://doi.org/10.1007/3-540-39568-7_5
50. Strackx, R., Piessens, F.: Ariadne: a minimal approach to state continuity. In: Holz, T., Savage, S. (eds.) USENIX Security, Austin, TX, USA, Aug. 10–12, 2016, pp. 875–892. USENIX (2016)
51. Suzuki, T., Emura, K., Ohigashi, T., Omote, K.: Verifiable functional encryption using intel SGX. Cryptology ePrint Archive, Report 2020/1221 (2020). https://eprint.iacr.org/2020/1221
52. Tramer, F., Zhang, F., Lin, H., Hubaux, J. P., Juels, A., Shi, E.: Sealed-glass proofs: using transparent enclaves to prove and sell knowledge. Cryptology ePrint Archive, Report 2016/635 (2016). http://eprint.iacr.org/2016/635
53. Tselekounis, I.: Cryptographic techniques for hardware security. PhD thesis, University of Edinburgh, UK (2018). http://ethos.bl.uk/OrderDetails.do?uin=uk.bl.ethos.763966
54. Wu, P., Shen, Q., Deng, R. H., Liu, X., Zhang, Y., Wu, Z.: ObliDC: an SGX-based oblivious distributed computing framework with formal proof. In: Galbraith, S.D., Russello, G., Susilo, W., Gollmann, D., Kirda, E., Liang, Z. (eds.) ASIACCS 19, Auckland, New Zealand, July 9–12, pp. 86–99. ACM (2019)
55. Yilek, S.: Resettable public-key encryption: how to encrypt on a virtual machine. In: Pieprzyk, J. (ed.) CT-RSA 2010. LNCS, vol. 5985, pp. 41–56. Springer, Heidelberg (2010). https://doi.org/10.1007/978-3-642-11925-5_4

Attacks and Cryptanalysis

Adventures in Crypto Dark Matter: Attacks and Fixes for Weak Pseudorandom Functions

Jung Hee Cheon[1,2], Wonhee Cho[1(✉)], Jeong Han Kim[3], and Jiseung Kim[3]

[1] Seoul National University, Seoul, Republic of Korea
{jhcheon,wony0404}@snu.ac.kr
[2] Crypto Lab Inc., Seoul, Republic of Korea
[3] School of Computational Sciences, Korea Institute for Advanced Study, Seoul, Republic of Korea
{jhkim,jiseungkim}@kias.re.kr

Abstract. A weak pseudorandom function (weak PRF) is one of the most important cryptographic primitives for its efficiency although it has lower security than a standard PRF.

Recently, Boneh et al. (TCC'18) introduced two types of new weak PRF candidates, which are called a basic Mod-2/Mod-3 and alternative Mod-2/Mod-3 weak PRF. Both use the mixture of linear computations defined on different small moduli to satisfy conceptual simplicity, low complexity (depth-2 ACC^0) and MPC friendliness. In fact, the new candidates are conjectured to be exponentially secure against any adversary that allows exponentially many samples, and a basic Mod-2/Mod-3 weak PRF is the only candidate that satisfies all features above. However, none of the direct attacks which focus on basic and alternative Mod-2/Mod-3 weak PRFs use their own structures.

In this paper, we investigate weak PRFs from two perspectives; attacks, fixes. We first propose direct attacks for an alternative Mod-2/Mod-3 weak PRF and a basic Mod-2/Mod-3 weak PRF when a circulant matrix is used as a secret key.

For an alternative Mod-2/Mod-3 weak PRF, we prove that the adversary's advantage is at least $2^{-0.105n}$, where n is the size of the input space of the weak PRF. Similarly, we show that the advantage of our heuristic attack to the weak PRF with a circulant matrix key is larger than $2^{-0.21n}$, which is contrary to the previous expectation that 'structured secret key' does not affect the security of a weak PRF. Thus, for an optimistic parameter choice $n = 2\lambda$ for the security parameter λ, parameters should be increased to preserve λ-bit security when an adversary obtains exponentially many samples.

Next, we suggest a simple method for repairing two weak PRFs affected by our attack while preserving the parameters.

Keywords: Cryptanalysis · Weak PRF

© International Association for Cryptologic Research 2021
J. A. Garay (Ed.): PKC 2021, LNCS 12711, pp. 739–760, 2021.
https://doi.org/10.1007/978-3-030-75248-4_26

1   Introduction

A pseudorandom function (PRF) proposed by Goldreich, Goldwasser and Micali [GGM86] is a keyed function which looks like a true random function. PRFs have been widely used as building blocks to construct several cryptographic primitives such as HMAC, digital signature and indistinguishability obfuscation [Gol86, BCK96, App14, Bel15, ABSV15, BR17].

Weak PRFs, which satisfy weaker security and higher efficiency than PRFs, are keyed functions whose input-output behaviors are indistinguishable from those of random functions when adversaries are limited to observing outputs mapped by randomly sampled inputs. Many cryptographic primitives and applications are built from weak PRFs because of its efficiency [DN02, MS07, Pie09, DKPW12, LM13, ASA17, BHI+20].

To construct more efficient weak PRFs, simple constructions are emphasized to minimize the circuit complexity and depth. Akavia *et al.* proposed a simple construction of weak PRFs which satisfies depth-3 ACC^0 circuit complexity with quasi-polynomial security [ABG+14].

As a line of work, Boneh *et al.* (TCC'18) proposed simple weak PRF candidates by mixing linear computations on different moduli [BIP+18]. Inspired by a paper [ABG+14], they provided a weak PRF which satisfies the following properties: conceptually simple structure, low complexity (depth-2 ACC^0 circuit complexity) and MPC-friendliness. In particular, the new candidates are the unique depth-2 weak PRFs conjectured to satisfy the exponential hardness beyond the polynomial hardness. Moreover, they provided two types of parameters: optimistic and conservative. A conservative parameter is set to be secure against the attacks for LPN problem, but it does not seem to be applicable to weak PRFs. Thus, an optimistic choice was additionally proposed.

We now briefly describe the construction of Mod-2/Mod-3 weak PRFs in [BIP+18]. For each Mod-2/Mod-3 weak PRF, a function $\mathcal{F} : \mathbb{Z}_2^n \times \mathbb{Z}_2^{m \times n} \to \mathbb{Z}_3$ with an input $\mathbf{x} \in \{0,1\}^n$ is defined as follows. (For details, see the construction 3.1)

- Basic Mod-2/Mod-3:
  For a "random" secret key $\mathbf{A} \in \mathbb{Z}_2^{m \times n}$, $\mathcal{F}(\mathbf{x}, \mathbf{A}) = \mathsf{map}(\mathbf{A} \cdot \mathbf{x})$, where map is a function from $\{0,1\}^m$ to $\mathbb{Z}_3$ mapping a binary vector $\mathbf{y} = (y_j)$ to an integer $\sum_{j=1}^m y_j \bmod 3$.[1]
- Circulant Mod-2/Mod-3:[2]
  Take $m = n$. Then, it is exactly the same as a basic Mod-2/Mod-3 except $\mathbf{A}$ is a circulant matrix.

---

[1] For well-definedness, $\mathbf{A} \cdot \mathbf{x}$ is interpreted as a binary vector.

[2] In the original paper [BIP+18], they used a Toeplitz matrix or a block-circulant matrix as a secret key of weak PRF for its efficiency. However, in this paper, we only deal with the case that a secret key of weak PRF is a circulant matrix which is the same as block-circulant matrix in the original paper. Indeed, they said that block-circulant matrix can be represented by a single vector'.

- Alternative Mod-2/Mod-3:
  Set $m = 1$. $\mathcal{F}(\mathbf{x}, \mathbf{k}) = (\langle \mathbf{k}, \mathbf{x} \rangle \bmod 2 + \langle \mathbf{k}, \mathbf{x} \rangle \bmod 3) \bmod 2$ for a random secret key $\mathbf{k} \in \{0, 1\}^n$.

However, there is no direct or concrete attack for weak PRFs on their own structures. Therefore, further cryptanalyses or security proofs are required to break or support their conjectures and concrete security.

1.1   This Work

In this paper, we investigate Mod-2/Mod-3 weak PRFs in two perspectives; attacks and fixes.

Attacks. Our concrete attacks mainly concentrate on two weak PRFs; an alternative and a circulant Mod-2/Mod-3 weak PRFs. As a result, we show that the advantage of an alternative Mod-2/Mod-3 weak PRF is $2^{-0.105n}$ with the size of input space n. It is computed as the conditional probability of input vectors given that the outputs are 'zero'. Similarly, we provide a heuristic attack with an advantage $2^{-0.21n}$ and experimental results of a circulant weak PRF. This result is contrary to the previous prediction that the parameters will not be much affected by the structure of a key. Our attacks are the first attacks using the structure of Mod-2/Mod-3 weak PRFs. Indeed, we first observe interesting features of certain secret keys of weak PRFs and statistically attack them using these features. As an example, a circulant matrix always preserves the number of nonzero entries h in each column, so $(1, ..., 1)$ is a left-eigenvector of a circulant matrix with an eigenvalue h.

As a result, we introduce new concrete parameters of weak PRFs in Table 1. As described in [BIP+18], we use two categories; optimistic and conservative parameters. The optimistic parameter is chosen by the fact that the authors of the paper speculate that the most efficient algorithm for solving LPN is not applicable to attack weak PRF candidates. The conservative one is the same as a parameter that is secure against LPN attacks, especially BKW attack [BKW03]. Moreover, we use two types of concrete parameter estimation; $\lambda = \log_2(T/\epsilon^2)$ and $\lambda = \log_2(T/\epsilon)$. The latter one is traditionally used to measure the concrete security of symmetric cryptography primitives [DS09], and the former one is proposed by Micciancio and Walter [MW18] for measuring the concrete security of decision primitives.

Our attacks mainly exploit the conditional probabilities based on structures of weak PRFs to distinguish weak PRF samples from uniform samples. More specifically, an adversary model to attack an alternative Mod-2/Mod-3 weak PRF computes $\Pr[x_i = 0 \mid \mathcal{F}_{\mathbf{k}}(\mathbf{x}) = 0 \bmod 2]$ for input $\mathbf{x} = (x_j) \in \{0, 1\}^n$. If the probability for some x_i is far from $1/2$ by $\frac{1}{2^{0.105n}}$, we conclude that pairs of inputs and outputs follow a distribution of an alternative weak PRF, not a uniform distribution. As a result, this simple attack satisfies the following interesting features:

- Support a full parallel computing: when δ processors are given, the total time complexity decreases from T_{total} to $T_{total}/\delta + O(\delta)$

Table 1. Changes of concrete parameters for 128-bit security to prevent our attacks with $m = n$. [‡]

Mod-2/Mod-3 weak PRFs			
Parameter choices		Alternative	Circulant key
[BIP+18]	Optimistic	–	256
	Conservative	384	384
Ours	$\log(T/\epsilon^2)$-bit security	610	305
	$\log(T/\epsilon)$-bit security	1220	610

[‡] We take concrete parameters according to the guidance of a paper [MW18]. For decision primitives, they recommended $\lambda = \log_2(T/\epsilon^2)$ rather than $\lambda = \log_2(T/\epsilon)$, with a cost T and an advantage ϵ. The latter is also widely used in crypto community. We include both results in Table 1. However, we mainly deal with the measure $\lambda = \log_2(T/\epsilon^2)$ in this paper.

- Require only $O(n)$ memory space because calculating an average does not need to store samples.
- Simply extend to Mod-p/Mod-q weak PRFs for any primes p and q: For an alternative Mod-p/Mod-q, we show that the bigger pq is, the more powerful our attack is. For example, an alternative and a circulant Mod-3/Mod-5 weak PRFs should be set as $n = 4000$ and $n = 2000$, respectively, for 128-bit security under the measure T/ϵ^2.

For more details, we refer Sects. 4.1 and 4.2.

Fixes. We suggest simple variants of weak PRFs to be secure against our attacks while preserving a depth of original weak PRFs and circuit class complexity ACC^0.

For an alternative case, our attack heavily relies on the number of nonzero entries in the secret key **k**, so we easily present a new alternative candidate to force the hamming weights of **k**. For instance, if we use the secret key with 310 nonzero entries, then it is secure against the statistical attack. Moreover, an adversary cannot search **k** by brute-force attack since $\binom{384}{310} \gg 2^{256}$.

On the other hand, for repairing a circulant Mod-2/Mod-3 weak PRF, we use two different vectors **a** and **b** to construct a secure circulant Mod-2/Mod-3 weak PRF. By the exploiting two secret vectors, we generate a new secret key **B** such that for $1 \leq i \leq n/2$, i-th row of **B** is rotation of the vector **a**, and for $n/2 < j \leq n$, j-th row vector is rotation of the vector **b**. Then, the fixed Mod-2/Mod-3 weak PRF with the secret key **B** is secure against our attack since a combination of two vectors can remove the structured weakness of circulant matrix that the number of nonzero entries in column vector is always the same. In other words, the vector of ones $(1, \cdots, 1)$ is not a left-eigenvector of **B** anymore. Moreover, we heuristically confirm that combining the two vector strategy is an appropriate approach for small n. Indeed, the experimental results show that the advantage of a fixed candidate is larger than $2^{-0.5n}$, which means that it achieves 128-bit security against all known attacks without a parameter blow-up. The size of PRF key of the fixed candidate is still smaller than that of random key, and it preserves depth-2 ACC^0 circuits and current parameter n. For more details, we refer Sect. 5.

Discussion and Open Questions. Both attacks that we propose require exponentially many samples. However, any of applications such as a secure multiparty computation only requires a polynomial number of samples of weak PRFs. Thus, they might be hard to affect any of the real world applications.

To overcome this situation, we discuss a few further works. Is there an application for requiring an exponential number of samples? If it exists, the application must consider parameters to be secure against our attacks. Moreover, it would be also interesting to extend our attack given a polynomial/sub-exponential number of samples? Or is there an application to be possible to amplify the number of samples?

One of the interesting approaches is to use the algebraic property of weak PRFs since our attack only uses a statistical weakness of weak PRFs. Thus, it still remains as an open problem that new algebraic or hybrid attacks against these candidates.

Moreover, a direct attack as asymptotic and concrete perspectives for a basic Mod-2/Mod-3 remains as an open question. Similarly, it would be interesting to prove or disprove the exponential hardness of circular Mod-2/Mod-3 weak PRF although the alternative one fails the exponential hardness due to the BKW algorithm.

Organization. We describe preliminaries about definitions of PRF and weak PRF, and some circuit complexities and results of k-xor problem in Sect. 2. We explicitly describe the construction of weak PRF candidates in Sect. 3, and provide cryptanalyses of an alternative Mod-2/Mod-3 weak PRF and a circulant weak PRF in Sect. 4, respectively. In Sect. 5, we suggest a method to fix the alternative and circulant Mod-2/Mod-3 weak PRFs.

2   Preliminaries

2.1   Notations

Matrices and vectors are written as bold capital letters, and bold lower-case letters respectively. Moreover, we assume that the vectors are column form in this paper, and i-th component of $\mathbf{x}$ will be denoted by x_i. The transpose of a matrix or vector is denoted by $\mathbf{A}^T$ or $\mathbf{x}^T$. Moreover, we denote an inner product between two vectors $\mathbf{x}$ and $\mathbf{y}$ by $\langle \mathbf{x}, \mathbf{y} \rangle$.

A square matrix $\mathbf{A}$ is called a circulant matrix which has a structure such that (i, j) entry of $\mathbf{A}$, $\mathbf{A}_{i,j}$ is given by $\mathbf{A}_{i,j} = a_{j-i \bmod n}$ with a dimension n. Thus, the circulant matrix is generated by a single vector $(a_1, a_2, \cdots a_n)$.

$\mathbf{I}_n$ is the n-dimensional identity matrix. Also, we denote the n-dimensional vector that all entries are zero by $\mathbf{0}^n$, and similarly, $\mathbf{1}^n$ is a vector that all entries are one. For the convenience of notation, we sometimes omit the subscript if it does not lead to any confusion.

For any positive integer n, $[n]$ is denoted by the set of integers $\{1, 2, \cdots, n\}$. All elements in $\mathbb{Z}_q$ are represented by integers in range $[0, q)$ for any positive integer q. For a vector $\mathbf{x}$, we use a notation $[\mathbf{x}]_q$ to denote an "entrywise" modulo q. i.e, $[\mathbf{x}]_q = ([x_i]_q)$ for $\mathbf{x} = (x_i)$. Let S be a finite set. Then, $s \xleftarrow{\$} S$ is denoted that an element s is uniformly sampled from the set S.

Definition 2.1 (Pseudorandom function (PRF) in [BIP+18]). *Let λ be the security parameter. A $(t(\lambda), \epsilon(\lambda))$-pseudorandom function family (PRF) is a collection of functions $\mathcal{F}_\lambda : \mathcal{X}_\lambda \times \mathcal{K}_\lambda \to \mathcal{Y}_\lambda$ with a domain $\mathcal{X}_\lambda$, a key space $\mathcal{K}_\lambda$ and an output space $\mathcal{Y}_\lambda$ such that for any adversary running time in $t(\lambda)$, it holds that*

$$\left| \Pr[\mathcal{A}^{\mathcal{F}_\lambda(\cdot, k)}(1^\lambda) = 1] - \Pr[\mathcal{A}^{f_\lambda(\cdot)}(1^\lambda) = 1] \right| \leq \epsilon(\lambda),$$

where $k \xleftarrow{\$} \mathcal{K}_\lambda$, and $f_\lambda \xleftarrow{\$} \mathsf{Funs}[\mathcal{X}_\lambda, \mathcal{Y}_\lambda]$.

In this paper, PRF is sometimes called strong PRF to be distinguished from the weak PRF in the below. The main difference between strong PRF and weak PRF is that an adversary is limited to obtaining randomly chosen input vectors.

Definition 2.2 (Weak PRF). *Let λ be the security parameter. A function $\mathcal{F}_\lambda : \mathcal{X}_\lambda \times \mathcal{K}_\lambda \to \mathcal{Y}_\lambda$ with a domain $\mathcal{X}_\lambda$, a key space $\mathcal{K}_\lambda$ and an output space $\mathcal{Y}_\lambda$ is called (ℓ, t, ϵ)-weak PRF for any adversary running time in $t(\lambda)$, it holds that*

$$\{(\mathbf{x}_i, \mathcal{F}_\lambda(\mathbf{x}_i, k))\}_{i \in [\ell]} \approx_\epsilon \{(\mathbf{x}_i, y_i)\}_{i \in [\ell]}$$

where a key $k \xleftarrow{\$} \mathcal{K}_\lambda$, $\mathbf{x}_i \xleftarrow{\$} \mathcal{X}_\lambda$, and $y_i \xleftarrow{\$} \mathcal{Y}_\lambda$. We denote $\approx_\epsilon$ by the advantage of any adversary is smaller than ϵ.

3 Construction of Weak PRF Candidates

In this section, we briefly review how to construct weak PRF candidates proposed by Boneh *et al.* [BIP+18]. All constructions consist of linear computations on different moduli, which are deemed to be simple and efficient.

3.1 Mod-2/Mod-3 Weak PRF Candidate

In this section, we provide a basic construction of Mod-2/Mod-3 weak PRF candidate. Mod-2/Mod-3 weak PRFs are easily extended to Mod-p/Mod-q constructions for arbitrary primes p and q.

Construction 3.1 (A basic Mod-2/Mod-3 weak PRF). For the security parameter λ, a weak PRF candidate is a collection of functions $\mathcal{F}_\lambda : \{0, 1\}^n \times \{0, 1\}^{m \times n} \to \mathbb{Z}_3$ with a domain $\{0, 1\}^n$, a key space $\{0, 1\}^{m \times n}$ and an output space $\mathbb{Z}_3$. For a fixed key $\mathbf{A} \in \{0, 1\}^{m \times n}$, we use a notation $\mathcal{F}_\mathbf{A} : \{0, 1\}^n \to \mathbb{Z}_3$ which defines as follows.

1. Computes $\mathbf{y} = [\mathbf{A} \cdot \mathbf{x}]_2$
2. Outputs $\mathsf{map}(\mathbf{y})$, where map is a function from $\{0,1\}^m$ to $\mathbb{Z}_3$ which maps a binary vector $\mathbf{y} = (y_j)$ to an integer $\sum_{j=1}^{m} y_j \bmod 3$.

Thus, we summarize $\mathcal{F}_{\mathbf{A}}(\mathbf{x}) = \mathsf{map}([\mathbf{A} \cdot \mathbf{x}]_2)$. This simple construction induced by mixed linear computations on different moduli might be secure against previous attacks. Moreover, the authors showed that a low-degree polynomial (rational function) approximation of map is hard, and standard learning algorithms cannot break these constructions. Furthermore, Conjecture 3.2 is proposed.

Conjecture 3.2 (Exponential Hardness of Mod-2/Mod-3 weak PRF). Let λ be the security parameter. Then, there exist constants $c_1, c_2, c_3, c_4 > 0$ such that for $n = c_1\lambda, m = c_2\lambda$, $\ell = 2^{c_3\lambda}$, and $t = 2^\lambda$, a function family $\{\mathcal{F}_\lambda\}$ defined as Mod-2/Mod-3 construction is an (ℓ, t, ϵ)-weak PRF for $\epsilon = 2^{-c_4\lambda}$.

Remark 3.3. For the improved efficiency of Mod-2/Mod-3 weak PRFs in real applications, a structured key $\mathbf{A}$ is used, not a random key from $\{0,1\}^{m \times n}$. Thus we expect the key size can be reduced when $\mathbf{A}$ is a block-circulant matrix or Toeplitz matrix.[3] Roughly speaking, a random key $\mathbf{A}$ requires mn key size, but the key size of a structured key $\mathbf{A}$ is $m + n$, much smaller than mn. A basic Mod-2/Mod-3 weak PRF with a circulant secret key $\mathbf{A}$ is called a circulant Mod-2/Mod-3 weak PRF.

Concrete Parameters. They proposed two types of parameters; optimized and conservative choices. The conservative choice, $m = n = 384$, is set to be robust against the BKW attack for LPN problem. However, the BKW attack does not seem to be applicable to this candidate, the optimized parameter, $m = n = 2\lambda = 256$, is also suggested to obtain 128-bit security.

3.2 Alternative Mod-2/Mod-3 Weak PRF Candidate

An alternative weak PRF is additionally proposed to obtain higher efficiency in a two-party secure computation setting.

Construction 3.4 (Alternative Mod-2/Mod-3 weak PRF). For a secret key $\mathbf{k} \in \{0,1\}^n$, an alternative Mod-2/Mod-3 weak PRF is defined that for any input $\mathbf{x} \in \{0,1\}^n$,

$$\mathcal{F}(\mathbf{k}, \mathbf{x}) = \langle \mathbf{k}, \mathbf{x} \rangle \bmod 2 + \langle \mathbf{k}, \mathbf{x} \rangle \bmod 3 \bmod 2.$$

For simplicity, we use a notation $\mathcal{F}_{\mathbf{k}}(\mathbf{x})$ instead of $\mathcal{F}(\mathbf{k}, \mathbf{x})$ on a key $\mathbf{k} \in \{0,1\}^n$.

Concrete Parameters. Similar to a basic Mod-2/Mod-3 weak PRF, they consider all known attacks to claim the security of the alternative candidate. Moreover, it resembles an LPN instance with a deterministic noise rate $1/3$, so the parameters are set as $m = n = 384$. For more details, see the original paper [BIP+18] or later section.

---

[3] In the original paper, the authors mentioned that a 'block-circulant matrix' can be represented by a single vector. Thus, a block-circulant matrix is the same as a circulant matrix in this paper.

4 Cryptanalysis of Weak PRF Candidates

We now introduce our analysis on two weak PRF candidates; the alternative Mod-2/Mod-3 and circulant Mod-2/Mod-3 weak PRFs. These attacks are also applicable to an alternative and a circulant Mod-p/Mod-q weak PRF for arbitrary primes p and q.

4.1 Cryptanalysis of an Alternative Mod-2/Mod-3 Weak PRF

We briefly recall the construction of the alternative Mod-2/Mod-3 weak PRF with the secret key $\mathbf{k} \in \{0,1\}^n$

$$\mathcal{F}_{\mathbf{k}}(\mathbf{x}) = (\langle \mathbf{k}, \mathbf{x} \rangle \bmod 2 + \langle \mathbf{k}, \mathbf{x} \rangle \bmod 3) \bmod 2.$$

We simply observe that $\mathcal{F}_{\mathbf{k}}(\mathbf{x}) = 0 \bmod 2$ if and only if $\langle \mathbf{k}, \mathbf{x} \rangle = 0, 1, 2 \bmod 6$. In other words, one can understand that $\mathcal{F}_{\mathbf{k}}(\mathbf{x})$ is an operation on the $\mathbb{Z}_6$ space.

On the other hand, since the secret key $\mathbf{k}$ and input vector $\mathbf{x}$ are made up of only 0 and 1, we conjecture that $\mathcal{F}_{\mathbf{k}}(\mathbf{x})$ would not cover the whole uniformly. Thus, we can present the statistical attack for the alternative alternative Mod-2/Mod-3 weak PRF.

Based on the intuition, we obtain the following theorem.

Theorem 1. *Let $\mathbf{k} \in \{0,1\}^n$ be the secret key of the alternative Mod-2/Mod-3 weak PRF and $\mathcal{F}_{\mathbf{k}}$ a function as defined above. If h is the hamming weight of $\mathbf{k}$, then we can show that there exists $j \in [n]$ such that*

$$\left| \Pr[x_j = 0 \mid k_j = 1 \text{ and } \mathcal{F}_{\mathbf{k}}(\mathbf{x}) = 0 \bmod 2] - \frac{1}{2} \right| \approx \frac{1}{2^{0.21h}}$$

Therefore, if the number of samples, ℓ, is $O(2^{0.21h})$, one can distinguish $\{(\mathbf{x}_i, \mathcal{F}_\lambda(\mathbf{x}_i, \mathbf{k}))\}_{i \in [\ell]}$ from the uniform samples $\{(\mathbf{x}_i, y_i)\}_{i \in [\ell]}$.

Then, our attack for alternative Mod-2/Mod-3 weak PRF is very simple. After an adversary collects $\ell = c_1 \cdot 2^{0.21n}$ samples whose output is 0 for some constant c_1, the distinguishing attack computes a conditional probability $\Pr[x_j = 0 \mid \mathcal{F}_{\mathbf{k}}(\mathbf{x}) = 0 \bmod 2]$ for each index $j \in [n]$. If there exists an index j such that it is apart from $1/2$ by $\frac{1}{2^{0.105n}}$, we conclude that an adversary has alternative Mod-2/Mod-3 weak PRF samples.

To compute the conditional probability, we exploit a simple lemma.

Lemma 4.1. *Let n be a positive integer. For all $0 \le a \le 5$, the following equation holds.*

$$\sum_{a+6k \le n} \binom{n}{a+6k} = \frac{1}{6} \left(\sum_{j=0}^{5} (w^j)^{6-a} \cdot (1+w^j)^n \right).$$

where w is 6-th root of unity, $\frac{1+\sqrt{3}i}{2}$.

Proof. Since w is 6-th root of unity, the following equations hold.

$$(1 + w^j)^n = \sum_{a=0}^{n} \binom{n}{a} (w^j)^a, \ 1 + w + w^2 + w^3 + w^4 + w^5 = 0.$$

Then, the equations imply that $\sum_{j=0}^{5} (w^j)^{6-a} \cdot (1 + w^j)^n$ can be rewritten as follows.

$$\sum_{j=0}^{5} (w^j)^{6-a} \cdot (1 + w^j)^n = \sum_{j=0}^{5} \sum_{k=0}^{n} \binom{n}{k} (w^j)^k (w^j)^{6-a}$$

$$= \sum_{k=0}^{n} \binom{n}{k} \{ \sum_{j=0}^{5} (w^j)^{6-a+k} \}$$

$$= \sum_{k \equiv a \pmod 6} \binom{n}{k} \cdot 6$$

$$= \sum_{a+6k \leq n} \binom{n}{a+6k} \cdot 6$$

$\square$

For the sake of explanation, suppose that the first h elements of $\mathbf{k}$ are all 1, and the others are zero. Then, we observe that

$$\langle \mathbf{k}, \mathbf{x} \rangle = x_1 + \cdots + x_h.$$

Note that a value x_i with $i > h$ has no effect on the result $\langle \mathbf{k}, \mathbf{x} \rangle$ since k_i is zero. Therefore, we only consider x_i for $i \in [h]$. For all $j \in [h]$, the conditional probability of x_j given by $\mathcal{F}_{\mathbf{k}}(\mathbf{x}) = 0 \bmod 2$ is that

$$\Pr[x_j = 0 \mid \mathcal{F}_{\mathbf{k}}(\mathbf{x}) = 0 \bmod 2] = \frac{\sum_{k=0}^{\lfloor \frac{h-1}{6} \rfloor} \binom{h-1}{6k} + \binom{h-1}{6k+1} + \binom{h-1}{6k+2}}{\sum_{k=0}^{\lfloor \frac{h}{6} \rfloor} \binom{h}{6k} + \binom{h}{6k+1} + \binom{h}{6k+2}}. \quad (1)$$

For events $A : [\mathcal{F}_{\mathbf{k}}(\mathbf{x}) = 0 \bmod 2]$, and $B : [x_j = 0]$, the left-hand side of the Eq. (1) equals to $\frac{\Pr[A \cap B]}{\Pr[A]}$. As we mentioned, it holds that $\mathcal{F}_{\mathbf{k}}(\mathbf{x}) = 0 \bmod 2$ if and only if $\langle \mathbf{k}, \mathbf{x} \rangle = 0, 1, 2 \bmod 6$. Moreover, for every $k \in \{0, \cdots, \lfloor \frac{h-1}{6} \rfloor\}$ and $a \in \{0, \cdots, 5\}$, $\binom{h}{6k+a}$ if and only if $\langle \mathbf{k}, \mathbf{x} \rangle = a \bmod 6$ because of $\langle \mathbf{k}, \mathbf{x} \rangle = \sum_{i=1}^{h} x_i$. Thus, $\Pr[A]$ equals to the denominator of the right-hand side of the Eq. (1).

On the other hand, for some j, $A \cap B : [x_j = 0 \ \& \ \mathcal{F}_{\mathbf{k}}(\mathbf{x}) = 0 \bmod 2]$. Hence, it holds that $\langle \mathbf{k}, \mathbf{x} \rangle = \sum_{i=1, i \neq j}^{h} x_i$ to satisfy the event $A \cap B$. Similarly, we also show that $\Pr[A \cap B]$ is the same as the numerator of the right-hand side of the Eq. (1) since the number of possible variables is $h - 1$ because of $x_j = 0$. As a result, with the Lemma 4.1 and the properties of 6-th root of unity w, we can calculate the conditional probability that we desired.

$$\Pr[x_j = 0 \mid \mathcal{F}_{\mathbf{k}}(\mathbf{x}) = 0 \bmod 2] = \frac{\sum_{k=0}^{\lfloor \frac{h-1}{6} \rfloor} \binom{h-1}{6k} + \binom{h-1}{6k+1} + \binom{h-1}{6k+2}}{\sum_{k=0}^{\lfloor \frac{h}{6} \rfloor} \binom{h}{6k} + \binom{h}{6k+1} + \binom{h}{6k+2}}$$

$$= \frac{\sum_{j=0}^{5}(1 + (w^j)^5 + (w^j)^4) \cdot (1 + w^j)^{h-1}}{\sum_{j=0}^{5}(1 + (w^j)^5 + (w^j)^4) \cdot (1 + w^j)^h}$$

$$= \frac{3 \cdot 2^{h-1} + 2w^5 \cdot (1+w)^{h-1} + 2w \cdot (1+w^5)^{h-1}}{3 \cdot 2^h + 2w^5 \cdot (1+w)^h + 2w \cdot (1+w^5)^h}$$

$$= \frac{3 \cdot 2^{h-1} + 2w^5 \cdot (w^5 i\sqrt{3})^{h-1} + 2w \cdot (-wi\sqrt{3})^{h-1}}{3 \cdot 2^h + 2w^5 \cdot (w^5 i\sqrt{3})^h + 2w \cdot (-wi\sqrt{3})^h}$$

$$= \frac{1}{2} + \frac{(w^5 i\sqrt{3})^{h-1} \cdot w^4 + (-wi\sqrt{3})^{h-1} \cdot w^2}{3 \cdot 2^h + 2w^5 \cdot (w^5 i\sqrt{3})^h + 2w \cdot (-wi\sqrt{3})^h}$$

where w is 6-th root of unity, $\frac{1+\sqrt{3}i}{2}$. Thus, we can obtain the following lemma.

Lemma 4.2. *Let h be the hamming weight of the secret key $\mathbf{k}$. For all $i \in [h]$,*

$$\Pr[x_i = 0 \mid \mathcal{F}_{\mathbf{k}}(\mathbf{x}) = 0 \bmod 2] = \begin{cases} \frac{1}{2} - \frac{(i\sqrt{3})^h}{3 \cdot 2^h + 2 \cdot (i\sqrt{3})^h} & h = 6k \\ \frac{1}{2} - \frac{(i\sqrt{3})^{h-1}}{3 \cdot 2^h + 6 \cdot (i\sqrt{3})^{h-1}} & h = 6k+1 \\ \frac{1}{2} & h = 6k+2 \\ \frac{1}{2} + \frac{3(i\sqrt{3})^{h-3}}{3 \cdot 2^h + 18 \cdot (i\sqrt{3})^{h-3}} & h = 6k+3 \\ \frac{1}{2} + \frac{9(i\sqrt{3})^{h-4}}{3 \cdot 2^h + 18 \cdot (i\sqrt{3})^{h-4}} & h = 6k+4 \\ \frac{1}{2} + \frac{18(i\sqrt{3})^{h-5}}{3 \cdot 2^h} & h = 6k+5 \end{cases}$$

Proof (of Lemma 4.2). The proof only requires straightforward (but tedious) computations, so we only deal with a case of $h = 6k$. Computations of the others are almost the same as the case $h = 6k$.

$$\Pr[x_i = 0 \mid \mathcal{F}_{\mathbf{k}}(\mathbf{x}) = 0 \bmod 2] = \frac{1}{2} + \frac{(w^5 i\sqrt{3})^{6k-1} \cdot w^4 + (-wi\sqrt{3})^{6k-1} \cdot w^2}{3 \cdot 2^{6k} + 2w^5 \cdot (w^5 i\sqrt{3})^{6k} + 2w \cdot (-wi\sqrt{3})^{6k}}$$

$$= \frac{1}{2} + \frac{(w^5 - w) \cdot (i\sqrt{3})^{6k-1}}{3 \cdot 2^{6k} + 2(w^5 + w) \cdot (i\sqrt{3})^{6k}}$$

$$= \frac{1}{2} + \frac{-(i\sqrt{3})^{6k}}{3 \cdot 2^{6k} + 2(i\sqrt{3})^{6k}}$$

$$= \frac{1}{2} - \frac{(i\sqrt{3})^h}{3 \cdot 2^h + 2 \cdot (i\sqrt{3})^h}$$

$\square$

Since the simple attack does not work if $h \equiv 2 \bmod 6$, another adversary is required. A new adversary computes a conditional probability of $x_i = x_j = 0$ with $i \neq j$ given by $\mathcal{F}_{\mathbf{k}}(\mathbf{x}) = 0$. Then, through similar computations from Lemma 4.2, we obtain the below lemma.

Lemma 4.3. *Let h be the hamming weight of the secret key* **k***. If $i \neq j \in [h]$ and $h \equiv 2 \bmod 6$,*

$$\Pr[x_i = 0, x_j = 0 \mid \mathcal{F}_{\mathbf{k}}(\mathbf{x}) = 0 \bmod 2] = \frac{\sum_{k=0}^{\lfloor \frac{h-2}{6} \rfloor} \binom{h-2}{6k} + \binom{h-2}{6k+1} + \binom{h-2}{6k+2}}{\sum_{k=0}^{\lfloor \frac{h}{6} \rfloor} \binom{h}{6k} + \binom{h}{6k+1} + \binom{h}{6k+2}}$$

$$= \frac{1}{4} - \frac{(i\sqrt{3})^{h-2}}{3 \cdot 2^h + 12(i\sqrt{3})^{h-2}}$$

According to Lemmas 4.2, 4.3, the advantage of an alternative Mod-2/Mod-3 weak PRF is larger than $c_h \cdot \left(\frac{\sqrt{3}}{2}\right)^h \approx \frac{1}{2^{0.21h}}$. Moreover, since **k** is chosen uniformly from the set $\{0,1\}^n$, we assume that h is $\frac{n}{2}$ without loss of generality. Thus, the advantage is larger than $\frac{1}{2^{0.105n}}$. As a result, to preserve 128-bit security, a parameter n should increase from 384 to 610 or 1220 under the measure $\log \frac{T}{\epsilon^2}$ or $\log \frac{T}{\epsilon}$ with a cost T and an advantage ϵ.

The Theorem 1 is proved by Lemma 4.2 and Lemma 4.3.

Compare to BKW Algorithm. The construction of the alternative Mod-2/Mod-3 weak PRF is quite similar to LPN problem with a noise rate 1/3. Thus, one expects that the algorithm proposed by Blum, Kalai, and Wasserman [BKW03], one of the current best attacks for LPN with a constant noise rate, can be applicable to alternative Mod-2/Mod-3 weak PRF.

The difference between conventional LPN instances and pseudo-LPN instances from alternative Mod-2/Mod-3 weak PRF is that the error terms of pseudo-LPN instances are of the form $\sum_i \mathbf{k}_i x_i \bmod 3 \bmod 2$, which means that the error terms are always correlated to the input **x**, and the secret key **k**. However, the error terms of conventional LPN instances are independent to the input, and the independence has implicitly used to analyze the BKW algorithm.

On the other hand, Bogos, Tramèr and Vaudenay [BTV16] mentioned that BKW algorithm heuristically works in spite of dependence of the error term. Therefore, BKW attack can be heuristically applied to analyze the alternative Mod-2/Mod-3 weak PRF. Therefore, it cannot achieve the exponential hardness conjecture like the basic Mod-2/Mod-3 weak PRF since the time complexity of BKW is sub-exponential in a dimension n. However, the BKW attack cannot impact on the concrete parameter since the alternative candidate already sets parameters to be secure against the BKW attack. The original paper already mentioned that a parameter $n = 384$ captures 128-bits security.

Unlike the BKW attack, our attack which exploits statistical properties takes exponential time in a dimension n, but when exponentially many samples are allowed, our attack can affect the concrete parameters. To be secure against our attack, the parameter n should be set at least 610 as in Table 1.

Remark 4.4. Our attack is easily extended to an alternative Mod-p/Mod-q weak PRF for arbitrary primes p and q. Following our proof, the adversary's advantage of an alternative Mod-p/Mod-q is larger than $c_h \cdot \left|\frac{w_{pq}+1}{2}\right|^h \approx \left(\cos\left(\frac{\pi}{pq}\right)\right)^h$ where

w_{pq} is pq-th root of unity. Therefore, our attach is getting more powerful as pq gets bigger. For example, the advantage of an alternative Mod-3/Mod-5 weak PRF is larger than $\left(\cos\left(\frac{\pi}{15}\right)\right)^h \approx \frac{1}{2^{0.032h}}$, so n should be increased to 4000 for the 128-bit security under a measure T/ϵ^2 if $h = n/2$.

Remark 4.5. Since our attack just computes conditional probabilities, there exist interesting features.

- Full parallel computations are allowed. Hence, if there are δ processors, total time complexity is reduced from $O(2^{0.21n})$ to $O(2^{0.21n}/\delta) + O(\delta)$.
- An adversary does not need to store many weak PRF samples. Thus, Our attack is a space efficient algorithm. It requires only $O(n)$ space even though our attack needs a lot of samples.

Remark 4.6. An alternative construction can be reinterpreted by operations on mod 6 space. However, an input space of this construction is only $\{0, 1\}^n$, not a full space $\mathbb{Z}_6^n$. This might be a statistical weakness of the alternative weak PRF.

4.2 Cryptanalysis of a Circulant Mod-2/Mod-3 Weak PRF

As stated in Remark 3.3, structured keys are widely used to provide higher efficiency. In this section, we provide a heuristic analysis of a circulant Mod-2/Mod-3 weak PRF candidate.[4] We briefly recall a circulant Mod-2/Mod-3 weak PRF. For a circulant matrix $\mathbf{A} \in \mathbb{Z}_2^{n \times n}$ with generated by a vector $\mathbf{a} \in \mathbb{Z}_2^n$,

$$\mathcal{F}_\mathbf{A}(\mathbf{x}) = \mathsf{map}(\mathbf{A} \cdot \mathbf{x}),$$

where map is a function from $\{0, 1\}^n$ to $\mathbb{Z}_3$ mapping a binary vector $\mathbf{y} = (y_j)$ to an integer $\sum_{j=1}^m y_j$ mod 3.

We first present several observations of a circulant Mod-2/Mod-3 weak PRF under the secret key $\mathbf{A}$.

- $\mathbf{1}^T \cdot \mathbf{A} = h(1, \cdots, 1)$
- $\mathbf{1}^T \cdot \mathbf{A} \cdot \mathbf{x} = h \cdot h_\mathbf{x}$ where $h_\mathbf{x}$ is the number of 1's in an input $\mathbf{x}$
- $\mathbf{1}^T \cdot [\mathbf{A} \cdot \mathbf{x}]_2 \equiv h \cdot h_\mathbf{x}$ mod 2
- If $h_\mathbf{x}$ is even, then the number of 1's in $[\mathbf{A} \cdot \mathbf{x}]_2$ is also even.

The key ingredient of the attack for a circulant weak PRF is that $[\mathbf{A} \cdot \mathbf{x}]_2$ preserves the parity of $\mathbf{x}$ if $h_\mathbf{x}$ is even. If $\mathcal{F}_\mathbf{A}(\mathbf{x})$ truly behaves a random element, it never keeps the parity even if $h_\mathbf{x}$ is even. Similar to Sect. 4.1, by limiting the parity of $[\mathbf{A} \cdot \mathbf{x}]_2$, we could distinguish a circulant Mod-2/Mod-3 weak PRF from uniform. Indeed, it might be conjectured that $\Pr[\mathcal{F}_\mathbf{A}(\mathbf{x}) \equiv 0 \bmod 3 \mid h_\mathbf{x} \text{ is even}]$ or $\Pr[\mathcal{F}_\mathbf{A}(\mathbf{x}) \equiv 2 \bmod 3 \mid h_\mathbf{x} \text{ is even}]$ is apart from $1/2$.

With the intuition, if $[\mathbf{A} \cdot \mathbf{x}]_2$ is component-wise independent, then we can directly compute values $\Pr[\mathcal{F}_\mathbf{A}(\mathbf{x}) \equiv 0 \bmod 3 \mid h_\mathbf{x} \text{ is even}]$ and $\Pr[\mathcal{F}_\mathbf{A}(\mathbf{x}) \equiv 2$

---

[4] As stated in Sect.1, a circulant matrix is exactly the same a block-circulant in [BIP+18].

mod 3 | $h_{\mathbf{x}}$ is even]. Then, we obtain that an adversary's advantage is larger than $c_n \cdot \left(\frac{\sqrt{3}}{2}\right)^n \approx \frac{1}{2^{0.21n}}$ for some very small constant c_n.

Unfortunately, no one could be sure whether the components of $[\mathbf{A} \cdot \mathbf{x}]_2$ behave independently since $\mathbf{A}$ is a circulant matrix. Therefore, we will give experimental results to support that the above conditional probabilities are almost the same as the results of Lemmas 4.7 and 4.8, where the lemmas are assumed to be independent of each component. (See experimental results 4.9.) As a result, we obtain the following theorem.

Theorem 2. *Let $\mathbf{A} \in \{0,1\}^{n \times n}$ be a circulant matrix used in a Mod-2/Mod-3 weak PRF as a secret key and $h_{\mathbf{x}}$ be the hamming weights of a vector $\mathbf{x}$. Then, we can heuristically show that*

$$\left| \Pr[\mathcal{F}_{\mathbf{A}}(\mathbf{x}) \equiv 0 \bmod 3 \mid h_{\mathbf{x}} \text{ is even}] - \frac{1}{3} \right| \approx \frac{1}{2^{0.21n}} \text{ if } n \neq 3 \bmod 6$$

$$\left| \Pr[\mathcal{F}_{\mathbf{A}}(\mathbf{x}) \equiv 2 \bmod 3 \mid h_{\mathbf{x}} \text{ is even}] - \frac{1}{3} \right| \approx \frac{1}{2^{0.21n}} \text{ if } n = 3 \bmod 6$$

Therefore, if the number of samples, $\ell = O(2^{0.42n})$, one can distinguish $\{(\mathbf{x}_i, \mathcal{F}_{\mathbf{A}}(\mathbf{x}_i))\}_{i \in [\ell]}$ from the uniform samples $\{(\mathbf{x}_i, y_i)\}_{i \in [\ell]}$.

Now, we give an analysis under the assumption that a vector is component-wise independent. For the avoidance of confusion, we newly define a random variable Y as follows. Let Y be a multivariate random variable that follows a distribution on $\{0,1\}^n$ that each entry is independently and uniformly sampled from $\{0,1\}$. Then, the conditional probability of $\mathbf{1}^T \cdot \mathbf{y} = 0 \bmod 3$ given that $\mathbf{y}$ is uniformly sampled from Y and $h_{\mathbf{y}}$ is even is

$$\Pr[\mathbf{1}^T \cdot \mathbf{y} = 0 \bmod 3 | \mathbf{y} \xleftarrow{\$} Y, h_{\mathbf{y}} \text{ is even}] = \frac{\sum_{k=0}^{\lfloor \frac{n}{6} \rfloor} \binom{n}{6k}}{\sum_{k=0}^{\lfloor \frac{n}{6} \rfloor} \binom{n}{6k} + \binom{n}{2+6k} + \binom{n}{4+6k}} \quad (2)$$

We first note that $h_{\mathbf{y}} = \mathbf{1}^T \cdot \mathbf{y} = \langle \mathbf{1}, \mathbf{y} \rangle$ since $\mathbf{y} \in \{0,1\}^n$, and will gain use the fact that $\binom{n}{6k+a}$ if and only if $\langle \mathbf{1}, \mathbf{y} \rangle = a \bmod 6$ for every $k \in \{0, \cdots, \lfloor \frac{n-1}{6} \rfloor\}$ and $a \in \{0, \cdots, 5\}$. For events $A : [\mathbf{y} \xleftarrow{\$} Y \& h_{\mathbf{y}} \text{ is even}]$, and $B : [\mathbf{1}^T \cdot \mathbf{y} = 0 \bmod 3]$, we easily observe that $\Pr[A]$ equals to the denominator of the right-hand side of the Eq. (2). Moreover, we easily verify that the probability $\Pr[A \cap B]$ equals to the numerator of the right-hand side of the Eq. (2). Therefore, with the Lemma 4.1 and the properties of 6-th root of unity w, we obtain the following.

$$\Pr[\mathbf{1}^T \cdot \mathbf{y} = 0 \bmod 3 | \mathbf{y} \xleftarrow{\$} Y, h_{\mathbf{y}} \text{ is even}] = \frac{\sum_{k=0}^{\lfloor \frac{n}{6} \rfloor} \binom{n}{6k}}{\sum_{k=0}^{\lfloor \frac{n}{6} \rfloor} \binom{n}{6k} + \binom{n}{2+6k} + \binom{n}{4+6k}}$$

$$= \frac{\sum_{k=0}^{5}(1+w^k)^n}{6 \cdot 2^{n-1}} = \frac{1}{3} + \frac{w^{2n}((-i\sqrt{3})^n + (-1)^n) + w^{4n}((i\sqrt{3})^n + (-1)^n)}{6 \cdot 2^{n-1}}$$

where w is 6-th root of unity, $\frac{1+i\sqrt{3}}{2}$. Similar to the above section, a straightforward computation leads us the following lemmas.

Lemma 4.7. *Let Y be a multivariate random variable that follows a distribution on $\{0,1\}^n$ that each entry is independently and uniformly sampled from $\{0,1\}$. Then, the conditional probability of $\mathbf{1}^T \cdot \mathbf{y} = 0 \bmod 3$ given that $\mathbf{y}$ is uniformly sampled from Y and $h_{\mathbf{y}}$ is even is that*

$$\Pr[\mathbf{1}^T \cdot \mathbf{y} = 0 \bmod 3 | \ \mathbf{y} \xleftarrow{\$} Y, h_{\mathbf{y}} \text{ is even}] = \begin{cases} \frac{1}{3} + \frac{2(i\sqrt{3})^n + 2}{6 \cdot 2^{n-1}} & n = 6k \\ \frac{1}{3} + \frac{3(i\sqrt{3})^{n-1} + 1}{6 \cdot 2^{n-1}} & n = 6k+1 \\ \frac{1}{3} - \frac{(i\sqrt{3})^n + 1}{6 \cdot 2^{n-1}} & n = 6k+2 \\ \frac{1}{3} + \frac{-2}{6 \cdot 2^{n-1}} & n = 6k+3 \\ \frac{1}{3} - \frac{(i\sqrt{3})^n + 1}{6 \cdot 2^{n-1}} & n = 6k+4 \\ \frac{1}{3} - \frac{3(i\sqrt{3})^{n-1} - 1}{6 \cdot 2^{n-1}} & n = 6k+5 \end{cases}$$

Proof (of Lemma 4.7). Repetitive computations are required to prove this lemma. Similar to the proof of Lemma 4.2, we only leave a proof of a case $n = 6k$ for readability.

$$\Pr[\mathbf{1}^T \cdot \mathbf{y} = 0 \bmod 3 \mid \mathbf{y} \xleftarrow{\$} Y, h_{\mathbf{y}} \text{ is even}] = \frac{\sum_{k=0}^{\lfloor \frac{n}{6} \rfloor} \binom{n}{6k}}{\sum_{k=0}^{\lfloor \frac{n}{6} \rfloor} \binom{n}{6k} + \binom{n}{6k+2} + \binom{n}{6k+4}}$$

$$= \frac{2^n + (1+w)^n + (1+w^2)^n + (1+w^4)^n + (1+w^5)^n}{3 \cdot 2^h}$$

$$= \frac{2^n + (w^5 i\sqrt{3})^n + (-w^4)^n + (-w^2)^n + (-wi\sqrt{3})^n}{3 \cdot 2^n}$$

$$= \frac{2^n + 2(i\sqrt{3})^n + 2}{3 \cdot 2^n} = \frac{1}{3} + \frac{2(i\sqrt{3})^n + 2}{6 \cdot 2^{n-1}}$$

$\square$

If $n \equiv 3 \bmod 6$, we require an extra analysis to point out a weakness of circulant Mod-2/Mod-3 weak PRF. However, we easily overcome this situation by computing a new conditional probability. Indeed, through similar computations of Lemma 4.7, we obtain the below lemma.

Lemma 4.8. *Let Y be a random variable defined on Lemma 4.7. If n is $6k+3$, then we have that*

$$\Pr[\mathbf{1}^T \cdot \mathbf{y} = 2 \bmod 3| \ \mathbf{y} \xleftarrow{\$} Y, h_{\mathbf{y}} \text{ is even}] = \frac{\sum_{k=0}^{\lfloor \frac{n}{6} \rfloor} \binom{n}{6k+2}}{\sum_{k=0}^{\lfloor \frac{n}{6} \rfloor} \binom{n}{6k} + \binom{n}{2+6k} + \binom{n}{4+6k}}$$

$$= \frac{1}{3} + \frac{w^{2n+4}((-i\sqrt{3})^n + (-1)^n) + w^{4n+2}((i\sqrt{3})^n + (-1)^n)}{6 \cdot 2^{n-1}}$$

$$= \frac{1}{3} - \frac{3(-i\sqrt{3})^{n-1} + (-1)^n}{6 \cdot 2^{n-1}}$$

Experiments 4.9. To support our expectation, we implement experiments in accordance with

1. Sample a random vector $\mathbf{a}$ from $\{0,1\}^n$.
2. Construct a circulant matrix $\mathbf{A}$ using the sampled vector $\mathbf{a}$.[5]
3. Compute $\mathcal{F}_\mathbf{A}(\mathbf{x})$ for sufficiently many $\mathbf{x}$'s.
4. Compute a conditional probability as done in the above two lemmas.
5. Go to 1 again.

Then, we can provide experimental results to support that $\Pr[\mathcal{F}_\mathbf{A}(\mathbf{x}) \equiv 0 \bmod 3 \mid h_\mathbf{x}$ is even$]$ and $\Pr[\mathcal{F}_\mathbf{A}(\mathbf{x}) \equiv 2 \bmod 3 \mid h_\mathbf{x}$ is even$]$ are almost the same as results of Lemmas 4.7 and 4.8.

In Fig. 1, we first regard (logarithms of) the averages of the above conditional probabilities for several n, as blue points. Then, we draw a trend line from them. The (logarithm) trend line is $0.2038n + 0.4537$ similar to $2^{-0.21n}$ induced by our computations.

We also conducted several experiments for a fixed n. For case $n \leq 18$, we ran experiments for all possible base vectors to demonstrate that our experiments are not lucky cases. For the same reason, 128 random base vectors were used to support our heuristic assumptions for $n = 32, 40$ and 50.

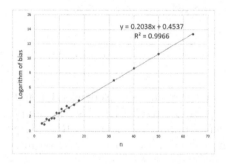

Fig. 1. Averages of (logarithm) biases according to n and its trend line.

During experiments, we observed some irregularities outside of our expectations. For example, under the case $n = 2^{18}$, there are $3.2\% = (8422/2^{18})$ base vectors that our assumption is invalid even though the analysis does not depend on the form of $\mathbf{A}$. Indeed, the value of red points drawn along the irregular cases in Fig. 2a is much smaller than that of the green points that follow our prediction. However, for these cases, we gathered $\mathbf{x}$'s with odd $h_\mathbf{x}$. Then, we observe that the maximum value M of $\{M_{\alpha,\beta}\}_{\alpha \in \{0,2\}, \beta \in \{odd, even\}}$, where $M_{\alpha,\beta}$ is defined as (3), is far from $1/3$ by at least $\frac{1}{2^{0.21n}}$ in Fig. 2b, which supports that our attacks succeed regardless of the base vector $\mathbf{a}$.

$$M_{\alpha,\beta} := \left| \Pr[\mathcal{F}_\mathbf{A}(\mathbf{x}) \equiv \alpha \bmod 3 \mid h_\mathbf{x} \text{ is } \beta] - \frac{1}{3} \right| \tag{3}$$

---

[5] We call $\mathbf{a}$ a base vector.

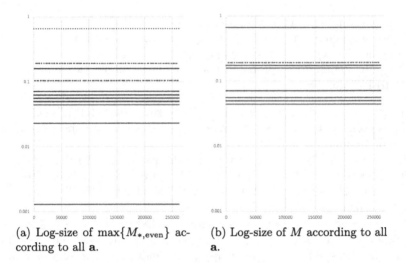

(a) Log-size of $\max\{M_{*,\mathrm{even}}\}$ according to all **a**.

(b) Log-size of M according to all **a**.

Fig. 2. Experimental results of all base vectors in $\{0,1\}^n$ with $n = 2^{18}$. The x-axis is the decimal representation of the all base vectors. Note that every binary vector with the length n can be represented by an integer $\leq 2^n$.

The Theorem 2 is proved by Lemma 4.7, Lemma 4.8 and experimental results 4.9.

Remark 4.10. The above mentioned Remarks 4.4 and 4.5 are also satisfied with a circulant Mod-p/Mod-q weak PRF. As an example, we observe that the advantage of a circulant Mod-3/Mod-5 weak PRF is larger than $\left(\cos\left(\frac{\pi}{15}\right)\right)^n \approx \frac{1}{2^{0.032n}}$ from the same computation, so n should be increased to 2000 for the 128-bit security under a measure $T/\epsilon^2 = 2^\lambda$.

5   How to Fix a Weakness of Mod-2/Mod-3 Weak PRFs

In this section, we suggest modified weak PRF candidates to prevent statistical attacks while preserving low depth and its circuit complexity. Thus, we think that fixed weak PRFs are still MPC friendly. Since our attacks use the biases of conditional probabilities, if the bias of the probability becomes smaller, our attacks become weaker.

An Alternative Mod-2/Mod-3 weak PRF. We are easily able to fix an alternative Mod-2/Mod-3 weak PRF since our attack heavily depends on the hamming weights of the secret key **k**. More specifically, under the current parameter $n = 384$, when we set the hamming weights $h = 310$ that is larger than $n/2$, it is secure against our statistical attacks. Moreover, this simple variant is secure against all known attacks presented by the original paper since they do not consider the hamming weights of the secret vector. Also, it is robust against brute-force attacks for finding the secret key because of $\log_2\binom{384}{310} \gg 200$. Thus, the fixed scheme preserves the depth-2 ACC^0 circuit complexity and current parameters.

A Circulant Mod-2/Mod-3 weak PRF. Our strategy is to break a weak structure of a circulant Mod-2/Mod-3 weak PRF that preserves a parity of $[\mathbf{Ax}]_2$ if $h_{\mathbf{x}}$ is even for any circulant matrix $\mathbf{A}$. To avoid a weakness, we inject an extra secret vector and generate a new secret key $\mathbf{B}$ with two secret vectors. We name $\mathbf{B}$ a semi-circulant key. Previously, a circulant secret key is generated by a single vector. For explanation, let $\mathbf{a}$ and $\mathbf{b}$ be secret vectors. Then, we construct a secret matrix $\mathbf{B}$ as follows. For simplicity's sake, assume that n is even.

- Set initial vectors such that the first row of $\mathbf{B}$ is $\mathbf{a}$ and $n/2$-th row of $\mathbf{B}$ is $\mathbf{b}$.
- For each $2 \leq i \leq n/2$, i-th row of $\mathbf{B}$ is $\rho_i(\mathbf{a})$, where $\rho_i(\mathbf{a})$ shifts one element to the right relative to the $\rho_{i-1}(\mathbf{a})$ with $\rho_1(\mathbf{a}) = \mathbf{a}$ and $\rho_{n+1}(\mathbf{a}) = \mathbf{a}$.
- Similarly, for each $n/2 < j \leq n$, j-th row of $\mathbf{B}$ is $\rho_j(\mathbf{b})$.

Then, we observe that each column of a matrix $\mathbf{B}$ does not preserve hamming weights, so vectors of ones $(1, \cdots, 1)$ is not a left-eigenvector of $\mathbf{B}$. Thus, we can easily fix a circulant Mod-2/Mod-3 weak PRF against all known attacks including our statistical attack. Moreover, the size of PRF key is still smaller than that of random key, and it preserves the current parameter n and depth-2 ACC^0 circuits.

To support that the simple modification to a semi-circulant key $\mathbf{B}$ is reasonable, we conducted experiments for several n and types of secret key; random $\mathbf{A}$ and semi-circulant $\mathbf{B}$. To construct a semi-circulant key $\mathbf{B}$, we randomly choose two vectors from $\{0, 1\}^n$. For $n = 16, 18$, we experimented with 128 different secret keys to compute (average of) logarithm biases of the statistical attack. Similarly, for $n = 24, 28$, we provided experimental results for 20 different secret keys. Moreover, for each case, 2^n samples were used to compute accurate $M = \max_{\alpha,\beta}\{M_{\alpha,\beta}\}_{\alpha \in \{0,2\}, \beta \in \{\text{odd, even}\}}$.

According to the above graph, we observe that a semi-circulant weak PRF with $\mathbf{B}$, behaves Mod-2/Mod-3 weak PRF with random secret key $\mathbf{A}$. Moreover, the fixed candidate is secure against all known attacks under the current parameters $n = m = 256$ since its advantage is already larger than $2^{-0.5n}$.

The fixed candidate would be also interesting since it almost preserves the advantage of a circulant Mod-2/Mod-3 weak PRF: a quasi-linear multiplication time. Since the semi-circulant matrix consists of two secret vectors with their rotations, by computing two circulant matrix-vector multiplications, we easily obtain outputs of the semi-circulant Mod-2/Mod-3 weak PRFs. Thus, the fixed candidate still allows a quasi-linear multiplication time although its real time is twice slower than the circulant Mod-2/Mod-3 weak PRF (Fig. 3).

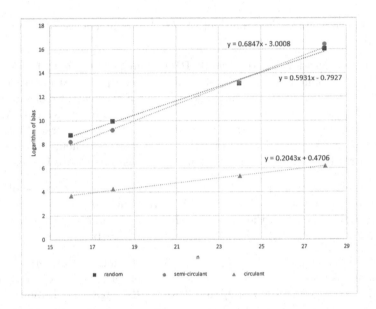

Fig. 3. Averages of (logarithm) biases according to n and types of secret keys and their trend lines.

Remark 5.1. We observe that the weakness of a circulant Mod-2/Mod-3 weak PRF might come from a structured property of $\mathbf{A}$. Indeed, we observe that if we break down the property using two secret vectors, then a Mod-2/Mod-3 weak PRF with secret key $\mathbf{B}$ is secure against our attack although a circulant with key $\mathbf{A}$ is vulnerable to our attack. Thus, we can make a hypothesis that a structured chaos of the secret key implies the security of weak PRF candidates.

Remark 5.2. The main idea of our revision of weak PRF candidates is to change the way secret keys are sampled (a single vector with high hamming weights, or a semi-circulant key) while preserving the parameters. Thus, it is more efficient than the basic revision that increases the key size.

Acknowledgments. We thank anonymous reviewers of PKC 2021 for insightful and helpful comments. In particular, we thank Venkata Koppula to shepherd our paper. Also, we would like to thank Minki Hhan for helpful discussions. The authors of Seoul National University were supported by Institute for Information & communication Technology Promotion (IITP) grant funded by the Korea government (MSIT) (No. 2016-6-00598, The mathematical structure of functional encryption and its analysis). Jeong Han Kim was partially supported by National Research Foundation of Korea (NRF) Grants funded by the Korean Government (MSIP) (NRF-2012R1A2A2A01018585 & 2017R1E1A1A03070701) and by a KIAS Individual Grant(CG046001) at Korea Institute of Advanced Study. Jiseung Kim was supported by a KIAS Individual Grant CG078201 at Korea Institute for Advanced Study.

A   Definitions about Circuit Class

In this section, we deal with definitions about the circuit class in [BIP+18].

Definition A.1 (in [BIP+18]). *For any integer m, the MOD_m gate outputs 1 if m divides the sum of its inputs, and 0 otherwise.*

Definition A.2 (Circuit Class ACC^0 in [BIP+18]). *For integers $m_1, \cdots, m_k > 1$, $\mathsf{ACC}^0[m_1, \cdots, m_k]$ is the set of languages $\mathcal{L}$ decided by some circuit family $\{C_n\}_{n \in \mathbb{N}}$ with constant depth, polynomial size, and consisting of unbounded fan-in AND, OR, NOT and $\mathsf{MOD}_{m_1}, \cdots, \mathsf{MOD}_{m_k}$ gates. Moreover, ACC^0 is denoted by the class of all languages that is in $\mathsf{ACC}^0[m_1, \cdots, m_k]$ for some $k \geq 0$ and integers $m_1, \cdots, m_k > 1$.*

B   Simple Non-adaptive Attack

In this section, we provide a simple non-adaptive attack of a basic Mod-2/Mod-3 weak PRF, which runs in polynomial time n. The attack is motivated by rank attack [CVW18, CHVW19].

Assume that adversary has exponentially many samples $(\mathbf{z}_i, v_i)$. The goal is to determine whether v_i is uniformly sampled from $\mathbb{Z}_3$ or sampled from a Mod-2/Mod-3 weak PRF.

Let s be an integer $> \max\{m, n\}$. Then, our attack is:

1. Find s^2 pairs of vectors $\{(\mathbf{x}_i, \mathbf{y}_j)\}_{i,j \in [s]}$ such that $\mathbf{z}_{i,j} = \mathbf{x}_i + \mathbf{y}_j$ for some $\mathbf{z}_{i,j}$ in a list of samples.
2. Construct a matrix $\mathbf{M} = (v_{i,j})$, where $v_{i,j}$ is a sample corresponding to a vector $\mathbf{z}_{i,j}$.
3. Compute a rank of $\mathbf{M}$.

For an analysis, we borrow a polynomial representation of $\mathcal{F}_\mathbf{A}(\mathbf{x})$ in [BIP+18].

$$\mathcal{F}_\mathbf{A}(\mathbf{x}) = \sum_{i=1}^{m} \left(\prod_{j=1}^{n} (1 + x_j)^{a_{i,j}} - 1 \right),$$

where a matrix $\mathbf{A} = (a_{i,j}) \in \{0.1\}^{m \times n}$ and a vector $\mathbf{x} = (x_i) \in \{0,1\}^n$. Note that since $a_{i,j}$ is 0 or 1, the following lemma is trivial.

Lemma B.1. *Mod-2/Mod-3 weak PRF is interpreted as a product of matrices. More precisely, for a key $\mathbf{A} = (a_{i,j}) \in \{0,1\}^{m \times n}$ and a vector $\mathbf{x} = (x_i) \in \{0,1\}^n$,*

$$\mathcal{F}_\mathbf{A}(\mathbf{x}) + n = \sum_{i=1}^{n} f_i(\mathbf{x}) = \mathbf{1}^T \cdot \prod_{i=1}^{n} (\mathbf{I} + \mathsf{diag}(x_i \mathbf{A}_i)) \cdot \mathbf{1}$$

where $\mathbf{A}_i$ is the i-th column of $\mathbf{A}$, and $f_i(\mathbf{x}) = \prod_{j=1}^{n}(1 + a_{i,j}x_j)$, and $\mathsf{diag}(x_i\mathbf{A}_i)$ is a diagonal matrix whose j-th diagonal entry is the same as j-th component of a vector $x_i\mathbf{A}_i$.

Based on the above lemma, we complete the non-adaptive attack. When $v_{i,j}$'s are truly random, a rank of $\mathbf{M}$ is s with high probability. However, if it is of the form $\mathsf{map}(\mathbf{A} \cdot ([\mathbf{x}_i + \mathbf{y}_j)]_2)$, then a matrix $\mathbf{M}$ is divided into a product of two matrices using Lemma B.1.

$$\mathbf{M} = \begin{pmatrix} \mathbf{1}^T \cdot \mathbf{H}(\mathbf{x}_1) \\ \mathbf{1}^T \cdot \mathbf{H}(\mathbf{x}_2) \\ \mathbf{1}^T \cdot \mathbf{H}(\mathbf{x}_3) \\ \vdots \\ \mathbf{1}^T \cdot \mathbf{H}(\mathbf{x}_\rho) \end{pmatrix} \cdot \Big(\mathbf{H}(\mathbf{y}_1) \cdot \mathbf{1}, \mathbf{H}(\mathbf{y}_2) \cdot \mathbf{1}, \mathbf{H}(\mathbf{y}_3) \cdot \mathbf{1}, \cdots, \mathbf{H}(\mathbf{y}_\rho) \cdot \mathbf{1} \Big)$$

Hence, a rank of $\mathbf{M}$ is bounded by $\min(m, n)$ with high probability. The attack runs in $O(n)$ time and space.

The rank attack only succeeds when an adversary is possible to use an oracle access to input queries. However, in the setting of weak PRF, inputs are selected randomly from $\{0,1\}^n$, our attack does not work anymore.

References

[ABG+14] Akavia, A., Bogdanov, A., Guo, S., Kamath, A., Rosen, A.: Candidate weak pseudorandom functions in ac0◯ mod2. In: Proceedings of the 5th conference on Innovations in Theoretical Computer Science, pp. 251–260 (2014)

[ABSV15] Ananth, P., Brakerski, Z., Segev, G., Vaikuntanathan, V.: From selective to adaptive security in functional encryption. In: Gennaro, R., Robshaw, M. (eds.) CRYPTO 2015, Part II. LNCS, vol. 9216, pp. 657–677. Springer, Heidelberg (2015). https://doi.org/10.1007/978-3-662-48000-7_32

[App14] Applebaum, B.: Bootstrapping obfuscators via fast pseudorandom functions. In: Sarkar, P., Iwata, T. (eds.) ASIACRYPT 2014, Part II. LNCS, vol. 8874, pp. 162–172. Springer, Heidelberg (2014). https://doi.org/10.1007/978-3-662-45608-8_9

[ASA17] Alperin-Sheriff, J., Apon, D.: Weak is better: Tightly secure short signatures from weak PRFs. IACR Cryptol. ePrint Arch. (2017)

[BCK96] Bellare, M., Canetti, R., Krawczyk, H.: Keying hash functions for message authentication. In: Koblitz, N. (ed.) CRYPTO 1996. LNCS, vol. 1109, pp. 1–15. Springer, Heidelberg (1996). https://doi.org/10.1007/3-540-68697-5_1

[Bel15] Bellare, M.: New proofs for NMAC and HMAC: security without collision resistance. J. Cryptol. 28(4), 844–878 (2015)

[BHI+20] Ball, M., Holmgren, J., Ishai, Y., Liu, T., Malkin, T.: On the complexity of decomposable randomized encodings, or: how friendly can a garbling-friendly PRF be? In: 11th Innovations in Theoretical Computer Science Conference, ITCS 2020. Schloss Dagstuhl-Leibniz-Zentrum für Informatik (2020)

[BIP+18] Boneh, D., Ishai, Y., Passelègue, A., Sahai, A., Wu, D.J.: Exploring crypto dark matter. In: Beimel, A., Dziembowski, S. (eds.) TCC 2018. LNCS, vol. 11240, pp. 699–729. Springer, Cham (2018). https://doi.org/10.1007/978-3-030-03810-6_25

[BKW03] Blum, A., Kalai, A., Wasserman, H.: Noise-tolerant learning, the parity problem, and the statistical query model. J. ACM (JACM) 50(4), 506–519 (2003)

[BR17] Bogdanov, A., Rosen, A.: Pseudorandom functions: three decades later. In: Lindell, Y. (ed.) Tutorials on the Foundations of Cryptography. ISC, pp. 79–158. Springer, Cham (2017). https://doi.org/10.1007/978-3-319-57048-8_3

[BTV16] Bogos, S., Tramer, F., Vaudenay, S.: On solving LPN using BKW and variants. Crypt. Commun. 8(3), 331–369 (2016). https://doi.org/10.1007/s12095-015-0149-2

[CHVW19] Chen, Y., Hhan, M., Vaikuntanathan, V., Wee, H.: Matrix PRFs: constructions, attacks, and applications to obfuscation. In: Hofheinz, D., Rosen, A. (eds.) TCC 2019, Part I. LNCS, vol. 11891, pp. 55–80. Springer, Cham (2019). https://doi.org/10.1007/978-3-030-36030-6_3

[CVW18] Chen, Y., Vaikuntanathan, V., Wee, H.: GGH15 beyond permutation branching programs: proofs, attacks, and candidates. In: Shacham, H., Boldyreva, A. (eds.) CRYPTO 2018, Part II. LNCS, vol. 10992, pp. 577–607. Springer, Cham (2018). https://doi.org/10.1007/978-3-319-96881-0_20

[DKPW12] Dodis, Y., Kiltz, E., Pietrzak, K., Wichs, D.: Message authentication, revisited. In: Pointcheval, D., Johansson, T. (eds.) EUROCRYPT 2012. LNCS, vol. 7237, pp. 355–374. Springer, Heidelberg (2012). https://doi.org/10.1007/978-3-642-29011-4_22

[DN02] Damgård, I., Nielsen, J.B.: Expanding pseudorandom functions; or: from known-plaintext security to chosen-plaintext security. In: Yung, M. (ed.) CRYPTO 2002. LNCS, vol. 2442, pp. 449–464. Springer, Heidelberg (2002). https://doi.org/10.1007/3-540-45708-9_29

[DS09] Dodis, Y., Steinberger, J.: Message authentication codes from unpredictable block ciphers. In: Halevi, S. (ed.) CRYPTO 2009. LNCS, vol. 5677, pp. 267–285. Springer, Heidelberg (2009). https://doi.org/10.1007/978-3-642-03356-8_16

[GGM86] Goldreich, O., Goldwasser, S., Micali, S.: How to construct random functions. J. ACM (JACM) 33(4), 792–807 (1986)

[Gol86] Goldreich, O.: Two remarks concerning the Goldwasser-Micali-Rivest signature scheme. In: Odlyzko, A.M. (ed.) CRYPTO 1986. LNCS, vol. 263, pp. 104–110. Springer, Heidelberg (1987). https://doi.org/10.1007/3-540-47721-7_8

[LM13] Lyubashevsky, V., Masny, D.: Man-in-the-middle secure authentication schemes from LPN and Weak PRFs. In: Canetti, R., Garay, J.A. (eds.) CRYPTO 2013, Part II. LNCS, vol. 8043, pp. 308–325. Springer, Heidelberg (2013). https://doi.org/10.1007/978-3-642-40084-1_18

[MS07] Maurer, U., Sjödin, J.: A fast and key-efficient reduction of chosen-ciphertext to known-plaintext security. In: Naor, M. (ed.) EUROCRYPT 2007. LNCS, vol. 4515, pp. 498–516. Springer, Heidelberg (2007). https://doi.org/10.1007/978-3-540-72540-4_29

[MW18] Micciancio, D., Walter, M.: On the bit security of cryptographic primitives. In: Nielsen, J.B., Rijmen, V. (eds.) EUROCRYPT 2018, Part I. LNCS, vol. 10820, pp. 3–28. Springer, Cham (2018). https://doi.org/10.1007/978-3-319-78381-9_1

[Pie09] Pietrzak, K.: A leakage-resilient mode of operation. In: Joux, A. (ed.) EUROCRYPT 2009. LNCS, vol. 5479, pp. 462–482. Springer, Heidelberg (2009). https://doi.org/10.1007/978-3-642-01001-9_27

Author Index

Printed in the United States
by Baker & Taylor Publisher Services